Ordnance Survey

STREET ATLAS
South Hampshire

Contents

III	Key to map symbols
IV	Key to map pages
VI	Administrative and post code boundaries
1	Street maps
215	Town maps of Andover and Basingstoke
216	Town maps of Farnborough and Newbury
217	Index of hospitals, railway stations, schools, shopping centres, street names and universities

PHILIP'S

First edition published 1991
Fourth edition published 1994
First colour edition published 1998
Reprinted 1998, 1999, 2000 twice by

George Philip Ltd, a division of
Octopus Publishing Group Ltd
2-4 Heron Quays, London E14 4JP

ISBN 0-540-07476-4 (hardback)
ISBN 0-540-07477-2 (spiral)

To the best of the Publishers' knowledge, the information in this atlas was
correct at the time of going to press. No responsibility can be accepted
for any errors or their consequences.

The representation in this atlas of a road, track or path is no evidence
of the existence of a right of way.

**The mapping between pages 1 and 216 (inclusive) in this atlas is
derived from Ordnance Survey® OSCAR® and Land-Line® data,
and Landranger® mapping.**

Ordnance Survey, OSCAR, Land-Line and Landranger are registered trade
marks of Ordnance Survey, the national mapping agency of Great Britain.

Printed and bound in Spain by Cayfosa

Digital Data

The exceptionally high-quality mapping
found in this book is available as digital
data in TIFF format, which is easily
convertible to other bit-mapped (raster)
image formats.

The index is also available in digital form
as a standard database table. It contains
all the details found in the printed index
together with the National Grid reference
for the map square in which each entry
is named and feature codes for places
of interest in eight categories such as
education and health.

For further information and to discuss
your requirements, please contact
Philip's on 020 7531 8440 or
george.philip@philips-maps.co.uk

Motorway (with junction number)	**British Rail station**
Primary route (dual carriageway and single)	**Underground station**
A road (dual carriageway and single)	**Docklands Light Railway station**
B road (dual carriageway and single)	**Private railway station**
Minor road (dual carriageway and single)	**Bus, coach station**
Other minor road	**Ambulance station**
Road under construction	**Coastguard station**
Pedestrianised area	**Fire station**
Railway	**Police station**
Tramway, miniature railway	**Accident and Emergency entrance to hospital**
Rural track, private road or narrow road in urban area	**Hospital**
Gate or obstruction to traffic (restrictions may not apply at all times or to all vehicles)	**Church, place of worship**
Path, bridleway, byway open to all traffic, road used as a public path	**Information centre** (open all year)
The representation in this atlas of a road, track or path is no evidence of the existence of a right of way	**Parking**
	Post Office
Adjoining page indicators	**Important buildings, schools, colleges, universities and hospitals**

Prim Sch

Acad	**Academy**	Mon	**Monument**
Cemy	**Cemetery**	Mus	**Museum**
C Ctr	**Civic Centre**	Obsy	**Observatory**
CH	**Club House**	Pal	**Royal Palace**
Coll	**College**	PH	**Public House**
Ent	**Enterprise**	Recn Gd	**Recreation Ground**
Ex H	**Exhibition Hall**	Resr	**Reservoir**
Ind Est	**Industrial Estate**	Ret Pk	**Retail Park**
Inst	**Institute**	Sch	**School**
Ct	**Law Court**	Sh Ctr	**Shopping Centre**
L Ctr	**Leisure Centre**	Sta	**Station**
LC	**Level Crossing**	TH	**Town Hall/House**
Liby	**Library**	Trad Est	**Trading Estate**
Mkt	**Market**	Univ	**University**
Meml	**Memorial**	YH	**Youth Hostel**

County and unitary authority boundaries

River Medway **Water name**

Stream

River or canal (minor and major)

Water

Tidal water

Woods

Houses

House **Non-Roman antiquity**

VILLA **Roman antiquity**

■ The dark grey border on the inside edge of some pages indicates that the mapping does not continue onto the adjacent page

■ The small numbers around the edges of the maps identify the 1 kilometre National Grid lines

The scale of the maps is 5.52 cm to 1 km (3½ inches to 1 mile)

0   ¼   ½   ¾   1 mile
0   250m   500m   750m   1 kilometre

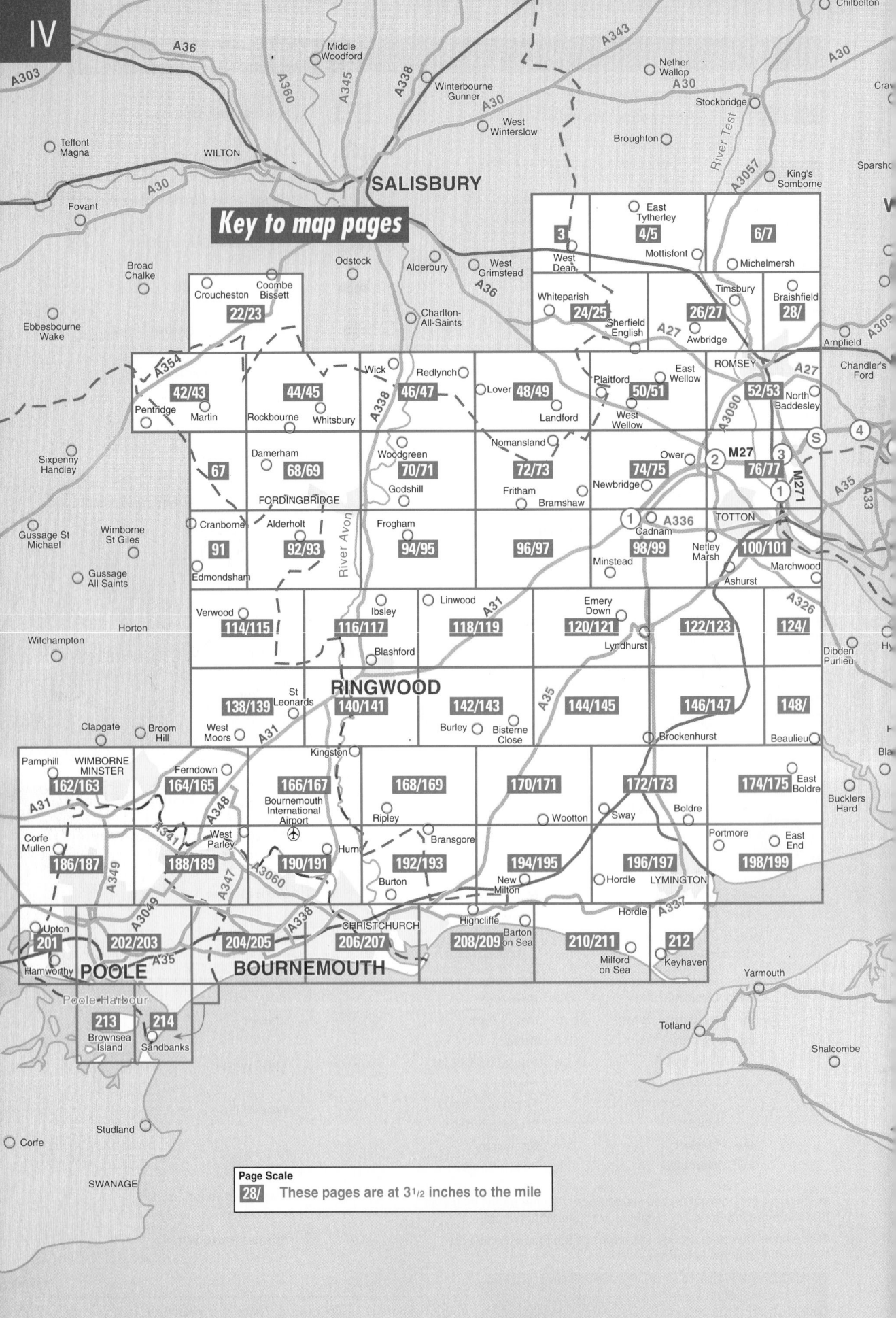

IV

Key to map pages

SALISBURY

3	
4/5	6/7
22/23	24/25	26/27	28/
42/43	44/45	46/47	48/49	50/51	52/53
67	68/69	70/71	72/73	74/75	76/77
91	92/93	94/95	96/97	98/99	100/101
114/115	116/117	118/119	120/121	122/123	124/
138/139	140/141	142/143	144/145	146/147	148/
162/163	164/165	166/167	168/169	170/171	172/173	174/175
186/187	188/189	190/191	192/193	194/195	196/197	198/199
201	202/203	204/205	206/207	208/209	210/211	212
213	214					

RINGWOOD

WIMBORNE MINSTER

POOLE

BOURNEMOUTH

CHRISTCHURCH

LYMINGTON

Page Scale
28/ These pages are at 3½ inches to the mile

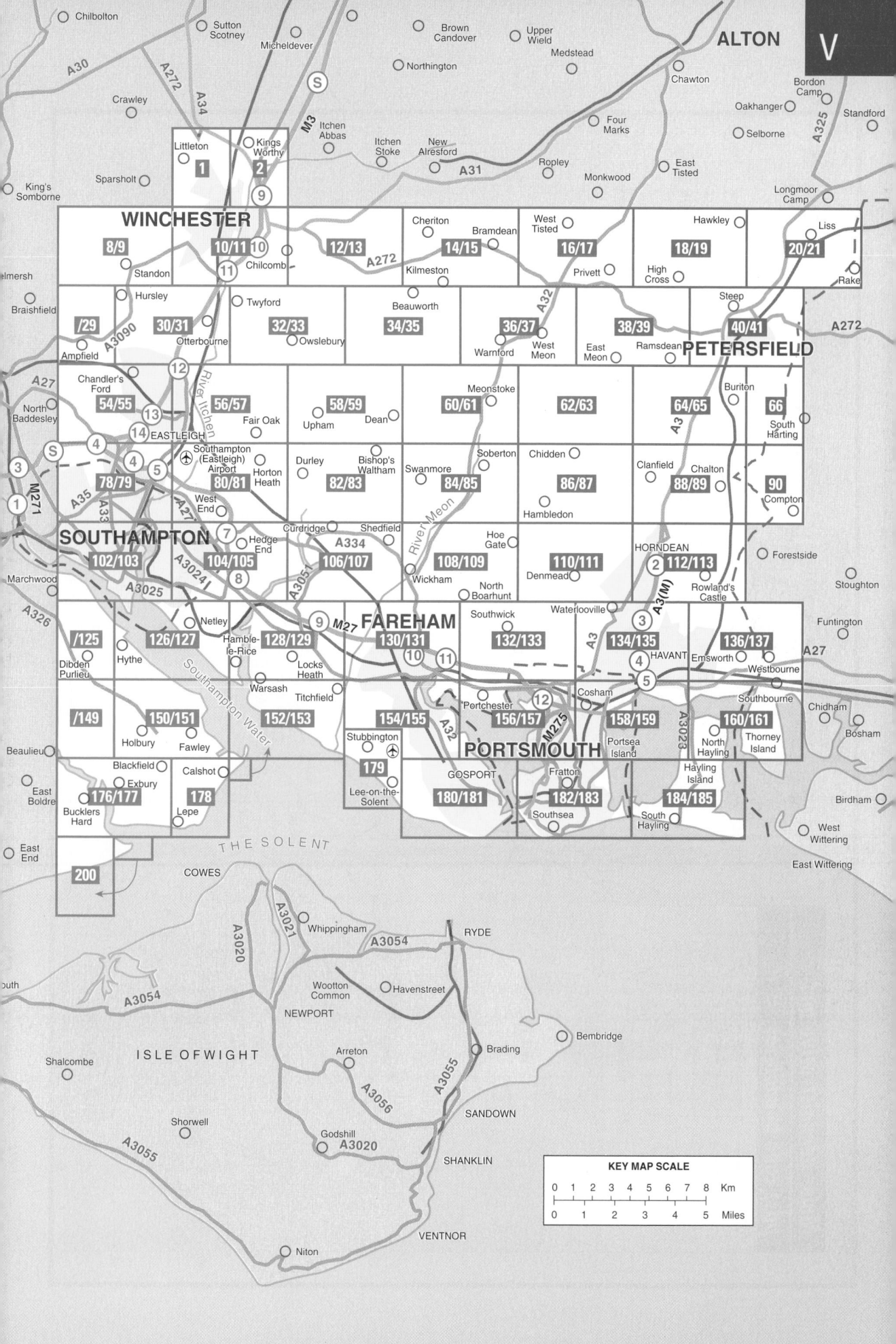

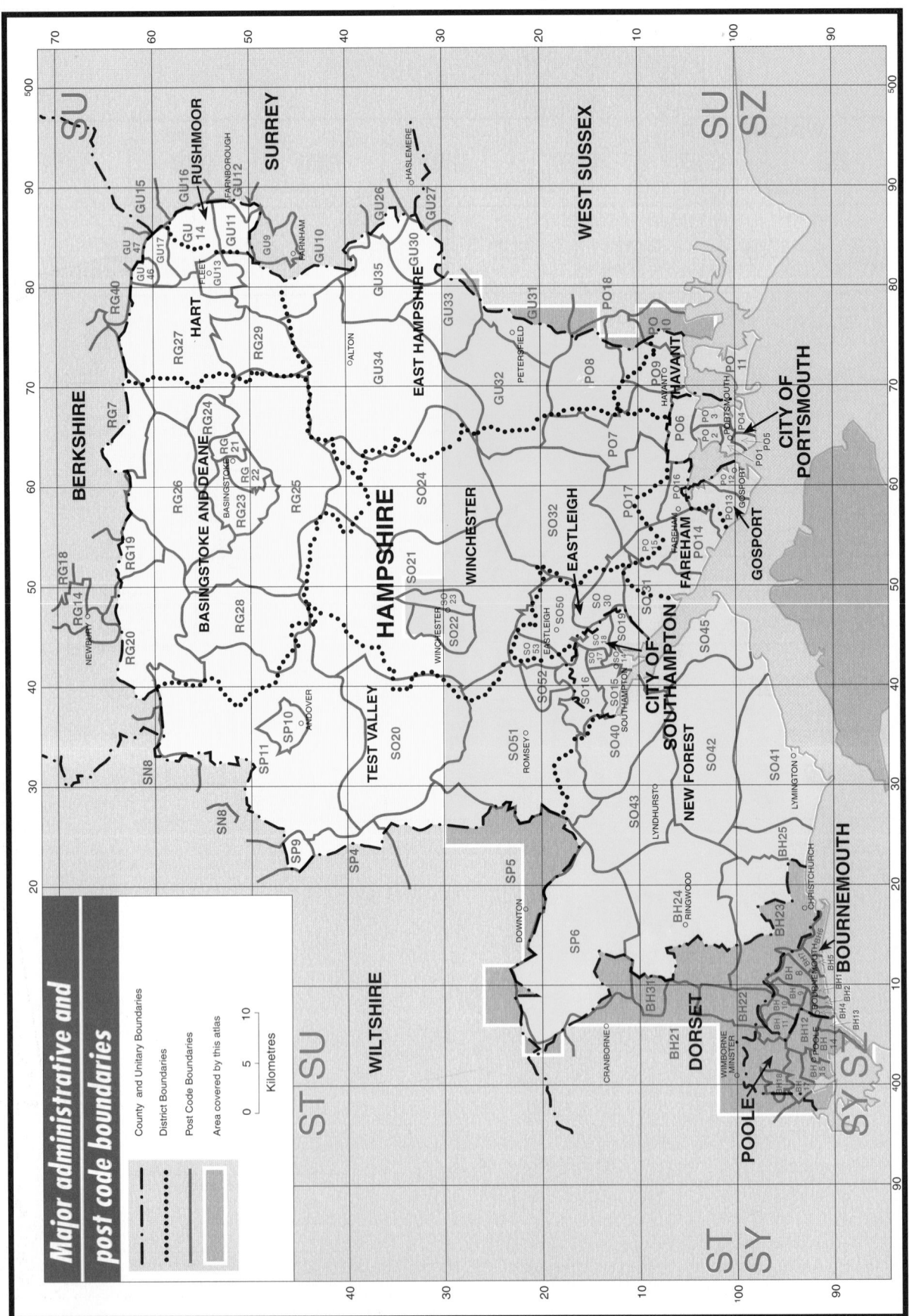

Major administrative and post code boundaries

County and Unitary Boundaries

District Boundaries

Post Code Boundaries

Area covered by this atlas

Kilometres

0   5   10

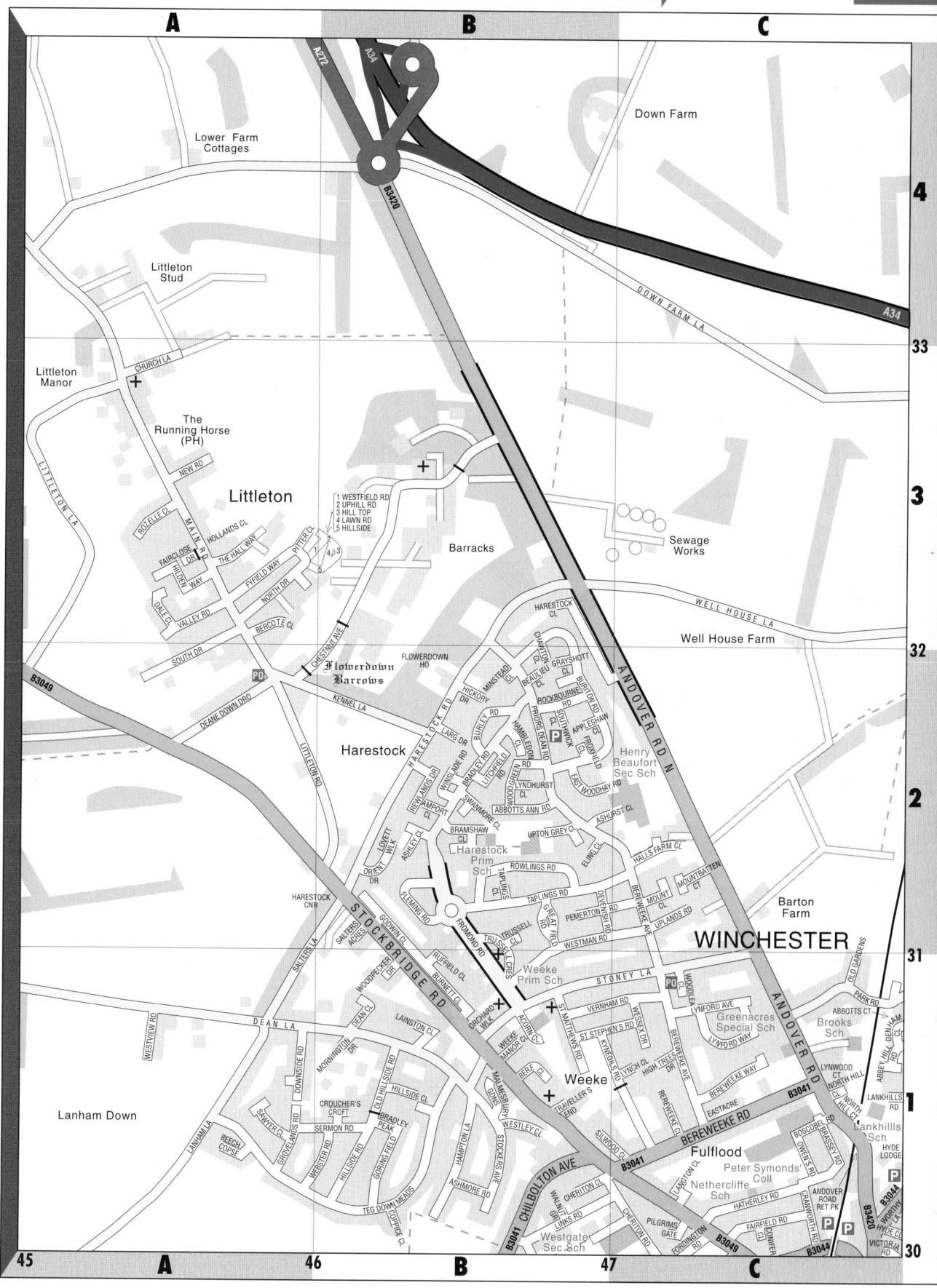

A   B   C

4

33

3

2

32

2

31

1

30

45   A   46   B   47   C   30

Down Farm

Lower Farm
Cottages

Littleton
Stud

Littleton
Manor

CHURCH LA

The
Running Horse
(PH)

NEW RD

Littleton

ROZELLE CL

MAIN RD

HOLLANDS CL

THE HALL WAY

FAIRCLOSE
DR

HILDEN
WAY

FYFIELD WAY

DALE CL

VALLEY RD

NORTH DR

SOUTH DR

BERCOTE CL

PITTER CL

1 WESTFIELD RD
2 UPHILL RD
3 HILL TOP
4 LAWN RD
5 HILLSIDE

Barracks

FLOWERDOWN
HO

Flowerdown
Barrows

LOCKSTREET AVE

PO

DEANE DOWN DRO.

KENNEL LA

LITTLETON RD

Harestock

HARESTOCK RD

LARG DR

HICKORY
DR

BURLEY
RD

BRADLEY
RD

WINGLADE RD

AMPORT

NEW LANDS DR

SWANMORE CL

ASHLEY CL

LOVET
WLK

ORIENT
DR

FLEMING RD

LITCHFIELD

WOODGREEN

LYNDHURST
CL

ABBOTTS ANN RD

BRAMSHAW
CL

TAPLINGS
CL

Harestock
Prim Sch

UPTON GREY CL

ROWLINGS RD

TAPLINGS RD

HARESTOCK
CNR

SALTERS LA

STOCKBRIDGE RD

GODWIN CL

SALTERS
ACRES

WOODPECKER
DR

RUFFIELD CL

BURNETT CL

FROMOND RD

TRUSSELL
CL

TRUSSELL CRES

GREAT
RD

FIELD

PEMERTON RD

WESTMAN RD

DEVPARK RD

BERWEEKE
AVE

MOUNT

MOUNTBATTEN
CT

HALLS FARM CL

ELING CL

ASHURST CL

MINSTEAD

CHARLTON CL

BEAULIEU

GRAYSHOTT
CL

ROCKBOURNE
RD

SOUTHWICK

PRIORS DEAN RD

APPLESHAW
RD

EAST WOODHAY

FROXFIELD

BURSTON RD

HAMBLEDON

HARESTOCK
CL

HENRY
Beaufort
Sec Sch

ANDOVER RD N

WELL HOUSE LA

Well House Farm

Sewage
Works

DEAN LA

WESTVIEW RD

MORNINGTON
DR

DOWNSIDE RD

DEAN CL

LAINSTON CL

HILLSIDE RD

OLD FIELD RD

SAWYER CL

BROXLANDS RD

WESTLEY RD

HILLSIDE RD

GORING FIELD

BRADLEY
PEAK

CROUCHER'S
CROFT

SERMON RD

LANHAM LA

BEECH
COPSE

ASHMORE RD

TEG DOWN MEADS

HAMPTON LA

MALMESBURY

GUNS

WEEKE
MANOR CL

ORCHARD
WLK

ACORN CL

BERE CL

STOKES AVE

WESTLEY CL

TRAVELLER'S
END

CHIL BOLTON AVE

WALNUT

CHERITON CL

LINKS RD

CHERITON RD

B3041

Westgate
Sec Sch

PILGRIMS'
GATE

Weeke
Prim Sch

St MATTHENS RD

St STEPHEN'S RD

VERNHAM RD

STONEY LA

WESSEX RD

KYMBOLS RD

LYNCH CL

HIGH TREES

LYNFORD AVE

LYNFORD WAY

Greenacres
Special Sch

BEREWEEKE WAY

BEREWEEKE AVE

EASTACRE

BEREWEEKE RD

B3041

Fulflood

LANGTON CL

Nethercliffe
Sch

HATHERLEY RD

FORDINGTON RD

B3049

SILWOOD CL

Weeke

Barton
Farm

WINCHESTER

PO

OLD GARDENS

PARK RD

ABBOTTS CT

Brooks
Sch

ANDOVER RD

LYNWOOD
CT

NORTH HILL

NORTH HILL CL

ABBEY HILL

DEN HAM

LANKHILLS
RD

Lankhills
Sch

HYDE
LODGE

B3041

BOSCOBEL RD

BRASSEY RD

OWENS RD

CRANWORTH RD

Peter Symonds'
Coll

Andover
Road
Ret Pk

FAIRFIELD RD

CONIFER RD

B3049

B3044

HYDE CL

VICTORIA
RD

B3420

WORTHY

P

P

P

P

Lanham Down

B3049

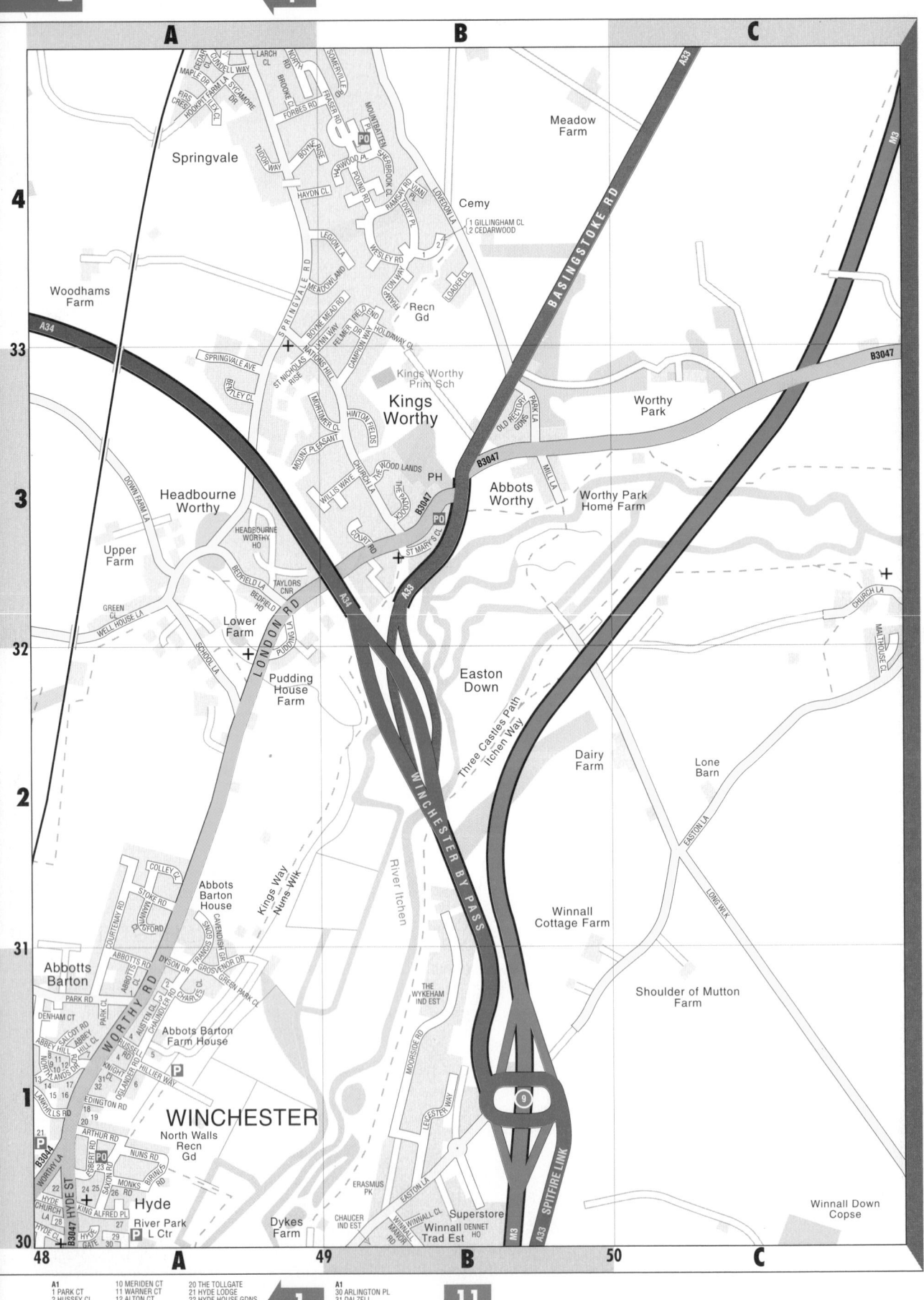

A   B   C

Springvale

Woodhams
Farm

Meadow
Farm

Cemy

1 GILLINGHAM CL
2 CEDARWOOD

A34

Kings
Worthy

Kings Worthy
Prim Sch

B3047

B3047

Worthy
Park

Headbourne
Worthy

PH

Abbots
Worthy

Worthy Park
Home Farm

Upper
Farm

Headbourne
Worthy Ho

Lower
Farm

A34

A33

Easton
Down

Pudding
House
Farm

Three Castles Path
Itchen Way

Dairy
Farm

Lone
Barn

WINCHESTER BY PASS

River Itchen

Kings Way
Nuns Wlk

Winnall
Cottage Farm

Abbots
Barton
House

Abbotts
Barton

THE
WYKEHAM
IND EST

Shoulder of Mutton
Farm

Abbots Barton
Farm House

WORTHY LA

WINCHESTER

North Walls
Recn
Gd

9

SPITFIRE LINK

Hyde

River Park
L Ctr

Dykes
Farm

ERASMUS
PK

CHAUCER
IND EST

Winnall
Trad Est

Superstore

DENNET
HO

M3

A33

Winnall Down
Copse

48   A   49   B   50   C

1

11

4

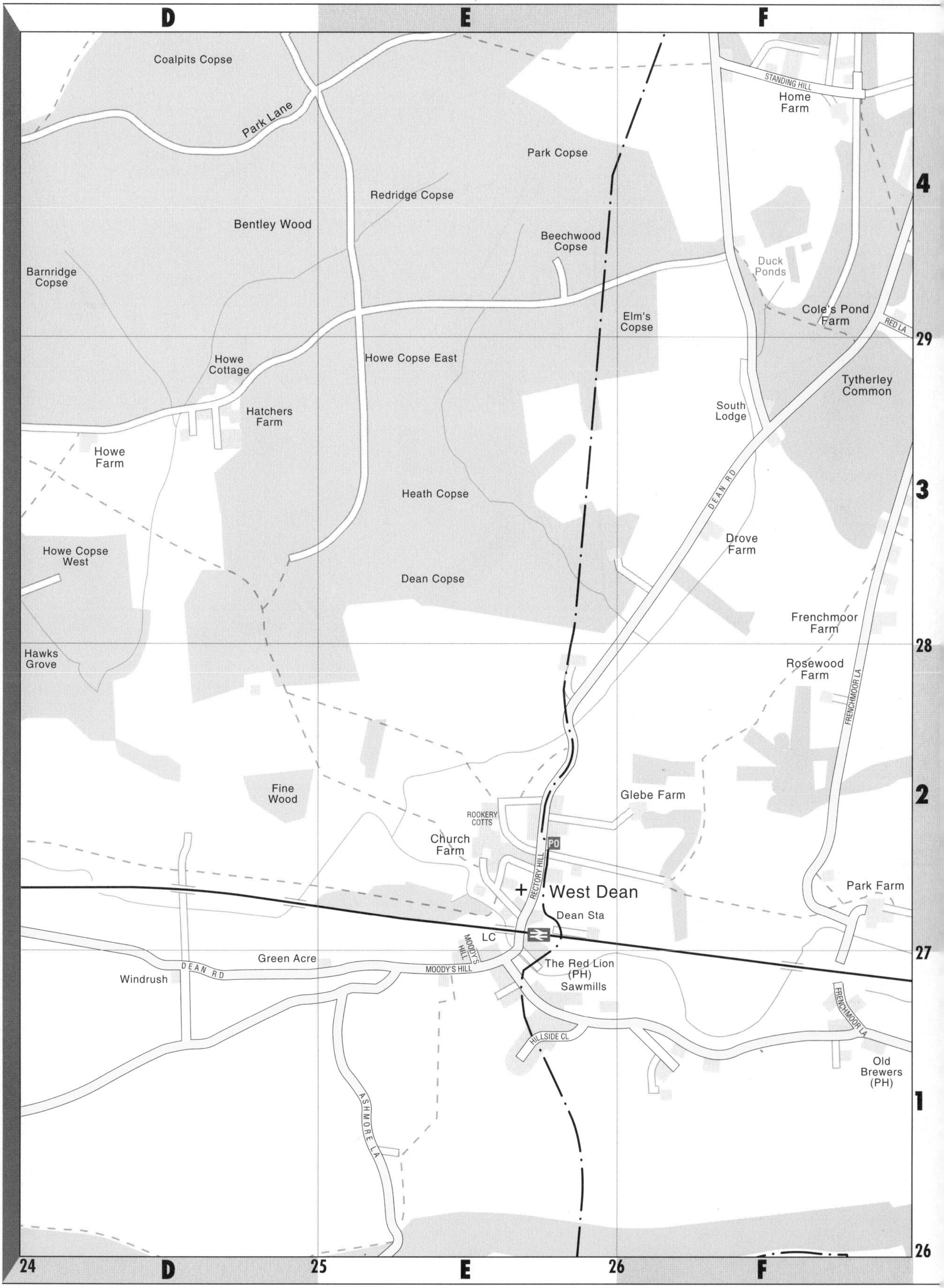

D
E
F
Coalpits Copse
Park Lane
STANDING HILL
Home Farm
Park Copse
Redridge Copse
Bentley Wood
Beechwood Copse
Duck Ponds
Barnridge Copse
Cole's Pond Farm
RED LA
Elm's Copse
Howe Cottage
Howe Copse East
Tytherley Common
Hatchers Farm
South Lodge
Howe Farm
Heath Copse
DEAN RD
Howe Copse West
Drove Farm
Dean Copse
Frenchmoor Farm
Hawks Grove
Rosewood Farm
FRENCHMOOR LA
Fine Wood
Glebe Farm
ROOKERY COTTS
Church Farm
PO
RECTORY HILL
West Dean
Park Farm
Dean Sta
LC
MOODY'S HILL
Green Acre
The Red Lion (PH)
Windrush
DEAN RD
MOODY'S HILL
Sawmills
FRENCHMOOR LA
HILLSIDE CL
Old Brewers (PH)
ASHMORE LA
4
3
2
1
29
28
27
26
24
25
26

24

4

West Tytherley
CE Prim Sch

Church
Farm

Stony
Batter

Stride's
Farm

Manor
Farm

East
Tytherley

NORTH LA

DEAN RD

Poplar
Farm

Lye
Farm

The Green

Sopp's
Farm

MANOR
RD

RED LA

THE COACH RD

White House

BONNER
COTTS

Oaklands
Farm

4

29

RED LA

PUG'S HOLE

BULLS DROVE

Drove

FRENCHMOOR LA

Lockerley Hall
Park

Frenchmoor

Lain
Copse

3

Upper Frenchmoor Copse

Lower
Frenchmoor
Copse

Bulls Drove

Lockerley
Hall

Pug's Hole

HOME FARM
BSNS CTR

28

Holbury Wood

The Star Inn
(PH)

2

Holbury
Farm

MARK WAY

HOLBURY LA

PARK
VIEW

Holbury Mill

Lockerley Water
Farm

27

Mill Farm

Manor
Farm

LC

River Dun

GLEBE MEADOW

East Dean

EAST DEAN RD

PO

1

Lockerley

Dean Hill Barn
Farm

Deangate
Farm

Top Green

PENOLE
GREEN

Butt's
Green

Dean Hill

Curlew's
Farm

Critchell's
Green

COOKS LA

BUTTS CL

26

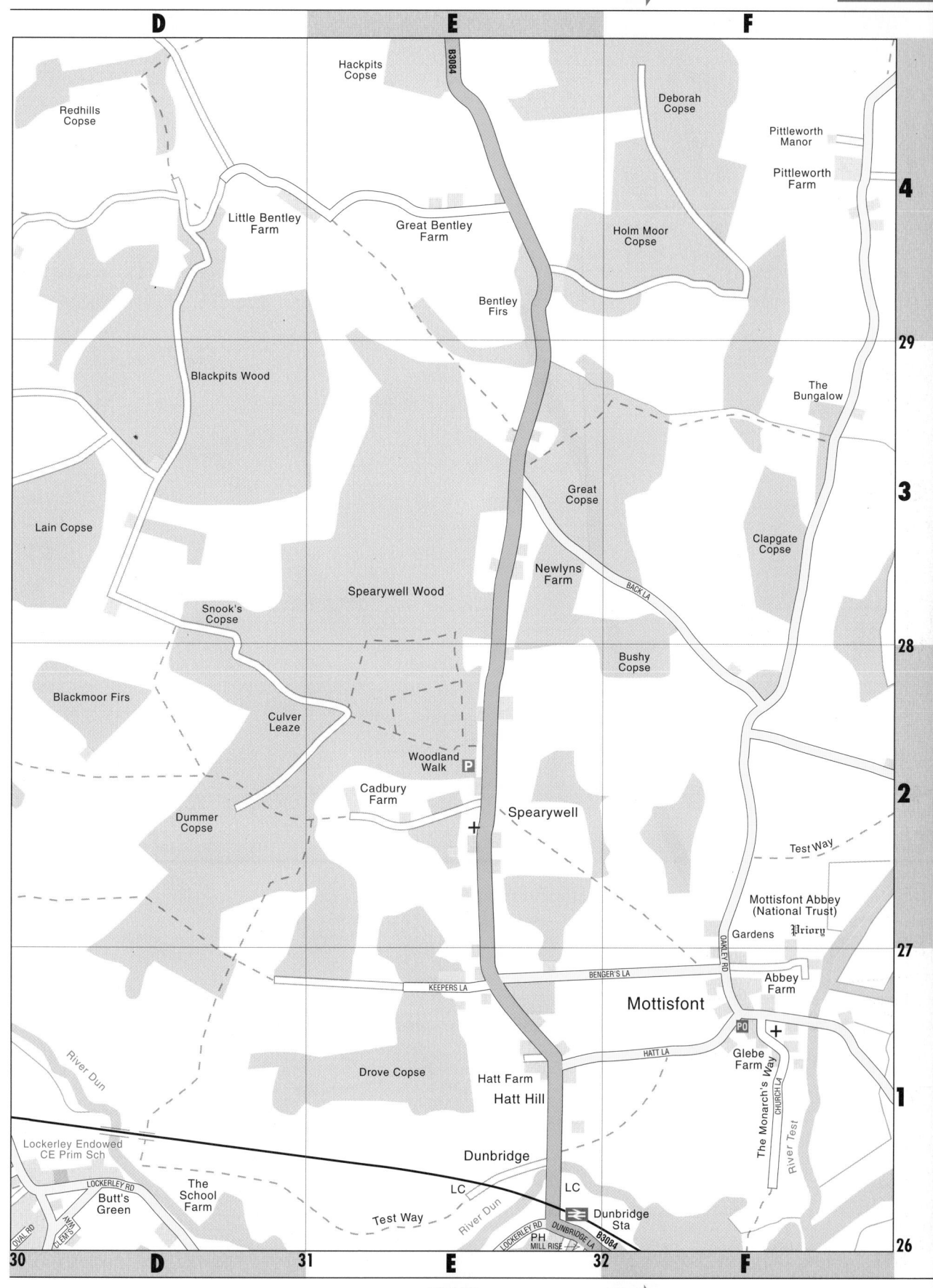

Redhills
Copse

Hackpits
Copse

B3084

Deborah
Copse

Pittleworth
Manor

Pittleworth
Farm

4

Little Bentley
Farm

Great Bentley
Farm

Holm Moor
Copse

Bentley
Firs

29

Blackpits Wood

The
Bungalow

Great
Copse

3

Lain Copse

Clapgate
Copse

Snook's
Copse

Spearywell Wood

Newlyns
Farm

BACK LA

28

Blackmoor Firs

Culver
Leaze

Bushy
Copse

Dummer
Copse

Woodland
Walk P

Cadbury
Farm

+

Spearywell

Test Way

Mottisfont Abbey
(National Trust)

Gardens   Priory

2

OAKLEY RD

27

KEEPERS LA   BENGER'S LA

Abbey
Farm

Mottisfont

River Dun

Drove Copse

Hatt Farm

Hatt Hill

HATT LA

PO

Glebe
Farm

+

The Monarch's Way

CHURCH LA

River Test

1

Lockerley Endowed
CE Prim Sch

LOCKERLEY RD

Butt's
Green

The
School
Farm

Dunbridge

LC

LC

River Dun

Test Way

PH
MILL RISE

LOCKERLEY RD

DUNBRIDGE LA

B3084

Dunbridge
Sta

26

5

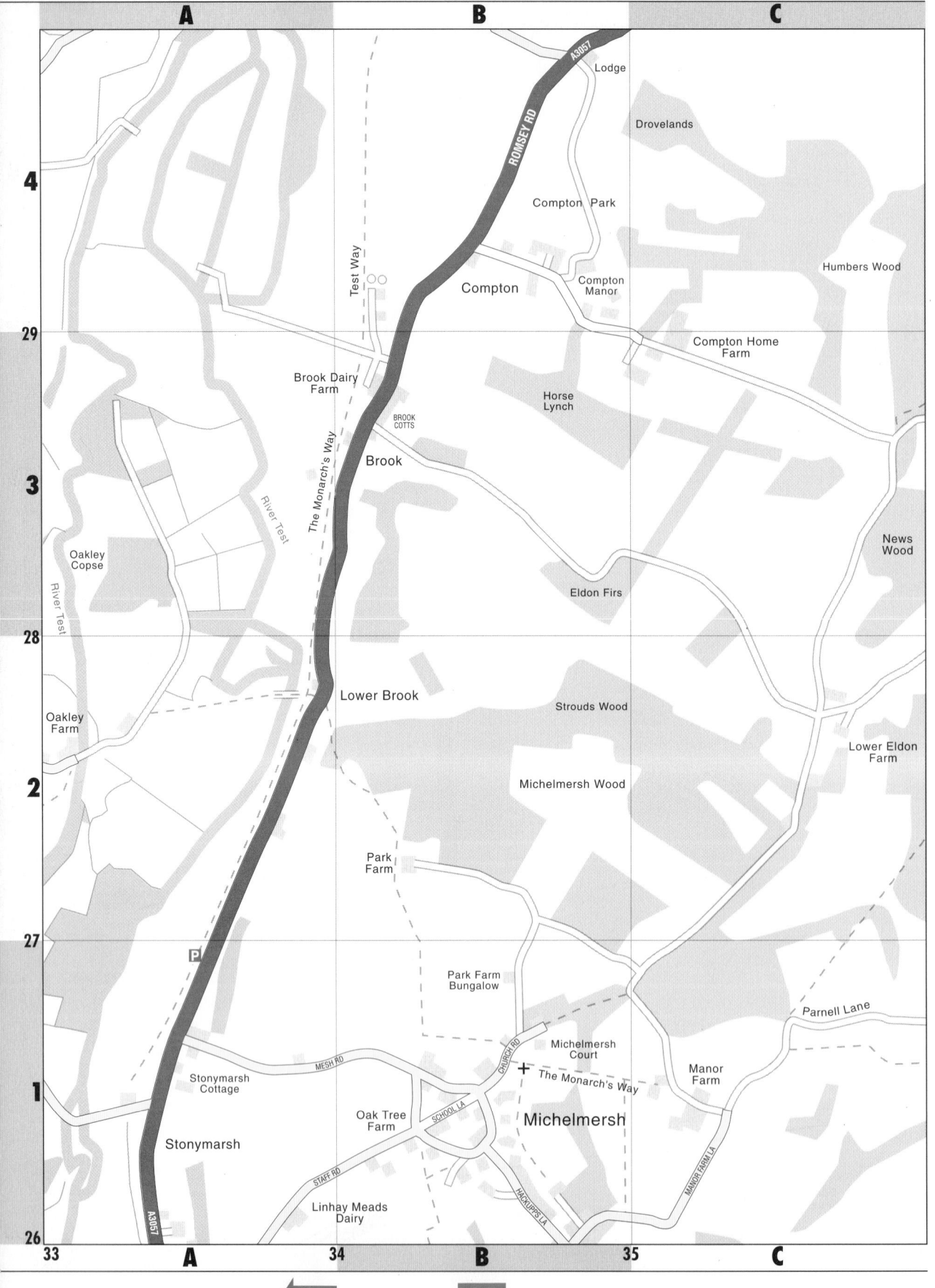

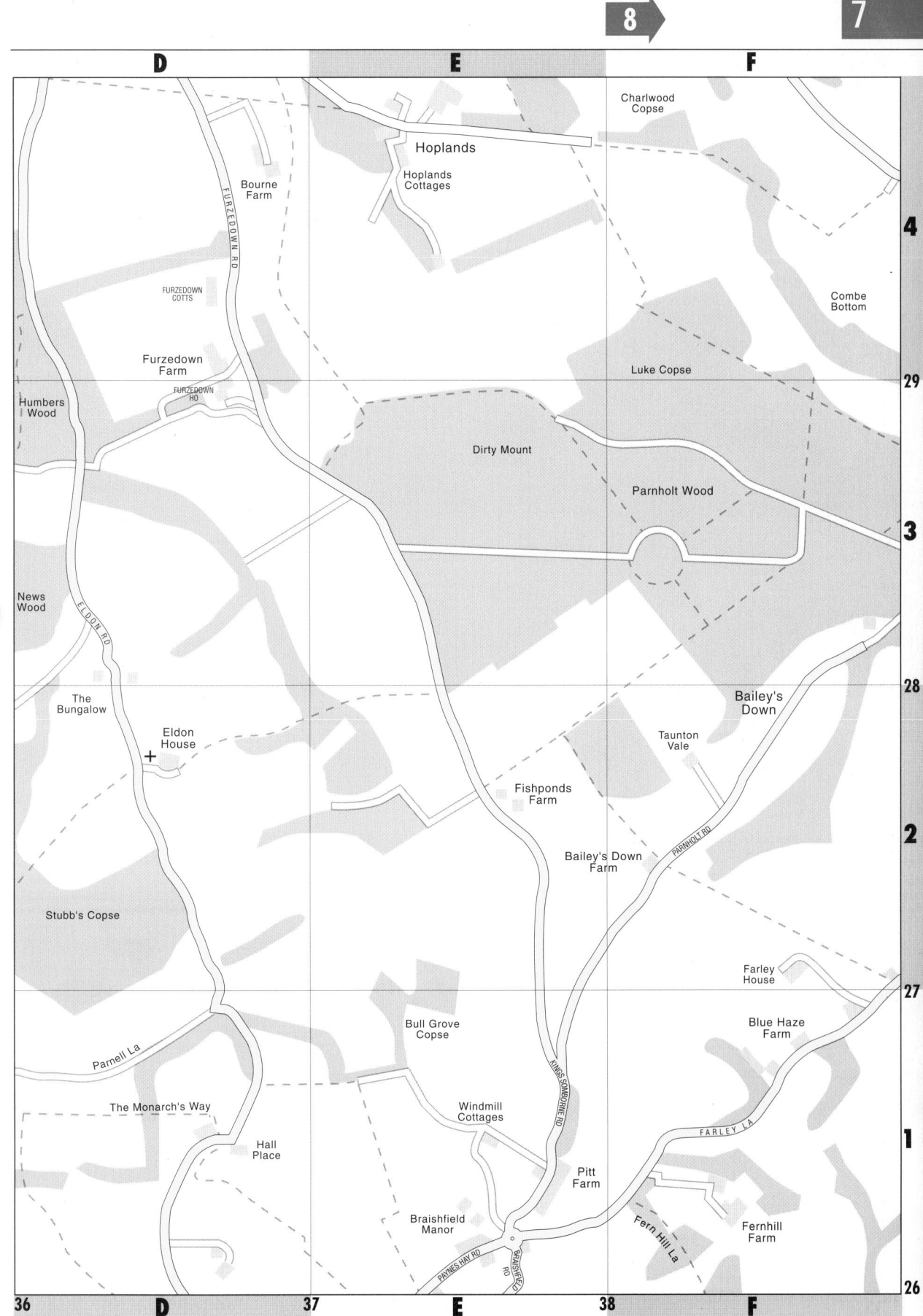

Charlwood
Copse

Hoplands

Hoplands
Cottages

4

Bourne
Farm

FURZEDOWN RD

Combe
Bottom

FURZEDOWN
COTTS

Luke Copse

29

Furzedown
Farm

FURZEDOWN
HO

Humbers
Wood

Dirty Mount

Parnholt Wood

3

News
Wood

ELDON RD

Bailey's
Down

28

The
Bungalow

Eldon
House

✛

Taunton
Vale

Fishponds
Farm

PARNHOLT RD

Bailey's Down
Farm

2

Stubb's Copse

Farley
House

27

Parnell La

Bull Grove
Copse

Blue Haze
Farm

The Monarch's Way

KINGS SOMBORNE RD

Windmill
Cottages

FARLEY LA

1

Hall
Place

Pitt
Farm

Fern Hill La

Fernhill
Farm

Braishfield
Manor

BRAISHFIELD RD

PAYNES HAY RD

26

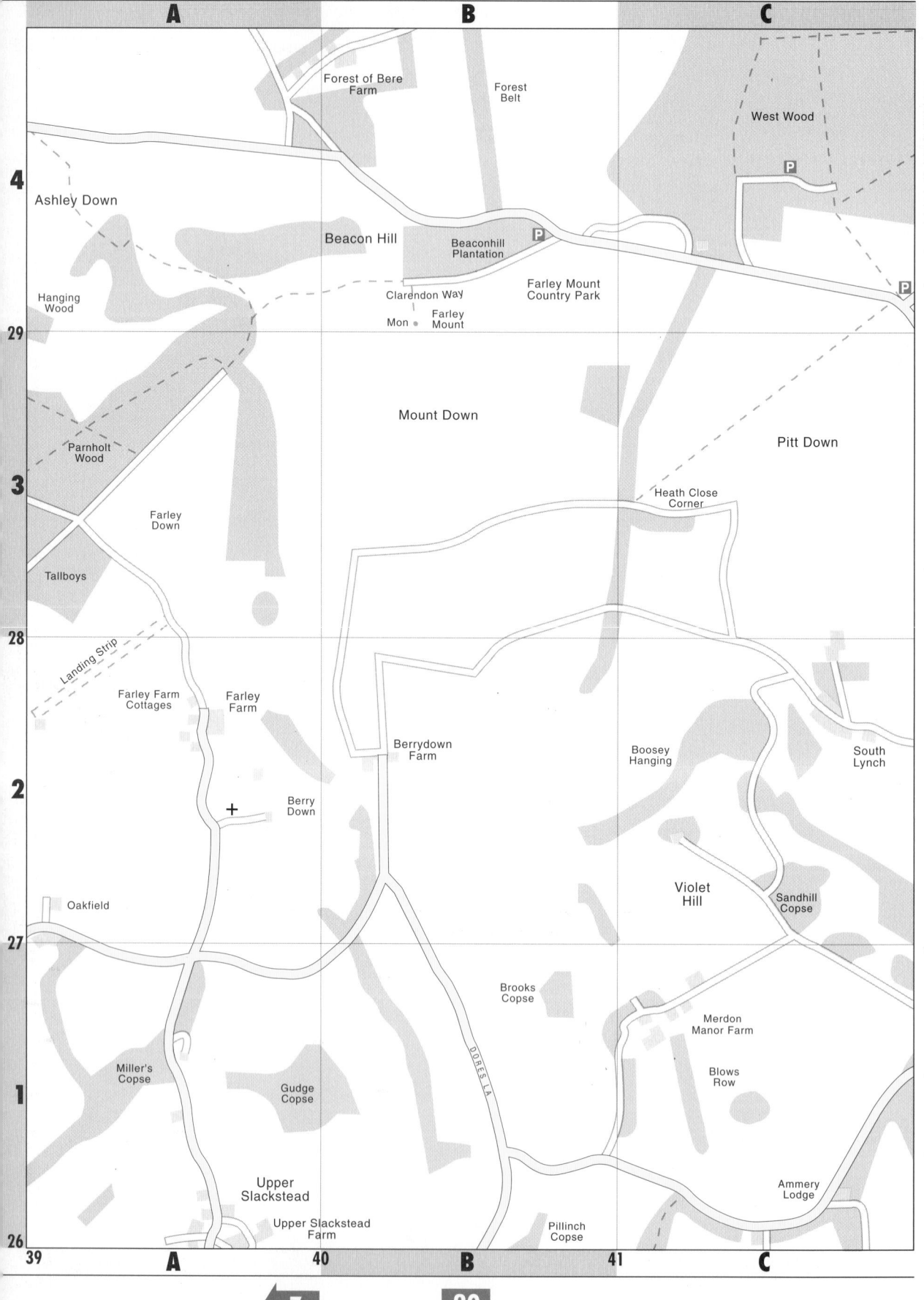

A   B   C

4

Ashley Down

Forest of Bere
Farm

Forest
Belt

West Wood

P

Beacon Hill

Beaconhill
Plantation

P

Farley Mount
Country Park

Hanging
Wood

P

Clarendon Way

Mon •

Farley
Mount

29

Mount Down

Pitt Down

Parnholt
Wood

3

Heath Close
Corner

Farley
Down

Tallboys

28

Landing Strip

Farley Farm
Cottages

Farley
Farm

Berrydown
Farm

Boosey
Hanging

South
Lynch

2

+

Berry
Down

Violet
Hill

Sandhill
Copse

Oakfield

27

Brooks
Copse

Merdon
Manor Farm

Miller's
Copse

Blows
Row

1

Gudge
Copse

DORES LA

Ammery
Lodge

Upper
Slackstead

Upper Slackstead
Farm

Pillinch
Copse

26

39   A   40   B   41   C

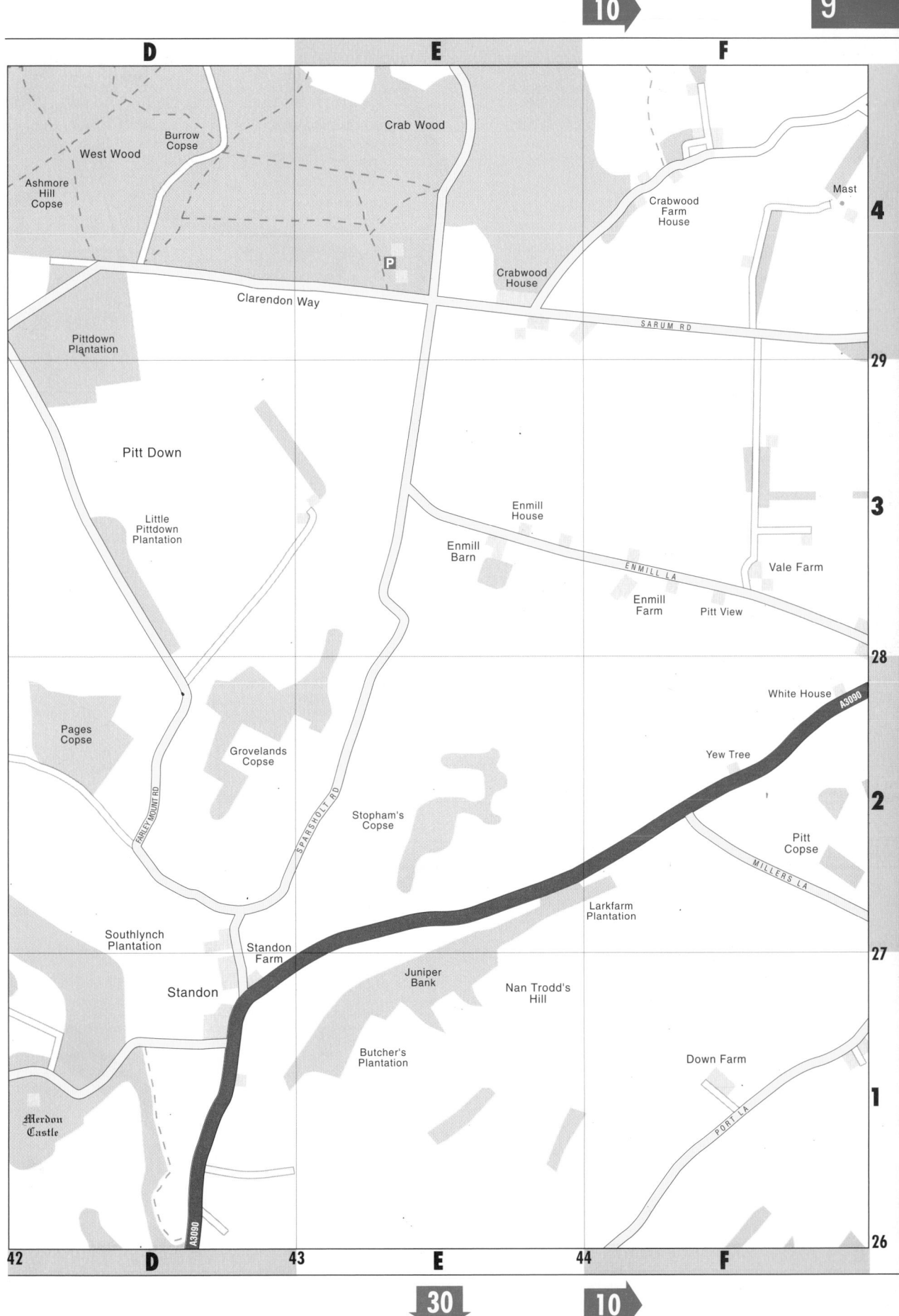

West Wood

Burrow
Copse

Crab Wood

Ashmore
Hill
Copse

Crabwood
Farm
House

Mast

4

P

Crabwood
House

Clarendon Way

SARUM RD

Pittdown
Plantation

29

Pitt Down

Little
Pittdown
Plantation

Enmill
House

3

Enmill
Barn

ENMILL LA

Vale Farm

Enmill
Farm

Pitt View

28

White House

A3090

Pages
Copse

Grovelands
Copse

Yew Tree

2

FARLEYMOUNT RD

SPARSHOLT RD

Stopham's
Copse

Pitt
Copse

MILLERS LA

Larkfarm
Plantation

Southlynch
Plantation

Standon
Farm

27

Standon

Juniper
Bank

Nan Trodd's
Hill

Butcher's
Plantation

Down Farm

1

Merdon
Castle

PORT LA

A3090

26

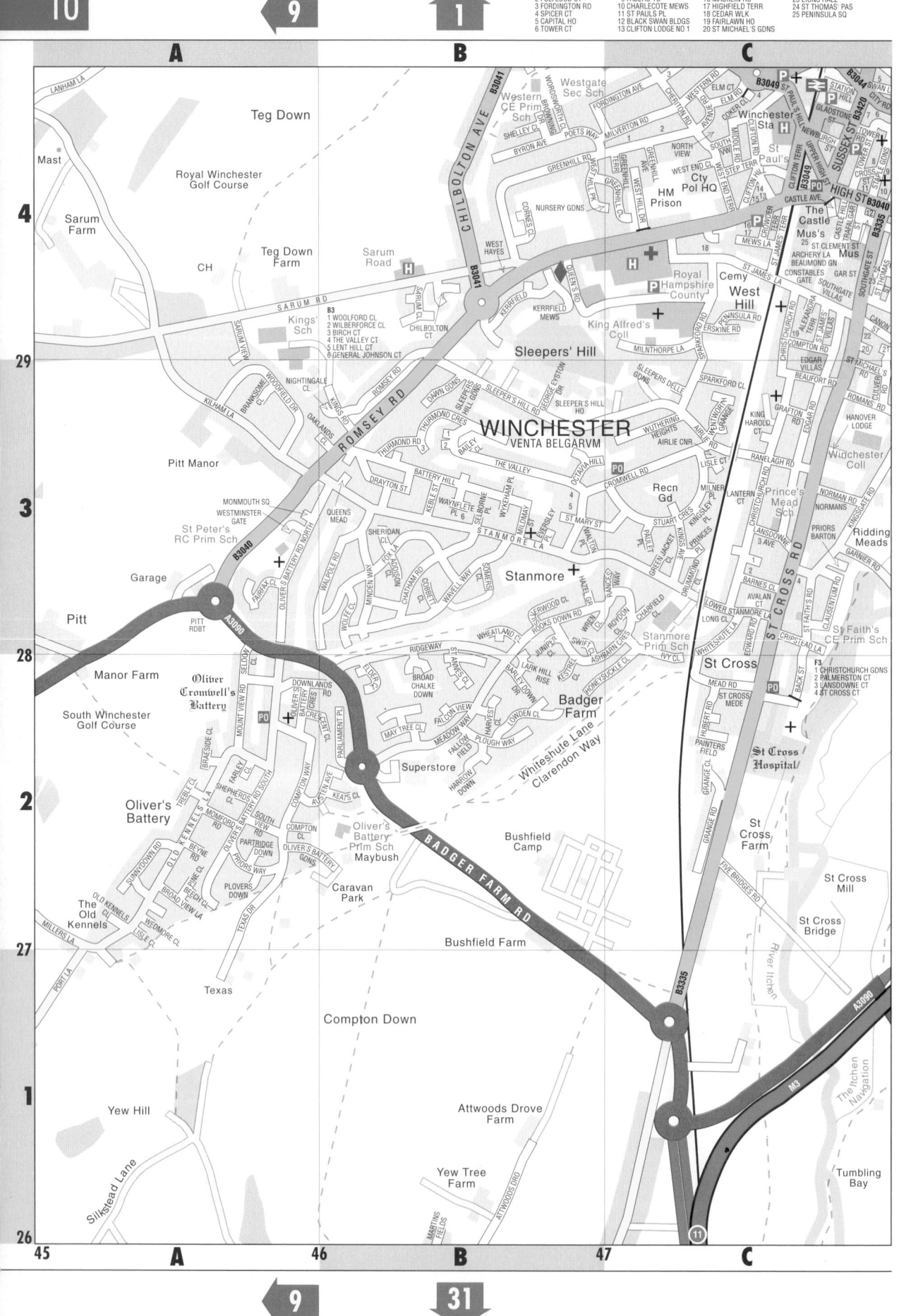

D4	7 PRINCESS CT	14 GODSON HO	21 ST JOHN'S HOSPITAL (N)	28 CULVER RD	D4	47 EASTON LANE BSNS PK	D4	
1 HOMERISE HO	8 PARK HO	15 GARDEN LA	22 CROSS KEYS PAS	29 CULVER MEWS	35 ST MARY MAGDALEN ALMSHOUSES		41 MAGDALEN MEWS	**11**
2 ARLINGTON PL	9 MERCHANTS PL	16 LAWN ST	23 ST CLEMENT ST	30 PASTERNOSTER ROW	36 WATERSMEET		42 MILDMAY CT	
3 MATILDA PL	10 PRINCE'S BLDGS	17 LAWN ST	24 ST THOMAS ST	31 PATERNOSTER HO	37 CHESIL TERR		43 ITCHEN CT	
4 DANEMARK CT	11 COSSACK LA	18 WINDSOR HO	25 KINGS HEAD YD	32 ST JOHN'S HOSPITAL (S)	38 THE CONSERVATORY		44 RIVERSIDE HO	
5 DE LUNN BLDGS	12 LOWER BROOK ST	19 GREYFRIARS	26 LITTLE MINSTER ST	33 HIGH ST	39 CHILCOMBE HTS		45 PARMITER HO	
6 RICHARD MOSS HO	13 COSSACK LANE HO	20 TANNER ST	27 MINSTER LA	34 BRIDGE ST	40 EARLSDOWN		46 COLSON CL	

2 **12**

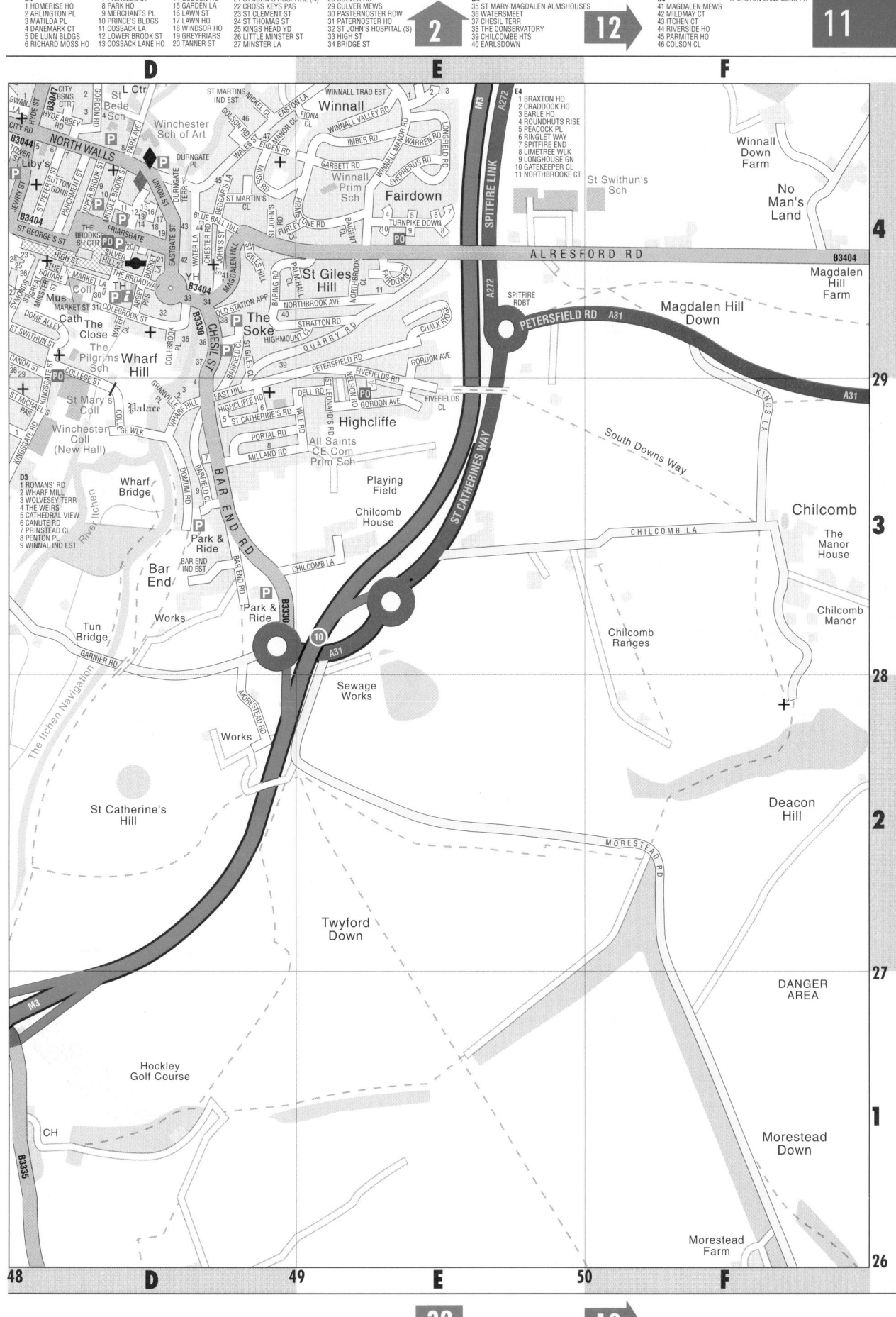

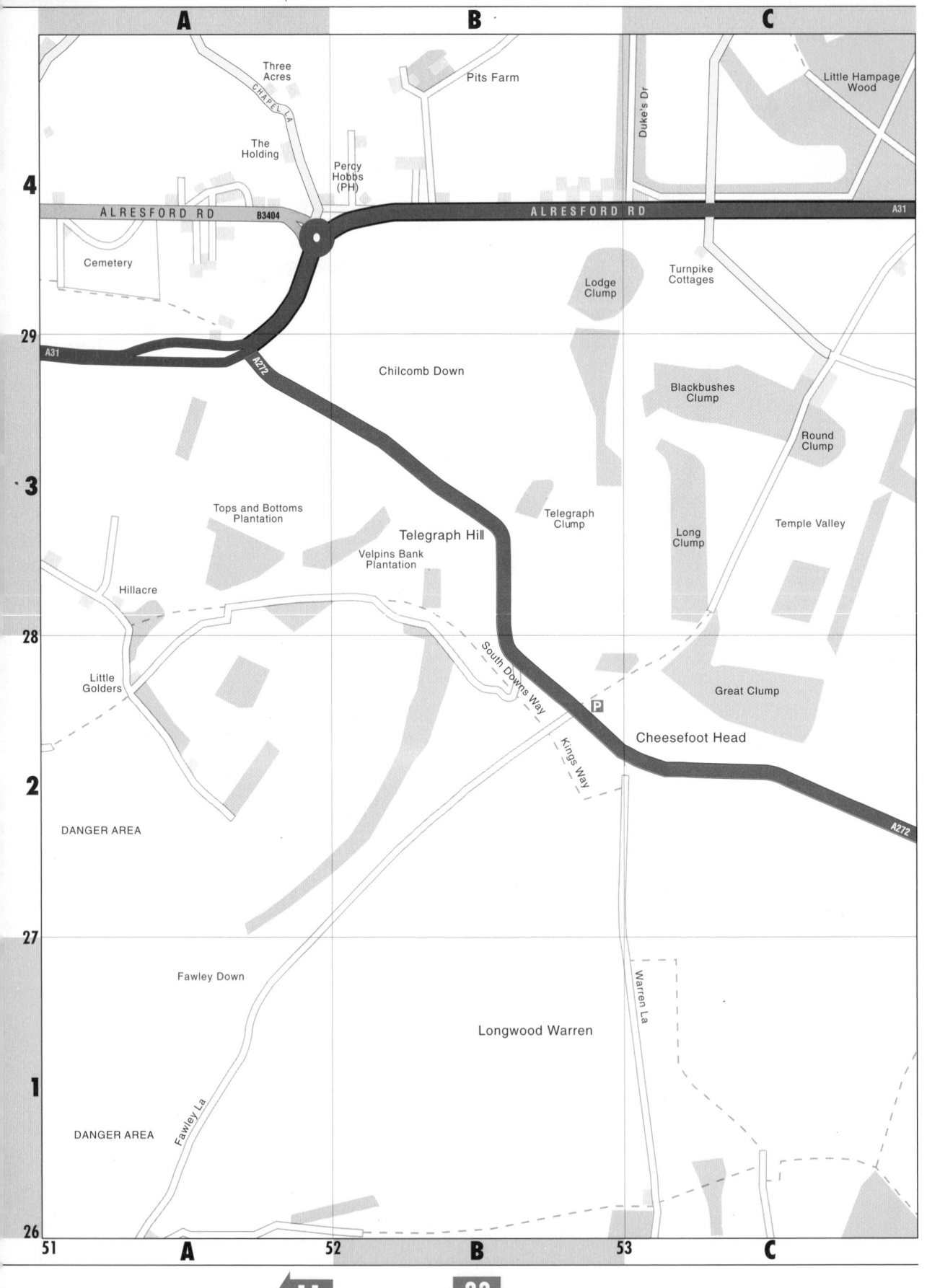

A   B   C

4

Three
Acres

CHAPEL LA

The
Holding

Percy
Hobbs
(PH)

Pits Farm

Duke's Dr

Little Hampage
Wood

ALRESFORD RD   B3404   ALRESFORD RD   A31

Cemetery

Lodge
Clump

Turnpike
Cottages

29

A31

A272

Chilcomb Down

Blackbushes
Clump

Round
Clump

3

Tops and Bottoms
Plantation

Velpins Bank
Plantation

Telegraph Hill

Telegraph
Clump

Long
Clump

Temple Valley

Hillacre

South Downs Way

28

Little
Golders

P

Great Clump

Cheesefoot Head

2

DANGER AREA

Kings Way

A272

27

Fawley Down

Warren La

Longwood Warren

1

DANGER AREA

Fawley La

26

51   A   52   B   53   C

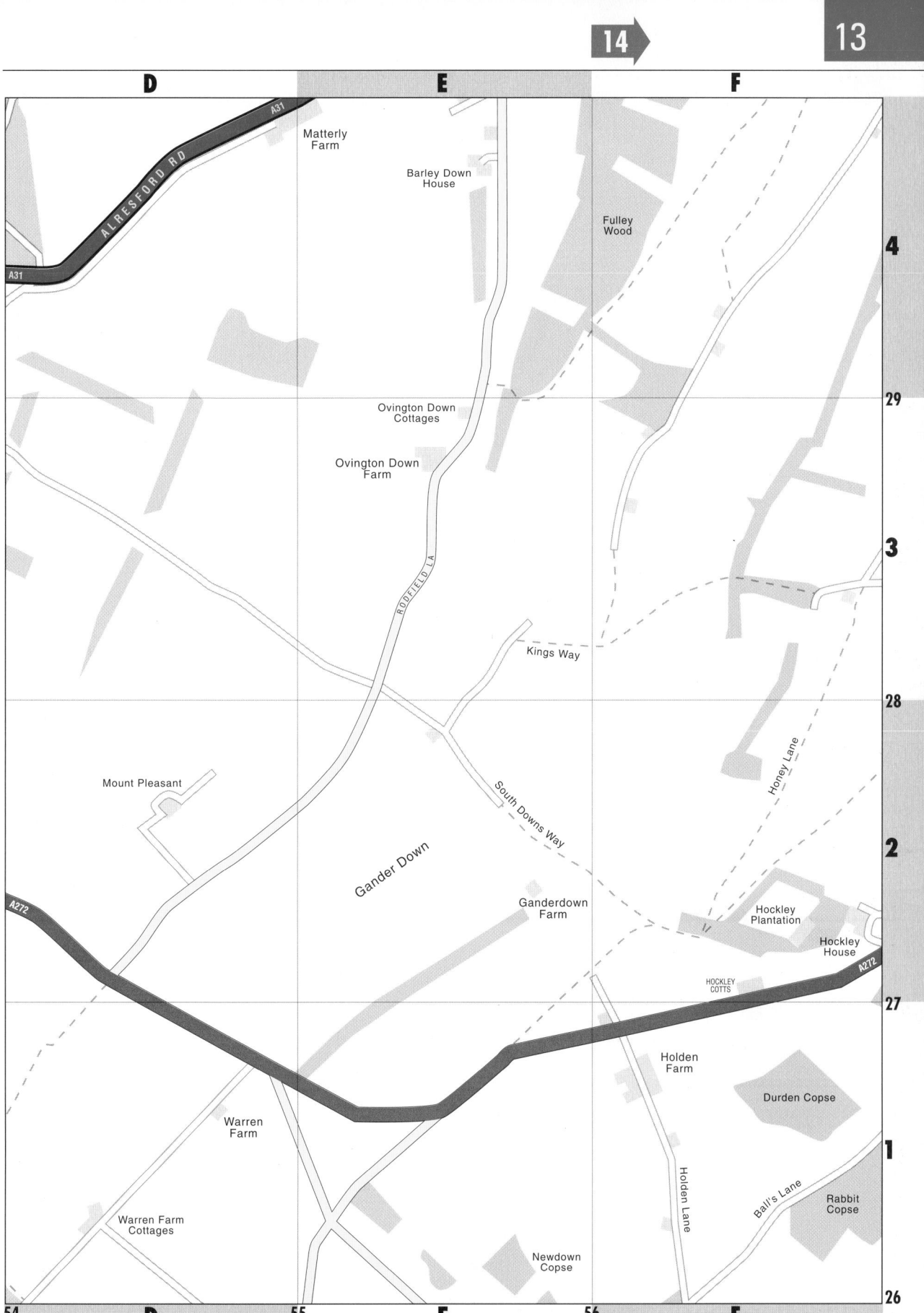

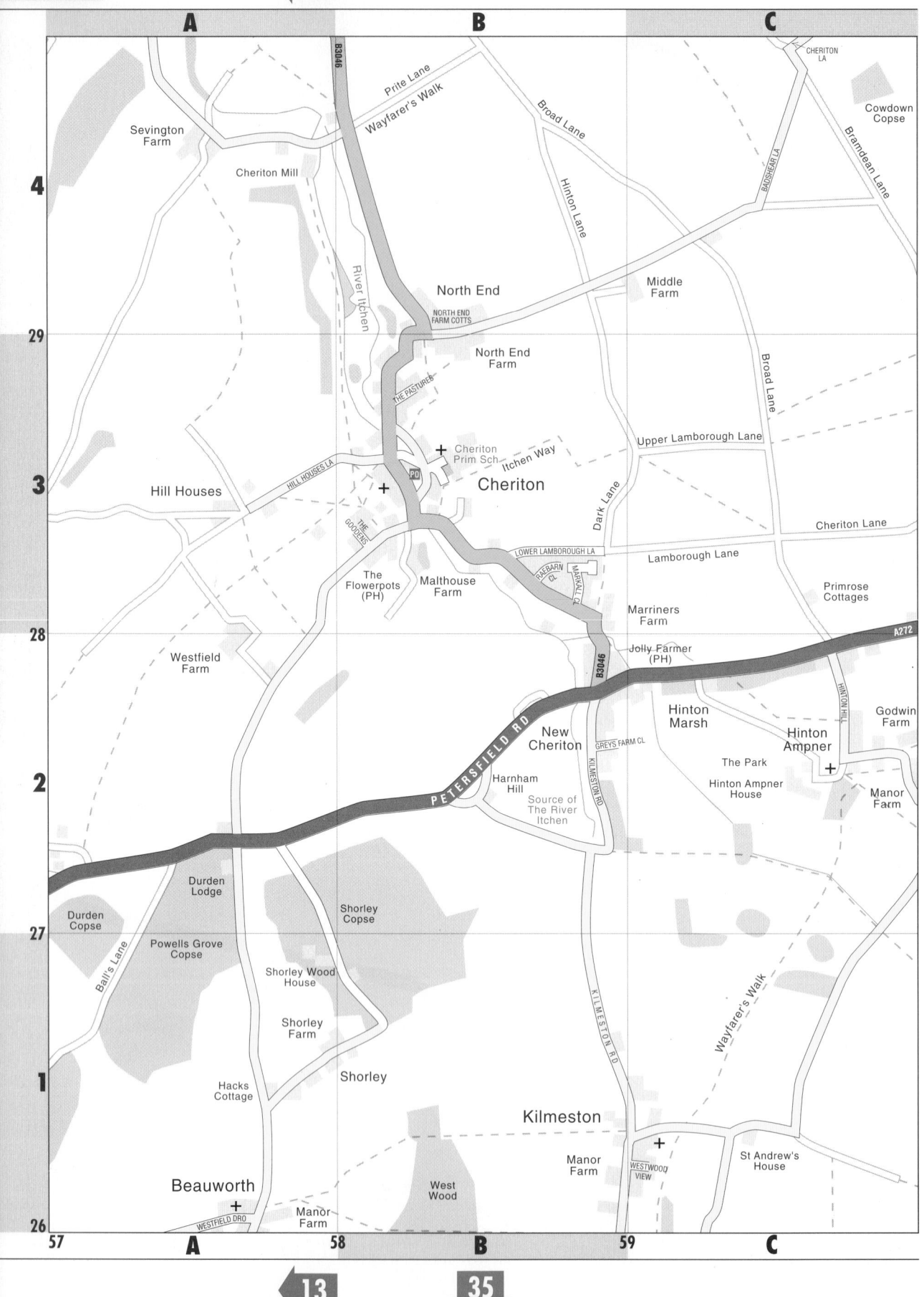

A B C

4

29

3

28

2

27

1

26

57 58 59

A B C

Sevington Farm
Cheriton Mill
Prite Lane
Wayfarer's Walk
Broad Lane
Hinton Lane
B3046
River Itchen
North End
NORTH END FARM COTTS
North End Farm
Middle Farm
Broad Lane
BADSHEAR LA
Bramdean Lane
CHERITON LA
Cowdown Copse
THE PASTURES
HILL HOUSES LA
Hill Houses
Cheriton Prim Sch
PO
Itchen Way
Cheriton
Upper Lamborough Lane
Dark Lane
Cheriton Lane
THE GOODENS
The Flowerpots (PH)
Malthouse Farm
LOWER LAMBOROUGH LA
RAEBARN CL
MARKALL CL
Lamborough Lane
Marriners Farm
Primrose Cottages
Westfield Farm
B3046
Jolly Farmer (PH)
A272
New Cheriton
PETERSFIELD RD
GREYS FARM CL
Hinton Marsh
Hinton Ampner
Godwin Farm
Hinton Hill
Harnham Hill
Source of The River Itchen
KILMESTON RD
The Park
Hinton Ampner House
Manor Farm
Durden Lodge
Shorley Copse
Ball's Lane
Durden Copse
Powells Grove Copse
Shorley Wood House
Shorley Farm
Shorley
Wayfarer's Walk
Hacks Cottage
Kilmeston
Beauworth
WESTFIELD DRO
Manor Farm
West Wood
Manor Farm
WESTWOOD VIEW
St Andrew's House

16

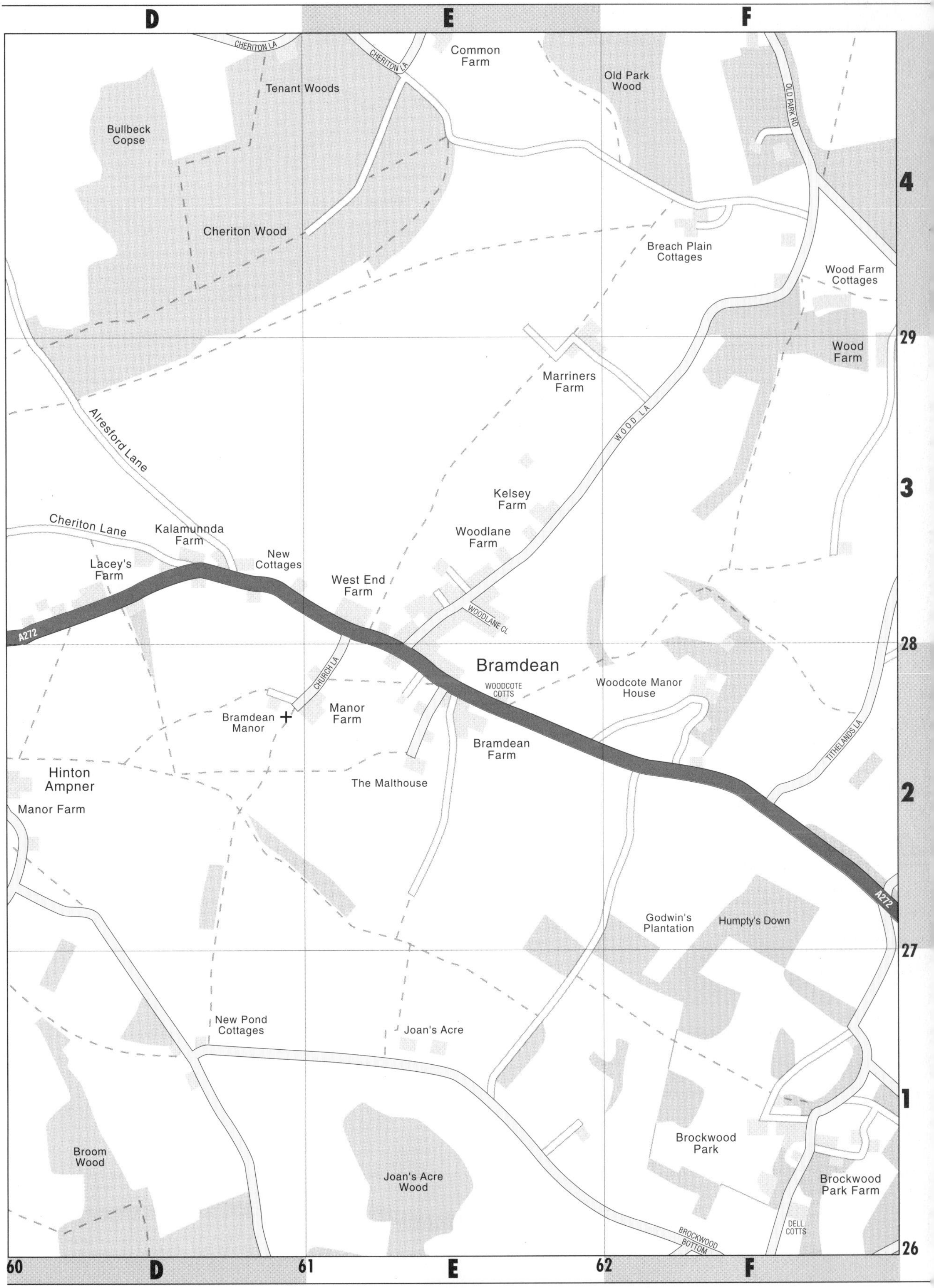
D
E
F
CHERITON LA
CHERITON LA
Common Farm
Tenant Woods
Old Park Wood
OLD PARK RD
Bullbeck Copse
4
Cheriton Wood
Breach Plain Cottages
Wood Farm Cottages
29
Wood Farm
Marriners Farm
Alresford Lane
WOOD LA
3
Kelsey Farm
Woodlane Farm
Cheriton Lane
Kalamunnda Farm
New Cottages
Lacey's Farm
West End Farm
WOODLANE CL
A272
28
Bramdean
CHURCH LA
WOODCOTE COTTS
Woodcote Manor House
Bramdean Manor
Manor Farm
Bramdean Farm
TITHELANDS LA
Hinton Ampner
The Malthouse
2
Manor Farm
A272
Godwin's Plantation
Humpty's Down
27
New Pond Cottages
Joan's Acre
1
Brockwood Park
Broom Wood
Joan's Acre Wood
Brockwood Park Farm
DELL COTTS
BROCKWOOD BOTTOM
26
60
D
61
E
62
F

36

16

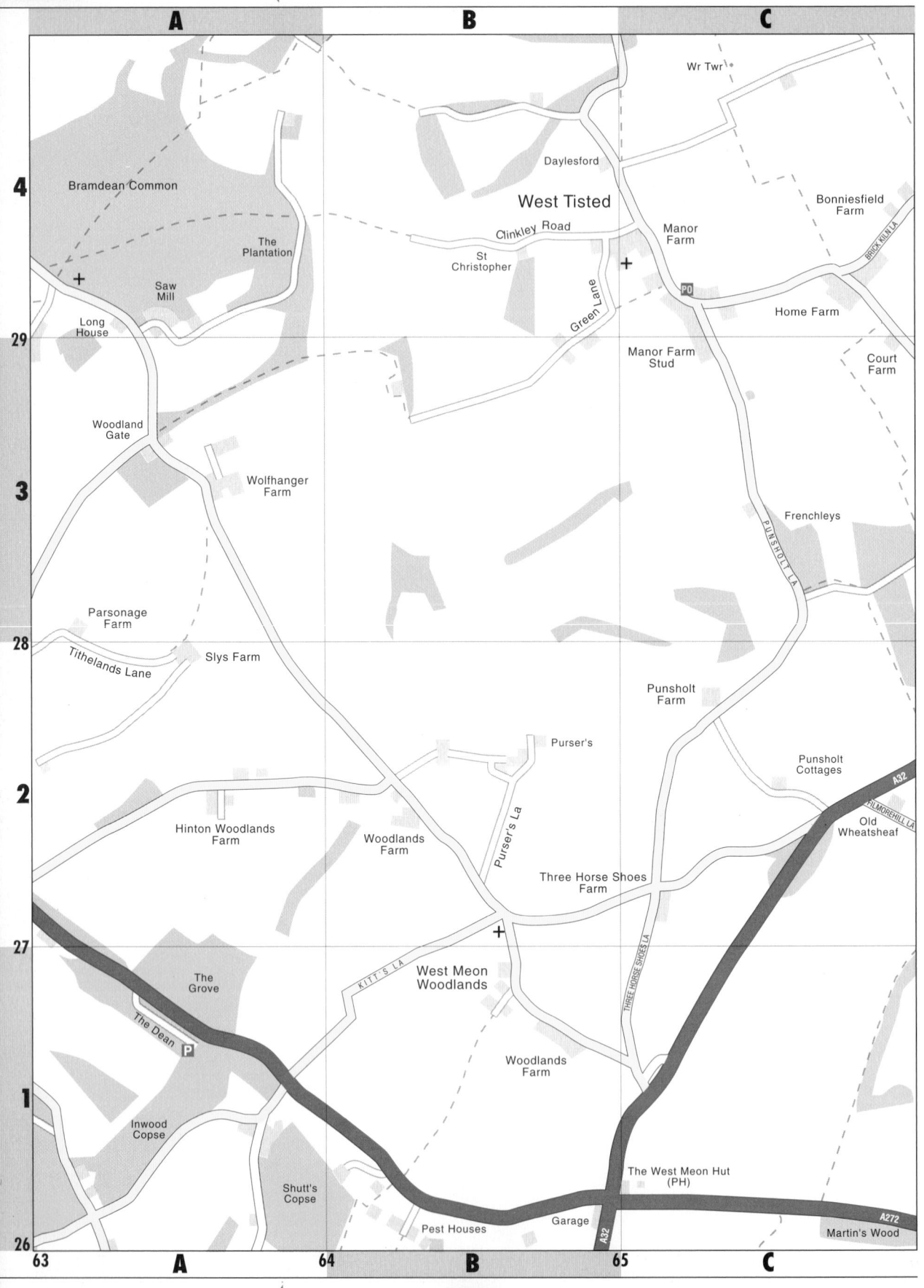

A   B   C

Wr Twr

Bramdean Common

Daylesford

West Tisted

4

The Plantation

Clinkley Road

Manor Farm

Bonniesfield Farm

St Christopher

BRICK KILN LA

Saw Mill

Green Lane

Home Farm

Long House

29

Manor Farm Stud

Court Farm

Woodland Gate

Wolfhanger Farm

3

Frenchleys

PUNSHOLT LA

Parsonage Farm

28

Punsholt Farm

Tithelands Lane

Slys Farm

Purser's

Punsholt Cottages

2

A32

Hinton Woodlands Farm

Woodlands Farm

Purser's La

Old Wheatsheaf

FILMOREHILL LA

Three Horse Shoes Farm

27

THREE HORSE SHOES LA

The Grove

KITT'S LA

West Meon Woodlands

The Dean

P

1

Inwood Copse

Woodlands Farm

The West Meon Hut (PH)

Shutt's Copse

A32

A272

Pest Houses

Garage

Martin's Wood

26

63   A   64   B   65   C

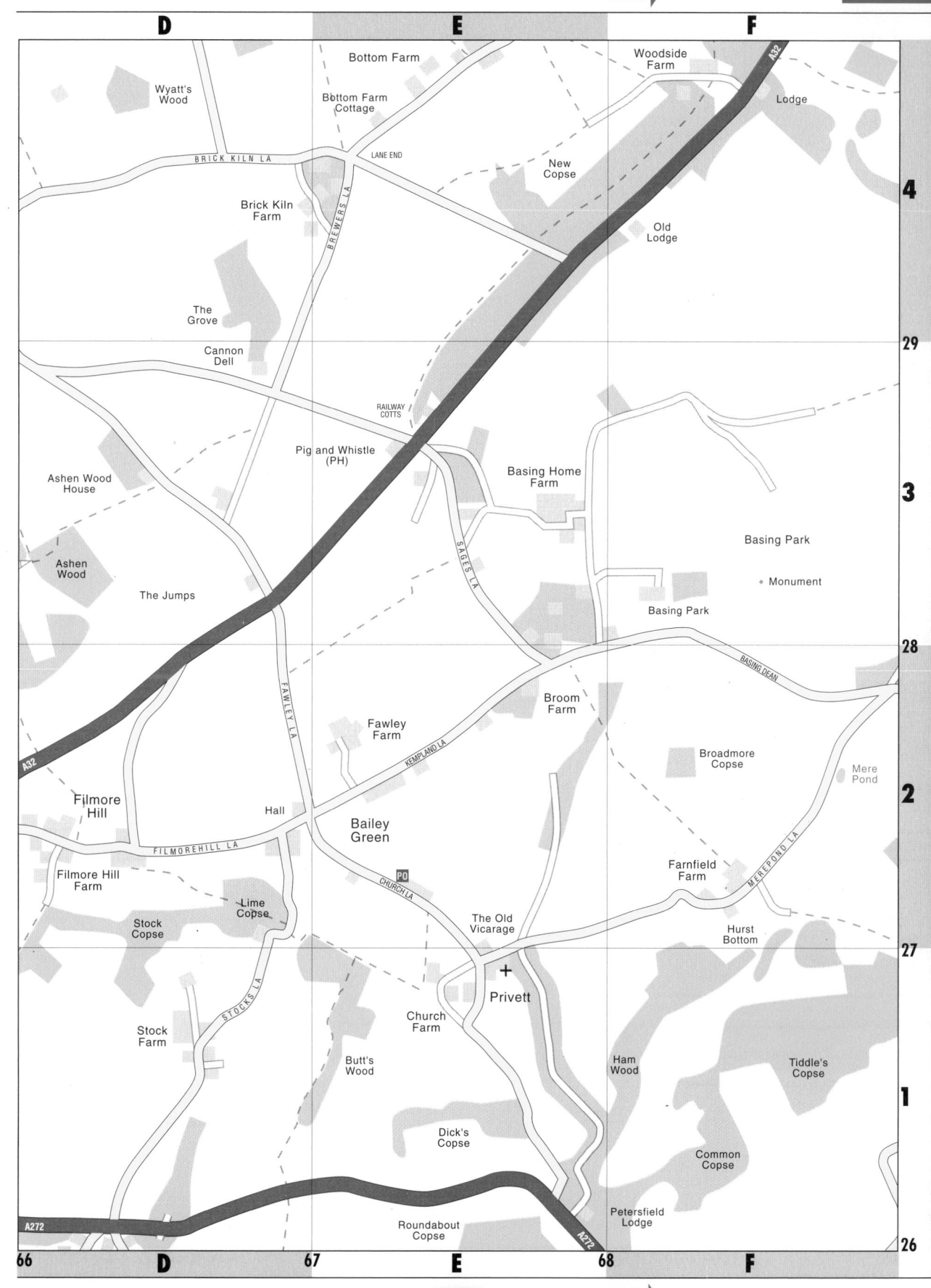

D   E   F

Wyatt's Wood

Bottom Farm

Woodside Farm

A32

Lodge

Bottom Farm Cottage

BRICK KILN LA

LANE END

New Copse

4

Brick Kiln Farm

BREWERS LA

Old Lodge

The Grove

29

Cannon Dell

RAILWAY COTTS

Pig and Whistle (PH)

Basing Home Farm

3

Ashen Wood House

SAGES LA

Basing Park

Monument

Ashen Wood

The Jumps

Basing Park

28

BASING DEAN

FAWLEY LA

Fawley Farm

Broom Farm

Broadmore Copse

Mere Pond

KEMPLAND LA

A32

Filmore Hill

Hall

Bailey Green

2

MEREPOND LA

Filmore Hill Farm

FILMOREHILL LA

PO

Farnfield Farm

CHURCH LA

Lime Copse

Hurst Bottom

Stock Copse

The Old Vicarage

27

STOCKS LA

✚ Privett

Stock Farm

Church Farm

Butt's Wood

Ham Wood

Tiddle's Copse

1

Dick's Copse

Common Copse

A272

Petersfield Lodge

A272

Roundabout Copse

26

66   D   67   E   68   F

17

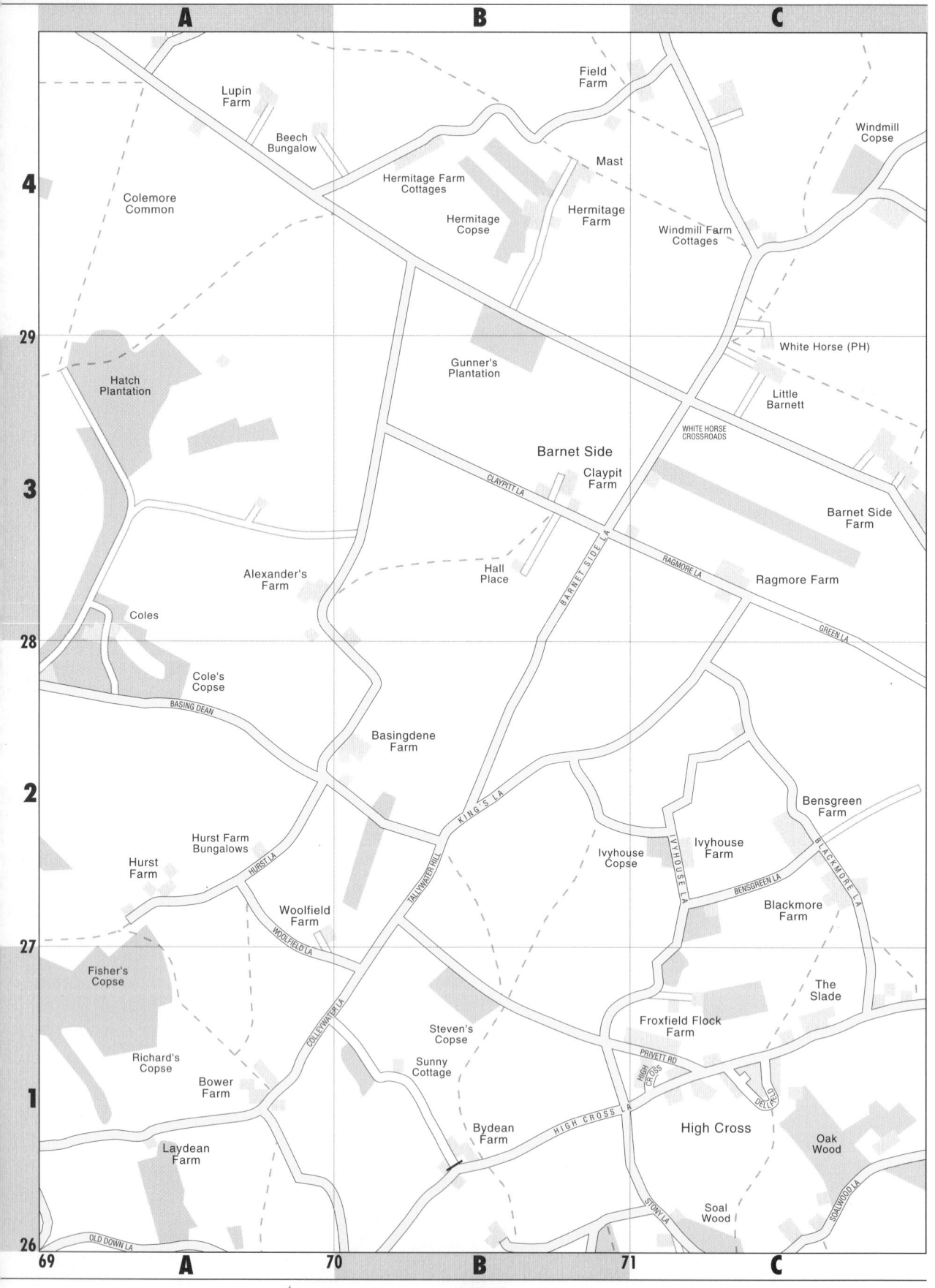

17

39

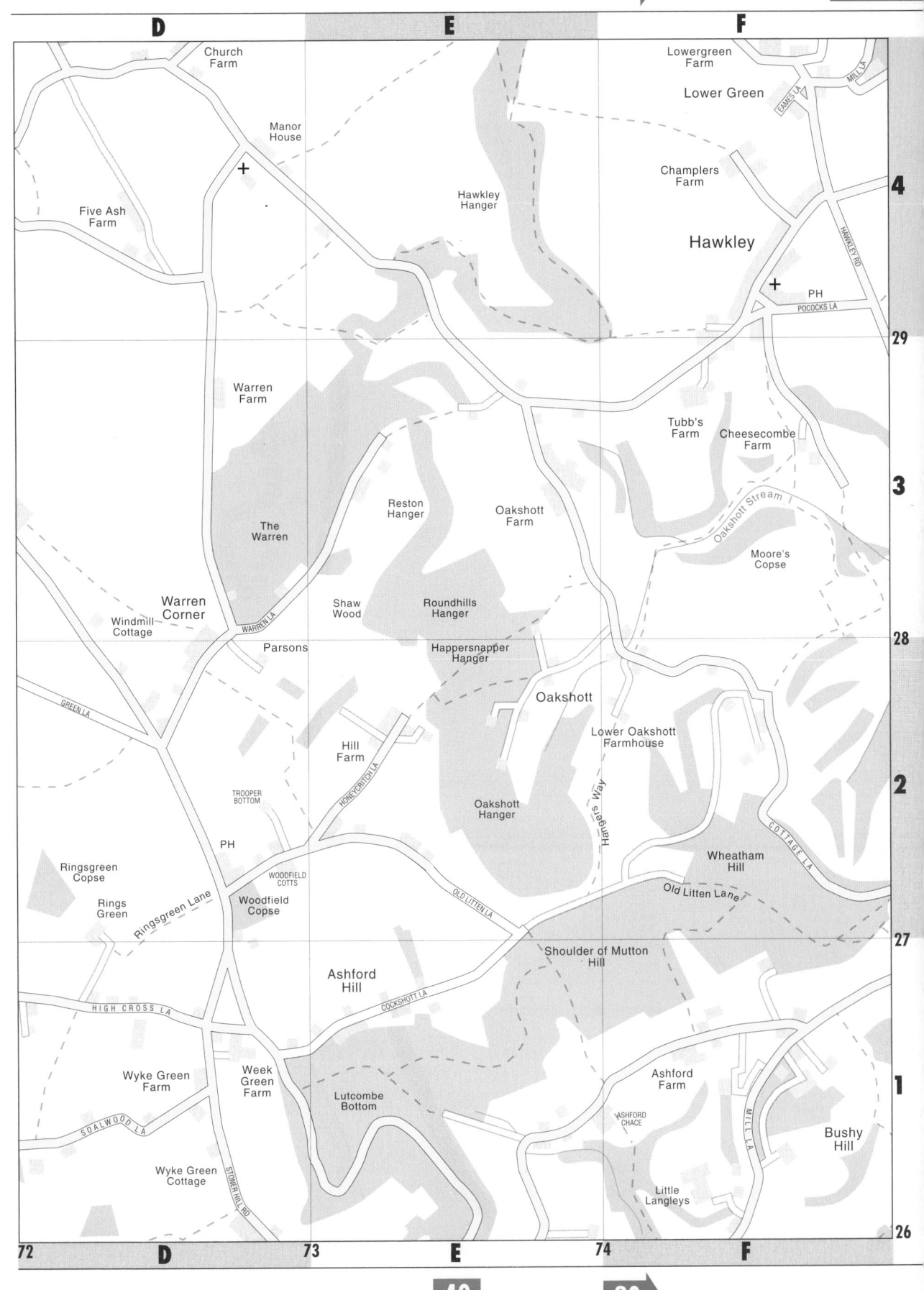

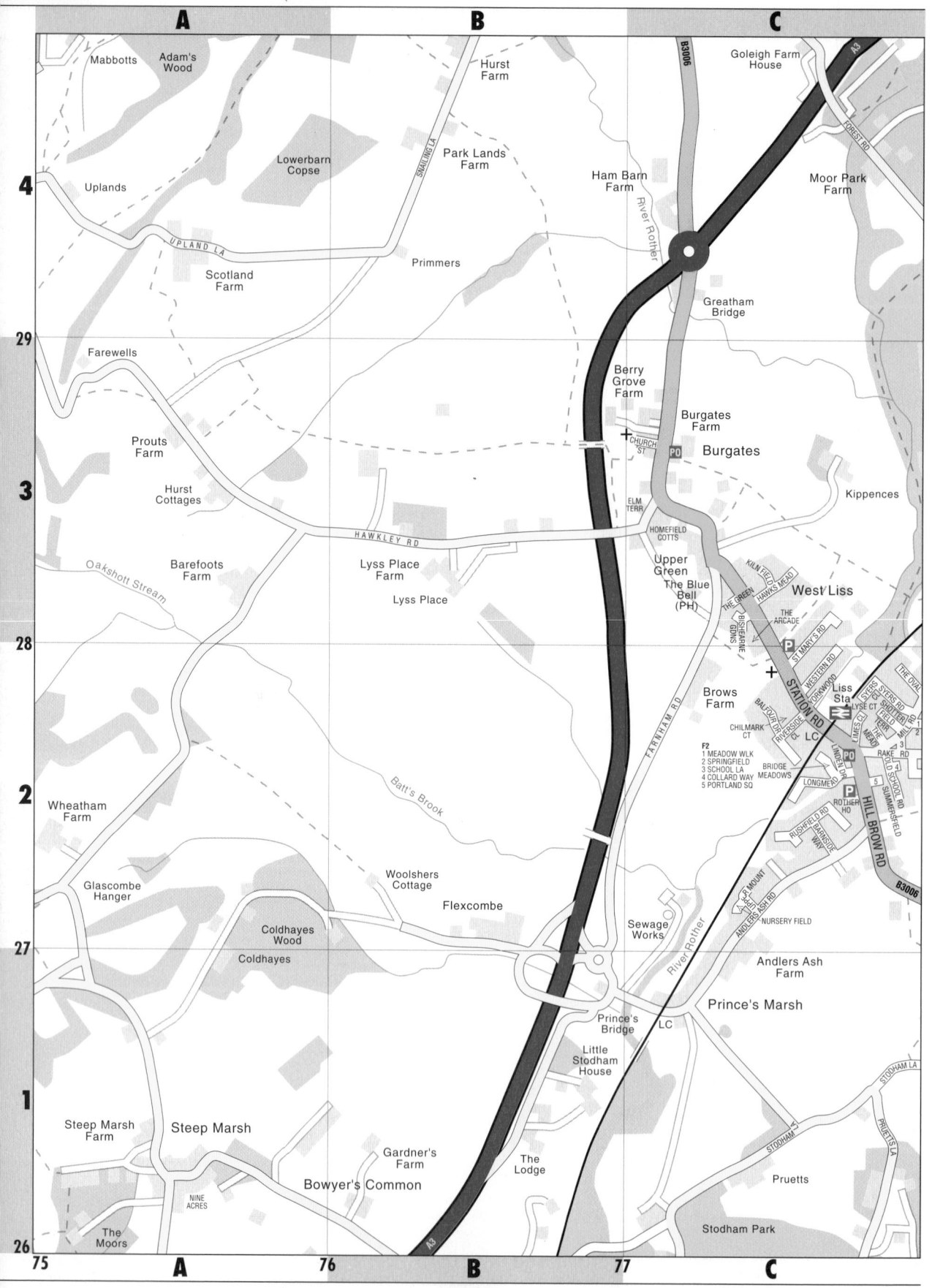

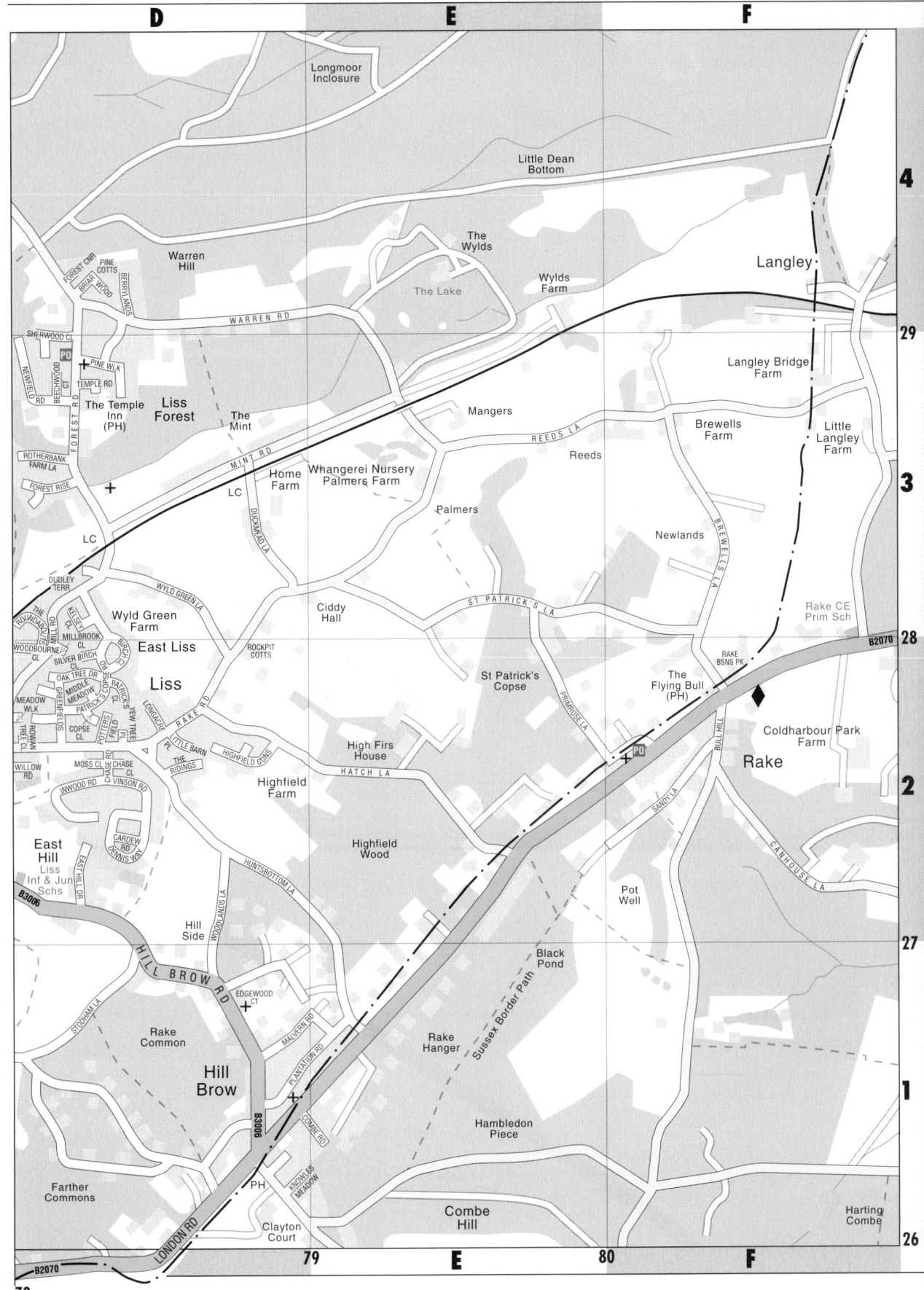

D　　　　　E　　　　　F

4

Longmoor
Inclosure

Little Dean
Bottom

The Wylds

Langley

Warren
Hill

The Lake

Wylds
Farm

29

WARREN RD

Langley Bridge
Farm

SHERWOOD CL

PINE WLK

Mangers

REEDS LA

Brewells
Farm

Little
Langley
Farm

The Temple
Inn (PH)

Liss
Forest

The
Mint

Reeds

ROTHERBANK
FARM LA

MINT RD

Whangerei Nursery
Palmers Farm

Home
Farm

Newlands

3

FOREST RISE

LC

Palmers

Rake CE
Prim Sch

LC

DUCKMEAD LA

BREWELLS LA

DUDLEY
TERR

WYLD GREEN LA

Ciddy
Hall

St Patrick's La

Wyld Green
Farm

Rake
BSNS PK

B2070

28

East Liss

ROCKPIT
COTTS

Liss

St Patrick's
Copse

The
Flying Bull
(PH)

RAKE RD

PRIMROSE LA

Coldharbour Park
Farm

High Firs
House

PO

Rake

HATCH LA

2

East
Hill

Highfield
Farm

Highfield
Wood

SANDY LA

PUB HILL

CANHOUSE LA

Liss
Inf & Jun
Schs

HUNTSBOTTOM LA

Pot
Well

B3006

27

Hill
Side

Black
Pond

HILL BROW RD

Sussex Border Path

STODHAM LA

EDGEWOOD
CT

Rake
Common

MALVERN RD

Rake
Hanger

1

Hill
Brow

PLANTATION RD

B3006

COMBE RD

Hambledon
Piece

Harting
Combe

Farther
Commons

PH

KNOWLES MEADOW

Combe
Hill

26

LONDON RD

Clayton
Court

B2070

78　　　　　79　　　　　E　　　　　80　　　　　F

A B C

The White Hart
(PH)

THE STYLES

Bishopstone

THE CROFT

NETTON CL.

NETTON ST.

STANLEY CL.

BUTT LA.

PH

Faulston House

FLAMSTONE ST.

MILL LA.

FAULSTON
COTTS

Flamstone Farm

River Ebble

Faulston

4

Croucheston
Farm

Corn Mill

Throope Hill

Throope
Bottom
Cottages

Croucheston

25

Faulston Hole

Croucheston Hollow

Faulston Drove

3

Bishopstone Hollow

Faulston Down

24

Croucheston Drove

2

A354

Faulston Down
Farm

Ox Drove

Knighton High
Wood

Croucheston Down
Farm

23

Toyd
Clump

Knighton Wood
Farm

1

Garage

Croucheston Down

Trinity House

Swayne's
Firs

Grim's Ditch

22

Granary

06 A 07 B 08 C

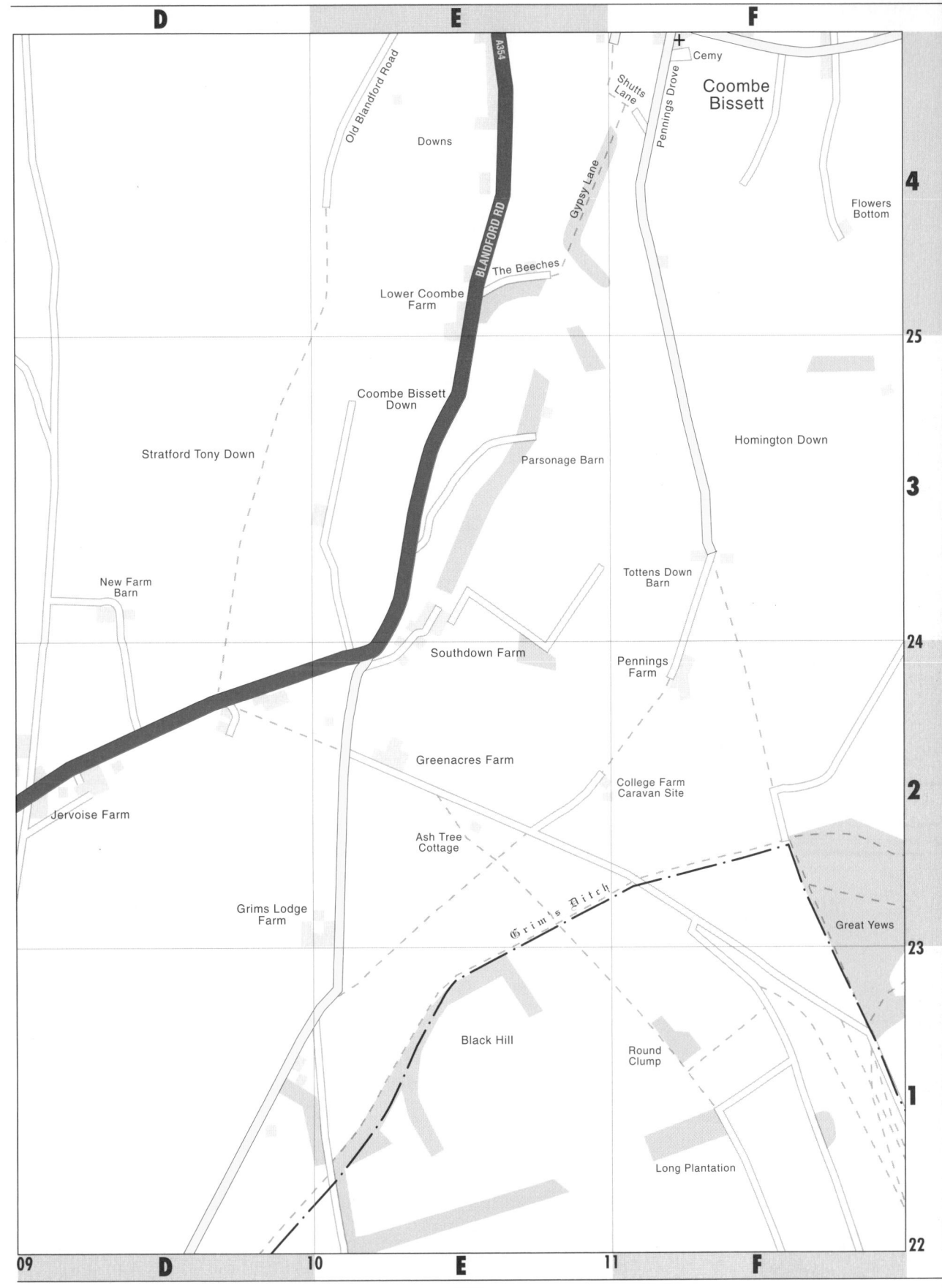

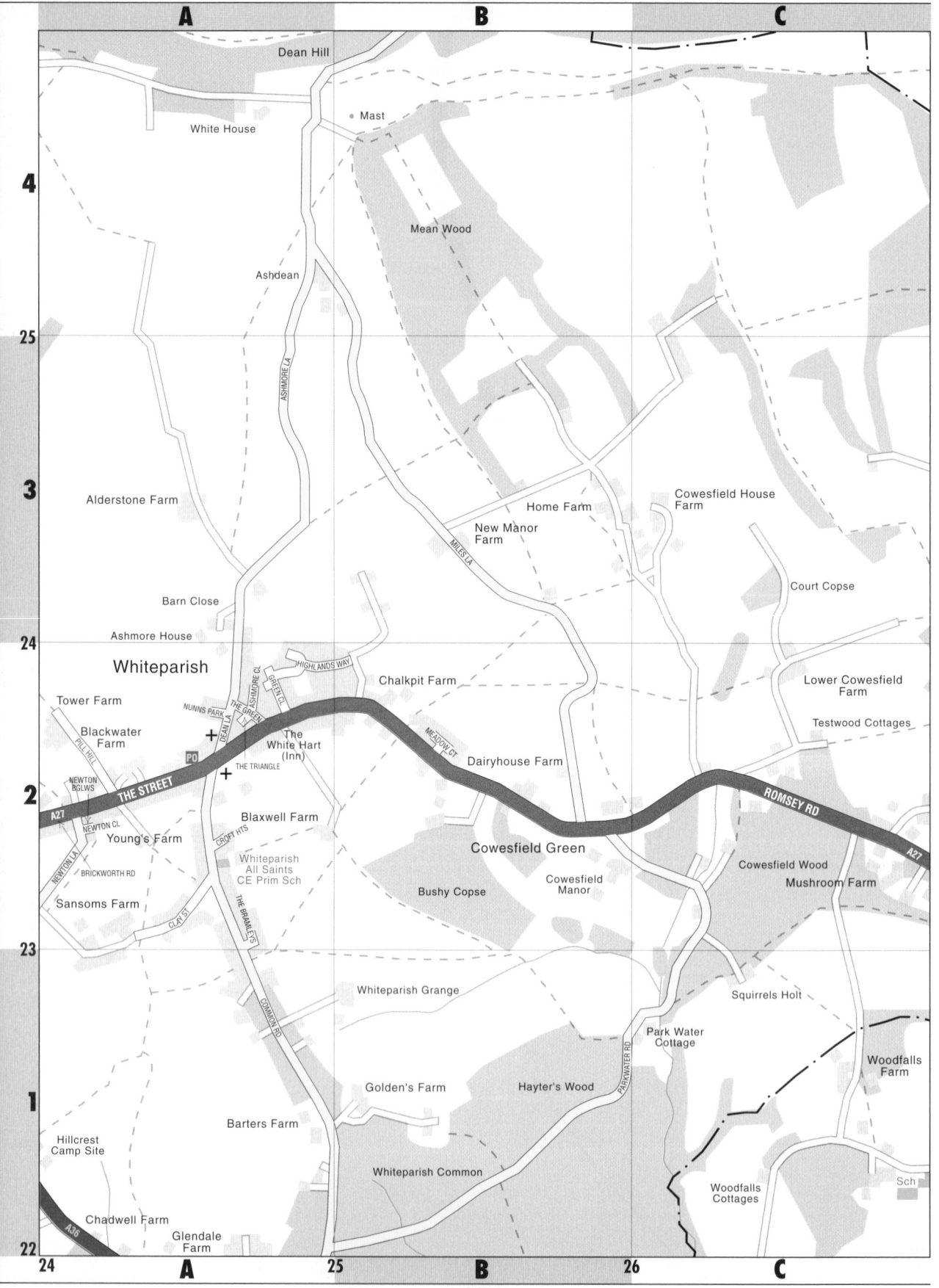

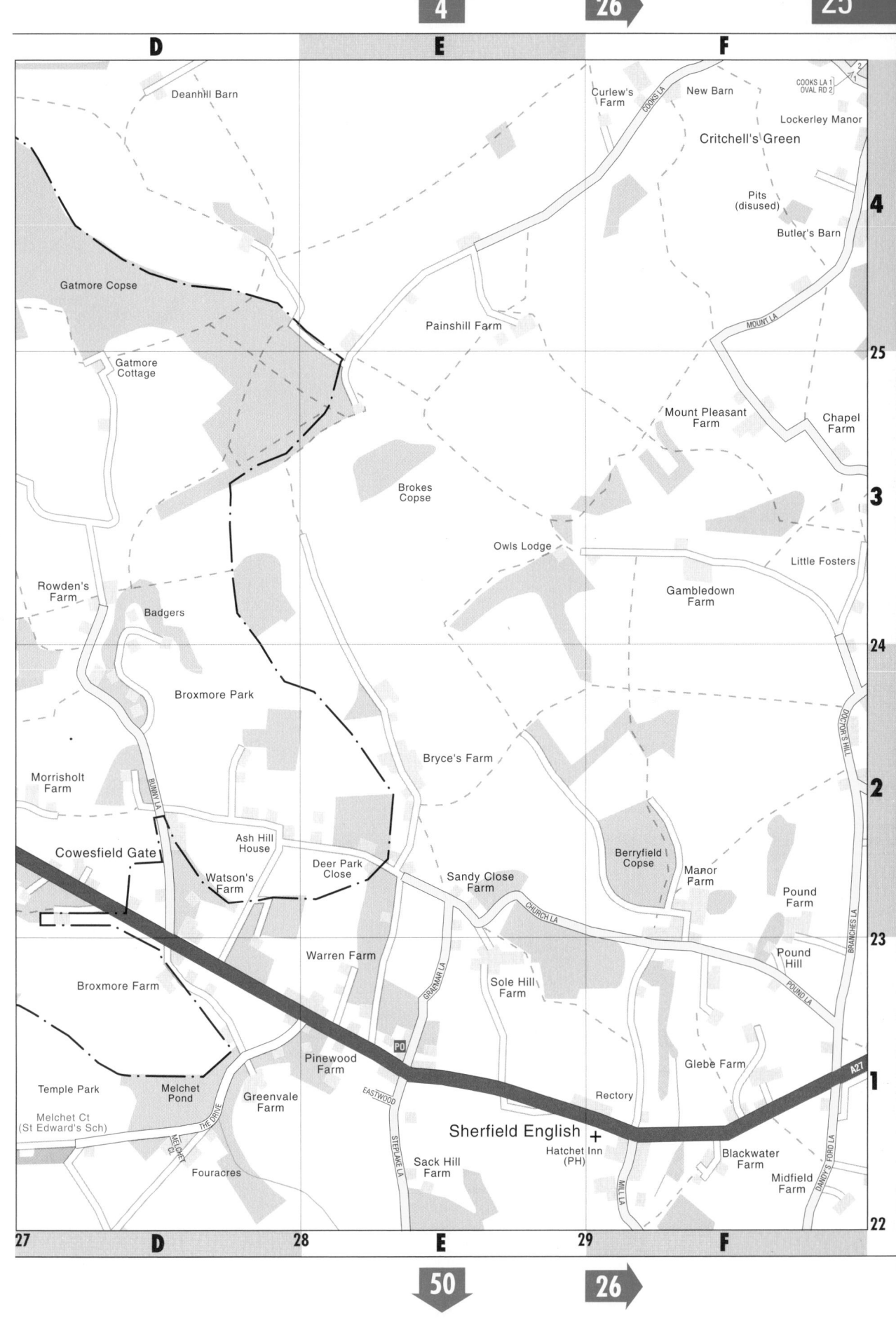

D

E

F

Deanhill Barn

Curlew's Farm

New Barn

COOKS LA 1
OVAL RD 2

Lockerley Manor

Critchell's Green

COOKS LA

Pits
(disused)

4

Butler's Barn

Gatmore Copse

MOUNT LA

25

Gatmore Cottage

Painshill Farm

Mount Pleasant Farm

Chapel Farm

Brokes Copse

3

Owls Lodge

Little Fosters

Rowden's Farm

Gambledown Farm

Badgers

24

Broxmore Park

DOCTOR'S HILL

Bryce's Farm

2

Morrisholt Farm

BUNNY LA

Berryfield Copse

Manor Farm

Pound Farm

Cowesfield Gate

Ash Hill House

Deer Park Close

Sandy Close Farm

BRANCHES LA

Watson's Farm

CHURCH LA

23

Warren Farm

Pound Hill

Broxmore Farm

GRAMMAR LA

Sole Hill Farm

POUND LA

A27

Pinewood Farm

PO

Glebe Farm

1

Temple Park

Melchet Pond

THE DRIVE

Greenvale Farm

EASTWOOD

Rectory

Sherfield English ✚

Blackwater Farm

DANDY'S FORD LA

Melchet Ct
(St Edward's Sch)

MELCHET CT

Hatchet Inn
(PH)

MILL LA

Midfield Farm

Fouracres

STEPLAKE LA

Sack Hill Farm

27

D

28

E

29

F

22

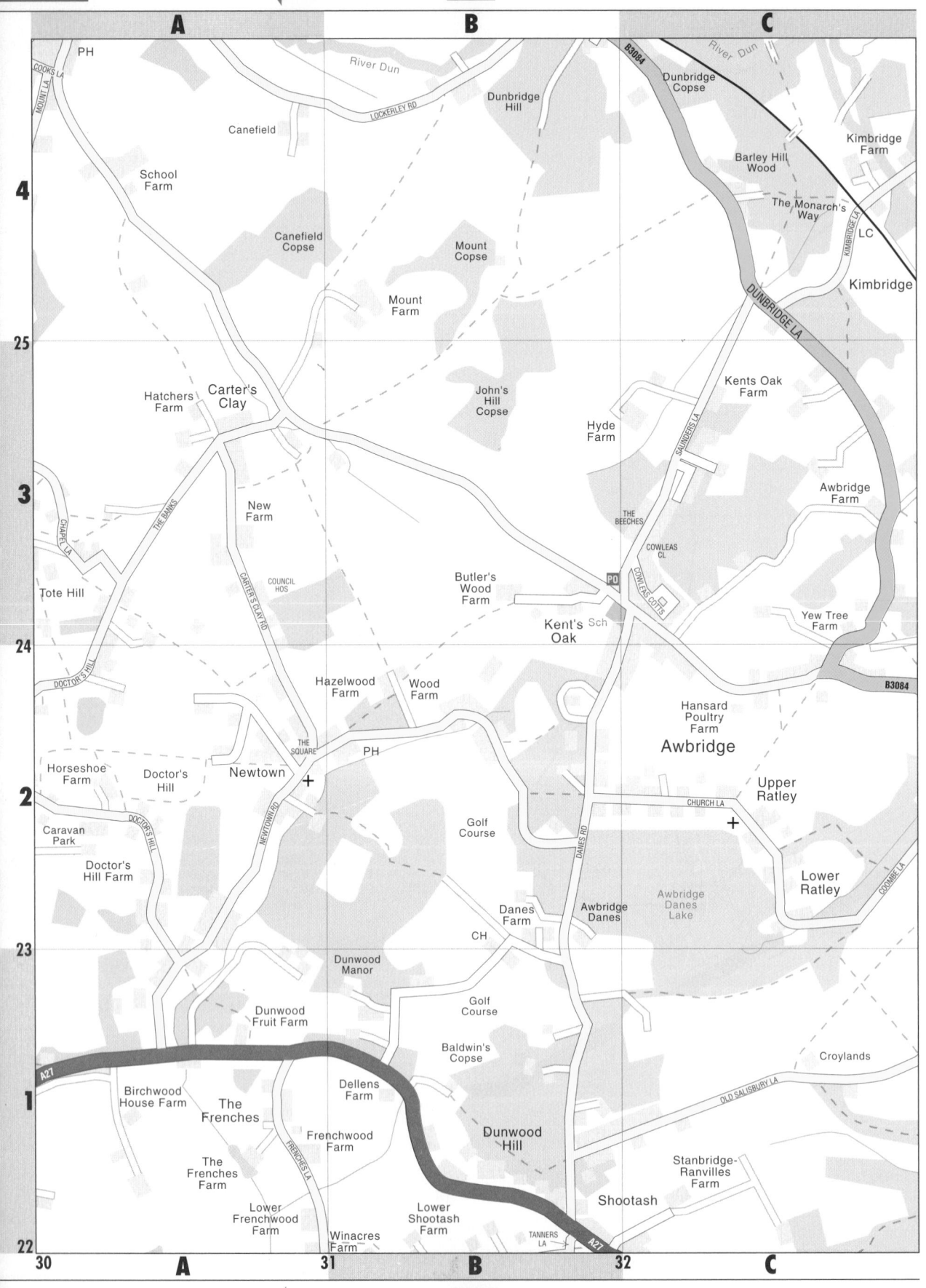

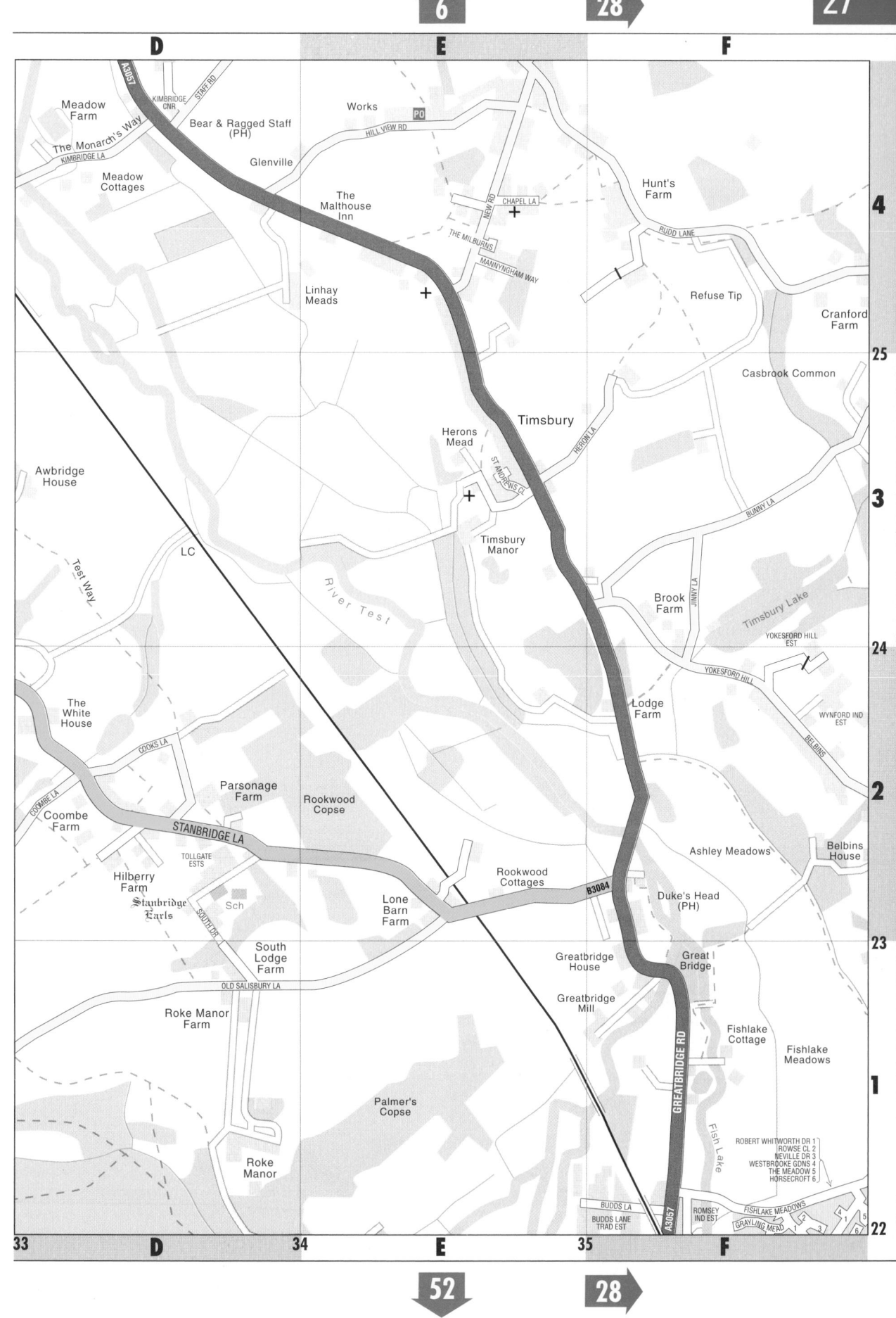

Meadow Farm
The Monarch's Way
KIMBRIDGE LA
Meadow Cottages

A3057
KIMBRIDGE CNR
STAFF RD
Bear & Ragged Staff (PH)
Glenville

The Malthouse Inn

Linhay Meads

Works
HILL VIEW RD
PO
NEW RD
CHAPEL LA
THE MILBURNS
MANNYNGHAM WAY

Hunt's Farm
RUDD LANE

Refuse Tip

Cranford Farm

Casbrook Common

4

25

Awbridge House

Test Way

LC

River Test

Herons Mead
ST ANDREWS CL

Timsbury

Timsbury Manor

HERON LA

Brook Farm

JINNY LA

Timsbury Lake

YOKESFORD HILL EST

YOKESFORD HILL

BUNNY LA

3

24

The White House
COOKS LA
COOMBE LA

Coombe Farm

Parsonage Farm

Rookwood Copse

STANBRIDGE LA
TOLLGATE ESTS

Hilberry Farm
Stanbridge Earls
Sch
SOUTH DR

South Lodge Farm
OLD SALISBURY LA

Roke Manor Farm

Lone Barn Farm

Rookwood Cottages

B3084

Lodge Farm

WYNFORD IND EST

BELBINS

Ashley Meadows

Belbins House

Duke's Head (PH)

Greatbridge House

Greatbridge Mill

Great Bridge

GREATBRIDGE RD

Fishlake Cottage

Fishlake Meadows

2

23

Palmer's Copse

Roke Manor

Fish Lake

ROBERT WHITWORTH DR 1
ROWSE CL 2
NEVILLE DR 3
WESTBROOKE GDNS 4
THE MEADOW 5
HORSECROFT 6

1

BUDDS LA
BUDDS LANE TRAD EST

A3057

ROMSEY IND EST

FISHLAKE MEADOWS
GRAYLING MEAD

22

33 **D** **34** **E** **35** **F**

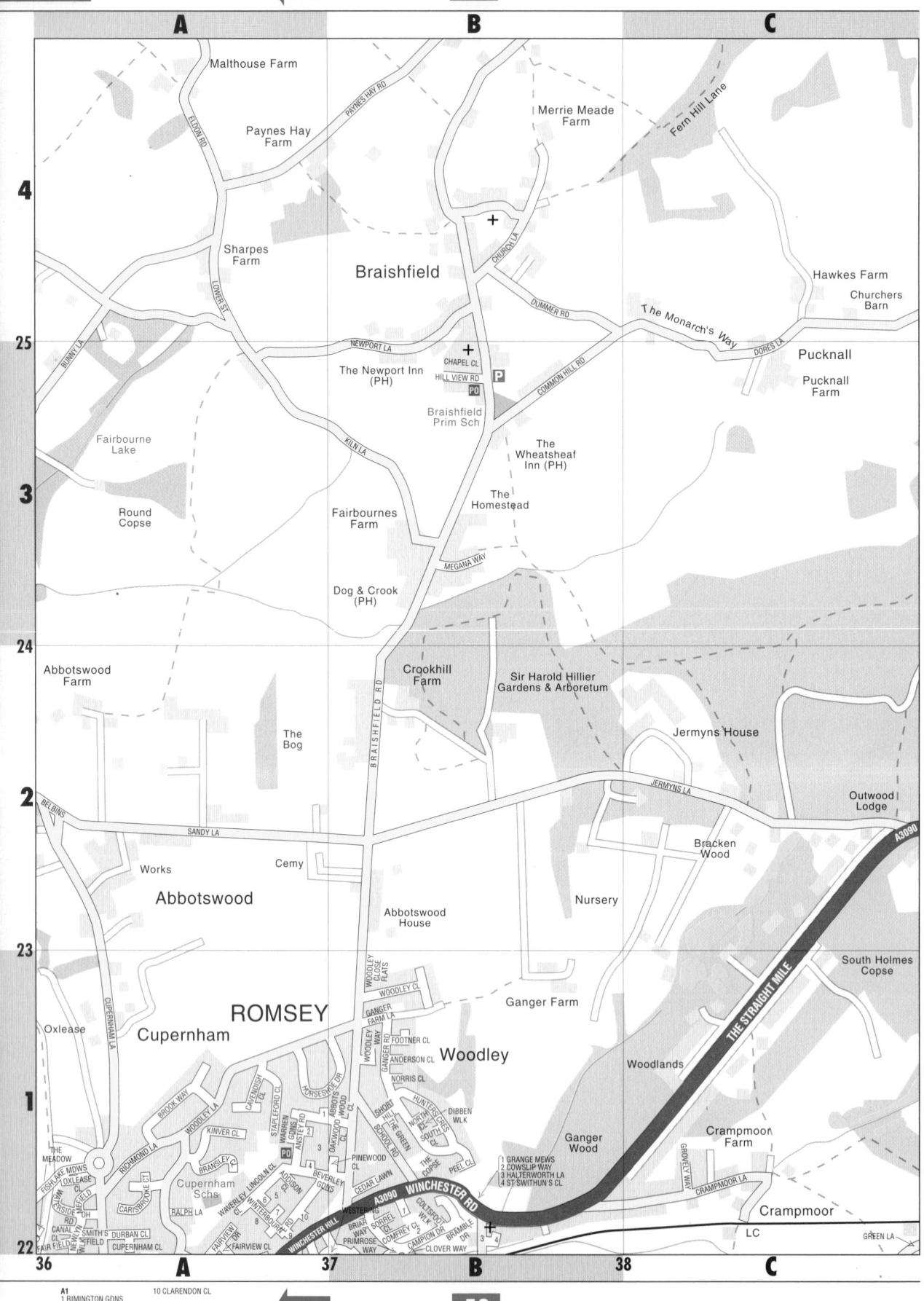

A
B
C

4

Malthouse Farm

Paynes Hay Farm

Merrie Meade Farm

Fern Hill Lane

ELDON RD

PAYNES HAY RD

Sharpes Farm

Braishfield

CHURCH LA

Hawkes Farm

Churchers Barn

DUMMER RD

The Monarch's Way

DORES LA

25

BUNNY LA

LOWER ST

NEWPORT LA

The Newport Inn (PH)

CHAPEL CL
HILL VIEW RD
P
PO

COMMON HILL RD

Pucknall

Pucknall Farm

Braishfield Prim Sch

Fairbourne Lake

KILN LA

The Wheatsheaf Inn (PH)

3

Round Copse

Fairbournes Farm

The Homestead

Dog & Crook (PH)

MEGANA WAY

24

Abbotswood Farm

BRAISHFIELD RD

Crookhill Farm

Sir Harold Hillier Gardens & Arboretum

The Bog

Jermyns House

2

BELBINS

SANDY LA

JERMYNS LA

Bracken Wood

Outwood Lodge

A3090

Works

Cemy

Abbotswood

Abbotswood House

Nursery

South Holmes Copse

23

CUPERNHAM LA

ROMSEY

Cupernham

WOODLEY CLOSE FLATS

WOODLEY CL

Ganger Farm

THE STRAIGHT MILE

Oxlease

BROOK WAY

WOODLEY LA

CAVENDISH CL

GANGER FARM LA

GANGER RD

FOOTNER CL

ANDERSON CL

NORRIS CL

Woodley

Woodlands

Ganger Wood

Crampmoor Farm

1

THE MEADOW

FISHLAKE MDWS

RICHMOND LA

KINVER CL

STAPLEFORD CL

WARREN GDNS

OAKWOOD

ABBOTS WOOD

SHORT

HUNTER CL
NORTH CL
SOUTH CL

DIBBEN WLK

THE GREEN

THE COPSE

PEEL CL

GROVELY WAY

CRAMPMOOR LA

Crampmoor

PO

BRAMLEY CL

CARISBROOKE

RALPH LA

BEVERLEY GDNS

PINEWOOD CL

CEDAR LAWN

SCHOOL RD

1 GRANGE MEWS
2 COWSLIP WAY
3 HALTERWORTH LA
4 ST SWITHUN'S CL

Cupernham Schs

DURBAN CL
CUPERNHAM CL

SMITH'S FIELD

WATERLEY

LINCOLN CL

ADDISON

WINTERBOURNE RD

FAIRVIEW DR

FAIRVIEW CL

WINCHESTER HILL

WESTERING

A3090 WINCHESTER RD

COLTSFOOT WLK

BRIAR WAY
SORREL CL
PRIMROSE WAY

COMFREY CL

CAMPION DR

BRAMBLE DR

CLOVER WAY

LC

GREEN LA

22

36
A
37
B
38
C

A1
1 RIMINGTON GDNS
2 HALDEN CL
3 SELBORNE CT
4 TAVISTOCK CL
5 WINCHESTER CT
6 SUTHERLAND CL
7 HOGARTH CL
8 WOODLANDS GDNS
9 SAVERNAKE CL

10 CLARENDON CL

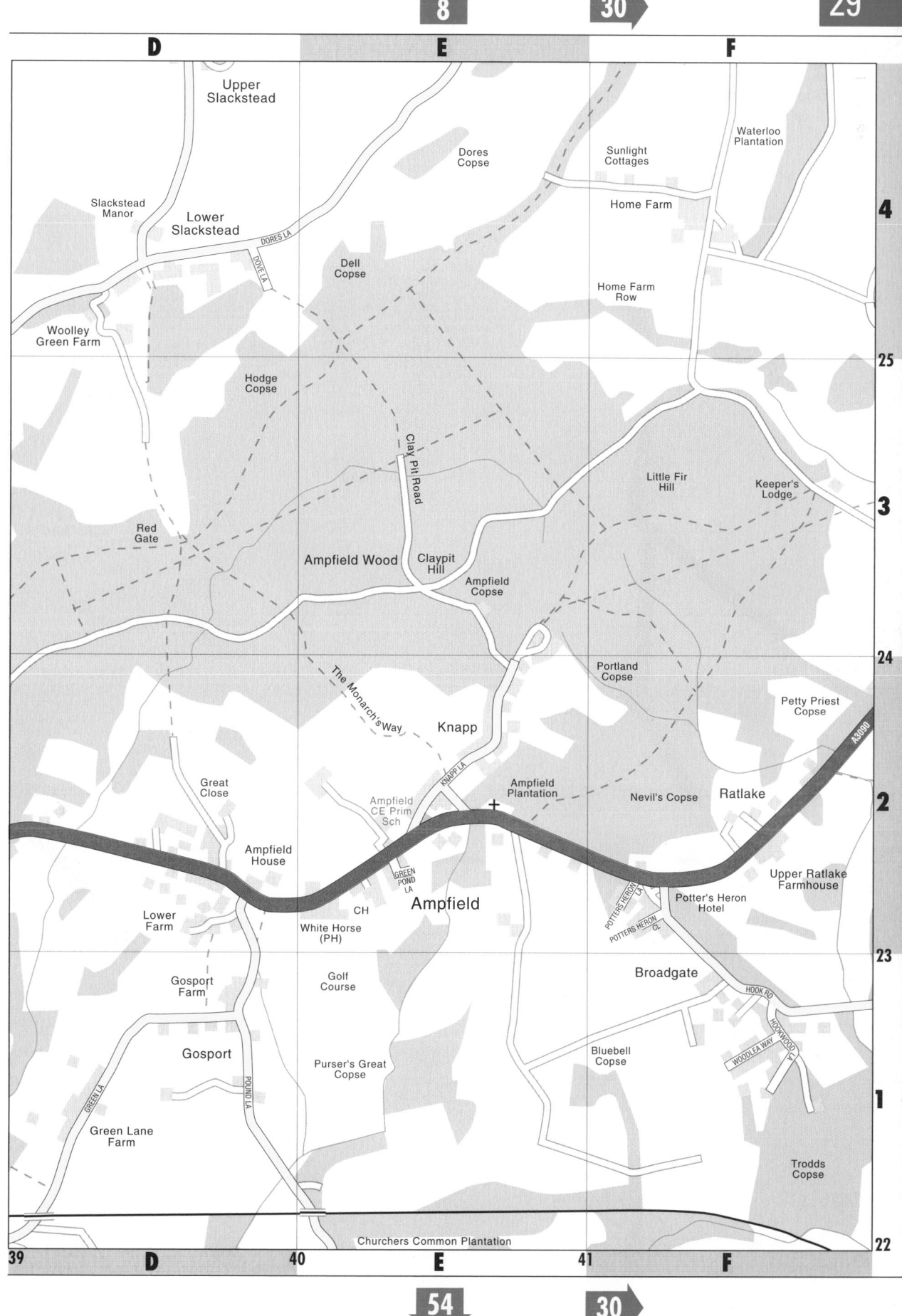

Upper Slackstead

Dores Copse

Sunlight Cottages

Waterloo Plantation

Slackstead Manor

Lower Slackstead

DORES LA

Home Farm

4

Woolley Green Farm

DOVE LA

Dell Copse

Home Farm Row

25

Hodge Copse

Clay Pit Road

Little Fir Hill

Keeper's Lodge

3

Red Gate

Ampfield Wood

Claypit Hill

Ampfield Copse

24

The Monarch's Way

Knapp

Portland Copse

Petty Priest Copse

A3090

Great Close

Ampfield CE Prim Sch

KNAPP LA

Ampfield Plantation

Nevil's Copse

Ratlake

2

Ampfield House

GREEN POND LA

Upper Ratlake Farmhouse

Lower Farm

CH

Ampfield

POTTERS HERON LA

Potter's Heron Hotel

White Horse (PH)

POTTERS HERON CL

23

Gosport Farm

Golf Course

Broadgate

HOOK RD

HOCKWOOD LA

Gosport

GREEN LA

POUND LA

Purser's Great Copse

Bluebell Copse

WOODLEA WAY

1

Green Lane Farm

Trodds Copse

22

Churchers Common Plantation

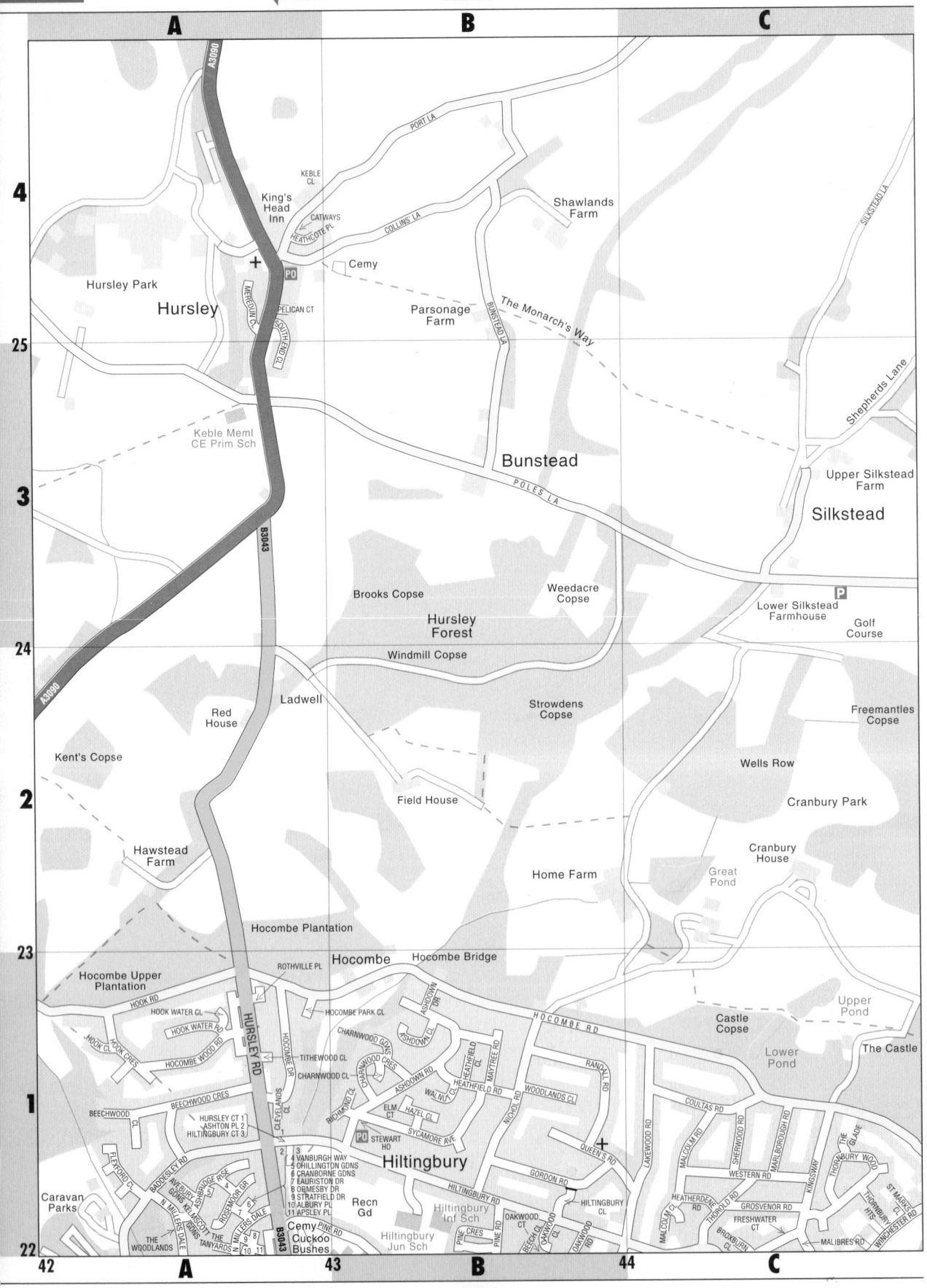

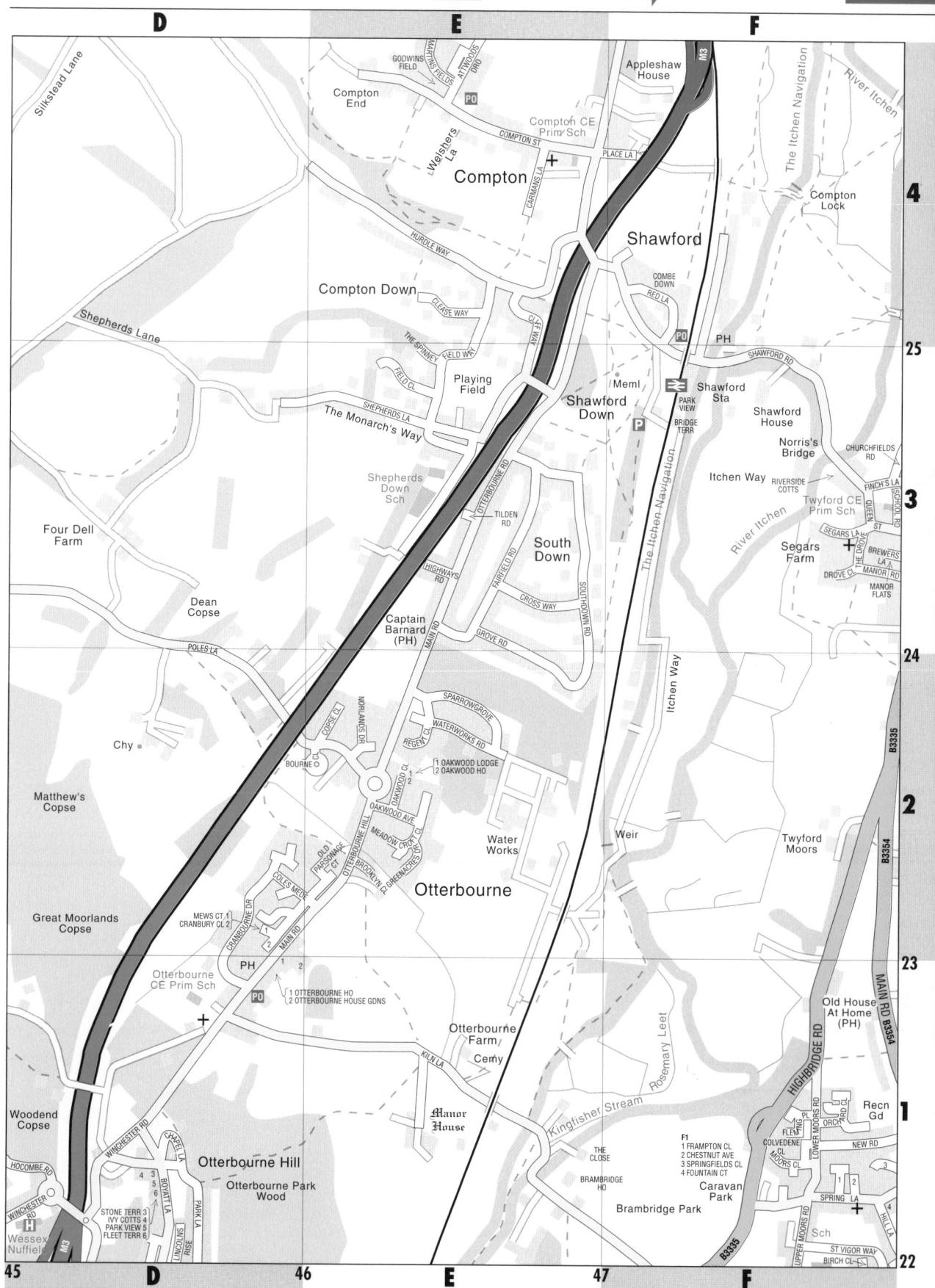

A   B   C

4

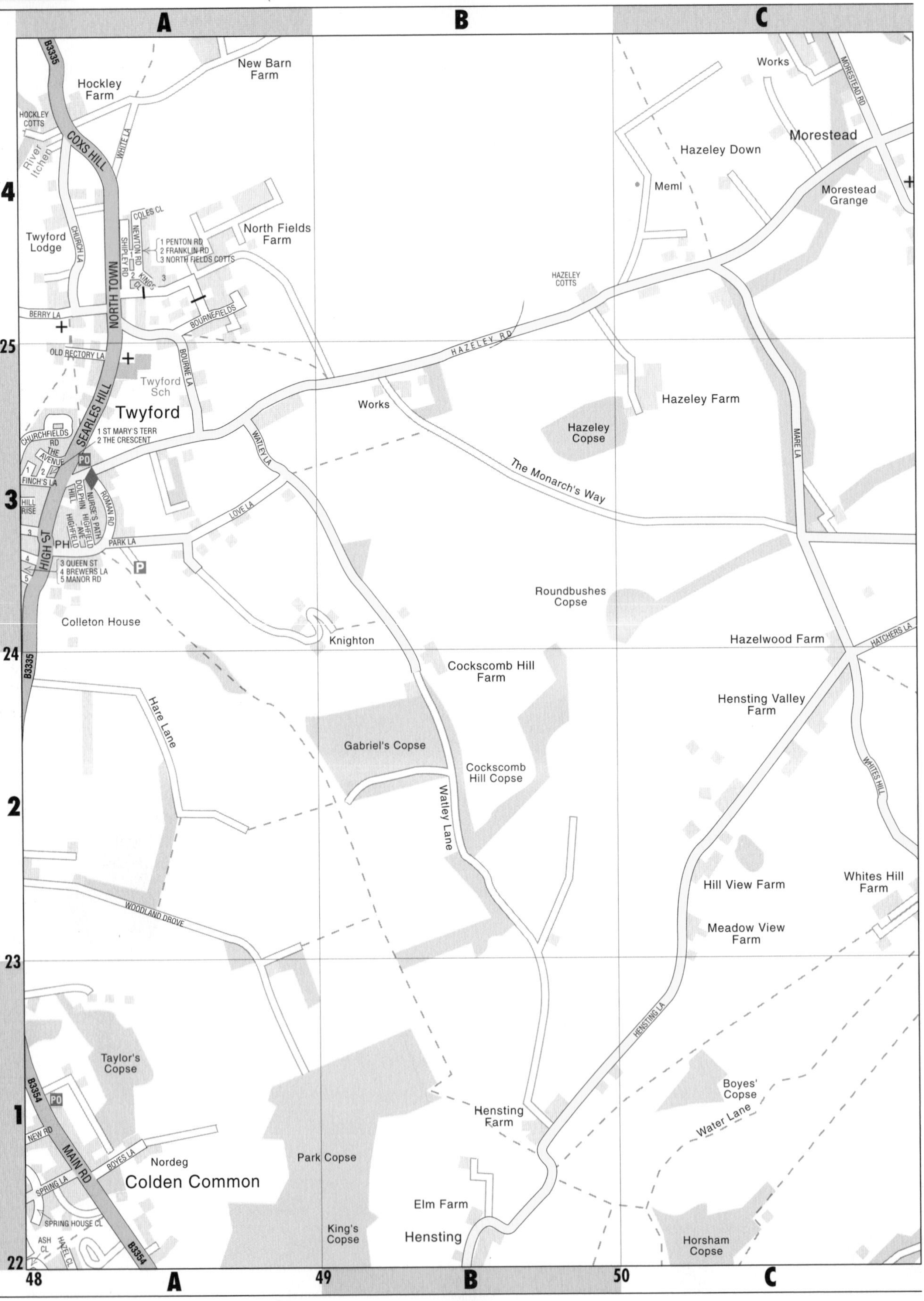

25

24

23

2

3

1

22

B3335

Hockley Farm
HOCKLEY COTTS
COXS HILL
River Itchen
WHITE LA
New Barn Farm
Twyford Lodge
CHURCH LA
COLES CL
NEWTON RD
SHIPLEY RD
KINGS CL
NORTH TOWN
North Fields Farm
1 PENTON RD
2 FRANKLIN RD
3 NORTH FIELDS COTTS
BERRY LA
OLD RECTORY LA
BOURNEFIELDS
BOURNE LA
Twyford Sch
Twyford
SEARLES HILL
CHURCHFIELDS RD
THE AVENUE
FINCH'S LA
HILL RISE
PH
HIGH ST
DOLPHIN HILL
NURSE'S PATH
HIGHFIELD AVE
ROMAN RD
WATLEY LA
LOVE LA
PARK LA
1 ST MARY'S TERR
2 THE CRESCENT
PO
3 QUEEN ST
4 BREWERS LA
5 MANOR RD
P
Colleton House
Knighton
B3335
Hare Lane
WOODLAND DROVE
Taylor's Copse
B3354
PO
NEW RD
MAIN RD
SPRING LA
BOYES LA
Nordeg
Colden Common
SPRING HOUSE CL
ASH CL
HAZEL CL
B3354

Works
Hazeley Down
Meml
MORESTEAD RD
Morestead
Morestead Grange
HAZELEY COTTS
HAZELEY RD
Works
Hazeley Copse
Hazeley Farm
The Monarch's Way
MARE LA
Roundbushes Copse
Hazelwood Farm
HATCHERS LA
Cockscomb Hill Farm
Gabriel's Copse
Cockscomb Hill Copse
Watley Lane
Hensting Valley Farm
WHITES HILL
Hill View Farm
Whites Hill Farm
Meadow View Farm
HENSTING LA
Boyes' Copse
Water Lane
Hensting Farm
Park Copse
Elm Farm
King's Copse
Hensting
Horsham Copse

4

25

3

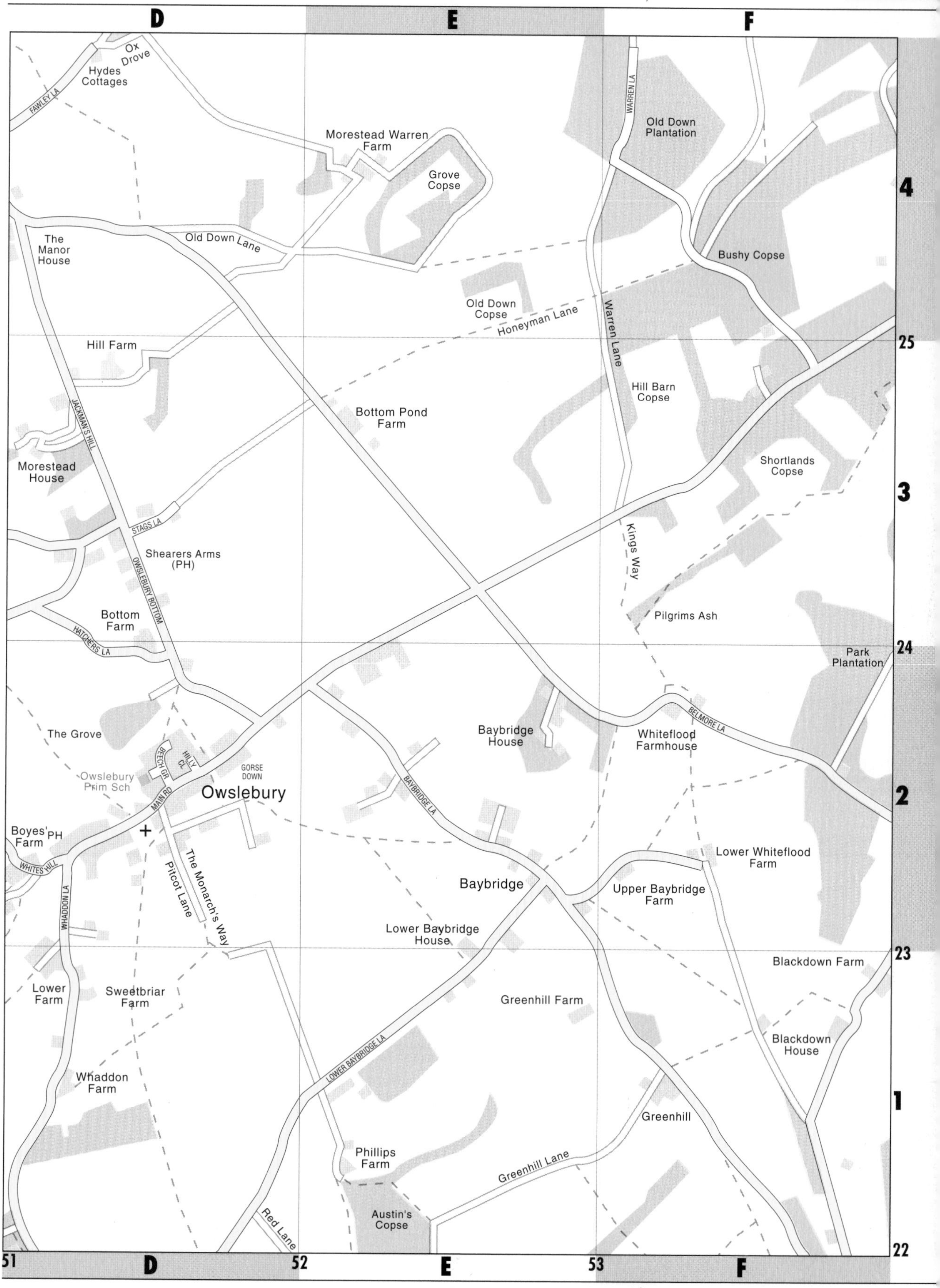

24

2

23

1

22

Ox Drove
Hydes Cottages
FAWLEY LA

Morestead Warren Farm
Grove Copse

Old Down Plantation
WARREN LA
Old Down Lane

The Manor House
Bushy Copse

Old Down Copse
Honeyman Lane
Warren Lane

Hill Farm
Hill Barn Copse

Bottom Pond Farm
JACKMAN'S HILL

Shortlands Copse

Morestead House

STAGS LA.

Shearers Arms (PH)
Kings Way

OWSLEBURY BOTTOM
HATCHERS LA.

Bottom Farm
Pilgrims Ash

Park Plantation

The Grove
BELMORE LA.

Baybridge House
Whiteflood Farmhouse

BEECH GR.
HILLY CL.
GORSE DOWN

Owslebury Prim Sch
MAIN RD

Owslebury

Boyes' Farm PH

The Monarch's Way
Pitcot Lane

Lower Whiteflood Farm

WHITES HILL

WHADDON LA.

BAYBRIDGE LA.

Baybridge

Upper Baybridge Farm

Lower Baybridge House

Blackdown Farm

Lower Farm

Sweetbriar Farm

Greenhill Farm

Blackdown House

Whaddon Farm

LOWER BAYBRIDGE LA.

Greenhill

Phillips Farm

Greenhill Lane

Red Lane

Austin's Copse

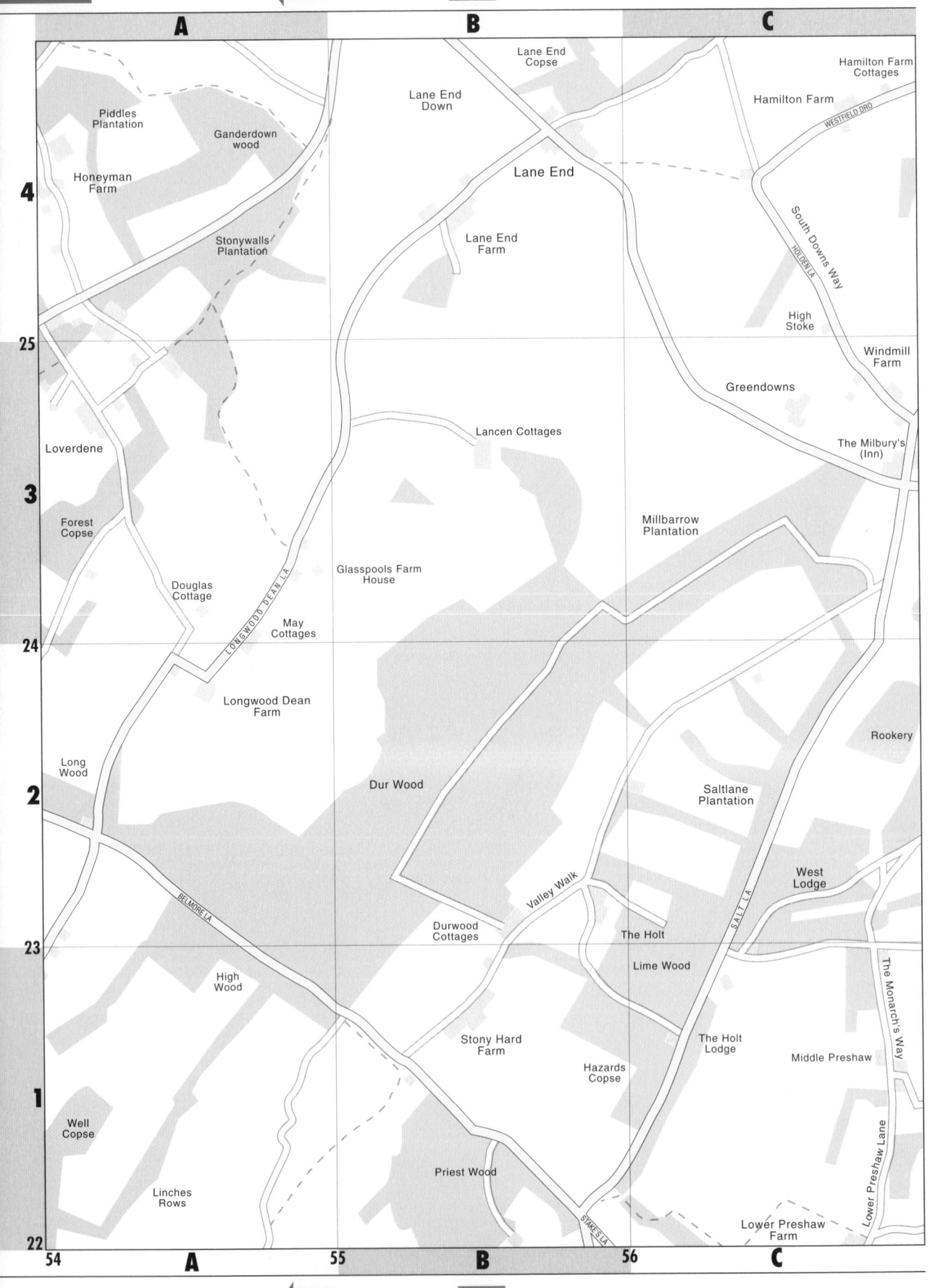

A B C

Piddles
Plantation

Ganderdown
wood

Honeyman
Farm

4

Stonywalls
Plantation

25

Loverdene

3

Forest
Copse

Douglas
Cottage

LONGWOOD DEAN LA

May
Cottages

24

Longwood Dean
Farm

Long
Wood

2

BELMORE LA

23

High
Wood

1

Well
Copse

Linches
Rows

22
54 A 55 B 56 C

Lane End
Copse

Lane End
Down

Lane End

Lane End
Farm

Lancen Cottages

Glasspools Farm
House

Dur Wood

Durwood
Cottages

Valley Walk

Stony Hard
Farm

Hazards
Copse

Priest Wood

STAKE'S LA

Hamilton Farm
Cottages

Hamilton Farm

WESTFIELD DRO

South Downs Way

HOLDER LA

High
Stoke

Windmill
Farm

Greendowns

The Milbury's
(Inn)

Millbarrow
Plantation

Rookery

Saltlane
Plantation

West
Lodge

SALT LA

The Holt

Lime Wood

The Holt
Lodge

Middle Preshaw

Lower Preshaw Lane

The Monarch's Way

Lower Preshaw
Farm

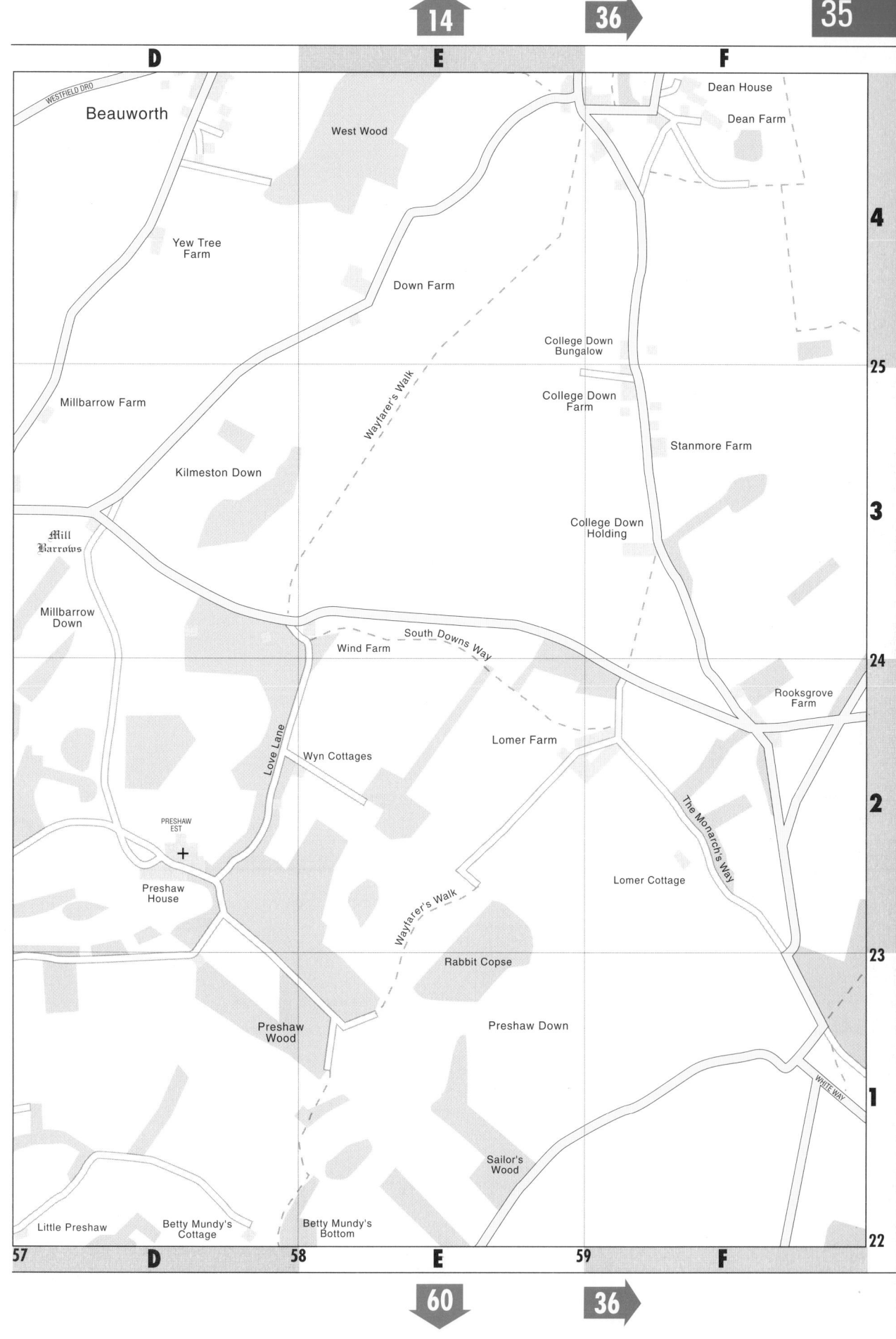

WESTFIELD DRO

Beauworth

West Wood

Dean House

Dean Farm

Yew Tree
Farm

Down Farm

College Down
Bungalow

Millbarrow Farm

College Down
Farm

Stanmore Farm

Wayfarer's Walk

Kilmeston Down

College Down
Holding

Mill
Barrows

Millbarrow
Down

South Downs Way

Wind Farm

Rooksgrove
Farm

Love Lane

Wyn Cottages

Lomer Farm

The Monarch's Way

PRESHAW
EST

Lomer Cottage

Preshaw
House

Wayfarer's Walk

Rabbit Copse

Preshaw
Wood

Preshaw Down

WHITE WAY

Little Preshaw

Betty Mundy's
Cottage

Betty Mundy's
Bottom

Sailor's
Wood

A

B

C

Brockwood Bottom

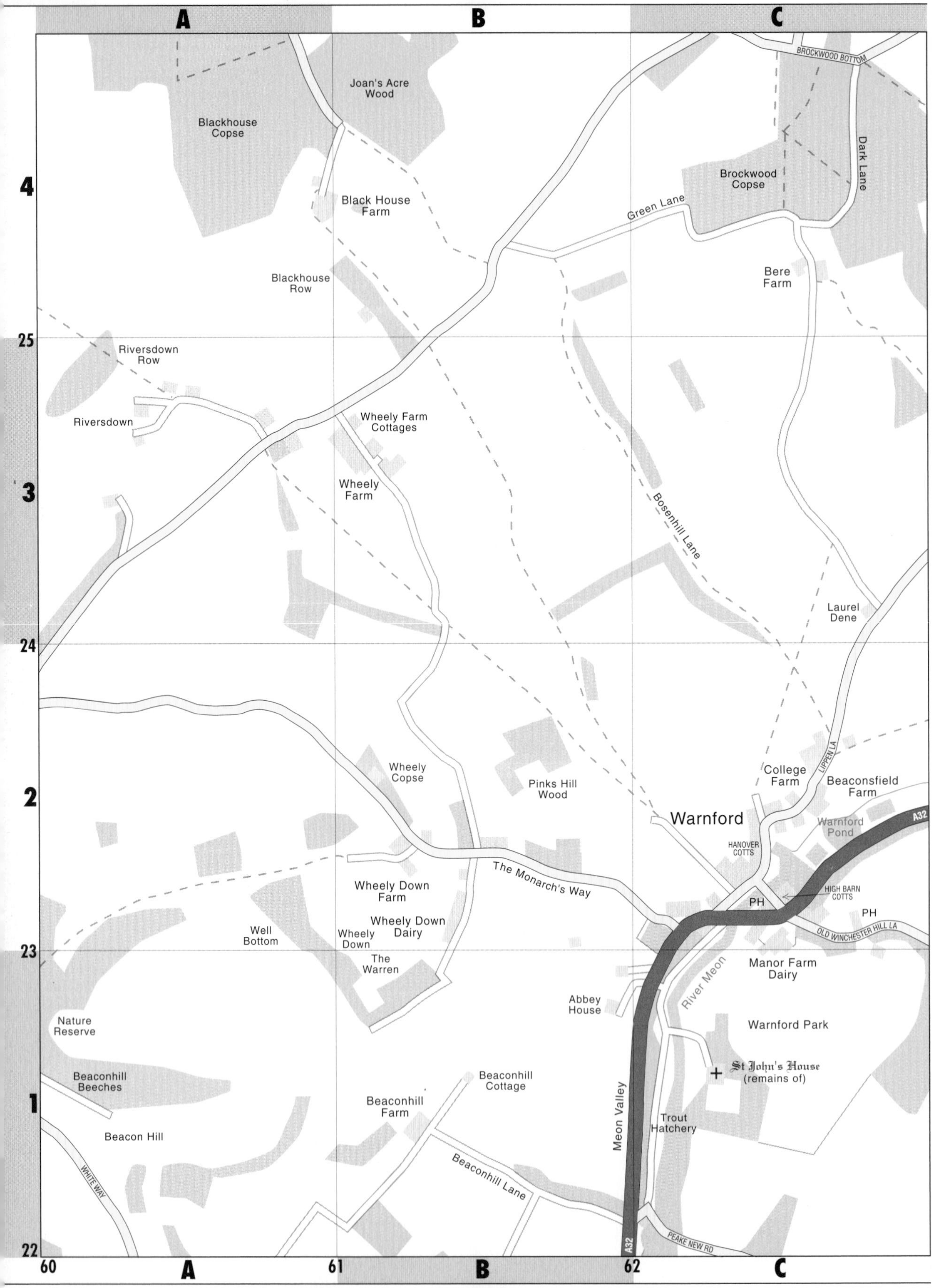

Joan's Acre
Wood

Blackhouse
Copse

Dark Lane

Brockwood
Copse

4

Black House
Farm

Green Lane

Bere
Farm

Blackhouse
Row

25

Riversdown
Row

Riversdown

Wheely Farm
Cottages

Bosenhill Lane

3

Wheely
Farm

Laurel
Dene

24

LIPPEN LA

Wheely
Copse

Pinks Hill
Wood

College
Farm

Beaconsfield
Farm

2

Warnford

Warnford
Pond

A32

HANOVER
COTTS

The Monarch's Way

High Barn
Cotts

PH

PH

Wheely Down
Farm

OLD WINCHESTER HILL LA

Well
Bottom

Wheely Down
Dairy

23

Wheely
Down

The
Warren

River Meon

Manor Farm
Dairy

Abbey
House

Nature
Reserve

Warnford Park

Beaconhill
Cottage

Beaconhill
Beeches

+

St John's House
(remains of)

1

Beaconhill
Farm

Meon Valley

Beacon Hill

Trout
Hatchery

WHITE WAY

Beaconhill Lane

22

A32

PEAKE NEW RD

60

A

61

B

62

C

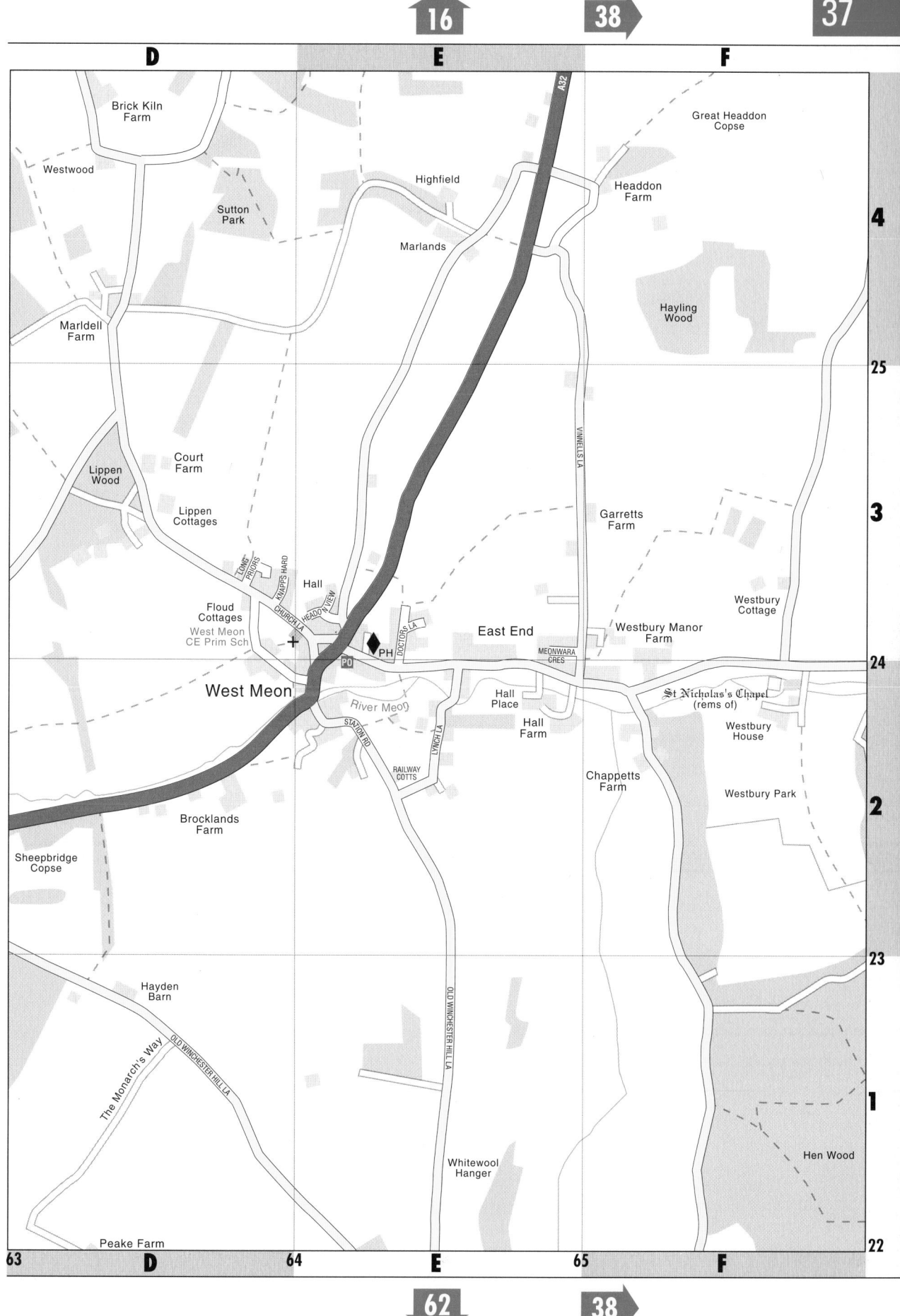

D
E
F

4

25

3

24

2

23

1

22

Brick Kiln Farm

Westwood

Sutton Park

Highfield

Marlands

Great Headdon Copse

Headdon Farm

Hayling Wood

A32

Marldell Farm

Court Farm

Lippen Wood

Lippen Cottages

Garretts Farm

VINNELLS LA

Westbury Cottage

LONG PRIORS

KNAPPS HARD

Hall

HEADDON VIEW

CHURCH LA

Floud Cottages

West Meon CE Prim Sch

DOCTORS LA

East End

Westbury Manor Farm

MEONWARA CRES

PO PH

St Nicholas's Chapel (rems of)

West Meon

River Meon

Hall Place

Hall Farm

Westbury House

STATION RD

LYNCH LA

RAILWAY COTTS

Chappetts Farm

Westbury Park

Sheepbridge Copse

Brocklands Farm

Hayden Barn

The Monarch's Way

OLD WINCHESTER HILL LA

OLD WINCHESTER HILL LA

Whitewool Hanger

Hen Wood

Peake Farm

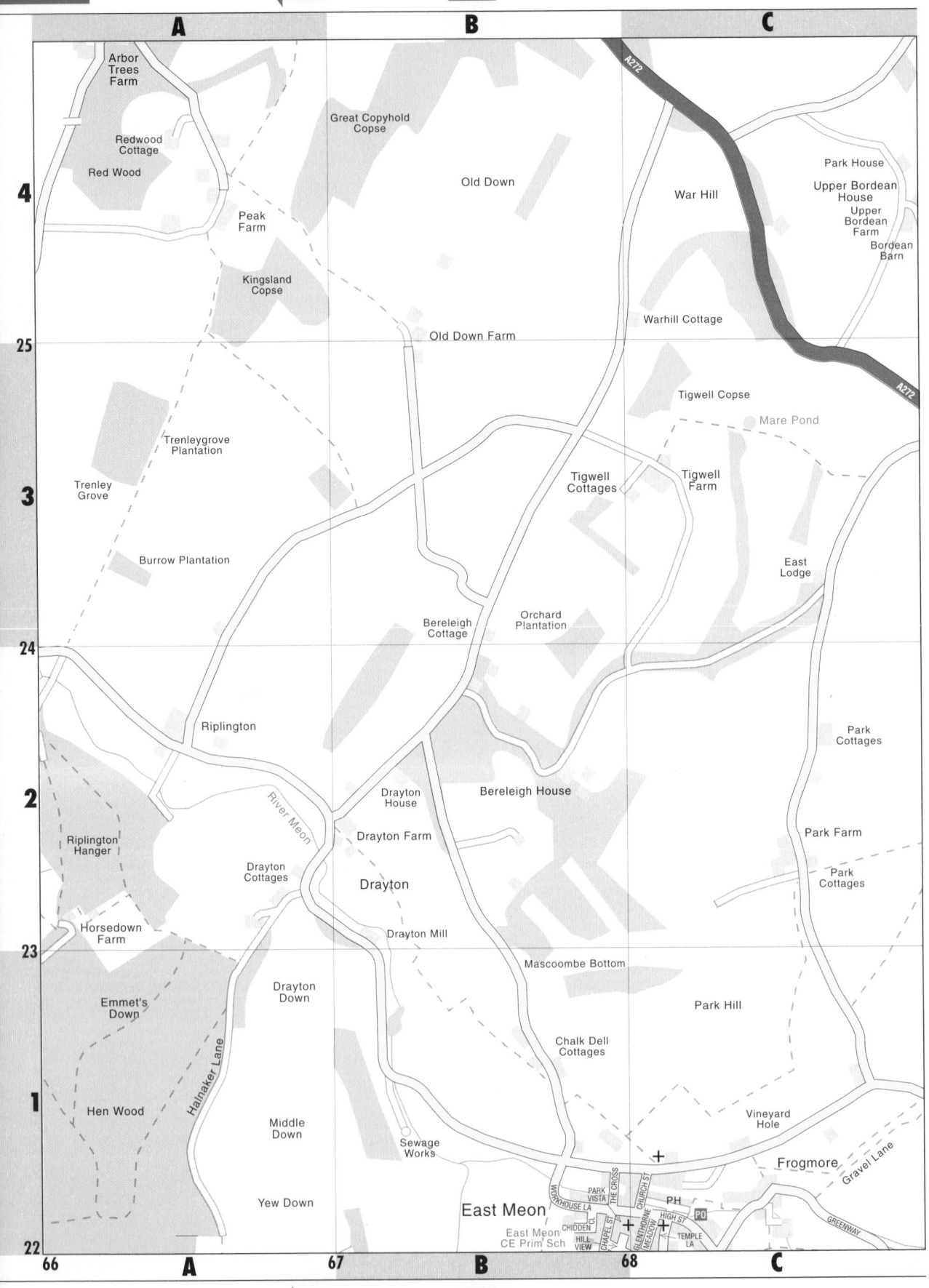

A   B   C

Arbor Trees Farm

Redwood Cottage

Red Wood

Peak Farm

Great Copyhold Copse

Old Down

War Hill

Park House

Upper Bordean House

Upper Bordean Farm

Bordean Barn

4

Kingsland Copse

Warhill Cottage

25

Old Down Farm

Tigwell Copse

Mare Pond

Trenleygrove Plantation

Trenley Grove

Tigwell Cottages

Tigwell Farm

3

Burrow Plantation

East Lodge

Bereleigh Cottage

Orchard Plantation

24

Riplington

Park Cottages

River Meon

Drayton House

Bereleigh House

2

Riplington Hanger

Drayton Farm

Park Farm

Drayton Cottages

Park Cottages

Drayton

Horsedown Farm

23

Drayton Mill

Mascoombe Bottom

Emmet's Down

Drayton Down

Park Hill

Chalk Dell Cottages

Halnaker Lane

1

Hen Wood

Middle Down

Vineyard Hole

Frogmore

Gravel Lane

Sewage Works

East Meon

PARK VISTA

THE CROSS

CHURCH ST

PH

PO

GREENWAY

Yew Down

East Meon CE Prim Sch

CHIDDEN CL

CHAPEL ST

HILL VIEW

GLENTHORNE MEADOW

HIGH ST

TEMPLE LA

22

66   A   67   B   68   C

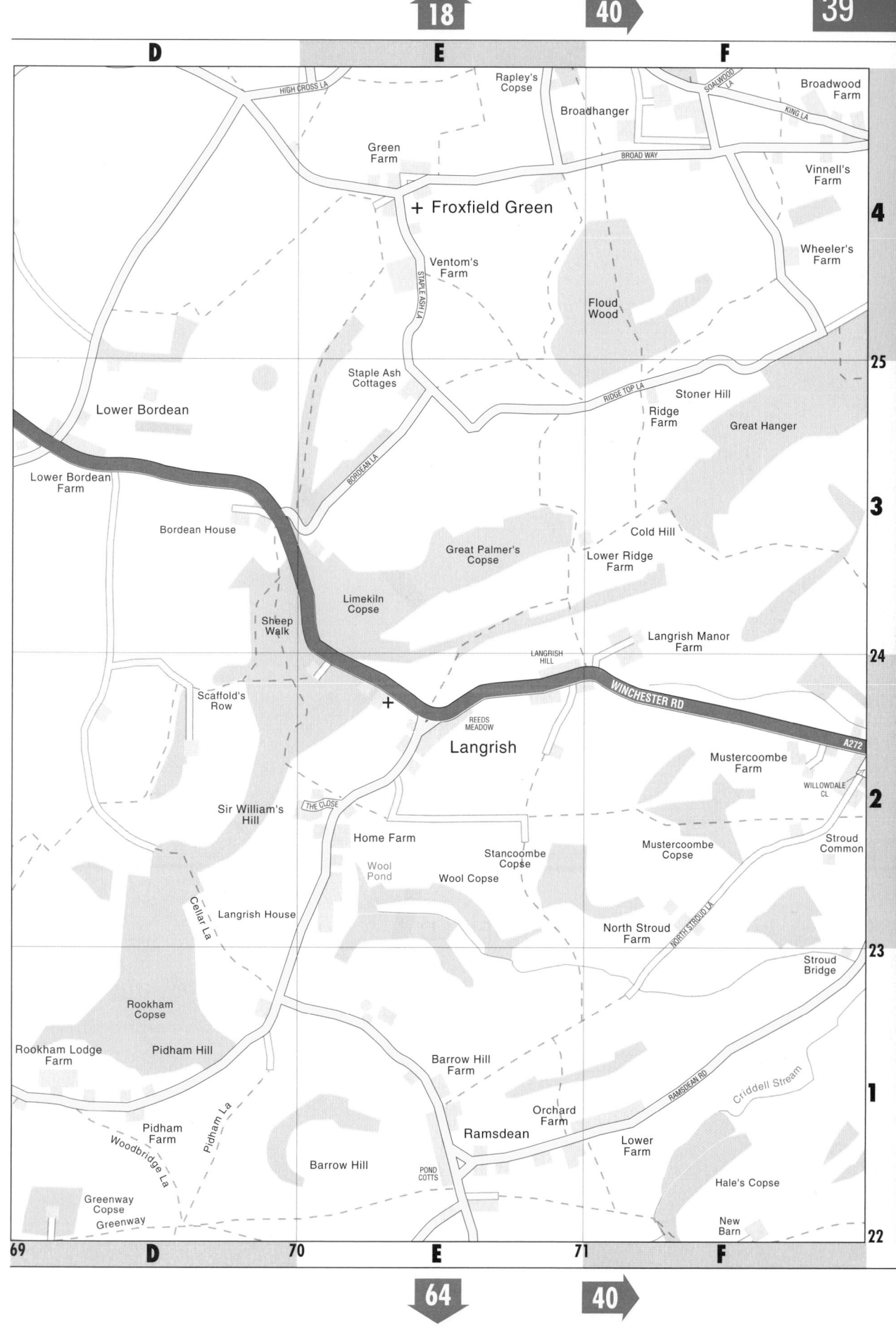

D
E
F

High Cross La

Rapley's Copse

Broadhanger

Broadwood Farm

SOALWOOD LA

KING LA

Green Farm

BROAD WAY

Vinnell's Farm

4

+ Froxfield Green

Ventom's Farm

STAPLE ASH LA

Floud Wood

Wheeler's Farm

Staple Ash Cottages

RIDGE TOP LA

Stoner Hill

25

Lower Bordean

Ridge Farm

Great Hanger

BORDEAN LA

Lower Bordean Farm

3

Bordean House

Cold Hill

Great Palmer's Copse

Lower Ridge Farm

Limekiln Copse

Sheep Walk

Langrish Manor Farm

LANGRISH HILL

24

Scaffold's Row

+

WINCHESTER RD

A272

REEDS MEADOW

Langrish

Mustercoombe Farm

WILLOWDALE CL

Sir William's Hill

THE CLOSE

Home Farm

Stancoombe Copse

Mustercoombe Copse

Stroud Common

2

Wool Pond

Wool Copse

NORTH STROUD LA

Cellar La

Langrish House

North Stroud Farm

23

Stroud Bridge

Rookham Copse

Rookham Lodge Farm

Pidham Hill

Barrow Hill Farm

RAMSDEAN RD

Criddell Stream

1

Pidham La

Orchard Farm

Pidham Farm

Woodbridge La

Barrow Hill

Ramsdean

Lower Farm

Greenway Copse

Greenway

POND COTTS

Hale's Copse

New Barn

22

69
D
70
E
71
F

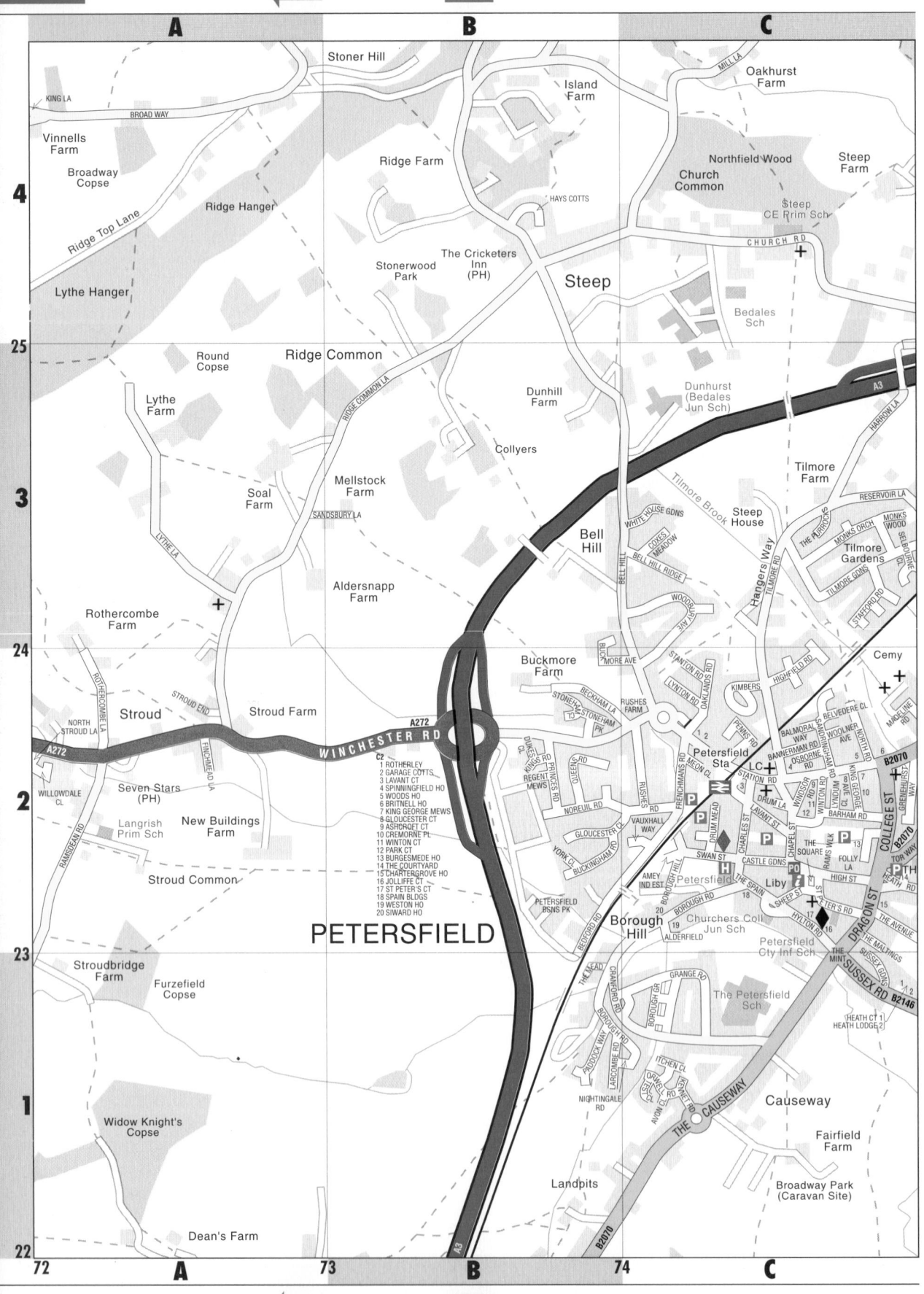

A · B · C

4

25

3

24

2

23

1

22

King La

Broad Way

Vinnells Farm

Broadway Copse

Ridge Hanger

Ridge Top Lane

Lythe Hanger

Stoner Hill

Ridge Farm

HAYS COTTS

Stonerwood Park

The Cricketers Inn (PH)

Island Farm

Steep

Oakhurst Farm

Northfield Wood

Church Common

Steep Farm

MILL LA

Steep CE Prim Sch

CHURCH RD

Bedales Sch

Round Copse

Ridge Common

Lythe Farm

RIDGE COMMON LA

Soal Farm

Mellstock Farm

SANDSBURY LA

LYTHE LA

Aldersnapp Farm

Dunhill Farm

Collyers

Dunhurst (Bedales Jun Sch)

A3

HARROW LA

RESERVOIR LA

Tilmore Farm

Bell Hill

WHITE HOUSE GDNS

COXES MEADOW

BELL HILL RIDGE

BELL HILL

Steep House

Tilmore Brook

Hangers Way

TILMORE RD

THE MIRRORS

MONKS ORCH

MONKS WOOD

SELBOURNE RD

Tilmore Gardens

TILMORE GDNS

STAFFORD RD

Rothercombe Farm

ROTHERCOMBE LA

Stroud End

Stroud Farm

NORTH STROUD LA

FINCHMEAD LA

A272

WINCHESTER RD

Buckmore Farm

BUCK MORE AVE

BECKHAM LA

STONEHAM PK

STONEHAM

RUSHES FARM

WOODROFFE

WOODBURY AVE

STANTON RD

LYNTON RD

OAKLANDS RD

KIMBERS

HIGHFIELD RD

PEMBS RD

Cemy

MAGDALENE RD

A272

Stroud

Seven Stars (PH)

RAMSDEAN RD

WILLOWDALE CL

Langrish Prim Sch

New Buildings Farm

Stroud Common

C2
1 ROTHERLEY
2 GARAGE COTTS
3 LAVANT CT
4 SPINNINGFIELD HO
5 WOODS HO
6 BRITNELL HO
7 KING GEORGE MEWS
8 GLOUCESTER CT
9 ASHCROFT CT
10 CREMORNE PL
11 WINTON CT
12 PARK CT
13 BURGESMEDE HO
14 THE COURTYARD
15 CHARTERGROVE HO
16 JOLLIFFE CT
17 ST PETER'S CT
18 SPAIN BLDGS
19 WESTON HO
20 SIWARD HO

PETERSFIELD

A272

STONEHAM CL

DUNSMEAD

KINGS RD

REGENT MEWS

QUEEN RD

S RD

NOREUIL RD

YORK CL

PRINCES RD

BUCKINGHAM RD

GLOUCESTER CL

VAUXHALL WAY

RUSHES RD

FRENCHMANS RD

STATION RD

BALMORAL WAY

BANNERMAN RD

BELVEDERE CL

WOOLNER AVE

NORTH RD

KING GEORGE

OSBORNE RD

B2070

GREENHURST WAY

TOR WAY

Petersfield Sta

LC

DRUM MEAD

LAVANT ST

CHARLES ST

WINDSOR CT

LYNDUM CL

WINTON CL

BARHAM RD

THE SQUARE

CHAPEL ST

RAMS WALK

FOLLY LA

COLLEGE ST

B2070

HEATH RD

PH

Petersfield BSNS PK

AMEY IND EST

SWAN ST

H

Petersfield

Liby

CASTLE GDNS

SHEEP ST

HIGH ST

ST PETER'S RD

DRAGON ST

THE AVENUE

THE MALTINGS

Borough Hill

BOROUGH RD

BEDFORD RD

ALDERFIELD

Churchers Coll Jun Sch

Petersfield Cty Inf Sch

HYLTON RD

SUSSEX RD

THE MINT

SUSSEX GDNS

B2146

Stroudbridge Farm

Furzefield Copse

THE MEAD

CRANFORD RD

Grange Rd

GRANGE RD

BOROUGH GR

The Petersfield Sch

HEATH CT
HEATH LODGE

Widow Knight's Copse

BOROUGHLY RD

PADDOCK WAY

LARCOMBE RD

NIGHTINGALE RD

ITCHEN CL

ORWELL CL

TEST CL

AVON CL

THE CAUSEWAY

Causeway

Fairfield Farm

Broadway Park (Caravan Site)

Dean's Farm

Landpits

B2070

A3

72 · A · 73 · B · 74 · C

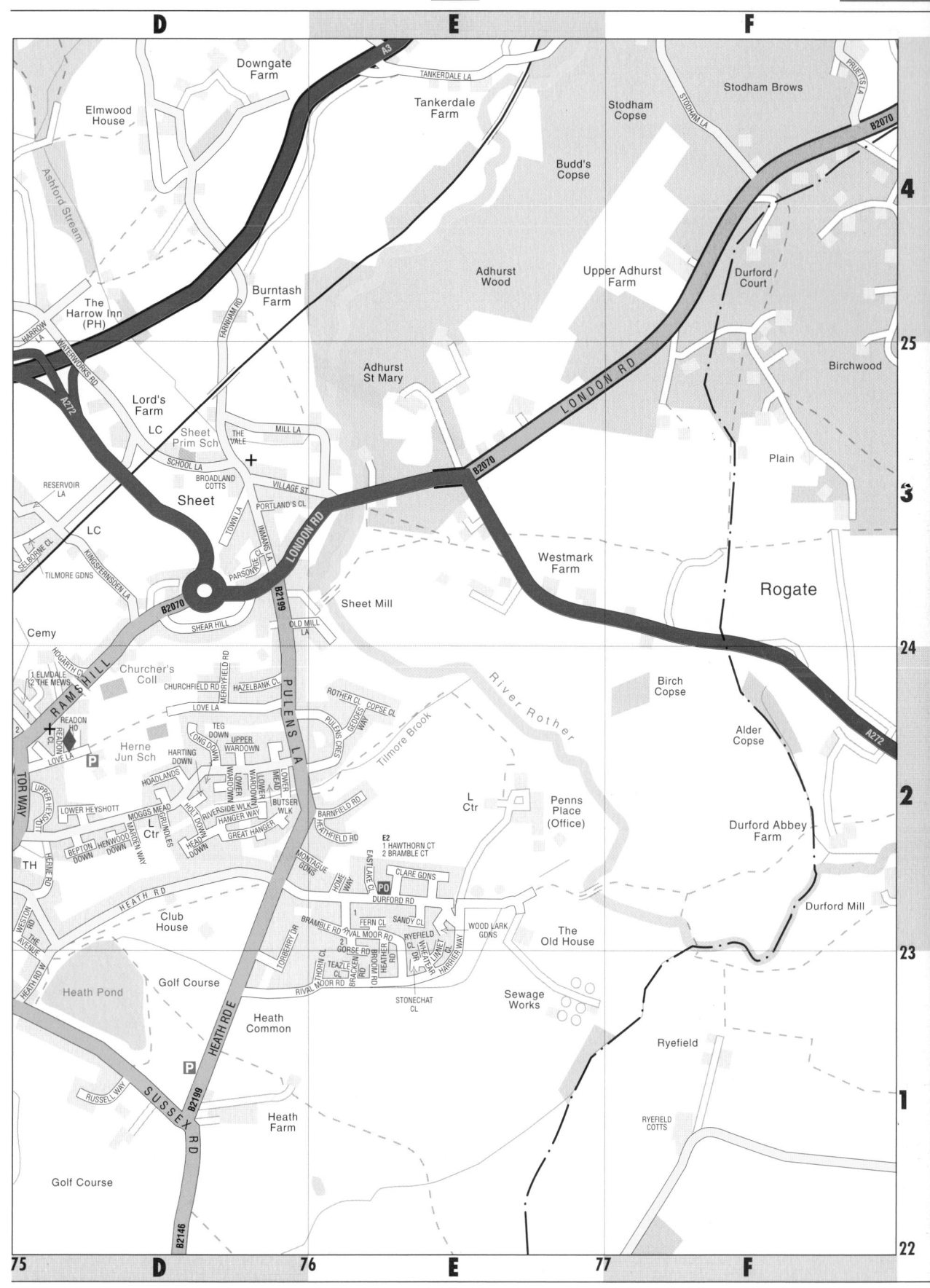

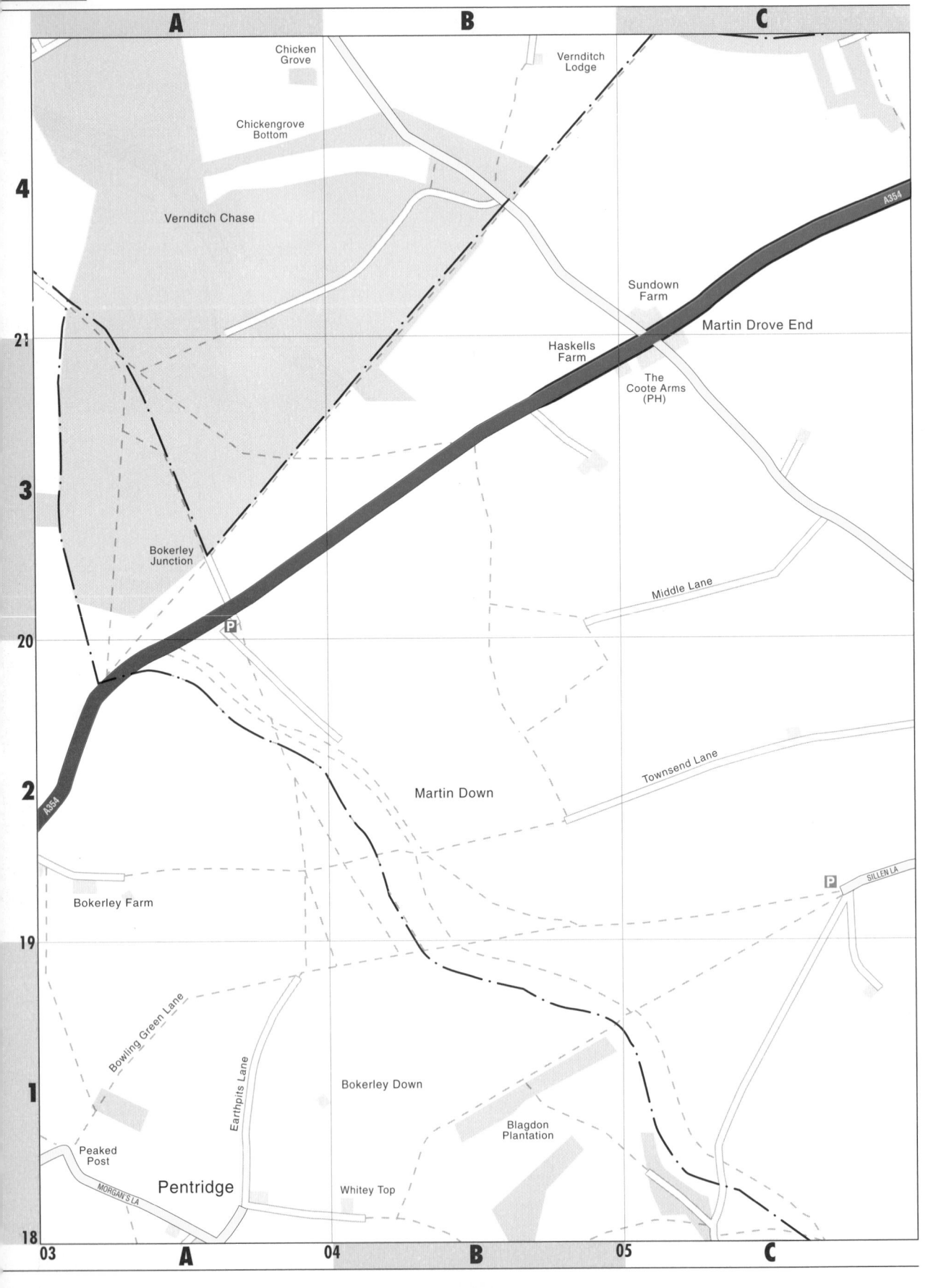

A   B   C

Chicken
Grove

Chickengrove
Bottom

Vernditch
Lodge

A354

4

Vernditch Chase

Sundown
Farm

Martin Drove End

21

Haskells
Farm

The
Coote Arms
(PH)

3

Bokerley
Junction

Middle Lane

P

20

2

A354

Townsend Lane

Martin Down

Bokerley Farm

P   SILLEN LA

19

Bowling Green Lane

Earthpits Lane

1

Bokerley Down

Blagdon
Plantation

Peaked
Post

Pentridge

MORGAN'S LA.

Whitey Top

18

03   A   04   B   05   C

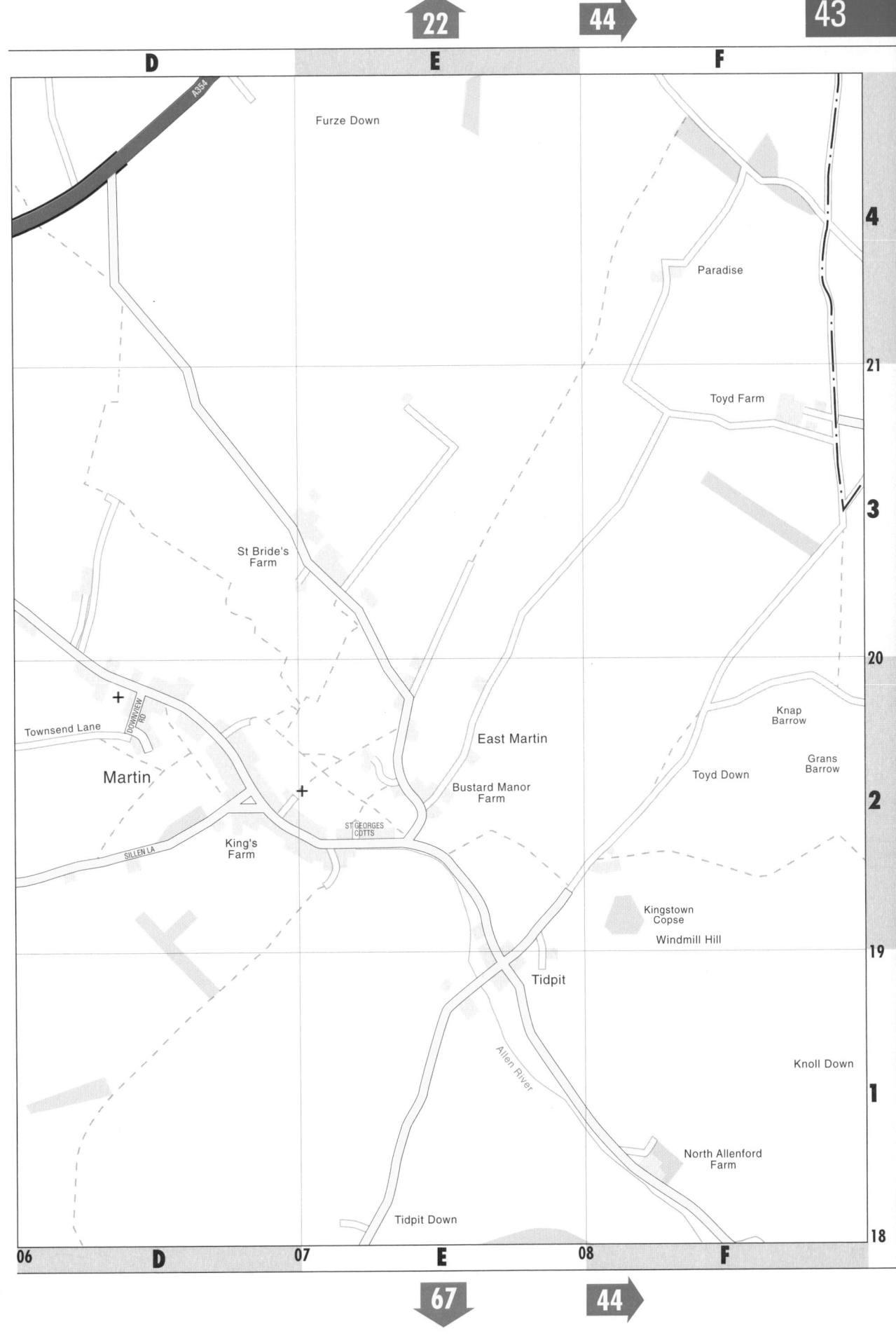

Furze Down

Paradise

Toyd Farm

St Bride's Farm

East Martin

Knap Barrow

Grans Barrow

Townsend Lane

Martin

Toyd Down

Bustard Manor Farm

King's Farm

ST GEORGES COTTS

SILLEN LA

Kingstown Copse

Windmill Hill

Tidpit

Allen River

Knoll Down

North Allenford Farm

Tidpit Down

A354

DOWNVIEW RD

4

21

3

20

2

19

1

18

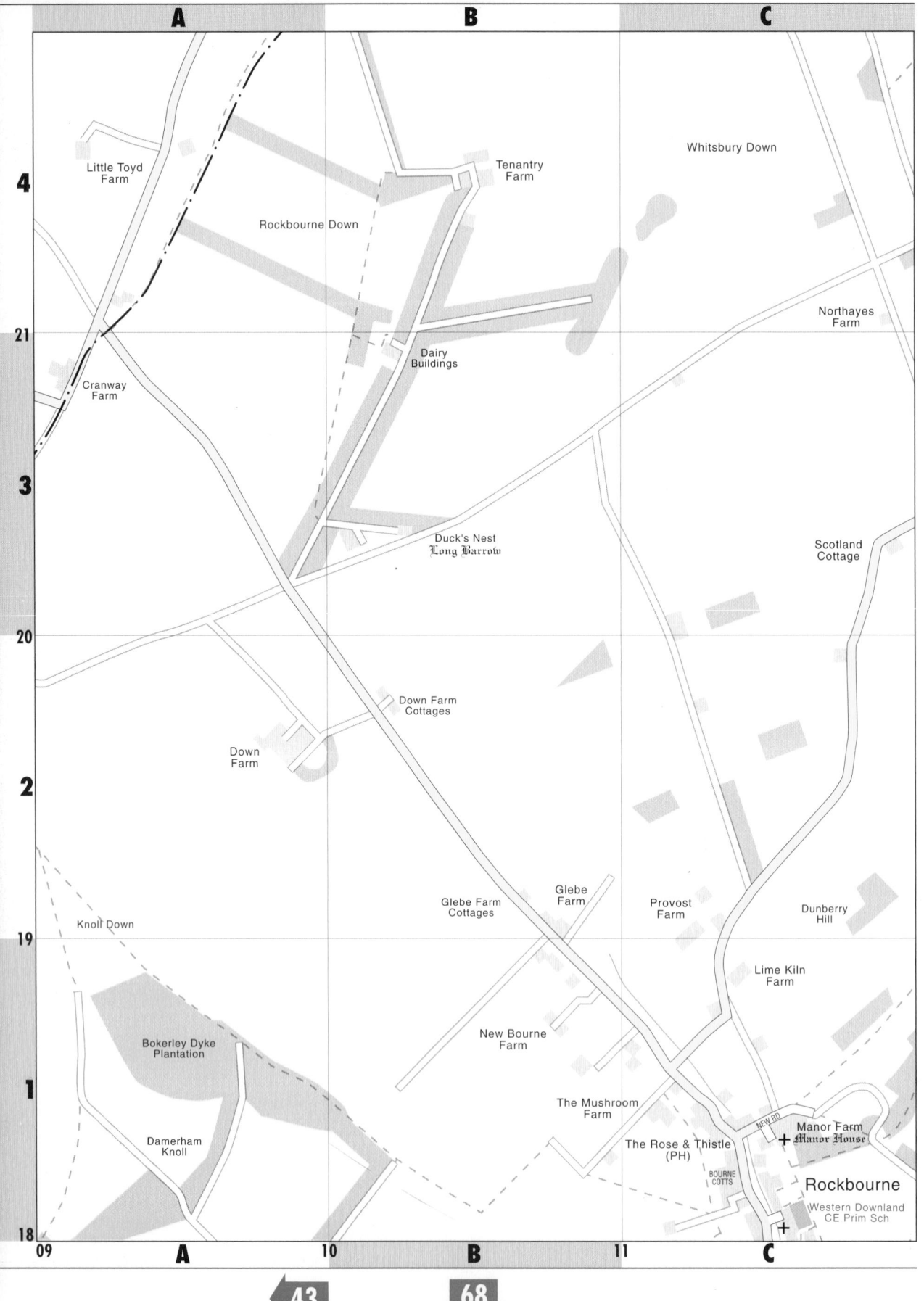

A   B   C

Little Toyd
Farm

Whitsbury Down

4

Rockbourne Down

Tenantry
Farm

Northayes
Farm

21

Dairy
Buildings

Cranway
Farm

3

Duck's Nest
Long Barrow

Scotland
Cottage

20

Down Farm
Cottages

Down
Farm

2

Glebe Farm
Cottages

Glebe
Farm

Provost
Farm

Dunberry
Hill

Knoll Down

19

Lime Kiln
Farm

Bokerley Dyke
Plantation

New Bourne
Farm

1

The Mushroom
Farm

NEW RD

Manor Farm
Manor House

Damerham
Knoll

The Rose & Thistle
(PH)

BOURNE
COTTS

Rockbourne

Western Downland
CE Prim Sch

18

09   A   10   B   11   C

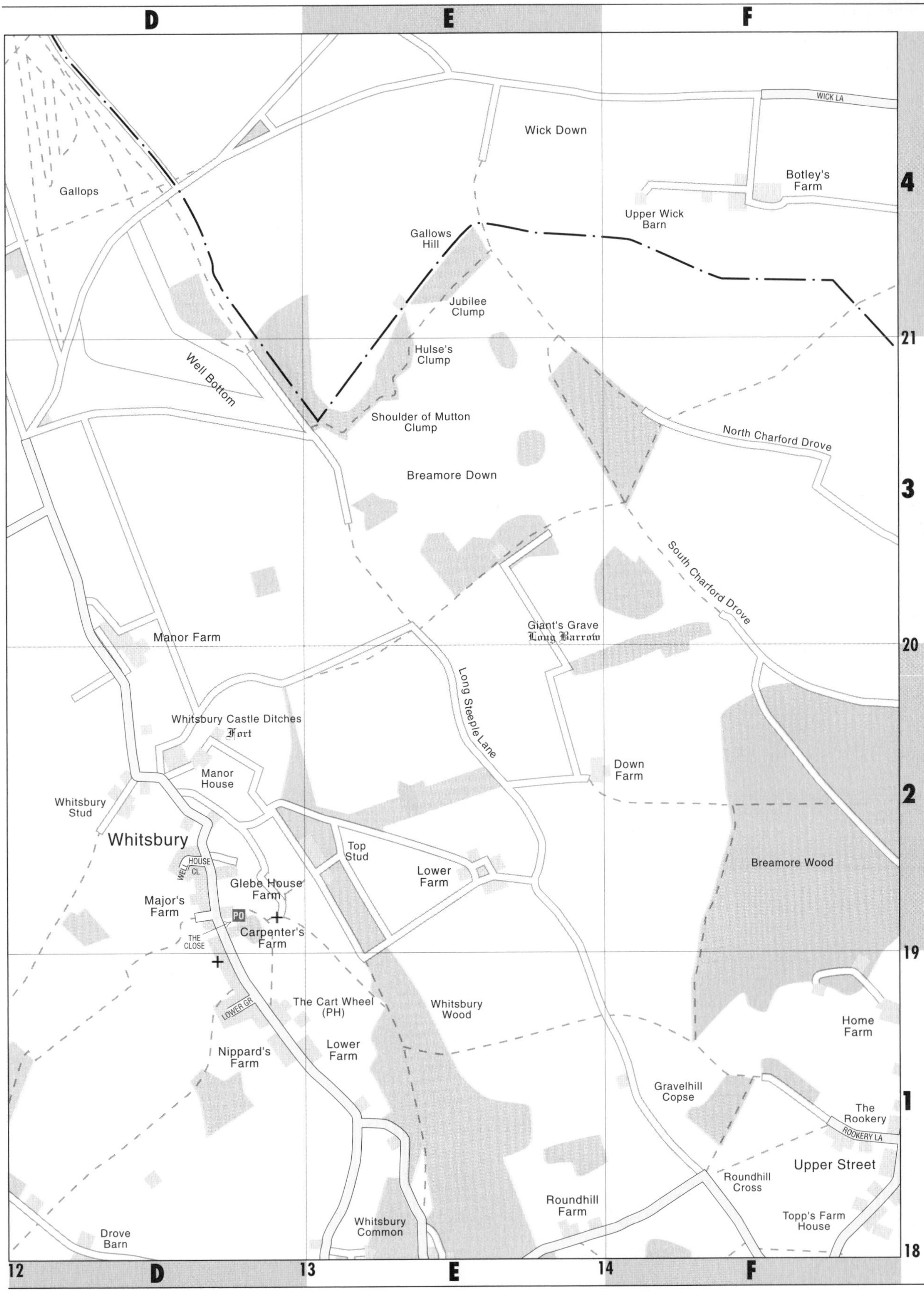

D **E** **F**

WICK LA

Wick Down

Botley's Farm

4

Upper Wick Barn

Gallops

Gallows Hill

Jubilee Clump

21

Well Bottom

Hulse's Clump

North Charford Drove

Shoulder of Mutton Clump

3

Breamore Down

South Charford Drove

Giant's Grave Long Barrow

Manor Farm

20

Whitsbury Castle Ditches Fort

Long Steeple Lane

Down Farm

2

Manor House

Breamore Wood

Whitsbury Stud

Whitsbury

Top Stud

Lower Farm

HOUSE CL WELL

Glebe House Farm

Major's Farm

PO

19

THE CLOSE

Carpenter's Farm

Home Farm

LOWER GR

The Cart Wheel (PH)

Whitsbury Wood

Lower Farm

Nippard's Farm

Gravelhill Copse

1

The Rookery

ROOKERY LA

Roundhill Cross

Upper Street

Drove Barn

Whitsbury Common

Roundhill Farm

Topp's Farm House

18

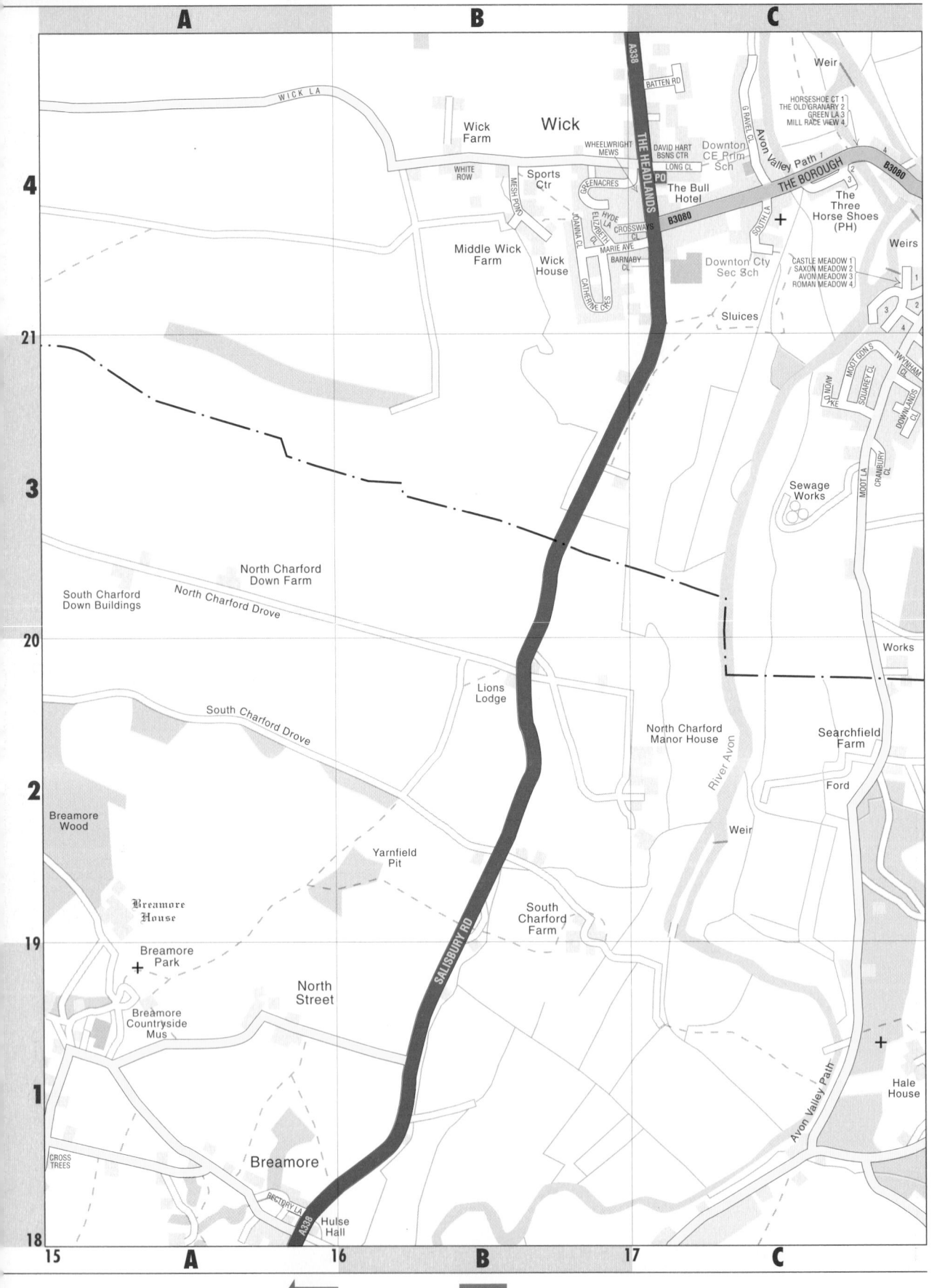

48

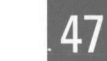

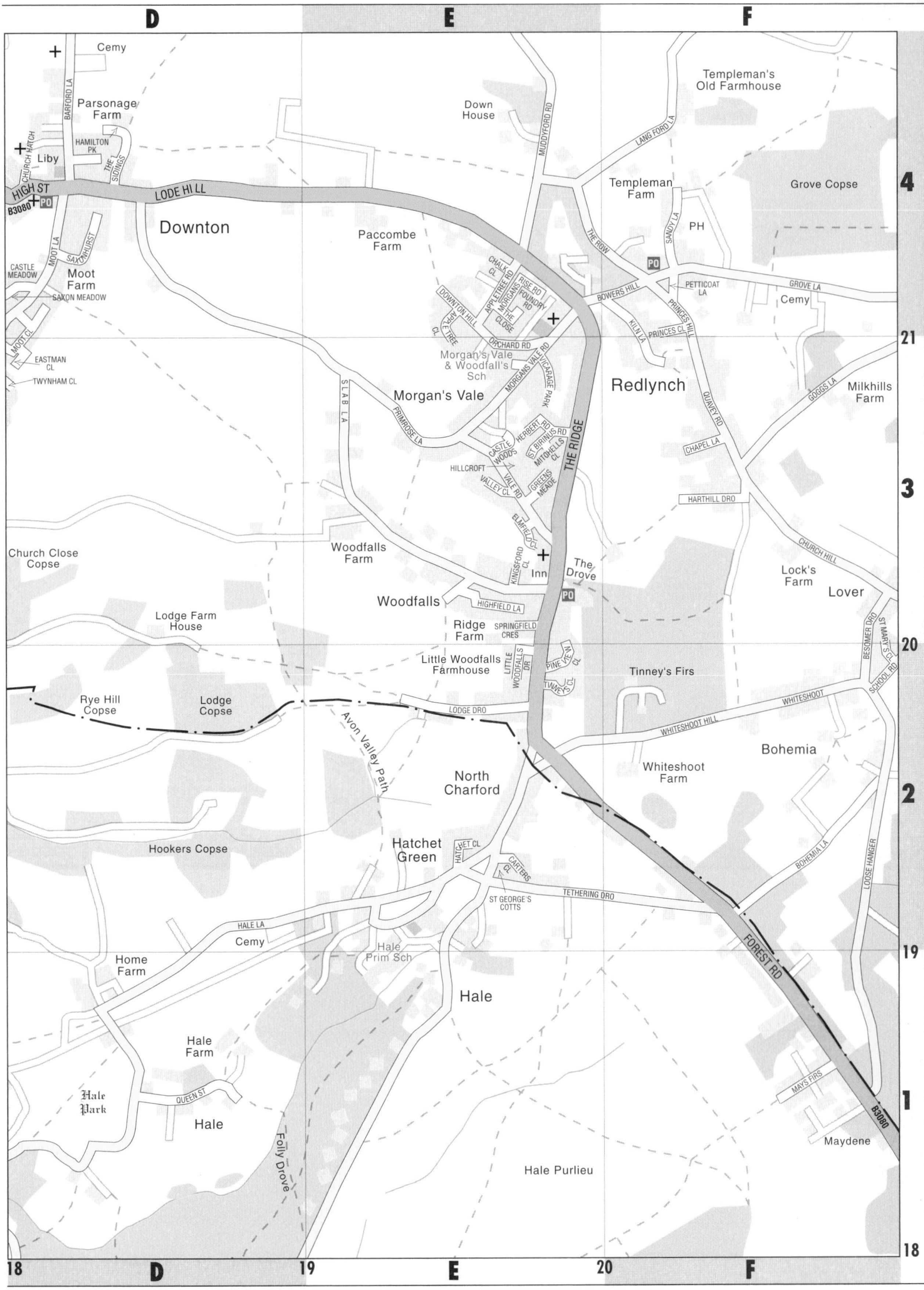

D
E
F
Cemy
Parsonage Farm
BARFORD LA
HAMILTON PK
CHURCH HATCH
Liby
THE SIDINGS
HIGH ST
B3080
PO
LODE HILL
Downton
MOOT LA
SAXONHURST
CASTLE MEADOW
Moot Farm
SAXON MEADOW
MOOT CL
EASTMAN CL
TWYNHAM CL
Down House
MUDDYFORD RD
Paccombe Farm
CHALK CL
APPLETREE RD
RISE RD
MORGANS RISE RD
FOUNDRY RD
THE CLOSE
DOWNTON HILL
APPLE TREE CL
ORCHARD RD
Morgan's Vale & Woodfall's Sch
MORGANS VALE RD
VICARAGE PARK
Morgan's Vale
PRIMROSE LA
SLAB LA
HERBERT RD
ST BIRINUS RD
MITCHELLS CL
CASTLE WOODS
HILLCROFT
VALE RD
VALLEY CL
GREENS MEADE
ELMFIELD CL
KINGSFORD CL
THE RIDGE
Inn
The Drove
Templeman's Old Farmhouse
LANG FORD LA
Templeman Farm
SANDY LA
PH
Grove Copse
THE ROW
BOWERS HILL
PETTICOAT LA
GROVE LA
Cemy
KILN LA
PRINCES HILL
PRINCES CL
Redlynch
QUAVEY RD
CHAPEL LA
GOGGS LA
Milkhills Farm
HARTHILL DRO
CHURCH HILL
Lock's Farm
Lover
Church Close Copse
Woodfalls Farm
Woodfalls
HIGHFIELD LA
Lodge Farm House
Ridge Farm
SPRINGFIELD CRES
Little Woodfalls Farmhouse
LITTLE WOODFALLS DR
PINE VIEW CL
TINNEYS CL
Tinney's Firs
BESOMER DRO
ST MARY'S CL
SCHOOL RD
WHITESHOOT
WHITESHOOT HILL
Rye Hill Copse
Lodge Copse
LODGE DRO
Avon Valley Path
Bohemia
Whiteshoot Farm
North Charford
Hookers Copse
Hatchet Green
HATCHET CL
CARTERS CL
ST GEORGE'S COTTS
TETHERING DRO
BOHEMIA LA
LOOSE HANGER
FOREST RD
HALE LA
Cemy
Hale Prim Sch
Home Farm
Hale
Hale Farm
Hale Park
QUEEN ST
Hale
Folly Drove
Hale Purlieu
MAYS FIRS
Maydene
B3080
4
21
3
20
2
19
1
18
18
19
20
D
E
F

71

48

47

Titchborne Farm

MOOR LA

Great Sherwood Copse

Redhills

Mollcroft Copse

Gill's Hole

Horse Pond Copse

Wall Copse

East Copse

Thorn's Copse

4

Lower Pensworth Farm

Newhouse

Bagfield Copse

GROVE LA

21

GOGG'S LA

Out Wood

River Blackwater

TIMBERLEY LA

Timbury Farm House

Shearwood Copse

Appsy Copse

Homan's Copse

Langley Wood

Round Copse

3

Badger's Copse

Brickkiln Cottages

Witterns Hill Farm

Lover

The Foresters Arms (PH)

VICARAGE RD

Langley Wood

COLE'S LA

CHURCH WLK

Cole's Copse

CHURCH HILL

Bishops Wood

Golf Course

PO

SCHOOL RD

The Mount

Redlynch CE Sch

Ford

20

BLACK LA

Moor Copse

Hamptworth Farm

HAMPTWORTH RD

Loosehanger Farm

Hamptworth Lodge

Home Farm

2

Loosehanger Copse

The Bog

Pimlico Firs

19

Loosehanger Common

Pimlico Bottom

1

Radnor Firs

LYBURN RD

Lyburn Farm

Quar Hill Plantation

Horse Common

B3080

Windyeats Farm

Cloven Hill Plantation

18

47   72

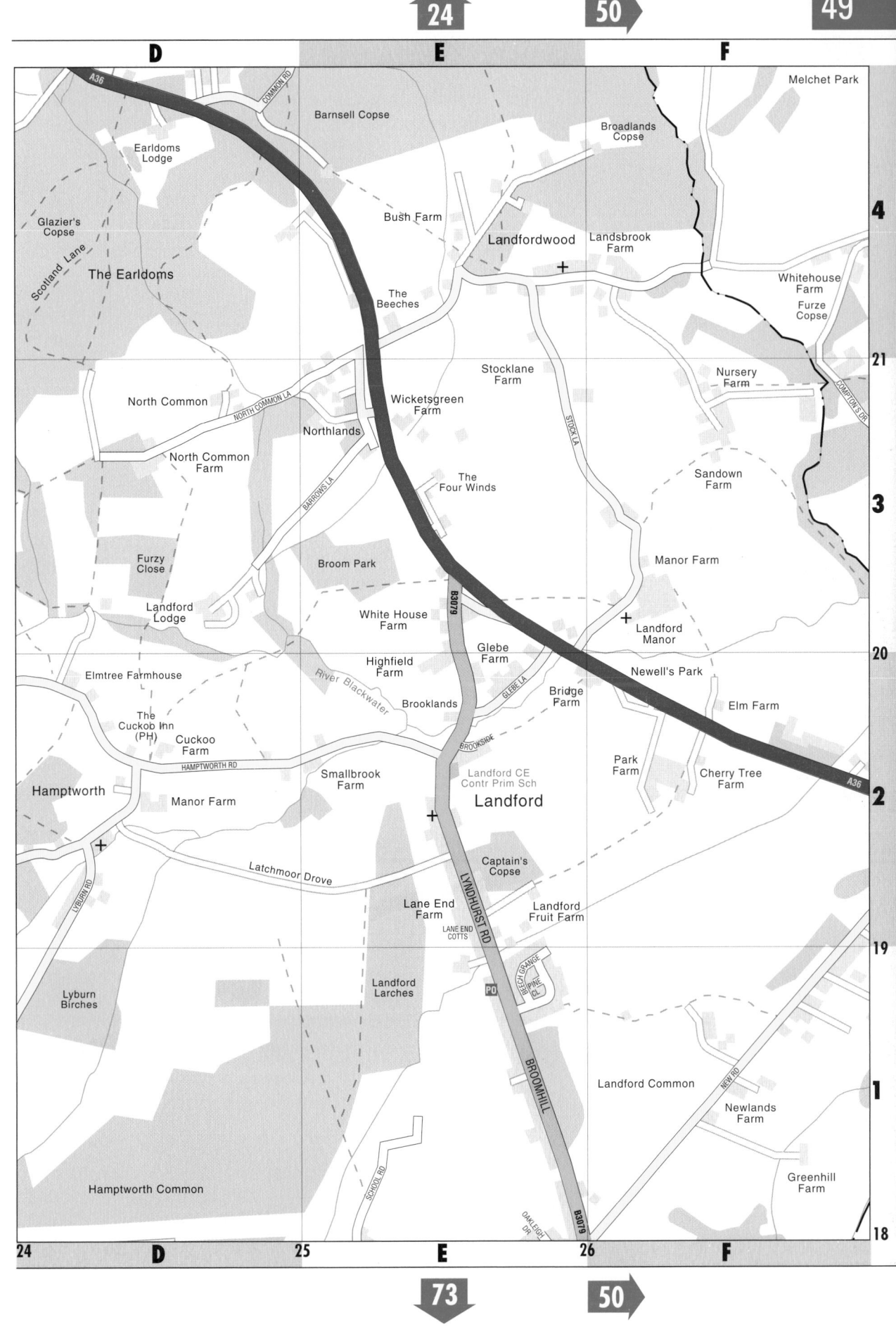

D
E
F

Melchet Park

A36

Barnsell Copse

Earldoms
Lodge

Broadlands
Copse

Glazier's
Copse

4

Scotland Lane

Bush Farm

Landfordwood

Landsbrook
Farm

The Earldoms

Whitehouse
Farm

The Beeches

Furze
Copse

21

NORTH COMMON LA

North Common

Wicketsgreen
Farm

Stocklane
Farm

Nursery
Farm

COMPTON'S DR

Northlands

STOCK LA

Sandown
Farm

North Common
Farm

BARRONS LA

The
Four Winds

3

Furzy
Close

Broom Park

Manor Farm

Landford
Lodge

White House
Farm

B3079

Landford
Manor

Elmtree Farmhouse

Highfield
Farm

Glebe
Farm

Newell's Park

20

River Blackwater

Brooklands

GLEBE LA

Bridge
Farm

Elm Farm

The
Cuckoo Inn
(PH)

Cuckoo
Farm

BROOKSIDE

Park
Farm

Cherry Tree
Farm

HAMPTWORTH RD

Smallbrook
Farm

Landford CE
Contr Prim Sch

A36

Hamptworth

Manor Farm

Landford

2

LYBURN RD

Latchmoor Drove

Captain's
Copse

LYNDHURST RD

Lane End
Farm

Landford
Fruit Farm

LANE END
COTTS

19

Lyburn
Birches

Landford
Larches

PO

BEECH GRANGE

PINE
CL

BROOMHILL

Landford Common

NEW RD

1

Newlands
Farm

SCHOOL RD

Greenhill
Farm

Hamptworth Common

OAKLEIGH
DR

B3079

18

24
D
25
E
26
F

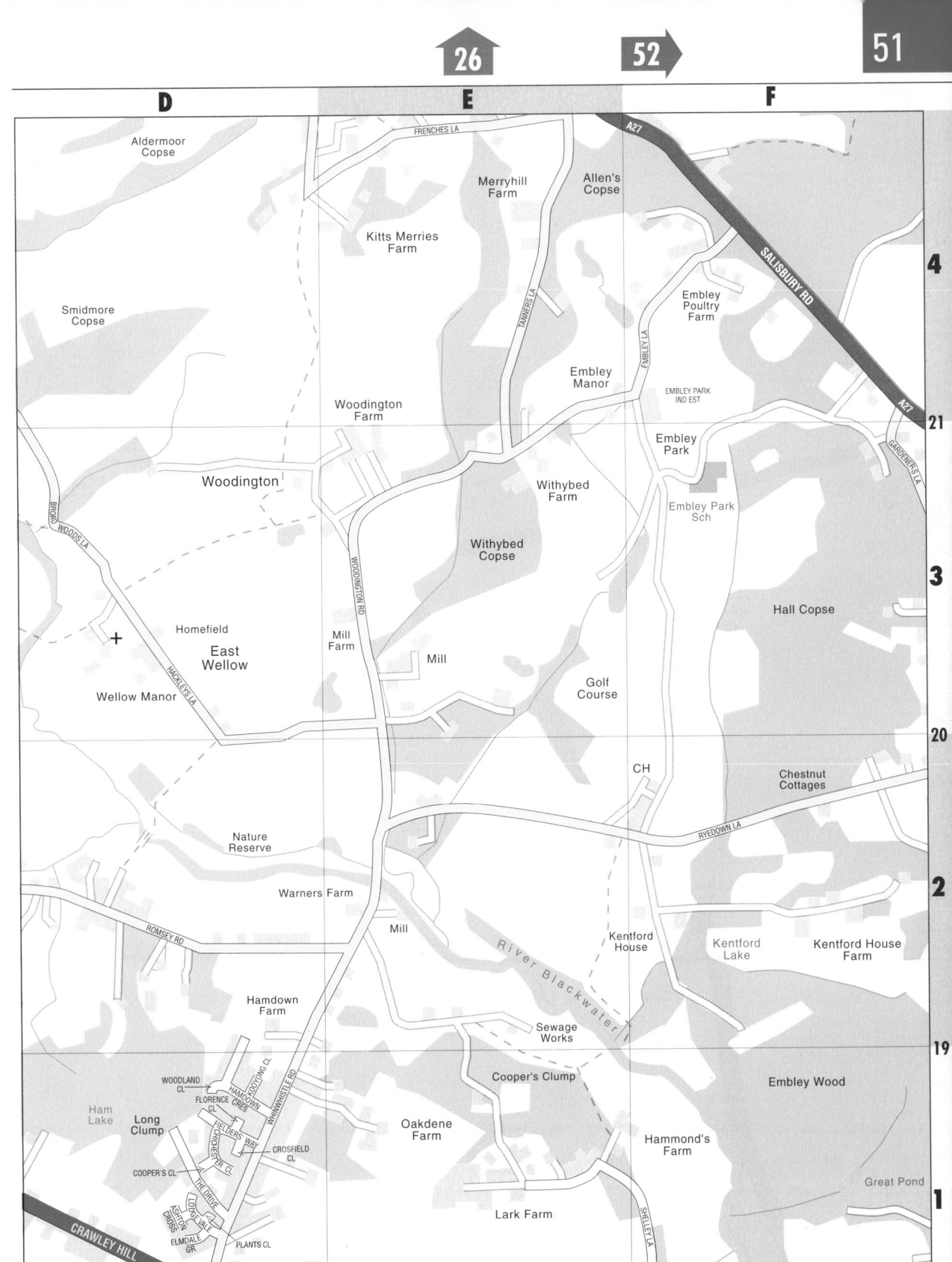

D
E
F

Aldermoor
Copse

FRENCHES LA

Merryhill
Farm

Allen's
Copse

A27

SALISBURY RD

Kitts Merries
Farm

Smidmore
Copse

TANNERS LA

Embley
Manor

Embley Poultry
Farm

EMBLEY LA

4

A27

Woodington
Farm

Embley
Park

EMBLEY PARK
IND EST

Woodington

BROAD WOODS LA

WOODINGTON RD

Withybed
Farm

Embley Park
Sch

GARDENER'S LA

21

Withybed
Copse

3

Hall Copse

Homefield

East
Wellow

HACKLEYS LA

Mill
Farm

Mill

Golf
Course

Wellow Manor

CH

Chestnut
Cottages

20

Nature
Reserve

RYEDOWN LA

Warners Farm

2

ROMSEY RD

Mill

Kentford
House

Kentford
Lake

Kentford House
Farm

River Blackwater

Hamdown
Farm

Sewage
Works

19

Cooper's Clump

Embley Wood

WOODLAND
CL

Ham
Lake

Long
Clump

KYOTING CL

HAMDOWN

WHINWHISTLE RD

FLORENCE
CL

FIELDERS WAY

Oakdene
Farm

Hammond's
Farm

HITCHENER CL

CROSFIELD
CL

COOPER'S CL

THE DRIVE

LODYCKALE

Great Pond

1

CRAWLEY HILL

ASHTON
CROSS

ELMDALE
GR

PLANTS CL

Lark Farm

SHELLEY LA

Blackhill

Blackhill
Farm

BLACKHILL RD

A36

Fighting Cocks
Farm

Shelley
Bungalow

Shelley Common

Romsey Common
Farm

18

30
D
31
E
32
F

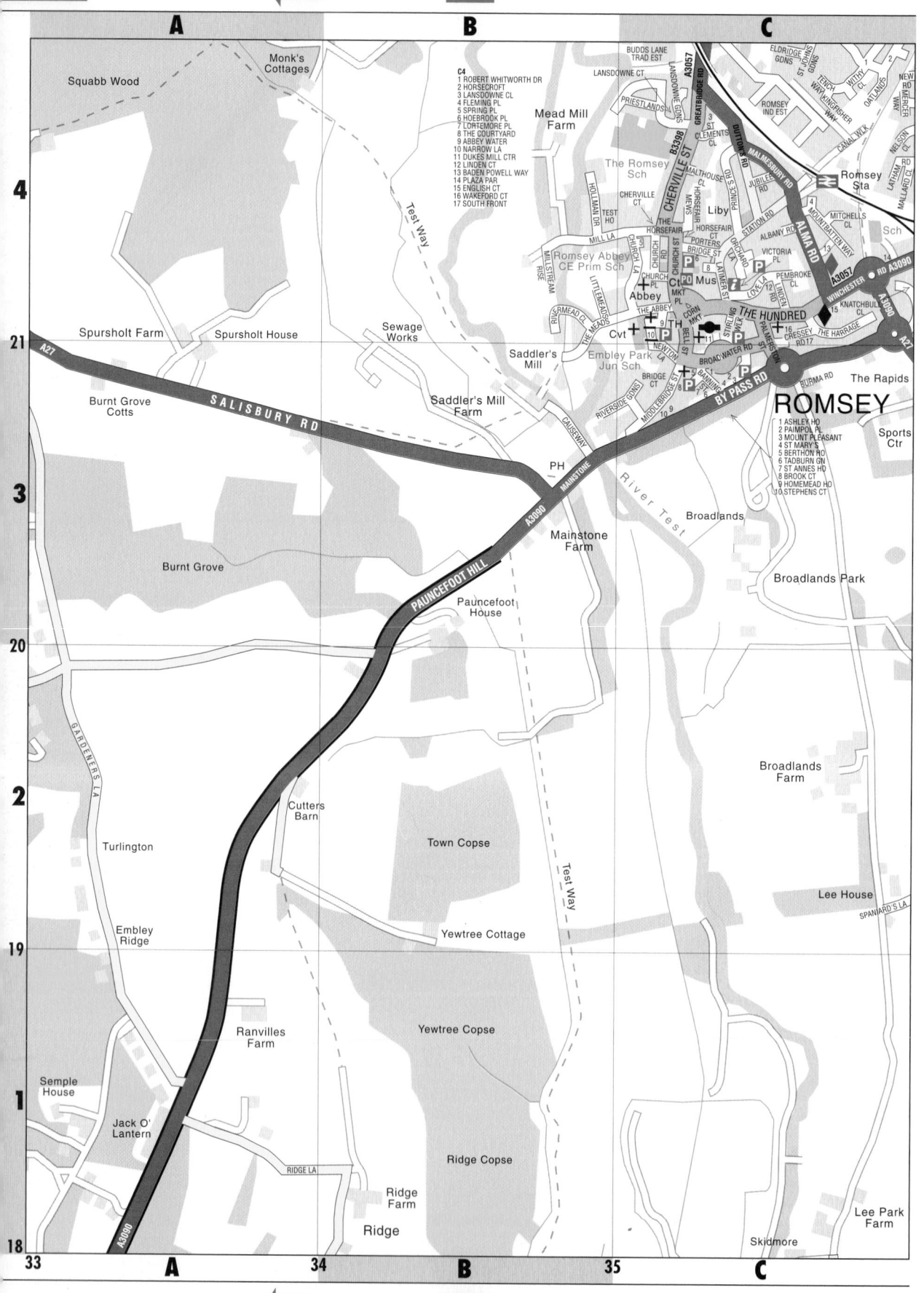

C4
1 ROBERT WHITWORTH DR
2 HORSECROFT
3 LANSDOWNE CL
4 FLEMING PL
5 SPRING PL
6 HOEBROOK PL
7 LORTEMORE PL
8 THE COURTYARD
9 ABBEY WATER
10 NARROW LA
11 DUKES MILL CTR
12 LINDEN CT
13 BADEN POWELL WAY
14 PLAZA PAR
15 ENGLISH CT
16 WAKEFORD CT
17 SOUTH FRONT

ROMSEY
1 ASHLEY HO
2 PAIMPOL PL
3 MOUNT PLEASANT
4 ST MARY'S
5 BERTHON HO
6 TADBURN GN
7 ST ANNES HO
8 BROOK CT
9 HOMEMEAD HO
10 STEPHENS CT

28
54

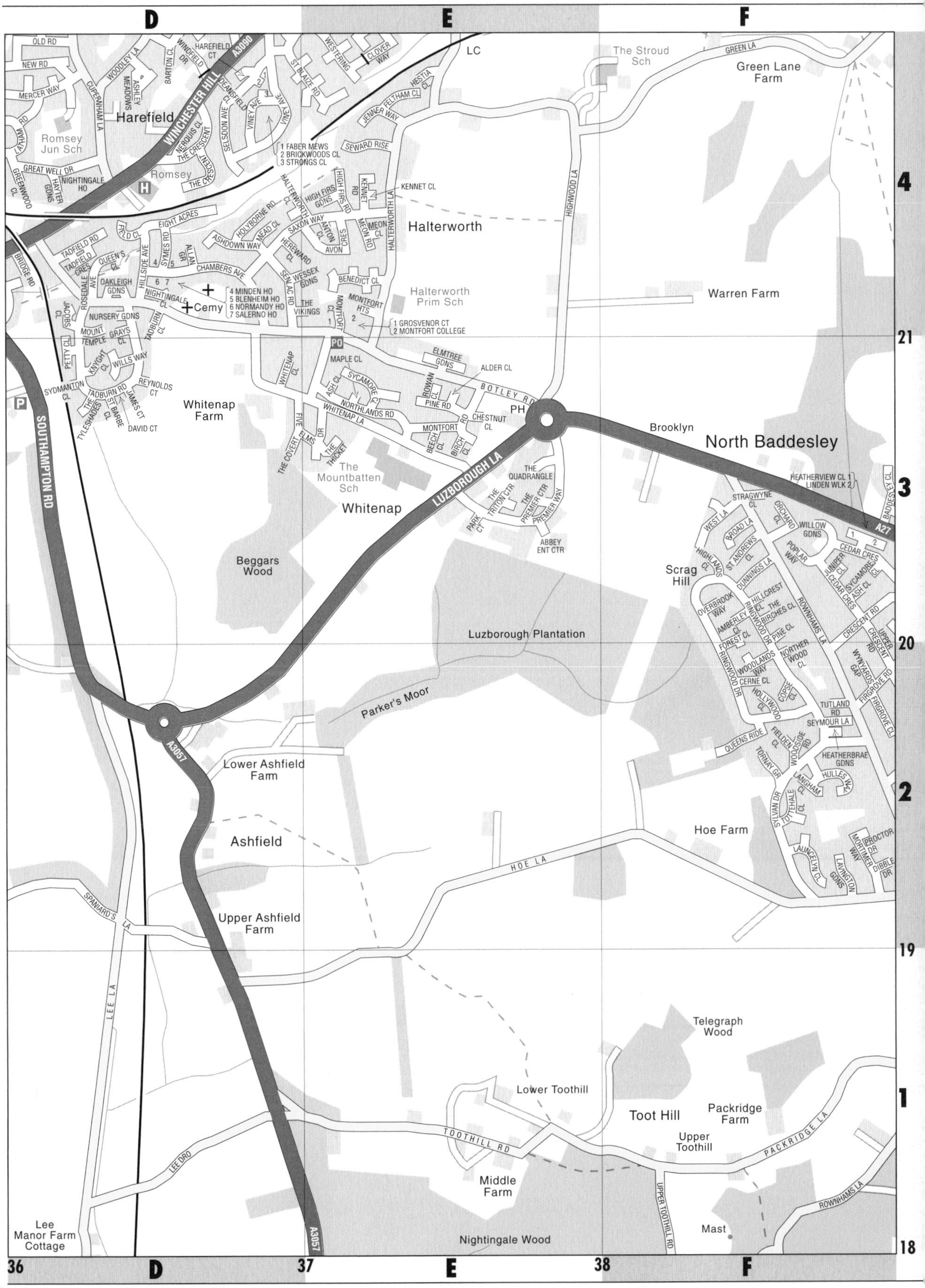
D
E
F
4
21
3
20
2
19
1
18
36
37
38
Harefield
Romsey Jun Sch
Romsey
WINCHESTER HILL
A3090
OLD RD
NEW RD
MERCER WAY
WOODLEY LA
CUPERNHAM LA
ASHLEY MEADOWS
BARTON CL
WINDFIELD DR
HAREFIELD CT
DEANSFIELD CL
SELSDON AVE
NEROUIS CL
THE CRESCENT
VINEY AVE
ST BLAIZE RD
WESTERING
CLOVER WAY
1 FABER MEWS
2 BRICKWOODS CL
3 STRONGS CL
GREAT WELL DR
NIGHTINGALE HO
HAYTER GDNS
GREENWOOD CL
LC
The Stroud Sch
GREEN LA
Green Lane Farm
HESTIA CL
FELTHAM CL
JENNER WAY
SEWARD RISE
HIGH FIRS RD
HIGH FIRS GDNS
KENNET RD
KENNET CL
HALTERWORTH CL
HALTERWORTH LA
HIGHWOOD LA
Halterworth
EIGHT ACRES
FIELD CL
HOLYBORNE RD
MEAD CL
ASHDOWN WAY
SAXON WAY
ANTON CL
AVON CRES
MEON RD
MEON CL
HEREWARD CL
TADFIELD RD
TADFIELD CRES
QUEEN'S AVE
ROSEDALE AVE
HILLSIDE AVE
SYMES RD
ALLAN GR
CHAMBERS AVE
OAKLEIGH GDNS
NIGHTINGALE CL
4 MINDEN HO
5 BLENHEIM HO
6 NORMANDY HO
7 SALERNO HO
Cemy
SEN AC RD
WESSEX GDNS
THE VIKINGS
BENEDICT CL
MONTFORT CL
MONTFORT HTS
1 GROSVENOR CT
2 MONTFORT COLLEGE
Halterworth Prim Sch
Warren Farm
BRIDGE RD
JACOBS CL
NURSERY GDNS
MOUNT TEMPLE
GRAYS CL
TADBURN CL
PETTY CL
KNIGHT CL
WILLS WAY
REYNOLDS CT
SYDMANTON CL
TADBURN RD
ST BARBE CL
JAMES CT
DAVID CT
THE TYLESHADES
P
PO
SOUTHAMPTON RD
Whitenap Farm
WHITENAP CL
MAPLE CL
SYCAMORE CL
ASH CL
NORTHLANDS RD
WHITENAP LA
ROWAN CL
PINE RD
ELMTREE GDNS
ALDER CL
BOTLEY RD
PH
CHESTNUT CL
MONTFORT
BEECH CL
BIRCH CL
FIVE ELMS DR
THE COVERT
THE THICKET
The Mountbatten Sch
Whitenap
LUZBOROUGH LA
THE QUADRANGLE
THE TRITON CTR
THE PREMIER CTR
PREMIER WAY
PARK CT
ABBEY ENT CTR
Brooklyn
North Baddesley
HEATHERVIEW CL 1
LINDEN WLK 2
BADDESLEY CL
A27
STRAGWYNE CL
ORCHARD CL
WEST LA
BROAD LA
WILLOW GDNS
CEDAR CRES
POPLAR WAY
JUNIPER CL
SYCAMORE CL
CEDAR CRES
ASH CL
Beggars Wood
Scrag Hill
HIGHLANDS CL
ST ANDREWS CL
DUNNINGS LA
OVERBROOK WAY
HILLCREST
AMBERLEY CL
THE BIRCHES CL
RINGWOOD DR
PINE CL
ROWNHAMS LA
CRESCENT RD
UPPER CRESCENT RD
Luzborough Plantation
FOREST CL
WOODLANDS WAY
NORTHER WOOD CL
CERNE CL
HOLLYWOOD CL
COPSE CL
WYNYARDS GAP
FIRGROVE RD
Parker's Moor
TUTLAND RD
SEYMOUR LA
QUEENS RIDE
FIELDEN CL
WOODSIDE RD
TORNAY GR
HEATHERBRAE GDNS
HULLES WAY
LANGHAM CL
SYLVAN DR
TOTTEHALE CL
A3057
Lower Ashfield Farm
Ashfield
Hoe Farm
HOE LA
LAUNCELYN CL
LAVINGTON GDNS
MORTIMER WAY
PROCTOR DR
DIBBLE DR
SPANIARD'S LA
Upper Ashfield Farm
LEE LA
Telegraph Wood
Lower Toothill
Toot Hill
Packridge Farm
Upper Toothill
TOOTHILL RD
PACKRIDGE LA
LEE DRO
Middle Farm
UPPER TOOTHILL RD
ROWNHAMS LA
Mast
Lee Manor Farm Cottage
Nightingale Wood

77
54

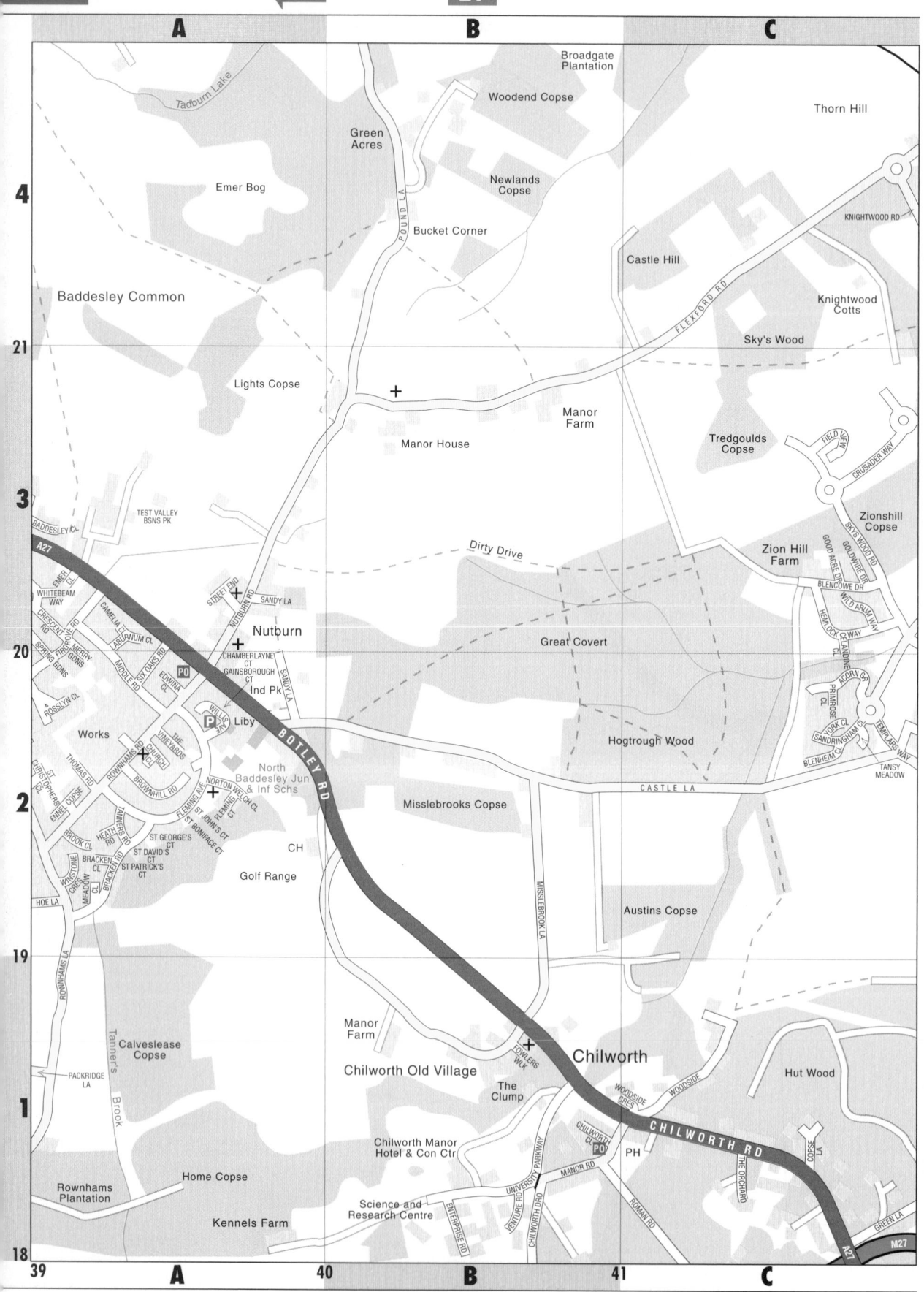

A   B   C

4

Thorn Hill

Tadburn Lake

Broadgate Plantation

Woodend Copse

Green Acres

Emer Bog

KNIGHTWOOD RD

Newlands Copse

POUND LA

Bucket Corner

Castle Hill

Knightwood Cotts

Baddesley Common

FLEXFORD RD

Sky's Wood

21

Lights Copse

Manor Farm

Tredgoulds Copse

CRUSADER WAY

FIELD VIEW

Manor House

3

SKY'S WOOD RD

Zionshill Copse

TEST VALLEY BSNS PK

Dirty Drive

Zion Hill Farm

GOLDWIRE DR

GOOD ACRE DR

BLENCOWE DR

WILD ARUM WAY

HEMLOCK CL

BADDESLEY CL

A27

WHITEBEAM WAY

EMER CL

CRESCENT RD

FIRSTHILL RD

MERRY GDNS

CAMELIA CT

LABURNUM CL

SANDY LA

STREET END

NUTBURN RD

CELANDINE WAY

ACORN CP

Nutburn

CHAMBERLAYNE CT

GAINSBOROUGH CT

Great Covert

PRIMROSE CL

SANDRINGHAM

20

SPRING GDNS

ROSSLYN CL

MIDDLE RD

SIX OAKS RD

EDWINA CL

PO

Ind Pk

SANDY LA

BLENHEIM CL

TEMPLARS WAY

Works

THE VINEYARDS

P

Liby

Hogtrough Wood

TANSY MEADOW

THOMAS RD

ROWNHAMS RD

BROWNHILL RD

CHURCH RD

North Baddesley Jun & Inf Schs

NORTON WELCH CL

FLEMING CT

Misslebrooks Copse

CASTLE LA

2

ST CHRISTOPHERS CL

EMBLEY CL

TANNERS RD

HEATH RD

BRACKEN CL

ST JOHN'S CT

ST BONIFACE CT

FLEMING AVE

CH

Austins Copse

BROOK CL

WYRSTONE CL

MEADOW CL

ORESTONE CL

ST GEORGE'S CT

ST DAVID'S CT

ST PATRICK'S CT

Golf Range

MISSLEBROOK LA

HOE LA

BOTLEY RD

19

ROWNHAMS LA

Tanner's Brook

Calveslease Copse

Manor Farm

Chilworth

FOWLERS WLK

Hut Wood

PACKRIDGE LA

Chilworth Old Village

WOODSIDE CRES

WOODSIDE

COPSE LA

THE ORCHARD

1

The Clump

CHILWORTH CL

PO

PH

CHILWORTH RD

Home Copse

Rownhams Plantation

Chilworth Manor Hotel & Con Ctr

VENTURE RD

CHILWORTH DRO

UNIVERSITY PARKWAY

MANOR RD

ROMAN RD

GREEN LA

A27

M27

Kennels Farm

Science and Research Centre

ENTERPRISE RD

18

39   A   40   B   41   C

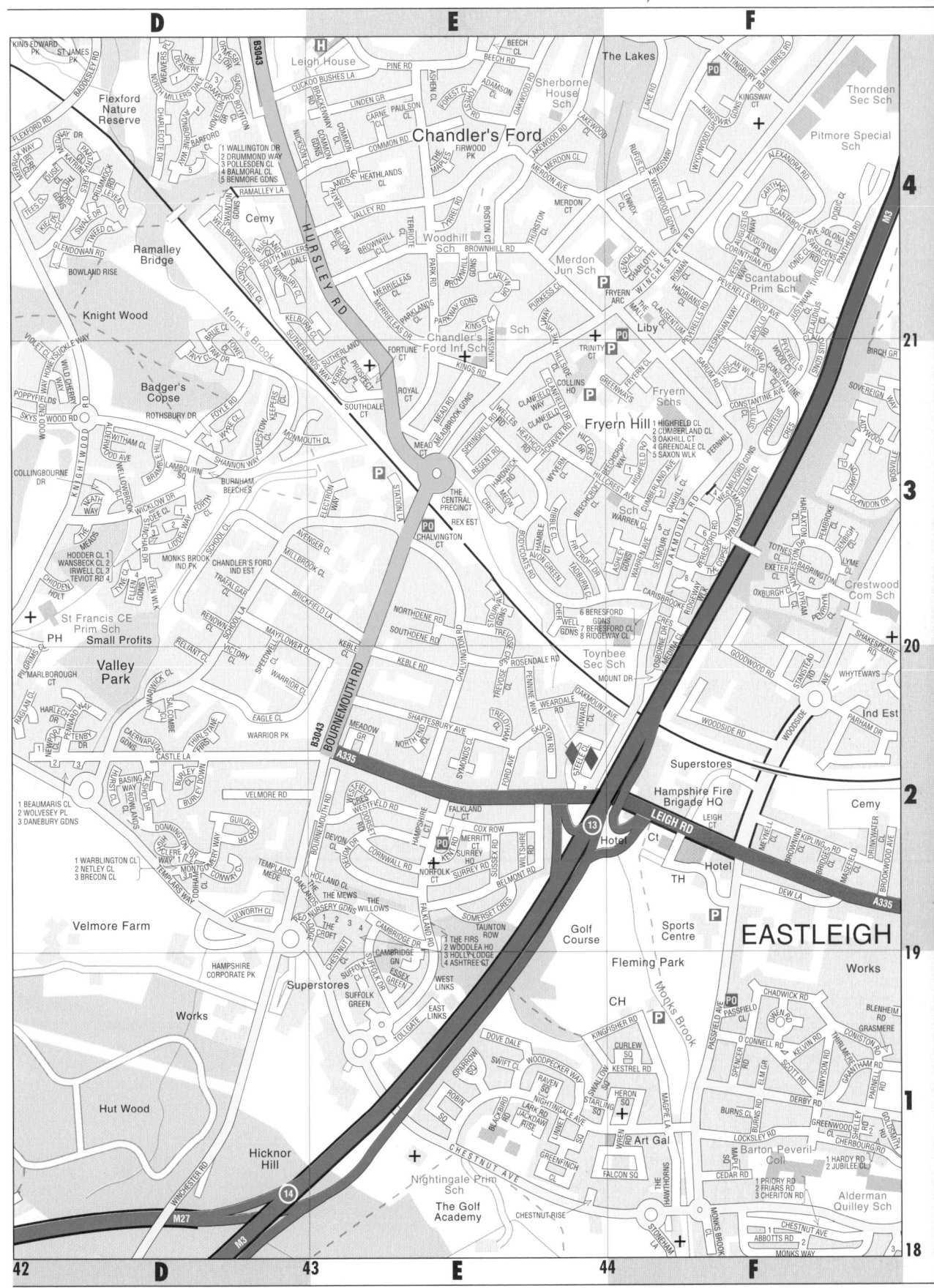

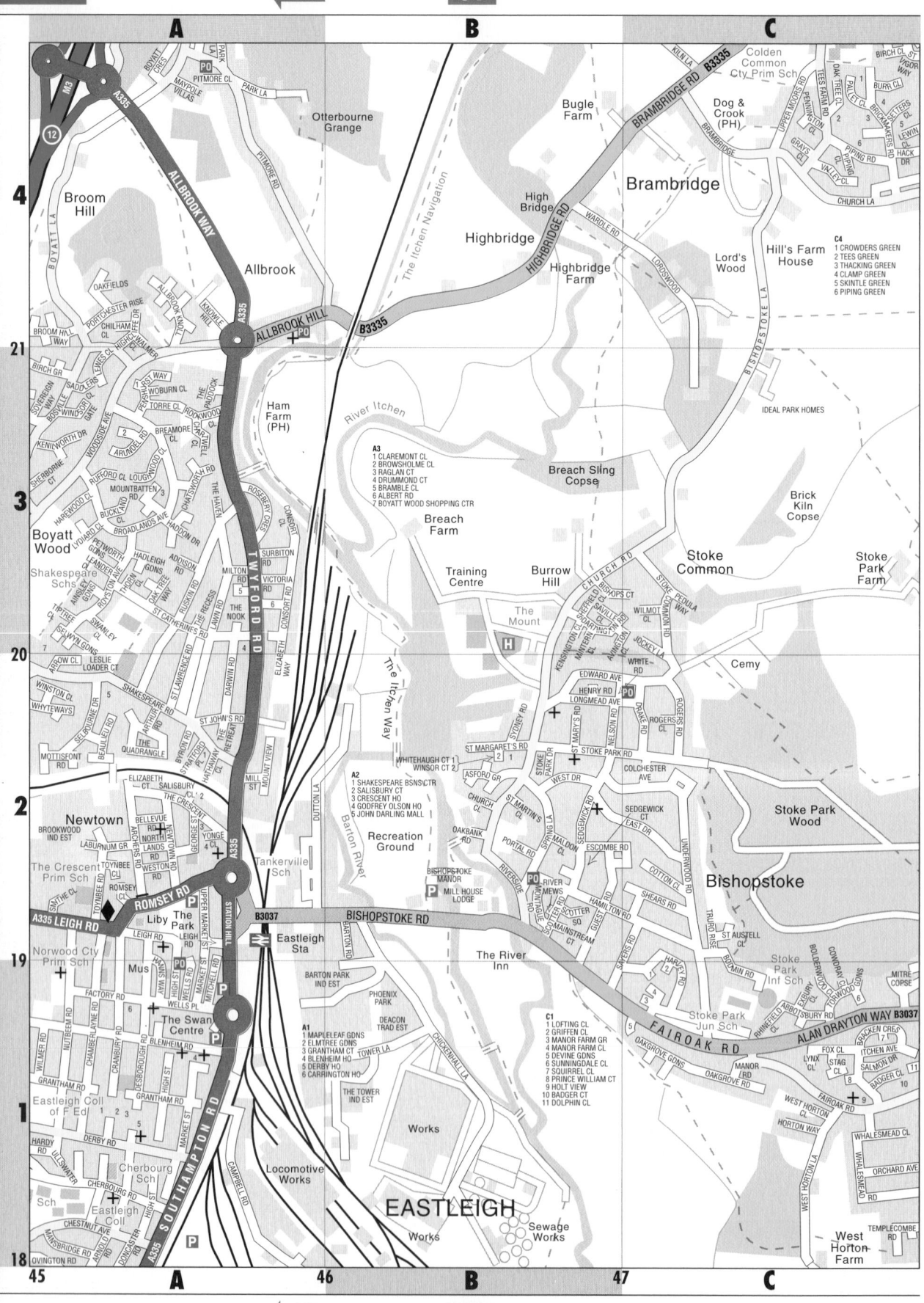

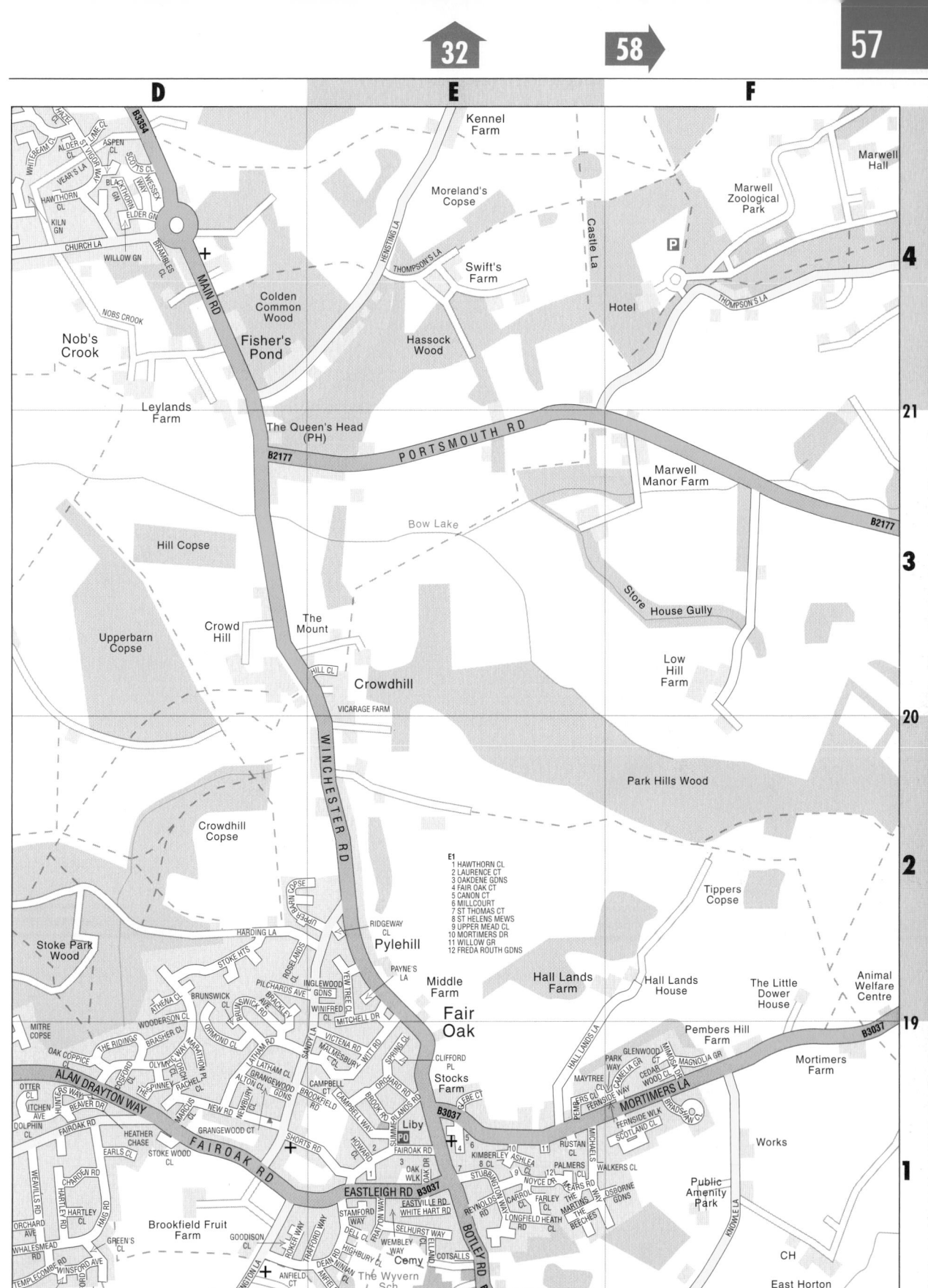

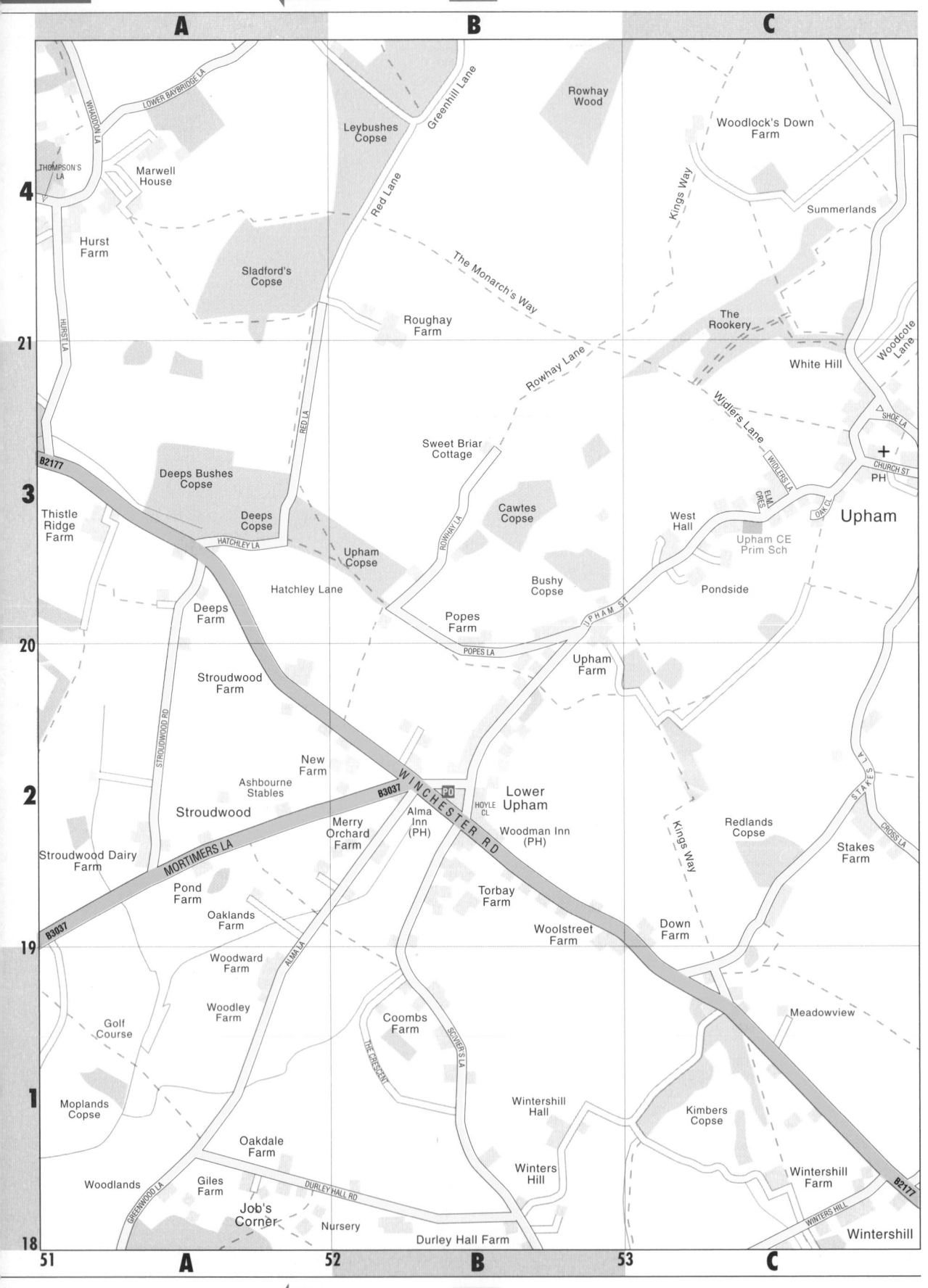

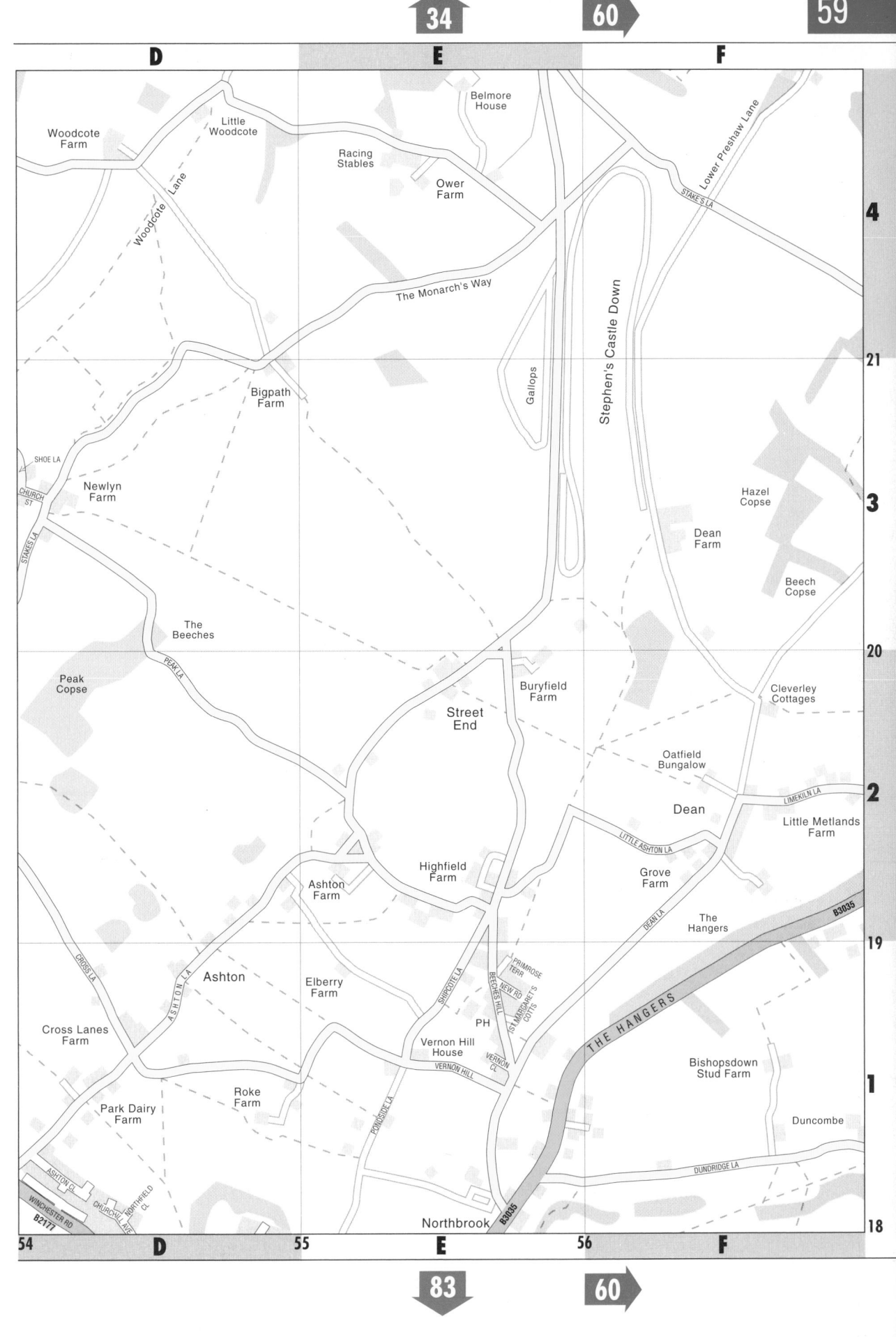

A **B** **C**

4

Sargeant's Copse

King's Copse

SAILORS LA

Downleaze Copse

Punch Bowl

Shellets Farm

Winters Down

LONE BARN LA

Littleton Copse

St Clair's Farm

STAKES LA

Corhampton Forest

21

Franklin Lane

Warners Cottage

BEACON HILL LA

Wyndham Lodge

CORHAMPTON LA

3

Bottom Copse

Franklin Farm

Corhampton Lane Farm

Wayfarer's Walk

Steynes Farm

B3035

Greenacres

Corhampton Down

Golf Course

Droxford Down

20

Club House

LIMEKILN LA

Hazel Holt

SHEEP POND LA

2

THE HANGERS

Hazel Holt Farm

Shepherds Down Farm

B3035

Galley Down

19

DUNDRIDGE LA

Shepherds Down

Peak Down

HACKETTS LA

Lycroft Farm

Wayfarer's Walk

1

Dundridge

Hampshire Bowman (PH)

PARK LA

Dundridge Farm

Swanmore Barn Farm

DAMSON HILL

Beechen Copse

Fir Down

Field Farm

Swanmore Park Farm

18

57 **A** **58** **B** **59** **C**

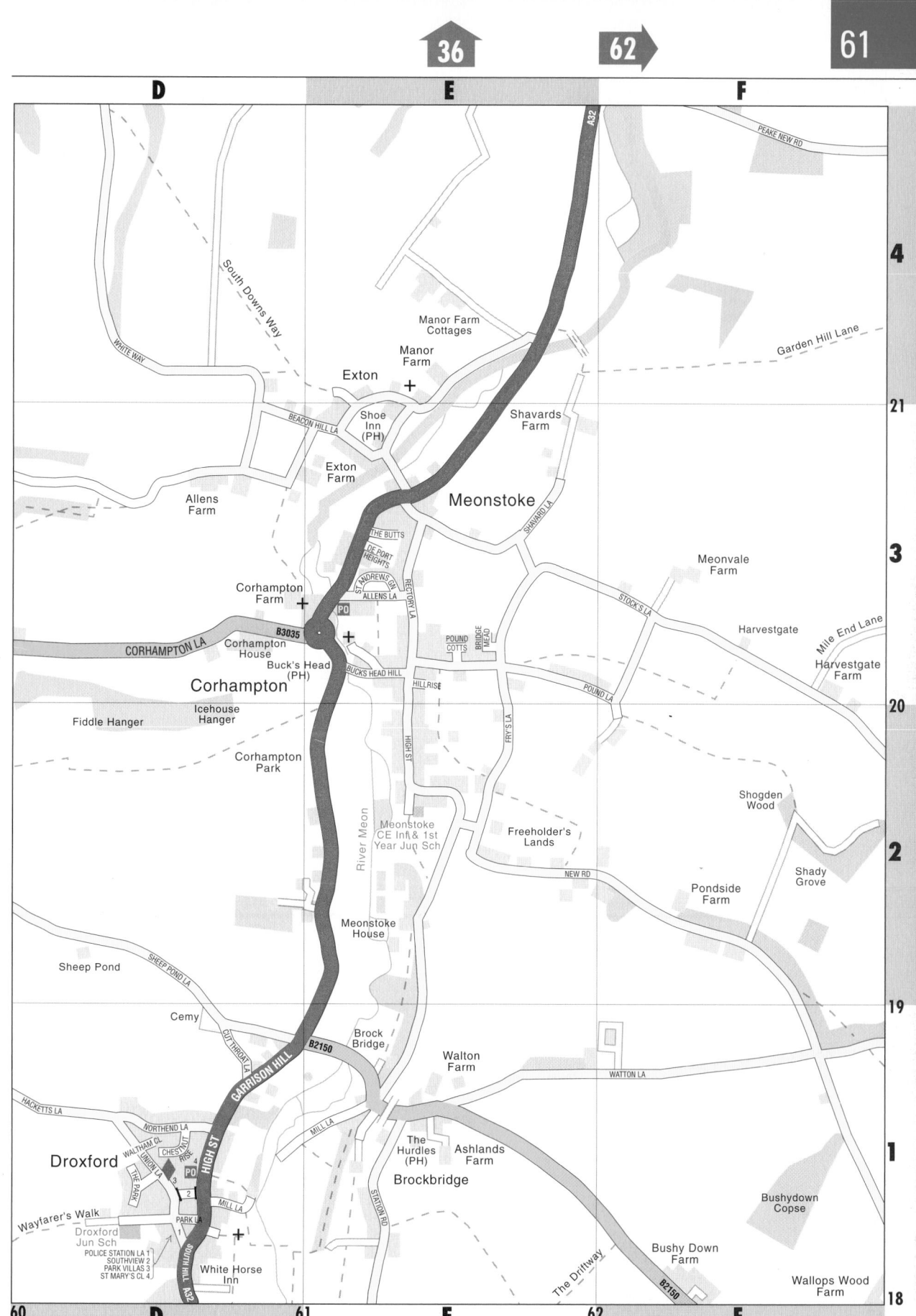

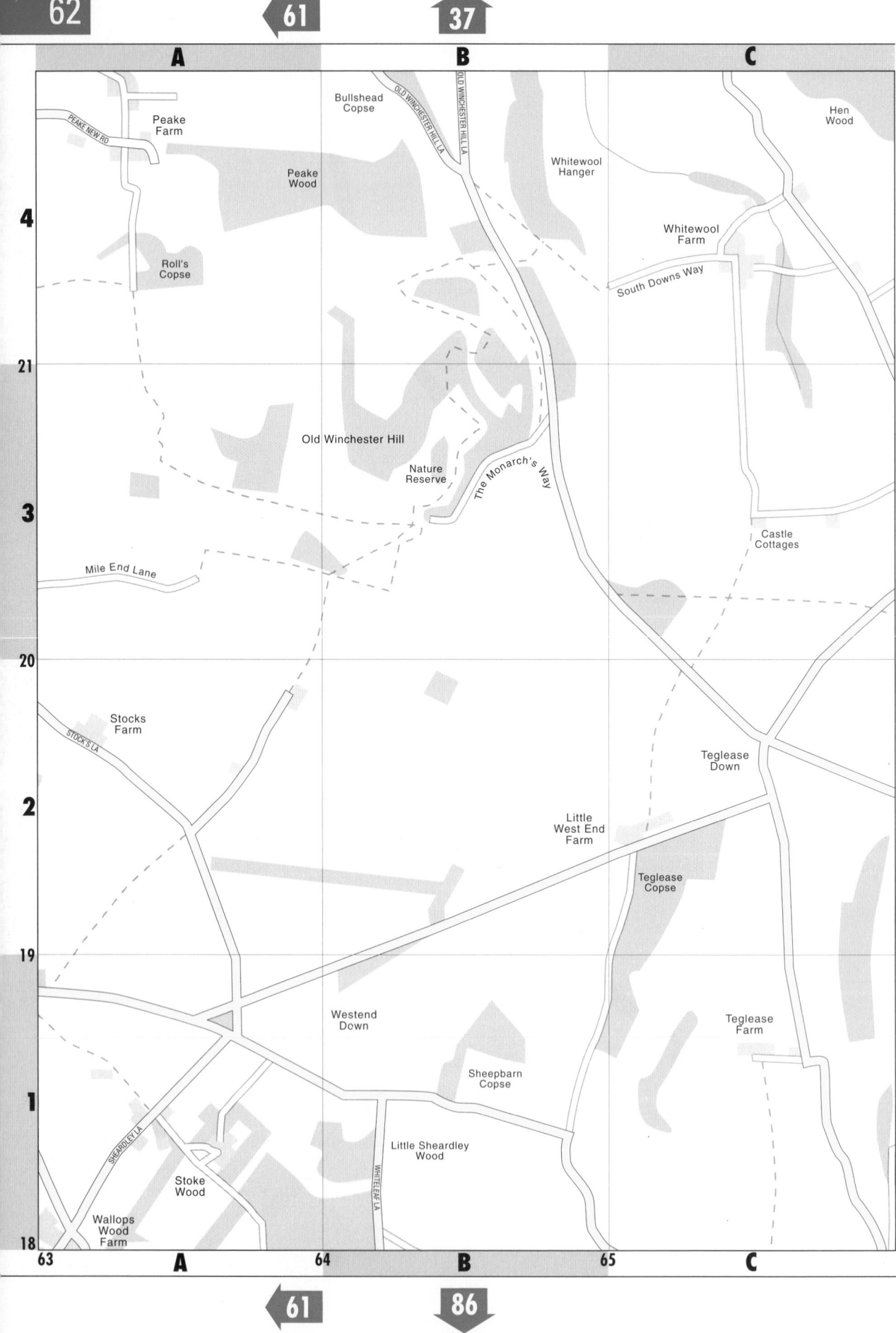

A
B
C

Peake New Rd

Peake
Farm

Bullshead
Copse

Old Winchester Hill La

Old Winchester Hill La

Hen
Wood

Whitewool
Hanger

Peake
Wood

4

Whitewool
Farm

Roll's
Copse

South Downs Way

21

Old Winchester Hill

The Monarch's Way

Nature
Reserve

Castle
Cottages

3

Mile End Lane

20

Stocks
Farm

Stock's La

Teglease
Down

2

Little
West End
Farm

Teglease
Copse

19

Westend
Down

Teglease
Farm

1

Sheepbarn
Copse

Sheardley La

Little Sheardley
Wood

Whiteleaf La

Stoke
Wood

Wallops
Wood
Farm

18

63
A
64
B
65
C

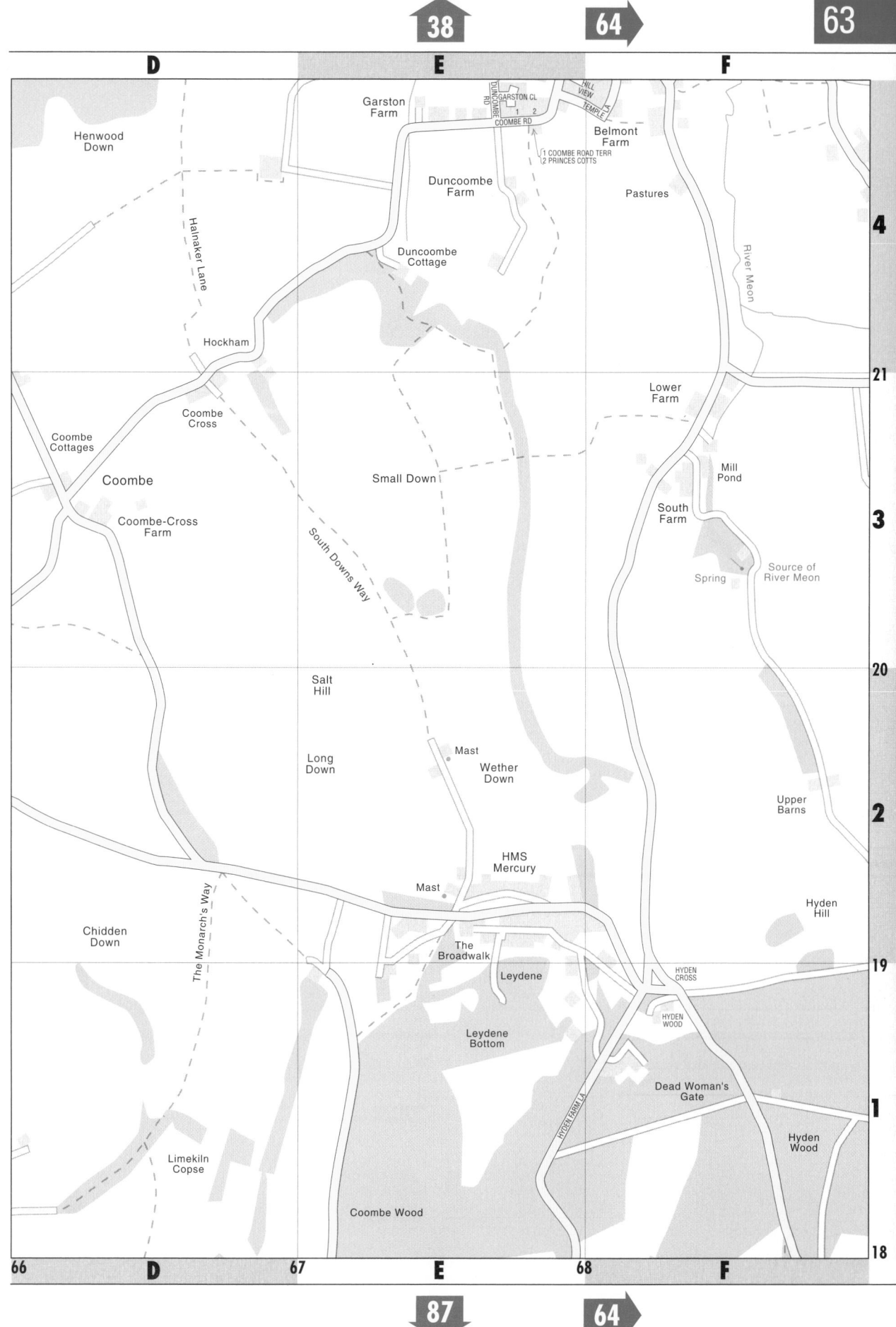

Henwood
Down

Garston
Farm

DUNCOOMBE RD
GARSTON CL
1 2
COOMBE RD
HILL VIEW
TEMPLE LA
Belmont
Farm

1 COOMBE ROAD TERR
2 PRINCES COTTS

Duncoombe
Farm

Pastures

River Meon

Halnaker Lane

Duncoombe
Cottage

4

Hockham

21

Lower
Farm

Coombe
Cross

Coombe
Cottages

Coombe

Small Down

Mill
Pond

South
Farm

3

Coombe-Cross
Farm

South Downs Way

Spring

Source of
River Meon

20

Salt
Hill

Long
Down

Mast

Wether
Down

Upper
Barns

2

The Monarch's Way

HMS
Mercury

Chidden
Down

Mast

Hyden
Hill

The
Broadwalk

Leydene

HYDEN
CROSS

19

HYDEN
WOOD

Leydene
Bottom

HYDEN FARM LA

Dead Woman's
Gate

1

Limekiln
Copse

Hyden
Wood

Coombe Wood

18

Kiln Cottages
Weston Farm
WYLDS LA
Weston
Trinity Barn
WESTON LA
Bopeep Copse
Copyhold Barn
New Barn
B2070
Quarry (disused)
Whiteland Copse
Refuse Tip
GREENWAY LA
Glebe Farm
PH
Hundry Copse
Refuse Tip
Bolinge Hill Farm
B2070 THE CAUSEWAY
Bolinge Hill Copse
Nursted House
Pilmead Row
Hoadlands Crundle
Round Copse
Furzefield Copse
Buriton
PETERSFIELD
GLEBE RD
SUMNER RD
HEATHERFIELD
HIGH ST
BONES LA
NORTH LA
PITCROFT LA
Buriton House
Mead Lane
KILN LA
SOUTH LA
Buriton Prim Sch
PO
Wooliff Pond
Appleton's Copse
War Down
Hangers Way
P
Fagg's Farm
Dean Bank
South Downs Way
Buriton Hanger
Milky Way
Cockshot Wood
Coulters Dean Farm
Ditcham Woods
Queen Elizabeth Country Park
Holt Down Plantation
Head Down Plantation
Ludgersham Copse
Gravelhill Bottom
Benhams Bushes
Queen Elizabeth Forest
Holt Down Plantation
Gorecombe Hole
Newbarn Hanger
New Barn
Head Down Hanger
Wolver Row
Oakham
Ditcham Woods
Oakham Bottom

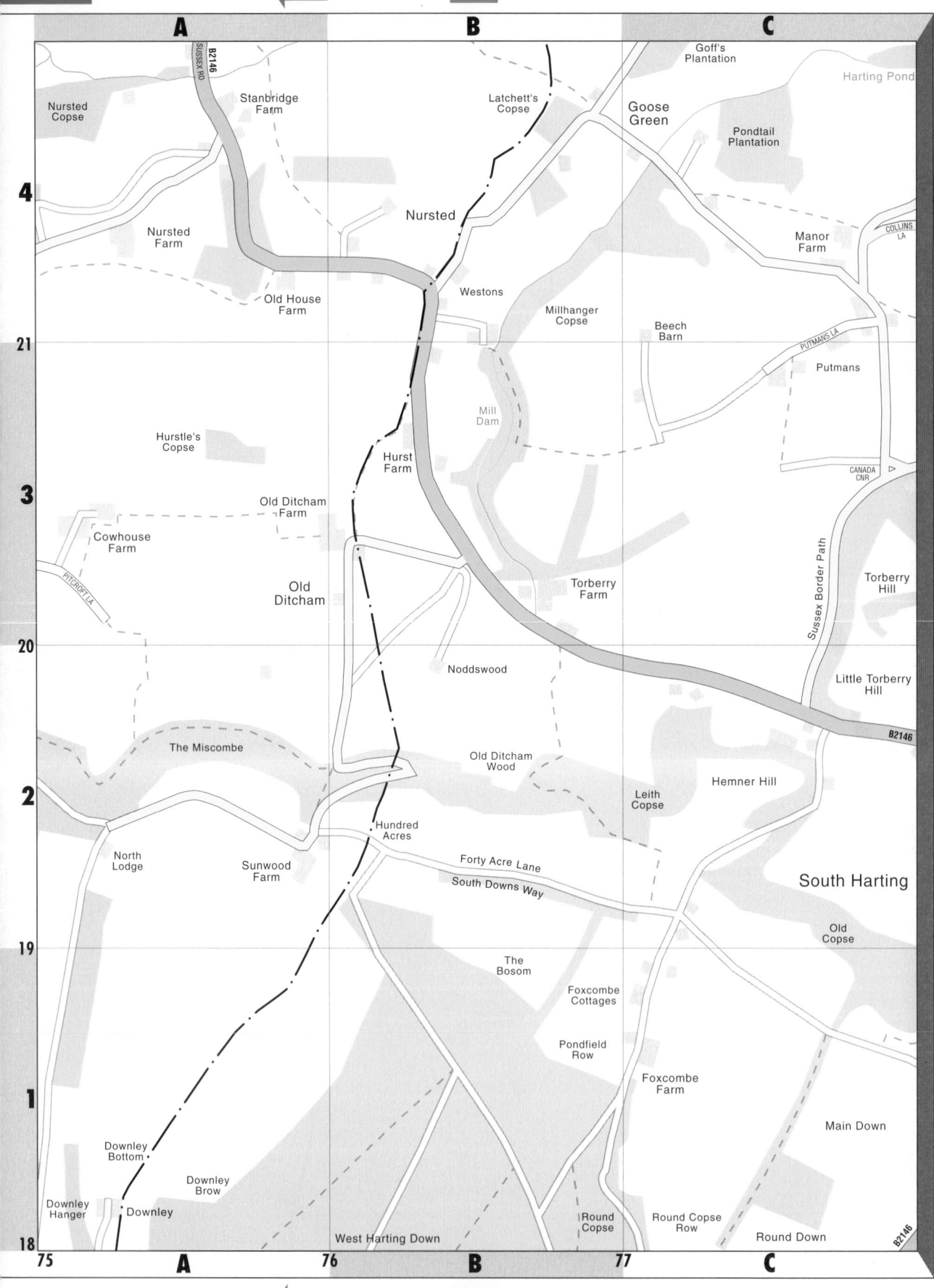

A
B
C

4

21

3

20

2

19

1

18

75
76
77

Nursted Copse

Stanbridge Farm

Latchett's Copse

Goff's Plantation

Harting Pond

Goose Green

Pondtail Plantation

SUSSEX RD
B2146

Nursted

Nursted Farm

Old House Farm

Westons

Millhanger Copse

Beech Barn

Manor Farm

COLLINS LA

PUTMANS LA

Putmans

Hurstle's Copse

Hurst Farm

Mill Dam

CANADA CNR

Old Ditcham Farm

Cowhouse Farm

PITCROFT LA

Old Ditcham

Torberry Farm

Torberry Hill

Sussex Border Path

Noddswood

Little Torberry Hill

The Miscombe

Old Ditcham Wood

Leith Copse

Hemner Hill

B2146

North Lodge

Sunwood Farm

Hundred Acres

Forty Acre Lane

South Downs Way

South Harting

Old Copse

The Bosom

Foxcombe Cottages

Pondfield Row

Foxcombe Farm

Main Down

Downley Bottom

Downley Brow

Downley Hanger

Downley

West Harting Down

Round Copse

Round Copse Row

Round Down

B2146

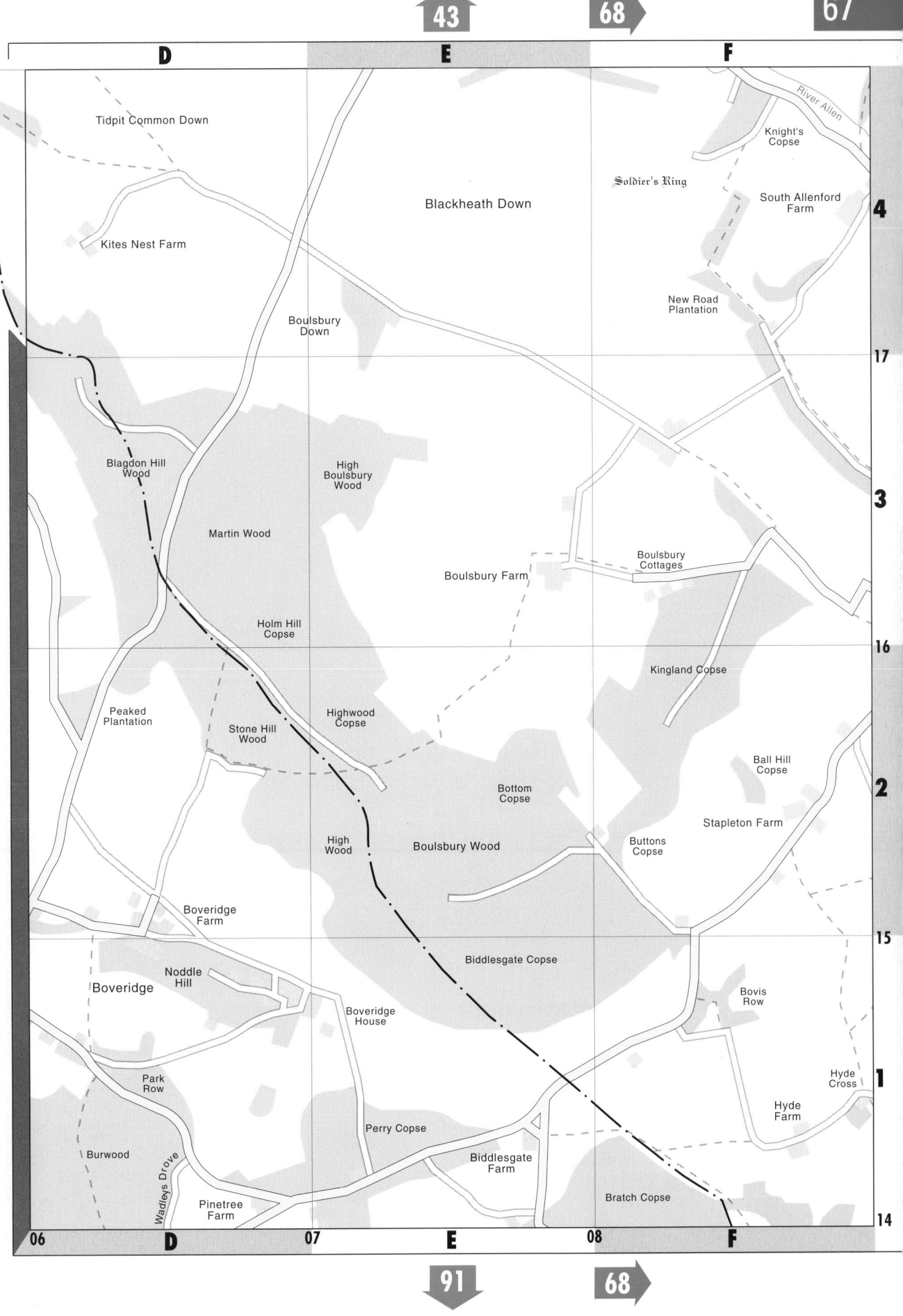

D
E
F

River Allen

Tidpit Common Down

Knight's Copse

Soldier's Ring

South Allenford Farm

4

Blackheath Down

Kites Nest Farm

New Road Plantation

Boulsbury Down

17

Blagdon Hill Wood

High Boulsbury Wood

3

Martin Wood

Boulsbury Cottages

Boulsbury Farm

Holm Hill Copse

16

Kingland Copse

Peaked Plantation

Highwood Copse

Stone Hill Wood

Ball Hill Copse

Bottom Copse

2

Stapleton Farm

High Wood

Boulsbury Wood

Buttons Copse

Boveridge Farm

15

Biddlesgate Copse

Noddle Hill

Boveridge

Bovis Row

Boveridge House

Hyde Cross

1

Park Row

Hyde Farm

Burwood

Perry Copse

Wadleys Drove

Biddlesgate Farm

Pinetree Farm

Bratch Copse

14

A   B   C

4

Knoll Farm

Little Bagland
Plantation

17

Allen River

ROCKBOURNE LA

The Belt

West Park

Littlemill
Bridge

Channel Hill
Farm

LITTLEMILL LA

North
End

Damerham

Mon

3

POUND LA

HIGH ST

WEST PARK LA

THE TERRACE

West Park Drive

Last Post

BROWNS LA

PO

East End

Court Farm

COURT HILL

Court Lodge

ELEVEN
CROSS

PH

16

FOUR
CNRS

Stony Lane

Manor
Farm
House

STEELS LA

CHURCH LA

Western Downland
CE Prim
Sch

Court Vale

Lower Breach
Copse

White's
Copse

MILL END

Hill
Farm

Courtwood
Farm

2

Manor
Farm

CORNPITS LA

South
End

Lower
Court
Wood

Ashley Farm

The
Marsh

15

Brinton
Lodge

Ashridge
Copse

Furze
Close
Copse

1

Hawkhill Ditch

Hawkhill Mill
Farm

Mill
Craft
Ctr

Lopshill
Pond

Pond
Copse

Bullhill
Copse

Andrew's
Copse

Alderholt
Bridge

P

Hill Copse

SANDLEHEATH RD

Avon
Farm

14

MINTYS HILL

THE
TERRACE

Marsh
Farm

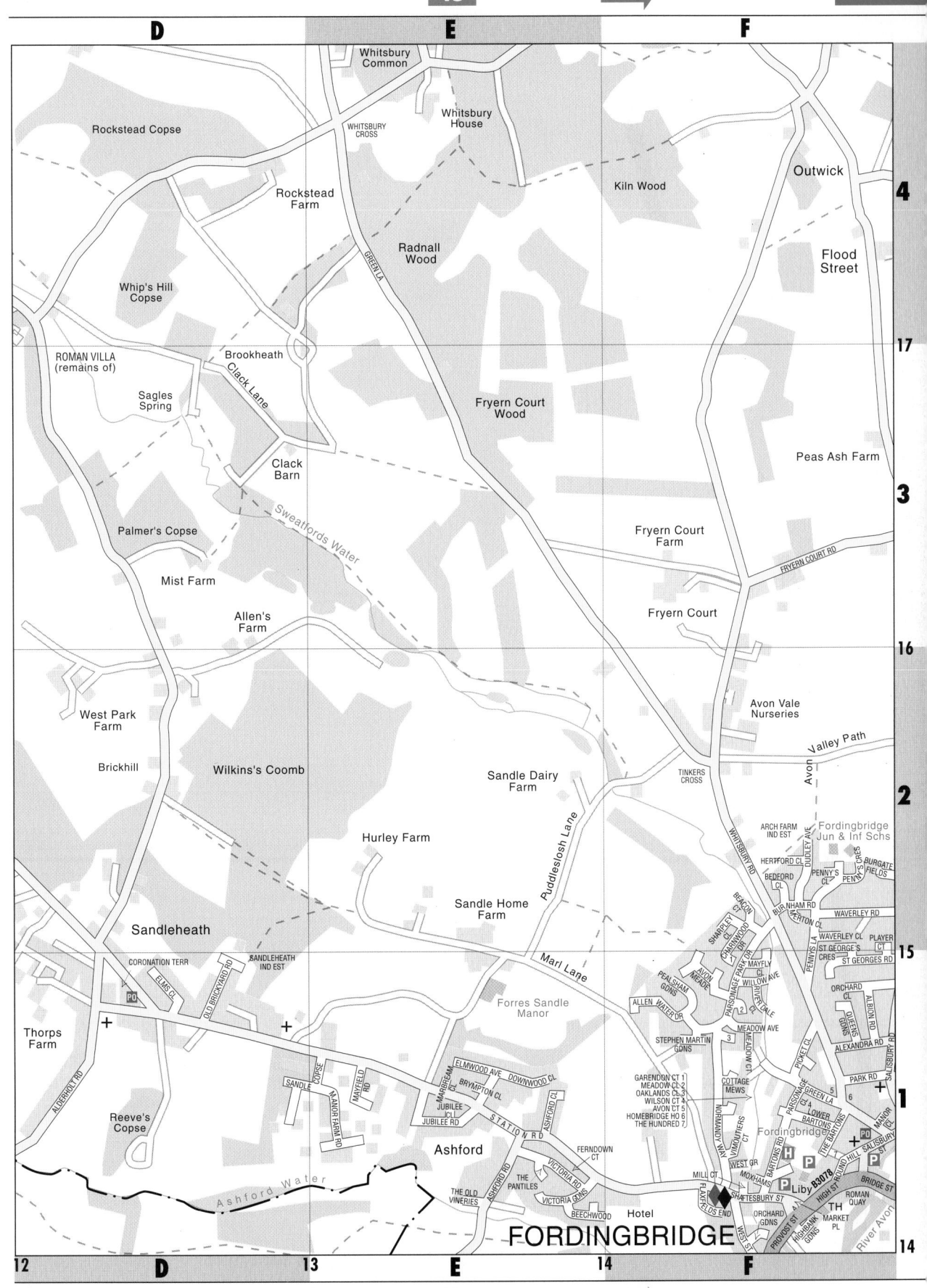

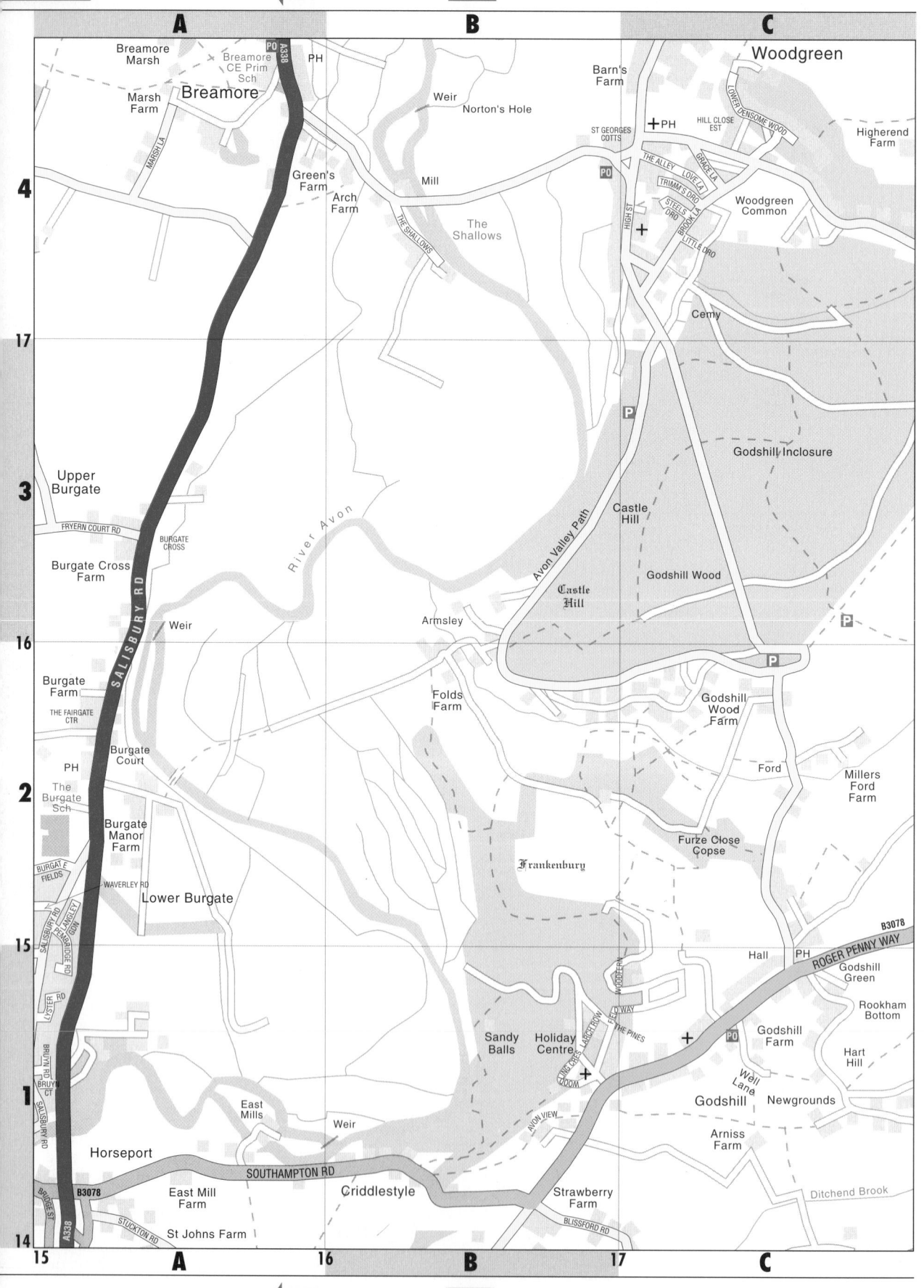

Breamore
Marsh

Breamore
CE Prim
Sch

PH

Barn's
Farm

Woodgreen

Marsh
Farm

Breamore

Weir

Norton's Hole

St Georges
Cotts

LOWER DENSOME WOOD

HILL CLOSE
EST

Higherend
Farm

+PH

4

Green's
Farm

Arch
Farm

Mill

PO

THE ALLEY LOVE LA

GRACE LA

TRIMM'S DRO

HIGH ST

STEEL'S
DRO

BROOK LA

Woodgreen
Common

The
Shallows

LITTLE DRO

THE SHALLOWS

17

Cemy

Godshill Inclosure

3

Upper
Burgate

FRYERN COURT RD

BURGATE
CROSS

River Avon

Avon Valley Path

Castle
Hill

Godshill Wood

Burgate Cross
Farm

SALISBURY RD

Weir

Armsley

Castle
Hill

P

16

Burgate
Farm

THE FAIRGATE
CTR

Folds
Farm

P

Godshill
Wood
Farm

Ford

Millers
Ford
Farm

PH

Burgate
Court

2

The
Burgate
Sch

Burgate
Manor
Farm

Frankenbury

Furze Close
Copse

BURGATE E
FIELDS

WAVERLEY RD

SALISBURY RD

LANGLEY RD

FLAMBRIDGE RD

Lower Burgate

15

LYSTER
RD

Hall

PH

ROGER PENNY WAY

B3078

Godshill
Green

BRUYN RD

BRUYN
CT

Sandy
Balls

KING CRES

ABBETSON

WOODFERN

FIELD WAY

THE PINES

Holiday
Centre

+

PO

Godshill
Farm

Rookham
Bottom

Hart
Hill

1

SALISBURY
RD

East
Mills

Weir

AVON VIEW

+

Well
Lane

Godshill

Newgrounds

Horseport

BRIDGE ST

B3078

SOUTHAMPTON RD

Criddlestyle

Strawberry
Farm

Arniss
Farm

Ditchend Brook

A338

East Mill
Farm

STUCKTON RD

St Johns Farm

BLISSFORD RD

14

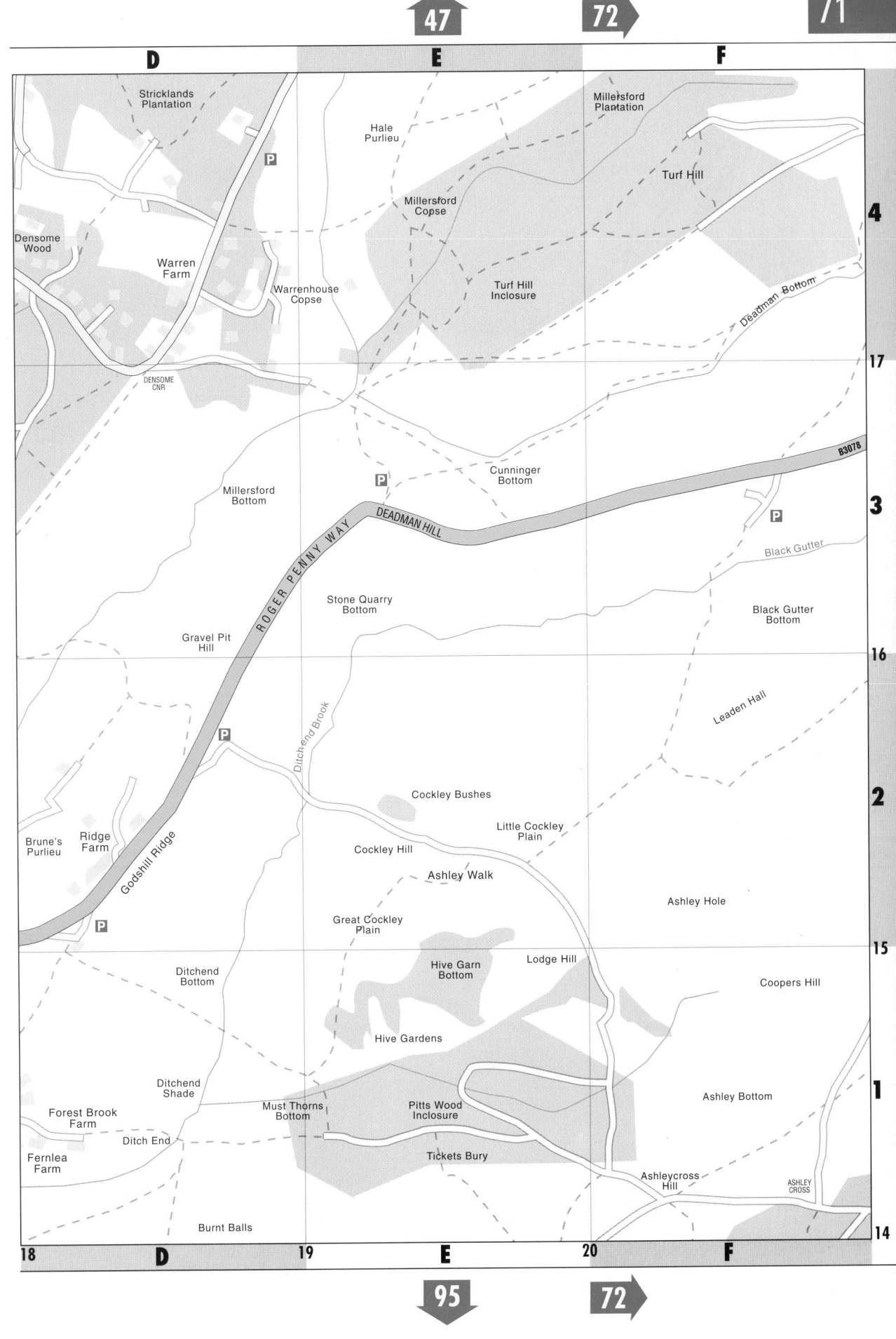

Stricklands
Plantation

P

Densome
Wood

Warren
Farm

Warrenhouse
Copse

DENSOME
CNR

Millersford
Bottom

Hale
Purlieu

Millersford
Copse

Turf Hill
Inclosure

Millersford
Plantation

Turf Hill

Deadman Bottom

4

17

Cunninger
Bottom

P

ROGER PENNY WAY

DEADMAN HILL

B3078

P

Black Gutter

3

Stone Quarry
Bottom

Gravel Pit
Hill

Black Gutter
Bottom

16

Ditchend Brook

Leaden Hall

P

Cockley Bushes

Little Cockley
Plain

2

Brune's
Purlieu

Ridge
Farm

Godshill Ridge

Cockley Hill

Ashley Walk

Great Cockley
Plain

Ashley Hole

P

Hive Garn
Bottom

Lodge Hill

Coopers Hill

15

Ditchend
Bottom

Hive Gardens

Ditchend
Shade

Forest Brook
Farm

Ditch End

Fernlea
Farm

Must Thorns
Bottom

Pitts Wood
Inclosure

Tickets Bury

Ashley Bottom

1

Ashleycross
Hill

ASHLEY
CROSS

Burnt Balls

14

Golden Cross
Jacob's Barrow

P

P

Pound
Bottom

Cloven Hill Plantation

Franchises
Common

Tinney's
Plantation

4

Rushy
Flat

Burnt Ground Wood

Franchises
Lodge

Franchises
Wood

17

B3080

ROGER PENNY WAY

Hope
Cottage

Firs Hill
Copse

B3078

Bramshaw
Telegraph

Tucker's
Hat

P

3

Black Gutter

Picket
Corner

Studley
Head

Bur
Bushes

Claypits Bottom

Studley
Wood

Homy Ridge

B3078

16

The Butts

2

Howen Bottom

Eyeworth Wood

Islands Thorns Inclosure

15

Crock Hill

Latchmore Brook

Eyeworth
Pond

Eyeworth
Lodge

P

Howen
Bushes

1

Fritham
Farm

Fritham
Bridge

The Royal Oak
(PH)

Fritham

Gorley Bushes

P

14

Tilhill

Foxbury
Plantation

Pearce's Copse

A36
SALISBURY RD

Shelley
Farm

SHELLEY LA

Shelley
Nursery

River Brackwater

Picnic
Area
P

A3090

4

Bricky Lake Lane

Allmoor Copse

Cooper's Lane

Home
Farm

CH

Golf Course

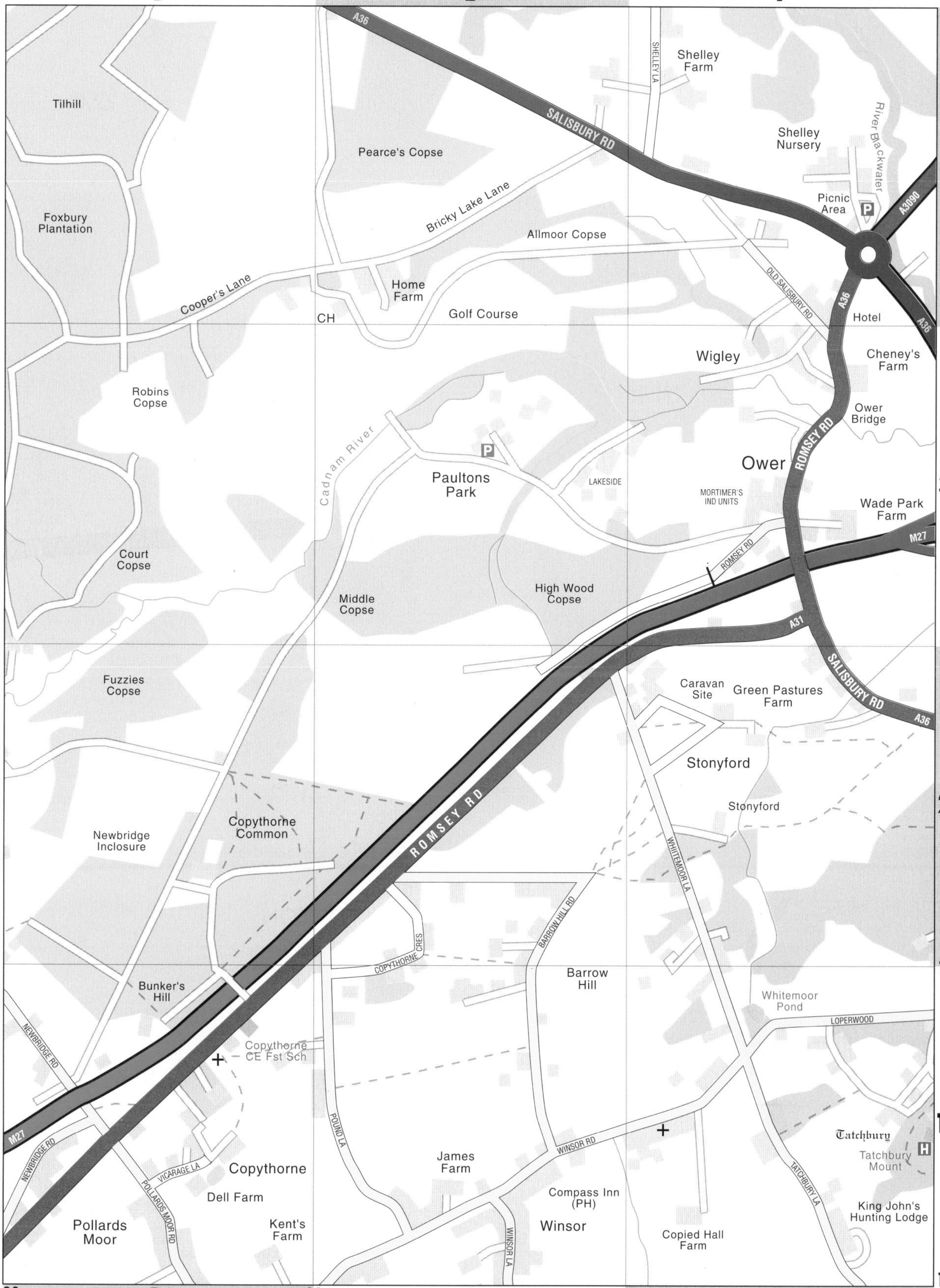

OLD SALISBURY RD

Hotel

A36

17

Wigley

Cheney's
Farm

Ower
Bridge

ROMSEY RD

Robins
Copse

Cadnam River

P

Paultons
Park

LAKESIDE

MORTIMER'S
IND UNITS

Ower

Wade Park
Farm

3

M27

Court
Copse

Middle
Copse

High Wood
Copse

ROMSEY RD

A31

SALISBURY RD

16

A36

Fuzzies
Copse

Caravan
Site

Green Pastures
Farm

Newbridge
Inclosure

Copythorne
Common

Stonyford

Stonyford

WHITEMOOR LA

2

BARROW HILL RD

COPYTHORNE CRES

ROMSEY RD

Bunker's
Hill

Barrow
Hill

Whitemoor
Pond

LOPERWOOD

15

NEWBRIDGE RD

Copythorne
CE Fst Sch

+

POUND LA

WINSOR RD

+

Tatchbury

Tatchbury
Mount
H

TATCHBURY LA

1

M27

VICARAGE LA

POLLARDS MOOR RD

Copythorne

Dell Farm

Kent's
Farm

James
Farm

WINSOR LA

Compass Inn
(PH)

Winsor

Copied Hall
Farm

King John's
Hunting Lodge

Pollards
Moor

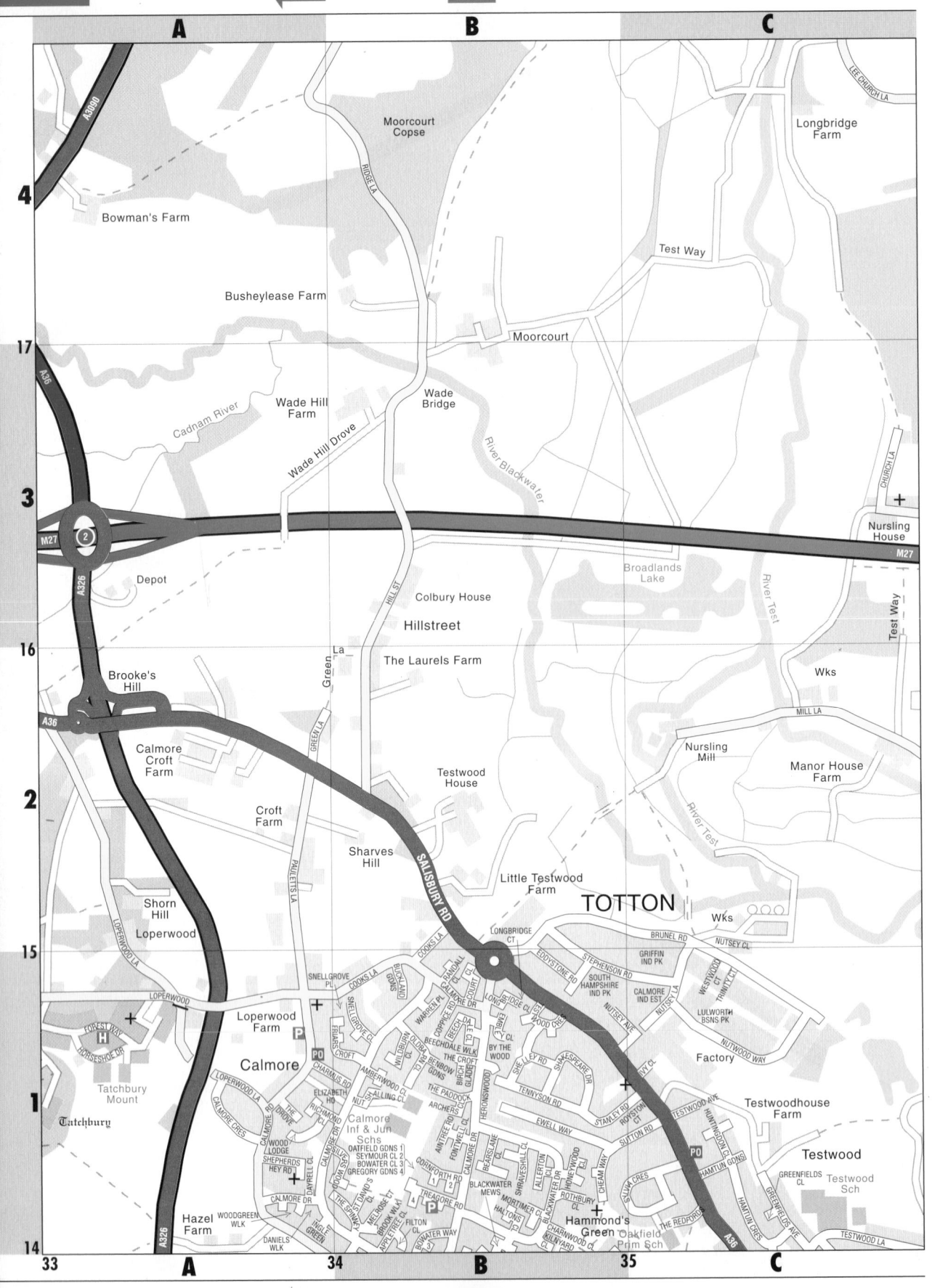

A   B   C

Moorcourt Copse

Longbridge Farm

4

A3090

Bowman's Farm

Test Way

Busheylease Farm

RIDGE LA

Moorcourt

17

A36

Cadnam River

Wade Hill Farm

Wade Bridge

Nursling House

Wade Hill Drove

River Blackwater

CHURCH LA

3

M27

A326

2

Depot

Colbury House

Broadlands Lake

River Test

M27

Test Way

Hillstreet

HILL ST

16

Green La

The Laurels Farm

Wks

MILL LA

Brooke's Hill

A36

Calmore Croft Farm

GREEN LA

Testwood House

Nursling Mill

Manor House Farm

2

Croft Farm

Sharves Hill

Little Testwood Farm

River Test

TOTTON

Wks

Shorn Hill

SALISBURY RD

PAULETTS LA

Loperwood

LOPERWOOD LA

Longbridge CT

BRUNEL RD

NUTSEY CL

15

SNELLGROVE PL

COOKS LA

STEPHENSON RD

Griffin IND PK

South Hampshire IND PK

Calmore IND EST

WESTWOOD CT

LULWORTH BSNS PK

LOPERWOOD

Loperwood Farm

P

PO

Calmore

FOREST WAY

H

HORSESHOE DR

Tatchbury Mount

Tatchbury

1

Calmore Inf & Jun Schs

Factory

NUTWOOD WAY

Testwoodhouse Farm

Testwood

Hazel Farm

WOODGREEN WLK

A326

Hammond's Green

A36

Oakfield Prim Sch

Greenfields CL

Testwood Sch

TESTWOOD LA

14

33   A   34   B   35   C

E
F

Nightingale Wood

M27

Service Area

Romsey Golf Course

Service Area

Parker's Farm

4

M271

CH

Rownhams

17

Upton

HORNS HILL

UPTON CRES

UPTON LA
UPTON LYMER LA
LYMER VILLAS

VICTORY WAY 1
LOREILLE CL 2
ST JOHNS CL 3

ADCOCK CT

PO

ROUTS WAY

ACORN DR

COLTS RD

PRINCE RD

HEDGEROW CL

ARMADA CL

ROWNHAMS LA

HAWN RD

ST JOHNS GLEBE

THE MEWS

BEACON CL
NUTFIELD RD
BALMORAL WAY
MANDY CL
HURRICANE DR

Rownhams House

HORNS DROVE
ROWNHAMS WAY

ROWNHAMS CH

3

GREENWOOD AVE

UKIN DR
BLAKE

CRAWFORD CL

LYME FIELD

BROADMEAD RD

TESTLANDS AVE

MILL LA

WINFRITH WAY

BARKER MILL CL

PHILLIPS

BROADWELL

BETTERIDGE

RUFUS CL

LAVERSTOKE CL

MICHELMERSH CL

WESTWAYS CL

Rownhams CE Prim Sch

JEFFRIES
HORSEBRIDGE WAY
TROWBRIDGE CL

RINGS DROVE

HALEOGEON

ROSSINGTON AVE

MARSHALLING AVE

FAIRWAY GDNS

FERNLEY
BRUGERS PL
RISEDALE AVE
HEDGEMAN
COLT CL
COTT CL

FAIRLAWN CL
EYEFORD
BREDWELL CL
MASSELEIGH AVE

EVOX CL

LENNOX CL

FORBES CL

MATHESON RD

CHISHOLM

BUCHANAN RD

ROSEBANK LODGE

WELCH WAY

ST CLOUD CL
LUCAS CL

EMMETT RD

SUTHERLAND RD

ARMSTRONG CT

LOGAN CL

DURBAN CL

ERSKINE

3

SHEPHERDS WAY

Four Horseshoes (PH)

WINSTANLEY RD

WILKS CL

BLANN

C BLANN

CRANMER DR

UFFIN CL

CHAMBERS CL

WATLEY CL

Nursling ST

Nursling CE Prim Sch

BROADMEAD FLATS

PO

Recn Gnd

P

TOOGOODS WAY

ROMSEY RD

VIKING CL

GRANGE

WELCH WAY

TOWNHILL

CAMERON

MENZIES

LORD'S HILL WAY

Oaklands Com Sch

CARDINGTON CT

PO

BLACKBERRY

HORSESHOE

CRANWELL

ERSKINE

16

Nursling

Home Covert

The Cedar Special Sch

Lord's Hill

Fairisle Inf & Jun Schs

PO

PO

Liby

PO

Adanac Farm

SOUTHAMPTON

FAIRISLE RD

ANDROMEDA RD

LORD'S HILL WAY

LORD'S HILL CTR W

PEGASUS CT

SATURN CL

NEPTUNE CT

MERCURY

GEMINI CL

MANSTON CT

EASTCHURCH

DORHAM

2

Yewtree Farm

YEWTREE LA

LLOYDS

FROGMORE LA

HERBERT'S LA

Tennis Ctr

TRIANGLE GDNS

DANEBURY WAY

PORTELET HO

ST BRELADE

GUERNSEY CL

BONIFACE CRES

ALDERNEY

SARNIA

JERSEY CL

HELIER RD

BROWNHILL

CORBIERE CL

ST MARTINS CL

BROZEL CL

JUPITER CL

UPPER BROWNHILL RD

KENNEDY RD

ROSEWALL RD

LANCASTER RD

ASHMEAD RD

RYLANDES CT

DOLTON RD

PO

2

Bargain Farm

BROWNHILL WAY

LOWER BROWNHILL RD

CLAMBOROUGH

SEAFIELD RD

WINDBURY RD

HOOLHAM

BARONS MEAD

WATTS CL

KERN CL

GREEN LA

Millbrook Com Sch

Maybush

ROWNHAMS RD

KINGSTON CT

SWINHAM CT

CONFORD CT

15

NEW COTTS

REDBRIDGE LA

COL BURN

HAYBURN

BLAKENEY RD

OSBORN AVE

CLANFORD RD

CLOVE AVE

ANERBY RD

MAPLIN RD

COLNE CT

LULWORTH

SELSEY

BREAM

HERFIELD CL

TETNEY

LULWORTH CL

Ordnance Survey Office

HARDWICKE CL

1

TEST VALLEY SNS CTR

Holy Family RC Prim Sch

Mansel Inf & Jun Schs

MANSEL RD W

CANVEY CT

THIRLMERE RD

MAYBUSH RD

GRASMERE CT

ENNERDALE

TINDALE

CRABWOOD RD

GLENCOYNE GDNS

CRABTREE

WIMPSON GDNS

TIMSBURY CRES

LOCKERLY CRES

BRAISHFIELD

1

YEOMAN PK

P

Playing Field

THORNESS CL

VELLAN CT

SEACOMBE RD

PORLOCK CL

CRANFORD CT

CULVER RD

KENDAL AVE

CROMER RD

STUDLAND RD

DURLSTON RD

SEDBERG HO

PEVENSEY

BIDEFORD

EVENLODE RD

ORWELL RD

MANSEL RD

WINDERMERE AVE

CRABWOOD RD

ULLSWATER RD

DERWENT RD

HAWSWATER CL

Recn Gnd

Newlands Inf & Jun Schs

BORROWDALE RD

PLAITFORD WLK 1
WIMBORNE HO 2
BLANDFORD HO 3

REDBRIDGE HILL

WALNUT CR

WALNUT CL

Western Com

H

1

GOVER RD

M271

BALLARD CL

KENDAL CT

STUDLAND CL

PERRAN RD

PLAND RD

INGLETON RD

SEDBERGH RD

WAVENEY GN

PO

TEME CRES

SWINHAM

TRIBLE

LOAKEY CL

PRIGHTON RD

HARBIN RD

BARTERS CL

14

Nature Reserve

STIRLING CL

36
D
37
E
38
F

A B C

4

Chilworth Common

Chilworth Tower

Dymer's Wood

Chilworth Common

Tanner's Brook

M27

Roman Rd

Heatherlands Rd

Pinelands Rd

Chilworth Rd

A27

Pine Way Little Oller

Pine Wlk Dene Cl Ling Maple Beech Ho

Hadrian Way Lindswood Wlk Pinehurst Dale

Roman Dr Pine Wlk Pine Cl Fitzroy Cl

The Ring Julian Cl Bassett Heath Ave

17

Lord's Wood

Castle Hill

Chilworth Ring

Bassett Dale Links View Way Birch Ho Pineford Cl

Saxholm Way Saxholm Dale Bassett Row

Golf Course Rd

Golf Course

Lordswood

Matheson Rd Sutherland Rd Sinclair Jun Sch Sinclair Inf Sch

Whitchat Cl Wryneck Cl Hampton Cl Brambling Cl Widgeon Cl Warbler Cl Tintagel Cl

Redstart Pl Firecrest Harrier Sheldrake Gdns Puffin Cl Dunvegan Dr

Kestrel Cl Plover Cl Fulmar Curlew Oakwood Schs Oakwood Dr Balmoral Cl Dunster Cl

Goldcrest Gdns Turnstone Gdns Osprey Melville Cl Coxford Rd Grafton Gdns

Lord's Hill Way Woburn Rd Abbotsfield Kelly Ct

CH Greenbank Cres Arundle Cres Ridgemount Ave

Ridgemount La 1 Chelwood Gate 2 Brampton Tower 3 Brampton Manor 4

Gables Rd Bassett Mews Beechmount Rd Beechmount

3

16

Pembrey Cl Kinloss Northolt Gdns Tangmere Dr Gatwick Cl Croydon Cl Caistor Cl

Abercrombie Gdns Lewis La Aldermoor Rd Cowdray Nulieu Ct Petworth Gdns Longleat Gdns

Branksbury Purbrook Cl Waltham Salerno Rd Taranto Rd Aldermoor Lordswood Ct

Palace Rd Dunkirk Cl Curzon Ct Dunkirk Rd

Vectis Ct 1 Redcourt 2 Fairlea Grange 3 Tower Gdns 4 The Mount 5 Bassett Wood Mews 7

Vermont Sch Holly Hill Dell Holly Hill Cl Redhill Cl

Vermont Cl The Firs Talbot Rd Little Oak A35

Chetwynd Rd Chetwynd Dr Bassett Cres E

Chilveston Cres Nightingale Ct Linden Rd Outer Circ Holly Oak Ct Holly Oak Rd

Peach Rd Springford Cl Langrish Cl Bradley Pl Lyburn Greywell Ave Shalden Cl Preston Cl Stella Ct

Arnheim Cl Dunkirk Rd

1 Greywell Ct 2 Pinelands Ct 3 Lyburn Ct

Sports Centre

Redhill Cres Red Hill Way Boldrewood Rd Underwood Rd Wykeham Cl

Avington Ct Shawford Cl Tudor Wood Bassett Green Cl Bassett Meadow

Oaklands Way

Red Lodge Sch

2

Conifer Rd Larch Rd Olive Rd Willow Rd Palm Rd Holly Oak Rd Mead Rd

The Polygon Sch (Annexe) Springford Gdns Springford Rd Winston Cl

The Pines Ct Arcadia Cl

Cemy Holly Brook

Winford Cres Seagarth La Maybush Ct Highclere Rd Thornhill Rd

Abingdon Gdns Butterfield Cl Beaumont Oak Tree Pointout Cl Pointout Rd

Sherwood Cl Burgess Gdns

Boldrewood Con Ctr Univ A35

1 Wellman Ct 2 Glencarron Way 3 Chestnut Lodge

Cutthorn

Burgess Rd A3035 Highfield Ave

Rowan Coxford Rd Vine Rd Tanner's Brook Aldermoor Princess Anne

Dale Valley Gdns Seymour Cl Seymour Rd Munton Maldwood

Winchester Rd Burgess Rd Winstone Bldgs Ashurst Cl Rockleigh Rd Wolverley Ct

Lordswood Gdns

Southampton Common The Lake Coronation Ave The Avenue

15

Birch Rd Thorndike Rd Rosoman Rd Ross Gdns Burns Pl Bindon Cl Bindon Rd Warren Cres

Sycamore Rd Chestnut Rd Tremona Rd Maundry Rd Elmwood Ct

The Barton Ctr Shirley Warren Southampton Gen

Chalybeate St James' Rd Northbrook Gdns Hollybrook Rd Malvern Rd

Hollybrook Gdns Dale Valley Cl Malvern Bsns Ctr Malvern Ind Est Norham Ave Norham Cl

Chester Ct Bellemoor Sec Sch (Boys) Pewsey Pl Warwick Rd Melrose Rd Pentire Ave

Luccombe Rd Luccombe Pl Hill La Leicester Rd Lincoln Ct Shanklin Cres

SOUTHAMPTON

Hill La

Southampton Common The Lake

1

A3057 Braishfield Cl Irving 1 Upton Ho 2 Sturminster Ho Redbridge Hill William Macleod Way

Coxford Arliss Rd Stoke Rd Bracken Pl Holland Rd Buckley Ct Winchester Rd

Conv Old Shirley Sch Anglesea Rd Redbridge Hill Beulah Rd

Romsey Rd Tebourba Way The Mount Medina Rd Sydney Rd Wordsworth Inf Sch

Briarswood Rd Worthy Ho Turners Rd Oak Ct St James' Rd St Winifred's Rd

Mordaunt Rd Shayer Rd Queen's Rd Bellemoor Rd

Colebrook Ave Bourne Ave Braemore Ave Tytyrol Rd Upper Shirley Ave Wilton Cres Wilton Gdns Wilton Ave

Upper Shirley Taunton Coll

Radway Rd Highfield Rd Oakmount Ave Oakmount Mansions

Alderman Rd Gallia A33

14

Brook Valley Percy Rd King Edward Ave Cecil Ave Clarendon Rd A3057

Hyde Cl Vaudrey Cl Howard's Salen Rd St James' Rd

Darlington Gdns Cranbourne Rd Kineton Rd

Cemetery Lake The Cowherds (PH)

39 A 40 B 41 C

D1
1 KINGFISHER CT
2 OMDURMAN CT
3 HIGHFIELD LODGE
4 BURLEY CT
5 CRANFORD HO
6 OAKDENE
7 ST ANNS CT
8 CHESTNUT CT
9 WESTBOURNE MANSIONS
10 LEIGH MANSIONS
11 LATIMER CT
12 COTSWOLD CT
13 PINEHURST
14 BROOKVALE CT
15 ABBOTTS CT
16 BENTLEY CT
17 WICKHAM HO
18 AUTUMN PL
19 MELBURY CT
20 SOVEREIGN CT
21 SANDRINGHAM CT
22 BERMUDA CT
23 HAMILTON CT
24 REGENT CT
25 WINN MANSIONS
26 CHELTENHAM CT
27 TENNYSON CT
28 WESTWOOD MANSIONS
29 ELM CT
30 GUARDIAN CT
31 BARRINGTON CT
32 SOMBORNE CT
33 CARRINGTON HO
34 SOBERTON HO
35 ADDIS SQ
36 PORTSWOOD CTR
37 TENNYSON HO
38 WICKHAM HO
39 WESTRIDGE CT

E1
1 WESTMARCH CT
2 THE NEWLANDS
3 KENSINGTON CT
4 MILL CT
5 GROSVENOR LODGE
6 RICHMOND HALL
7 GROSVENOR HALL
8 GROSVENOR MEWS
9 SHAMROCK VILLAS

F1
1 JULIAN CT
2 CAMELLIA CT
3 CASTLE HTS
4 CASTLE CT
5 THE BROADWAY
6 PARKLANDS

A · B · C

4

17

3

16

2

15

1

14

WIDE LA

A335

SOUTHAMPTON RD A335

MITCHELL WAY

TICHBORNE RD
OVINGTON RD
YOBK RD
DONCASTER RD
ARNOLD RD
SOUTH ST

CAMPBELL RD

LC

West Horton Farm

A335

TINKER VALLEY

Southampton (Eastleigh) Airport

SPITFIRE LOOP

Decoy Covert

River Itchen

The Itchen Navigation (disused)
Itchen Way

Hog Wood

Allington Manor Farm BSNS CTR

Allington Manor Sch

HOGWOOD LA

Railway Cottage

Milkmead Copse

SEDDUL-BAHR

ALLINGTON LA

Itchen Valley Country Park

High Hill

WHITE HARMONY ACRES IND EST

Oaklands House

High Wood

Visitor Ctr

M27

Water Works

OAKTREE CARAVAN PARK

Winslowe House

Moorgreen Farm

Gaters Mill

A27 MANSBRIDGE RD

Garden Ctr

ROMILL CL

OAK VALE

QUOB LA

Quob Farm

Brookside Way

THE DRIVE

RAYMOND CL

GOLDEN CL

Southampton Arms (PH)

WELLINGTON

STOUR CL 1
CREEDY GDNS 2
WEBBURN GDNS 3

TORRIDGE GDNS

RYE CL

THAMES RD

BARNSLAND

HICKORY

REDWOOD

CHESTNUT CL

HORNBEAM GDNS

LIME GDNS

HOLLY

ELM GDNS

WILLOW CL

QUOB LA

St James Sch

Moorgreen

Sch

Townhill Park

Schs

ATLANTIC PARK VIEW

ROSTRON CL

CARPATHIA

LINDEN CT
TAMAR CT

TRESILLIAN GDNS

HAYLE RD

ARUN RD

WALDON RD

KENWYN RD

HELFORD GDNS

LAMBOURN

OKEMENT RD

WELLAND RD

EDEN RD

HATCH MEAD

CRANWELL CRES

SNYDON RD

CHARNWOOD CRES

BARBE BAKER AVE

ARCH CL

1 LANCASTER CT
2 HALIFAX CT
3 WELLINGTON CT
4 LINCOLN CT

The King's Sch (Prim)

MEGAN RD

TRICIA CL

CHAPEL RD

GLENN RD

VICTORIA WLK

LITTLE QUOB LA

LONG CT

CATHERINE CL

CATHERINE GDNS

MOORGREEN RD

MONARCH WAY

Moorgreen

Liby

Hatch Grange

CHAPEL CL

AVON WAY

Hatch Bottom

TYNE WAY

PRINCESS CL

BALTIC RD

West End

OLD SCHOOL GDNS

H

CAMELLIA GDNS

BAILEY GN

GASCOMBE GDNS

HARBOURNE GDNS

OLD IVY LA

IVY LA

TOWNHILL WAY

THE CIRCLE

SWAYTHLING RD

CHURCH HILL

B3035

MUDLANDS

GLENLEA DR

High St

P

TRENT WAY

WOODLEA GDNS

SEVERN WAY

BOTLEY RD B3035

KINGSDOWN WAY

MIDDLETON CL

BENHAMS RD

DYNELEY AVE

HALLET CL

PAULET CL

PO

Cudbush La

DUNBURY CT

ROUNDHILL CL

PINEWOOD

DERWENT CL

WINDERMERE RD

HEDGEROW GDNS

GRASMERE

ROTHER CL

MOOR CL

SHIPSCOMBE DR

EDELVALE RD

MORROW CL

GONCE CL

ENNERDALE RD

BARLE CL

CLIFTON GDNS

COOPERS CL

CHALK HILL

ULLSWATER AVE

ULLSWATER AVE

CLAN CL

MANNS CL

BEECHWOOD RISE

Sch

EPPING CL

NOTTAL

KESTREL RD

GORSELANDS RD

ALPINE CL

WHEATCROFT DR

WILDERNESS HTS

SEATON CL

ELIZABETH CT

SEPTEMBER CL

WEST END RD

ORCHARDS WAY

UPPER NEW RD

WINTON CT

MALLARDS RD

TOWER PL

WOODLAND MEWS

BEACON RD

ELIZABETH CT

RUNNYMEDE

SHOTTERS HILL CL

HOPE RD

HILLDENE

CRABWOOD CT

HILLDOWNE

SOUTHERN RD

WESTERN RD

LITTLEWOOD GDNS

KENWORTH GDNS

WESTGATE MEWS

TELEGRAPH RD

The Hampshire Health & Tennis Club

Dog Kennel Farm

CAVERSHAM CL

WARDEN CL

A27

Midanbury

CHESTER RD

CLEVELAND RD

PORTVIEW RD

WYCLIFFE RD

LYTHAM RD

EXETER RD

LYNHAM RD

WAKEFIELD RD

CORNWALL RD

LITTLE DIP

WELBURN CL

DIBLEY CL

1
2
3
4
5

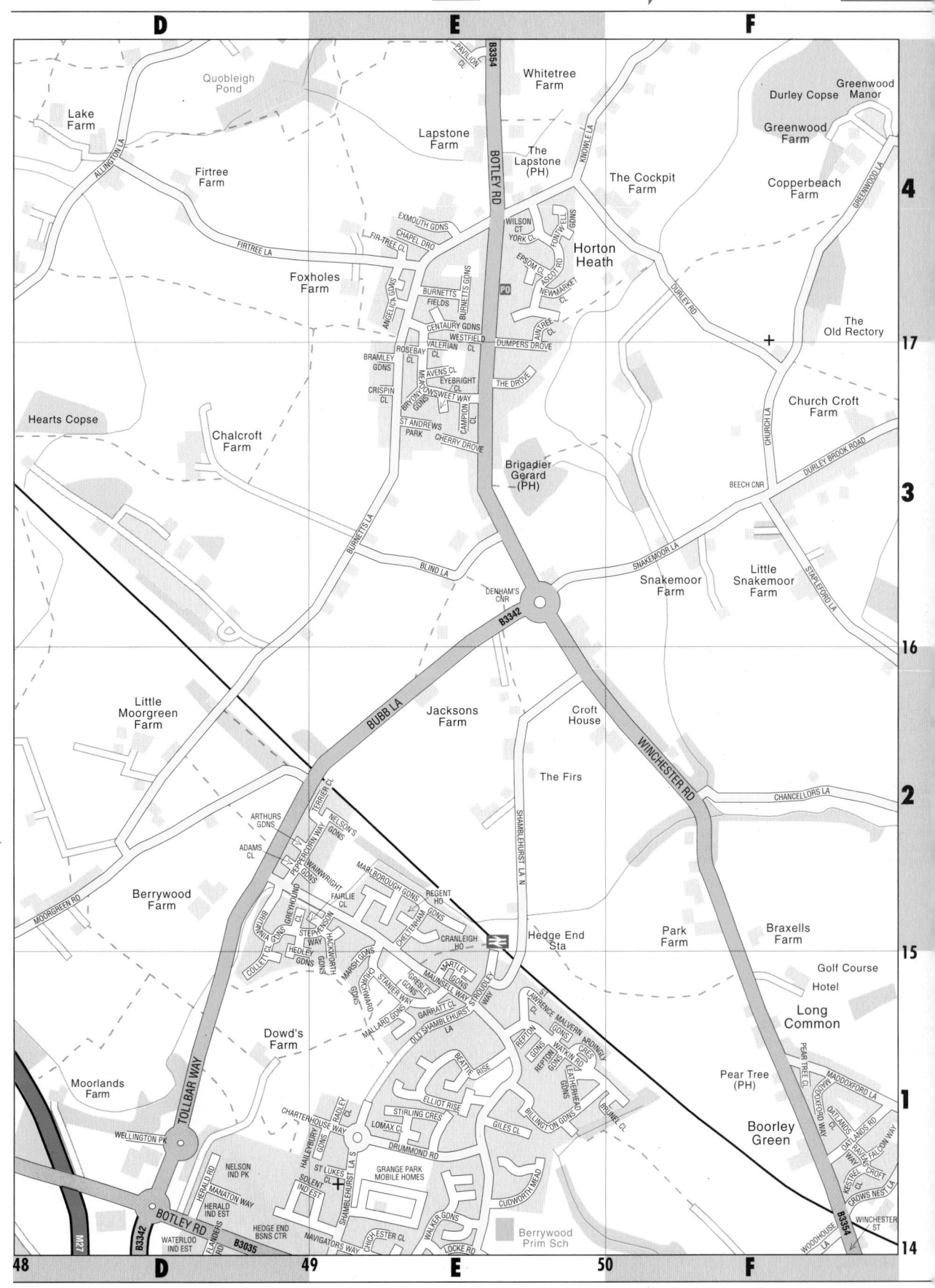

D
E
F

4

17

3

16

2

15

1

14

48
D
49
E
50
F

Quobleigh
Pond

Lake
Farm

Firtree
Farm

ALLINGTON LA

FIRTREE LA

FIR-TREE CL

CHAPEL DRO

EXMOUTH GDNS

Foxholes
Farm

Lapstone
Farm

Whitetree
Farm

BOTLEY RD

B3354

PAVILION CL

The
Lapstone
(PH)

KNOWLE LA

The Cockpit
Farm

Durley Copse

Greenwood
Farm

Greenwood
Manor

Copperbeach
Farm

GREENWOOD LA

WILSON
CT
YORK CL

EPSOM CL
SCOTT RD

FONTWELL

SANDY

NEWMARKET
CL

Horton
Heath

PO

BURNETTS
FIELDS

BURNETTS GDNS

ANGELICA GDNS

CENTAURY GDNS

ROSEBAY
CL

BRAMLEY
GDNS

CRISPIN
CL

St Andrews
Park

MEADOWSWEET WAY

BRYONY CL

VALERIAN
CL

WESTFIELD

AVENS CL

EYEBRIGHT
CL

CAMPION
CL

AINTREE
CL

DUMPERS DROVE

THE DROVE

CHERRY DROVE

DURLEY RD

The
Old Rectory

Church Croft
Farm

CHURCH LA

DURLEY BROOK ROAD

BEECH CNR

Hearts Copse

Chalcroft
Farm

BURNETTS LA

BLIND LA

DENHAM'S
CNR

B3342

Brigadier
Gerard
(PH)

SNAKEMOOR LA

Snakemoor
Farm

Little
Snakemoor
Farm

STANFORD LA

Little
Moorgreen
Farm

BUBB LA

Jacksons
Farm

Croft
House

The Firs

WINCHESTER RD

CHANCELLORS LA

MOORGREEN RD

Berrywood
Farm

ARTHURS
GDNS

ADAMS
CL

TERRIER CL

NELSON'S
GDNS

PEPPERCORN WAY

WAINWRIGHT
GDNS

MARLBOROUGH GDNS

FAIRLIE
CL

REGENT
HO

CRANLEIGH
HO

SHAMBLEHURST LA N

Hedge End
Sta

Park
Farm

Braxells
Farm

Golf Course

Hotel

Long
Common

Dowd's
Farm

COLLETT CL

BRUNEL CL

GREYHOUND
GDNS

STEPHENSON
WAY

HEDLEY
GDNS

HACKWORTH
GDNS

RICHWARD GDNS

MARSH GDNS

STANIER WAY

MALLARD GDNS

HARTLEY
GDNS

MAUNSELL WAY

CHELTENHAM
GDNS

GRESLEY
GDNS

GARRATT CL

OLD SHAMBLEHURST
LA

STROUDLEY
WAY

LAWRENCE
GDNS

MALVERN
GDNS

ARDINGLY
CRES

REPTON
GDNS

WATKIN RD

REPTON
GDNS

LEATHERHEAD
GDNS

BILLINGTON GDNS

Moorlands
Farm

TOLLBAR WAY

WELLINGTON PK

CHARTERHOUSE WAY

HALYBURY

RADLEY
CL

LOMAX CL

STIRLING CRES

BEATTIE RISE

ELLIOT RISE

GILES CL

DRUMMOND RD

Pear Tree
(PH)

PEAR TREE CL

MADDOXFORD WAY

MADDOXFORD LA

OATLANDS
RD

GATCLANDS
WAY

FALCON WAY

KESTREL CL

Boorley
Green

CROWS NEST LA

B3354

WOODHOUSE LA

WINCHESTER
ST

M27

B3342

BOTLEY RD

B3035

HERALD RD

MANATON WAY

NELSON
IND PK

HERALD
IND EST

WATERLOO
IND EST

FLANDERS RD

HEDGE END
BSNS CTR

NAVIGATORS WAY

ST LUKES
CL

SOLENT
IND EST

SHAMBLEHURST LA S

Grange Park
Mobile Homes

CHICHESTER CL

WALKER GDNS

LOCKE RD

CUDWORTH MEAD

Berrywood
Prim Sch

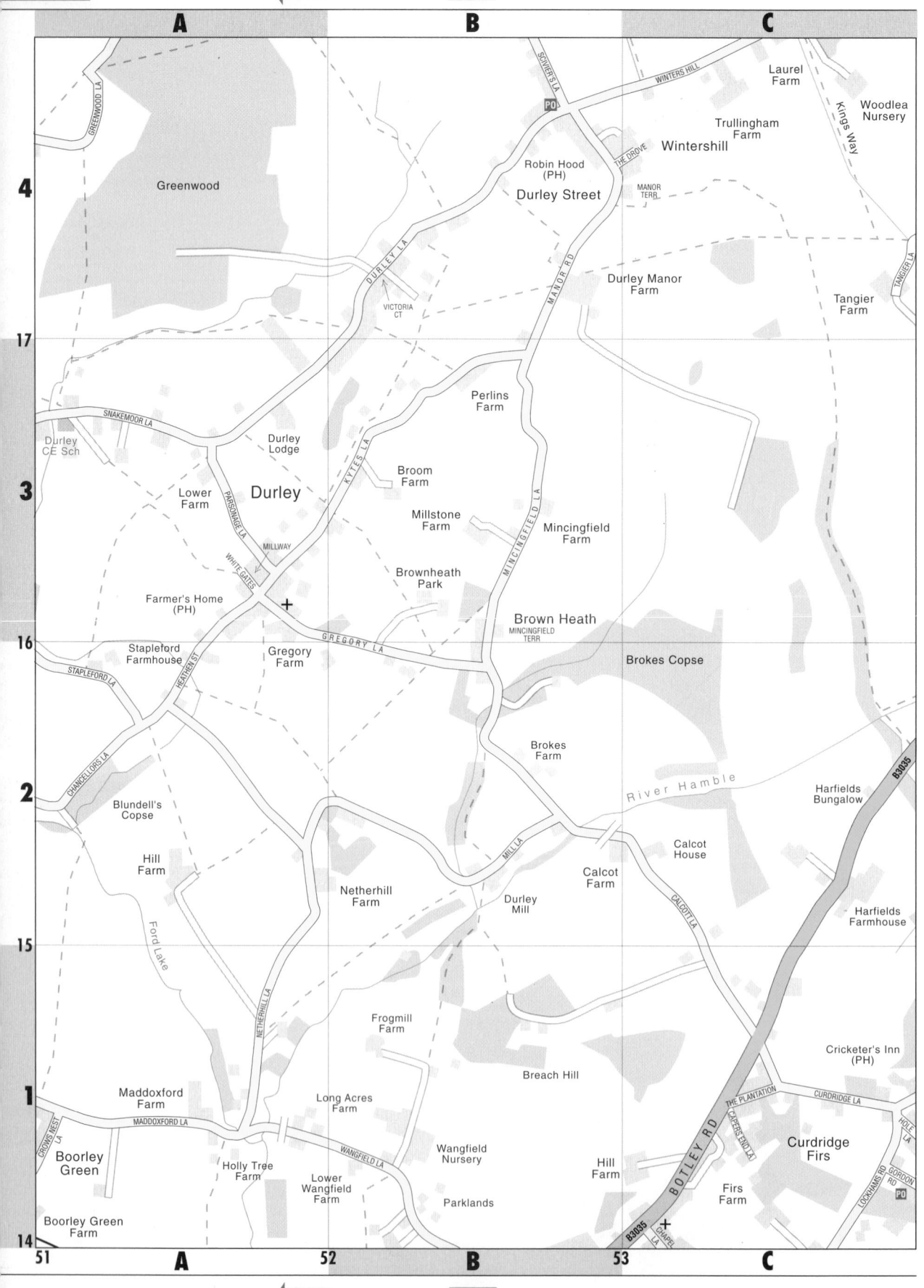

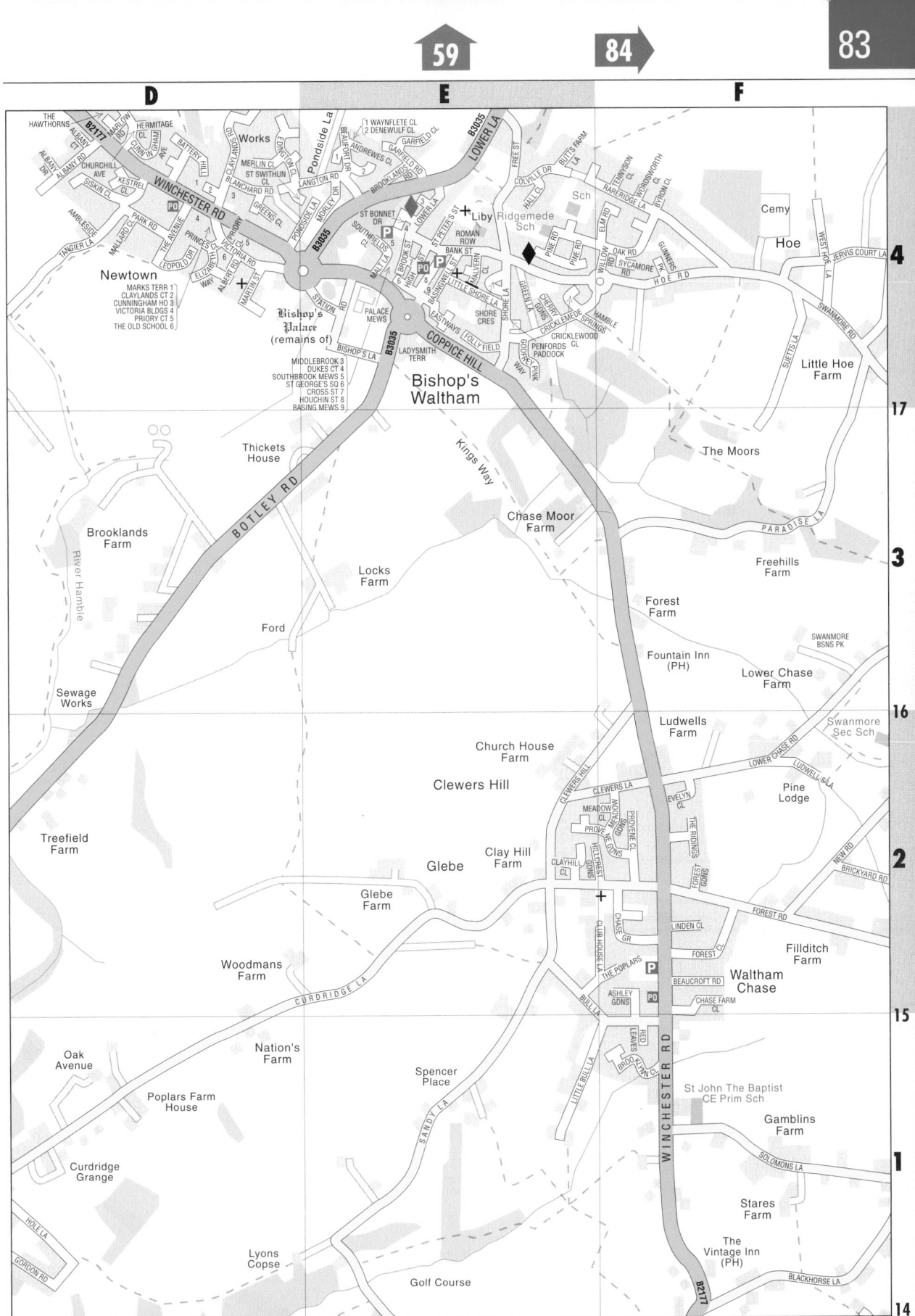

D　　　　　　　　　　E　　　　　　　　　　F

THE HAWTHORNS
B2177
Works
Pondside La
1 WAYNFLETE CL
2 DENEWULF CL
B3035
LOWER LA
HERMITAGE CL
ALBANY RD
ALBANY DR
CHURCHILL AVE
KESTREL CL
SISKIN CL
MERLIN CL
ST SWITHUN CL
BLANCHARD RD
GREENS CL
LANGTON RD
EDMON LA
MOSLEY DR
BEAUFORT DR
ANDREWES CL
BROOKLANDS
GARFIELD RD
LOWER LA
HIGH ST
ST PETER'S ST
BANK ST
FREE ST
COLVILLE DR
BUTTS FARM LA
HALL
TENNYSON
RANERIDGE LA
WORDSWORTH
BYRON CL
WINCHESTER RD
PO
TANGIER LA
AMBLESIDE
PARK RD
THE AVENUE
PRINCESS RD
LEOPOLD DR
VICTORIA RD
ELIZABETH WAY
ALBERT RD
MARTIN ST
B3035
STATION RD
ST BONNET DR
SOUTHFIELDS CL
MALT LA
BRICK ST
ROMAN ROW
LITTLE SHORE LA
SHORE LA
ST GEORGE'S CL
BASINGWELL ST
MAVERN CL
PINE RD
PINE RD
OAK RD
WILLOW CL
ELM RD
GUNNERS PK
SYCAMORE RD
HOE RD
Sch
Liby
Ridgemede Sch
Cemy
Hoe
WEST HOE LA
JERVIS COURT LA
4

Newtown
MARKS TERR 1
CLAYLANDS CT 2
CUNNINGHAM HO 3
VICTORIA BLDGS 4
PRIORY CT 5
THE OLD SCHOOL 6
Bishop's
Palace
(remains of)
MIDDLEBROOK 3
DUKES CT 4
SOUTHBROOK MEWS 5
ST GEORGE'S SQ 6
CROSS ST 7
HOUCHIN ST 8
BASING MEWS 9
PALACE MEWS
P
P
PO
EASTWAYS
FOLLY FIELD
SHORE CRES
GODFREY WAY
CHERRY GDNS
CRICKLEMEDE SPRINGS
PINK
CRICKLEWOOD CL
PENFORDS PADDOCK
GREEN LA
HAMBLE
SUETTS LA
SWANMORE RD
Little Hoe
Farm
17

BISHOP'S LA
LADYSMITH TERR
COPPICE HILL
B3035
Bishop's
Waltham
Kings Way
The Moors
PARADISE LA

Thickets
House
BOTLEY RD
Chase Moor
Farm
Freehills
Farm
3

Brooklands
Farm
Locks
Farm
Forest
Farm
SWANMORE BSNS PK
Lower Chase
Farm
River Hamble
Ford
Fountain Inn
(PH)

Sewage
Works
Ludwells
Farm
LOWER CHASE RD
LUDWELL LA
Swanmore
Sec Sch
16

Church House
Farm
Clewers Hill
CLEWERS HILL
CLEWERS LA
MEADOW CL
MOUNTAIN CL
PROVENE GDNS
EVELYN CL
THE RIDINGS
FOREST GDNS
NEW RD
Pine
Lodge
BRICKYARD RD
2

Treefield
Farm
Glebe
Clay Hill
Farm
CLAYHILL CL
HILL CREST
HILL GDNS
PROVENE CL
+
FOREST RD
Filditch
Farm

Glebe
Farm
CLUB HOUSE LA
CHASE GR
LINDEN CL
FOREST CL
Waltham
Chase

Woodmans
Farm
CURDRIDGE LA
THE POPLARS
ASHLEY GDNS
BULL LA
P
PO
BEAUCROFT RD
CHASE FARM CL
15

Oak
Avenue
Nation's
Farm
Spencer
Place
SANDY LA
LITTLE BULL LA
RED LEAVES CL
BROOK CL
WINCHESTER RD
St John The Baptist
CE Prim Sch
Gamblins
Farm
SOLOMONS LA
1

Poplars Farm
House
Curdridge
Grange
HOLE LA
GORDON RD
Lyons
Copse
Golf Course
The
Vintage Inn
(PH)
B2177
Stares
Farm
BLACKHORSE LA
14

54　　　　D　　　55　　　E　　　56　　　F

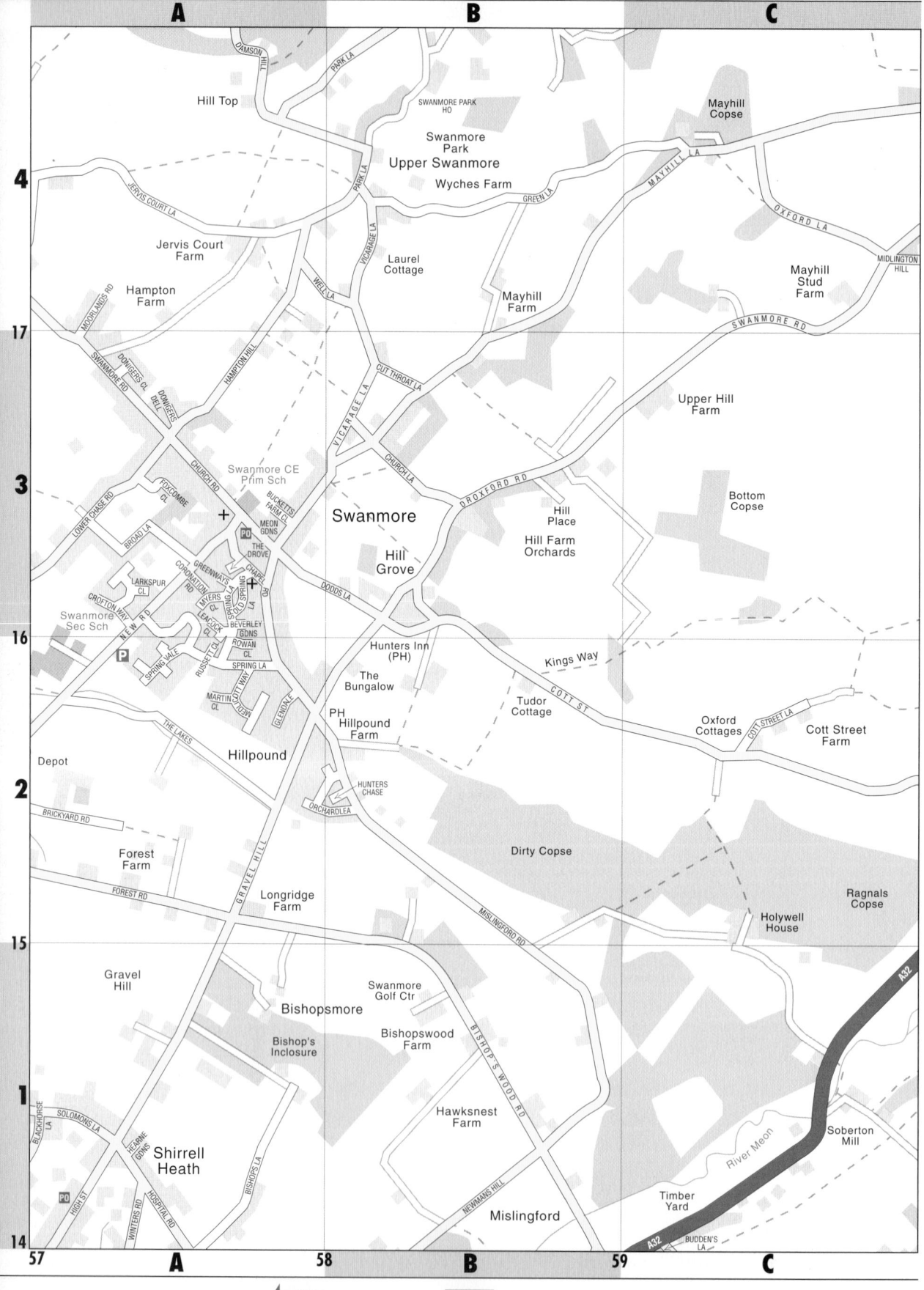

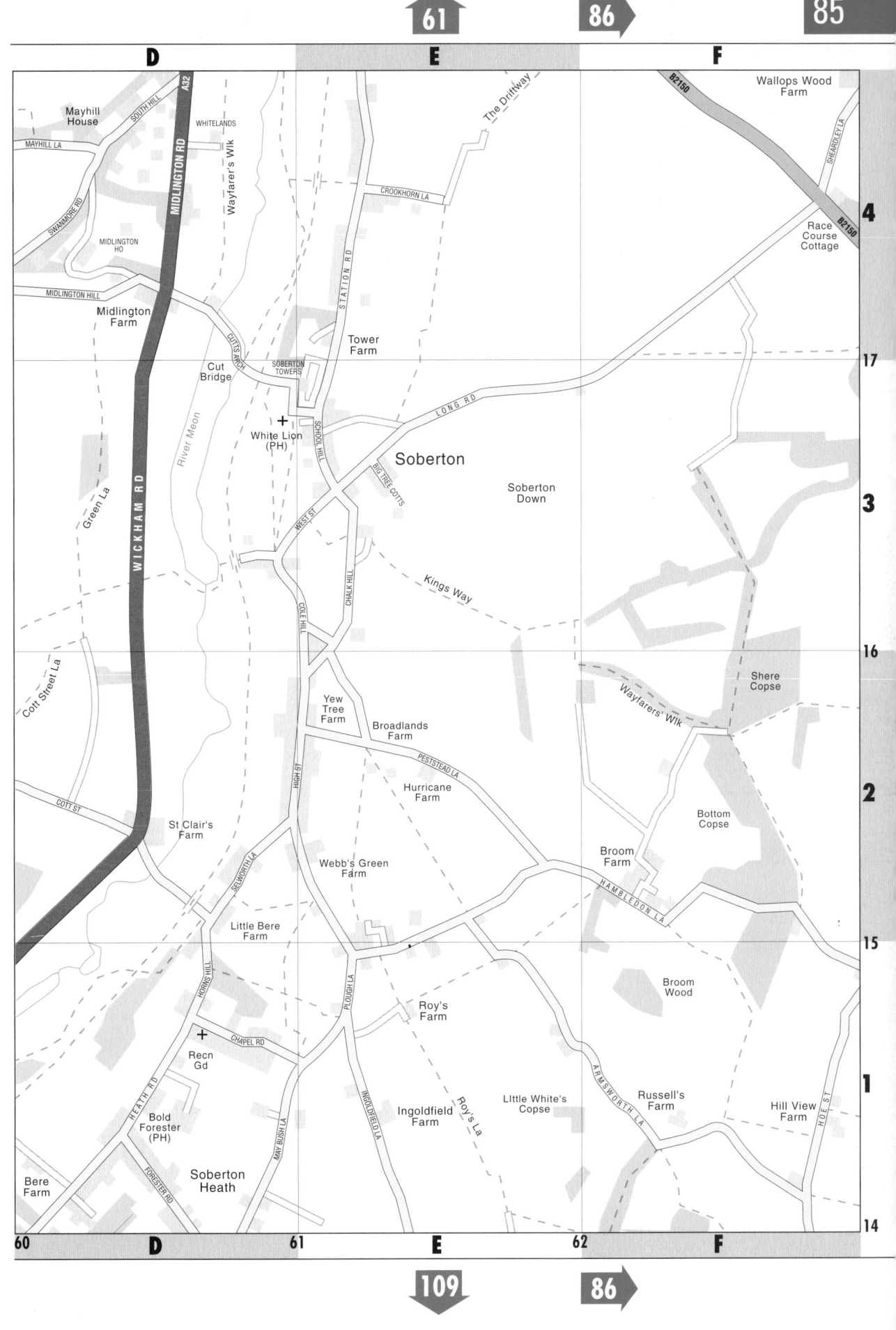

Mayhill
House

MAYHILL LA

SWANMORE RD

SOUTH HILL

MIDLINGTON RD

WHITELANDS

Wayfarer's Wlk

The Driftway

Wallops Wood
Farm

B2150

SHEARDLEY LA

CROOKHORN LA

MIDLINGTON HILL

Midlington
HO

STATION RD

Race
Course
Cottage

B2150

4

Midlington
Farm

Cut
Bridge

CUTTS ARCH

SOBERTON
TOWERS

Tower
Farm

+

White Lion
(PH)

Cut
Bridge

River Meon

Green La

WICKHAM RD

SCHOOL HILL

LONG RD

17

Soberton

Soberton
Down

WEST ST

CHALK HILL

BIG TREE COTTS

Kings Way

3

COLE HILL

Cott Street La

Yew
Tree
Farm

Broadlands
Farm

PESTSTEAD LA

Hurricane
Farm

Waytarers' Wlk

Shere
Copse

16

COTT ST

St Clair's
Farm

HIGH ST

Webb's Green
Farm

Bottom
Copse

Broom
Farm

HAMBLEDON LA

2

SELWORTH LA

Little Bere
Farm

Roy's
Farm

Broom
Wood

15

HORNS HILL

PLOUGH LA

CHAPEL RD

+

Recn
Gd

ARMSWORTH LA

Russell's
Farm

Hill View
Farm

HOE ST

1

HEATH RD

Bold
Forester
(PH)

MAY BUSH LA

FORESTER RD

Soberton
Heath

INGOLDFIELD LA

Ingoldfield
Farm

Roy's La

Little White's
Copse

Bere
Farm

14

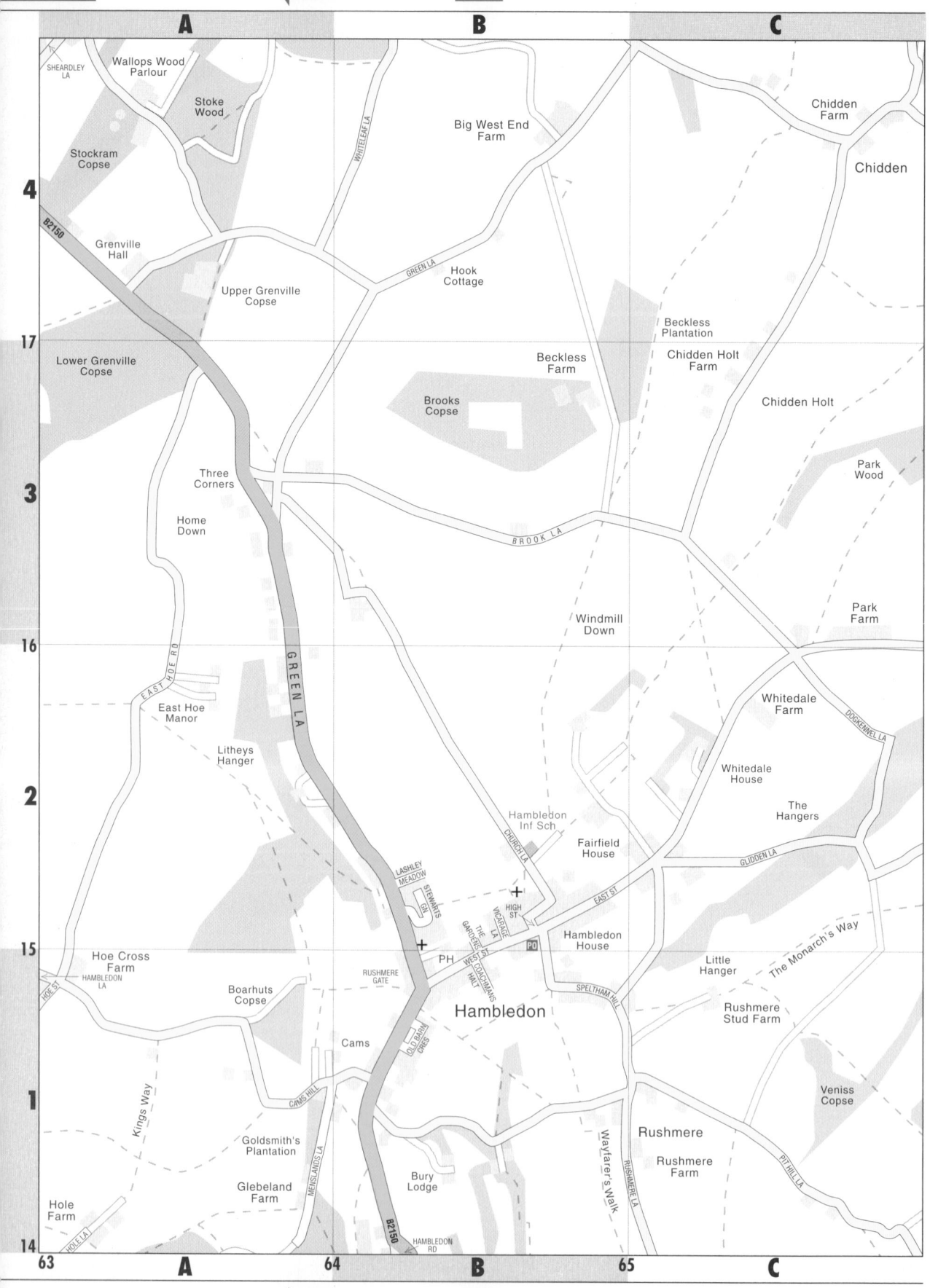

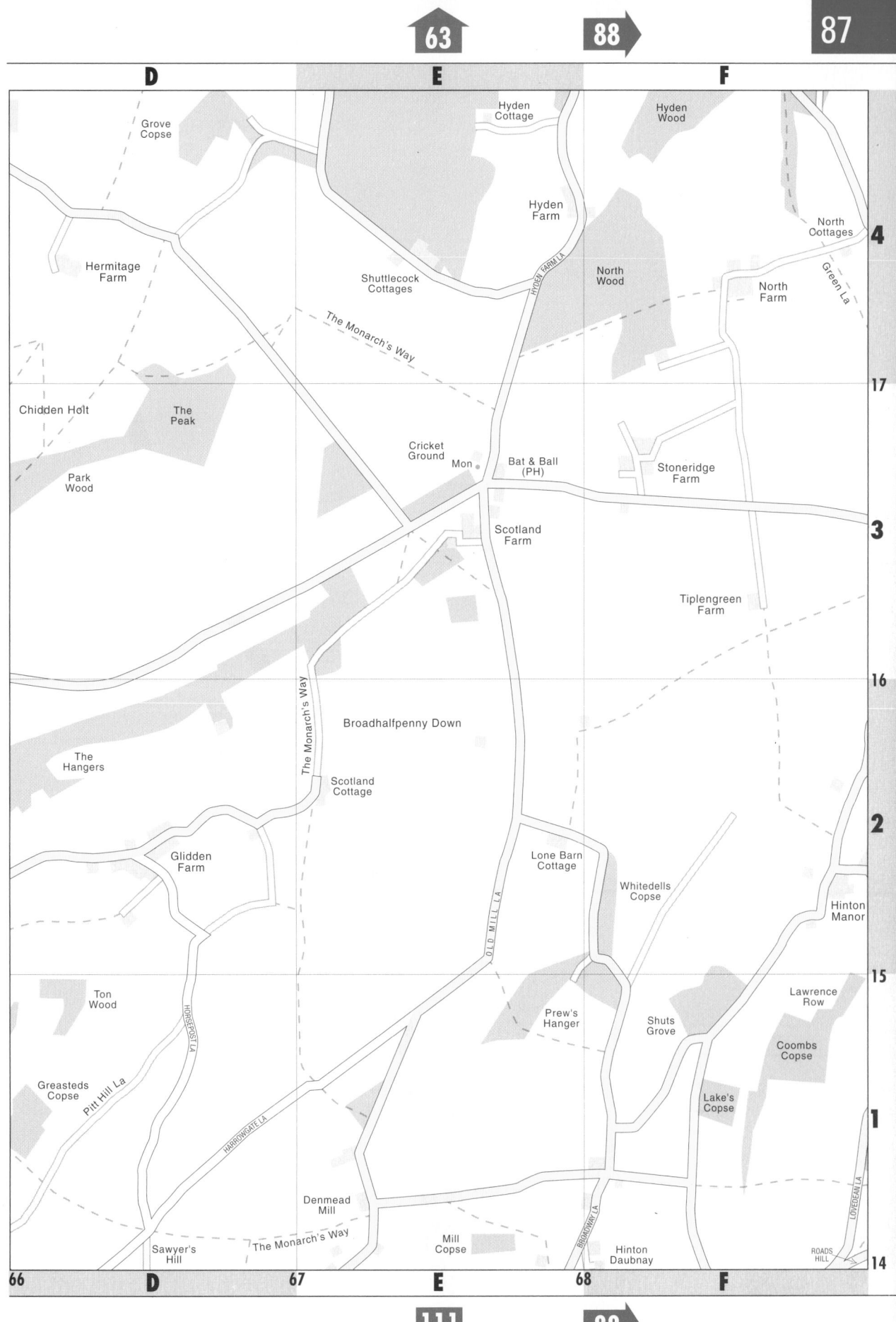

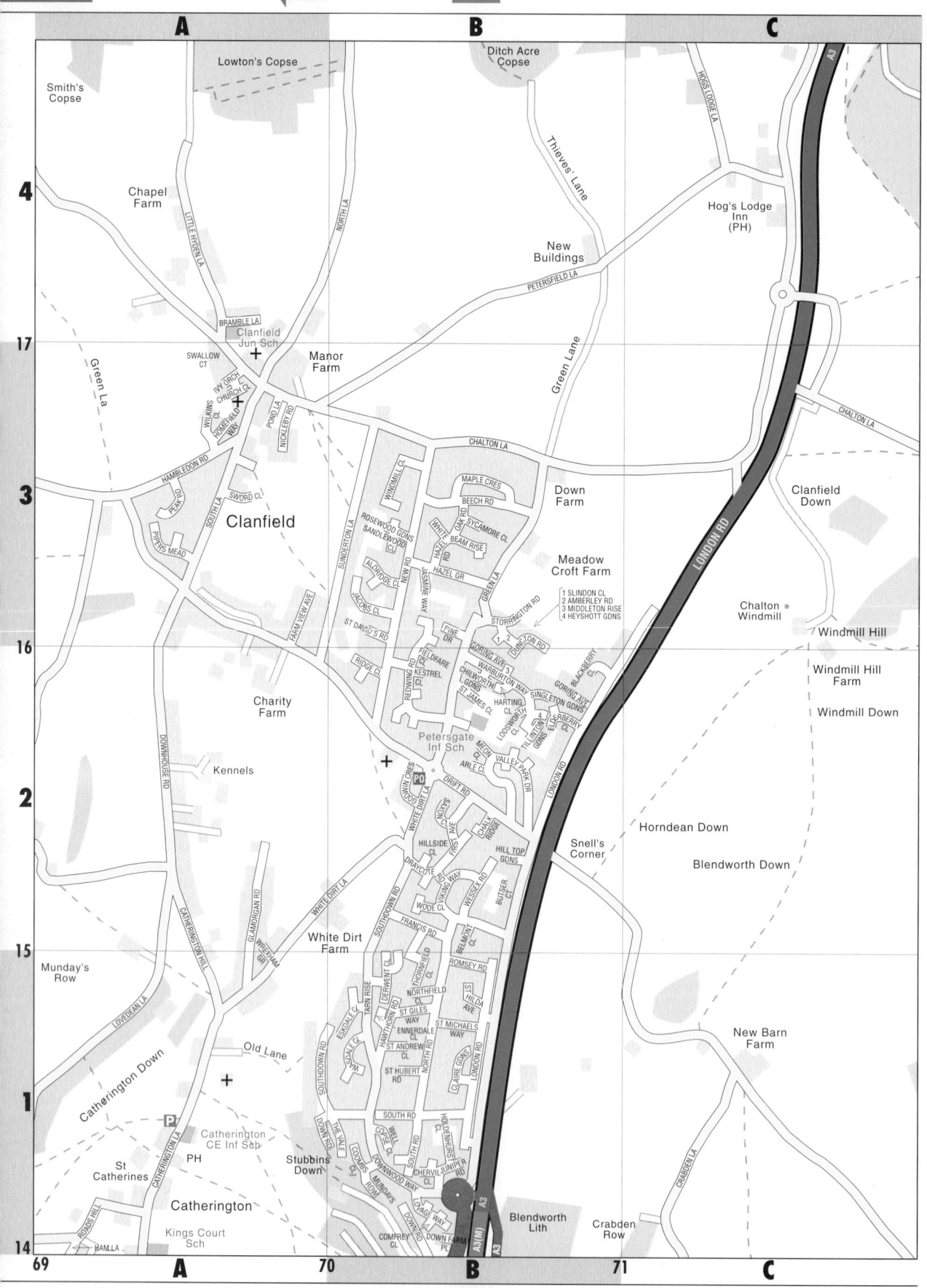

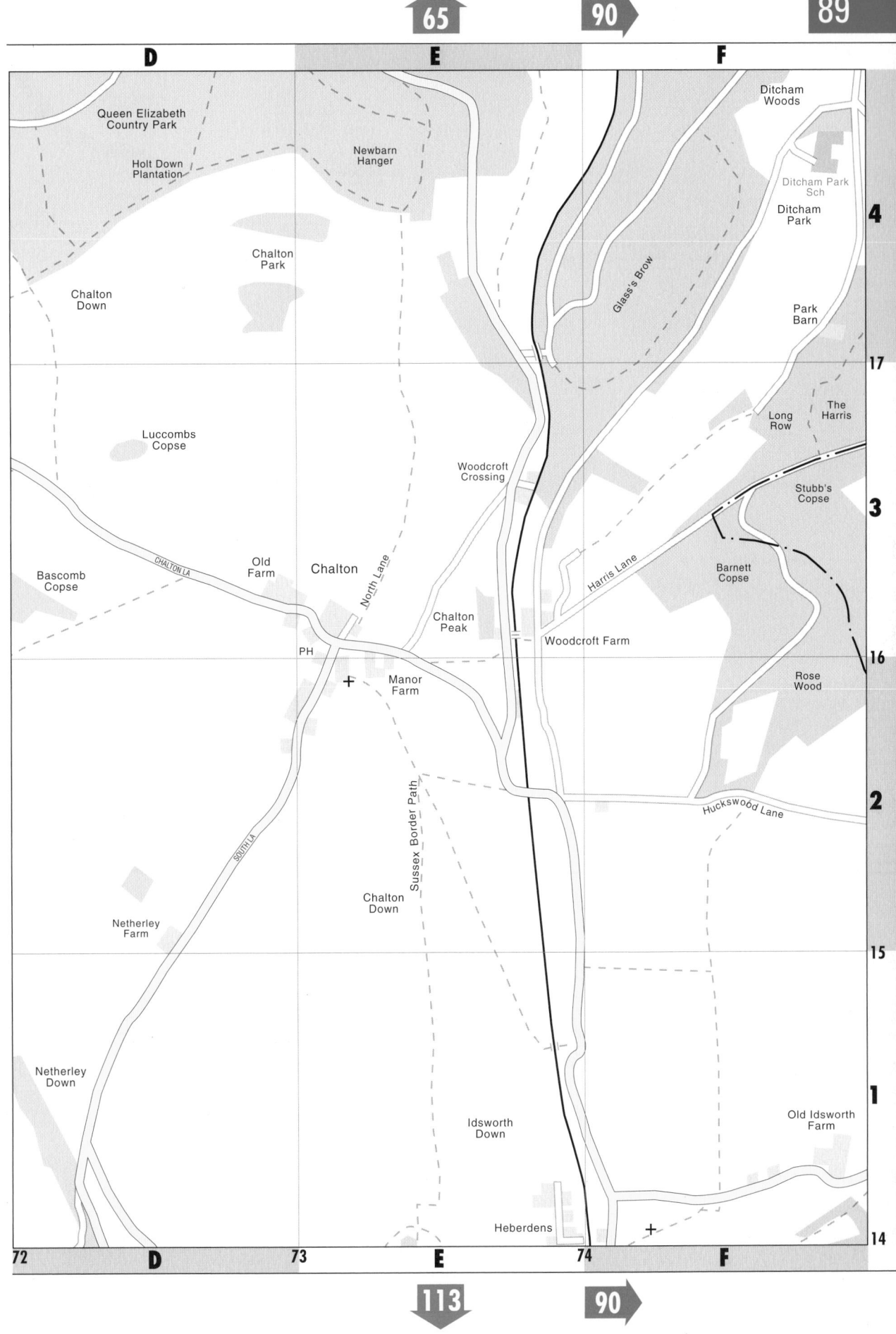

Queen Elizabeth
Country Park

Ditcham
Woods

Holt Down
Plantation

Newbarn
Hanger

Ditcham Park
Sch

Ditcham
Park

4

Chalton
Park

Chalton
Down

Glass's Brow

Park
Barn

17

Luccombs
Copse

Long
Row

The
Harris

Woodcroft
Crossing

Stubb's
Copse

3

Bascomb
Copse

CHALTON LA

Old
Farm

Chalton

North Lane

Harris Lane

Barnett
Copse

Chalton
Peak

Woodcroft Farm

16

PH

Manor
Farm

Rose
Wood

Sussex Border Path

Huckswood Lane

2

SOUTH LA

Chalton
Down

Netherley
Farm

15

Netherley
Down

1

Idsworth
Down

Old Idsworth
Farm

Heberdens

14

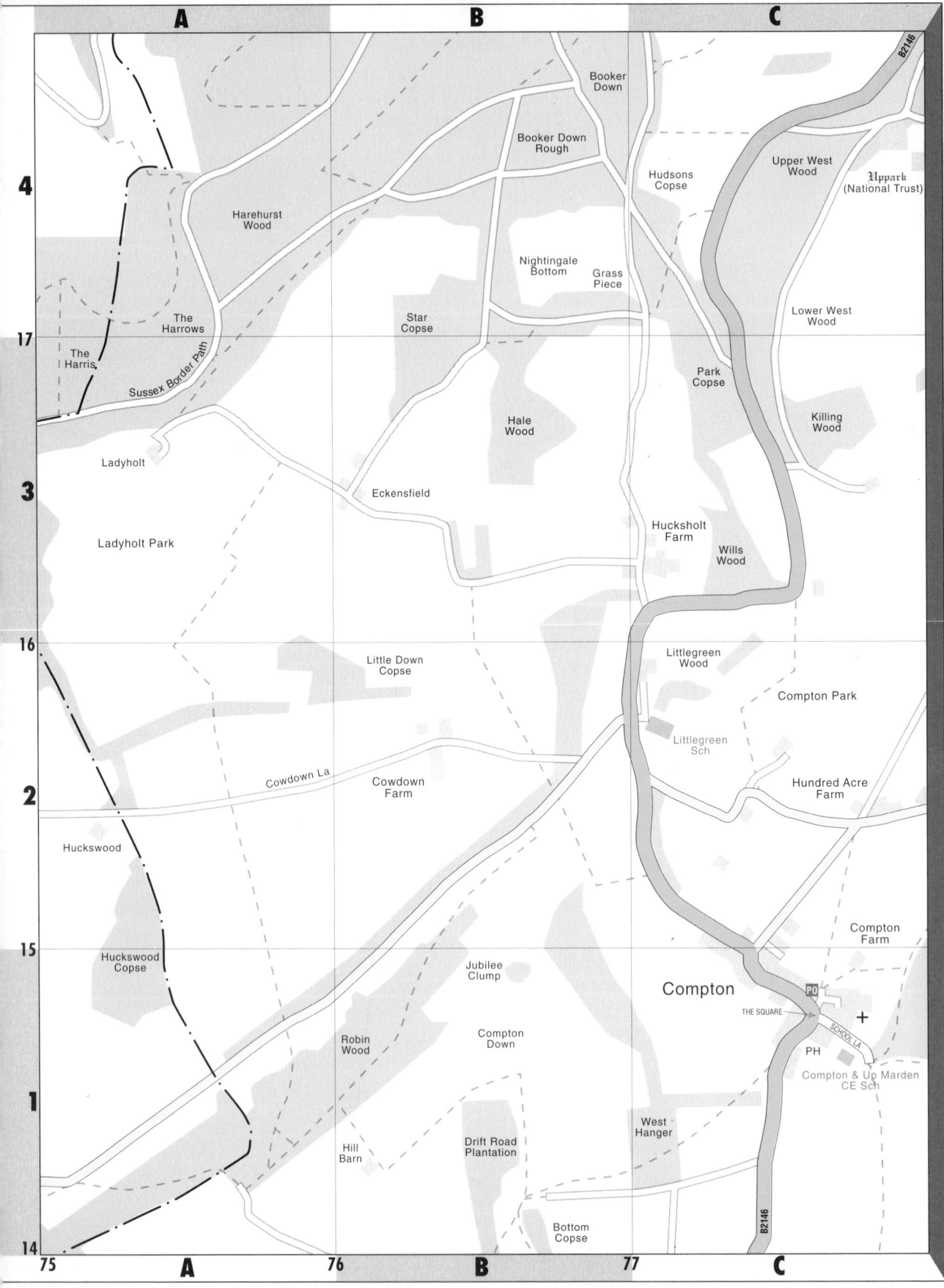

A   B   C

4

Booker
Down

Booker Down
Rough

Hudsons
Copse

Upper West
Wood

Uppark
(National Trust)

Harehurst
Wood

Nightingale
Bottom

Grass
Piece

Lower West
Wood

17

The Harrows

Star
Copse

Park
Copse

Killing
Wood

The Harris

Sussex Border Path

Hale
Wood

Ladyholt

Eckensfield

Hucksholt
Farm

Wills
Wood

3

Ladyholt Park

16

Little Down
Copse

Littlegreen
Wood

Compton Park

Littlegreen
Sch

Cowdown La

Cowdown
Farm

Hundred Acre
Farm

2

Huckswood

15

Huckswood
Copse

Jubilee
Clump

Compton
Down

Compton

PO

Compton
Farm

THE SQUARE

SCHOOL LA

Robin
Wood

PH

Compton & Up Marden
CE Sch

1

Hill
Barn

Drift Road
Plantation

West
Hanger

B2146

Bottom
Copse

14

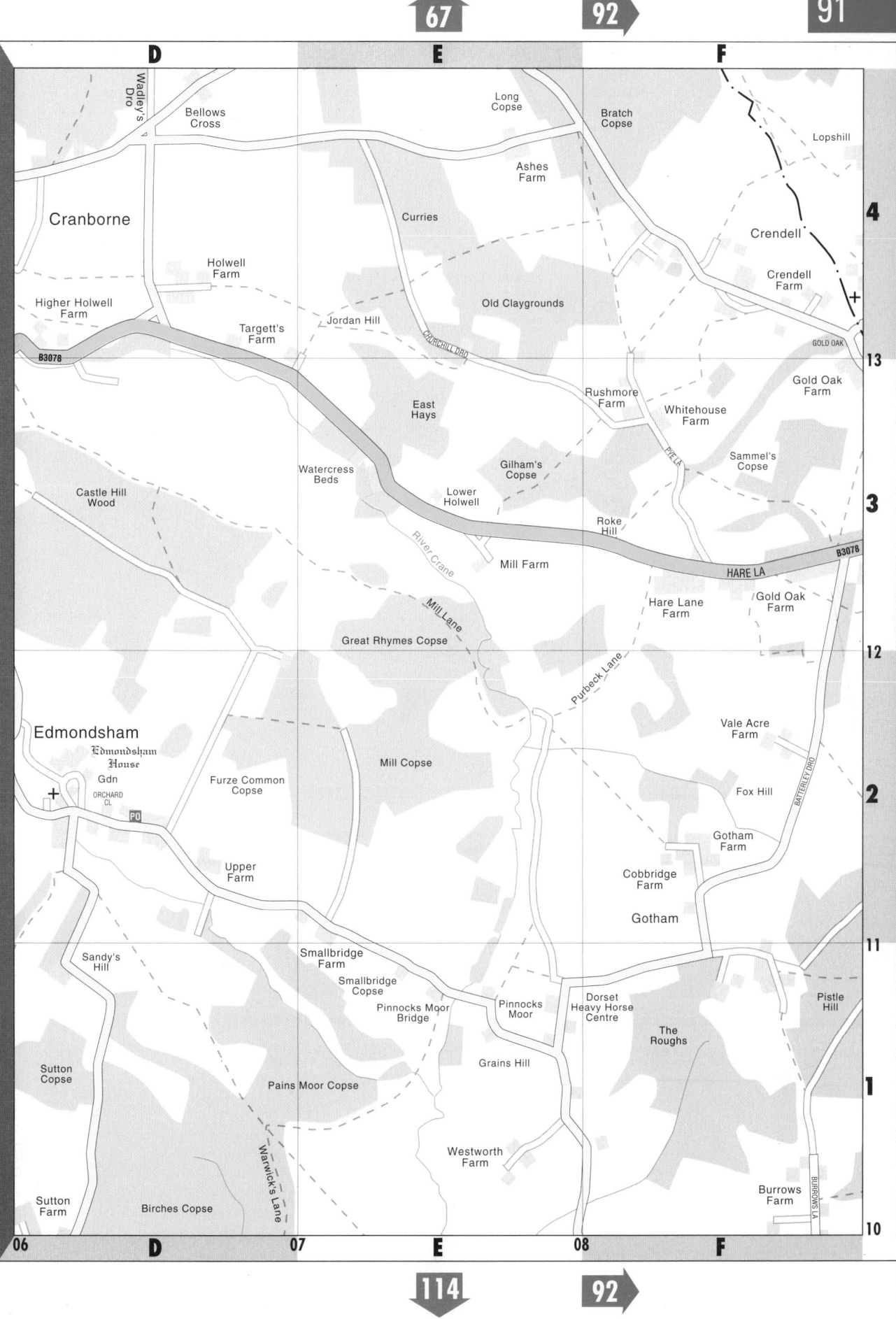

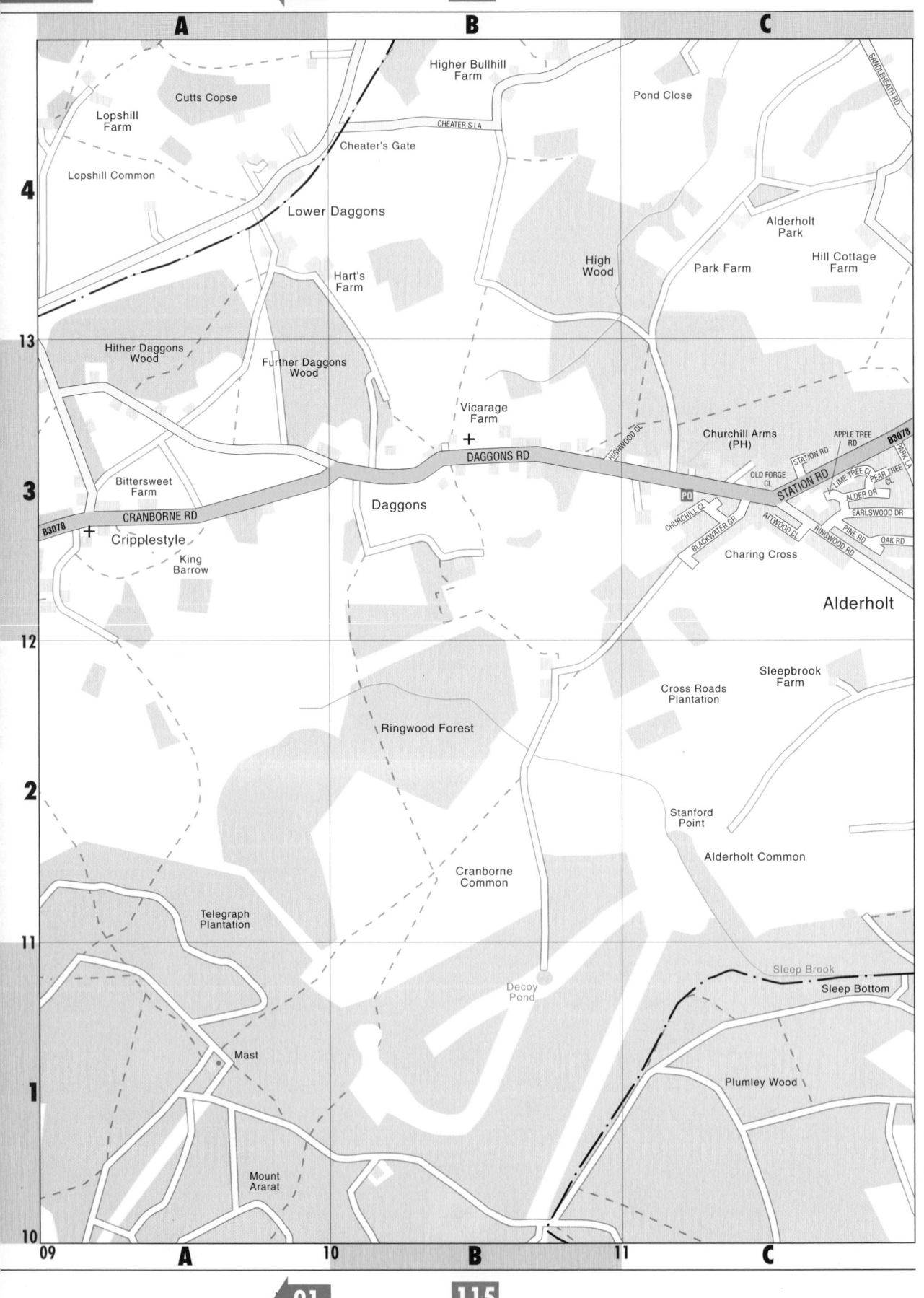

D **E** **F**

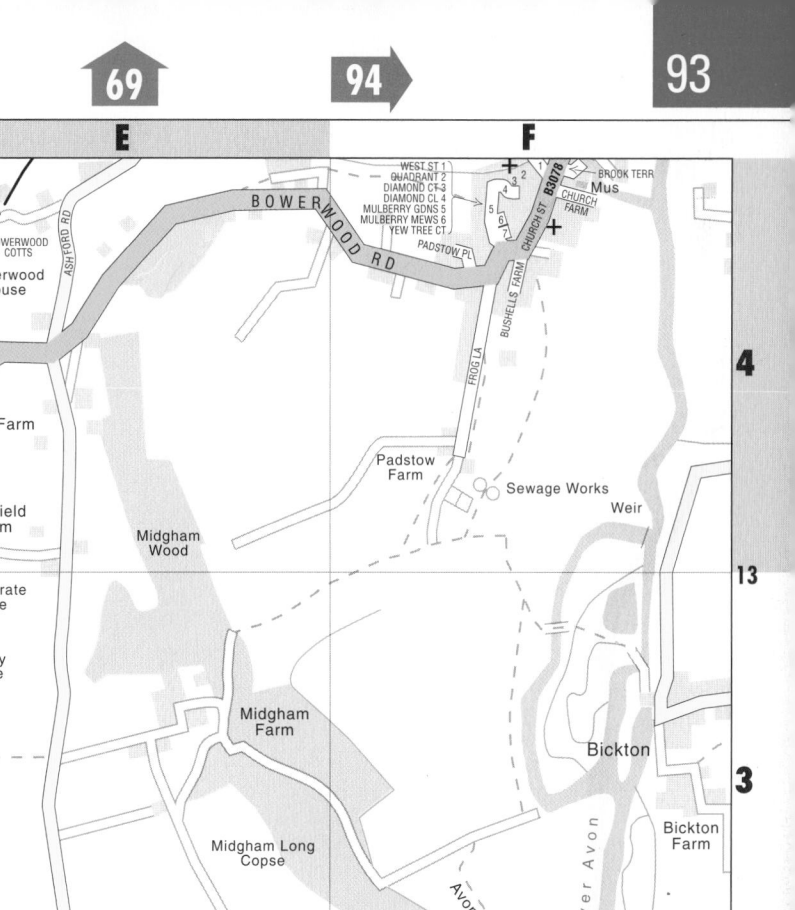

Hill Farm

SANDLEHEATH RD

Home Farm

BOWERWOOD COTTS

Bowerwood House

ASHFORD RD

BOWERWOOD RD

WEST ST 1
QUADRANT 2
DIAMOND CL 3
DIAMOND CL 4
MULBERRY GDNS 5
MULBERRY MEWS 6
YEW TREE CT 7

BROOK TERR

CHURCH FARM

Mus

PADSTOW PL

CHURCH ST

B3078

BUSHELLS FARM

FORDINGBRIDGE RD

New Farm

Padstow Farm

FROG LA

Sewage Works

Weir

4

Salisbury Arms Farm

SANDLEHEATH RD

PRESSEYS CNR

Cross Farm

STATION RD

Bonfire Hill

Highfield Farm

Wolvercrate Copse

Midgham Wood

13

Camel Green

Sch

COPPERS CL
DOWN LOOP CL
POSSUM WAY
WINIMOR
HAYTERS HILL
TREE HILL
FIR HILL
CAMEL GREEN RD
SILVERDALE CRES
TUDOR CL
BIRCHWOOD DR
GREEN CL
GILBERT CL
HILLBURY PK
WREN GDNS
KESTREL WAY
SAXON WAY

ANTELL'S WAY
SOUTH
BRAMBLE CL
BEECH CL
ASH CL
PARK LA
EARLSWOOD DR
OAK RD
BROOMFIELD DR
FERN CL
HAZEL CL

Hilbury Copse

Hillbury Farm

HILLBURY RD

Midgham Farm

Bickton

3

Bickton Farm

River Avon

Avon Valley Path

Midgham Long Copse

RINGWOOD RD

Oak Tree Farm

Drove End Farm

12

Sleepbrook Farm

Alderholt Common

East Moor Copse

Warren Park Farm

NORTH END LA

2

Whitefield Bottom

Plumley Wood

Bleakhill Farm

LOMER LA

HARBRIDGE DRO

Bleak Hill

North End Farmhouse

11

Cobley Wood Farm

Harbridge Green

CHURCHFIELD LA

North Plumley Farmhouse

Cobley Hill

1

Hamer Copse

Hamer

KENT LA

Kent

Kent Hill

Harbridge

Harbridge House

10

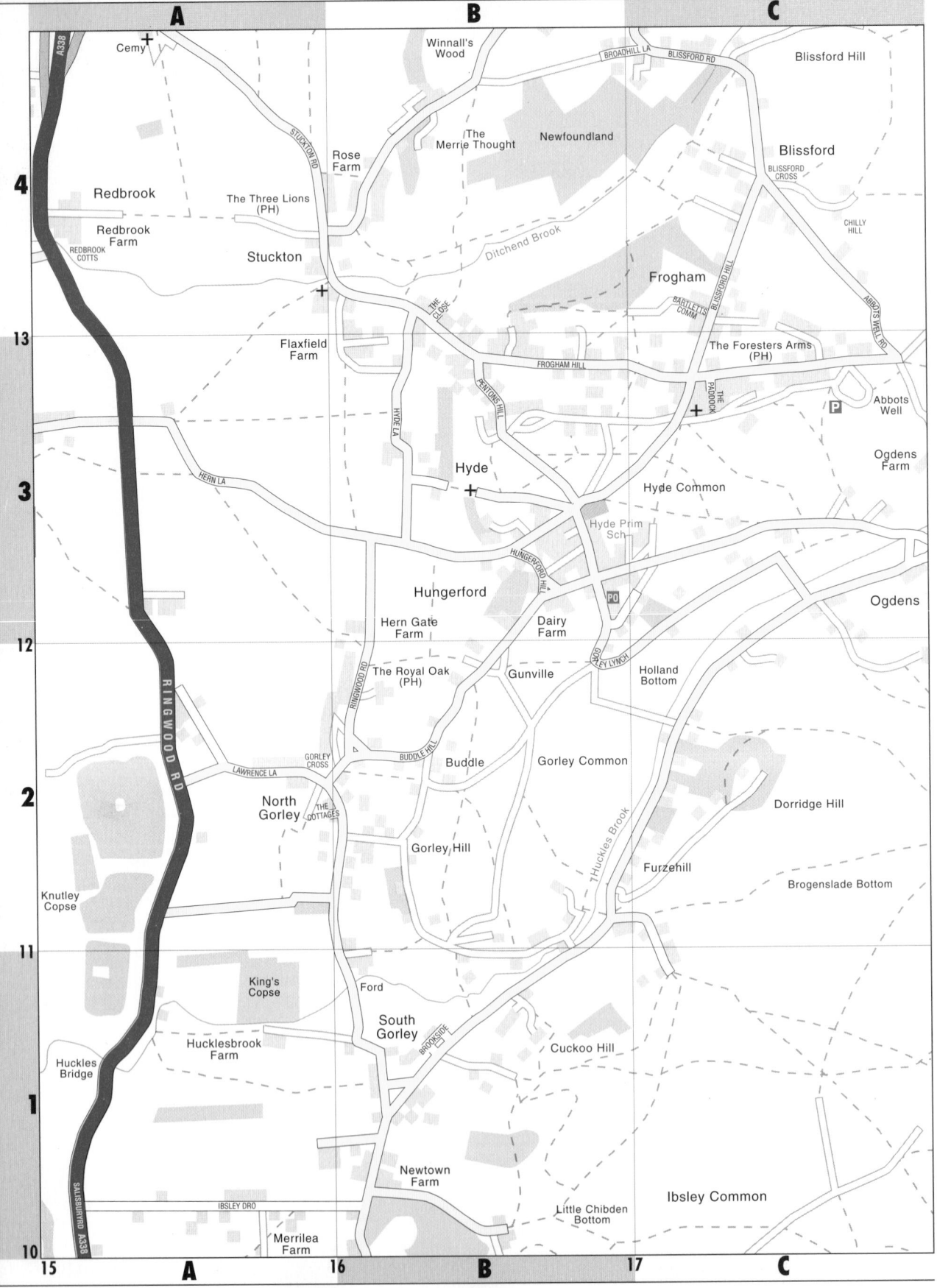

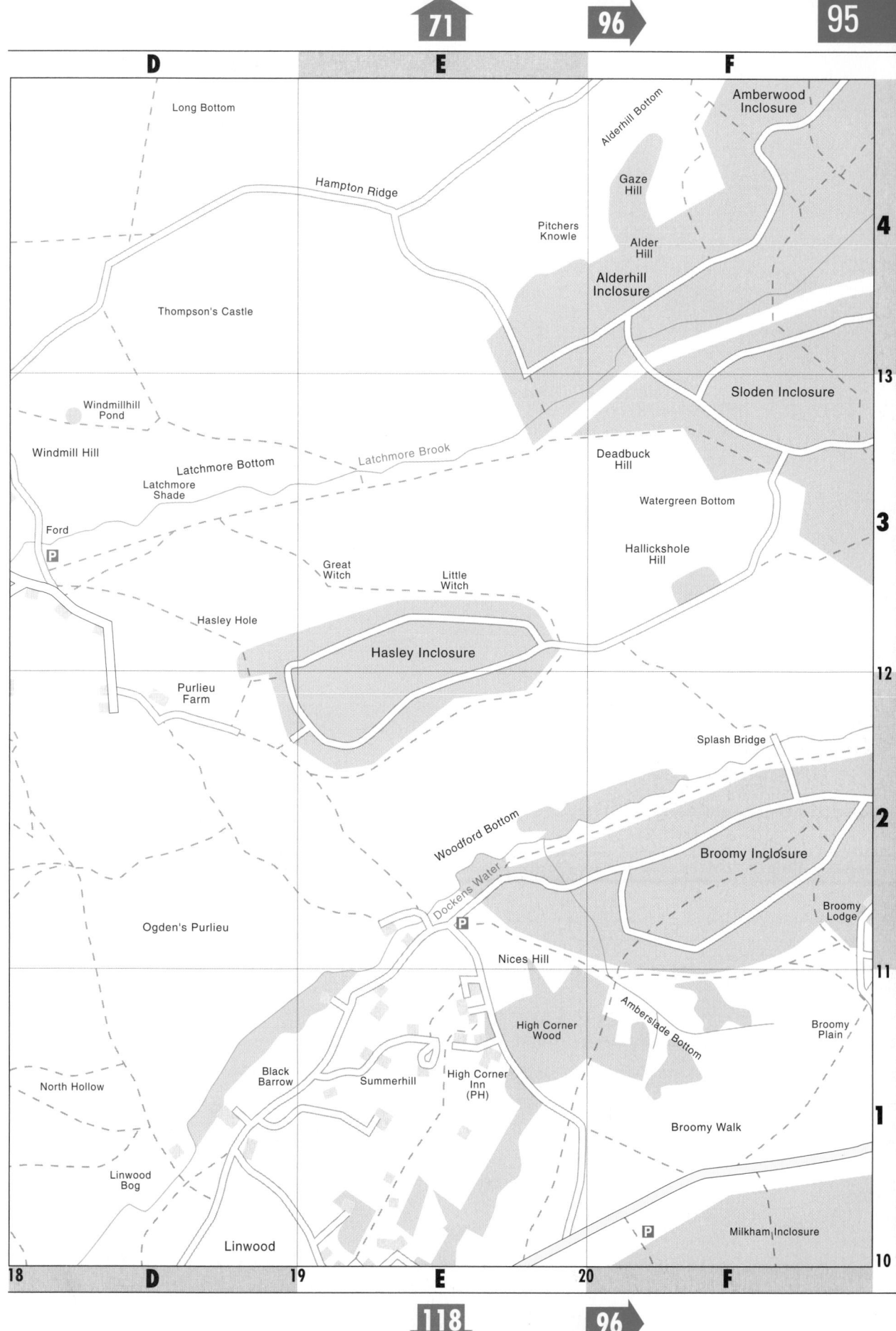

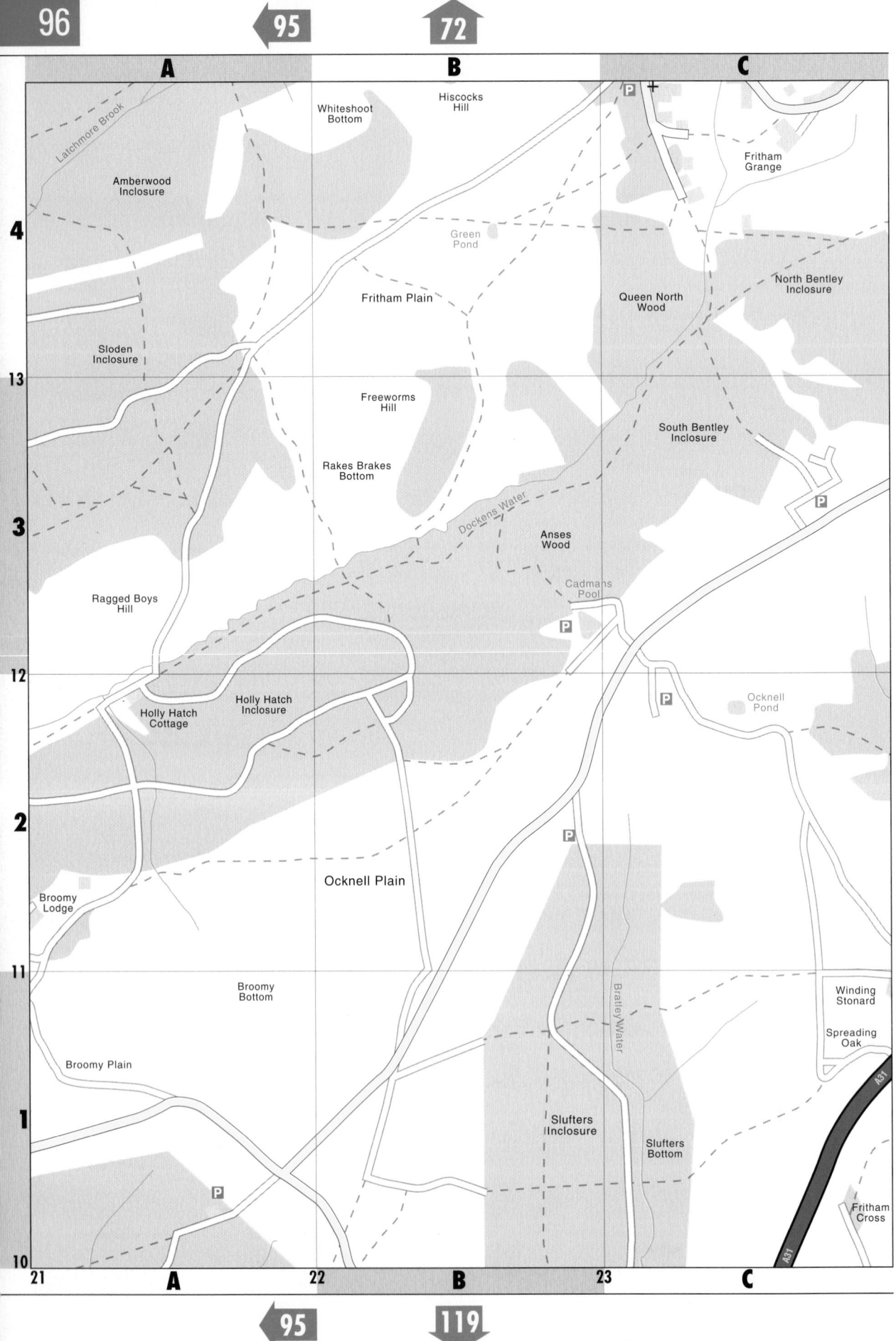

Latchmore Brook

Amberwood
Inclosure

Whiteshoot
Bottom

Hiscocks
Hill

Fritham
Grange

4

Green
Pond

North Bentley
Inclosure

Fritham Plain

Queen North
Wood

Sloden
Inclosure

13

Freeworms
Hill

South Bentley
Inclosure

Rakes Brakes
Bottom

P

Dockens Water

3

Anses
Wood

Cadmans
Pool

Ragged Boys
Hill

P

12

P

Holly Hatch
Cottage

Holly Hatch
Inclosure

Ocknell
Pond

P

2

Ocknell Plain

Broomy
Lodge

11

Broomy
Bottom

Winding
Stonard

Braiiey Water

Spreading
Oak

Broomy Plain

A31

1

Slufters
Inclosure

Slufters
Bottom

P

Fritham
Cross

10

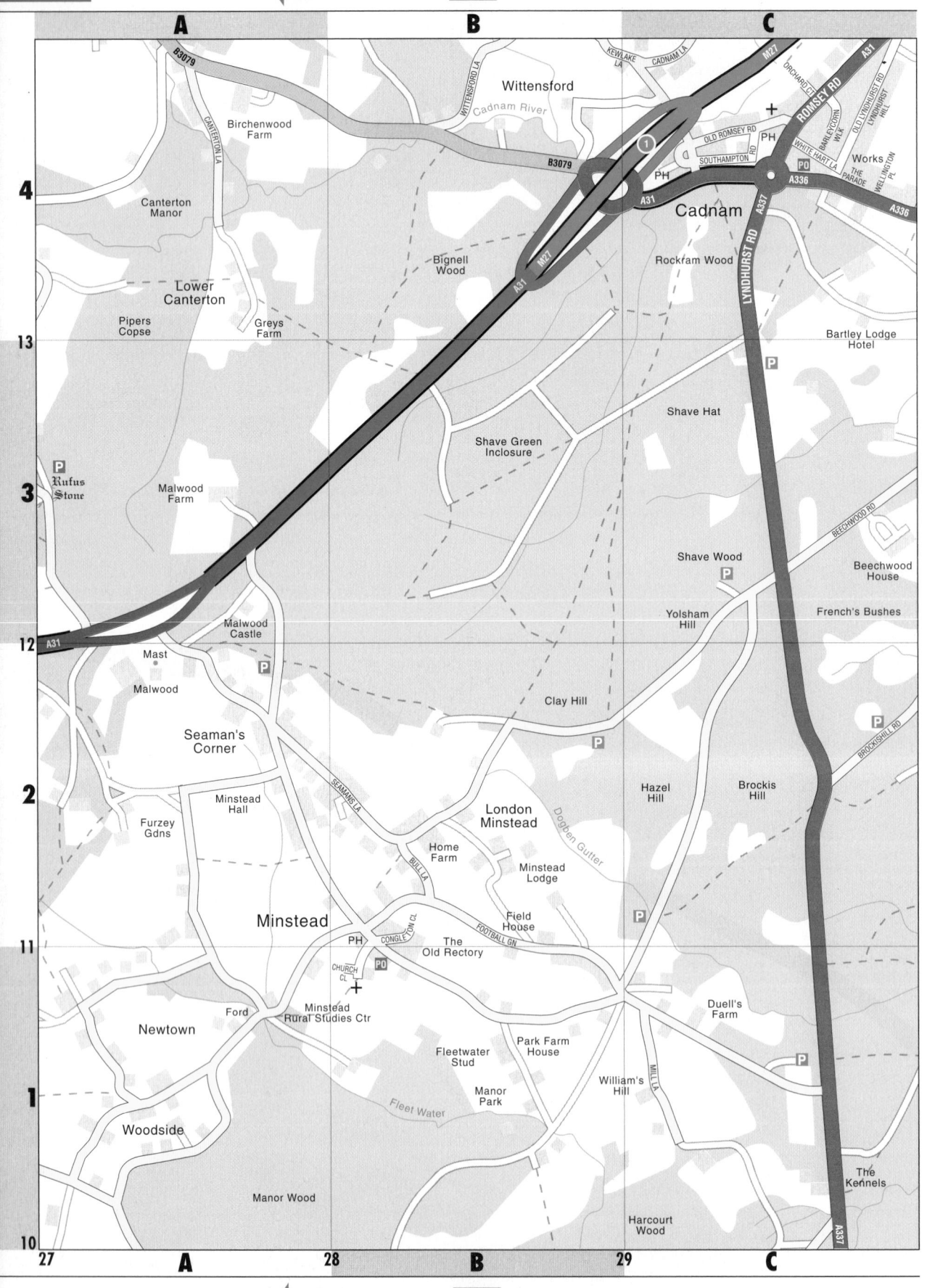

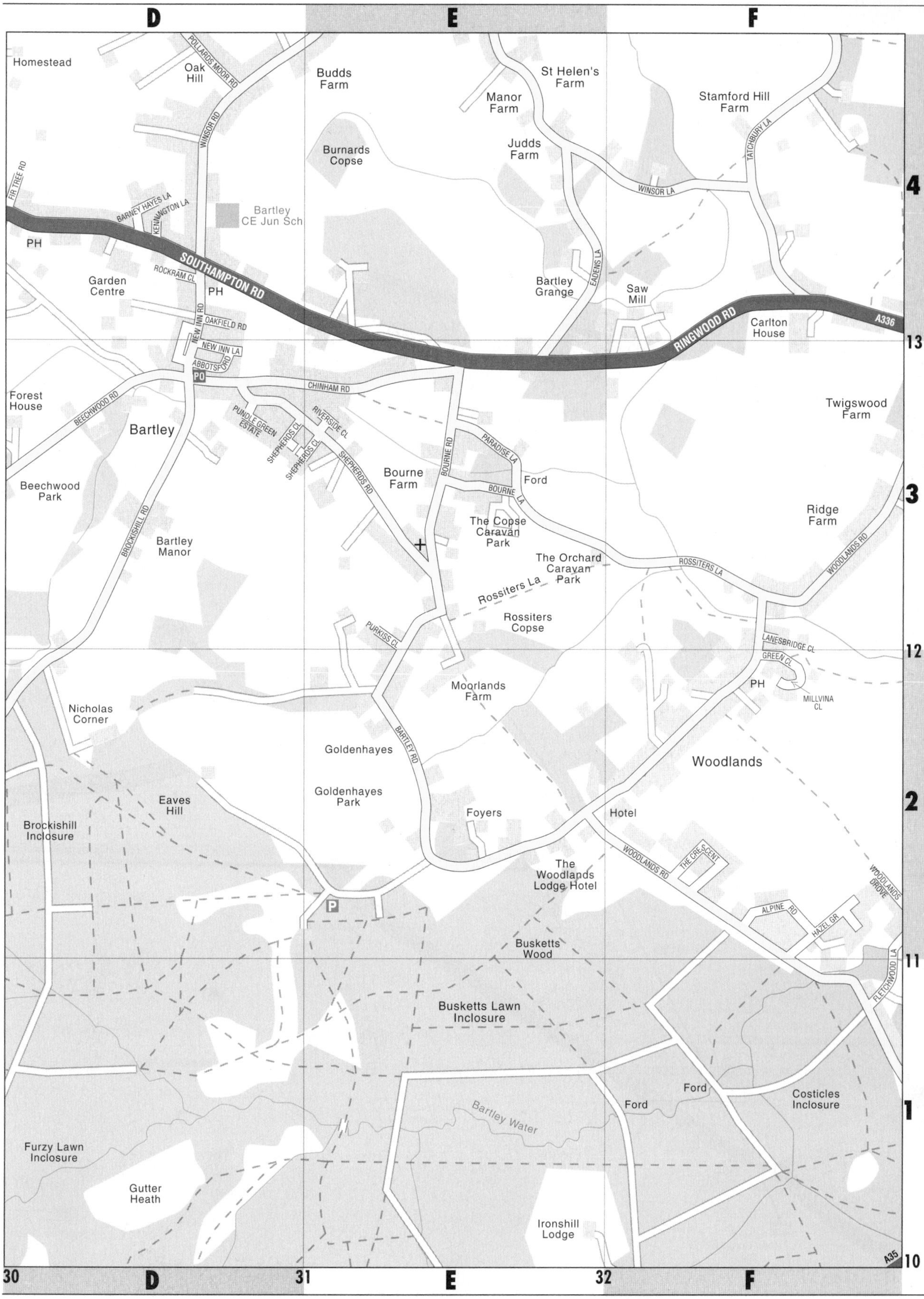

D E F

Homestead

Oak Hill

POLLARDS MOOR RD

Budds Farm

St Helen's Farm

Manor Farm

Stamford Hill Farm

TATCHBURY LA

WINSOR RD

Burnards Copse

Judds Farm

WINSOR LA

4

FIR TREE RD

BARNEY HAYES LA

KENNINGTON LA

Bartley CE Jun Sch

PH

SOUTHAMPTON RD

ROCKRAM CL

PH

Garden Centre

Bartley Grange

EADENS LA

Saw Mill

RINGWOOD RD

Carlton House

A336

13

NEW INN RD

OAKFIELD RD

NEW INN LA

ABBOTS FD

PO

CHINHAM RD

Twigswood Farm

Forest House

BEECHWOOD RD

Bartley

PUNDLE GREEN ESTATE

SHEPHERDS CL

RIVERSIDE CL

Bourne Farm

BOURNE RD

PARADISE LA

Ford

BOURNE

WOODLANDS RD

3

Beechwood Park

BROCKISHILL RD

SHEPHERDS RD

The Copse Caravan Park

Ridge Farm

Bartley Manor

The Orchard Caravan Park

ROSSITERS LA

Rossiters La

Rossiters Copse

LANESBRIDGE CL

GREEN CL

12

PURKISS CL

Moorlands Farm

PH

MILLVINA CL

Nicholas Corner

BARTLEY RD

Goldenhayes

Goldenhayes Park

Woodlands

2

Eaves Hill

Foyers

Hotel

WOODLANDS RD

THE CRESCENT

WOODLANDS DROVE

Brockishill Inclosure

The Woodlands Lodge Hotel

ALPINE RD

HAZEL GR

P

Busketts Wood

FLETCHWOOD LA

11

Busketts Lawn Inclosure

Ford

Ford

Costicles Inclosure

1

Bartley Water

Ford

Furzy Lawn Inclosure

Gutter Heath

Ironshill Lodge

A35

10

30 D 31 E 32 F

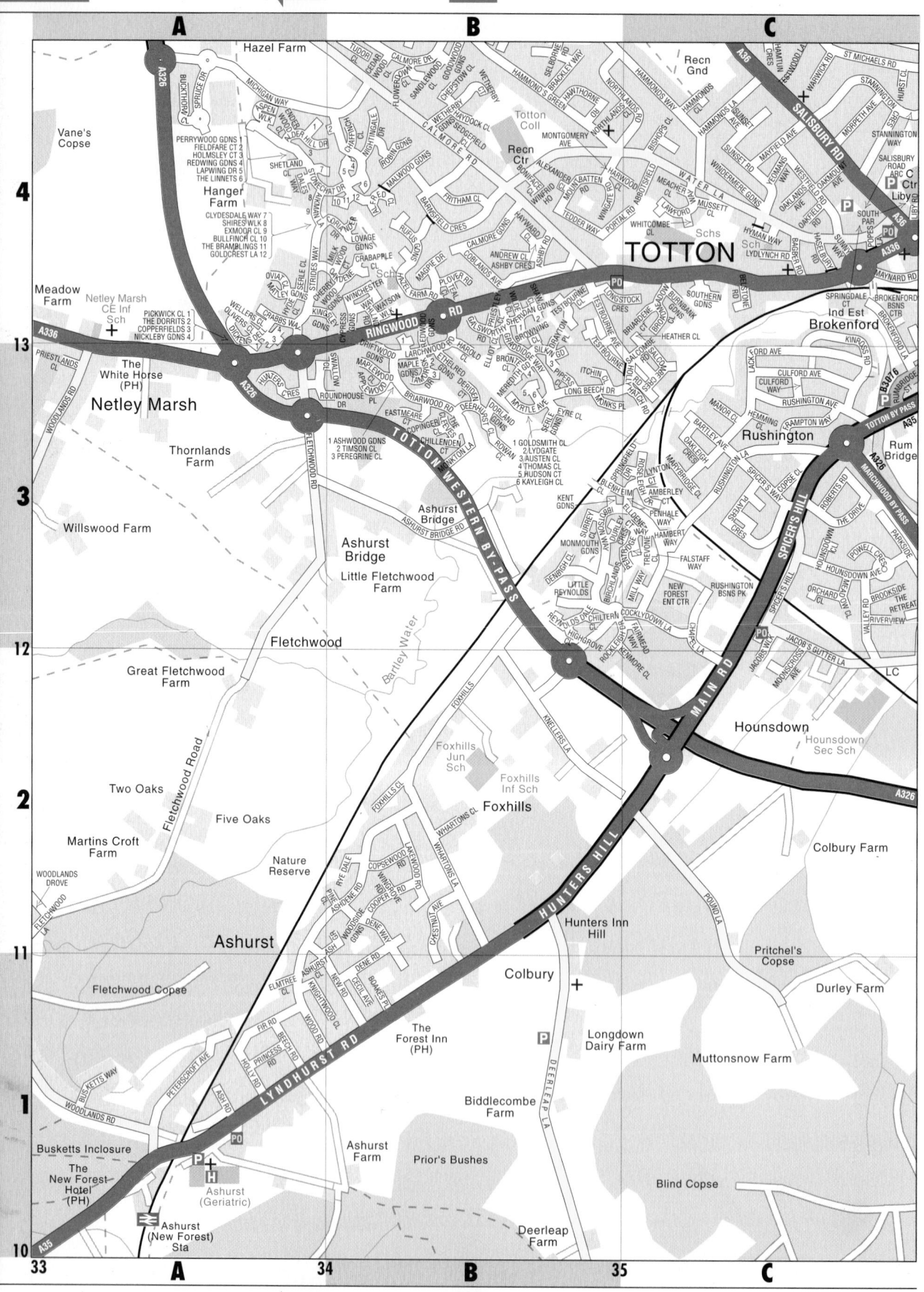

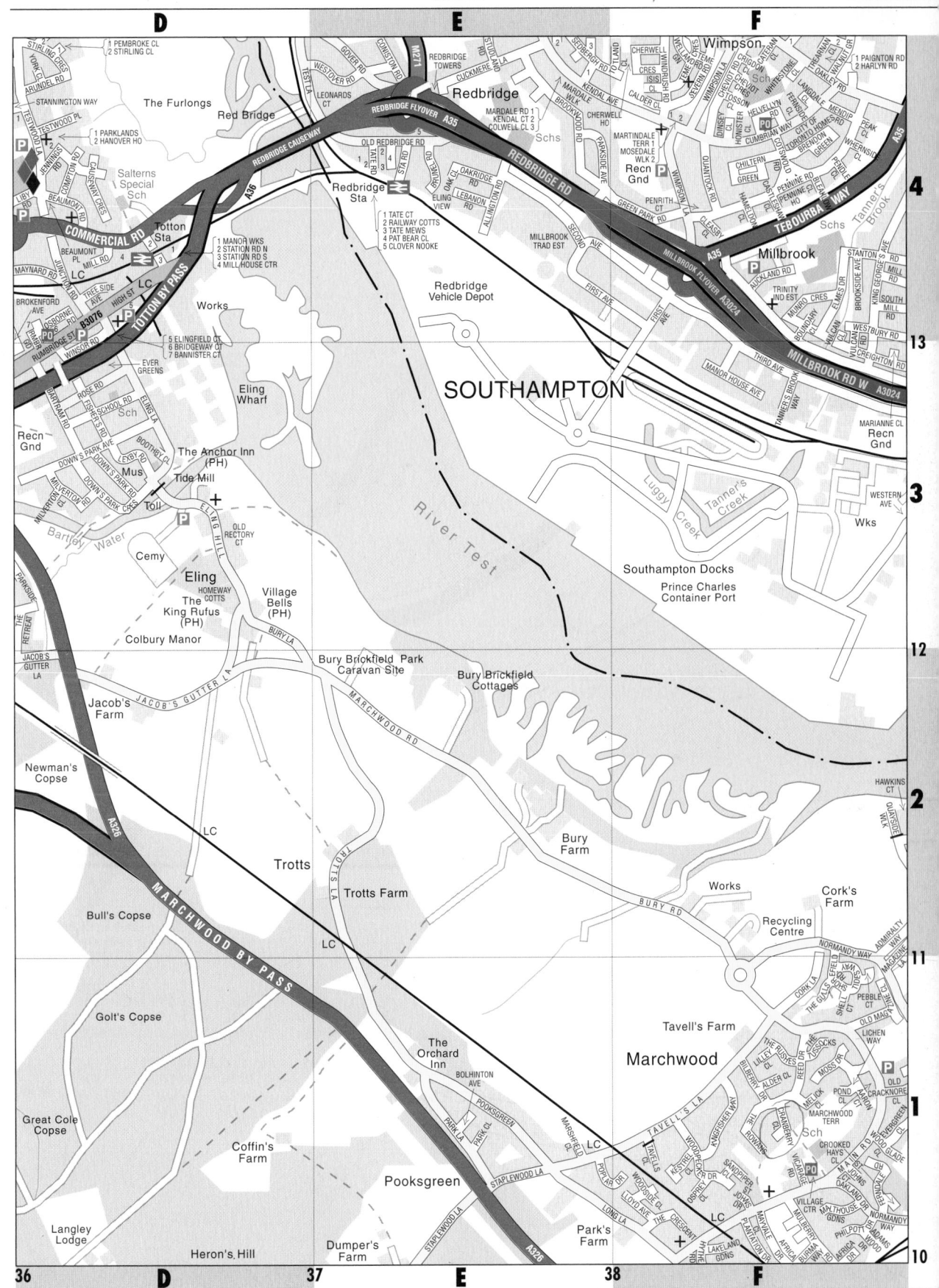

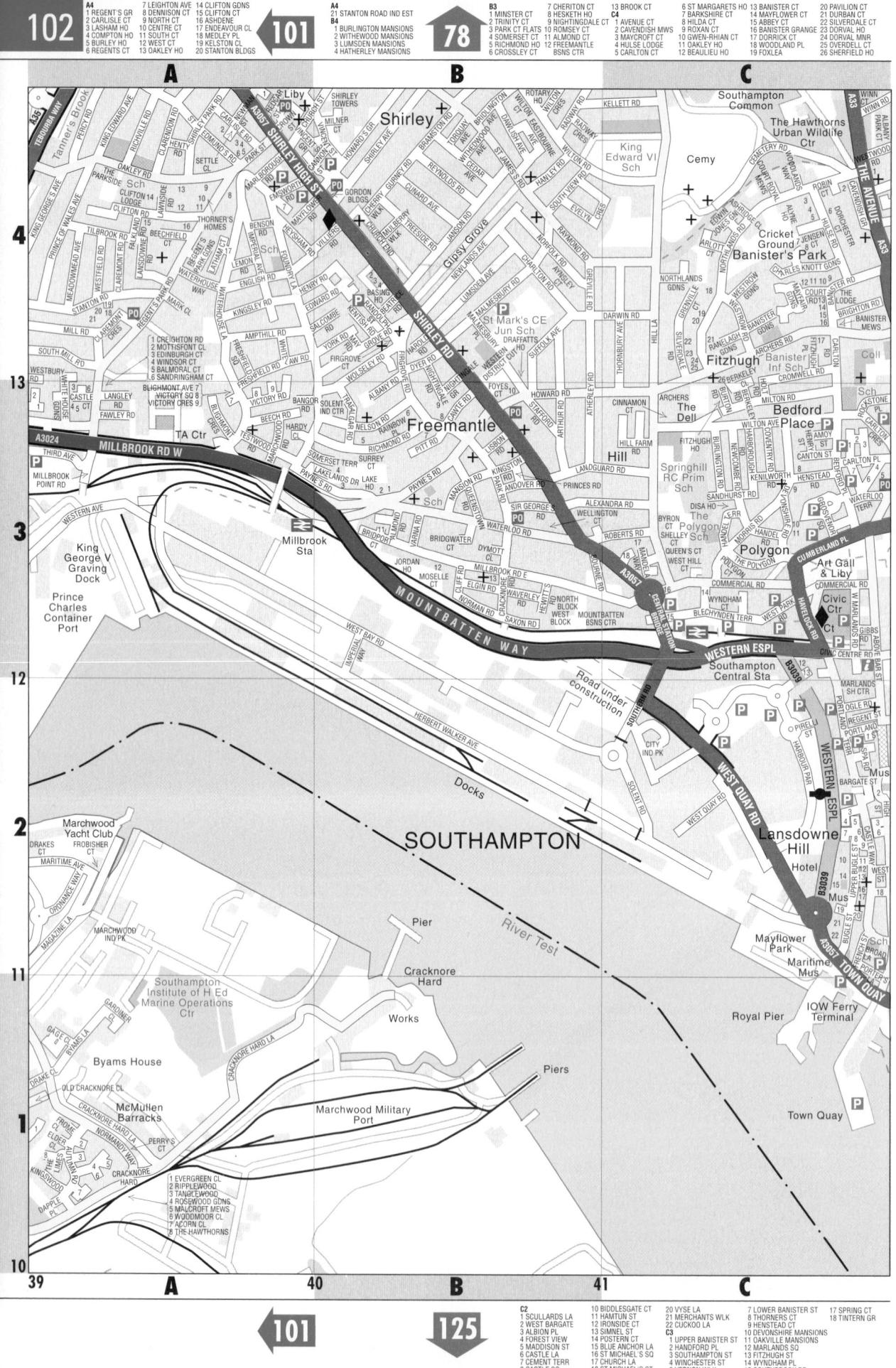

A4
1 REGENT'S GR
2 CARLISLE CT
3 LASHAM HO
4 COMPTON HO
5 BURLEY HO
6 REGENTS CT

7 LEIGHTON AVE
8 DENNISON CT
9 NORTH CT
10 CENTRE CT
11 SOUTH CT
12 WEST CT
13 OAKLEY HO

14 CLIFTON GDNS
15 CLIFTON CT
16 ASHDENE
17 ENDEAVOUR CL
18 MEDLEY PL
19 KELSTON CL
20 STANTON BLDGS

101

A4
21 STANTON ROAD IND EST
B4
1 BURLINGTON MANSIONS
2 WITHEWOOD MANSIONS
3 LUMSDEN MANSIONS
4 HATHERLEY MANSIONS

78

B3
1 MINSTER CT
2 TRINITY CT
3 PARK CT FLATS
5 SOMERSET CT
5 RICHMOND HO
6 CROSSLEY CASTLE

7 CHERITON CT
8 HESKETH HO
9 NIGHTINGDALE CT
10 ROMSEY CT
11 ALMOND CT
12 FREEMANTLE
     BSNS CTR

13 BROOK CT
C4
1 AVENUE CT
2 CAVENDISH MWS
3 MAYCROFT CT
4 HULSE LODGE
5 CARLTON'S CT

6 ST MARGARETS HO
7 BARKSHIRE CT
8 HILDA CT
9 ROXAN CT
10 GWEN-RHIAN CT
11 OAKLEY HO
12 BEAULIEU HO

13 BANISTER CT
14 MAYFLOWER CT
15 ABBEY CT
16 BANISTER GRANGE
17 DORRICK CT
18 WOODLAND PL
19 FOXLEA

20 PAVILION CT
21 DURBAN CT
22 SILVERDALE CT
23 DORVAL HO
24 DORVAL MNR
25 OVERDELL CT
26 SHERFIELD HO

101

125

C2
1 SCULLARDS LA
2 WEST BARGATE
3 ALBION PL
4 FOREST VIEW
5 MADDISON ST
6 CASTLE LA
7 CEMENT TERR
8 CASTLE SQ
9 LANSDOWNE HILL

10 BIDDLESGATE CT
11 HAMTUN ST
12 IRONSIDE CT
13 SIMNEL ST
14 POSTERN CT
15 BLUE ANCHOR LA
16 ST MICHAEL'S SQ
17 CHURCH LA
18 ST MICHAEL'S ST
19 WESTGATE ST

20 VYSE LA
21 MERCHANTS WLK
22 CUCKOO LA
C3
1 UPPER BUGLE ST
2 HANDFORD PL
3 SOUTHAMPTON ST
4 WINCHESTER ST
5 VERNON WLK
6 SALISBURY ST

7 LOWER BANISTER ST
8 THORNERS CT
9 HENSTEAD CT
10 DEVONSHIRE MANSIONS
11 OAKVILLE MANSIONS
12 MARLANDS SQ
13 FITZHUGH ST
14 WYNDHAM PL
15 SOUTHBROOK CL
16 FOURPOSTS HILL

17 SPRING CT
18 TINTERN GR

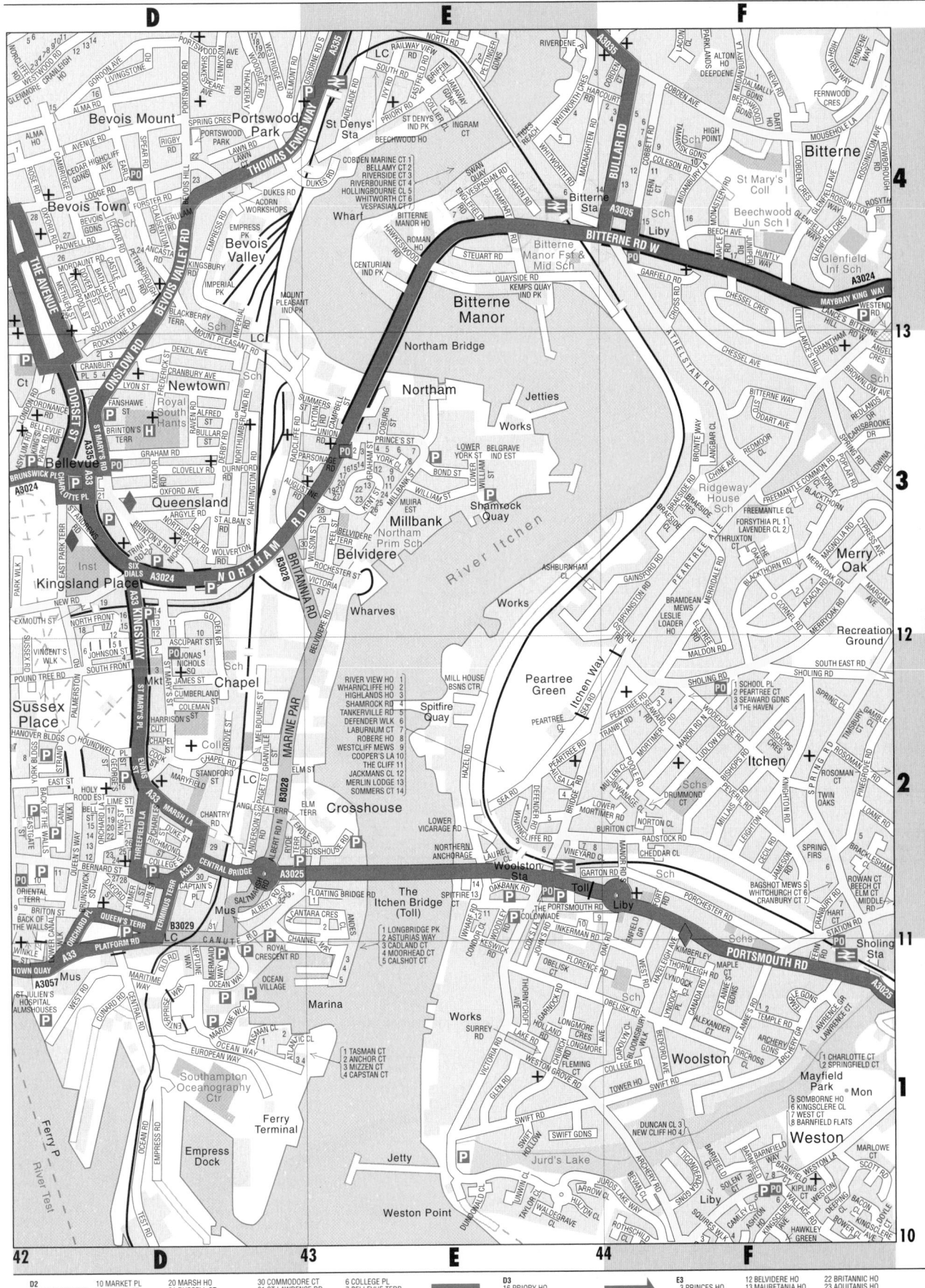

D4
1 CLIFFORD DIBBEN MEWS
2 BUCKINGHAM CT
3 LINGDALE PL
4 MINSTEAD CT
5 WINDSOR CT
6 BALMORAL CT

7 WESSEX CT
8 RANELAGH CT
9 KINTERBURY CT
10 ELFIN CT
11 WESTWOOD CT
12 CANDLEMAS PL
13 PARKLAND PL

14 CHERRY CT
15 CAMBRIDGE CT
16 ST ANNES MEWS
17 HYNES CT
18 BARTLETT HO
19 ST ANDREWS HO
20 ST GEORGES HO

21 WOODSIDE CT
22 ASCUPART HO
23 BEVOIS MANSIONS
24 BEVOIS MEWS
25 DARNAN HO
26 CHARLES WYATT HO
27 TEMPLAR CT

28 LAMWARD MANSIONS

F4
1 MIDANBURY WLK
2 KELLY CT
3 FLORENCE CT
4 DEAN CT
5 BINDON CT
6 CAUSEWAY CT

F4
1 ABBEYFIELD HO
2 BIRCHWOOD CT
3 CHRISTINE CT
4 MIDANBURY CT
5 WELLOW CT
6 THE GATEHOUSE

13 WINDSOR CT
14 MANOR PARK HO
15 COBBETT CT
16 ROSEBROOK CT
17 JUNIPER CT

79

104

103

D2
1 ALBION TOWERS
2 JOHNSON ST
3 KINGSLAND SQ
4 KINGSLAND HO
5 BROAD GN
6 COSSACK GN
7 EAST BARGATE
8 BARGATE CT
9 HIGH ST

10 MARKET PL
11 TALBOT CT
12 HOLYROOD HO
13 ORCHARD HO
14 CHANDOS CT
15 QUEENS HO
16 EAST STREET CTR
17 KING'S HO
18 CHALLIS CT
19 ALL SAINTS HO

20 MARSH HO
21 RUSSELL ST
22 ELDON HO
23 ST JAMES HO
24 ST BERNARD HO
25 CANUTE HO
26 CHANDOS ST
27 LATIMER GATE
28 JESSIE TERR
29 CITY COMMERCE CTR

30 COMMODORE CT
31 ST LAWRENCE RD
32 CONSULATE HO
33 BRIDGE TERR
D3
1 SOUTHCLIFFE HO
2 THE CRANBURY
3 CRANBURY TERR
4 CRANBURY TOWERS
5 ST SWITHUNS CT

6 COLLEGE PL
7 BELLEVUE TERR
8 LOWER ALFRED ST
9 RADCLIFFE CT
10 JOSIAN WLK
11 CLIFFORD ST
12 WINTON ST
13 CRAVEN ST
14 NORTH FRONT
15 WOOLLEY HO

126

104

D3
16 PRIORY HO
17 LEWIS HO
18 KINGSLAND HO
19 THE CARRONADES
20 ST MATTHEWS CT
21 COMPTON WLK
E3
1 NORTHAM BSNS CTR
2 PRINCES CT

E3
3 PRINCES HO
4 GRAHAM HO
5 CLARENCE HO
6 CHURCH HO
7 YORK HO
8 AVON HO
9 TEVIOT HO
10 SOLWAY HO
11 FORTH HO

12 BELVIDERE HO
13 MAURETANIA HO
14 MILLBANK HO
15 KENILWORTH CL
16 NORMAN HO
17 SAXON HO
18 CHARLEJOY GDNS
19 ARUNDEL HO
20 ARMADALE WAY
21 WARWICK HO

22 BRITANNIC HO
23 AQUITANIS HO
24 CLYDE HO
25 TRENT HO
26 SHANNON HO
27 KENT HO
28 HILDA PL
29 CABLE ST
30 GUILDFORD ST

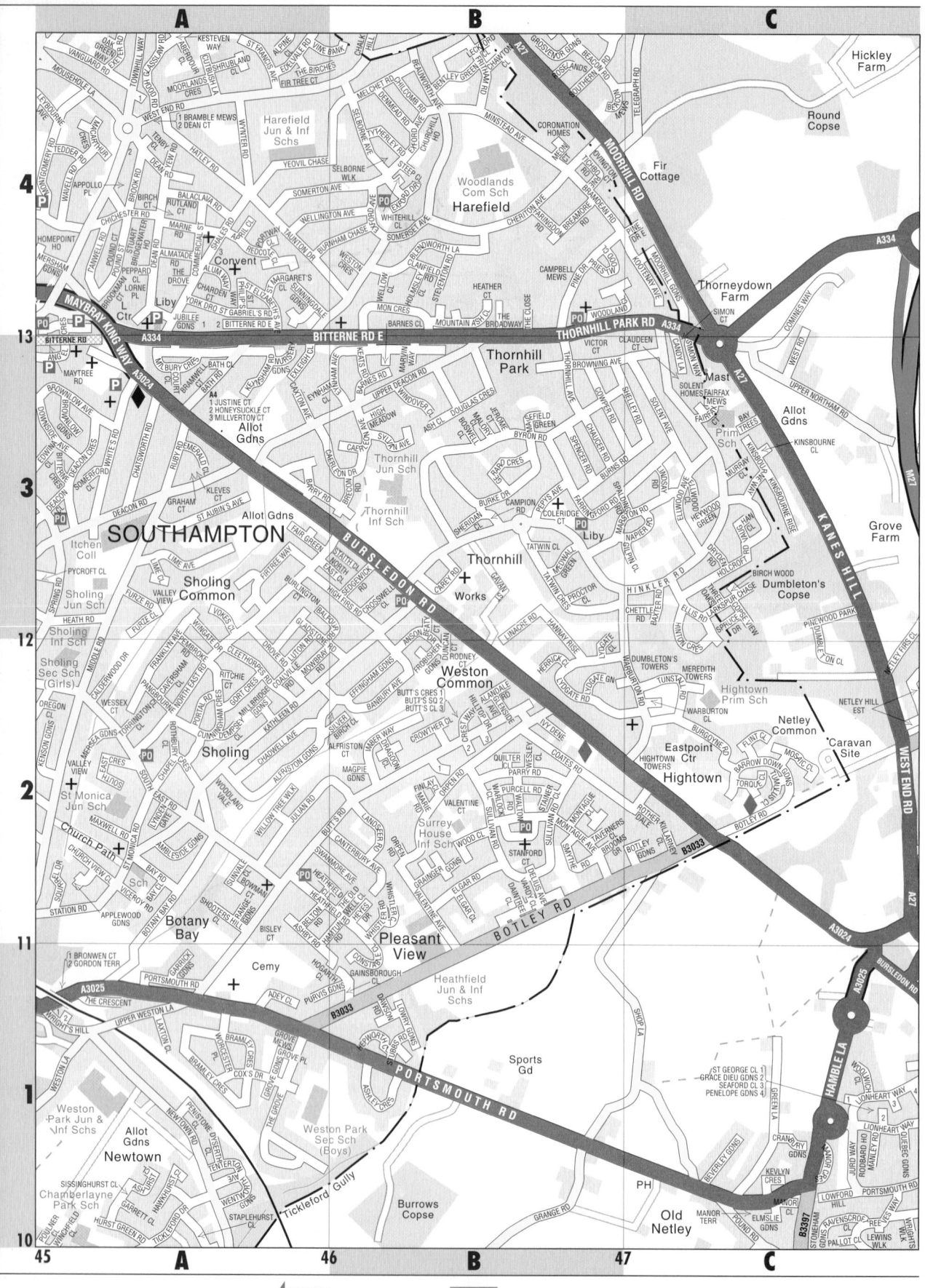

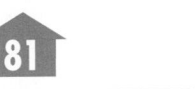

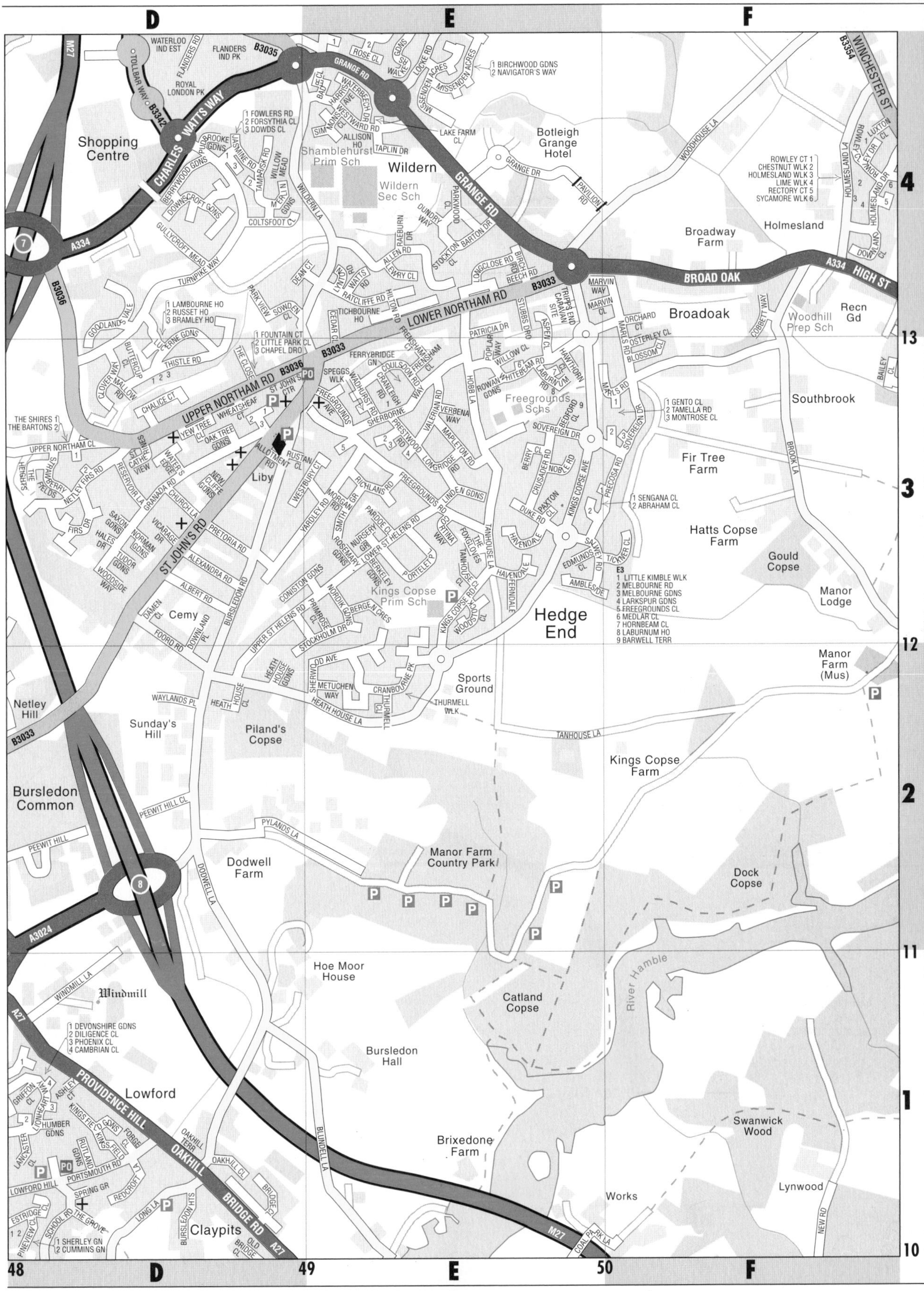
D
E
F
WATERLOO IND EST
FLANDERS RD
FLANDERS IND PK
B3035
TOLLBAR WAY
ROYAL LONDON PK
B3342
M27
GRANGE RD
ROSE CL
WALKER GDNS
LOCKE RD
SENDEN ACRES
MISSENDEN ACRES
1 BIRCHWOOD GDNS
2 NAVIGATOR'S WAY
WATERBEECH DR
HARRIS AVE
WESTWARD RD
ALLISON HO
TAPLIN DR
LAKE FARM CL
Botleigh Grange Hotel
GRANGE DR
PAVILION RD
WOODHOUSE LA
B3354
WINCHESTER ST
Shopping Centre
CHARLES WATTS WAY
1 FOWLERS RD
2 FORSYTHIA CL
3 DOWDS CL
BROOKE GDNS
JASMINE RD
TAMARISK RD
WILLOW MEAD
MERLIN GDNS
BERRYWOOD GDNS
DOWNSCROFT GDNS
COLTSFOOT CL
Shamblehurst Prim Sch
Wildern
Wildern Sec Sch
WILDERN LA
DUNDRY WAY
PARKWOOD CL
BARTON DR
ROWLEY CT 1
CHESTNUT WLK 2
HOLMESLAND WLK 3
LIME WLK 4
RECTORY CT 5
SYCAMORE WLK 6
HOLMESLAND LA
HOLMESLAND DR
LUXTON CL
DOWD CL
4
Broadway Farm
Holmesland
A334
GULLYCROFT MEAD
TURNPIKE WAY
DEAN CT
LYNTON RD
WATTS RD
RABURN DR
ALLEN RD
FEWRY CL
STOCKTON CL
LONGCLOSE RD
BIRCH RD
BEECH RD
B3033
MARVIN WAY
MARVIN CL
BROAD OAK
HIGH ST
Recn Gd
PARK VIEW
SOWDEN CL
RATCLIFFE RD
HILTON RD
TICHBOURNE HO
CEDAR CL
LOWER NORTHAM RD
STUBBS DRO
TRIPPS END CARAVAN SITE
ORCHARD CT
Broadoak
COBBETT WAY
Woodhill Prep Sch
B3036
GOODLANDS VALE
1 LAMBOURNE HO
2 RUSSET HO
3 BRAMLEY HO
LUCERNE GDNS
1 FOUNTAIN CT
2 LITTLE PARK CL
3 CHAPEL DRO
THE CLOSE
FRENSHAM CL
PATRICIA DR
ASPEN CL
MARLS RD
OSTERLEY CL
BLOSSOM CL
13
BUTTERCUP CL
THISTLE RD
CLOVER WAY
MALLOW RD
UPPER NORTHAM RD
PO
FERRYBRIDGE GN
SPEGGS WLK
COULSDON RD
RENSHAM CL
POPLAR WAY
WILLOW CL
HAWTHORN
BAILEY CL
CHALICE CT
WHEATSHEAF CT
ST JOHN'S CTR
FREEGROUNDS AVE
WADHURST RD
CRANLEIGH RD
HOBB LA
ROWAN GDNS
WHITEBEAM RD
LABURNUM RD
Freegrounds Schs
1 GENTO CL
2 TAMELLA RD
3 MONTROSE CL
Southbrook
THE SHIRES 1
THE BARTONS 2
UPPER NORTHAM CL
YEW TREE CL
OAK TREE GDNS
ST CATHERINES VIEW
WATERS EDGE
SHERBORNE
PRESTWOOD RD
VALERIAN RD
VERBENA WAY
MAPLETON RD
BEDFORD CL
SOVEREIGN DR
SOVEREIGN DR
Fir Tree Farm
BROOK LA
ALLOTMENT RD
RUSTAN CL
Liby
LONGRIDGE RD
HEIGHTS
STRAWBERRY FIELDS
NETLEY FIRS RD
RESERVOIR LA
GRANADA RD
NEW CLIFFE GDNS
WESTBURY CT
RICHLANS RD
FREEGROUNDS RD
BERRY CL
CRUSADER RD
NOBLE RD
PRECOSA RD
1 SENGANA CL
2 ABRAHAM CL
3
CHURCH LA
MORGAN RD
LINDEN GDNS
KINGS COPSE AVE
FIRS DR
SAXON GDNS
VICARAGE DR
PRETORIA RD
SMITH GR
PARDOE CL
LOWER ST HELENS RD
CORTINA WAY
FOXGLOVES
DUKE RD
PAXTON CL
Hatts Copse Farm
HALES DR
NORMAN GDNS
ST JOHN'S RD
YARDLEY RD
NURSERY GR
ROSEMARY GDNS
BERKELEY GDNS
TANHOUSE LA
HAVENDALE
SALWEY RD
TICKNER CL
Gould Copse
TUDOR GDNS
ALEXANDRA RD
PORTELET PL
TANHOUSE CL
EDMUNDS CL
WOODSIDE WAY
ALBERT RD
CONISTON GDNS
NORDIK GDNS
HAVENDALE
AMBLESIDE
E3
1 LITTLE KIMBLE WLK
2 MELBOURNE RD
3 MELBOURNE GDNS
4 LARKSPUR GDNS
5 FREEGROUNDS CL
6 MEDLAR CL
7 HORNBEAM CL
8 LABURNUM HO
9 BARWELL TERR
Manor Lodge
BURSLEDON RD
Kings Copse Prim Sch
KINGS COPSE RD
WOODSTOCK CL
FERNDALE
DAMEN CL
Cemy
DOWNLAND PL
UPPER ST HELENS RD
PRIMROSE CL
BERGEN CRES
Hedge End
FOORD RD
STOCKHOLM DR
12
Manor Farm (Mus)
HEATH HOUSE GDNS
SHERWOOD AVE
Sports Ground
METUCHEN WAY
CRANBOURNE PK
Netley Hill
WAYLANDS PL
HEATH HOUSE CL
THURMELL CL
THURMELL WLK
Sunday's Hill
HEATH HOUSE LA
Piland's Copse
TANHOUSE LA
B3033
Kings Copse Farm
Bursledon Common
PEEWIT HILL CL
2
PYLANDS LA
PEEWIT HILL
Dodwell Farm
Manor Farm Country Park
Dock Copse
8
DODWELL LA
A3024
11
Hoe Moor House
River Hamble
WINDMILL LA
Windmill
Catland Copse
A27
1 DEVONSHIRE GDNS
2 DILIGENCE CL
3 PHOENIX CL
4 CAMBRIAN CL
Bursledon Hall
PROVIDENCE HILL
Lowford
ASHLEY CT
GRIFFON CL
LIONHEART WAY
HUMBER GDNS
KINGS FIELD
KINGS FIELD GDNS
FORGE
1
Swanwick Wood
LANCASTER CL
RUTLAND GDNS
PO
PORTSMOUTH RD
OAKHILL
OAKHILL TERR
OAKHILL CL
BLUNDELL LA
Brixedone Farm
LOWFORD HILL
SPRING GR
REDCROFT LA
BRIDGE CL
Works
Lynwood
ESTRIDGE CL
SCHOOL RD
THE GROVE
LONG LA
BURSLEDON HTS
BRIDGE RD
Claypits
M27
COAL PARK LA
NEW RD
PINEVIEW CL
1 SHERLEY GN
2 CUMMINS GN
OLD BRIDGE CL
A27
10
48
49
50
D
E
F

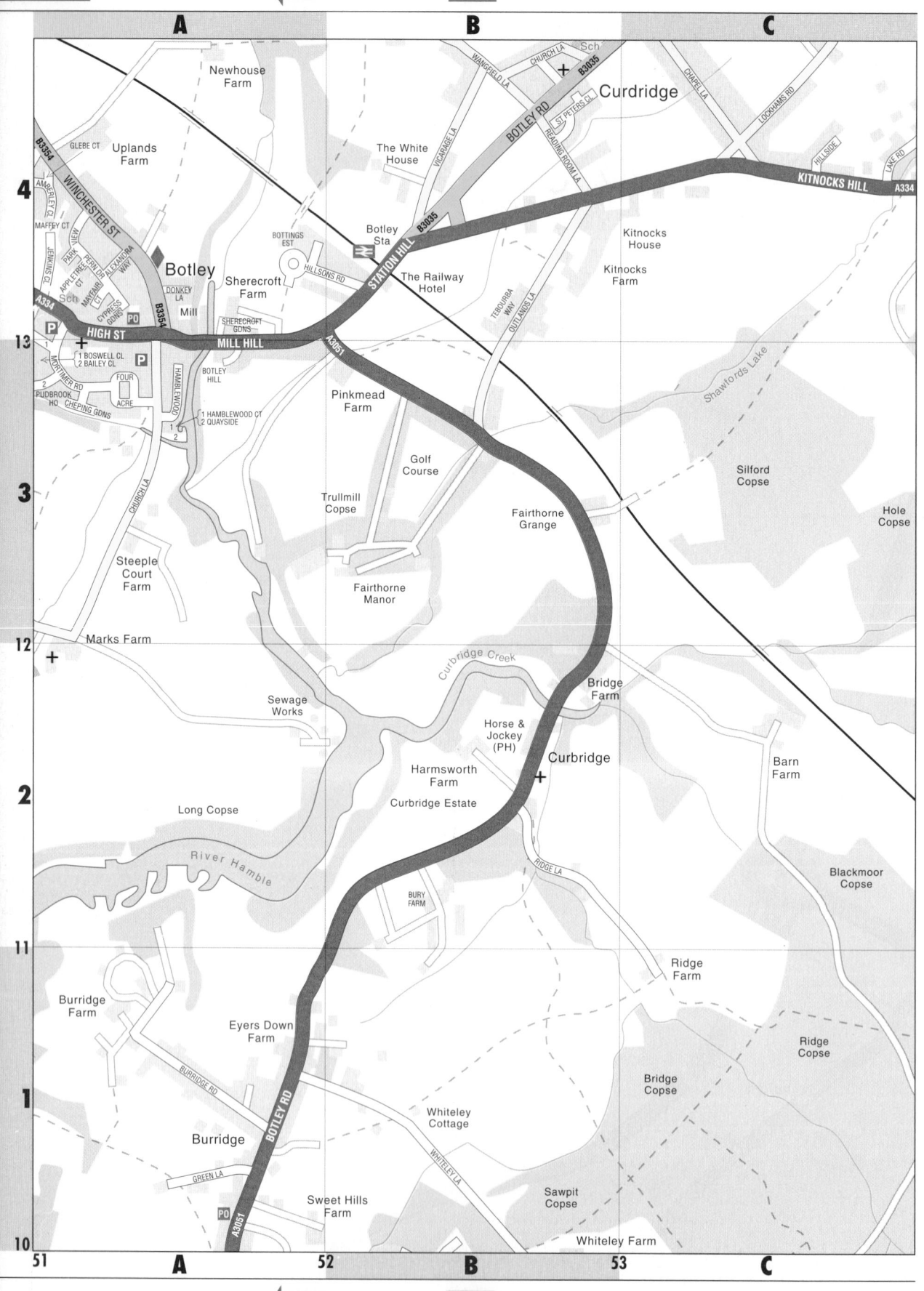
A | B | C

4

Newhouse Farm

GLEBE CT
Uplands Farm
B3354
AMBERLEY CL
MAFFEY CT
PARK VIEW
FERN RD
JENKINS CL
WINCHESTER ST
APPLETREE CL
MAYFIELD CT
ALEXANDRA WAY
Botley
Sch
DONKEY LA
CYPRESS GDNS
Mill
PO
B3354
A334

The White House
VICARAGE LA
WANGFIELD LA
CHURCH LA   Sch
BOTLEY RD
B3035   +
Curdridge
ST PETERS CL
READING ROOM LA
CHAPEL LA
LOCKHAMS RD
LAKE RD
HILLSIDE
KITNOCKS HILL   A334

Bottings EST
Botley Sta
B3035
Sherecroft Farm
HILLSONS RD
STATION HILL
The Railway Hotel
Kitnocks House
Kitnocks Farm

13
P   +
HIGH ST
1 BOSWELL CL
2 BAILEY CL
P
MORTIMER RD
PUDBROOK HO
CHEPING GDNS
FOUR ACRE
HAMBLEWOOD
MILL HILL
SHERECROFT GDNS
A3051
Botley Hill
1 HAMBLEWOOD CT
2 QUAYSIDE
1
2
TEBOURBA WAY
OUTLANDS LA

Pinkmead Farm

3
CHURCH LA
Golf Course
Trullmill Copse
Fairthorne Grange
Silford Copse
Hole Copse

Steeple Court Farm
Fairthorne Manor

12
+
Marks Farm
Curbridge Creek
Bridge Farm

Sewage Works
Horse & Jockey (PH)
Curbridge
+
Barn Farm

2
Harmsworth Farm
Curbridge Estate
Long Copse
River Hamble
RIDGE LA
Blackmoor Copse

BURY FARM

11
Ridge Farm
Burridge Farm
BURRIDGE RD
Ridge Copse

1
Eyers Down Farm
BOTLEY RD
Bridge Copse
Whiteley Cottage
WHITELEY LA

Burridge
GREEN LA
PO
A3051
Sweet Hills Farm
Sawpit Copse

10
Whiteley Farm

51 | A | 52 | B | 53 | C

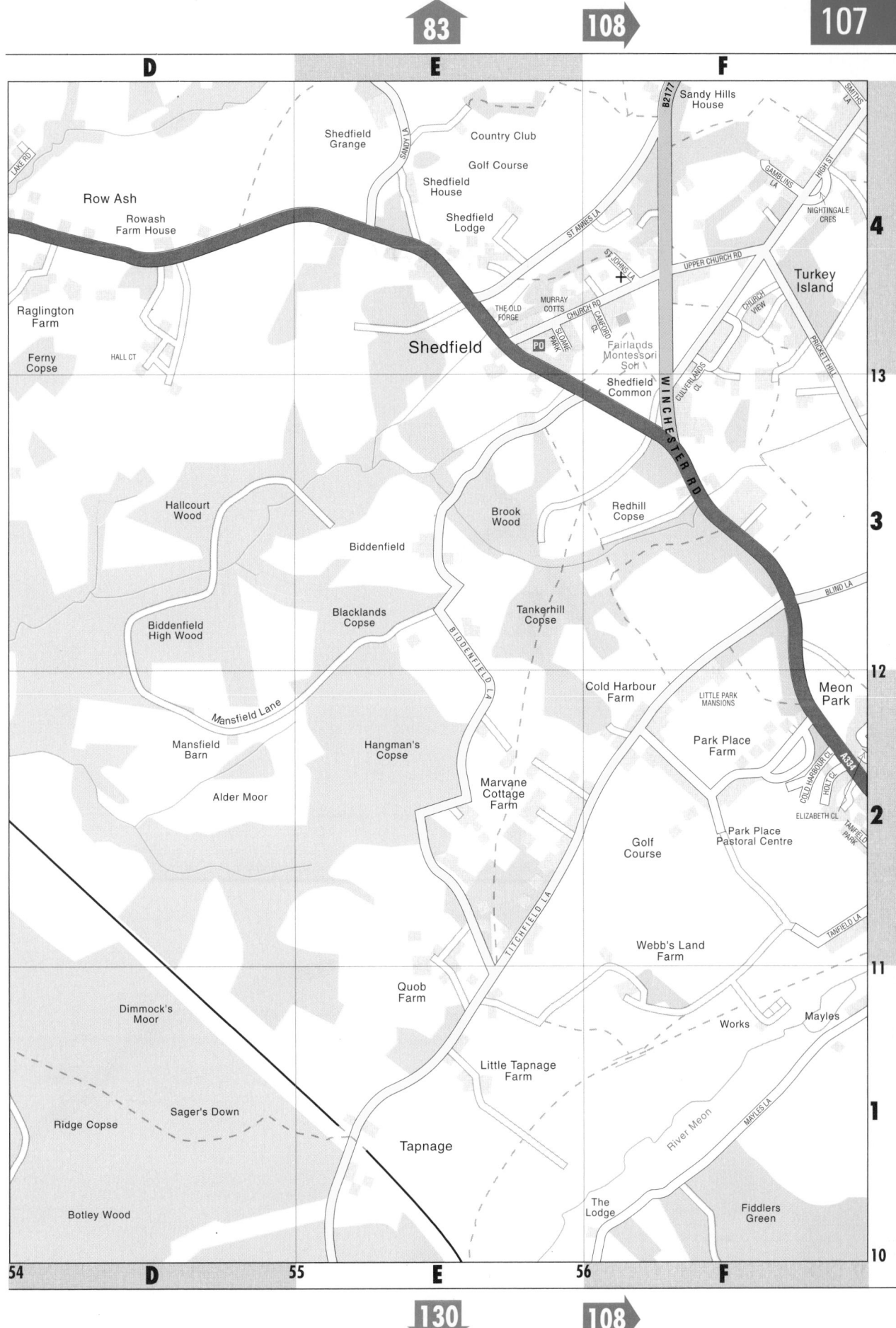

LAKE RD
Row Ash
Rowash Farm House
Raglington Farm
Ferny Copse
HALL CT
SANDY LA
Shedfield Grange
Shedfield House
Shedfield Lodge
Country Club
Golf Course
ST ANNES LA
ST JOHN'S LA
THE OLD FORGE
MURRAY COTTS
CHURCH RD
SLOANE PARK
CANFORD CL
PO
Shedfield
Fairlands Montessori Sch
Shedfield Common
B2177
Sandy Hills House
SMITHS LA
HIGH ST
GAMBLINS LA
NIGHTINGALE CRES
UPPER CHURCH RD
Turkey Island
CHURCH VIEW
CULVERLANDS CL
PRICKETT HILL
WINCHESTER RD
4
13
Hallcourt Wood
Biddenfield
Brook Wood
Redhill Copse
Blacklands Copse
Tankerhill Copse
BIDDENFIELD LA
BLIND LA
3
Biddenfield High Wood
Mansfield Lane
Mansfield Barn
Hangman's Copse
Alder Moor
Marvane Cottage Farm
Cold Harbour Farm
LITTLE PARK MANSIONS
Park Place Farm
Meon Park
A334
COLD HARBOUR CT
HOLT CT
ELIZABETH CL
TANFIELD PARK
12
2
Golf Course
Park Place Pastoral Centre
TITCHFIELD LA
Webb's Land Farm
TANFIELD LA
Quob Farm
11
Dimmock's Moor
Little Tapnage Farm
Works
Mayles
Ridge Copse
Sager's Down
Tapnage
River Meon
MAYLES LA
1
Botley Wood
The Lodge
Fiddlers Green
10

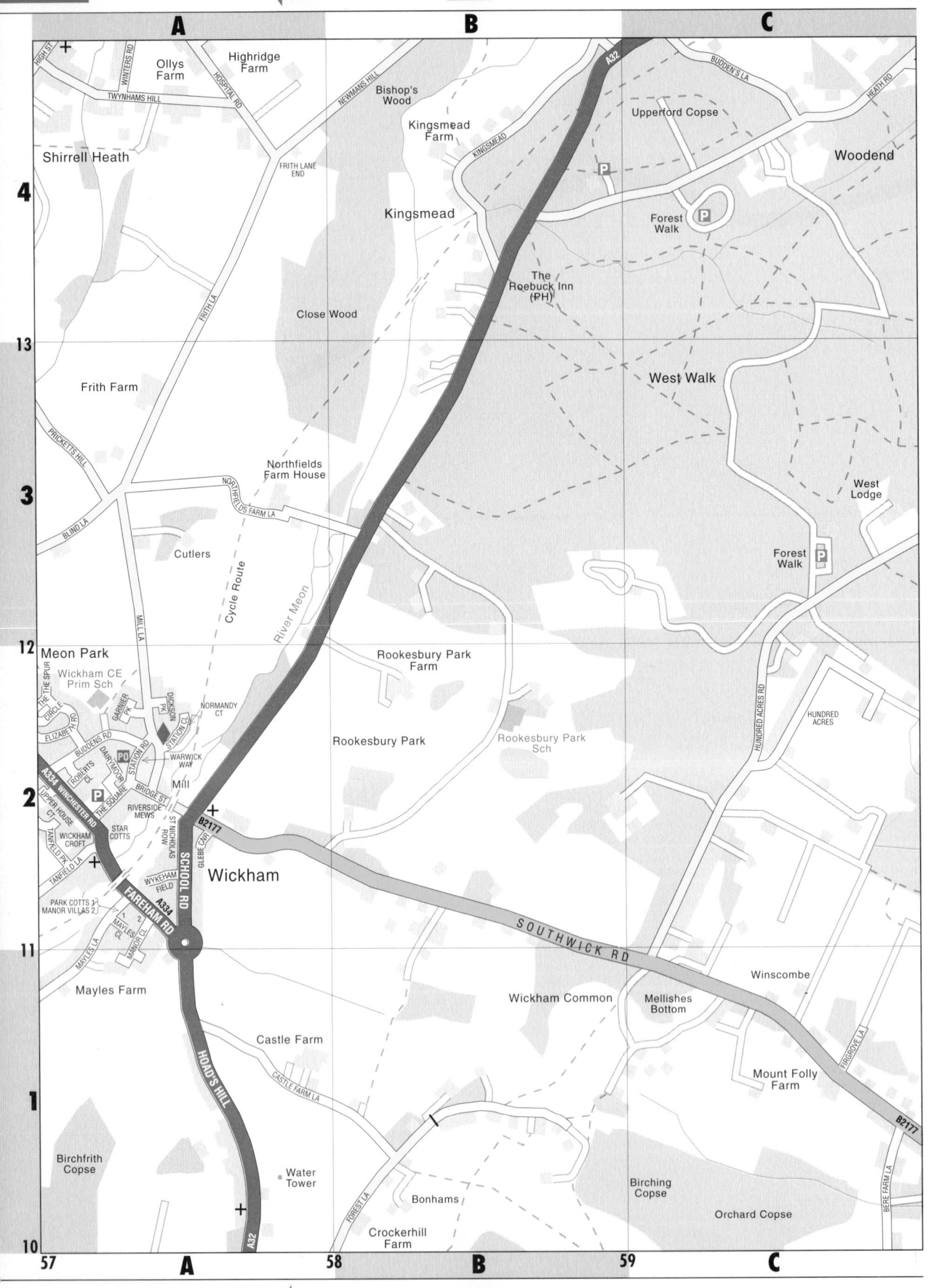

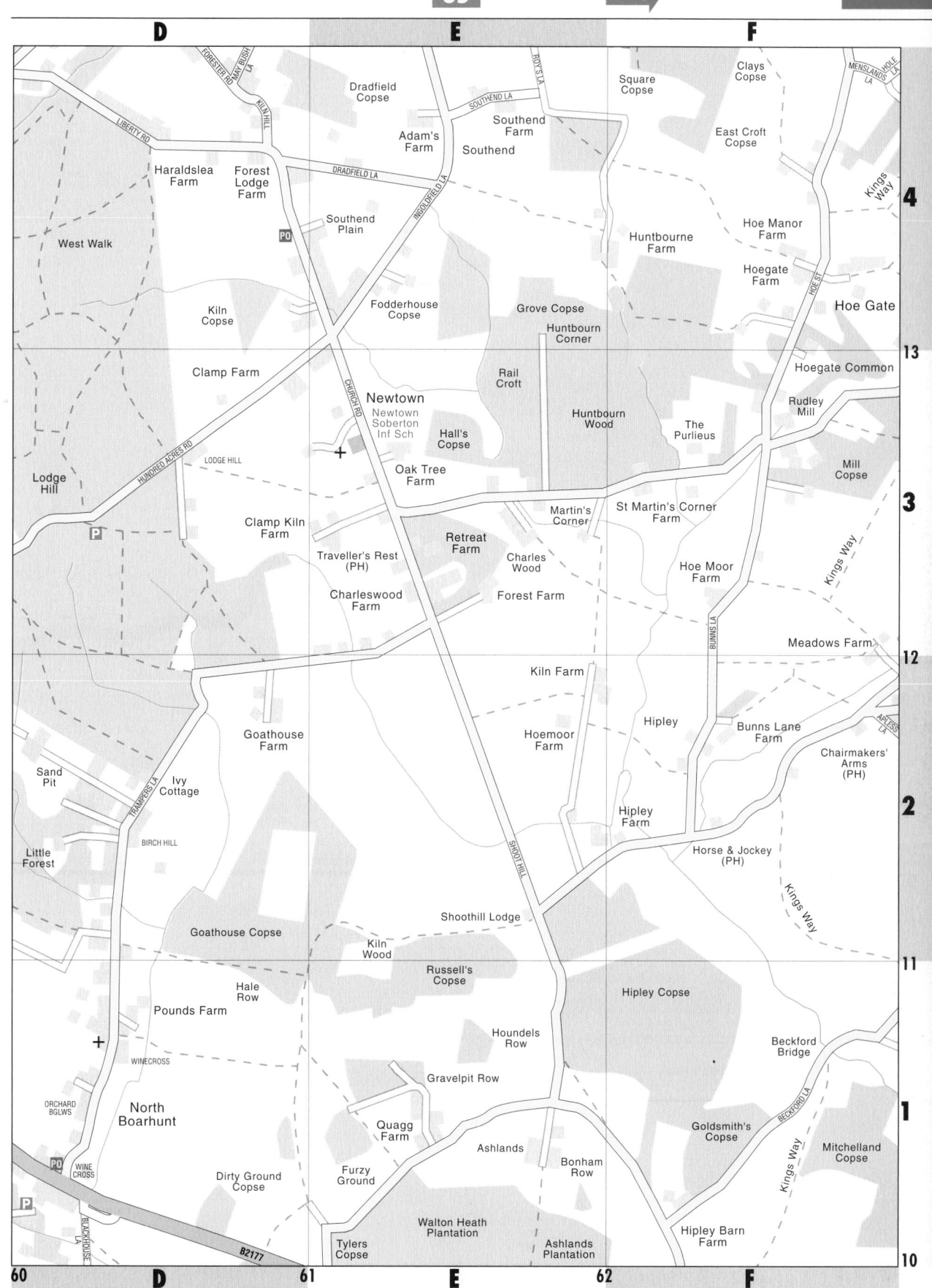

109
86

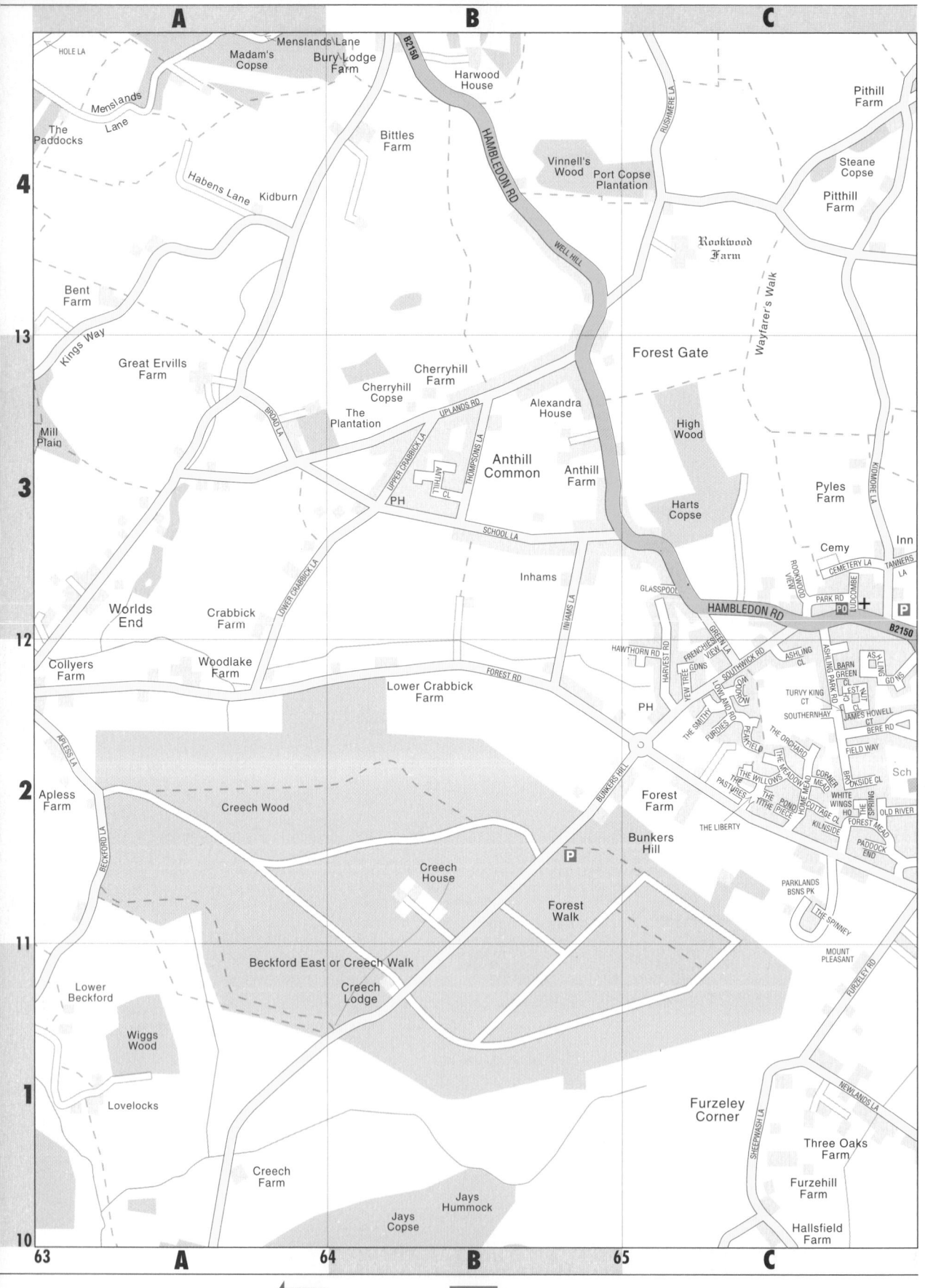

A   B   C

HOLE LA

Menslands Lane
Madam's Copse
Bury Lodge Farm

Menslands Lane

The Paddocks

Habens Lane   Kidburn

Bittles Farm

HAMBLEDON RD

B2150

Harwood House

Vinnell's Wood
Port Copse Plantation

RUSHMERE LA

Pithill Farm

Steane Copse

Pitthill Farm

WELL HILL

4

Rookwood Farm

Bent Farm

Kings Way

13

Great Ervills Farm

Cherryhill Copse

Cherryhill Farm

The Plantation

BROAD LA

UPLANDS RD

UPPER CRABBICK LA

ANTHILL CL

THOMPSONS LA

Alexandra House

Forest Gate

Wayfarer's Walk

High Wood

Pyles Farm

KIDMORE LA

Mill Plain

PH

Anthill Common

Anthill Farm

Harts Copse

Inn

Cemy

CEMETERY LA

TANNERS LA

3

LOWER CRABBICK LA

SCHOOL LA

Inhams

INHAMS LA

GLASSPOOL

ROOKWOOD VIEW

PARK RD

PO

LUDCOMBE

P

HAMBLEDON RD

B2150

Worlds End

Crabbick Farm

12

Collyers Farm

Woodlake Farm

Lower Crabbick Farm

FOREST RD

HAWTHORN RD

HARVEST RD

YEW TREE

GREEN LA

FRENCHIES VIEW

GDNS

SOUTHWICK RD

ASHLING CL

ASHLING PARK RD

BARN GREEN CL

AS- LING GD INS

LONG

TURVY KING CT

SOUTHERNHAY

JAMES HOWELL CT

BERE RD

FIELD WAY

Sch

APLESS LA

PH

THE SMITH

LOW ANN RD

PURDIES

PEAKFIELD

THE ORCHARD

BROOKSIDE CL

2

Apless Farm

BECKFORD LA

Creech Wood

BUNKERS HILL

Forest Farm

THE MEADOW

CORNER MEAD

WHITE WINGS

THE WILLOWS

THE PASTURES

HOME MEAD

THE POND

COTTAGE CL

THE TITHE PIECE

KILNSIDE

THE SPRING

OLD RIVER

FOREST MEAD

Creech House

P

Forest Walk

Bunkers Hill

THE LIBERTY

PADDOCK END

PARKLANDS BSNS PK

THE SPINNEY

11

Lower Beckford

Beckford East or Creech Walk

Creech Lodge

MOUNT PLEASANT

FURZELEY RD

Wiggs Wood

1

Lovelocks

Furzeley Corner

NEWLANDS LA

SHEEPWASH LA

Three Oaks Farm

Creech Farm

Jays Copse

Jays Hummock

Furzehill Farm

Hallsfield Farm

10

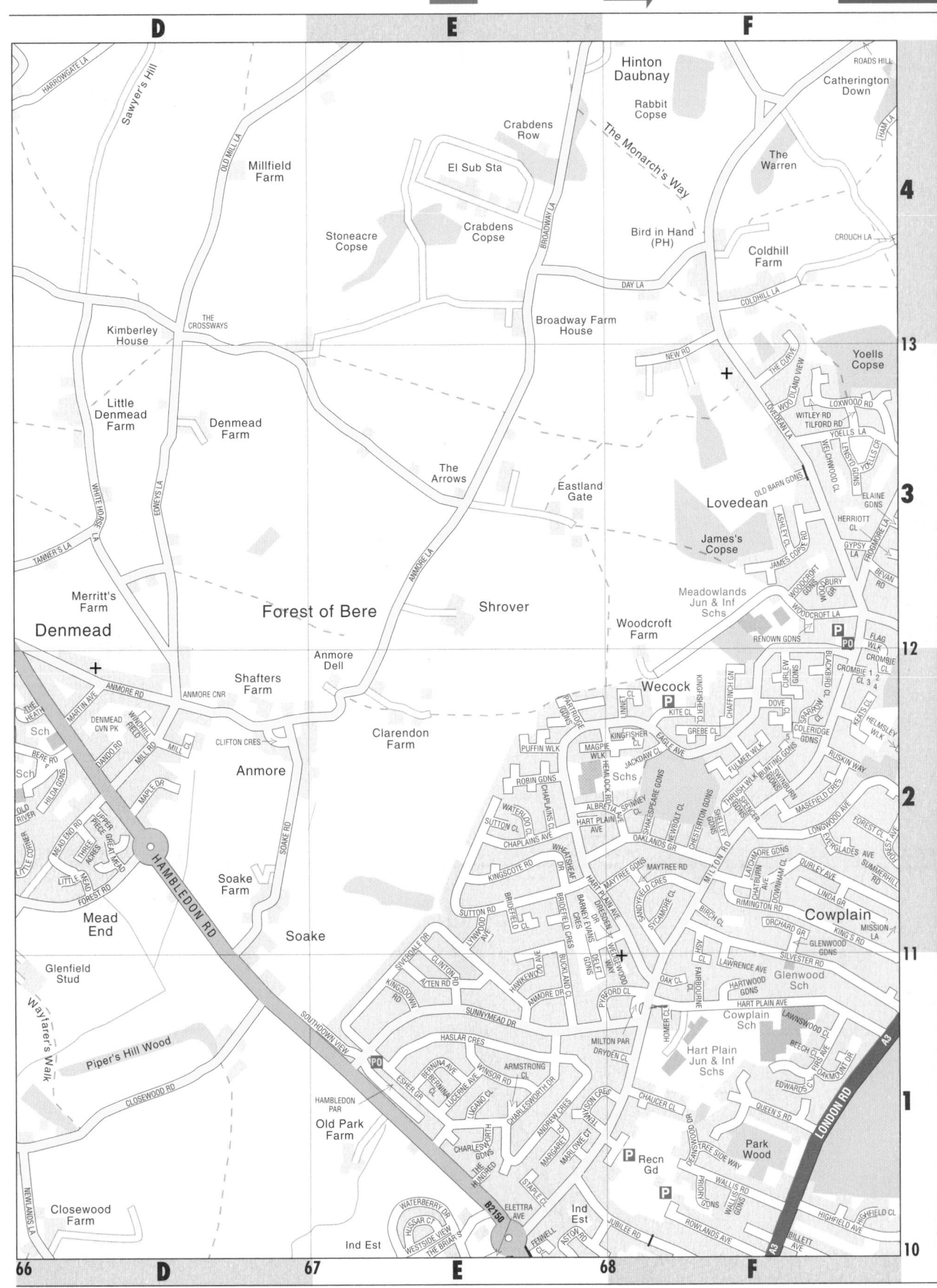

F2
1 THAMES CT
2 AVON CT
3 HAMBLE CT
4 ITCHEN CT
5 PATRICK HOWARD -DOBSON CT

← 111
88 ↑

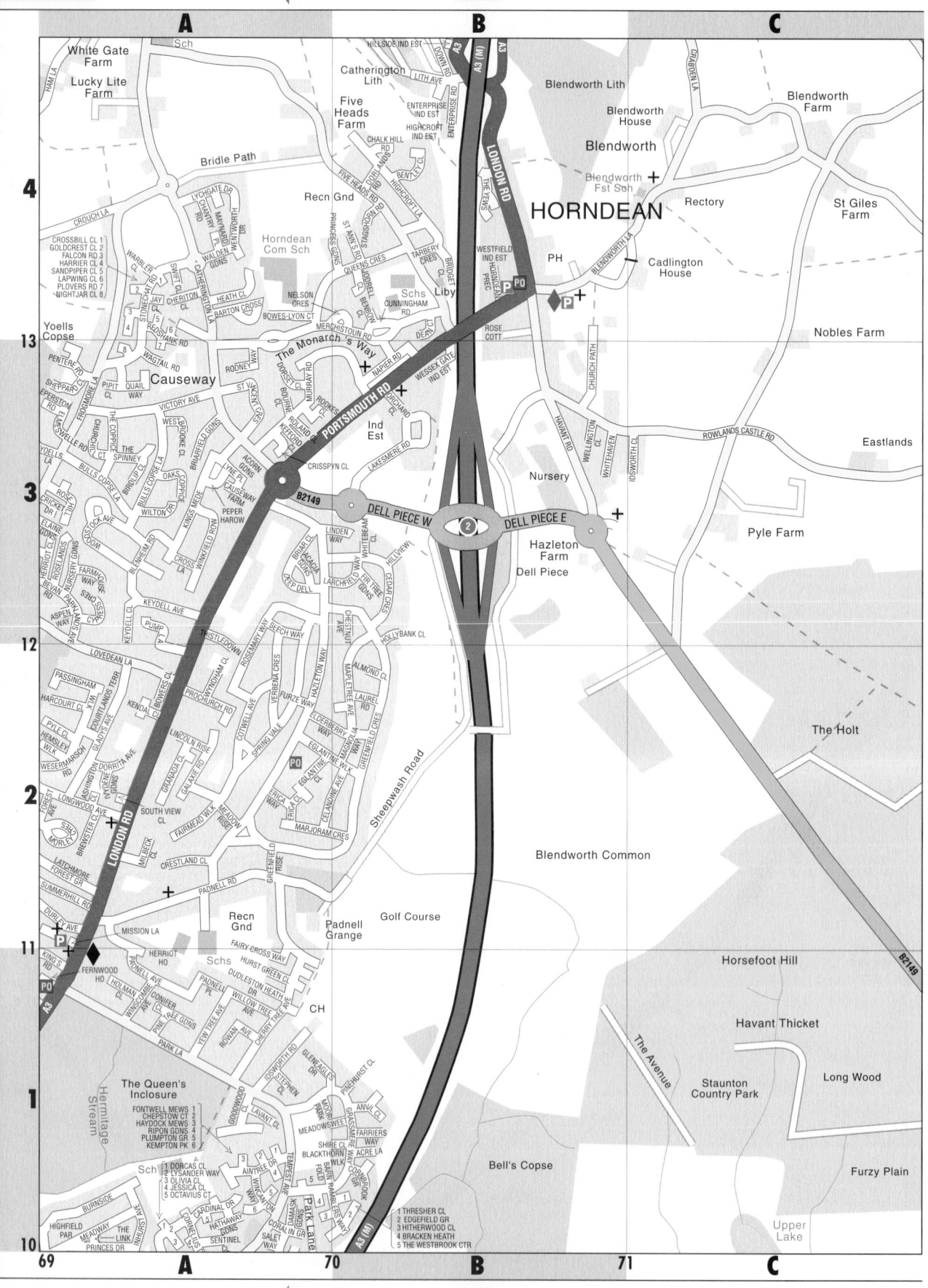

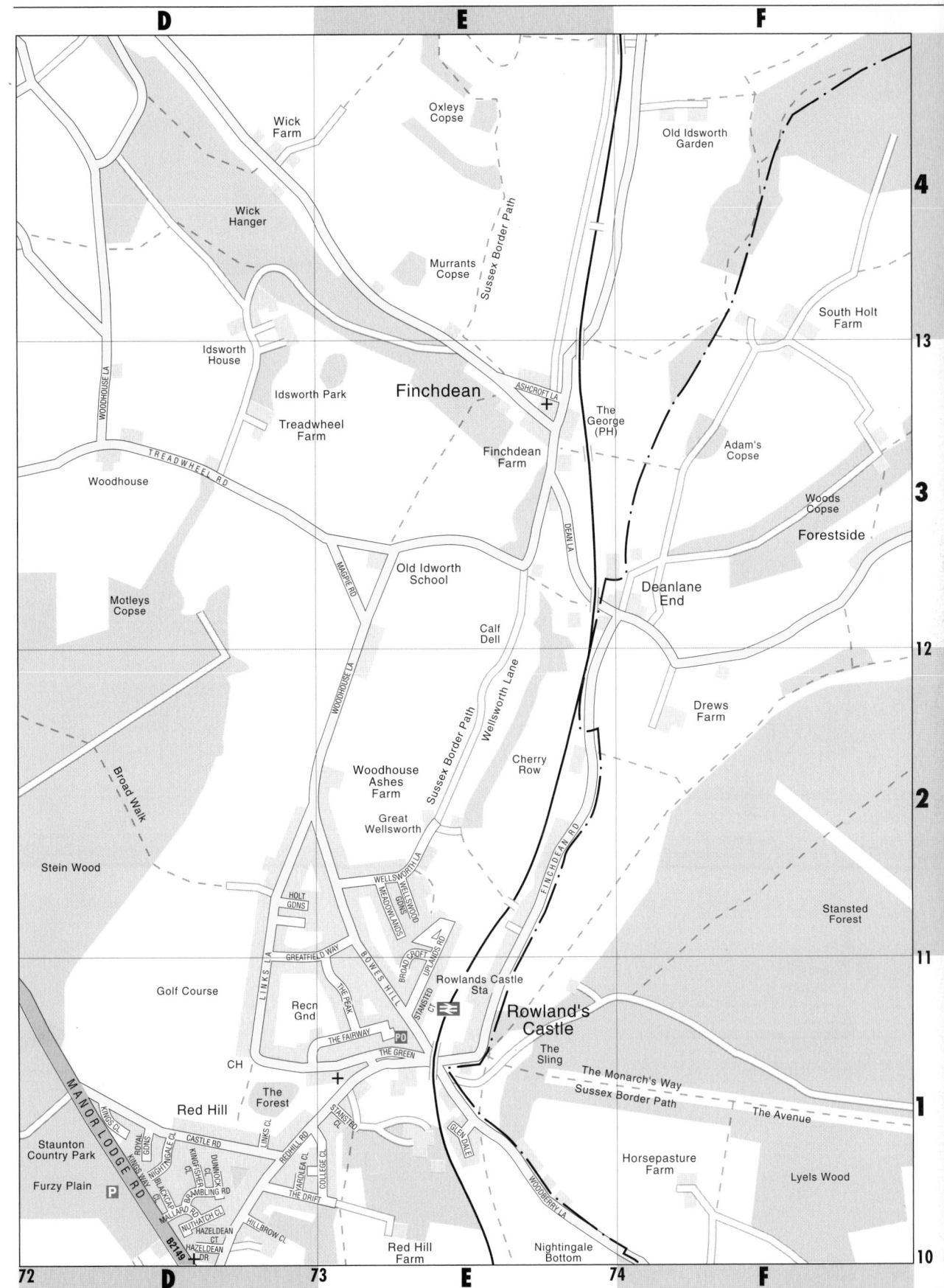

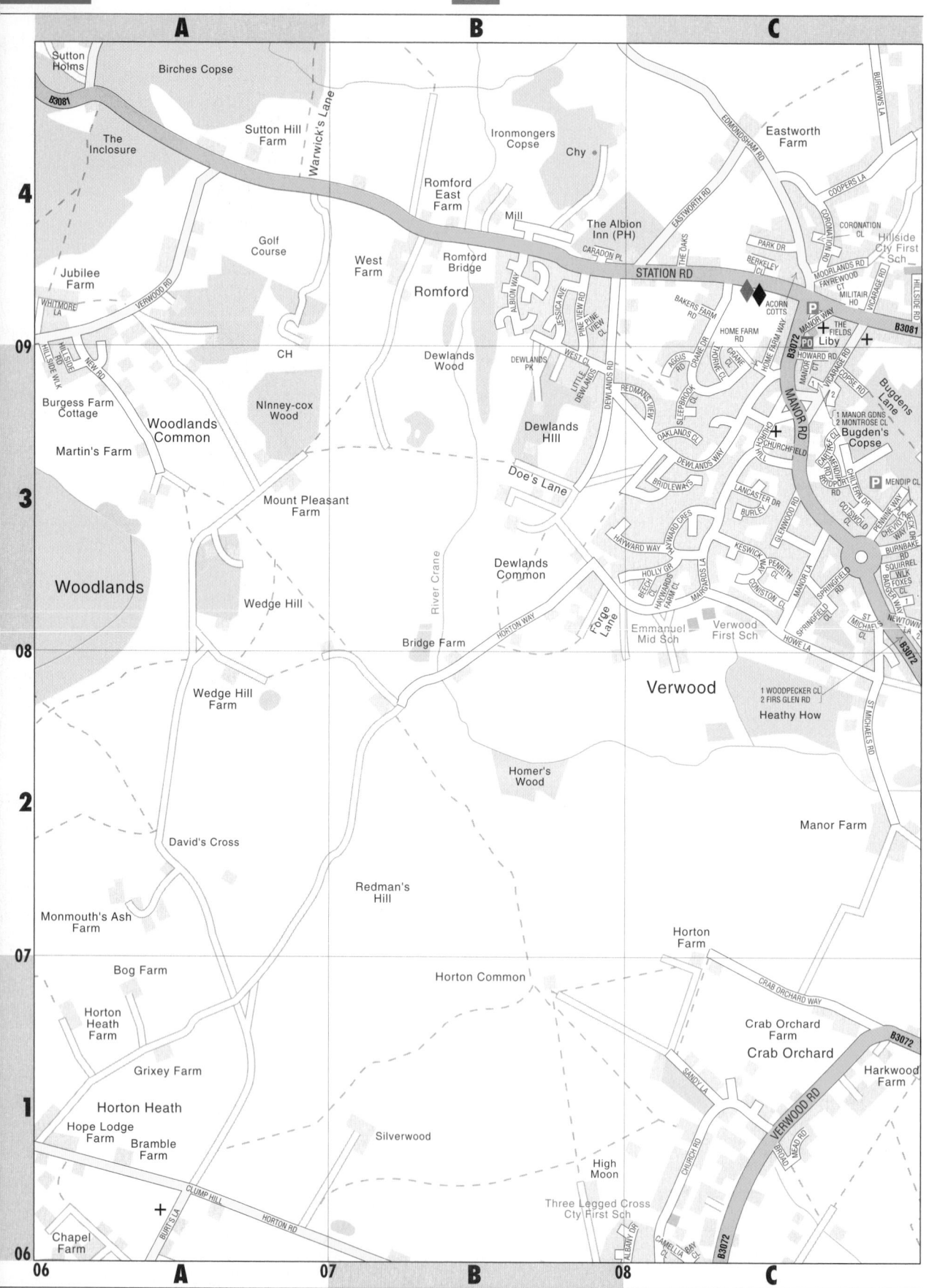

D
E
F

4

Wiggs
Copse

Boveridge Heath

Plumley Wood

Stephen's
Castle

Harefield Plantation

Stephen's Castle
Nature Reserve

Wild Church
Bottom

Bailey's Plantation

09

HILLSIDE RD

+
HEATHLANDS
CL

ST STEPHENS LA

STRATHMORE DR

NOON
GDNS

NOON
HILL
DR

Noon Hill
Farm

Noon Hill

Numbers

NEWTOWN RD

SHARD CL

SHERWOOD DR

FOXHILLS

NOON HILL RD

Reservoir
Cottage

CRESCENT RD

BLACK HILL

RINGWOOD RD

SOUTHERNHAY
RD

3

Hainault
Farm

BUGDENS LA

RAYMOND CL

VERWOOD IND EST

SANDY LA

THE CHASE

Ringwood Forest

BURNBAKE RD

FERNE RD

STANLEY
CL

NEWTOWN RD

PADDOCK
GR
ORCHARD
CT

OWL'S THE LA

LAKE RD

MEADOW
DR

LOMBARDY DR

ASHFERN DR

BLACKTHORN WAY

HUNTERS CL

THE GROVE

BITTERNE
WAY

THE KINGFISHERS

NIGHTINGALE

WYM MOOVWY

WHITEBEAM
WAY

PINE WAY

LAVENDER
CL

BARBERRY
WAY

THE FORESIDE

THE FORESIDE

BELMONT CL

THE CURLEWS

OTTERS
CL

CLAYLAKE
DR

FAIRWOOD RD

LABURNUM CL

ACACIA AVE

ROSEBERY

08

NEWTOWN LA

FIRS GLEN RD

THOMAS
LOCKYER
CL

LAKE RD

BURN CL

WOODLINKEN DR

MAGNOLIA CL

WISTERIA DR

WOODLINKEN WAY

ENT CL
PK

Cemy

PARKLAND
CL

Ebblake
Bridge

Chatsworth

MANOR RD

BINGHAM RD

BINGHAM CL

BINGHAM DR

MONMOUTH DR

MONMOUTH
CL

BROOK DR

ROWAN DR

WOODLINKEN DR

THE FORELEE
CTR

Ind
Est

BLACK MOOR RD

BRUNEL RD

FOREST CL

Potterne
Hill

POTTERNE
WAY

P

Potterne
Farm

Ebblake

BESSEMER

Ebblake Stream

2

Potterne
Poultry Farm

VERWOOD RD

B3072

Potterne
Wood

Gravel Pit

07

Cottage
Farm

English
Farm

Rushmoor
Pond

B3081

1

Withy Bed

Golf Course

Lower Common

Moors River

Moors Valley
Country Park

Kingsmere
Station

Kings Farm
CH

06

A   B   C

4

Gravel Pit

Turmer Hill

Harbridge Farm

Ibsley Bridge

Turmer

Avon Valley Path

Weir

Plumley Farm

Harbridge Lodge

PH

Lower Turmer

Hamer Brook

09

Nea Farm

Turmer Brook

Mill Stream

SHEPHERDS LA

Shepherds Cottage

Dog Kennel Wood

Riverbank Covert

3

Home Wood

SHEPHERDS HILL

Ellingham

Whitehoe Cottages

CHESTNUT AVE

Old Somerley

New Barn Cottages

ELLINGHAM DR

Ellingham Farm

ELLINGHAM CROSS

SALISBURY RD

ELLINGHAM DROVE

NEA DR

Somerley Park

The Bothy

New Bridge

08

Nursery Cottages

Broad Close Covert

Somerley

Gravel Works

Old Laundry Cottage

2

Park Cottage

Ringwood Forest

River Avon

Meadow Lake

Blashford Farm

The Belt

A338

07

Gravel Pit

DUNCOMBE DR

ASHLEY DR

Dockens Water

SALISBURY RD

B30 81

Sunderton Wood

Weir

Lifeland Copse

Upper Hurst Farm

1

VERWOOD RD.

Duncombe Lodge

Ashley Farm

King Stream

Gouldings Farm

A338

B30 81

Baker's Hanging

Up Mead

Hurst Old Farm

06

Lin Brook

12   A   13   B   14   C

SALISBURY RD
A338

Cottage Plantation

Whitefield Plantation

Great Bottom

Ibsley Manor Farm

NEW RD
PO

Summerlug Hill

Linwood Bog

4

Ibsley

Cross Lanes Farm

CUFFNELLS CL

Mockbeggar Farm

Mockbeggar

Digden Bottom

Hearns Plantation

+

MOCKBEGGAR LA

CROSS LANES

09

Ibsley House

Avon Valley Path

Newlands Plantation

Dockens Water

Rodens Bottom

Fir Walk

Gravel Pit

Moyles Court Sch
Ford

Rockford Common

Big Whitemoor Bottom

3

Works

ELLINGHAM DROVE

New Buildings

Little Whitemoor Bottom

Alice Lisle Inn (PH)

Rockford

Rockford Green

Waterslade

08

Blashford Lakes Study Ctr

Gravel Pit

Water Slade Bottom

Ivy Lake

IVY LA
P

Bigsburn Hill

2

Rockford Farm

Highwood

Highwood Copse

LINFORD HO

SNAILS LA

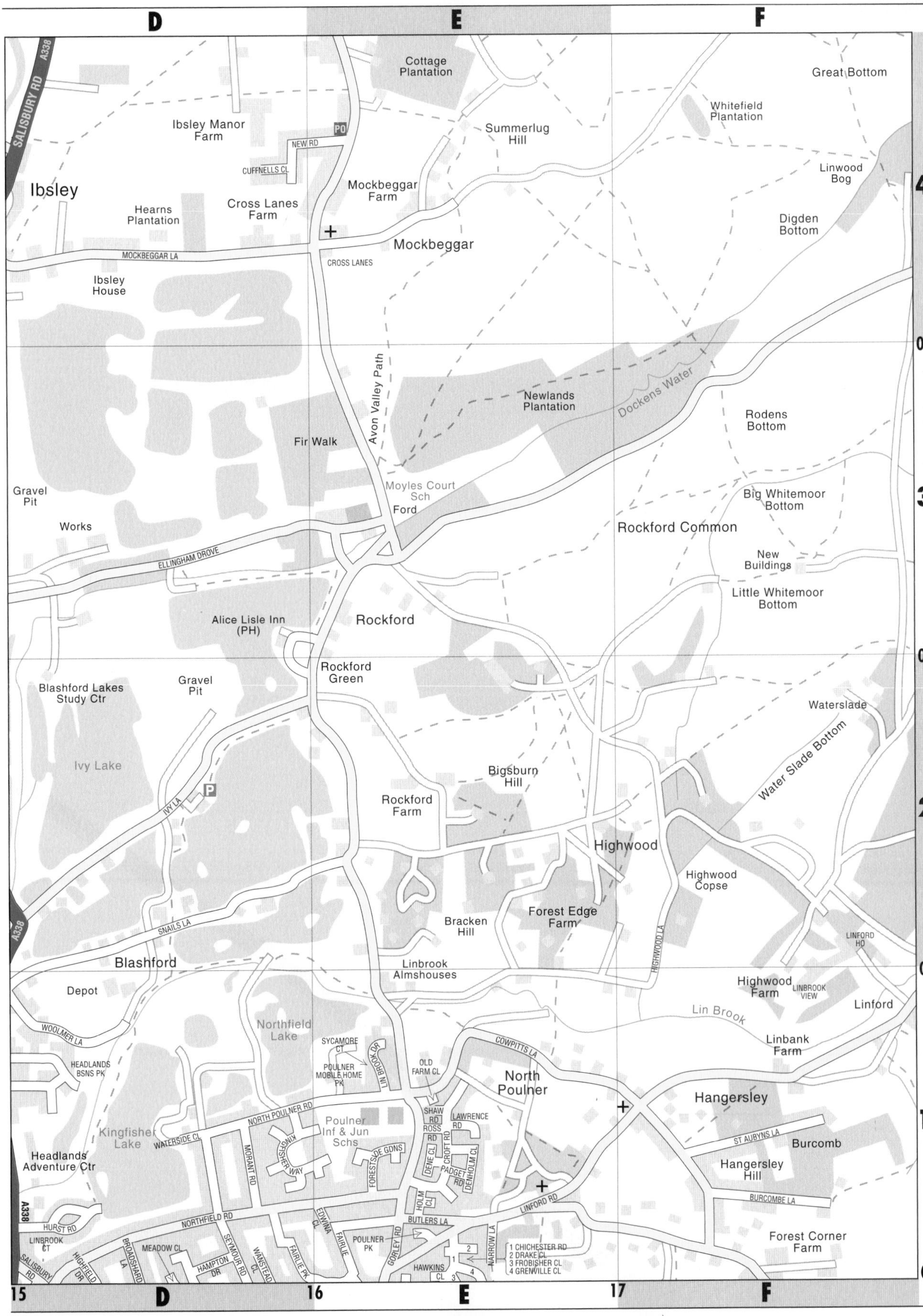

Bracken Hill

Forest Edge Farm

HIGHWOOD LA

Blashford

Linbrook Almshouses

Highwood Farm

LINBROOK VIEW

Linford

07

Depot

Lin Brook

Linbank Farm

WOOLMER LA

Northfield Lake

SYCAMORE CT

COWPITTS LA

HEADLANDS BSNS PK

POULNER MOBILE HOME PK

OLD FARM CL

North Poulner

+

Hangersley

1

Kingfisher Lake

WATERSIDE CL

NORTH POULNER RD

MORANT RD

SMITH SWAY

Poulner Inf & Jun Schs

FORESTSIDE GDNS

LIN BROOK DR

SHAW RD
ROSS

LAWRENCE RD

CROFT RD

DENE CL

PADGET RD

DENHOLM CL

ST AUBYNS LA

Burcomb

Headlands Adventure Ctr

A338

SALISBURY RD

HURST RD

LINBROOK CT

HIGHFIELD DR

BROADSHARD LA

MEADOW CL

HAMPTON DR

SEYMOUR RD

WANSTEAD RD

FAIRLIE

EDVINA

FAIRLIE PK

NORTHFIELD RD

Poulner PK

GORLEY RD

HOLM CL

BUTLERS LA

HAWKINS CL

NARROW LA

LINFORD RD

1 CHICHESTER RD
2 DRAKE CL
3 FROBISHER CL
4 GRENVILLE CL

+

Hangersley Hill

BURCOMBE LA

Forest Corner Farm

06

117
95

117
142

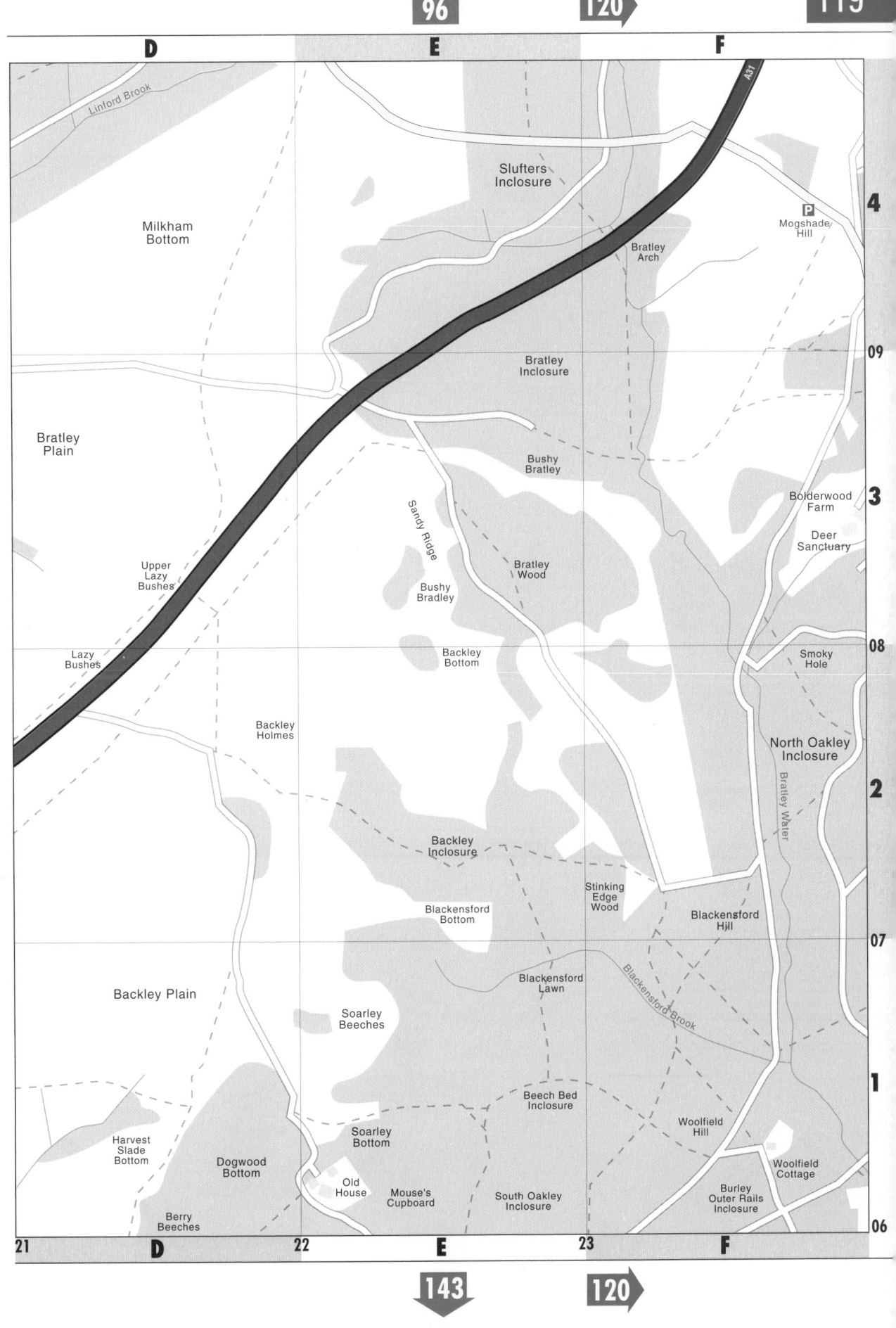

D
E
F

Linford Brook

Milkham
Bottom

Slufters
Inclosure

A31

Bratley
Arch

Mogshade
Hill

4

09

Bratley
Inclosure

Bratley
Plain

Bushy
Bratley

Bolderwood
Farm

Deer
Sanctuary

3

Sandy Ridge

Bratley
Wood

Upper
Lazy
Bushes

Bushy
Bradley

Lazy
Bushes

Backley
Bottom

Smoky
Hole

08

Backley
Holmes

North Oakley
Inclosure

Bratley Water

2

Backley
Inclosure

Stinking
Edge
Wood

Blackensford
Bottom

Blackensford
Hill

07

Backley Plain

Blackensford
Lawn

Blackensford Brook

Soarley
Beeches

1

Beech Bed
Inclosure

Woolfield
Hill

Harvest
Slade
Bottom

Soarley
Bottom

Dogwood
Bottom

Woolfield
Cottage

Old
House

Mouse's
Cupboard

South Oakley
Inclosure

Burley
Outer Rails
Inclosure

Berry
Beeches

06

21
D
22
E
23
F

119
97

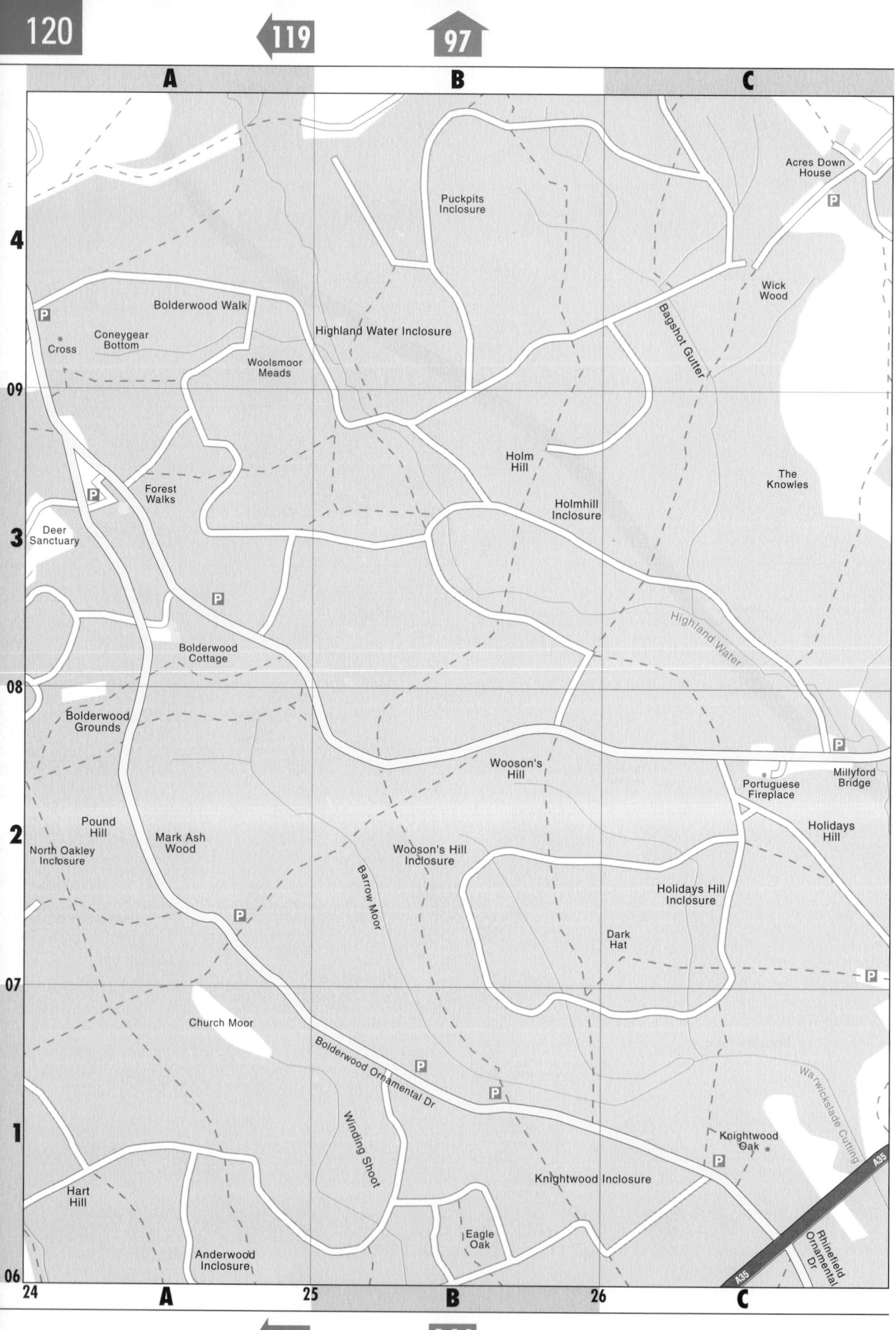

119
144

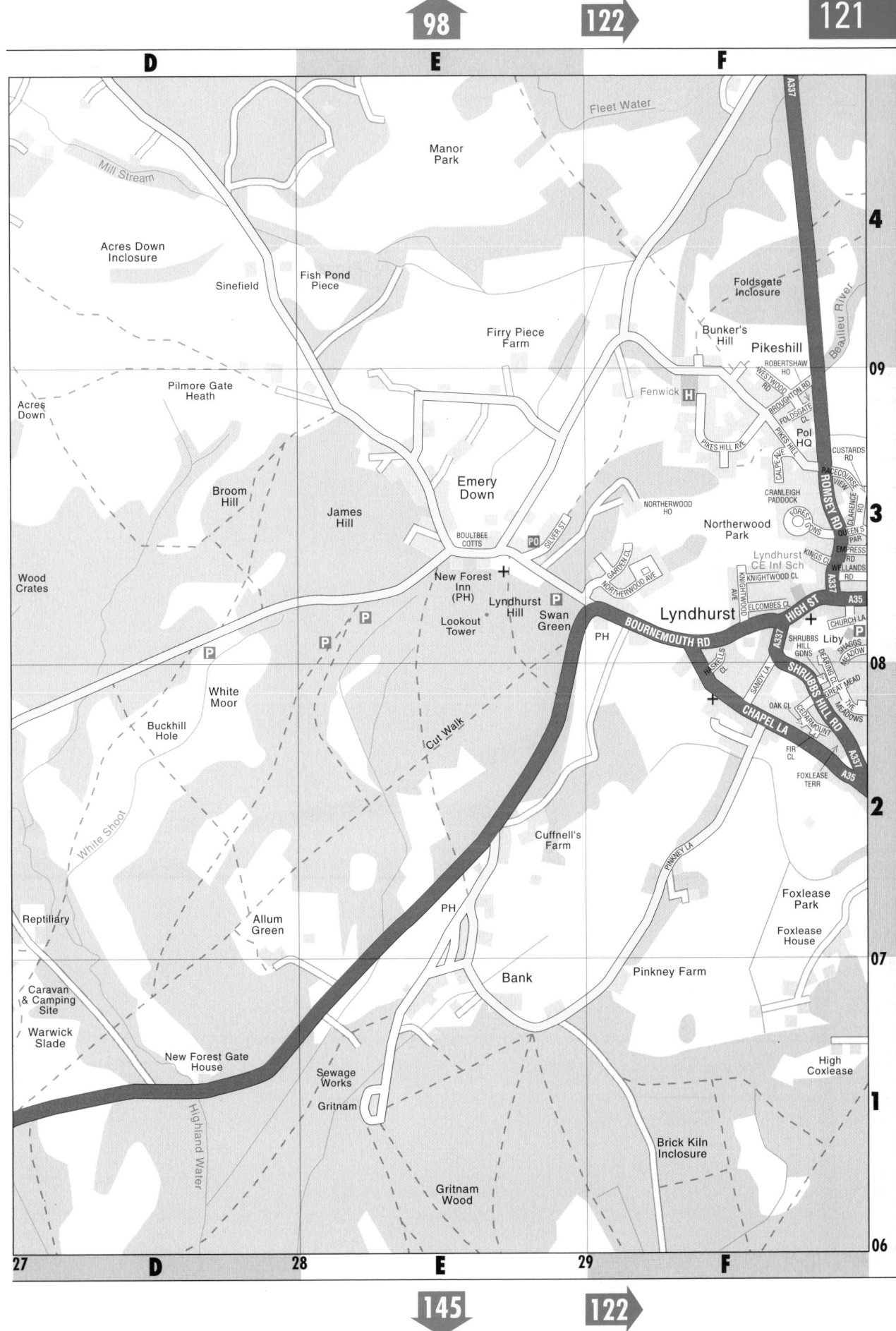

Fleet Water

Mill Stream

Manor
Park

4

Acres Down
Inclosure

Sinefield

Fish Pond
Piece

Foldsgate
Inclosure

Beaulieu River

A337

Bunker's
Hill

Pikeshill

09

Firry Piece
Farm

Fenwick H

ROBERTSHAW
HO

WESTWOOD
RD

BROUGHTON RD

FOLDSGATE
CL

Pol
HQ

CUSTARDS
RD

PIKES HILL AVE

PIKES HILL

CALE AVE

Acres
Down

Pilmore Gate
Heath

RACECOURSE
VIEW

KINGS CL

QUEEN'S
PK

CLARENCE
RD

3

Emery
Down

Broom
Hill

James
Hill

BOULTBEE
COTTS

SILVER ST

NORTHERWOOD
HO

Northerwood
Park

CRANLEIGH
PADDOCK

FOREST
GDNS

ROMSEY RD

A337

EMPRESS
RD

WELLANDS
RD

Wood
Crates

New Forest
Inn (PH)

PO

Lyndhurst
Hill

GARDEN CL

NORTHERWOOD AVE

Lyndhurst
CE Inf Sch

KNIGHTWOOD CL

KNIGHTWOOD
AVE

ELCOMBES CL

HIGH ST

A35

Lookout
Tower

Swan
Green

P

Lyndhurst

Liby

CHURCH LA

P

P

PH

BOURNEMOUTH RD

A337

SHRUBBS
HILL
GDNS

DEANING CL

SMAGGS
MEADOW

08

White
Moor

P

P

P

HASPELLS CL

SANDY LA

SHRUBBS HILL RD

GREAT MEAD

THE
MEADOWS

Buckhill
Hole

CHAPEL LA

OAK CL

ESCARMOUNT

A337

GREAT MEAD

Cut Walk

FIR
CL

A35

2

FOXLEASE
TERR

Reptiliary

Allum
Green

Cuffnell's
Farm

Foxlease
Park

PH

Foxlease
House

PINKNEY LA

07

Caravan
& Camping
Site

Warwick
Slade

New Forest Gate
House

Bank

Pinkney Farm

High
Coxlease

Highland Water

White Shoot

Sewage
Works

Gritnam

1

Brick Kiln
Inclosure

Gritnam
Wood

06

A   B   C

Fox Hill

Redbridge Hill

Ironshill Inclosure

Rushpole Wood

Lodgehill Inclosure

Whitebridge Hill

4

Fair Cross

Lodgehill Cottage

Beaulieu River

Mallard Wood

Dunces Arch Inclosure

09

A35

Golf Course

CH

Dunces Arch

THE CUSTARDS

Beaulieu River

3

Custards

Fox Hill

Row Hill

Longwater Lawn

PEMBERTON RD

QUEENS RD

PRINCES RD

SOUTHAMPTON RD

1 QUEEN'S PAR
2 EMPRESS RD

WELLANDS RD

PRINCES CT

PO

HIGH ST

A35

P

Meml

Cemy

B3056

RUFUS CT

Hotel Mus

Bolton's Bench

White Moor

P

SHAGGS MEADOW

THE MEADOWS

GOSPORT LA

08

P

The Bench

The Ridge

Goose Green

A35

BEAULIEU RD

Brooklands

A337

2

Irons Hill Walk

B3056

Clayhill

Matley Ridge

BEECHEN LA

HILARY CL

PARK CL

Pondhead Inclosure

Pondhead

The Crown & Stirrup (PH)

Parkhill (Hotel)

CLAY HILL

Parkhill Lawn

Holmhill Passage

07

Beechen La

Little Holmhill Inclosure

1

Park Ground Inclosure

Park Hill

Denny Inclosure

Little Holmhill

P

A337

06

30 A 31 B 32 C

D E F

Camp and Caravan Site

Ashurst Wood

Churchplace Inclosure

Church Place

Langley Cottage

Nature Quest

Langley Wood

DEERLEAP LA

4

The Homestead

NEW COTTS

Deerleap Inclosure

09

Home Farm

Ashurst Lodge

Longdown Inclosure

Ashurst Walk

Peel Hill

3

Fulliford Bog

Beaulieu River

08

Matley Heath

Matley Holms

Matley Wood

Fulliford Passage

Withycombe Shade

2

King's Passage

Decoy Pond Farm

Caravan and Camping Site

Matley Bog

07

Matley Passage

Church Place

Black Down

Caravan and Camping Site

1

Hotel

Stag Park

Shatterford Bottom

Beaulieu Road Sta

STATION COTTS

Denny Wood

B3056

06

33 D 34 E 35 F

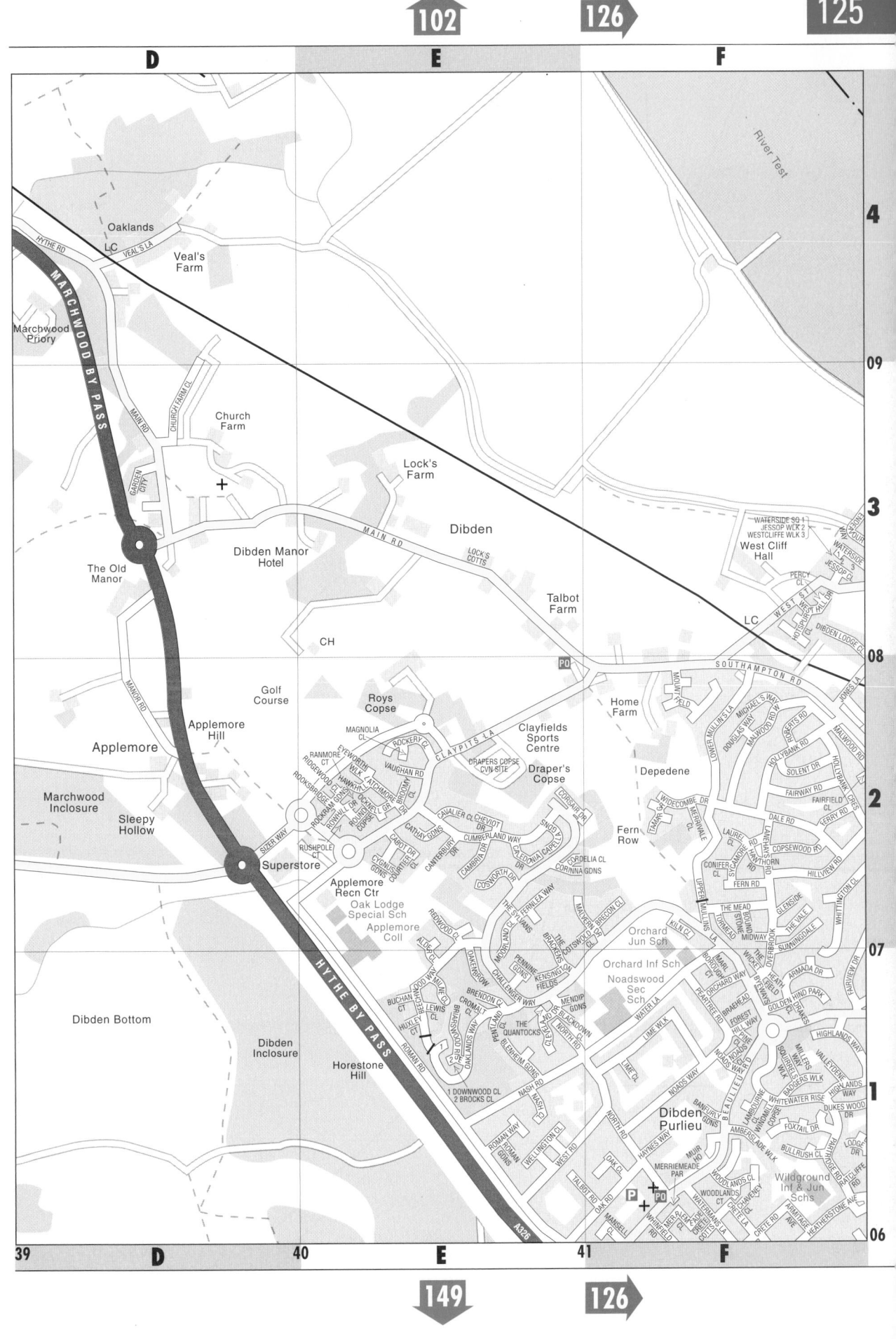

D E F

4

09

3

Dibden

8

2

07

1

06

39 D 40 E 41 F

River Test

Oaklands
LC
VEAL'S LA
Veal's
Farm

HYTHE RD

Marchwood
Priory

MARCHWOOD BY PASS

Church Farm CL
MAIN RD
GARDEN CITY

Church
Farm

Lock's
Farm

WATERSIDE SQ 1
JESSOP WLK 2
WESTCLIFFE WLK 3
WATERSIDE

Dibden

MAIN RD

West Cliff
Hall

Dibden Manor
Hotel

LOCK'S
COTTS

PERCY
CL

WEST ST

JESSOP CL

DIBDEN LODGE CL

The Old
Manor

Talbot
Farm

LC

CH

PO

SOUTHAMPTON RD

JONES LA

Golf
Course

MANOR RD

Applemore
Hill

Roys
Copse

MAGNOLIA CL

Clayfields
Sports
Centre

Home
Farm

MOUNT FIELD

LOWER MULLIN'S LA
MICHAEL'S WAY
DOUGLAS WAY
MAJWOOD RD W

HOLLYBANK RD
ROBERTS RD
SOLENT DR

MALWOOD RD W
HOLLYPARK CRES

Applemore

Marchwood
Inclosure

Sleepy
Hollow

SIZER WAY

RANMORE
CT
EYEWORTH
WLK
RIDGEWOOD GDNS
ROOKSBRIDGE

ROCKERY CL
CLAYPITS LA
VAUGHAN RD
LATCHMORE GR
HAWKHILL
COOMES CL
REDHILL DR
ROUND
ROWHILL DR
ROOKSMORE GDNS

DRAPERS COPSE
CVN SITE

Draper's
Copse

Depedene

Fern
Row

FAIRWAY RD
FAIRFIELD CL
DALE RD
TERRY RD

TAMAR
WIDECOMBE DR
MERRIVALE

LANEHAYS RD
CAMBODE RD
LAUREL CL
COPSEWOOD RD

Superstore

RUSHPOLE
CT

CABOT DR
CYGNUS
GDNS
COURTLEIGH
CL

CANTERBURY
CL
CATHAY GDNS

CAVALIER CL
CHEVIOT
DR

CUMBERLAND WAY

CAMBRIA DR

COSWORTH DR

CORSAIR DR

SNO'S

CORDELIA CL
CALEDONIA CL
CAPEL
CORINNA GDNS

CONIFER
CL
FERN RD
CAMORE RD
HAWTHORN
HILLVIEW CL

UPPER MULLIN'S LA
GLENSIDE
THE VALE
WHITTINGTON CL

Applemore
Recn Ctr

Oak Lodge
Special Sch

Applemore
Coll

REDWOOD CL

ALDOS

MOOR LAND CL

THE ST
FERNLEA WAY
EVANS

MALVERN
THE BRACKENS
COTSWOLD CL
BRECON CL

KILN CL
BROOKLYNE
HEATH
WICKEL RD

THE MEAD
BOUND
TORMEAD
MIDWAY
DEERBROOK

SUNNINGDALE

OAKENBROW

BRENDON CT

REDWOOD GR
PENNINE
KENSINGTON
FIELDS

Orchard Jun Sch
Orchard Inf Sch
Noadswood Sec Sch

ORCHARD WAY

BRAESIDE
PEARTREE RD

BRAMFIELD
FOREST
HILL WAY

ARMADA DR

FAIRVIEW DR

BUCHAN
CT
MILNE CL
AXFORD
LEWIS
CL
HUXLEY CL

CROMALT
CL
OAKLANDS WAY
BRIARSWOOD RISE

CHALLENGER WAY

LAPLAND
GDNS

MENDIP
GDNS

THE
QUANTOCKS

MARL
BROOK
GDNS
OLD BLACKDOWN
NORTH RD

KILN CL
WATER LA
LIME WLK

MILLERS
WICKEL
DRAKES

GOLDEN HIND PARK
SQUIRRELS WLK
BADGERS WLK

HIGHLANDS WAY

VALLEYDENE

Dibden Bottom

Dibden
Inclosure

HYTHE BY PASS

ROMAN RD

Horestone
Hill

1 DOWNWOOD CL
2 BROCKS CL

NASH RD

NASH CT

ROMAN WAY
ROMAN GDNS

WELLINGTON CL

WEST RD

OAK CL

NORTH RD

HAYNES WAY

LIME CL

NOADS WAY

MUIR
HO

WHITEWATER RISE

LAMBOURNE
WINDMILL
FOXTAIL DR

AMBERSLADE WLK

BANBURY
GDNS

BEAULIEU

BULLRUSH DR

DUKES WOOD
DR

HIGHLANDS WAY

HEATHERSTONE AVE

Dibden
Purlieu

TALBOT RD

P

PO

OAK RD

WHINFIELD
RD

MANSELL CL

WOODLANDS CL
WOODLANDS CT

CHAVEY

CREE
COTTS

WOODLANDS
CL

Wildground
Inf & Jun
Schs

RATCLIFFE
RD

ARMITAGE
AVE

LODGE DR

MERRIEMEADE
PAR

A326

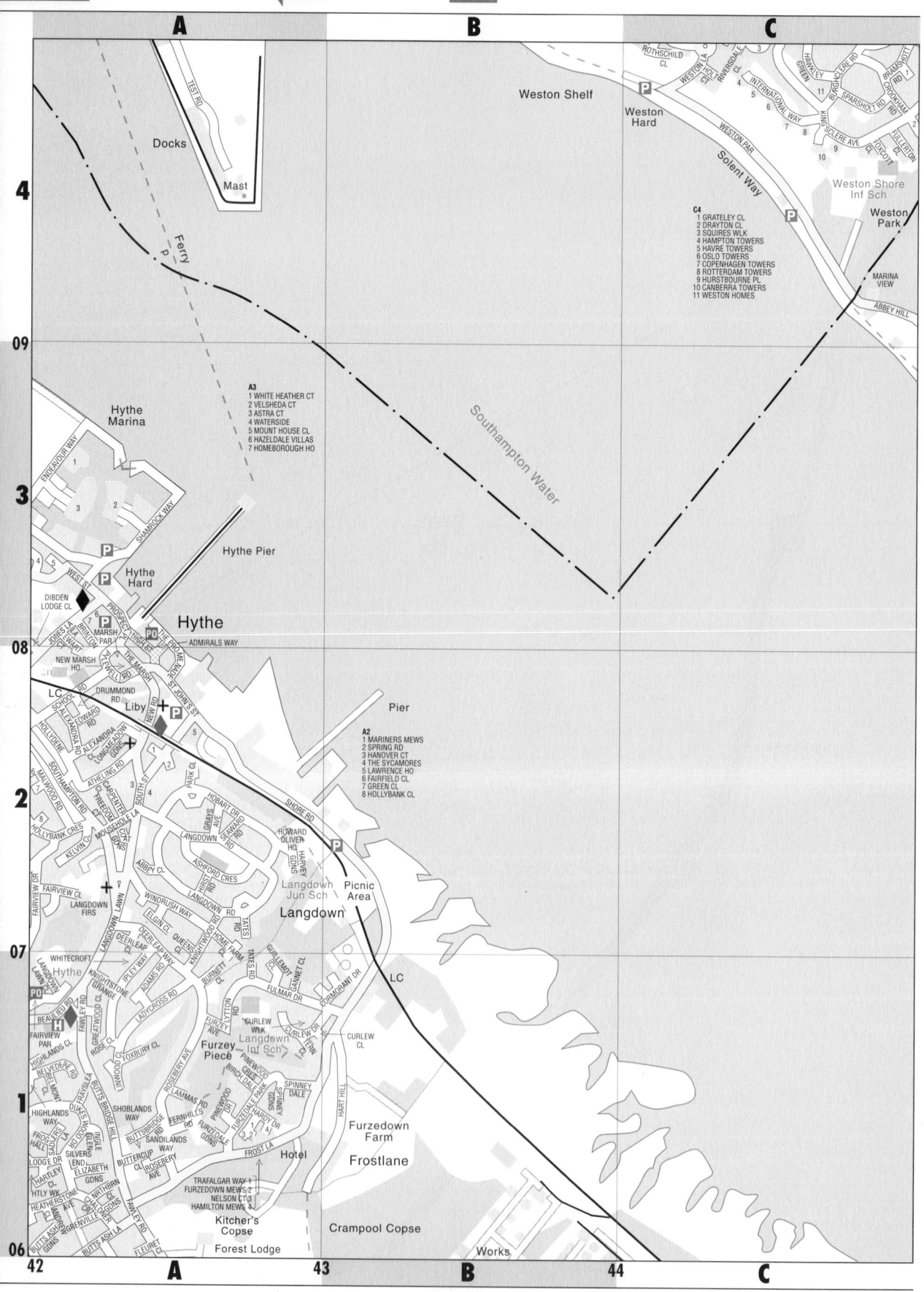

A   B   C

Weston Shelf

Weston Hard

Solent Way

Weston Shore Inf Sch

Weston Park

Marina View

Abbey Hill

C4
1 GRATELEY CL
2 DRAYTON CL
3 SQUIRES WLK
4 HAMPTON TOWERS
5 HAVRE TOWERS
6 OSLO TOWERS
7 COPENHAGEN TOWERS
8 ROTTERDAM TOWERS
9 HURSTBOURNE PL
10 CANBERRA TOWERS
11 WESTON HOMES

Docks

Mast

Ferry

Hythe Marina

A3
1 WHITE HEATHER CT
2 VELSHEDA CT
3 ASTRA CT
4 WATERSIDE
5 MOUNT HOUSE CL
6 HAZELDALE VILLAS
7 HOMEBOROUGH HO

Southampton Water

Hythe Pier

DIBDEN LODGE CL

Hythe Hard

Hythe

ADMIRALS WAY

NEW MARSH HO

Liby

Pier

A2
1 MARINERS MEWS
2 SPRING RD
3 HANOVER CT
4 THE SYCAMORES
5 LAWRENCE HO
6 FAIRFIELD CL
7 GREEN CL
8 HOLLYBANK CL

Langdown Jun Sch

Langdown

Picnic Area

WHITECROFT

Hythe

LC

Langdown Inf Sch

CURLEW CL

Furzey Piece

Furzedown Farm

Frostlane

Fairview Par

Highlands Way

Shoblands Way

Hotel

TRAFALGAR WAY
FURZEDOWN MEWS
NELSON CT
HAMILTON MEWS

Kitcher's Copse

Crampool Copse

Forest Lodge

Works

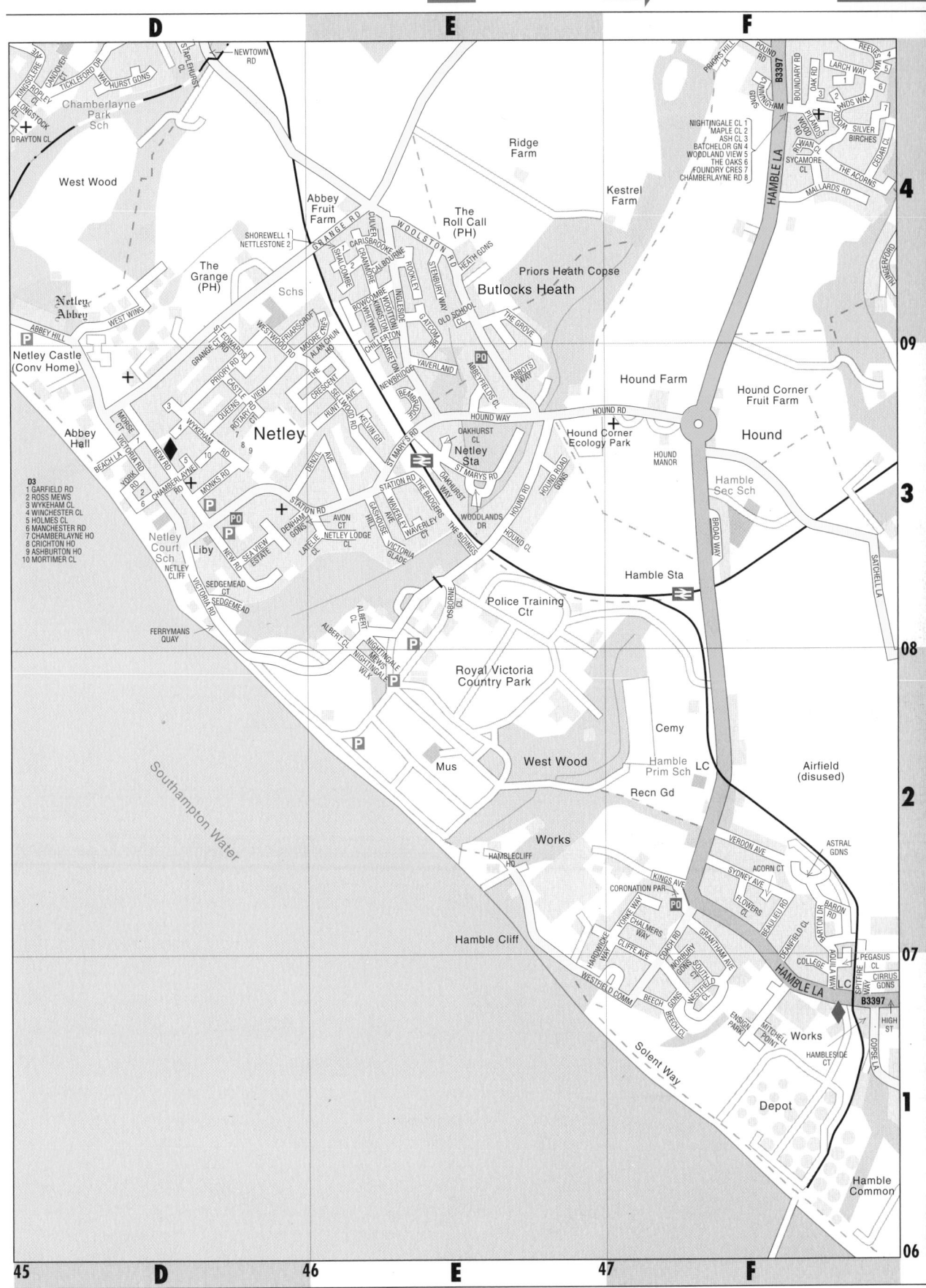

4

09

3

08

2

07

1

06

D3
1 GARFIELD RD
2 ROSS MEWS
3 WYKEHAM CL
4 WINCHESTER CL
5 HOLMES CL
6 MANCHESTER RD
7 CHAMBERLAYNE HO
8 CRICHTON HO
9 ASHBURTON HO
10 MORTIMER CL

NIGHTINGALE CL 1
MAPLE CL 2
ASH CL 3
BATCHELOR GN 4
WOODLAND VIEW 5
THE OAKS 6
FOUNDRY CRES 7
CHAMBERLAYNE RD 8

SHORWELL 1
NETTLESTONE 2

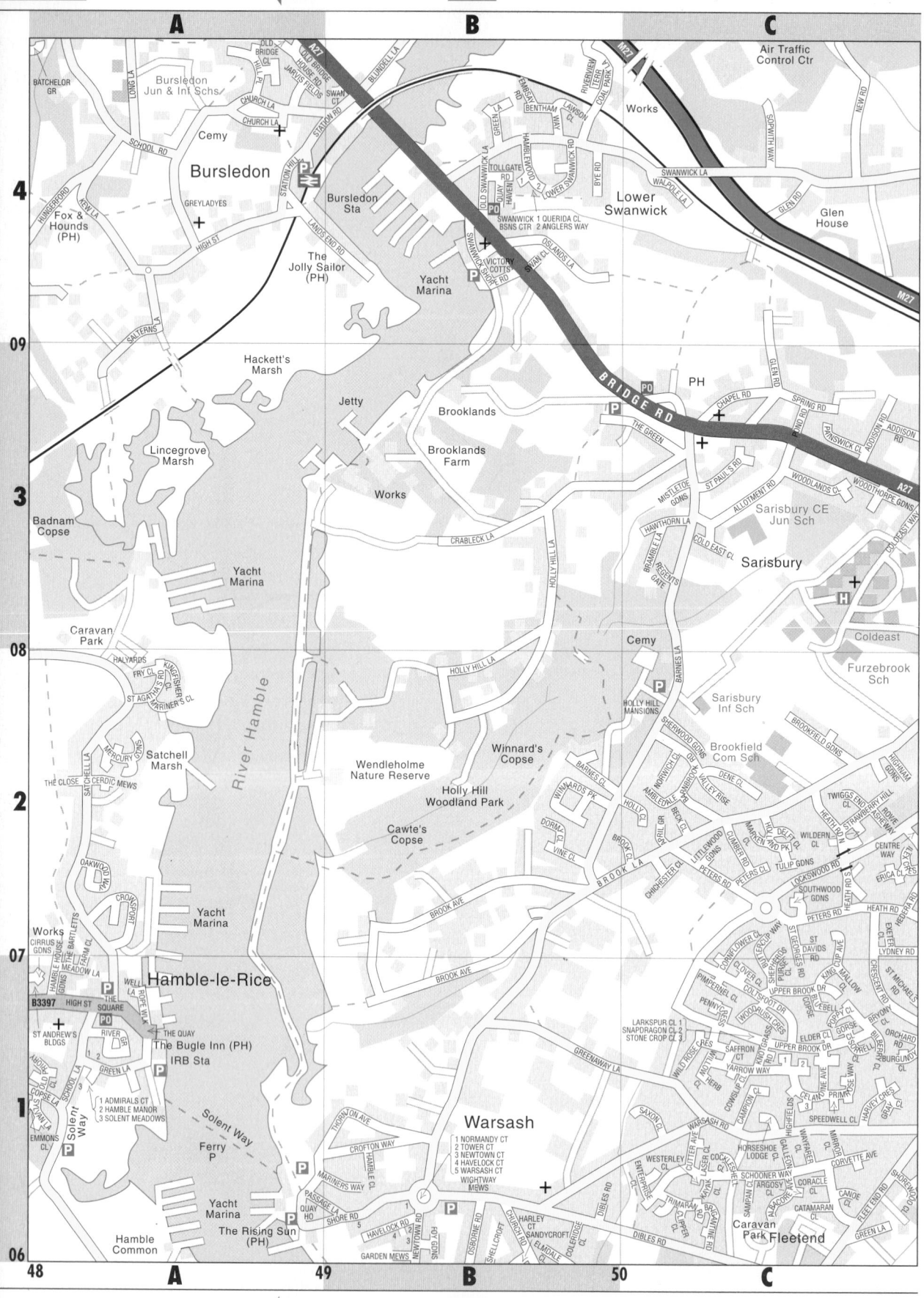
A   B   C

4

Batchelor
Gr

Bursledon Jun & Inf Schs

Cemy

Bursledon

Greyladyes

Fox &
Hounds
(PH)

High St

Bursledon
Sta

The
Jolly Sailor
(PH)

Yacht
Marina

Tollgate

SWANWICK 1 QUERIDA CL
BSNS CTR 2 ANGLERS WAY

VICTORY
COTTS

**Lower
Swanwick**

Glen
House

09

Hackett's
Marsh

Jetty

Brooklands

BRIDGE RD

PH

Chapel Rd

3

Lincegrove
Marsh

Badnam
Copse

Yacht
Marina

Works

Brooklands
Farm

CRABLECK LA

HOLLY HILL LA

St Paul's Rd

Allotment Rd

Woodlands Cl

Woodthorpe Gdns

Sarisbury CE
Jun Sch

Sarisbury

08

Caravan
Park

Halyards

River Hamble

HOLLY HILL LA

Cemy

Holly Hill
Mansions

Sarisbury
Inf Sch

Coldeast

Furzebrook
Sch

2

Satchell
Marsh

Wendleholme
Nature Reserve

Holly Hill
Woodland Park

Winnard's
Copse

Cawte's
Copse

Yacht
Marina

Brookfield
Com Sch

07

Works
CIRRUS
GDNS

Hamble-le-Rice

B3397 HIGH ST

THE
SQUARE

BROOK AVE

BROOK AVE

Southwood
Gdns

1

The Bugle Inn (PH)
IRB Sta

1 ADMIRALS CT
2 HAMBLE MANOR
3 SOLENT MEADOWS

Solent Way

Ferry
P

Yacht
Marina

Hamble
Common

The Rising Sun
(PH)

THORNTON AVE

CROFTON WAY

MARINERS WAY

Warsash

1 NORMANDY CT
2 TOWER CT
3 NEWTOWN CT
4 HAVELOCK CT
5 WARSASH CT
WIGHTWAY
MEWS

GREENAWAY LA

Caravan
Park **Fleetend**

06

48   A   **49**   B   **50**   C

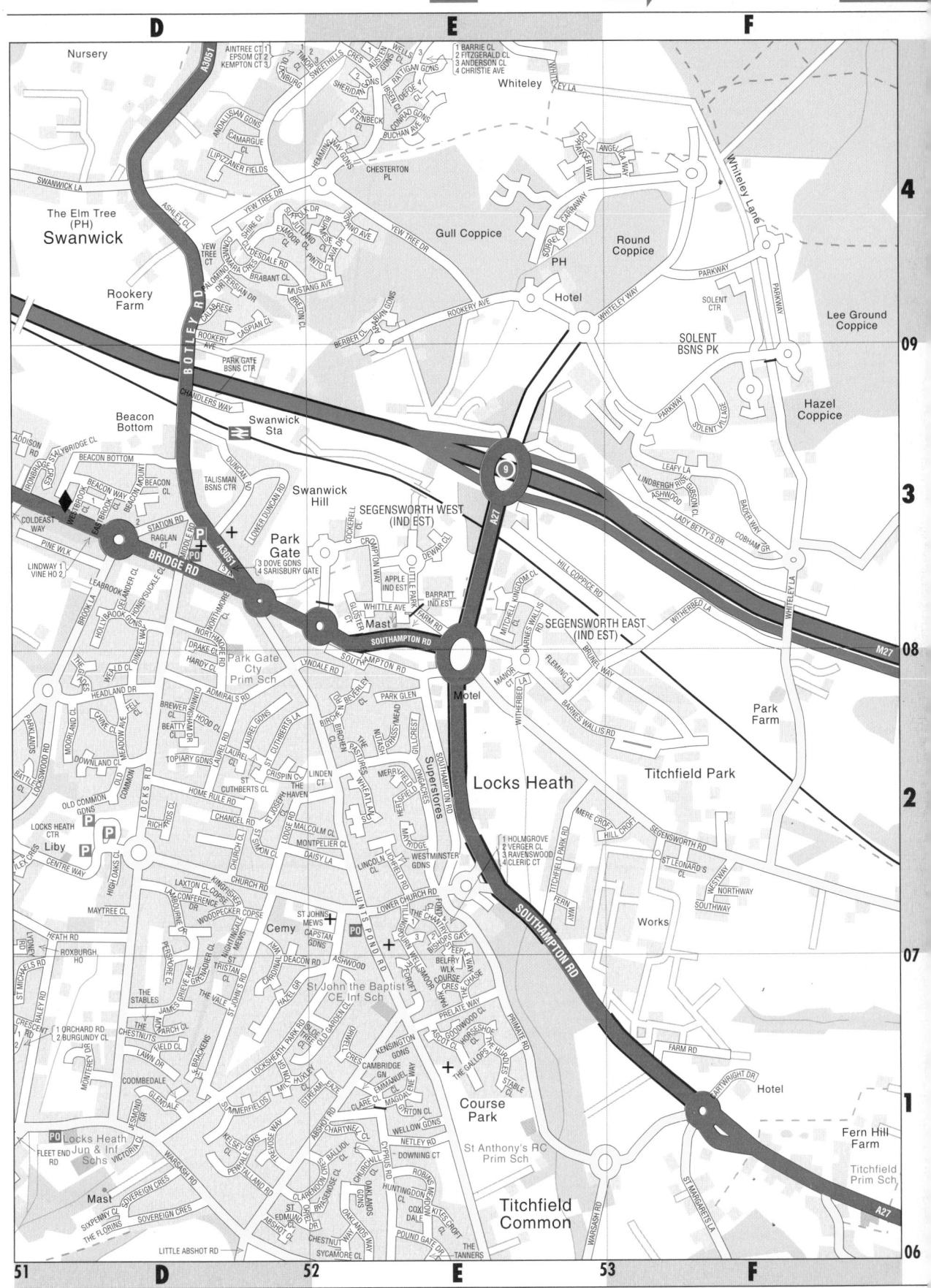

129
107

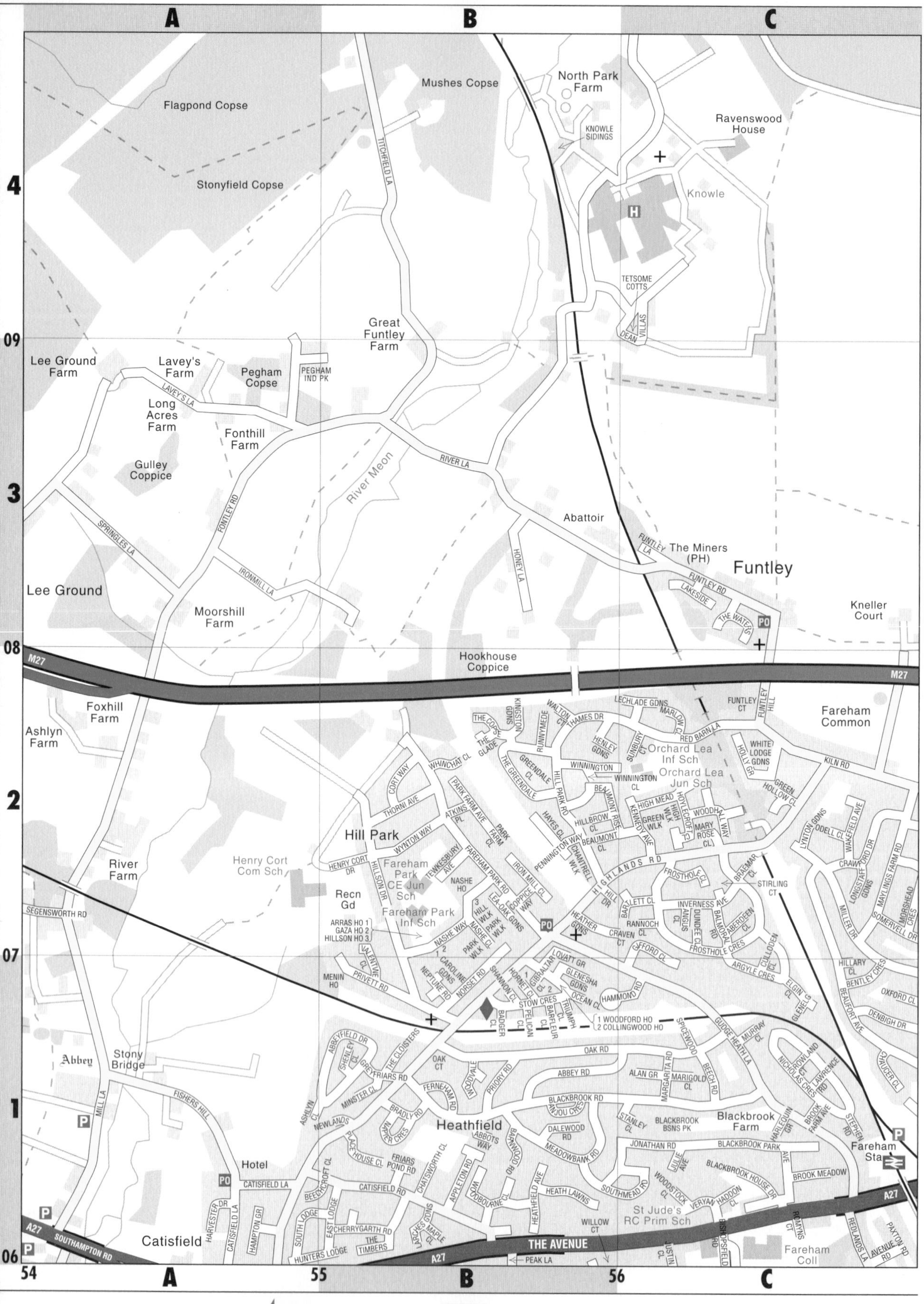
A
B
C
4
09
3
08
2
07
1
06
54
55
56
Flagpond Copse
Mushes Copse
North Park Farm
KNOWLE SIDINGS
Ravenswood House
Stonyfield Copse
TITCHFIELD LA
Knowle
TETSOME COTTS
DEAN VILLAS
Great Funtley Farm
Lee Ground Farm
Lavey's Farm
LAVEY'S LA
Pegham Copse
PEGHAM IND PK
Long Acres Farm
Fonthill Farm
Gulley Coppice
River Meon
RIVER LA
FONTLEY RD
SPRINGLES LA
IRONMILL LA
HONEY LA
Abattoir
FUNTLEY LA
The Miners (PH)
Funtley
FUNTLEY RD
LAKESIDE
THE WATERS
PO
Kneller Court
Lee Ground
Moorshill Farm
Hookhouse Coppice
M27
Foxhill Farm
Ashlyn Farm
Fareham Common
FUNTLEY CT
FUNTLEY HILL
LECHLADE GDNS
MARLOW CL
RED BARN LA
WALTON CT
THAMES DR
KINGSTON GDNS
RUNNYMEDE
HENLEY GDNS
SUNBURY CT
THE COPSE
THE GLADE
Orchard Lea Inf Sch
Orchard Lea Jun Sch
WHITE LODGE GDNS
HOLLY GR
KILN RD
WHINCHAT CL
GREENDALE CL
THE GREENDALE
WINNINGTON
WINNINGTON CL
GREEN HOLLOW CL
CORT WAY
THORNI AVE
PARK FARM AVE
HILL PARK RD
BEAUMONT RISE
HIGH MEAD
HOYLECROFT CL
WOODHALL WAY
KENNEDY AVE
GREEN WLK
HIGH WLK
MARY ROSE CL
HILLBROW CL
BEAUMONT CL
HAYES CL
ATKINS PL
PARK FARM CL
Hill Park
WYNTON WAY
TEWKESBURY AVE
LYNTON GDNS
ODELL CL
WAKEFIELD AVE
CRAWFORD DR
MAYLINGS FARM RD
Henry Cort Com Sch
HENRY CORT DR
HILLSON DR
Fareham Park CE Jun Sch
NASHE HO
FAREHAM PARK RD
IRON MILL CL
PENNINGTON WAY
CHANTRELL WLK
HIGHLANDS RD
FROSTHOLE CL
BRAEMAR CL
STIRLING CT
LONGSTAFF GDNS
MORSHEAD CRES
River Farm
Recn Gd
Fareham Park Inf Sch
HILL WLK
LEA-OAK GDNS
COPPICE WAY
PARK WLK
HILL DR
BARTLETT CL
INVERNESS AVE
ANGUS CL
DUNDEE CL
BALMORAL RD
ABERDEEN CL
MILLER DR
SOMERVELL DR
SEGENSWORTH RD
ARRAS HO 1
GAZA HO 2
HILLSON HO 3
NASHE WAY
NASHE CL
PARK WLK
HEATHER GDNS
CRAVEN CT
RANNOCH CL
FROSTHOLE CRES
CULLODEN CL
ARGYLE CRES
VALENTINE CL
CAROLINE GDNS
NORSET RD
GIFFORD CL
HILLARY CL
BENTLEY CRES
OXFORD CL
MENIN HO
PRIVETT RD
NEPTUNE RD
SHANNON CT
HORNET CL
GIBRALTAR CL
LOVATT GR
GLENESHA GDNS
OCEAN CL
HAMMOND RD
ELGIN CL
GLENEAGLES
BEAUFORT AVE
DENBIGH DR
STOW CRES
PELICAN CL
BARFLEUR CL
TRIUMPH CL
BADGER CL
1 WOODFORD HO
2 COLLINGWOOD HO
SPICEWOOD
GUDGE HEATH LA
MURRAY CL
ROWLAND CL
NICHOLAS CRES
LAWRENCE AVE
CHAUCER CL
ABBEYFIELD DR
SHENLEY CL
THE CLOISTERS
Abbey
Stony Bridge
FRIARS RD
OAK CT
OAK RD
WOODVALE
PRIORY RD
ABBEY RD
ALAN GR
MARGARITA RD
MARIGOLD CL
BEECH RD
MINSTER CL
FERNEHAM RD
BLACKBROOK RD
ANJOU CRES
STANLEY CL
BLACKBROOK BSNS PK
Blackbrook Farm
BROOK FARM AVE
STEPHEN RD
FISHERS HILL
MILL LA
P
ASHLYN CL
NEWLANDS
BRADLY RD
NAPIER CRES
Heathfield
ABBOTS WAY
BARNWOOD RD
DALEWOOD RD
JONATHAN RD
BLACKBROOK PARK AVE
HARLEQUIN GR
Fareham Sta
PLACE HOUSE CL
FRIARS POND RD
CHATSWORTH CL
MEADOWBANK RD
JULIE AVE
BLACKBROOK HOUSE DR
BROOK MEADOW
Hotel
PO
CATISFIELD LA
BEECHCROFT CL
CATISFIELD RD
APPLETON RD
WOODBOURNE CL
HEATHFIELD AVE
HEATH LAWNS
SOUTHMEAD RD
WOODSTOCK CL
VERYAN
HADDON CL
A27
HARVESTER DR
CATISFIELD LA
HAMPTON GR
SOUTH LODGE
EAST LODGE
CHERRYGARTH RD
LARCHES GDNS
MAPLE CL
WILLOW CT
St Jude's RC Prim Sch
BISHOPSFIELD RD
ROMYNS CT
REDLANDS LA
PAXTON RD
AVENUE RD
Catisfield
SOUTHAMPTON RD
HUNTERS LODGE
THE TIMBERS
THE AVENUE
PEAK LA
AUSTIN CL
Fareham Coll

129
154

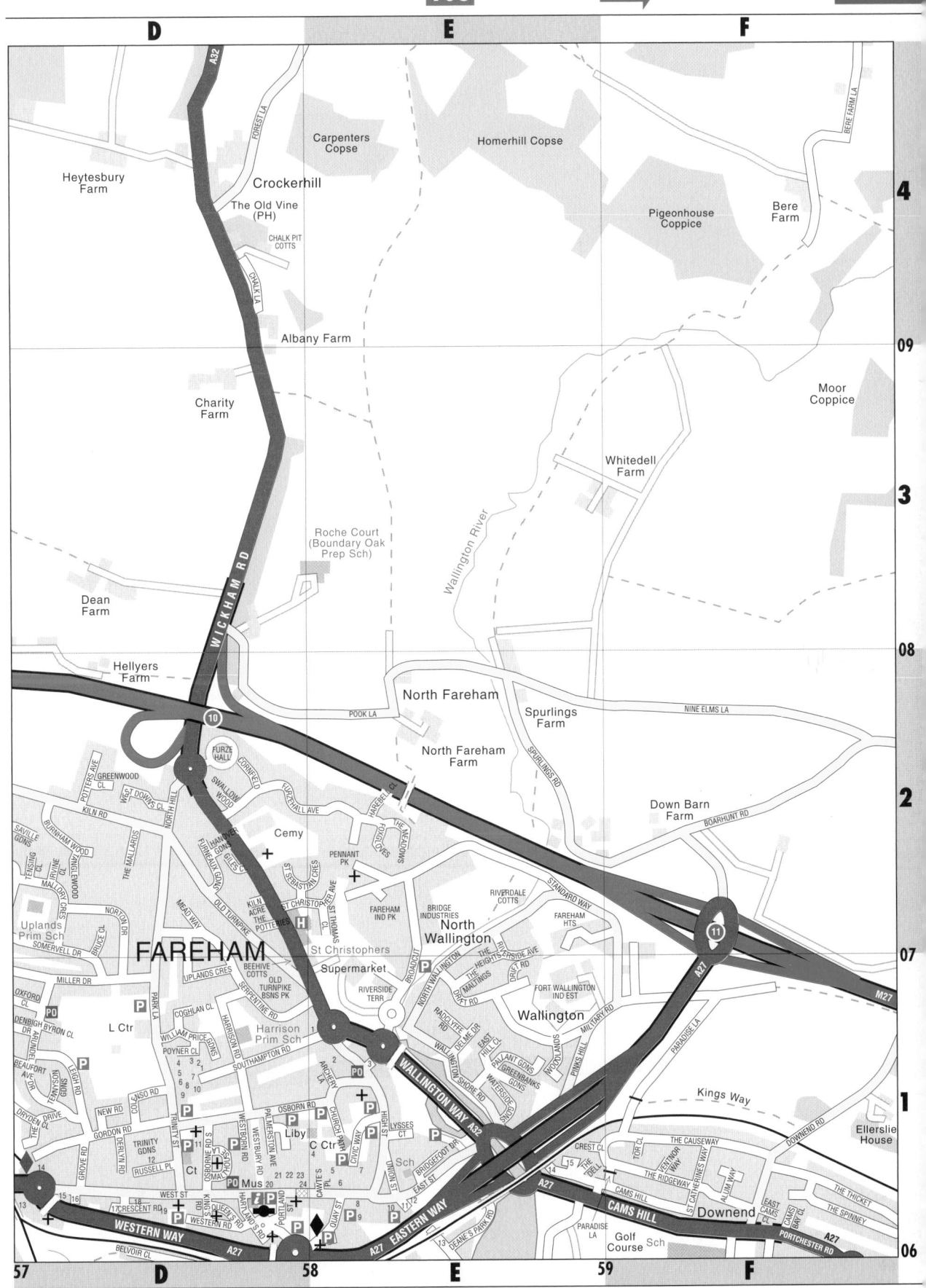

D1
1 ASHWOOD LODGE
2 ELMWOOD LODGE
3 BEECHWOOD LODGE
4 REDWOOD LODGE
5 PINEWOOD LODGE
6 CEDARWOOD LODGE
7 BIRCHWOOD LODGE
8 NORTHWOOD SQ
9 DARREN CT
10 KELLY CT
11 VICTORIA HO
12 MEADOW TERR
13 WEST END COTTS
14 WESTERN CT
15 DELME CT
16 MAYTREE RD
17 THE GILLIES
18 BURY HO
19 HOMEFAYRE HO
20 SAVOY BLDGS
21 DELME SQ
22 WESTBURY MALL
23 WESTBURY SQ
24 THACKERAY MALL

E1
1 TIVERTON CT
2 FERN COTTS
3 WALLINGTON HILL
4 THACKERAY SQ
5 OSBORN SQ
6 OSBORN MALL
7 CROOD CT
8 WESTQUAY HO
9 ADELAIDE PL

E1
10 MADISON CT
11 BATH LA
12 CEDAR CT
13 BATH LA (LOWER)
14 WALLINGTON SHORE RD
15 CHARLEMONT DR

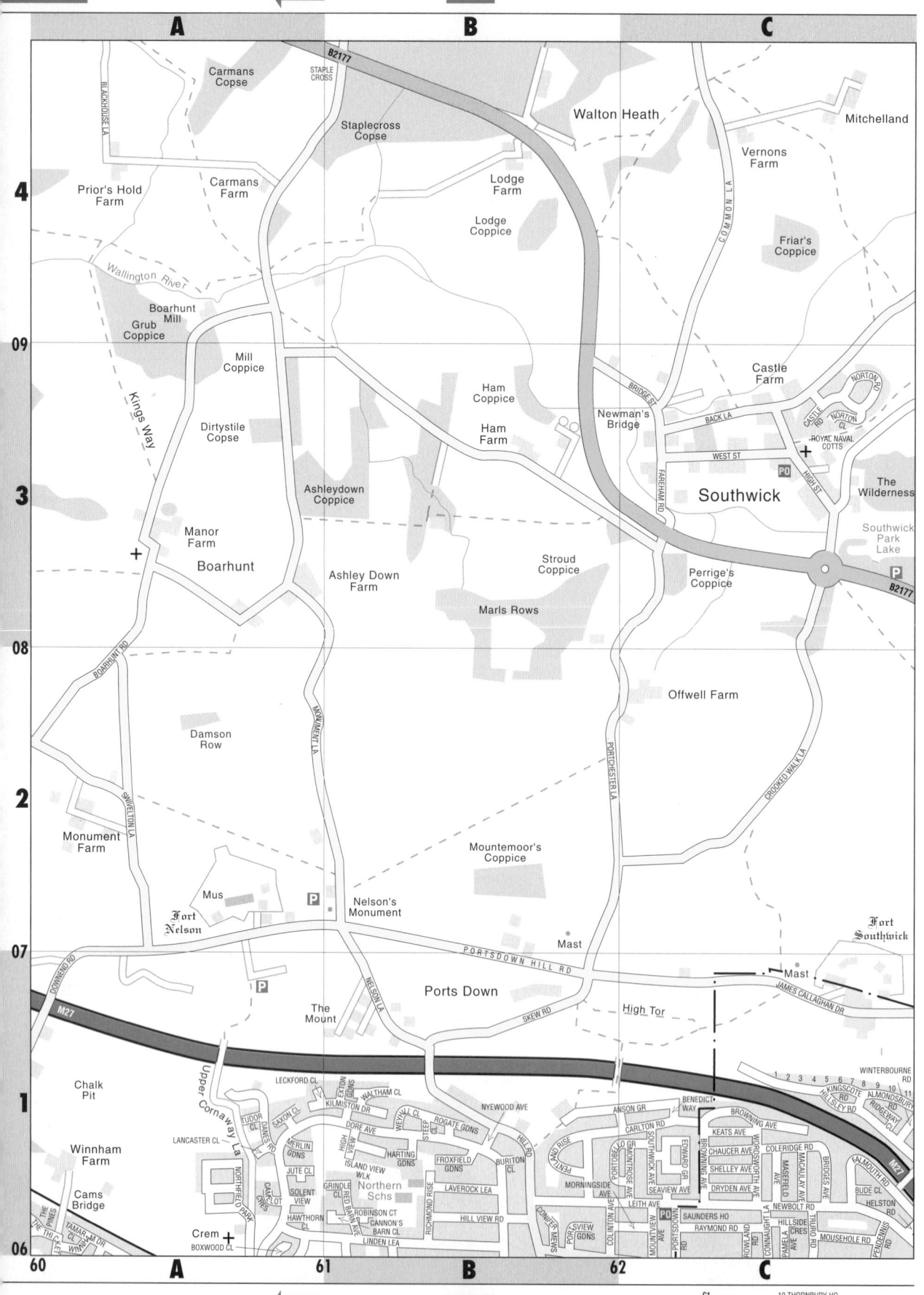

C1
1 TRINIDAD HO
2 ST LUCIA HO
3 BERMUDA HO
4 ST KITTS HO
5 ANTIGUA HO
6 FOXCOTE HO
7 KINGSCOTE HO
8 ALMONDSBURY HO
9 OAKLANDS HO
10 THORNBURY HO
11 PARKFIELD HO

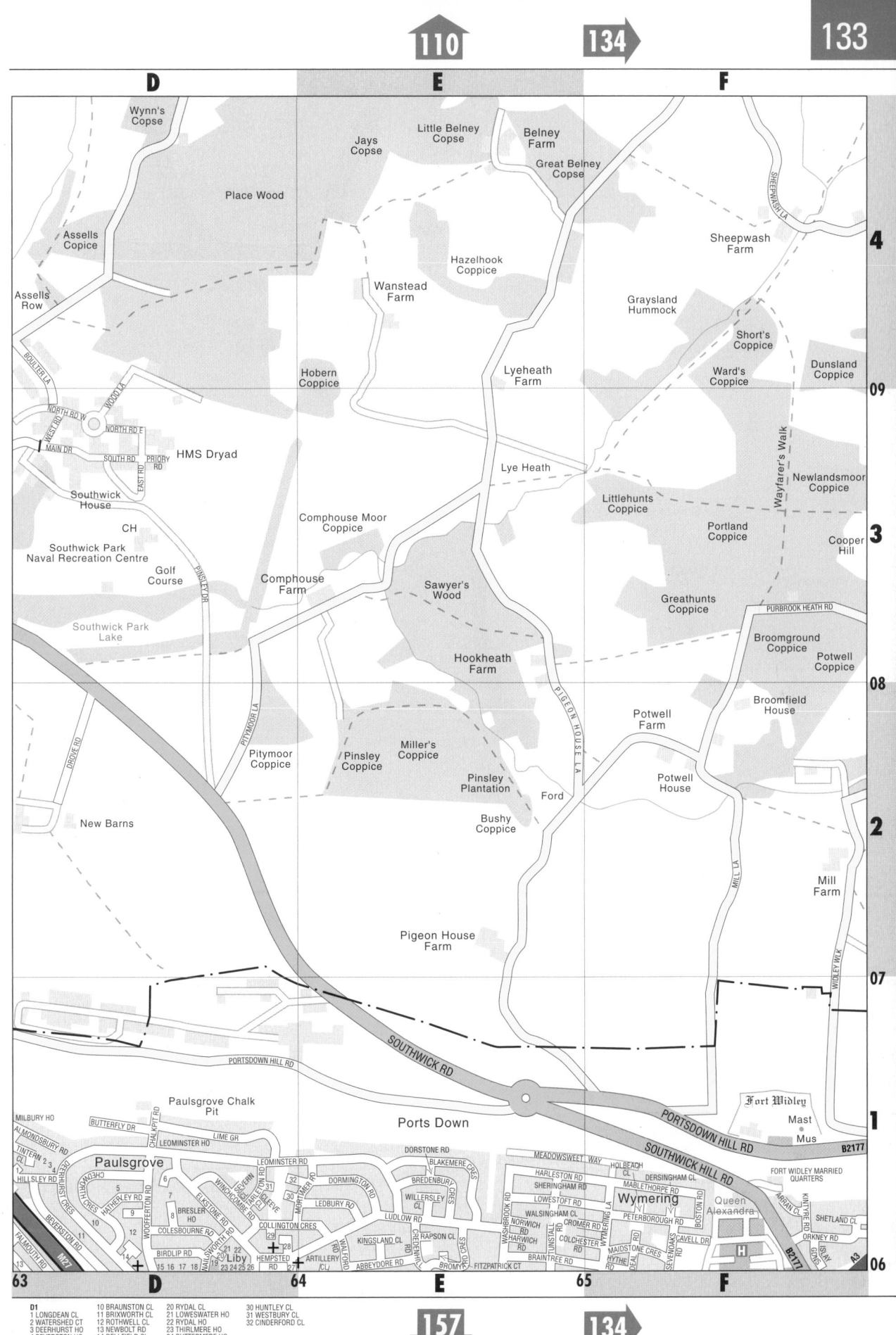

D E F

4

09

3

08

2

07

1

06

Wynn's Copse

Place Wood

Assells Copice

Assells Row

BOULTER LA

NORTH RD W
WEST RD
WOOD LA
NORTH RD E
MAIN DR
SOUTH RD
EAST RD
PRIORY RD

HMS Dryad

Southwick House

CH

Southwick Park Naval Recreation Centre

Golf Course

PINSLEY DR

Southwick Park Lake

GROVE RD

New Barns

Jays Copse

Little Belney Copse

Belney Farm

Great Belney Copse

Hazelhook Coppice

Wanstead Farm

Hobern Coppice

Lyeheath Farm

Lye Heath

Comphouse Moor Coppice

Comphouse Farm

Sawyer's Wood

PITYMOOR LA

Pitymoor Coppice

Pinsley Coppice

Miller's Coppice

Hookheath Farm

Pinsley Plantation

Bushy Coppice

Ford

PIGEON HOUSE LA

Pigeon House Farm

SHEEPWASH LA

Sheepwash Farm

Grayland Hummock

Short's Coppice

Ward's Coppice

Dunsland Coppice

WAYFARER'S WALK

Littlehunts Coppice

Newlandsmoor Coppice

Portland Coppice

Cooper Hill

Greathunts Coppice

PURBROOK HEATH RD

Broomground Coppice

Potwell Coppice

Broomfield House

Potwell Farm

Potwell House

MILL LA

Mill Farm

WIDLEY WLK

SOUTHWICK RD

PORTSDOWN HILL RD

PORTSDOWN HILL RD

SOUTHWICK HILL RD

Fort Widley

Mast

Mus

B2177

FORT WIDLEY MARRIED QUARTERS

PORTSDOWN HILL RD

Paulsgrove Chalk Pit

Ports Down

MILBURY HO
ALMONDSBURY RD
BUTTERFLY DR
CHALKPIT RD
LEOMINSTER HO
LIME GR

Paulsgrove

TINTERN CL
HILLSLEY RD
FALMOUTH RD
M27
BEVERSTON RD
DEERHURST CRES
NORTH RD
HATHERLEY RD
WOOFFERTON RD
SEVERN RD
WINCHCOMBE RD
ELMSTONE RD
BRESLER HO
COLESBOURNE RD
BIRDLIP RD
COLLINGTON CRES
Liby

LEOMINSTER RD
DORMINGTON RD
LEDBURY RD
LUDLOW RD
HEMPSTED RD
ARTILLERY CL
KINGSLAND CL
ABBEYDORE RD

DORSTONE RD
BLAKEMERE CRES
BREDENBURY CRES
WILLERSLEY CL
RAPSON CL
BROMY
FITZPATRICK CT
BRAINTREE RD

MEADOWSWEET WAY
HOLBEACH
HARLESTON RD
DERSINGHAM CL
SHERINGHAM RD
LOWESTOFT RD
MABLETHORPE RD
WALSINGHAM CL
NORWICH
CROMER RD
HARWICH RD
WYMERING RD
COLCHESTER RD
HYTHE RD
MAIDSTONE CRES
DEAL RD
SEVENOAKS
WASHBROOK RD
TINSTALL RD
CREDENHILL

Wymering

PETERBOROUGH RD
BOSTON RD
MABLETHORPE RD
CAVELL DR

Queen Alexandra

H

ARRAN CL
KINTYRE RD
ISLAY GDNS
ORKNEY RD
SHETLAND CL

B2177

A3

63 D 64 E 65 F

D1
1 LONGDEAN CL
2 WATERSHED CT
3 DEERHURST HO
4 BEVERSTON HO
5 NASEBY CL
6 AUSTIN CT
7 CAMCROSS CL
8 WITHINGTON CL
9 DESBOROUGH CL

10 BRAUNSTON CL
11 BRIXWORTH CL
12 ROTHWELL CL
13 NEWBOLT RD
14 DELLFIELD CL
15 ULLSWATER HO
16 ESKDALE HO
17 POTTERDALE HO
18 GRASMERE HO
19 CONISTON HO

20 RYDAL CL
21 LOWESWATER HO
22 RYDAL HO
23 THIRLMERE HO
24 BUTTERMERE HO
25 WASTWATER HO
26 SEATHWAITE HO
27 LUDLOW HO
28 ST MICHAEL'S CT
29 EDWARD'S CL

30 HUNTLEY CL
31 WESTBURY CL
32 CINDERFORD CL

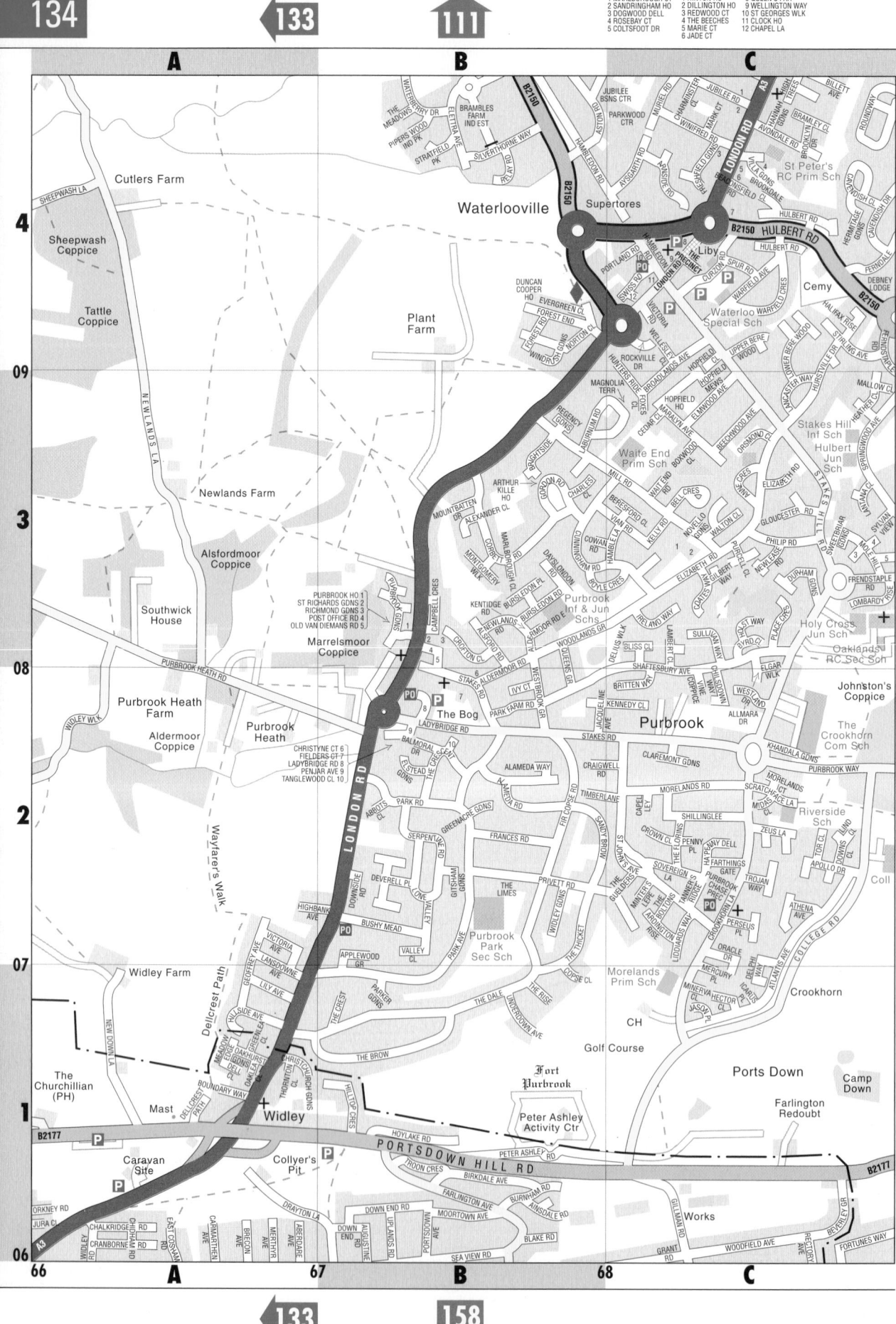

133
111

C3
1 MARLBOROUGH CT
2 SANDRINGHAM HO
3 DOGWOOD DELL
4 ROSEBAY CT
5 COLTSFOOT DR

C4
1 HINTON HO
2 DILLINGTON HO
3 REDWOOD CT
4 THE BEECHES
5 MARIE CT
6 JADE CT

7 HOMEWATER HO
8 QUEEN'S PAR
9 WELLINGTON WAY
10 ST GEORGES WLK
11 CLOCK HO
12 CHAPEL LA

133
158

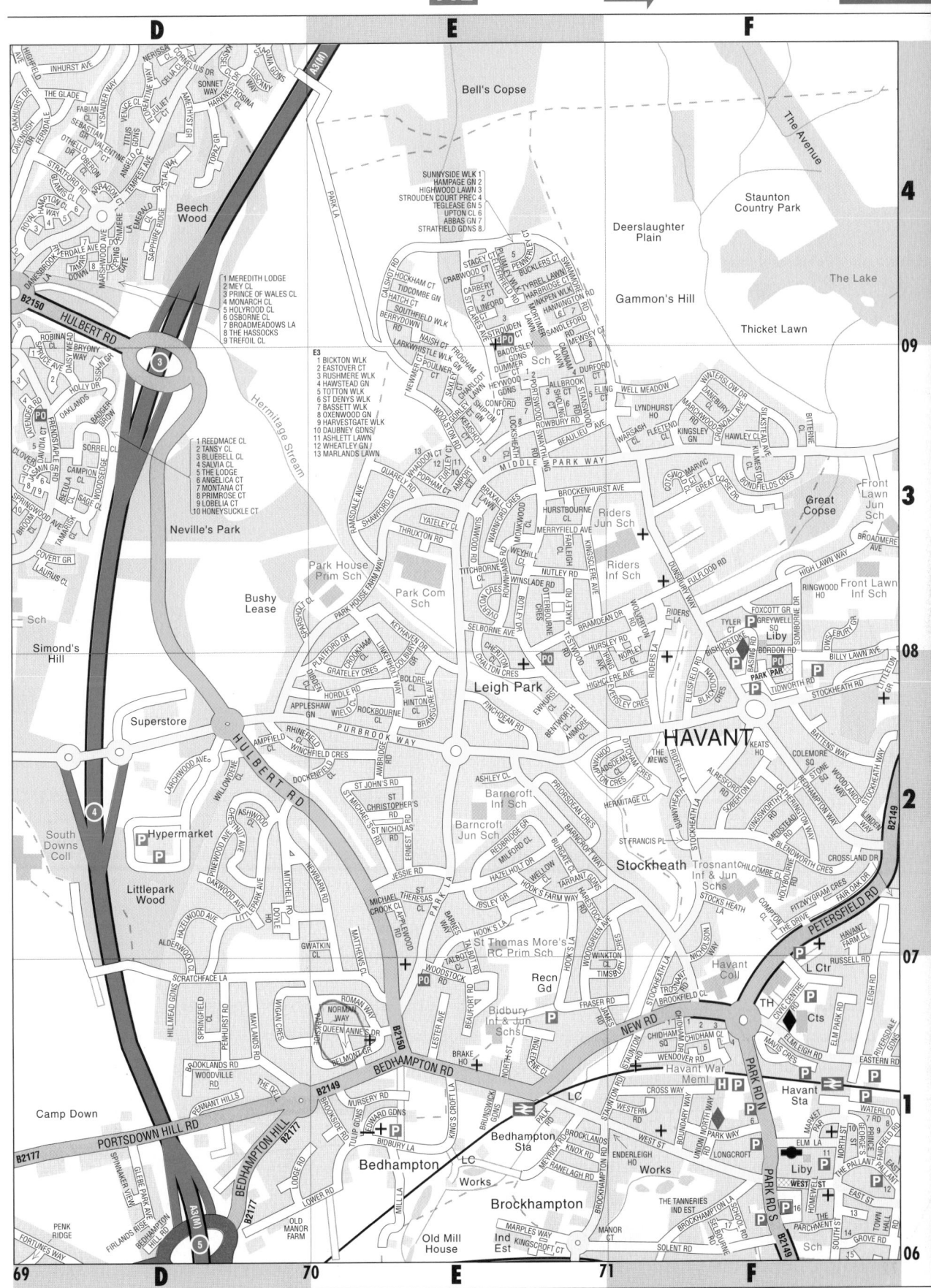

4

09

3

08

2

07

1

06

69   D   70   E   71   F

F1
1 CHIDHAM WLK
2 WHYKE CT
3 COMPTON CT
4 WESTBOURNE CT
5 THE FORUM
6 POTASH TERR
7 WELLINGTON CT
8 EAST VIEW TERR
9 MANOR CL
10 NORTH STREET ARC
11 MERIDIAN CTR
12 EMPIRE CT
13 TWITTENS WAY
14 GROVE CT
15 SLINDON GDNS
16 BULBECK RD
17 CLARENDON RD

136

A3
1 HOUGHTON CL
2 SYDMONTON CT
3 FOUR MARKS GN
4 WYEFORD CL
5 ITCHEN RD
6 WARNBOROUGH CT

7 HEDGE END WLK
8 SCOTNEY CT
9 TIPTOE GN
10 SOPLEY CT
11 MONXTON GN
12 YALDHURST CT
13 WOODHAY WLK

← **135**

113

A3
14 IFORD CT
15 BURLEY CL
16 CHILBOLTON CT
17 HURN CT
18 SHALDON CT
19 TYTHERLEY GN

A3
20 HOLBURY CT
21 MUSCLIFFE CT
22 WARBROOK CT
23 FREEFOLK GN
24 BRADLEY CT
25 KIMPTON CT

26 BLACKMOOR WLK
27 ANDOVER HO
28 SOUTHAMPTON HO
29 BOURNEMOUTH HO
30 WINCHESTER HO
31 FURZEDOWN CRES
32 HILTINGBURY AVE

33 CURDRIDGE CL
34 TISTED CT
35 WOOLMER CT
36 WHITE OAK WLK
37 ALDERSHOT HO
38 LIPHOOK HO
39 GOSPORT HO

40 NEWNHAM CT
41 BRAMSHAW CT
42 SUMMERLANDS WLK
43 WHERWELL CT
44 PENWOOD GN
45 HAZELEY CT
46 WORTHY CT

47 ROPLEY RD
48 FAWLEY CT
49 ASHE RD
50 KITWOOD GN
51 STANFORD CT
52 DEANE CT
53 PASSFIELD WLK

54 FROYLE CT

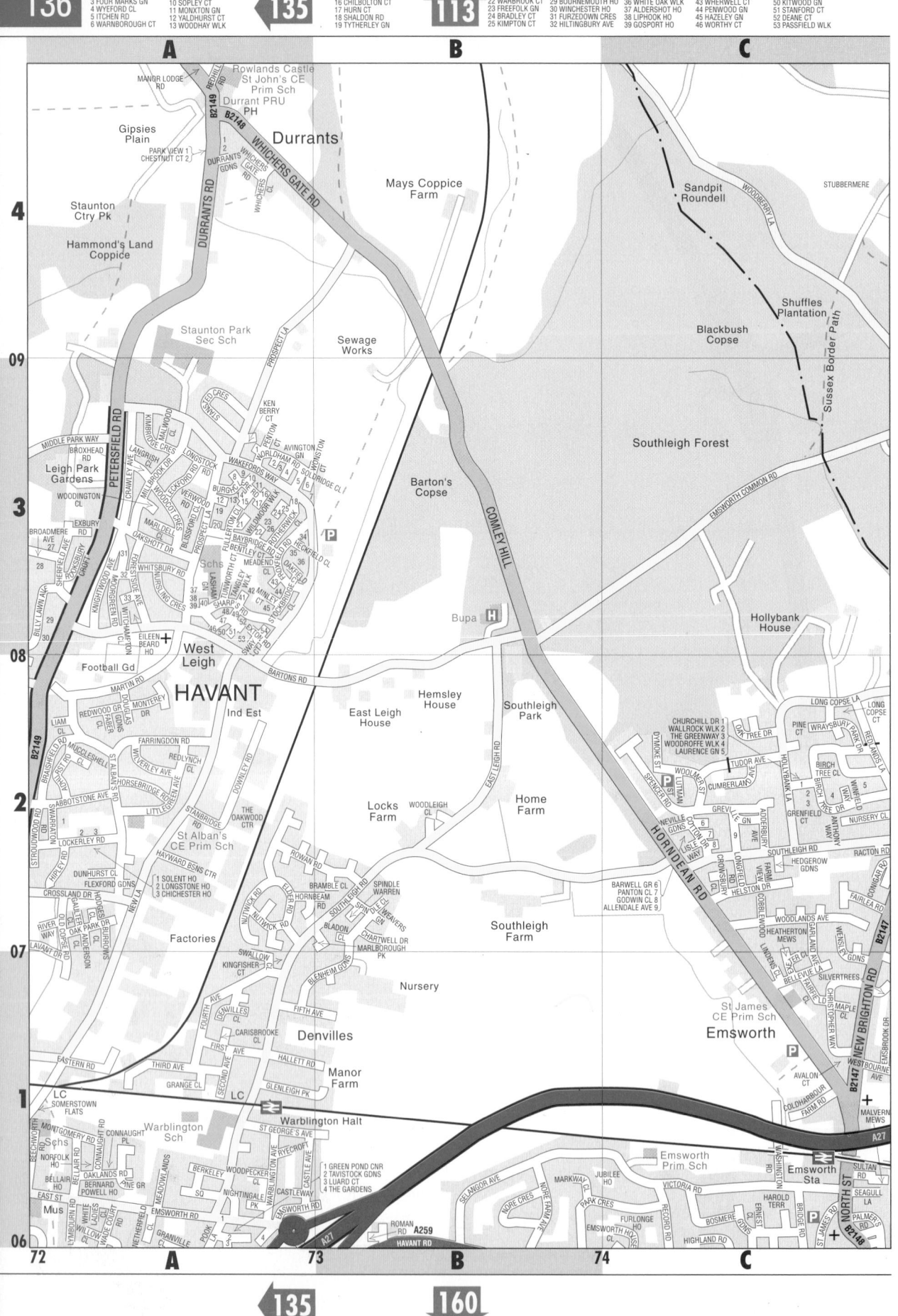

← **135**

160

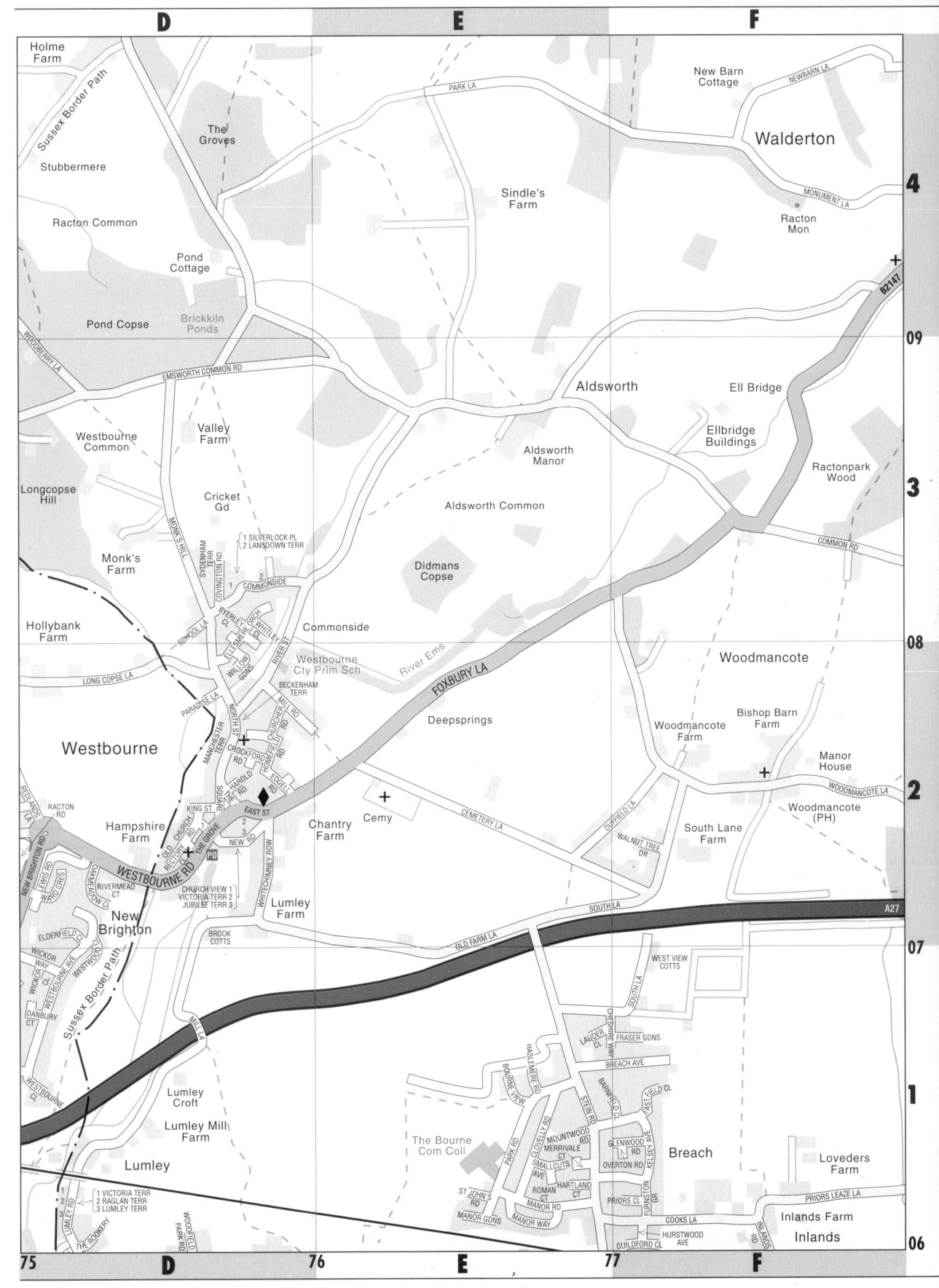

D E F

Holme Farm

Sussex Border Path

The Groves

Stubbermere

Racton Common

Pond Cottage

Pond Copse

Brickkiln Ponds

WOODBERRY LA

EMSWORTH COMMON RD

PARK LA

Sindle's Farm

New Barn Cottage

NEWBARN LA

Walderton

MONUMENT LA

Racton Mon

B2147

09

Aldsworth

Ell Bridge

Ellbridge Buildings

Ractonpark Wood

COMMON RD

3

Westbourne Common

Valley Farm

Longcopse Hill

Cricket Gd

MONK'S HILL

Monk's Farm

Hollybank Farm

LONG COPSE LA

SYDENHAM TERR

COVINGTON RD

1 SILVERLOCK PL
2 LANSDOWN TERR

2
1

COMMONSIDE

SCHOOL LA

BYERLEY
ELLESMERE ORCH
WHITLEY CL

WILLOW GDNS

River Ems

Aldsworth Manor

Aldsworth Common

Didmans Copse

Woodmancote

08

Westbourne

PARADISE LA

MANCHESTER TERR

NORTH ST

Westbourne Cty Prim Sch

Commonside

BECKENHAM TERR

MILL RD

CHURCH RD

FOXBURY LA

Deepsprings

Woodmancote Farm

Bishop Barn Farm

Manor House

WOODMANCOTE LA

Woodmancote (PH)

RED LANDS

NEW BRIGHTON RD

RACTON RD

CAMERON RD

Hampshire Farm

KING ST

OLD RECTORY

THE GROVE

SQUARE

CROCKFORD RD

HOMEFIELD

EDGELL

HAROLD

EAST ST

NEW RD

WESTBOURNE RD

Chantry Farm

Cemy

+

CEMETERY LA

DUFFIELD LA

WALNUT TREE DR

South Lane Farm

+

2

LEWIS RD

WYKE CRES

ELDERFIELD

WICKOR WAY

WICKOR CL

WESTBOURNE AVE

WESTWOOD CL

DANBURY CT

RIVERMEAD CT

New Brighton

Sussex Border Path

WHITECHIMNEY ROW

CHURCH VIEW 1
VICTORIA TERR 2
JUBILEE TERR 3

Lumley Farm

BROOK COTTS

OLD FARM LA

SOUTH LA

A27

WEST VIEW COTTS

07

WESTBOURNE CL

MILL LA

Lumley Croft

Lumley Mill Farm

Lumley

The Bourne Com Coll

PARK RD

HASLEMERE RD

BOURNE VIEW

STEIN RD

CLOVELLY RD

MOUNTWOOD RD

MERRIVALE CT

SMALLCUTS AVE

ROMAN CT

HARTLAND CT

MANOR RD

CHESTER WAY

LAUDER CL

SOUTH LA

FRASER GDNS

BREACH AVE

BARNFIELD CL

GLENWOOD RD

OVERTON RD

KELSEY AVE

EYST FIELD CL

FURNISTON

Breach

PRIORS CL

Loveders Farm

PRIORS LEAZE LA

INLANDS RD

Inlands Farm

Inlands

1

LUMLEY RD

THE ROOKERY

WOODFIELD PARK RD

1 VICTORIA TERR
2 RAGLAN TERR
3 LUMLEY TERR

1
2
3

ST JOHN'S RD

MANOR GDNS

MANOR WAY

GUILDFORD CL

HURSTWOOD AVE

COOKS LA

06

75 D 76 E 77 F

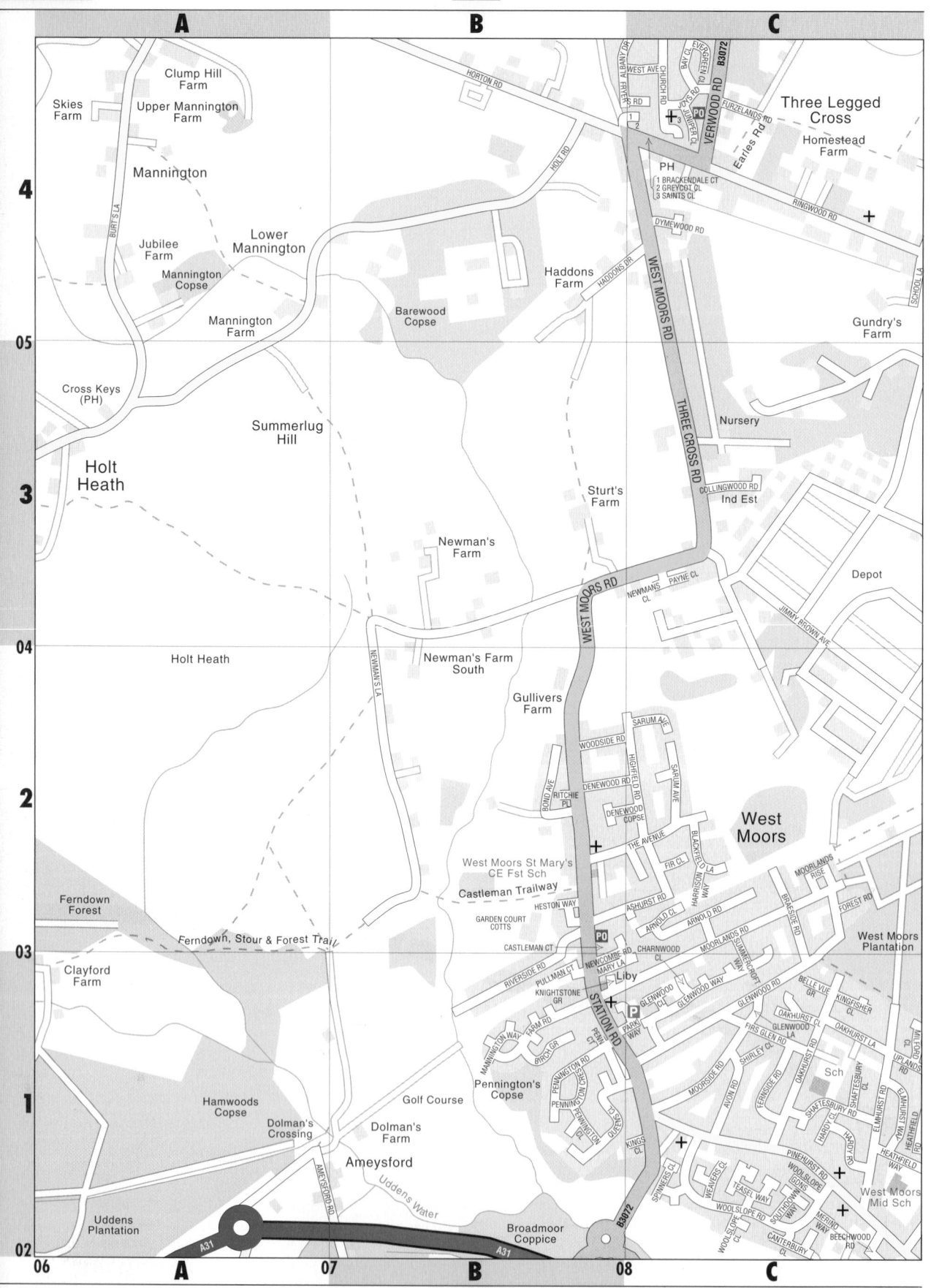

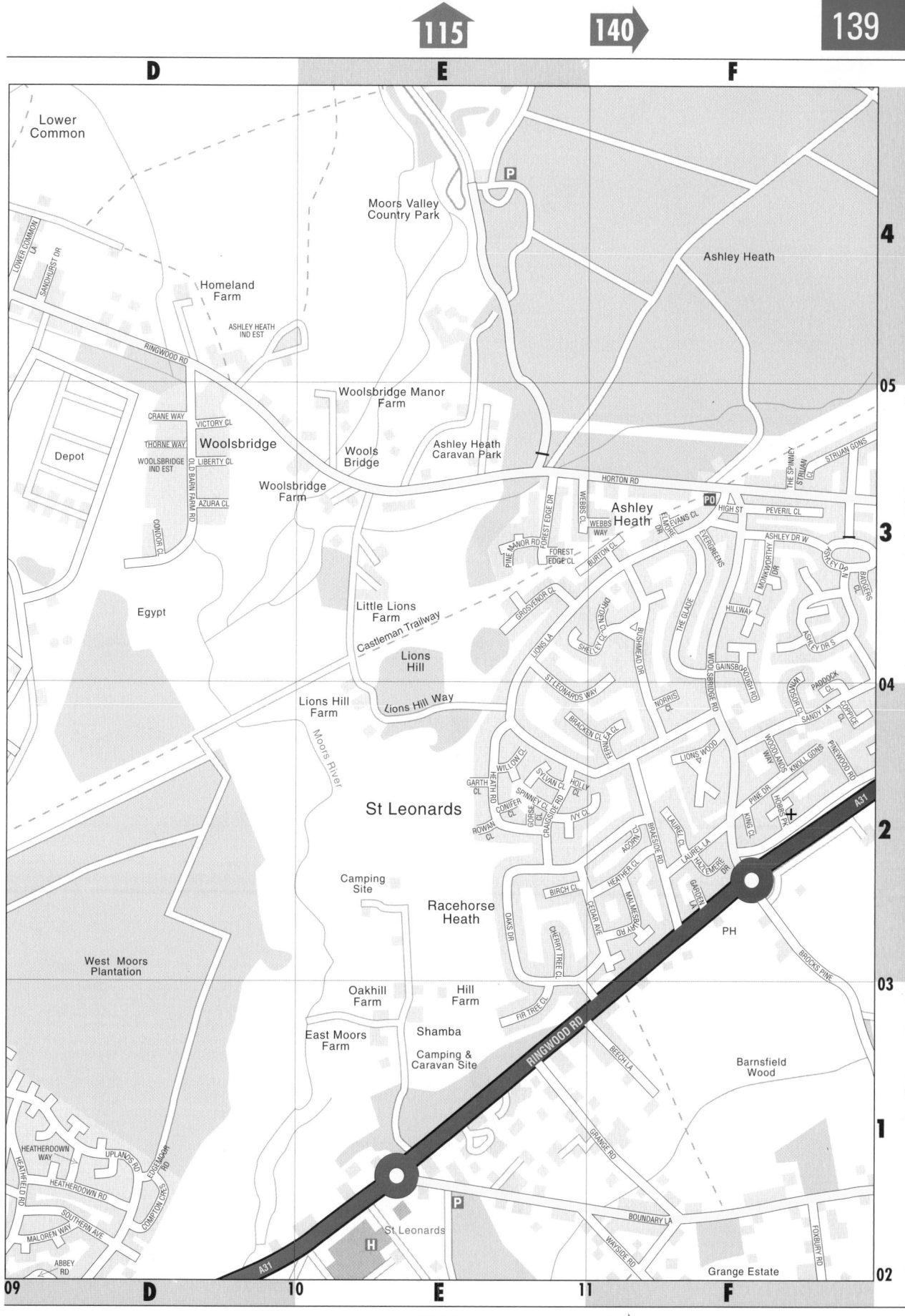

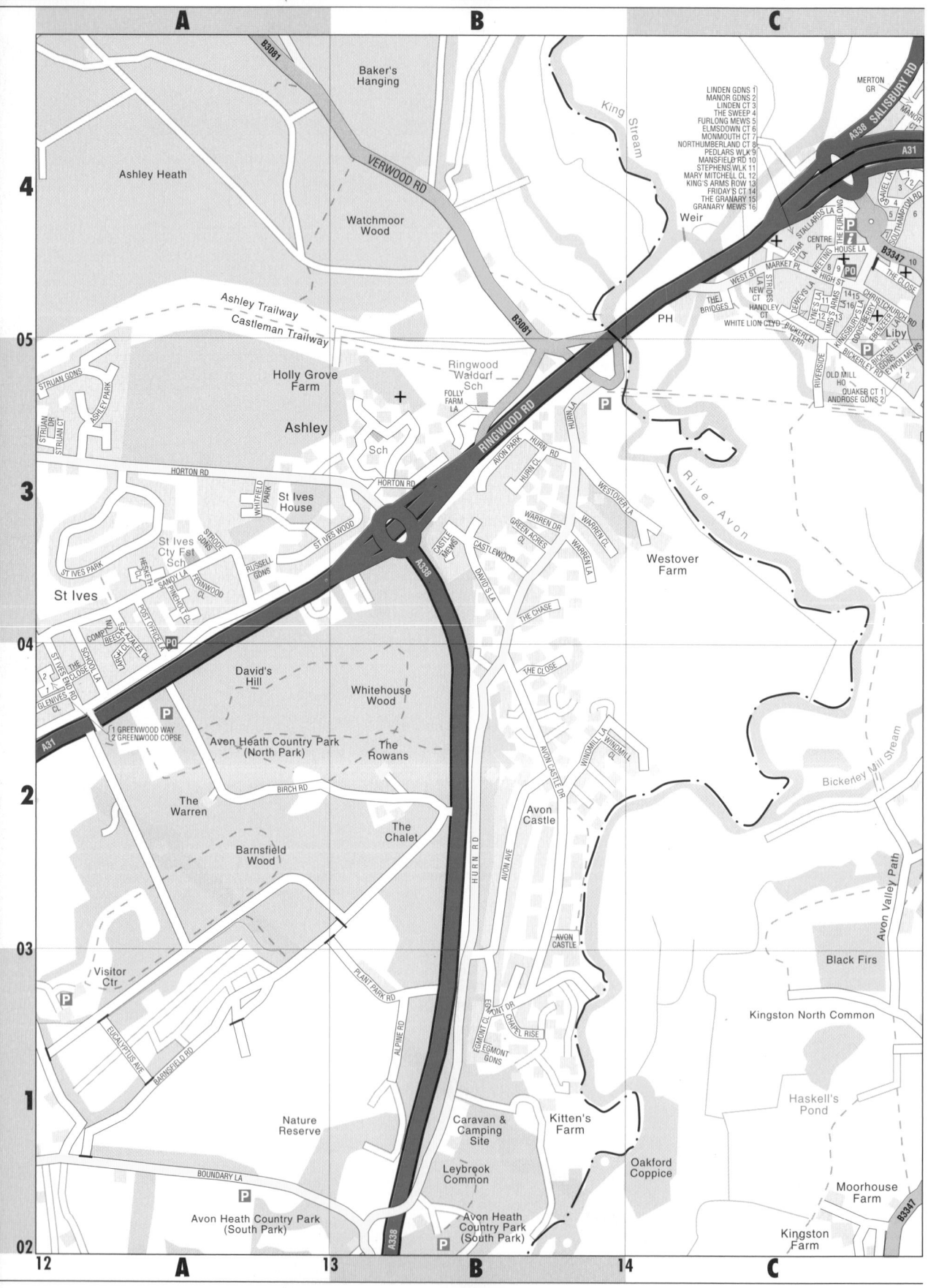

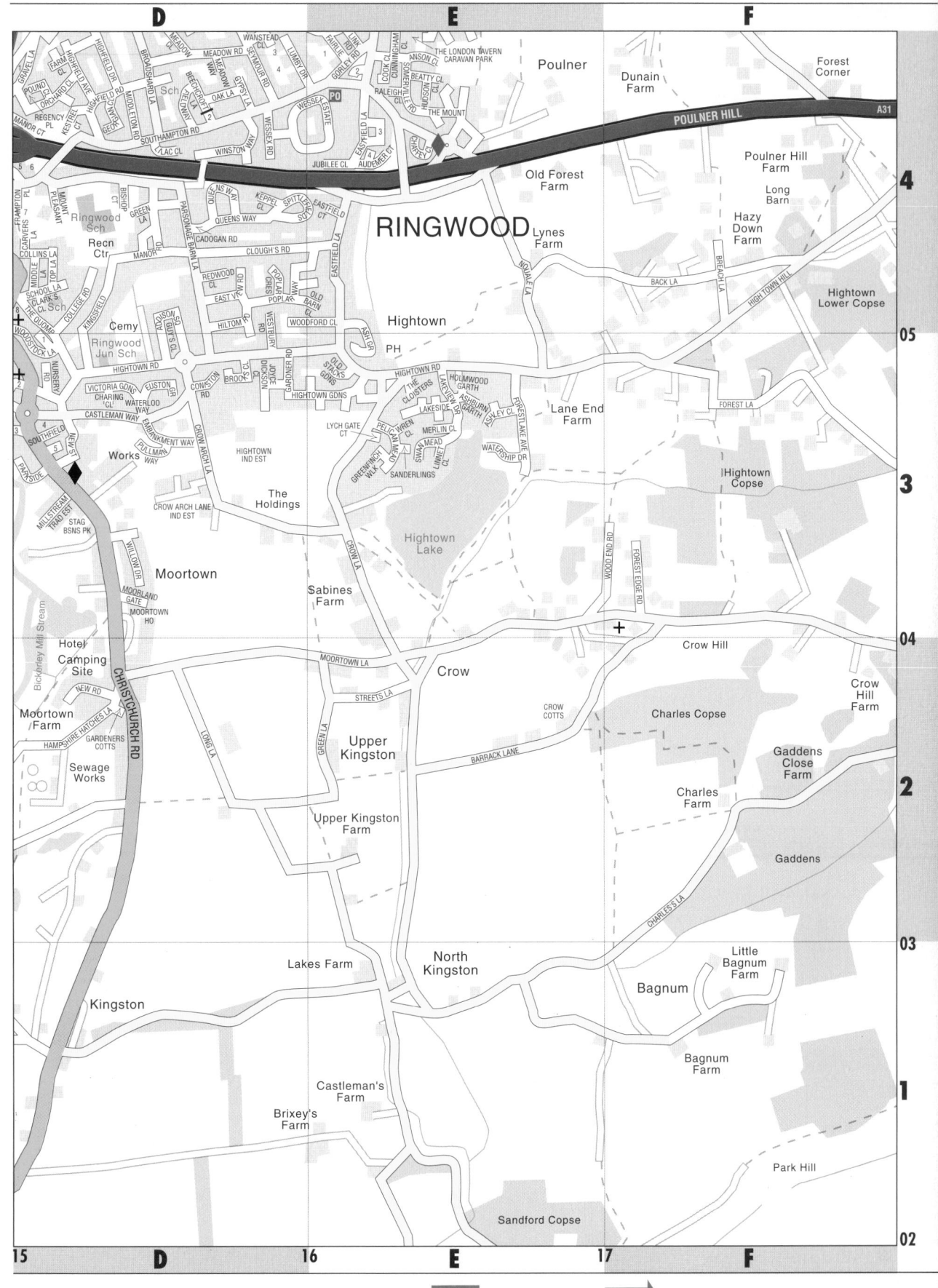

D3
1 HARRY BARROW CL
2 COXSTONE LA
3 DUCK ISLAND LA
4 MINTYS YD
5 SOUTHFIELD MEWS

D4
1 SOMERLEY VIEW
2 BEECHCROFT MEWS
3 LUMBY DRIVE CARAVAN PARK
4 CAVENDISH CORNER CARAVAN PARK
5 ORCHARD MEAD
6 ORCHARD MOUNT

7 CARVERS IND EST
8 ELM COTTS

E4
1 PILGRIM PARK HOMES CARAVAN PARK
2 WHITEHART FIELDS
3 MERRYWEATHER EST
4 PIPERS ASH

117

142

141

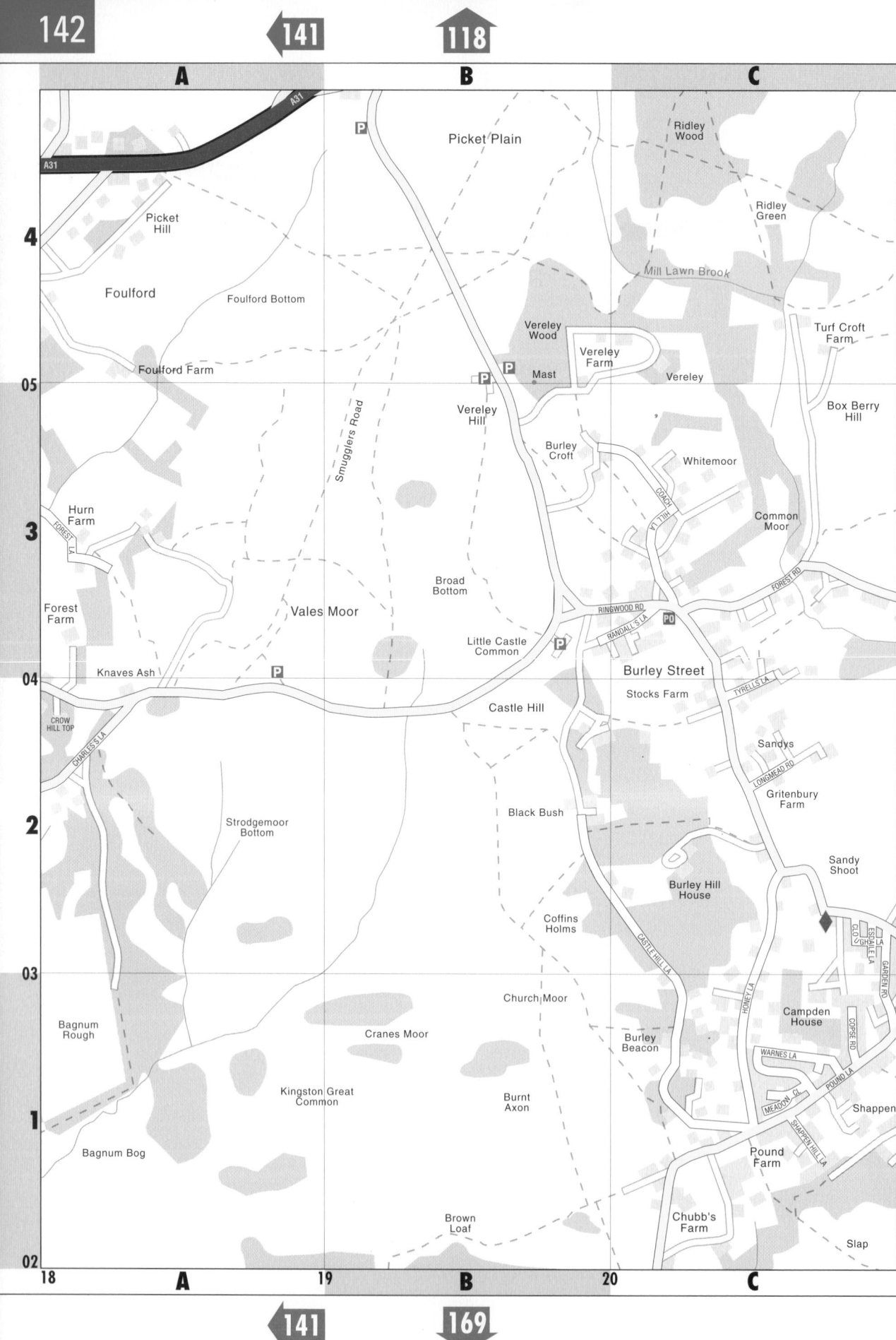

D · **E** · **F**

Burley Outer Rails Inclosure

Stir Dudley's Ride

Berry Wood

4

Burley Lodge

South Oakley Inclosure

Springwood Cottages

Turf Croft

Southmead Cottage

05

Burley Walk

White Moor Bottom

Depot

Great Early

Burley New Inclosure

Black Hill

3

Burley Moor

Lucy Hill

Brookside Farm

FOREST RD

WOOD'S CNR

Cockroad Hill

North Farm

Little Early

04

Burley Grange

Mill Lawn House

Redrise Hill

MILL LA

Mill Lawn

Burley Manor Hotel

Mill Lawn Brook

BURLEY LAWN

2

Burley Lawn

Fords

CHAPEL LA

Burley Rocks

Burley

Shoot Wood

THE MALL

The Queens Head Hotel

BEECHWOOD LA

DOVEYS

LESTER SQ

BISTERNE CL

Creek Bottom

03

HOWARD CL

CHURCH LA

Burley Prim Sch

CH

Bisterne Close

Rock Hills

POUND LA

PO

The White Buck Inn

SOUTHFIELD LA

BENNETTS LA

COTT LA

YH

Shappen Farm

MOORHILL RD

Golf Course

The Burrows

Hotel

1

Pigsty Hill

Clay Hill

STATION RD

Turf Hill

Cot Bottom

Shappen Hill

Shappen Bottom

Broadoak Bottom

Holman's Bottom

02

21 **D** 22 **E** 23 **F**

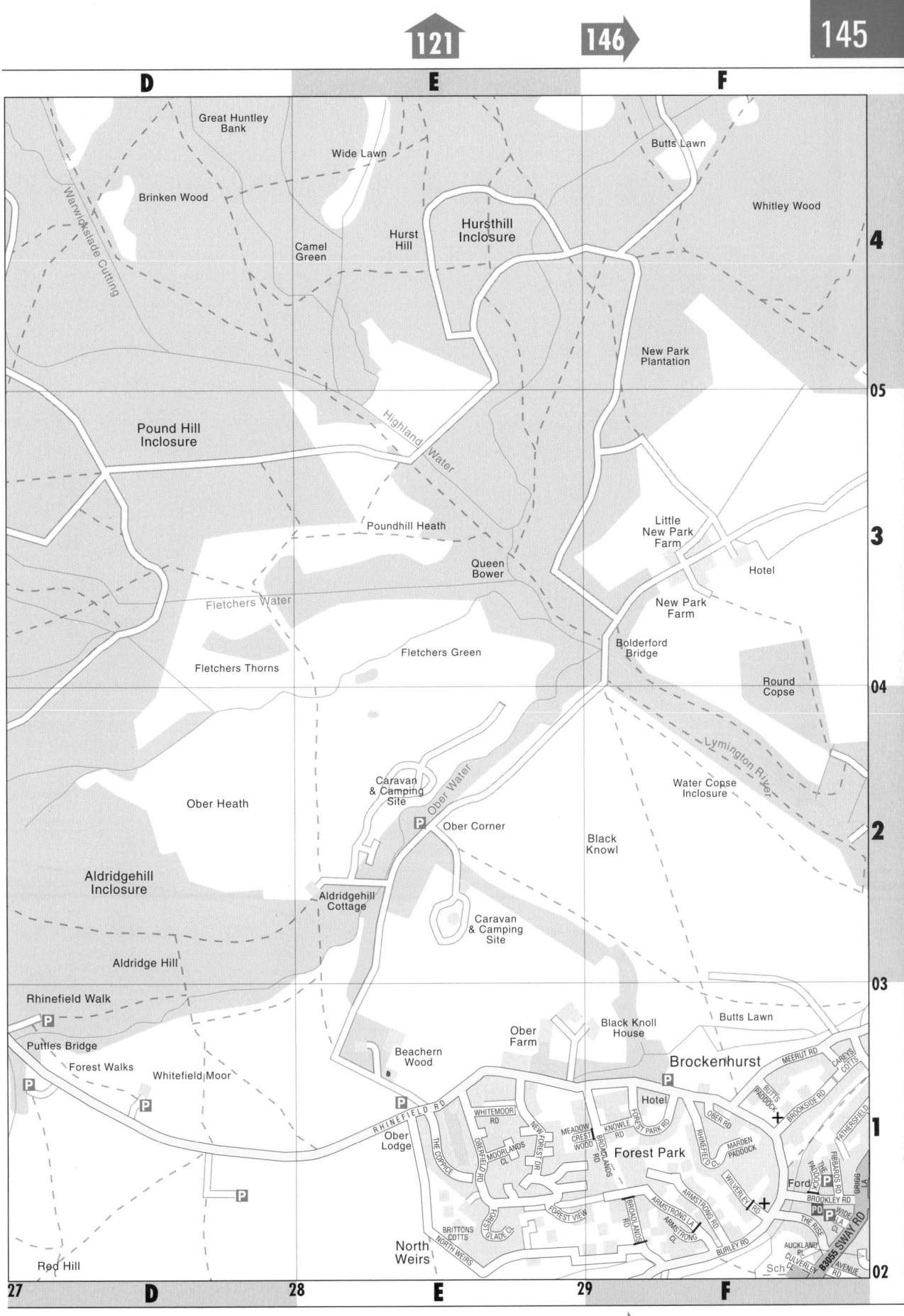

D
E
F

Great Huntley Bank

Wide Lawn

Butts Lawn

Brinken Wood

Hurst Hill

Hursthill Inclosure

Whitley Wood

4

Warwickslade Cutting

Camel Green

New Park Plantation

05

Highland Water

Pound Hill Inclosure

Little New Park Farm

Poundhill Heath

Hotel

3

Queen Bower

New Park Farm

Fletchers Water

Bolderford Bridge

Fletchers Green

Round Copse

Fletchers Thorns

04

Ober Water

Lymington River

Ober Heath

Caravan & Camping Site

Water Copse Inclosure

P

Ober Corner

2

Black Knowl

Aldridgehill Inclosure

Aldridgehill Cottage

Caravan & Camping Site

Aldridge Hill

03

Rhinefield Walk

Black Knoll House

Butts Lawn

P

Ober Farm

Brockenhurst

Puttles Bridge

Beachern Wood

MEERUT RD

CAREYS COTTS

P

Forest Walks

Hotel

BUTTS PADDOCK

BROOKSIDE RD

FATHERSFIELD

P

Whitefield Moor

RHINEFIELD RD

WHITEMOOR RD

MEADOW CREST WOOD

KNOWLE RD

FOREST PARK RD

OBER RD

RHINEFIELD CL

MARDEN PADDOCK

Ford

RIBBARDS RD

GRIGG LA

1

Ober Lodge

THE COPPICE

NEW FOREST DR

DEERFIELD RD

MOORLANDS RD

BROADLANDS RD

Forest Park

WILVERLEY RD

THE PADDOCK

B3055 SWAY RD

P

FOREST GLADE CL

FOREST VIEW

ARMSTRONG RD

ARMSTRONG LA

ARMSTRONG CL

BROADLANDS RD

BURLEY RD

THE RISE

WIDE LA

AUCKLAND RL

CULVERLEY CL

AVENUE RD

P

BRITTONS COTTS

North Weirs

NORTH WEIRS

Sch

02

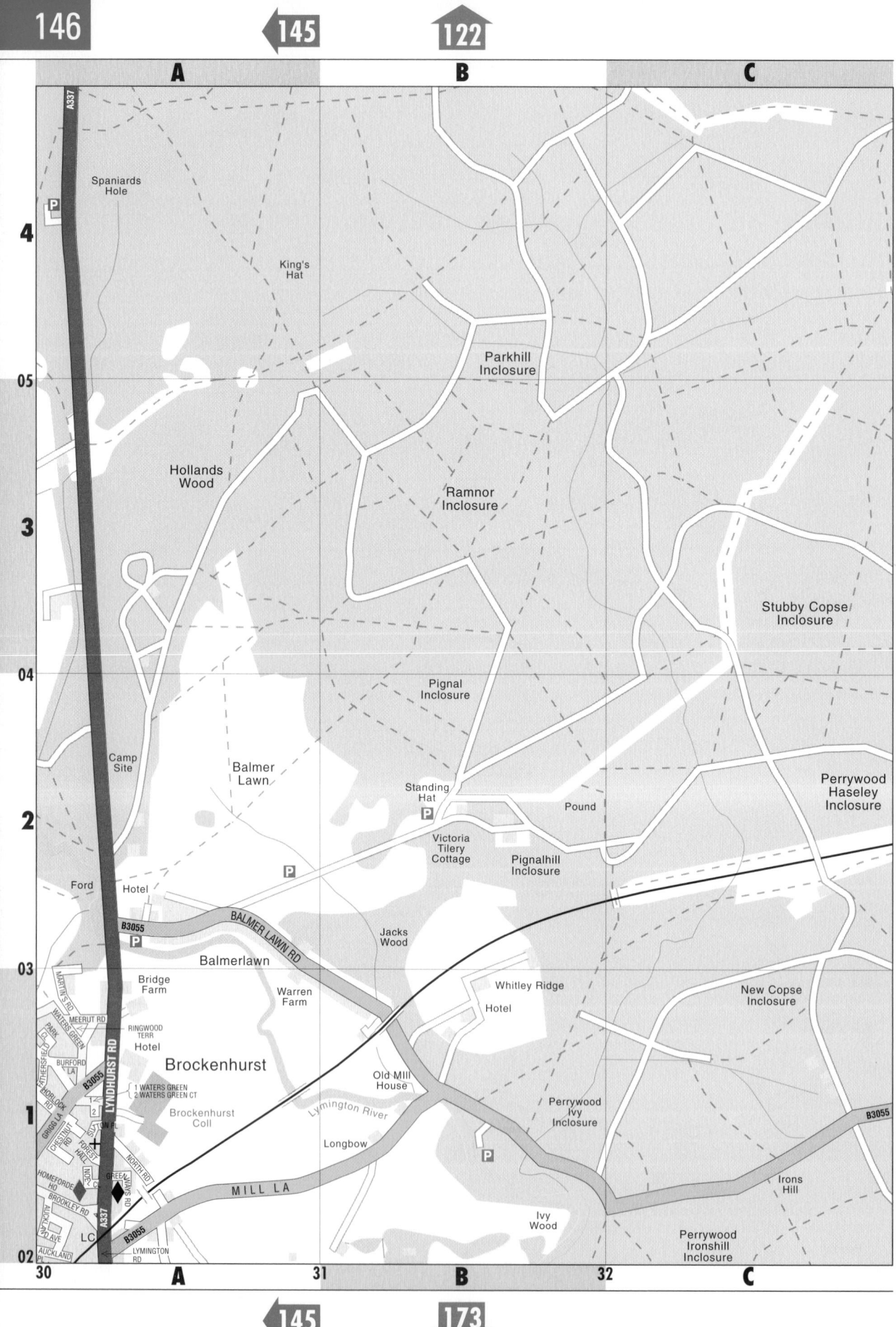

A   B   C

A337

P

Spaniards Hole

4

King's Hat

Parkhill Inclosure

05

Hollands Wood

Ramnor Inclosure

3

Stubby Copse Inclosure

04

Pignal Inclosure

Camp Site

Balmer Lawn

Standing Hat
P

Pound

Perrywood Haseley Inclosure

2

Victoria Tilery Cottage

Pignalhill Inclosure

Ford

Hotel

P

B3055

BALMER LAWN RD

Jacks Wood

Balmerlawn

03

Bridge Farm

Warren Farm

Whitley Ridge

Hotel

New Copse Inclosure

RINGWOOD TERR
Hotel

MARTIN'S RD
WATERS GREEN
PARK CLOSE
MEERUT RD
Brockenhurst

B3055
LYNDHURST RD
BURFORD LA
FETHERSTON RD
HORLOCK RD
GRIGG LA
CHESTNUT RD
ADDISON PL
FOREST PARK HALL
NORTH RD
GREENWAYS RD

1 WATERS GREEN
2 WATERS GREEN CT

Brockenhurst Coll

Old Mill House

Lymington River

Longbow

Perrywood Ivy Inclosure

P

B3055

1

HOMEFORDE HO
BROOKLEY RD
AUCKLAND AVE
A337
B3055
LYMINGTON RD

MILL LA

Ivy Wood

Irons Hill

Perrywood Ironshill Inclosure

LC

AUCKLAND PL

02

30   A   31   B   32   C

D   E   F

4

Denny
Wood

Denny
Lodge

Woodfidley
Passage

Stephill
Bottom

B3056

B3056

Furzy
Brow

05

Bishop of
Winchester's
Purlieu

Denny Lodge
Inclosure

Penny
Moor

3

Woodfidley

Rowbarrow

04

LC

Frame Heath
Inclosure

Frame
Wood

2

03

Ladycross
Inclosure

Moon
Hill

Ladycross
Lodge

1

Worts Gutter

Hawkhill
Inclosure

Lodge
Heath

B3055

Stockley
Inclosure

Little
Wood

02

33   D   34   E   35   F

A **B** **C**

4

King's Hat Cottage

Buck Hill

Ferny Crofts (Scout Ctr)

King's Hat Inclosure

Gurnetfields Furzebrake

Ford

Starpole Pond

B3056

05

Culverley Old Farm

P

Pig Bush

Culverley Farm

Foxhunting Inclosure

P

NORTH LA

3

Gurnet Fields

North Gate

P

Shepton Water

Honey Hill

Shepton Bridge

Penerley Water

The House in the Wood

Halfpenny Green

Penerley Wood

Beaulieu River

04

Little Honeyhill Wood

Penerley Gate

Penerley Farm

Little Goswell Copse

Hides Hill La

Penerley Lodge

Hartford Bridge

Tantany Wood

Leygreen Farm

Hides Close

2

Stubbs Wood

Black Bridge

Hartford Copse

P

03

Abbotstanding Wood

Wood La

P

The National Motor Mus

P

Beaulieu Abbey (remains of)

Palace House

+

Works Gutter

FURZEY LA

P

1

Furzey Lodge

Hotel

Mill

PALACE LA

B3054

Pit Copse

PONDSIDE FLATS 1
DITTON COTTS 2
CLITHEROE COTTS 3

P PO

HIGH ST

B3056

B3054

Beaulieu

Beaulieu Prim Sch

02

36 **A** 37 **B** 38 **C**

D E F

4

05

3

04

2

03

1

02

39 D 40 E 41 F

Dibden Inclosure

The Noads

Crabhat Inclosure

Harford House

Hartford Heath

BEAULIEU RD

Solent Way

Beaulieu Heath

Fawley Inclosure

Flash Pond

Stonyford Pond

Holbury Purlieu

Nature Reserve

HYTHE BY PASS

A326

B3054

A326

PRU

BEAULIEU RD
LUNEDALE RD
WHINFIELD RD
SOLENT RD
MONKS WLK
CRETE COTTS
CRETE RD
VILLIERS RD
HEATHERSTONE AVE
CORBOULD RD
BEVERLEY RD
ARNWOOD AVE
BUTTS ASH LA
BARCLAY CL
BARCLAY MEWS
HAYLEY CL
FOREST FRONT
FOREST MEADOW
ROMAN RD

Great Goswell Copse

Hilltop Farm

Hill Top

Hilltop Wood

Hilltop House

Boarman Pond

Royal Oak (PH)

Moonhills Gate

Moonhills Copse

MOONHILLS LA

PALACE LA

Home Farm

Carpenters Cottage

DOCK LA

Otterwood

SUMMER LA

Otterwood Gate

Otterwood Farm House

Stock Water

Cowleys La

Cowleys Copse

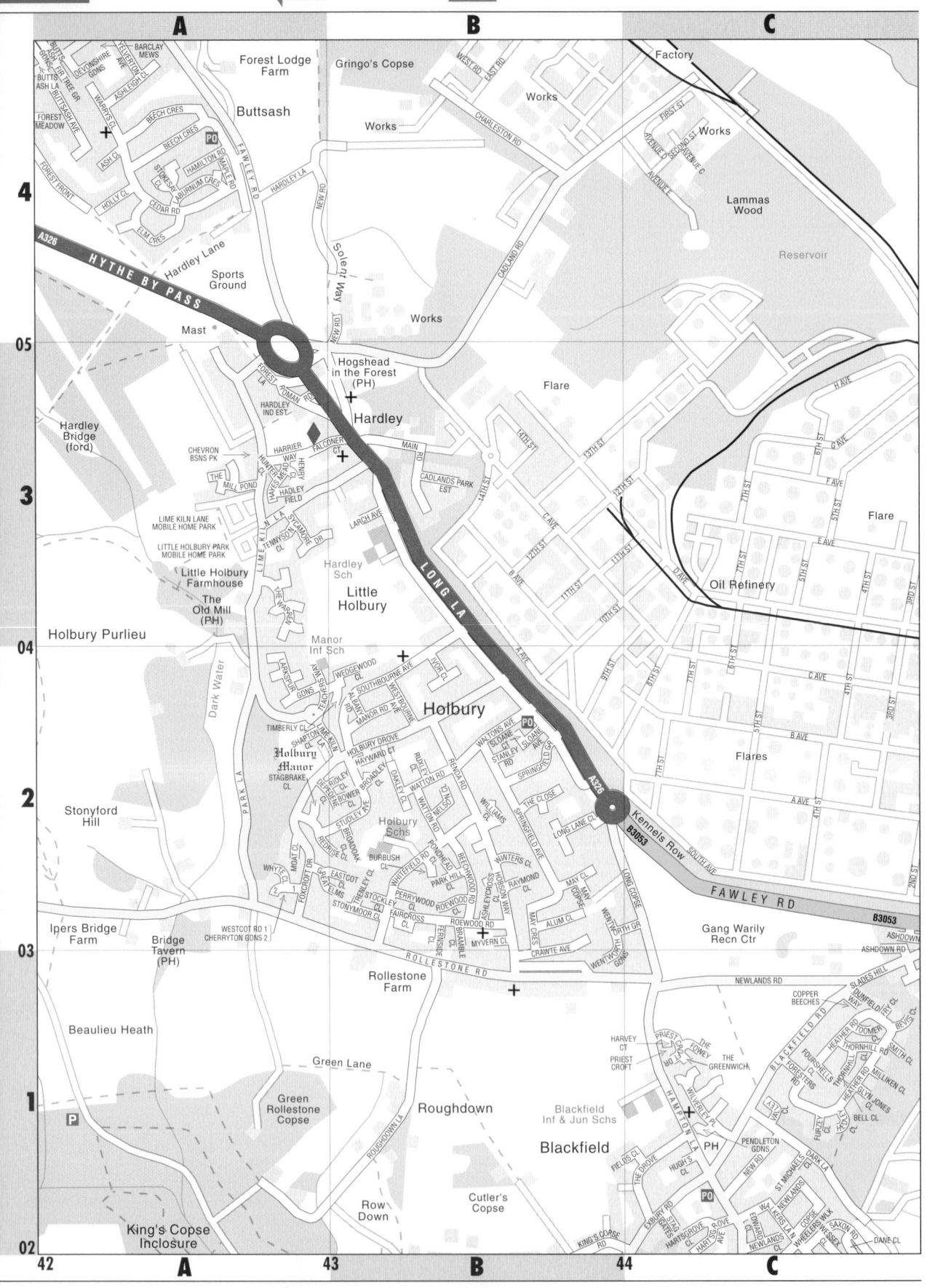

D   E   F

Jetty

Southampton Water

Cadland Creek

4

Pier

Marine Terminal

05

Foreshore N

Foreshore S
PL P.H. RD
North Trestle Rd
Burma Rd
Pier

3

Jetty Rd
Burma Rd S
South Trestle Rd
Pier

Cadland Rd
Old AGWI Rd

Bitumen Rd
Agitator Rd
Seps 4 Rd

04
Flume Rd

Ashlett Creek

2

Marsh La
Rye Paddock La
Churchfields
Copthorne Cotts

The Jolly Sailor (PH)

Hamlet Ct
Church La
Sherring Cl
Copthorne La
Copthorne La
Admirals Cl

Fawley

Orchard Cl
Woodville Rd
Edgeville Ave
Linda Rd
PO
Ashlett Cl
Ashlett Rd
Stonehills

A Ave
Forest Edge
The Paddocks
The Square
Liby

Fawley
Inf Sch
Church La
Fawley
BSNS CTR
School Rd
School Rd
Denny Cl
Falvit Fields
Cassot Rd
1 2
The Lane
Whites La
Stonehills

Ashlett

Fawley Rd
FAWLEY BY PASS

03

The Pentagon
Chapel La
Blackfield Rd
P
Meadow Way
Charles Ley Ct
Ashlett Mews 1
Rhyme Hall Mews 2

Stone Hill Farm

Stonehills

Northern Rd
Eastern Rd

Northern Access Rd

1

Fields Farm

Central Way N
Switch House Rd
Halfway Rd
Western Rd
Boiler Rd
Wright Way
Channel Mouth Rd

Fawley
Power Station

Fields Heath

Badminston La
Badminston Farm

Swing Bridge

Chy

Tom's Down

Badminston Common

Badminston Drove
B3053

Ashlett La
Southern Rd
Quayside Rd

02

45   **D**   46   **E**   47   **F**

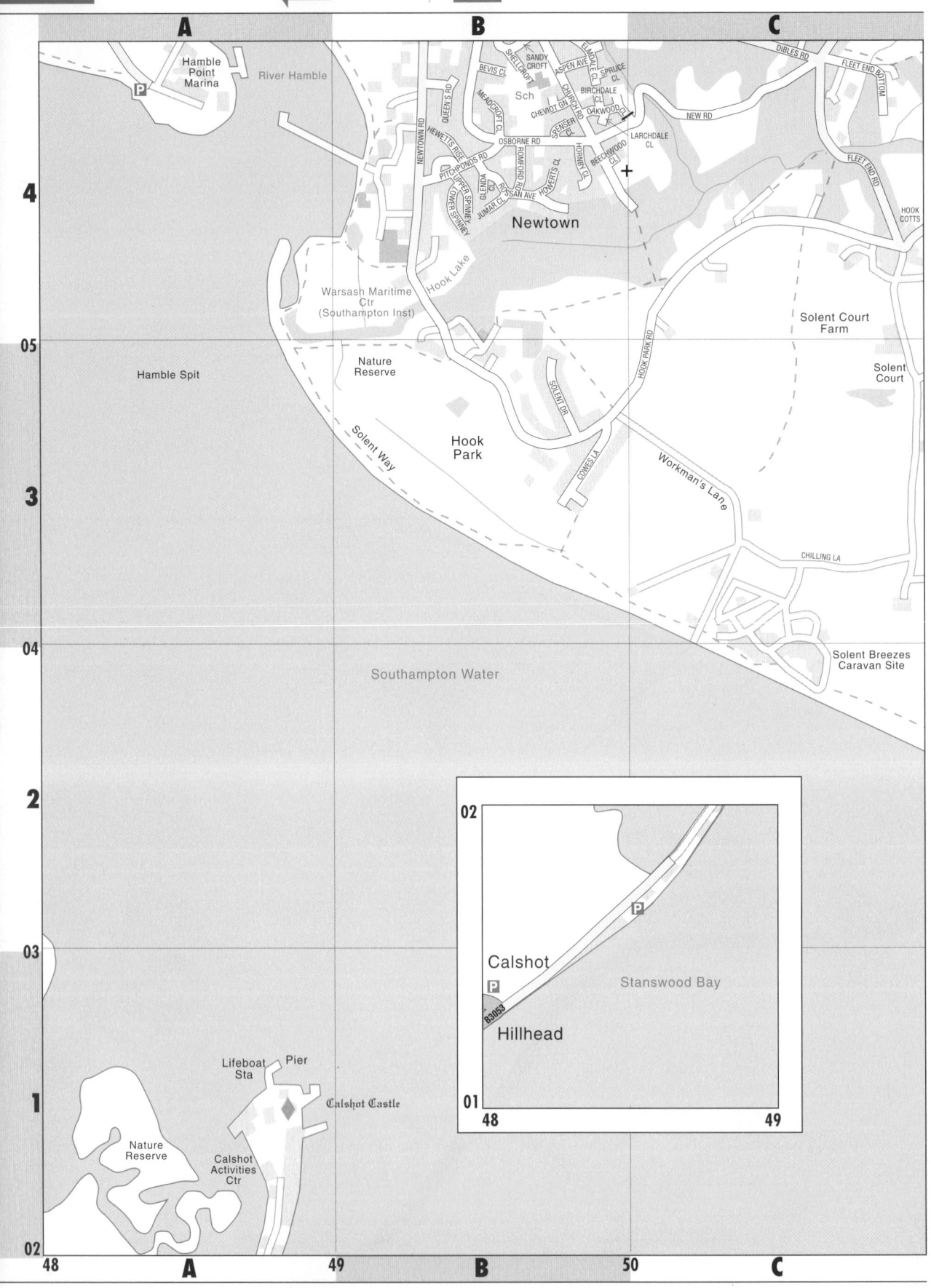

A   B   C

Hamble
Point
Marina

River Hamble

Newtown

DIBLES RD

FLEET END BOTTOM

Sch

NEW RD

FLEET END RD

HOOK
COTTS

4

Warsash Maritime
Ctr
(Southampton Inst)

Hook Lake

Solent Court
Farm

Solent
Court

05

Hamble Spit

Nature
Reserve

HOOK PARK RD

SOLENT DR

Hook
Park

Solent Way

COMBS LA

Workman's Lane

3

CHILLING LA

04

Southampton Water

Solent Breezes
Caravan Site

2

02

P

03

Calshot

P

Stanswood Bay

P

B3053

Hillhead

1

Lifeboat
Sta

Pier

Calshot Castle

01

48   49

Nature
Reserve

Calshot
Activities
Ctr

02

48   A   49   B   50   C

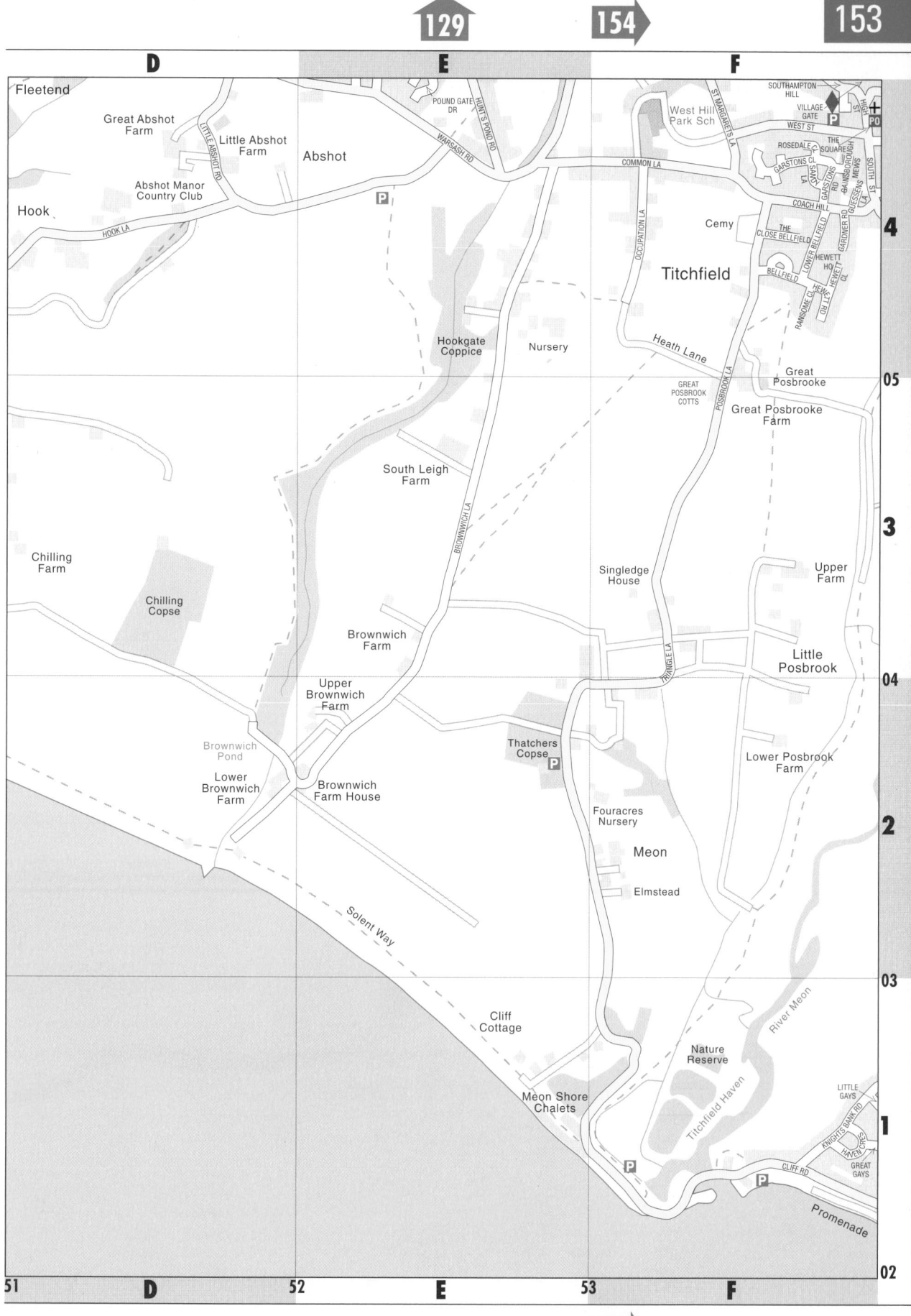

Fleetend

Great Abshot Farm
Little Abshot Farm
Abshot
Abshot Manor Country Club
Hook
HOOK LA
LITTLE ABSHOT RD

POUND GATE DR
HUNTS POND RD
WARSASH RD

SOUTHAMPTON HILL
West Hill Park Sch
VILLAGE GATE
WEST ST
THE SQUARE
ROSEDALE CL
GARSTONS CL
GARSTONS RD
BAINSBOROUGH
QUEENS MEWS
ST MARGARETS LA

COMMON LA

COACH HILL
Cemy
THE CLOSE BELLFIELD
Bellfield
LOWER BELLFIELD
HEWETT RD
HEWETT CL
GARDNER RD
RAMSDALE CL

Titchfield

Hookgate Coppice
Nursery

Heath Lane
POSBROOK LA
GREAT POSBROOK COTTS
Great Posbrooke
Great Posbrooke Farm

South Leigh Farm

Chilling Farm
Chilling Copse

BROWNWICH LA

Singledge House

Upper Farm

Little Posbrook

Brownwich Farm

TRIANGLE LA

Upper Brownwich Farm

Brownwich Pond
Lower Brownwich Farm
Brownwich Farm House

Thatchers Copse

Lower Posbrook Farm

Fouracres Nursery

Meon
Elmstead

Solent Way

Cliff Cottage

Nature Reserve

River Meon

Meon Shore Chalets

Titchfield Haven

LITTLE GAYS

KNIGHTS BANK RD
HAVEN CRES
CLIFF RD
GREAT GAYS

Promenade

05
4
3
04
2
03
1
02

51   D   52   E   53   F

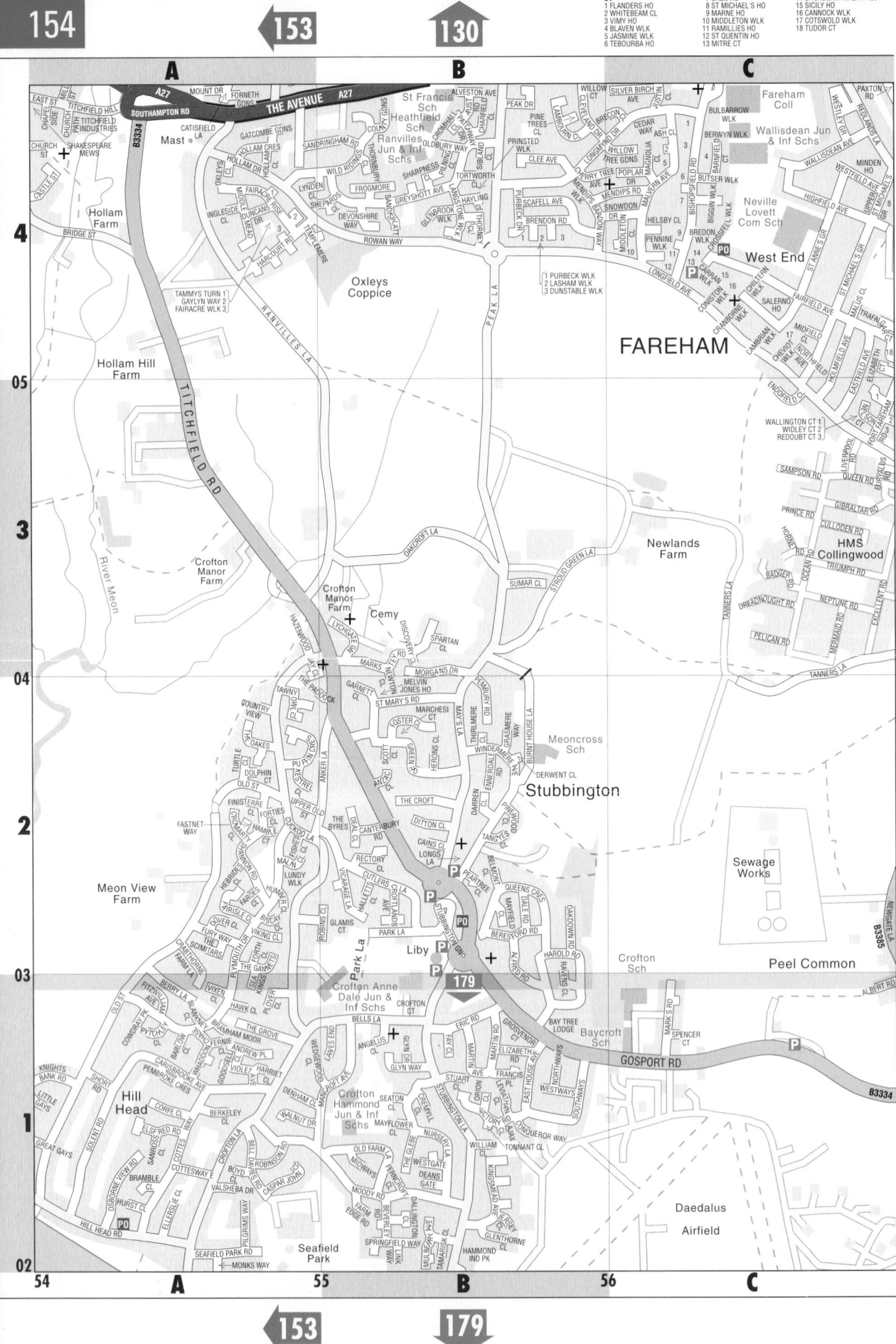

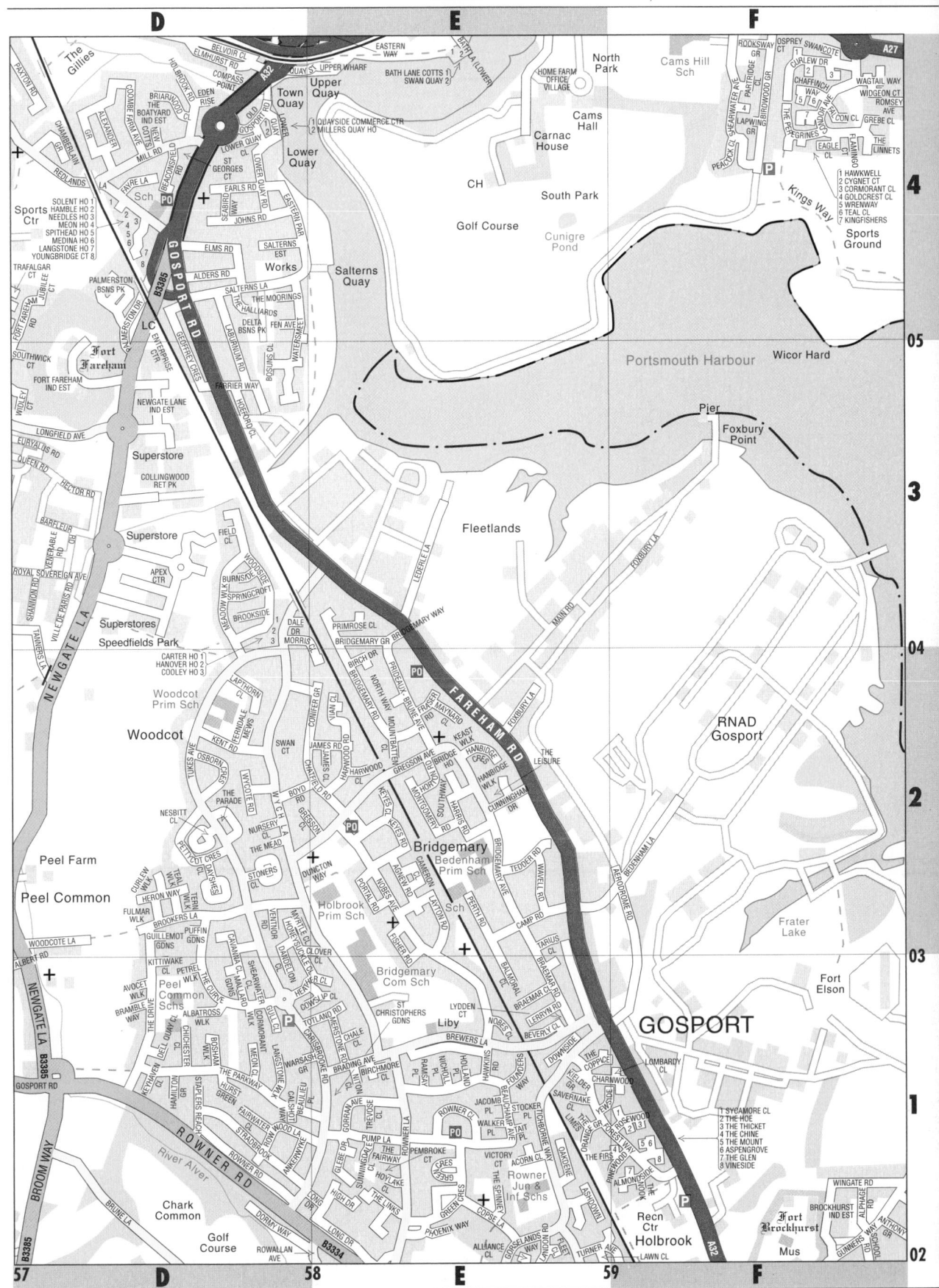

155
132

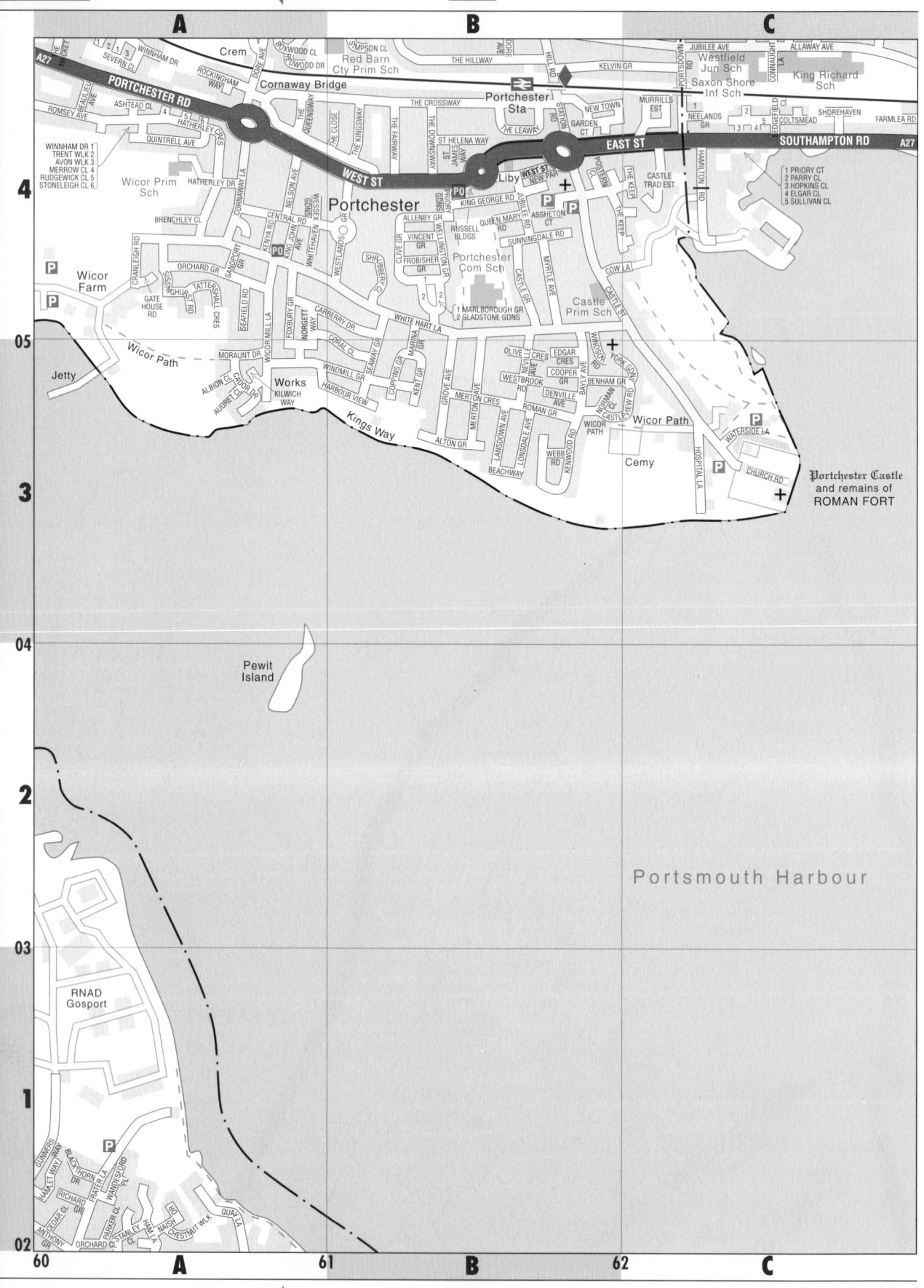

D4
1 PADDOCK WLK
2 WATERSEDGE RD
3 DELLFIELD CL
4 BELNEY HO
5 WINDERMERE HO
6 PAULSGROVE ENT CTR

E4
1 ARTILLERY CL
2 DOWNTON HO
3 COTSWOLD
4 MELLOR CL
5 MALDON RD
6 HADLEIGH RD

7 HOCKLEY CL
8 PEBMARSH CL
9 WYMERING MANOR CL
10 BLACKWATER CL
F4
1 GLEBEFIELD GDNS
2 TANKERTON CL

F4
3 DYMCHURCH HO
4 ODEON BLDGS
5 NEPTUNE HO
6 MALLOW CL
7 ELIZABETH CT
8 STUART CT
9 TUDOR CT

F4
9 WINDSOR CT
10 ODEON BLDGS
11 CHIPSTEAD HO
12 CHIPSTEAD HO
13 NORTHERN BLDGS
14 ALDROKE ST

15 BEATRICE MEWS
16 ORFORD CT
17 GLENLEIGH CT
18 GLENLEIGH AVE
19 MEGAN CT
20 SELWYN CT
21 VINE CT

133 158 **157**

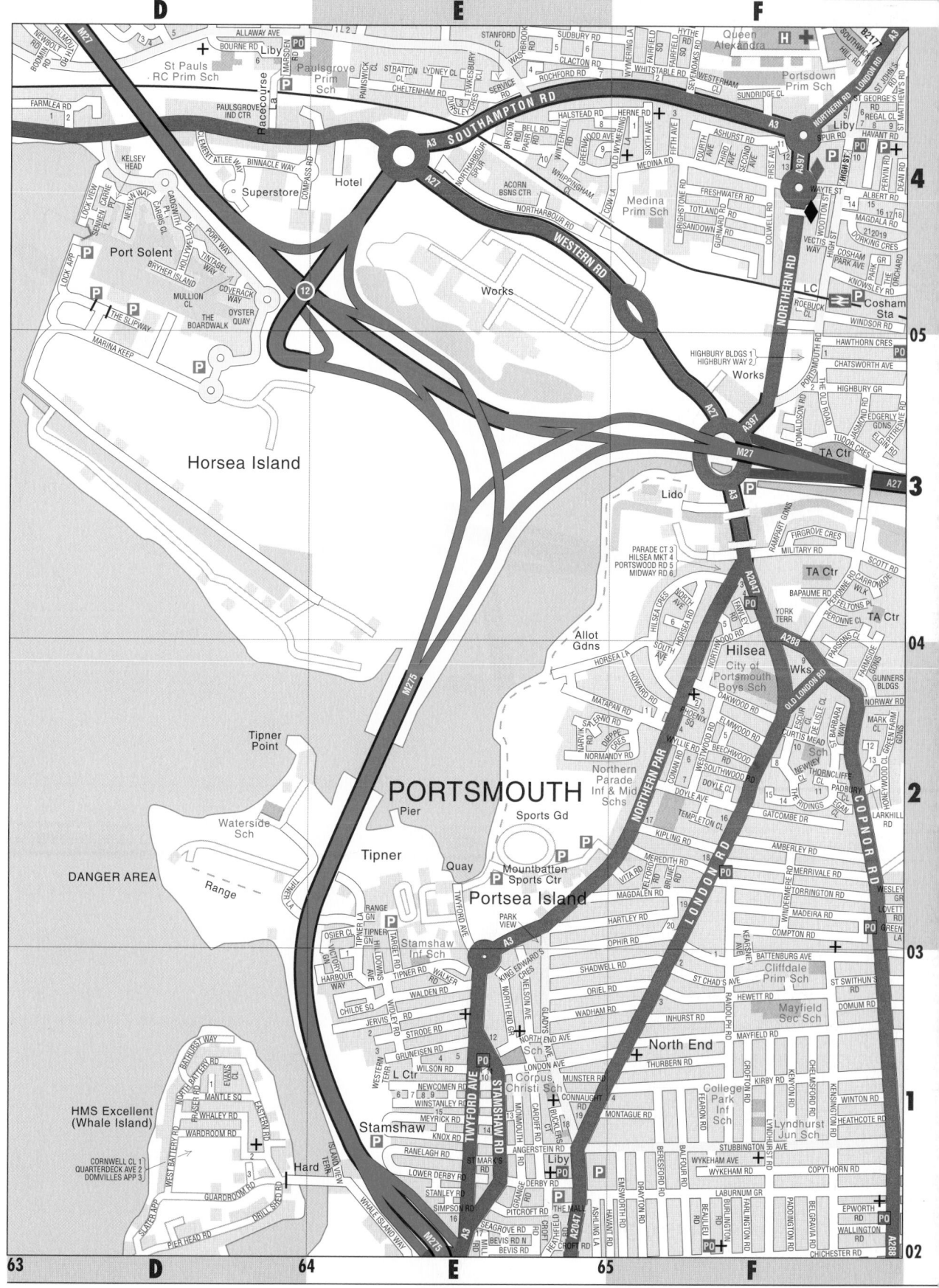

E1
1 SOMERVILLE PL
2 SCOTT HO
3 HASTINGS HO
4 OAK LODGE
5 STAMPSEY CT
6 BILL STILLWELL CT
7 SMEATON ST
8 NEWCOMEN CT
9 SHADWELL CT

10 EDEN TERR
11 PENROSE CL
12 HARRISON HO
13 WEYMOUTH HO
14 STAMSHAW HO
15 MEYRICK HO
16 ST JOHN'S CT
17 ST NICHOLAS FLATS
18 WHITES CT
19 THE PROMENADE

182 158

F1
1 BURGUNDY TERR
2 SHACKLETON HO
3 VERNON CT
4 KIRBY CT
F2
1 FALKLANDS RD
2 ST FRANCIS CT
3 DAME ELIZABETH KELLY CT
4 CORONATION EVENTIDE HOMES

5 EASTWOOD RD
6 GERARD HO
7 LORING HO
8 OLDGATE GDNS
9 WALBERANT BLDGS
10 KNIGHTSTONE CT
11 GARRICK HO
12 BREECH CL
13 BENHAM DR
14 WHITECROSS GDNS

15 BALDERTON CL
16 DOYLE CT
17 PARK ROYAL
18 KIPLING BLDGS
19 MAGDALEN CT
20 BRIGHAM CL

158

A4
1 WALBERTON CT
2 DOMEY CT
3 PARK MANSIONS
4 WIDLEY CT

157   134

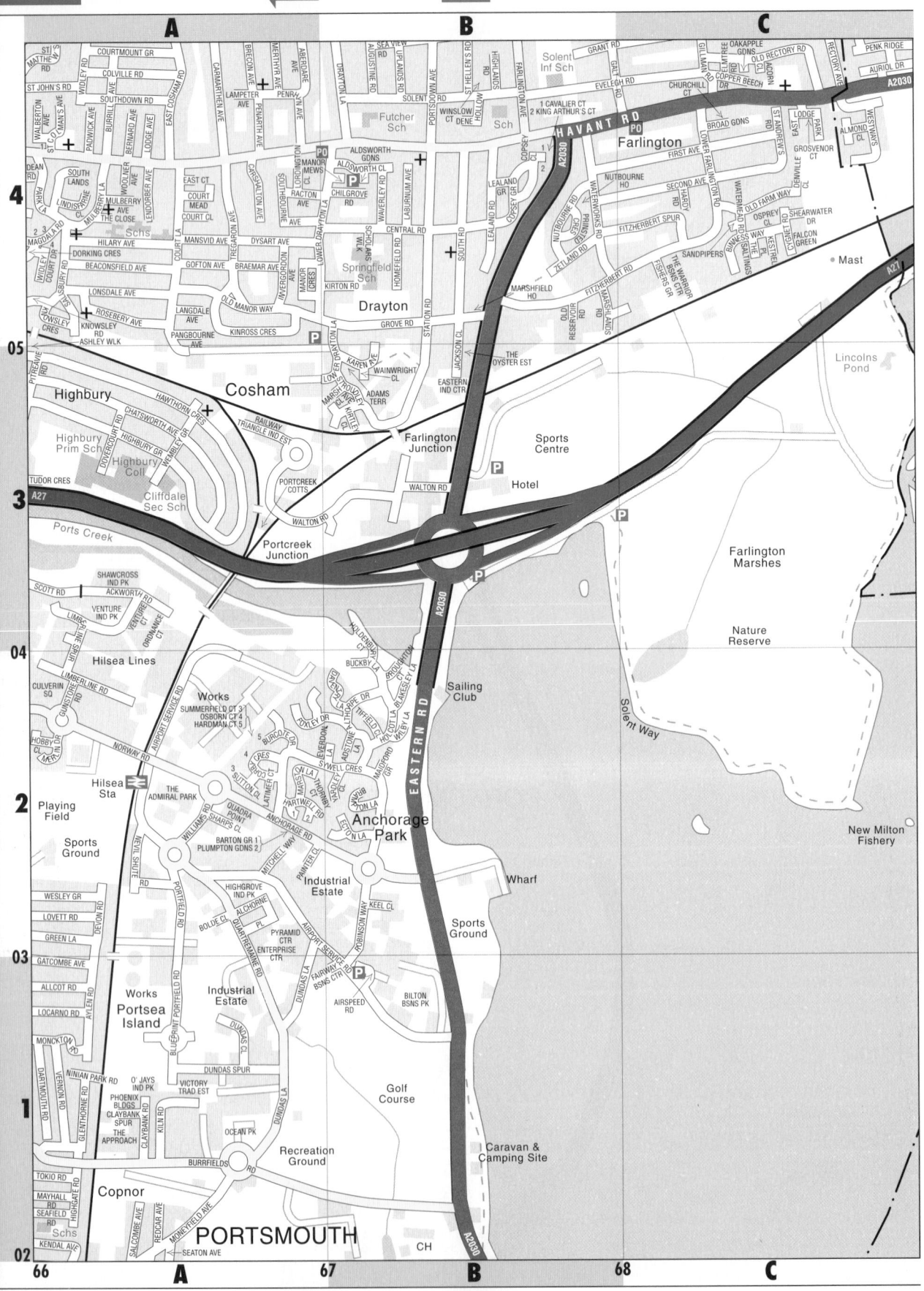

D   E   F

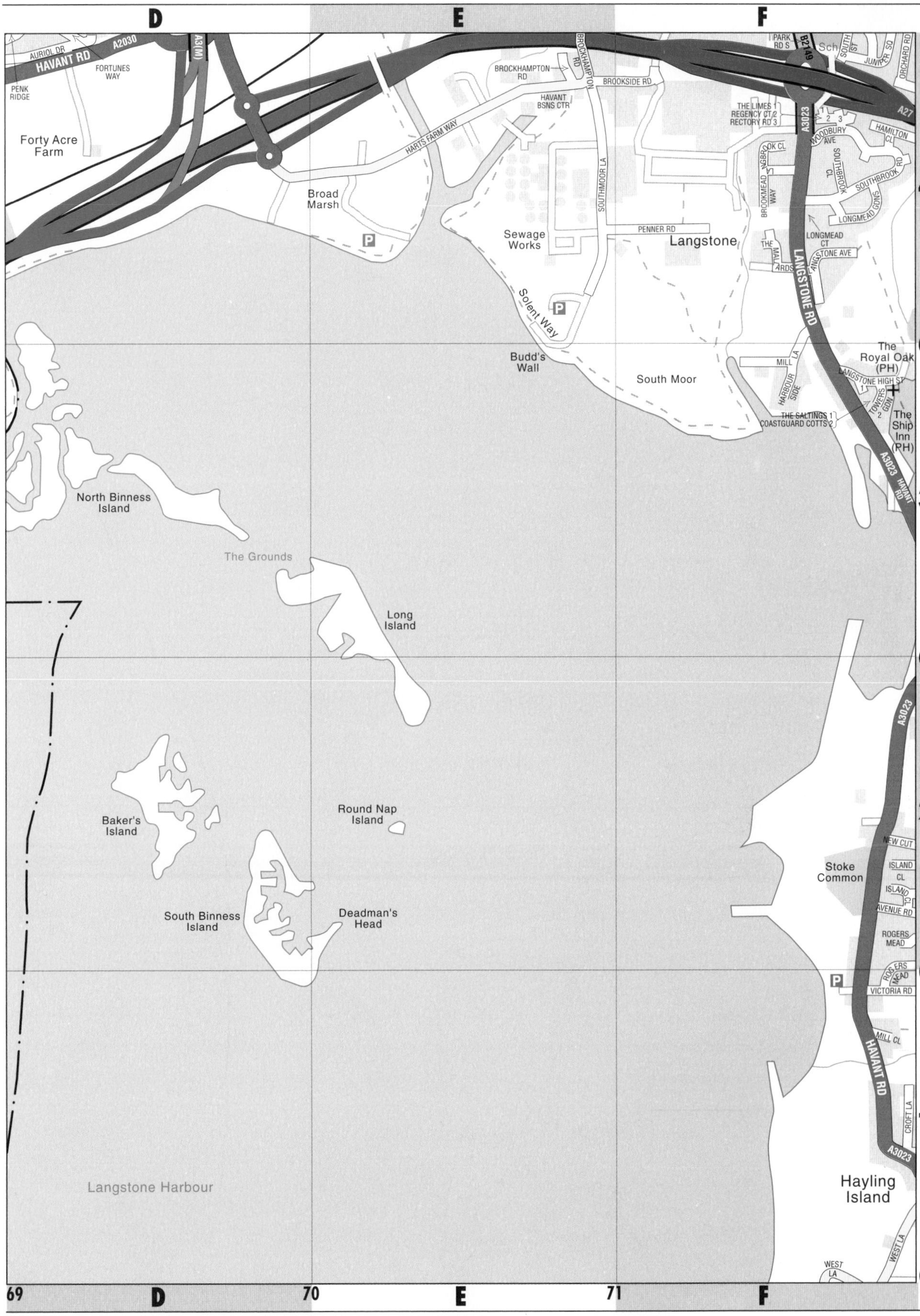

AURIOL DR
HAVANT RD A2030
A3(M)
FORTUNES WAY
PENK RIDGE

PARK RD S
B2149
Sout...
ORCHARD RD
JUNR

BROCKHAMPTON RD
BROCKHAMPTON RD
BROOKSIDE RD
A27
A2023

Forty Acre Farm

HARTS FARM WAY

HAVANT BSNS CTR

THE LIMES
REGENCY CT
RECTORY RD 3

HAMILTON CL
WOODBURY AVE
SOUTHBROOK
SOUTHBROOK RD

Broad Marsh

P

SOUTHMOOR LA

Sewage Works

PENNER RD

Langstone

NGBROOK
BROOKMEAD
WAY
OK CL
LONGMEAD CT
LONGMEAD GDNS
LONGMEAD
THE
MALL
ARDS
NGSTONE AVE

4

Solent Way

P

Budd's Wall

South Moor

LANGSTONE RD

MILL
HARBOUR
SIDE
LANGSTONE HIGH ST
LANGSTONE
NTERS
GDN

The Royal Oak (PH)

05

THE SALTINGS 1
COASTGUARD COTTS 2

The Ship Inn (PH)

A3023 HAVANT RD

North Binness Island

The Grounds

3

Long Island

A3023

04

Baker's Island

Round Nap Island

2

Stoke Common

NEW CUT
ISLAND CL
ISLAND
AVENUE RD
ROGERS MEAD

South Binness Island

Deadman's Head

ROGERS MEAD
VICTORIA RD

P

03

HAVANT RD

Langstone Harbour

CROFT LA

Hayling Island

A3023

1

WEST LA
WEST LA

02

69   D   70   E   71   F

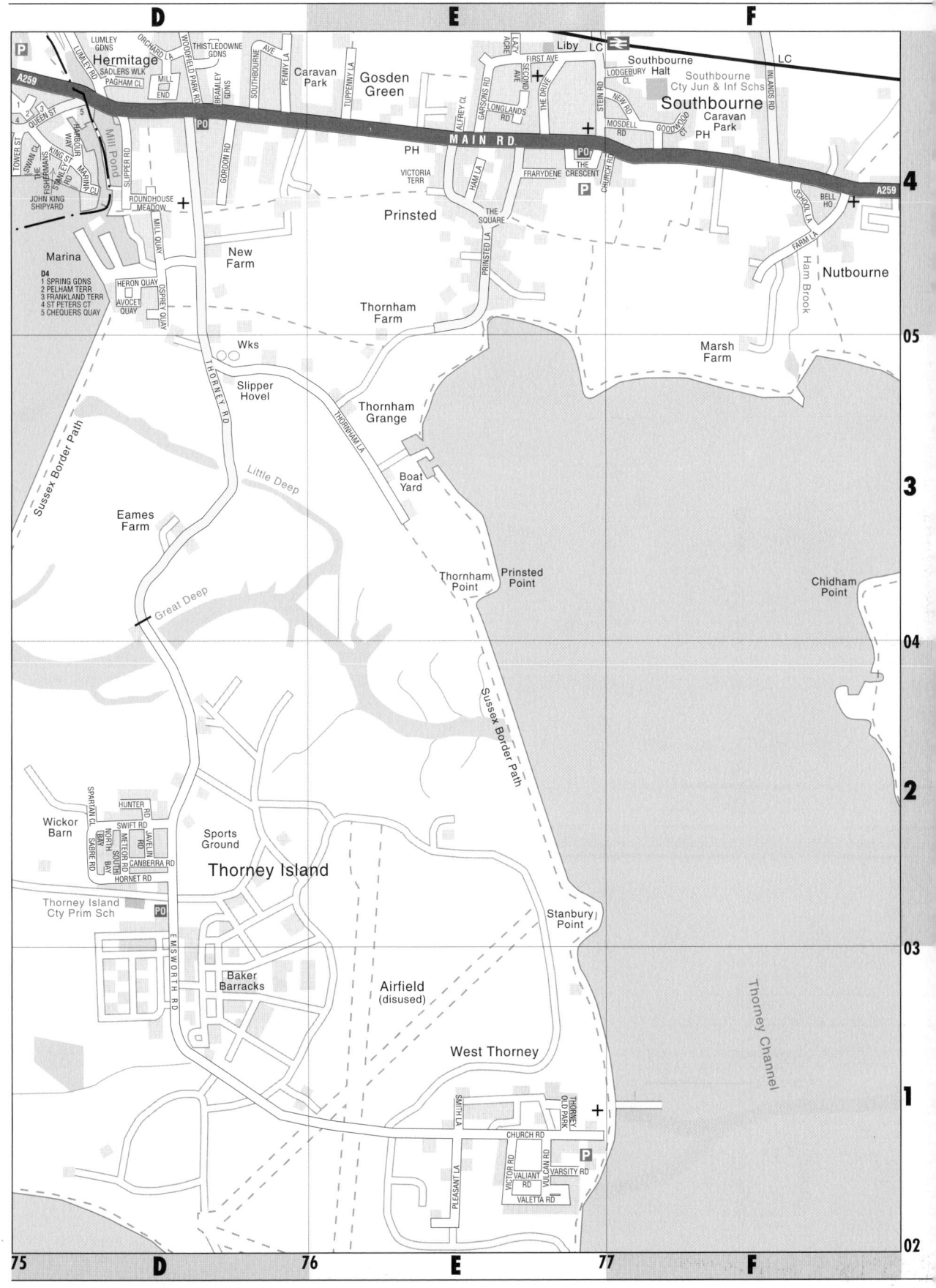

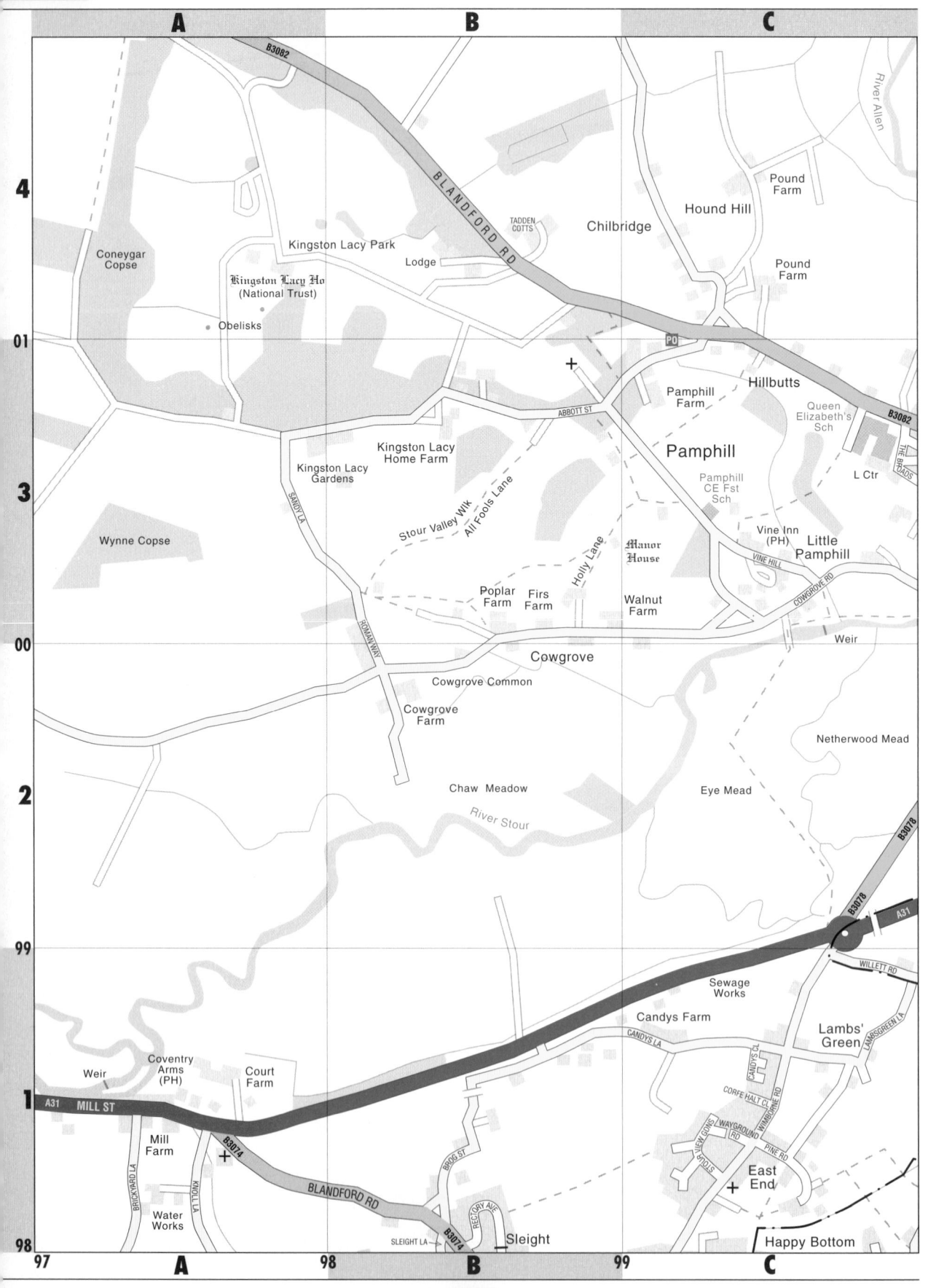

A   B   C

4

Coneygar
Copse

Kingston Lacy Park

Lodge

Kingston Lacy Ho
(National Trust)

Obelisks

TADDEN
COTTS

Chilbridge

Hound Hill

Pound
Farm

Pound
Farm

Hillbutts

01

PO

Pamphill
Farm

Queen
Elizabeth's
Sch

THE BEADS

ABBOTT ST

Pamphill

Kingston Lacy
Home Farm

Kingston Lacy
Gardens

Pamphill
CE Fst
Sch

L Ctr

3

SANDY LA

Stour Valley Wlk

All Fools Lane

Vine Inn
(PH)

Little
Pamphill

Wynne Copse

Holly Lane

Manor
House

VINE HILL

COWGROVE RD

Poplar
Farm

Firs
Farm

Walnut
Farm

ROMAN WAY

Weir

00

Cowgrove

Cowgrove Common

Netherwood Mead

Cowgrove
Farm

2

Chaw Meadow

Eye Mead

River Stour

99

B3078

B3078

A31

WILLETT RD

Sewage
Works

Candys Farm

Lambs'
Green

LAMBSGREEN LA

CANDYS LA

CANDYS CL

Weir

Coventry
Arms
(PH)

Court
Farm

CORFE HALT CL

WIMBORNE RD

1

A31   MILL ST

Mill
Farm

B3074

BRICKYARD LA

KNOLL LA

BLANDFORD RD

BOG ST

RECTORY AVE

STOUR VIEW GDNS

WAYGROUND RD

PINE RD

East
End

Water
Works

SLEIGHT LA

B3074

Sleight

Happy Bottom

98

97   98   99

A   B   C

164 ▶

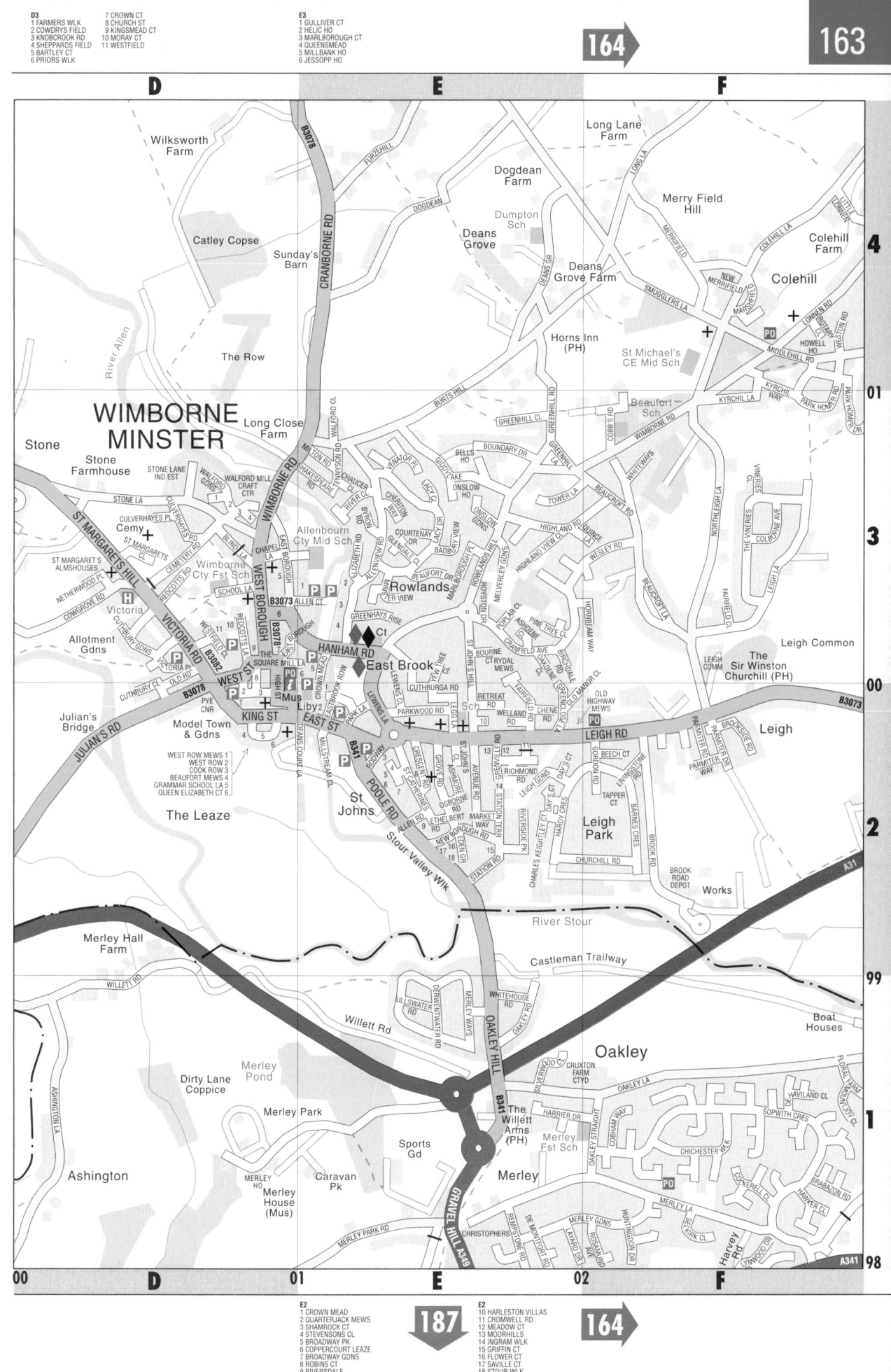

187

164 ▶

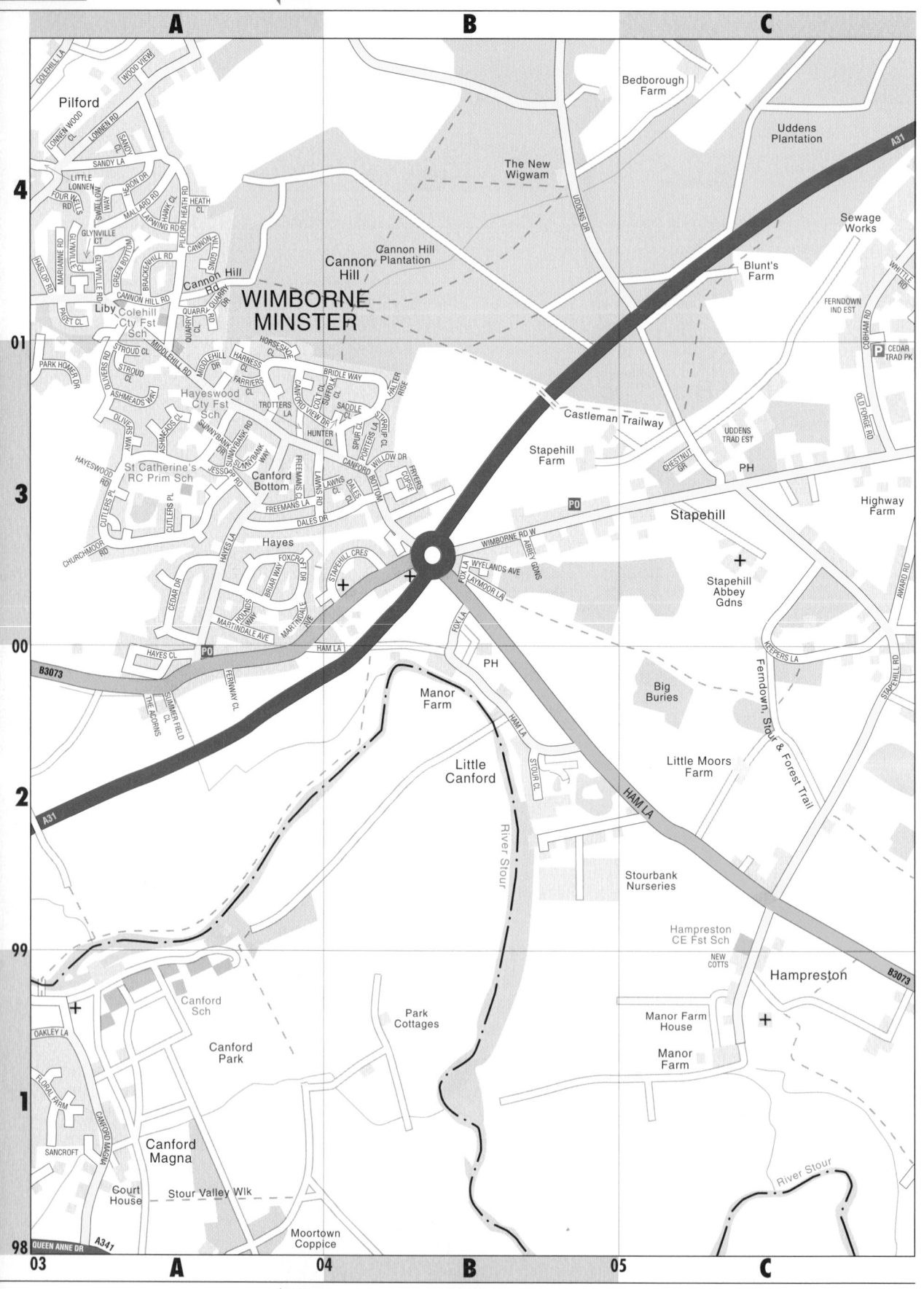

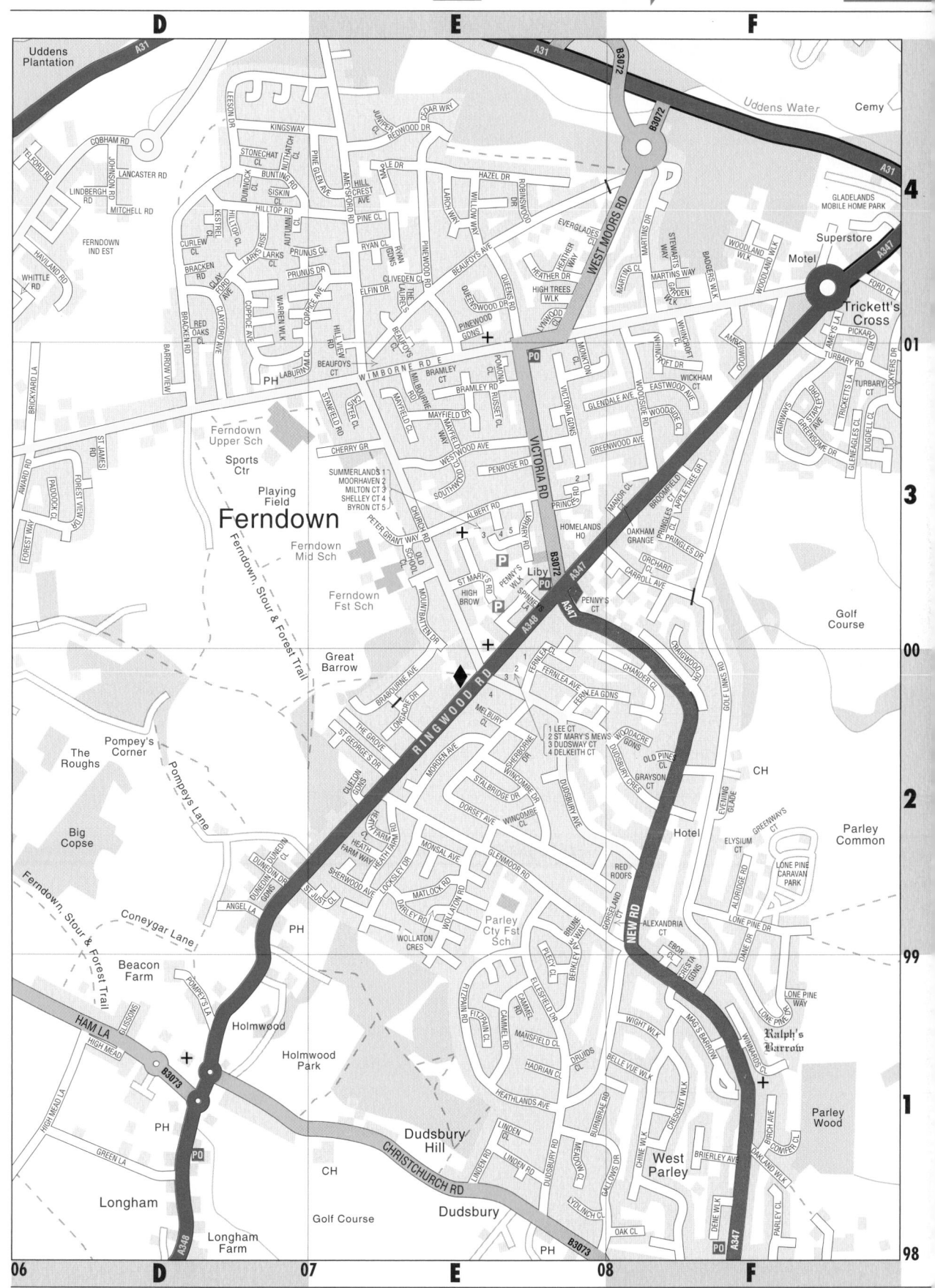

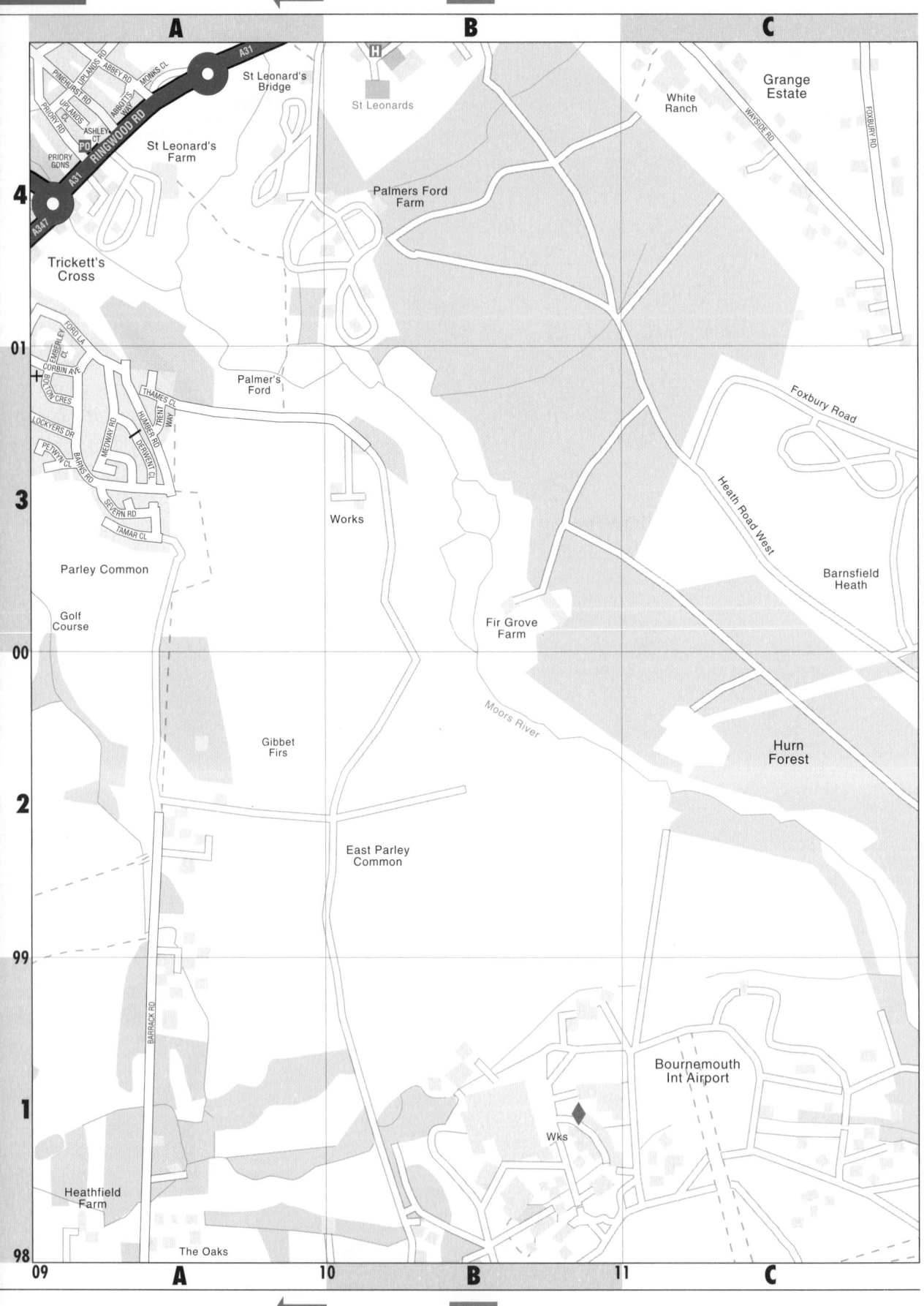

165 139

A   **B**   **C**

St Leonard's Bridge
St Leonards
White Ranch
Grange Estate
FOXBURY RD

UPLANDS RD ABBEY RD MONKS CL
A31
PINEHURST RD ASHLEY CT ABBOTTS WAY
UPLANDS CL
PRIORY RD PO
PRIORY GDNS RINGWOOD RD
A31
A347

St Leonard's Farm
Palmers Ford Farm
WAYSIDE RD

Trickett's Cross

01

AMBERLEY CL FORD LA
BURTON CRES CORBIN AVE
LOCKYERS DR HUMBER RD THAMES CL
PETWYN CL MEDWAY RD TRENT WAY
BARNES RD DERWENT CL
SEVERN RD
TAMAR CL

Palmer's Ford
Foxbury Road

Works
Heath Road West
Barnsfield Heath

3

Parley Common

Golf Course
Fir Grove Farm

00
Moors River
Hurn Forest

Gibbet Firs

2
East Parley Common

99
BARRACK RD

1
Bournemouth Int Airport
Wks

Heathfield Farm

98
The Oaks

09   **A**   10   **B**   11   **C**

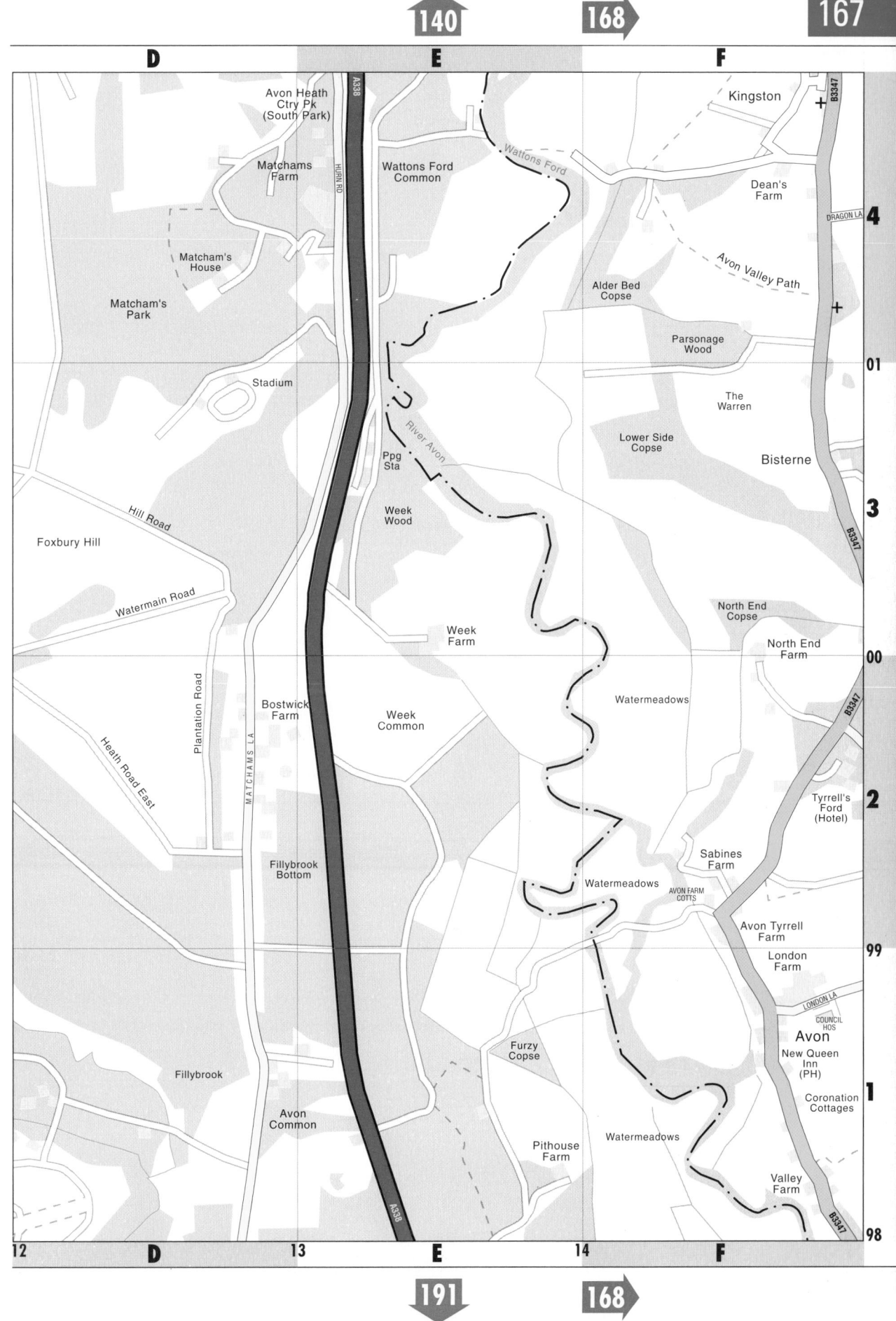

D   E   F

Kingston

Avon Heath
Ctry Pk
(South Park)

Matchams
Farm

Wattons Ford
Common

Dean's
Farm

Matcham's
House

Alder Bed
Copse

Parsonage
Wood

Matcham's
Park

Stadium

The
Warren

Lower Side
Copse

Bisterne

Hill Road

Foxbury Hill

River Avon

Ppg
Sta

Week
Wood

Watermain Road

North End
Copse

Week
Farm

North End
Farm

Plantation Road

Bostwick
Farm

Week
Common

Watermeadows

Heath Road East

Tyrrell's
Ford
(Hotel)

Fillybrook
Bottom

Sabines
Farm

Watermeadows

AVON FARM
COTTS

Avon Tyrrell
Farm

London
Farm

LONDON LA

COUNCIL
HOS

Furzy
Copse

Avon

New Queen
Inn
(PH)

Fillybrook

Coronation
Cottages

Avon
Common

Pithouse
Farm

Watermeadows

Valley
Farm

MATCHAMS LA

HURN RD

A338

B3347

DRAGON LA

Avon Valley Path

Wattons Ford

4

01

3

00

2

99

1

98

12   D   13   E   14   F

A   **B**   **C**

Wilkin's Farm

Sandford

DRAGON LA

4

Keepers Copse

Selfsown Firs

Upper Bisterne Farm

Three Corner Copse

01

Bisterne Manor

Hain Hill

Broad Heath

3

Gardens Cottage

Ripley Wood

Ringwood Lodge

B3347

Lower Bisterne Farm

Summergates

Ripley

00

Bunnybrook

North Ripley Farm

Blackberry Farm

Whistlers Copse

ANNA LA

Ball's Copse

Ford

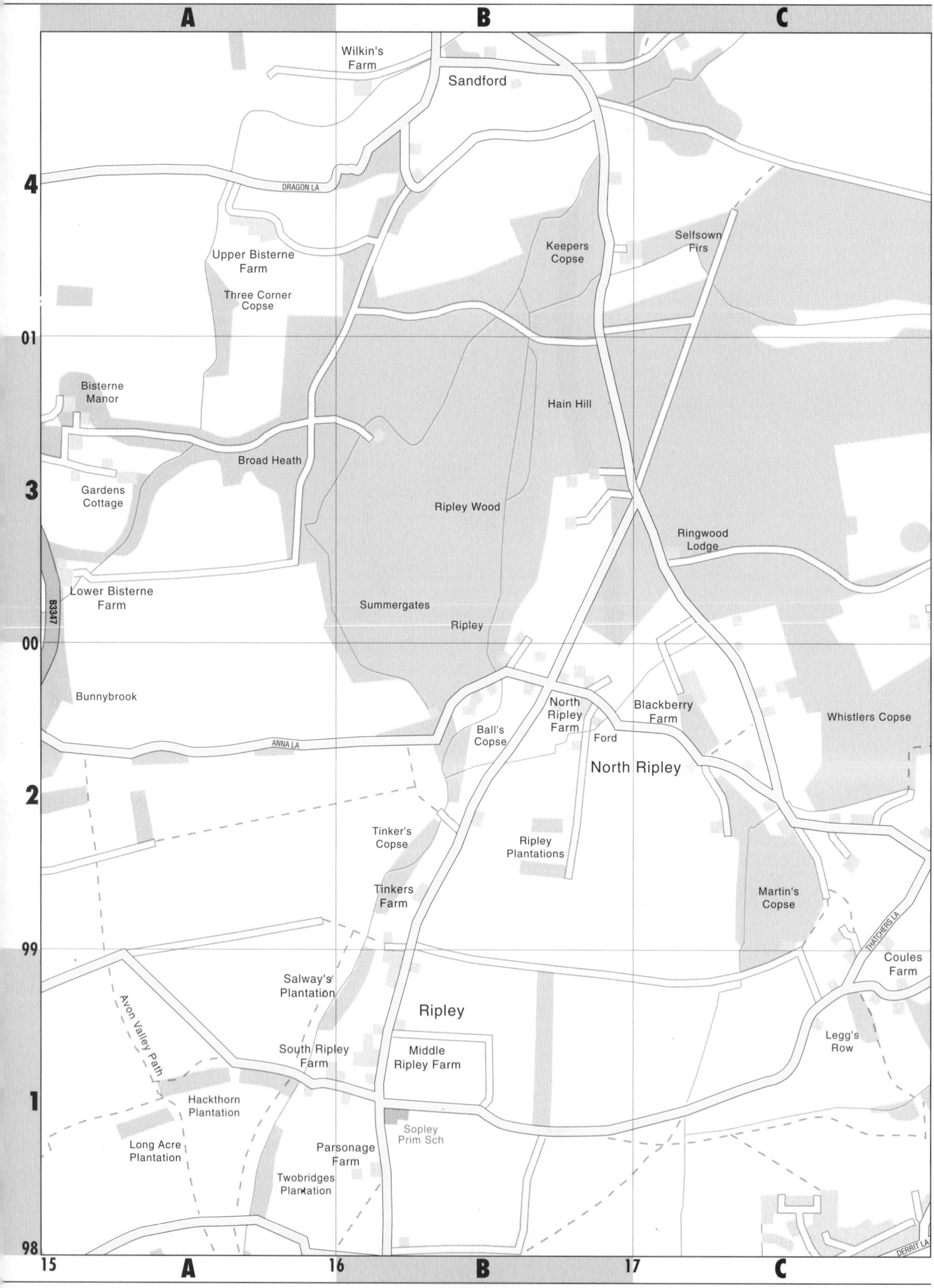

North Ripley

2

Tinker's Copse

Ripley Plantations

Martin's Copse

Tinkers Farm

THATCHERS LA

99

Coules Farm

Salway's Plantation

Ripley

Avon Valley Path

South Ripley Farm

Middle Ripley Farm

Legg's Row

1

Hackthorn Plantation

Long Acre Plantation

Parsonage Farm

Sopley Prim Sch

Twobridges Plantation

DERRIT LA

98
15   **A**   **16**   **B**   **17**   **C**

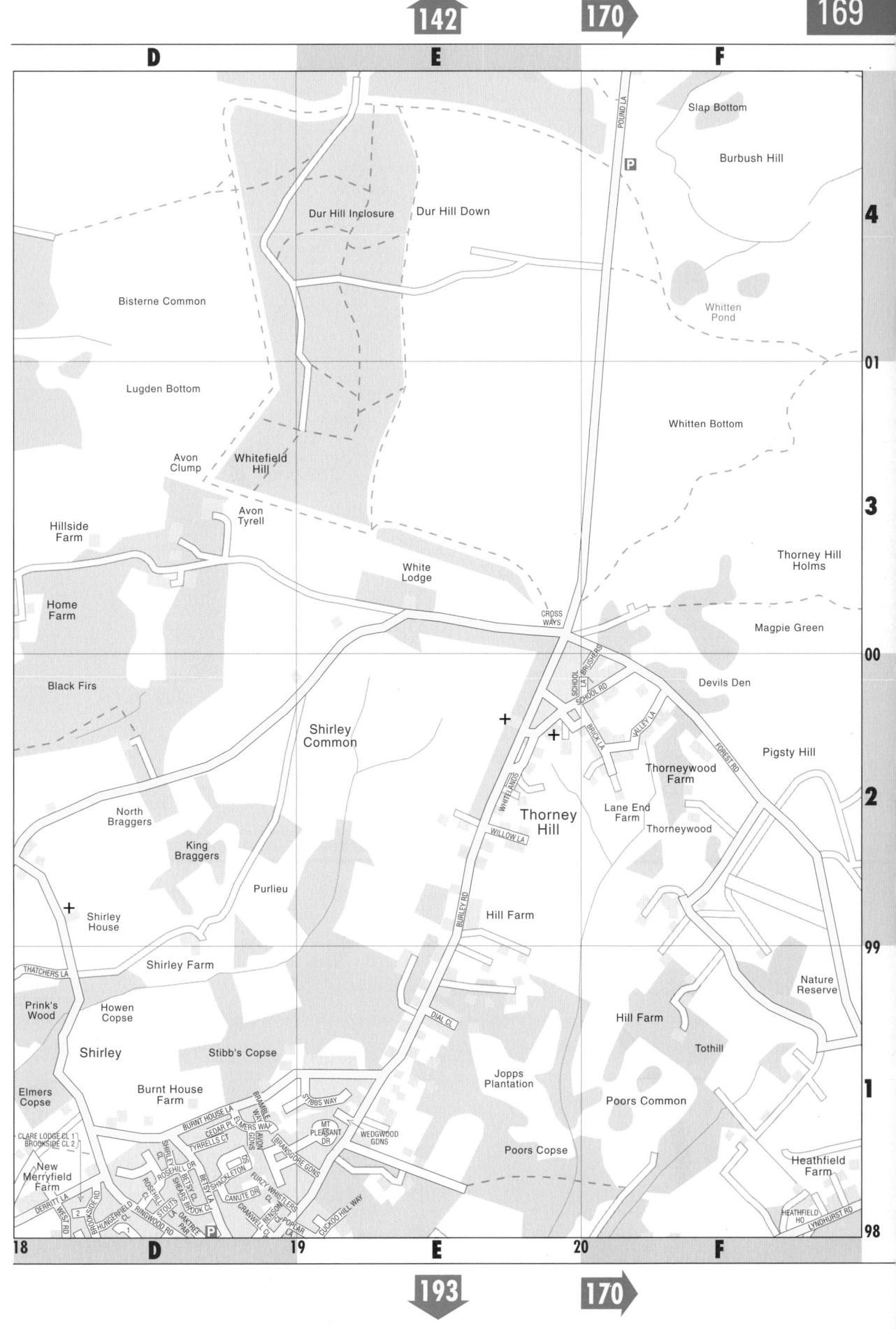

169
143

169
194

D E F

4
01
3
00
2
99
1
98

30 D 31 E 32 F

Brockenhurst Sta
LYMINGTON RD
A337
1 AVENUE RD
2 EAST BANK RD
3 WOODSIDE

Brockenhurst Park
Brockenhurst Park Stables
Bakers Copse

Perrywood Ironshill Inclosure
Furze Hill
Dilton
Dilton Copse

Tile Barn Farm
TILEBARN LA
CHURCH LA

Newlands Copse

Holly Bush Farm
Dawkins Bottom
Setley
Roydon Manor
Dilton Gardens

The Filly Inn
Setley Farm
Setley Common
Calveslease Copse

Lymington River
Howe Copse

Blazemore Farm

Sandy Down
SANDY DOWN
Sandy Down
Heywood Farm

COBBLERS CNR
HURSTLY LA
LOWER SANDY DOWN LA
The Old Mill House

Race Plain

The Hobler (PH)
Heywood Manor
Rodlease Rough
ROYDEN LA
RODLEASE LA
CHURCH LA

Battramsley Lodge
Boldre Grange
Great Oaks Farm
Dunsford Farm
Rodlease House
Slade Farm

JEALOUS LA
Battramsley
Battramsley Farm
Boldre
Pilley
William Gilpin CE Prim Sch
GILPIN CL
BURNT HOUSE LA
HUDSON DAVIES CL

Shirley Holms
SHIRLEY HOLMS
Passford Water
Battramsley Cross
Battramsley House
A337
The Red Lion (PH)
Hill House Sch
ROPE HILL
TWEEDLA
BOLDRE LA
SHALLOW LA
PILLEY HILL
SCHOOL LA
Fleur-de-lys Inn

173
147

A **B** **C**

Lodge Heath

Stockley Inclosure

Stockley Cottage

B3055

Hawkhill Inclosure

P

B3055

4

Dilton Common

01

Dilton Farm

Hatchet Moor

Beaulieu Heath

P

3

Little Dilton Farm

B3054

Two Bridges Bottom

00

Greenmoor

Sheffield Copse

Deep Moor

Crockford Stream

2

Whitemoor Rough

P

99

Crockford Bridge

Allot Gdns

Lower Crockford Bottom

Pilley Bailey

Fords

P

WOOD HOUSE LA

Bull Hill

1

PILLEY BAILEY

Pilley GN

MAY LA

PILLEY ST

PO

LUCKY LA

JORDANS LA

HOLLY LA

BULL HILL

Norley Inclosure

Wormstall Wood

BURNT HOUSE LA

Pilley

P

Norley Farm

98

WARBORNE LA

B3054

NORLEYWOOD RD

33 **A** **34** **B** **35** **C**

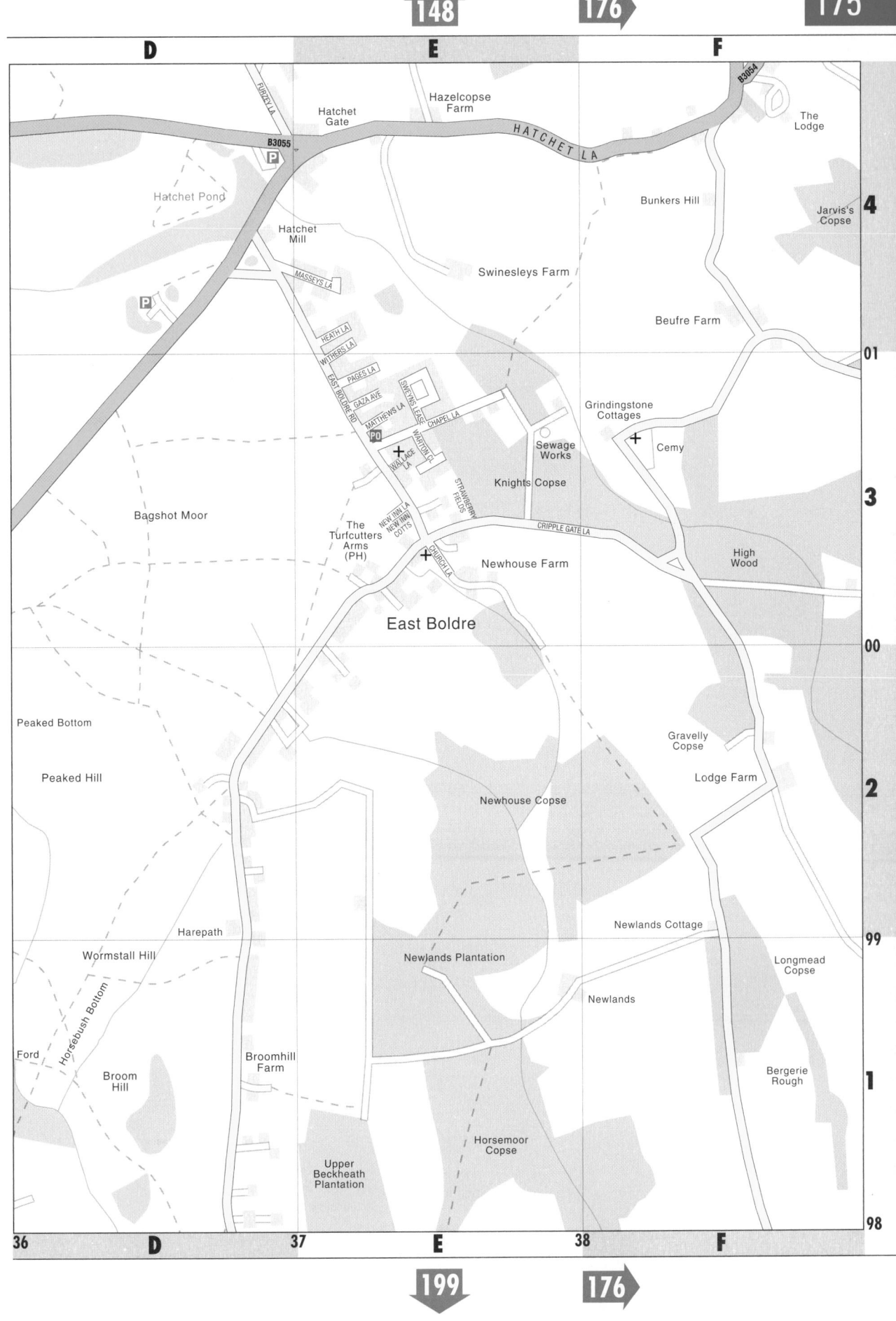

D E F

B3055

B3054

The Lodge

Hatchet Gate

Hazelcopse Farm

HATCHET LA

Bunkers Hill

Jarvis's Copse

4

Hatchet Pond

P

P

Hatchet Mill

MASSEYS LA

Swinesleys Farm

Beufre Farm

P

HEATH LA

WITHERS LA

PAGES LA

EAST BOLDRE RD

GAZA AVE

MATTHEWS LA

SMETONS LEASE

CHAPEL LA

WHARTON LA

STRAWBERRY FIELDS

Grindingstone Cottages

01

PO

WALLACE LA

Sewage Works

Knights Copse

Cemy

3

Bagshot Moor

NEW INN LA

NEW INN COTTS

The Turfcutters Arms (PH)

CHURCH LA

CRIPPLE GATE LA

High Wood

Newhouse Farm

East Boldre

00

Peaked Bottom

Peaked Hill

Gravelly Copse

Lodge Farm

2

Newhouse Copse

Newlands Cottage

99

Harepath

Wormstall Hill

Newlands Plantation

Longmead Copse

Horsebush Bottom

Newlands

Ford

Broomhill Farm

Broom Hill

Bergerie Rough

1

Upper Beckheath Plantation

Horsemoor Copse

98

36 D 37 E 38 F

Carpenters
Dock

Oxleys

THE HUMMICKS

Oxleys
Copse

DOCK LA

Landing
Stage

Bailey's
Hard

Spearbed
Copse

Sims
Wood

Stock
Copse

Cowleys Lane

SUMMER LA

Steerleys
Copse

Keeping
Copse

Solent Way

Keeping
Marsh

Keeping
Farm

Keeping

Marina

Gilbury
Hard

Dungehill
Copse

Beaulieu River

Jetty

Ashen
Wood

Little
Purnel

Quay

Hotel

Mus

P

Bucklers
Hard

Clobb
Gorse

Clobb
Copse

Foul
Bush

Solent Way

Salternshill
Copse

Tylers
Copse

Old Park Wood

Clobb
Farm

Salternshill

99

Lodge
Plantation

Coopers Wood

Kitchers
Rough

Drokes

Shadebush
Copse

Landing
Stages

St Leonards
Grange

Gins

GINS LA

Chapel
Tithe Barn

St Leonard's
Farm

WARREN LA

D E F

Row Down
KING'S COPSE RD
East Stock Copse
Kings Copse Inclosure
Meadow Close Copse
Gatewood Bridge
Blackwell Common
Cemy
Ford
JANES CL
WHEELERS WLK
NORMAN RD
WALKER'S LANE N
WIESSEX RD
LOXING
CEDRIC RD
SAXON RD
DANE CL
HAMPTON GDNS
HAMPTON CL
NORTHAMPTON LA
HOLLY RD
HAMPTON LA
Blackfield
Recn Gd
WHITEHAVEN HOME PK
THORNBURY AVE
CHAPEL LA
WALKER'S LANE S
GREEN LA
4
MOPLEY CL
NICHOLAS RD
CLARE GDNS
MOPLEY
FOREST GATE

THE GLADE
LEA RD
SHERWOOD WAY
BOWLANDL
KING'S RIDE
CHALEWOOD RD
BERNWOOD
ST FRANCIS RD
ST DUNSTAN'S RD
Langley
FOXHAYES LA
4 5
FOXGLADE LA
FORG'E RD

1 THE MEWS
2 FOXY PADDOCK
3 FOXLANDS
4 FOX'S WLK
5 FOXGLADE

FORESTERS GATE
CHARM WOOD
WYCHWOOD DR
S LEY RD
LANGLEY LODGE GDNS
PH

Gatewood Hill
Gatewood Farm House
WEST COMMON
WEST COMMON
HOME FARM LA
LEFE RD
Nursery
SUMMER LA
Whitefield Farm
HOMER MOBILE HOME PARK
West Common
Yard Wood
Main Drive
Nursery
Dark Water
3
Exbury Bridge
Chale Wood
East Wood
Whitefield Rough
Witchers Copse
Exbury Gdns
NEW COTTS
CRESCENT COTTS
Exbury House
PO
Recn Grd
Exbury
00
East Hill Farm
St Mary's Spring
Upper Exbury
The Green
2
Salterns Copse
Haxland Pits
Lepe Farm
Grassy Copse
Pophams Wood
Aldermoor
The Moor
99
Lower Exbury House
Three Stones
Little Haxland Copse
Inchmery House
Lepe House
Lower Exbury
Quay
Groynes
1

98
42 D 43 E 44 F

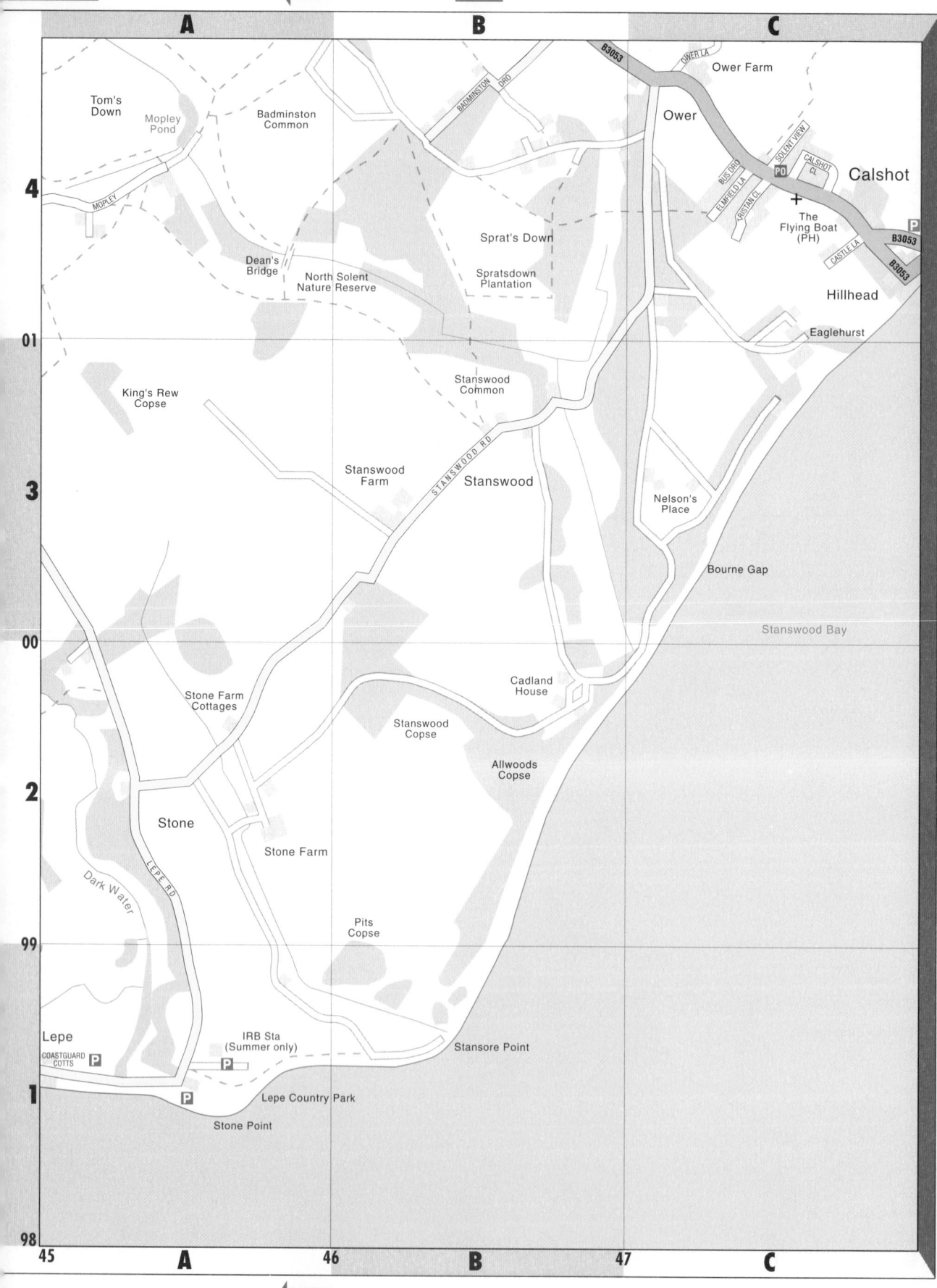

A   B   C

Tom's
Down

Mopley Pond

Badminston
Common

B3053

OWER LA

Ower Farm

Ower

SOLENT VIEW

PO

CALSHOT CL

Calshot

MOPLEY

BUS DRO

ELMFIELD LA

KRISTAL CL

The
Flying Boat
(PH)

Dean's
Bridge

North Solent
Nature Reserve

Sprat's Down

Spratsdown
Plantation

Hillhead

CASTLE LA

B3053

B3053

Eaglehurst

4

01

King's Rew
Copse

Stanswood
Common

3

Stanswood
Farm

STANSWOOD RD

Stanswood

Nelson's
Place

Bourne Gap

00

Stanswood Bay

Stone Farm
Cottages

Stanswood
Copse

Cadland
House

2

Stone

Stone Farm

Allwoods
Copse

LEPE RD

Dark Water

Pits
Copse

99

Lepe

COASTGUARD
COTTS

P

IRB Sta
(Summer only)

P

Stansore Point

1

P

Lepe Country Park

Stone Point

98

45   46   47

A   B   C

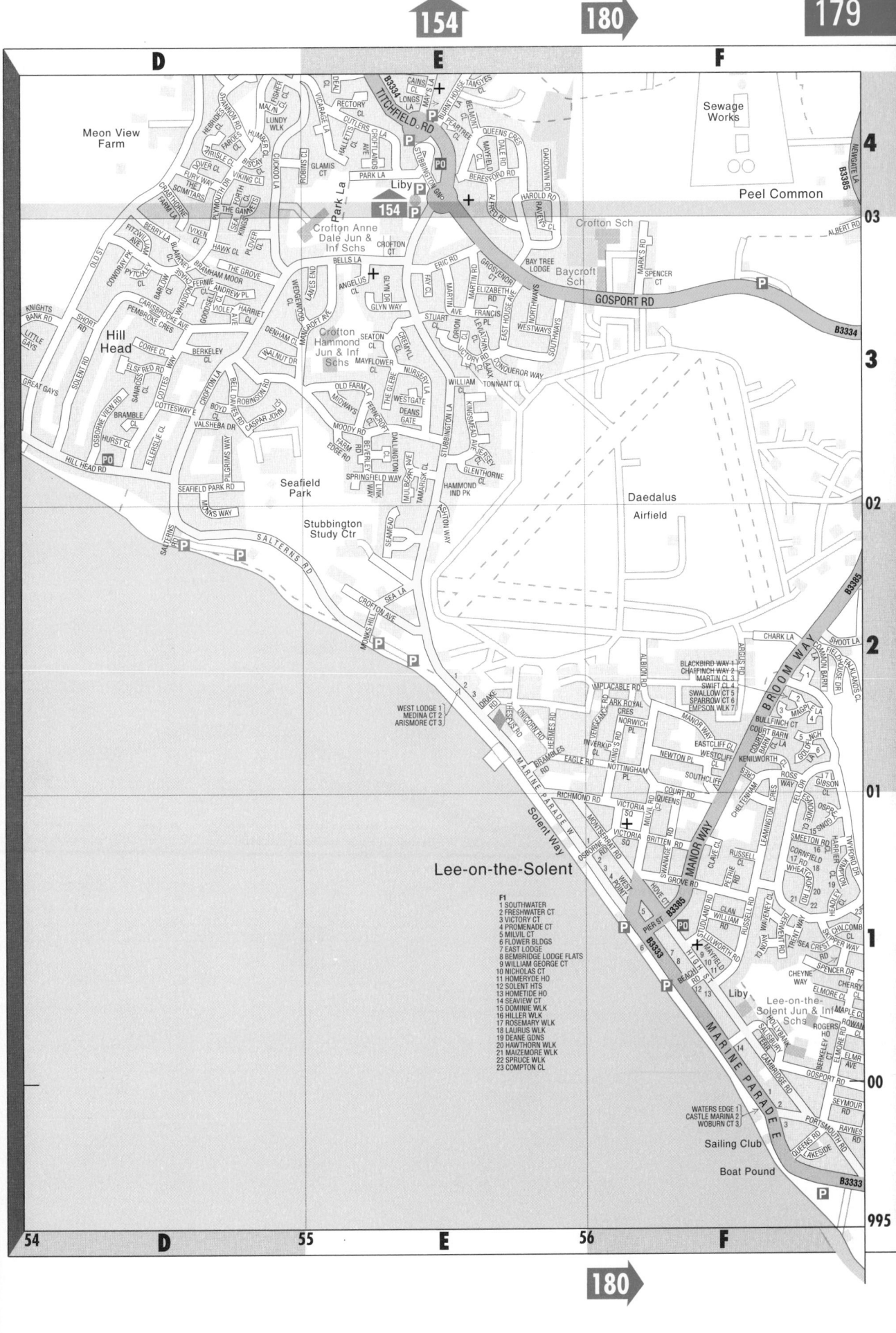

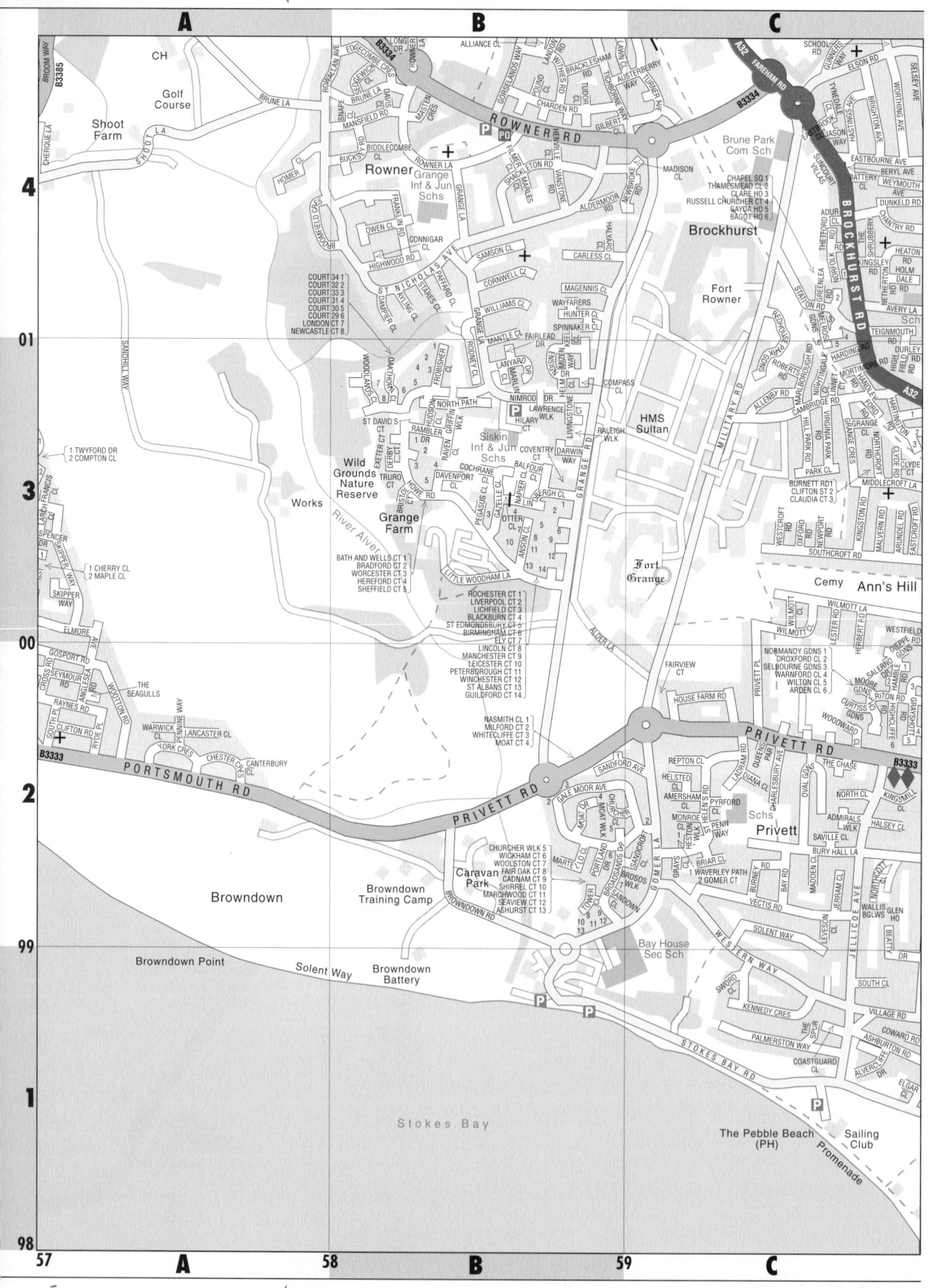

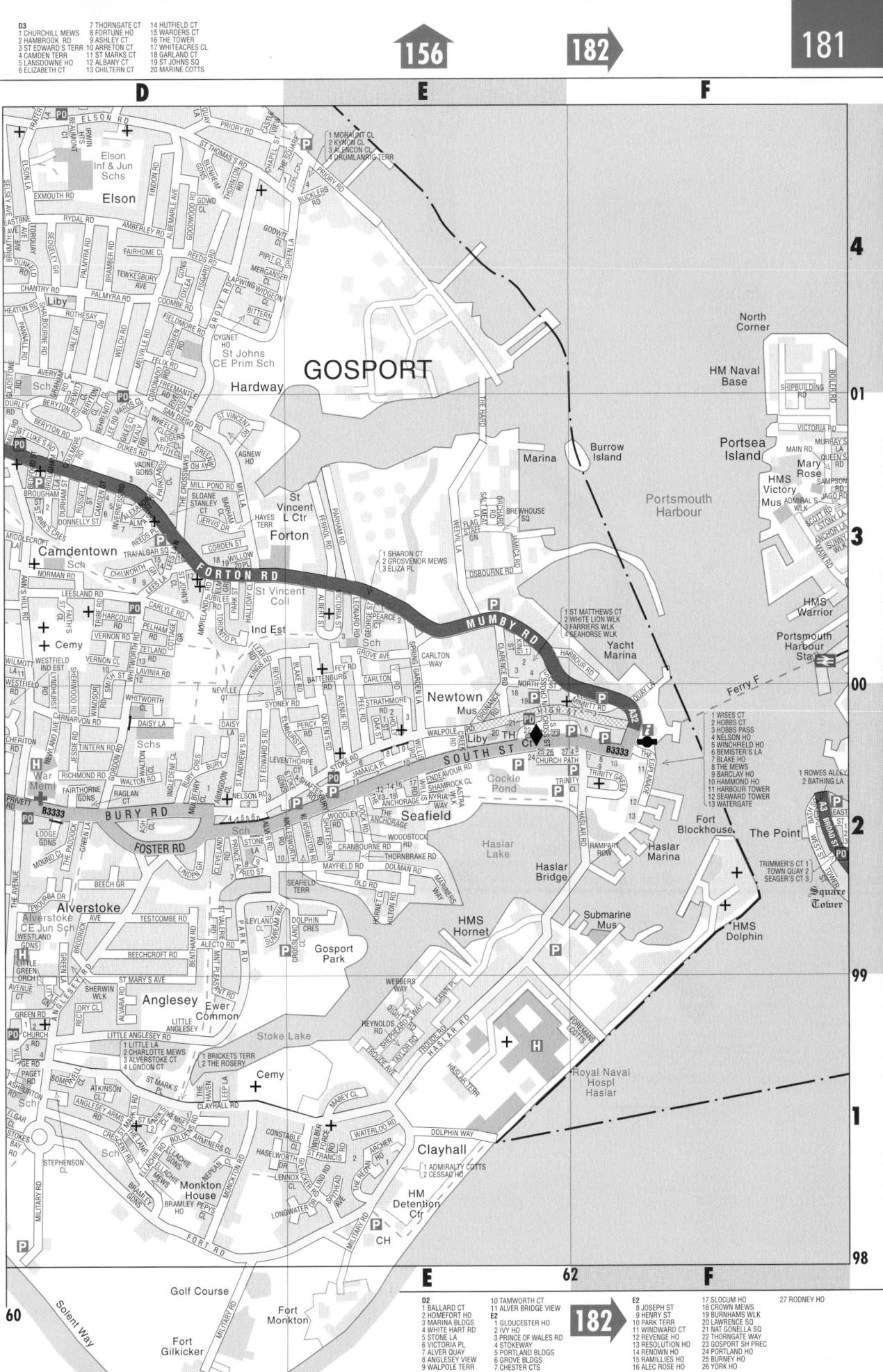

156   182   181

D3
1 CHURCHILL MEWS
2 HAMBROOK RD
3 ST EDWARD S TERR
4 CAMDEN TERR
5 LANSDOWNE HO
6 ELIZABETH CT
7 THORNGATE CT
8 FORTUNE HO
9 ASHLEY CT
10 ARRETON CT
11 ST MARKS CT
12 ALBANY CT
13 CHILTERN CT
14 HUTFIELD CT
15 WARDERS CT
16 THE TOWER
17 WHITEACRES CL
18 GARLAND CT
19 ST JOHNS SQ
20 MARINE COTTS

D2
1 BALLARD CT
2 HOMEFORT HO
3 MARINA BLDGS
4 WHITE HART RD
5 STONE LA
6 VICTORIA PL
7 ALVER QUAY
8 ANGLESEY VIEW
9 WALPOLE TERR
10 TAMWORTH CT
11 ALVER BRIDGE VIEW

E2
1 GLOUCESTER HO
2 IVY HO
3 PRINCE OF WALES RD
4 STOKEWAY
5 PORTLAND BLDGS
6 GROVE BLDGS
7 CHESTER CTS

E2
8 JOSEPH ST
9 HENRY ST
10 PARK TERR
11 WINDWARD CT
12 REVENGE HO
13 RESOLUTION HO
14 RENOWN HO
15 RAMILLIES HO
16 ALEC ROSE HO
17 SLOCUM HO
18 CROWN MEWS
19 BURNHAMS WLK
20 LAWRENCE SQ
21 NAT GONELLA SQ
22 THORNGATE WAY
23 GOSPORT SH PREC
24 PORTLAND HO
25 BURNEY HO
26 YORK HO
27 RODNEY HO

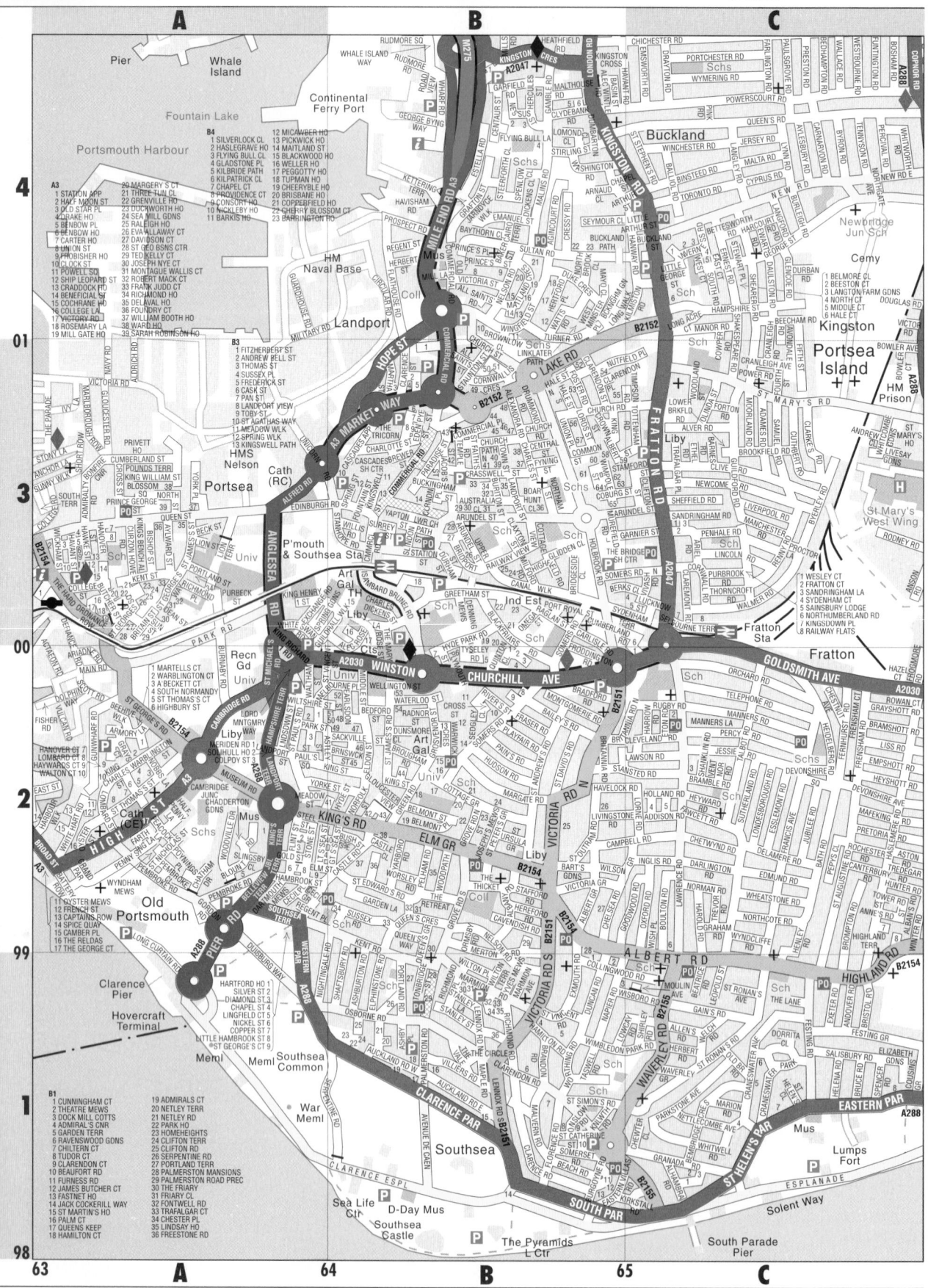

B3
14 ARUNDELWAY SH ARC
15 GUILDHALL SQ
16 DOROTHY DYMOND ST
17 HARRY LAW HALL
18 DUGALD DRUMMOND ST
19 WILMCOTE HO

20 WILMCOTE GDNS
21 OMEGA HO
22 MAXSTOKE CL
23 REDNAL HO
24 FLADHURST HO
25 WINDSOR HO
26 DALE PARK HO

27 EAST SURREY ST
28 ANGMERING HO
29 CAMBERRA HO
30 MELBOURNE HO
31 PERTH HO
32 DARWIN HO
33 SYDNEY HO

34 SETTLERS CL
35 DURBAN HO
36 NICHOLSON GDNS
37 CLANFIELD HO
38 FAREHAM HO
39 HORNDEAN HO
40 BURSLEDON HO

157

B3
41 PETERSFIELD HO
42 CHALTON HO
43 SPICER ST
44 CATSFIELD HO
45 TITCHFIELD HO
46 BLENDWORTH HO

47 DROXFORD HO
48 ROGATE HO
49 LOWER WINGFIELD ST
50 CORNWALLIS RD
51 NORTH ST
52 DHEKELIA CT
53 SELHURST HO

54 REIGATE HO
55 REDHILL HO
56 BOXGROVE HO
57 MIDHURST HO
58 CROWN CT
59 KING ALBERT CT
60 FITZROY HO

61 LORDS CT
62 HARLEY WLK
63 WIMPOLE CT
64 WIGMORE HO
65 LITTLE COBURG ST

A3
1 STATION APP
2 HALF MOON ST
3 OLD STAR PL
4 DRAKE HO
5 BENBOW PL
6 BENBOW HO
7 CARTER HO
8 UNION ST
9 FROBISHER HO
10 CLOCK ST
11 POWELL CL
12 SHIP LEOPARD ST
13 CRADDOCK PL
14 BENEFICIAL ST
15 COCHRANE HO
16 COLLEGE LA
17 VICTORY RD
18 ROSEMARY LA
19 MILL GATE HO

20 MARGERY'S CT
21 THREE TUN CL
22 GRENVILLE HO
23 DUCKWORTH HO
24 SEA MILL GDNS
25 RALEIGH HO
26 EVA ALLAWAY CT
27 DAVIDSON CT
28 ST GEO BSNS CTR
29 TED KELLY CT
30 JOSEPH NYE CT
31 MONTAGUE WALLIS CT
32 ROBERT MACK CT
33 FRANK JUDD CT
34 RICHMOND HO
35 DELAVAL HO
36 FOUNDRY CT
37 WILLIAM BOOTH HO
38 WARD HO
39 SARAH ROBINSON HO

B4
1 SILVERLOCK CL
2 HASLEGRAVE HO
3 FLYING BULL LA
4 GLADSTONE PL
5 KILBRIDE PATH
6 KILPATRICK CL
7 CHAPEL CT
8 PROVIDENCE CT
9 CONSORT HO
10 NICKLEBY HO
11 BARKIS HO

12 MICAWBER HO
13 PICKWICK HO
14 MAITLAND CL
15 BLACKWOOD HO
16 WELLER HO
17 PEGGOTTY HO
18 TUPMAN HO
19 CHEERYBLE HO
20 BRISBANE HO
21 COPPERFIELD HO
22 CHERRY BLOSSOM CT
23 BARRINGTON HO

B3
1 FITZHERBERT ST
2 ANDREW BELL ST
3 THOMAS ST
4 SUSSEX PL
5 FREDERICK ST
6 CASK ST
7 PAN ST
8 LANDPORT VIEW
9 ST AGATHAS WAY
10 MEADOW WLK
11 SPRING WLK
12 KINGSWELL PATH

B2
1 COTTERIDGE HO
2 FORBURY RD
3 BLACKFRIARS CL
4 ARTHUR POPE HO
5 HANDSWORTH HO
6 LADYWOOD HO
7 HYDE PARK HO
8 ALDWELL ST
9 LOWER FORBURY RD

10 MORECOMBE CT
11 EDGBASTON HO
12 TIPTON HO
13 GROSVENOR HO
14 CANNOCK LAWN
15 LOUIS FLAGG HO
16 FRANK MILES HO
17 HOMERISE HO
18 HOMESEA HO
19 ROSLYN HO

B2
20 CHIVERS CL
21 MILVERTON HO
22 CHANCTONBURY HO
23 GROVE HO
24 WINDSOR LA
25 EASTFIELDS
26 HEATHERLEY CT
27 PORTLAND TERR
28 KEYES CT

29 HILLBOROUGH CRES
30 THE CLOSE
31 GREYFRIARS CT
32 QUEEN'S PL
33 SUSSEX TERR
34 SUSSEX PL
35 WOODPATH HO
36 WILBERFORCE RD
37 PARK CT
38 BUSH HO

39 RAVEN CROFT
40 BARN ST W
41 SOUTH ST
42 GLOUCESTER TERR
43 GLOUCESTER PL
44 OCKENFOLD CL
45 PRINCE REGENT CT
46 ELDON CT
47 STRATFORD HO
48 ATHERSTONE WLK

49 OLDBURY HO
50 CALDECOTE WLK
51 LONGBRIDGE HO
52 LEAMINGTON HO
53 PICTON HO
54 PONSONBY HO

C1
1 MANSION HO
2 MANSION CT
3 ROSTREVOR LA
4 CRANESWATER GATE
5 CRANESWATER MEWS
6 NORMAN CT
7 DOLPHIN CT
8 CRESTA CT

C2
1 CUMBERLAND BSNS CTR
2 PRIORY CT
3 EMBASSY CT
4 GRENVILLE RD
5 NORLAND RD
6 BRANDON CT
7 WHITE CLOUD PK
8 WHITE CLOUD PL

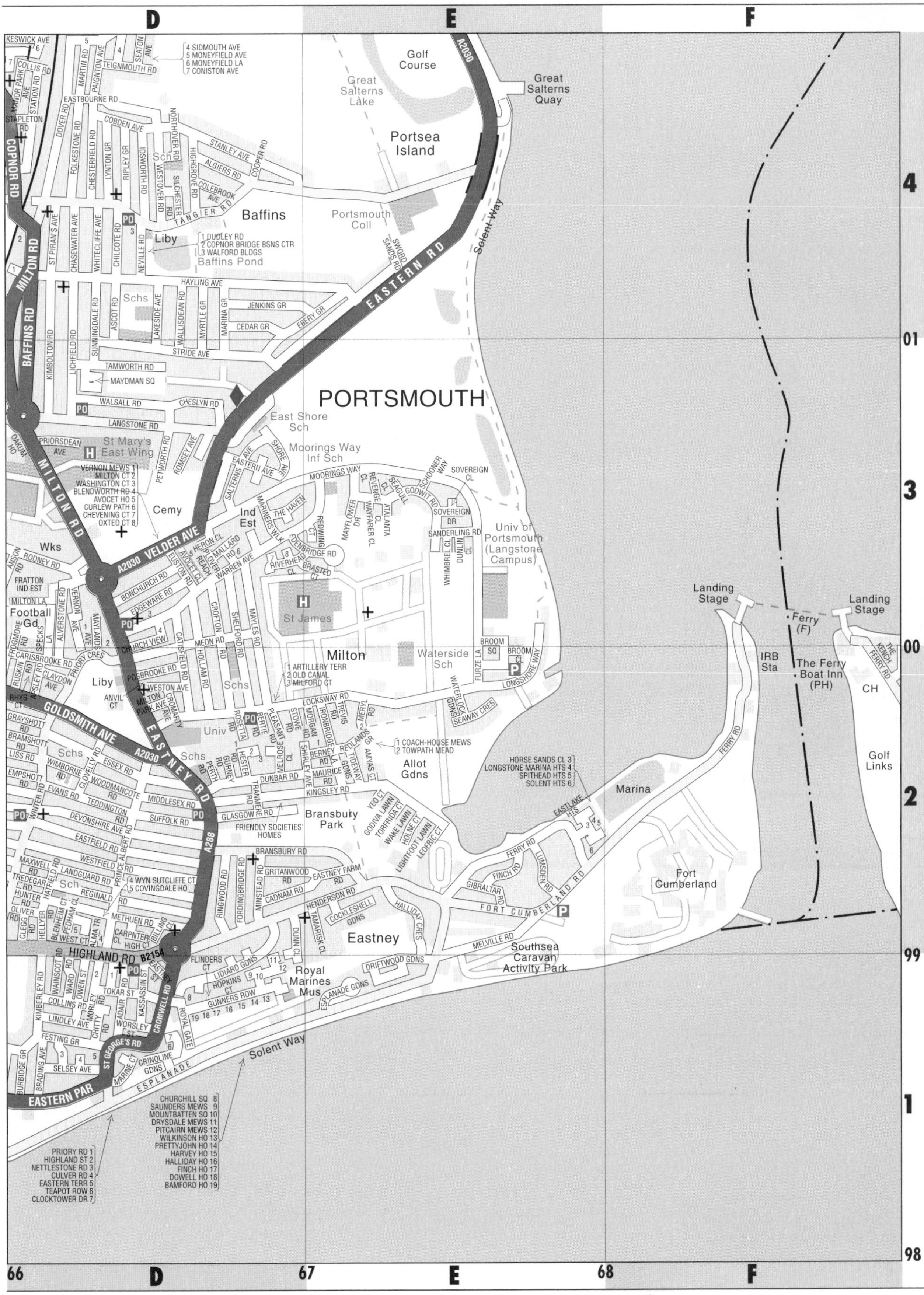
D
E
F
4
3
2
1
01
00
99
98
66
67
68
PORTSMOUTH
Golf Course
Great Salterns Lake
Great Salterns Quay
Portsea Island
Portsmouth Coll
Baffins
Baffins Pond
Liby
Schs
Sch
A2030
EASTERN RD
Solent Way
COPNOR RD
MILTON RD
BAFFINS RD
4 SIDMOUTH AVE
5 MONEYFIELD AVE
6 MONEYFIELD LA
7 CONISTON AVE
1 DUDLEY RD
2 COPNOR BRIDGE BSNS CTR
3 WALFORD BLDGS
EASTBOURNE RD
TEIGNMOUTH RD
COBDEN AVE
STANLEY AVE
ALGIERS RD
COLEBROOK AVE
TANGIER RD
HAYLING AVE
JENKINS GR
CEDAR GR
EBERY GR
STRIDE AVE
TAMWORTH RD
MAYDMAN SQ
WALSALL RD
CHESLYN RD
LANGSTONE RD
East Shore Sch
Moorings Way Inf Sch
St Mary's East Wing
PRIORSDEAN AVE
VERNON MEWS 1
MILTON CT 2
WASHINGTON CT 3
BLENDWORTH RD 4
AVOCET HO 5
CURLEW PATH 6
CHEVENING CT 7
OXTED CT 8
Cemy
Wks
Ind Est
A2030 VELDER AVE
RODNEY RD
FRATTON IND EST
MILTON LA
Football Gd
MOORINGS WAY
SOVEREIGN CL
SOVEREIGN DR
SANDERLING RD
Univ of Portsmouth (Langstone Campus)
St James
Milton
Waterside Sch
BROOM SQ
BROOM CL
LONGSHORE WAY
EDENBRIDGE RD
Landing Stage
Ferry (F)
IRB Sta
The Ferry Boat Inn (PH)
CH
Golf Links
Liby
GOLDSMITH AVE
EASTNEY RD
A2030
A288
1 ARTILLERY TERR
2 OLD CANAL
3 MILFORD CT
LOCKSWAY RD
SEAWAY CRES
1 COACH-HOUSE MEWS
2 TOWPATH MEAD
Allot Gdns
HORSE SANDS CL 3
LONGSTONE MARINA HTS 4
SPITHEAD HTS 5
SOLENT HTS 6
Marina
FERRY RD
Fort Cumberland
FORT CUMBERLAND RD
Univ
Schs
DUNBAR RD
KINGSLEY RD
Bransbury Park
FRIENDLY SOCIETIES' HOMES
MIDDLESEX RD
SUFFOLK RD
GLASGOW RD
BRANSBURY RD
GRITANWOOD RD
EASTNEY FARM RD
CADNAM RD
HENDERSON RD
COCKLESHELL GDNS
HALLIDAY CRES
GIBRALTAR RD
FINCH RD
LUMSDEN RD
MELVILLE RD
Southsea Caravan Activity Park
Eastney
4 WYN SUTCLIFFE CT
5 COVINGDALE HO
HIGHLAND RD B2154
Royal Marines Mus
DRIFTWOOD GDNS
ESPLANADE GDNS
GUNNERS ROW
EASTERN PAR
ESPLANADE
Solent Way
CHURCHILL SQ 8
SAUNDERS MEWS 9
MOUNTBATTEN SQ 10
DRYSDALE MEWS 11
PITCAIRN MEWS 12
WILKINSON HO 13
PRETTYJOHN HO 14
HARVEY HO 15
HALLIDAY HO 16
FINCH HO 17
DOWELL HO 18
BAMFORD HO 19
PRIORY RD 1
HIGHLAND ST 2
NETTLESTONE RD 3
CULVER RD 4
EASTERN TERR 5
TEAPOT ROW 6
CLOCKTOWER DR 7

THE KENCH

The Kench

Sinah Farm

Pier

Hotel

Sinah Common

Golf Links

Gunner Point

Ferry Rd

Club House

Bay Hayling Bay

NORTH SHORE RD

WARREN LA

SINAH LA

PARK RD

HARBOUR RD

LIME GR

LINKS LA

ST CATHERINES RD

ST AUBIN'S PARK

ST CATHERINES CT

ST GEORGE'S RD

ST THOMAS AVE

STAUNTON AVE

FERNHURST CL

RICHMOND DR

RICHMOND CL

ST HELEN'S RD

THE GORSEWAY

GORSEWAY

WEST MEAD CL

STAMFORD AVE

BACON LA

WINSTON AVE

MEGAN CT

GREEN LA

JAMES CL

STATION RD

FURNISS WAY

PRINCES WAY

NEWTOWN LA

CHARDON CL

GLEBE CL

GILBERT MEAD

SYCAMORE

NEWTOWN LA

GRAYLAND CL

SPINNAKER

FADMAS REACH

LEXDEN GDNS

WOODLANDS LA

BRIGHTS LA

SALTMARSH LA

OLD RD

GARDENS

DOVER CT

ATHERLEY RD

MANOR RD

HIGWORTH LA

WEST LA

DAW LA

A3023

Camp Site

Higworth Caravan Site

Higworth Caravan Site

Newtown

Rook Farm

SOUTHLEIGH GR

ST MARY'S RD

HILDEN CT

WALNUT TREE CL

BRIARWOOD GDNS

ELWELL GREEN

OAKWOOD CT

ELM CLOSE ESTATE

BENWELL CT

West Town

HOLLOW LA

SOUTH RD

GARDEN CL

WESTFIELD AVE

VICTORIA AVE

ORCHARD CL

ALEXANDRA AVE

TUDOR CL

ST JOHNS CL

SOLENTON LA

OLD TIMBERS

BEACH RD

A3023

Westfield

The Beach

South Hayling

Hotel

PH

SEA FRONT

BAY VIEW CT

NORFOLK CRES

CHICHESTER AVE

BAY VIEW MEWS   1
WARD CT   2
STAMFORD LODGE   3
ROPLEY CT   4
NORFOLK MEWS   5
FAIRMEAD CT   6
OCEAN CT   7
NICHOLAS CT   8
PADWICK CT   9
ANNES CT   10
VICTORIA CT   11
MARK ANTHONY CT   12
WESTFIELD OAKS   13

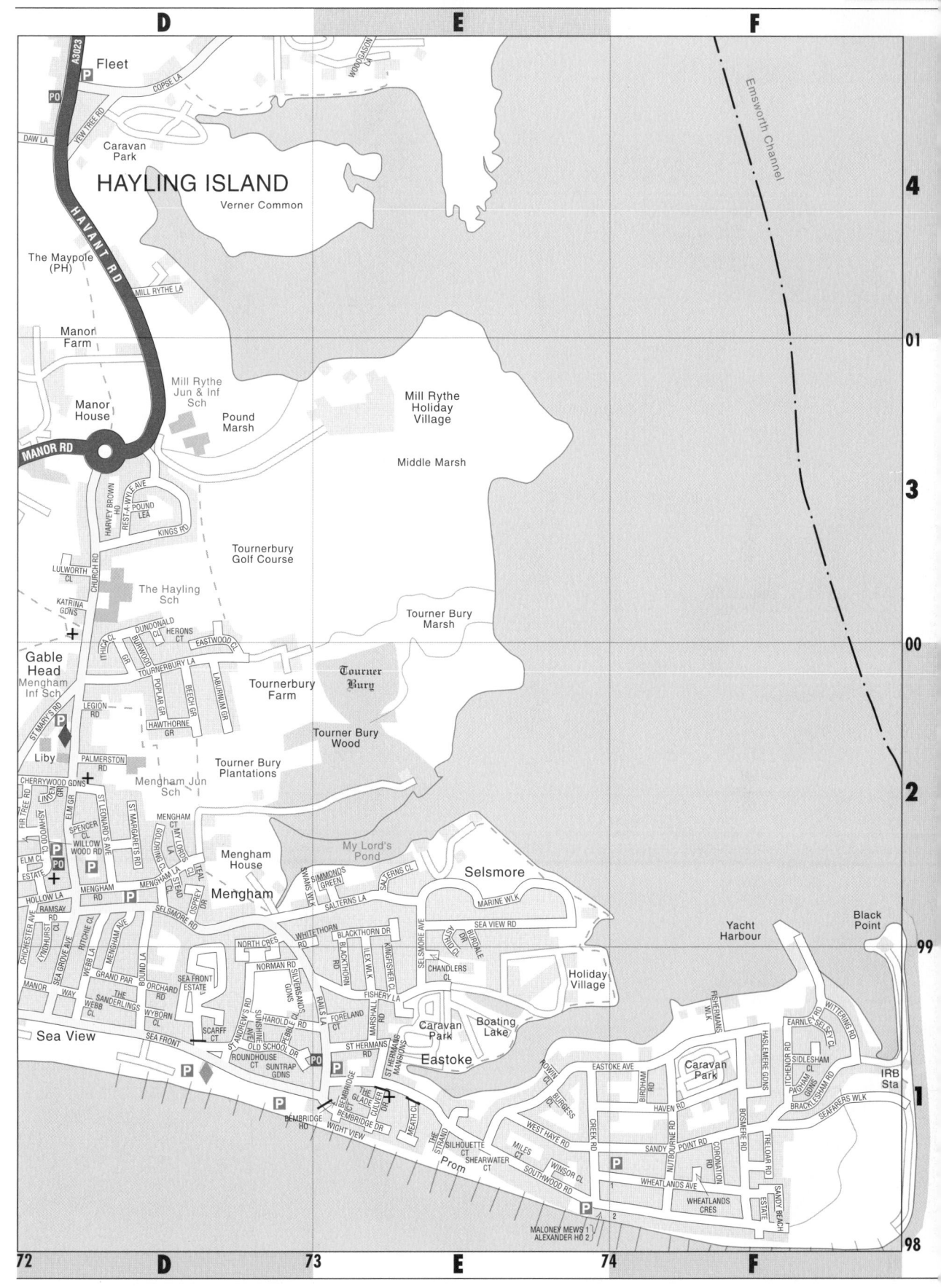

HAYLING ISLAND

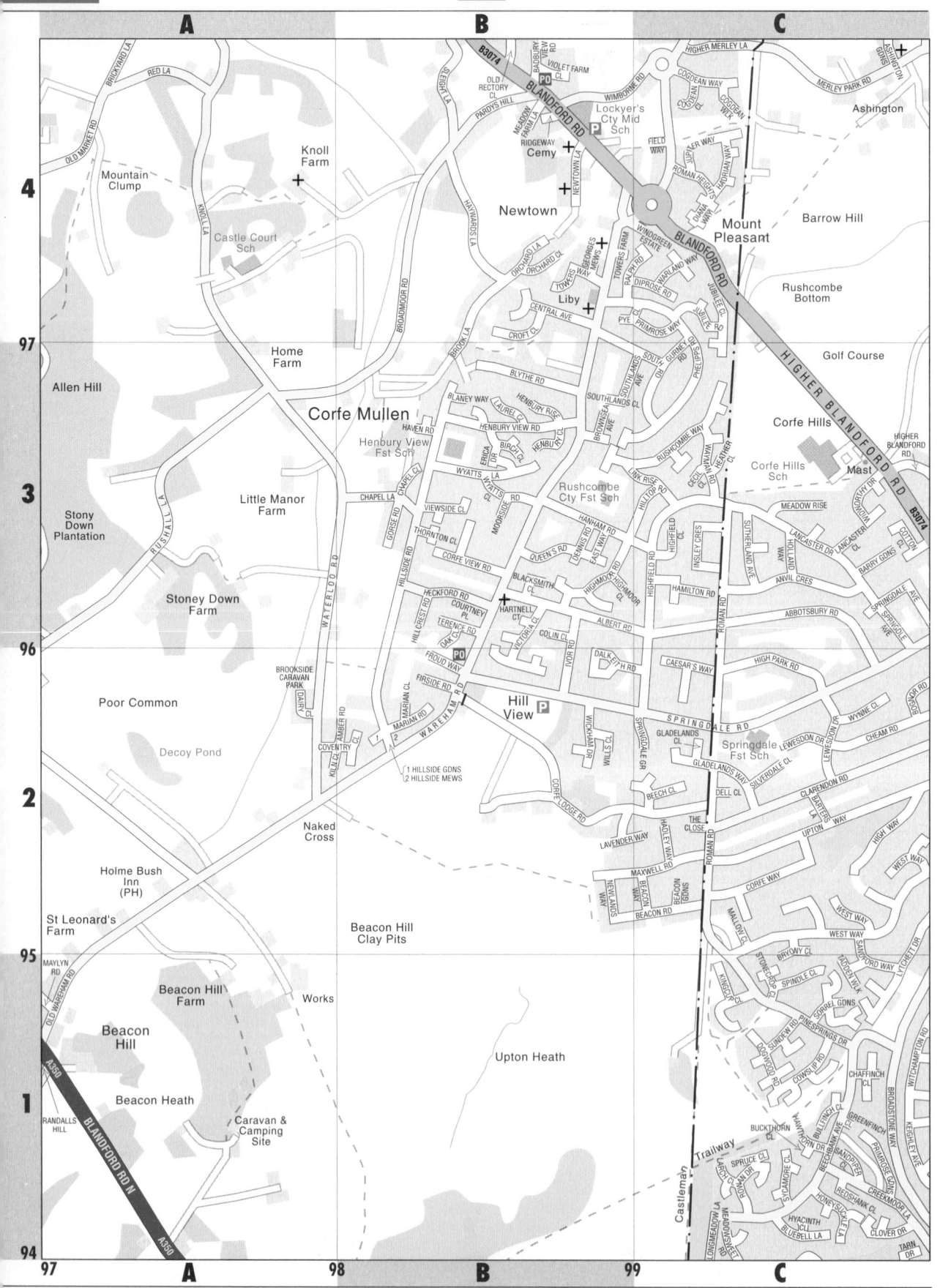

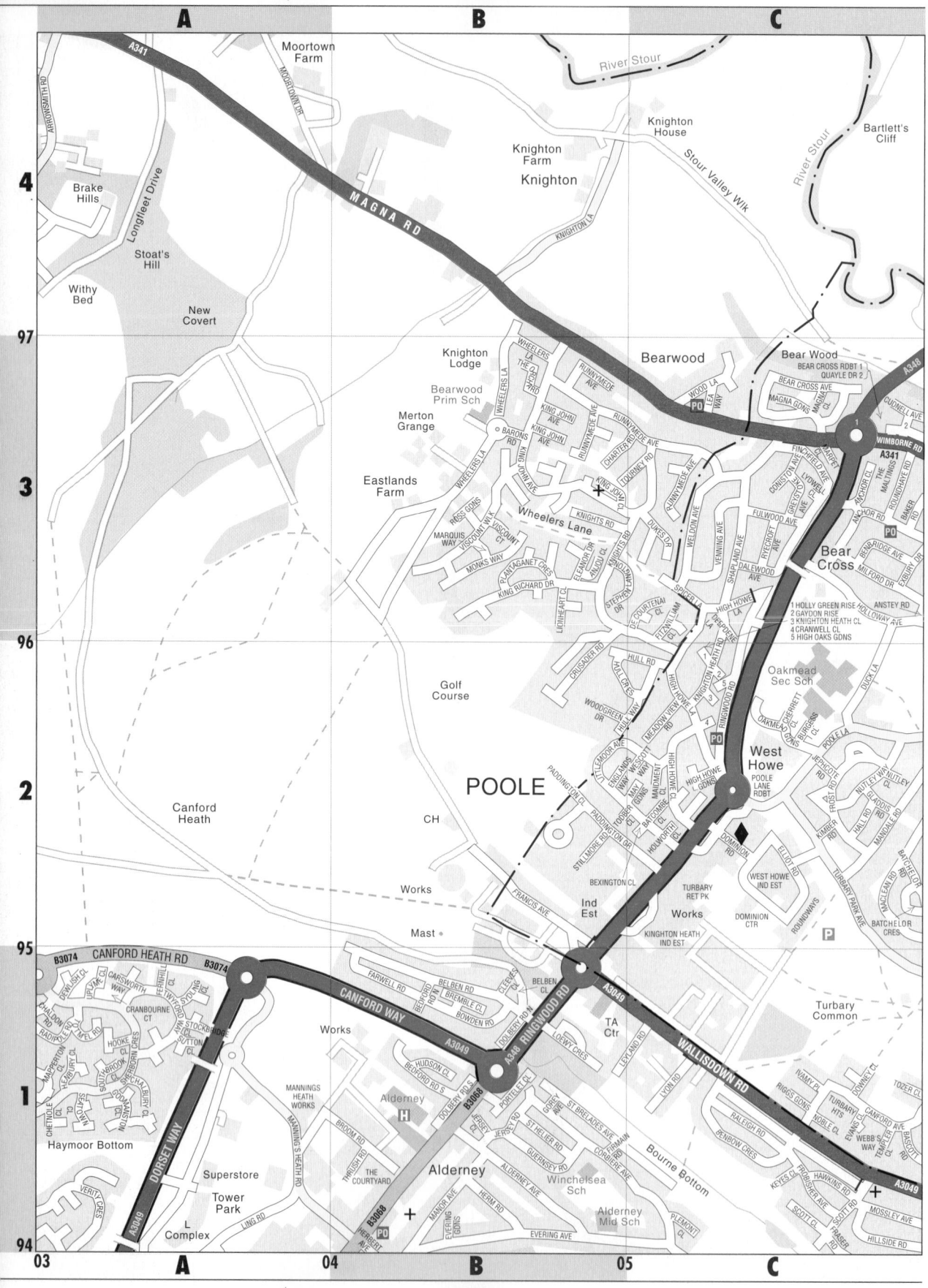

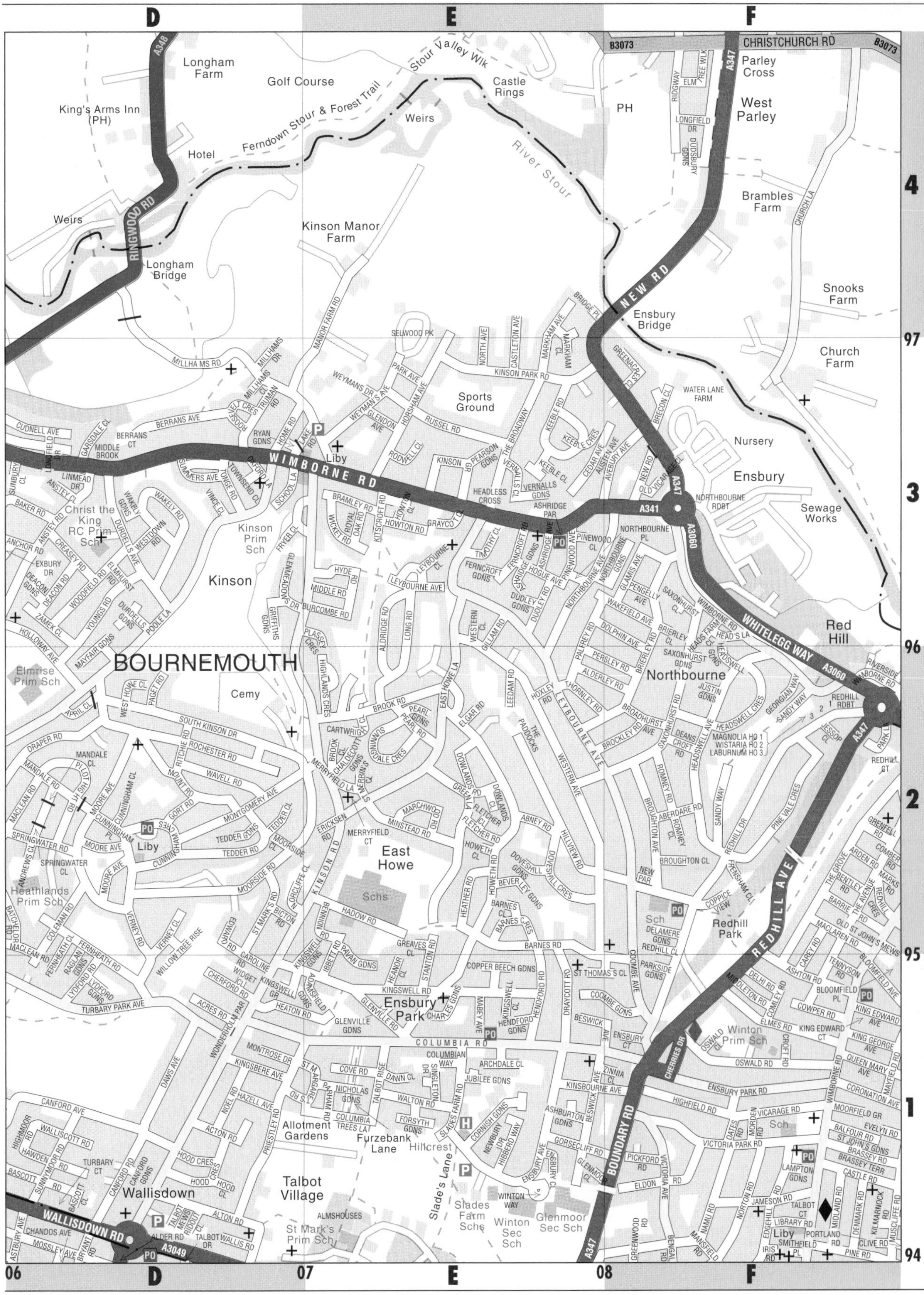
D
E
F
B3073
CHRISTCHURCH RD
B3073
A348
Longham Farm
Golf Course
Stour Valley Wlk
Castle Rings
Parley Cross
West Parley
PH
King's Arms Inn (PH)
Ferndown Stour & Forest Trail
Weirs
Hotel
River Stour
RINGWOOD RD
Weirs
Kinson Manor Farm
Brambles Farm
CHURCH LA
4
Longham Bridge
NEW RD
Snooks Farm
Ensbury Bridge
Church Farm
97
SELWOOD PK
MANOR FARM RD
NORTH AVE
CASTLETON AVE
MARKHAM AVE
KINSON PARK RD
WATER LANE FARM
Sports Ground
Nursery
BERRANS AVE
CUDNELL AVE
MIDDLE BROOK
Liby
WIMBORNE RD
Ensbury
HEADLESS CROSS
A347
A341
NORTHBOURNE RDBT
Sewage Works
3
Christ the King RC Prim Sch
Kinson Prim Sch
ASHRIDGE PAR
PO
NORTHBOURNE PL
A3060
Kinson
LEYBOURNE AVE
WHITELEGG WAY
Red Hill
BOURNEMOUTH
96
Elmrise Prim Sch
Cemy
Northbourne
LEYBOURNE AVE
WESTERN AVE
THE PADDOCKS
REDHILL RDBT
SOUTH KINSON DR
ROCHESTER RD
WAVELL RD
MAGNOLIA HO 1
WISTARIA HO 2
LABURNUM HO 3
REDHILL CT
2
MONTGOMERY AVE
Liby
TEDDER RD
MOORSIDE RD
KINSON RD
MERRYFIELD CT
East Howe
Schs
REDHILL AVE
Heathlands Prim Sch
Sch
Redhill Park
BARNES RD
95
TURBARY PARK AVE
COPPER BEECH GDNS
Ensbury Park
COLUMBIA RD
Winton Prim Sch
KING EDWARD AVE
1
ENSBURY PARK RD
HIGHFIELD RD
VICTORIA PARK RD
Allotment Gardens
Furzebank Lane
Hillcrest
Slade's Lane
Talbot Village
Wallisdown
BOUNDARY RD
Sch
WALLISDOWN RD
A3049
ALMSHOUSES
St Mark's Prim Sch
Slades Farm Schs
Winton Sec Sch
Glenmoor Sec Sch
Liby
94
06
D
07
E
08
F

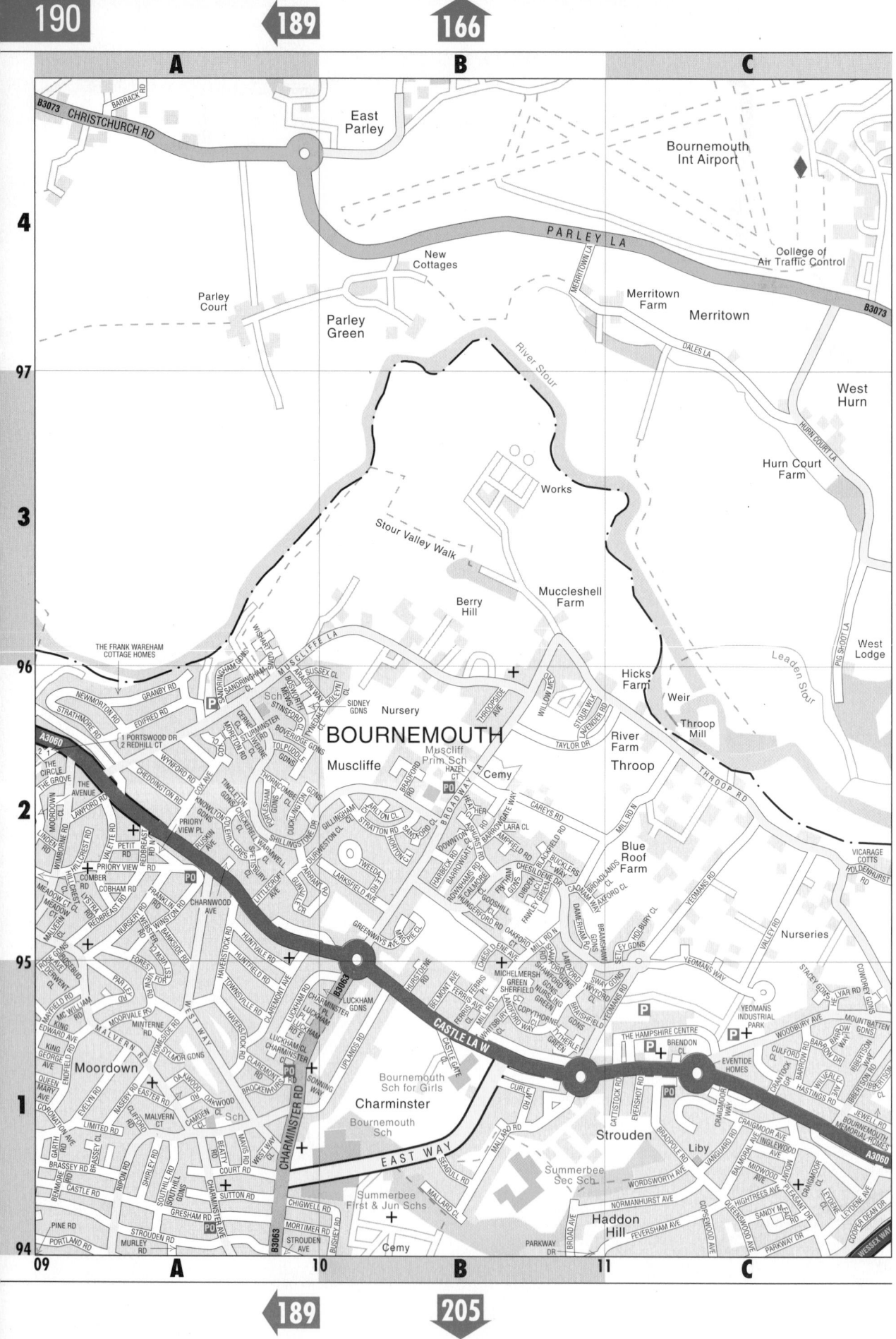

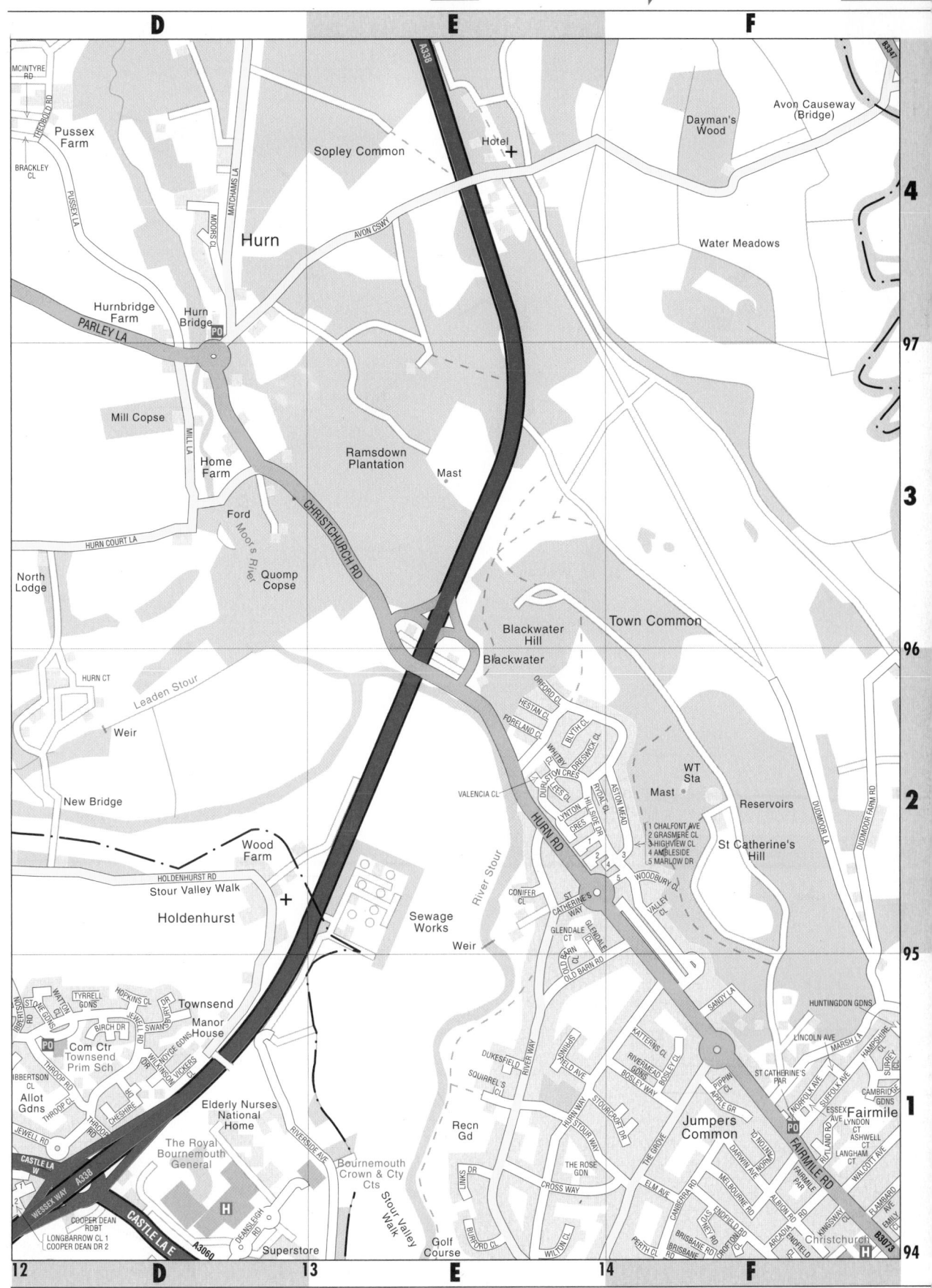

191
168

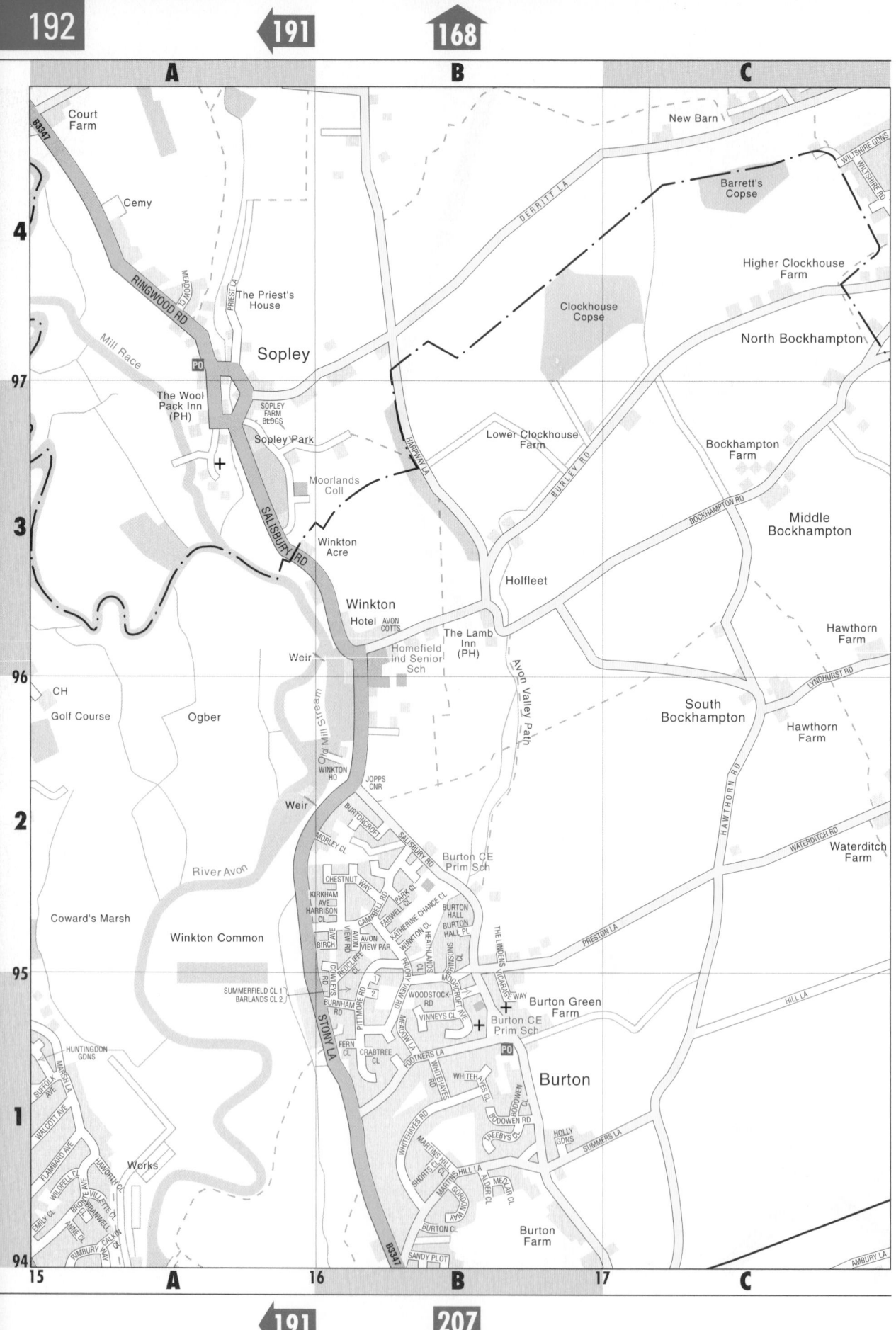

191
207

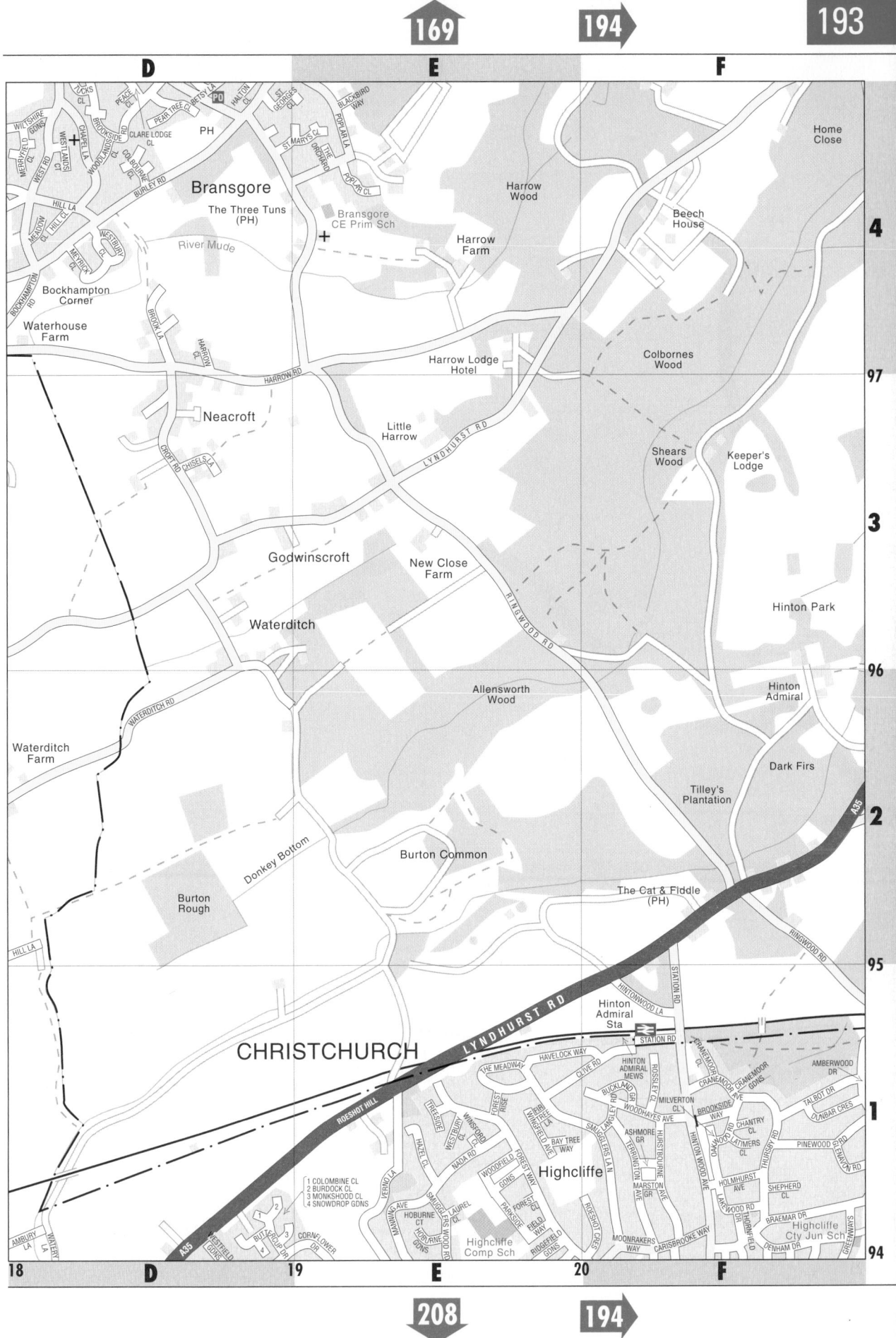

D E F

4

97

Bransgore

The Three Tuns
(PH)
Bransgore
CE Prim Sch

River Mude

Harrow
Wood

Harrow
Farm

Home
Close

Beech
House

Bockhampton
Corner

Waterhouse
Farm

Neacroft

Harrow Lodge
Hotel

Colbornes
Wood

3

Little
Harrow

Shears
Wood

Keeper's
Lodge

Godwinscroft

New Close
Farm

Waterditch

Hinton Park

96

Allensworth
Wood

Hinton
Admiral

Waterditch
Farm

Dark Firs

Tilley's
Plantation

2

Donkey Bottom

Burton Common

The Cat & Fiddle
(PH)

95

Burton
Rough

Hill La

CHRISTCHURCH

Hinton
Admiral
Sta

Amberwood
Dr

Highcliffe

1 COLOMBINE CL
2 BURDOCK CL
3 MONKSHOOD CL
4 SNOWDROP GDNS

Highcliffe

Highcliffe
Cty Jun Sch

94

18 D 19 E 20 F

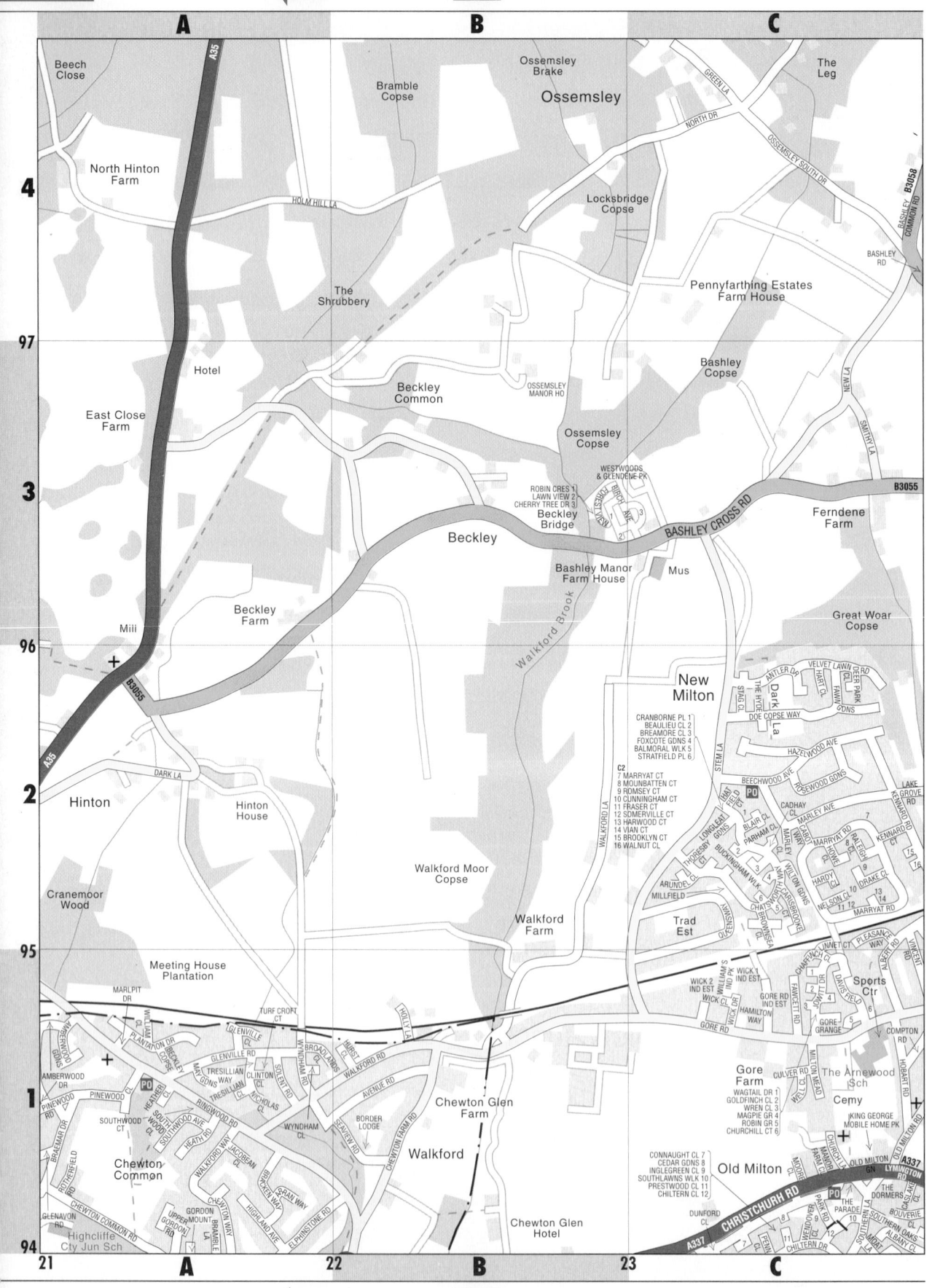

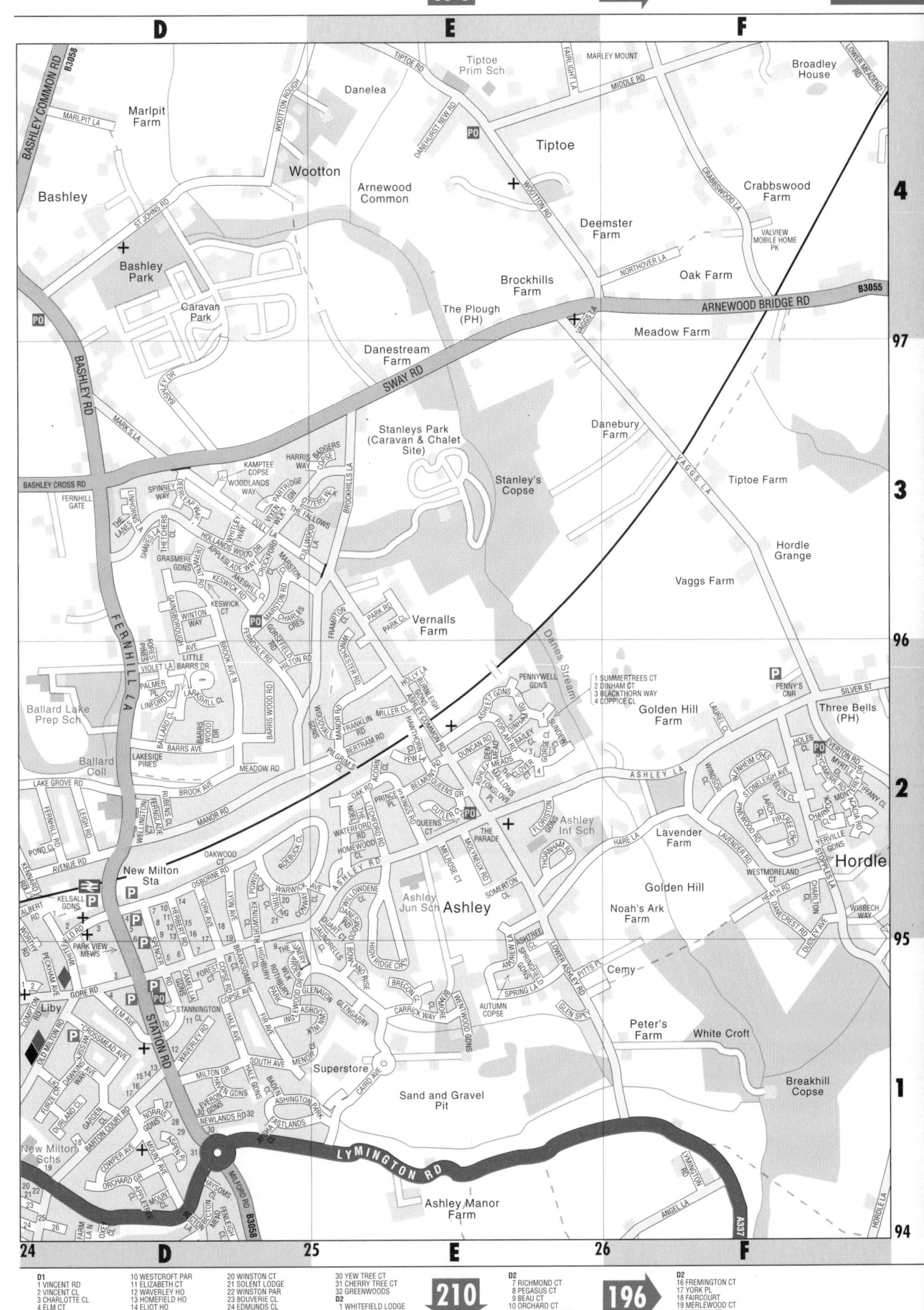

210 196

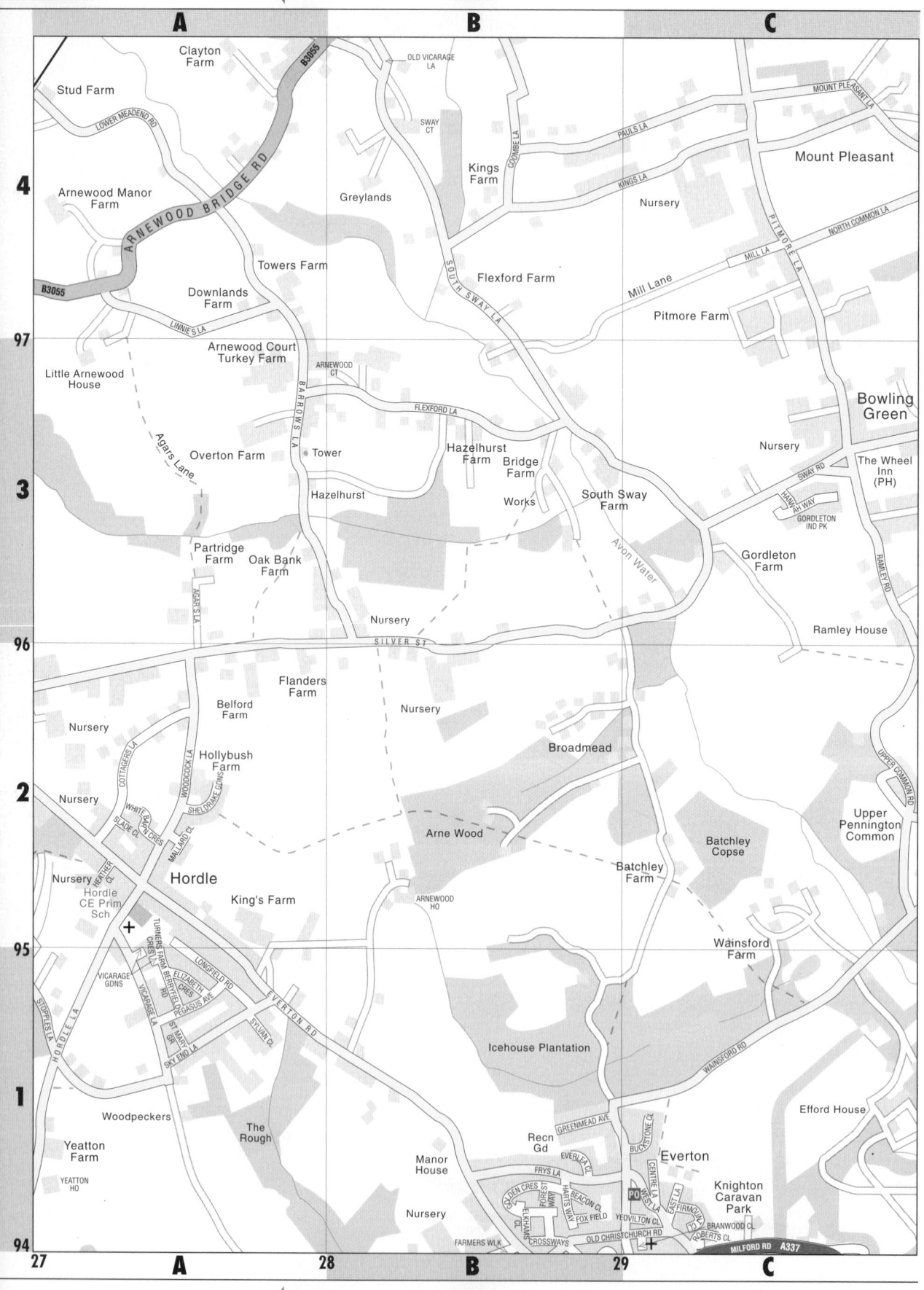

A   B   C

Clayton
Farm

Stud Farm

Old Vicarage
La

Sway
Ct

Mount Pleasant La

Mount Pleasant

Lower Meadend Rd

Coombe La

Pauls La

Kings La

B3055

4

Arnewood Manor
Farm

Greylands

Kings
Farm

Nursery

North Common La

Pitmore La

Towers Farm

Flexford Farm

Mill Lane

Mill La

Pitmore Farm

B3055

Downlands
Farm

South Sway La

97

Linnie's La

Arnewood Court
Turkey Farm

Arnewood
Ct

Bowling
Green

Little Arnewood
House

Nursery

Flexford La

The Wheel
Inn
(PH)

Agars Lane

Barrows La

Overton Farm

Tower

Hazelhurst
Farm

Bridge
Farm

South Sway
Farm

Sway Rd

Gordleton
Ind Pk

3

Hazelhurst

Works

Hannah Way

Ramley Rd

Partridge
Farm

Oak Bank
Farm

Avon Water

Gordleton
Farm

Agars La

Ramley House

96

Silver St

Nursery

Flanders
Farm

Belford
Farm

Nursery

Broadmead

Upper Common Rd

Woodcock La

Cottagers La

Hollybush
Farm

Nursery

Shellrake Gdns

White Lion Cres

Arne Wood

Batchley
Copse

Upper
Pennington
Common

2

Nursery

Slade Cl

Mallard Cl

Heather Cl

Batchley
Farm

Nursery
Hordle
CE Prim
Sch

Hordle

King's Farm

Arnewood
Ho

Wainsford
Farm

95

Turners Farm
Cres

Longfield Rd

Elizabeth
Cres

Everton Rd

Wainsford Rd

Vicarage
Gdns

Vicarage La

Berryfield Rd

Pegasus Ave

St Mary
Gr

Sylvan Cl

Stopples La

Hordle La

Sky End La

Icehouse Plantation

Efford House

1

Woodpeckers

The
Rough

Greenmead Ave

Everton

Knighton
Caravan
Park

Yeatton
Farm

Manor
House

Recn
Gd

Buckstone Cl

Centre La

East La

Everlea Cl

Yeovilton Cl

Yeatton
Ho

Frys La

Beacon Cl

Forest Way

Fox Field

East Firmount Cl

Branwood Cl

Nursery

Cyden Cres

Harts Way

PO

Roberts Cl

Elkhams

Old Christchurch Rd

Milford Rd   A337

Farmers Wlk

Crossways

94

27   A   28   B   29   C

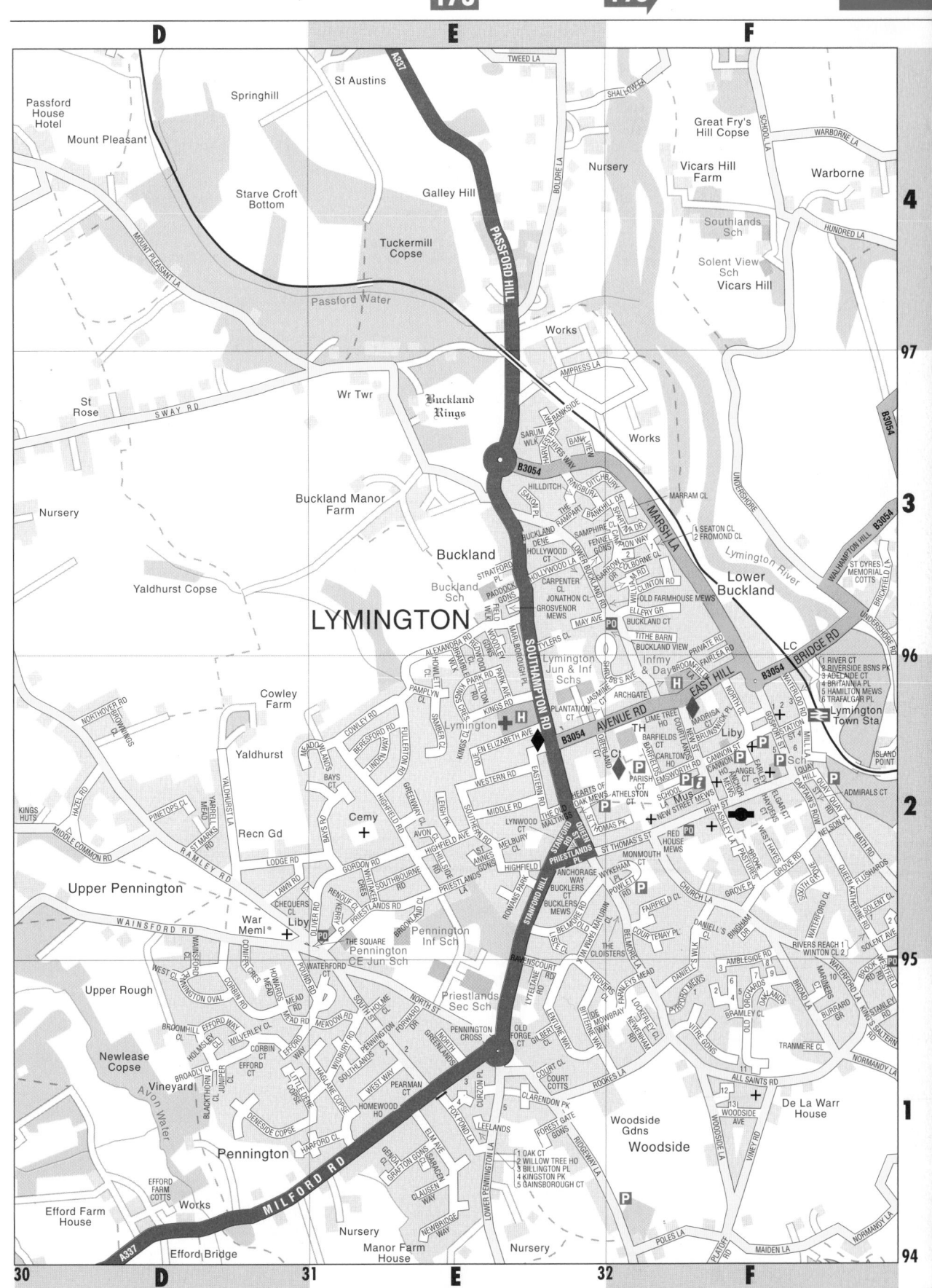

F1
1 PYRFORD GDNS
2 VICTORIA PL
3 GOLD MEAD CL
4 PEARMAIN DR
5 PEARTREE CT
6 PIPPIN CL
7 WORCESTER PL
8 BROADMEAD CL
9 RUSSET CL
10 MONKS CT
11 CONFERENCE PL
12 CHURCH MEAD
13 WOODSIDE CL

A **B** **C**

Norley Inclosure

NORLEYWOOD RD

Bull
Hill
Farm

B3054

SWEDISH
HOS

Norleywood

THATCHERS LA

JOYS LA

BROOK HILL

4

WARBORNE LA

JORDANS LA

Brick Kiln
Clump

Carters
Farm

Portmore

Ford

HUNDRED LA

Newtown Park
Farm

Pleasure
Copse

Winter's
Wood

97

WALHAMPTON HILL

Newtown
Park

South
Baddesley

Plummers Water

B3054

Portmore
Pond

Walhampton
Sch

South Baddesley
CE Prim Sch

B3054

3

WALHAMPTON
HILL

SNOOKS LA

Pike
Lake

Solent Way

Dod's
Pond

MONUMENT LA

Snooks
Farm

Shotts
Copse

Pylewell
Park

Pylewell Home
Farm

96

Mon

MILL LA

Walhampton

SHOTTS LA

Pylewell
House

LINDERSHORE RD

SOUTH BADDESLEY RD

Bampton's
Farm

2

Marina

P

Country
Club

Lisle Court
Farm

Lymington Pier
Station

1 2

LISLE COURT RD

SOLEN AVE

BATH RD

Ferry
Terminal

1 SOLENT VIEW
2 HOLBEIN LODGE

Lisle
Court

SPRINGFIELD CL

SPRING RD

MAYFLOWER CL

95

P

IRB Sta

STANLEY RD

KINGS SALTERN RD

WESTFIELD RD

Lymington River

Yacht
Haven

COASTGUARD
COTTS

1

NORMANDY LA

Waterford

Normandy
Farm

94

A 34 **B** 35 **C**

Solent Way

199
176

199

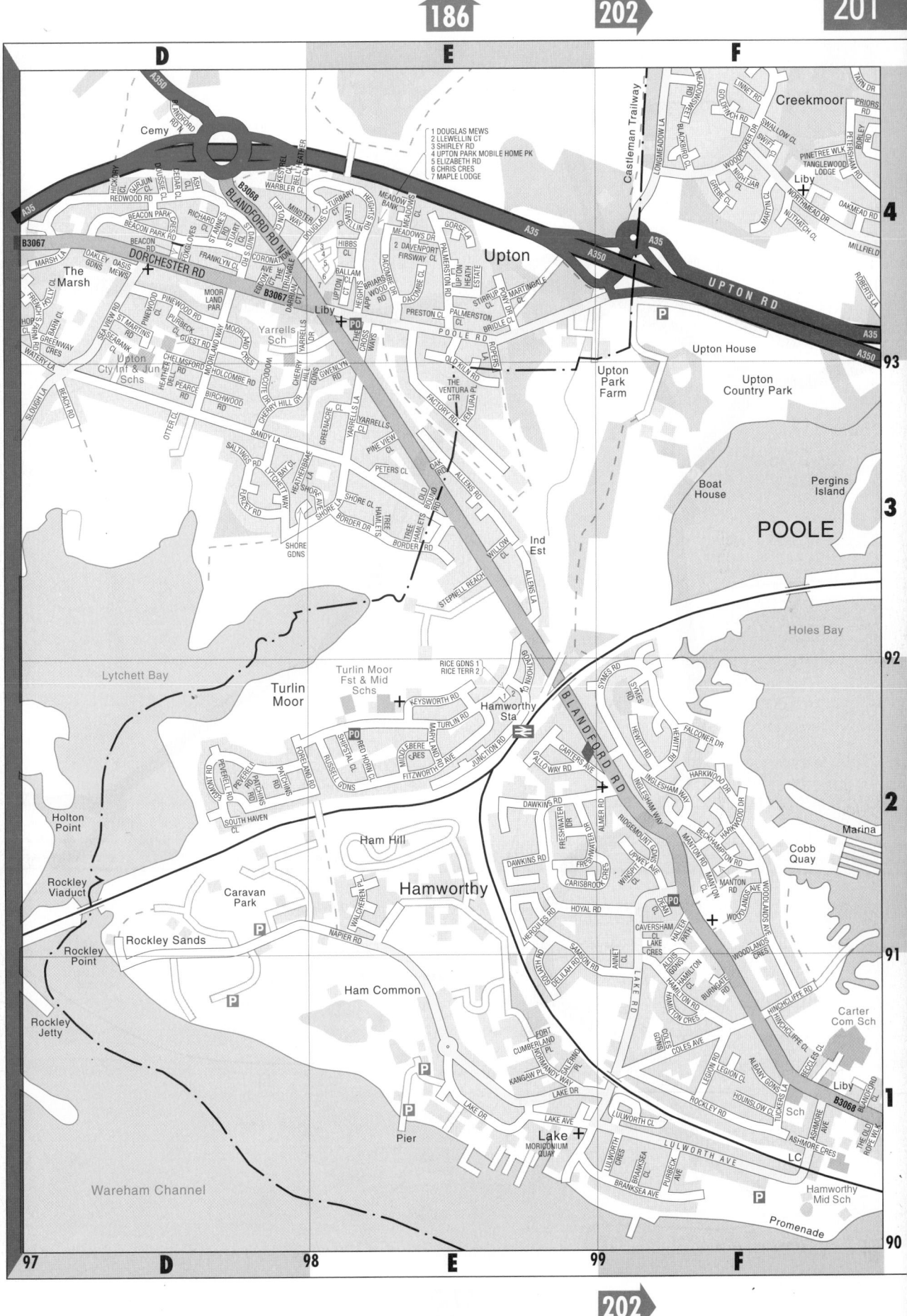

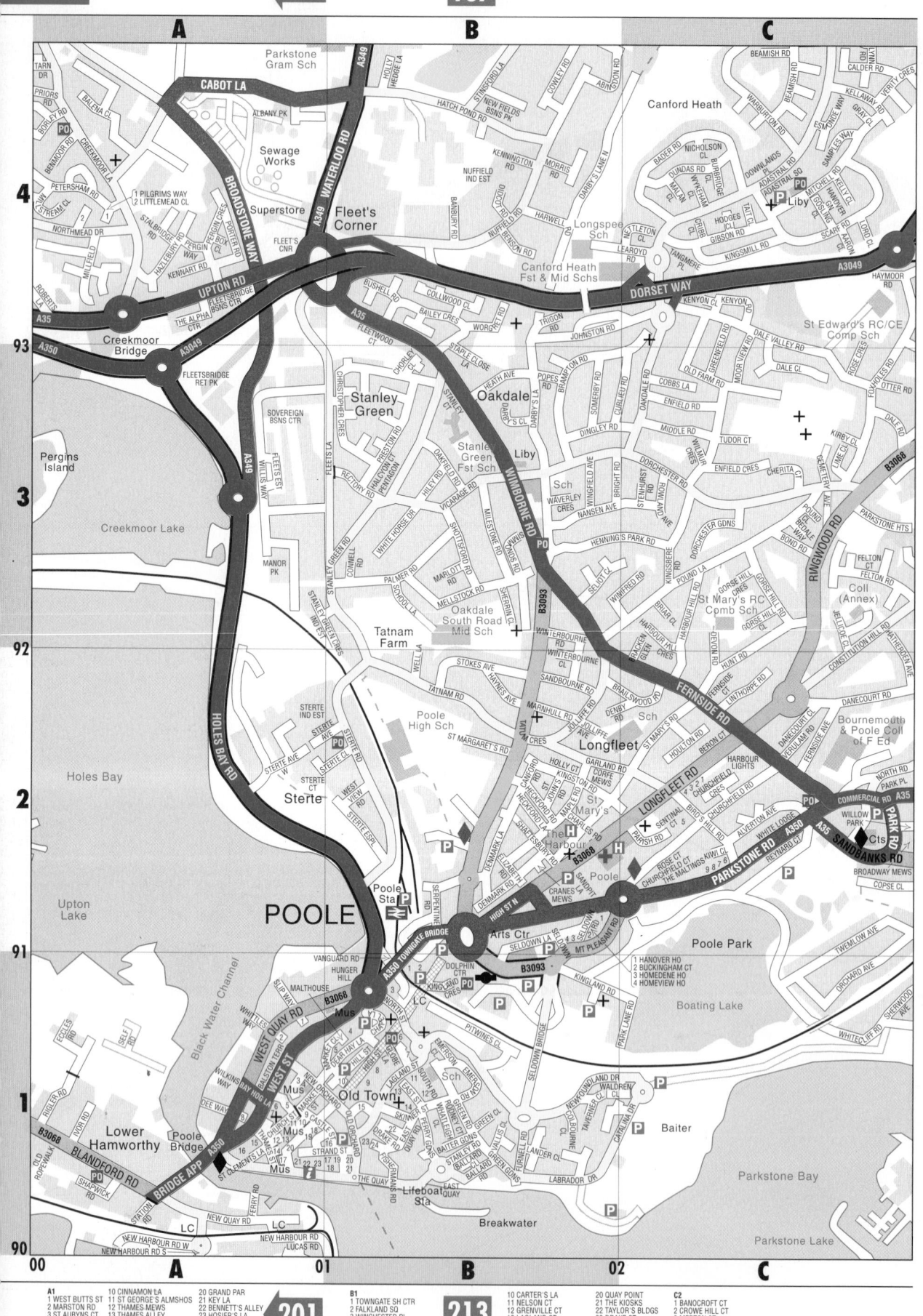

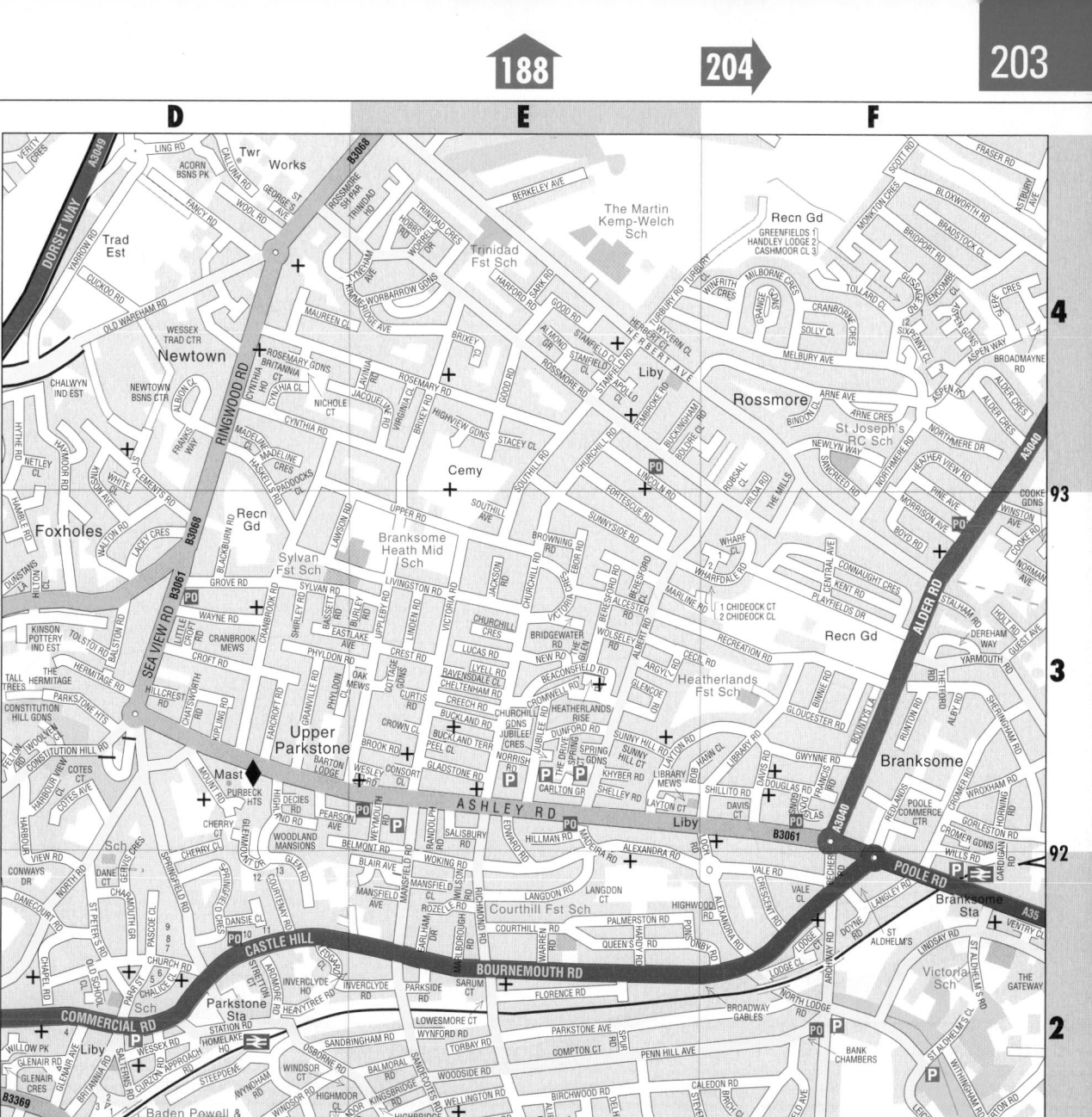

D2
1 TENNYSON RD
2 MENTONE RD
3 CLARENCE RD
4 BRANDWOOD CT
5 PARR HO
6 FRINTON CT
7 ST PETER'S CT
8 SINCLAIR CT
9 ELDON CT
10 WESTBURY CT
11 CHALBURY CT
12 HIGHFIELD HO
13 FAR ENDS

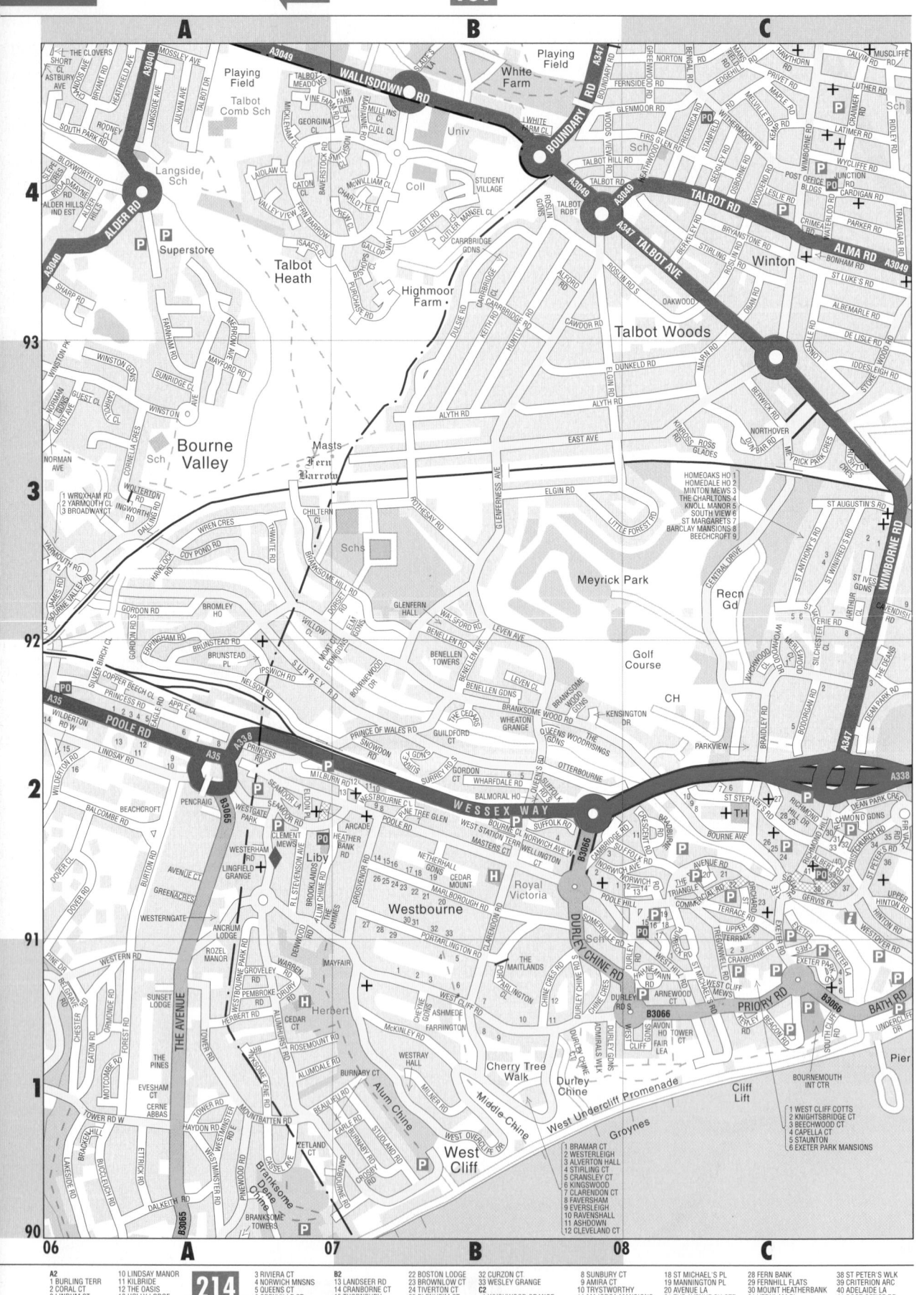

A2
1 BURLING TERR
2 CORAL CT
3 LINDUM CT
4 DARWIN CT
5 EAGLHURST
6 PRINCES CT
7 MARLBOROUGH CT
8 BARONS CT
9 RUTLAND MANOR
10 LINDSAY MANOR
11 KILBRIDE
12 THE OASIS
13 HOLLY LODGE
14 MELTON CT
15 LINDSAY PK
16 PINE PARK MNSNS
B2
1 THE MEWS
2 ST MICHAEL'S

3 RIVIERA CT
4 NORWICH MNSNS
5 QUEENS CT
6 GRENVILLE CT
7 QUARRY CHASE
8 WEST MANSIONS
9 ANGLEWOOD MNS
10 BICKNELL CT
11 BENNETT HO
12 MILBURN CL
B2
13 LANDSEER RD
14 CRANBORNE CT
15 THORNBURY
16 WOLVERLEY CT
17 STOURTON CT
18 ALINGTON
19 CLIVE CT
20 KENT HO
21 MARLBOROUGH CT

22 BOSTON LODGE
23 BROWNLOW CT
24 TIVERTON CT
25 BLENHEIM CT
26 BELMOUR LODGE
27 LANGTON DENE
28 BRIARFIELD
29 BEVERLEY GRANGE
30 BEECHFIELD
31 BEAU CT

32 CURZON CT
33 WESLEY GRANGE
C2
1 WYCHWOOD GRANGE
2 FAIRTHORN CT
3 BOURNE PINES
4 NORWICH CT
5 HORSESHOE CT
6 MEYRICK PARK MANSIONS
7 DURRANT RD

8 SUNBURY CT
9 AMIRA CT
10 TRYSTWORTHY
11 MAJORCA MANSIONS
12 ORCHARD WLK
13 UPPER NORWICH RD
14 PARK GATE MEWS
15 WEST HILL PL
16 ST MICHAEL'S MEWS
17 SOUTH VIEW PL

18 ST MICHAEL'S PL
19 MANNINGTON PL
20 AVENUE LA
21 THE AVENUE SH CTR
22 ORCHARD WLK
23 EDMONSHAM HO
24 BOURNE CT
25 HAMPSHIRE CT
26 HAMPSHIRE
27 ST STEPHEN'S WAY

28 FERN BANK
29 FERNHILL FLATS
30 MOUNT HEATHERBANK
31 VERULAM PL
32 GRANVILLE PL
33 YELVERTON RD
34 BURLINGTON ARC
35 OLD CHRISTCHURCH LA
36 ST PETER'S CRES
37 THE ARCADE

38 ST PETER'S WLK
39 CRITERION ARC
40 ADELAIDE LA
41 POST OFFICE RD

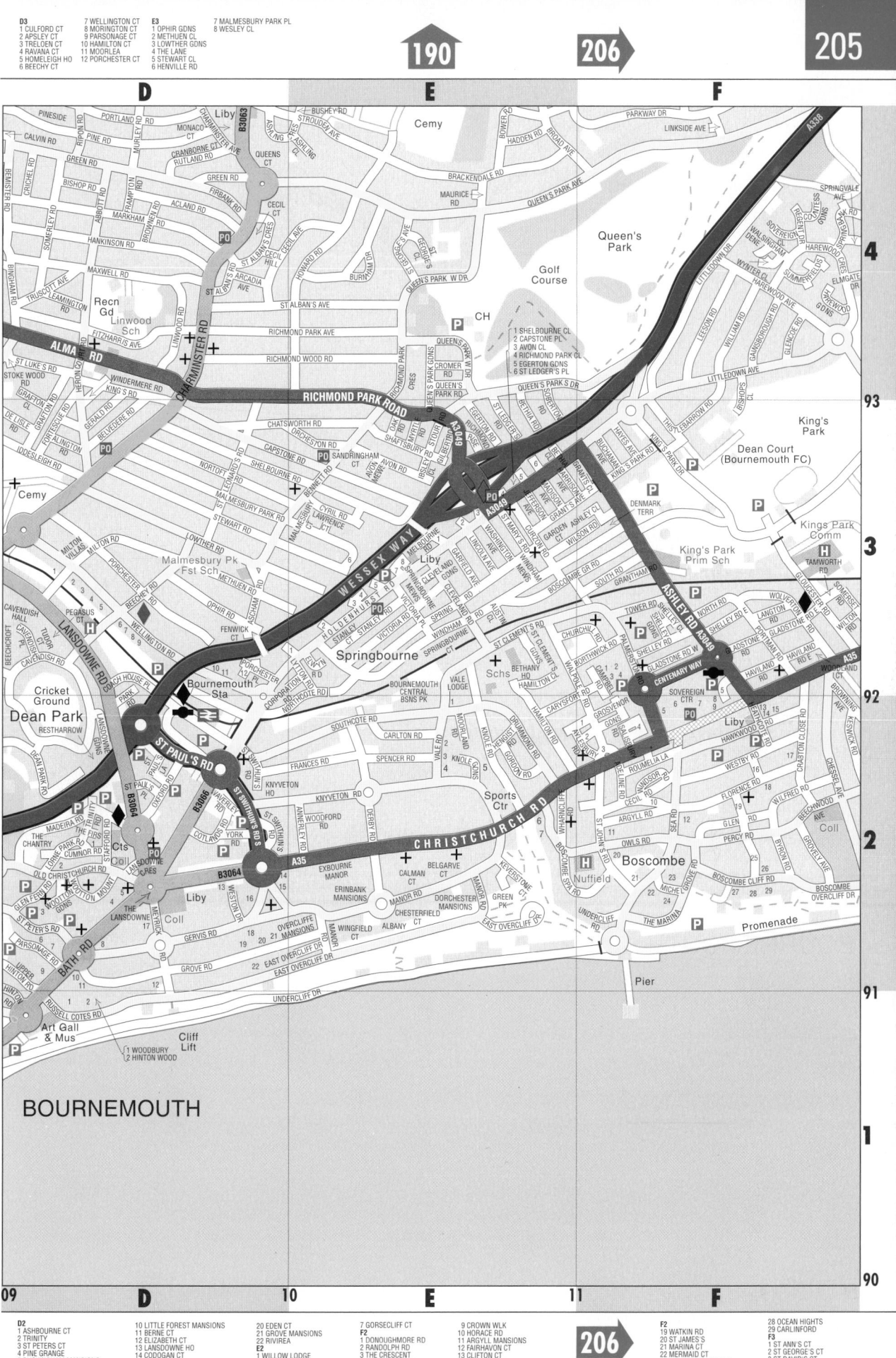

BOURNEMOUTH

Queen's Park

Golf Course

King's Park

Dean Court (Bournemouth FC)

Springbourne

Boscombe

Dean Park
Cricket Ground

Pier

Promenade

Art Gall & Mus

Cliff Lift

206

A3
1 LASCELLES CT
2 MARLBOROUGH MANSIONS
3 WARWICK PL
4 COLONNADE RD W
5 COLONNADE RD
6 COLVILLE RD

7 HARCOURT MEWS
8 WHITINGHAM CT
9 CROMWELL PL
10 STOURVALE PL
11 GAINSBOROUGH CT
12 SEABOURNE PL
13 DEAN'S RD

205 ←

A3
14 PARKWOOD LA
B2
1 ST MICHAELS CT
2 CARBERY ROW
3 CARBERY LA
4 STOURWOOD MANSIONS

191 ↑

205 ←

C2
1 FOXHOLES
2 BELLE VUE GDNS
3 BRACKEN LODGE
4 BOLTON CT
5 THE PARADE
6 SOUTHBOURNE CROSS ROADS
7 BELLE VUE MANSIONS
8 INGARTH
9 AUDRAYTON CT

10 CLIFF HO

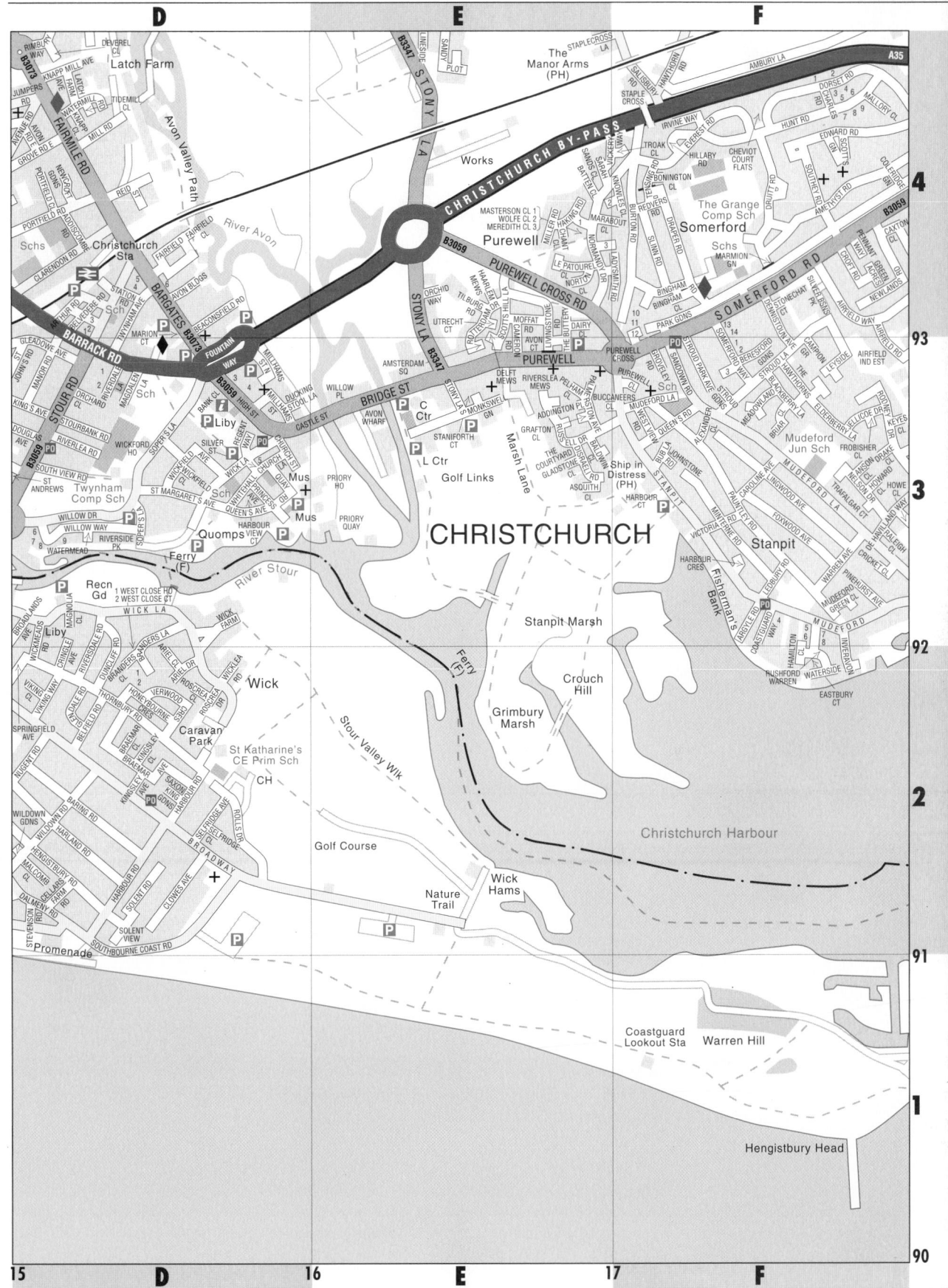

D3
1 HOMESTOUR HO
2 ORCHARD MEWS
3 POUND LA
4 SAXON SQ SH CTR
5 PRIORY VIEW CT
6 MARINA VIEW

7 THE MOORINGS
8 SWAN GN
9 KINGFISHERS
D4
1 WINSTON CT
2 KENILWORTH CT
3 ARTHUR LA

4 MULBERRY CT
5 GILBERT CT
6 CENTENARY HO

F3
1 FRANCESCA LODGE
2 GILLION CT
3 ROSEDALE CL
4 GREEN LOANING
5 ALDERBURY CT
6 CHALBURY CT

F3
7 BADBURY CT
8 DUDSBURY CT
F4
1 SOUTHDOWN CT
2 MALVERN CT
3 PURBECK CT

F4
4 MENDIP CT
5 CHILTERN CT
6 COTSWOLD CT
7 QUANTOCK CT
8 PENNINE CT
9 WENLOCK CT

10 STRETE MOUNT
11 PUREWELL CT
12 COURT CL
13 FRANCESCA GRANGE
14 FRANCESCA CT

192

208

207

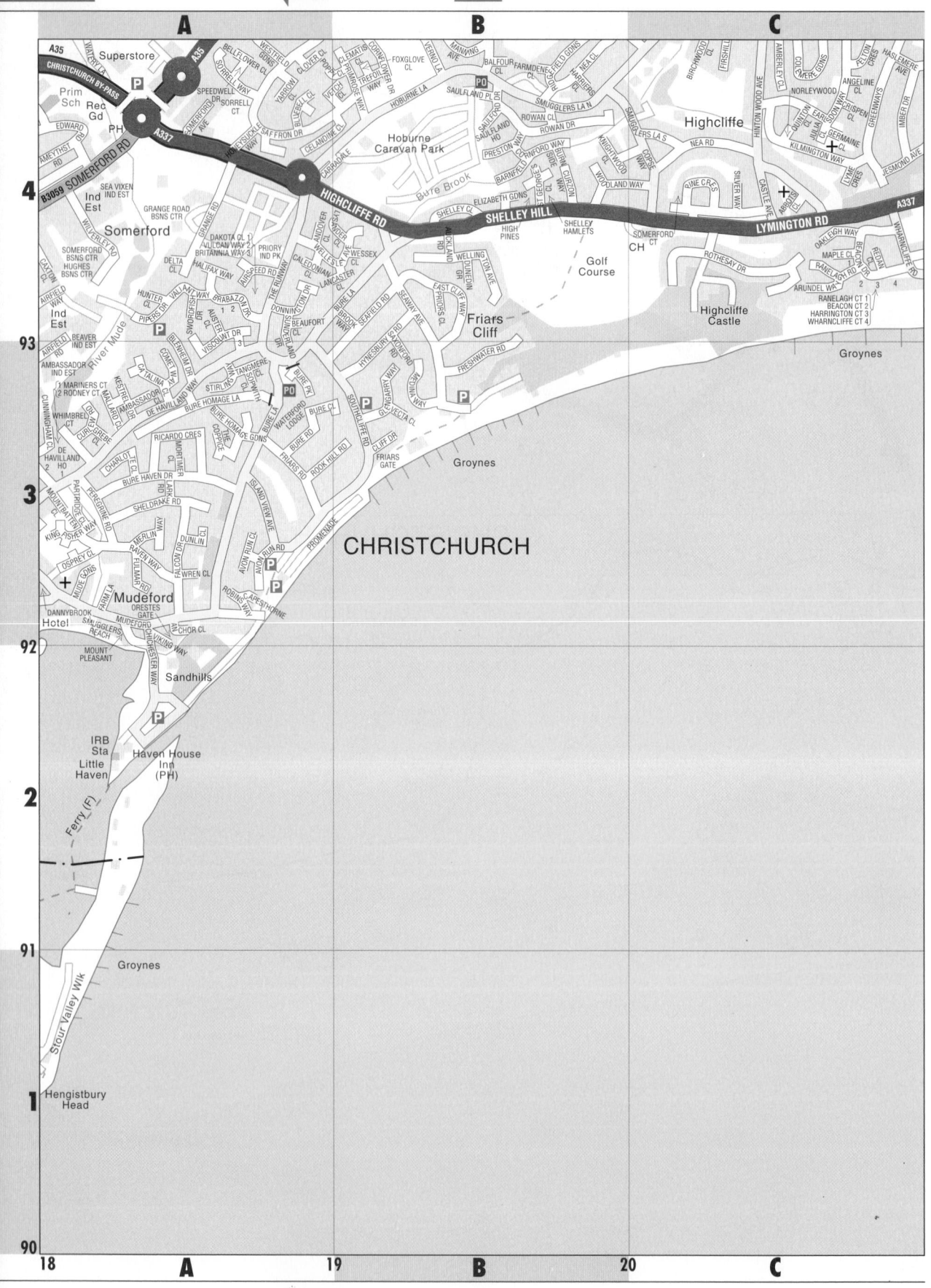

CHRISTCHURCH

D   E   F

HASLEMERE PL
KINGSBERE GDNS
HASLEMERE AVE
MERLEY RD
GORDON MOUNT
ELPHINSTONE RD
GROSVENOR CT
CHEWTON COMMON RD
HOLME RD
CHRISTCHURCH RD
A337
DUNFORD CL
CHILTERN DR
HWOOD AVE
ELDON CL
ELDON DR
THREE ACRE DR
PARKLAND
SOUTHERN LA
WOOD
MOORLAND AVE
MAIN RD
MOAT LA
MOORLAND AVE

LEN CL
EAST CL
KINGSTON PARK
BYRON RD
WAVENDON AVE
HEATHY CL
BARTON DR
BARTON COURT AVE

LYMINGTON RD
Liby
PO
P
SEATON CL
POPLAR
CHEWTON CL
HIGHCLIFFE CNR
MONTAGU RD
BLUE DR
ANDREE
STUART RD
BREARLEY
LORAINE AVE
STUDLEY
ABINGDON DR
GLENDRIVE
THE DE
THE CRESCENT
CUL-DE-SAC
ROCKBOURNE GDNS
SELLWOOD WAY
BRAMSHAW WAY
BURLEY
FIELD PL
TO DE
STUDLEY CT
WESTERN AVE
BARTON LA
SEACROFT AVE
HENGISTBURY RD
SEAFIELD RD
KEYSWORTH AVE
ARNOLDS CL
SEAWARD AVE
BLYTHSWOOD CT

STANLEY RD
WORTLEY RD
MONTAGU PK
WATERFORD GDNS
WATERFORD RD
HIGHCLIFFE LODGE
MARYVAN
THE LAWNS
GLENSIDE
THE PARK
BARTONSIDE RD
PINECLIFFE
EAST AVE
SEAVIEW RD
ISLAND VIEW RD
SALENT RD
SOUTHCLIFFE RD
BSO
BOPLEY
ELLINGHAM
RNEACROFT CL
CARLTON AVE
VECTIS RD
NAISH RD
FAIRFIELD RD
SEAFIELD CL
WHITE KNIGHTS
GROVE RD

ELMWOOD WAY
WHARNCLIFFE GDNS
WHARNCLIFFE RD
MARINA CT
PALMA CT
High Cliff
P
PH
THE PARK
Naish Holiday Village
MARINE CT
PURBECK RD
CLEVELAND CL
POWERSCOURT RD
MARINE DRIVE W
CLIFFE RD
BARTON WOOD RD
WOODLANDS
PO
CHANNEL CT
BARTON HO
WHITE HORSES
MARINE DR
BEACH AVE
SANDMARTIN CL
CHRISTCHURCH BAY RD
SEAWARD AVE

1 TRACEY CT
2 DIANA CT
3 CLAIRE CT

Groynes

Barton Cliff
HARBOUR CT
PEARCE-SMITH CT
WESTMINSTER CT 1
CRESCENT CT 2
CLIFF TERR 3
P
PO
FIRST MARINE AVE
CRESCENT DR
CLIFF CRES

Groynes
Barton on Sea

D4
1 LAVENDER VILLAS
2 BUCKINGHAM CT
3 CASTLE CT
4 CARISBROOKE CT
5 WINDSOR CT
6 HURST CT
7 BALMORAL CT
8 MERTON CT
9 BERMUDA CT
10 EXETER CT
11 PEMBROKE CT
12 HERTFORD CT
13 FRANCES CT
14 ROSEMARY CT
15 KENNETH CT
16 ALAN CT
17 WILLIAM CT
18 PENELOPE CT
19 STELLA CT

4

93

3

92

2

91

1

90

21   D   22   E   23   F

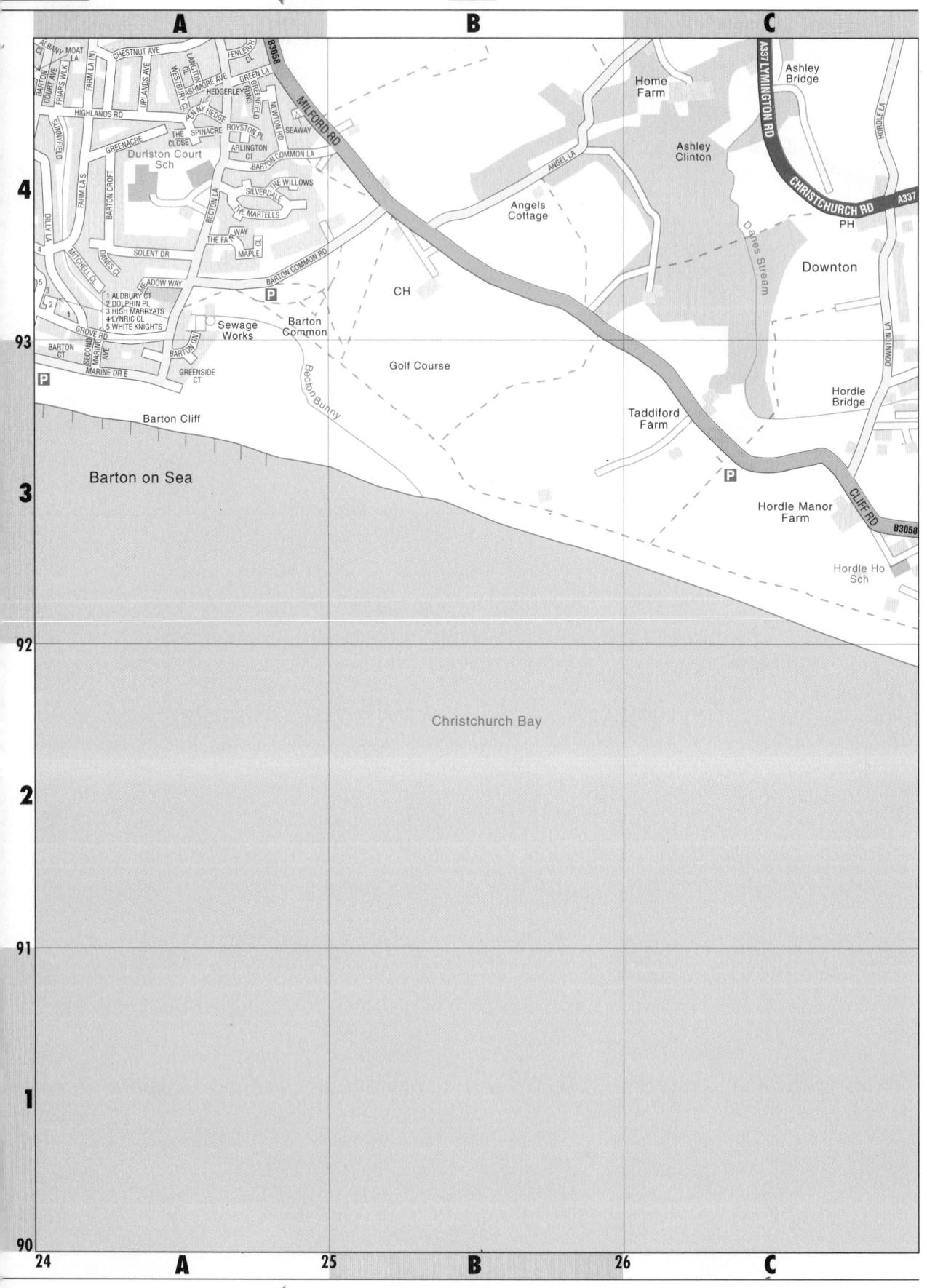

209

195

A **B** **C**

4

93

3

92

2

91

1

90

Barton on Sea

Christchurch Bay

ALBANY MOAT CT
FARM LA INN
FRIARS WLK
BARTON COURT AVE
UPLANDS AVE
CHESTNUT AVE
LANGTON CT
WESTBURY CL
BASHMORE AVE
HEDGERLEY
FENLEIGH CL
GREEN LA
NEWTON RD
GREENFIELD
GREENACRE
HIGHLANDS RD
SUNNYFIELD
DAHLIA LA
FARM LA S
THE HEDGE
THE CLOSE
SPINACRE
ROYSTON PL
ARLINGTON CT
SEAWAY
MILFORD RD
B3058
Durlston Court Sch
BECTON LA
BARTON CROFT
SILVERDALE
THE WILLOWS
THE MARTELLS
MITCHELL CL
DANES CL
SOLENT DR
MEADOW WAY
THE FA WAY
MAPLE CL
BARTON COMMON RD
BARTON COMMON LA
CH
1 ALDBURY CT
2 DOLPHIN PL
3 HIGH MARRYATS
4 LYNRIC CL
5 WHITE KNIGHTS
Sewage Works
Barton Common
Barton Common
Golf Course
GROVE RD
BARTON CT
SECOND MARINE AVE
MARINE DR E
GREENSIDE CT
Becton Bunny
Barton Cliff

Home Farm
Ashley Clinton
Angel La
Angels Cottage
Danes Stream
A337 LYMINGTON RD
Ashley Bridge
HORDLE LA
CHRISTCHURCH RD
A337
PH
Downton
Hordle Bridge
DOWNTON LA
Taddiford Farm
Hordle Manor Farm
CLIFF RD
B3058
Hordle Ho Sch

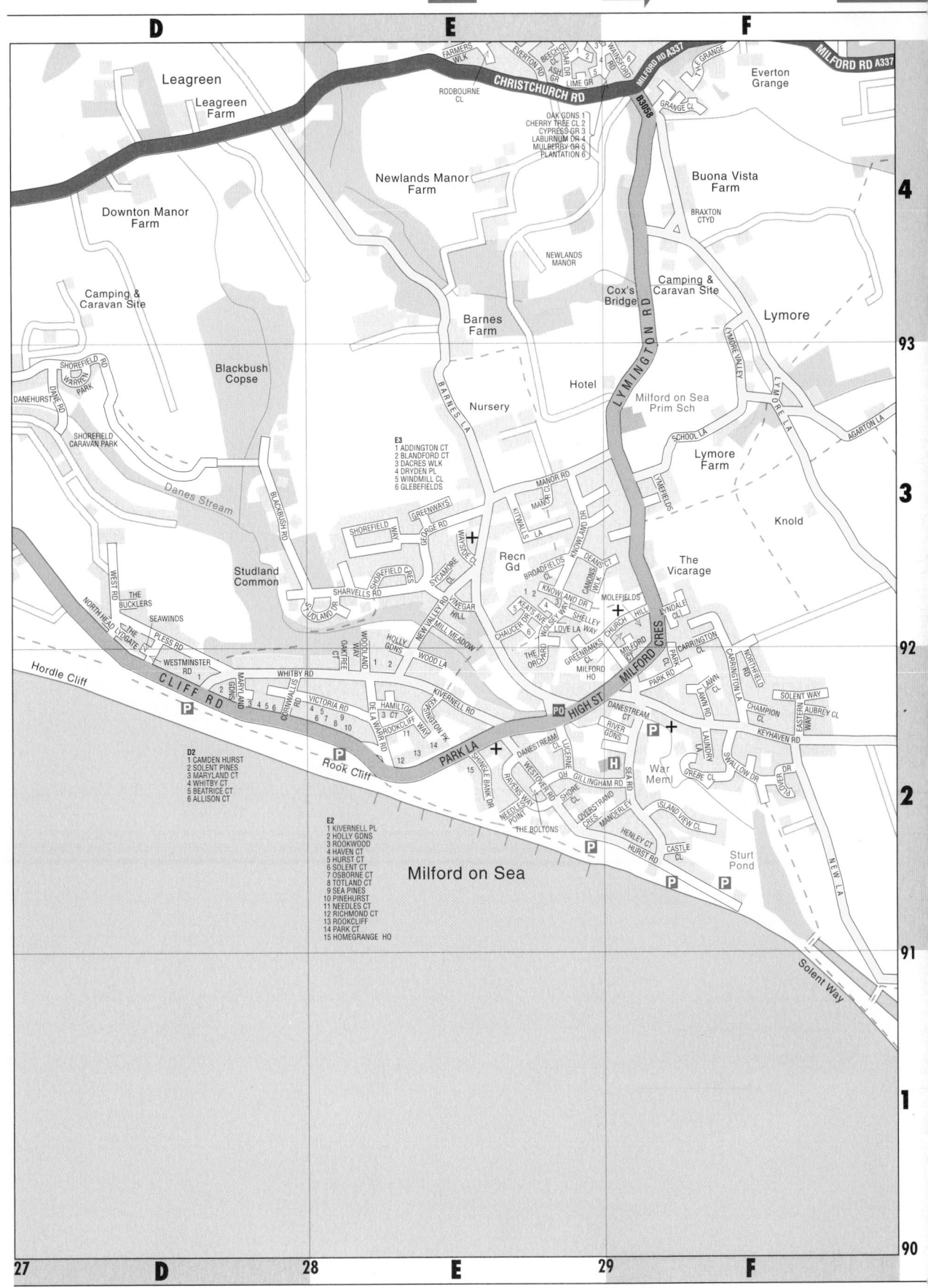

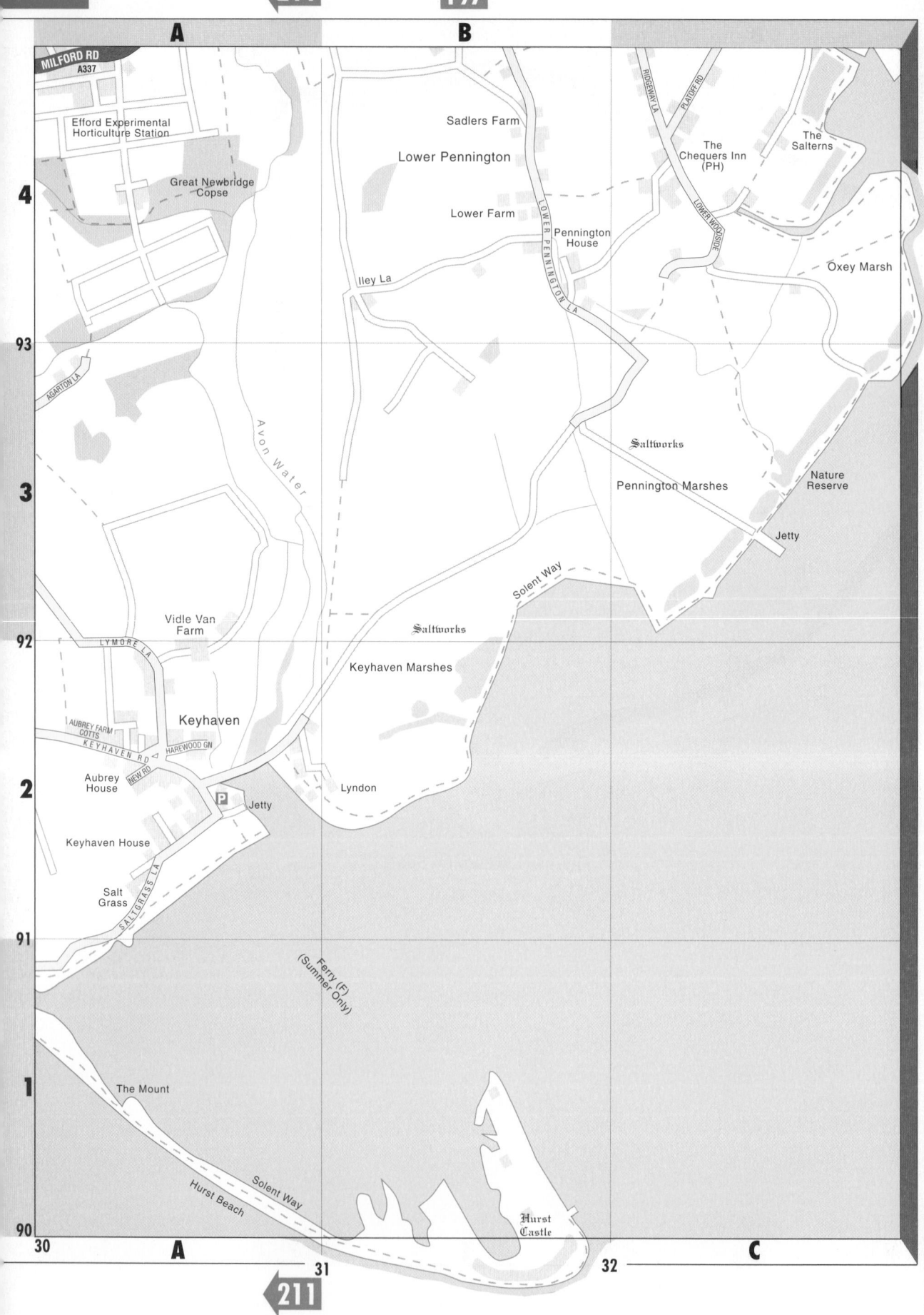

MILFORD RD
A337

Efford Experimental
Horticulture Station

Great Newbridge
Copse

Sadlers Farm

Lower Pennington

Lower Farm

Pennington House

Iley La

Lower Pennington La

The Chequers Inn
(PH)

The
Salterns

RIDGEWAY LA
PLATFORD RD
LOWER WOODSIDE

Oxey Marsh

4

93

Agarton La

Avon Water

Saltworks

Pennington Marshes

Nature
Reserve

3

Jetty

Solent Way

Vidle Van
Farm

Saltworks

Lymore La

92

Keyhaven Marshes

Aubrey Farm
Cotts

Keyhaven

Keyhaven Rd

Harewood Gn

Aubrey
House

New Rd

Lyndon

2

P

Jetty

Keyhaven House

Saltgrass La

Salt
Grass

91

Ferry (F)
(Summer Only)

1

The Mount

Solent Way

Hurst Beach

Hurst
Castle

90

30

A

31

B

32

C

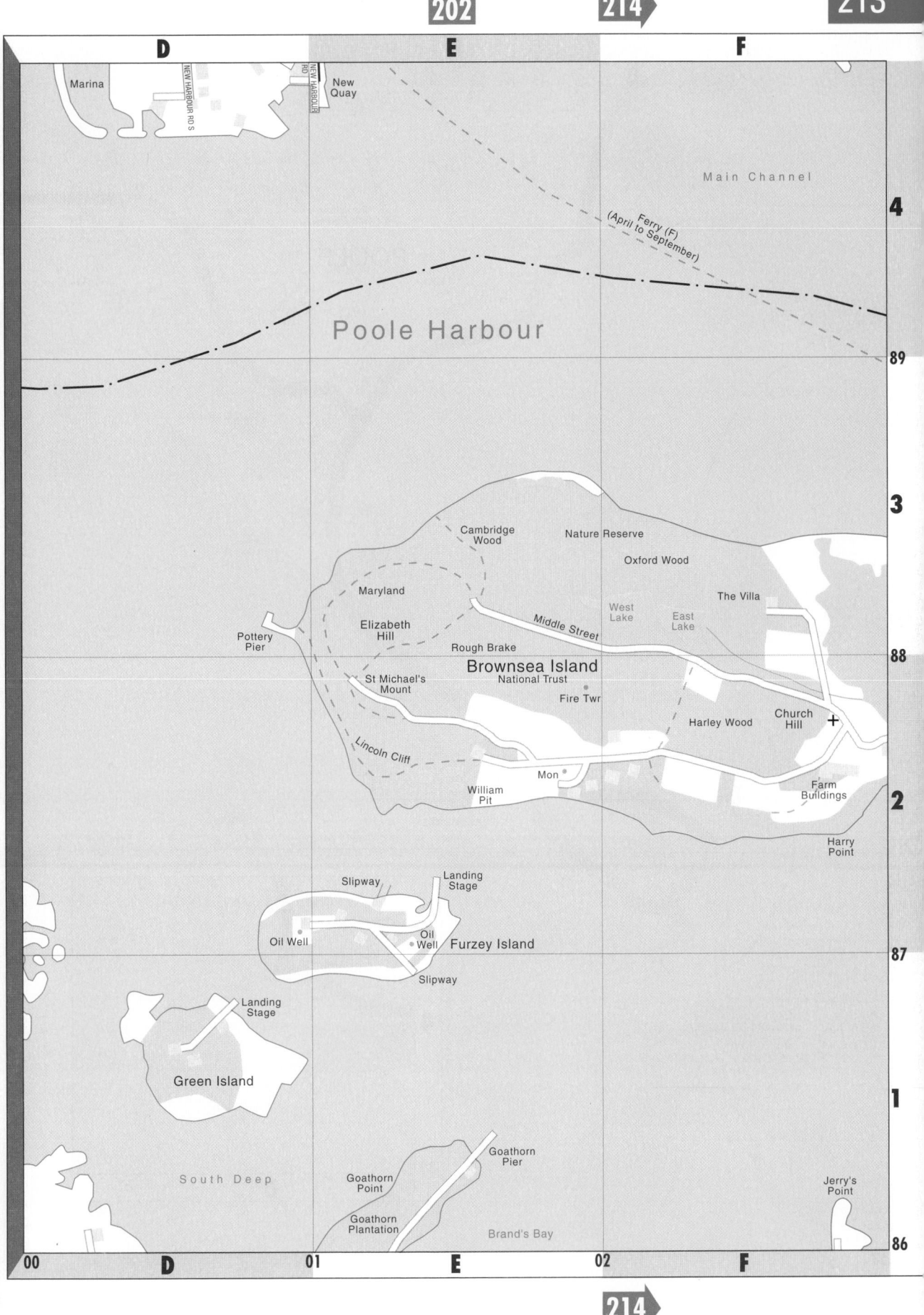

D   E   F

Marina

New Harbour Rd S

New Quay

NEW HARBOUR RD

Main Channel

4

Ferry (F)
(April to September)

Poole Harbour

89

3

Cambridge Wood

Nature Reserve

Oxford Wood

Maryland

West Lake

East Lake

The Villa

Elizabeth Hill

Middle Street

Pottery Pier

Rough Brake

88

St Michael's Mount

Brownsea Island
National Trust

Fire Twr

Harley Wood

Church Hill

+

Lincoln Cliff

Mon

Harry Point

William Pit

Farm Buildings

2

Slipway

Landing Stage

Oil Well

Oil Well

Furzey Island

87

Landing Stage

Green Island

1

South Deep

Goathorn Pier

Goathorn Point

Jerry's Point

Goathorn Plantation

Brand's Bay

86

00   D   01   E   02   F

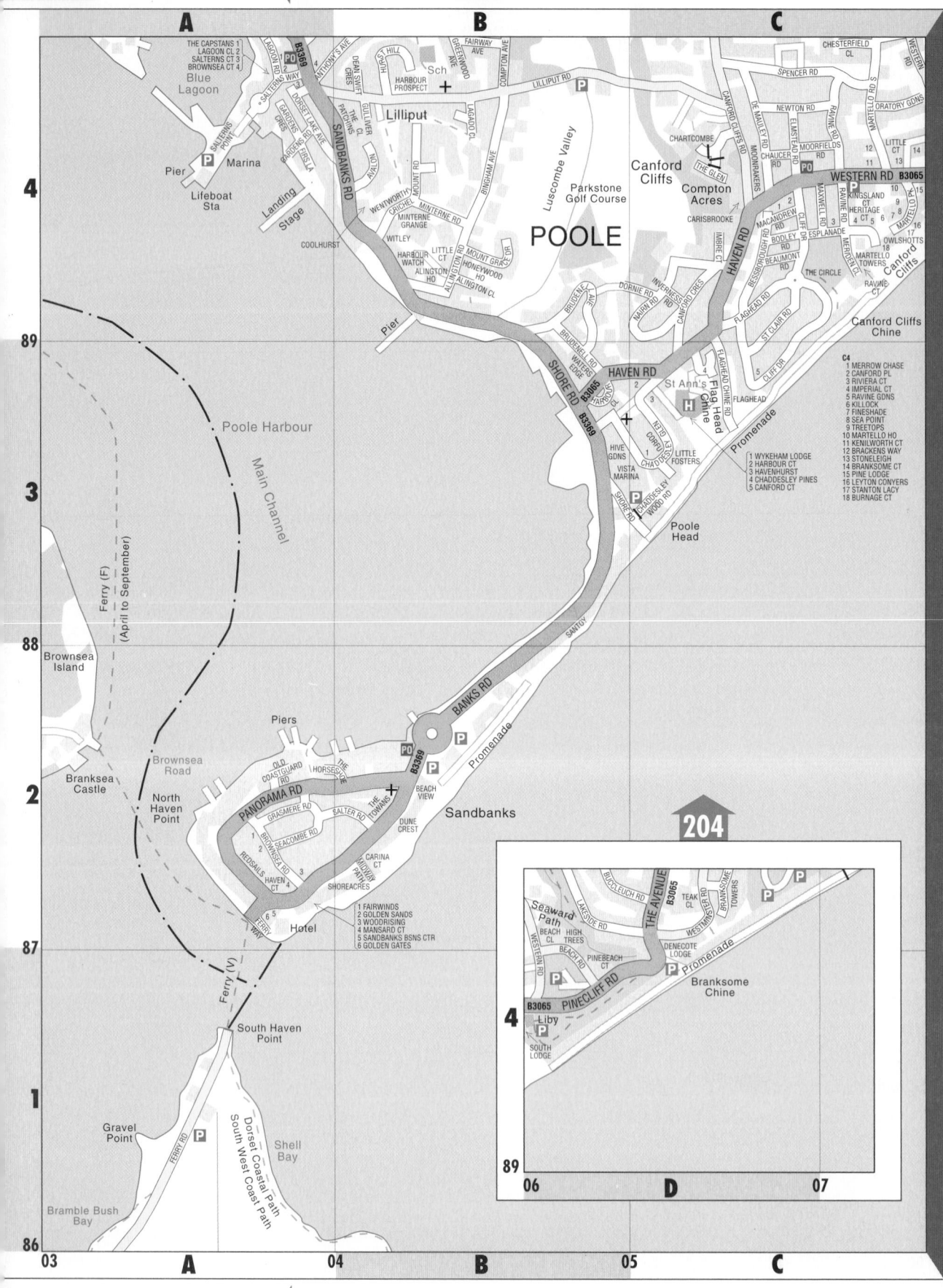

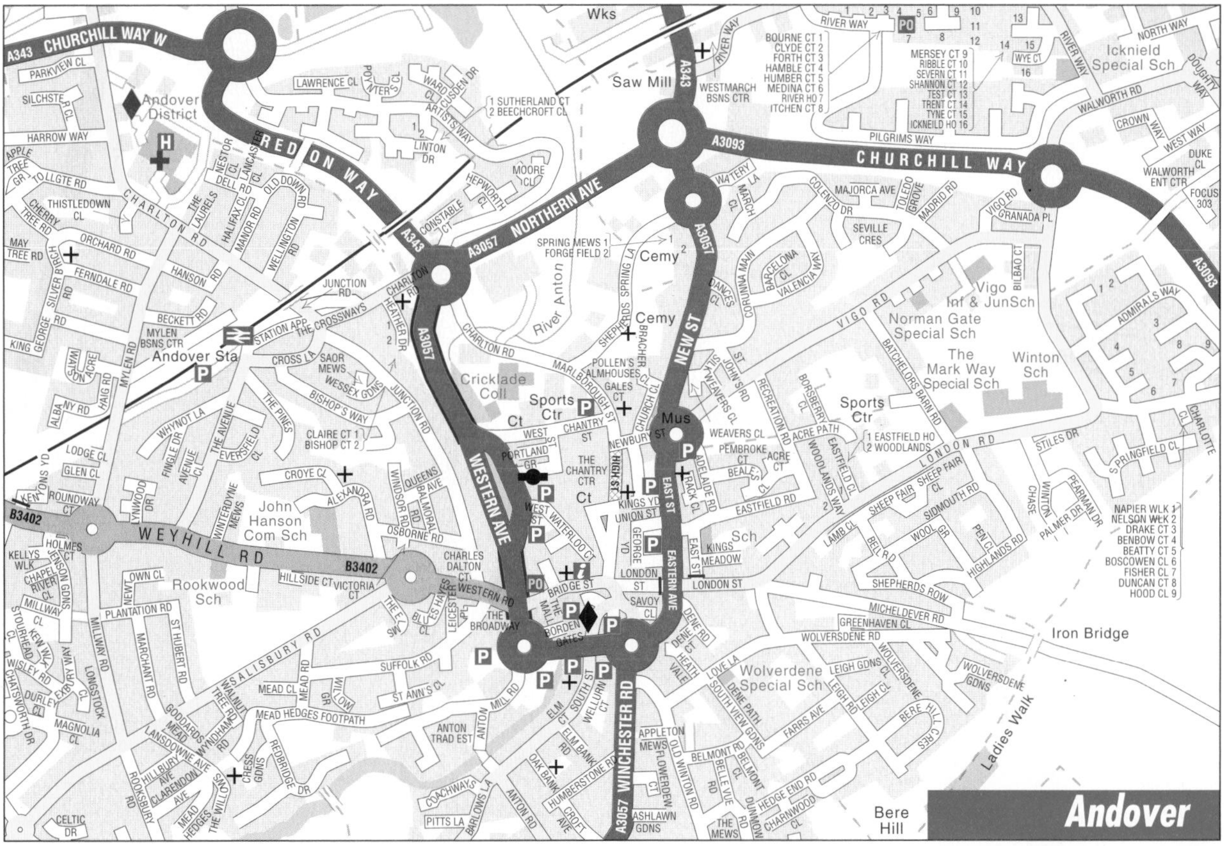
Andover
A343 CHURCHILL WAY W
Andover District
RED ON WAY
NORTHERN AVE
A3057
A343
A3093
CHURCHILL WAY
Wks
Saw Mill
Icknield Special Sch
RIVER WAY
WESTMARCH BSNS CTR
BOURNE CT 1
CLYDE CT 2
FORTH CT 3
HAMBLE CT 4
HUMBER CT 5
MEDINA CT 6
RIVER HO 7
ITCHEN CT 8
MERSEY CT 9
RIBBLE CT 10
SEVERN CT 11
SHANNON CT 12
TEST CT 13
TRENT CT 14
TYNE CT 15
ICKNEILD HO 16
PILGRIMS WAY
NORTH WAY
WALWORTH RD
WALWORTH ENT CTR
FOCUS 303
1 SUTHERLAND CT
2 BEECHCROFT CL
SPRING MEWS 1
FORGE FIELD 2
Cemy
River Anton
Vigo Inf & JunSch
Norman Gate Special Sch
The Mark Way Special Sch
Winton Sch
Andover Sta
MYLEN BSNS CTR
STATION APP
THE CROSSWAYS
Cricklade Coll
Sports Ctr
Ct
Mus
WESTERN AVE
NEW ST
EAST ST
EASTERN AVE
HIGH ST
VIGO RD
LONDON RD
John Hanson Com Sch
Rookwood Sch
WEYHILL RD
B3402
CLAIRE CT 1
BISHOP CT 2
CHARLES DALTON CT
1 EASTFIELD HO
2 WOODLANDS
NAPIER WLK 1
NELSON WLK 2
DRAKE CT 3
BENBOW CT 4
BEATTY CT 5
BOSCOWEN CL 6
FISHER CL 7
DUNCAN CT 8
HOOD CL 9
SHEPHERDS ROW
MICHELDEVER RD
Iron Bridge
Wolverdene Special Sch
Ladies Walk
A3057 WINCHESTER RD
SALISBURY RD
MEAD HEDGES FOOTPATH
ANTON TRAD EST
Bere Hill

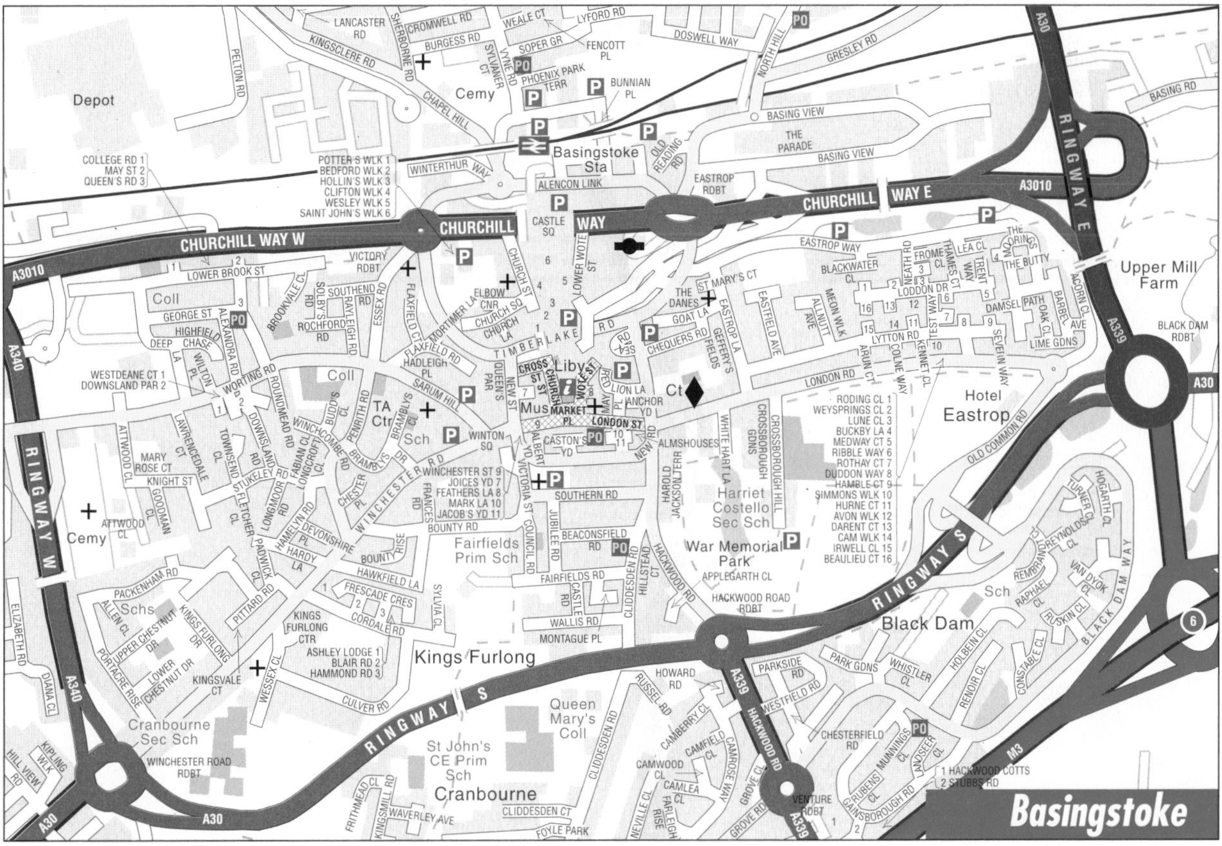
Basingstoke
Depot
Cemy
Basingstoke Sta
BASING VIEW
THE PARADE
EASTROP RDBT
CHURCHILL WAY E
A3010
CHURCHILL WAY W
CHURCHILL WAY
RINGWAY E
RINGWAY W
RINGWAY S
A30
A339
A340
M3
COLLEGE RD 1
MAY ST 2
QUEEN'S RD 3
POTTER'S WLK 1
BEDFORD WLK 2
HOLLIN'S WLK 3
CLIFTON WLK 4
WESLEY WLK 5
SAINT JOHN'S WLK 6
VICTORY RDBT
CASTLE SQ
Upper Mill Farm
BLACK DAM RDBT
Coll
Liby
Mus
Ct
TA Ctr
Sch
Hotel Eastrop
WESTDEANE CT 1
DOWNSLAND PAR 2
WINCHESTER ST 9
JOICES YD 7
FEATHERS LA 8
MARK LA 10
JACOB'S YD 11
RODING CL 1
WEYSPRINGS CL 2
LUNE CL 3
BUCKBY LA 4
MEDWAY CT 5
RIBBLE WAY 6
ROTHAY CT 7
DUDDON WAY 8
HAMBLE CT 9
SIMMONS WLK 10
HURNE CT 11
AVON WLK 12
DARENT CT 13
CAM WLK 14
IRWELL CL 15
BEAULIEU CT 16
Harriet Costello Sec Sch
War Memorial Park
Fairfields Prim Sch
HACKWOOD ROAD RDBT
Black Dam
Kings Furlong
ASHLEY LODGE 1
BLAIR RD 2
HAMMOND RD 3
Queen Mary's Coll
Cranbourne Sec Sch
WINCHESTER ROAD RDBT
St John's CE Prim Sch
Cranbourne
VENTURE RDBT
1 HACKWOOD COTTS
2 STUBBS RD

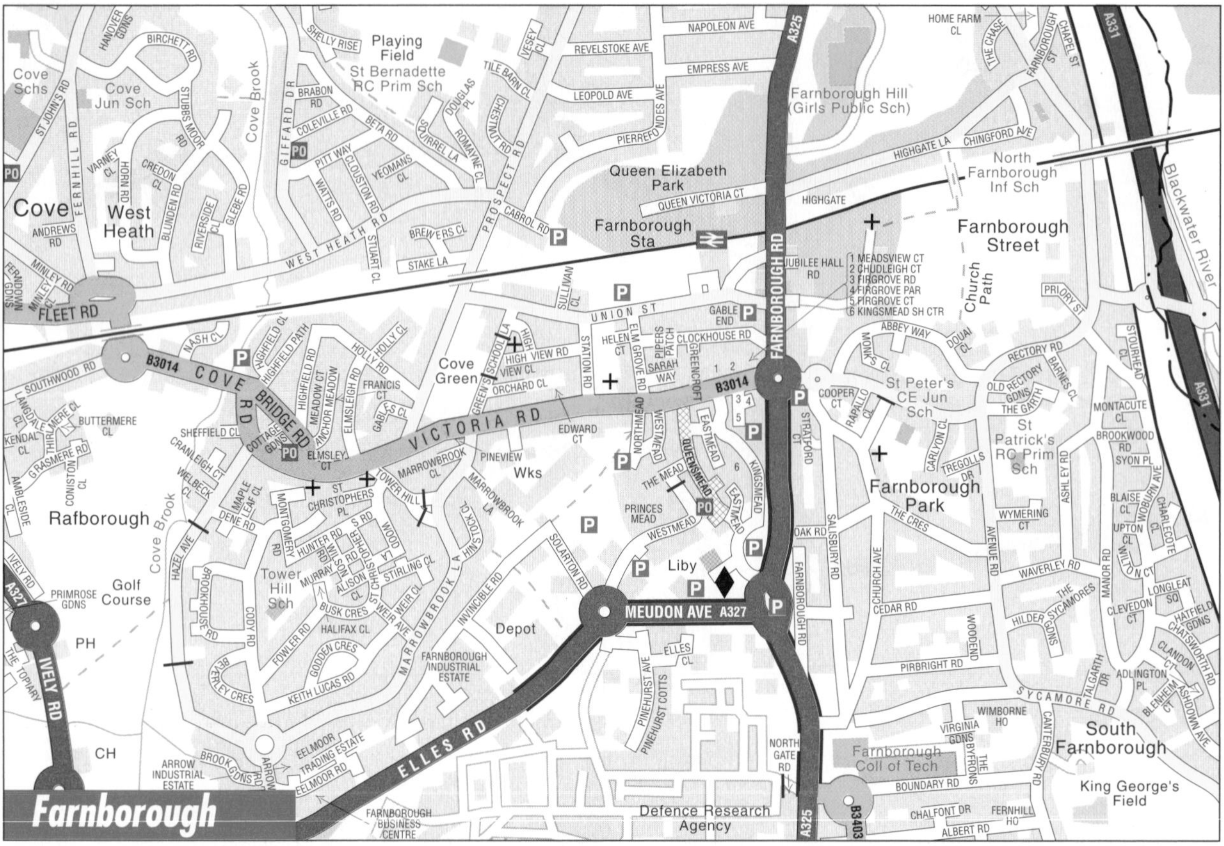
Farnborough
Cove
West Heath
Cove Schs
Cove Jun Sch
Playing Field
St Bernadette RC Prim Sch
Queen Elizabeth Park
Farnborough Sta
Farnborough Hill (Girls Public Sch)
North Farnborough Inf Sch
Farnborough Street
Blackwater River
Church Path
Cove Green
St Peter's CE Jun Sch
St Patrick's RC Prim Sch
Farnborough Park
Rafborough
Golf Course
Tower Hill Sch
Wks
Depot
Liby
Farnborough Industrial Estate
Arrow Industrial Estate
Eelmoor Trading Estate
Farnborough Business Centre
Defence Research Agency
Farnborough Coll of Tech
South Farnborough
King George's Field
CH
PH
FLEET RD
VICTORIA RD
COVE RD
MEUDON AVE
ELLES RD
IVELY RD
FARNBOROUGH RD
WEST HEATH RD
UNION ST
SYCAMORE RD
HIGHGATE LA
A325
A327
A331
B3014
B3403
1 MEADSVIEW CT
2 CHUDLEIGH CT
3 FIRGROVE RD
4 FIRGROVE PAR
5 FIRGROVE CT
6 KINGSMEAD SH CTR

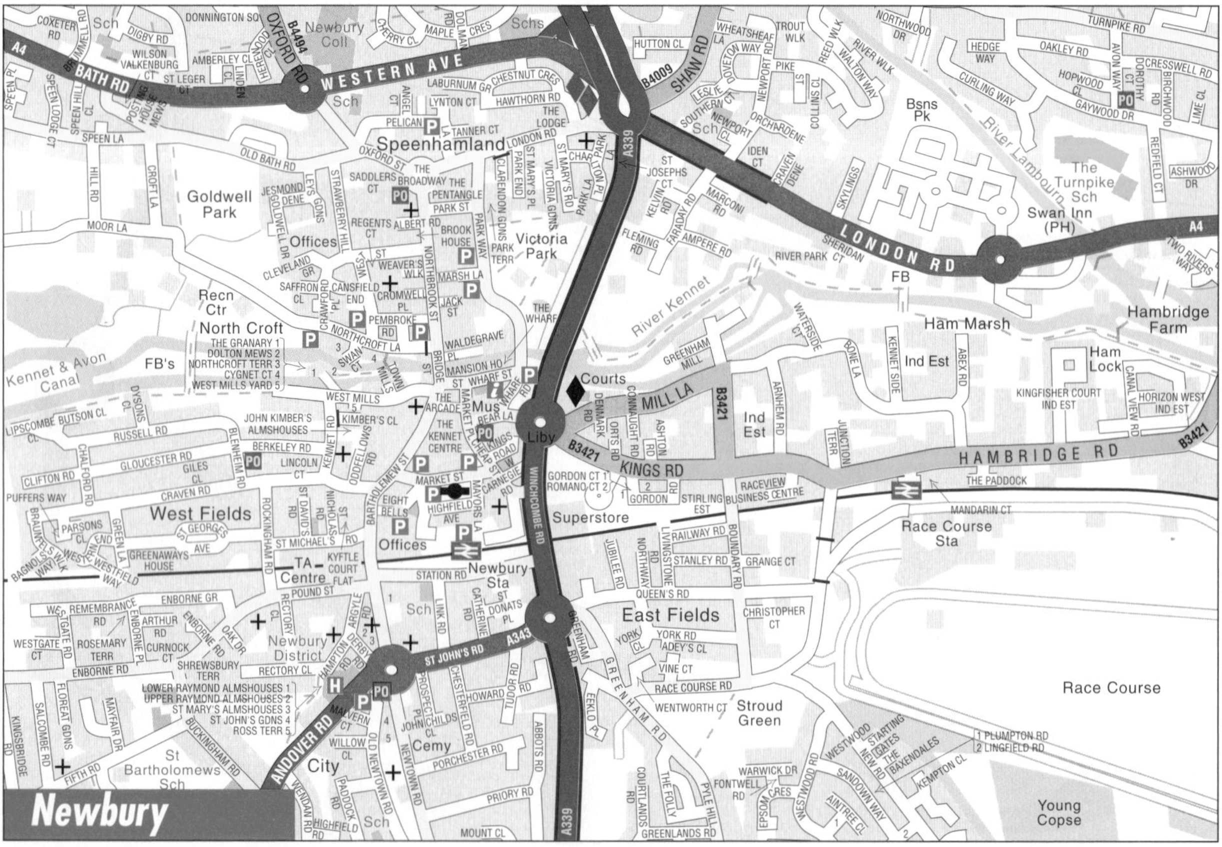
Newbury
Newbury Coll
Speenhamland
Goldwell Park
Victoria Park
Offices
Recn Ctr
North Croft
FB's
Kennet & Avon Canal
River Kennet
River Lambourn
Mus
Liby
Courts
West Fields
TA Centre
Newbury Sta
Newbury District
Superstore
East Fields
Stroud Green
City
Cemy
St Bartholomews Sch
Bsns Pk
The Turnpike Sch
Swan Inn (PH)
Ham Marsh
Ind Est
Hambridge Farm
Ham Lock
Race Course Sta
Race Course
Young Copse
BATH RD
WESTERN AVE
OXFORD RD
LONDON RD
KINGS RD
HAMBRIDGE RD
MILL LA
ANDOVER RD
ST JOHN'S RD
A4
A339
A343
B4494
B4009
B3421
1 THE GRANARY
2 DOLTON MEWS
3 NORTHCROFT TERR
4 CYGNET CT
5 WEST MILLS YARD
1 LOWER RAYMOND ALMSHOUSES
2 UPPER RAYMOND ALMSHOUSES
3 ST MARY'S ALMSHOUSES
4 ST JOHN'S GDNS
5 ROSS TERR
1 PLUMPTON RD
2 LINGFIELD RD

Street names are listed alphabetically and show the locality, the Postcode District, the page number and
a reference to the square in which the name falls on the map page

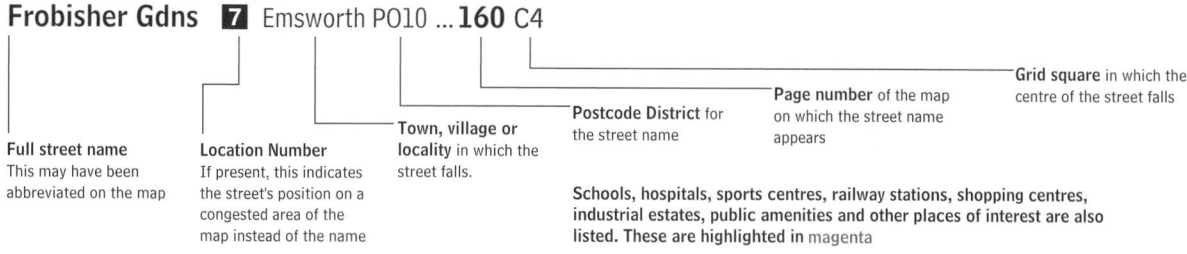

Full street name
This may have been
abbreviated on the map

Location Number
If present, this indicates
the street's position on a
congested area of the
map instead of the name

Town, village or
locality in which the
street falls.

Postcode District for
the street name

Page number of the map
on which the street name
appears

Grid square in which the
centre of the street falls

Schools, hospitals, sports centres, railway stations, shopping centres,
industrial estates, public amenities and other places of interest are also
listed. These are highlighted in magenta

Abbreviations used in the index

App **Approach**	Cl **Close**	Ent **Enterprise**	La **Lane**	Rdbt **Roundabout**
Arc **Arcade**	Comm **Common**	Espl **Esplanade**	N **North**	S **South**
Ave **Avenue**	Cnr **Corner**	Est **Estate**	Orch **Orchard**	Sq **Square**
Bvd **Boulevard**	Cotts **Cottages**	Gdns **Gardens**	Par **Parade**	Strs **Stairs**
Bldgs **Buildings**	Ct **Court**	Gn **Green**	Pk **Park**	Stps **Steps**
Bsns Pk **Business Park**	Ctyd **Courtyard**	Gr **Grove**	Pas **Passage**	St **Street, Saint**
Bsns Ctr **Business Centre**	Cres **Crescent**	Hts **Heights**	Pl **Place**	Terr **Terrace**
Bglws **Bungalows**	Dr **Drive**	Ho **House**	Prec **Precinct**	Trad Est **Trading Estate**
Cswy **Causeway**	Dro **Drove**	Ind Est **Industrial Estate**	Prom **Promenade**	Wlk **Walk**
Ctr **Centre**	E **East**	Intc **Interchange**	Ret Pk **Retail Park**	W **West**
Cir **Circus**	Emb **Embankment**	Junc **Junction**	Rd **Road**	Yd **Yard**

Town and village index

Abbotswood 28 A2	Compton .... 90 Cl	Havant 135 F2	Netley Marsh 100 A3
Alderholt 92 C3	Compton (Winchester) .. 31 E4	Hawkley 19 F4	New Milton 194 C2
Ampfield 29 E2	Coombe Bisset 23 F4	Hayling Island 185 D4	Newbridge 74 C2
Ashurst 100 A2	Corfe Mullen 186 B3	Hedge End 105 E3	Nomansland 73 E4
Awbridge 26 C2	Cosham 158 A3	High Cross 18 C1	North Baddesley 53 F3
Bartley 99 D3	Cowplain 111 F2	Highcliffe 208 C4	North Boarhunt 109 D1
Barton on Sea 209 F3	Cranbourne 91 D4	Hill Brow .... 21 DI	North Hayling 160 B2
Beaulieu .... 148 Cl	Croucheston 22 A4	Hoe Gate 109 F4	Nursling 77 E3
Beauworth 35 D4	Curdridge 106 C4	Holbury 150 B2	Oakley .... 163 FI
Bishop's Waltham 83 E4	Damerham 68 B3	Holt Heath 138 A3	Otterbourne 31 E2
Bishopstoke 56 C2	Dean 59 F2	Hordle 195 F2	Ower 75 F3
Bisterne Close 143 E1	Denmead 111 D3	Horndean 112 B4	Owslebury 33 D2
Blackfield 177 F4	Dibden Purlieu 125 F1	Horton Heath 81 E4	Pamphill 162 C3
Blashford 117 D2	Downton 47 D4	Hurn 191 D4	Pentridge .... 42 AI
Boldre .... 173 EI	Droxford .... 61 DI	Hursley 30 A4	Petersfield 40 B2
Botley 106 A4	Durley 82 A3	Hythe 126 A3	Plaitford 50 A2
Bournemouth 206 A2	East Boldre 175 E3	Ibsley 117 D4	Poole 202 A2
Braishfield 28 B4	East Dean .... 4 AI	Keyhaven 212 A2	Portchester 156 B4
Bramdean 15 E2	East End 199 D4	Kilmeston .... 14 BI	Portmore 198 A4
Bramshaw 73 F2	East Meon .... 38 BI	Kings Worthy 2 B3	Portsea Island 182 C3
Bransgore 193 D4	East Tytherley 4 C4	Kingston 167 F4	Portsmouth 157 E2
Breamore 70 A4	East Wellow 51 D3	Landford 49 E2	Privett 17 E1
Broadstone 187 D2	Eastleigh 55 F2	Langrish 39 E2	Purbrook 134 C2
Brockenhurst .... 145 FI	Edmondsham 91 D2	Langstone 159 F4	Rake 21 F2
Brook .... 74 AI	Emery Down 121 E3	Lee-on-the-Solent 179 E1	Ramsdean 39 E1
Brown Sea Island 213 E2	Emsworth .... 136 CI	Lepe 178 A1	Redlynch 47 F3
Bucklers Hard 176 B2	Exbury 177 D3	Linwood 118 A4	Ringwood 141 E4
Buriton 65 E3	Fair Oak .... 57 EI	Liss 21 D2	Ripley 168 B1
Burley 143 D2	Fareham 131 D2	Littleton 1 A3	Rockbourne .... 44 Cl
Bursledon 128 A4	Fawley 151 D2	Lockerley .... 4 Cl	Rogate 41 F3
Burton .... 192 BI	Ferndown 165 D3	Locks Heath 129 E2	Romsey 52 C3
Cadnam 98 C4	Finchdean 113 E3	Lover 48 A3	Rowland's Castle .... 113 EI
Calshot 178 C4	Fordingbridge .... 69 FI	Lymington 197 D2	Rownhams 77 F4
Chalton 89 E3	Fratton 182 C2	Lyndhurst 121 F3	Sandbanks 214 B2
Chandler's Ford 55 E4	Fritham .... 72 CI	Marchwood .... 101 FI	Shawford 31 F4
Cheriton 14 B3	Frogham 94 C4	Martin 43 D2	Shedfield 107 E4
Chidden 86 C4	Froxfield Green 39 E4	Meonstoke 61 E3	Sherfield English .... 25 EI
Chilcomb 12 A3	Godshill 70 C1	Michelmersh .... 6 BI	Soberton 85 E3
Chilworth .... 54 BI	Gosport 181 E4	Milford on Sea 211 E2	Sopley 192 A4
Christchurch 207 E3	Hamble-le-Rice 128 A1	Minstead 98 A2	South Harting 66 C2
Clanfield 88 A3	Hambledon .... 86 BI	Mottisfont .... 5 FI	South Hayling .... 184 CI
Colden Common .... 32 AI	Hamworthy 201 E2	Netley 127 D3	Southampton 102 B2
			Southbourne 161 F4
			Southsea 182 B1
			Southwick 132 C3
			St Leonards 139 E2
			Standon 9 D1
			Steep 40 B4
			Stubbington 154 B2
			Swanmore 84 B3
			Swanwick 129 D4
			Sway 172 A1
			Thorney Island 161 D2
			Three Legged Cross 138 C4
			Timsbury 27 E3
			Titchfield 153 F4
			Totton 100 C4
			Twyford 32 A3
			Upham 58 C3
			Upton 201 E4
			Verwood 114 C2
			Walderton 137 F4
			Warnford 36 C2
			Warsash 128 B1
			Waterlooville 134 B4
			West Dean 3 E2
			West End 80 C1
			West Meon 37 D2
			West Moors 138 C2
			West Parley 189 F4
			West Tisted 16 B4
			West Wellow 50 C2
			Westbourne 137 D2
			Whiteparish 24 A2
			Whitsbury 45 D2
			Wick 46 B4
			Wickham 108 A2
			Wimborne Minster 163 D3
			Winchester 10 B3
			Woodgreen 70 C4
			Woodlands 114 A3
			Wootton 171 D1

1st St SO45 151 D2
2nd St SO45 151 D2
3rd St SO45 150 C2
4th St SO45 150 C2
5th St SO45 150 C2
6th St Fawley SO45 150 C2
Fawley SO45 150 C3
7th St SO45 150 C2
8th St SO45 150 C2
9th St SO45 150 B2
10th St SO45 150 B3
11th St SO45 150 B3
12th St SO45 150 B3
13th St SO45 150 B3
14th St SO45 150 B3
A Ave SO45 150 B2
A'beckett Ct PO1 182 A2
Aaron Cl BH17 202 C4
Aaron Ct SO40 101 F1
Abbas Gr PO9 135 E4
Abbey Cl SO45 126 A2
Abbey Ct 15 SO15 102 C4
Abbey Ent Ctr SO51 53 E3
Abbey Gdns BH21 164 B3
Abbey Hill SO31 127 D4
Abbey Hill Cl SO23 2 A1
Abbey Hill Rd SO23 1 C1
Abbey Pas SO23 11 D4
Abbey Rd Fareham PO15 130 B1
West Moors BH22 166 A4
Abbey The SO51 52 C4
Abbey Water 9 SO51 52 C4
Abbeyfield Dr PO15 130 B1
Abbeyfield House 7 SO18 103 F4
Abbeyfields Cl SO31 127 E3
Abbots Cl Christchurch BH23 208 C4
Waterlooville PO7 134 B2
Abbots Way Fareham PO15 130 B1
Netley SO31 127 E3
Abbots Well Rd SP6 94 C4
Abbotsbury Rd
Bishopstoke SO50 56 C1
Corfe Mullen BH18 186 C3
Abbotsfield SO40 100 C4
Abbotsfield Cl SO16 78 B3
Abbotsford SO40 99 D3
Abbotstone Ave PO9 136 A2
Abbotswood Cl SO51 28 B1
Abbotswood GM Jun Sch
SO40 100 C4
Abbott Rd BH9 205 D4
Abbott St BH21 162 B3
Abbotts Ann Rd SO22 1 B2
Abbotts Cl SO23 2 A1
Abbotts Ct
15 Southampton SO17 79 D1
Winchester SO22 1 C1
Abbotts Dro SO51 50 C1
Abbotts Rd Eastleigh SO50 55 F1
Winchester SO23 2 A1
Abbotts Way Southampton SO17 79 D1
West Moors BH22 166 A4
Abercrombie Gdns SO16 78 A2
Aberdare Ave PO6 158 A4
Aberdare Rd BH10 189 F2
Aberdeen Cl PO15 130 C2
Aberdeen Rd SO17 79 E1
Aberdour Cl SO18 104 A4
Abingdon Cl PO12 181 D2
Abingdon Dr BH23 209 E4
Abingdon Gdns SO16 78 C2
Abingdon Rd BH17 202 B4
Abinger Rd BH7 206 A3
Abney Rd BH10 189 E2
Above Bar St SO14 102 C3
Abraham Cl SO30 105 E3
Abshot Cl PO14 129 D1
Abshot Rd PO14 129 E1
Acacia Ave BH31 115 E3
Acacia Gdns PO8 112 A3
Acacia Rd Hordle SO41 195 F2
Southampton SO19 103 F3
Ackworth Rd PO3 158 A3
Acland Rd BH9 205 D4
Acorn Bsns Ctr PO6 157 E4
Acorn Bsns Pk BH12 203 D4
Acorn Cl Christchurch BH23 206 C4
Cosham PO6 158 C4
Gosport PO13 155 E1
Marchwood SO40 102 A1
New Milton BH25 195 E2
St Leonards BH24 139 F2
Acorn Cotts BH31 114 C4
Acorn Ct SO31 127 F2
Acorn Dr SO16 77 F4
Acorn Gdns PO8 112 A3
Acorn Gr SO52 54 C2
Acorn Workshops SO14 103 D4
Acorns The Bursledon SO31 127 F4
Wimborne Minster BH21 164 A2
Acre La PO7 112 B1
Acres Rd BH11 189 D1
Actaeon Rd PO1 182 A2
Acton Rd BH10 189 D1
Ad Astro Fst Sch BH17 187 F1
Adair Rd PO4 183 D1
Adames Rd PO1 182 C3
Adams Cl SO30 81 D2
Adams Rd SO45 126 A1
Adams Terr PO6 158 B3
Adams Wood Dr SO40 101 F1
Adamsfield Gdns BH10 189 E1
Adamson Cl SO53 55 E4
Adastral Rd BH17 202 C4
Adastral Sq BH17 202 C4
Adcock Ct SO16 77 F4
Adderbury Ave PO10 136 C2
Addington Ct 1 SO41 211 E3
Addington Pl BH23 207 E3
Addis Sq 35 SO17 79 D1
Addiscombe Rd BH23 207 D4
Addison Cl Romsey SO51 28 A1
Winchester SO22 10 B3
Addison Rd Brockenhurst SO42 172 C4
Eastleigh SO50 56 A3
Locks Heath SO31 128 C3
Portsmouth PO5 182 C2
Addison Sq BH24 141 D4
Adelaide Cl BH23 206 C4
Adelaide Ct SO41 197 F2
Adelaide La 40 BH1 204 C2
Adelaide Pl 9 PO16 131 E1
Adelaide Rd SO17 103 E4
Adeline Rd BH5 205 F2
Adey Cl SO19 104 A1
Adhurst Rd PO9 136 A2
Adlam's La SO41 172 A1
Admiral Park The PO3 158 A2
Admiral's Cnr 4 PO5 182 B1
Admiral's Wlk PO1 181 F3
Admirals Cl SO45 151 D2
Admirals Ct
Hamble-le-Rice SO31 128 A1
Lymington SO41 197 F2
19 Portsmouth PO5 182 B1
Admirals Rd SO31 129 D2
Admirals Way SO45 126 A3
Admirals Wlk
Bournemouth BH2 204 B1
Gosport PO12 180 C2
Admiralty Cotts PO12 181 E1
Admiralty Rd
Bournemouth BH6 206 C2
Portsmouth PO1 182 A3
Admiralty Way SO40 101 F2
Adsdean Cl PO9 135 F2
Adstone La PO3 158 B2
Adur Cl PO12 180 C4
Aerodrome Rd PO13 155 F2
Africa Dr SO40 124 C4
Agar's La SO41 196 A3
Agarton La SO41 211 F3
Aggis Farm Rd BH31 114 C3
Agincourt Rd PO2 182 B4
Agitator Rd SO45 151 E2
Agnew House PO12 181 D3
Agnew Rd PO13 155 E2
Aikman La SO40 100 A4
Ailsa La SO19 103 E2
Ainsdale Rd PO6 134 B1
Ainsley Gdns SO50 56 A3
Aintree Cl SO50 81 E4
Aintree Ct SO31 129 D4
Aintree Dr PO7 112 A1
Aintree Rd SO40 76 B1
Airetons Cl BH18 187 E2
Airfield Ind Est BH23 207 F3
Airfield Rd BH23 207 F3
Airfield Way BH23 207 F4
Airlie Cnr SO22 10 C3
Airlie Rd SO22 10 C3
Airport Service Rd PO3 158 A2
Airspeed Rd
Christchurch BH23 208 A4
Portsmouth PO3 158 B1
Ajax Cl PO14 179 E3
Akeshill Cl BH25 195 D3
Alameda Rd PO7 134 B2
Alameda Way PO7 134 B2
Alan Chun House SO31 127 E4
Alan Ct 16 BH23 209 D4
Alan Drayton Way SO50 56 C1
Alan Gr PO15 130 C1
Alandale Rd SO19 104 B2
Albacore Ave SO31 128 C1
Albany BH1 205 E2
Albany Cl BH25 194 C1
Albany Ct
Bishop's Waltham SO32 83 D4
12 Gosport PO12 181 D3
Albany Dr
Bishop's Waltham SO32 83 D4
Three Legged Cross BH21 114 C1
Albany Gdns BH15 201 F1
Albany Park Ct SO17 102 C4
Albany Pk BH17 202 A4
Albany Rd
Bishop's Waltham SO32 83 D4
Holbury SO45 150 B2
Portsmouth PO5 182 B2
Romsey SO51 52 C4
Southampton SO15 102 B3
Albatross Wlk PO13 155 D1
Albemarle Ave PO12 181 D4
Albemarle Rd BH3 204 C4
Albermarle Ct SO17 79 E2
Albert Cl SO31 127 E3
Albert Gr PO5 182 B2
Albert Rd
Bishop's Waltham SO32 83 D4
Bournemouth BH1 204 C2
Corfe Mullen BH21 186 B3
Cosham PO6 157 F4
6 Eastleigh SO50 56 A3
Ferndown BH22 165 E3
Hedge End SO30 105 D3
New Milton BH25 194 C1
Poole BH12 203 E3
Portsmouth PO4, PO5 182 C1
Stubbington PO14 179 F3
Albert Rd N SO14 103 D2
Albert Rd S SO14 103 D2
Albert St PO12 181 E3
Albion Cl Poole BH12 203 D4
Portchester PO16 156 A3
Albion Pl 3 SO14 102 C2
Albion Rd Christchurch BH23 191 F1
Fordingbridge SP6 69 F1
Lee-on-the-Solent PO13 179 F2
Albion Towers 1 SO14 103 D2
Albion Way BH31 114 B4
Albretia Ave PO8 111 F2
Albury Pl SO53 30 A1
Alby Rd BH12 203 F3
Alcantara Cres SO14 103 D2
Alcester Rd BH12 203 E3
Alchorne Pl PO3 158 A2
Aldbury Ct 1 BH25 210 A4
Alder Cl Burton BH23 192 B1
Colden Common SO21 57 D4
Hythe SO45 125 E2
Marchwood SO40 101 F1
Romsey SO51 53 E3
Alder Cres BH12 203 F4
Alder Dr SP6 92 C3
Alder Hill Dr SO40 100 A4
Alder Hills BH12 204 A4
Alder Hills Ind Est BH12 204 A4
Alder La PO13 180 B3
Alder Rd Poole BH12 203 F3
Southampton SO16 78 A2
Alderbury Ct 5 BH23 207 F3
Alderfield GU32 40 C2
Alderholt Rd SP6 69 D1
Alderley Rd BH10 189 F2
Alderman Quilley Sch SO50 55 F1
Alderman Quilley Sch The
SO50 56 A1
Aldermoor Ave SO16 78 A2
Aldermoor Cl SO16 78 B2
Aldermoor Rd Gosport PO13 180 B4
Southampton SO16 78 A2
Waterlooville PO7 134 B2
Aldermoor Rd E PO7 134 B3
Alderney Ave BH12 188 B1
Alderney Cl SO16 77 F2
Alderney Hospl BH12 188 B1
Alderney Mid Sch BH12 188 B1
Alders Rd PO16 155 D4
Aldershot House 37 PO9 136 A3
Alderwood Ave SO53 55 D3
Alderwood Cl PO9 135 D2
Aldis Gdns BH15 201 F1
Aldrich Rd PO1 182 A3
Aldridge Cl PO8 88 B3
Aldridge Rd Bournemouth BH10 189 E3
Ferndown BH22 165 F2
Aldroke St 14 PO6 157 F4
Aldsworth Cl PO6 158 B4
Aldsworth Gdns PO6 158 B4
Aldwell St 8 PO5 182 B2
Alec Rose House 16 PO12 181 E2
Alec Rose La PO1 182 B3
Alec Wintle House PO2 182 B4
Alecto Rd PO12 181 D2
Alencon Cl PO12 181 E4
Alexander Cl
Christchurch BH23 207 F3
Totton SO40 100 B4
Waterlooville PO7 134 B3
Alexander Ct SO19 103 F1
Alexander Gr PO16 155 D4
Alexander House PO11 185 F1
Alexandra Ave PO11 184 C1
Alexandra Cl SO45 126 A2
Alexandra Lodge 6 BH1 205 D2
Alexandra Rd
Bournemouth BH6 206 B3
Chandler's Ford SO53 55 F4
Fordingbridge SP6 69 F1
Hedge End SO30 105 D3
Hythe SO45 126 A2
Lymington SO41 197 E3
Poole BH14 203 F2
Portsmouth PO1 182 B3
Southampton SO15 102 C3
Alexandra St PO12 181 D3
Alexandra Terr SO23 10 C4
Alexandra Way SO30 106 A4
Alexandria Ct BH22 165 F2
Alford Rd BH3 204 B4
Alfred Cl SO40 100 B4
Alfred Rd Portsmouth PO1 182 A3
Stubbington PO14 154 B2
Alfred Rose Ct SO18 79 F2
Alfred St SO14 103 D3
Alfrey Cl PO10 161 E4
Alfriston Ct SO19 104 B2
Alfriston Gdns SO19 104 A2
Algiers Rd PO3 183 D4
Alhambra Rd PO4 182 C1
Alington 18 BH4 204 B2
Alington Cl BH14 214 B4
Alington House BH14 214 B4
Alington Rd BH3 205 D3
Alipore Cl BH14 203 E2
Alipore Hts BH14 203 E2
All Saints CE Com Prim Sch
SO23 11 D3
All Saints House 19 SO14 103 D2
All Saints Rd SO41 197 F1
All Saints' Rd PO1 182 B4
All Saints' St PO1 182 B3
Allan Gr SO51 53 D4
Allaway Ave Cosham PO6 157 D4
Portchester PO6 157 D4
Allbrook Ct PO9 135 E3
Allbrook Hill Eastleigh SO50 56 A4
Otterbourne SO50 56 A4
Allbrook Knoll SO50 56 A4
Allbrook Way SO50 56 A4
Allcot Rd PO3 158 A1
Allen Ct BH21 163 E3
Allen Rd Hedge End SO30 105 E4
Wimborne Minster BH21 163 E2
Allen Water Dr SP6 69 F1
Allen's Rd PO4 182 C1
Allenbourn Cty Mid Sch BH21 163 E3
Allenby Cl BH17 187 D1
Allenby Gr PO16 156 B4
Allenby Rd Broadstone BH17 187 D1
Gosport PO12 180 C3
Allendale Ave PO10 136 C2
Allens La Hamworthy BH16 201 E3
Meonstoke SO32 61 E3
Allens Rd Hamworthy BH16 201 E3
Upton BH16 201 E3
Allenview Rd BH21 163 E3
Allerton Cl SO40 76 B1
Alliance Cl PO13 180 B4
Allington La SO30 80 C3
Allington Manor Farm
Bsns Ctr SO50 80 C4
Allington Manor Sch SO50 80 C4
Allington Rd Poole BH14 214 B4
Southampton SO15 101 E4
Allison Ct 6 SO41 211 D2
Allison House SO30 105 E4
Allmara Dr PO7 134 C2
Allotment Rd Hedge End SO30 105 D3
Locks Heath SO31 128 C3
Alma House SO14 103 D4
Alma La SO32 58 A1
Alma Rd Bournemouth BH9 205 D4
Romsey SO51 52 C4
Southampton SO14 103 D4
Alma St PO12 181 D3
Alma Terr PO4 183 D2
Almatade Rd SO18 104 A4
Almer Rd BH15 201 F2
Almond Cl Cosham PO6 158 C4
Waterlooville PO8 112 B2
Almond Ct 11 SO15 102 B3
Almond Gr BH12 203 E4
Almond Rd SO15 102 B3
Almondsbury House 8 PO6 132 C1
Almondsbury Rd PO6 132 C1
Almondside PO13 155 F1
Almshouses BH10 189 E1
Alpha Ctr The BH17 202 A4
Alphage Rd PO12 155 F1
Alpine Cl SO18 104 A4
Alpine Rd Ashurst SO40 99 F2
St Leonards BH24 140 B1
Alresford Rd
Chilcomb SO21, SO23 12 B4
Havant PO9 135 F2
Winchester SO21, SO23 11 E4
Alsford Rd PO7 134 B3
Alswitha Terr 27 SO23 2 A1
Alten Rd PO7 111 E1
Althorpe Dr PO3 158 B2
Alton Cl SO50 57 D1
Alton Ct 12 SO23 2 A1
Alton Gr PO16 156 B3
Alton House SO18 103 F4
Alton Rd Bournemouth BH10 189 D1
Poole BH14 203 E2
Alton Rd E BH14 203 E1
Alum Chine Rd BH4 204 A2
Alum Cl SO45 150 B2
Alum Way Portchester PO16 131 F1
Southampton SO18 104 A4
Alumdale Rd BH4 204 A1
Alumhurst Rd BH4 204 A1
Alvandi Gdns 12 BH25 195 D2
Alvara Rd PO12 181 D1
Alver Bridge View 11 PO12 181 D2
Alver Quay 7 PO12 181 D2
Alver Rd Gosport PO12 181 D2
Portsmouth PO1 182 C3
Alvercliffe Dr PO12 180 C1
Alverstoke CE Jun Sch PO12 181 D2
Alverstoke Ct PO12 181 D1
Alverstoke Inf Sch PO12 181 D1
Alverstone Rd PO4 183 D3
Alverton Ave BH15 202 C2
Alverton Hall BH4 204 B1
Alveston Ave PO14 154 B4
Alyne House SO15 102 C4
Alyth Rd BH3 204 B3
Ambassador Cl BH23 208 A3
Ambassador Ind Est BH23 208 A3
Amber Rd BH21 186 B2
Amberley Cl Botley SO30 106 A4
Christchurch BH23 208 C4
North Baddesley SO52 53 F3
Amberley Ct
8 Bournemouth BH1 205 D2
Totton SO40 100 C3
Amberley Rd Clanfield PO8 88 B3
Gosport PO12 181 D4
Portsmouth PO2 157 F2
Amberslade Wlk SO45 125 F1
Amberwood BH22 165 F3
Amberwood Cl SO40 76 B1
Amberwood Dr BH23 193 F1
Amberwood Gdns BH23 194 A1
Ambledale SO31 128 C2
Ambleside
Bishop's Waltham SO32 83 D4
Christchurch BH23 191 F2
Hedge End SO30 105 E3
Ambleside Gdns SO19 104 A2
Ambleside Rd SO41 197 F2
Ambury La BH23 207 F4
Amersham Cl PO12 180 C2
Amesbury Rd BH6 206 B3
Amethyst Gr PO7 135 D4
Amethyst Rd BH23 207 F4
Amey Ind Est GU32 40 C2
Ameys La BH22 165 F4
Ameysford Rd BH22 165 E4
Amira Ct 9 BH2 204 C2
Amoy St SO15 102 C3
Ampfield CE Prim Sch SO51 29 E2
Ampfield Cl PO9 135 D2
Ampfield Rd BH8 190 B2
Amport Cl SO22 1 B2
Amport Ct PO9 135 E3
Ampress La SO41 197 E3
Ampthill Rd SO15 102 A4
Amsterdam Sq BH23 207 E3
Amyas Ct PO4 183 E2
Ancasta Rd SO14 103 D4
Anchor Cl Bournemouth BH11 188 C3
Christchurch BH23 208 A3
Anchor Ct SO14 103 D1
Anchor La PO1 182 A3
Anchor Mews SO41 197 F2
Anchor Rd BH11 188 C3
Anchorage Rd PO3 158 A2
Anchorage The PO12 181 E2
Anchorage Way SO41 197 E2
Ancrum Lodge BH4 204 A2
Andalusian Gdns SO31 129 D4
Andbourne Ct BH6 206 C2
Anderby Rd SO16 77 E1
Anderson Cl Havant PO9 136 A2
Romsey SO51 28 B1
Swanwick PO15 129 E4
Anderson's Rd SO14 103 D2
Anderwood Dr SO41 172 A1
Andes Cl SO14 103 E2
Andes Rd SO16 77 D2
Andlers Ash Rd GU33 20 C2
Andover Cl BH23 208 A4
Andover House 27 PO9 136 A3
Andover Rd Portsmouth PO4 182 C1
Southampton SO15 102 B3
Winchester SO21, SO22, SO23 1 C1
Andover Rd N SO22 1 C2
Andover Road Ret Pk SO23 1 C1
Andree Ct BH23 209 D4
Andrew Bell St 2 PO1 182 B3
Andrew Cl Hythe SO45 126 A1
Portsmouth PO1 182 C3
Totton SO40 100 B4
Andrew Cres PO7 111 E1
Andrew La BH25 195 E1
Andrew Pl PO14 179 D3
Andrewes Cl SO32 83 E4
Andrews Cl BH11 189 D2
Andromeda Rd SO16 77 F2
Androse Gdns BH24 140 C3
Anfield Cl SO50 57 E1
Anfield Ct SO50 57 D1
Angel Cres SO19 104 A3
Angel Ct SO41 197 F2
Angel La Barton on Sea BH25 210 B4
Ferndown BH22 165 D2
Angelica Ct PO7 135 D3
Angelica Gdns SO50 81 E4
Angelica Way PO15 129 F4
Angeline Cl BH23 208 C4
Angelo Cl PO7 135 D4
Angelus Cl PO14 179 E3
Angerstein Rd PO2 157 E1
Anglers Way SO31 128 B4
Anglesea Ct SO15 78 A1
Anglesea Rd
Lee-on-the-Solent PO13 180 A2
Portsmouth PO1 182 A3
Southampton SO15 78 A1
Anglesea Terr SO14 103 D2
Anglesey Arms Rd PO12 181 D1
Anglesey Rd PO12 181 D1
Anglesey View 8 PO12 181 D2
Anglewood Mnsns 9 BH4 204 B2
Anglo-European Coll of
Chiropractic BH5 206 A2
Angmering House 28 PO1 182 B3
Angus Cl PO15 130 C2
Anjou Cl BH11 188 B3
Anjou Cres PO15 130 B1
Anker La PO14 154 B2
Ankerwyke PO13 155 D1
Anmore Cl PO9 135 E2
Anmore Cnr PO7 111 D2
Anmore Dr PO7 111 E1
Anmore La PO7 111 E3
Anmore Rd PO7 111 D2
Ann's Hill Rd PO12 181 D3
Anna La BH23 168 A2
Annandale Ct BH6 206 B2
Anne Cl BH23 192 A1
Anne Cres PO7 134 C3
Annerley Rd BH1 205 E2
Annes Ct PO11 184 C1
Annet Cl BH15 201 F1
Anson Cl Christchurch BH23 207 F3
Gosport PO13 180 B3
Ringwood BH24 141 E4
Anson Dr SO19 104 B3
Anson Gr PO16 132 C1
Anson Rd PO4 183 D3
Anstey Cl BH11 189 D3
Anstey Rd Bournemouth BH11 189 D3
Romsey SO51 28 A1
Antell's Way SP6 93 D3
Anthill Cl PO7 110 B3
Anthony Gr PO12 156 A1
Anthony Way PO10 136 C2
Anthony's Ave BH14 203 E1
Antigua House 5 PO6 132 C1
Antler Dr BH25 194 C2
Anton Cl SO51 53 E4

Anvil Cl PO7 .... 112 B1
Anvil Cres BH18 .... 186 C3
Anvil Ct PO4 .... 183 D2
Anzac Cl PO14 .... 154 B2
Apex Ctr PO14 .... 155 D3
Apless La PO7 .... 110 A2
Apollo Cl BH12 .... 203 E4
Apollo Dr PO7 .... 134 C2
Apollo Rd SO53 .... 55 F4
Apple Cl BH12 .... 204 A2
Apple Gr BH23 .... 191 F1
Apple Ind Est PO15 .... 129 E3
Apple Tree Cl SP5 .... 47 E4
Apple Tree Gr BH22 .... 165 F3
Apple Tree Rd SP6 .... 92 C3
Applemore Coll SO45 .... 125 E2
Applemore Recn Ctr SO45 ... 125 E2
Appleshaw Cl SO22 .... 1 B1
Appleshaw Gn PO9 .... 135 E2
Appleslade Way BH25 .... 195 D3
Appleton Rd Fareham PO15 .. 130 B1
  Southampton SO18 .... 79 F1
Appletree Cl Bournemouth BH6 206 B3
  New Milton BH25 .... 195 D1
  Totton SO40 .... 76 B1
Appletree Ct SO30 .... 106 A4
Appletree Rd SP5 .... 47 E4
Applewood Gdns SO19 ...... 104 A2
Applewood Gr PO7 .... 134 B2
Applewood Pl SO40 .... 100 B3
Applewood Rd PO9 .... 135 E2
Appollo Pl SO18 .... 104 A4
Approach Rd BH14 .... 203 D2
Approach The PO3 .... 158 A1
April Cl Bournemouth BH11 . 189 D2
  Southampton SO18 .... 104 A4
April Gr SO31 .... 128 C2
Apsley Cres BH17 .... 187 E1
Apsley Ct BH8 .... 205 D3
Apsley Pl SO53 .... 30 A1
Apsley Rd PO4 .... 183 D2
Aquila Way SO51 .... 127 F1
Aquitanis House SO14 .... 103 E3
Arabian Gdns PO15 .... 129 E4
Aragon Way BH9 .... 190 A2
Arbour SO22 .... 10 C4
Arcade BH4 .... 204 A2
Arcade The
  BH1 Bournemouth BH1 ..... 204 C2
  Liss GU33 .... 20 C3
Arcadia Ave BH8 .... 205 D4
Arcadia Cl SO16 .... 78 B2
Arcadia Rd BH23 .... 191 F1
Arch Farm Ind Est SP6 .... 69 F2
Archdale Cl BH10 .... 189 E1
Archer House PO12 .... 181 E1
Archers SO15 .... 102 C3
Archers Cl SO40 .... 76 B1
Archers Rd Eastleigh SO50 .. 56 A2
  Southampton SO15 .... 102 C4
Archery Gdns SO19 .... 103 F1
Archery Gr SO19 .... 103 F1
Archery La Fareham PO16 ... 131 E1
  Winchester SO22 .... 10 C4
Archery Rd SO19 .... 103 F1
Archgate SO41 .... 197 F2
Archway Rd BH14 .... 203 F2
Arden Cl Gosport PO12 ...... 180 C2
  Southampton SO18 .... 80 A1
Arden Rd BH9 .... 189 F2
Arden Wlk BH25 .... 195 D1
Ardingly Cres SO30 .... 81 E1
Ardington Rise PO7 .... 134 C2
Ardmore Rd BH14 .... 203 D2
Ardnave Cres SO16 .... 78 C3
Argosy Cl SO31 .... 128 C1
Argus Rd PO13 .... 179 F2
Argyle Cres PO15 .... 130 C1
Argyle Rd Christchurch BH23 207 F3
  Southampton SO14 .... 103 D3
Argyll Mansions BH5 .... 205 F2
Argyll Rd Bournemouth BH5 . 205 F2
  Poole BH12 .... 203 E3
Ariadne Rd PO1 .... 182 A2
Ariel Cl BH6 .... 207 D2
Ariel Dr BH6 .... 207 D2
Ariel Rd PO1 .... 182 C3
Arismore Ct PO13 .... 179 F2
Ark Royal Cres PO13 .... 179 F2
Arle Cl PO8 .... 88 B2
Arley Rd BH14 .... 203 D1
Arlington Ct BH25 .... 210 A4
Arlington Pl
  Winchester SO23 .... 2 A1
  Winchester SO23 .... 11 D4
Arliss Rd SO15 .... 78 A1
Arlott Ct SO15 .... 102 C4
Armada Cl SO16 .... 77 F4
Armada Dr SO45 .... 125 F1
Armadale House SO14 ...... 103 E3
Arminers Cl PO12 .... 181 D1
Armitage Ave SO45 .... 125 F1
Armory La PO1 .... 182 A2
Armstrong Cl
  Brockenhurst SO42 .... 145 F1
  Waterlooville PO7 .... 111 E1
Armstrong Ct SO16 .... 77 F3
Armstrong La SO42 .... 145 F1
Armstrong Rd SO42 .... 145 F1
Armsworth La SO32 .... 85 F1
Arnaud Cl PO2 .... 182 B4
Arne Ave PO3 .... 203 F4
Arne Cres BH12 .... 203 F4
Arnewood Bridge Rd SO41 . 196 A4
Arnewood Ct
  Bournemouth BH2 .... 204 C1
  Sway SO41 .... 196 B3
Arnewood House SO41 ..... 196 B2

Arnewood Rd BH6 .... 206 B3
Arnewood Sch The BH25 ... 194 C1
Arnheim Cl BH16 .... 78 B2
Arnheim Rd SO16 .... 78 B2
Arnold Cl BH22 .... 138 C2
Arnold Rd Eastleigh SO50 ... 80 A4
  Southampton SO17 .... 79 E1
  West Moors BH22 .... 138 C2
Arnolds Cl BH25 .... 209 F4
Arnside Rd PO7 .... 134 C4
Arnwood Ave SO45 .... 149 F4
Aragon Cl PO7 .... 135 D4
Arran Cl PO6 .... 133 F1
Arran Way BH23 .... 194 A1
Arras House PO15 .... 130 B2
Arreton SO31 .... 127 E3
Arreton Ct PO12 .... 181 D3
Arrow Cl Eastleigh SO50 ..... 56 A2
Arrowsmith Ct BH18 .... 187 D2
Arrowsmith La BH21 .... 187 F4
Arrowsmith Rd BH21 .... 187 F4
Arters Lawn SO40 .... 124 B3
Arthur Cl BH2 .... 204 C3
Arthur Kille House PO7 ..... 134 B3
Arthur La BH21 .... 207 D4
Arthur Pope House PO5 .... 182 B2
Arthur Rd Christchurch BH23 207 F4
  Eastleigh SO50 .... 56 A2
  Southampton SO15 .... 102 B3
  Winchester SO23 .... 2 A1
Arthur St PO2 .... 182 C4
Arthurs Gdns SO30 .... 81 D2
Artillery Cl PO6 .... 157 E4
Artillery Terr PO4 .... 183 D2
Arun Rd SO18 .... 80 A1
Arun Way SO51 .... 50 B2
Arundel Cl BH25 .... 194 C2
Arundel Ct Inf Sch PO1 ..... 182 B3
Arundel Ct Jun Sch PO1 .... 182 B3
Arundel Dr PO16 .... 131 D1
Arundel House PO13 .... 103 E3
Arundel Rd Eastleigh SO50 .. 56 A3
  Gosport PO12 .... 180 C3
  Totton SO40 .... 101 D4
Arundel St PO1 .... 182 B3
Arundel Way PO21 .... 208 C4
Arundel Way Sh Arc PO1 ... 182 B3
Ascham Rd BH8 .... 205 D3
Ascot Cl PO14 .... 129 E1
Ascot Rd Broadstone BH18 . 187 D2
  Fair Oak SO50 .... 81 E4
  Portsmouth PO3 .... 183 D4
Ascupart House SO17 .... 103 D4
Ascupart St SO14 .... 103 D2
Asford Gr SO30 .... 56 B2
Ash Cl Alderholt SP6 .... 93 D3
  Bursledon SO31 .... 127 F4
  Colden Common SO21 .... 32 A1
  Fareham PO14 .... 154 C4
  Gosport PO12 .... 181 D2
  Hythe SO45 .... 150 A4
  North Baddesley SO52 .... 53 F3
  Romsey SO51 .... 53 E3
  Southampton SO19 .... 104 B3
  Upton BH16 .... 201 D4
  Waterlooville PO8 .... 111 F1
Ash Gr Ashurst SO40 .... 100 B2
  Hordle SO41 .... 211 E4
  Ringwood BH24 .... 141 E4
Ash Rd SO40 .... 100 A1
Ash Tree Rd SO18 .... 79 F1
Ashbarn Cres SO22 .... 10 C3
Ashbourne Ct BH1 .... 205 D2
Ashbourne Rd BH5 .... 206 A3
Ashbridge Rise SO53 .... 30 A1
Ashburn Garth BH24 .... 141 E3
Ashburton Gdns BH10 ..... 189 E1
Ashburton House SO31 .... 127 D3
Ashburton Rd Gosport PO12 180 C1
  Portsmouth PO5 .... 182 B1
Ashby Cres SO40 .... 100 B4
Ashby Pl PO5 .... 182 B1
Ashby Rd Southampton SO19 104 A2
  Totton SO40 .... 100 B4
Ashcroft Ct GU32 .... 40 C2
Ashcroft La PO8 .... 113 E3
Ashdene SO15 .... 102 A4
Ashdene Cl BH21 .... 163 E3
Ashdene Rd SO40 .... 100 B2
Ashdown Bournemouth BH2 204 B1
  Fawley SO45 .... 150 C2
  Gosport PO13 .... 155 E1
Ashdown Cl
  Chandler's Ford SO53 .... 30 B1
  Poole BH17 .... 187 F1
Ashdown Dr SO53 .... 30 B1
Ashdown Rd Blackfield SO45 150 C1
  Chandler's Ford SO53 .... 30 B1
Ashdown Sch BH17 .... 187 F1
Ashdown Way SO51 .... 53 D4
Ashdown Wlk BH25 .... 195 E1
Ashe Rd PO9 .... 136 A3
Ashen Cl SO53 .... 55 E4
Ashford Chace GU32 .... 19 F1
Ashford Cl SP6 .... 69 E1
Ashford Cres SO45 .... 126 A2
Ashford Rd Bournemouth BH6 206 B4
  Fordingbridge SP6 .... 93 E4
Ashington Cl PO8 .... 112 A2
Ashington Gdns BH21 ...... 186 C4
Ashington La BH21 .... 163 D1
Ashington Park BH25 .... 195 D1
Ashlea Cl SO50 .... 57 E1
Ashleigh Cl SO45 .... 150 A4
Ashlett Cl SO45 .... 151 E2
Ashlett Gdns SO45 .... 195 E2

Ashlett Lawn PO9 .... 135 E3
Ashlett Mews SO45 .... 151 D2
Ashlett Rd SO45 .... 151 E2
Ashley Arnewood Ct PO9 .. 195 D1
Ashley Cl Bournemouth BH1 205 F3
  Havant PO9 .... 135 E2
  Horndean PO8 .... 111 F3
  Ringwood BH24 .... 141 E3
  Swanwick SO31 .... 129 D4
  Winchester SO22 .... 1 B2
Ashley Common Rd BH25 .. 195 E2
Ashley Cres SO19 .... 104 B1
Ashley Cross SP6 .... 71 F1
Ashley Ct Bursledon SO31 .. 105 D1
  Gosport PO12 .... 181 D3
  West Moors BH22 .... 166 A4
Ashley Dr Ibsley BH24 ...... 116 B2
  St Leonards BH24 .... 116 B2
Ashley Dr N BH24 .... 139 F3
Ashley Dr S BH24 .... 139 F3
Ashley Dr W BH24 .... 139 F3
Ashley Gdns
  Chandler's Ford SO53 .... 55 F3
  Sheffield SO53 .... 83 F2
Ashley Heath Ind Est BH21 . 139 D4
Ashley House SO51 .... 52 C3
Ashley Inf Sch BH25 .... 195 E2
Ashley Jun Sch BH25 .... 195 E2
Ashley La Hordle SO41 ...... 195 E2
  Lymington SO41 .... 197 F2
  New Milton BH25 .... 195 F2
Ashley Meadows SO51 .... 53 D4
Ashley Meads BH25 .... 195 E2
Ashley Park BH24 .... 140 A3
Ashley Rd
  Bournemouth BH1, BH7 ... 205 F3
  New Milton BH25 .... 195 E2
  Poole BH14 .... 203 E3
Ashley Wlk PO6 .... 158 A3
Ashleycross Cl SO45 .... 150 B2
Ashling Cl Bournemouth BH8 205 E4
  Denmead PO7 .... 110 C2
Ashling Cres BH8 .... 205 D4
Ashling Gdns PO7 .... 110 C2
Ashling La PO2 .... 157 E1
Ashling Park Rd PO7 .... 110 C2
Ashlyn Cl PO15 .... 130 B1
Ashmead Rd SO16 .... 77 F2
Ashmeads Cl BH21 .... 164 A3
Ashmeads Way BH23 .... 164 A3
Ashmede BH4 .... 204 B1
Ashmore BH21 .... 163 E2
Ashmore Ave
  Barton on Sea BH25 .... 210 A4
  Hamworthy BH15 .... 201 F1
Ashmore Cl SP5 .... 24 A2
Ashmore Cres BH15 .... 201 F1
Ashmore Gr BH23 .... 193 F1
Ashmore La West Dean SP5 . 24 A3
  Whiteparish SP5 .... 24 A3
Ashmore Rd SO22 .... 1 B1
Ashridge Ave BH10 .... 189 E3
Ashridge Cl SO15 .... 102 C4
Ashridge Gdns BH10 .... 189 E3
Ashridge Par BH10 .... 189 E3
Ashtead Cl PO16 .... 156 A4
Ashton Cl SO32 .... 59 D1
Ashton Cross SO51 .... 51 D1
Ashton Ct BH25 .... 195 D2
Ashton House SO19 .... 103 F1
Ashton La SO32 .... 59 D1
Ashton Pl SO53 .... 30 A1
Ashton Rd BH9 .... 189 F1
Ashton Way PO14 .... 179 E2
Ashtree Cl BH25 .... 195 E1
Ashtree Ct SO53 .... 55 E2
Ashurst Bridge Rd
  Netley Marsh SO40 .... 100 B3
  Totton SO40 .... 100 B3
Ashurst Cl Ashurst SO40 ... 100 A1
  Southampton SO19 .... 104 A1
  Winchester SO22 .... 1 B2
Ashurst Ct PO12 .... 180 B2
Ashurst Hospl (Geriatric)
  SO40 .... 100 A1
Ashurst (New Forest) Sta
  SO40 .... 100 A1
Ashurst Rd Bournemouth BH8 190 B2
  Cosham PO6 .... 157 F4
  West Moors BH22 .... 138 C2
Ashwell Ct BH23 .... 191 F1
Ashwood
  Swanwick, Whiteley PO15 . 129 E3
  Titchfield SO31 .... 129 E1
Ashwood Cl Havant PO9 ... 135 D2
  South Hayling PO11 .... 185 D2
Ashwood Dr BH18 .... 187 E2
Ashwood Gdns
  Southampton SO16 .... 78 C2
  Totton SO40 .... 100 B4
Ashwood Lodge PO16 ...... 131 D1
Aspen Ave SO31 .... 152 B4
Aspen Cl Colden Common SO21 32 A1
  Hedge End SO30 .... 105 E4
Aspen Dr BH31 .... 115 D3
Aspen Gdns BH12 .... 203 F4
Aspen Holt SO16 .... 79 D3
Aspen Pl BH25 .... 195 D1
Aspen Rd BH12 .... 203 F4
Aspen Way Poole BH12 ..... 203 F4
  Waterlooville PO8 .... 112 A3
Aspen Wlk SO40 .... 100 A4
Aspengrove PO13 .... 155 F1
Asquith Cl BH23 .... 207 E3
Assheton Ct PO16 .... 156 B4
Astbury Ave BH12 .... 189 D1
Aster Rd SO16 .... 79 E2
Astley St PO5 .... 182 B2

Aston Mead BH23 .... 191 F2
Aston Rd Portsmouth PO4 . 182 C2
  Waterlooville PO7 .... 134 B4
Astra Ct SO45 .... 126 A3
Astra Wlk PO12 .... 181 E2
Astral Gdns SO31 .... 127 F2
Astrid Cl PO11 .... 185 E2
Asturias Way SO14 .... 103 E2
Atalanta Cl PO4 .... 183 E3
Atheling Rd SO45 .... 126 A2
Athelney Ct BH1 .... 205 D2
Athelstan Rd
  Bournemouth BH6 .... 206 C3
  Southampton SO19 .... 103 F3
Athelston Ct SO41 .... 197 E2
Athena Ave PO7 .... 134 C2
Athena Cl SO50 .... 57 D2
Atherfield Rd SO16 .... 77 F2
Atherley Rd
  South Hayling PO11 .... 184 C3
  Southampton SO15 .... 102 B3
Atherley Sch SO16 .... 77 D3
Atherstone Wlk PO5 .... 182 B2
Atkins Pl SO53 .... 130 B2
Atkinson Cl PO12 .... 181 D1
Atlantic Cl SO14 .... 103 D1
Atlantic Park View SO18 .... 80 A1
Atlantis Ave PO7 .... 134 C1
Attwood Cl SP6 .... 92 C3
Attwoods Dro SO21 .... 10 B1
Aubrey Cl SO41 .... 211 F2
Aubrey Farm Cotts SO41 .. 212 A2
Auckland Ave SO42 .... 146 A1
Auckland Pl SO42 .... 146 A1
Auckland Rd
  Christchurch BH23 .... 208 B4
  Southampton SO15 .... 101 F4
Auckland Rd E PO5 .... 182 B1
Auckland Rd W PO5 .... 182 B1
Audemer Ct BH23 .... 141 E4
Audrayton Ct BH6 .... 206 C2
Audret Cl BH23 .... 156 A3
Augustine Rd Cosham PO6 . 158 B4
  Southampton SO14 .... 103 D3
Augustus Cl SO53 .... 55 F4
Augustus Way SO53 .... 55 F4
Auriol Dr PO9 .... 159 D4
Aust Rd PO14 .... 154 B4
Austen Ave
  Bournemouth BH10 .... 189 F3
  Winchester SO22 .... 10 B2
Austen Cl Totton SO40 ..... 100 B3
  Winchester SO23 .... 2 A1
Austen Gdns PO15 .... 129 E4
Auster Cl BH23 .... 208 A4
Austerberry Way PO13 ..... 180 C4
Austin Ave BH14 .... 203 D1
Austin Cl BH1 .... 205 E3
Austin Ct PO7 .... 133 D1
Australia Cl PO1 .... 182 B3
Autumn Cl BH22 .... 165 D4
Autumn Copse BH25 .... 195 E1
Autumn Pl SO17 .... 79 D1
Autumn Rd SO40 .... 102 A1
Avalan Ct 10 C3
Avalon BH14 .... 214 B4
Avalon Ct PO10 .... 136 C1
Avebury Ave BH10 .... 189 F3
Avebury Gdns SO53 .... 30 A1
Avenger Cl SO53 .... 55 D3
Avens Cl SO50 .... 81 E3
Avenue Cl SO45 .... 150 C4
Avenue Campus (Univ of
  Southampton) SO17 .... 79 D1
Avenue Ct Gosport PO12 .. 181 D1
  Poole BH13 .... 204 A2
  Southampton SO17 .... 102 C4
Avenue De Caen PO5 .... 182 B1
Avenue E SO45 .... 150 C4
Avenue La BH2 .... 204 C2
Avenue Rd
  Bournemouth BH2 .... 204 C2
  Brockenhurst SO42 .... 172 C4
  Christchurch BH23 .... 206 C4
  Christchurch, Walkford BH23 194 B1
  Fareham PO14 .... 130 C1
  Gosport PO12 .... 181 D2
  Lymington SO41 .... 197 F2
  New Milton BH25 .... 195 D2
  North Hayling PO11 .... 160 A2
  Southampton SO14 .... 103 D4
  Wimborne Minster BH21 . 163 D2
  Winchester SO22 .... 10 C4
Avenue Sh Ctr The BH2 .... 204 C2
Avenue The
  Bishop's Waltham SO32 .... 83 D4
  Bournemouth BH9 .... 189 F2
  Fareham PO14 .... 130 C1
  Gosport PO12 .... 181 D2
  Petersfield GU31 .... 40 C2
  Poole BH13 .... 204 A1
  Southampton SO17 .... 102 C4
  Twyford SO21 .... 32 A3
  West Moors BH22 .... 138 C2
Avery La PO12 .... 181 D4
Avington Cl SO50 .... 56 B3
Avington Ct SO16 .... 78 C2
Avington Gn PO9 .... 136 A3
Avocet Cl PO4 .... 183 D3
Avocet House PO4 .... 183 D3
Avocet Quay PO10 .... 161 D4
Avocet Wlk PO15 .... 155 D3
Avon Ave BH24 .... 140 B2
Avon Bldgs BH23 .... 207 D4
Avon Castle BH24 .... 140 B2
Avon Castle Dr BH24 .... 140 B2

Avon Cl Bournemouth BH8 . 205 E3
  Lee-on-the-Solent PO13 ... 179 F1
  Lymington SO41 .... 197 E2
  Petersfield GU32 .... 40 C1
Avon Cotts BH23 .... 192 B3
Avon Cres SO51 .... 53 E4
Avon Cswy BH23 .... 191 E4
Avon Ct Christchurch BH23 207 E3
  Fordingbridge SP6 .... 69 F1
  Netley SO31 .... 127 E3
  Waterlooville PO8 .... 111 F2
Avon Dyke SP5 .... 46 C3
Avon Farm Cotts BH23 .... 167 F2
Avon Gdns BH23 .... 169 D1
Avon Gr SO53 .... 55 E3
Avon Heath Ctry Pk
  (North Pk) BH24 .... 140 A2
Avon Heath Ctry Pk
  (South Pk) BH24 .... 167 E4
Avon House Bournemouth BH2 204 C1
  Southampton SO14 .... 103 E3
Avon Meade SP6 .... 69 F1
Avon Meadow SP5 .... 46 C4
Avon Mews BH8 .... 205 E3
Avon Park BH24 .... 140 B3
Avon Rd Bournemouth BH8 205 E3
  Southampton SO18 .... 79 F1
  West Moors BH22 .... 138 C1
Avon Rd E BH23 .... 207 D4
Avon Rd W BH23 .... 206 C4
Avon Run Cl BH23 .... 208 A3
Avon Run Rd BH23 .... 208 A3
Avon View SP6 .... 70 B1
Avon View Par BH23 .... 192 B2
Avon View Rd BH23 .... 192 B2
Avon Way SO30 .... 80 C1
Avon Wharf BH23 .... 207 E3
Avon Wlk PO15 .... 156 A4
Avonborne Way SO53 .... 55 D4
Avonbourne Sch BH7 ...... 206 A4
Avoncliffe Rd BH6 .... 206 C2
Avondale Ct SO17 .... 79 D1
Avondale Rd Portsmouth PO1 182 C4
  Waterlooville PO7 .... 134 C4
Avonlea Sch BH24 .... 141 D4
Award Rd BH21 .... 164 C3
Awbridge Prim Sch SO51 ... 26 B3
Awbridge Rd PO9 .... 135 E2
Axford Cl BH8 .... 190 B2
Aylen Rd PO3 .... 158 A1
Aylesbury Rd
  Bournemouth BH1 .... 205 F2
  Portsmouth PO2 .... 182 C4
Ayling Cl PO13 .... 180 B4
Aylward St PO1 .... 182 A3
Aynsley Ct SO15 .... 102 B4
Aysgarth Rd PO7 .... 134 C4
Aysha Cl PO1 .... 195 D1
Azalea Cl BH24 .... 140 A3
Azura Cl BH21 .... 139 D3

B Ave Fawley SO45 .... 150 B3
  Fawley SO45 .... 150 C2
Back La Mottisfont SO51 ...... 5 F3
  Ringwood BH24 .... 141 F4
  Southwick PO17 .... 132 C3
  Sway SO41 .... 172 B1
Back of the Walls
  Southampton SO14 .... 103 D1
  Southampton SO14 .... 103 D2
Back St SO23 .... 10 C2
Bacon Cl SO19 .... 103 F1
Bacon La PO11 .... 184 C2
Badbury Cl BH18 .... 187 E2
Badbury Ct BH7 .... 207 F3
Badbury View BH21 .... 163 E3
Badbury View Rd BH21 .... 186 B4
Baddesley Cl SO52 .... 53 F3
Baddesley Gdns PO9 .... 135 E4
Baddesley Rd SO53 .... 30 A1
Baden Cl BH25 .... 195 D1
Baden Powell & St Peter's
  CE Mid Sch BH14 .... 203 D2
Baden Powell Way SO51 .... 52 C4
Bader Cl SO30 .... 105 E4
Bader Rd BH17 .... 202 C4
Bader Way PO15 .... 129 F3
Badger Brow PO7 .... 135 D3
Badger Cl Bishopstoke SO50 56 C1
  Fareham PO15 .... 130 B1
Badger Ct SO50 .... 56 C1
Badger Rd PO14 .... 154 C3
Badger Way BH31 .... 114 C3
Badger Wood Pl SO18 .... 79 F1
Badgers Cl St Leonards BH24 139 F3
  Sway SO41 .... 172 B1
Badgers Copse BH25 .... 195 E3
Badgers The SO31 .... 127 E3
Badgers Wlk Ferndown BH22 165 F4
  Hythe SO45 .... 125 F1
Badminton Dro SO45 .... 178 B4
Badminton La SO45 .... 151 E1
Badshear La SO24 .... 14 C4
Baffins Pl PO3 .... 183 D4
Bagber Rd SO40 .... 100 C4
Bagot House PO12 .... 180 C3
Bagshot Mews SO19 .... 103 F2
Baigent Cl SO23 .... 11 E4
Bailey Cl Botley SO30 ...... 106 A3
  New Milton BH25 .... 195 E2
  Winchester SO22 .... 10 B3
Bailey Cres BH15 .... 202 B4
Bailey Gn SO18 .... 80 A1
Bailey's Rd PO5 .... 182 B2

Baiter Gdns BH15 202 B1
Baker Rd BH11 189 D3
Baker St PO1 182 B4
Bakers Dro SO16 77 F3
Bakers Farm Rd BH31 114 C4
Balaclava Rd SO18 104 A4
Balcombe Rd BH13 204 A2
Balderton Cl 15 PO2 157 F2
Baldwin Cl BH23 207 E3
Balena Cl BH17 202 A4
Balfour Cl Christchurch BH23 208 B4
Gosport PO13 180 B3
Balfour Dr GU33 20 C2
Balfour Rd Bournemouth BH9 189 F1
Portsmouth PO2 157 F1
Southampton SO19 104 B3
Ball La 18 BH15 202 B1
Ballam Cl BH16 201 E4
Ballard Cl New Milton BH25 195 D2
Poole BH15 202 B1
Southampton SO16 77 E1
Ballard Coll BH25 195 D2
Ballard Ct 1 PO12 181 D2
Ballard Lake Prep Sch BH25 195 D2
Ballard Rd BH15 202 B1
Balliol Cl PO14 129 E1
Balliol Rd PO2 182 C4
Balmer Lawn Rd SO42 146 A2
Balmoral Ave BH8 190 C1
Balmoral Cl
Chandler's Ford SO53 55 D4
Gosport PO13 155 E1
Southampton SO16 78 B3
Balmoral Ct
7 Christchurch BH23 209 D4
6 Southampton SO17 103 D4
Southampton, Millbrook SO15 102 A3
Balmoral Dr PO7 134 B2
Balmoral House BH2 204 B2
Balmoral Rd Fareham PO15 130 C2
Poole BH14 203 E2
Balmoral Way
Petersfield GU32 40 C2
Rownhams SO16 77 F3
Balmoral Wlk BH25 194 C2
Balston Rd BH14 203 D3
Balston Terr BH15 202 A1
Baltic Rd SO30 80 C1
Bamford House PO4 183 D1
Banbury Ave SO19 104 B2
Banbury Rd BH17 202 B4
Banfurly Gdns SO45 125 F1
Bangor Rd SO15 102 A3
Banister Ct 13 SO15 102 C4
Banister Gdns SO15 102 C4
Banister Grange 16 SO15 102 C4
Banister Inf Sch SO15 102 C4
Banister Mews SO15 102 C4
Banister Rd SO15 102 C4
Bank Chambers BH14 203 F2
Bank Cl BH23 207 D3
Bank Side SO18 79 E2
Bank St SO32 83 E4
Bankhill Dr SO41 197 E3
Banks Rd BH13 214 B2
Banks The SO51 26 A3
Bankside SO41 197 E3
Bankside Rd BH9 190 A2
Bankview SO41 197 E3
Bannerman Rd GU32 40 C2
Banning St SO51 52 C3
Bannister Ct SO40 101 D4
Banocroft Ct 1 BH15 202 C2
Banstead Rd BH18 187 D3
Bapaume Rd PO3 157 F3
Bar End Ind Est SO23 11 D3
Bar End Rd SO23 11 D3
Bar Gate & Guildhall(Mus)
SO14 102 C2
Barbe Baker Ave SO30 80 B1
Barberry Way BH31 115 E3
Barbers Gate 15 BH15 202 A1
Barbers Piles 8 BH15 202 A1
Barbers Wharf 16 BH15 202 A1
Barclay House PO12 181 F2
Barclay Mansions BH2 204 C3
Barclay Mews Hythe SO45 149 F4
Hythe SO45 150 A4
Bardon Way PO14 154 B4
Barfield Cl SO23 11 D3
Barfields SO41 197 F2
Barfields Ct SO41 197 F2
Barfleur Cl PO15 130 B1
Barfleur Rd PO14 155 D3
Barford Cl SO53 55 D4
Barford La SP5 47 D4
Bargate Ctr 8 SO14 103 D2
Bargate St SO14 102 C2
Bargates BH23 207 D4
Barham Cl PO12 181 D3
Barham Rd GU32 40 C2
Baring Rd Bournemouth BH6 207 D2
Winchester SO23 11 D4
Barker Mill Cl SO16 77 F3
Barkis House 11 PO1 182 B4
Barkshire Ct 7 SO15 102 C4
Barlands Cl BH23 192 B1
Barle Cl SO18 80 A1
Barley Down Dr SO22 10 B2
Barleycorn Wlk SO40 98 C4
Barlow Cl PO14 179 D3
Barn Cl Emsworth PO10 160 B4
Upton BH16 201 D4
Barn Fold PO7 112 B1
Barn Rd BH18 187 D2
Barnaby Cl SP5 46 B4
Barnbrook Rd SO31 128 C2
Barncroft Inf Sch PO9 135 E2
Barncroft Jun Sch PO9 135 E2
Barncroft Way PO9 135 E2
Barnes Cl Bournemouth BH10 189 E2
Locks Heath SO31 128 B2
Southampton SO19 104 B3
West Wellow SO51 50 C2
Winchester SO23 10 C3
Barnes Cres
Bournemouth BH10 189 E2
Wimborne Minster BH21 163 F2
Barnes La Locks Heath SO31 128 C2
Milford on Sea SO41 211 E3
Barnes Rd Bournemouth BH10 189 E2
Portsmouth PO1 182 C3
Southampton SO19 104 B3
Barnes Wallis Rd PO15 129 E2
Barnes Way PO9 135 E2
Barnet Side La GU32 18 B3
Barney Evans Cres PO8 111 E2
Barney Hayes La SO40 99 D4
Barnfield BH23 208 B4
Barnfield Cl Southampton SO19 103 F1
Southbourne PO10 137 F1
Barnfield Ct Fareham PO14 154 C4
Southampton SO19 103 F1
Barnfield Flats SO19 103 F1
Barnfield Rd Petersfield GU31 41 E2
Southampton SO19 103 F1
Barnfield Way SO19 103 F1
Barns Rd BH22 166 A3
Barnsfield Cres SO40 100 B4
Barnside Way GU33 20 C2
Barnsland SO30 80 B2
Barnwood Rd PO15 130 B1
Baron Rd SO31 127 F2
Barons Ct 8 BH12 204 A2
Barons Mead SO16 77 F2
Barons Rd BH11 188 B3
Barrack Lane BH24 141 E2
Barrack Rd Christchurch BH23 206 C4
Ferndown BH22 166 A1
Barratt Ind Est PO15 129 E3
Barrie Cl PO15 129 E4
Barrie Rd BH9 189 F2
Barrington Cl SO50 55 F3
Barrington Ct 31 SO17 79 D1
Barrington House 23 PO1 182 B4
Barrow Down Gdns SO19 104 C2
Barrow Dr BH8 190 C1
Barrow Hill Rd SO40 75 E2
Barrow Rd BH8 190 C1
Barrow View BH22 165 D3
Barrow Way BH8 190 C1
Barrowgate Rd BH8 190 B2
Barrowgate Way BH8 190 B2
Barrows La Landford SP5 49 E3
Sway SO41 196 A3
Barrs Ave BH25 195 D2
Barrs Wood Dr BH25 195 D2
Barrs Wood Rd BH25 195 D2
Barry Gdns BH18 186 C3
Barry Rd SO19 104 A3
Barters Cl SO16 77 F1
Barters La BH18 186 C2
Bartholomew Cl 25 SO23 2 A1
Bartlett Cl PO15 130 C2
Bartlett Dr BH7 206 A4
Bartlett House 18 SO17 103 D4
Bartletts Comm SP6 94 C4
Bartletts The SO31 128 A1
Bartley Ave SO40 100 C3
Bartley CE Jun Sch SO40 99 D4
Bartley Ct 5 BH21 163 D3
Bartley Rd SO40 99 E2
Barton Cl SO51 53 D4
Barton Common La BH25 210 A4
Barton Common Rd BH25 210 A4
Barton Court Ave BH25 210 A4
Barton Court Rd BH25 195 D1
Barton Cres SO18 79 F1
Barton Croft BH25 210 A4
Barton Ct BH25 210 A3
Barton Ctr The SO16 78 A1
Barton Dr Barton on Sea BH25 209 F4
Hamble-le-Rice SO31 127 F2
Hedge End SO30 105 E4
Barton Gn BH25 210 A3
Barton Gr PO3 158 A2
Barton House BH25 209 F4
Barton La BH25 209 F4
Barton Lodge BH12 203 D3
Barton Park Ind Est SO50 56 B1
Barton Peveril Coll SO50 55 F1
Barton Rd SO50 56 B2
Barton Way BH25 209 F4
Barton Wood Rd BH25 209 F4
Bartons Rd
Fordingbridge SP6 69 F1
Havant PO9 136 A2
Bartons The
Fordingbridge SP6 69 F1
Hedge End SO30 105 D3
Bartonside Rd BH25 209 E4
Bartram Rd SO40 101 D3
Barwell Gr PO10 136 C2
Barwell Terr SO30 105 E3
Bascott Cl BH11 189 D1
Bascott Rd BH11 189 D1
Bashley Common Rd BH25 195 D4
Bashley Cross Rd BH25 194 C3
Bashley Dr BH25 195 D3
Bashley Rd BH25 195 D3
Basin St PO2 182 B4
Basing Dean GU34 17 F2
Basing House SO15 102 B4
Basing Mews SO32 83 E4
Basing Rd PO9 135 F3
Basing Way SO53 55 D2
Basingstoke Rd SO23 2 B4
Basingwell St SO32 83 E4
Bassett Ave SO16 78 C3
Bassett Cl SO16 78 C2
Bassett Cres E SO16 78 C2
Bassett Cres W SO16 78 C2
Bassett Ct SO16 78 C2
Bassett Dale SO16 78 C3
Bassett Gdns SO16 78 C2
Bassett Gn SO16 79 D3
Bassett Green Cl SO16 79 D3
Bassett Green Ct SO16 79 D3
Bassett Green Dr SO16 79 D3
Bassett Green Inf Sch SO16 79 D2
Bassett Green Jun Sch SO16 79 D2
Bassett Green Rd SO16 79 D3
Bassett Heath Ave SO16 78 C3
Bassett Meadow SO16 78 C2
Bassett Mews SO16 78 C3
Bassett Rd BH12 203 D3
Bassett Row SO16 78 C3
Bassett Wlk 7 PO9 135 E3
Bassett Wood Dr SO16 79 D3
Bassett Wood Mews SO16 78 C2
Bassett Wood Rd SO16 79 D3
Batchelor Cres BH11 188 C2
Batchelor Gn SO31 127 F4
Batchelor Rd BH11 188 C2
Batcombe Cl BH11 188 C2
Bath & Wells Ct PO13 180 B3
Bath Cl SO18 104 A3
Bath Hill Ct 9 BH1 205 D2
Bath La 11 PO16 131 E1
Bath La (lower) 13 PO16 131 E1
Bath Lane Cotts PO16 155 E4
Bath Rd Bournemouth BH1 205 D2
Emsworth PO10 160 C4
Lymington SO41 197 F2
Portsmouth PO4 182 C2
Southampton SO18 104 A3
Bath Sq PO1 181 F2
Bath St SO14 103 D4
Bathing La PO1 181 F2
Bathurst Way PO2 157 D1
Batten Cl BH23 207 E4
Batten Rd SP5 46 C4
Battenburg Ave PO2 157 F1
Battenburg Rd PO12 181 E3
Battens Way PO9 135 F2
Batterley Dro BH21 91 F2
Battery Cl PO12 180 C4
Battery Hill
Bishop's Waltham SO32 83 D4
Winchester SO22 10 B3
Battery Row PO1 182 A2
Battle Cl SO31 129 D2
Battramsley Cross SO41 173 E1
Baverstock Rd BH12 204 A4
Baxter Rd SO19 104 C3
Bay Cl Southampton SO19 104 A2
Three Legged Cross BH21 138 C4
Upton BH16 201 D3
Bay Hog La BH15 202 A1
Bay House Sec Sch PO12 180 C2
Bay Rd Gosport PO12 180 C2
Southampton SO19 104 A2
Bay Tree Lodge PO14 179 E3
Bay Tree Way BH23 193 E1
Bay Trees SO19 104 C3
Bay View Ct PO11 184 B1
Bay View Mews PO11 184 B1
Baybridge La SO21 33 E2
Baybridge Rd PO9 136 A3
Baycroft Sch PO14 179 F3
Bayly Ave PO16 156 B3
Bays Ct SO41 197 E2
Bays Rd SO41 197 E2
Bayswater House 27 PO5 182 B2
Baythorn Cl PO2 182 B4
Beach Ave BH25 209 F4
Beach Cl BH13 214 D4
Beach La SO31 127 D3
Beach Rd Emsworth PO10 160 C4
Lee-on-the-Solent PO13 179 F1
Poole BH13 214 D4
Portsmouth PO5 182 B1
South Hayling PO11 184 C2
Upton BH16 201 D3
Beach View BH13 214 B2
Beachcroft BH13 204 A2
Beachway PO16 156 B3
Beacon Bottom SO31 129 D3
Beacon Cl Hordle SO41 196 B1
Locks Heath SO31 129 D3
Rownhams SO16 77 E3
Beacon Ct Christchurch BH23 208 C4
Fordingbridge SP6 69 F2
Beacon Dr BH23 208 C4
Beacon Gdns BH18 186 C2
Beacon Hill La
Droxford SO32 60 C3
Meonstoke SO32 61 E3
Beacon Mews SO30 104 B4
Beacon Mount SO31 129 D3
Beacon Park Cres BH16 201 D4
Beacon Park Rd BH16 201 D4
Beacon Rd
Bournemouth BH2 204 C1
Broadstone BH18 186 C2
Upton BH16 201 D4
West End SO30 104 B4
Beacon Sq PO10 160 C4
Beacon Way Broadstone BH18 186 C2
Locks Heath SO31 129 D3
Beaconsfield Ave PO6 158 A4
Beaconsfield Rd
Christchurch BH23 207 D4
Fareham PO16 155 D4
Poole BH12 203 E3
Waterlooville PO7 134 C4
Bealing Cl SO16 79 D2
Beamish Rd BH17 202 C4
Bear Cross Ave BH11 188 C3
Bear Cross Rdbt BH11 188 C3
Bearslane Cl SO40 76 B1
Bearwood Prim Sch BH11 188 B3
Beatrice Ct 5 SO41 211 D2
Beatrice Mews 15 PO6 157 F4
Beatrice Rd Portsmouth PO4 182 C1
Southampton SO15 102 B4
Beatrice Royal Art Gal SO50 55 F1
Beattie Rise SO30 81 E1
Beatty Cl Locks Heath SO31 129 D2
Ringwood BH24 141 E4
Beatty Dr PO12 180 C2
Beatty Rd BH9 190 A1
Beaty Ct SO19 104 B3
Beau Ct 31 Bournemouth BH4 204 B2
9 New Milton BH25 195 D2
Beauchamp Ave PO13 155 E1
Beauchamps Gdns BH7 206 A4
Beaucroft La BH21 163 F3
Beaucroft Rd Shedfield SO32 83 F2
Wimborne Minster BH21 163 F3
Beaufort Ave PO16 130 C1
Beaufort Cl BH23 208 A4
Beaufort Dr
Bishop's Waltham SO32 83 E4
Wimborne Minster BH21 163 E3
Beaufort Mews BH21 163 D2
Beaufort Rd Bournemouth BH6 206 B3
Havant PO9 135 E1
10 Portsmouth PO5 182 B1
Winchester SO23 10 C3
Beaufort Sch BH21 163 F3
Beaufoys Ave BH22 165 E4
Beaufoys Cl BH22 165 E4
Beaufoys Ct BH22 165 E3
Beaulieu Abbey SO42 148 C1
Beaulieu Ave
Christchurch BH23 206 C4
Havant PO9 135 E3
Portchester PO16 156 A4
Beaulieu Cl New Milton BH25 194 C2
Southampton SO16 78 A3
Winchester SO22 1 B2
Beaulieu House 12 SO15 102 C4
Beaulieu Pl PO13 155 D1
Beaulieu Prim Sch SO42 148 C1
Beaulieu Rd Beaulieu SO42 149 E3
Bournemouth BH4 204 A1
Christchurch BH23 206 C4
Eastleigh SO50 56 A2
Hamble-le-Rice SO31 127 F2
Hythe SO45 125 F1
Lyndhurst SO42 122 B2
Lyndhurst SO43 122 B2
Marchwood SO40 124 C3
Portsmouth PO2 157 F1
Beaulieu Road Sta SO42 123 E1
Beaumaris Cl SO53 55 D2
Beaumond Gn SO22 10 C4
Beaumont Cl Fareham PO15 130 B2
Southampton SO16 78 C2
Beaumont Ct PO12 181 D4
Beaumont Pl SO40 101 D4
Beaumont Rd Poole BH13 214 C4
Totton SO40 101 D4
Beaumont Rise PO15 130 B2
Beauworth Ave SO18 104 B4
Beaver Dr SO50 57 D1
Beaver Ind Est BH23 208 A3
Beccles Cl BH15 201 F1
Becher Rd BH14 203 F2
Beck Cl SO31 128 C2
Beck St PO1 182 A3
Beckenham Terr PO10 137 D2
Beckford La PO17 109 F1
Beckham La GU32 40 B2
Beckhampton Rd BH15 201 F2
Beckley Copse BH23 194 A1
Becton La BH25 210 A4
Becton Mead BH25 195 D1
Bedale Way BH15 202 C3
Bedales Sch GU32 40 C4
Bedenham La PO13 155 F2
Bedenham Prim Sch PO13 155 E2
Bedfield House SO23 2 A3
Bedfield La SO23 2 A3
Bedford Ave SO19 103 F1
Bedford Cl Fordingbridge SP6 69 F2
Havant PO9 160 A4
Hedge End SO30 105 E3
Bedford Cres BH7 206 B4
Bedford Pl SO15 102 C3
Bedford Rd GU32 40 B2
Bedford Rd N BH12 188 B1
Bedford Rd S BH12 188 B1
Bedford St Gosport PO12 181 D3
Portsmouth PO5 182 B2
Bedhampton Hill PO9 135 D1
Bedhampton Rd Havant PO9 135 E1
Portsmouth PO2 182 C4
Bedhampton Sta PO9 135 E1
Bedhampton Way PO9 135 F2
Bedwell Cl SO16 77 F3
Beech Ave Bournemouth BH6 206 B2
Christchurch BH23 206 B4
Southampton SO18 103 F4
Beech Cl Alderholt SP6 93 D3
Broadstone BH18 186 C2
Chandler's Ford SO53 30 B1
Hamble-le-Rice SO31 127 F1
Beech Cl Continued
Hordle SO41 211 E4
Romsey SO51 53 E3
Verwood BH31 114 C3
Waterlooville PO8 111 F1
Winchester SO22 10 A2
Beech Cnr SO32 81 F3
Beech Copse SO22 1 A1
Beech Cres SO45 150 A4
Beech Ct Southampton SO19 103 F2
Wimborne Minster BH21 163 F2
Beech Gdns SO31 127 F1
Beech Gr Gosport PO12 181 D2
Owslebury SO21 33 D2
South Hayling PO11 185 D2
Beech Grange SP5 49 E1
Beech House SO16 78 C4
Beech La BH24 139 F1
Beech Rd Ashurst SO40 100 A1
Chandler's Ford SO53 55 E4
Clanfield PO8 88 B3
Fareham PO15 130 C1
Hedge End SO30 105 E4
Southampton SO15 102 A3
Beech Way PO8 112 A3
Beech Wood Cl BH18 187 D2
Beecham Rd PO1 182 C4
Beechbank Ave BH17 186 C1
Beechcroft BH1 205 D3
Beechcroft Cl
Chandler's Ford SO53 55 E3
Fareham PO15 130 B1
Beechcroft La BH24 141 D4
Beechcroft Mews 2 BH24 141 D4
Beechcroft Rd PO12 181 D2
Beechcroft Way SO53 55 E4
Beechdale Cl SO40 76 B1
Beechdale Wlk SO40 76 B1
Beechen La SO43 122 A2
Beeches Hill SO32 59 E1
Beeches The Awbridge SO51 26 C3
Bournemouth BH7 206 A4
Fair Oak SO50 57 E1
4 Waterlooville PO7 134 C4
West Wellow SO51 50 B2
Beechey Ct 6 BH8 205 D3
Beechey Rd BH8 205 D3
Beechfield 30 BH4 204 B2
Beechfield Ct SO15 102 A4
Beechmount SO16 78 C3
Beechmount Rd SO16 78 C3
Beechwood SP6 69 E1
Beechwood Ave
Bournemouth BH5 205 F2
New Milton BH25 194 C2
Waterlooville PO7 134 C3
Beechwood Cl
Chandler's Ford SO53 30 A1
Locks Heath SO31 152 B4
Beechwood Cres SO53 30 A1
Beechwood Ct
Bournemouth BH2 204 C1
Liss GU33 21 D3
Beechwood Gdns
Bournemouth BH5 206 A2
Southampton SO18 103 F4
Beechwood House SO14 103 E4
Beechwood Jun Sch SO18 103 F4
Beechwood La BH24 143 D2
Beechwood Lodge 3 PO16 131 D1
Beechwood Rd Cadnam SO40 99 D3
Holbury SO45 150 B2
Portsmouth PO2 157 F2
West Moors BH22 138 C1
Beechwood Rise SO18 80 B1
Beechwood Way SO45 125 E1
Beechworth Rd PO9 136 A1
Beehive Cotts PO16 131 D1
Beehive Wlk PO1 182 A2
Beeston Ct PO1 182 C4
Beggar's La SO23 11 D4
Begonia Rd SO16 79 D2
Behrendt Cl PO12 181 D3
Belben Cl BH12 188 B1
Belben Rd BH12 188 B1
Belbins SO51 27 F2
Belfield Rd BH6 207 D2
Belfry Wlk PO14 129 E1
Belgarve Ct BH1 205 E2
Belgrave Ind Est
Southampton, Millbank SO14 103 E3
Southampton, Portswood SO17 79 E1
Belgrave Rd Poole BH13 204 A1
Southampton SO17 79 E1
Belgravia Rd PO2 157 F1
Bell Cl SO45 150 C1
Bell Cres PO7 134 C3
Bell Davies Rd PO14 179 D3
Bell Heather Cl BH16 201 D4
Bell Hill GU32 40 C3
Bell Hill Ridge GU32 40 C3
Bell House PO18 161 F4
Bell La 18 BH15 202 A1
Bell Rd PO6 157 E4
Bell St Romsey SO51 52 C4
Southampton SO14 103 D2
Bellair House PO9 136 A1
Bellair Rd PO9 136 A1
Bellamy Ct SO17 103 E4
Belle Vue Cl BH6 206 B2
Belle Vue Cres BH6 206 C2
Belle Vue Gdns 2 BH6 206 C2
Belle Vue Gr BH22 138 C1
Belle Vue Mansions 7 BH6 206 C2
Belle Vue Rd
Bournemouth BH6 206 C2
Poole BH14 203 E2
Belle Vue Wlk BH22 165 F1

Bellemoor Rd SO15 78 B1
Bellemoor Sec Sch (Boys) SO15 78 B1
Belleview Terr PO5 182 A2
Bellevue La PO10 136 C1
Bellevue Rd Eastleigh SO50 56 A2
Southampton SO15 103 D3
Bellevue Terr 7 SO14 103 D3
Bellfield PO14 153 F4
Bellflower Cl BH23 208 A4
Bells House BH21 163 E3
Bells La PO14 179 E3
Belmont Ave BH8 190 B1
Belmont Cl Horndean PO8 88 B2
Hythe SO45 126 A1
Stubbington PO14 154 B2
Verwood BH31 115 D3
Belmont Gr PO9 135 E1
Belmont Pl PO5 182 B2
Belmont Rd
Chandler's Ford SO53 55 E2
New Milton BH25 195 E2
Poole BH14 203 E3
Southampton SO17 103 D4
Belmont St PO5 182 B2
Belmore Cl PO1 182 C4
Belmore La
Lymington SO41 197 F2
Owslebury SO21 33 F2
Upham SO32 34 A2
Belmore Rd SO41 197 E2
Belmour Lodge 26 BH4 204 B2
Belney House 4 PO6 157 D4
Belstone Rd SO40 100 C4
Belton Rd SO19 104 A2
Belvedere Cl GU32 40 C2
Belvedere Rd
Bournemouth BH3 205 D3
Christchurch BH23 207 D4
Hythe SO45 126 A1
Belvidere House 12 SO14 103 E3
Belvidere Rd SO14 103 E3
Belvidere Terr SO14 103 E3
Belvoir Cl PO16 155 D4
Bembridge SO31 127 E3
Bembridge Cl SO16 79 E3
Bembridge Cres PO4 182 C1
Bembridge Ct PO11 185 E1
Bembridge Dr PO11 185 E1
Bembridge House PO11 185 D1
Bembridge Lodge Flats
8 PO13 179 F1
Bemister Rd BH9 205 D4
Bemister's La PO12 181 F2
Benbow Cl PO8 112 B4
Benbow Cres BH12 188 C1
Benbow Gdns SO40 76 B1
Benbow House 6 PO1 182 A3
Benbow Pl 5 PO1 182 A3
Benbridge Ave BH11 188 C3
Bencraft Ct SO16 79 D3
Bendigo Rd BH23 206 C4
Benedict Cl SO51 53 E4
Benedict Way PO16 132 C1
Beneficial St 14 PO1 182 A3
Benellen Ave BH4 204 B2
Benellen Gdns BH4 204 B2
Benellen Rd BH4 204 B3
Benellen Towers BH4 204 B2
Bengal Rd BH9 204 C4
Benger's La SO51 5 E1
Benham Dr 13 PO3 157 F2
Benham Gr PO16 156 B3
Benhams Farm Cl 8 SO18 80 A1
Benhams Rd SO18 80 A1
Benjamin Ct BH23 206 C4
Benmoor Rd BH17 202 A4
Benmore Cl BH25 195 E1
Benmore Gdns SO53 55 D4
Benmore Rd BH9 190 A1
Bennett House 11 BH4 204 B2
Bennett Rd BH8 205 E3
Bennett's Alley 22 BH15 202 A1
Bennetts La BH24 143 E1
Bennion Rd BH10 189 E2
Benridge Cl BH18 187 D2
Bensgreen La GU32 18 C2
Benson Cl BH23 169 D1
Benson Rd Poole BH17 202 B4
Southampton SO15 102 A4
Bentham Rd PO12 181 D2
Bentham Way SO31 128 B4
Benthem Ct SO16 79 D2
Bentley Cl Horndean PO8 112 B4
Kings Worthy SO23 2 A3
Bentley Cres PO16 130 C1
Bentley Ct Havant PO9 136 A3
16 Southampton SO17 79 D1
Bentley Gr SO18 104 B4
Bentley Rd BH9 189 F2
Bentworth Cl PO9 135 E2
Benwell Ct PO11 184 C2
Bepton Down GU31 41 D2
Berber Cl PO15 129 E4
Bercote Cl SO22 1 A3
Bere Cl
Broadstone BH17 187 E1
North Baddesley SO53 55 D4
Winchester SO22 1 B1
Bere Farm La PO17 131 F4
Bere Rd PO7 110 C2
Beresford Cl
Chandler's Ford SO53 55 F3
Poole BH12 203 E3
Waterlooville PO7 134 C3
Beresford Gdns
Chandler's Ford SO53 55 F3
Christchurch BH23 207 F3
Beresford Rd
Bournemouth BH6 206 A2
Chandler's Ford SO53 55 F3
Lymington SO41 197 E2
Poole BH12 203 E3
Portsmouth PO2 157 F1
Stubbington PO14 154 B2
Bereweeke Ave SO22 1 C1
Bereweeke Cl SO22 1 C1
Bereweeke Rd SO22 1 C1
Bereweeke Way SO22 1 C1
Bergen Cres SO30 105 E3
Berkeley Ave BH12 203 E4
Berkeley Cl Southampton SO15 102 C4
Stubbington PO14 179 D3
Verwood BH31 114 C4
Berkeley Ct PO13 179 F1
Berkeley Gdns SO30 105 E3
Berkeley Rd
Bournemouth BH3 204 C4
Southampton SO15 102 C3
Berkeley Sq PO9 136 A1
Berkley Ave BH22 165 E1
Berkshire Cl PO1 182 C3
Bermuda Ct
9 Christchurch BH23 209 D4
22 Southampton SO17 79 D1
Bermuda House 3 PO6 132 C1
Bernard Ave PO6 158 A4
Bernard Powell House PO9 136 A1
Bernard St SO14 103 D2
Bernard Cl BH23 206 C4
Berne Ct 11 BH1 205 D2
Berney Rd PO4 183 E2
Bernina Ave PO7 111 E1
Bernina Cl PO7 111 E1
Bernwood Gr SO45 177 F4
Beron Ct BH15 202 C2
Berrans Ave BH11 189 D3
Berrans Ct BH11 189 D3
Berry Cl SO30 105 E3
Berry La Stubbington PO14 179 D3
Twyford SO21 32 A4
Berrydown Rd PO9 135 E4
Berryfield Rd SO41 196 A1
Berrylands GU33 21 D4
Bernards Cl BH23 206 C4
Berrywood Gdns SO30 105 D4
Berrywood Prim Sch SO30 81 E1
Berthon House SO51 52 C3
Bertie Rd PO4 183 D2
Bertram Rd BH25 195 E2
Berwick Rd BH3 204 C3
Berwyn Ct BH18 187 D2
Berwyn Wlk PO14 154 C4
Beryl Ave PO12 180 C4
Beryton Cl PO12 181 D3
Beryton Rd PO12 181 D3
Besomer Dro SP5 47 F3
Bessborough Rd BH13 214 C4
Bessemer Cl BH31 115 E2
Beswick Ave BH10 189 E1
Bethany House BH1 205 E3
Bethany Jun CE Sch BH1 205 E3
Bethia Cl BH8 205 E3
Bethia Rd BH8 205 E3
Betsy Cl BH23 169 D1
Betsy La BH23 169 D1
Betteridge Dr SO16 77 E3
Bettesworth Rd PO1 182 C4
Bettiscombe Cl BH17 187 F1
Betula Cl PO7 135 D3
Beulah Rd SO16 78 A1
Bevan Cl SO19 103 F1
Bevan Rd PO8 112 A3
Beverley Cl PO14 129 E2
Beverley Gdns
Bournemouth BH10 189 E2
Bursledon SO31 104 C1
Romsey SO51 28 B1
Swanmore SO32 84 A3
Beverley Gr PO6 134 C1
Beverley Grange 29 BH4 204 B2
Beverley Hts SO18 79 F2
Beverley Rd Hythe SO45 149 F4
Stubbington PO14 179 E3
Beverly Cl PO13 155 E1
Beverston House 4 PO6 133 D1
Beverston Rd PO6 133 D1
Bevis Cl Blackfield SO45 150 C1
Locks Heath SO31 152 B4
Bevis Rd Gosport PO12 181 D3
Portsmouth PO2 157 E1
Bevis Rd N PO2 157 E1
Bevois Gdns SO14 103 D4
Bevois Hill SO14 103 D4
Bevois Mansions 23 SO14 103 D4
Bevois Mews 24 SO14 103 D4
Bevois Town Prim Sch SO14 103 D4
Bevois Valley Rd SO14 103 D4
Bexington Cl BH11 188 C2
Beyne Rd SO22 10 A2
Bickerley Gdns BH24 140 C3
Bickerley Rd BH24 140 C3
Bickerley Terr BH24 140 C4
Bicknell Ct 10 BH4 204 B2
Bicknell Sch BH7 206 A4
Bickton Wlk 1 PO9 135 E3
Bicton Rd BH11 189 D2
Bidbury Inf Sch PO9 135 E1
Bidbury Jun Sch PO9 135 E1
Bidbury La PO9 135 E1
Biddenfield La Shedfield SO32 107 E3
Wickham PO17 107 E3
Biddlecombe Cl PO13 180 B4
Biddlesgate Ct 10 SO14 102 C2
Bideford Cl SO16 77 F1
Big Tree Cotts SO32 85 E3
Biggin Wlk PO14 154 C4
Bilberry Cl SO31 128 C1
Bilberry Ct 8 SO22 10 C4
Bilberry Dr SO40 101 F1
Bill Stillwell Ct 6 PO2 157 E1
Billett Ave PO7 134 C4
Billing Cl PO4 183 D2
Billington Gdns SO30 81 E1
Billington Pl SO41 197 E1
Billy Lawn Ave PO9 135 F3
Bilton Bsns Pk PO3 158 B1
Bindon Cl Poole BH12 203 F4
Southampton SO16 78 A1
Bindon Ct 5 SO18 103 F4
Bindon Rd SO16 78 A1
Bingham Ave BH14 214 B4
Bingham Cl
Christchurch BH23 207 F4
Verwood BH31 115 D2
Bingham Dr Lymington SO41 197 F2
Verwood BH31 115 D2
Bingham Rd
Bournemouth BH9 205 D4
Christchurch BH23 207 F4
Verwood BH31 115 D2
Binnacle Way PO6 157 D4
Binness Way PO6 158 C4
Binnie Rd BH12 203 F3
Binstead Cl SO16 79 E3
Binsteed Rd PO2 182 C4
Birch Ave Burton BH23 192 B2
Ferndown BH22 165 F1
New Milton BH25 194 B3
Birch Cl Colden Common SO21 56 C4
Corfe Mullen BH21 186 B3
Liss GU33 21 D2
Poole BH14 203 F2
Romsey SO51 53 E3
Southampton SO16 78 A1
St Leonards BH24 139 E2
Waterlooville PO8 111 F2
Birch Ct Southampton SO18 104 A4
3 Winchester SO22 10 B3
Birch Dale SO45 126 A1
Birch Dr Bournemouth BH8 191 D1
Gosport PO13 155 E2
Birch Gr Eastleigh SO50 56 A3
West Moors BH22 138 B1
Birch Hill PO17 109 D2
Birch House SO16 78 C4
Birch Rd Chilworth SO16 79 D4
Hedge End SO30 105 E4
Southampton SO16 78 A2
St Leonards BH24 140 A2
Birch Tree Cl PO10 136 C2
Birch Tree Dr PO10 136 C2
Birch Wood SO19 104 C3
Birchdale Cl SO31 152 B4
Birchdale Rd BH21 163 E3
Birchen Cl SO31 129 E2
Birchen Rd SO31 129 E2
Birches Cl The SO52 53 F3
Birches The SO18 104 A4
Birchglade SO40 76 B1
Birchlands SO40 100 B3
Birchmore Cl PO13 155 E1
Birchwood Cl BH23 208 C4
Birchwood Ct 8 SO18 103 F4
Birchwood Dr SP6 93 D3
Birchwood Gdns SO30 105 E4
Birchwood Lodge 7 PO16 131 D1
Birchwood Mews BH14 203 E2
Birchwood Rd Poole BH14 203 E2
Upton BH16 201 D3
Birchy Hill SO41 172 B1
Bird's Hill Rd BH15 202 C2
Birdham Rd PO11 185 F1
Birdlip Cl PO8 112 A3
Birdlip Rd PO6 133 D1
Birds Hill Gdns 5 BH15 202 C2
Birdwood Gr PO16 155 F4
Birinus Rd SO23 2 A1
Birkdale Ave PO6 134 B1
Birkdale Ct BH18 187 D3
Birkdale Rd BH18 187 D3
Birmingham Ct PO13 180 B3
Biscay Cl PO14 154 A2
Bishearne Gdns GU33 20 C3
Bishop Ct BH24 141 D4
Bishop Rd BH9 205 D4
Bishop St PO1 182 A3
Bishop's La SO32 83 E4
Bishop's Palace SO32 83 E4
Bishop's Waltham Inf Sch SO32 83 E4
Bishop's Wood Rd PO17 84 B1
Bishops Cl Bournemouth BH7 205 F4
Poole BH12 204 B4
Totton SO40 100 C4
Bishops Cres SO19 103 F2
Bishops Ct SO50 56 B3
Bishops Gate PO14 129 E2
Bishops La SO32 84 A1
Bishops Rd SO19 103 F2
Bishopsfield Rd PO14 154 C4
Bishopstoke La SO50 56 C4
Bishopstoke Manor SO50 56 B2
Bishopstoke Rd Eastleigh SO50 56 B2
Havant PO9 135 F3
Bisley Ct SO19 104 A2
Bisterne Cl BH24 143 F1
Bittern Cl PO12 181 D4
Bitterne CE Inf & Jun Sch SO19 103 F3
Bitterne Cl PO9 135 F3
Bitterne Cres SO19 104 A3
Bitterne Manor House SO18 103 E4
Bitterne Manor Prim Sch SO18 103 E4
Bitterne Park Inf Sch SO17 79 E1
Bitterne Park Jun Sch SO17 79 E1
Bitterne Park Sec Sch SO18 79 F1
Bitterne Park Triangle SO18 79 E1
Bitterne Rd SO19 104 A3
Bitterne Rd E SO18 104 B4
Bitterne Rd W SO18 103 F4
Bitterne Sta SO18 103 E4
Bitterne Way Lymington SO41 197 E1
Southampton SO19 103 F3
Verwood BH31 115 D3
Bitumen Rd SO45 151 D2
Black Hill BH31 115 D3
Black La SP5 48 A2
Black Moor Rd BH31 115 E2
Black Swan Bldgs 12 SO22 10 C4
Blackberry Cl PO8 88 B2
Blackberry La BH23 207 F3
Blackberry Terr SO14 103 D4
Blackbird Cl Broadstone BH17 201 F4
Waterlooville PO8 111 F2
Blackbird Rd SO50 55 E1
Blackbird Way
Bransgore BH23 193 E4
Lee-on-the-Solent PO13 179 F2
Blackbrook Bsns Pk PO15 130 C1
Blackbrook House Dr PO15 130 C1
Blackbrook Park Ave PO15 130 C1
Blackbrook Rd PO15 130 B1
Blackburn Ct PO13 180 B3
Blackburn Rd BH12 203 D3
Blackbush Rd SO41 211 D3
Blackbushe Cl SO16 77 F3
Blackcap Cl PO9 113 D1
Blackdown Cl SO45 125 E1
Blackdown Cres PO9 135 F2
Blackfield Inf & Jun Schs SO45 150 C1
Blackfield La BH22 138 C2
Blackfield Rd Blackfield SO45 150 C1
Bournemouth BH8 190 B2
Blackfriars Cl 3 PO1 182 B2
Blackfriars Rd PO1 182 B3
Blackhill Rd SO51 74 C4
Blackhorse La SO32 83 F1
Blackhouse La PO17 109 D1
Blackmoor Wlk 26 PO9 136 A3
Blackmore La GU32 18 C2
Blacksmith Cl BH21 186 B3
Blackthorn Cl Lymington SO41 197 D1
Southampton SO19 103 F3
Blackthorn Dr Gosport PO12 156 A1
South Hayling PO11 185 E2
Blackthorn Gn SO21 57 D4
Blackthorn Rd
South Hayling PO11 185 E1
Southampton SO19 103 F3
Blackthorn Way
New Milton BH25 195 E2
Verwood BH31 115 D3
Blackthorn Wlk PO7 112 B1
Blackwater Cl 10 PO6 157 E4
Blackwater Dr Oakley BH21 187 E4
Totton SO40 76 B1
Blackwater Gr SP6 92 C3
Blackwater Mews SO40 76 B1
Blackwood House 15 PO1 182 B4
Bladon Cl PO9 136 B2
Bladon Rd SO16 78 B1
Blair Ave BH14 203 E2
Blair Cl BH25 194 C2
Blake Cl SO16 77 E3
Blake Dene Rd BH14 203 D1
Blake Hill Ave BH14 203 E1
Blake Hill Cres BH14 203 E1
Blake House PO12 181 F2
Blake Rd Cosham PO6 134 B1
Gosport PO12 181 E3
Blakemere Cres PO6 133 E1
Blakeney Rd SO16 77 E1
Blakesley La PO3 158 B2
Blanchard Rd SO32 83 D4
Blandford Cl BH15 201 F1
Blandford Ct 2 SO41 211 E3
Blandford House SO16 77 F1
Blandford Rd
Coombe Bissett SP5 23 E4
Corfe Mullen BH21 186 B4
Hamworthy BH15 201 E2
Pamphill BH21 162 B4
Upton BH16 201 E2
Blandford Rd N BH16 201 D4
Blaney Way BH21 186 B3
Blankney Cl PO14 179 D3
Blann Cl SO16 77 E3
Blashford Lakes Study Ctr BH24 117 D2
Blaven Wlk 4 PO14 154 C4
Bleaklow Cl SO16 101 F4
Blechynden Terr SO15 102 C3
Blencowe Dr SO52 54 C3
Blendworth Cres PO9 135 F2
Blendworth Fst Sch PO8 112 C4
Blendworth House 16 PO1 182 B3
Blendworth La Horndean PO8 112 C4
Southampton SO18 104 B4
Blendworth Rd PO4 183 D3
Blenheim Ave SO17 79 D1
Blenheim Cl
North Baddesley SO52 54 C2
Totton SO40 100 C3
Blenheim Cres SO41 195 F2
Blenheim Ct
25 Bournemouth BH4 204 B2
Portsmouth PO4 183 D2
Southampton SO17 79 D1
Blenheim Dr BH23 208 A3
Blenheim Gdns Gosport PO12 181 D4
Havant PO9 136 B1
Hythe SO45 125 E1
Southampton SO17 79 D1
Blenheim House
4 Eastleigh SO50 56 A1
Romsey SO51 53 D4
Blenheim Rd Eastleigh SO50 56 A1
Waterlooville PO8 112 A3
Blighmont Ave SO15 102 A3
Blighmont Cres SO15 102 A3
Blind La Fair Oak SO30 81 E3
West End SO30 81 E3
Wickham PO17 107 F3
Wimborne Minster BH21 163 D3
Bliss Cl PO7 134 C3
Blissford Cl PO9 136 A3
Blissford Cross SP6 94 C4
Blissford Hill SP6 94 C4
Blissford Rd SP6 94 C4
Bloomfield Pl BH9 189 F1
Bloomsbury Wlk SO19 103 F1
Blossom Cl SO30 105 F3
Blount Rd PO1 182 A2
Bloxworth Rd BH12 203 F4
Blue Anchor La 15 SO14 102 C2
Blue Ball Hill SO23 11 D4
Bluebell Cl Christchurch BH23 208 A4
Waterlooville PO7 135 D3
Bluebell Copse SO31 128 C1
Bluebell La BH17 186 C1
Bluebell Rd SO16 79 E2
Blueprint Portfield Rd PO3 158 A1
Blundell La SO31 105 E1
Blyth Cl Christchurch BH23 191 E2
Southampton SO16 77 E1
Blythe Rd BH21 186 B3
Blythswood Ct BH25 209 F4
Boakes Pl SO40 100 B1
Boardwalk The PO6 157 D4
Boarhunt Cl PO1 182 B3
Boarhunt Rd PO17 131 F2
Boatyard Ind Est The PO16 155 D4
Bob Hann Cl BH12 203 E3
Bockhampton Rd
Bransgore BH23 192 C3
Burton BH23 192 C3
Bodley Rd BH13 214 C4
Bodmin Rd Bishopstoke SO50 56 C1
Portchester PO6 157 D4
Bodorgan Rd BH2 204 C2
Bodowen Cl BH23 192 B1
Bodowen Rd BH23 192 B1
Bodycoats Rd SO53 55 E3
Bognor Rd BH18 186 C2
Bohemia La SP5 47 F2
Boiler Rd Fawley SO45 151 F1
Portsmouth PO1 181 F4
Bolde Cl PO3 158 A2
Boldens Rd PO12 181 D1
Bolderwood Cl SO50 56 C1
Bolderwood Ornamental Dr SO43 120 B1
Boldre Cl Barton on Sea BH25 209 E4
Havant PO9 135 E2
Poole BH12 203 E4
Boldre La SO41 197 E4
Boldrewood Con Ctr (Univ of Southampton) SO16 78 C2
Boldrewood Rd SO16 78 C2
Boleyn CL BH9 190 A2
Bolhinton Ave SO40 101 E1
Bolton Cl BH6 206 C2
Bolton Cres BH22 166 A3
Bolton Ct 4 BH6 206 C2
Bolton Rd BH6 206 C2
Boltons The
Milford on Sea SO41 211 E2
Waterlooville PO7 134 C2
Bonchurch Cl SO16 79 E3
Bonchurch Rd PO4 183 D3
Bond Ave BH22 138 B2
Bond Cl SO41 172 A2
Bond Rd Poole BH15 202 C3
Southampton SO18 79 F1
Bond St SO14 103 E3
Bondfields Cres PO9 135 F3
Bones La GU31 65 E3
Bonfire Cnr PO1 182 A3
Bonham Rd BH3 204 C4
Boniface Cl SO40 100 B4
Boniface Cres SO16 77 F2
Bonington Cl BH23 207 F4
Bonner Cotts SP5 4 C4
Boothby Cl SO40 101 D3
Border Dr BH16 201 E3
Border Lodge BH23 194 B1
Border Rd Hamworthy BH16 201 E3
Upton BH16 201 E3
Bordon Rd PO9 135 F3
Boredean La Froxfield GU32 39 E3
Langrish GU32 39 E3
Boreham Rd BH6 206 B3
Borley Rd BH17 202 A4
Borough Gr GU32 40 C1
Borough Hill GU32 40 C2
Borough Rd Petersfield GU32 40 B1
Petersfield GU32 40 C2
Borough The SP5 46 C4
Borrowdale Rd SO16 77 F1
Borthwick Rd BH1 205 F3
Boscobel Rd SO22 1 C1
Boscombe Cliff Rd BH5 205 F2
Boscombe Gr Rd BH1 205 E3

Boscombe Overcliff Dr BH5 .. **206** A2
Boscombe Spa Rd BH5 .... **205** E2
Bosham Rd PO2 .... **182** C4
Bosham Wlk PO13 .... **155** D1
Bosley Cl BH23 .... **191** F1
Bosley Way BH23 .... **191** F1
Bosmere Gdns PO10 .... **136** C1
Bosmere Jun Sch PO9 .... **159** F4
Bosmere Rd PO11 .... **185** F1
Bossington Cl SO16 .... **77** F3
Boston Ct SO53 .... **55** E4
Boston Lodge **22** BH4 .... **204** B2
Boston Rd PO6 .... **133** F1
Bosuns Cl PO16 .... **155** D3
Bosville SO50 .... **56** A3
Boswell Cl Botley SO30 .... **106** A3
  Southampton SO19 .... **104** B3
Bosworth Mews BH9 .... **190** A2
Botany Bay Rd SO19 .... **104** A2
Botley Dr PO9 .... **135** E3
Botley Gdns SO19 .... **104** C2
Botley Hill SO30 .... **106** A3
Botley Rd
  Bishop's Waltham SO32 .... **82** C1
  Curdridge SO32 .... **82** C1
  Fair Oak SO50 .... **57** E1
  Fair Oak, Wildern SO50 .... **81** E4
  Hedge End SO30 .... **81** D1
  North Baddesley SO52 .... **53** E3
  Romsey SO51 .... **53** E3
  Southampton SO19 .... **104** B2
  Swanwick SO31 .... **129** D4
  West End SO30 .... **81** D1
Botley Sta SO30 .... **106** B4
Bottings Est SO30 .... **106** A4
Bottom La SO51 .... **50** C2
Boulnois Ave BH14 .... **203** F2
Boultbee Cotts SO43 .... **121** E3
Boulter La PO17 .... **133** D4
Boulton Rd PO5 .... **182** C2
Bound Cl PO11 .... **185** D1
Boundary Cl SO15 .... **101** F4
Boundary Dr BH21 .... **163** E3
Boundary La BH24 .... **139** F1
Boundary Rd
  Bournemouth BH10 .... **189** F1
  Bursledon SO31 .... **127** F4
Boundary Way Havant PO9 ... **135** F1
  Waterlooville PO7 .... **134** A1
Boundstone SO45 .... **125** F2
Boundway SO41 .... **171** F1
Bountys La BH12 .... **203** F3
Bourne Ave Bournemouth BH2 .. **204** C2
  Southampton SO15 .... **78** B1
Bourne Cl Bournemouth BH4 .... **204** B2
  Horndean PO8 .... **112** A3
  Otterbourne SO21 .... **31** D2
  West Wellow SO51 .... **50** B2
Bourne Com Coll The PO10 .. **137** E1
Bourne Cotts SP6 .... **44** C1
Bourne Ct
  24 Bournemouth BH2 .... **204** C2
  Wimborne Minster BH21 ..... **163** E3
Bourne La Netley Marsh SO40 .. **99** E3
  Twyford SO21 .... **32** A3
Bourne Pines **3** BH1 .... **204** C2
Bourne Rd Cosham PO6 .... **157** D4
  Netley Marsh SO40 .... **99** E3
  Southampton SO15 .... **102** B3
Bourne Valley Rd BH12 .... **204** A3
Bourne View PO10 .... **137** E1
Bournefields SO21 .... **32** A4
Bournemouth Ave PO12 ...... **181** D4
Bournemouth Central
  Bsns Pk BH1 .... **205** E3
Bournemouth Coll
  of Art & Design BH12 ... **204** B4
Bournemouth Crown & Cty
  Cts BH7 .... **191** E1
Bournemouth House **29** PO9 .. **136** A3
Bournemouth Int Airport
  BH23 .... **190** C4
Bournemouth Int Ctr BH2 .... **204** C1
Bournemouth Memorial
  Homes BH8 .... **190** C1
Bournemouth Nuffield
  Hospl BH8 .... **205** D3
Bournemouth & Poole Coll
  Annexe The BH1 .... **205** D2
Bournemouth & Poole Coll
  of F Ed BH14 .... **202** C2
Bournemouth & Poole Coll
  of F Ed (Annex) BH14 .... **202** C3
Bournemouth & Poole
  Coll The BH1 .... **205** D2
Bournemouth Rd
  Chandler's Ford SO53 .... **55** E2
  Chilworth SO16 .... **55** E2
  Lyndhurst SO43 .... **121** F3
  Poole BH14 .... **203** E2
Bournemouth Sch BH8 .... **190** B1
Bournemouth Sch for Girls
  BH8 .... **190** B1
Bournemouth Sta BH1 .... **205** D2
Bournemouth Univ BH12 .... **204** B4
Bournewood Dr BH4 .... **204** B2
Bourton Gdns BH7 .... **206** A4
Bouverie Cl **23** BH25 .... **195** D1
Boveridge Gdns BH9 .... **190** A2
Bovington BH17 .... **187** F1
Bowater Cl SO40 .... **76** B1
Bowater Way SO40 .... **76** B1
Bowcombe SO31 .... **127** E4
Bowden La SO17 .... **79** E1

Bowden Rd BH12 .... **188** B1
Bower Cl Holbury SO45 .... **150** B2
  Southampton SO19 .... **103** F1
Bower Rd BH8 .... **205** E4
Bowers Cl PO8 .... **112** A2
Bowers Hill SP5 .... **47** F4
Bowerwood Cotts SP6 .... **93** E4
Bowerwood Rd SP6 .... **93** E4
Bowes Hill PO9 .... **113** E2
Bowes-Lyon Ct BH8 .... **205** E4
Bowland Rise New Milton BH25 .. **195** E1
  North Baddesley SO53 .... **55** D4
Bowland Way SO45 .... **177** F4
Bowler Ave PO1 .... **182** C3
Bowler Ct PO1 .... **182** C3
Bowman Ct SO19 .... **104** A2
Box PO17 .... **202** A4
Boxgrove House **56** PO1 ... **182** B3
Boxwood Cl Portchester PO16 .. **132** A1
  Waterlooville PO7 .... **134** C3
Boyatt Cres SO50 .... **56** A4
Boyatt La Eastleigh SO50 .... **56** A4
  Otterbourne SO50 .... **56** A4
Boyatt Wood Sh Ctr **7** SO50 .. **56** A3
Boyd Cl PO14 .... **179** D3
Boyd Rd Gosport PO13 .... **155** D2
  Poole BH12 .... **203** F3
Boyes La PO21 .... **32** A1
Boyle Cres PO7 .... **134** B3
Boyne Mead Rd SO23 .... **2** B4
Boyne Rise SO23 .... **2** A4
Boynton Cl SO53 .... **55** D4
Brabant Cl PO15 .... **129** D4
Brabazon Dr BH23 .... **208** A4
Brabazon Rd BH21 .... **163** F1
Brabourne Ave BH22 .... **165** E2
Bracken Cl
  North Baddesley SO52 .... **54** A2
  St Leonards BH24 .... **139** E2
Bracken Cres SO50 .... **56** C1
Bracken Glen BH15 .... **202** C3
Bracken La SO16 .... **78** A1
Bracken Lodge **3** BH6 ...... **206** C2
Bracken Pl SO16 .... **79** D4
Bracken Rd Bournemouth BH6 .. **206** B2
  Ferndown BH22 .... **165** D4
  North Baddesley SO52 .... **54** A2
  Petersfield GU31 .... **41** E1
Bracken Way BH23 .... **194** A1
Brackendale BH21 .... **138** C4
Brackendale Rd BH8 .... **205** E4
Brackenhill BH13 .... **204** A1
Brackenhill Rd BH21 .... **164** A4
Brackens The Hythe SO45 ... **125** E2
  Locks Heath SO31 .... **129** D1
Brackens Way **12** BH13 .... **214** C4
Brackenway Rd SO53 .... **55** E4
Bracklesham Cl SO19 .... **103** F2
Bracklesham Rd Gosport PO13 .. **180** B4
  South Hayling PO11 .... **185** F1
Brackley Ave SO50 .... **57** D2
Brackley Cl BH23 .... **191** D4
Brackley Way SO40 .... **100** B4
Bradbourne Rd BH22 .... **204** C2
Bradford Ct PO13 .... **180** B3
Bradford Rd Bournemouth BH9 .. **190** B2
  Portsmouth PO5 .... **182** B2
Brading Ave Gosport PO13 .. **155** E1
  Portsmouth PO4 .... **183** D1
Brading Cl SO16 .... **79** E3
Bradley Ct **24** PO9 .... **136** A3
Bradley Gn SO16 .... **78** A2
Bradley Peak SO22 .... **1** B1
Bradley Rd SO22 .... **1** B2
Bradly Rd PO15 .... **130** B1
Bradpole Rd BH8 .... **190** C1
Bradshaw Cl SO50 .... **57** F1
Bradstock Cl BH12 .... **203** F4
Braehead SO45 .... **125** F1
Braemar Ave Bournemouth BH6 .. **207** D2
  Cosham PO6 .... **158** A4
Braemar Cl Bournemouth BH6 .. **207** D2
  Fareham PO15 .... **130** C2
  Gosport PO13 .... **155** E1
Braemar Dr BH23 .... **193** F1
Braemar Rd PO13 .... **155** E1
Braeside Cl Southampton SO19 .. **103** F3
  Winchester SO22 .... **10** A2
Braeside Cres SO19 .... **103** F3
Braeside Rd Southampton SO19 **103** F3
  St Leonards BH24 .... **139** F2
  West Moors BH22 .... **138** C2
Braidley Rd BH2 .... **204** C2
Brailswood Rd BH15 .... **202** C2
Braintree Rd PO6 .... **133** E1
Braishfield Cl SO16 .... **77** F1
Braishfield Gdns BH8 .... **190** B1
Braishfield Prim Sch SO51 ... **28** B3
Braishfield Rd
  Abbotstock SO51 .... **28** B2
  Braishfield SO51 .... **28** B2
  Havant PO9 .... **136** A2
  Romsey SO51 .... **28** B2
Brake House PO9 .... **135** E1
Bramar Cl BH4 .... **204** B1
Bramber Rd PO12 .... **181** D4
Bramble Cl Alderholt SP6 ...... **93** D3
  5 Eastleigh SO50 .... **56** A3
  Havant PO9 .... **136** B2
  Holbury SO45 .... **150** B2
  Stubbington PO14 .... **179** D3
Bramble Ct **2** GU31 .... **41** E2
Bramble Dr BH25 .... **28** B1
Bramble Hill SO53 .... **55** D3
Bramble La Christchurch BH23 .. **194** A1
  Clanfield PO8 .... **88** A4
  Locks Heath SO31 .... **128** C3
Bramble Mews SO18 .... **104** A4

Bramble Rd Petersfield GU31 .. **41** E2
  Portsmouth PO4 .... **182** C2
Bramble Way Bransgore BH23 .. **169** D1
  Gosport PO13 .... **155** D1
Bramble Wlk SO41 .... **197** E3
Brambles Cl SO21 .... **129** D4
Brambles Farm Ind Est PO7 .. **134** B4
Brambles Rd PO13 .... **179** E2
Brambling Cl SO16 .... **78** A3
Brambling Rd PO9 .... **113** D1
Bramblings The SO40 .... **100** B4
Brambridge SO50 .... **56** C4
Brambridge House SO21 .... **31** E1
Brambridge Rd SO21, SO50 .. **56** C4
Bramdean Dr PO9 .... **135** F3
Bramdean Mews SO19 .... **103** F3
Bramdean Rd SO18 .... **104** B4
Bramham Moor PO14 .... **179** D3
Bramley Cl Lymington SO41 .. **197** F1
  Waterlooville PO7 .... **134** C4
Bramley Cres SO19 .... **104** A1
Bramley Ct BH22 .... **165** E3
Bramley Gdns Fair Oak SO50 .. **81** E3
  Gosport PO12 .... **181** D1
  Hermitage PO10 .... **161** D4
Bramley House Gosport PO12 . **181** D1
  Hedge End SO30 .... **105** D3
Bramley Rd
  Bournemouth BH10 .... **189** E3
  Ferndown BH22 .... **165** E3
Bramleys The SP5 .... **24** A2
Brampton La PO3 .... **158** B2
Brampton Manor SO16 .... **78** C3
Brampton Rd BH15 .... **202** B3
Brampton Tower SO16 .... **78** C3
Bramshaw Cl SO22 .... **1** B2
Bramshaw Gdns BH8 .... **190** B2
Bramshaw Way BH25 .... **209** E4
Bramshott Rd Portsmouth PO4 .. **182** C2
  Southampton SO19 .... **126** C4
Bramston Rd SO15 .... **102** B4
Bramwell Ct SO18 .... **104** A3
Branches La SO51 .... **25** F2
Branders Cl BH6 .... **207** D2
Branders La BH6 .... **207** D3
Brandon Ct **6** PO5 .... **182** C2
Brandon Rd PO5 .... **182** B1
Brandwood Ct **4** BH14 .... **203** D2
Branksea Ave BH15 .... **201** F1
Branksea Cl BH15 .... **201** F1
Branksome Ave SO15 .... **78** B1
Branksome Cl
  New Milton BH25 .... **195** D1
  Winchester SO22 .... **10** A3
Branksome Ct **14** BH13 ... **214** C4
Branksome Dene Rd BH4 .... **204** A1
Branksome Hill Rd
  Bournemouth BH4 .... **204** A3
  Poole BH12 .... **204** A3
Branksome Sta BH12 .... **203** F2
Branksome Towers BH13 .... **214** C4
Branksome Wood Gdns BH2 .. **204** B2
Branksome Wood Rd
  Bournemouth BH2, BH4 ..... **204** B2
  Poole BH12 .... **204** B2
Bransbury Cl SO16 .... **78** B2
Bransbury Rd PO4 .... **183** D2
Bransgore Ave PO9 .... **135** F3
Bransgore CE Prim Sch BH23 .. **193** E4
Bransgore Gdns BH23 .... **169** E1
Bransley Cl SO51 .... **28** A1
Branwell Cl BH23 .... **192** A1
Branwood Cl SO41 .... **196** C1
Brasenose Cl PO14 .... **129** E1
Brasher Cl SO50 .... **57** D1
Brassey Cl BH9 .... **190** A1
Brassey Rd Bournemouth BH9 .. **190** A1
  Winchester SO22 .... **1** C1
Brassey Terr BH9 .... **189** F1
Brasted Ct PO4 .... **183** E3
Braunston Cl PO6 .... **133** D1
Braxall Lawn PO9 .... **135** E3
Braxton Ctyd SO41 .... **211** F4
Braxton House **1** SO23 .... **11** E4
Breach Ave PO6 .... **137** F1
Breach La BH24 .... **141** F4
Breamore CE Prim Sch SP6 .. **70** A4
Breamore Cl Eastleigh SO50 .. **56** A3
  New Milton BH25 .... **194** C2
Breamore Countryside Mus
  SP6 .... **46** A1
Breamore House SP6 .... **46** A2
Breamore Rd SO18 .... **104** B4
Brean Cl SO16 .... **77** F1
Brearley Ct BH23 .... **209** D4
Brecon Ave PO6 .... **158** A4
Brecon Cl Bournemouth BH10 .. **189** F3
  Chandler's Ford SO53 .... **55** D2
  Fareham PO14 .... **154** C4
  Hythe SO45 .... **125** F2
  New Milton BH25 .... **195** E1
Brecon Rd SO19 .... **104** B3
Bredenbury Cres PO6 .... **133** E1
Bredon Wlk PO14 .... **154** C4
Bredy Cl PO17 .... **187** E1
Breech Cl **12** PO3 .... **157** F2
Bremble Cl BH12 .... **188** B1
Brenchley Ct SO16 .... **156** A4
Brendon Cl Bournemouth BH8 .. **190** C1
  Hythe SO45 .... **125** E1
Brendon Gr SO16 .... **101** F4
Brendon Rd SO40 .... **154** B4
Brent Ct PO10 .... **160** C4
Brentwood Cres SO18 .... **80** A1
Breton Cl PO15 .... **129** D4

Brewells La GU33 .... **21** F2
Brewer Cl SO31 .... **129** D2
Brewer St PO1 .... **182** B3
Brewers La Gosport PO13 .... **155** E1
  West Tisted SO24 .... **17** E4
Brewhouse Sq PO12 .... **181** E3
Brewster Cl PO8 .... **112** A2
Briar Cl Christchurch BH23 .. **207** F3
  Gosport PO13 .... **180** C2
  Poole BH15 .... **202** C3
  Waterlooville PO8 .... **112** A3
Briar Way Romsey SO51 .... **28** B1
  Wimborne Minster BH21 .... **164** A3
Briar Wood GU33 .... **21** D4
Briar's The PO7 .... **111** E1
Briardene Ct SO40 .... **100** C4
Briarfield **28** BH4 .... **204** B2
Briarfield Gdns PO8 .... **112** A3
Briarswood SO16 .... **78** A1
Briarswood Rd BH16 .... **201** E4
Briarswood Rise SO45 .... **125** E1
Briarwood Cl PO16 .... **155** D4
Briarwood Gdns PO11 .... **184** C2
Briarwood Rd SO40 .... **100** B3
Brick Kiln La SO24 .... **17** D4
Brickets Terr PO12 .... **181** D1
Brickfield La Boldre SO41 ... **197** F3
  Chandler's Ford SO53 .... **55** E3
Brickfield Rd ST01 .... **79** E1
Brickmakers Rd SO41 .... **56** C4
Brickwoods Cl SO51 .... **53** D4
Brickworth Rd SP5 .... **24** A2
Brickyard La Broadstone BH21 .. **162** A1
  Ferndown BH21 .... **165** D3
Brickyard Rd SO32 .... **84** A2
Bridefield Cl PO8 .... **111** E2
Bridefield Cres PO8 .... **111** E2
Bridge App BH15 .... **202** A1
Bridge Cl SO31 .... **105** D1
Bridge Cotts SO51 .... **50** C2
Bridge Ct SO51 .... **53** C3
Bridge House PO13 .... **155** E2
Bridge Industries PO16 ...... **131** E2
Bridge Mead SO32 .... **61** E3
Bridge Meadows GU33 .... **20** C2
Bridge Pl BH10 .... **189** E4
Bridge Rd Boldre SO41 .... **197** F3
  Bursledon SO31 .... **128** B3
  Emsworth PO10 .... **136** C1
  Locks Heath SO31 .... **128** B3
  Lymington SO41 .... **197** F3
  Romsey SO51 .... **53** D4
  Southampton SO19 .... **103** C2
  Swanwick SO31 .... **128** B3
Bridge Sh Ctr The PO1 .... **182** C3
Bridge St Christchurch BH23 .. **207** E3
  Fordingbridge SP6 .... **69** F1
  Southwick PO17 .... **132** C3
  Titchfield PO14 .... **154** A4
  Wickham PO17 .... **108** A2
  34 Winchester SO23 .... **11** D4
Bridge Terr
  Compton(Hants) SO21 .... **31** F3
  33 Southampton SO14 .... **103** D2
Bridgefoot Dr PO16 .... **131** E1
Bridgefoot Hill PO16 .... **131** E1
Bridgefoot Path PO10 .... **160** C4
Bridgemary Ave PO13 .... **155** E2
Bridgemary Com Sch PO13 .. **155** E1
Bridgemary Gr PO13 .... **155** E3
Bridgemary Rd PO13 .... **155** E2
Bridgemary Way PO13 .... **155** E3
Bridgers Cl SO16 .... **77** F3
Bridges Ave PO6 .... **132** C1
Bridges Cl SO50 .... **55** F2
Bridges The BH24 .... **140** C4
Bridgeside Cl PO1 .... **182** B3
Bridget Cl PO8 .... **112** B4
Bridgewater Rd BH12 .... **203** E3
Bridgeway Ct SO40 .... **101** D4
Bridgwater Ct SO15 .... **102** B3
Bridle Cl BH16 .... **201** E4
Bridle Cres BH7 .... **206** B4
Bridle Way BH21 .... **164** B3
Bridleways BH31 .... **114** C3
Bridlington Ave SO15 .... **102** B4
Bridport Ct SO15 .... **102** B3
Bridport Rd Poole BH12 ..... **203** F4
  Verwood BH31 .... **114** C3
Bridport St PO1 .... **182** B3
Brierley Cl BH10 .... **189** F3
Brierley Rd BH10 .... **189** F2
Brigantine Rd SO31 .... **128** C1
Brigham Cl **20** PO2 .... **157** F2
Brighstone Cl SO16 .... **79** E3
Bright Rd BH15 .... **202** B3
Brightlands Ave BH6 .... **206** C3
Brighton Ave PO12 .... **180** C4
Brighton Rd
  Southampton SO15 .... **102** C4
  Sway SO41 .... **172** A1
Brights La PO11 .... **184** C2
Brightside PO7 .... **134** B3
Brightside Rd SO16 .... **77** F1
Brightstone Rd PO6 .... **157** F4
Brindle Cl SO16 .... **79** D3
Brinsons Cl BH23 .... **192** B2
Brinton La SO45 .... **126** A3
Brinton's Rd SO14 .... **103** D3
Brinton's Terr SO14 .... **103** D3
Brisbane House **20** PO1 .... **182** B4
Brisbane Rd BH23 .... **191** F1
Bristol Ct PO13 .... **180** B3
Bristol Rd PO4 .... **182** C1
Britain St PO1 .... **182** A3
Britannia Ct BH12 .... **203** D4

Britannia Gdns SO30 .... **81** D2
Britannia Pl SO41 .... **197** F2
Britannia Rd Poole BH14 .... **203** D2
  Portsmouth PO5 .... **182** B2
  Southampton SO14 .... **103** D3
Britannia Rd N PO5 .... **182** B2
Britannia Way BH23 .... **208** A4
Britannic House **22** SO14 .. **103** E3
Britnell House **6** GU31 ...... **40** C2
Briton St PO13 .... **103** D2
Briton Rd PO13 .... **179** F1
Britten Rd PO13 .... **134** C2
Britten Way PO7 .... **134** C2
Brittons Cotts SO42 .... **145** E1
Brixey Cl BH12 .... **203** E4
Brixey Rd BH12 .... **203** E4
Brixworth Cl **11** PO6 .... **133** D1
Broad Ave BH8 .... **205** E4
Broad Chalke Down SO22 ..... **10** B2
Broad Croft PO9 .... **113** E2
Broad Gdns PO6 .... **158** C4
Broad Gn **5** SO14 .... **103** D2
Broad La Denmead PO7 ...... **110** A3
  Lymington SO41 .... **197** F1
  North Baddesley SO52 .... **53** F3
  Southampton SO14 .... **102** C2
  Swanmore SO32 .... **84** A3
Broad Mead Rd GU23 .... **114** C1
Broad Oak SO30 .... **105** F4
Broad St PO1 .... **181** F2
Broad View La SO22 .... **10** A2
Broad Way Froxfield GU32 .... **39** F4
  Hamble-le-Rice SO31 .... **127** F3
Broad Woods La SO51 .... **51** D3
Broadbent Cl SO16 .... **77** F3
Broadcut PO16 .... **131** E1
Broadfields Cl SO41 .... **211** E3
Broadhill La SP6 .... **94** B4
Broadhurst Ave BH10 .... **189** F2
Broadland Cotts GU32 .... **41** D3
Broadlands SO51 .... **52** C3
Broadlands Ave
  Bournemouth BH6 .... **206** C2
  Eastleigh SO50 .... **56** A3
  Waterlooville PO7 .... **134** C4
Broadlands Cl
  Bournemouth BH8 .... **190** B2
  Christchurch BH23 .... **194** A1
Broadlands Rd
  Brockenhurst SO42 .... **145** F1
  Southampton SO17 .... **79** D2
Broadlands SO45 .... **150** B2
Broadly Cl SO41 .... **197** D1
Broadmayne Rd BH12 .... **204** A4
Broadmead Cl **8** SO41 ..... **197** F1
Broadmead Flats SO16 .... **77** E3
Broadmeadow Rd SO16 .... **77** E3
Broadmeadows La PO7 ...... **135** D4
Broadmere Ave PO9 .... **135** F3
Broadmoor Rd BH21 .... **186** B4
Broadoak Cl SO45 .... **150** B2
Broads The BH21 .... **162** C3
Broadsands Dr PO12 .... **180** B2
Broadsands Wlk PO12 .... **180** C2
Broadshard La BH24 .... **141** D4
Broadstone Cty Fst Sch
  BH18 .... **187** D2
Broadstone Cty Mid Sch
  BH18 .... **187** E3
Broadstone Way
  Broadstone BH17 .... **202** A4
  Broadstone, Fleet's Cnr BH18 .. **186** C1
Broadwater Ave BH14 .... **203** E1
Broadwater Rd Romsey SO51 .. **52** C3
  Southampton SO18 .... **79** F2
Broadway BH6 .... **207** D2
Broadway Cl BH12 .... **204** A3
Broadway Gables BH14 .... **203** F2
Broadway Rd **7** BH21 .... **163** E2
Broadway La
  Bournemouth BH8 .... **190** B2
  Horndean PO8 .... **111** E4
Broadway Mews BH14 .... **202** C2
Broadway Pk **5** BH21 .... **163** E2
Broadway The
  Bournemouth BH10 .... **189** E3
  5 Southampton, Bitterne Pk SO18 .. **79** F1
  Southampton, Portswood SO17 .. **79** D1
  Southampton, Thornhill Pk SO18 .. **104** B4
  Winchester SO23 .... **11** D4
Brockenhurst Ave PO9 .... **135** E3
Brockenhurst CE Prim Sch
  SO42 .... **172** C4
Brockenhurst Coll SO42 ..... **146** A1
Brockenhurst Rd BH9 .... **190** A1
Brockenhurst Sta SO42 ...... **173** D4
Brockhampton La PO9 .... **135** F1
Brockhampton Rd PO9 ...... **135** E1
Brockhills La BH25 .... **195** E3
Brockhurst Ind Est PO12 .... **155** F1
Brockhurst Inf Sch PO12 .... **180** C4
Brockhurst Jun Sch PO12 ... **181** D4
Brockhurst Rd PO12 .... **180** C4
Brockishill Rd SO40 .... **99** D3
Brocklands PO9 .... **135** E1
Brockley Rd BH10 .... **189** F2
Brocks Cl SO45 .... **125** E1
Brocks Pine BH24 .... **139** F2
Brockwood Bottom SO32 ..... **36** C4
Brodrick Ave PO12 .... **181** D2
Brog St BH21 .... **162** B1
Brokenford Ave SO40 .... **101** D4
Brokenford Bsns Ctr SO40 .. **100** C4
Brokenford La SO40 .... **100** C4
Brombys The **7** BH15 .... **202** B1
Bromley House BH12 .... **204** A3

Bromley Rd SO18 .... 79 F1
Brompton Rd PO4 .... 182 C2
Bromyard Cres PO6 .... 133 E1
Bronte Ave BH23 .... 192 A1
Bronte Cl SO40 .... 100 B3
Bronte Way SO19 .... 103 F3
Bronwen Ct SO19 .... 104 A1
Brook Ave Locks Heath SO31 ..... 128 B2
  New Milton SO41 .... 195 D2
Brook Ave N BH25 .... 195 D2
Brook Cl Bournemouth BH10 ...... 189 E2
  Locks Heath SO31 .... 128 C2
  North Baddesley SO52 .... 54 A2
Brook Cnr SO43 .... 74 A1
Brook Cotts
  King's Somborne SO51 .... 6 B3
  Westbourne PO10 .... 137 D2
Brook Ct Romsey SO51 .... 52 C3
  13 Southampton SO15 .... 102 B3
Brook Dr BH31 .... 115 D2
Brook Farm Ave PO15 .... 130 C1
Brook Gdns PO10 .... 160 B4
Brook Hill SO41 .... 198 C4
Brook La Botley SO30 .... 105 F3
  Bransgore BH23 .... 193 D4
  Corfe Mullen BH21 .... 186 B3
  Hambledon PO7 .... 86 B3
  Locks Heath SO31 .... 128 C2
  Woodgreen SP6 .... 70 C4
Brook Meadow PO15 .... 130 C1
Brook Rd Bournemouth BH10 ..... 189 E2
  Fair Oak SO50 .... 57 E1
  Lymington SO41 .... 197 F1
  Poole BH12 .... 203 E3
  Southampton SO18 .... 104 A4
  Wimborne Minster BH21 .... 163 F2
  Brook Road Depot BH21 .... 163 F2
Brook St SO32 .... 83 E4
Brook Terr SP6 .... 93 F4
Brook Valley SO16 .... 78 A1
Brook Way
  Christchurch BH23 .... 208 B4
  Romsey SO51 .... 28 A1
Brook Wlk SO40 .... 76 B1
Brookdale Cl
  Broadstone BH18 .... 187 D1
  Waterlooville PO7 .... 134 C4
Brooke Cl SO23 .... 2 A4
Brookers La PO13 .... 155 D1
Brookfield Cl PO9 .... 135 F1
  Brookfield Com Sch SO31 .... 128 C2
Brookfield Gdns SO31 .... 128 C2
Brookfield Pl SO17 .... 79 D1
Brookfield Rd Fair Oak SO50 ..... 57 E1
  Portsmouth PO1 .... 182 C3
Brookfields SO51 .... 50 B2
Brookland Cl SO41 .... 197 E2
Brooklands Bournemouth BH4 ... 204 A2
  Lyndhurst SO43 .... 122 A2
Brooklands Rd
  Bishop's Waltham SO32 .... 83 E4
  Havant PO9 .... 135 D1
Brookley Rd SO42 .... 146 A1
Brooklyn Cl SO21 .... 31 E2
Brooklyn Ct 15 BH25 .... 194 C4
Brooklyn Dr PO7 .... 134 C4
Brooklynn Cl SO32 .... 83 F1
Brookman Ct SO18 .... 104 A4
Brookmead Way PO9 .... 159 F4
Brooks Cl BH24 .... 141 D3
  Brooks Sch SO22 .... 1 C1
Brookside Gosport PO13 .... 155 D3
  Ibsley SP6 .... 94 B1
  Landford SP5 .... 49 E2
  Totton SO40 .... 100 C3
Brookside Ave SO15 .... 101 F4
Brookside Cl Bransgore BH23 ... 169 D1
  Denmead PO7 .... 110 C2
Brookside Cvn Pk BH21 .... 186 A2
Brookside House SO18 .... 79 F2
Brookside Rd
  Bransgore BH23 .... 193 D4
  Brockenhurst SO42 .... 145 F1
  Havant, Bedhampton PO9 .... 135 F2
  Wimborne Minster BH21 .... 163 F2
Brookside Way
  Christchurch BH23 .... 193 F1
  Southampton SO18 .... 79 F2
  West End SO30 .... 80 C2
Brookvale Ct 14 SO17 .... 79 D1
Brookvale Rd SO17 .... 79 D1
Brookwood Ave SO50 .... 55 F2
  Brookwood Ind Est SO50 .... 56 A2
Brookwood Rd SO16 .... 101 E4
Broom Cl Portsmouth PO4 .... 183 C2
  Waterlooville PO7 .... 135 D3
Broom Hill SO41 .... 199 D4
Broom Hill Way SO50 .... 56 A4
Broom Rd
  Petersfield GU31 .... 41 E1
  Poole BH12 .... 188 B1
Broom Sq PO4 .... 183 C2
Broom Way
  Lee-on-the-Solent PO13 .... 179 F2
  Stubbington PO13 .... 179 F2
Broomfield Ave PO9 .... 189 F1
Broomfield Cres PO13 .... 180 A4
Broomfield Ct BH22 .... 165 F3
Broomfield Dr SP6 .... 93 D3
Broomfield La SO41 .... 197 F2
Broomhill SP5 .... 49 E1
Broomhill Cl SO41 .... 197 D1
Brooms Gr SO19 .... 104 B2
Broomy Cl SO45 .... 125 E2
Brougham La PO12 .... 181 D3
Brougham Rd PO5 .... 182 B2
Brougham St PO12 .... 181 D3
Broughton Ave BH10 .... 189 F2

Broughton Cl
  Bournemouth BH10 .... 189 F2
  4 Southampton SO16 .... 78 A1
Broughton Ct PO3 .... 158 B2
Broughton Rd SO43 .... 121 F3
Brow The PO7 .... 134 B1
Browndown Rd PO13 .... 180 B2
Brownhill Cl BH9 .... 205 D4
Brownhill Cl SO53 .... 55 E4
Brownhill Ct SO16 .... 77 F2
Brownhill Gdns SO53 .... 55 E4
Brownhill Rd
  Brockenhurst BH25 .... 170 C2
  Chandler's Ford SO53 .... 55 E4
  North Baddesley SO52 .... 54 A2
Brownhill Way Nursling SO16 .... 77 E2
  Southampton SO16 .... 77 E2
Browning Ave
  Bournemouth BH5 .... 206 A2
  Portchester PO16 .... 132 C1
  Southampton SO19 .... 104 B3
Browning Cl Eastleigh SO50 ...... 55 F2
  Totton SO40 .... 100 B4
Browning Dr SO22 .... 10 B4
Browning Rd BH12 .... 203 E3
Brownings Cl SO41 .... 197 D2
Brownlow Ave SO19 .... 104 A3
Brownlow Cl PO1 .... 182 B4
Brownlow Ct 23 BH4 .... 204 B2
Brownlow Gdns SO19 .... 104 A3
Browns La Beaulieu SO41 .... 199 E3
  Damerham SP6 .... 68 A3
Brownsea Ave BH21 .... 186 B3
Brownsea Cl BH25 .... 194 C2
Brownsea Ct BH14 .... 214 A4
  Brownsea Island (NT) BH15 .... 213 E2
Brownsea View Ave BH14 .... 203 E1
Brownsea View Cl BH14 .... 203 E1
Brownsholme Cl 2 SO50 .... 56 A3
Broxburn Cl SO53 .... 30 C1
Broxhead Rd PO9 .... 136 A3
Bruce Cl PO16 .... 131 D2
Bruce Rd PO4 .... 182 C1
Brudenell Ave BH13 .... 214 B4
Brudenell Rd BH13 .... 214 B3
Brue Cl SO53 .... 55 D4
Brune La Gosport PO13 .... 180 A4
  Stubbington PO13 .... 155 D1
  Brune Park Com Sch PO13 ...... 180 C4
Brune Way BH22 .... 165 E2
Brunei House SO16 .... 79 D3
Brunel Cl Hedge End SO30 .... 81 F1
  Verwood BH31 .... 106 C2
Brunel Rd Portsmouth PO2 ...... 157 F2
  Southampton SO15 .... 101 E4
  Totton SO40 .... 76 C2
Brunel Way PO15 .... 129 E2
Brunstead Pl BH12 .... 204 A2
Brunstead Rd BH12 .... 204 A2
Brunswick Cl SO50 .... 57 D2
Brunswick Gdns PO9 .... 135 E1
Brunswick Pl
  Lymington SO41 .... 197 F2
  Southampton SO15 .... 103 D3
Brunswick Rd SO50 .... 57 D2
Brunswick Sq SO14 .... 103 D2
Brunswick St PO5 .... 182 B2
Brushers BH23 .... 169 F2
Bruyn Ct SP6 .... 70 A1
Bruyn Rd SP6 .... 70 A1
Bryanston Rd SO19 .... 103 F3
Bryanstone Rd BH3 .... 204 C4
Bryant Rd BH12 .... 204 A4
Bryher Island PO6 .... 157 D4
Brympton Cl SP6 .... 69 E1
Bryony Cl Broadstone BH18 ..... 186 C2
  Locks Heath SO31 .... 128 C1
Bryony Gdns SO50 .... 81 E3
Bryony Way PO7 .... 135 D4
Bryson Rd PO6 .... 157 E4
Bub La BH23 .... 207 F3
Bubb La SO32 .... 81 E2
Buccaneers Cl BH23 .... 207 F3
Buccleuch Rd BH13 .... 204 A1
Bucehayes Cl BH23 .... 209 D4
Buchan Ave PO15 .... 129 E4
Buchan Ct SO45 .... 125 E1
Buchanan Ave BH7 .... 205 F3
Buchanan Rd SO16 .... 77 F3
Buckby La PO3 .... 158 B2
Bucketts Farm Cl SO32 .... 84 A3
Buckingham Ct
  2 Christchurch BH23 .... 209 D4
  Poole BH15 .... 202 B2
  2 Southampton SO17 .... 103 D4
Buckingham Gr PO1 .... 182 B4
Buckingham Mansions
  5 BH1 .... 205 D2
Buckingham Rd
  Petersfield GU32 .... 40 B2
  Poole BH12 .... 203 E4
Buckingham St PO1 .... 182 B3
Buckingham Wlk BH25 .... 194 C2
Buckland Cl
  Eastleigh SO50 .... 56 A3
  Waterlooville PO7 .... 111 E1
Buckland Ct SO41 .... 197 F3
Buckland Dene SO41 .... 197 E3
Buckland Gdns SO40 .... 76 B1
Buckland Gr BH23 .... 193 F1
Buckland Path PO2 .... 182 B4
Buckland Rd BH12 .... 203 E3
Buckland St SO41 .... 197 F3
Buckland St PO2 .... 182 C4
Buckland Terr BH12 .... 203 E3
Buckland View SO41 .... 197 F3

Bucklers Ct Havant PO9 .... 135 E4
  Lymington SO41 .... 197 E2
  Portsmouth PO1 .... 157 E1
Bucklers Hard Maritime
  Mus SO42 .... 176 B3
Bucklers Mews SO41 .... 197 E2
Bucklers Rd PO12 .... 181 E4
Bucklers The SO41 .... 211 D3
Bucklers Way BH8 .... 190 B2
Bucklershard Rd SO42 .... 176 B3
Buckley Ct SO16 .... 78 A1
Buckmore Ave GU32 .... 40 B2
Bucks Head Hill SO32 .... 61 E3
Bucksey Rd PO13 .... 180 B4
Buckstone Cl SO41 .... 196 C1
Buckthorn Cl Broadstone BH17 . 186 C1
  Totton SO40 .... 100 A4
Budden's La PO17 .... 108 C4
Buddens Rd PO17 .... 108 A2
Buddle Hill SP6 .... 94 B2
Budds La SO51 .... 27 F1
  Budds Lane Trad Est SO51 .... 27 F1
Bude PO6 .... 132 C1
Bugdens La BH31 .... 115 D3
Bugle St SO14 .... 102 C2
Bulbarrow Wlk PO14 .... 154 C4
Bulbeck Rd 13 PO9 .... 135 F1
Buldowne Wlk SO41 .... 172 A2
Bull Hill Boldre SO41 .... 174 A1
  Rake GU33 .... 21 F3
Bull La Minstead SO43 .... 98 B2
  17 Poole BH15 .... 202 B1
  Shedfield SO32 .... 83 E2
Bullar Rd SO18 .... 103 F4
Bullar St SO14 .... 103 D3
Bullfinch Cl Broadstone BH17 ... 186 C1
  Totton SO40 .... 100 B4
Bullfinch Ct PO13 .... 179 F2
Bullrush Cl SO45 .... 125 F1
Bulls Copse La PO8 .... 112 A3
Bulls Dro SP5 .... 4 A3
Bunkers Hill PO7 .... 110 B2
Bunns La PO7 .... 109 F3
Bunny La Michelmersh SO51 .... 27 F3
  Sherfield English SO51 .... 25 D2
Bunstead La SO21 .... 30 B4
Bunting Gdns PO8 .... 111 F2
Bunting Rd BH11 .... 165 D4
BUPA Hospl PO9 .... 136 B3
Burbidge Gr PO4 .... 183 D1
Burbush Cl SO45 .... 150 B2
Burcombe La BH24 .... 117 F1
Burcombe Rd BH10 .... 189 E3
Burcote Dr PO3 .... 158 A2
Burdale Dr PO11 .... 185 E2
Burdock Cl BH23 .... 193 D1
Bure Cl BH23 .... 208 A3
Bure Haven Dr BH23 .... 208 A3
Bure Homage Gdns BH23 .... 208 A3
Bure Homage La BH23 .... 208 A3
Bure La BH23 .... 208 A3
Bure Pk BH23 .... 208 A3
Bure Rd BH23 .... 208 A3
Burford Cl BH23 .... 191 E1
Burford Ct 15 BH1 .... 205 D2
Burford La SO42 .... 146 A1
Burgate Cl PO9 .... 135 E2
Burgate Cross SP6 .... 70 A3
Burgate Fields SP6 .... 70 A2
  Burgate Sch The SP6 .... 70 A2
Burgesmede House 13 GU32 ... 40 C2
Burgess Cl Bournemouth BH11 . 188 C2
  South Hayling PO11 .... 185 E1
Burgess Gdns SO16 .... 78 C2
Burgess Rd SO16, SO17 .... 79 D2
Burghclere Rd Havant PO9 ...... 136 A3
  Southampton SO19 .... 104 C2
Burgoyne Rd Portsmouth PO5 .. 182 B1
  Southampton SO19 .... 104 C2
Burgundy Cl SO31 .... 128 C1
Burgundy Terr 1 PO2 .... 157 F1
Buriton Cl PO16 .... 132 B1
Buriton Ct SO19 .... 103 F2
  Buriton Prim Sch GU31 .... 65 E3
Buriton Rd SO22 .... 1 B2
Buriton St PO1 .... 182 B3
Burke Dr SO19 .... 104 B3
Burleigh Rd Bournemouth BH6 . 206 B3
  Portsmouth PO1 .... 182 C3
Burley Cl Barton on Sea BH25 ... 209 E4
  Chandler's Ford SO53 .... 55 D2
  15 Havant PO9 .... 136 A3
  Verwood BH31 .... 114 C3
Burley Ct 4 SO17 .... 79 D1
Burley Down SO53 .... 55 D2
Burley House 5 SO16 .... 102 A4
Burley Lawn BH24 .... 143 D2
  Burley Prim Sch BH24 .... 143 D2
Burley Rd Bransgore BH23 ...... 193 D4
  Brockenhurst SO42 .... 172 C4
  Burton BH23 .... 192 B3
  Poole BH12 .... 203 E3
  Winchester SO22 .... 1 B2
Burling Terr 1 BH12 .... 204 A2
Burlington Arc 34 BH1 .... 204 C2
Burlington Ct SO19 .... 104 A3
Burlington Mans 1 SO15 .... 102 B4
Burlington Rd
  Portsmouth PO2 .... 157 F1
  Southampton SO15 .... 102 C3

Burnaby Rd Bournemouth BH4 .. 204 B1
  Portsmouth PO1 .... 182 A2
Burnage Ct 18 BH13 .... 214 C4
Burnbake Rd BH31 .... 115 D3
Burnbank Gdns SO40 .... 100 C4
Burnbrae Rd PO12 .... 165 E1
Burnett Ave BH23 .... 206 C4
Burnett Cl Hythe SO45 .... 126 A1
  Southampton SO19 .... 79 F1
  Winchester SO22 .... 1 B1
Burnett Rd Christchurch BH23 .. 206 C4
  Gosport PO12 .... 180 C3
Burnetts Fields SO50 .... 81 E4
Burnetts Gdns SO50 .... 81 E3
Burnetts La Fair Oak SO50 .... 81 E3
  West End SO30,SO32 .... 81 E3
Burney House 25 PO12 .... 181 E2
Burney Rd PO12 .... 180 C2
Burngate Rd BH15 .... 201 F1
Burnham Beeches SO53 .... 55 D3
Burnham Chase SO18 .... 104 B4
Burnham Dr BH8 .... 205 E4
Burnham Rd Burton BH23 .... 192 B3
  Cosham PO6 .... 134 B1
  Fordingbridge SP6 .... 69 F2
Burnham Wood PO16 .... 131 D2
Burnhams Wlk 19 PO12 .... 181 E2
Burnleigh Gdns BH25 .... 195 E2
Burns Cl SO53 .... 55 F1
Burns Pl SO16 .... 78 A1
Burns Rd Bournemouth BH6 ..... 206 B4
  Eastleigh SO50 .... 55 F1
  Southampton SO19 .... 104 B3
Burnside Christchurch BH23 ..... 208 B4
  Gosport PO13 .... 155 D3
  Waterlooville PO7 .... 112 A1
Burnt House La Boldre SO41 .... 174 A1
  Bransgore BH23 .... 169 D1
  Stubbington PO14 .... 154 B2
Burr Cl SO21 .... 56 C4
Burrard Gr SO41 .... 197 F1
Burrfields Rd PO3 .... 158 A1
Burridge Rd SO31 .... 106 A1
Burrill Ave PO6 .... 158 A4
Burrows Cl PO7 .... 136 A2
Burrows La BH31 .... 114 C4
Burt Cl SO21 .... 56 C4
Burt's La Holt Heath BH21 .... 138 A4
  Verwood BH31 .... 138 A4
  Burton CE Prim Sch BH23 .... 192 B2
Burton Hall BH23 .... 192 B2
  St Leonards BH24 .... 139 F3
Burton Hall Pl BH23 .... 192 B2
Burton Rd Christchurch BH23 ... 207 F4
  Poole BH13 .... 204 A2
  Southampton SO15 .... 102 C3
Burtoncroft BH23 .... 192 B2
Burts Hill BH21 .... 163 E3
Burwood Gr PO11 .... 185 D2
Bury Cres PO12 .... 181 D2
Bury Ct PO12 .... 181 D2
Bury Farm SO30 .... 106 B2
Bury Hall La PO12 .... 180 C2
Bury House 18 PO16 .... 131 D1
Bury La SO40 .... 101 D3
Bury Rd Gosport PO12 .... 181 D2
  Marchwood SO40 .... 101 F2
  Poole BH13 .... 203 F1
Bus Dro SO45 .... 178 C4
Bush House 38 PO5 .... 182 B2
Bush St E PO5 .... 182 B2
Bush St W 40 PO5 .... 182 B2
Bushell Rd BH15 .... 202 B4
Bushells Farm SP6 .... 93 F4
Bushey Rd BH8 .... 190 B1
Bushmead Dr BH24 .... 139 F3
Bushy Mead PO7 .... 134 B2
Busket La SO23 .... 11 D4
Busketts Way SO40 .... 100 A1
Butcher St PO1 .... 182 A3
Butcher's Cnr SO43 .... 73 F2
Bute Dr BH23 .... 209 D4
Butlers Cl SO51 .... 4 C1
Butlers La BH24 .... 117 E1
Butser Ct PO8 .... 88 B2
Butser Wlk Fareham PO14 .... 154 C4
Butser Cl PO8 .... 88 B2
Butt La SP5 .... 22 A4
Butt's Cl SO19 .... 104 B2
Butt's Cres SO19 .... 104 B2
Butt's Rd SO19 .... 104 B2
Butt's Sq SO19 .... 104 B2
Buttercup Cl Hedge End SO30 .. 105 D3
  Hythe SO45 .... 126 A1
Buttercup Dr BH23 .... 193 D1
Buttercup Way SO31 .... 128 C2
Butterfield Rd SO16 .... 78 C2
Butterfly Dr PO6 .... 133 D1
Buttery The BH23 .... 207 E4
Button's La 19 Poole BH15 ...... 202 B1
  West Wellow SO51 .... 50 C2
Butts Ash Gdns SO45 .... 126 A1
Butts Ash La SO45 .... 149 F4
Butts Bridge Hill SO45 .... 126 A1
Butts Farm La SO32 .... 83 E4
Butts Paddock SO42 .... 145 F1

Butts The SO32 .... 61 E3
Buttsash Ave SO45 .... 150 A4
Buttsbridge Rd SO45 .... 126 A1
By Pass Rd SO51 .... 52 C3
By the Wood SO40 .... 76 B1
Byams La SO40 .... 102 A1
Bye Rd SO31 .... 128 B4
Byerley Cl PO10 .... 137 D3
Byerley Rd PO1 .... 182 C3
Byeways SO45 .... 125 F1
Byrd Cl PO7 .... 134 C3
Byres The PO14 .... 154 B2
Byron Ave SO22 .... 10 B4
Byron Cl
  Bishop's Waltham SO32 .... 83 E3
  Fareham PO16 .... 131 D1
Byron Ct Ferndown BH22 .... 165 E3
  Southampton SO15 .... 102 C3
Byron House 16 BH25 .... 195 D1
Byron Rd Barton on Sea BH25 .. 209 F4
  Bournemouth BH5 .... 205 F2
  Eastleigh SO50 .... 56 A2
  Portsmouth PO2 .... 182 C4
  Southampton SO19 .... 104 B3
  Wimborne Minster BH21 .... 163 E3

C Ave SO45 .... 150 C2
Cable St 29 SO14 .... 103 E3
Cabot Dr SO45 .... 125 E2
Cabot La BH17 .... 202 A4
Cabot Way PO25 .... 194 C2
Cadgwith Pl PO6 .... 157 D4
Cadhay Cl BH25 .... 194 C2
Cadland Ct SO14 .... 103 E1
Cadland Rd Fawley, Hardley SO45 150 B4
  Fawley SO45 .... 151 D3
Cadlands Park Est SO45 .... 150 B3
Cadnam Ct PO12 .... 180 B2
Cadnam La SO40 .... 74 C1
Cadnam Lawn PO9 .... 135 E4
Cadnam Rd PO4 .... 183 D2
Cadnam Way BH8 .... 190 B2
Cadogan Rd BH24 .... 141 D4
Cador Dr PO16 .... 156 A3
Caen House 2 PO14 .... 154 C4
Caerleon Ave SO19 .... 104 B3
Caerleon Dr SO19 .... 104 B3
Caernarvon Gdns SO53 .... 55 D2
Caesar's Way BH18 .... 186 C2
Cains Cl SO31 .... 154 B2
Caird Ave BH25 .... 195 E1
Cairns Cl BH23 .... 206 C4
Cairo Terr PO2 .... 182 B4
Caister Cl PO12 .... 165 E3
Caistor Cl SO16 .... 78 A2
Calabrese SO31 .... 129 D4
Calbourne SO31 .... 127 E4
Calcott La SO32 .... 82 C2
Caldecote Wlk 50 PO5 .... 182 B2
Calder Cl SO31 .... 101 F4
Calder Rd BH17 .... 202 C4
Calderwood Dr SO19 .... 104 A3
Caledon Rd BH14 .... 203 F2
Caledonia Dr SO45 .... 125 E2
Caledonian Cl BH23 .... 208 A4
Calkin Cl SO21 .... 192 A1
Calluna Rd BH12 .... 203 D4
Calman Ct PO1 .... 205 E2
Calmore Cl BH8 .... 190 B2
Calmore Cres SO40 .... 76 A1
Calmore Dr SO40 .... 76 A1
Calmore Gdns SO40 .... 100 B4
  Calmore Ind Est SO40 .... 76 C1
Calmore Inf Sch SO40 .... 76 B1
Calmore Jun Sch SO40 .... 76 B1
Calmore Rd SO40 .... 100 B4
Calpe Ave SO43 .... 121 F3
Calvin Rd BH9 .... 204 C4
Camargue Cl SO31 .... 129 D4
Camber Pl PO1 .... 182 A2
Cambria Dr SO45 .... 125 E2
Cambrian Cl SO31 .... 105 D1
Cambrian Wlk PO14 .... 154 C4
Cambridge Ct 15 SO14 .... 103 D4
Cambridge Dr SO53 .... 55 E2
Cambridge Gdns BH23 .... 191 F1
Cambridge Gn
  Chandler's Ford SO53 .... 55 E1
  Titchfield SO41 .... 129 E1
Cambridge Junc PO1 .... 182 A2
Cambridge Rd
  Bournemouth BH2 .... 204 B2
  Gosport PO12 .... 180 C3
  Lee-on-the-Solent PO13 .... 179 F1
  Portsmouth PO1 .... 182 A2
  Southampton SO14 .... 103 D4
Camcross Cl 7 PO6 .... 133 D1
Camden Cl BH9 .... 190 A1
Camden Hurst 1 SO41 .... 211 D2
Camden St PO12 .... 181 D3
Camden Terr 4 PO12 .... 181 D3
Camel Green Rd SP6 .... 93 D3
Camelia Cl SO52 .... 54 A3
Camelia Gdns SO18 .... 80 A1
Camelia Gr SO50 .... 57 F1
Camellia Cl BH21 .... 114 C1
Camellia Ct 2 SO18 .... 79 F1

Camellia Gdns BH25 195 D1
Camelot Cres PO16 132 A1
Cameron Cl PO13 155 E2
Cameron Ct SO16 77 F3
Cameron Rd BH23 207 E4
Camley Cl SO19 103 F1
Cammel Rd BH22 165 E1
Camp Rd PO13 155 E2
Campbell Cres PO7 134 B3
Campbell Ct SO50 57 E1
Campbell Mews SO18 104 B4
Campbell Rd Bournemouth BH1 205 F3
Burton BH23 192 B2
Eastleigh SO50 56 A1
Portsmouth PO5 182 C2
Campbell St SO14 103 E3
Campbell Way SO50 57 E1
Campion Cl Fair Oak SO50 81 E3
Locks Heath SO31 128 C1
Waterlooville PO7 135 D3
Campion Dr SO51 28 B1
Campion Gr BH23 207 F3
Campion Rd SO19 104 B3
Campion Way
Kings Worthy SO23 2 B4
Lymington SO41 197 F3
Cams Bay Cl PO16 131 F1
Cams Hill Hambledon PO7 86 A1
Portchester PO16 131 F1
Cams Hill Sch PO16 155 F4
Canada Cnr GU31 66 C3
Canada Pl SO16 78 C2
Canada Rd Southampton SO19 103 F1
West Wellow SO51 50 B1
Canal Cl SO51 28 A1
Canal Wlk Portsmouth PO1 182 B3
Romsey SO51 52 C4
Southampton SO14 103 D2
Canberra House [29] PO1 182 B3
Canberra Rd
Christchurch BH23 191 F1
Nursling SO16 77 D2
Thorney Island PO10 161 D2
Canberra Towers [10] SO19 126 C4
Candlemas Pl [12] SO17 103 D4
Candover Ct SO19 127 D4
Candy La SO19 104 C3
Candys Cl BH21 162 C1
Candys La BH21 162 C1
Canford Ave BH11 189 D1
Canford Bottom BH21 164 B3
Canford Cl Shedfield SO32 107 F4
Southampton SO16 77 E1
Canford Cliffs Ave BH14 203 F1
Canford Cliffs Rd BH13 203 F1
Canford Cres BH13 214 C4
Canford Ct BH13 214 C3
Canford Gdns BH12 189 D1
Canford Heath Fst & Mid Schs BH17 202 B4
Canford Heath Rd
Broadstone BH17 187 F1
Poole BH17 187 F1
Canford Magna BH21 164 A1
Canford Pl [2] BH13 214 C4
Canford Rd Bournemouth BH11 189 D1
Poole BH15 202 B2
Canford Sch BH21 164 A1
Canford View Dr BH21 164 A3
Canford Way BH12 188 B1
Canhouse La GU33 21 F2
Cannock Lawn [14] PO5 182 B2
Cannock Wlk [16] PO14 154 C4
Cannon Cl BH18 187 D1
Cannon Hill Gdns BH21 164 A4
Cannon Hill Rd BH21 164 A4
Cannon House SO41 197 F2
Cannon St Lymington SO41 197 F2
Southampton SO15 102 B4
Cannon's Barn Cl PO16 132 B1
Canoe Cl SO31 128 C1
Canon Ct [5] SO50 57 E1
Canon St SO23 10 C4
Canons Wlk SO41 211 E3
Cantell Sec Sch SO16 79 D2
Canterbury Ave SO19 104 B2
Canterbury Cl
Lee-on-the-Solent PO13 180 A2
West Moors BH22 138 C1
Canterbury Dr SO45 125 E2
Canterbury Rd
Portsmouth PO4 182 C2
Stubbington PO14 154 B2
Canterton La SO43 98 A4
Canton St SO15 102 C3
Canute Dr BH23 169 D1
Canute House [25] SO14 103 D2
Canute Rd Southampton SO14 103 D2
[6] Winchester SO23 11 D3
Canvey Ct SO16 77 F1
Capel Ley PO7 134 C2
Capella Ct BH2 204 C1
Capella Gdns SO45 125 E2
Capers End La SO32 82 C1
Capesthorne BH23 208 A3
Capital House [5] SO22 10 C4
Capon Cl SO18 79 F2
Capstan Ct SO14 103 D1
Capstan Gdns SO31 129 E2
Capstans The BH14 214 A4
Capstone Pl BH8 205 E3
Capstone Rd BH8 205 D3
Captain's Pl SO14 103 D2
Captain's Row SO41 197 F2
Captains Row PO1 182 A2
Caradon Pl BH31 114 B4
Carberry Dr PO16 156 B4
Carbery Ave BH6 206 B3
Carbery Ct PO9 135 E4
Carbery Gdns BH6 206 C3
Carbery La [3] BH6 206 B2
Carbery Row [2] BH6 206 B2
Carbis Cl PO6 157 D4
Cardew Rd GU33 21 D2
Cardiff Rd PO2 157 E1
Cardigan Rd
Bournemouth BH9 204 C4
Poole BH12 203 F2
Cardinal Dr PO7 112 A1
Cardinal Way SO31 129 D1
Cardington Ct SO16 77 F2
Carey Rd Bournemouth BH9 189 F2
Southampton SO19 104 B3
Careys Cotts SO42 145 F1
Careys Rd BH8 190 B2
Carina Ct BH13 214 B2
Carisbrook Cres BH15 201 E2
Carisbrooke Netley SO31 127 E4
Poole BH13 214 C4
Carisbrooke Ave PO14 179 D3
Carisbrooke Cl PO9 136 A1
Carisbrooke Cres SO53 55 F3
Carisbrooke Ct
[4] Christchurch BH23 209 D4
New Milton BH25 194 C2
Romsey SO51 28 A1
Carisbrooke Dr SO19 103 F3
Carisbrooke Rd Gosport PO13 155 E1
Portsmouth PO4 183 D2
Carisbrooke Way BH23 193 F1
Carless Cl PO13 180 B4
Carlinford [29] BH5 205 F2
Carlisle Ct [2] SO16 102 A4
Carlisle Rd Portsmouth PO1 182 B3
Southampton SO16 102 A4
Carlton Ave BH25 209 F4
Carlton Cres SO15 102 C3
Carlton Ct [5] SO15 102 C4
Carlton Gr BH12 203 E3
Carlton House SO41 197 F2
Carlton Pl SO15 102 C3
Carlton Rd Bournemouth BH1 205 E2
Gosport PO12 181 E3
Portchester PO16 132 C1
Southampton SO15 102 C4
Carlton Way PO12 181 E3
Carlyle Rd Bournemouth BH6 206 B3
Gosport PO12 181 D3
Carlyn Dr SO53 55 E4
Carmans La SO21 31 E4
Carmarthen Ave PO6 158 A4
Carnarvon Rd
[4] Bournemouth BH1 205 F2
Gosport PO12 181 D2
Portsmouth PO2 182 C4
Carnation Rd SO16 79 E2
Carne Cl SO53 55 E4
Carne Pl PO6 157 D4
Caroline Ave BH23 207 F3
Caroline Gdns PO15 130 B1
Caroline Rd BH11 189 D2
Carolyn Cl SO19 103 F1
Carpathia Cl SO18 80 A1
Carpenter Cl Hythe SO45 126 A2
Lymington SO41 197 E3
Portsmouth PO4 183 D2
Carradale BH23 208 A4
Carran Wlk PO14 154 C4
Carraway PO15 129 E4
Carrbridge Cl BH3 204 B4
Carrbridge Gdns BH3 204 B4
Carrbridge Rd BH3 204 B4
Carrick Way BH25 195 E1
Carrington Cl SO41 211 F3
Carrington House
[6] Eastleigh SO50 56 A1
[33] Southampton SO17 79 D1
Carrington La SO41 211 F2
Carrol Cl SO50 57 E1
Carroll Ave BH22 165 F3
Carroll Cl BH12 204 A3
Carronade Wlk PO3 157 F3
Carronades The [19] SO14 103 D3
Carshalton Ave PO6 158 A4
Carsworth Way BH17 188 A1
Carter Com Sch BH15 201 F1
Carter House Gosport PO13 155 D3
[7] Portsmouth PO1 182 A3
Carter's Clay Rd SO51 26 A3
Carter's La [10] BH15 202 B1
Carters Ave BH15 201 E2
Carters Cl SP6 47 E2
Carthage Cl SO53 55 F4
Cartref Cl BH31 114 C3
Cartwright Cl BH10 189 E2
Cartwright Dr PO15 129 F1
Carvers Ind Est [7] BH24 141 D4
Carvers La BH24 141 D4
Carysfort Rd BH1 205 E2
Cascades App PO1 182 B3
Cascades Sh Ctr PO1 182 B3
Cashmoor Cl BH12 203 F4
Cask St [6] PO1 182 B3
Caslake Cl BH25 194 C1
Caspar John Cl PO14 179 D3
Caspian Cl SO31 129 D4
Cassel Ave BH13 204 A1
Castle Ave Christchurch BH23 208 C4
Havant PO9 136 A1
Winchester SO23 10 C4
Castle Cl Milford on Sea SO41 211 F2
Portsmouth PO5 182 B2
Castle Court Sch BH21 186 A4
Castle Ct
[3] Christchurch BH23 209 D4
[4] Southampton, Bitterne Pk SO18 79 F1
Southampton, Millbrook SO15 102 A3
Castle Farm La PO17 108 A1
Castle Gate Cl BH8 190 B1
Castle Gdns GU32 40 C2
Castle Gr PO16 156 B4
Castle Hill Poole BH14 203 D2
Winchester SO22 10 C4
Castle Hill La BH24 142 C2
Castle Hts [3] SO18 79 F1
Castle La Chandler's Ford SO53 55 D2
Fawley SO45 178 C4
North Baddesley SO52 54 C2
[6] Southampton SO14 102 C2
Castle La E BH7 206 B4
Castle La W BH8, BH9 190 B1
Castle Marina PO13 179 F1
Castle Meadow SP5 46 C4
Castle Mews BH24 140 B3
Castle Par BH7 206 B4
Castle Prim Sch PO16 156 B4
Castle Rd Bournemouth BH9 190 A1
Netley SO31 127 D3
Portsmouth PO5 182 B2
Rowland's Castle PO9 113 D1
Southampton SO18 79 F1
Southwick PO17 132 C3
Castle Sq [8] SO14 102 C2
Castle St Christchurch BH23 207 E3
Poole BH15 202 B1
Portchester PO16 156 B4
Southampton SO14 103 D4
Titchfield PO14 154 A4
Castle Trad Est PO16 156 C4
Castle View PO12 181 D4
Castle View Rd PO16 156 C3
Castle Way SO14 102 C2
Castle Woods SP5 47 E3
Castledene Cres BH14 203 D1
Castlemain Ave BH6 206 B3
Castleman Ct BH22 138 B2
Castleman Way BH24 141 D3
Castlemans La PO11 160 A1
Castleshaw Cl SO16 101 F4
Castleton Ave BH10 189 E3
Castleway PO9 136 A1
Castlewood BH24 140 B3
Catalina Cl BH23 208 A3
Catalina Dr BH15 202 C1
Catamaran Cl SO31 128 C1
Cateran Cl SO16 101 F4
Cathay Gdns SO45 125 E2
Cathedral View [5] SO23 11 D3
Catherine Cl SO30 80 C1
Catherine Cres SP5 46 B4
Catherine Gdns SO30 80 C1
Catherington CE Inf Sch PO8 88 A1
Catherington Hill PO8 88 A2
Catherington La
Horndean PO8 112 A4
Waterlooville PO8 112 A4
Catherington Way PO9 135 F2
Catisfield House [44] PO1 182 B3
Catisfield La PO15 130 A1
Catisfield Rd Fareham PO15 130 B1
Portsmouth PO4 183 D2
Caton Cl BH12 204 A4
Cattistock Rd BH8 190 C1
Catways SO21 30 A4
Causeway SO51 52 B3
Causeway Cres SO40 101 D4
Causeway Ct [6] SO18 103 F4
Causeway Farm PO8 112 A3
Causeway The
Petersfield GU31 40 C1
Portchester PO16 131 F1
Cavalier Cl SO45 125 E2
Cavalier Ct PO6 158 B4
Cavan Cres BH17 187 D1
Cavanna Cl PO13 155 D1
Cavell Dr PO6 133 F1
Cavendish Cl Romsey SO51 28 A1
Waterlooville PO7 134 C4
Cavendish Corner Cvn Pk
[4] BH24 141 D4
Cavendish Dr PO7 134 C4
Cavendish Gr
Southampton SO17 102 C4
Winchester SO23 2 A2
Cavendish Hall BH1 205 D3
Cavendish Mews [2] SO15 102 C4
Cavendish Pl BH1 205 D3
Cavendish Rd
Bournemouth BH1 205 D3
Portsmouth PO5 182 B2
Caversham Cl
Hamworthy BH15 201 F2
Southampton SO19 104 A2
West End SO30 80 B1
Cawdor Rd BH3 204 B4
Cawte Rd SO15 102 B3
Cawte's Pl PO16 131 E1
Caxton Ave SO19 104 A3
Caxton Cl BH23 208 A4
Cecil Ave Ashurst SO40 100 B1
Bournemouth BH8 205 E4
Southampton SO15, SO16 78 A1
Cecil Cl BH21 186 C3
Cecil Ct BH8 205 D4
Cecil Gr PO5 182 A2
Cecil Hill BH8 205 D4
Cecil Pl PO5 182 A2
Cecil Rd Bournemouth BH5 205 F2
Poole BH12 203 E3
Southampton SO19 103 F2
Cecil Villas SO17 79 E1
Cedar Ave Bournemouth BH10 189 E3
Christchurch BH23 206 B4
Southampton SO15 102 B4
St Leonards BH24 139 F2
Cedar Cl Bursledon SO31 127 F4
Gosport PO12 156 A1
Hedge End SO30 105 E4
Kings Worthy SO23 2 A4
Upton BH16 201 D4
Waterlooville PO7 134 C3
Cedar Cres
North Baddesley SO52 53 F3
Waterlooville PO8 112 B3
Cedar Ct Bournemouth BH4 204 A1
[12] Fareham PO16 131 E1
Cedar Dr Hordle SO41 211 E4
Wimborne Minster BH21 164 A3
Cedar Gdns
Barton on Sea BH25 194 C1
Southampton SO14 103 D4
Cedar Gr PO3 183 D4
Cedar Lawn SO51 28 B1
Cedar Mount BH4 204 B2
Cedar Pl BH23 169 D1
Cedar Rd Eastleigh SO50 55 F1
Hythe SO45 150 A4
Southampton SO14 103 D4
Cedar Specl Sch The SO16 77 F2
Cedar Trad Pk BH21 164 C3
Cedar Way Fareham PO14 154 C4
Ferndown BH22 165 E4
Cedar Wlk [18] SO22 10 C4
Cedar Wood Cl Fair Oak SO50 57 F1
Totton SO40 100 B4
Cedarmount SO43 121 F2
Cedars The BH4 204 B2
Cedarwood SO23 2 B4
Cedarwood Lodge [6] PO16 131 D1
Cedric Cl SO45 177 F4
Celandine Ave
Locks Heath SO31 128 C1
Waterlooville PO8 112 A2
Celandine Cl
Christchurch BH23 208 A4
North Baddesley SO52 54 C3
Celia Cl PO7 135 D4
Cellars Farm Rd BH6 207 D2
Cement Terr [7] SO14 102 C2
Cemetery Ave BH15 202 C3
Cemetery La Denmead PO7 110 C3
Westbourne PO10 137 E2
Cemetery Rd
Southampton SO15 102 C4
Wimborne Minster BH21 163 D3
Centaur St PO2 182 B4
Centenary Cl SO41 172 B1
Centenary House [6] BH23 207 D4
Centenary Way BH1, 205 F3
Central Ave Corfe Mullen BH21 186 B4
Poole BH12 203 F3
Central Bridge SO14 103 D2
Central Dr BH2 204 C3
Central Prec The SO53 55 E3
Central Rd Cosham PO6 158 B4
Portchester PO16 156 A4
Southampton SO14 103 D1
Central St PO1 182 B3
Central Station Bridge SO15 102 C3
Central Way N SO45 151 F1
Centre La SO41 196 C1
Centre Pl BH24 140 C4
Centre Way SO31 129 D2
Centurian Ind Pk SO18 103 E4
Cerdic Mews SO31 128 A2
Cerne Abbas BH13 204 A1
Cerne Cl Bournemouth BH9 190 A2
North Baddesley SO52 53 F2
West End SO18 80 A1
Cessac House PO12 181 E1
Chadderton Gdns PO1 182 A2
Chaddesley Glen BH13 214 C3
Chaddesley Pines BH13 214 C3
Chaddesley Wood Rd BH13 214 C3
Chadwell Ave SO19 104 A2
Chadwick Rd SO50 55 F1
Chafen Rd SO18 103 E4
Chaffey Cl BH24 141 E4
Chaffinch Cl Broadstone BH18 186 C1
New Milton BH25 194 C1
Totton SO40 100 B4
Chaffinch Gn PO8 111 F2
Chaffinch Way
Lee-on-the-Solent PO13 179 F2
Portchester PO16 155 F4
Chalbury Cl BH17 188 A1
Chalbury Ct
[6] Christchurch BH23 207 F3
[11] Poole BH14 203 D2
Chaldecott Gdns BH10 189 E2
Chaldon Rd BH17 187 F1
Chale Cl PO13 155 E1
Chalewood Rd SO45 177 F4
Chalfont Ave BH23 191 E2
Chalfont Ct [6] SO16 78 A1
Chalice Cl BH14 203 D2
Chalice Ct SO30 105 D3
Chalk Cl SP5 47 E4
Chalk Hill Soberton SO32 85 E3
West End SO18 80 B1
Chalk Hill Rd PO8 112 B4
Chalk La PO17 131 D4
Chalk Pit Cotts PO17 131 D4
Chalk Ridge PO8 88 B2
Chalkpit Rd PO6 133 D1
Chalkridge Rd PO6 134 A1
Challenger Way SO45 125 E1
Challis Ct [18] SO14 103 D2
Chalmers Way SO31 127 F2
Chaloner Cres SO45 126 A1
Chalton Cres PO9 135 E2
Chalton House [42] PO1 182 B3
Chalton La PO8 88 B3
Chalvington Ct SO53 55 E3
Chalvington Rd SO53 55 E2
Chalwyn Ind Est BH12 203 D4
Chalybeate Cl SO16 78 A1
Chalybeate Hospl SO16 78 A1
Chamberlain Gr PO14 155 D4
Chamberlain Hall SO16 79 D2
Chamberlain Rd SO17 79 D2
Chamberlayne Ct SO52 54 A2
Chamberlayne House
[7] SO31 127 D3
Chamberlayne Park Sch
SO19 104 A1
Chamberlayne Park Sch
SO19 127 D4
Chamberlayne Rd
Bursledon SO31 127 F4
Eastleigh SO50 56 A1
Netley SO31 127 D3
Chambers Ave SO51 53 D4
Chambers Cl SO16 77 E3
Champion Cl SO41 211 F2
Chancel Rd SO31 129 D2
Chancellors La SO32 81 F2
Chanctonbury House [22] PO5 182 B2
Chander Cl BH22 165 F2
Chandler's Ford Ind Est SO53 55 D3
Chandler's Ford Inf Sch SO53 55 E3
Chandler's Ford Inf Sch (Annexe SO53 55 E4
Chandlers Cl
Bournemouth BH7 206 A4
South Hayling PO11 185 E1
Chandlers Way SO31 129 D3
Chandos Ave BH12 204 A4
Chandos House [14] SO14 103 D2
Chandos St [26] SO14 103 D2
Channel Ct
Barton on Sea BH25 209 F4
Bournemouth BH6 206 B2
Channel Mouth Rd SO45 151 F1
Channel Way SO14 103 E2
Channels Farm Rd SO16 79 E3
Chant Cl BH23 207 E4
Chantrell Wlk PO15 130 B2
Chantry Cl BH23 193 F1
Chantry Rd Gosport PO12 181 D4
Horndean PO8 112 A4
Southampton SO14 103 D2
Chantry The
Bournemouth BH1 205 D2
Locks Heath PO14 129 E2
Chapel Cl Braishfield SO51 28 B3
Corfe Mullen BH21 186 B3
Chapel Cres SO19 104 A2
Chapel Ct [7] PO1 182 B4
Chapel Dro Fair Oak SO50 81 E4
Hedge End SO30 105 D3
Chapel La Blackfield SO45 177 F4
Bransgore BH23 193 D4
Burley BH24 143 D2
Chilcomb SO21, SO23 12 A4
Corfe Mullen BH21 186 B3
Curdridge SO32 106 C4
East Boldre SO42 175 E3
Fawley SO45 151 D1
Lockerley SO51 26 A3
Lyndhurst SO43 121 F2
Michelmersh SO51 27 E4
Nomansland SP5 73 E4
Otterbourne SO50 31 D1
Poole BH15 202 B1
Redlynch SP5 47 F3
Sherfield English SO51 26 A3
Sway SO41 172 B1
Totton SO40 100 C3
[13] Waterlooville PO7 134 C4
Wimborne Minster BH21 163 D3
Chapel Rd Locks Heath SO31 128 C3
Poole BH14 203 D2
Soberton SO32 85 D1
Southampton SO14 103 D2
Swanmore SO32 84 A3
West End SO30 80 C1
Chapel Rise BH24 140 B1
Chapel Sq PO12 180 C4
Chapel St East Meon GU32 38 B1
Gosport PO12 181 D4
Petersfield GU32 40 C2
Portsmouth PO2 182 A2
Southampton SO14 103 D2
Chapelside PO14 154 A4
Chaplains Ave PO8 111 E2
Chaplains Cl PO8 111 E2
Charborough Rd BH18 187 D2
Charden Ct SO18 104 A4
Charden Rd Bishopstoke SO50 57 D1
Gosport PO13 180 B4
Charfield Cl Fareham PO14 154 B4
Winchester SO22 10 C3
Charing Cl BH24 141 D3
Chark La PO13 179 F2
Charlcot Lawn PO9 135 E3
Charlecote Dr SO53 55 D4
Charlecote Mews [10] SO22 10 C4
Charlemont Dr [15] PO16 131 E1
Charles Cl Waterlooville PO7 134 B3
Winchester SO23 2 A1
Charles Cres BH25 195 D3
Charles Dickens Inf Sch PO1 182 B4
Charles Dickens Jun Sch PO1 182 B4
Charles Dickens St PO1 182 B3
Charles Gdns BH10 189 E1

Charles Keightley Ct BH21 ...... 163 E2
Charles Knott Gdns SO15 ...... 102 C4
Charles Ley St SO45 ...... 151 D2
Charles Rd Christchurch BH23 ...... 207 F4
 Poole BH15 ...... 202 B2
Charles St Petersfield GU32 ...... 40 C2
 Portsmouth PO1 ...... 182 B3
 Southampton SO14 ...... 103 D2
Charles Watts Way SO30 ...... 105 D4
Charles Wyatt House 26 SO14 103 D4
Charles's La BH24 ...... 141 F2
Charlesbury Ave PO12 ...... 180 C2
Charleston Cl PO11 ...... 184 C2
Charleston Rd SO45 ...... 150 B4
Charlesworth Dr PO7 ...... 111 E1
Charlesworth Gdns PO7 ...... 111 E1
Charliejoy Gdns 18 SO14 ...... 103 E3
Charlotte Cl Christchurch BH23 208 A3
 3 New Milton BH25 ...... 195 D1
 Poole BH12 ...... 204 B4
Charlotte Ct
 Chandler's Ford SO53 ...... 55 F4
 Southampton SO19 ...... 103 F1
Charlotte Mews PO12 ...... 181 D1
Charlotte Pl SO14 ...... 103 D3
Charlotte St PO1 ...... 182 B3
Charlton Cl Bournemouth BH9 .... 190 B2
 Hordle SO41 ...... 195 F2
Charlton Rd SO15 ...... 102 B4
Charltons The BH2 ...... 204 C3
Charminster Ave BH9 ...... 190 A1
Charminster Cl
 Bournemouth BH8 ...... 190 A1
 Waterlooville PO7 ...... 134 C4
Charminster Pl BH8 ...... 190 B1
Charminster Rd BH8 ...... 205 D4
Charmouth Gr BH14 ...... 203 D2
Charmouth Terr 5 SO16 ...... 78 A1
Charmus Rd SO40 ...... 76 A1
Charmwen Cres SO30 ...... 80 B1
Charnock Cl PO13 ...... 155 F1
Charnwood Ave BH9 ...... 190 A2
Charnwood Cl
 Chandler's Ford SO53 ...... 30 B1
 Totton SO40 ...... 76 B1
 West Moors BH22 ...... 138 C1
Charnwood Cres SO53 ...... 30 B1
Charnwood Dr SP6 ...... 69 F2
Charnwood Gdns SO53 ...... 30 B1
Charnwood Way SO45 ...... 177 F4
Chartcombe BH13 ...... 214 C4
Charter Rd BH11 ...... 188 B3
Chartergrove House 15 SO31 .. 40 C2
Charterhouse Way SO30 ...... 81 E1
 Titchfield PO14 ...... 129 E1
Chartwell Cl Eastleigh SO50 ...... 56 A3
Chartwell Dr PO9 ...... 136 B2
Chase Cl GU33 ...... 21 D2
Chase Farm Cl SO32 ...... 83 F2
Chase Gr SO32 ...... 83 F2
Chase Rd GU33 ...... 21 D2
Chase The Gosport PO12 ...... 180 C2
 St Leonards BH24 ...... 140 B3
 Titchfield PO14 ...... 129 E1
 Verwood BH31 ...... 115 E3
Chaseside BH7 ...... 206 A4
Chasewater Ave PO3 ...... 183 D4
Chatburn Ave PO8 ...... 111 F2
Chatfield Rd PO13 ...... 155 E2
Chatham Dr PO1 ...... 182 A2
Chatham Rd SO22 ...... 10 B3
Chatsworth Ave PO6 ...... 158 A3
Chatsworth Cl PO15 ...... 130 B1
Chatsworth Rd
 Bournemouth BH8 ...... 205 E3
 Eastleigh SO50 ...... 56 A3
 Poole BH14 ...... 203 D1
 Southampton SO19 ...... 104 A3
Chatsworth Way BH25 ...... 194 C2
Chaucer Ave PO6 ...... 132 C1
Chaucer Cl Fareham PO16 .... 130 C1
 Waterlooville PO7 ...... 111 F1
 Wimborne Minster BH21 ...... 163 E3
Chaucer Dr SO41 ...... 211 E3
Chaucer Ind Est SO23 ...... 2 B1
Chaucer Rd Poole BH13 ...... 214 C4
 Southampton SO19 ...... 104 B3
Chaundler Rd SO23 ...... 2 A1
Chaveney Cl SO45 ...... 125 F1
Chawton Cl Southampton SO18 . 104 B4
 Winchester SO22 ...... 1 B2
Cheam Rd BH18 ...... 186 C2
Cheam Way SO40 ...... 76 B1
Cheater's La SP6 ...... 92 B4
Cheddar Cl SO19 ...... 103 F2
Cheddington Rd BH9 ...... 190 A2
Chedington Cl BH17 ...... 187 F1
Chedworth Cres PO6 ...... 133 D1
Cheeryble House 19 PO1 ...... 182 B4
Chelmsford Rd
 Portsmouth PO2 ...... 157 F1
 Upton BH16 ...... 201 D4
Chelsea Rd PO5 ...... 182 B2
Cheltenham Cres PO13 ...... 179 F2
Cheltenham Ct 28 SO17 ...... 79 D1
Cheltenham Gdns SO30 ...... 81 E2
Cheltenham Rd Cosham PO6 .... 157 E4
 Poole BH12 ...... 203 E3
Chelveston Cres SO16 ...... 78 A2
Chelwood Gate SO16 ...... 78 C3
Chene Rd BH21 ...... 163 E2
Cheping Gdns SO30 ...... 106 A3
Chepstow Cl
 North Baddesley SO53 ...... 55 D3
 Totton SO40 ...... 100 B4
Chepstow Court PO7 ...... 112 A1
Chequers Cl SO41 ...... 197 E2

Chequers Quay 5 PO10 ...... 161 D4
Cherbourg Prim Sch SO50 ...... 56 A1
Cherbourg Rd SO50 ...... 56 A1
Cherford Rd BH11 ...... 189 D1
Cherita Ct BH15 ...... 202 C3
Cheriton Ave
 Bournemouth BH7 ...... 206 B4
 Southampton SO18 ...... 104 B4
Cheriton Cl Havant PO9 ...... 135 E2
 Horndean PO8 ...... 112 A4
 Winchester SO22 ...... 1 B1
Cheriton Ct 7 SO15 ...... 102 B3
Cheriton La SO24 ...... 15 D4
Cheriton Prim Sch SO24 ...... 14 B3
Cheriton Rd Eastleigh SO50 ...... 55 F1
 Gosport PO12 ...... 180 C2
 Southampton SO17 ...... 10 C4
Cheriton Way BH21 ...... 163 E3
Cherque La PO13 ...... 180 A4
Cherrett Cl BH11 ...... 188 C2
Cherries Dr BH9 ...... 189 F1
Cherry Blossom Ct 22 PO1 .. 182 B4
Cherry Cl
 Lee-on-the-Solent PO13 ...... 180 A3
 Poole BH14 ...... 203 D2
Cherry Ct Poole BH14 ...... 203 D3
 14 Southampton SO17 ...... 103 D4
Cherry Drove SO50 ...... 81 E3
Cherry Gdns SO32 ...... 83 E4
Cherry Gr BH22 ...... 165 E3
Cherry Hill Gdns BH16 ...... 201 D3
Cherry Hill Gr BH16 ...... 201 D3
Cherry Tree Ave
 Fareham PO14 ...... 154 B4
 Waterlooville PO8 ...... 112 A1
Cherry Tree Cl Hordle SO41 .... 211 E4
 St Leonards BH24 ...... 139 E2
Cherry Tree Ct 31 BH25 ...... 195 D1
Cherry Tree Dr BH25 ...... 194 C3
Cherry Wlk SO15 ...... 102 B4
Cherrygarth Rd PO15 ...... 130 B1
Cherryton Gdns SO45 ...... 150 A2
Cherrywood Gdns
 South Hayling PO11 ...... 185 D2
 Totton SO40 ...... 100 B4
Chervil Cl PO8 ...... 88 B1
Cherville Ct SO51 ...... 52 C4
Cherville St SO51 ...... 52 C4
Cherwell Cres SO16 ...... 101 F4
Cherwell Gdns SO53 ...... 55 E3
Cherwell House SO16 ...... 101 F4
Cheshire Dr BH8 ...... 191 D1
Cheshire Way PO10 ...... 137 E1
Chesil St SO23 ...... 11 D4
Chesil Terr 37 SO23 ...... 11 D4
Chesildene Ave BH8 ...... 190 B2
Chesildene Dr BH8 ...... 190 B2
Chesley Rd PO3 ...... 183 D3
Chessel Ave Bournemouth BH5 . 205 F2
 Southampton SO19 ...... 103 F3
Chessel Cres SO19 ...... 103 F4
Chester Cres SO19 ...... 180 A2
Chester Ct SO16 ...... 78 B1
Chester Cts 7 PO12 ...... 181 E2
Chester Pl 34 PO5 ...... 182 B1
Chester Rd Poole BH13 ...... 204 A1
 Southampton SO18 ...... 80 A1
 Winchester SO23 ...... 11 D4
Chesterfield Cl BH13 ...... 214 C4
Chesterfield Ct BH1 ...... 205 E2
Chesterfield Rd PO3 ...... 183 D4
Chesterton Gdns PO8 ...... 111 F2
Chesterton Pl SO31 ...... 129 E4
Chestnut Ave Ashurst SO40 .... 100 B2
 Barton on Sea BH25 ...... 210 A4
 Bournemouth BH6 ...... 206 B2
 Chandler's Ford SO53 ...... 55 E1
 Christchurch BH23 ...... 206 B4
 2 Colden Common SO21 ...... 31 F1
 Eastleigh SO50, SO53 ...... 55 E1
 Havant PO9 ...... 135 D2
 Ibsley BH24 ...... 116 A3
 Littleton SO22 ...... 1 A2
 Portsmouth PO4 ...... 182 C2
 Waterlooville PO8 ...... 112 B3
Chestnut Cl
 Chandler's Ford SO53 ...... 55 E2
 Denmead PO7 ...... 110 C2
 Romsey SO51 ...... 53 E3
 West End SO30 ...... 80 B2
Chestnut Ct
 Rowland's Castle PO9 ...... 136 A4
 8 Southampton SO17 ...... 79 D1
Chestnut Gr BH21 ...... 164 C3
Chestnut Lodge SO16 ...... 78 C2
Chestnut Rd
 Brockenhurst SO42 ...... 146 A1
 Southampton SO16 ...... 78 A1
Chestnut Rise Droxford SO32 .... 61 D1
 Eastleigh SO50 ...... 55 E1
Chestnut Way Burton BH23 ... 192 B2
 Titchfield PO14 ...... 129 E1
Chestnut Wlk Botley SO30 ...... 105 F4
 Gosport PO12 ...... 156 A1
Chestnuts The SO31 ...... 129 D1
Chetnole Cl BH17 ...... 188 A1
Chettle Rd SO19 ...... 104 C3
Chetwode Way BH17 ...... 187 D1
Chetwynd Dr SO16 ...... 78 C2
Chetwynd Rd Portsmouth PO4 .. 182 C2
 Southampton SO16 ...... 78 C3
Chevening Ct PO4 ...... 183 D3
Cheviot Court Flats BH23 ...... 207 F4
Cheviot Cres SO16 ...... 101 F4
Cheviot Dr SO45 ...... 125 E2
Cheviot Gn SO31 ...... 152 B4
Cheviot Rd SO16 ...... 101 F4
Cheviot Way BH31 ...... 114 C4

Cheviot Wlk PO14 ...... 154 C4
Cheviots BH14 ...... 203 E2
Chevron Bsns Pk SO45 ...... 150 A3
Chewter Cl PO4 ...... 182 C1
Chewton Common Rd BH23 .. 209 D4
Chewton Farm Rd BH23 ...... 194 B1
Chewton Lodge BH23 ...... 209 D4
Chewton Way BH23 ...... 194 A1
Cheyne Gdns BH4 ...... 204 B1
Cheyne Way PO13 ...... 179 F1
Chichester Ave PO11 ...... 185 D2
Chichester Cl Gosport PO13 .... 155 D1
 Hedge End SO30 ...... 81 E1
 Locks Heath SO31 ...... 128 C2
 West Wellow SO51 ...... 51 D1
Chichester House PO9 ...... 136 A2
Chichester Rd
 North Hayling PO11 ...... 160 B1
 Portsmouth PO2 ...... 182 C4
 Ringwood BH24 ...... 117 E1
 Southampton SO18 ...... 104 A4
Chichester Way BH23 ...... 208 A3
Chichester Wlk BH21 ...... 163 F1
Chickenhall La SO50 ...... 56 B1
Chickerell Cl BH9 ...... 190 A2
Chidden Cl GU32 ...... 38 B1
Chidden Holt SO53 ...... 55 D3
Chideock Cl BH12 ...... 203 F3
Chideock Ct BH12 ...... 203 F3
Chidham Cl PO9 ...... 135 F1
Chidham Dr PO9 ...... 135 F1
Chidham Rd PO6 ...... 134 A1
Chidham Sq PO9 ...... 135 F1
Chidham Wlk 1 PO9 ...... 135 F1
Chigwell Rd BH8 ...... 190 A1
Chilbolton Ave SO22 ...... 10 B4
Chilbolton Ct 16 Havant PO9 .. 136 A3
 Winchester SO22 ...... 10 B4
Chilcomb Cl PO13 ...... 179 F1
Chilcomb Rd SO18 ...... 104 B4
Chilcombe Cl PO9 ...... 135 F2
Chilcombe Hts 38 SO23 ...... 11 D3
Chilcombe La Chilcomb SO23 ... 11 F3
 Winchester SO23 ...... 11 E3
Chilcombe Rd BH6 ...... 206 A3
Chilcote Rd PO3 ...... 183 D4
Childe Sq PO2 ...... 157 E1
Chilfrome Cl BH17 ...... 187 E1
Chilgrove Rd PO6 ...... 158 B4
Chilham Cl SO30 ...... 56 A4
Chillenden Ct SO40 ...... 100 B3
Chillerton SO31 ...... 127 E4
Chilling La SO31 ...... 152 C3
Chillington Gdns SO53 ...... 30 A1
Chilly Hill SP5 ...... 94 C4
Chilmark Ct GU33 ...... 20 C2
Chilsdown Way PO7 ...... 134 C2
Chiltern Cl
 Barton on Sea BH25 ...... 194 C1
 Poole BH12 ...... 204 A3
 Totton SO40 ...... 100 B3
Chiltern Ct
 5 Christchurch BH23 ...... 207 F4
 13 Gosport PO12 ...... 181 D3
 7 Portsmouth PO5 ...... 182 B1
Chiltern Dr Barton on Sea BH25 209 F4
 Verwood BH31 ...... 114 C3
Chiltern Gr SO16 ...... 101 F4
Chiltern Wlk PO14 ...... 154 C4
Chilworth Cl SO16 ...... 54 B1
Chilworth Gdns PO8 ...... 88 B2
Chilworth Gr PO12 ...... 181 D3
Chilworth Manor Hotel
 & Con Ctr SO16 ...... 54 B1
Chilworth Rd SO16 ...... 54 C1
Chimes The BH4 ...... 204 A2
Chine Ave SO19 ...... 103 F3
Chine Cl SO31 ...... 129 D2
Chine Cres BH2 ...... 204 B1
Chine Crescent Rd BH2 ...... 204 B1
Chine The PO13 ...... 155 F1
Chine Wlk BH22 ...... 165 F1
Chinham Rd SO40 ...... 99 E3
Chipstead House 12 PO6 ...... 157 F4
Chipstead Rd 11 PO6 ...... 157 F4
Chisels La PO13 ...... 193 D3
Chisholm Cl SO16 ...... 77 F3
Chiswell Rd BH17 ...... 187 E1
Chitty Rd PO4 ...... 183 D1
Chivers Cl 20 PO5 ...... 182 B2
Chorley Cl BH15 ...... 202 B3
Chris Cres BH8 ...... 201 E4
Christ the King RC
 Prim Sch BH11 ...... 189 D3
Christchurch Bay Rd BH25 .. 209 E4
Christchurch By-Pass BH23 .. 207 E4
Christchurch Cty Jun Sch
 BH23 ...... 207 D4
Christchurch Cty Prim Sch
 BH23 ...... 207 D4
Christchurch Gdns
 Waterlooville PO7 ...... 134 A1
 1 Winchester SO23 ...... 10 C3
Christchurch Hospl BH23 ...... 206 C4
Christchurch Rd
 Barton on Sea BH25 ...... 209 E4
 Bournemouth BH1, BH7 .... 205 E4
 Ferndown BH22 ...... 165 E1
 Hordle SO41 ...... 211 E4
 Hurn BH23 ...... 191 E3
 Ringwood BH24 ...... 141 D2
 Winchester SO23 ...... 10 C3
 Winchester SO23 ...... 10 C4
Christchurch Sta BH23 ...... 207 D4
Christie Ave PO15 ...... 129 E4
Christine Ct 9 SO18 ...... 103 F4
Christopher Cres BH15 ...... 202 B3
Christopher Way PO10 ...... 136 C1

Christophers BH21 ...... 163 E1
Christyne Ct PO7 ...... 134 B2
Church Cl Bishopstoke SO50 .... 56 B2
 Clanfield PO8 ...... 88 A3
 Locks Heath SO31 ...... 129 D2
 Minstead SO43 ...... 98 B1
 North Baddesley SO52 ...... 54 A2
Church End SO15 ...... 102 B4
Church Farm SP6 ...... 93 F4
Church Farm Cl SO45 ...... 125 D3
Church Hatch SP5 ...... 47 D4
Church Hill Milford on Sea SO41 211 F2
 Redlynch SP5 ...... 47 F3
 Verwood BH31 ...... 114 C3
 West End SO18,SO30 ...... 80 B1
Church La Awbridge SO51 ...... 26 C2
 Boldre SO41 ...... 173 F1
 Botley SO30 ...... 106 A3
 Braishfield SO51 ...... 28 B4
 Bramdean SO24 ...... 15 E2
 Brockenhurst SO42 ...... 173 D4
 Burley BH24 ...... 143 D2
 Bursledon SO31 ...... 128 A4
 Christchurch BH23 ...... 207 D3
 Colden Common SO21 ...... 56 C4
 Curdridge SO32 ...... 106 B4
 Damerham SP6 ...... 68 B2
 Durley SO32 ...... 81 F3
 East Boldre SO42 ...... 175 E3
 Fawley SO45 ...... 151 D2
 Ferndown BH22 ...... 189 F4
 Froxfield GU34 ...... 17 E2
 Hambledon PO7 ...... 86 B2
 Havant PO9 ...... 160 A4
 Hedge End SO30 ...... 105 D3
 Itchen Abbas SO21 ...... 2 C3
 Kings Worthy SO23 ...... 2 B3
 Littleton SO22 ...... 1 A3
 Lymington SO41 ...... 197 F2
 Lyndhurst SO43 ...... 121 F3
 Mottisfont SO51 ...... 5 F1
 New Milton BH25 ...... 194 C1
 North Hayling PO11 ...... 160 B2
 Nursling SO16 ...... 76 C3
 Plaitford SO51 ...... 50 A3
 Romsey SO51 ...... 52 C4
 Sherfield English SO51 ...... 25 E2
 17 Southampton SO14 ...... 102 C2
 Southampton, Highfield SO17 .. 79 D1
 Swanmore SO32 ...... 84 B3
 Sway SO41 ...... 172 A1
 Twyford SO21 ...... 32 A4
 West Meon GU32 ...... 37 E3
Church Mead 12 SO41 ...... 197 F1
Church Path
 3 Emsworth PO10 ...... 160 C4
 Fareham PO4, PO16 ...... 131 E1
 Gosport PO12 ...... 181 E2
 Horndean PO8 ...... 112 B3
 Titchfield PO14 ...... 154 A4
Church Path N PO1 ...... 182 B3
Church Pl SO51 ...... 52 C4
Church Rd Bishopstoke SO50 .... 56 B3
 Bournemouth BH6 ...... 206 C2
 Ferndown BH22 ...... 165 E3
 Gosport PO12 ...... 181 D1
 Locks Heath SO31 ...... 129 D2
 Locks Heath, Newtown SO31 ... 152 B4
 Michelmersh SO51 ...... 6 B1
 Poole BH14 ...... 203 D2
 Portchester PO16 ...... 156 C3
 Portsmouth PO1 ...... 182 B3
 Romsey SO51 ...... 52 C4
 Shedfield SO32 ...... 107 F4
 Soberton SO17 ...... 109 E3
 South Hayling PO11 ...... 185 D3
 Southampton SO19 ...... 103 E1
 Southbourne PO10 ...... 161 F4
 Steep GU32 ...... 40 C4
 Swanmore SO32 ...... 84 A3
 Thorney Island PO10 ...... 161 E1
 Three Legged Cross BH21 ...... 114 C1
 Westbourne PO10 ...... 137 D2
Church St Christchurch BH23 .. 207 D3
 East Meon GU32 ...... 38 C1
 Fordingbridge SP6 ...... 93 F4
 Liss GU33 ...... 20 C3
 Poole BH15 ...... 202 A1
 Portsmouth PO1 ...... 182 B3
 Romsey SO51 ...... 52 C4
 Southampton SO15 ...... 78 B1
 Titchfield PO14 ...... 154 A4
 Upham SO32 ...... 58 C3
 8 Wimborne Minster BH21 .... 163 D4
Church View
 Portsmouth PO4 ...... 183 D3
 Shedfield SO32 ...... 107 F4
 Westbourne PO10 ...... 137 D2
Church View Cl SO19 ...... 104 A2
Church Wlk SP5 ...... 48 A3
Churcher Cl PO12 ...... 180 B2
Churcher Rd PO10 ...... 137 D2
Churcher Wlk PO12 ...... 180 B2
Churcher's Coll GU31 ...... 41 D2
Churchers Coll Jun Sch GU32 . 40 C2
Churchfield BH31 ...... 114 C3
Churchfield Cres BH15 ...... 202 C2
Churchfield Ct BH15 ...... 202 C2
Churchfield La BH24 ...... 93 F1
Churchfield Rd
 Petersfield GU31 ...... 41 D2
 Poole BH15 ...... 202 C2
Churchfields SO45 ...... 151 D2
Churchfields Rd SO21 ...... 32 A3
Churchill Ave SO59 ...... 59 D1
Churchill Cl Alderholt SP6 ...... 92 C3
 Titchfield PO14 ...... 129 E1
Churchill Cres BH12 ...... 203 E3

Churchill Ct Cosham PO6 ...... 158 C4
 New Milton BH25 ...... 194 C1
 Waterlooville PO8 ...... 112 A3
Churchill Dr PO10 ...... 136 C2
Churchill Dro PO11 ...... 91 E4
Churchill Gdns BH12 ...... 203 E3
Churchill House SO14 ...... 104 B4
Churchill Mews 1 PO12 ...... 181 D3
Churchill Rd Bournemouth BH1 . 205 E3
 Poole BH21 ...... 203 E3
 Wimborne Minster BH21 ...... 163 F2
Churchill Sq PO4 ...... 183 D1
Churchmoor Rd BH21 ...... 164 A3
Churchward Gdns SO30 ...... 81 E1
Cinderford Cl 31 PO6 ...... 133 D1
Cinnamon Ct SO15 ...... 102 C3
Cinnamon La 10 BH15 ...... 202 A1
Circle The Bournemouth BH9 ... 190 A2
 Poole BH13 ...... 214 C4
 Portsmouth PO5 ...... 182 B1
 Wickham PO17 ...... 108 A2
Circular Rd PO1 ...... 182 B4
Cirrus Gdns SO31 ...... 127 F1
City Bsns Ctr SO23 ...... 11 D4
City Commerce Ctr 29 SO14 ... 103 D2
City Ind Pk SO15 ...... 102 C2
City of Portsmouth Boys
 Sch PO2 ...... 157 F2
City of Portsmouth Girls'
 Sch PO1 ...... 182 C3
City of Toronto Homes SO16 . 101 F4
City Rd SO23 ...... 10 C4
Civic Centre Rd Havant PO9 .... 135 F1
 Southampton SO14 ...... 102 C3
Civic Way PO16 ...... 131 E1
Clacton Rd PO6 ...... 157 E4
Claire Ct BH23 ...... 209 D4
Claire Gdns PO8 ...... 88 B1
Clamp Gr 4 SO21 ...... 56 C4
Clandon Dr SO50 ...... 55 F3
Clanfield Cl SO53 ...... 55 E3
Clanfield Dr SO53 ...... 55 E3
Clanfield House 37 PO1 ...... 182 B3
Clanfield Jun Sch PO8 ...... 88 A4
Clanfield Rd SO18 ...... 104 B4
Clanfield Way SO53 ...... 55 E3
Clanwilliam Rd PO13 ...... 179 F1
Clare Cl PO14 ...... 129 E1
Clare Gdns Blackfield SO45 ..... 177 F4
 Petersfield GU31 ...... 41 E2
Clare House PO12 ...... 180 C4
Clare Lodge Cl BH23 ...... 169 D1
Claremont Ave BH9 ...... 190 A1
Claremont Cl 1 SO50 ...... 56 A3
Claremont Cres SO15 ...... 102 A4
Claremont Gdns PO7 ...... 134 C2
Claremont Rd
 Bournemouth BH9 ...... 190 A1
 Portsmouth PO1 ...... 182 C3
 Southampton SO15 ...... 102 A4
Clarence Espl PO5 ...... 182 B1
Clarence House 5 SO14 ...... 103 E3
Clarence Par PO5 ...... 182 B1
Clarence Park Rd BH7 ...... 206 A3
Clarence Rd Gosport PO12 ...... 181 E3
 Lyndhurst SO43 ...... 121 F3
 3 Poole BH14 ...... 203 D2
 Portsmouth PO5 ...... 182 B1
Clarence St PO1 ...... 182 B3
Clarendon Cl
 Broadstone BH18 ...... 187 D2
 10 Romsey SO51 ...... 28 A1
Clarendon Cres PO14 ...... 129 E1
Clarendon Ct
 Bournemouth BH2 ...... 204 B1
 9 Portsmouth PO5 ...... 182 B1
Clarendon Pk SO45 ...... 197 E1
Clarendon Pl PO1 ...... 182 B3
Clarendon Rd
 Bournemouth BH4 ...... 204 B2
 Broadstone BH18 ...... 186 C2
 Christchurch BH23 ...... 207 D4
 17 Havant PO9 ...... 135 F1
 Portsmouth PO5 ...... 182 B1
 Southampton SO16 ...... 102 A4
Clarendon St PO1 ...... 182 B3
Clark's Cl BH24 ...... 141 D4
Clarke's Rd PO1 ...... 182 C3
Claude Ashby Cl SO18 ...... 79 F2
Claudeen Cl SO18 ...... 79 F3
Claudeen Ct SO19 ...... 104 C3
Claudia Ct PO12 ...... 180 C3
Claudius Cl SO53 ...... 55 F4
Claudius Gdns SO53 ...... 55 F4
Clausen Way SO41 ...... 197 E1
Clausentum Cl SO53 ...... 55 F4
Clausentum Rd
 Southampton SO14 ...... 103 D4
 Winchester SO23 ...... 10 C3
Clave Cl PO13 ...... 179 F1
Claxton St PO1 ...... 182 B3
Clay Hill SO43 ...... 122 A2
Clay St SP5 ...... 24 A2
Claybank Rd PO3 ...... 158 A1
Claybank Spur PO3 ...... 158 A1
Claydon Ave PO4 ...... 183 D2
Clayfields Sports Ctr SO45 .... 125 E2
Clayford Ave BH22 ...... 165 D4
Clayford Cl BH17 ...... 187 E1
Clayhall Rd PO12 ...... 181 D1
Clayhill Cl SO32 ...... 83 E2
Clayhill SO32 ...... 83 D4
Claylake Dr BH31 ...... 115 D3
Claylands Cl SO32 ...... 83 D4
Claylands Rd SO32 ...... 83 D4
Claypit La GU32 ...... 18 B3

Claypits La SO45 .... 125 E2
Cleasby Cl SO16 .... 101 F4
Cleasby Grange 28 BH5 .... 205 F2
Clease Way SO21 .... 31 E4
Clee Ave PO14 .... 154 B4
Cleethorpes Rd SO19 .... 104 A2
Cleeve Cl PO6 .... 133 D1
Cleeves Cl BH12 .... 188 B1
Cleeves The SO40 .... 100 B3
Clegg Rd PO4 .... 183 D2
Clem's Way SO51 .... 5 D1
Clematis Cl BH23 .... 208 B4
Clement Atlee Way PO6 .... 157 D4
Clement Mews BH4 .... 204 A2
Cleric Ct PO14 .... 129 E2
Cleveland Cl BH25 .... 209 E4
Cleveland Ct
  Bournemouth BH2 .... 204 B1
  7 Southampton SO18 .... 80 A1
Cleveland Dr Fareham PO14 ... 154 B4
  Hythe SO45 .... 125 E1
Cleveland Gdns BH1 .... 205 E3
Cleveland Rd
  Bournemouth BH1 .... 205 E3
  Gosport PO12 .... 181 D2
  Portsmouth PO5 .... 182 C2
  Southampton SO18 .... 79 F1
Clevelands Cl SO53 .... 30 A1
Clewers Hill SO32 .... 83 E2
Clewers La SO32 .... 83 F2
Cliff Cres BH25 .... 209 F4
Cliff Dr Christchurch BH23 .... 208 B3
  Poole BH13 .... 214 C3
Cliff House 10 BH6 .... 206 C2
Cliff Rd Milford on Sea SO41 .. 211 D2
  Southampton SO15 .... 102 B3
  Stubbington PO14 .... 153 F1
Cliff Terr BH25 .... 209 F3
Cliff The SO19 .... 103 E2
Cliff Way SO21 .... 31 E4
Cliffdale Prim Sch PO2 .... 157 F1
Cliffdale Sec Sch PO6 .... 158 A3
Cliffe Ave SO31 .... 127 E2
Cliffe Rd BH25 .... 209 F4
Clifford Dibben Mews
  1 SO14 .... 103 D4
Clifford Pl SO50 .... 57 E1
Clifford Rd BH9 .... 190 A1
Clifford St **11** SO14 .... 103 D3
Clifton Cres PO7 .... 111 E2
Clifton Ct
  13 Bournemouth BH5 .... 205 F2
  19 New Milton BH25 .... 195 D1
  13 Southampton SO15 ...... 102 A4
Clifton Gdns Ferndown PO1 ... 165 E2
  14 Southampton SO15 ...... 102 A4
  West End SO18 .... 80 B1
Clifton Hill SO22 .... 10 C4
Clifton Lodge SO15 .... 102 A4
Clifton Lodge No 1 13 SO22 ... 10 C4
Clifton Lodge No 2 14 SO22 ... 10 C4
Clifton Rd
  Bournemouth BH6 .... 206 B2
  Lee-on-the-Solent PO13 ...... 180 A2
  Poole BH14 .... 203 F1
  25 Portsmouth PO5 .... 182 B1
  Southampton SO15 .... 102 A4
  Winchester SO22 .... 10 C4
Clifton St Gosport PO12 .... 180 C3
  Portsmouth PO1 .... 182 C3
Clifton Terr **24**
  Portsmouth PO5 .... 182 B1
  Winchester SO22 .... 10 C4
Clinghan Rd BH6 .... 206 B4
Clinton Cl BH23 .... 194 A1
Clinton Rd Lymington SO41 .... 197 F3
  Waterlooville PO7 .... 111 E1
Clipper Cl SO31 .... 128 C1
Clitheroe Cotts SO42 .... 148 C1
Clive Ct 18 BH4 .... 204 B2
Clive Gr PO16 .... 156 B4
Clive Rd Bournemouth BH9 .... 189 F1
  Christchurch BH23 .... 193 F1
  Portsmouth PO1 .... 182 C3
Cliveden Cl BH22 .... 165 E4
Clock House 12 PO7 .... 134 C4
Clock St 10 PO1 .... 182 A3
Clocktower Dr PO4 .... 183 D1
Cloisters The Fareham PO15 .. 130 B1
  Lymington SO41 .... 197 F2
  Ringwood BH24 .... 141 E3
  Southampton SO16 .... 79 D2
Close Bellfield The PO14 .... 153 F4
Close The
  Barton on Sea BH25 .... 210 A4
  Broadstone BH18 .... 186 C2
  Colden Common SO21 .... 31 E1
  Cosham PO6 .... 158 A4
  Fordingbridge SP6 .... 94 B4
  Hamble-le-Rice SO31 .... 128 A2
  Hedge End SO30 .... 105 D3
  Holbury SO45 .... 150 B2
  Langrish GU32 .... 39 E2
  Portchester PO16 .... 156 B4
  30 Portsmouth PO5 .... 182 B2
  Redlynch SP5 .... 47 E4
  Ringwood BH24 .... 140 C4
  Southampton SO18 .... 104 B4
  St Leonards, Avon Castle BH24 .. 140 B4
  St Leonards, St Ives BH24 ... 140 A4
  Sway SO41 .... 172 A1
  Whitsbury SP6 .... 45 D2
Closewood Rd PO7 .... 111 D1
Clough La BH24 .... 142 C2
Clough's Rd BH24 .... 141 D4

Clovelly Rd Emsworth PO10 .... 160 C4
  North Hayling PO11 .... 160 B2
  Portsmouth PO4 .... 183 D2
  Southampton SO14 .... 103 D3
  Southbourne PO10 .... 137 E1
Clover Cl Christchurch BH23 .. 208 A4
  Gosport PO13 .... 155 E2
  Locks Heath SO31 .... 128 C1
Clover Ct New Milton BH25 .... 195 E2
  Waterlooville PO7 .... 135 D3
Clover Dr BH17 .... 186 C1
Clover Nooke SO15 .... 101 E4
Clover Way Hedge End SO30 .. 105 D3
  Romsey SO51 .... 53 E4
Clovers The BH12 .... 204 A4
Clowes Ave BH6 .... 207 D2
Club House La SO32 .... 83 F2
Clump Hill BH21 .... 114 A1
Clyde Ct PO12 .... 180 C3
Clyde House 24 SO14 .... 103 D3
Clyde Rd Broadstone BH17 .... 187 D1
  Gosport PO12 .... 180 C3
Clydebank Rd PO2 .... 182 B4
Clydesdale Rd PO15 .... 129 D4
Clydesdale Way SO40 .... 100 A4
Coach Hill Cl SO53 .... 55 D4
Coach Hill La BH24 .... 142 C3
Coach House Pl BH1 .... 205 D3
Coach Rd SO31 .... 127 F2
Coach Rd The
  East Tytherley SP5 .... 4 C4
  West Tytherley SP5 .... 4 B4
Coach-House Mews PO4 .... 183 E2
Coachmans Copse SO18 .... 80 A1
Coachmans Halt PO7 .... 86 B1
Coal Park La SO31 .... 128 B4
Coalville Rd SO19 .... 104 A2
Coastguard Cl PO12 .... 180 C1
Coastguard Cotts Exbury SO45 .. 178 A1
  Havant PO9 .... 159 F3
  Lymington SO41 .... 198 A1
Coastguard Way BH23 .... 207 F3
Coat Gdns SO45 .... 126 A2
Coates Rd SO19 .... 104 B2
Coates Way PO7 .... 134 C3
Cobb's Rd BH21 .... 163 F3
Cobbett Cl SO22 .... 10 B3
Cobbett Ct 15 SO18 .... 103 F4
Cobbett Rd SO18 .... 103 F4
Cobbett Way SO30 .... 105 F4
Cobblers Cnr SO41 .... 173 D2
Cobblewood PO10 .... 136 C2
Cobbs La PO15 .... 202 C3
Cobden Ave Portsmouth PO3 .. 183 D4
  Southampton SO18 .... 103 F4
Cobden Cres SO18 .... 103 F4
Cobden Ct SO18 .... 103 F4
Cobden Gdns SO18 .... 79 F1
Cobden Hts SO18 .... 79 F1
Cobden Marine Ct SO17 .... 103 E4
Cobden Rise SO18 .... 79 F1
Cobden St PO12 .... 181 D3
Cobham Gr PO15 .... 129 F3
Cobham Rd Bournemouth BH9 .. 190 A2
  Ferndown BH21 .... 165 D4
Cobham Way BH21 .... 163 F1
Coburg House 6 SO14 .... 103 E3
Coburg St Portsmouth PO1 .... 182 B3
  Southampton SO14 .... 103 E3
Cochrane Cl PO13 .... 180 B3
Cochrane House 15 PO1 .... 182 A3
Cockerell Cl Locks Heath PO15 .. 129 E3
  Oakley BH21 .... 163 F1
Cockleshell Cl SO31 .... 128 C1
Cockleshell Gdns PO4 .... 183 E2
Cocklydown La SO40 .... 100 B3
Cockshott La GU32 .... 19 E1
Codogan Cl BH1 .... 205 D2
Cogdean Cl BH21 .... 186 C4
Cogdean Way BH21 .... 186 C4
Cogdean Wlk BH21 .... 186 C4
Cogdeane Rd BH17 .... 187 E1
Coghlan Cl PO16 .... 131 D1
Coker Cl SO22 .... 10 C4
Colborne Ave BH21 .... 163 F3
Colborne Cl SO41 .... 197 F3
Colbourne Cl Bransgore BH23 .. 193 D4
  Poole BH15 .... 202 B1
Colbourne Ct 6 SO23 .... 2 A1
Colburn Cl SO16 .... 77 E1
Colbury Gr PO9 .... 135 E3
Colchester Ave SO50 .... 56 C2
Colchester Rd PO6 .... 133 F1
Cold East Cl SO31 .... 128 C3
Cold Harbour Cl PO17 .... 107 F2
Coldeast Hospl SO31 .... 128 C3
Coldeast Way SO31 .... 128 C3
Colden Common Cty
  Prim Sch SO21 .... 56 C4
Coldharbour Farm Rd PO10 .. 136 C1
Coldharbour La SO16 .... 77 D4
Coldhill La PO8 .... 111 F4
Cole Hill SO32 .... 85 E3
Cole's La SP5 .... 48 C3
Colebrook Ave
  Portsmouth PO3 .... 183 D4
  Southampton SO15 .... 78 B1
Colebrook Pl SO23 .... 11 D4
Colebrook St SO23 .... 11 D4
Colehill Cres BH9 .... 190 A2
Colehill Cty Fst Sch BH21 .... 164 A4
Colehill La BH21 .... 163 F4
Coleman Rd BH11 .... 189 D2
Coleman St SO14 .... 103 D4
Colemore Rd BH7 .... 206 B4
Colemore Sq PO9 .... 135 F2

Colenso Rd PO16 .... 131 D1
Coleridge Cl SO31 .... 128 B1
Coleridge Ct SO19 .... 104 B3
Coleridge Gdns PO8 .... 111 F2
Coleridge Gn BH23 .... 207 F4
Coleridge Rd PO6 .... 132 C1
Coles Ave BH15 .... 201 F1
Coles Cl SO21 .... 32 A4
Coles Gdns BH15 .... 201 F1
Coles Mede SO21 .... 31 D2
Colesbourne Rd PO6 .... 133 D1
Coleson Rd SO18 .... 103 F4
Coleville Ave SO45 .... 151 D2
Colin Cl BH21 .... 186 B3
Colinton Ave PO16 .... 132 B1
Collard Way **4** GU33 .... 20 C2
College Cl
  Hamble-le-Rice SO31 .... 127 F1
  Rowland's Castle PO9 .... 113 E1
College La **16** PO1 .... 182 A3
Coll of Air Traffic Control
  BH23 .... 190 C4
College Park Inf Sch PO2 ...... 157 F1
College Pl **6** SO15 .... 103 D3
College Rd
  Bournemouth BH5 .... 206 A2
  Portsmouth PO2 .... 182 A3
  Ringwood BH24 .... 141 D4
  Southampton SO19 .... 103 F1
  Waterlooville PO7 .... 134 C2
College St
  Petersfield GU31, GU32 .... 40 C2
  Portsmouth PO1 .... 182 A3
  Southampton SO14 .... 103 D2
  Winchester SO23 .... 11 D3
College Wlk SO23 .... 11 D3
Collett Cl SO30 .... 81 D1
Colley Cl SO23 .... 2 A2
Colleywater La GU34 .... 18 A2
Collier Cl SO17 .... 103 E4
Collingbourne Ave BH6 .... 206 B4
Collingbourne Dr SO53 .... 55 D3
Collington Cres PO6 .... 133 D1
Collingwood House PO15 ...... 130 B1
Collingwood Rd
  Portsmouth PO5 .... 182 B1
  West Moors BH21 .... 138 C3
Collingwood Ret Pk PO14 ..... 155 D3
Collins House SO53 .... 55 E3
Collins' La SO21 .... 30 B4
Collins La Ringwood BH24 ..... 141 D4
  South Harting GU31 .... 66 C4
Collins Rd PO4 .... 183 D1
Collis Rd PO3 .... 183 D4
Collwood Cl BH15 .... 202 B4
Collyers Rd SO42 .... 172 C4
Colne Ave SO16 .... 77 E1
Colne Ct SO16 .... 77 F1
Colombine Cl BH23 .... 193 D1
Colonnade Rd **5** BH5 .... 206 A3
Colonnade Rd W **4** BH5 ..... 206 A3
Colonnade The SO19 .... 103 E2
Colpoy St PO5 .... 182 A2
Colson Cl **46** SO23 .... 11 D4
Colson Rd SO23 .... 11 D4
Colt Cl Rownhams SO16 .... 77 F3
  Wimborne Minster BH21 ..... 164 A3
Colts Rd SO16 .... 77 F4
Coltsfoot Cl SO30 .... 105 D4
Coltsfoot Dr Locks Heath SO31 .. 128 C1
  5 Waterlooville PO7 .... 134 C3
Coltsfoot Wlk SO51 .... 28 B1
Coltsmead PO6 .... 156 C4
Columbia Rd BH10 .... 189 E1
Columbia Trees La BH10 .... 189 E1
Columbian Way BH10 .... 189 E1
Colvedene Cl SO21 .... 31 F1
Colville Cl BH5 .... 206 A3
Colville Dr SO32 .... 83 E4
Colville Rd
  6 Bournemouth BH5 .... 206 A3
  Cosham PO6 .... 158 A4
Colwell Cl SO16 .... 101 E4
Colwell Rd PO6 .... 157 F4
Combe Down SO21 .... 31 F4
Combe Rd GU33 .... 21 D1
Comber Rd BH9 .... 190 A2
Comet Way BH23 .... 208 A3
Comfrey Cl Horndean PO8 ...... 88 B1
  Romsey SO51 .... 28 B1
Comines Way SO18 .... 104 C4
Comley Hill PO9 .... 136 B3
Comley Rd BH9 .... 189 F1
Commercial Pl PO1 .... 182 B3
Commercial Rd
  Bournemouth BH2 .... 204 C2
  Poole BH14 .... 203 D2
  Portsmouth PO1 .... 182 B3
  Southampton SO15 .... 102 C3
  Totton SO40 .... 101 D4
Commercial St SO18 .... 104 A4
Commodore Ct **30** SO14 ... 103 D2
Common Barn La PO13 .... 179 F2
Common Cl SO53 .... 55 E4
Common Gdns SO53 .... 55 E4
Common Hill Rd SO51 .... 28 B3
Common La Southwick PO17 .. 132 C4
  Titchfield PO14 .... 153 F4
Common Rd
  Chandler's Ford SO53 .... 55 E4
  Westbourne BH21 .... 137 F3
  Whiteparish SP5 .... 24 A1
Common St PO1 .... 182 B4
Commonside PO10 .... 137 D3
Compass Cl PO13 .... 180 B3
Compass Point PO16 .... 155 D4
Compass Rd PO6 .... 157 D4
Compton Acres BH13 .... 214 C4

Compton Ave BH14 .... 203 E1
Compton Beeches BH24 .... 140 A3
Compton CE Prim Sch SO21 .. 31 E4
Compton Cl SO50 .... 55 F3
  Havant PO9 .... 135 F2
  23 Lee-on-the-Solent PO13 .. 179 F1
  Winchester SO22 .... 10 A2
Compton Cres SO22 .... 139 D1
Compton Ct **3** Havant PO9 .. 135 F1
  Poole BH14 .... 203 E2
Compton Dr BH14 .... 203 E1
Compton Gdns BH14 .... 203 E1
Compton House **4** SO16 ... 102 A4
Compton Rd New Milton BH25 .. 195 D1
  Portsmouth PO2 .... 157 F2
  Totton SO40 .... 101 D4
  Winchester SO23 .... 10 C4
Compton St SO21 .... 31 E4
Compton & Up Marden
  CE Sch PO18 .... 90 C1
Compton Way SO22 .... 10 A2
Compton Wlk **21** SO14 ...... 103 D3
Compton's Dr SO51 .... 50 A3
Conan Rd PO2 .... 157 F2
Condor Ave PO16 .... 155 F4
Condor Cl Southampton SO19 .. 103 E2
  West Moors BH21 .... 139 D3
Coney Gn **4** SO23 .... 2 A1
Conference Dr SO31 .... 129 D2
Conference Pl **11** SO41 ..... 197 F1
Conford Ct PO9 .... 135 E3
Congleton Cl SO43 .... 98 B2
Conifer Ave BH14 .... 203 D1
Conifer Cl Christchurch BH23 .. 191 E2
  Ferndown BH22 .... 165 F1
  Hythe SO45 .... 125 F2
  St Leonards BH24 .... 139 E2
  Waterlooville PO8 .... 112 A1
  Winchester SO22 .... 1 C1
Conifer Cres SO41 .... 197 D2
Conifer Gr PO13 .... 155 E2
Conifer Mews PO16 .... 132 B1
Conifer Rd SO16 .... 78 A2
Conigar Rd PO10 .... 136 C2
Coniston Ave
  Bournemouth BH11 .... 188 C3
  Portsmouth PO3 .... 183 D4
Coniston Cl BH31 .... 114 C3
Coniston Gdns SO30 .... 105 E3
Coniston House **19** PO6 .... 133 D1
Coniston Rd Eastleigh SO50 ... 55 F1
  Ringwood BH24 .... 141 D3
  Southampton SO16 .... 101 E4
Coniston Wlk PO14 .... 154 C4
Connaught Cl BH25 .... 194 C1
Connaught Cres BH12 .... 203 F3
Connaught Hall SO18 .... 79 E2
Connaught La PO6 .... 156 C4
Connaught Pl PO9 .... 136 A1
Connaught Rd
  Bournemouth BH5 .... 206 A3
  Havant PO9 .... 136 A1
  Portsmouth PO2 .... 157 E1
Connell Rd BH15 .... 202 B3
Connemara Cres PO15 .... 129 D4
Connigar Cl PO13 .... 180 B4
Conqueror Way PO14 .... 179 E3
Conrad Gdns PO15 .... 129 E4
Conservatory The **38** SO23 .. 11 D4
Consort Cl Eastleigh SO50 ... 56 A3
  Poole BH12 .... 203 E3
Consort House **9** PO1 ..... 182 B4
Consort Rd SO50 .... 56 A3
Constable Cl Gosport PO12 .. 181 E1
  Southampton SO19 .... 104 B1
Constables Gate SO22 .... 10 C4
Constantine Ave SO53 .... 55 F3
Constantine Cl SO53 .... 55 F3
Constitution Hill Gdns BH14 .. 203 D3
Constitution Hill Rd BH14 .... 203 D3
Consulate House **32** SO14 .. 103 D2
Convent Ct PO10 .... 160 C4
Convent La PO10 .... 160 C4
Conway Cl Chandler's Ford SO53 .. 55 D2
  New Milton BH25 .... 195 D2
Conway Ct **20** BH25 .... 195 D2
Conways Dr BH14 .... 203 D2
Cook Cl BH24 .... 141 E4
Cook Row BH21 .... 163 D2
Cook St SO14 .... 103 D2
Cooke Gdns BH12 .... 203 F3
Cooke Rd BH12 .... 203 F3
Cooks La Awbridge SO51 ..... 27 D2
  Lockerley SO51 .... 25 F4
  Southbourne PO10 .... 137 E1
Cooley House PO13 .... 155 D3
Coolhurst BH14 .... 214 B4
Coombe Ave BH10 .... 189 F2
Coombe Farm Ave PO16 ..... 155 D4
Coombe Gdns BH10 .... 189 F1
Coombe La SO41 .... 196 B4
Coombe Rd East Meon GU32 .. 63 E4
  Gosport PO12 .... 181 D4
Coombe Road Terr GU32 ...... 63 E4
Coombedale SO31 .... 129 D1
Coombs Cl PO8 .... 88 B1
Cooper Dean Dr BH8 .... 206 B3
Cooper Dean Rdbt BH7, BH8 .. 191 D1
Cooper Gr PO16 .... 156 B3
Cooper Rd Ashurst SO40 ..... 100 B2
  Portsmouth PO3 .... 183 D4
Cooper's Cl West End SO18 ... 80 B1
  West Wellow SO51 .... 51 D1
Cooper's La SO19 .... 103 E2
Coopers La BH31 .... 114 C4
Copeland Dr BH14 .... 203 D1
Copeland Rd SO16 .... 77 E1

Copenhagen Towers **7** SO19 .. 126 C4
Copinger Cl SO40 .... 100 B3
Copnor Bridge Bsns Ctr PO3 .. 183 D4
Copnor Inf & Jun Sch PO3 .... 158 A1
Copnor Rd PO2 .... 157 F2
Copper Beech Cl BH12 .... 204 A4
Copper Beech Dr PO6 .... 158 C4
Copper Beech Gdns BH10 ... 189 E1
Copper Beeches SO45 .... 150 C1
Copper St PO5 .... 182 A2
Coppercourt Leaze **6** BH21 .. 163 E2
Copperfield House **21** PO1 .. 182 B4
Copperfield Rd SO16 .... 79 D3
Copperfields SO40 .... 100 A4
Coppers Cl SP6 .... 93 D3
Coppice Ave BH22 .... 165 D4
Coppice Cl New Milton BH25 .. 195 E2
  St Leonards BH24 .... 139 F2
  Winchester SO22 .... 1 B1
Coppice Hill SO32 .... 83 E4
Coppice Rd SO40 .... 76 B1
Coppice The
  Brockenhurst SO42 .... 145 E1
  Christchurch BH23 .... 208 A3
  Gosport PO13 .... 155 E1
  Waterlooville PO8 .... 112 A3
Coppice View BH10 .... 189 F2
Coppice Way PO15 .... 130 B2
Coppins Gr PO16 .... 156 B3
Copse Ave BH25 .... 195 D1
Copse Cl Liss GU33 .... 21 D2
  North Baddesley SO52 .... 53 F2
  Otterbourne SO21 .... 31 E2
  Petersfield GU31 .... 41 E2
  Poole BH14 .... 202 C2
  Totton SO40 .... 100 C3
  Waterlooville PO7 .... 134 B1
Copse Cvn Pk The SO40 ...... 99 E3
Copse La Chilworth SO16 ..... 54 C1
  Gosport PO13 .... 155 E1
  Hamble-le-Rice SO31 .... 127 F1
  North Hayling PO11 .... 160 A1
Copse Rd Burley BH24 .... 142 C1
  New Milton BH25 .... 195 D1
  Southampton SO18 .... 80 A1
  Verwood BH31 .... 114 C3
Copse The Chandler's Ford SO53 .. 55 F3
  Fareham PO15 .... 130 B2
  Romsey SO51 .... 28 B1
Copse View SO19 .... 104 C3
Copse Way BH23 .... 208 C4
Copsewood Ave BH8 .... 190 C1
Copsewood Rd Ashurst SO40 .. 100 B2
  Hythe SO45 .... 125 F2
  Southampton SO18 .... 79 F1
Copsey Cl PO6 .... 158 B4
Copsey Gr PO6 .... 158 B4
Copthorne Cotts SO45 ...... 151 E2
Copthorne La SO45 .... 151 E2
Copthorn Rd PO2 .... 157 F1
Copythorne CE Fst Sch SO40 .. 75 D1
Copythorne Cl BH8 .... 190 B1
Copythorne Cres SO40 .... 75 E2
Coracle Cl SO31 .... 128 C1
Coral Cl PO16 .... 156 B3
Coral Ct **2** BH12 .... 204 A2
Coralin Gr PO7 .... 112 A1
Coram Cl **3** SO23 .... 2 A1
Corbar Rd BH23 .... 206 C4
Corbett Rd PO7 .... 134 B3
Corbiere Ave BH12 .... 188 C1
Corbiere Cl SO16 .... 77 F2
Corbin Ave BH22 .... 166 A3
Corbin Ct SO41 .... 197 D1
Corbin Rd SO41 .... 197 D1
Corbould Rd SO45 .... 149 F4
Corby Cres PO3 .... 158 A2
Cordelia Cl SO45 .... 125 E2
Corfe Cl PO14 .... 179 D3
Corfe Halt Cl BH21 .... 162 C1
Corfe Hills Sch BH18 .... 186 C3
Corfe Lodge Rd BH18 .... 186 B2
Corfe Mews BH15 .... 202 B2
Corfe View Rd
  Corfe Mullen BH21 .... 186 B3
  Poole BH14 .... 203 E2
Corfe Way BH18 .... 186 C2
Corfu BH13 .... 214 C3
Corhampton Cres PO9 ...... 135 E2
Corhampton La Droxford SO32 .. 60 B3
  Meonstoke SO32 .... 61 D3
Corhampton Rd BH6 .... 206 B3
Coriander Dr SO40 .... 100 B4
Coriander Way PO15 .... 129 E4
Corinna Gdns SO45 .... 125 E2
Corinthian Rd SO53 .... 55 F4
Cork La SO40 .... 101 F1
Cormorant Cl PO16 .... 155 F4
Cormorant Dr SO45 .... 126 B1
Cormorant Wlk PO13 .... 155 D1
Corn Market SO51 .... 52 C4
Cornaway La PO16 .... 156 A4
Cornbrook Gr PO7 .... 112 A1
Cornel Rd SO19 .... 103 F3
Cornelia Cres BH12 .... 204 A3
Cornelius Dr PO7 .... 112 A1
Corner Mead PO7 .... 110 C2
Cornerways St **7** BH25 .. 195 D1
Cornes Cl SO22 .... 10 B4
Cornfield PO16 .... 131 D2
Cornfield Rd PO13 .... 179 F1
Cornflower Cl SO31 .... 128 C2
Cornflower Dr BH23 .... 208 B4
Cornford Way BH23 .... 208 B4
Cornforth Rd SO40 .... 76 B1
Cornish Gdns BH10 .... 189 E1
Cornpits La SP6 .... 68 B2
Cornwall Cl **4** SO18 .... 80 A1

Cornwall Cres SO18 ...... 79 F1
Cornwall Rd
　Chandler's Ford SO53 ...... 55 E2
　Portsmouth PO1 ...... 182 C3
　Southampton SO18 ...... 79 F1
Cornwallis Cres PO1 ...... 182 B3
Cornwallis House 49 PO1 ...... 182 B3
Cornwallis Rd SO41 ...... 211 D2
Cornwell Cl Gosport PO13 ...... 180 B4
　Portsmouth PO2 ...... 157 D1
Coronado Rd PO12 ...... 181 D4
Coronation Ave
　Bournemouth BH9 ...... 189 F1
　Upton BH16 ...... 201 D4
Coronation Cl BH31 ...... 114 C4
Coronation Eventide
　Homes 4 PO2 ...... 157 F2
Coronation Homes SO18 ...... 104 B4
Coronation Par SO31 ...... 127 F2
Coronation Rd
　South Hayling PO11 ...... 185 F1
　Swanmore SO32 ...... 84 A3
　Verwood BH31 ...... 114 C4
Coronation Terr SP6 ...... 69 D1
Corporation Rd BH1 ...... 205 E3
Corpus Christi RC Prim Sch
　Bournemouth BH5 ...... 206 A3
　Portsmouth PO2 ...... 157 E1
Corsair Dr SO45 ...... 125 E2
Corscombe Cl BH17 ...... 187 F1
Cort Way PO15 ...... 130 B2
Cortina Way SO30 ...... 105 E3
Corvette Ave SO31 ...... 128 C1
Cosford Cl SO50 ...... 57 D1
Cosham Park Ave PO6 ...... 157 F4
Cosham Sta PO6 ...... 157 F4
Cossack Gn 6 SO14 ...... 103 D2
Cossack La 11 SO23 ...... 11 D4
Cossack Lane House 13 SO23 ...... 11 D4
Cosworth Dr SO45 ...... 125 E2
Cotes Ave SO31 ...... 203 D3
Cotes Ct BH14 ...... 203 D3
Cotlands Rd BH1 ...... 205 D2
Cotsalls SO50 ...... 57 E1
Cotswold Cl Havant PO9 ...... 135 F3
　Hythe SO45 ...... 125 E2
　Verwood BH31 ...... 114 C3
Cotswold Ct
　6 Christchurch BH23 ...... 207 F4
　12 Southampton SO17 ...... 79 D1
Cotswold House 3 PO6 ...... 157 E4
Cotswold Rd SO16 ...... 101 F4
Cotswold Wlk 17 PO14 ...... 154 C4
Cott La BH24 ...... 143 D1
Cott St SO32 ...... 84 B2
Cott Street La SO32 ...... 84 C2
Cottage Cl PO7 ...... 110 C2
Cottage Gdns BH12 ...... 203 E3
Cottage Gr Gosport PO12 ...... 181 D3
　Portsmouth PO5 ...... 182 B2
Cottage Grove Prim Sch PO5 ...... 182 B2
Cottage La GU32 ...... 19 F2
Cottage Mews SP6 ...... 69 F1
Cottage View PO1 ...... 182 B3
Cottagers La SO41 ...... 196 A2
Cottages The SP6 ...... 94 A2
Cotteridge House 1 PO1 ...... 182 B2
Cottes Way PO14 ...... 179 D3
Cottesway E PO14 ...... 179 D3
Cotton Cl Bishopstoke SO50 ...... 56 C2
　Corfe Mullen BH18 ...... 186 C3
Cotton Dr PO10 ...... 136 C2
Cotwell Ave PO14 ...... 112 A2
Coulmere Rd PO12 ...... 181 D3
Coulsdon Rd SO30 ...... 105 E3
Coultas Rd SO53 ...... 30 C1
Council Hos Lockerley SO51 ...... 26 A1
　Sopley BH23 ...... 167 F1
Countess Cl BH21 ...... 187 F4
Countess Gdns BH6 ...... 205 F4
Country View Stubbington PO14 ...... 154 A2
　West Wellow SO51 ...... 50 C2
County Gdns PO14 ...... 154 B4
Course Park Cres PO14 ...... 129 E1
Court 29 PO13 ...... 180 B3
Court 30 PO13 ...... 180 B3
Court 31 PO13 ...... 180 B3
Court 32 PO13 ...... 180 B3
Court 33 PO13 ...... 180 B3
Court 34 PO13 ...... 180 B3
Court Barn Cl PO13 ...... 179 F2
Court Barn La PO13 ...... 179 F2
Court Cl 12 Christchurch BH23 ...... 207 F4
　Cosham PO6 ...... 158 A4
　Lymington SO41 ...... 197 E1
　Southampton SO18 ...... 104 A3
　Totton SO40 ...... 76 B1
Court Cotts SO41 ...... 197 E1
Court Hill SP6 ...... 68 C3
Court Lane Inf Sch PO6 ...... 158 A4
Court Lane Jun Sch PO6 ...... 158 A4
Court Mead PO6 ...... 158 A4
Court Rd Bournemouth BH9 ...... 190 A1
　Kings Worthy SO23 ...... 2 B3
　Lee-on-the-Solent PO13 ...... 179 F2
　Southampton SO15 ...... 102 C4
Court Royal Mews SO15 ...... 102 C4
Courtenay Dr BH21 ...... 163 E3
Courtenay Pl SO41 ...... 197 F2
Courtenay Rd Poole BH14 ...... 203 D2
　Winchester SO23 ...... 2 A1
Courthill Fst Sch BH14 ...... 203 E2
Courthill Rd BH14 ...... 203 E2
Courtier Cl SO45 ...... 125 E2
Courtland Gdns SO16 ...... 79 D3
Courtlands SO41 ...... 197 F2
Courtlands Terr PO8 ...... 112 A2

Courtleigh Manor 6 BH5 ...... 205 E2
Courtmount Gr PO6 ...... 158 A4
Courtney Pl BH21 ...... 186 B3
Courtyard The
　Christchurch BH23 ...... 207 E3
　14 Petersfield GU31 ...... 40 C2
　Poole BH12 ...... 188 B3
　8 Romsey SO51 ...... 52 C4
Cousins Gr PO4 ...... 182 C1
Cove Rd BH10 ...... 189 E1
Covena Rd BH6 ...... 206 C3
Coventry Cl BH23 ...... 193 F1
Coventry Cres BH17 ...... 187 D1
Coventry Ct Gosport PO13 ...... 180 B3
　7 Winchester SO23 ...... 2 A1
Coventry Rd SO15 ...... 102 C3
Coverack Way PO6 ...... 157 D4
Covert Gr PO7 ...... 135 D3
Covert The SO51 ...... 53 D3
Covingdale House PO4 ...... 183 D2
Covington Rd PO10 ...... 137 D3
Cow La Cosham PO6 ...... 157 E4
　Portchester PO16 ...... 156 B4
Cowan Rd PO7 ...... 134 B3
Coward Rd PO12 ...... 180 C1
Cowdray Cl Bishopstoke SO50 ...... 56 C1
　Southampton SO16 ...... 78 A2
Cowdray Pk PO14 ...... 179 D3
Cowdrey Gdns BH8 ...... 190 C1
Cowdrys Field 2 BH21 ...... 163 D3
Cowell Dr BH7 ...... 206 A4
Cowes Cl SO31 ...... 152 B3
Cowgrove Rd BH21 ...... 162 C3
Cowleas Cl SO51 ...... 26 C3
Cowleas Cotts SO51 ...... 26 C3
Cowley Cl SO16 ...... 77 F1
Cowley Rd Lymington SO41 ...... 197 E2
　Poole BH17 ...... 202 B4
Cowleys Rd BH23 ...... 192 B1
Cowper Ave BH25 ...... 195 D1
Cowper Rd Bournemouth BH9 ...... 189 F1
　Portsmouth PO1 ...... 182 C4
　Southampton SO19 ...... 104 B3
Cowpitts La BH24 ...... 117 E1
Cowplain Sch PO8 ...... 111 F1
Cowslip Cl Gosport PO13 ...... 155 E1
　Locks Heath SO31 ...... 128 C1
Cowslip Rd BH18 ...... 186 C1
Cowslip Way SO51 ...... 28 B1
Cox Ave BH9 ...... 190 A2
Cox Cl BH9 ...... 190 A2
Cox Dale PO14 ...... 129 E1
Cox Row SO53 ...... 55 E2
Cox's Dr SO19 ...... 104 A1
Cox's La SO19 ...... 103 E2
Coxes Meadow GU32 ...... 40 C3
Coxford Cl SO16 ...... 78 A1
Coxford Dro SO16 ...... 78 A1
Coxford Rd SO16 ...... 78 A2
Coxs Hill SO21 ...... 32 A4
Coxstone La 2 BH24 ...... 141 D3
Coy Pond Rd PO4 ...... 204 A3
Crab Orchard Way BH21 ...... 114 C1
Crabapple Cl SO40 ...... 100 B4
Crabbs Way SO40 ...... 100 A4
Crabbswood La SO41 ...... 195 F4
Crabden La PO8 ...... 88 C1
Crableck La SO31 ...... 128 B3
Crabthorne Farm La PO14 ...... 154 A2
Crabton Close Rd BH5 ...... 205 F2
Crabtree SO16 ...... 77 F1
Crabtree Cl BH23 ...... 192 B1
Crabwood Cl SO16 ...... 77 F1
Crabwood Ct PO9 ...... 135 E4
Crabwood Dr SO30 ...... 80 C1
Crabwood Rd SO16 ...... 77 F1
Craddock House
　13 Portsmouth PO1 ...... 182 A3
　2 Winchester SO23 ...... 11 E4
Craigmoor Ave BH8 ...... 190 C1
Craigmoor Cl BH8 ...... 190 C1
Craigmoor Way BH8 ...... 190 C1
Craigside Rd BH24 ...... 139 E2
Craigwell Rd PO7 ...... 134 B2
Craigwood Dr BH22 ...... 165 F2
Crampmoor La SO51 ...... 28 C1
Cranberry Cl SO40 ...... 101 F1
Cranborne Cres BH12 ...... 203 F4
Cranborne Ct
　Bournemouth BH9 ...... 205 D4
　14 Bournemouth, Westbourne
　BH4 ...... 204 B2
Cranborne Gdns SO53 ...... 30 A1
Cranborne Pl BH25 ...... 194 C2
Cranborne Rd
　Alderholt SP6, BH21 ...... 92 A3
　Bournemouth BH2 ...... 204 C1
　Cosham PO6 ...... 134 A1
　Wimborne Minster BH21 ...... 163 E4
Cranborne Wlk PO14 ...... 154 C4
Cranbourne Cl SO15 ...... 78 B1
Cranbourne Ct BH17 ...... 188 A1
Cranbourne Dr SO21 ...... 31 D2
Cranbourne Pk SO30 ...... 105 E2
Cranbourne Rd PO12 ...... 181 E2
Cranbrook Mews BH12 ...... 203 D3
Cranbrook Rd BH12 ...... 203 D3
Cranbury Ave SO14 ...... 103 D3
Cranbury Cl Downton SP5 ...... 46 C3
　Otterbourne SO21 ...... 31 D2
Cranbury Gdns SO31 ...... 104 C1
Cranbury Pl SO14 ...... 103 D3
Cranbury Rd Eastleigh SO50 ...... 56 A1
　Southampton SO19 ...... 103 F2

Cranbury Terr 3 SO14 ...... 103 D3
Cranbury The 2 SO14 ...... 103 D3
Cranbury Towers 4 SO14 ...... 103 D3
Crane Cl BH31 ...... 114 C3
Crane Dr BH31 ...... 114 C4
Crane Way BH31 ...... 139 D3
Cranemoor Ave BH23 ...... 193 F1
Cranemoor Cl BH23 ...... 193 F1
Cranemoor Gdns BH23 ...... 193 F1
Cranes Mews BH15 ...... 202 B2
Craneswater Ave PO4 ...... 182 C1
Craneswater Gate 4 PO4 ...... 182 C1
Craneswater Jun Sch PO4 ...... 182 C1
Craneswater Mews 5 PO4 ...... 182 C1
Craneswater Park PO4 ...... 182 C1
Cranfield Ave BH21 ...... 163 E3
Cranford Gdns SO53 ...... 55 D4
Cranford House 5 SO17 ...... 79 D1
Cranford Rd GU32 ...... 40 C1
Cranford Way SO17 ...... 79 D1
Cranleigh Ave PO1 ...... 182 C3
Cranleigh Cl BH6 ...... 206 C3
Cranleigh Ct BH6 ...... 206 C3
Cranleigh Gdns BH6 ...... 206 C3
Cranleigh House
　Hedge End SO30 ...... 81 E2
　Southampton SO17 ...... 103 D4
Cranleigh Paddock SO43 ...... 121 F3
Cranleigh Rd
　Bournemouth BH6 ...... 206 C3
　Hedge End SO30 ...... 105 E3
　Portchester PO16 ...... 156 A4
　Portsmouth PO1 ...... 182 C3
Cranmer Dr SO16 ...... 77 F3
Cranmer Rd BH9 ...... 204 C4
Cranmore SO31 ...... 127 E4
Cransley Ct BH4 ...... 204 B1
Crantock Gr BH8 ...... 190 C1
Cranwell Cl
　Bournemouth BH11 ...... 188 C2
　Bransgore BH23 ...... 169 E1
Cranwell Ct SO16 ...... 77 F3
Cranworth Rd SO22 ...... 1 C1
Crasswell St PO1 ...... 182 B3
Craven Cr PO15 ...... 130 C2
Craven Rd SO53 ...... 55 E1
Craven St 13 SO14 ...... 103 D3
Crawford Cl SO16 ...... 77 E3
Crawford Dr PO16 ...... 130 C2
Crawley Ave PO9 ...... 136 A3
Crawley Hill SO51 ...... 50 C1
Crawshaw Rd BH14 ...... 203 D1
Crawte Ave SO45 ...... 150 B1
Creasey Rd BH11 ...... 189 D3
Credenhill Rd PO6 ...... 133 E1
Creech Rd BH12 ...... 203 D3
Creedy Gdns SO18 ...... 80 A2
Creek End PO10 ...... 160 C4
Creek Rd Gosport PO12 ...... 181 E2
　South Hayling PO11 ...... 185 E1
Creekmoor La BH17 ...... 202 A4
Creighton Rd SO15 ...... 101 F3
Cremorne Pl 10 GU32 ...... 40 C2
Cremyll Cl PO14 ...... 179 E3
Crescent Cl SO22 ...... 10 A1
Crescent Cotts SO45 ...... 177 D3
Crescent Ct BH25 ...... 209 F4
Crescent Dr BH25 ...... 209 F4
Crescent House 3 SO50 ...... 56 A2
Crescent Prim Sch The SO50 ...... 56 A2
Crescent Rd
　Bournemouth BH2 ...... 204 C2
　Fareham PO14 ...... 131 D1
　Gosport PO12 ...... 181 D1
　Locks Heath SO31 ...... 128 C1
　North Baddesley SO52 ...... 53 F3
　Poole BH14 ...... 203 F2
　Verwood BH31 ...... 115 D3
　Wimborne Minster BH21 ...... 163 E2
Crescent The
　Barton on Sea BH25 ...... 209 E4
　3 Bournemouth BH7 ...... 205 F2
　Eastleigh SO50 ...... 56 A2
　Marchwood SO40 ...... 101 F1
　Netley SO31 ...... 127 E3
　Netley Marsh SO40 ...... 99 F2
　Romsey SO51 ...... 53 D4
　Southampton SO19 ...... 104 A1
　Southbourne PO10 ...... 161 E4
　Twyford SO21 ...... 32 A3
　Uphham SO32 ...... 58 B1
　Waterlooville PO7 ...... 134 B2
Crescent Wlk BH22 ...... 165 F1
Cressey Rd SO51 ...... 52 C4
Cressy Rd PO2 ...... 182 B4
Crest Cl PO15 ...... 131 E1
Crest Rd BH12 ...... 203 E3
Crest The PO7 ...... 134 B1
Crest Way SO19 ...... 104 B2
Cresta Ct 8 PO4 ...... 182 C1
Cresta Gdns PO4 ...... 165 F1
Crestland Cl PO8 ...... 112 A2
Crestwood Com Sch SO50 ...... 55 F3
Crete Cotts SO45 ...... 125 F1
Crete La SO45 ...... 125 F1
Crete Rd SO45 ...... 125 F1
Cribb Cl BH17 ...... 202 C4
Crichel Mount Rd BH14 ...... 214 B4
Crichel Rd BH9 ...... 205 D4
Crichton House 8 SO31 ...... 127 D3
Cricket Cl BH23 ...... 207 F3
Cricket Dr PO8 ...... 112 A3
Cricklemede SO32 ...... 83 E4
Cricklewood Cl SO32 ...... 83 E4
Crigdon Cl SO16 ...... 101 F4
Crimea Rd BH9 ...... 204 C4
Cringle Ave BH6 ...... 207 D2
Crinoline Gdns PO4 ...... 183 D1

Cripple Gate La Beaulieu SO42 ...... 175 E3
　East Boldre SO42 ...... 175 E3
Cripstead La SO23 ...... 10 C3
Crispen Cl BH23 ...... 208 C4
Crispin Cl Fair Oak SO50 ...... 81 E3
　Locks Heath SO31 ...... 129 D2
Crisspyn Cl PO8 ...... 112 A3
Criterion Arc 39 BH1 ...... 204 C2
Crittall Cl SO41 ...... 172 B1
Crockford Cl BH25 ...... 195 D3
Crockford Rd SO10 ...... 137 D2
Croft Cl PO11 ...... 186 B4
Croft Hts SP5 ...... 24 A2
Croft La PO11 ...... 159 F1
Croft Rd Bournemouth BH9 ...... 189 F1
　Bransgore BH23 ...... 193 D3
　Christchurch BH23 ...... 207 F4
　Poole BH12 ...... 203 D3
　Portsmouth PO2 ...... 157 E1
　Ringwood BH24 ...... 117 E1
Croft The Chandler's Ford SO53 ...... 55 E2
　Crouchecton SP5 ...... 22 B4
　Stubbington PO14 ...... 154 B2
　Totton SO40 ...... 76 B1
Croftlands Ave PO14 ...... 154 B2
Crofton Anne Dale Jun
　& Inf Schs PO14 ...... 179 E3
Crofton Ave PO13 ...... 179 E2
Crofton Cl Christchurch BH23 ...... 191 F1
　Southampton SO17 ...... 79 D1
　Waterlooville PO7 ...... 134 B3
Crofton Ct PO14 ...... 179 E3
Crofton Hammond Jun
　& Inf Schs PO14 ...... 179 E3
Crofton La PO14 ...... 179 D3
Crofton Rd
　Portsmouth, Milton PO4 ...... 183 D3
　Portsmouth, North End PO2 ...... 157 F1
Crofton Sch PO14 ...... 179 E3
Crofton Way Locks Heath SO31 ...... 128 B1
　Swanmore SO32 ...... 84 A3
Cromalt Cl SO45 ...... 125 E1
Cromarty Ave PO4 ...... 183 D2
Cromarty Cl PO14 ...... 154 A2
Cromarty Rd SO16 ...... 77 F3
Crombie Cl PO8 ...... 111 F2
Cromer Gdns BH12 ...... 203 F3
Cromer Rd Bournemouth BH8 ...... 205 E4
　Cosham PO6 ...... 133 F1
　Poole BH12 ...... 203 F3
　Southampton SO16 ...... 77 E1
Cromhall Cl PO14 ...... 154 B4
Crompton Way PO15 ...... 129 E3
Cromwell Pl 9 BH5 ...... 206 A3
Cromwell Rd
　Bournemouth BH5 ...... 206 A3
　Poole BH12 ...... 203 E3
　Portsmouth PO4 ...... 183 D1
　Southampton SO15 ...... 102 C4
　11 Wimborne Minster BH21 ...... 163 E2
　Winchester SO23 ...... 10 C3
Crondall Ave PO9 ...... 135 F3
Crood Ct 7 PO16 ...... 131 E1
Crooked Hays Cl SO40 ...... 101 F1
Crooked Walk La PO17 ...... 132 C2
Crookham Cl PO9 ...... 135 E2
Crookham Rd SO19 ...... 126 C4
Crookhorn Com
　Sch The PO7 ...... 134 C2
Crookhorn La Soberton SO32 ...... 85 E4
　Waterlooville PO7 ...... 134 C2
Crosby Rd BH4 ...... 204 B1
Crosfield Cl SO51 ...... 51 D1
Cross Keys Pas 22 SO23 ...... 11 D4
Cross La SO32 ...... 59 D1
Cross Lanes BH24 ...... 117 E4
Cross Rd
　Lee-on-the-Solent PO13 ...... 180 A2
　Southampton SO19 ...... 103 F4
Cross St
　Bishop's Waltham SO32 ...... 83 E4
　Portsmouth PO5 ...... 182 B2
　Portsmouth, Portsea PO1 ...... 182 A3
　Winchester SO23 ...... 10 C4
Cross The Burley BH24 ...... 143 D2
　East Meon GU32 ...... 38 B1
Cross Trees SP6 ...... 46 A1
Cross Way Christchurch BH23 ...... 191 E1
　Compton(Hants) SO21 ...... 31 E3
　Havant PO9 ...... 135 F1
Cross Ways BH23 ...... 169 E3
Crossbill Cl PO8 ...... 112 A4
Crossfell Wlk PO14 ...... 154 C4
Crosshouse Rd SO14 ...... 103 E2
Crossland Cl PO12 ...... 181 E2
Crossland Dr PO9 ...... 136 A2
Crossley Ct 6 SO15 ...... 102 B3
Crossmead Ave BH25 ...... 195 D1
Crossway The PO16 ...... 156 B4
Crossways SO41 ...... 196 B1
Crossways Cl SP5 ...... 46 C4
Crossways The Denmead PO7 ...... 111 D4
　Gosport PO12 ...... 181 D3
　Upton BH16 ...... 201 E4
Crosswell Cl SO19 ...... 104 B3
Crouch La PO8 ...... 112 A4
Croucher's Croft SO22 ...... 1 B1
Crow Arch La BH24 ...... 141 D3
Crow Arch Lane Ind Est
　BH24 ...... 141 D3
Crow Cotts BH24 ...... 141 E2
Crow Hill Top BH24 ...... 142 A2
Crow La BH24 ...... 141 E3
Crowder Terr SO22 ...... 10 C4
Crowders Gr 1 SO21 ...... 56 C4
Crowe Hill Ct 2 BH15 ...... 202 C2
Crown Cl Poole BH12 ...... 203 E3
　Waterlooville PO7 ...... 134 C2

Cor – Cur 227

Crown Ct
　58 Portsmouth PO1 ...... 182 B3
　7 Wimborne Minster BH21 ...... 163 E3
Crown Mead 1 BH21 ...... 163 E2
Crown Mews 8 PO12 ...... 181 E2
Crown St Portsmouth PO1 ...... 182 B3
　Southampton SO15 ...... 102 A4
Crown Wlk 9 BH7 ...... 205 F2
Crows Nest La SO32 ...... 81 F1
Crowsbury Cl PO10 ...... 136 C2
Crowsbury Cl PO10 ...... 136 C2
Crowsbury SO31 ...... 128 A2
Crowther Cl SO19 ...... 104 B2
Croydon Cl SO16 ...... 78 A2
Crummock Rd SO53 ...... 55 D4
Crusader Rd
　Bournemouth BH11 ...... 188 B2
　Hedge End SO30 ...... 105 E3
Crusader Way SO52 ...... 54 C3
Cruse Cl SO41 ...... 172 A1
Cruxton Farm Ctyd BH21 ...... 163 E1
Crystal Way PO7 ...... 135 D4
Cucklington Gdns BH9 ...... 190 A2
Cuckmere La SO16 ...... 101 E4
Cuckoo Bushes La SO53 ...... 55 E4
Cuckoo Hill Way BH23 ...... 169 E1
Cuckoo La
　22 Southampton SO14 ...... 102 C2
　Stubbington PO14 ...... 154 A2
Cuckoo Rd BH12 ...... 203 D4
Cudnell Ave BH11 ...... 189 D3
Cudworth Mead SO30 ...... 81 E1
Cuffnells Cl BH24 ...... 117 D4
Cul-de-sac PO4 ...... 209 E4
Culford Ave SO40 ...... 100 C3
Culford Cl BH8 ...... 190 C1
Culford Ct 1 BH8 ...... 205 D4
Culford Way SO40 ...... 100 C3
Cull Cl SO40 ...... 204 B4
Cull La BH25 ...... 195 D3
Culliford Cres BH17 ...... 187 F1
Culloden Cl PO15 ...... 130 C1
Culloden Rd PO14 ...... 154 C3
Cullwood La BH25 ...... 195 E4
Culver SO31 ...... 127 E4
Culver Cl SO16 ...... 77 E1
Culver Dr PO11 ...... 185 E1
Culver Mews 29 SO23 ...... 11 D4
Culver Rd New Milton BH25 ...... 194 C1
　Portsmouth PO4 ...... 183 D1
　28 Winchester SO23 ...... 11 D4
Culverhayes Pl BH21 ...... 163 D3
Culverhayes Rd BH21 ...... 163 D3
Culverin Sq PO3 ...... 158 A2
Culverlands Cl SO32 ...... 107 F4
Culverley Cl SO42 ...... 145 F1
Culverwell Gdns 21 SO23 ...... 10 C4
Culvery Gdns SO18 ...... 80 A1
Cumber Rd SO31 ...... 128 C2
Cumberland Cl
　Chandler's Ford SO53 ...... 55 F3
　Emsworth PO10 ...... 136 C2
Cumberland Bsns Ctr 1 PO1 ...... 182 C2
Cumberland Ct SO53 ...... 55 F3
Cumberland House(Mus &
　Aquarium) PO5 ...... 182 C1
Cumberland Inf Sch PO4 ...... 183 D2
Cumberland Pl SO15 ...... 102 C3
Cumberland Rd PO1 ...... 182 C3
Cumberland St
　Portsmouth PO1 ...... 182 A3
　Southampton SO14 ...... 103 D2
Cumberland Way SO45 ...... 125 E2
Cumbrian Way SO16 ...... 101 F4
Cummins Gn SO31 ...... 105 D1
Cumnor Rd BH1 ...... 205 D2
Cunard Ave SO15 ...... 102 B4
Cunard Rd SO14 ...... 103 D1
Cundell Way SO23 ...... 2 A4
Cunningham Ave SO32 ...... 83 D4
Cunningham Cl
　Bournemouth BH11 ...... 189 D2
　Christchurch BH23 ...... 208 A3
　Ringwood BH24 ...... 141 E4
Cunningham Cres
　Bournemouth BH11 ...... 189 D2
　Southampton SO19 ...... 104 A3
Cunningham Ct
　10 New Milton BH25 ...... 194 C2
　1 Portsmouth PO5 ...... 182 B1
Cunningham Dr Gosport PO13 ...... 155 E2
　Locks Heath SO31 ...... 129 D2
Cunningham Gdns SO31 ...... 127 F4
Cunningham House SO32 ...... 83 D4
Cunningham Pl BH9 ...... 189 D2
Cunningham Rd
　Horndean PO8 ...... 112 B4
　Waterlooville PO7, PO8 ...... 134 B3
Cupernham Cl SO51 ...... 28 A1
Cupernham Inf Sch SO51 ...... 28 A1
Cupernham Jun Sch SO51 ...... 28 A1
Cupernham La
　Abbotswood SO51 ...... 28 A1
　Romsey SO51 ...... 28 A1
Curdridge Cl 33 PO9 ...... 136 A3
Curdridge La Curdridge SO32 ...... 83 E2
　Shedfield SO32 ...... 83 E2
Curdridge Prim Sch SO32 ...... 106 B4
Curlew Cl Emsworth PO10 ...... 160 C4
　Ferndown BH22 ...... 165 D3
　Hythe SO45 ...... 126 B1
　Southampton SO16 ...... 78 A3
Curlew Dr Hythe SO45 ...... 126 A1
　Portchester PO16 ...... 155 F4
Curlew Gdns PO8 ...... 111 F2
Curlew Path PO4 ...... 183 D3

Curlew Rd Bournemouth BH8 190 B1
Christchurch BH23 208 A3
Curlew Sq SO50 55 F1
Curlew Wlk Gosport PO13 155 D2
Hythe SO45 126 A1
Curlews The BH31 115 D3
Curlieu Rd BH15 202 B3
Curtis Mead PO2 157 F2
Curtis Rd BH12 203 E3
Curtiss Gdns PO12 180 C2
Curve The Gosport PO13 155 D1
Horndean PO8 111 F3
Curzon Ct
32 Bournemouth BH4 204 B2
Southampton SO16 78 B2
Curzon Howe Rd PO1 182 A3
Curzon Pl SO41 197 E1
Curzon Rd Bournemouth BH1 205 E3
Poole BH14 203 D2
Waterlooville PO7 134 C4
Curzon Way BH23 208 B4
Custards Rd SO43 121 F3
Custards The SO43 122 A3
Cut Throat La Droxford SO32 61 D1
Swanmore SO32 84 B3
Cutbush La Southampton SO18 80 A2
Southampton SO18 104 A4
West End SO18 80 A2
Cuthbert Rd PO1 182 C3
Cuthburga Rd BH21 163 E2
Cuthbury Cl BH21 163 D2
Cuthbury Gdns BH21 163 D3
Cutler Cl New Milton BH25 195 E2
Poole BH12 204 B4
Cutlers La PO14 154 B2
Cutlers Pl BH21 164 A3
Cutter Ave SO31 128 C1
Cutts Arch Droxford SO32 85 D3
Soberton SO32 85 D3
Cygnet Ct PO16 155 F4
Cygnet House PO12 181 D4
Cygnet Rd PO6 158 C4
Cygnus Gdns SO45 125 E2
Cynthia Cl BH12 203 D4
Cynthia House BH12 203 D4
Cynthia Rd BH12 203 D4
Cypress Ave SO19 103 F3
Cypress Cres PO8 112 A3
Cypress Gdns Botley SO30 106 A4
Totton SO40 100 B4
Cypress Gr SO41 211 E4
Cyprus Rd Portsmouth PO2 182 C4
Titchfield PO14 129 E1
Cyril Rd BH8 205 E3

D Ave SO45 150 C3
D-Day Mus PO5 182 B1
Dacombe Cl BH16 201 E4
Dacombe Dr BH16 201 E4
Dacres Wlk 3 SO41 211 E3
Daffodil Rd SO16 79 E2
Daggons Rd SP6 92 B3
Dahlia Rd SO17 79 D2
Daintree Cl SO19 104 B2
Dairy Cl Broadstone BH21 186 A2
Christchurch BH23 207 E4
Dairy La SO16 77 D3
Dairymoor PO17 108 A2
Daisy La Gosport PO12 181 D2
Locks Heath SO31 129 E2
Daisy Mead PO7 135 D4
Daisy Rd SO16 79 D2
Dakota Cl BH23 208 A4
Dale Cl Littleton SO22 1 A3
Poole BH15 202 C3
Dale Dr PO13 155 D3
Dale Park House 26 PO1 182 B3
Dale Rd Hythe SO45 125 F2
Poole BH15 202 C3
Southampton SO16 78 B1
Stubbington PO14 154 B2
Dale The PO7 134 B1
Dale Valley Cl SO16 78 B1
Dale Valley Gdns SO16 78 B1
Dale Valley Rd Poole BH15 202 C4
Southampton SO16 78 B2
Dales Cl BH21 164 B3
Dales Dr BH21 164 A3
Dales La BH23 190 C4
Dales Way SO40 100 A4
Dalewood Ave BH11 188 C3
Dalewood Rd PO15 130 B1
Dalkeith Rd Broadstone BH21 186 B2
Poole BH13 204 A1
Dalling Rd BH12 204 A3
Dallington Cl PO14 179 E3
Dalmally Gdns SO18 103 F4
Dalmeny Rd BH6 207 D2
Dalzell 31 SO23 2 A1
Damask Gdns PO7 112 A1
Dame Elizabeth
Kelly Ct 3 PO2 157 F2
Damen Cl SO30 105 D3
Damerham Rd BH8 190 B2
Dampier Cl PO13 180 B4
Damson Hill SO32 60 A1
Danbury Ct PO10 137 D1
Dances Way PO11 184 C2
Dandelion Cl PO13 155 D1
Dando Rd PO7 111 D2
Dandy's Ford La SO51 25 F1
Dane Cl SO45 150 C1
Dane Ct BH14 203 D2
Dane Dr BH22 165 F2
Dane Rd SO41 211 D3
Danebury Cl PO9 135 F3
Danebury Gdns SO53 55 D2
Danebury Way SO16 77 E2
Danecourt Cl BH14 202 C2
Danecourt Rd BH14 202 C2
Danecrest Rd SO41 195 F2
Danehurst SO41 211 D3
Danehurst New Rd SO41 195 E4
Danemark Ct 4 SO23 11 D4
Danes Cl BH25 210 A4
Danes Rd Awbridge SO51 26 B2
Portchester PO16 132 A1
23 Winchester SO23 2 A1
Danesbrook La PO7 135 D4
Danesbury Ave BH6 206 C2
Danestream Cl SO41 211 E2
Danestream Ct SO41 211 F2
Daneswood Rd BH25 195 E2
Daniel Gdns 14 BH15 202 B1
Daniell's Cl SO41 197 F2
Daniell's Wlk SO41 197 F2
Daniels Wlk SO40 76 A1
Dannybrook BH23 208 A3
Dansie Cl BH14 203 D2
Dapple Pl SO40 102 A1
Darby's Cl BH15 202 B3
Darby's Cnr BH17 187 E1
Darby's La BH15 202 B3
Darby's La N BH17 202 B4
Dark La Blackfield SO45 150 C1
Bransgore BH23 194 A2
Darley Rd BH22 165 E2
Darlington Gdns SO15 78 B1
Darlington Rd PO4 182 C2
Darnan House 25 SO14 103 D4
Darracott Rd BH5 206 A3
Darren Cl PO14 154 B2
Darren Ct 9 PO16 131 D1
Darrian Ct BH16 201 D4
Dart House SO18 103 F4
Dart Rd SO18 80 A2
Dartington Rd SO50 56 B3
Dartmouth Mews PO5 182 A2
Dartmouth Rd PO3 158 A1
Darwin Ave BH23 191 F1
Darwin Ct 4 BH12 204 A2
Darwin House 32 PO1 182 B3
Darwin Rd Eastleigh SO50 56 A2
Southampton SO15 102 C4
Darwin Way PO13 180 B3
Daubney Gdns 10 PO9 135 E3
Daulston Rd PO1 182 C4
Davenport Cl Gosport PO13 180 B3
Upton BH16 201 E4
Daventry La PO3 158 B2
David Ct SO51 53 D3
David Hart Bsns Ctr SP5 46 C4
David's La BH24 140 B3
Davidia Ct PO7 135 D3
Davidson Ct 27 PO1 182 A3
Davis Cl PO13 180 B4
Davis Ct BH12 203 F3
Davis Field BH25 194 C1
Davis Rd BH12 203 F3
Daw La PO11 184 C4
Dawkins Rd BH15 201 E2
Dawkins Way BH25 195 D1
Dawlish Ave SO15 102 B4
Dawn Chorus BH14 203 D2
Dawn Cl BH10 189 E1
Dawn Gdns SO22 10 B3
Dawnay Cl SO16 79 E3
Daws Ave BH11 189 D1
Dawson Rd SO19 104 B1
Day La PO8 111 F4
Day's Ct BH21 163 E2
Daylesford Cl BH14 203 D1
Dayrell Cl SO40 76 A1
Dayshes Cl PO13 155 D2
Dayslondon Rd PO7 134 B3
De Courtenai Cl BH11 188 C3
De Grouchy La SO17 79 D1
De Haviland Cl BH21 163 F1
De Havilland House BH23 208 A3
De Havilland Way BH23 208 A3
De La Warr Rd SO41 211 E2
De Lisle Cl PO2 157 F2
De Lisle Rd BH3 204 C4
De Lunn Bldgs 5 SO23 11 D4
De Mauley Rd BH13 214 C4
De Montfort Rd BH21 163 E1
De Mowbray Way SO41 197 E1
De Port Hts SO32 61 E3
De Redvers Rd BH14 203 E1
Deacon Cl SO19 104 A3
Deacon Cres SO19 104 A3
Deacon Gdns BH11 189 D3
Deacon Rd Bournemouth BH11 189 D3
Locks Heath SO31 129 D1
Southampton SO19 104 A3
Deacon Trad Est SO50 56 B1
Deadman Hill SP 6 71 E3
Deal Cl PO14 154 B2
Deal Rd PO6 133 F1
Dean Cl Hamworthy BH15 201 F2
Winchester SO22 1 B1
Dean Court
(Bournemouth FC) BH7 205 F3
Dean Ct Hedge End SO30 105 E4
Horndean PO8 112 B4
Southampton SO18 104 A4
4 Southampton, Bitterne
Manor SO18 103 F4
Dean La
Bishop's Waltham SO32 59 F2
Rowland's Castle PO8 113 E3
Sparsholt SO22 1 A1
Whiteparish SP5 24 A2
Dean La Continued
Winchester SO22 1 A1
Dean Park Cres BH1 204 C2
Dean Park Rd BH1 204 C2
Dean Rd Cosham PO6 157 F4
Fair Oak SO50 57 E1
Southampton SO18 104 A4
West Dean SP5 3 D1
West Tytherley SP5 3 F3
Dean St PO1 182 A3
Dean Sta SP5 3 E2
Dean Swift Cres BH14 214 B4
Dean Villas PO17 130 C4
Dean's Rd 13 BH5 206 A3
Deane Ct 52 PO9 136 A3
Deane Down Dro SO22 1 A2
Deane Gdns 19 PO13 179 F1
Deane's Park Rd PO16 131 E1
Deanery The SO53 55 D4
Deanfield Cl SO31 127 F1
Deans Court La BH21 163 E2
Deans Ct SO41 211 E3
Deans Gate PO14 179 E3
Deans Gr BH21 163 E4
Deans The BH1 204 C2
Deanscroft Rd BH10 189 F2
Deansfield Cl SO51 53 D4
Deansleigh Rd BH7 191 D1
Deanswood Dr PO7 111 F1
Dear Hay La BH15 202 B1
Dearing Cl SO43 121 F2
Debney Lodge PO7 134 C4
Decies Rd BH14 203 D3
Dee Cl SO53 55 D3
Dee Way BH15 202 A1
Deep Dell PO8 112 A3
Deepdene SO18 103 F4
Deepdene La BH11 188 C3
Deeping Cl SO19 103 F1
Deeping Gate PO7 135 D4
Deer Park Cl BH25 194 C2
Deer Sanctuary BH24 119 F3
Deerhurst Cl SO40 100 B3
Deerhurst House 3 PO6 133 D1
Deerleap Cl SO45 126 A2
Deerleap La SO40 100 B1
Deerleap Way Hythe SO45 126 A2
New Milton BH25 195 D3
Defender Rd SO19 103 E2
Defender Wlk SO19 103 E2
Defiance Rd PO1 182 A2
Defoe Cl PO15 129 E4
Delamere Gdns BH10 189 F2
Delamere Rd PO4 182 C2
Delaval House 35 PO1 182 A3
Delft Cl SO31 128 C2
Delft Gdns PO8 111 E1
Delft Mews BH23 207 E3
Delhi Cl BH14 203 E2
Delhi Rd BH9 189 F1
Delilah Rd BH15 201 E1
Delius Ave SO19 104 B2
Delius Wlk PO7 134 C3
Delkeith Ct BH22 165 E2
Dell Cl Broadstone BH18 186 C2
Fair Oak SO50 57 E1
Waterlooville PO7 134 A1
Dell Cotts SO24 15 F1
Dell Piece East PO8 112 B3
Dell Piece West PO8 112 B3
Dell Quay Cl PO13 155 D1
Dell Rd Southampton SO18 79 F1
Winchester SO23 11 E3
Dell The Barton on Sea BH25 209 E4
Havant PO9 135 D1
Portchester PO16 131 E1
Southampton FC SO15 102 C3
Dellcrest Path PO7 134 A1
Dellfield GU32 18 C1
Dellfield Cl
14 Cosham PO6 133 D1
3 Cosham PO6 157 D4
Delme Ct 15 PO16 131 D1
Delme Dr PO16 131 E1
Delme Sq 21 PO16 131 D1
Delph Rd BH21 187 E4
Delphi Way PO7 134 C1
Delta Bsns Pk PO16 155 D4
Delta Cl BH23 208 A4
Dempsey Cl SO19 104 A2
Denbigh Cl Eastleigh SO50 55 F3
Totton SO40 100 B3
Denbigh Dr PO16 130 C1
Denbigh Gdns SO16 78 C2
Denby Rd BH15 202 C2
Dene Cl Chilworth SO16 78 C4
Locks Heath SO31 128 C2
Ringwood BH24 117 E1
Dene Hollow PO6 158 B4
Dene Rd SO40 100 B1
Dene Way SO40 100 B2
Dene Wlk BH22 165 F1
Denecote Lodge BH13 214 D4
Deneside Copse SO41 197 D1
Deneve Ave BH17 187 E1
Denewood Copse BH22 138 B2
Denewood Rd BH22 138 B2
Denewulf Cl SO32 83 E4
Denham Cl Broadstone BH17 187 F2
Stubbington PO14 179 D3
Winchester SO23 1 C1
Denham Ct SO23 2 A1
Denham Dr BH23 193 F1
Denham Gdns SO31 127 D3
Denham's Cnr SO32 81 E3
Denhill Cl PO11 184 C3
Denholm Cl BH24 117 E1
Denison Rd BH17 187 E1
Denmark La BH15 202 B2
Denmark Rd
Bournemouth BH9 189 F1
Poole BH15 202 B2
Denmark Terr BH1 205 F3
Denmead BH25 195 E2
Denmead Cvn Pk PO7 111 D2
Denmead Inf Sch PO7 111 D2
Denmead Jun Sch PO7 111 D2
Denmead Rd
Bournemouth BH6 206 B4
Southampton SO18 104 B4
Dennet House SO23 2 B1
Dennetts La 19 BH15 202 A1
Denning Mews PO1 182 B3
Dennis Rd BH21 186 B3
Dennis Way GU33 21 D2
Dennison Ct 8 SO15 102 A4
Dennistoun Ave BH23 207 F4
Denny Cl SO45 151 D2
Densome Cnr SP 6 71 D3
Denville Ave PO16 156 B3
Denville Cl PO6 158 C4
Denvilles Cl PO9 136 A1
Denwood Rd BH4 204 A2
Denzil Ave Netley SO31 127 E3
Southampton SO14 103 D3
Depedene Cl SO45 150 B2
Derby Ct PO13 180 B3
Derby House 5 SO50 56 A1
Derby Rd Bournemouth BH1 205 E2
Eastleigh SO50 55 F1
Portsmouth PO2 157 E1
Southampton SO14 103 D3
Dereham Way BH12 203 F3
Deridene Ct SO40 100 B3
Derlyn Rd PO16 131 D1
Derritt La Bransgore BH23 192 B4
Sopley BH23 192 B4
Dersingham Cl PO6 133 F1
Derwent Cl Bournemouth BH9 190 A1
Ferndown BH22 166 A3
Horndean PO8 88 B1
Stubbington PO14 154 B2
West End SO18 80 A1
Derwent Rd
Lee-on-the-Solent PO13 179 F1
New Milton BH25 195 D3
Southampton SO16 77 F1
Derwentwater Rd BH21 163 E1
Desborough Cl 9 PO6 133 D1
Desborough Rd SO50 56 A1
Devenish Rd SO22 1 B2
Deverel Cl BH23 207 D4
Deverell Pl PO7 134 B2
Devine Gdns 5 SO50 56 C1
Devon Cl SO53 55 E2
Devon Dr SO53 55 E2
Devon Rd Christchurch BH23 206 C4
Poole BH15 202 C3
Portsmouth PO3 158 A2
Devonshire Ave PO4 183 D2
Devonshire Gdns
Bursledon SO31 105 D1
Hythe SO45 150 A4
Devonshire Inf Sch PO4 182 C2
Devonshire Mansions
10 SO15 102 C3
Devonshire Rd SO15 102 C3
Devonshire Sq PO4 182 C2
Devonshire Way PO14 154 B4
Dew La SO50 55 F2
Dewar Cl PO15 129 E3
Deweys La BH24 140 C4
Dewlands Pk BH31 114 B3
Dewlands Rd BH31 114 B3
Dewlands Way BH31 114 C3
Dewlish Cl BH17 188 A1
Dewsbury Ct 3 SO18 80 A1
Dhekelia Ct 52 PO1 182 B3
Dial Cl BH23 169 E1
Diamond Cl SP6 93 F4
Diamond Ct SP6 93 F4
Diamond St PO5 182 A2
Diana Cl PO12 180 C2
Diana Ct BH23 209 D4
Diana Way BH21 186 C4
Dibben Wlk SO51 28 B1
Dibble Dr SO52 53 F2
Dibden Cl Bournemouth BH8 190 B2
Havant PO9 135 E2
Dibden Lodge Cl SO45 125 F3
Dibles Rd SO31 128 C1
Dickens Cl PO2 182 B4
Dickens Dell SO40 100 A4
Dickens Mus PO1 182 B4
Dickens Rd BH6 206 B4
Dickson Pk PO17 108 A2
Didcot Rd Poole BH17 202 B4
Southampton SO15 78 B1
Dieppe Cres PO2 157 F2
Dieppe Gdns PO12 180 C2
Dight Rd PO12 181 E1
Diligence Cl SO31 105 D1
Dillington House 2 PO7 134 C4
Dilly La BH25 210 A4
Dimond Cl SO18 79 F1
Dimond Hill SO18 79 F1
Dimond Rd SO18 79 F1
Dingle Rd BH5 206 A2
Dingle Way SO31 129 D3
Dingley Rd BH15 202 B3
Dinham Ct BH25 195 E2
Dinham Rd BH25 195 E2
Dinsey Cl SO16 101 F4
Diprose Rd BH21 186 C4
Disa House SO15 102 C3
Discovery Cl PO14 154 B3
Disraeli Rd BH23 207 E3
Ditcham Cres PO9 135 F2
Ditcham Park Sch GU31 89 F4
Ditchbury SO41 197 E3
Ditton Cl PO14 154 B2
Ditton Cotts SO42 148 C1
Dock La SO42 149 D1
Dock Mill Cotts 3 PO5 182 B1
Dock Rd PO12 181 E2
Dockenfield Cl PO9 135 E2
Doctor's Hill SO51 26 A2
Doctors La GU32 37 E3
Dodds La SO32 84 B3
Dodwell La SO31 105 D2
Doe Copse Way BH25 194 C2
Dogdean BH21 163 E4
Dogkennel La PO7 86 C2
Dogwood Dell 8 PO7 134 C3
Dogwood Rd BH18 186 C1
Dolbery Rd N BH12 188 B1
Dolbery Rd S BH12 188 B1
Dolman Rd PO12 181 E2
Dolphin Ave BH10 189 F3
Dolphin Cl 11 SO50 56 C1
Dolphin Cres PO12 181 E2
Dolphin Ct
7 Portsmouth PO5 182 C1
Stubbington PO14 154 A2
Dolphin Ctr BH15 202 B1
Dolphin Hill SO21 32 A3
Dolphin Pl 2 BH25 210 A4
Dolphin Way Gosport PO12 181 E1
Portsmouth PO1 182 A2
Dolton Rd SO16 77 F2
Dome Al SO23 11 D4
Domey Ct 2 PO6 158 A4
Dominie Wlk 15 PO13 179 F1
Dominion Ctr BH11 188 C2
Dominion Rd BH11 188 C2
Domum Rd Portsmouth PO2 157 F1
Winchester SO23 11 D3
Domvilles App PO2 157 D1
Donaldson Rd PO6 157 F3
Doncaster Rd SO50 80 A4
Donigers Cl SO32 84 A3
Donigers Dell SO32 84 A3
Donkey La SO30 106 A4
Donnelly Rd BH6 206 C3
Donnelly St PO12 181 D3
Donnington Ct 19 SO23 2 A1
Donnington Dr
Chandler's Ford SO53 55 D2
Christchurch BH23 208 A4
Donnington Gr SO17 79 E1
Donoughmore Rd 1 BH1 205 F2
Dorcas Cl PO7 112 A1
Dorchester Ct SO15 102 C4
Dorchester Gdns BH15 202 C3
Dorchester Mansions BH1 205 E2
Dorchester Rd Poole BH15 202 C3
Upton BH16 201 D4
Dore Ave PO16 132 B1
Dores La Braishfield SO51 29 D4
Hursley SO51 29 D4
Doric Cl SO53 55 F4
Dorking Cres PO6 157 F4
Dorland Gdns SO40 100 B3
Dorlands Rd PO8 112 B4
Dormers The BH25 194 C1
Dormington Rd PO6 133 E1
Dormy Cl SO31 128 B2
Dormy Way PO13 155 D1
Dornie Rd BH13 214 C4
Dornmere La PO7 135 D4
Dorothy Dymond St 16 PO1 182 B3
Dorrick Ct 17 SO15 102 C4
Dorrien Rd PO12 181 D4
Dorrita Ave PO8 112 A2
Dorrita Cl PO4 182 C1
Dorrits The SO40 100 A4
Dorset Ave BH22 165 E2
Dorset Cl PO8 112 A3
Dorset Grange BH23 206 C4
Dorset Heavy Horse Ctr
BH21 91 E1
Dorset Lake Ave BH14 214 A4
Dorset Lake Manor BH14 203 D1
Dorset Rd Bournemouth BH4 204 B3
Chandler's Ford SO53 55 E2
Christchurch BH23 207 F4
Dorset St SO14 103 D3
Dorstone Rd PO6 133 E1
Dorval House 23 SO15 102 C4
Dorval Manor 24 SO15 102 C4
Douglas Ave BH23 207 D3
Douglas Cl BH16 201 E4
Douglas Cres SO19 104 B3
Douglas Gdns Havant PO9 136 A2
Poole BH12 203 F3
Douglas Mews
Bournemouth BH6 206 B3
Upton BH16 201 E4
Douglas Rd Bournemouth BH6 206 C2
Poole BH12 203 F3
Douglas Way SO45 125 F2
Doulton Gdns BH14 203 D1
Doussie Cl BH16 201 D4
Dove Cl PO8 111 F2
Dove Dale SO50 55 E1
Dove Gdns SO31 129 D3
Dove La SO51 29 D4
Dover Cl Poole BH13 204 A2
Stubbington PO14 154 A2
Dover Ct PO11 184 C3
Dover Rd Poole BH13 204 A2
Portsmouth PO3 183 D4
Dover St SO14 103 D4
Dovercourt Rd PO6 158 A3

Doveshill Cres BH10 .... 189 E2
Doveshill Gdns BH10 .... 189 E2
Doveys Cl BH24 .... 143 D2
Dowds Cl SO30 .... 105 D4
Dowell House PO4 .... 183 D1
Dowlands Cl BH10 .... 189 E2
Dowlands Rd BH10 .... 189 E2
Down End PO6 .... 134 B1
Down End Rd PO6 .... 134 B1
Down Farm La SO23 .... 1 C4
Down Farm Pl PO8 .... 88 B1
Down Lodge SP6 .... 93 D3
Down Rd Horndean PO8 .... 88 A1
Horndean PO8 .... 112 B4
Down's Park Ave SO40 .... 101 D3
Down's Park Cres SO40 .... 101 D3
Down's Park Rd SO40 .... 101 D3
Downend Rd PO16 .... 131 F1
Downey Cl BH11 .... 188 C1
Downham Cl PO11 .... 111 F2
Downhouse Rd PO8 .... 88 A2
Downing Ct PO14 .... 129 E1
Downland Cl Botley SO30 .... 105 F4
Locks Heath SO31 .... 129 D2
Downland Pl SO30 .... 105 D3
Downlands Cl SP5 .... 46 C3
Downlands Pl BH17 .... 202 C4
Downlands Rd SO22 .... 10 A2
Downley Rd PO9 .... 136 A2
Downs Cl PO7 .... 134 C2
Downscroft Gdns SO30 .... 105 D4
Downside PO13 .... 155 E1
Downside Ave SO19 .... 104 A3
Downside Rd
Waterlooville PO7 .... 134 B2
Winchester SO22 .... 1 A1
Downsway The PO16 .... 156 B4
Downton CE Prim Sch SP5 .... 46 C4
Downton Cl BH8 .... 190 B2
Downton Cty Sec Sch SP5 .... 46 C4
Downton Hill SP5 .... 47 E4
Downton House 2 PO6 .... 157 E4
Downton La SO41 .... 210 C4
Downton Rd SO18 .... 79 F1
Downview Rd SP6 .... 43 D2
Downwood Cl
Fordingbridge SP6 .... 69 E1
Hythe SO45 .... 125 E1
Downwood Way PO8 .... 88 B1
Doyle Ave PO2 .... 157 F2
Doyle Cl PO2 .... 157 F2
Doyle Ct 16 Portsmouth PO2 ... 157 F2
Southampton SO19 .... 103 F1
Doyle House PO9 .... 135 D2
Doyne Rd BH14 .... 203 F2
Dradfield La SO32 .... 109 E4
Draffatts House SO15 .... 102 B4
Dragon La BH23 .... 168 A4
Dragon St GU31,GU32 .... 40 C2
Dragoon Cl SO19 .... 104 B2
Dragoon Way BH23 .... 206 C4
Drake Cl Christchurch BH23 ..... 207 F3
Locks Heath SO31 .... 129 D3
Marchwood SO40 .... 102 A1
New Milton BH25 .... 194 C2
Ringwood BH24 .... 117 E1
Drake Ct 28 BH15 .... 202 B1
Drake House 4 PO1 .... 182 A3
Drake Rd Bishopstoke SO50 ..... 56 C2
Lee-on-the-Solent PO13 .... 179 E2
Poole BH15 .... 202 B1
Drakes Cl SO45 .... 125 F1
Drakes Ct SO40 .... 102 A2
Draper Rd Bournemouth BH11 .. 189 D2
Christchurch BH23 .... 207 F4
Drapers Copse Cvn Site
SO45 .... 125 E1
Draycote Rd PO8 .... 88 B2
Draycott Rd BH10 .... 189 E1
Drayton Cl 2 SO19 .... 126 C4
Drayton La PO6 .... 134 A1
Drayton Pl SO40 .... 100 B4
Drayton Rd PO2 .... 157 F1
Drayton St SO22 .... 10 B3
Dreadnought Rd PO14 .... 154 C3
Dresden Dr PO8 .... 111 F2
Dreswick Ct BH23 .... 191 E2
Drew Cl BH12 .... 204 B4
Drift Rd Clanfield PO8 .... 88 B2
Fareham PO16 .... 131 C1
Drift The PO9 .... 113 D1
Driftwood Gdns
Portsmouth PO4 .... 183 E1
Totton SO40 .... 100 B3
Drill Shed Rd PO2 .... 157 D1
Drinkwater Cl SO50 .... 55 F2
Drive The Fareham PO16 .... 131 D1
Gosport PO13 .... 155 D1
Havant PO9 .... 135 F2
Plaitford SO51 .... 25 D1
Poole BH12 .... 203 E3
Sherfield English SO51 .... 25 D1
Southbourne PO10 .... 161 E4
Totton SO40 .... 100 C4
West End SO30 .... 80 A2
West Wellow SO51 .... 51 D1
Drove Cl SO21 .... 31 F3
Drove Rd Southampton SO19 .. 104 A2
Southwick PO17 .... 133 D2
Drove The Blackfield SO45 .... 150 C1
Durley SO32 .... 82 B4
Fair Oak SO50 .... 81 E3
Southbourne SO18 .... 104 A4
Swanmore SO32 .... 84 A3
Totton SO40 .... 76 A1
Twyford SO21 .... 31 F3
West End SO30 .... 80 C2
West Wellow SO51 .... 50 C2

Droxford Cl PO12 .... 180 C2
Droxford House 47 PO1 .... 182 B3
Droxford Jun Sch SO32 .... 61 D1
Droxford Rd
Bournemouth BH6 .... 206 A3
Swanmore SO32 .... 84 B3
Druids Cl BH22 .... 165 E1
Druitt Rd BH23 .... 207 F4
Drum La GU32 .... 40 C2
Drum Mead GU32 .... 40 C2
Drumlanrig Terr PO12 .... 181 E4
Drummond Cl SO22 .... 10 C3
Drummond Ct
4 Eastleigh SO50 .... 56 A3
Southampton SO19 .... 103 F2
Drummond Rd
Bournemouth BH1 .... 205 E2
Hedge End SO30 .... 81 E1
Hythe SO45 .... 126 A2
Portsmouth PO1 .... 182 B3
Drummond Way SO53 .... 55 D4
Drury Rd BH11 .... 204 A1
Dryden Ave PO6 .... 132 C1
Dryden Cl Fareham PO16 .... 131 D1
St Leonards BH24 .... 139 F3
Waterlooville PO7 .... 111 F1
Dryden Pl 4 SO41 .... 211 E3
Dryden Rd SO19 .... 104 C3
Drysdale Mews PO4 .... 183 D1
Duart Ct SO41 .... 195 E2
Duck Island La 3 BH24 .... 141 D3
Duck La BH11 .... 188 C2
Ducking Stool La BH23 .... 207 D3
Duckmead La GU33 .... 21 D3
Duckworth House 23 PO1 .... 182 A3
Duddon Cl SO18 .... 80 A1
Duddleston Heath Dr PO8 ..... 112 A1
Dudley Ave Fordingbridge SP6 .. 69 F2
Hordle SO41 .... 195 F2
Dudley Gdns BH10 .... 189 E3
Dudley Pl 29 BH25 .... 195 D1
Dudley Rd Bournemouth BH10 .. 189 E3
Portsmouth PO3 .... 183 D4
Dudley Terr GU33 .... 21 D3
Dudmoor Farm Rd BH23 .... 191 F2
Dudmoor La BH23 .... 191 F2
Dudsbury Ave BH22 .... 165 E2
Dudsbury Cres BH22 .... 165 F2
Dudsbury Ct 8 BH23 .... 207 F3
Dudsbury Gdns BH22 .... 189 F4
Dudsbury Rd BH22 .... 165 E1
Dudsway Ct BH22 .... 165 E2
Duffield La PO10 .... 137 F2
Dugald Drummond St 18 PO1 182 B3
Dugdell Cl BH22 .... 165 F3
Duisburg Way PO5 .... 182 A1
Duke Cres PO1 .... 182 B4
Duke Rd SO30 .... 105 E3
Duke St SO14 .... 103 D2
Dukes Cl GU32 .... 40 B2
Dukes Cl SO32 .... 83 E4
Dukes Dr BH11 .... 188 C3
Dukes Mill Ctr 11 SO51 .... 52 C4
Dukes Rd Gosport PO12 .... 181 D3
Southampton SO14 .... 103 E4
Dukes Wood Dr SO45 .... 126 A1
Dukesfield BH23 .... 191 E1
Dulsie Rd BH3 .... 204 B4
Dumbarton Cl PO2 .... 182 B4
Dumbleton Cl SO19 .... 104 C2
Dumbleton's Towers SO19 ...... 104 C2
Dummer Ct PO9 .... 135 E3
Dummer Rd SO51 .... 28 B4
Dumpers Drove SO50 .... 81 E3
Dumpton Sch BH21 .... 163 E4
Dunbar Cl SO16 .... 77 F3
Dunbar Cres BH23 .... 193 F1
Dunbar Rd Bournemouth BH3 .. 204 C3
Portsmouth PO4 .... 183 D2
Dunbridge La Awbridge SO51 .. 26 C4
Mottisfont SO51 .... 26 C4
Dunbridge Sta SO51 .... 5 E1
Duncan Cl SO19 .... 103 F1
Duncan Cooper House PO7 .... 134 B4
Duncan Ct SO19 .... 104 B3
Duncan Rd Locks Heath SO31 .. 129 D3
New Milton BH25 .... 195 E2
Portsmouth PO5 .... 182 B1
Duncans Dr PO14 .... 154 A4
Duncliff Rd BH6 .... 207 D2
Duncombe Dr BH24 .... 116 B2
Duncombe Rd GU32 .... 63 E4
Duncton Rd PO8 .... 88 B3
Duncton Way PO13 .... 155 E2
Dundas Cl PO3 .... 158 A1
Dundas La PO3 .... 158 A1
Dundas Rd BH17 .... 202 C4
Dundas Spur PO3 .... 158 A1
Dundee Cl PO15 .... 130 C2
Dundee Rd SO17 .... 79 E1
Dundonald Cl
South Hayling SO41 .... 185 D3
Southampton SO19 .... 103 E1
Dundridge La
Bishop's Waltham SO32 .... 60 B1
Droxford SO32 .... 60 B4
Dundry Way SO30 .... 105 E4
Dune Crest BH13 .... 214 B2
Dunedin Cl BH22 .... 165 D2
Dunedin Dr BH22 .... 165 D2
Dunedin Gdns BH22 .... 165 D2
Dunedin Gr BH23 .... 208 B4
Dunfield Way SO45 .... 150 C1
Dunford Cl Barton on Sea BH25 209 F4
Southampton SO19 .... 194 C1
Dunford Rd BH12 .... 203 E3
Dunhurst (Bedales Jun Sch)
GU32 .... 40 C3

Dunhurst Cl PO9 .... 136 A2
Dunkeld Rd Bournemouth BH3 .. 204 C3
Gosport PO12 .... 181 D4
Dunkirk Cl SO16 .... 78 B2
Dunkirk Rd SO16 .... 78 B2
Dunlin Cl Christchurch BH23 ..... 208 A3
Portsmouth PO4 .... 183 E3
Dunn Cl PO4 .... 183 D2
Dunnings La SO52 .... 53 F3
Dunnock Cl Ferndown BH22 .... 165 D4
Rowland's Castle PO9 .... 113 D1
Dunsbury Way PO9 .... 135 F3
Dunsmore Cl PO5 .... 182 B2
Dunstable Wlk PO14 .... 154 B4
Dunstans La BH15 .... 203 D3
Dunster Cl SO16 .... 78 B3
Dunvegan Dr SO16 .... 78 B3
Dunvegan Rd SO16 .... 78 B3
Dunvegan Way SO16 .... 78 B3
Dunyeats Rd BH18 .... 187 D2
Dunyeats Rdbt BH18 .... 187 E3
Durban Cl SO51 .... 28 A1
Durban Ct 21 SO15 .... 102 C4
Durban House 35 PO1 .... 182 B3
Durban Rd PO1 .... 182 C4
Durdells Ave BH11 .... 189 D3
Durdells Gdns BH11 .... 189 D3
Durford Ct PO9 .... 135 E3
Durford Rd GU31 .... 41 E2
Durham Gdns PO7 .... 134 C3
Durham St Gosport PO12 .... 181 D3
Portsmouth PO1 .... 182 B3
Durland Cl BH25 .... 195 D1
Durley Ave PO8 .... 111 F2
Durley Brook Road SO32 .... 81 F3
Durley CE Sch SO32 .... 82 A3
Durley Chine BH2 .... 204 B1
Durley Chine Rd BH2 .... 204 B1
Durley Chine Rd S BH2 .... 204 B1
Durley Cres SO40 .... 100 B3
Durley Gdns BH2 .... 204 B1
Durley Hall Rd SO32 .... 58 B1
Durley La SO32 .... 82 B4
Durley Rd Bournemouth BH2 .... 204 C1
Durley SO32,SO50 .... 81 F4
Fair Oak SO50 .... 81 F4
Gosport PO12 .... 181 D3
Durley Rd S BH2 .... 204 B1
Durlston Court Sch BH25 .... 210 A4
Durlston Cres BH23 .... 191 E2
Durlston Rd Poole BH14 .... 203 E1
Southampton SO16 .... 77 F1
Durnford Rd SO14 .... 103 D3
Durngate Pl SO23 .... 11 D4
Durngate Terr SO23 .... 11 D4
Durnstown SO41 .... 172 B1
Durrant PRU PO9 .... 136 A4
Durrant Rd
7 Bournemouth BH2 .... 204 C2
Poole BH14 .... 203 E2
Durrant Way SO41 .... 172 A1
Durrants Gdns PO9 .... 136 A4
Durrants Rd PO9 .... 136 A4
Durrington Pl BH7 .... 206 A3
Durrington Rd BH7 .... 206 A4
Dursley Cres PO6 .... 157 E4
Durweston Cl BH9 .... 190 A2
Dutton La SO50 .... 56 A2
Dutton's Rd SO51 .... 52 C4
Dyer Rd SO15 .... 102 B4
Dymchurch House 3 PO6 ...... 157 F4
Dymewood Rd BH21 .... 138 C4
Dymoke St PO10 .... 136 C2
Dymott Cl SO15 .... 102 B3
Dyneley Gn SO18 .... 80 A1
Dyram Cl SO50 .... 55 F3
Dysart Ave PO6 .... 158 A4
Dyserth Cl SO19 .... 104 A1
Dyson Dr SO23 .... 2 A1

E Ave SO45 .... 150 C3
Eadens La SO40 .... 99 E4
Eagle Ave PO8 .... 111 F2
Eagle Cl Chandler's Ford SO53 .. 55 D2
Portchester PO16 .... 155 F4
Eagle House Sch BH14 .... 203 D2
Eagle Rd
Lee-on-the-Solent PO13 .... 179 E2
Poole BH14 .... 204 A2
Eaglhurst 5 BH12 .... 204 A2
Eames La GU33 .... 19 F4
Earle House 1 SO23 .... 11 E4
Earle Rd BH4 .... 204 B1
Earley St SO41 .... 197 F2
Earlham Dr BH14 .... 203 E2
Earls Cl SO50 .... 57 D1
Earls Rd Fareham PO16 .... 155 D4
Southampton SO14 .... 103 D4
Earlsdon St PO5 .... 182 B2
Earlsdon Way BH23 .... 208 C4
Earlsdown 40 SO23 .... 11 D4
Earlswood SP6 .... 92 C3
Earnley Rd PO11 .... 185 F1
East Ave BH25 .... 209 E4
East Avenue BH3 .... 204 B3
East Bank Rd SO42 .... 173 D4
East Bargate 7 SO14 .... 103 D2
East Boldre Rd SO42 .... 175 E3
East Borough BH21 .... 163 D3
East Cams Cl PO16 .... 131 F1
East Cl BH25 .... 209 E4
East Cliff Way BH23 .... 208 B4
East Cosham Rd PO6 .... 158 A4
East Ct Cosham PO6 .... 158 A4
Portsmouth PO1 .... 182 C4
East Dean Rd SO51 .... 4 C1
East Dr SO50 .... 56 C2
East Field Cl PO10 .... 137 F1

East Hill SO41 .... 197 F2
East Hill Cl PO16 .... 131 F1
East Hill Dr GU33 .... 21 D2
East Hoe Rd PO7 .... 86 A2
East Horton Golf Ctr SO50 ...... 57 F1
East House Ave PO14 .... 179 E3
East Howe La BH10 .... 189 E2
East La SO41 .... 196 C1
East Leigh Rd PO9 .... 136 B2
East Links SO51 .... 55 E1
East Lodge Fareham PO15 ...... 130 B1
7 Lee-on-the-Solent PO13 ... 179 F1
East Lodge Park PO6 .... 158 C4
East Meon CE Prim Sch GU32 . 38 B1
East Overcliff Dr BH1 .... 205 E2
East Pallant PO9 .... 135 F1
East Park Terr SO14 .... 103 D3
East Quay BH15 .... 202 B1
East Quay Rd BH15 .... 202 B1
East Rd Fawley SO45 .... 150 B4
Southwick PO17 .... 133 D3
East Shore Ctr PO3 .... 183 D3
East St Fareham PO14, PO16 ... 131 E1
Hambledon PO7 .... 86 B2
Havant PO9 .... 135 F1
Poole BH15 .... 202 B1
Portchester PO16 .... 156 C4
Portsmouth PO1 .... 182 A2
Southampton SO14 .... 103 D2
Titchfield PO14 .... 154 A4
Westbourne PO10 .... 137 D2
Wimborne Minster BH21 .... 163 E2
East Street Ctr 16 SO14 .... 103 D2
East Surrey St 27 PO1 .... 182 B3
East View Rd BH24 .... 141 D4
East View Terr 8 PO7 .... 135 F1
East Way Bournemouth BH8 .... 190 B1
Corfe Mullen BH21 .... 186 B3
East Woodhay Rd SO22 .... 1 B2
Eastacre 1 C1
Eastbourne Ave Gosport PO12 .. 180 C4
Eastbourne Rd PO3 .... 183 D4
Eastbrook Cl Gosport PO12 .... 180 C4
Locks Heath SO31 .... 129 D3
Eastbrook Row BH21 .... 163 E2
Eastbury Ct BH23 .... 207 F2
Eastchurch Cl SO16 .... 77 F2
Eastcot Cl SO45 .... 150 B2
Eastcott Cl BH7 .... 206 A4
Eastcroft Rd PO12 .... 180 C3
Easter Rd BH9 .... 190 A1
Eastern Ave PO4 .... 183 D3
Eastern Ind Ctr PO6 .... 158 B3
Eastern Par Fareham PO16 ..... 155 D4
Portsmouth PO4 .... 182 C1
Eastern Rd Fawley SO45 .... 151 F1
Havant PO9 .... 136 A1
Lymington SO41 .... 197 E2
Portsmouth PO3, PO6 .... 158 B2
Portsmouth, Whale Is PO2 ...... 157 D1
Eastern Terr PO4 .... 183 D1
Eastern Villas Rd PO4 .... 182 B1
Eastern Way Fareham PO16 .... 131 E1
Milford on Sea SO41 .... 211 F2
Eastfield Ave PO14 .... 154 C4
Eastfield Cl BH24 .... 141 E4
Eastfield La BH24 .... 141 E4
Eastfield Rd Portsmouth PO4 .. 183 D2
Southampton SO17 .... 103 E4
Eastfields 25 PO5 .... 182 B2
Eastgate St
Southampton SO14 .... 103 D2
Winchester SO23 .... 11 D4
Eastlake Ave BH12 .... 203 E3
Eastlake Cl GU31 .... 41 E2
Eastlake Hts PO4 .... 183 E2
Eastlands BH25 .... 195 D1
Eastleigh Coll SO50 .... 56 A1
Eastleigh Coll of F Ed SO50 .... 56 A1
Eastleigh Rd SO50 .... 57 E1
Eastleigh Sta SO50 .... 56 A2
Eastleigh Town Mus SO50 ...... 56 A1
Eastman Cl SP5 .... 47 D3
Eastmeare Ct SO40 .... 100 B3
Eastney Farm Rd PO4 .... 183 E2
Eastney Rd PO4 .... 183 D1
Eastney St PO4 .... 183 D1
Eastoke Ave PO11 .... 185 E1
Easton La SO21 .... 2 C2
Easton Lane Bsns Pk 47 SO23 .. 11 D4
Eastover Ct 2 PO9 .... 135 E3
Eastville Rd SO50 .... 57 E1
Eastways SO32 .... 83 E4
Eastwood Cl PO11 .... 185 D3
Eastwood Rd 8 SO22 .... 157 F2
Eastworth Rd BH31 .... 114 C4
Eaton Rd BH13 .... 204 A1
Ebden Rd SO23 .... 11 D4
Ebenezer La BH24 .... 140 C4
Ebery Gr PO3 .... 183 E4
Ebor Cl BH22 .... 165 F1
Ebor Rd BH12 .... 203 E3
Eccles Rd BH15 .... 202 A1
Ecton La PO3 .... 158 B2
Eddystone Rd SO40 .... 76 B1
Edelvale Rd SO18 .... 80 A1
Eden Ct 20 BH1 .... 205 D2
Eden Gr BH21 .... 163 E2
Eden La SO41 .... 80 A1
Eden Rise PO16 .... 155 D2
Eden Terr 10 PO2 .... 157 E1
Eden Wlk SO53 .... 55 D3
Edenbridge Rd PO4 .... 183 E3

Edgar Cres PO16 .... 156 B3
Edgar Rd SO23 .... 10 C3
Edgar Villas SO23 .... 10 C3
Edgarton Rd BH17 .... 187 E2
Edgbaston House 11 PO5 ...... 182 B2
Edgecombe Cres PO13 .... 180 B4
Edgehill Rd Bournemouth BH9 .. 189 F1
Southampton SO18 .... 79 F1
Edgell Rd PO10 .... 137 D2
Edgerly Gdns PO6 .... 157 F3
Edgeware Rd PO4 .... 183 D3
Edgewood Ct GU33 .... 21 D1
Edifred Rd BH9 .... 190 A2
Edinburgh Cl SO15 .... 102 A3
Edinburgh Rd PO1 .... 182 B3
Edington Cl SO32 .... 83 D4
Edington Rd SO23 .... 2 A1
Edmondsham House & Gdn
BH31 .... 91 D2
Edmondsham Rd BH31 .... 114 C4
Edmonsham House 28 PO4 .... 204 C2
Edmund Rd PO4 .... 182 C2
Edmunds Cl
Barton on Sea BH25 .... 195 D1
Hedge End SO30 .... 105 E3
Edneys La PO7 .... 111 D3
Edward Ave SO50 .... 56 B2
Edward Cl SO45 .... 150 C1
Edward Gdns PO9 .... 135 E1
Edward Gr PO16 .... 132 C1
Edward Rd
Bournemouth BH11 .... 189 D2
Christchurch BH23 .... 207 F4
Hythe SO45 .... 126 A2
Poole BH14 .... 203 E3
Southampton SO15 .... 102 B4
Winchester SO23 .... 10 C3
Edward's Cl 28 PO6 .... 133 D1
Edwards Cl PO11 .... 111 F2
Edwin Jones Gn SO15 .... 102 C4
Edwina Cl
North Baddesley SO52 .... 54 A2
Ringwood BH24 .... 117 E1
Southampton SO19 .... 104 A3
Edwina Dr BH17 .... 187 D1
Edwina House SO18 .... 79 F2
Effingham Gdns SO19 .... 104 B2
Efford Ct SO41 .... 197 D1
Efford Farm Cotts SO41 .... 197 D1
Efford Way SO41 .... 197 D1
Egan Cl PO2 .... 157 F2
Egbert Rd SO23 .... 2 A1
Egdon Ct BH16 .... 201 D4
Egdon Dr BH21 .... 187 F4
Egerton Gdns BH8 .... 205 E3
Egerton Rd BH8 .... 205 E3
Eglantine Cl PO8 .... 112 A2
Eglantine Wlk PO8 .... 112 B2
Egmont Cl BH24 .... 140 B1
Egmont Dr BH24 .... 140 B1
Egmont Gdns BH24 .... 140 B1
Egmont Rd BH16 .... 201 D2
Eight Acres SO51 .... 53 D4
Eileen Beard House PO9 .... 136 A3
Elaine Gdns PO8 .... 112 A3
Elan Cl SO18 .... 80 A1
Elcombes Cl SO43 .... 121 F3
Elder Cl Locks Heath SO31 ...... 128 C1
Marchwood SO40 .... 102 A1
Winchester SO22 .... 10 B2
Elder Gn SO21 .... 57 D4
Elder Rd PO9 .... 136 A2
Elderberry Cl PO8 .... 88 B2
Elderberry La PO8 .... 207 F3
Elderberry Way PO8 .... 112 B2
Elderfield Cl PO10 .... 137 D2
Elderfield Rd PO9 .... 135 E4
Eldon Ave BH25 .... 209 F4
Eldon Cl BH25 .... 209 F4
Eldon Ct 9 Poole BH14 .... 203 D2
48 Portsmouth PO5 .... 182 B2
Eldon House 22 SO14 .... 103 D2
Eldon Pl BH4 .... 204 A2
Eldon Rd Bournemouth BH9 .... 189 F1
Braishfield SO20, SO51 .... 7 D3
King's Somborne SO20 .... 7 D3
Eldon St PO5 .... 182 B2
Eldridge Gdns SO51 .... 52 C4
Eleanor Dr BH11 .... 188 B3
Electron Way SO53 .... 55 E3
Elettra Ave PO7 .... 134 B4
Eleven Cross SP6 .... 68 A3
Elfin Cl SO17 .... 103 D4
Elfin Dr BH22 .... 165 E4
Elgar Cl Gosport PO12 .... 181 D1
Portchester PO6 .... 156 C4
Southampton SO19 .... 104 B2
Elgar Ct SO41 .... 197 F2
Elgar Rd Bournemouth BH10 ... 189 E2
Southampton SO19 .... 104 B2
Elgar Wlk PO7 .... 134 C3
Elgin Cl Fareham PO15 .... 130 C1
Hythe SO45 .... 126 A2
Elgin Rd
Bournemouth BH2, BH4 .... 204 B3
Cosham PO6 .... 157 F3
Poole BH14 .... 203 E1
Southampton SO15 .... 102 B3
Eling Cl SO22 .... 1 B2
Eling Hill SO40 .... 101 D3
Eling Inf Sch SO40 .... 101 D3
Eling La SO40 .... 101 D3
Eling Mus SO40 .... 101 D3
Eling Tide Mill SO40 .... 101 D3

Eling View SO15 .... 101 E4
Elingfield Ct SO40 .... 101 D4
Eliot House
14 New Milton BH25 .... 195 D1
Southampton SO17 .... 79 E1
Elise Cl BH7 .... 206 A4
Eliza Pl PO12 .... 181 E3
Elizabeth Ave BH23 .... 206 C4
Elizabeth Cl Downton SP5 .... 46 B4
West End SO30 .... 80 B1
Wickham PO17 .... 107 F2
Elizabeth Cres SO41 .... 196 A1
Elizabeth Ct
12 Bournemouth BH1 .... 205 D2
6 Cosham PO6 .... 157 F4
Eastleigh SO50 .... 56 A2
Fareham PO14 .... 154 C4
6 Gosport PO12 .... 181 D3
11 New Milton BH25 .... 195 D1
Southampton, Aldermoor SO16 .. 78 A2
Southampton, Portswood SO17 .. 79 E1
West End SO30 .... 80 B1
Elizabeth Gdns
Christchurch BH23 .... 208 B4
Hythe SO45 .... 126 A1
Portsmouth PO4 .... 182 C1
Elizabeth House SO40 .... 76 B1
Elizabeth Rd Poole BH15 .. 202 B2
Stubbington SO14 .... 179 E3
Upton BH16 .... 201 E4
Waterlooville PO7 .... 134 C3
Wickham PO17 .... 108 A2
Wimborne Minster BH21 .. 163 E3
Elizabeth Way
Bishop's Waltham SO32 .. 83 D4
Eastleigh SO50 .... 56 A3
Elkhams Cl SO41 .... 196 B1
Elkstone Rd PO6 .... 133 D2
Ellachie Gdns PO12 .... 181 D1
Ellachie Mews PO12 .... 181 D1
Ellachie Rd PO12 .... 181 D1
Elland Cl SO50 .... 57 E1
Elldene Ct SO40 .... 100 C3
Ellen Gdns SO50 .... 55 D3
Ellen Wren House SO18 .. 79 F2
Ellerslie Cl PO14 .... 179 D3
Ellery Gr SO41 .... 197 F3
Ellesfield Dr BH22 .... 165 E1
Ellesmere Orch PO10 .. 137 D3
Ellingham Cross BH24 .. 116 C3
Ellingham Dr BH24 .... 116 B3
Ellingham Dro BH24 .... 117 D3
Ellingham Rd BH25 .... 209 E4
Elliot Cl SO40 .... 100 B4
Elliot Rd BH11 .... 188 C2
Elliot Rise SO30 .... 81 E1
Ellis Rd SO19 .... 104 C3
Ellisfield Rd PO9 .... 135 F2
Ellwood Ave SO19 .... 104 C3
Ellwood Cl SO19 .... 104 C3
Elm Ave Christchurch BH23 .. 191 F1
Lymington SO41 .... 197 E1
New Milton BH25 .... 195 D1
Elm Cl SO16 .... 78 C2
Elm Close Est PO11 .... 184 C2
Elm Cotts **8** BH24 .... 141 D4
Uppham SO32 .... 58 C3
Elm Ct Chandler's Ford SO53 .. 30 B1
4 New Milton BH25 .... 195 D1
Southampton, Sholing SO19 .. 103 F2
29 Southampton, Westwood Pk
SO17 .... 79 D1
Winchester SO22 .... 10 C4
Elm Gdns Bournemouth BH4 .. 204 B3
West End SO30 .... 80 B2
Elm Gr Eastleigh SO50 .... 55 F1
Gosport PO12 .... 181 D3
Portsmouth PO5 .... 182 B2
South Hayling PO11 .... 185 D2
Elm La PO9 .... 135 F1
Elm Park Rd PO9 .... 135 F1
Elm Rd Bishop's Waltham SO32 .. 83 F4
Havant PO9 .... 160 A4
Winchester SO22 .... 10 C4
Elm St Portsmouth PO1 .... 182 A2
Southampton SO14 .... 103 D2
Elm Terr Liss GU33 .... 20 C3
Southampton SO14 .... 103 D2
Elm Tree Wlk BH22 .... 189 F4
Elmdale GU31 .... 41 D2
Elmdale Ct SO31 .... 152 B4
Elmdale Gr SO51 .... 51 D1
Elmers Way BH23 .... 169 D1
Elmes Dr SO15 .... 101 F4
Elmes Rd BH9 .... 189 F1
Elmeswelle Rd PO8 .... 112 A4
Elmfield Cl SP5 .... 47 E3
Elmfield La SO45 .... 178 C4
Elmgate Dr BH7 .... 206 A4
Elmhurst Rd
Bournemouth BH11 .... 189 D3
Fareham PO16 .... 155 D4
Gosport PO12 .... 181 D2
West Moors BH22 .... 138 C1
Elmhurst Way BH22 .... 138 C1
Elmleigh Rd PO9 .... 135 F1
Elmore Ave PO13 .... 180 A3
Elmore Cl PO13 .... 179 F1
Elmore Dr BH24 .... 139 F3
Elmore Rd PO13 .... 179 F1
Elmrise Prim Sch BH11 .. 189 D2
Elms Ave BH14 .... 203 D1
Elms Cl Fordingbridge SP6 .. 69 D1
Poole BH14 .... 203 D1

Elms Rd PO16 .... 155 D4
Elms Way BH6 .... 206 C2
Elmsdown Ct BH24 .... 140 C4
Elmsleigh Ct SO17 .... 79 D2
Elmsleigh Gdns SO16 .... 79 D2
Elmslie Gdns SO31 .... 104 C1
Elmstead Rd BH13 .... 214 C4
Elmtree Cl SO40 .... 100 A1
Elmtree Gdns **2** Eastleigh SO50 56 A1
Romsey SO51 .... 53 E3
Elmtree Rd PO6 .... 158 C4
Elmwood Ave Fordingbridge SP6 69 E1
Waterlooville PO7 .... 134 C3
Elmwood Ct SO16 .... 78 A1
Elmwood Lodge **2** PO16 .. 131 D1
Elmwood Rd PO2 .... 157 F2
Elmwood Way BH23 .... 209 D4
Elphinstone Rd
Christchurch BH23 .... 194 A1
Portsmouth PO5 .... 182 B1
Elsfred Rd PO14 .... 179 D3
Elson Inf Sch PO12 .... 181 D4
Elson Jun Sch PO12 .... 181 D4
Elson La PO12 .... 181 D4
Elson Rd PO12 .... 181 D4
Elstead Gdns PO7 .... 134 B2
Elstree Rd SO19 .... 103 F3
Eltham Cl BH7 .... 206 A4
Elvin Cl SO41 .... 195 F2
Elwell Gn PO11 .... 184 C2
Elwyn Rd BH1 .... 205 E3
Ely Cl PO13 .... 180 B3
Elysium St BH22 .... 165 F2
Emanuel St PO2 .... 182 B4
Embankment Way BH24 .. 141 D3
Embassy Ct **8** PO4 .... 182 C2
Emberley Ct BH22 .... 166 A3
Embley Cl SO40 .... 76 B1
Embley La SO51 .... 51 F4
Embley Park Ind Est SO51 .. 51 F1
Embley Park Jun Sch SO51 .. 52 C4
Embley Park Sch SO51 .... 51 F3
Embsay Rd SO31 .... 128 B4
Emer Cl SO52 .... 54 A3
Emerald Cl Southampton SO19 .. 104 A3
Waterlooville PO7 .... 135 D4
Emerson Cl BH15 .... 202 B1
Emerson Rd BH15 .... 202 B1
Emily Cl BH23 .... 192 A1
Emmanuel Cl PO14 .... 154 C4
Emmanuel Mid Sch BH31 .. 114 C3
Emmett Rd SO16 .... 77 F3
Emmons Cl SO31 .... 128 A1
Empire Ct **12** PO9 .... 135 F1
Empress Pk SO14 .... 103 D4
Empress Rd
Lyndhurst SO43 .... 121 F3
Southampton, Bevois
Valley SO14 .... 103 D4
Southampton, Old Docks SO14 .. 103 D1
Empshott Rd PO4 .... 182 C2
Empson Wlk PO13 .... 179 F2
Emsbrook Dr PO10 .... 136 C1
Emsworth Common Rd PO10 .136 C3
Emsworth House Cl PO10 .. 136 C1
Emsworth Prim Sch PO10 .. 136 C1
Emsworth Rd Havant PO9 .. 136 A1
Lymington SO41 .... 197 F2
Portsmouth PO2 .... 157 F1
Southampton SO15 .... 102 A4
Thorney Island PO10 .... 161 D1
Emsworth Sta PO10 .... 136 C1
Encombe Cl BH12 .... 203 F4
Endeavour Cl **17** SO15 .... 102 A4
Endeavour Rd PO12 .... 181 E2
Endeavour Way SO45 .... 126 A3
Enderleigh House PO9 .. 135 F1
Enderwood Cl SO40 .... 100 A4
Endfield Cl BH23 .... 191 F1
Endfield Rd Bournemouth BH9 .. 190 A1
Christchurch BH23 .... 191 F1
Endle St SO14 .... 103 D2
Endofield Cl PO14 .... 154 C3
Enfield Cres BH15 .... 202 C3
Enfield Gr SO19 .... 103 F2
Enfield Rd BH15 .... 202 C3
Englands Way BH11 .... 188 B2
Englefield Rd SO18 .... 103 E4
English Cl **18** SO51 .... 52 C4
English Rd SO15 .... 102 A4
Enmill La SO22 .... 9 F3
Ennel Copse SO52 .... 54 A2
Ennerdale Cl PO8 .... 88 B1
Ennerdale Gdns SO18 .... 80 A1
Ennerdale Rd
Southampton SO16 .... 77 F1
Stubbington PO14 .... 154 B2
Ensbury Ave BH10 .... 189 E1
Ensbury Cl BH10 .... 189 E1
Ensbury Ct BH10 .... 189 F1
Ensbury Park Rd BH9 .... 189 F1
Ensign Dr PO13 .... 180 B3
Ensign Park SO31 .... 127 F1
Enterprise Cl SO31 .... 128 C1
Enterprise Ctr Fareham PO14 .. 155 D3
Portsmouth PO3 .... 158 A2
Enterprise Ind Est PO8 .. 112 B4
Enterprise Rd Chilworth SO16 .. 54 B1
Horndean PO8 .... 112 B4
Enterprise Way SO14 .... 103 D1
Eperston Rd PO8 .... 112 A3
Epiphany CE Prim Sch BH9 .. 190 A2
Epping Cl SO18 .... 80 A1
Epsom Cl SO50 .... 81 E4
Epsom Ct PO5 .... 129 E4
Epworth Rd PO2 .... 157 F1
Erasmus Pk SO23 .... 2 B1
Eric Rd PO14 .... 179 D4

Erica Cl Locks Heath SO31 .. 128 C2
Waterlooville PO8 .... 112 A2
Erica Dr BH21 .... 186 B3
Erica Way PO8 .... 112 A2
Ericksen Rd BH11 .... 189 E2
Erinbank Mansions BH1 .. 205 E2
Erpingham Rd BH12 .... 204 A3
Erskine Ct SO16 .... 77 F3
Erskine Rd SO40 .... 100 A1
Escombe Rd SO50 .... 56 B2
Escur Cl PO2 .... 157 F2
Esdaile La BH24 .... 142 C2
Esher Gr PO7 .... 111 E1
Eskdale Cl PO8 .... 88 B1
Eskdale House **16** PO6 .... 133 D1
Esmond Cl PO10 .... 160 C4
Esmonde Cl PO13 .... 179 F1
Esmonde Way BH17 .... 202 C4
Esplanade Poole BH13 .... 214 C4
Portsmouth PO4 .... 183 D1
Esplanade Gdns PO4 .... 183 E1
Esplanade The PO12 .... 181 F2
Essex Ave BH23 .... 191 F1
Essex Gr SO53 .... 55 E1
Essex Rd PO4 .... 183 D2
Esslemont Rd PO4 .... 182 C2
Estella Rd PO2 .... 182 B4
Estridge Cl SO31 .... 105 D1
Ethel Rd PO1 .... 182 C3
Ethelbert Rd PO21 .... 163 E2
Ethelburt Ave SO16 .... 79 D4
Ethelred Gdns SO40 .... 100 B3
Eton Gdns BH4 .... 204 B2
Eton Rd PO5 .... 182 C2
Ettrick Rd BH13 .... 204 A1
Eucalyptus Ave BH24 .... 140 A1
European Way SO14 .... 103 D1
Euryalus Rd PO14 .... 155 D3
Euston Gr BH24 .... 141 D3
Euston Rd PO4 .... 183 D3
Eva Allaway Ct **26** PO1 .... 182 A3
Evans Cl Bournemouth BH11 .. 188 C1
Portsmouth PO2 .... 157 D1
St Leonards BH24 .... 139 F3
Evans Rd PO4 .... 183 D2
Evans St SO14 .... 103 D2
Evelegh Rd PO6 .... 158 B4
Evelyn Cl SO32 .... 83 F2
Evelyn Cres SO15 .... 102 B4
Evelyn Rd BH9 .... 190 A1
Evening Glade BH22 .... 165 F2
Evenlode Rd SO16 .... 77 F1
Everdon La PO3 .... 158 B2
Everest Rd BH23 .... 207 F4
Everglades Ave PO8 .... 111 F2
Everglades BH22 .... 165 E4
Evergreen Rd Marchwood SO40 101 F1
Three Legged Cross BH21 .. 138 C4
Waterlooville PO7 .... 134 B4
Evergreens St Leonards BH24 .. 139 F3
Totton SO40 .... 101 D3
Evering Ave BH12 .... 188 B1
Evering Gdns BH12 .... 188 B1
Everlea Cl SO41 .... 196 B1
Everon Gdns BH25 .... 195 D1
Evershot Rd BH8 .... 190 C1
Eversleigh Rd PO4 .... 182 B4
Eversley Cres PO9 .... 135 F2
Eversley Pl SO22 .... 10 B3
Everton Rd SO41 .... 196 A1
Evesham Cl Bournemouth BH7 .. 206 A4
Southampton SO19 .... 79 D3
Evesham Ct BH13 .... 204 A1
Ewart Ct SO45 .... 126 A3
Ewart Rd PO1 .... 182 C4
Ewell Way SO40 .... 76 B1
Ewhurst Cl PO9 .... 135 E2
Exbourne Manor BH1 .. 205 E2
Exbury Cl SO50 .... 56 C1
Exbury Dr BH11 .... 188 C3
Exbury Gdns SO45 .... 177 D3
Exbury Rd Blackfield SO45 .. 150 C1
Havant PO9 .... 136 A3
Excellent Rd PO14 .... 154 C3
Excelsior Rd BH14 .... 203 E2
Exchange Rd PO1 .... 182 A3
Exeter Cl Eastleigh SO50 .. 55 F3
Emsworth PO10 .... 136 C1
Locks Heath SO31 .... 128 C2
Southampton SO18 .... 80 A1
Exeter Cres BH2 .... 204 C2
Exeter Ct
10 Christchurch BH23 .... 209 D4
Gosport PO13 .... 180 B3
Exeter La BH2 .... 204 C1
Exeter Park Mansions BH2 .. 204 C1
Exeter Park Rd BH2 .... 204 C1
Exeter Rd Bournemouth BH2 .. 204 C2
Portsmouth PO4 .... 182 C1
Southampton SO18 .... 104 A4
Exford Ave SO18 .... 104 B4
Exford Dr SO18 .... 104 B4
Exleigh Cl SO18 .... 104 A3
Exmoor Cl Swanwick PO15 .. 129 D4
Totton SO40 .... 100 A4
Exmoor Rd SO14 .... 103 D3
Exmouth Gdns SO50 .... 81 E4
Exmouth Rd Gosport PO12 .. 181 D4
Portsmouth PO5 .... 182 B1
Exmouth St SO14 .... 103 D3
Exon Cl BH16 .... 201 E4
Exton Rd Bournemouth BH6 .. 206 B4
Havant PO9 .... 136 A3
Eyebright Cl SO50 .... 81 E3

Eyeworth Wlk SO45 .... 125 E2
Eynham Ave SO19 .... 104 B3
Eynham Cl SO19 .... 104 B3
Eynon Mews BH24 .... 140 C3
Eyre Cl SO40 .... 100 B3
Fair Field SO51 .... 28 A1
Fair Gr SO19 .... 104 A3
Fair Isle Cl PO14 .... 154 A2
Fair Lea BH2 .... 204 C1
Fair Oak Ct **4** Fair Oak SO50 .. 57 E1
Gosport PO12 .... 180 B2
Fair Oak Dr PO9 .... 135 F2
Fair Oak Cty Jun Sch SO50 .. 57 E1
Fair Oak Inf Sch SO50 .... 57 E1
Fairacre Rise PO14 .... 154 A4
Fairacre Wlk PO14 .... 154 A4
Fairbourne Cl PO8 .... 111 F1
Fairclose Dr SO22 .... 1 A3
Faircourt **18** BH25 .... 195 D2
Faircross Cl SO45 .... 150 B2
Fairdown Cl SO23 .... 11 E4
Fairfax Cl SO22 .... 10 A3
Fairfax Ct SO19 .... 104 C3
Fairfax Mews SO19 .... 104 C3
Fairfield Ave PO14 .... 154 C4
Fairfield Cl Christchurch BH23 . 207 D4
Hythe SO45 .... 125 F2
Lymington SO41 .... 197 F2
Wimborne Minster BH21 .. 163 F3
Fairfield Inf Sch PO9 .... 136 A1
Fairfield Rd
Barton on Sea BH25 .... 209 F4
Compton(Hants) SO21 .... 31 E3
Havant PO9 .... 135 F1
Wimborne Minster BH21 .. 163 E2
Winchester SO21, SO22 .... 1 C1
Fairfield Sq PO6 .... 157 F4
Fairgate Ctr The SP6 .... 70 A2
Fairhavon Ct **12** BH5 .... 205 F2
Fairhome Cl PO12 .... 181 D4
Fairisle Inf Sch SO16 .... 77 F3
Fairisle Jun Sch SO16 .... 77 F3
Fairisle Rd SO16 .... 77 F2
Fairlands Montessori Sch
SO32 .... 107 F4
Fairlawn Cl SO16 .... 77 F3
Fairlawn House **19** SO22 .... 10 C4
Fairlea Grange SO16 .... 78 C2
Fairlea Rd Emsworth PO10 .. 136 C2
Lymington SO41 .... 197 F3
Fairlead Dr PO13 .... 180 B3
Fairlie BH24 .... 117 E1
Fairlie Cl SO30 .... 81 E2
Fairlie Pk BH24 .... 117 D1
Fairlight La SO41 .... 195 E4
Fairmead Ct PO11 .... 184 C2
Fairmead Way SO40 .... 100 C3
Fairmead Wlk PO8 .... 112 A2
Fairmile Par BH23 .... 191 F1
Fairmile Rd BH23 .... 191 F1
Fairoak Rd Bishopstoke SO50 .. 57 D1
Fair Oak SO50 .... 57 D1
Fairthorn Ct **2** BH2 .... 204 C2
Fairthorne Gdns PO12 .... 181 D2
Fairview Cl Hythe SO45 .... 126 A2
Romsey SO51 .... 28 A1
Fairview Cres BH18 .... 187 D3
Fairview Ct PO12 .... 180 C2
Fairview Dr Broadstone BH18 .. 187 D3
Hythe SO45 .... 126 A2
Romsey SO51 .... 28 A1
Fairview Par BH25 .... 126 A1
Fairview Pk BH14 .... 203 E2
Fairview Rd BH18 .... 187 D3
Fairwater Cl PO13 .... 155 D1
Fairway Ave PO14 .... 214 B4
Fairway Bsns Ctr PO3 .... 158 B1
Fairway Dr BH23 .... 206 C3
Fairway Gdns SO16 .... 77 F3
Fairway Rd SO45 .... 125 F2
Fairway The
Barton on Sea BH25 .... 210 A4
Gosport PO13 .... 155 E1
Portchester PO16 .... 156 B4
Rowland's Castle PO9 .... 113 E1
Fairways PO12 .... 165 F3
Fairwinds BH13 .... 214 A2
Fairwood Rd BH31 .... 115 E3
Fairy Cross Way PO8 .... 112 A1
Falaise Rd SO16 .... 78 B2
Falcon Cl PO16 .... 155 F4
Falcon Dr BH23 .... 208 A3
Falcon Gr PO3 .... 158 C4
Falcon Rd PO8 .... 112 A4
Falcon Sq SO50 .... 55 F1
Falcon View SO22 .... 10 B2
Falcon Way SO32 .... 81 F1
Falconer Ct SO45 .... 150 B3
Falconer Dr BH15 .... 201 F2
Falkland Ct SO53 .... 55 E2
Falkland Rd
Chandler's Ford SO53 .... 55 E2
Southampton SO15 .... 102 A4
Falklands Cl PO13 .... 179 F2
Falklands Rd **1** PO2 .... 157 F2
Fallow Field SO22 .... 10 B2

Fallows The BH25 .... 195 D3
Falstaff Way SO40 .... 100 C3
Fancy Rd BH12 .... 203 D4
Fanshawe St SO14 .... 103 D3
Far Ends **18** BH14 .... 203 D2
Far Meadow Way PO10 .. 160 B4
Farcroft Rd BH12 .... 203 D3
Fareham Coll PO14 .... 130 C1
Fareham House **38** PO1 .. 182 B3
Fareham Hts PO16 .... 131 E2
Fareham Ind Pk PO16 .... 131 E2
Fareham Park CE Jun Sch
PO15 .... 130 B2
Fareham Park Inf Sch PO15 .. 130 B2
Fareham Park Rd PO15 .... 130 B2
Fareham Rd Gosport PO13 .. 155 E2
Southwick PO17 .... 132 C3
Wickham PO17 .... 108 A2
Fareham Sta PO16 .... 130 C1
Faringdon Ct **18** SO23 .... 2 A1
Faringdon Rd SO18 .... 104 B4
Farleigh Cl PO9 .... 135 E3
Farley Cl Fair Oak SO50 .... 57 E1
Winchester SO22 .... 10 A2
Farley Ct SO15 .... 78 B1
Farley La SO51 .... 8 B1
Farley Mount Ctry Pk SO21 .. 8 B4
Farley Mount Rd SO21 .... 9 D2
Farlington Ave PO6 .... 134 B1
Farlington Marshes (Nature
Reserve) PO6 .... 158 C3
Farlington Rd PO2 .... 157 F1
Farm Cl Hamble-le-Rice SO31 .. 128 A1
Ringwood BH24 .... 141 D4
Farm Edge Rd PO14 .... 179 E3
Farm La Christchurch BH23 .. 208 A3
Southbourne PO18 .... 161 F4
Farm La (N) BH25 .... 210 A4
Farm La S BH25 .... 210 A4
Farm Rd Titchfield PO15 .... 129 F1
West Moors BH22 .... 138 B1
Farm View PO10 .... 136 C2
Farm View Ave PO8 .... 88 A3
Farmdene Cl BH23 .... 208 B4
Farmers Wlk Hordle SO41 .. 211 E4
1 Wimborne Minster BH21 .. 163 D3
Farmery Cl SO18 .... 79 E2
Farmhouse Way PO8 .... 112 A3
Farmlea Rd PO6 .... 157 D4
Farmside Gdns PO3 .... 157 F2
Farnham Rd Liss GU33 .... 20 C2
Poole BH14 .... 204 A4
Steep GU32 .... 41 D4
Farnleys Mead SO41 .... 197 E1
Faroes Cl PO14 .... 154 A2
Farrier Way PO16 .... 155 D3
Farriers Cl BH21 .... 164 A3
Farriers Way PO7 .... 112 B1
Farriers Wlk PO12 .... 181 E3
Farringdon Rd PO9 .... 136 A2
Farringford Rd SO19 .... 104 B3
Farrington BH4 .... 204 B1
Farthing La PO1 .... 182 A2
Farthings Gate PO7 .... 134 C2
Farwell Cl BH23 .... 192 B2
Farwell Rd BH12 .... 188 B1
Fastnet Cl SO16 .... 77 F3
Fastnet House **13** PO5 .... 182 B1
Fastnet Way PO14 .... 154 A2
Fathersfield SO42 .... 145 F1
Fathoms Reach PO11 .... 184 C2
Faulston Cotts SP5 .... 22 B4
Faversham BH2 .... 204 B1
Fawcett Rd
Barton on Sea BH25 .... 194 C1
Portsmouth PO4 .... 182 C2
Fawley Bsns Ctr SO45 .... 151 D2
Fawley By Pass SO45 .... 151 D2
Fawley Cl BH8 .... 190 B2
Fawley Gr BH8 .... 190 B2
Fawley Inf Sch SO45 .... 151 D2
Fawley La Froxfield GU34 .... 17 D2
Owslebury SO21 .... 33 D4
Fawley Rd Fawley SO45 .... 150 C2
Hythe SO45 .... 150 A4
Portsmouth PO2 .... 157 F3
Southampton SO15 .... 102 A3
Fawn Gdns BH25 .... 194 C2
Fay Cl PO14 .... 179 E3
Fayre La PO16 .... 155 D4
Fayrewood Ct BH31 .... 114 C4
Fearon Rd PO2 .... 157 F1
Felix Rd PO12 .... 181 D4
Fell Cl SO31 .... 129 D2
Fell Dr PO13 .... 179 F2
Felmer Dr SO23 .... 2 B4
Feltham Cl SO51 .... 53 E4
Felton Cres BH23 .... 208 C4
Felton Ct BH14 .... 202 C3
Felton Rd BH14 .... 202 C3
Feltons Pl PO3 .... 157 F3
Fen Ave PO16 .... 155 D4
Fenleigh Cl BH25 .... 195 D1
Fennel Gdns SO41 .... 197 E3
Fennell Cl PO7 .... 111 E1
Fenton Rd BH6 .... 206 B3
Fenwick Ct BH8 .... 205 D3
Fenwick Hospl SO43 .... 121 F3
Fern Bank **28** BH2 .... 204 C4
Fern Barrow BH12 .... 204 A4
Fern Cl Alderholt SP6 .... 93 D3
Burton BH23 .... 192 B1
Petersfield GU31 .... 41 E2
Fern Cotts **2** PO16 .... 131 E2
Fern Ct SO18 .... 103 F4
Fern Rd Hythe SO45 .... 125 D2
Southampton SO19 .... 103 F1
Fern Way PO15 .... 129 E2

Ferncroft Cl PO14 179 E3
Ferncroft Gdns BH10 189 E3
Ferncroft Rd BH10 189 E3
Ferndale Hedge End SO30 105 E3
Waterlooville PO7 135 D4
Ferndale Mews PO13 155 D2
Ferndale Rd Marchwood SO40 101 F1
New Milton BH25 195 D3
Ferndene Way SO18 103 F4
Ferndown Ct SP6 69 E1
Ferndown Fst Sch BH22 165 E3
Ferndown Ind Est BH21 164 C4
Ferndown Mid Sch BH22 165 E3
Ferndown Upper Sch BH22 165 D3
Ferneham Rd PO15 130 B1
Fernglade BH25 195 D2
Fernheath Cl BH11 189 D2
Fernheath Rd BH11 189 D2
Fernhill SO53 55 F3
Fernhill Cl BH17 188 A1
Fernhill Flats 29 BH2 204 C2
Fernhill Gate BH25 195 D3
Fernhill La BH25 195 D2
Fernhill Rd BH25 195 D2
Fernhills Rd SO45 126 A1
Fernhurst Cl PO11 184 B2
Fernhurst Jun Sch PO4 182 C2
Fernhurst Rd PO4 182 C2
Fernie Cl PO14 179 D3
Fernlea Ave BH22 165 E2
Fernlea Cl Ferndown BH22 165 E2
St Leonards BH24 139 F2
Fernlea Gdns Ferndown BH22 165 E2
Southampton SO16 78 C2
Fernlea Way SO45 125 E2
Fernside Ave BH14 202 C2
Fernside Cl Holbury SO45 150 B2
Southampton SO16 101 F4
Fernside Ct BH15 202 C2
Fernside Rd Bournemouth BH9 204 C4
Poole BH15 202 C2
West Moors BH22 138 C1
Fernside Way SO50 57 F1
Fernside Wlk SO50 57 F1
Fernway Cl BH21 164 A2
Fernwood Cl BH24 140 A3
Fernwood Cres SO18 103 F4
Ferny Crofts (Scout Ctr)
SO42 148 A4
Fernyhurst Ave SO16 77 F3
Ferris Ave BH8 190 B1
Ferris Cl BH8 190 B1
Ferris Pl BH8 190 B1
Ferrol Rd PO12 181 E3
Ferry Rd Bournemouth BH6 206 C2
Hamworthy BH15 202 A1
Hythe SO45 125 F2
Poole BH19 214 A1
Portsmouth PO4 183 E2
Portsmouth PO4 183 F2
South Hayling PO11 184 A2
Ferry Way BH13 214 A2
Ferrybridge Gr SO30 105 E3
Ferrymans Quay SO31 127 D3
Festing Gr PO4 183 D1
Festing Rd PO4 182 C1
Feversham Ave BH8 190 C1
Fey Rd PO12 181 E3
Fibbards Rd SO42 145 F1
Field Cl Compton(Hants) SO21 31 E3
Gosport PO13 155 D3
Locks Heath SO31 129 D1
Romsey SO51 53 D4
Southampton SO16 79 E3
Field End SO23 2 B4
Field Pl BH25 209 E4
Field View SO52 54 C3
Field Way Christchurch BH23 193 E1
Compton(Hants) SO21 31 E3
Corfe Mullen BH21 186 C4
Denmead PO7 110 C2
Fordingbridge SP6 70 B1
Field Wlk SO41 197 E3
Fielden Cl SO52 53 F2
Fielders Ct PO7 134 B2
Fielders' Way SO51 51 D1
Fieldfare Cl PO8 88 B2
Fieldfare Ct SO40 100 B4
Fieldhouse Dr PO13 179 F2
Fieldmore Rd PO12 181 D4
Fields Cl SO45 150 C1
Fields The BH31 114 C4
Fieldway BH24 141 D4
Fifth Ave Cosham PO6 157 F4
Havant PO9 136 A1
Fifth St PO1 182 C3
Filmer Cl PO13 180 B4
Filmorehill La GU34 17 D2
Filton Cl SO40 76 B1
Filton Rd SO41 197 E2
Finch House PO4 183 D1
Finch Rd PO4 183 E2
Finch's La SO21 31 F3
Finchdean Rd Havant PO9 135 E2
Rowland's Castle PO9 113 E2
Finches The SO17 79 D1
Finchfield Ave BH11 188 C3
Finchmead La GU32 40 A2
Finchwood Farm Ind Units
PO11 160 A1
Findon Rd PO12 181 D4
Fineshade 7 BH13 214 C4
Finisterre Cl PO14 154 A2
Finlay Cl SO19 104 B2
Fiona Cl SO23 11 E4
Fir Ave BH25 195 D1
Fir Cl Lyndhurst SO43 121 F2
West Moors BH22 138 C2
Fir Copse Rd PO7 134 B2
Fir Croft Dr SO53 55 E3
Fir Rd SO40 100 A1
Fir Tree Cl Fair Oak SO50 81 E4
St Leonards BH24 139 E1
Fir Tree Ct SO18 104 A4
Fir Tree Gdns PO8 112 B3
Fir Tree Gr SO45 150 A4
Fir Tree Hill SP6 93 D3
Fir Tree La BH23 193 E1
Fir Tree Rd Cadnam SO40 99 D4
South Hayling PO11 185 D2
Fir Vale Rd BH1 204 C2
Firbank Rd BH9 205 D4
Firecrest Cl SO16 78 A3
Firgrove Cl SO52 53 F2
Firgrove Cres PO3 157 F3
Firgrove Ct SO15 102 B4
Firgrove La PO17 108 C1
Firgrove Rd
North Baddesley SO52 54 A3
Southampton SO15 102 B4
Firlands Rise PO9 135 D1
Firmain Rd BH12 188 B1
Firmount Cl SO41 196 C1
Firs Ave PO8 111 F1
Firs Cres SO23 2 A4
Firs Dr SO30 105 D3
Firs Glen Rd
Bournemouth BH9 204 C4
Verwood BH31 115 D2
West Moors BH22 138 C1
Firs La BH14 214 A4
Firs The Bournemouth BH1, 205 D2
Chandler's Ford SO53 55 E2
Gosport PO13 155 E1
Southampton SO16 78 C2
Firshill BH23 208 C4
Firside Rd BH21 186 B2
First Ave Cosham PO6 157 F4
Cosham, Farlington PO6 158 C4
Havant PO9 136 A1
Horndean PO8 88 B2
Southampton SO15 101 E4
Southbourne PO10 161 E4
First Marine Ave BH25 209 F4
First St SO45 150 C4
Firsway BH16 201 E4
Firtree Cres SO41 195 F2
Firtree La SO50 81 D4
Firtree Way SO19 104 A3
Firwood Pk (Cvn Pk) SO53 55 E4
Fisgard Rd PO12 181 D4
Fisher Cl PO14 154 A2
Fisher Rd Gosport PO13 155 E2
Portsmouth PO1 182 A2
Fisher's Rd SO40 101 D3
Fisherman's Ave BH5,BH6 206 A2
Fisherman's Wlk BH5 206 A2
Fishermans Rd BH15 202 B1
Fishermans The PO10 161 D4
Fishermans Wlk PO11 185 F1
Fishers Gr PO6 158 C4
Fishers Hill PO15 130 A1
Fishery La PO11 185 E1
Fishlake Meadows SO51 28 A1
Fitzgerald Cl PO15 129 E4
Fitzharris Ave BH9 205 D4
Fitzherbert Rd PO6 158 B4
Fitzherbert Spur PO6 158 C4
Fitzherbert St 1 PO1 182 B3
Fitzhugh House SO15 102 C3
Fitzhugh Pl SO15 102 C4
Fitzhugh St 13 SO15 102 C3
Fitzmaurice Rd BH23 206 C4
Fitzpain Cl BH22 165 E1
Fitzpain Rd BH22 165 E1
Fitzpatrick Ct PO6 133 E1
Fitzroy Cl SO16 78 C4
Fitzroy Wlk 60 PO1 182 B3
Fitzwilliam Ave PO14 179 D3
Fitzwilliam Cl BH11 188 C3
Fitzworth Ave BH16 201 E2
Fitzwygram Cres PO9 135 F2
Five Bridges Rd SO22 10 C2
Five Elms Dr SO51 53 E3
Five Heads Rd PO8 112 B4
Five Post La PO12 181 D3
Fivefields Cl SO23 11 E4
Fivefields Rd SO23 11 E4
Flag Staff Gn PO12 181 E3
Flag Wlk PO8 111 F2
Flaghead BH13 214 C3
Flaghead Chine Rd BH13 214 C3
Flaghead Rd BH13 214 C4
Flambard Ave BH23 192 A1
Flambard Rd BH14 203 E2
Flamborough Cl SO16 77 E2
Flamingo Ct PO16 155 F4
Flamston St SP5 22 A4
Flanders House 1 PO14 154 C4
Flanders Ind Pk SO30 105 D4
Flanders Rd SO30 105 D4
Flathouse Rd PO1 182 B4
Flaxfields End SP6 69 F1
Fleet Cl PO13 155 E1
Fleet End Bottom SO31 152 C4
Fleet End Rd SO31 152 C4
Fleet Terr SO50 31 D1
Fleet's Cnr BH17 202 A4
Fleetend Cl PO9 135 F3
Fleets Est BH15 202 A3
Fleets La BH15 202 B3
Fleetsbridge Bsns Ctr BH17 202 A4
Fleetsbridge Ret Pk BH17 202 A3
Fleetwood Ct BH15 202 B4
Fleming Ave SO52 54 A2
Fleming Cl PO14 129 E2
Fleming Ct
North Baddesley SO52 54 A2
Southampton SO19 103 E1
Fleming Pl
Colden Common SO21 31 F1
4 Romsey SO51 52 C4
Fleming Rd SO17 79 E2
Fletcher Cl BH10 189 E2
Fletcher Rd BH10 189 E2
Fletchwood La SO40 99 F1
Fletchwood Rd SO40 100 A3
Fleuret Cl SO45 126 A1
Flexford Cl SO53 30 A1
Flexford Gdns PO9 136 A2
Flexford La SO41 196 B3
Flexford Rd SO52 54 C4
Flinders Ct PO4 183 D1
Flint Cl SO19 104 C2
Flint St PO5 182 A2
Floating Bridge Rd SO14 103 E2
Floral Farm BH21 164 A1
Florence Cl SO51 51 D1
Florence Ct 3 SO18 103 F4
Florence Rd Bournemouth BH5 205 F2
Poole BH14 203 E2
Portsmouth PO5 182 B1
Southampton SO19 103 E1
Florentine Way PO7 135 D4
Florin Mall 7 BH7 205 F2
Florins The Locks Heath PO14 129 D1
Waterlooville PO7 134 C2
Floriston Gdns BH25 195 E2
Flower Bldgs 6 PO13 179 F1
Flower Ct 16 BH21 163 E2
Flowerdown Cl SO40 100 B4
Flowerdown House SO22 1 B2
Flowers Cl SO31 127 F2
Flowers La SO51 50 B3
Flum' E Rd SO45 151 E2
Flushards SO41 197 F2
Flying Bull Cl 3 PO2 182 B4
Flying Bull Inf Sch PO2 182 B4
Flying Bull Jun Sch PO2 182 B4
Flying Bull La PO2 182 B4
Foldsgate Cl SO43 121 F3
Folkestone Rd PO3 183 D4
Folly Farm La BH24 140 B3
Folly Field SO32 83 E4
Folly La GU32 40 C2
Font Cl PO14 129 E2
Fontley Rd PO15 130 A3
Fontmell Rd BH18 187 E2
Fontwell Cl SO40 76 B1
Fontwell Gdns SO50 81 E4
Fontwell Mews PO7 112 A1
Fontwell Rd 32 PO5 182 B1
Foord Rd SO30 105 D2
Football Gr SO43 98 B2
Footner Cl SO51 28 B1
Footners La BH23 192 B1
Forbes Cl SO16 77 F3
Forbes Rd SO23 2 A4
Forbury Rd 2 PO1 182 B2
Ford Ave SO53 55 E2
Ford Cl BH22 165 F4
Ford La BH22 166 A4
Ford Rd PO12 180 C3
Fordingbridge Hospl SP6 69 F1
Fordingbridge Inf Sch SP6 69 F2
Fordingbridge Jun Sch SP6 69 F2
Fordingbridge Rd
Alderholt SP6 93 D4
Fordingbridge SP6 93 D4
Portsmouth PO4 183 D2
Fordington Ave SO22 10 C4
Fordington Rd 3 SO22 10 C4
Foreland Cl BH23 191 E2
Foreland Ct PO11 185 E1
Foreland Rd BH16 201 E2
Forelle Ctr The BH31 115 E2
Foremans Cotts PO12 181 F1
Foreshore N SO45 151 D3
Foreshore S SO45 151 D3
Forest Ave PO8 112 A2
Forest Cl Chandler's Ford SO53 55 E4
Christchurch BH23 193 E1
North Baddesley SO52 53 F3
Shedfield SO32 83 F2
Verwood BH31 115 E2
Waterlooville PO8 111 F2
Forest Cnr GU33 21 D4
Forest Ct BH25 195 D1
Forest Edge SO45 151 D2
Forest Edge Cl BH24 139 E3
Forest Edge Dr BH24 139 E3
Forest Edge Rd BH24 141 F3
Forest Edge Sch SO40 100 C4
Forest End PO7 134 B4
Forest Front SO45 150 A4
Forest Gate SO45 177 F4
Forest Gate Gdns SO41 197 E1
Forest Gdns Lyndhurst SO43 121 F3
Shedfield SO32 83 F2
Forest Glade Cl SO42 145 E1
Forest Hall SO42 146 A1
Forest Hill Way SO45 125 F1
Forest Hills Dr SO18 79 F2
Forest La Fareham PO17 131 D4
Holbury SO45 150 A3
Ringwood BH24 141 F3
Forest Mead PO7 110 C2
Forest Meadow SO45 150 A4
Forest Park Rd SO42 145 F1
Forest Pines BH25 195 D2
Forest Rd Bransgore BH23 169 F2
Burley BH24 142 C3
Chandler's Ford SO53 55 E4
Denmead PO7 110 B2
Forest Rd Continued
Greatham GU33 20 C4
Liss GU33 21 D3
Nomansland SP5 73 E4
Poole BH13 204 A1
Redlynch SP5 47 F2
Shedfield SO32 83 F2
Swanmore SO32 83 F2
Waterlooville PO7 134 B4
West Moors BH22 138 C2
Woodgreen SP6 47 F2
Forest Rise
Christchurch BH23 193 E1
Liss GU33 21 D3
Forest View
Brockenhurst SO42 145 E1
New Milton BH25 194 B3
4 Southampton SO14 102 C2
Forest View Cl BH9 190 A1
Forest View Dr BH21 165 D3
Forest View Rd BH9 190 A1
Forest Way Christchurch BH23 193 E1
Ferndown BH21 165 D3
Gosport PO13 155 F1
Hordle SO41 196 B1
Netley Marsh SO40 76 A1
Forester Rd SO32 85 D1
Foresters Gate SO45 177 E4
Foresters Rd SO45 150 C1
Forestlake Ave BH24 141 E3
Forestside Ave PO9 136 A3
Forestside Gdns BH24 117 E1
Forestside The BH31 115 E3
Forge Cl SO31 105 D1
Forge Rd SO45 177 F4
Forneth Gdns PO15 154 A4
Forres Sandle Manor SP6 69 E1
Forster Rd SO14 103 D4
Forsyth Gdns BH10 189 E1
Forsythia Cl SO30 105 D4
Forsythia Pl SO19 103 F3
Fort Brockhurst PO12 155 F1
Fort Cumberland Pl BH15 201 E1
Fort Cumberland Rd PO4 183 E2
Fort Fareham Ind Est PO14 155 D3
Fort Fareham Rd PO14 154 C3
Fort Nelson PO16 132 A2
Fort Nelson Mus PO17 132 A2
Fort Rd Gosport PO12 181 D1
Southampton SO19 103 F2
Fort Wallington Ind Est PO16 131 E1
Fort Widley Married
Quarters PO6 133 F1
Fortescue Rd
Bournemouth BH3 205 D3
Poole BH12 203 E3
Forth Cl North Baddesley SO53 55 D3
Stubbington PO14 154 A2
Forth House 11 SO14 103 E3
Forties Cl PO14 154 A2
Forton Rd Gosport PO12 181 D3
Portsmouth PO1 182 C3
Fortune Ct SO53 55 E3
Fortune House 8 PO12 181 D3
Fortunes Way PO9 134 C1
Forum The 5 PO9 135 F1
Forward Dr SO41 197 E1
Foster Cl PO14 154 B2
Foster Rd Gosport PO12 181 D2
Portsmouth PO1 182 B3
Founders Way PO13 155 E1
Foundry Cres SO31 127 F4
Foundry Ct 36 PO1 182 A3
Foundry La SO15 102 A4
Foundry Lane Prim Sch SO15 102 A4
Foundry Rd SP5 47 E4
Fountain Ct
4 Colden Common SO21 31 F1
Hedge End SO30 105 D3
Fountain St PO1 182 B3
Fountain Way BH23 207 D3
Four Acre SO30 106 A3
Four Cnrs SP6 68 A2
Four Marks Gn 3 PO9 136 A3
Four Wells Rd BH21 164 A4
Fourposts Hill 16 SO15 102 C3
Fourshells Cl SO45 150 C1
Fourth Ave Cosham PO6 157 F4
Havant PO9 136 A1
Fourth St PO1 182 C3
Fowey Cl SO53 55 D3
Fowey The SO45 150 C1
Fowlers Rd SO30 105 D4
Fowlers Wlk SO16 54 B1
Fox Cl SO50 56 C1
Fox Field SO41 196 B1
Fox La Ferndown BH21 164 B3
Winchester SO22 10 B3
Fox Pond La SO41 197 E1
Fox's Wlk 4 SO45 177 F4
Foxbury Cl SO45 126 A1
Foxbury Gr PO16 156 A4
Foxbury La Gosport PO13 155 E2
Gosport PO13 155 F3
Westbourne PO10 137 E2
Foxbury Rd BH24 166 C4
Foxbury Special Sch The
PO13 155 E2
Foxcombe Cl SO32 84 A3
Foxcote Gdns BH25 194 C2
Foxcote House 6 PO6 132 C1
Foxcott Cl SO19 126 C4
Foxcott Gr PO9 135 F3
Foxcroft Dr Holbury SO45 150 A2
Wimborne Minster BH21 164 A3
Foxes Cl Verwood BH31 114 C3
Waterlooville PO7 134 C3
Foxes La SO51 50 C3
Foxglade 5 SO45 177 F4
Foxglove Cl BH23 208 B4
Foxglove Pl BH25 195 E2
Foxgloves Fareham PO16 131 E2
Upton BH16 201 D4
Foxgloves The SO30 105 E3
Foxhayes La SO45 177 F4
Foxhills Ashurst SO40 100 B2
Verwood BH31 115 D3
Foxhills Cl SO40 100 B2
Foxhills Inf Sch SO40 100 B2
Foxhills Jun Sch SO40 100 B2
Foxholes 1 BH6 206 C2
Foxholes Rd
Bournemouth BH6 206 C2
Poole BH15 202 C3
Foxlands 3 SO45 177 F4
Foxlea 19 SO15 102 C4
Foxlea Gdns PO12 181 D4
Foxlease Terr SO43 121 F2
Foxley Dr PO3 158 A2
Foxtail Dr SO45 125 F1
Foxwood Ave BH23 207 F3
Foxy Paddock 2 SO45 177 F4
Foy Gdns SO31 128 B1
Foyes Ct SO15 102 B3
Foyle Rd SO53 55 D3
Frampton Cl
1 Colden Common SO21 31 F1
New Milton BH25 195 E3
Frampton Pl BH24 141 D4
Frampton Rd BH9 205 D4
Frampton Way
Kings Worthy SO23 2 B4
Totton SO40 100 C3
Frances Ct 13 BH23 209 D4
Frances Rd Bournemouth BH1 205 E2
Waterlooville PO7 134 B2
Francesca Ct 14 BH23 207 F4
Francesca Grange 13 BH23 207 F4
Francesca Lodge 1 BH23 207 F3
Francis Ave Bournemouth BH11 188 B2
Portsmouth PO4 182 C2
Francis Cl PO13 180 A3
Francis Gdns SO23 2 A2
Francis Pl PO14 179 E3
Francis Rd Horndean PO8 88 B2
Poole BH12 203 F3
Franconia Dr SO16 77 D2
Frank Judd Ct 33 PO1 182 A3
Frank Miles House 16 PO5 182 B2
Frank Wareham
Cottage Homes The BH9 190 A2
Frankland Cres BH14 203 F2
Frankland Terr 3 PO10 161 D4
Franklin Rd Bournemouth BH9 190 A2
Gosport PO13 180 B4
New Milton BH25 195 E2
Twyford SO21 32 A4
Franklyn Ave SO19 104 A2
Franklyn Cl BH16 201 D4
Franks Way BH12 203 D4
Frankston Rd BH6 206 B2
Frarydene PO10 161 E4
Fraser Cl SO16 77 F3
Fraser Ct 11 BH25 194 C2
Fraser Gdns PO10 137 F1
Fraser Rd Gosport PO13 155 E2
Havant PO9 135 E1
Kings Worthy SO23 2 B4
Poole BH12 203 F4
Portsmouth PO5 182 B2
Portsmouth,Whale Is PO2 157 D1
Frater La PO12 156 A1
Fratton Ct PO1 182 C3
Fratton Ind Est PO4 183 D3
Fratton Park
Portsmouth FC PO4 183 D3
Fratton Rd PO1 182 C3
Fratton Sta PO1 182 C3
Fratton Way SO50 57 E1
Frayslea SO45 126 A1
Freda Rd BH23 206 C3
Freda Routh Gdns 12 SO50 57 E1
Frederica Rd BH9 204 C4
Frederick St
5 Portsmouth PO1 182 B3
Southampton SO14 103 D3
Free St SO32 83 E4
Freedom Ct SO45 126 A2
Freefolk Gn 23 PO9 136 A3
Freegrounds Ave SO30 105 E3
Freegrounds Cl SO30 105 E3
Freegrounds Cty Inf Sch SO30 105 E3
Freegrounds Jun Sch SO30 105 E3
Freegrounds Rd SO30 105 E3
Freemans Cl BH21 164 A3
Freemans La BH21 164 A3
Freemantle Bsns Ctr 12 SO15 102 B3
Freemantle CE Inf Sch SO15 102 B3
Freemantle Cl SO19 103 F3
Freemantle Common Rd
SO19 103 F3
Freemantle Rd PO12 181 D4
Freestone Rd 38 PO5 182 B1
Fremington Ct 16 BH25 195 D2
French Rd BH17 187 D1
French St Portsmouth PO1 182 A2
Southampton SO14 102 C2
French's Farm Rd BH16 201 D4
Frenches La SO51 51 E4
Frenchmans Rd GU32 40 C2
Frenchmoor La East Dean SP5 3 F1
West Tytherley SP5 3 F2
Frendstaple Rd PO7 135 D3

Frensham Cl
Bournemouth BH10 ..... 189 F2
Hedge End SO30 ..... 105 E3
Frensham Ct Hedge End SO30 .. 105 E3
Portsmouth PO4 ..... 182 C2
Frensham Rd PO4 ..... 182 C2
Freshfield Gdns PO7 ..... 134 C4
Freshfield Rd SO15 ..... 102 A4
Freshfield Sq SO15 ..... 102 A4
Freshwater Ct
Chandler's Ford SO53 ..... 30 C1
2 Lee-on-the-Solent PO13 ..... 179 F1
Freshwater Dr BH15 ..... 201 E2
Freshwater Rd
Christchurch BH23 ..... 208 B3
Cosham PO6 ..... 157 F4
Frewen Liby PO1 ..... 182 A2
Friars Croft SO40 ..... 76 B1
Friars Gate BH23 ..... 208 B3
Friars Pond Rd PO15 ..... 130 B1
Friars Rd Christchurch BH23 ..... 208 A3
Eastleigh SO50 ..... 55 F1
Friars Way SO18 ..... 79 E2
Friars Wlk BH25 ..... 210 A4
Friarscroft SO31 ..... 127 D4
Friarsgate SO23 ..... 11 D4
Friary Cl 31 PO5 ..... 182 B1
Friary The 30 PO5 ..... 182 B1
Friday's Ct BH24 ..... 140 C4
Friendly Societies' Homes
PO4 ..... 183 D2
Frinton Ct 6 BH14 ..... 203 D2
Frith La SO17 ..... 108 A4
Frith Lane End PO17 ..... 108 A4
Fritham Cl SO40 ..... 100 B4
Fritham Gdns BH8 ..... 190 B2
Fritham Rd SO18 ..... 104 B4
Frobisher Ave BH12 ..... 188 C1
Frobisher Cl
Christchurch BH23 ..... 207 F3
Gosport PO13 ..... 180 B3
Ringwood BH24 ..... 117 E1
Frobisher Ct SO40 ..... 102 A2
Frobisher Gdns
7 Emsworth PO10 ..... 160 C1
Southampton SO19 ..... 104 B2
Frobisher Gr PO16 ..... 156 B4
Frobisher Gr 9 PO1 ..... 182 A3
Froddington Rd PO1 ..... 182 B2
Frog La SP6 ..... 93 F4
Froghall SO45 ..... 126 A1
Frogham Gn PO9 ..... 135 E3
Frogham Hill SP6 ..... 94 B3
Frogmore PO14 ..... 154 B4
Frogmore La Horndean PO8 ..... 112 A3
Nursling SO16 ..... 77 E2
Waterlooville PO8 ..... 112 A3
Frogmore Rd PO4 ..... 183 D2
Frome Cl SO40 ..... 102 A1
Fromond Cl SO41 ..... 197 F3
Fromond Rd SO22 ..... 1 B2
Front Lawn Inf Sch PO9 ..... 135 F3
Front Lawn Jun Sch PO9 ..... 135 F3
Frost La SO45 ..... 126 A1
Frost Rd BH11 ..... 188 C2
Frosthole Cl PO15 ..... 130 C2
Frosthole Cres PO15 ..... 130 C2
Froud Way BH21 ..... 186 B2
Froude Ave PO12 ..... 181 E1
Froude Rd PO12 ..... 181 E1
Froxfield CE Inf Sch GU32 ..... 18 C1
Froxfield Cl SO22 ..... 1 B2
Froxfield Gdns PO16 ..... 132 B1
Froxfield Rd PO9 ..... 136 A3
Froyle Cl 54 PO9 ..... 136 A3
Fry Cl Blackfield SO45 ..... 150 C1
Hamble-le-Rice SO31 ..... 128 A2
Fry's La 2 ..... 61 E2
Fryer Cl BH11 ..... 189 D3
Fryern Arc SO53 ..... 55 F4
Fryern Cl SO53 ..... 55 F3
Fryern Court Rd SP6 ..... 69 F3
Fryern Inf Sch SO53 ..... 55 F3
Fryern Jun Sch SO53 ..... 55 F3
Fryers Copse BH21 ..... 164 B3
Fryers Rd BH21 ..... 138 B4
Frys La SO41 ..... 196 B1
Fuchsia Gdns SO16 ..... 78 B1
Fulflood Ct 2 SO22 ..... 10 C1
Fulflood Rd PO9 ..... 135 F3
Fullerton Cl Havant PO9 ..... 136 A3
Southampton SO19 ..... 126 C4
Fullerton Rd SO41 ..... 197 E2
Fulmar Cl SO16 ..... 78 A3
Fulmar Dr BH23 ..... 126 A1
Fulmar Rd BH23 ..... 208 A3
Fulmar Wlk PO13 ..... 155 D2
Fulmer Wlk PO8 ..... 111 F2
Fulwood Ave BH11 ..... 188 C3
Funtington Rd PO2 ..... 182 C4
Funtley Ct PO16 ..... 130 C2
Funtley Hill PO16 ..... 130 C2
Funtley La PO17 ..... 130 C3
Funtley Rd PO15, PO17 ..... 130 C3
Furdies PO7 ..... 110 C2
Furley Cl SO23 ..... 11 D4
Furlong Mews BH24 ..... 140 C4
Furlong The BH24 ..... 140 C4
Furlonge House PO10 ..... 136 C1
Furneaux Gdns PO16 ..... 131 D2
Furnell Rd PO5 ..... 182 B1
Furness Rd 11 PO5 ..... 182 B1
Furniss Way PO11 ..... 184 B2
Furston Gr PO10 ..... 137 F1
Fury Way PO14 ..... 154 A2

Furze Cl SO19 ..... 104 A3
Furze Croft BH25 ..... 195 D1
Furze Hall PO16 ..... 131 D2
Furze Hill Dr BH14 ..... 203 E1
Furze La PO4 ..... 183 E2
Furze Rd SO19 ..... 104 A3
Furze Way PO4 ..... 112 A2
Furzebrook Cl BH17 ..... 187 F2
Furzedale Gdns SO45 ..... 126 A1
Furzedale Park SO45 ..... 126 A1
Furzedown Cotts SO20 ..... 7 D4
Furzedown Cres 31 PO9 ..... 136 A3
Furzedown House SO20 ..... 7 D3
Furzedown Mews SO45 ..... 126 A1
Furzedown Rd
King's Somborne SO20 ..... 7 D4
Southampton SO17 ..... 79 D1
Furzehall Ave PO16 ..... 131 D2
Furzehill BH21 ..... 163 E4
Furzelands Rd BH21 ..... 138 C4
Furzeley Rd PO7 ..... 110 C1
Furzey Ave SO45 ..... 126 A1
Furzey Cl SO45 ..... 150 C1
Furzey Gdns SO43 ..... 98 A2
Furzley Ct PO9 ..... 135 E3
Furzley La SO51 ..... 74 B3
Furzley Rd SO51, SO40 ..... 74 C2
Furzy Whistlers Cl BH23 ..... 169 D1
Futcher Sch PO6 ..... 158 B4
Fyeford Cl SO16 ..... 77 F3
Fyning St PO1 ..... 182 B3

G Ave SO45 ..... 150 C3
Gables Ct SO16 ..... 78 C3
Gage Cl SO40 ..... 102 A1
Gain's Rd PO4 ..... 182 C1
Gainsborough Ave BH25 ..... 195 D3
Gainsborough Cl SO19 ..... 104 B1
Gainsborough Ct
11 Bournemouth BH5 ..... 206 A3
Lymington SO41 ..... 197 E1
North Baddesley SO52 ..... 54 A2
Gainsborough Mews PO14 ..... 153 F4
Gainsborough Rd
Bournemouth BH7 ..... 205 F4
St Leonards BH24 ..... 139 F3
Gainsford Rd SO19 ..... 103 F3
Galaxie Rd PO8 ..... 112 A2
Gale Moor Ave PO12 ..... 180 B2
Galleon Cl SO31 ..... 128 C1
Gallia Ct SO15 ..... 78 C1
Gallop Way BH12 ..... 204 B4
Gallops The PO14 ..... 129 E1
Galloway Rd BH15 ..... 201 E2
Gallows Dr BH22 ..... 165 F1
Galsworthy Rd SO40 ..... 100 B4
Galt Rd PO6 ..... 158 B4
Galton Ave BH23 ..... 206 C3
Gamble Cl SO19 ..... 103 F2
Gamble Rd PO2 ..... 182 B4
Gamblins La SO32 ..... 107 F4
Gang Warily Recn Ctr SO45 ..... 150 C2
Ganger Farm La SO51 ..... 28 B1
Ganger Rd SO51 ..... 28 B1
Gannet Cl Hythe SO45 ..... 126 A1
Southampton SO16 ..... 78 A3
Gannets The PO14 ..... 154 A2
Gar St SO22 ..... 10 C4
Garage Cotts 2 GU32 ..... 40 C2
Garbett Rd SO23 ..... 11 E4
Garden City SO45 ..... 125 D3
Garden Cl Lyndhurst SO43 ..... 121 F3
New Milton BH25 ..... 195 D1
South Hayling PO11 ..... 184 C1
Garden Court Cotts BH12 ..... 138 B2
Garden Ct Bournemouth BH1 ..... 205 D4
Porchester PO16 ..... 156 B4
Garden House 17 BH1 ..... 205 D2
Garden La Portsmouth PO5 ..... 182 B2
St Leonards BH24 ..... 139 F2
15 Winchester SO23 ..... 11 D4
Garden Mews SO31 ..... 128 B1
Garden Rd BH24 ..... 142 C2
Garden Terr 5 PO5 ..... 182 B1
Garden Wlk BH22 ..... 165 F4
Gardeners Cotts BH24 ..... 141 D2
Gardeners La Awbridge SO51 ..... 52 A2
Romsey SO51 ..... 52 A2
Gardens Cres BH14 ..... 214 A4
Gardens Ct 8 BH15 ..... 202 C2
Gardens The Hambledon PO7 ..... 86 B2
Havant PO9 ..... 136 A1
Gardiner Ct SO40 ..... 102 A1
Gardner Ct BH23 ..... 206 C4
Gardner Rd Christchurch BH23 ..... 206 C4
Ringwood BH24 ..... 141 D3
Titchfield PO14 ..... 153 F4
Garendon Ct SP6 ..... 69 F1
Garfield Ave BH1 ..... 205 E3
Garfield Cl SO32 ..... 83 E4
Garfield Rd
Bishop's Waltham SO32 ..... 83 E4
1 Netley SO31 ..... 127 D3
Portsmouth PO2 ..... 182 B4
Southampton SO19 ..... 103 F4
Waterlooville PO7 ..... 135 D4
Garland Ave PO10 ..... 136 C2
Garland Ct 18 PO12 ..... 181 D3
Garland Rd BH15 ..... 202 B2
Garnett Cl PO14 ..... 154 B2
Garnier Pk PO17 ..... 108 A2
Garnier Rd SO23 ..... 11 D3
Garnier St PO1 ..... 182 C3
Garnock Rd SO19 ..... 103 E1
Garratt Cl SO30 ..... 105 E2
Garrett Cl SO19 ..... 104 A1

Garrick Gdns SO19 ..... 104 A1
Garrick House 11 PO2 ..... 157 F2
Garrison Hill SO32 ..... 61 D1
Garrow Dr SO41 ..... 197 F3
Garsdale Cl BH11 ..... 189 D3
Garsons Rd PO10 ..... 161 E4
Garston Cl GU32 ..... 63 E4
Garstons Cl PO14 ..... 153 F4
Garstons Rd PO14 ..... 153 F4
Garth BH24 ..... 139 E2
Garth Rd BH9 ..... 190 A1
Garton Rd SO19 ..... 103 E2
Gashouse Hill SO31 ..... 127 E3
Gatcombe PO8 ..... 88 A2
Gatcombe Ave PO3 ..... 158 A1
Gatcombe Dr PO2 ..... 157 F2
Gatcombe Gdns
Fareham PO14 ..... 154 A4
West End SO30 ..... 80 A1
Gatcombe Park Inf Sch PO2 .. 157 F2
Gate House Rd PO16 ..... 156 A4
Gatehouse The 12 SO18 ..... 103 F4
Gatekeeper Cl 10 SO23 ..... 11 E4
Gateway The BH13 ..... 203 F2
Gatwick Cl SO16 ..... 78 A2
Gaulter Cl PO9 ..... 136 A2
Gavan St SO19 ..... 104 B3
Gawn Pl PO12 ..... 181 E1
Gayda House PO12 ..... 180 C3
Gaydon Rise BH11 ..... 188 C2
Gaylyn Way PO14 ..... 154 A4
Gaza Ave SO42 ..... 175 E3
Gaza House PO15 ..... 130 B2
Gazelle Cl PO13 ..... 180 B3
Gazing La SO51 ..... 50 C2
Gazings The SO51 ..... 50 C2
Geddes Way GU31 ..... 41 E2
Gemini Cl SO16 ..... 77 F2
General Johnson Ct 6 SO22 .... 10 B3
Geneva Ave BH6 ..... 206 B3
Genoa Cl SO41 ..... 197 E1
Gento Cl SO30 ..... 105 F3
Geoffrey Ave PO7 ..... 134 A1
Geoffrey Cres PO16 ..... 155 D3
George Byng Way PO2 ..... 182 B4
George Ct The PO1 ..... 182 A2
George Eyston Dr SO22 ..... 10 B3
George Rd SO41 ..... 211 E3
George St Eastleigh SO50 ..... 56 A2
Gosport PO13 ..... 181 E3
Portsmouth PO1, PO2 ..... 182 C4
Georges Mews BH21 ..... 186 B4
Georgian Cl BH24 ..... 141 D4
Georgian Way BH10 ..... 189 F2
Georgina Cl PO14 ..... 204 B4
Gerald Rd BH3 ..... 205 D3
Gerard Cres SO19 ..... 104 B3
Gerard House 6 PO2 ..... 157 F2
Germaine Cl BH23 ..... 208 C4
Gervis Cres BH14 ..... 203 D2
Gervis Pl BH2 ..... 204 C2
Gervis Rd BH1 ..... 205 D2
Gibbs Rd SO14 ..... 102 C3
Gibraltar Cl PO15 ..... 130 B1
Gibraltar Rd Gosport PO14 ..... 154 C3
Portsmouth PO4 ..... 183 E2
Gibson Cl
Lee-on-the-Solent PO13 ..... 179 F2
Swanwick PO15 ..... 129 F3
Gibson Rd BH17 ..... 202 C4
Giddylake BH21 ..... 163 E3
Gifford Cl PO15 ..... 130 C2
Gilbert Cl Alderholt SP6 ..... 93 D3
Gosport PO13 ..... 180 B4
Lymington SO41 ..... 197 E1
Gilbert Ct 5 BH23 ..... 207 D4
Gilbert Mead PO11 ..... 184 C2
Gilbert Rd BH1 ..... 205 E3
Gilbert Way PO7 ..... 134 C3
Gilbury Cl SO18 ..... 79 F2
Giles Cl Fareham PO16 ..... 131 D2
Gosport PO13 ..... 181 D3
Hedge End SO30 ..... 81 E1
Giles Hill SO23 ..... 11 D4
Giles La SP5 ..... 50 A2
Gilkicker Rd PO12 ..... 181 E1
Gillam Rd BH10 ..... 189 E3
Gillcrest PO14 ..... 129 E2
Gillett Rd PO12 ..... 204 B4
Gillies The 17 PO16 ..... 131 D1
Gillingham Cl
Bournemouth BH9 ..... 190 B2
Kings Worthy SO23 ..... 2 B4
Gillingham Rd SO41 ..... 211 E2
Gillion Ct 2 BH23 ..... 207 F3
Gillman Rd PO6 ..... 134 C1
Gilpin Cl Boldre SO41 ..... 173 F1
Southampton SO19 ..... 104 C3
Gilpin Hill SO41 ..... 172 A1
Gins La SO42 ..... 176 C1
Girton Cl PO14 ..... 129 E1
Gitsham Gdns PO7 ..... 134 B2
Gladdis Rd BH11 ..... 188 C2
Glade The Blackfield SO45 ..... 177 F4
Chandler's Ford SO53 ..... 30 C1
Fareham PO15 ..... 130 B2
South Hayling PO11 ..... 185 E1
St Leonards BH24 ..... 139 F3
Waterlooville PO7 ..... 135 D4
Gladelands Cl BH18 ..... 186 C2
Gladelands Mobile Home Pk
BH22 ..... 165 F4
Gladelands Way BH18 ..... 186 C2
Glades The SO31 ..... 129 D2
Gladstone Cl BH23 ..... 207 E3
Gladstone Gdns PO16 ..... 156 B4
Gladstone Hill SO22 ..... 10 C4
Gladstone Pl 4 PO2 ..... 182 B4

Gladstone Rd
Bournemouth BH7 ..... 205 F3
Gosport PO12 ..... 181 D4
Poole BH12 ..... 203 E3
Southampton SO19 ..... 104 A3
Gladstone Rd E BH7 ..... 205 F3
Gladstone Rd W BH1 ..... 205 F3
Gladys Ave Portsmouth PO2 ..... 157 E1
Waterlooville PO8 ..... 112 A2
Glamis Ave BH10 ..... 189 F3
Glamis Cl PO7 ..... 135 D4
Glamis Ct PO14 ..... 154 B2
Glamorgan Rd PO8 ..... 88 A2
Glasgow Rd PO4 ..... 183 D2
Glasslaw Rd SO18 ..... 104 A4
Glasspool PO7 ..... 110 C3
Gleadowe Ave BH23 ..... 206 C3
Glebe Cl PO11 ..... 184 C3
Glebe Cnr PO17 ..... 108 A2
Glebe Ct Botley SO30 ..... 106 A4
Fair Oak SO50 ..... 57 E1
Southampton SO17 ..... 79 D1
Glebe Dr PO13 ..... 155 E1
Glebe La SP5 ..... 49 E2
Glebe Meadow SP5 ..... 4 A1
Glebe Park Ave PO9 ..... 135 D1
Glebe Rd GU31 ..... 65 E3
Glebe The PO14 ..... 179 E3
Glebefield Gdns 1 PO6 ..... 157 F4
Glebefields 6 SO41 ..... 211 E3
Glen BH25 ..... 209 E4
Glen Dale PO9 ..... 113 E1
Glen Eyre Cl SO16 ..... 79 D2
Glen Eyre Dr SO16 ..... 79 D3
Glen Eyre Hall SO16 ..... 79 D3
Glen Eyre Rd SO16 ..... 78 C3
Glen Eyre Way SO16 ..... 79 D2
Glen Fern Rd BH1 ..... 205 D2
Glen House PO12 ..... 180 C2
Glen Rd Bournemouth BH5 ..... 205 F2
Locks Heath SO31 ..... 128 C3
Poole BH14 ..... 203 D2
Southampton SO19 ..... 103 E1
Swanwick SO31 ..... 128 C4
Glen Spey BH25 ..... 195 E1
Glen The Gosport PO13 ..... 155 F1
Poole BH14 ..... 203 E3
Poole, Canford Cliffs BH13 ..... 214 C4
Glenair Ave BH14 ..... 203 D2
Glenair Cres BH14 ..... 203 D2
Glenair Rd BH14 ..... 203 D2
Glenavon BH25 ..... 195 E1
Glenavon Rd BH23 ..... 193 F1
Glenbrook Wlk PO14 ..... 154 B4
Glencarron Way SO16 ..... 78 C2
Glencoe Rd Bournemouth BH7 .. 205 F4
Poole BH14 ..... 203 E3
Portsmouth PO1 ..... 182 C4
Glencoyne Gdns SO16 ..... 77 F1
Glenda Cl SO31 ..... 152 B4
Glendale Locks Heath SO31 ..... 129 D1
Swanmore SO32 ..... 84 A2
Glendale Cl Christchurch BH23 .. 191 E2
Wimborne Minster BH21 ..... 163 E3
Glendale Ct BH21 ..... 191 E2
Glendale Rd BH6 ..... 207 D2
Glendon Ave BH10 ..... 189 E3
Glendowan Rd SO53 ..... 55 D4
Glendrive BH25 ..... 209 E4
Gleneagles BH23 ..... 206 C3
Gleneagles Ave PO14 ..... 203 E1
Gleneagles Cl BH22 ..... 165 F3
Gleneagles Dr PO7 ..... 112 A1
Glenelg PO15 ..... 130 C1
Glenesha Gdns PO15 ..... 130 B1
Glenfern Hall BH4 ..... 204 B3
Glenferness Ave BH3, BH4 ..... 204 B3
Glenfield Ave SO18 ..... 103 F4
Glenfield Cres SO18 ..... 103 F4
Glenfield Inf Sch SO18 ..... 103 F4
Glenfield Way SO18 ..... 103 F4
Glengariff Rd BH14 ..... 203 E2
Glengarry BH25 ..... 195 E1
Glengarry Way BH23 ..... 208 B3
Glenhurst Sch PO9 ..... 136 A1
Glenives Cl BH24 ..... 140 A2
Glenlea Cl SO30 ..... 80 B1
Glenlea Dr SO30 ..... 80 B1
Glenleigh Ave 18 PO6 ..... 157 F4
Glenleigh Ct 17 PO6 ..... 157 F4
Glenleigh Pk PO9 ..... 136 A1
Glenmeadows Dr BH10 ..... 189 D3
Glenmoor Cl BH10 ..... 189 E1
Glenmoor Rd
Bournemouth BH9 ..... 204 C4
Ferndown BH22 ..... 165 E2
Glenmoor Sec Sch BH10 ..... 189 E1
Glenmore Ct SO17 ..... 103 D4
Glenmount Dr BH14 ..... 203 D2
Glenn Rd SO30 ..... 80 B1
Glenroyd Gdns BH6 ..... 206 C2
Glenside Barton on Sea BH25 ... 209 D4
Hythe SO45 ..... 125 F2
Glenside Ave SO19 ..... 104 B2
Glenside Cl SO30 ..... 80 B1
Glenthorne Cl PO14 ..... 179 E3
Glenthorne Meadow GU32 ..... 38 C1
Glenthorne Rd PO3 ..... 158 A1
Glenville Cl BH23 ..... 194 A1
Glenville Gdns BH10 ..... 189 E1
Glenville Rd
Bournemouth BH10 ..... 189 E1
Christchurch BH23 ..... 194 A1
Glenwood Ave SO16 ..... 79 D3
Glenwood Cl SO50 ..... 57 F1
Glenwood Ct SO50 ..... 57 F1
Glenwood Gdns PO8 ..... 111 F2
Glenwood La BH22 ..... 138 C1

Glenwood Rd
Southbourne PO10 ..... 137 F1
Verwood BH31 ..... 114 C3
West Moors BH22 ..... 138 C1
Glenwood Sch PO8 ..... 111 F1
Glenwood Way BH22 ..... 138 C1
Glidden Cl PO1 ..... 182 B3
Glidden La PO7 ..... 86 C2
Glissons BH22 ..... 165 D1
Globe La BH15 ..... 202 B1
Gloster Ct PO14 ..... 129 E3
Gloucester Cl GU32 ..... 40 B2
Gloucester Cl 8 GU32 ..... 40 C2
Gloucester House 1 PO12 ..... 181 E2
Gloucester Pl 43 PO5 ..... 182 B2
Gloucester Rd
Bournemouth BH7 ..... 205 F3
Poole BH12 ..... 203 F3
Portsmouth PO1 ..... 182 A3
Waterlooville PO7 ..... 134 C3
Gloucester Terr 22 PO1 ..... 182 B2
Gloucester View PO5 ..... 182 B2
Glyn Dr PO14 ..... 179 E3
Glyn Jones Cl SO45 ..... 150 C1
Glyn Way PO14 ..... 179 E3
Glynville Cl BH21 ..... 164 A4
Glynville Ct BH21 ..... 164 A4
Glynville Rd BH21 ..... 164 A4
Goathorn Cl BH16 ..... 201 E2
God's House Tower (Mus)
SO14 ..... 103 D1
Goddard Cl SO51 ..... 50 C2
Godfrey Olson House 4 SO50 .. 56 A2
Godfrey Pink Way SO32 ..... 83 E4
Godiva Lawn PO4 ..... 183 E2
Godmanston Cl BH17 ..... 188 A1
Godshill Cl BH8 ..... 190 B2
Godson House 14 SO23 ..... 11 D4
Godwin Cl Emsworth PO10 ..... 136 C2
Winchester SO22 ..... 1 B1
Godwin Cres PO8 ..... 88 B2
Godwins Field SO21 ..... 31 E4
Godwit Cl PO4 ..... 181 D4
Godwit Rd PO4 ..... 183 E3
Gofton Ave PO6 ..... 158 A4
Goggs La SP5 ..... 47 F3
Gold Mead Cl 3 SO41 ..... 197 F1
Gold Oak La 91 F4
Gold St PO5 ..... 182 A2
Goldcrest Cl Horndean PO8 ..... 112 A4
Portchester PO16 ..... 155 F4
Goldcrest Gdns SO16 ..... 78 A3
Goldcrest La SO40 ..... 100 B4
Golden Cres SO41 ..... 196 B1
Golden Ct SO30 ..... 80 C2
Golden Gates BH13 ..... 214 A2
Golden Gr SO14 ..... 103 D3
Golden Hind Park SO45 ..... 125 F1
Golden Sands BH13 ..... 214 A2
Goldfinch Cl BH25 ..... 194 C1
Goldfinch La PO13 ..... 179 F2
Goldfinch Rd BH17 ..... 201 F4
Goldring Cl PO11 ..... 185 D2
Goldsmith Ave PO4 ..... 182 C2
Goldsmith Cl SO40 ..... 100 B4
Goldsmith Inf Sch PO4 ..... 182 C2
Goldsmith Rd SO50 ..... 55 F1
Goldwire Dr SO52 ..... 54 C3
Golf Course Rd SO16 ..... 78 C3
Golf Links Rd Broadstone BH18 187 D3
Ferndown BH22 ..... 165 F2
Goliath Rd BH15 ..... 201 E1
Gomer Ct PO12 ..... 180 C2
Gomer Inf Sch PO12 ..... 180 C2
Gomer Jun Sch PO12 ..... 180 C2
Gomer La PO12 ..... 180 C2
Good Acre Dr SO52 ..... 54 C3
Good Rd BH12 ..... 203 E4
Goodens The SO24 ..... 14 B3
Goodison Cl SO50 ..... 57 D1
Goodlands Vale SO30 ..... 105 D4
Goodsell Cl PO14 ..... 179 D3
Goodwin Cl SO16 ..... 77 E1
Goodwood Cl Gosport PO12 ..... 181 D4
Titchfield PO14 ..... 129 E1
Waterlooville PO8 ..... 112 A1
Goodwood Ct PO10 ..... 161 F4
Goodwood Gdns SO40 ..... 100 B4
Goodwood Rd Eastleigh SO50 .... 55 F2
Gosport PO12 ..... 181 D4
Portsmouth PO5 ..... 182 C2
Gooseberry La BH24 ..... 140 C4
Gordleton Ind Pk SO41 ..... 196 C3
Gordon Ave Southampton SO14 103 D4
Winchester SO23 ..... 11 E3
Gordon Bldgs SO15 ..... 102 B4
Gordon Cl BH4 ..... 204 B2
Gordon Mount PO12 ..... 209 D4
Gordon Rd Bournemouth BH1 .. 205 E2
Chandler's Ford SO53 ..... 30 B1
Christchurch BH23 ..... 209 D4
Curdridge SO32 ..... 83 D1
Fareham PO16 ..... 131 D1
Gosport PO12 ..... 181 D2
Hermitage PO10 ..... 161 D4
Lymington SO41 ..... 197 E2
Poole BH12 ..... 204 A3
Portsmouth PO1 ..... 182 A2
Waterlooville PO7 ..... 134 B3
Wimborne Minster BH21 ..... 163 F2
Winchester SO23 ..... 11 D4
Gordon Rd S BH12 ..... 204 A3
Gordon Terr SO19 ..... 104 A1
Gordon Way BH23 ..... 192 B1
Gore Grange BH25 ..... 194 C1
Gore Rd BH25 ..... 194 C1
Gore Rd Ind Est BH25 ..... 194 C1
Gorey Ave BH12 ..... 188 B1

Goring Ave P08 .... 88 B2
Goring Field SO22 .... 1 B1
Gorleston Rd BH12 .... 203 F3
Gorley Cross SP6 .... 94 A2
Gorley Ct P09 .... 135 E3
Gorley Lynch SP6 .... 94 B2
Gorley Rd BH24 .... 117 E1
Gorran Ave P013 .... 155 E1
Gorse Cl Locks Heath SO31 .... 128 C1
    New Milton BH25 .... 195 E2
    St Leonards BH24 .... 139 E2
Gorse Down SO21 .... 33 D2
Gorse Hill Cl BH15 .... 202 C3
Gorse Hill Cres BH15 .... 202 C3
Gorse Hill Rd BH15 .... 202 C3
Gorse La BH16 .... 201 E4
Gorse Rd Corfe Mullen BH21 .... 186 B3
    Petersfield GU31 .... 41 E2
Gorsecliff Ct 7 BH5 .... 205 E2
Gorsecliff Rd BH10 .... 189 E1
Gorsefield Rd BH25 .... 195 D2
Gorseland Ct BH22 .... 165 F2
Gorselands Rd SO18 .... 80 A1
Gorselands Way P013 .... 180 B4
Gorseway P011 .... 184 B2
Gorseway The P011 .... 184 B2
Gort Cres SO19 .... 104 A2
Gort Rd Bournemouth BH11 .... 189 D2
    Broadstone BH17 .... 187 D1
Gosling Cl BH17 .... 202 C4
Gosport House 39 P09 .... 136 A3
Gosport La SO43 .... 122 A2
Gosport Rd
    Fareham P014, P016 .... 155 D4
    Lee-on-the-Solent P013 .... 179 F1
    Stubbington P014 .... 179 F3
Gosport Sh Prec 23 P012 .... 181 E2
Gosport St SO41 .... 197 F2
Gough Cres BH17 .... 187 D1
Gover Rd SO16 .... 101 E4
Grace Dieu Gdns SO31 .... 104 C1
Grace La SP6 .... 70 C4
Graddidge Way SO40 .... 100 B3
Graemar La SO51 .... 25 E1
Grafton Cl Bournemouth BH3 ... 205 D4
    Christchurch BH23 .... 207 E3
Grafton Gdns Lymington SO41 .. 197 E1
    Southampton SO16 .... 101 F3
Grafton Rd Bournemouth BH3 .. 205 D3
    Winchester SO23 .... 10 C3
Grafton St P02 .... 182 B4
Graham Ct SO19 .... 104 A3
Graham House 4 SO14 .... 103 E3
Graham Rd Gosport P012 .... 181 D4
    Portsmouth P04 .... 182 C2
    Southampton SO14 .... 103 D3
Graham St SO14 .... 103 E3
Grainger Gdns SO19 .... 104 B2
Grammar School La BH21 ..... 163 D2
Granada Cl P08 .... 112 A2
Granada Rd Hedge End SO30 .. 105 D3
    Portsmouth P04 .... 182 C1
Granary Mews BH24 .... 140 C4
Granary The BH24 .... 140 C4
Granby Gr SO17 .... 79 D2
Granby Rd BH9 .... 190 A2
Grand Ave BH6 .... 206 B2
Grand Par 20 Poole BH15 .... 202 A1
    Portsmouth P01 .... 182 A4
    South Hayling P011 .... 185 D1
Grange Cl Gosport P012 .... 180 C3
    Havant P09 .... 136 A1
    Hordle SO41 .... 211 F4
    Southampton SO18 .... 79 F2
    Winchester SO23 .... 10 C2
Grange Cres P012 .... 180 C3
Grange Ct
    16 Bournemouth BH1 .... 205 D2
    Netley SO31 .... 127 D4
Grange Dr SO30 .... 105 E4
Grange Gdns BH12 .... 203 F4
Grange Inf Sch P013 .... 180 B4
Grange Jun Sch P013 .... 180 B4
Grange La P013 .... 180 B4
Grange Mews SO51 .... 28 B1
Grange Park Mobile Homes
    SO30 .... 81 E1
Grange Rd Bournemouth BH6 .. 206 B2
    Broadstone BH18 .... 187 D2
    Christchurch BH23 .... 208 A4
    Gosport P013 .... 180 B3
    Hedge End SO30 .... 105 E4
    Netley SO31 .... 127 E4
    Petersfield GU32 .... 40 C1
    Portsmouth P02 .... 157 E1
    Southampton SO15 .... 78 A1
    St Leonards BH24 .... 139 F1
    Winchester SO23 .... 10 C2
Grange Road Bsns Ctr BH23 .. 208 A4
Grange Sch The BH23 .... 207 F4
Grange The Hordle SO41 ..... 211 F4
    8 Southampton SO15 ..... 78 A1
Grangewood Ct SO50 .... 57 D1
Grangewood Gdns SO50 ..... 57 D1
Grant Rd P06 .... 158 B4
Grant's Ave BH1 .... 205 E3
Grantham Ave SO31 .... 127 F2
Grantham Ct 3 SO50 .... 56 A1
Grantham Rd
    Bournemouth BH1 .... 205 E3
    Eastleigh SO50 .... 56 A1
    Southampton SO19 .... 103 F3
Grantley Rd 14 BH5 .... 205 F2
Grants Cl BH1 .... 205 F3
Granville Cl P09 .... 136 A1
Granville Pl
    32 Bournemouth BH1 .... 204 C2
    Winchester SO23 .... 11 D3

Granville Rd Bournemouth BH5 . 206 A3
    Poole BH12 .... 203 D3
Granville St SO14 .... 103 D2
Grasdean Cl 5 SO18 .... 80 A1
Grasmere SO50 .... 55 F1
Grasmere Cl Christchurch BH23 191 E2
    West End SO18 .... 80 A1
Grasmere Ct SO16 .... 77 F1
Grasmere Gdns BH25 .... 195 D3
Grasmere House 18 P06 ..... 133 D1
Grasmere Rd
    Bournemouth BH5 .... 206 A2
    Poole BH12 .... 214 A2
Grasmere Way P014 .... 154 B2
Grassmere Way P07 .... 112 B1
Grassymead P014 .... 129 E2
Grateley Cl 1 SO19 .... 126 C4
Grateley Cres P09 .... 135 E2
Gravel Cl SP5 .... 46 C4
Gravel Hill Broadstone BH18 ... 187 E3
    Oakley BH18 .... 187 E3
    Shedfield SO32 .... 84 A2
    Swanmore SO32 .... 84 A2
Gravel La SP5 .... 140 C4
Gray Cl Locks Heath SO31 ..... 128 C1
    Poole BH17 .... 202 C4
Gray's Yd 24 BH15 .... 202 B1
Graycot Cl BH10 .... 189 E3
Grayland Cl P011 .... 184 C2
Grays Ave SO45 .... 126 A2
Grays Cl Colden Common SO21 ... 56 C4
    Gosport P012 .... 180 C2
    Romsey SO51 .... 53 D4
Grays Ct P01 .... 182 A2
Grayshott Cl SO22 .... 1 B2
Grayshott Rd Gosport P012 ... 180 C2
    Portsmouth P04 .... 182 C2
Grayson Ct P012 .... 165 F2
Great Copse Dr P09 .... 135 F3
Great Elms Cl SO45 .... 150 A2
Great Field Rd SO22 .... 1 B1
Great Gays P014 .... 179 D3
Great Hanger GU31 .... 41 D2
Great Mead Denmead P07 ..... 111 D2
    Lyndhurst SO43 .... 121 F2
Great Minster St SO23 .... 11 C4
Great Posbrook Cotts P014 .. 153 F3
Great Southsea St P05 .... 182 B2
Great Well Dr SO51 .... 53 D4
Greatbridge Rd
    Awbridge SO51 .... 27 F1
    Romsey SO51 .... 53 D4
Greatfield Way P09 .... 113 D2
Greatwood Cl SO45 .... 126 A1
Greaves Cl BH10 .... 189 E2
Grebe Cl Broadstone BH17 .... 201 F4
    Christchurch BH23 .... 208 A3
    Milford on Sea SO41 .... 211 F2
    Portchester P016 .... 155 F4
    Waterlooville P08 .... 111 F2
Green Acres BH23 .... 207 F4
Green Acres Cl BH24 .... 140 B3
Green Bottom BH21 .... 164 A4
Green Cl 7 Hythe SO45 .... 126 A2
    Kings Worthy SO23 .... 2 A3
    Netley Marsh SO40 .... 99 F2
    Poole BH15 .... 202 B1
    Whiteparish SP5 .... 24 A2
Green Cres P013 .... 155 E1
Green Dr SP6 .... 93 D3
Green Farm Gdns P03 .... 157 F2
Green Gdns BH15 .... 202 B1
Green Hollow Cl P016 .... 130 C2
Green Jacket Cl SO22 .... 10 C3
Green La Ampfield SO51 .... 29 D1
    Barton on Sea BH25 .... 210 A4
    Bishop's Waltham SO32 .... 83 E4
    Blackfield SO45 .... 177 F4
    Bournemouth BH10 .... 189 E2
    Bursledon SO31 .... 104 C1
    Chilworth SO16 .... 54 C1
    Clanfield P08 .... 88 B3
    Denmead P07 .... 110 C2
    Downton SP5 .... 46 C4
    Ferndown BH22 .... 165 D1
    Fordingbridge SP6 .... 69 F1
    Froxfield GU32 .... 18 C3
    Gosport P012 .... 181 E4
    Gosport, Alverstoke P012 ... 181 D2
    Hamble-le-Rice SO31 .... 128 A1
    Hambledon P07 .... 86 A2
    Locks Heath SO31 .... 128 C1
    New Milton BH25 .... 194 C4
    Ower SO40 .... 76 A2
    Portsmouth P03 .... 158 A2
    Ringwood BH24 .... 141 D4
    Ringwood, Upper Kingston
        BH24 .... 141 E2
    Rockbourne SP6 .... 69 E4
    Soberton P07 .... 86 A3
    South Hayling P011 .... 184 C2
    Southampton SO16 .... 77 F1
    Swanmore SO32 .... 84 B4
    Swanwick SO31 .... 106 A1
    Swanwick, Lwr Swanwick SO31 . 128 B4
    Whitsbury SP6 .... 69 E4
Green Loaning 4 BH23 .... 207 F3
Green Park Cl SO23 .... 2 A1
Green Park Rd SO16 .... 101 F4
Green Pk BH1 .... 205 E2
Green Pond Cnr P09 .... 136 A1
Green Pond La SO51 .... 29 E2
Green Rd
    Bournemouth BH9 .... 205 D4
    Gosport P012 .... 181 D1
    Poole BH15 .... 202 B1
    Portsmouth P05 .... 182 B2
    Stubbington P014 .... 154 B2

Green The Liss GU33 .... 20 C3
    Locks Heath SO31 .... 128 C3
    Romsey SO51 .... 28 B1
    Rowland's Castle P09 .... 113 E1
    Whiteparish SP5 .... 24 A2
Green Wlk P015 .... 130 C2
Green's Cl SO50 .... 57 D1
Greenacre BH25 .... 210 A4
Greenacre Cl BH16 .... 201 E3
Greenacre Gdns P07 .... 134 B2
Greenacres
    Chandler's Ford SO53 .... 55 F3
    Poole BH13 .... 204 A2
Greenacres Downton SP5 ..... 46 B4
Greenacres Cl BH10 .... 189 F3
Greenacres Dr SO21 .... 31 E2
Greenacres Special Sch SO22 ... 1 C1
Greenaway La SO31 .... 128 B1
Greenbank Cres SO16 .... 78 C3
Greenbanks Cl SO41 .... 211 E2
Greenbanks Gdns P016 .... 131 E1
Greenclose La SO41 .... 163 E2
Greendale Cl
    Chandler's Ford SO53 .... 55 F3
    Fareham P015 .... 130 A2
Greendale The P015 .... 130 B2
Greenfield Gdns BH25 .... 210 A4
Greenfield Rd BH15 .... 202 C4
Greenfield Rise P08 .... 112 A2
Greenfields Liss GU33 .... 21 D2
    Poole BH13 .... 203 F4
Greenfields Ave SO40 .... 76 C1
Greenfields Cl SO40 .... 76 C1
Greenfinch Cl Broadstone BH17 186 C1
    Eastleigh SO50 .... 55 E1
Greenfinch Wlk BH24 .... 141 E3
Greenhayes BH18 .... 187 E1
Greenhays Rise BH21 .... 163 E3
Greenhill Ave SO22 .... 10 C4
Greenhill Cl
    Wimborne Minster BH21 ..... 163 E3
    Winchester SO22 .... 10 C4
Greenhill La Rownhams SO16 ... 77 F4
    Wimborne Minster BH21 ..... 163 E3
Greenhill Rd
    Wimborne Minster BH21 ..... 163 E3
    Winchester SO22 .... 10 B4
Greenhill Terr SO22 .... 10 C4
Greenlea Cl P07 .... 134 A1
Greenlea Cres SO16 .... 79 E3
Greenlea Rd P012 .... 180 C4
Greenmead Ave SO41 .... 196 B1
Greens Cl SO32 .... 83 D4
Greens Meade SP5 .... 47 E3
Greenside Ct BH25 .... 210 A3
Greensleeves Ave BH18 ..... 187 D3
Greensome Dr BH22 .... 165 F3
Greenway GU32 .... 38 C1
Greenway Cl SO41 .... 197 E2
Greenway Cres SO16 .... 201 D4
Greenway La GU31 .... 65 E3
Greenway Rd P012 .... 181 D3
Greenway The P010 .... 136 C2
Greenways
    Chandler's Ford SO53 .... 55 F3
    Christchurch BH23 .... 208 C4
    Milford on Sea SO41 .... 211 E3
    Southampton SO16 .... 79 E3
    Swanmore SO32 .... 84 A3
Greenways Ave BH8 .... 190 B2
Greenways Ct BH22 .... 165 F2
Greenways Rd SO42 .... 146 A1
Greenwich The SO45 .... 150 C3
Greenwood Ave Cosham P06 ... 157 E4
    Ferndown BH22 .... 165 F3
    Poole BH14 .... 214 B4
    Rownhams SO16 .... 77 E3
Greenwood Cl Eastleigh SO50 ... 55 F1
    Fareham P016 .... 131 D2
    Romsey SO51 .... 53 D4
Greenwood Copse BH24 ..... 140 A2
Greenwood La SO32 .... 82 A4
Greenwood Rd BH9 .... 204 C4
Greenwood Way BH24 .... 140 A2
Greenwoods 32 BH25 .... 195 D1
Greetham St P01 .... 182 B3
Gregory Gdns SO40 .... 76 B1
Gregory La SO32 .... 82 B3
Gregson Ave P013 .... 155 E2
Gregson Cl P013 .... 155 E2
Grenadier Cl SO31 .... 129 D1
Grendon Cl SO16 .... 79 D3
Grenehurst Way GU31 .... 40 C2
Grenfell Rd BH9 .... 189 F2
Grenfield Ct P010 .... 136 C2
Grenville Cl BH24 .... 117 E1
Grenville Ct
    6 Bournemouth BH4 .... 204 B2
    12 Poole BH15 .... 202 B1
    Southampton, SO15 .... 102 C4
    Southampton, Bitterne Pk SO18 ... 79 F2
Grenville Gdns SO45 .... 126 A1
Grenville House 22 P01 ..... 182 A3
Grenville Rd
    4 Portsmouth P05 .... 182 C2
    Wimborne Minster BH21 ..... 163 E2
Gresham Rd BH9 .... 190 A1
Gresley Gdns SO30 .... 81 E1
Greville Gn P010 .... 136 C2
Greville Rd SO15 .... 102 B4
Greycot Cl BH21 .... 138 C4
Greyfriars 19 SO23 .... 11 D4
Greyfriars Ct 31 P05 .... 182 B2
Greyfriars Rd P015 .... 130 B1
Greyhound Cl SO30 .... 81 D2
Greyladyes SO31 .... 128 A4
Greys Farm Cl SO24 .... 14 B2
Greyshott Ave P014 .... 154 B4
Greystoke Ave BH11 .... 188 C3
Greywell Ave SO16 .... 78 B2

Greywell Ct SO16 .... 78 B2
Greywell Sq P09 .... 135 F2
Griffen Cl SO50 .... 56 C1
Griffin Ct Southampton SO17 ... 103 E4
    15 Wimborne Minster BH21 ... 163 E2
Griffin Ind Pk P040 .... 76 C1
Griffin Wlk P013 .... 180 B3
Griffiths Gdns BH10 .... 189 D3
Griffon Cl SO31 .... 105 D1
Grigg La SO42 .... 146 A1
Grindle Cl P016 .... 132 B1
Gritanwood Rd P04 .... 183 D2
Grosvenor Ct 19 BH1 .... 205 D2
Grosvenor Cl Southampton SO17 79 E1
    St Leonards BH24 .... 139 E3
Grosvenor Ct
    2 Bournemouth BH1 .... 205 E2
    Christchurch BH23 .... 209 D4
    Cosham P06 .... 158 C4
    Romsey SO51 .... 53 E4
    7 Southampton SO17 .... 79 E1
    Stubbington P014 .... 179 E3
Grosvenor Dr SO23 .... 2 A1
Grosvenor Gdns
    Bournemouth BH1 .... 205 F2
    Southampton SO17 .... 79 E1
    West End SO30 .... 104 B4
Grosvenor House 13 P05 ..... 182 B2
Grosvenor Lodge 5 SO17 ..... 79 E1
Grosvenor Mews
    Gosport P012 .... 181 E3
    Lymington SO41 .... 197 E3
    8 Southampton SO17 ..... 79 E1
Grosvenor Rd
    Bournemouth BH4 .... 204 B2
    Chandler's Ford SO53 .... 30 C1
    Southampton SO17 .... 79 E1
Grosvenor Sq SO15 .... 102 C3
Grosvenor St P05 .... 182 B2
Grove Ave Gosport P012 .... 181 E3
    Portchester P016 .... 156 B3
Grove Bldgs 6 P012 .... 181 E2
Grove Ct 14 P09 .... 135 F1
Grove Gdns SO19 .... 104 A3
Grove La SP5 .... 47 F4
Grove Mansions 21 BH1 ..... 205 D2
Grove Mews SO19 .... 104 A1
Grove Pastures SO41 .... 197 F2
Grove Pl Lymington SO41 .... 197 F2
    Southampton SO19 .... 104 A1
Grove Rd Barton on Sea BH25 ... 210 A4
    Bournemouth BH1 .... 205 D2
    Compton(Hants) SO21 .... 31 E3
    Cosham P06 .... 158 A4
    Fareham P016 .... 131 D1
    Gosport P012 .... 181 E4
    Havant P09 .... 135 F1
    Lee-on-the-Solent P013 .... 179 F1
    Lymington SO41 .... 197 F2
    Poole BH12 .... 203 D3
    Southampton SO15 .... 102 B4
    Wimborne Minster BH21 ..... 163 E2
Grove Rd E BH23 .... 207 D4
Grove Rd N P05 .... 182 B2
Grove Rd S P05 .... 182 B2
Grove Rd W BH23 .... 206 C4
Grove St SO14 .... 103 D3
Grove The Bournemouth BH9 ... 189 F1
    Bursledon SO31 .... 105 D1
    Christchurch BH23 .... 191 F1
    Ferndown BH22 .... 165 E2
    Netley SO31 .... 127 E4
    Southampton SO19 .... 104 A1
    Stubbington P014 .... 179 D3
    Verwood BH31 .... 115 D3
    Westbourne BH10 .... 137 D2
Grovelands Rd SO22 .... 1 A1
Groveley Rd Bournemouth BH4 . 204 A1
    Christchurch BH23 .... 207 F3
Groveley Way SO51 .... 28 C1
Grovely Ave BH5 .... 205 F2
Groves Down SO51 .... 50 C2
Grundles GU31 .... 41 D2
Gruneisen Rd P02 .... 157 E1
Guardhouse Rd P01 .... 182 A4
Guardian Ct 30 SO17 .... 79 D1
Guardroom Rd P02 .... 157 D1
Gudge Heath La P015 .... 130 C1
Guelders The P07 .... 134 C2
Guernsey Cl SO16 .... 77 F2
Guernsey Rd BH12 .... 188 B1
Guessens La P014 .... 153 F4
Guest Ave BH12 .... 204 A3
Guest Cl BH12 .... 204 A3
Guest Rd Bishopstoke SO50 ... 56 B2
    Upton BH16 .... 201 D4
Guildford Cl Bournemouth BH4 . 204 B2
    Gosport P012 .... 180 B3
Guildford Dr SO53 .... 55 D2
Guildford Rd P01 .... 182 C3
Guildford St 30 SO14 .... 103 E3
Guildhall Cl 4 BH15 .... 202 A1
Guildhall Sq 13 P01 .... 182 B3
Guildhall Wlk P01 .... 182 B3
Guildhill Rd BH6 .... 206 C2
Guillemot Cl SO45 .... 126 A1
Guillemot Gdns P013 .... 155 D2
Gull Cl P013 .... 155 D1
Gulliver Cl BH12 .... 214 B4
Gulliver Ct 1 BH21 .... 163 E3
Gulls The SO40 .... 101 F1
Gullycroft Mead SO30 ..... 105 D4
Gunners Bldgs P03 .... 157 F2
Gunners Pk SO32 .... 83 F4
Gunners Row P04 .... 183 D1
Gunners Way P012 .... 155 F1
Gunstore Rd P03 .... 158 A2

Gunville Cres BH9 .... 190 A2
Gunwharf Rd P01 .... 182 A2
Gurjun Cl BH16 .... 201 D4
Gurkha Mus The SO22 .... 10 C4
Gurnard Rd P06 .... 157 F4
Gurnays Mead SO51 .... 50 C2
Gurney Rd Corfe Mullen BH21 ... 186 C3
    Portsmouth P02 .... 183 D2
    Southampton SO15 .... 102 B4
Gussage Rd BH12 .... 203 F4
Gutner La BH16 .... 160 B1
Guy's Cl BH24 .... 141 D3
Gwatkin Cl P09 .... 135 E2
Gwen-Rhian Ct 10 SO15 ..... 102 C4
Gwenlyn Rd BH16 .... 201 E3
Gwynne Rd BH12 .... 203 F3
Gypsy La BH24 .... 141 D4

H Ave SO45 .... 150 C3
Ha'penny Dell P07 .... 134 C2
Haarlem Mews BH23 .... 207 E4
Hack Dr SO21 .... 56 C4
Hacketts La SO32 .... 60 C1
Hackleys La SO51 .... 51 D3
Hackupps La SO51 .... 6 B1
Hackworth Gdns SO30 ..... 81 E2
Hadden Cl BH8 .... 205 E4
Haddon Cl P015 .... 130 C1
Haddon Dr SO50 .... 56 A3
Haddons Dr BH21 .... 138 B4
Hadleigh Gdns SO50 .... 56 A3
Hadleigh Rd 6 P06 .... 157 E4
Hadley Field SO45 .... 150 A3
Hadley Way BH18 .... 186 C2
Hadow Rd BH10 .... 189 E2
Hadrian Cl BH22 .... 165 E1
Hadrian Way Chilworth SO16 ... 78 C4
    Corfe Mullen BH21 .... 186 C4
Hadrians Cl SO53 .... 55 F4
Haglane Copse SO41 .... 197 E1
Hahnemann Rd BH2 .... 204 C1
Haig Ave BH13 .... 203 F1
Haig Rd SO50 .... 57 D1
Haileybury Gdns SO30 ..... 81 E1
Haking Rd BH23 .... 207 E4
Halcyon Ct BH15 .... 202 B3
Halden Cl 2 SO51 .... 28 A1
Hale Ave BH25 .... 195 D1
Hale Cl P01 .... 182 C4
Hale Gdns BH25 .... 195 D1
Hale La SP6 .... 47 D2
Hale Prim Sch SP6 .... 47 E2
Hale St N P01 .... 182 B3
Hale St S P01 .... 182 B3
Hales Dr SO30 .... 105 D3
Halewood Way BH23 .... 206 C4
Half Moon St 2 P01 .... 182 A3
Halfpenny La P01 .... 182 A2
Halfway Rd SO45 .... 151 F1
Halifax Ct SO30 .... 80 B1
Halifax Rise P07 .... 134 C4
Halifax Way BH23 .... 208 A4
Hall Cl SO32 .... 83 E4
Hall Ct SO32 .... 107 D4
Hall Lands La SO50 .... 57 E1
Hall Rd BH11 .... 188 C2
Hall Way The SO22 .... 1 A3
Hallet Cl SO18 .... 80 A1
Hallett Rd P09 .... 136 A1
Halletts Cl P014 .... 154 B2
Halliards The P016 .... 155 D4
Halliday Cl P012 .... 181 D3
Halliday Cres P04 .... 183 E2
Halliday House P04 .... 183 D1
Halsey Cl P012 .... 180 C2
Halstead Rd Cosham P06 ..... 157 E4
    Southampton SO18 .... 79 F1
Halstock Cres BH17 .... 187 E1
Halter Path BH15 .... 201 F2
Halter Rise BH21 .... 164 B3
Halterworth Cl SO51 .... 53 D4
Halterworth La SO51 .... 53 E4
Halterworth Prim Sch SO51 ... 53 E4
Halton Cl BH23 .... 193 D4
Haltons Cl SO40 .... 76 B1
Halyards P013 .... 180 B4
Halyards SO31 .... 128 A2
Ham Cl P07 .... 156 A1
Ham La Ferndown BH21 .... 164 C2
    Horndean P08 .... 112 A4
    Southbourne P010 .... 161 E4
    Wimborne Minster BH21 ..... 164 B2
Hambert Way SO40 .... 100 C3
Hamble Cl SO31 .... 128 B1
Hamble Ct
    Chandler's Ford SO53 .... 55 E3
    Stubbington P014 .... 154 A2
    3 Waterlooville P08 ..... 111 F2
Hamble House P014 .... 155 D4
Hamble House Gdns SO31 ... 128 A1
Hamble La Bursledon SO31 ... 127 F4
    Hamble-le-Rice SO31 .... 127 F4
    Waterlooville P07 .... 134 C3
Hamble Manor SO31 .... 128 A1
Hamble Prim Sch SO31 .... 127 F2
Hamble Rd Gosport P012 ..... 180 C2
    Poole BH15 .... 203 D3
Hamble Sec Sch SO31 .... 127 F4
Hamble Springs SO32 .... 83 E4
Hamblecliff House SO31 ..... 127 E2
Hambledon Gdns BH6 .... 206 B3
Hambledon Inf Sch P07 ..... 86 B2
Hambledon La SO32 .... 85 F2

Hambledon Par PO7 111 E1
Hambledon Rd Clanfield PO8 88 A3
Denmead PO7 111 D2
Hambledon PO7 110 B4
Waterlooville PO7, PO8 111 D2
Hambleside Ct SO31 127 F1
Hambleton Rd BH7 206 A4
Hamblewood Botley SO30 106 A3
Swanwick SO31 128 B4
Hamblewood Ct SO30 106 A3
Hambrook Rd 2 PO12 181 D3
Hambrook St PO5 182 A2
Hamdown Cres SO51 51 D1
Hameldon Cl SO16 101 F4
Hamilton Cl Bournemouth BH1 205 E3
Christchurch BH23 207 F2
Hamworthy BH15 201 F1
Havant PO9 159 F4
Hamilton Cres BH15 201 F1
Hamilton Ct
10 Bournemouth BH8 205 D3
Milford on Sea SO41 211 E2
18 Portsmouth PO5 182 B1
23 Southampton SO17 79 D1
Hamilton Gr PO13 155 D1
Hamilton Mews Hythe SO45 126 A1
Lymington SO41 197 F2
Hamilton Pk SP5 47 D4
Hamilton Rd Bishopstoke SO50 56 B2
Bournemouth BH1 205 E2
Corfe Mullen BH21 186 C3
Hamworthy BH15 201 F1
Hythe SO45 150 A4
Portchester PO6 156 C4
Portsmouth PO5 182 B1
Hamilton Way BH25 194 C1
Hamlet Ct SO45 151 D2
Hamlet Way PO12 156 A1
Hammond House PO12 181 F2
Hammond Ind Pk PO14 179 E3
Hammond Rd PO15 130 C1
Hammond's Gr SO40 100 B4
Hammonds Cl SO40 100 C4
Hammonds La SO40 100 C4
Hammonds Way SO40 100 C4
Hampage Gn PO9 135 E4
Hampden La BH6 206 A3
Hampreston CE Fst Sch BH21 164 C2
Hampshire Cl BH23 191 F1
Hampshire Ct
26 Bournemouth BH2 204 C2
Chandler's Ford SO53 55 E2
Hampshire Ctr The BH8 190 C1
Hampshire Hatches La BH24 141 D2
Hampshire Health & Tennis Club The SO30 80 C1
Hampshire House 25 BH2 204 C2
Hampshire St PO1 182 C4
Hampshire Terr PO1 182 A2
Hampton Cl Blackfield SO45 177 F4
Waterlooville PO7 135 D4
Hampton Dr BH24 117 D1
Hampton Gdns SO45 177 F4
Hampton Gr PO15 130 A1
Hampton Hill SO32 84 A3
Hampton La Blackfield SO45 150 C1
Winchester SO22 1 B1
Hampton Towers 4 SO19 126 C4
Hamptworth Rd SP5 48 B2
Hamtun Cres SO40 76 C1
Hamtun Gdns SO40 76 C1
Hamtun Rd SO19 104 B2
Hamtun St 11 SO14 102 C2
Hamworthy Fst Sch BH15 201 F1
Hamworthy Mid Sch BH15 201 F1
Hamworthy Sta BH16 201 E2
Hanbidge Cres PO13 155 E2
Hanbidge Wlk PO13 155 E2
Handel Rd SO15 102 C3
Handel Terr SO15 102 C3
Handford Pl 2 SO15 102 C3
Handley Ct BH24 140 C4
Handley Lodge BH12 203 F4
Handley Rd PO12 180 C3
Handsworth House 5 PO5 182 B2
Hanger Way GU31 41 D2
Hangers The SO32 59 F1
Hanham Rd Corfe Mullen BH21 186 B3
Wimborne Minster BH21 163 E3
Hankinson Rd BH9 205 D4
Hanley Rd SO15 102 B4
Hann Rd SO16 77 F3
Hannah Gdns PO7 134 C4
Hannah Way SO41 196 C3
Hannay Rise SO19 104 B3
Hannington Pl BH7 206 A3
Hannington Rd
Bournemouth BH7 206 A3
Havant PO9 135 E4
Hanns Way SO50 56 A1
Hanover Bldgs SO14 103 D2
Hanover Cotts SO32 36 C2
Hanover Ct 3 Hythe SO45 126 A2
Portsmouth PO1 182 A2
Hanover Gdns PO16 131 D2
Hanover Gn BH17 202 C4
Hanover House Gosport PO13 155 D3
Poole BH15 202 B2
Totton SO40 101 D4
Hanover Lodge SO22 10 C3
Hanover St PO1 182 A3
Hants Corporate Pk SO53 55 D1
Hanway Rd PO1, PO2 182 C4
Harbeck Rd BH8 190 B2
Harborough Rd SO15 102 C3
Harbour Cl BH13 214 B3
Harbour Cres BH23 207 F3
Harbour Ct
Barton on Sea BH25 209 F4
Christchurch BH23 207 F3
Poole BH13 214 C3
Harbour Hill Cres BH15 202 C3
Harbour Hill Rd BH15 202 C3
Harbour Hospl The BH15 202 B2
Harbour Lights BH15 202 C2
Harbour Par SO15 102 C2
Harbour Prospect BH14 214 B4
Harbour Rd Bournemouth BH6 207 D2
Gosport PO12 181 F3
South Hayling PO11 184 B2
Harbour Tower PO12 181 F2
Harbour View PO16 156 B3
Harbour View Cl BH14 203 D3
Harbour View Ct BH23 207 D3
Harbour View Rd BH14 203 D2
Harbour Watch BH14 214 B4
Harbour Way Emsworth PO10 161 D4
Portsmouth PO2 157 E1
Harbour Wlk PO1 182 A2
Harbourne Gdns SO18 80 A1
Harbourside PO9 159 F3
Harbridge Ct PO9 135 E4
Harbridge Dro BH24 93 E2
Harcombe Cl BH17 187 F2
Harcourt Cl PO8 112 A2
Harcourt Mews 7 BH5 206 A3
Harcourt Rd
Bournemouth BH5 206 A3
Fareham PO14 154 A4
Gosport PO12 181 D3
Portsmouth PO1 182 C4
Southampton SO18 103 F4
Hard The Gosport PO12 181 E3
Portsmouth PO1 182 A3
Harding La SO50 57 D2
Harding Rd PO12 180 C3
Hardley Ind Est SO45 150 A3
Hardley La SO45 150 A4
Hardley Sch SO45 150 B3
Hardman Ct PO3 158 A2
Hardwick Rd SO53 55 E3
Hardwicke Cl SO16 77 F1
Hardwicke Way SO31 127 F2
Hardy Cl Locks Heath SO31 129 D2
New Milton BH25 194 C2
Southampton SO15 102 A3
West Moors BH22 138 C1
Hardy Cres BH21 163 E2
Hardy Dr SO45 126 A1
Hardy Rd Cosham PO6 158 C4
Eastleigh SO50 56 A1
Poole BH14 203 E2
West Moors BH22 138 C1
Hare La Alderholt BH21 91 F3
Hordle SO41 195 F2
New Milton BH25 195 F2
Harebell Cl PO16 131 E2
Harefield Ct SO51 53 D4
Harefield Inf Sch SO18 104 A4
Harefield Jun Sch SO18 104 A4
Harefield Rd SO17 79 E2
Hares Gn BH7 206 A4
Harestock Cl SO22 1 B3
Harestock Cnr SO22 1 B2
Harestock Prim Sch SO22 1 B2
Harestock Rd Havant PO9 135 E2
Winchester SO22 1 B2
Harewood Ave BH7 206 A3
Harewood Cl SO50 56 A3
Harewood Cres BH7 205 F4
Harewood Gdns BH7 205 F4
Harewood Gn SO41 212 A2
Harewood Pl BH7 206 A3
Harford Cl SO41 197 E1
Harford Rd BH12 203 E4
Harkness Dr PO7 135 D4
Harkwood Dr BH15 201 F2
Harland Cres SO15 78 B1
Harland Rd BH6 207 D2
Harlaxton Cl SO50 55 F3
Harlech Dr SO53 55 D2
Harlequin Gr PO15 130 C1
Harleston Rd PO6 133 E1
Harleston Villas 10 BH21 163 E2
Harley Ct SO31 128 B1
Harley Wlk 62 PO1 182 B3
Harlyn Rd SO16 77 F1
Harness Cl BH21 164 A3
Harold Cl SO40 100 B3
Harold Rd Portsmouth PO4 182 C2
South Hayling PO11 185 D1
Southampton SO15 102 B4
Stubbington PO14 154 B2
Westbourne PO10 137 D2
Harold Terr PO10 136 C1
Harpway La Burton BH23 192 B3
Sopley BH23 192 B3
Harrage The SO51 52 C4
Harrier Cl Horndean PO8 112 A4
Lee-on-the-Solent PO13 179 F1
Southampton SO16 78 A3
Harrier Dr BH21 163 E1
Harrier Way Fawley SO45 150 A3
Petersfield GU31 41 E1
Harriers Cl BH23 208 B4
Harriet Cl PO14 179 D3
Harrington Ct BH23 208 C4
Harris Ave SO30 105 E4
Harris Rd PO13 155 E2
Harris Way BH25 195 D3
Harrison Ave BH1 205 E3
Harrison Cl BH23 192 B2
Harrison House 12 PO2 157 E1
Harrison Prim Sch PO16 131 D1
Harrison Rd Fareham PO16 131 D1
Southampton SO17 79 E2
Harrison Way BH22 138 C2
Harrison's Cut SO14 103 D2
Harrow Cl BH23 193 D4
Harrow Down SO22 10 B2
Harrow La GU32 40 C3
Harrow Rd Bransgore BH23 193 D3
Portsmouth PO5 182 C2
Harrowgate La PO7,PO8 87 D1
Harry Barrow Cl 1 BH24 141 D3
Harry Law Hall 17 PO1 182 B3
Hart Cl BH25 194 C2
Hart Ct SO19 103 F2
Hart Hill SO45 126 B1
Hart Plain Ave PO8 111 F2
Hart Plain Jun & Inf Schs PO7,PO8 111 F1
Hartford House PO1 182 A2
Harthill Dro SP5 47 F3
Harting Cl PO8 88 B2
Harting Down GU31 41 D2
Harting Gdns PO16 132 B1
Harting Rd BH6 206 B4
Hartington Rd Gosport PO12 180 C3
Southampton SO14 103 D3
Hartland Ct PO10 137 E1
Hartland's Rd PO16 131 D1
Hartley Ave SO17 79 D2
Hartley Cl Bishopstoke SO50 57 D1
Hythe SO45 126 A1
Hartley Rd Bishopstoke SO50 57 D1
Portsmouth PO2 157 F2
Hartley Wlk SO45 126 A1
Hartnell Ct BH21 186 B3
Harts Farm Way PO9 159 E4
Harts Way SO41 196 B1
Hartsbourne Dr BH7 206 A4
Hartsgrove Ave SO45 150 C1
Hartsgrove Cl SO45 150 C1
Hartwell Rd PO3 158 A2
Hartwood Gdns PO8 111 F1
Harvest Cl SO22 10 B2
Harvest Rd PO7 110 C2
Harvester Dr PO15 130 A1
Harvester Way SO41 197 E3
Harvestgate Wlk 9 PO9 135 E3
Harvesting La GU32 64 B3
Harvey Brown House PO11 185 D3
Harvey Cres SO31 128 C1
Harvey Ct SO45 150 C1
Harvey Gdns SO45 126 A2
Harvey House PO4 183 D1
Harvey Rd Bishopstoke SO50 56 C1
Bournemouth BH5 206 A3
Oakley BH21 187 F4
Harwell Rd BH17 202 B4
Harwich Rd PO6 133 E1
Harwood Cl Gosport PO13 155 E2
Totton SO40 100 B4
Harwood Ct 13 BH25 194 C2
Harwood Pl SO23 2 B4
Harwood Rd PO13 155 E2
Haselbury Rd SO40 100 C4
Haselworth Dr PO12 181 D1
Haselworth Prim Sch PO12 181 D2
Haskells Cl SO43 121 F2
Haskells Rd BH12 203 D4
Haslar Cres PO7 111 E1
Haslar Rd PO12 181 E1
Haslar Terr PO12 181 E1
Haslegrave House 2 PO2 182 B4
Haslemere Ave BH23 209 D4
Haslemere Gdns PO11 185 F1
Haslemere Pl BH23 209 D4
Haslemere Rd Portsmouth PO4 182 C2
Southbourne PO10 137 E1
Hasler Rd BH17 187 E1
Haslop Rd BH21 164 A4
Hassocks The PO7 135 D4
Hastings Ave PO12 180 C4
Hastings House 3 PO2 157 E1
Hastings Rd Bournemouth BH8 190 C1
Broadstone BH17 187 D1
Hatch Ct PO9 135 E4
Hatch La GU33 21 E2
Hatch Mead SO30 80 B1
Hatch Pond Rd BH17 202 B4
Hatchers La SO21 33 D3
Hatchet Cl SP6 47 E2
Hatchet La Beaulieu SO42 175 E4
East Boldre SO42 175 E4
Hatchley La SO21 58 A3
Hatfield Ct BH25 194 C2
Hatfield Gdns BH7 206 A4
Hatfield Rd PO4 183 D2
Hathaway Cl SO50 56 A2
Hathaway Gdns PO7 112 A1
Hathaway Rd BH6 206 B2
Hatherden Ave BH14 202 C3
Hatherley Cres PO16 156 A4
Hatherley Dr PO16 156 A4
Hatherley Mans 4 SO15 102 B4
Hatherley Rd Cosham PO6 133 D1
Winchester SO22 1 C1
Hatley Rd SO18 104 A4
Hatt La SO51 5 F1
Havant Bsns Ctr PO9 159 E4
Havant Coll PO9 135 F1
Havant Farm Cl PO9 135 F2
Havant Rd Cosham PO6 158 B4
Emsworth PO10 160 C4
Horndean PO8 112 B3
North Hayling PO11 159 F1
Portsmouth PO2 182 C4
Havant St PO1 182 A3
Havant Sta PO9 135 F1
Havant War Meml Hospl PO9 135 F1
Havant-By-Pass PO9 160 A4
Havelock Ct SO31 128 B1
Havelock Rd Locks Heath SO31 128 B1
Poole BH12 204 A3
Portsmouth PO5 182 B2
Southampton SO14 102 C3
Havelock Way BH23 193 E1
Haven Cres PO14 153 F1
Haven Ct
4 Milford on Sea SO41 211 E2
Poole BH13 214 A2
Haven Gdns BH25 195 D1
Haven Rd Corfe Mullen BH21 186 B3
Poole BH13 214 C4
South Hayling PO11 185 F1
Haven The Eastleigh SO50 56 A3
Gosport PO12 181 D1
Locks Heath SO31 129 D2
Portsmouth PO4 183 D3
Southampton SO19 103 F2
Havendale SO30 105 E3
Havenhurst BH13 214 C3
Havenstone Way SO18 79 E2
Haverstock Rd BH9 190 A2
Haviland Rd
Bournemouth BH1, BH7 205 F3
Ferndown BH21 165 D4
Haviland Rd E BH7 205 F3
Haviland Rd W 5 BH7 205 F3
Havisham Rd PO2 182 B4
Havre Towers 5 SO19 126 C4
Hawden Rd BH11 189 D1
Hawfinch Cl SO16 78 A3
Hawk Cl Stubbington PO14 179 D3
Wimborne Minster BH21 164 A4
Hawkchurch Gdns BH17 187 F1
Hawke St PO1 182 A3
Hawker Cl BH21 163 F1
Hawkeswood Rd SO18 103 E4
Hawkewood Ave PO7 111 E1
Hawkhill SO45 125 E2
Hawkhurst Cl SO19 104 A1
Hawkins Cl BH24 117 E1
Hawkins Ct SO40 101 F2
Hawkins Rd Gosport PO13 155 E1
Poole BH12 188 C1
Hawkley Gr SO19 126 C4
Hawkley Rd Hawkley GU33 20 B3
Liss GU33 20 B3
Hawks Mead GU33 20 C3
Hawkwell PO16 155 F4
Hawkwood Rd BH5 205 F2
Hawley Cl PO9 135 F3
Haworth Cl BH23 192 A1
Hawstead Gn 4 PO9 135 E3
Hawswater Cl SO16 77 F1
Hawthorn Cl
Colden Common SO21 57 D4
1 Fair Oak SO50 57 E1
Hedge End SO30 105 E3
New Milton BH25 195 E2
Hawthorn Cres PO6 158 A3
Hawthorn Ct 1 GU31 41 E2
Hawthorn Dr Broadstone BH17 186 C1
Sway SO41 172 A1
Hawthorn La SO31 128 C3
Hawthorn Rd
Bournemouth BH9 204 C4
Burton BH23 192 C2
Denmead PO7 110 C2
Horndean PO8 88 B1
Hythe SO45 125 F2
Southampton SO17 79 D1
Hawthorn Wlk 20 PO13 179 F1
Hawthorne Gr PO11 185 D2
Hawthorne Rd SO40 100 B4
Hawthorns The
Bishop's Waltham SO32 83 D4
Christchurch BH23 207 F3
Eastleigh SO50 55 F1
Marchwood SO40 102 A1
Southampton SO15 102 C4
Hayburn Rd SO16 77 E1
Haydens Ct SO41 197 F2
Haydn Cl SO23 2 A4
Haydock Cl SO40 100 B4
Haydock Mews PO7 112 A1
Haydon Rd BH13 204 A1
Hayes Ave BH7 205 F3
Hayes Cl Fareham PO15 130 B2
Wimborne Minster BH21 164 A2
Hayes La BH21 164 A3
Hayes Mead SO45 150 A3
Hayes Terr PO12 181 D3
Hayeswood Cty Fst Sch BH21 164 A3
Hayeswood Rd BH21 164 A3
Hayle Rd SO18 80 A1
Hayley Cl SO45 149 F4
Hayling Ave PO3 183 D4
Hayling Cl PO14 154 B4
Hayling Sch The PO11 185 D3
Haymoor Mid Sch BH17 187 F1
Haymoor Rd BH15 203 D4
Haynes Ave BH15 202 B2
Haynes Way SO45 125 F1
Hays Cotts GU32 40 B4
Haysoms Cl BH25 195 D1
Hayter Gdns SO51 53 D4
Hayters Way SP6 93 D3
Hayward Bsns Ctr PO9 136 A2
Hayward Cl SO40 100 B4
Hayward Cres BH31 114 C3
Hayward Ct SO45 150 B2
Hayward Way BH31 114 C3
Haywards Ct PO1 182 A2
Haywards Farm Cl BH31 114 C3
Haywards La BH21 186 B4
Hazel Cl Alderholt SP6 93 D3
Chandler's Ford SO53 30 B1
Christchurch BH23 193 E1
Colden Common SO21 32 A1
Hazel Ct Bournemouth BH9 190 B2
27 New Milton BH25 195 D1
Portsmouth PO4 182 C2
Hazel Dr BH22 165 E4
Hazel Farm Rd SO40 100 B4
Hazel Gr Ashurst SO40 99 F2
Clanfield PO8 88 B3
Locks Heath SO31 129 D1
Winchester SO22 10 B3
Hazel Rd Clanfield PO8 88 B3
Lymington SO41 197 D2
Southampton SO19 103 E2
Hazel Wood Inf Sch SO40 100 B4
Hazelbank Cl GU31 41 D2
Hazeldale Villas 6 SO45 126 A3
Hazeldean Ct PO9 113 D1
Hazeldean Dr PO9 113 D1
Hazeldene BH18 187 D2
Hazeldown Rd SO16 77 F3
Hazeleigh Ave SO19 103 F1
Hazeley Cotts SO21 32 B4
Hazeley Gn 45 PO9 136 A3
Hazeley Rd SO21 32 B3
Hazelholt Dr PO9 135 E2
Hazell Ave BH10 189 D1
Hazelton Cl BH7 206 A4
Hazelwood PO14 154 A3
Hazelwood Ave Havant PO9 135 D2
New Milton BH25 194 C2
Hazelwood Dr BH31 115 D2
Hazelwood Rd SO18 80 A1
Hazlebury Rd BH17 202 A4
Hazlemere Dr BH24 139 F2
Hazleton Way PO8 112 A2
Head Down GU31 41 D2
Head's La BH10 189 F3
Headbourne Worthy House SO23 2 A3
Headland Dr SO31 129 D2
Headlands Adventure Ctr BH24 117 D1
Headlands Bsns Pk BH24 117 D1
Headlands The SP5 46 C4
Headless Cross BH10 189 E3
Headley Cl PO13 179 F1
Headon View GU32 37 E3
Heads Farm Cl BH10 189 F3
Headswell Ave BH10 189 F2
Headswell Cres BH10 189 F2
Headswell Gdns BH10 189 F2
Heanor Cl BH10 189 E1
Hearne Gdns SO32 84 A1
Hearts Of Oak Mews SO41 197 E2
Heath Ave BH15 202 B3
Heath Cl Fair Oak SO50 57 E1
Horndean PO8 112 A4
Wimborne Minster BH21 164 A4
Heath Ct GU31 40 C1
Heath Farm Cl BH22 165 E2
Heath Farm Rd BH22 165 E2
Heath Farm Way BH22 165 E2
Heath Gdns SO31 127 E4
Heath House Cl SO30 105 D2
Heath House Gdns SO30 105 D2
Heath House La SO30 105 E2
Heath La SO42 175 E4
Heath Lawns PO15 130 B1
Heath Lodge GU31 40 C1
Heath Rd Christchurch BH23 194 A1
Hordle SO41 195 F2
Locks Heath SO31 129 D2
North Baddesley SO52 54 A2
Petersfield GU31 41 D2
Soberton SO32 85 D1
Southampton SO19 104 A3
St Leonards BH24 139 E2
Heath Rd E GU31 41 D1
Heath Rd N SO31 128 C2
Heath Rd S SO31 128 C2
Heath Rd W GU31 41 D1
Heath The PO7 111 D2
Heathcote Pl SO21 30 A4
Heathcote Rd
Bournemouth BH5 205 F2
Chandler's Ford SO53 55 E3
Portsmouth PO2 157 F1
Heathen St SO32 82 A2
Heather Chase SO50 57 D1
Heather Cl Bournemouth BH8 190 B2
Christchurch BH23 194 A1
Corfe Mullen BH21 186 C3
Gosport PO13 155 D1
Hordle SO41 196 A2
St Leonards BH24 139 F2
Totton SO40 100 C4
Waterlooville PO7 134 C3
Heather Ct SO18 104 B4
Heather Dell BH16 201 D3
Heather Dr BH22 165 E4
Heather Gdns PO15 130 B2
Heather Lodge 2 BH25 195 D2
Heather Rd Blackfield SO45 150 C1
Bournemouth BH10 189 E2
Petersfield GU31 41 E2
Heather View Rd BH12 203 F4
Heather Way BH22 165 E4
Heatherbank Rd BH4 204 B2
Heatherbrae Gdns SO52 53 F2
Heatherbrae La BH16 201 D3
Heatherdeane Rd SO17 79 D1
Heatherdene Rd SO53 30 C1
Heatherdown Rd BH22 139 D1
Heatherdown Way BH22 139 D1
Heatherfield GU31 65 E3

Heatherlands Fst Sch BH12 ...... 203 F3
Heatherlands Rd SO16 .... 78 C4
Heatherlands Rise BH12 .... 203 E3
Heatherlea Rd BH6 .... 206 B2
Heatherley Ct 26 PO5 .... 182 B2
Heatherstone Ave SO45 .... 125 F1
Heatherton Mews PO10 .... 136 C1
Heatherview Cl SO52 .... 53 F3
Heathfield SO45 .... 125 F1
Heathfield Ave Fareham PO15 .. 130 B1
  Poole BH12 .... 204 A4
Heathfield Cl
  Chandler's Ford SO53 .... 30 B1
  Southampton SO19 .... 104 A2
Heathfield House BH23 .... 169 F1
Heathfield Inf Sch SO19 .... 104 B1
Heathfield Jun Sch SO19 .... 104 B2
Heathfield Rd
  Chandler's Ford SO53 .... 30 B1
  Petersfield GU31 .... 41 E2
  Portsmouth PO2 .... 157 E1
  Southampton SO19 .... 104 B2
  West Moors BH22 .... 139 D1
Heathfield Specl Sch PO14 ..... 154 B4
Heathfield Way BH22 .... 138 C1
Heathlands Ave SO15 .... 165 E1
Heathlands Cl Burton BH23 ..... 192 B2
  Chandler's Ford SO53 .... 55 E4
  Verwood BH31 .... 115 D3
Heathlands Prim Sch BH11 ... 189 D2
Heathlands Rd SO53 .... 55 E4
Heathwood Ave BH25 .... 209 F4
Heathwood Rd BH9 .... 204 C4
Heathy Cl BH25 .... 209 F4
Heaton Rd Bournemouth BH10 . 189 D1
  Gosport PO12 .... 181 D4
Heavytree Rd BH14 .... 203 D2
Hebrides Cl SO14 .... 154 A2
Heckfield Cl PO9 .... 136 A3
Heckford La BH15 .... 202 B2
Heckford Rd
  Corfe Mullen BH21 .... 186 B3
  Poole BH15 .... 202 B2
Hector Cl PO7 .... 134 C1
Hector Rd PO14 .... 155 D3
Hedera Rd SO31 .... 128 C2
Hedge End Bsns Ctr SO30 .... 81 D1
Hedge End Sta SO30 .... 81 E2
Hedge End Wlk 7 PO9 .... 136 A3
Hedgerley BH25 .... 210 A4
Hedgerow Cl SO16 .... 77 F4
Hedgerow Dr SO18 .... 80 A1
Hedgerow Gdns PO10 .... 136 C2
Hedley Cl SO45 .... 150 C1
Hedley Gdns SO30 .... 81 D2
Heidelberg Rd PO4 .... 182 C2
Heights App BH16 .... 201 E4
Heights Rd BH16 .... 201 E4
Heights The Fareham PO16 ..... 131 E1
  Hedge End SO30 .... 105 D3
Helena Rd PO4 .... 182 C1
Helford Gdns SO18 .... 80 A1
Helic House 2 BH21 .... 163 E3
Hellyer Rd PO4 .... 183 D2
Helm Cl PO13 .... 180 B3
Helsby Rd PO14 .... 154 C4
Helsted Cl PO12 .... 180 C2
Helston Dr PO10 .... 136 C2
Helston Rd PO6 .... 132 C1
Helvellyn Rd SO16 .... 101 F4
Helyar Rd BH8 .... 190 C1
Hemdean Gdns SO30 .... 80 B1
Hemlock Rd PO8 .... 111 F2
Hemlock Way SO52 .... 54 C3
Hemming Cl SO40 .... 100 C3
Hemmingway Gdns PO15 .... 129 E4
Hempsted Rd PO6 .... 133 D1
Hemsley Wlk PO8 .... 112 A2
Henbury Cl Corfe Mullen BH21 . 186 B3
  Poole BH17 .... 188 A1
Henbury Rise BH21 .... 186 B3
Henbury View Fst Sch BH21 .. 186 B3
Henbury View Rd BH21 .... 186 B3
Henderson Rd PO4 .... 183 E2
Hendford Gdns BH10 .... 189 E1
Hendford Rd BH10 .... 189 E1
Hengist Rd BH1 .... 205 E2
Hengistbury Rd
  Barton on Sea BH25 .... 209 F4
  Bournemouth BH6 .... 207 D2
Henley Cl SO41 .... 211 F2
Henley Gdns
  Bournemouth BH7 .... 206 A4
  Fareham BH22 .... 130 B2
Henley Rd PO4 .... 182 C2
Henning's Park Rd BH15 .... 202 C3
Henry Beaufort Sec Sch SO22 .. 1 C2
Henry Cl SO45 .... 150 A3
Henry Cort Com Sch PO15 ..... 130 A2
Henry Cort Dr PO15 .... 130 B2
Henry Rd Bishopstoke SO50 ..... 56 B2
  Southampton SO15 .... 102 B4
Henry St 9 Gosport PO12 .... 181 E2
  Southampton SO15 .... 102 C3
Henstead Ct 9 SO15 .... 102 C3
Henstead Rd SO15 .... 102 C3
Hensting La
  Colden Common SO21 .... 32 C1
  Owslebury SO21 .... 58 C1
Henty Rd SO16 .... 102 A4
Henville Cl PO13 .... 180 B4
Henville Rd 6 BH8 .... 205 E3
Henwood Down GU31 .... 41 D2
Hepworth Cl SO19 .... 104 B1
Herald Ind Est SO30 .... 81 D1
Herald Rd SO30 .... 81 D1
Herbert Ave BH12 .... 203 E4
Herbert Ct BH12 .... 203 E4

Herbert Hospl BH4 .... 204 A1
Herbert Rd Bournemouth BH4 .. 204 A1
  Gosport PO12 .... 180 C3
  New Milton BH25 .... 195 D2
  Poole BH13 .... 204 A1
  Portsmouth PO4 .... 182 C1
  Redlynch SP5 .... 47 E3
Herbert St PO1 .... 182 B4
Herbert Walker Ave SO15 ...... 102 B2
Herberton Rd BH6 .... 206 B3
Hercules Rd BH15 .... 201 E2
Hercules St PO2 .... 182 B4
Hereford Ct PO13 .... 180 B3
Hereford Rd PO5 .... 182 B2
Hereward Cl SO51 .... 53 D4
Heritage Ct BH13 .... 214 C4
Herm Rd BH12 .... 188 B1
Hermes Rd PO13 .... 179 E2
Hermitage Cl
  Bishop's Waltham SO32 .... 83 D4
  Havant PO9 .... 135 F2
Hermitage Gdns PO7 .... 134 C4
Hermitage Rd BH14 .... 203 D3
Hermitage The BH14 .... 203 D3
Hern La SP6 .... 94 A3
Herne Jun Sch GU31 .... 41 D2
Herne CI Cosham PO6 .... 157 F4
  Petersfield GU31 .... 41 D2
Heron Court Rd BH3, BH9 ...... 205 D4
Heron Dr BH21 .... 164 A4
Heron La SO51 .... 27 E3
Heron Quay PO10 .... 161 D4
Heron Sq SO50 .... 55 F1
Heron Way PO13 .... 155 D2
Herons Cl PO14 .... 154 B2
Herons Ct PO11 .... 185 D3
Heronswood SO40 .... 76 B1
Herrick Cl SO19 .... 104 B2
Herriot Cl PO8 .... 112 A3
Herriot House PO8 .... 112 A1
Herstone Cl BH17 .... 187 F1
Hertford Cl SP6 .... 69 F2
Hertford Ct 12 BH23 .... 209 D4
Hertford Pl PO1 .... 182 B4
Hertsfield PO14 .... 129 E2
Hesketh Cl BH24 .... 140 A3
Hesketh House 8 SO15 .... 102 B3
Hestan Cl SO31 .... 191 E2
Hester Rd PO4 .... 183 D2
Hestia Cl SO51 .... 53 E4
Heston Way SO31 .... 138 B2
Heston Wlk PO12 .... 180 C2
Hewett Cl PO14 .... 153 F4
Hewett House PO14 .... 153 F4
Hewett Rd Portsmouth PO2 .... 157 F1
  Titchfield PO14 .... 153 F4
Hewetts Rise SO31 .... 152 B4
Hewitt Cl PO12 .... 181 D4
Hewitt Rd BH15 .... 201 F2
Hewitt's Rd SO15 .... 102 B3
Heyes Dr SO19 .... 104 B2
Heysham Rd
  Broadstone BH18 .... 187 D2
  Southampton SO15 .... 102 A4
Heyshott Gdns PO8 .... 88 B2
Heyshott Rd PO4 .... 182 C2
Heytesbury Rd BH6 .... 206 B3
Heyward Rd PO4 .... 182 C2
Heywood Gdns PO9 .... 135 E3
Heywood Gr SO19 .... 104 C3
Hibberd Way BH10 .... 189 E1
Hibbs Cl BH16 .... 201 E4
Hickory Cl BH16 .... 201 D4
Hickory Dr SO22 .... 1 B2
Hickory Gdns SO30 .... 80 B2
High Barn Cotts SO32 .... 36 C2
High Cross SO32 .... 18 C1
High Cross La GU32 .... 18 B1
High Ct PO4 .... 183 D2
High Dr PO13 .... 155 E1
High Firs Gdns SO51 .... 53 E4
High Firs Rd Romsey SO51 .... 53 E4
  Southampton SO19 .... 104 B3
High Howe Cl BH11 .... 188 C2
High Howe Gdns BH11 .... 188 C2
High Howe La BH11 .... 188 C2
High Lawn Way PO9 .... 135 F3
High Marryats 3 BH25 .... 210 A4
High Mead Fareham PO15 .... 130 C2
  Ferndown BH22 .... 165 D1
High Meadow SO19 .... 104 B3
High Oaks Cl SO31 .... 129 D2
High Oaks Gdns BH11 .... 188 C2
High Park Rd BH18 .... 186 C2
High Pines BH23 .... 208 B4
High Point SO18 .... 103 F4
High Rd SO16 .... 79 E2
High Ridge Cres BH25 .... 195 E1
High St Beaulieu SO42 .... 148 C1
  Bishop's Waltham SO32 .... 83 E4
  Botley SO30 .... 106 A4
  Buriton GU31 .... 65 E3
  Bursledon SO31 .... 128 A4
  Christchurch BH23 .... 207 D3
  Cosham PO6 .... 157 F4
  Damerham SP6 .... 68 B3
  Downton SP5 .... 47 D2
  Droxford SO32 .... 61 D1
  East Meon GU32 .... 38 C1
  Eastleigh SO50 .... 56 A1
  Fareham PO14, PO16, PO17 .... 131 E1
  Fordingbridge SP6 .... 69 F1
  Gosport PO12 .... 181 E2

High St Continued
  Hamble-le-Rice SO31 .... 128 A1
  Hambledon PO7 .... 86 B2
  Hythe SO45 .... 126 A3
  Lee-on-the-Solent PO13 .... 179 F1
  Lymington SO41 .... 197 F2
  Lyndhurst SO43 .... 121 F3
  Meonstoke SO32 .... 61 E2
  Milford on Sea SO41 .... 211 E2
  Petersfield GU32 .... 40 C2
  Poole BH15 .... 202 B1
  Portsmouth PO1 .... 182 A2
  Ringwood BH24 .... 140 C4
  Shedfield SO23 .... 107 F4
  Soberton SO32 .... 85 D2
  9 Southampton SO14 .... 103 D2
  Southwick PO17 .... 132 C3
  St Leonards BH24 .... 139 F3
  Titchfield PO14 .... 153 F4
  Totton SO40 .... 101 D4
  Twyford SO21 .... 32 A3
  West End SO30 .... 80 B1
  Wimborne Minster BH21 .... 163 D2
  Winchester SO21, SO23 .... 10 C4
  33 Winchester SO21, SO23 ..... 11 D4
  Woodgreen SP6 .... 70 C4
High St N BH15 .... 202 B2
High Town Hill BH24 .... 141 F4
High Trees Poole BH13 .... 214 C4
  Waterlooville PO7 .... 134 C4
High Trees Dr SO22 .... 1 C1
High Trees Wlk BH22 .... 165 E4
High View PO16 .... 132 B1
High View Way SO18 .... 103 F4
High Way BH18 .... 186 C2
High Wlk PO15 .... 130 C2
Highbank Ave PO7 .... 134 B2
Highbank Gdns PO6 .... 69 F1
Highbridge Rd
  Colden Common SO21 .... 31 F1
  Colden Common SO50, SO21 ... 56 B4
  Poole BH14 .... 203 E2
  Twyford SO21 .... 31 F1
Highbury Bldgs PO6 .... 157 F3
Highbury Cl Fair Oak SO50 ...... 57 E1
  New Milton BH25 .... 195 D1
Highbury Coll PO6 .... 158 A3
Highbury Gr PO6 .... 158 A3
Highbury Prim Sch PO6 .... 158 A3
Highbury St PO1 .... 182 A2
Highbury Way PO6 .... 157 F3
Highclere Ave PO9 .... 135 F2
Highclere Rd SO16 .... 78 B2
Highclere Way SO53 .... 55 D2
Highcliff Ave SO14 .... 103 D4
Highcliffe Cnr BH23 .... 209 D4
Highcliffe Comp Sch BH23 .... 193 E1
Highcliffe Cty Jun Sch
  Christchurch BH23 .... 193 F1
  Christchurch BH23 .... 194 A1
Highcliffe Dr SO50 .... 56 A4
Highcliffe Rd
  Christchurch BH23 .... 208 B4
  Gosport PO12 .... 180 C2
  Winchester SO23 .... 11 D3
Highcroft Ind Est PO8 .... 112 B4
Highcroft La PO8 .... 112 B4
Highcrown Mews SO17 .... 79 C1
Highcrown St SO17 .... 79 D1
Higher Blandford Rd BH18 .... 186 C3
Higher Merley La BH21 .... 186 C4
Highfield Lymington SO41 .... 197 E2
  Twyford SO21 .... 32 A3
Highfield Ave Fareham PO14 .. 154 C4
  Lymington SO41 .... 197 E2
  Ringwood BH24 .... 141 D4
  Southampton SO15 .... 78 C2
  Twyford SO21 .... 32 A3
  Waterlooville PO7 .... 111 F1
Highfield Campus (Univ of
  Southampton) SO17 .... 79 D2
Highfield CE Jun Sch SO17 ...... 79 D1
Highfield CE Prim Sch SO17 .... 79 D1
Highfield Cl
  Chandler's Ford SO53 .... 55 F3
  Corfe Mullen BH21 .... 186 C3
  Southampton SO17 .... 79 D1
  Sway SO41 .... 172 A1
  Waterlooville PO7 .... 111 F1
Highfield Cres SO17 .... 79 D1
Highfield Dr BH24 .... 141 D4
Highfield Gdns Liss GU33 .... 21 D2
  Sway SO41 .... 172 A1
Highfield Hall SO17 .... 79 D1
Highfield House 12 BH14 .... 203 D2
Highfield La Redlynch SP5 .... 47 E3
  Southampton SO17 .... 79 D1
Highfield Lodge 3 SO17 .... 79 D1
Highfield Par PO8 .... 112 A1
Highfield Rd
  Bournemouth BH9 .... 189 F1
  Chandler's Ford SO53 .... 55 F3
  Corfe Mullen BH21 .... 186 C3
  Gosport PO12 .... 180 C3
  Lymington SO41 .... 197 E2
  Petersfield GU32 .... 40 C2
  Portsmouth PO1 .... 182 B3
  Ringwood BH24 .... 141 D4
  Southampton SO17 .... 79 D1
  West Moors BH22 .... 138 C2
Highfield Terr 17 SO22 .... 10 C4
Highfields SO31 .... 128 C1
Highgate Rd PO3 .... 158 A1
Highgrove Cl SO40 .... 100 B3
Highgrove Ind Pk PO3 .... 158 A2
Highgrove Rd PO3 .... 183 D4
Highland Ave BH23 .... 194 A1
Highland Cl PO10 .... 160 C4

Highland Rd Emsworth PO10 .. 136 C1
  Poole BH14 .... 203 D3
  Portsmouth PO4 .... 183 D1
  Wimborne Minster BH21 .... 163 E3
Highland St PO4 .... 183 D1
Highland Terr PO4 .... 182 C2
Highland View Cl BH21 .... 163 E3
Highlands Cl Hythe SO45 .... 126 A1
  North Baddesley SO52 .... 53 F3
Highlands Cres BH10 .... 189 E2
Highlands House SO19 .... 103 E2
Highlands Rd
  Barton on Sea BH25 .... 210 A4
  Cosham PO6 .... 158 B4
  Fareham PO15, PO16 .... 130 B2
Highlands Way Hythe SO45 .... 125 F1
  Whiteparish SP5 .... 24 A2
Highmoor Cl
  Corfe Mullen BH21 .... 186 B3
  Poole BH14 .... 203 D2
Highmoor Rd
  Bournemouth BH11 .... 189 D1
  Corfe Mullen BH21 .... 186 B3
  Poole BH14 .... 203 E2
Highnam Gdns SO31 .... 128 C2
Hightown Gdns BH24 .... 141 E3
Hightown Ind Est BH24 .... 141 D3
Hightown Prim Sch SO19 ...... 104 C2
Hightown Rd BH24 .... 141 E3
Hightown Towers SO19 .... 104 C2
Hightrees Ave BH8 .... 190 C1
Highview Cl BH23 .... 191 F2
Highview Gdns BH12 .... 203 E4
Highways Rd SO21 .... 31 E3
Highwood Cl SP6 .... 92 B3
Highwood La
  North Baddesley SO51 .... 53 E4
  Ringwood BH24 .... 117 F2
Highwood Lawn PO9 .... 135 E4
Highwood PRU SO42 .... 172 C4
Highwood Rd
  Brockenhurst SO42 .... 172 C4
  Gosport PO13 .... 180 B4
  Poole BH14 .... 203 F2
Higworth La PO11 .... 184 C3
Hilary Ave PO6 .... 158 A4
Hilary Cl SO43 .... 122 A2
Hilary Ct PO13 .... 180 B3
Hilary Rd BH17 .... 187 E1
Hilda Cl 8 SO15 .... 102 C4
Hilda Gdns PO7 .... 111 D2
Hilda Pl 28 SO14 .... 103 E3
Hilda Rd BH12 .... 203 F4
Hilden Ct PO11 .... 184 C2
Hilden Way SO22 .... 1 A3
Hiley Rd BH15 .... 202 B3
Hill Brow Rd Hill Brow GU33 .... 21 D1
  Liss GU33 .... 21 D1
Hill Cl Bransgore BH23 .... 193 D4
  Fair Oak SO50 .... 57 E3
Hill Close Est SP6 .... 70 C4
Hill Coppice Rd PO15 .... 129 E3
Hill Croft PO15 .... 129 F2
Hill Dr PO15 .... 130 B2
Hill Farm Rd SO15 .... 102 C3
Hill Head Rd PO14 .... 179 D3
Hill House Sch SO41 .... 173 E1
Hill Houses La SO24 .... 14 A3
Hill La Bransgore BH23 .... 193 D4
  Burton BH23 .... 192 C1
  Colden Common SO21 .... 31 F1
  Southampton SO15 .... 78 C1
Hill Park Rd Fareham PO15 .... 130 B2
  Gosport PO12 .... 180 C3
Hill Pl SO31 .... 128 A4
Hill Rd PO16 .... 132 B1
Hill Rise SO21 .... 32 A3
Hill St Ower SO51, SO40 .... 76 B3
  Poole BH15 .... 202 B1
Hill Top SO22 .... 1 B3
Hill View GU32 .... 38 B1
Hill View Prim Sch BH10 .... 189 F2
Hill View Rd Braishfield SO51 .. 28 B3
  Ferndown BH22 .... 165 E3
  Michelmersh SO51 .... 27 E4
  Portchester PO16 .... 132 B1
Hill Wlk PO15 .... 130 B2
Hillary Cl PO16 .... 130 C1
Hillary Rd BH23 .... 207 F4
Hillborough Cres 20 PO5 .... 182 B2
Hillbourne Fst & Mid Schs
  BH17 .... 187 D1
Hillbourne Rd BH17 .... 187 D1
Hillbrow Cl Fareham PO15 ...... 130 B2
  Rowland's Castle PO9 .... 113 D1
Hillbrow Rd BH6 .... 206 A3
Hillbury Pk SP6 .... 93 D3
Hillbury Rd SP6 .... 93 D3
Hillcrest Ave
  Chandler's Ford SO53 .... 55 F3
  Ferndown BH22 .... 165 E4
Hillcrest Cl Bournemouth BH9 . 190 A2
  North Baddesley SO52 .... 53 F3
Hillcrest Dr SO53 .... 55 E3
Hillcrest Gdns SO32 .... 83 E2
Hillcrest Hospl BH10 .... 189 E1
Hillcrest Rd Bournemouth BH9 . 190 A2
  Corfe Mullen BH21 .... 186 B3
Hillcroft SP5 .... 47 E3
Hilldene Way SO30 .... 80 C1
Hillditch SO41 .... 197 E3
Hilldown Rd SO17 .... 79 D1
Hilldowns Ave PO2 .... 157 E1
Hiller Wlk 16 PO13 .... 179 F1
Hillgrove Rd SO18 .... 79 F2
Hillier Way SO23 .... 2 A1
Hillman Rd BH14 .... 203 E3

Hillmead Gdns PO9 .... 135 D1
Hillrise SO32 .... 61 E3
Hillside Curdridge SO32 .... 106 C4
  Littleton SO22 .... 1 B3
Hillside Ave Romsey SO51 .... 53 D4
  Southampton SO18 .... 79 F1
  Waterlooville PO7 .... 134 A1
Hillside Cl Chandler's Ford SO53 . 55 E3
  Horndean BH23 .... 88 B2
  West Dean SP5 .... 3 E1
  Winchester SO22 .... 1 B1
Hillside Cres PO6 .... 132 C1
Hillside Cty First Sch BH31 .... 114 C4
Hillside Dr BH23 .... 191 E2
Hillside Gdns BH21 .... 186 B2
Hillside Ind Est PO8 .... 112 A4
Hillside Mews BH21 .... 186 B2
Hillside Rd Corfe Mullen BH21 . 186 B3
  Lymington SO41 .... 197 E2
  Poole BH12 .... 188 C1
  Verwood BH31 .... 114 C4
  Winchester SO22 .... 1 B1
  Woodlands BH21 .... 114 A3
Hillside Wlk BH21 .... 114 A3
Hillsley Rd PO6 .... 132 C1
Hillson Dr PO15 .... 130 B2
Hillson House PO15 .... 130 B2
Hillsons Rd SO30 .... 106 B4
Hilltop Cl BH22 .... 165 D4
Hilltop Cres PO6 .... 134 B1
Hilltop Dr SO19 .... 104 B2
Hilltop Gdns PO8 .... 88 B2
Hilltop Rd Corfe Mullen BH21 . 186 C3
  Ferndown BH22 .... 165 D4
Hillview PO8 .... 112 B3
Hillview Rd Bournemouth BH10 . 189 E2
  Hythe SO45 .... 125 F2
Hillway BH24 .... 139 F3
Hillway The
  Chandler's Ford SO53 .... 55 E4
  Portchester PO16 .... 156 B4
Hilly Cl SO21 .... 33 D2
Hillyfields SO16 .... 77 E2
Hilsea Cres PO2 .... 157 F3
Hilsea Mkt PO2 .... 157 F3
Hilsea Sta PO2 .... 158 A2
Hiltingbury Ave 32 PO9 .... 136 A3
Hiltingbury Cl SO53 .... 30 B1
Hiltingbury Ct SO53 .... 30 A1
Hiltingbury Inf Sch SO53 .... 30 B1
Hiltingbury Jun Sch SO53 .... 30 B1
Hiltingbury Rd SO53 .... 30 B1
Hiltom Rd BH24 .... 141 D4
Hilton Cl BH15 .... 203 D3
Hilton Rd Gosport PO12 .... 181 E2
  Hedge End SO30 .... 105 E4
  New Milton BH25 .... 195 D2
Hinchliffe Cl BH15 .... 201 F1
Hinchliffe Rd BH15 .... 201 F1
Hinkler Rd SO19 .... 104 C3
Hinton Admiral Mews BH23 .. 193 F1
Hinton Admiral Sta BH23 ...... 193 F1
Hinton Ampner House SO24 .... 14 C2
Hinton Cl PO9 .... 135 E2
Hinton Cres SO19 .... 104 C2
Hinton Hill SO24 .... 14 C2
Hinton House 1 PO7 .... 134 C4
Hinton Rd BH1 .... 204 C2
Hinton Wood BH1 .... 205 D1
Hinton Wood Ave BH23 .... 193 F1
Hintonwood La BH23 .... 193 F1
Hipley Rd PO9 .... 136 A2
Hirst Rd SO45 .... 126 A2
Hispano Ave PO15 .... 129 E4
Hive Gdns BH13 .... 214 B3
Hives Way SO41 .... 197 E3
HMS Victory PO1 .... 181 F3
HMS Warrior PO1 .... 181 F3
Hoad's Hill PO17 .... 108 A1
Hoadlands GU31 .... 41 D2
Hobart Dr SO45 .... 126 A2
Hobart Rd BH25 .... 194 C1
Hobb La SO30 .... 105 E3
Hobbs Ct PO12 .... 181 F2
Hobbs Pass PO12 .... 181 F2
Hobbs Pk BH24 .... 139 F2
Hobbs Rd BH12 .... 203 E4
Hobby Cl PO3 .... 158 A2
Hobson Way SO45 .... 150 B2
Hoburne Ct BH23 .... 193 E1
Hoburne Gdns BH23 .... 193 E1
Hoburne La BH23 .... 208 B4
Hockham Cty Inf PO6 .... 135 E4
Hockley Cl 7 PO6 .... 157 E4
Hockley Cotts Cheriton SO24 .... 13 F2
  Twyford SO21 .... 32 A1
Hockley Golf Course SO23 .... 11 D1
Hocombe Dr SO53 .... 30 A1
Hocombe Park Cl SO53 .... 30 A1
Hocombe Rd SO53 .... 30 B1
Hocombe Wood Rd SO53 .... 30 A1
Hodder Cl SO53 .... 55 D3
Hodges Cl Havant PO9 .... 136 A2
  Poole BH17 .... 202 C4
Hoe La SO52 .... 53 E2
Hoe Rd SO32 .... 83 F4
Hoe St PO7 .... 109 F4
Hoe The PO13 .... 155 F1
Hoebrook Pl 6 SO51 .... 52 C4
Hoeford Cl PO16 .... 155 D3
Hogarth Cl Petersfield GU32 .... 41 D2
  7 Romsey SO51 .... 28 A1
  Southampton SO19 .... 104 B1
Hogs Lodge La PO8 .... 88 C4
Hogue Ave BH10 .... 189 E3

Hogwood La SO30 .... 80 C3
Holbeach Cl PO6 .... 133 F1
Holbein Lodge SO41 .... 198 A2
Holbrook Prim Sch PO13 ..... 155 E2
Holbrook Rd Fareham PO16 .. 155 D4
Portsmouth PO1 .... 182 B3
Holbury Cl BH8 .... 190 C2
Holbury Ct 20 PO9 .... 136 A3
Holbury Dro SO45 .... 150 B2
Holbury Inf & Jun
Schs SO45 .... 150 B2
Holbury La
East Tytherley SO51 .... 4 B2
Lockerley SO51 .... 4 B2
Holcombe Rd BH16 .... 201 D3
Holcot La PO3 .... 158 B2
Holcroft Rd SO19 .... 104 C3
Holdaway Cl SO23 .... 2 B4
Holden La SO24 .... 34 C4
Holdenbury Ct PO3 .... 158 B2
Holdenhurst Ave BH7 .... 206 B4
Holdenhurst Cl PO8 .... 88 B1
Holdenhurst Rd
Bournemouth BH8 .... 205 E3
Bournemouth, Holdenhurst BH8 191 D2
Hole La Curdridge SO32 .... 83 D1
Soberton PO7 .... 110 A4
Holes Bay Rd BH15 .... 202 A2
Holes Cl SO41 .... 195 F2
Holkham Cl SO16 .... 77 F2
Hollam Cl PO14 .... 154 A4
Hollam Cres PO14 .... 154 A4
Hollam Dr PO14 .... 154 A4
Hollam Rd PO4 .... 183 D2
Holland Cl SO53 .... 55 D2
Holland Pk SO31 .... 128 C2
Holland Pl Gosport PO13 ...... 155 E1
Southampton SO16 .... 78 A1
Holland Rd
Portsmouth PO5 .... 182 C2
Southampton SO19 .... 103 E1
Totton SO40 .... 100 B4
Holland Way BH18 .... 186 C3
Hollands Cl SO22 .... 1 A3
Hollands Wood Dr BH25 ...... 195 D3
Hollies Cl SO41 .... 172 A1
Hollies The SO51 .... 50 C2
Hollingbourne Cl SO18 .... 103 E4
Hollman Dr SO51 .... 52 B4
Hollow La PO11 .... 184 C2
Holloway Ave BH11 .... 188 C3
Holly Cl Hythe SO45 .... 150 A4
Locks Heath SO31 .... 128 C2
St Leonards RH24 .... 139 F2
Upton BH16 .... 201 D4
Holly Ct BH15 .... 202 B2
Holly Dell SO16 .... 78 C3
Holly Dr PO7 .... 135 D3
Holly Gdns Burton BH23 ...... 192 B1
2 Milford on Sea SO41 .... 211 E2
Milford on Sea SO41 .... 211 E3
West End SO30 .... 80 B2
Holly Gr Fareham PO16 .... 130 C2
Verwood BH31 .... 114 C3
Holly Green Rise BH11 .... 188 C2
Holly Hatch Rd SO40 .... 100 C3
Holly Hedge La BH17 .... 202 B4
Holly Hill SO16 .... 78 C3
Holly Hill Cl SO16 .... 78 C3
Holly Hill La SO31 .... 128 B3
Holly Hill Mansions SO31 .... 128 C2
Holly Hill Woodland Pk SO31 128 B2
Holly La Boldre SO41 .... 174 A1
Christchurch BH23 .... 194 B1
New Milton BH25 .... 195 E2
Holly Lodge
Chandler's Ford SO53 .... 55 E2
13 Poole BH12 .... 204 A2
Southampton SO17 .... 79 D1
Holly Oak Ct SO16 .... 78 A2
Holly Oak Rd SO16 .... 78 A2
Holly Rd Ashurst SO40 .... 100 A1
Blackfield SO45 .... 177 F4
Holly St PO12 .... 181 E2
Hollybank PO13 .... 179 F1
Hollybank Cl 8 Hythe SO45 .. 126 A2
Waterlooville PO8 .... 112 B3
Hollybank Cres SO45 .... 125 F2
Hollybank La PO10 .... 136 C2
Hollybank Rd SO45 .... 125 F2
Hollybrook Ave SO16 .... 78 B2
Hollybrook Cl SO16 .... 78 A1
Hollybrook Gdns SO31 .... 129 D3
Hollybrook Inf Sch SO16 ...... 78 B2
Hollybrook Jun Sch SO16 ..... 78 B2
Hollybrook Rd SO16 .... 78 B1
Hollydene SO45 .... 126 A2
Hollywell Dr PO6 .... 157 D4
Hollywood Cl SO52 .... 53 F2
Hollywood Ct SO41 .... 197 E3
Hollywood La SO41 .... 197 E3
Holm Cl BH24 .... 117 E1
Holm Hill La BH23 .... 194 B4
Holman Cl PO8 .... 112 A1
Holmdale Rd PO12 .... 180 C4
Holme Cl SO41 .... 197 E1
Holme Rd BH23 .... 209 D4
Holmes Cl 5 SO31 .... 127 D3
Holmesland Dr SO30 .... 105 F4
Holmesland La SO30 .... 105 F4
Holmesland Wlk SO30 .... 105 F4
Holmfield Ave
Bournemouth BH7 .... 206 B4
Fareham PO14 .... 154 C4
Holmgrove PO14 .... 129 E2

Holmhurst Ave BH23 .... 193 F1
Holmsley Cl Lymington SO41 . 197 D1
Southampton SO18 .... 104 B4
Holmsley Ct SO40 .... 100 A4
Holmsley Pass BH24 .... 170 B4
Holmsley Rd
Brockenhurst BH25 .... 170 C1
New Milton BH25 .... 170 C1
Holmwood Garth BH24 .... 141 E3
Holne Ct PO4 .... 183 E2
Holnest Rd BH17 .... 187 E1
Holst Way PO7 .... 134 C3
Holt Cl PO17 .... 107 F2
Holt Ct SO19 .... 126 C4
Holt Down SO31 .... 41 D2
Holt Gdns PO9 .... 113 D2
Holt Rd Poole BH12 .... 203 F3
Southampton SO15 .... 102 C3
Verwood BH31 .... 138 B4
Holt View SO50 .... 56 C1
Holworth Cl BH11 .... 188 C2
Holy Cross Jun Sch PO7 ..... 134 C3
Holy Family RC Prim Sch
SO16 .... 77 E1
Holy Rood Est SO14 .... 103 D2
Holyborne Rd SO51 .... 53 D4
Holybourne Rd PO9 .... 135 F2
Holyrood Ave SO17 .... 79 D1
Holyrood Cl PO7 .... 135 D4
Holyrood House 12 SO14 ..... 103 D2
Holywell BH17 .... 188 C2
Home Farm Bsns Ctr SP5 ..... 4 C3
Home Farm Cl SO45 .... 126 A2
Home Farm La SO45 .... 177 F3
Home Farm Office Village
PO16 .... 155 E4
Home Farm Rd BH31 .... 114 C3
Home Farm Way BH31 .... 114 C3
Home Field Dr SO16 .... 77 E3
Home Mead PO7 .... 110 C2
Home Rd BH11 .... 189 D3
Home Rule Rd SO31 .... 129 D2
Home Way GU31 .... 41 E2
Homeborough House
7 SO45 .... 126 A3
Homebridge House SP6 .... 69 F1
Homedale House BH2 .... 204 C3
Homedene House BH15 .... 202 B2
Homefayre House 19 PO16 .. 131 D1
Homefield SO51 .... 28 A1
Homefield Cotts GU33 .... 20 C3
Homefield Ind Prep Sch BH6 . 206 C3
Homefield Ind Senior Sch
BH23 .... 192 B3
Homefield Rd Cosham PO6 ... 158 B4
Westbourne PO10 .... 137 D2
Homefield Way PO8 .... 88 A3
Homeforde House SO42 .... 146 A1
Homefort House 2 PO12 .... 181 D2
Homegrange House 16 SO41 . 211 E2
Homegrove House 23 PO5 ... 182 B2
Homeheights 22 PO5 .... 182 B1
Homelake House BH14 .... 203 D2
Homelands Est BH23 .... 206 C3
Homelands House BH22 ...... 165 E3
Homeleigh House 5 BH8 .... 205 D3
Homemead House SO51 .... 52 C3
Homemill House 6 BH25 .... 195 D2
Homeoaks House BH2 .... 204 C3
Homepoint House SO18 ...... 104 A4
Homer Cl Gosport PO13 ...... 180 A4
Waterlooville PO8 .... 111 F1
Homer Mobile Home Park
SO45 .... 177 F3
Homerise House 1 SO23 ..... 11 D4
Homerose House 17 PO5 .... 182 B2
Homeryde House 11 PO13 ... 179 F1
Homesea House 18 PO5 ..... 182 B2
Homeside Rd BH9 .... 190 A1
Homespinney House SO18 ..... 79 E1
Homestour House 1 BH23 ... 207 D3
Hometide House 13 PO13 ... 179 F1
Homeview House BH15 .... 202 B2
Homewater House 7 PO4 ... 134 C4
Homeway Cotts SO40 .... 101 D3
Homewell PO9 .... 135 F1
Homewood Cl BH25 .... 195 E2
Homewood House SO41 .... 197 E1
Honey La Burley BH24 .... 142 C1
Fareham PO15 .... 130 B3
Honeybourne Cres BH6 ...... 207 D3
Honeycritch La GU32 .... 19 E2
Honeysuckle Cl Gosport PO13 155 D2
Locks Heath SO31 .... 129 D3
Winchester SO22 .... 10 C2
Honeysuckle Ct
Southampton SO18 .... 104 A4
Waterlooville PO7 .... 135 D2
Honeysuckle La BH17 .... 186 C1
Honeysuckle Rd SO16 .... 79 E2
Honeysuckle Way
Christchurch BH23 .... 208 A4
North Baddesley SO53 .... 55 D3
Honeywood Cl
Portsmouth PO3 .... 157 F2
Totton SO40 .... 76 B1
Honeywood House BH14 .... 214 B4
Honister Cl SO16 .... 101 F4
Hood Cl
Bournemouth BH10 .... 189 D1
Locks Heath SO31 .... 129 D2
Hood Cres BH10 .... 189 D1
Hood Rd SO18 .... 104 A4
Hook Cl SO53 .... 30 A1
Hook Cotts SO31 .... 152 C4
Hook Cres SO53 .... 30 A1
Hook La PO14 .... 153 D4

Hook Park Rd SO31 .... 152 C3
Hook Rd Ampfield SO51 .... 29 F1
Chandler's Ford SO51 .... 29 F1
Hook Water Cl SO53 .... 30 A1
Hook Water Rd SO53 .... 30 A1
Hook with Warsash CE Prim
Sch SO31 .... 152 B4
Hook's Farm Way PO9 .... 135 E2
Hook's La PO9 .... 135 E2
Hooke Cl BH17 .... 188 A1
Hookpit Farm La SO23 .... 2 A4
Hookwood La SO51 .... 29 F1
Hop Cl BH16 .... 201 D4
Hope Lodge Sch
Southampton SO17 .... 79 D1
Southampton SO18 .... 103 F4
Hope Rd SO30 .... 80 C1
Hope St PO1 .... 182 B3
Hopfield Cl PO7 .... 134 C4
Hopfield House PO7 .... 134 C4
Hopfield Mews PO7 .... 134 C4
Hopkins Cl Bournemouth BH8 191 D1
Portchester PO6 .... 156 C4
Hopkins Ct PO4 .... 183 D1
Horace Rd 10 BH5 .... 205 F2
Hordle CE Prim Sch SO41 .... 196 A2
Hordle House Sch SO41 ...... 210 C3
Hordle La SO41 .... 196 A1
Hordle Rd PO9 .... 135 E2
Horlock Rd SO42 .... 146 A1
Hornbeam Cl SO30 .... 80 B2
Hornbeam Gdns SO30 .... 80 B2
Hornbeam Rd PO9 .... 136 A2
Hornbeam Way BH21 .... 163 F3
Hornby Cl SO31 .... 152 B4
Hornchurch Rd SO16 .... 77 F2
Horndean CE Jun Sch PO8 .. 112 B4
Horndean Com Sch PO8 ..... 112 A4
Horndean House 39 PO1 .... 182 B3
Horndean Inf Sch PO8 .... 112 B4
Horndean Prec PO8 .... 112 B4
Horndean Rd PO10 .... 136 C2
Hornet Cl Fareham PO15 .... 130 B1
Gosport PO12 .... 181 E2
Hornet Rd Gosport PO14 .... 154 C3
Thorney Island PO10 .... 161 D2
Horning Rd BH12 .... 203 F3
Horns Drove SO16 .... 77 F3
Horns Hill Nursling SO16 ..... 77 E3
Soberton SO16 .... 85 D1
Horsa Cl BH6 .... 206 C2
Horsa Ct BH6 .... 206 C2
Horsa Rd BH6 .... 206 C2
Horse Sands Cl PO4 .... 183 E2
Horsea La PO2 .... 157 F2
Horsea Rd PO2 .... 157 F3
Horsebridge Rd PO9 .... 136 A2
Horsebridge Way SO16 .... 77 F3
Horsecroft Cl SO51 .... 52 C4
Horsefair Ct SO51 .... 52 C4
Horsefair Mews SO51 .... 52 C4
Horsefair The SO51 .... 52 C4
Horsepost La PO7 .... 87 D1
Horseshoe Cl Titchfield PO14 129 E1
Wimborne Minster BH21 .... 164 A3
Horseshoe Ct
4 Bournemouth BH1 .... 204 C2
Downton SP5 .... 46 C4
Horseshoe Dr
Netley Marsh SO40 .... 76 A1
Romsey SO51 .... 28 A1
Horseshoe Lodge SO31 ...... 128 C1
Horseshoe The BH13 .... 214 B2
Horsham Ave BH10 .... 189 E3
Horton Cl BH9 .... 190 B2
Horton Rd Gosport PO13 .... 155 E2
St Leonards BH24 .... 139 F3
Verwood BH21 .... 114 A1
Horton Way Bishopstoke SO50 56 C1
Verwood BH21 .... 114 B3
Hosier's La 28 BH15 .... 202 A1
Hosker Rd BH5 .... 206 A3
Hospital La SO16 .... 156 C3
Hospital Rd SO32 .... 108 A4
Hotspur Cl SO45 .... 125 F3
Houchin St SO32 .... 83 E4
Houghton Cl 1 PO9 .... 136 A3
Houlton Rd BH15 .... 202 C2
Hound Cl SO31 .... 127 E3
Hound Manor SO31 .... 127 F3
Hound Rd SO31 .... 127 E3
Hound Road Gdns SO31 ...... 127 E3
Hound Way SO31 .... 127 E3
Hounds Way BH21 .... 164 A3
Houndwell Pl SO14 .... 103 D2
Hounsdown Ave SO40 .... 100 C3
Hounsdown Cl SO40 .... 100 C3
Hounsdown Sec Sch SO40 ... 100 C2
Hounslow Cl BH15 .... 201 F1
House Farm Rd PO12 .... 180 C2
Hove Ct SO13 .... 179 F1
Hoveton Gr SO53 .... 55 D4
Howard Cl Burley BH24 ...... 143 D2
Chandler's Ford SO53 .... 55 E2
Christchurch BH23 .... 207 F3
Fair Oak SO50 .... 57 E1
Southampton SO18 .... 79 F2
Howard Oliver House SO45 .. 126 A2
Howard Rd Bournemouth BH8 205 E4
Portsmouth PO2 .... 157 F2
Southampton SO15 .... 102 B3
Verwood BH31 .... 114 C3
Howard's Gr SO15 .... 102 B4
Howards Mead SO41 .... 197 D1
Howe Cl Christchurch BH23 .. 207 F3
New Milton BH25 .... 194 C3
Howe La BH31 .... 114 C3
Howe Rd PO13 .... 180 B3

Howell House BH21 .... 163 F4
Howerts Cl SO31 .... 152 B4
Howeth Cl BH10 .... 189 E2
Howeth Rd BH10 .... 189 E2
Howlett Cl SO41 .... 197 E2
Howton Cl BH10 .... 189 E1
Howton Rd BH10 .... 189 E1
Hoxley Rd BH10 .... 189 E2
Hoyal Rd BH15 .... 201 E2
Hoylake Cl PO13 .... 155 E1
Hoylake Rd PO6 .... 134 B1
Hoyle Cl SO32 .... 58 B2
Hoylecroft Cl PO15 .... 130 C2
Hubert Rd SO23 .... 10 C2
Hudson Ct Gosport PO13 .... 180 B3
Poole BH12 .... 188 B1
Hudson Ct SO40 .... 100 B3
Hudson Davies Cl SO41 ...... 173 F1
Hudson Rd PO5 .... 182 B2
Hugh's Cl SO45 .... 150 C1
Hughes Bsns Ctr BH23 ...... 208 A4
Hulbert Jun Sch PO7 .... 134 C4
Hulbert Rd Havant PO9 ...... 135 D2
Waterlooville PO7 .... 134 C4
Hull Cres BH11 .... 188 C2
Hull Rd BH11 .... 188 C2
Hull Way BH11 .... 188 C2
Hulles Way SO52 .... 53 F2
Hulse Lodge 4 SO15 .... 102 C4
Hulse Rd SO15 .... 102 C4
Hulton Cl SO19 .... 103 E1
Humber Cl PO14 .... 154 A2
Humber Gdns SO31 .... 105 D1
Hummicks The SO42 .... 176 B4
Hundred Acres PO17 .... 108 C2
Hundred Acres Rd
Soberton PO17 .... 108 C3
Wickham PO17 .... 108 C3
Hundred La SO41 .... 198 A4
Hundred The
Fordingbridge SP6 .... 69 F1
Romsey SO51 .... 52 C4
Waterlooville PO7 .... 111 E1
Hunger Hill BH15 .... 202 B1
Hungerford Cl BH23 .... 169 D1
Hungerford SO31 .... 128 A4
Hungerford Hill SP6 .... 94 B3
Hungerford Rd BH8 .... 190 B2
Hunt Ave SO31 .... 127 E3
Hunt Rd Christchurch BH23 .. 207 F4
Poole BH15 .... 202 C2
Hunter Cl Christchurch BH23 208 A4
Gosport PO13 .... 180 B4
Holbury SO45 .... 150 A3
Wimborne Minster BH21 .... 164 B3
Hunter Ct 10 SO15 .... 78 A1
Hunter Rd Portsmouth PO4 .. 183 D2
Thorney Island PO10 .... 161 D2
Hunters Chase SO32 .... 84 B2
Hunters Cl BH31 .... 115 E3
Hunters Cres Romsey SO51 .. 28 B1
Totton SO40 .... 100 A3
Hunters Hill SO40 .... 100 B2
Hunters Lodge PO15 .... 130 B1
Hunters Ride PO7 .... 134 C3
Hunters Way SO50 .... 57 D1
Huntfield Rd BH9 .... 190 A1
Huntingdon Cl
Titchfield PO14 .... 129 E1
Totton SO40 .... 76 C1
Huntingdon Dr BH21 .... 163 F1
Huntingdon Gdns BH23 .... 192 A1
Huntley Cl 20 PO6 .... 133 D1
Huntly Rd BH3 .... 204 B4
Huntly Way SO18 .... 103 F4
Hunton Cl SO16 .... 78 B2
Hunts La SO21 .... 31 F4
Hunts Pond Rd PO14 .... 129 E2
Huntsbottom La
Hill Brow GU33 .... 21 D2
Liss GU33 .... 21 D2
Huntvale Rd BH9 .... 190 A2
Hurdle Way SO21 .... 31 E4
Hurdles The
Christchurch BH23 .... 206 C4
Titchfield PO14 .... 129 E1
Hurlingham Gdns SO16 .... 79 D3
Hurn Cl BH24 .... 140 B3
Hurn Court La BH23 .... 190 C3
Hurn Ct 17 Havant PO9 ..... 136 A3
Hurn BH23 .... 191 D2
Hurn La BH24 .... 140 B3
Hurn Rd Christchurch BH23 . 191 E2
Hurn BH23 .... 191 E2
St Leonards BH24 .... 140 B2
Hurn Way BH23 .... 191 E1
Hurricane Dr SO16 .... 77 F3
Hursley Cl BH7 .... 206 B4
Hursley Ct SO53 .... 30 A1
Hursley Dr SO45 .... 177 F1
Hursley Rd
Chandler's Ford SO53 .... 55 E4
Havant PO9 .... 135 E3
Hurst Castle SO41 .... 212 B1
Hurst Cl Chandler's Ford SO53 55 D2
Christchurch BH23 .... 194 B1
Stubbington PO14 .... 179 D3
Totton SO40 .... 100 A3
Hurst Ct 6 Christchurch BH23 209 D4
5 Milford on Sea SO41 ...... 211 E2
Hurst Green Cl PO8 .... 112 A1
Hurst Green Rd SO19 .... 104 A1
Hurst Hill BH14 .... 214 B4
Hurst La Colden Common SO21 58 A4
Froxfield GU34 .... 18 A2

Hurst Rd Milford on Sea SO41 211 F2
Ringwood BH24 .... 117 D1
Hurstbourne Ave BH23 ...... 193 F1
Hurstbourne Cl PO9 .... 135 E3
Hurstbourne Pl 9 SO19 .... 126 C4
Hurstdene Rd BH8 .... 190 B1
Hurstly La SO41 .... 173 D2
Hurstville Dr PO7 .... 134 C4
Hurstwood Ave PO10 .... 137 F1
Hussar Cl BH23 .... 206 C4
Hussar Ct PO7 .... 111 E1
Hussey Cl 2 SO23 .... 2 A1
Hutfield Ct 14 PO12 .... 181 D3
Hutwood Rd SO16 .... 79 D4
Huxley Cl SO31 .... 129 D1
Huxley Ct SO45 .... 125 E1
Hyacinth Cl BH17 .... 186 C1
Hyde Abbey Rd SO23 .... 11 D4
Hyde Church La SO23 .... 2 A1
Hyde Church Path 26 SO23 ... 2 A1
Hyde Cl Southampton SO15 .. 78 B1
Sway SO41 .... 172 A1
Totton SO40 .... 100 A4
Winchester SO23 .... 1 C1
Hyde Gate SO23 .... 2 C1
Hyde House Gdns 22 SO23 .... 2 A1
Hyde La Downton SP5 .... 46 B4
Fordingbridge SP6 .... 94 B3
Hyde Lodge Winchester SO22 . 1 C1
21 Winchester SO23 .... 2 A1
Hyde Park House 7 PO1 .... 182 B2
Hyde Park Rd PO1 .... 182 B3
Hyde Prim Sch SP6 .... 94 B3
Hyde Rd BH10 .... 189 E3
Hyde St Portsmouth PO5 .... 182 B2
Winchester SO23 .... 2 A1
Hyde The BH25 .... 194 C2
Hyden Cross PO8 .... 63 F1
Hyden Farm La PO8 .... 87 E4
Hyden Wood PO8 .... 63 F1
Hylton Rd GU32 .... 40 C2
Hyman Way SO40 .... 100 C4
Hynes Ct 17 SO17 .... 103 D4
Hynesbury Rd BH23 .... 208 B4
Hythe-By-Pass SO45 .... 149 F4
Hythe-By-Pass SO45 .... 150 A4
Hythe Hospl SO45 .... 126 A1
Hythe Prim Sch SO45 .... 126 A2
Hythe Rd Cosham PO6 .... 157 F4
Marchwood SO40 .... 124 C4
Poole BH15 .... 203 D4

Ibbertson Cl BH8 .... 190 C1
Ibbertson Rd BH8 .... 190 C1
Ibbertson Way BH8 .... 190 C1
Ibbett Rd BH10 .... 189 E2
Ibbotson Way SO40 .... 100 B3
Ibsen Cl PO15 .... 129 E4
Ibsley Cl BH8 .... 205 E3
Ibsley Dro PO14 .... 94 A1
Ibsley Gr PO9 .... 135 E2
Icarus Pl PO7 .... 134 C1
Iddesleigh Rd BH3 .... 205 D3
Ideal Park Homes SO50 ...... 56 C3
Idsworth Rd
Portsmouth PO3 .... 183 D4
Waterlooville PO8 .... 112 A1
Iford Bridge Home Pk BH6 .. 206 B4
Iford Cl BH6 .... 206 B3
Iford Ct 14 PO9 .... 136 A3
Iford Gdns BH7 .... 206 B4
Iford La BH6 .... 206 C3
Ilex Cres SO31 .... 128 C2
Ilex Wlk PO11 .... 185 E1
Imber Dr BH23 .... 208 C4
Imber Rd SO23 .... 11 E4
Imber Way SO19 .... 104 B2
Imbre Cl BH13 .... 214 C4
Imperial Ave SO15 .... 102 A4
Imperial Ct 4 BH13 .... 214 C4
Imperial Pk SO14 .... 103 D4
Imperial Rd SO14 .... 103 D4
Imperial Way SO15 .... 102 B3
Implacable Rd PO13 .... 179 F2
Ingarth 8 BH6 .... 206 C2
Ingle Glen SO45 .... 126 A1
Ingle Gr SO40 .... 76 A1
Ingledene Cl Gosport PO12 .. 181 D2
Havant PO9 .... 135 E1
Inglegreen Cl BH25 .... 194 C1
Inglesham Way BH15 .... 201 F2
Ingleside SO31 .... 127 E4
Ingleside Cl PO14 .... 154 A4
Ingleton Rd SO16 .... 77 E1
Inglewood Ave BH8 .... 190 C1
Inglewood Dr BH25 .... 195 D1
Inglewood Gdns SO50 .... 57 E2
Inglis Rd PO5 .... 182 C2
Ingoldfield La SO32 .... 109 E4
Ingram Ct SO17 .... 103 E4
Ingram Wlk 14 BH21 .... 163 E2
Ingworth Rd BH12 .... 204 A3
Inhams La PO7 .... 110 B3
Inhurst Ave PO7 .... 135 D4
Inhurst Rd PO2 .... 157 F1
Inkerman Rd SO19 .... 103 E2
Inkpen Wlk PO9 .... 135 E4
Inlands Rd PO10 .... 161 F4
Inmans La GU32 .... 41 D3
Insley Cres BH18 .... 186 C3
International Way SO19 ...... 126 C4
Inveravon BH23 .... 207 F2
Inverclyde House BH14 ...... 203 D2
Inverclyde Rd BH14 .... 203 D2
Invergordon Ave PO6 .... 158 A4
Inverkip Cl PO13 .... 179 F2
Inverleigh Rd BH6 .... 206 B3
Inverness Ave PO15 .... 130 C2

Inverness Rd Gosport PO12 ...... 181 D3
  Poole BH13 .... 214 C4
  Portsmouth PO1 .... 182 C4
Inwood Rd GU33 .... 21 D2
Ionic Cl SO53 .... 55 F4
IOW Ferry Terminal SO14 .... 102 C1
Iping Ave PO9 .... 135 F2
Ipley Way SO45 .... 126 A1
Ipswich Rd BH4 .... 204 A2
Ireland Way PO7 .... 134 C3
Iris Rd Bournemouth BH9 .... 189 F1
  Southampton SO16 .... 79 D2
Iron Mill Cl PO15 .... 130 B2
Ironbridge Cres SO31 .... 129 D3
Ironbridge La PO4 .... 183 E2
Ironmill La PO15 .... 130 A3
Ironside Ct 12 SO14 .... 102 C2
Irvine Cl PO16 .... 131 D2
Irvine Way PO7 .... 207 F4
Irving Rd Bournemouth BH6 .... 206 B3
  Southampton SO16 .... 77 F1
Irwell Cl SO53 .... 55 D3
Irwin Hts PO12 .... 181 D4
Isaacs Cl BH12 .... 204 A4
Isambard Brunel
  Jun Sch PO2 .... 182 C4
Isambard Brunel Rd PO1 .... 182 B3
Isis Cl SO16 .... 101 F4
Island Cl PO11 .... 160 A2
Island Point SO41 .... 197 F2
Island View SO41 .... 172 A2
Island View Ave BH23 .... 208 A3
Island View Cl SO41 .... 211 F2
Island View Cl BH25 .... 209 E4
Island View Terr PO2 .... 157 E1
Island View Wlk PO16 .... 132 B1
Islay Gdns PO6 .... 133 F1
Itchen Ave SO50 .... 56 C1
Itchen Cl Petersfield GU32 .... 40 C1
  West Wellow SO51 .... 50 B2
Itchen Coll SO19 .... 104 A3
Itchen Ct 4 Waterlooville PO8 .. 111 F2
  43 Winchester SO23 .... 11 D4
Itchen Rd PO9 .... 136 A3
Itchen Valley Ctry Pk SO30 ..... 80 B3
Itchen View SO19 .... 79 F2
Itchenor Rd PO11 .... 185 F1
Itchenside Cl SO18 .... 79 F2
Itchin Cl SO40 .... 100 B3
Ithlca Cl PO11 .... 185 D2
Ivamy Pl BH11 .... 188 C1
Ivanhoe Rd SO15 .... 78 B1
Ivor Cl SO45 .... 150 B2
Ivor Rd Broadstone BH21 .... 186 B2
  Poole BH15 .... 202 A1
Ivy Cl St Leonards BH24 .... 139 E2
  Totton SO40 .... 76 C1
  Winchester SO22 .... 10 C3
Ivy Cotts SO50 .... 31 D1
Ivy Ct PO7 .... 134 B2
Ivy Dene SO19 .... 104 B2
Ivy House 2 PO12 .... 181 D2
Ivy La Portsmouth PO1 .... 182 A3
  Ringwood BH24 .... 117 D2
  West End SO18 .... 80 B1
Ivy Orch PO8 .... 88 A3
Ivy Rd Oakley BH21 .... 187 E4
  Southampton SO17 .... 103 E4
Ivyhouse La GU32 .... 18 C2
Iwerne Cl BH9 .... 190 A2

J Ave SO45 .... 151 D3
Jack Cockerill Way 14 PO5 .... 182 B1
Jackdaw Cl PO8 .... 111 F2
Jackdaw Rise SO50 .... 55 E1
Jacklin Ct BH18 .... 187 D3
Jackman's Hill SO21 .... 33 D3
Jackmans Cl SO19 .... 103 E2
Jackson Cl PO6 .... 158 B3
Jackson Rd BH12 .... 203 E3
Jacmar Ct 8 BH25 .... 195 D1
Jacob's Gutter La SO40 .... 101 D2
Jacob's St PO1 .... 182 B3
Jacobean Ct BH23 .... 194 A1
Jacobs Cl Clanfield PO8 .... 88 B3
  Romsey SO51 .... 53 D4
Jacobs Wlk SO40 .... 100 C3
Jacomb Pl PO13 .... 155 E1
Jacqueline Ave PO7 .... 134 B2
Jacqueline Rd BH12 .... 203 E4
Jade Ct 6 PO7 .... 134 C4
Jago Rd PO1 .... 181 F1
Jamaica Pl PO12 .... 181 E2
James Butcher Ct 12 PO5 ...... 182 B1
James Callaghan Dr PO17 ..... 132 C1
James Cl Gosport PO13 .... 155 E2
  South Hayling PO11 .... 184 C2
James Copse Rd PO8 .... 111 F3
James Cl SO51 .... 53 D3
James Grieve Ave SO31 .... 129 D1
James Howell Ct PO7 .... 110 C4
James Rd Gosport PO13 .... 155 E2
  Havant PO9 .... 135 F1
  Poole BH12 .... 204 A3
James St SO14 .... 103 D2
Jameson Rd Bournemouth BH9 .. 189 F1
  Southampton SO19 .... 103 F2
Jamica Rd PO12 .... 181 E3
Janaway Gdns SO17 .... 103 E4
Janes Cl SO41 .... 177 F4
Janred Ct BH25 .... 209 F4
Janson Rd SO15 .... 102 B4
Jarndyce Wlk PO2 .... 182 B4
Jarvis Fields SO31 .... 128 A4
Jasmine Cl SO41 .... 197 F2
Jasmine Gr PO7 .... 135 D3
Jasmine Rd SO30 .... 105 D4
Jasmine Way PO8 .... 88 B3

Jasmine Wlk 5 PO14 .... 154 C4
Jasmond Rd PO6 .... 157 F3
Jason Pl PO7 .... 134 C1
Jason Way PO12 .... 180 C4
Java Dr PO15 .... 129 E4
Javelin Rd PO10 .... 161 D2
Jay Cl Horndean PO8 .... 112 A4
  Stubbington PO14 .... 154 A3
Jay's Ct BH23 .... 209 D4
Jealous La SO41 .... 173 D1
Jefferson Ave BH1 .... 205 E3
Jeffries Cl SO16 .... 77 F3
Jellicoe Ave PO12 .... 180 C2
Jellicoe Dr BH14 .... 202 C3
Jellicoe Dr BH23 .... 207 F3
Jenkins Cl SO30 .... 106 A4
Jenkins Gr PO3 .... 183 D4
Jenner Way SO51 .... 53 E4
Jennings Rd Poole BH14 .... 203 E1
  Totton SO40 .... 101 D4
Jensen Ct SO15 .... 102 C4
Jephcote Rd BH11 .... 188 C2
Jermyns La Abbotswood SO51 .. 28 C2
  Ampfield SO51 .... 28 C2
Jerome Ct SO19 .... 104 B3
Jerram Ct PO12 .... 180 C2
Jerrett's La SO16 .... 77 E2
Jersey Cl Poole BH12 .... 188 B1
  Southampton SO16 .... 77 F2
  Stubbington PO14 .... 179 E3
Jersey Rd Poole BH12 .... 188 B1
  Portsmouth PO2 .... 182 C4
Jervis Court La
  Bishop's Waltham SO32 .... 84 A4
  Swanmore SO32 .... 84 A4
Jervis Dr PO12 .... 181 D3
Jervis Rd PO2 .... 157 E1
Jesmond Ave BH23 .... 208 C4
Jesmond Gr SO31 .... 129 D1
Jessamine Rd SO16 .... 78 A1
Jessica Ave BH31 .... 114 B4
Jessica Cl PO7 .... 112 A1
Jessie Rd Gosport PO12 .... 181 D2
  Havant PO9 .... 135 E2
  Portsmouth PO4 .... 182 C2
Jessie Terr 28 SO14 .... 103 D2
Jessop Cl Bournemouth BH10 .. 189 F2
  Hythe SO45 .... 125 F3
Jessop Rd BH21 .... 164 A3
Jessop Wlk SO45 .... 125 F3
Jessopp House 6 BH21 .... 163 E3
Jetty Rd SO45 .... 151 D3
Jewell Rd BH8 .... 191 D1
Jewry St SO23 .... 11 D4
Jimmy Brown Ave BH22 .... 138 C3
Jinny La SO51 .... 27 E3
Joanna Cl SP5 .... 46 B4
Jockey La SO50 .... 56 C3
Jodrell Cl PO8 .... 112 B4
John Darling Mall SO50 .... 56 A2
John King Shipyard PO10 ...... 161 D4
John St SO14 .... 103 D2
John's Rd SO19 .... 103 E2
Johns Rd PO16 .... 155 D4
Johnson Rd BH21 .... 165 D4
Johnson St 2 SO14 .... 103 D2
Johnston Rd BH15 .... 202 B4
Johnstone Rd BH23 .... 207 F3
Jolliffe Ave BH15 .... 202 B2
Jolliffe Ct 16 GU32 .... 40 C2
Jolliffe Rd BH15 .... 202 B2
Jonas Nichols Sq SO14 .... 103 D2
Jonathan Rd PO15 .... 130 C1
Jonathon Cl SO41 .... 197 F3
Jones La SO45 .... 126 A3
Jopps Cnr BH23 .... 192 B2
Jordan House SO15 .... 102 B3
Jordans La Boldre SO41 .... 198 A4
  Sway SO41 .... 172 B1
Joseph Nye Ct 30 PO1 .... 182 A3
Joseph St 8 PO12 .... 181 E2
Josian Wlk 10 SO14 .... 103 D3
Jowitt Dr PO15 .... 194 C1
Joyce Dickson Cl BH24 .... 141 D3
Joys La SO41 .... 198 C4
Joys Rd BH21 .... 138 C4
Jubilee Ave PO16 .... 156 C4
Jubilee Bsns Ctr PO7 .... 134 C4
Jubilee Cl Corfe Mullen BH21 .. 186 C4
  Eastleigh SO50 .... 55 F1
  Fordingbridge SP6 .... 69 E1
  Ringwood BH24 .... 141 E4
Jubilee Cres BH23 .... 203 E3
Jubilee Ct PO14 .... 155 D4
Jubilee Gdns
  Bournemouth BH10 .... 189 E1
  Southampton SO14 .... 104 A4
Jubilee House PO10 .... 136 C1
Jubilee Rd Corfe Mullen BH21 .. 186 C4
  Fordingbridge SP6 .... 69 E1
  Gosport PO12 .... 181 D3
  Poole BH12 .... 203 E3
  Portchester PO16 .... 156 B4
  Portsmouth PO4 .... 182 C2
  Romsey SO51 .... 52 C4
  Waterlooville PO8 .... 111 F1
Jubilee Terr Portsmouth PO5 .. 182 A2
  Westbourne PO10 .... 137 D2
Julia Cl BH21 .... 208 C4
Julian Cl Lee-on-the-Solent PO13 .. 179 F2
  New Milton BH25 .... 195 D2
Julian Ct SO16 .... 78 C3
Julian Ct 1 SO18 .... 79 F1
Julian Rd SO19 .... 104 A2
Julian's Rd Pamphill BH21 ..... 163 D2
  Wimborne Minster BH21 .... 163 D2
Julie Ave PO15 .... 130 C1
Juliet Ct PO7 .... 135 D4
Julius Cl SO53 .... 55 F3

Julyan Ave BH12 .... 204 A4
Jumar Cl SO31 .... 152 B4
Jumpers Ave BH23 .... 206 C4
Jumpers Rd BH23 .... 206 C4
Junction Rd
  Bournemouth BH9 .... 204 C4
  Hamworthy BH16 .... 201 E2
  Totton SO40 .... 101 D4
Juniper Cl Ferndown BH22 .... 165 E4
  Lymington SO41 .... 197 D1
  North Baddesley SO52 .... 53 F3
  Three Legged Cross BH21 ..... 138 C4
  Winchester SO22 .... 10 B3
Juniper Ct 17 SO18 .... 103 F4
Juniper Flats BH23 .... 206 C4
Juniper Rd Horndean PO8 .... 88 B1
  Southampton SO18 .... 103 F4
Juniper Sq PO9 .... 159 F4
Jupiter Cl SO16 .... 77 F2
Jupiter Way BH21 .... 186 C4
Jura Cl PO6 .... 133 F1
Jurd Way SO31 .... 104 C1
Jurds Lake Way SO19 .... 103 F1
Justin Cl PO14 .... 154 C4
Justin Gdns BH10 .... 189 F2
Justine Cl SO18 .... 104 A4
Justinian Cl SO53 .... 55 F4
Jute Cl PO15 .... 132 A1
Jutland Cl PO15 .... 129 D4

Kamptee Copse BH25 .... 195 D3
Kanes Hill SO19 .... 104 C3
Kanes Hill Prim Sch SO19 ...... 104 C3
Kangaw Pl PO19 .... 201 E1
Karen Ave PO6 .... 158 B3
Kassassin St PO4 .... 183 D1
Kassel Cl PO7 .... 135 D4
Katherine Chance Cl BH23 ... 192 B2
Kathleen Rd SO19 .... 104 A2
Katrina Gdns PO11 .... 185 D3
Katrine Cres SO53 .... 55 D4
Katterns Cl BH23 .... 191 F1
Kayak Cl SO31 .... 128 C1
Kayleigh Cl SO40 .... 100 B3
Kealy Rd PO12 .... 181 D3
Kearsney Ave PO2 .... 157 F2
Keast Wlk PO13 .... 155 E2
Keats Ave Milford on Sea SO41 .. 211 E3
  Portchester PO6 .... 132 C1
Keats Cl Waterlooville PO8 ..... 111 F2
  Winchester SO21, SO22 .... 10 B2
Keats House Havant PO9 .... 135 F2
  17 New Milton BH25 .... 195 D1
Keats Rd SO19 .... 104 B3
Keble Cl Chandler's Ford SO53 .. 55 E2
  Hursley SO21 .... 30 A1
Keble Meml CE
  Prim Sch SO51 .... 30 A3
Keble Rd SO53 .... 55 E2
Keble St SO22 .... 10 B3
Keeble Cl BH10 .... 189 E3
Keeble Cres BH10 .... 189 E3
Keeble Rd BH10 .... 189 E3
Keel Cl Gosport PO13 .... 180 B3
  Portsmouth PO3 .... 158 B2
Keep The PO16 .... 156 B4
Keepers Cl SO53 .... 55 D3
Keepers La Ferndown BH21 ... 164 C3
  Mottisfont SO51 .... 5 E1
Kefford Ct PO8 .... 112 A3
Keighley Ave BH18 .... 186 C1
Keith Cl PO12 .... 181 D3
Keith Rd BH3 .... 204 B4
Kelburn Cl SO53 .... 55 D4
Kellaway Rd BH17 .... 202 C4
Kellett Rd SO15 .... 102 C4
Kelly Cl BH17 .... 202 C4
Kelly Ct
  10 Fareham PO16 .... 131 D1
  2 Southampton, Bitterne SO18 .. 103 F4
  Southampton, Lordswood SO16 .. 78 B3
Kelly House SO18 .... 79 F2
Kelly Rd PO7 .... 134 C3
Kelmscott Gdns SO53 .... 30 A1
Kelsall Gdns BH25 .... 195 D2
Kelsey Ave PO10 .... 137 F1
Kelsey Cl Liss GU33 .... 21 D3
  Locks Heath PO14 .... 129 D1
Kelsey Head PO6 .... 157 D4
Kelston Ct 19 SO15 .... 102 A4
Kelvin Cl SO45 .... 126 A2
Kelvin Gr Netley SO31 .... 127 E3
  Portchester PO16 .... 156 B4
Kelvin Rd SO50 .... 55 F1
Kemp Rd BH9 .... 204 C4
Kempland La GU34 .... 17 E2
Kemps Quay Ind Pk SO18 ..... 103 E4
Kempton Ct SO15 .... 129 E4
Kempton Pk PO7 .... 112 A1
Kemshott Ct PO9 .... 135 E3
Ken Berry Ct PO9 .... 136 A3
Ken Rd BH6 .... 206 C2
Kench The PO11 .... 183 F2
Kendal Ave Portsmouth PO3 .. 158 A1
  Southampton SO16 .... 101 E4
Kendal Cl Chandler's Ford SO53 .. 55 F4
  Waterlooville PO8 .... 112 A2
Kendal Ct SO16 .... 77 E1
Kenilworth Cl
  Lee-on-the-Solent PO13 .... 179 F2
  New Milton BH25 .... 195 D2
Kenilworth Ct
  2 Christchurch BH23 .... 207 D4
  11 Poole BH13 .... 214 C4
  8 Winchester SO23 .... 2 A1
Kenilworth Dr SO50 .... 56 A3
Kenilworth Gdns SO30 .... 80 C1
Kenilworth House 15 SO14 ... 103 E3

Kenilworth Rd
  Portsmouth PO5 .... 182 B1
  Southampton SO15 .... 102 C3
Kenmore Cl SO40 .... 100 C3
Kennard Ct BH25 .... 194 C2
Kennard Rd BH25 .... 194 C2
Kennart Rd BH17 .... 202 A4
Kennedy Ave PO15 .... 130 C2
Kennedy Cl PO7 .... 134 C2
Kennedy Cres PO12 .... 180 C1
Kennedy Rd SO16 .... 77 F2
Kennel La 2 .... 1 B2
Kennet Cl Gosport PO12 .... 181 D1
  Romsey SO51 .... 53 E4
  West End SO18 .... 80 A2
Kennet Rd Petersfield GU32 ... 40 C1
  Romsey SO51 .... 53 E4
Kenneth Ct 16 BH23 .... 209 D4
Kennington La SO40 .... 99 D4
Kennington Rd BH17 .... 202 B4
Kensington Ct 3 SO17 .... 79 E1
Kensington Dr BH2 .... 204 B2
Kensington Fields SO45 .... 125 E1
Kensington Gdns PO14 .... 129 E1
Kensington Pk SO41 .... 211 E2
Kensington Rd Gosport PO12 .. 181 E2
  Portsmouth PO2 .... 157 F1
Kenson Gdns SO19 .... 104 A2
Kent Gdns SO40 .... 100 B3
Kent Gr PO16 .... 156 B3
Kent House
  20 Bournemouth BH4 .... 204 B2
  27 Southampton SO14 .... 103 E3
Kent La BH24 .... 93 C1
Kent Rd Chandler's Ford SO53 .. 55 E2
  Gosport PO13 .... 155 D2
  Poole BH12 .... 203 F3
  Portsmouth PO5 .... 182 B2
  Southampton SO17 .... 79 E1
Kent St Portsmouth PO1 .... 182 A3
  Southampton SO14 .... 103 E3
Kentidge Rd PO7 .... 134 B3
Kentish Rd SO15 .... 102 B4
Kenwood Rd PO16 .... 156 B3
Kenwyn Cl SO18 .... 80 A1
Kenya Rd PO16 .... 156 A4
Kenyon Cl BH15 .... 202 C4
Kenyon Rd Poole BH15 .... 202 C4
  Portsmouth PO2 .... 157 F1
Keppel Cl BH24 .... 141 D4
Kerley Rd BH2 .... 204 C1
Kern Cl SO16 .... 77 F2
Kerrfield SO22 .... 10 B4
Kerrfield Mews SO22 .... 10 B4
Kerry Cl Chandler's Ford SO53 .. 55 E3
  Lymington SO41 .... 197 E2
Kesteven Way SO18 .... 104 A4
Kestrel Cl
  Bishop's Waltham SO32 .... 83 D4
  Botley SO30 .... 81 F1
  Clanfield PO8 .... 88 B2
  Ferndown BH22 .... 165 D4
  Marchwood SO40 .... 101 F1
  Southampton SO16 .... 78 A3
  Stubbington PO14 .... 154 A2
  Upton BH16 .... 201 D4
  Winchester SO22 .... 10 B2
Kestrel Ct BH24 .... 141 D4
Kestrel Dr BH23 .... 208 A3
Kestrel Pl PO6 .... 158 C4
Kestrel Rd SO50 .... 55 F1
Kestrel Way SP6 .... 93 D3
Keswick Ave PO3 .... 183 D4
Keswick Ct BH25 .... 195 D3
Keswick Rd
  Bournemouth BH5 .... 206 A2
  New Milton BH25 .... 195 D3
  Southampton SO19 .... 103 E1
Keswick Way BH31 .... 114 C3
Kettering Terr PO2 .... 182 B4
Keverstone Ct BH1 .... 205 E2
Kevlyn Cres SO31 .... 104 C1
Kew La SO31 .... 128 A4
Kewlake La SO40 .... 74 B1
Key La 21 BH15 .... 202 A1
Keydell Ave PO8 .... 112 A3
Keydell Cl PO8 .... 112 A3
Keyes Cl Christchurch BH23 .. 207 F3
  Poole BH15 .... 188 C1
Keyes Ct PO13 .... 155 E2
Keyes Rd PO13 .... 155 E2
Keyhaven Cl PO13 .... 155 D1
Keyhaven Dr PO9 .... 135 E3
Keyhaven Rd SO41 .... 211 F2
Keynsham Rd SO19 .... 104 A3
Keysworth Ave BH25 .... 209 F4
Keysworth Rd BH16 .... 201 D2
Khandala Gdns PO7 .... 134 C2
Khartoum Rd SO17 .... 79 D1
Khyber Rd BH12 .... 203 E3
Kidmore La PO7 .... 110 C3
Kielder Cl SO53 .... 55 D4
Kielder Gr PO13 .... 155 E1
Kilbride 11 BH12 .... 204 A2
Kilbride Path 5 PO2 .... 182 B4
Kilham La SO22 .... 10 A3
Killarney Cl SO19 .... 104 C2
Killock Rd BH13 .... 214 C4
Kilmarnock Rd BH9 .... 189 F1
Kilmeston Cl PO9 .... 135 F3
Kilmeston Rd Cheriton SO24 .. 14 B2
  Kilmeston SO24 .... 14 B2
Kilmington Way BH23 .... 208 C4
Kilmiston Dr PO16 .... 132 B1
Kilmiston Rd PO1 .... 182 C4
Kiln Acre PO16 .... 131 D2

Kiln Cl Broadstone BH21 .... 186 B2
  Hythe SO45 .... 125 F2
Kiln Field GU33 .... 20 C3
Kiln Gn SO21 .... 57 D4
Kiln Hill SO32 .... 109 D4
Kiln La Braishfield SO51 .... 28 B3
  Buriton SO21 .... 65 E3
  Colden Common SO50 .... 31 E1
  Otterbourne SO21 .... 31 E1
  Redlynch SP5 .... 47 F4
Kiln Rd Fareham PO16, PO17 .. 131 D2
  Portsmouth PO3 .... 158 A1
Kilnside PO7 .... 110 C2
Kilnyard Cl SO40 .... 76 B1
Kilpatrick Cl 6 PO2 .... 182 B4
Kilwich Way PO16 .... 156 A3
Kimber Rd BH11 .... 188 C2
Kimberley Cl
  Christchurch BH23 .... 206 C4
  Fair Oak SO50 .... 57 E1
Kimberley Ct SO19 .... 103 F1
Kimberley Rd
  Bournemouth BH6 .... 206 B3
  Poole BH14 .... 203 D2
  Portsmouth PO4 .... 183 D1
Kimbers GU32 .... 40 C2
Kimbolton Rd PO3 .... 183 D3
Kimbridge Cnr SO51 .... 27 D4
Kimbridge Cres PO9 .... 136 A3
Kimbridge La SO51 .... 27 D4
Kimmeridge Ave BH12 .... 203 E4
Kimpton Cl PO13 .... 179 F1
Kimpton Ct 28 PO7 .... 136 A3
Kineton Rd SO15 .... 78 C1
King Albert Ct 59 PO1 .... 182 B3
King Albert St PO1 .... 182 B3
King Alfred Pl SO23 .... 2 A1
King Alfred Terr 29 SO23 .... 2 A1
King Alfred's Coll SO22 .... 10 C4
King Arthur's Ct PO6 .... 158 B4
King Charles St PO1 .... 182 A2
King Cl BH24 .... 139 F2
King Cup Ave SO31 .... 128 C2
King Edward Ave
  Bournemouth BH9 .... 190 A1
  Southampton SO16 .... 102 A4
King Edward Ct BH9 .... 189 F1
King Edward Pk(Cvn Pk) SO53 .. 56 F4
King Edward VI Sch SO15 ..... 102 C4
King Edward's Cres PO2 .... 157 E1
King Fisher Way BH23 .... 208 A3
King George Ave
  Bournemouth BH9 .... 189 F1
  Petersfield GU32 .... 40 C2
King George Mews 7 GU32 ... 40 C2
King George Mobile
  Home Pk BH25 .... 194 C1
King George Rd PO16 .... 156 B4
King George's Ave SO15 .... 101 F4
King Harold Ct SO22 .... 10 C3
King Henry 1 St PO1 .... 182 A3
King John Ave
  Bournemouth BH11 .... 188 B3
  Portchester PO16 .... 156 A4
King John Cl BH11 .... 188 B3
King La GU32 .... 39 F4
King Richard 1 Rd PO1 .... 182 A2
King Richard Dr BH11 .... 188 B3
King Richard Sch PO6 .... 156 C4
King St Emsworth PO10 .... 161 D4
  Gosport PO12 .... 181 E3
  Portsmouth PO5 .... 182 B2
  Southampton SO14 .... 103 D2
  Westbourne PO10 .... 137 D2
  Wimborne Minster BH21 .... 163 D2
King William St PO1 .... 182 A3
King's Arms La BH24 .... 140 C4
King's Arms Row BH24 .... 140 C4
King's Ave BH23 .... 206 C3
King's Cl SO53 .... 55 E4
King's Copse Rd SO45 .... 177 E4
King's Cres BH14 .... 203 F1
King's Croft La PO9 .... 135 E1
King's House 17 SO14 .... 103 D2
King's La GU32 .... 18 B2
King's Park Dr BH7 .... 205 F3
King's Park Prim Sch BH1 ..... 205 F3
King's Park Rd
  Bournemouth BH7 .... 205 F3
  Southampton SO15 .... 103 D3
King's Rd Bournemouth BH3 .. 205 D4
  Emsworth PO10 .... 160 C4
  Fareham PO16 .... 131 D1
  Lee-on-the-Solent PO13 .... 179 F2
  Portsmouth PO5 .... 182 B2
  Winchester SO22, SO23 .... 10 B3
King's Saltern Rd SO41 .... 198 A1
King's Sch (Prim) The SO30 ... 80 C2
King's Terr 1 PO10 .... 160 C4
Kingcup Cl BH18 .... 186 C1
Kingdom Cl PO15 .... 129 E3
Kingfisher Cl
  Bournemouth BH6 .... 206 C3
  Hamble-le-Rice SO31 .... 128 A2
  Rowland's Castle PO9 .... 113 D1
  South Hayling PO11 .... 185 E1
  West Moors BH22 .... 138 C1
Kingfisher Copse SO31 .... 129 D2
Kingfisher Ct Havant PO9 ...... 136 A1
  1 Southampton SO17 .... 79 D1
Kingfisher Rd SO50 .... 55 F1
Kingfisher Way
  Marchwood SO40 .... 101 F1
  Ringwood BH24 .... 117 D1
  Romsey SO51 .... 52 C4

Kingfishers
9 Christchurch BH23 .... 207 D3
Portchester PO16 .... 155 F4
Kingfishers The BH31 .... 115 D3
Kinghton Heath
Ind Est BH11 .... 188 C2
Kingland Cres BH15 .... 202 B1
Kingland Rd BH15 .... 202 B1
Kings Ave
Hamble-le-Rice SO31 .... 127 F2
Poole BH14 .... 203 E1
Winchester SO22 .... 10 C3
Kings Bench Alley PO1 .... 182 A3
Kings Cl Lymington SO41 ...... 197 E2
Lyndhurst SO43 .... 121 F3
Rowland's Castle PO9 .... 113 D1
Twyford SO21 .... 32 A4
West Moors BH22 .... 138 C1
Kings Copse Ave SO30 .... 105 E3
Kings Copse Prim Sch SO30 .. 105 E3
Kings Copse Rd SO30 .... 105 E3
Kings Court Sch PO8 .... 88 A1
Kings Cres SO41 .... 197 E2
Kings Field SO31 .... 105 D1
Kings Field Gdns SO31 .... 105 D1
Kings Head Yd **25** SO23 .... 11 D4
Kings Huts SO41 .... 197 D2
Kings La Chilcomb SO23 .... 11 F3
Sway SO41 .... 196 C4
Kings Mede PO8 .... 112 A3
Kings Park Com Hospl BH7 ... 205 F3
Kings Rd Chandler's Ford SO53 .. 55 E3
Gosport PO12 .... 181 E2
Lymington SO41 .... 197 E2
New Milton BH25 .... 195 E2
Petersfield GU32 .... 40 B2
South Hayling PO11 .... 185 D3
Kings Ride SO45 .... 177 F4
Kings' Sch SO22 .... 10 A4
Kings Sch The SO50 .... 57 E1
Kings Somborne Rd SO51 .... 7 E1
Kings Way PO9 .... 113 D1
Kings Worthy Prim Sch SO23 ... 2 B3
Kingsbere Ave BH10 .... 189 D1
Kingsbere Gdns BH23 .... 209 D4
Kingsbere Rd BH15 .... 202 C3
Kingsbridge Rd BH14 .... 203 E2
Kingsbury Rd SO14 .... 103 D4
Kingsbury's La BH24 .... 140 C4
Kingsclere Ave Havant PO9 .. 135 E3
Southampton SO19 .... 126 C4
Kingsclere Cl SO19 .... 103 F1
Kingscote House **7** PO6 ..... 132 C1
Kingscote Rd Cosham PO6 .... 132 C1
Waterlooville PO8 .... 111 E2
Kingscroft Ct PO9 .... 135 E1
Kingsdale Ct **7** SO22 .... 10 C4
Kingsdown Pl PO1 .... 182 C3
Kingsdown Rd PO7 .... 111 E1
Kingsdown Way SO18 .... 80 A1
Kingsey Ave PO10 .... 160 C4
Kingsfernsden La GU32 .... 41 D3
Kingsfield Lymington SO41 .. 198 A1
Ringwood BH24 .... 141 D4
Kingsfold Ave SO18 .... 79 F2
Kingsford Cl SP5 .... 47 E3
Kingsgate Rd SO23 .... 10 C3
Kingsgate St SO23 .... 11 D3
Kingsland Cl PO6 .... 133 E1
Kingsland Ct Poole BH13 ...... 214 C4
4 Southampton SO14 .... 103 D2
Kingsland House **18** SO14 .. 103 D3
Kingsland Mkt SO14 .... 103 D2
Kingsland Sq **3** SO14 .... 103 D2
Kingsleigh Fst Sch BH10 ...... 189 E1
Kingsleigh Jun Sch BH10 ..... 189 E2
Kingsleigh Sec Sch BH10 ..... 189 E1
Kingsley Ave BH6 .... 207 D2
Kingsley Cl BH6 .... 207 D2
Kingsley Gdns SO40 .... 100 A4
Kingsley Gn PO9 .... 135 F3
Kingsley Pl SO22 .... 10 C3
Kingsley Rd Gosport PO12 .... 180 C4
Portsmouth PO4 .... 183 E2
Southampton SO15 .... 102 A4
Kingsmead PO17 .... 108 B4
Kingsmead Ave PO14 .... 179 E3
Kingsmead Ct
12 Southampton SO15 .... 78 A1
9 Wimborne Minster BH21 .. 163 D3
Kingsmill Cl PO12 .... 180 C2
Kingsmill Rd BH17 .... 202 C4
Kingston SO31 .... 127 E4
Kingston Cres PO2 .... 182 B4
Kingston Cross PO2 .... 182 B4
Kingston Ct SO16 .... 77 F1
Kingston Gdns PO15 .... 130 B2
Kingston Lacy House (NT)
BH21 .... 162 A4
Kingston Pk SO41 .... 197 E1
Kingston Rd Gosport PO12 ... 180 C3
Poole BH15 .... 202 B2
Portsmouth PO1, PO2 .... 182 C4
Southampton SO19 .... 102 B3
Kingsway Chandler's Ford SO53 .. 55 F4
Ferndown BH22 .... 165 D4
North Hayling PO11 .... 160 A2
Southampton SO14 .... 103 D3
Kingsway Cl BH23 .... 191 F1
Kingsway Ct SO53 .... 55 F4
Kingsway Gdns SO53 .... 55 F4
Kingsway The PO16 .... 156 B4
Kingswell Cl BH10 .... 189 E1
Kingswell Gdns BH10 .... 189 D1
Kingswell Gr BH10 .... 189 D1

Kingswell Path **13** PO1 .... 182 B3
Kingswell Rd BH10 .... 189 E1
Kingswell St PO1 .... 182 B3
Kingswood
Bournemouth BH4 .... 204 B1
Marchwood SO40 .... 102 A1
Kingsworthy Rd PO9 .... 135 F2
Kinloss Ct SO16 .... 78 A3
Kinnell Cl PO10 .... 160 C4
Kinross Cres PO6 .... 158 A4
Kinross Rd Bournemouth BH3 .. 204 C3
Totton SO40 .... 100 C3
Kinsbourne Ave BH10 .... 189 E1
Kinsbourne Cl SO19 .... 104 C3
Kinsbourne Rise SO19 .... 104 C3
Kinsbourne Way SO19 .... 104 C3
Kinson Ave BH15 .... 203 D4
Kinson Gr BH10 .... 189 E3
Kinson Park Rd BH10 .... 189 E3
Kinson Pottery Ind Est BH14 .. 203 D3
Kinson Prim Sch BH11 .... 189 D3
Kinson Rd BH10 .... 189 E2
Kinterbury Ct **9** SO17 .... 103 D4
Kintyre Rd PO6 .... 133 F1
Kinver Cl SO51 .... 28 A1
Kiosks The **21** BH15 .... 202 B1
Kipling Bldgs **18** PO2 .... 157 F2
Kipling Cl SO19 .... 103 F1
Kipling Rd Eastleigh SO50 ... 55 F2
Poole BH14 .... 203 D3
Portsmouth PO2 .... 157 F2
Kirby Cl BH15 .... 202 C3
Kirby Cl **4** PO2 .... 157 F1
Kirby Rd PO2 .... 157 F1
Kirby Way BH6 .... 206 B2
Kirkham Ave BH23 .... 192 B4
Kirkstall Rd PO4 .... 182 C1
Kirkway PO8 .... 187 D2
Kirtley Cl PO6 .... 158 B3
Kirton Rd PO6 .... 158 B4
Kitchener Cres BH17 .... 187 D1
Kitchener Rd SO17 .... 79 E1
Kitchers Cl SO41 .... 172 A1
Kite Cl PO8 .... 111 F2
Kites Croft Cl PO14 .... 129 E1
Kitnocks Hill SO32 .... 106 C4
Kitscroft Rd BH10 .... 189 E3
Kitt's La GU10 .... 16 B1
Kittiwake Cl
Bournemouth BH6 .... 206 C3
Gosport PO13 .... 155 D1
Kitwalls La SO41 .... 211 E3
Kitwood Gn **50** PO9 .... 136 A3
Kivernell Pl **1** SO41 .... 211 E2
Kivernell Rd SO41 .... 211 E2
Kiwi Cl BH15 .... 202 C2
Kleves Ct SO19 .... 104 A3
Knapp Cl BH23 .... 207 D4
Knapp La SO51 .... 29 E2
Knapp Mill Ave BH23 .... 207 D4
Knapps Hard GU32 .... 37 D3
Knatchbull Cl SO51 .... 52 C4
Knellers La SO40 .... 100 B2
Knight Cl SO23 .... 2 A1
Knighton Heath Cl BH11 ...... 188 C2
Knighton Heath Rd BH11 ..... 188 C2
Knighton La BH21 .... 188 B4
Knighton Park BH25 .... 209 F4
Knighton Rd SO19 .... 103 F2
Knights Bank Rd PO14 .... 153 F1
Knights Rd BH11 .... 188 B3
Knightsbridge Ct BH2 .... 204 C1
Knightstone Ct **10** PO2 .... 157 F2
Knightstone Gr BH22 .... 138 B1
Knightstone Grange SO45 ... 126 A1
Knightwood Ave
Havant PO9 .... 136 A3
Lyndhurst SO43 .... 121 F3
Knightwood Cl Ashurst SO40 .. 100 A1
Christchurch BH23 .... 208 B4
Lyndhurst SO43 .... 121 F3
Knightwood Oak SO43 .... 120 C1
Knightwood Rd
Chandler's Ford SO52 .... 55 D3
Hythe SO45 .... 126 A2
North Baddesley SO52 .... 55 D3
Knobcrook Rd **3** BH21 .... 163 D3
Knole Ct **5** BH1 .... 205 E2
Knole Gdns BH1 .... 205 E2
Knole Rd BH1 .... 205 E2
Knoll Gdns BH24 .... 139 F2
Knoll La BH21 .... 186 A4
Knoll Manor BH2 .... 204 C3
Knotgrass Rd SO31 .... 128 C1
Knowland Dr SO41 .... 211 E3
Knowle Hill SO50 .... 56 A4
Knowle Hospl PO17 .... 130 C4
Knowle La SO50 .... 57 F1
Knowle Rd SO42 .... 145 F1
Knowle Sidings PO17 .... 130 B4
Knowles Cl BH23 .... 207 F4
Knowles Meadow GU33 .... 21 D1
Knowlton Gdns BH9 .... 190 A2
Knowlton Rd BH17 .... 187 F1
Knowsley Cres PO6 .... 158 A4
Knowsley Rd PO6 .... 157 F4
Knox Rd Havant PO9 .... 135 E1
Portsmouth PO2 .... 157 E1
Knyght Cl SO51 .... 53 D3
Knyveton House BH1 .... 205 D2
Knyveton Rd BH1 .... 205 E2
Kootenay Ave SO18 .... 104 C4
Kooyong Cl SO51 .... 51 D1
Kynegils Rd SO22 .... 1 C1
Kynon Cl PO12 .... 181 E4
Kyrchil La BH21 .... 163 F3
Kyrchil Way BH21 .... 163 F4
Kytes La SO32 .... 82 B3

Labrador Dr BH15 .... 202 B1
Laburnum Ave PO6 .... 158 B4
Laburnum Cl Ferndown BH22 .. 165 D3
North Baddesley SO52 .... 54 A3
Verwood BH31 .... 115 C3
Laburnum Cres SO45 .... 150 A4
Laburnum Ct SO19 .... 103 E2
Laburnum Dr SO41 .... 211 F4
Laburnum Gr Eastleigh SO50 .. 56 A2
Portsmouth PO2 .... 157 F1
South Hayling PO11 .... 185 D2
Laburnum House
Bournemouth BH10 .... 189 F2
Hedge End SO30 .... 105 E3
Laburnum Rd
Fareham PO16 .... 155 D3
Hedge End SO30 .... 105 E3
Southampton SO16 .... 79 E2
Waterlooville PO7 .... 134 B3
Lacey Cres BH15 .... 203 D3
Lackford Ave SO40 .... 100 C3
Lacon Cl SO18 .... 103 F4
Lacy Cl BH21 .... 163 E3
Lacy Dr BH21 .... 163 E3
Ladram Rd PO12 .... 180 C2
Lady Betty's Dr PO15 .... 129 F3
Ladybridge Rd PO7 .... 134 B2
Ladycross Rd SO45 .... 126 A1
Ladysmith Rd BH23 .... 207 F4
Ladysmith Terr SO32 .... 83 E4
Ladywood SO50 .... 55 F3
Ladywood House **6** PO1 .... 182 B2
Lagado Cl BH14 .... 214 B4
Lagland Ct **13** BH15 .... 202 B1
Lagland St BH15 .... 202 B1
Lagoon Cl BH14 .... 214 A4
Lagoon Rd BH14 .... 214 A4
Laidlaw Cl BH12 .... 204 A4
Lake Ave BH15 .... 201 E4
Lake Cres BH15 .... 201 F2
Lake Dr BH15 .... 201 E1
Lake Farm Cl SO30 .... 105 E4
Lake Grove Rd BH25 .... 195 D2
Lake House SO15 .... 102 B3
Lake Rd
Chandler's Ford SO53 .... 55 F4
Curdridge SO32 .... 106 C4
Hamworthy BH15 .... 201 F1
Portsmouth PO1 .... 182 B3
Southampton SO19 .... 103 E1
Verwood BH31 .... 115 D3
Lakeland Gdns SO40 .... 101 F1
Lakelands Dr SO15 .... 102 B3
Lakes The SO32 .... 84 A2
Lakeside
Fareham PO16 .... 130 C3
Lee-on-the-Solent PO13 ...... 179 F1
Ower SO51 .... 75 E3
Ringwood BH24 .... 141 E3
Lakeside Ave
Portsmouth PO3 .... 183 D4
Rownhams SO16 .... 77 F3
Lakeside Pines BH25 .... 195 D2
Lakeside Rd BH13 .... 204 A1
Lakesmere Rd PO8 .... 112 B3
Lakeview Dr BH24 .... 141 E3
Lakewood Cl SO53 .... 55 E4
Lakewood Rd Ashurst SO40 .. 100 B2
Chandler's Ford SO53 .... 30 C1
Christchurch BH23 .... 193 F1
Lambert Cl PO7 .... 134 C3
Lambourn Cl PO14 .... 154 B4
Lambourn Sq SO53 .... 55 D3
Lambourne Cl SO45 .... 125 F1
Lambourne Dr SO31 .... 129 D2
Lambourne House SO30 ...... 105 D3
Lambourne Rd SO18 .... 80 A1
Lambs Cl BH17 .... 187 E1
Lambsgate La BH21 .... 162 C1
Lammas Rd SO45 .... 126 A1
Lamorbey Ave SO50 .... 55 F3
Lampeter Ave PO6 .... 158 A4
Lampton Gdns BH9 .... 189 F1
Lamward Mansions **28** SO14 .. 103 D4
Lancaster Cl Burseldon SO31 .. 105 D1
Christchurch BH23 .... 208 B4
Corfe Mullen BH18 .... 186 C3
Lee-on-the-Solent PO13 ...... 180 A2
Portchester PO16 .... 132 A1
Lancaster Ct SO30 .... 80 B1
Lancaster Dr
Corfe Mullen BH18 .... 186 C3
Verwood BH31 .... 114 C3
Lancaster Rd Ferndown BH21 .. 165 D4
Southampton SO16 .... 77 F2
Lancaster Way PO7 .... 134 C3
Lance's Hill SO18 .... 103 F4
Lancer Cl BH23 .... 206 C4
Lander Cl BH15 .... 202 B1
Landford CE Contr
Prim Sch SP5 .... 49 E2
Landford Gdns BH8 .... 190 B1
Landford Way BH8 .... 190 B1
Landguard Rd
Portsmouth PO4 .... 183 D2
Southampton SO15 .... 102 B3
Landon Rd PO13 .... 180 B4
Landport St Portsmouth PO1 .. 182 A2
Portsmouth PO1 .... 182 B3
Landport Terr PO1 .... 182 A2
Landport View **8** PO1 .... 182 B3
Lands End Rd SO31 .... 128 B4
Landsdowne St PO5 .... 182 A2
Landseer Rd
13 Bournemouth BH4 .... 204 B2
Southampton SO19 .... 104 B2
Lane End SO24 .... 17 E4
Lane End Cotts SP5 .... 49 E2
Lane End Rd PO12 .... 160 C4

Lane The
4 Bournemouth BH8 .... 205 E3
Fawley SO45 .... 151 D2
Gosport PO12 .... 181 D1
Portsmouth PO4 .... 182 C1
Lanehays Rd SO45 .... 125 F2
Lanes End PO14 .... 179 E3
Lanes The BH25 .... 195 D3
Lanesbridge Cl SO40 .... 99 F3
Langar Cl SO19 .... 103 F3
Langbrook Cl PO9 .... 159 F4
Langdale Ave PO6 .... 158 A4
Langdale Cl SO16 .... 101 F4
Langdon Cl BH14 .... 203 E2
Langdon Rd BH14 .... 203 E2
Langdown Firs SO45 .... 126 A2
Langdown Inf Sch SO45 .... 126 A1
Langdown Jun Sch SO45 ...... 126 A1
Langdown Lawn SO45 .... 126 A2
Langdown Lawn Cl SO45 ..... 126 A1
Langdown Rd SO45 .... 126 A2
Langford La SP5 .... 47 F4
Langford Rd PO1 .... 182 C4
Langham Ct BH23 .... 191 F1
Langham Ct SO52 .... 53 F2
Langhorn Rd SO16 .... 79 E2
Langley Gdn SP6 .... 70 A2
Langley Lodge Gdns SO45 ... 177 F4
Langley Rd Christchurch BH23 .. 193 F1
Poole BH14 .... 203 F2
Portsmouth PO2 .... 182 C4
Southampton SO15 .... 102 A3
Langrish Cl PO9 .... 136 A3
Langrish Hill GU32 .... 39 E2
Langrish Prim Sch GU32 ...... 40 A2
Langrish Rd SO16 .... 78 A2
Langside Ave BH12 .... 204 A4
Langside Sch BH12 .... 204 A4
Langstone Ave PO9 .... 159 F4
Langstone High St PO9 .... 159 F3
Langstone House PO14 .... 155 D4
Langstone Inf Sch PO3 .... 183 D4
Langstone Jun Sch PO3 .... 183 D4
Langstone Rd Havant PO9 ... 159 F4
Portsmouth PO3 .... 183 D3
Langstone Wlk
Fareham PO14 .... 154 B4
Gosport PO13 .... 155 D1
Langton Cl
Barton on Sea BH25 .... 210 A4
Winchester SO22 .... 1 C1
Langton Dene **27** BH25 ...... 204 B2
Langton Farm Gdns PO1 ...... 182 C4
Langton Rd
Bishop's Waltham SO32 .... 83 E4
Bournemouth BH7 .... 206 B2
Lanham La Sparsholt SO22 ... 10 A4
Winchester SO22 .... 1 A1
Lankhills Sch SO22 .... 1 C1
Lankhills Rd SO23 .... 2 A1
Lansdell Ct **6** BH15 .... 202 C2
Lansdowne Ave PO16 .... 156 B3
Lansdowne Terr PO10 .... 137 D3
Lansdowne Ave
Waterlooville PO7 .... 134 A1
Winchester SO22 .... 10 C3
Lansdowne Cl **3** SO51 .... 52 C4
Lansdowne Cres Romsey SO51 .. 52 C4
3 Winchester SO22 .... 10 C3
Lansdowne Gdns
Bournemouth BH1 .... 205 D2
Romsey SO51 .... 52 C4
Lansdowne Hill **9** SO14 .... 102 C2
Lansdowne House
13 Bournemouth BH1 .... 205 D2
5 Gosport PO12 .... 181 D3
Lansdowne Rd
Bournemouth BH1 .... 205 D2
Southampton SO15 .... 102 A4
Lansdowne The BH1 .... 205 D2
Lantana Cl PO7 .... 134 C3
Lantern Ct SO22 .... 10 C3
Lanyard Dr PO13 .... 180 B3
Lapthorn Cl PO13 .... 155 D2
Lapwing Cl Gosport PO12 .... 181 D4
Horndean PO8 .... 112 A4
Lapwing Dr SO40 .... 100 B4
Lapwing Gr PO16 .... 155 F4
Lapwing Rd BH21 .... 164 A4
Lara Cl BH8 .... 190 B2
Larch Ave SO45 .... 150 B3
Larch Cl Broadstone BH17 ... 186 C1
Hordle SO41 .... 195 F2
Kings Worthy SO23 .... 2 A4
Lee-on-the-Solent PO13 ...... 180 A3
St Leonards BH24 .... 140 A2
West End SO30 .... 80 B1
Larch Rd SO16 .... 78 A2
Larch Row SP6 .... 70 B1
Larch Way Bursledon SO31 .. 127 F4
Ferndown BH22 .... 165 E4
Larchdale Cl SO31 .... 152 B4
Larches Gdns PO15 .... 130 B1
Larchfield Way PO8 .... 112 B3
Larchwood Ave PO9 .... 135 D2
Larchwood Rd SO40 .... 100 B3
Larcombe Rd GU32 .... 40 B1
Larg Dr SO22 .... 1 B2
Lark Hill Rise SO22 .... 10 B2
Lark Rd Christchurch BH23 .. 208 A3
Eastleigh SO50 .... 55 E1
Larkhill Rd PO3 .... 157 F2
Larks Cl BH22 .... 165 D4
Larks Rise BH22 .... 165 D4
Larksfield Ave BH9 .... 190 B2
Larkshill CI BH25 .... 195 D2
Larkspur Chase SO19 .... 104 C3

Larkspur Cl Locks Heath SO31 .. 128 C1
Swanmore SO32 .... 84 A3
Larkspur Dr SO40 .... 124 C4
Larkspur Gdns Hedge End SO30 .. 105 E3
Holbury SO45 .... 150 A2
Larkwhistle Wlk PO9 .... 135 E4
Lascelles Ct **1** BH7 .... 206 A3
Lascelles Rd BH7 .... 206 A3
Laser Cl SO31 .... 128 C1
Lasham Gn PO9 .... 136 A3
Lasham House **3** SO16 ...... 102 A4
Lasham Wlk PO14 .... 154 B4
Lashley Meadow PO7 .... 86 B2
Latch Farm Ave BH23 .... 207 D4
Latchmore Dr SO45 .... 125 E2
Latchmore Forest Gr PO8 .... 112 A2
Latchmore Gdns PO8 .... 111 F2
Latelie Cl SO31 .... 127 E3
Latham Cl SO50 .... 57 D1
Latham Ct SO15 .... 102 A4
Latham Rd Fair Oak SO50 .... 57 D1
Romsey SO51 .... 53 D4
Latimer Ct Portsmouth PO3 .. 158 A2
11 Southampton SO17 .... 79 D1
Latimer Gate **27** SO14 .... 103 D2
Latimer Rd BH9 .... 204 C4
Latimer St Romsey SO51 ...... 52 C4
Southampton SO14 .... 103 D2
Latimers Cl BH23 .... 193 F1
Lauder Cl PO10 .... 137 F1
Launcelyn Cl SO52 .... 53 F2
Launceston Dr SO50 .... 55 F3
Laundry La SO41 .... 211 F2
Laundry Rd SO16 .... 78 A1
Laurel Cl Christchurch BH23 .. 193 E1
Corfe Mullen BH21 .... 186 B3
Hordle SO41 .... 195 F2
Hythe SO45 .... 125 F2
Locks Heath SO31 .... 129 D2
Southampton SO19 .... 103 E2
St Leonards BH24 .... 139 F2
Laurel Dr BH18 .... 187 E2
Laurel Gdns Broadstone SO30 .. 187 E2
Locks Heath SO31 .... 129 D2
Laurel La PH24 .... 139 F2
Laurel Rd Locks Heath SO31 .. 129 D2
Waterlooville PO8 .... 112 B2
Laurels The
Brockenhurst SO42 .... 172 C4
Ferndown BH22 .... 165 E4
Laurence Ct **2** SO50 .... 57 E1
Laurence Gn PO10 .... 136 C2
Lauriston Dr SO53 .... 30 A1
Laurus Cl PO7 .... 135 D3
Laurus Wlk **18** PO13 .... 179 F1
Lavant Cl PO8 .... 112 A1
Lavant Ct **3** GU32 .... 40 C2
Lavant Dr PO9 .... 136 A2
Lavant St GU32 .... 40 C2
Lavender Cl
Southampton SO19 .... 103 F3
Verwood BH31 .... 115 C3
Lavender Rd
Bournemouth BH8 .... 190 B2
Hordle SO41 .... 195 F2
Waterlooville PO7 .... 135 D3
Lavender Villas **1** BH23 ..... 209 D4
Lavender Way BH18 .... 186 B2
Laverock Lea PO16 .... 132 B1
Laverstock BH5 .... 205 F2
Laverstoke Cl SO16 .... 77 F3
Lavey's La PO15 .... 130 A3
Lavington Gdns SO52 .... 53 F2
Lavinia Rd Gosport PO12 .... 181 D3
Poole BH14 .... 203 E4
Lawford Rd BH9 .... 190 A2
Lawford Way SO40 .... 100 C4
Lawn Cl Gosport PO13 .... 180 B4
Milford on Sea SO41 .... 211 F2
Lawn Ct SO17 .... 103 D4
Lawn Dr SO31 .... 129 D1
Lawn House **17** SO23 .... 11 D4
Lawn Rd Eastleigh SO50 ...... 56 A3
Littleton SO22 .... 1 B2
Lymington SO41 .... 197 E2
Milford on Sea SO41 .... 211 F2
Southampton SO17 .... 103 D4
Lawn St **16** SO23 .... 11 D4
Lawn View BH25 .... 194 B3
Lawns Cl BH21 .... 164 B3
Lawns Rd BH21 .... 164 A3
Lawns The BH23 .... 209 D4
Lawnside Rd SO15 .... 102 A4
Lawnswood Cl PO8 .... 111 F1
Lawrence Ave
Bournemouth BH8 .... 205 E3
Southampton SO19 .... 103 F1
Lawrence Dr BH13 .... 203 F1
Lawrence Gr SO19 .... 103 F1
Lawrence House **5** SO45 ... 126 A2
Lawrence La SP6 .... 94 A2
Lawrence Rd Fareham PO15 .. 130 C1
Portsmouth PO5 .... 182 C2
Ringwood BH24 .... 117 E1
Lawrence Sq **20** PO12 .... 181 E2
Lawrence Wlk PO13 .... 180 B3
Lawson Cl SO31 .... 128 B4
Lawson Ct **9** SO15 .... 78 A1
Lawson Rd Poole BH12 .... 203 D3
Portsmouth PO5 .... 182 C2
Laxton Cl Locks Heath SO31 .. 129 D2
Southampton SO19 .... 104 A1
Layard Dr BH21 .... 163 E1
Laymoor La BH21 .... 164 B3
Layton Ct BH12 .... 203 E3
Layton Rd Gosport PO13 .... 155 E2
Poole BH12 .... 203 E3

Lazy Acre PO10 ...... 161 E4
Le Patourel Cl BH23 ...... 207 E4
Lea Rd SO45 ...... 177 F4
Lea Way BH11 ...... 188 C3
Lea-Oak Gdns PO15 ...... 130 B2
Leabrook SO31 ...... 129 D3
Leacock Cl SO32 ...... 84 A3
Leafy La PO15 ...... 129 F3
Lealand Gr PO6 ...... 158 B4
Lealand Rd PO6 ...... 158 B4
Leamington Cres PO13 ...... 179 F1
Leamington House 52 PO5 ...... 182 B2
Leamington Rd BH9 ...... 205 D4
Leander Cl SO50 ...... 56 A3
Leaphill Rd BH7 ...... 206 A3
Lear Rd PO12 ...... 181 D3
Learoyd Rd BH17 ...... 202 C4
Leaside Way SO16 ...... 79 E3
Leatherhead Gdns SO30 ...... 81 E1
Leaway The PO16 ...... 156 B4
Lebanon Rd SO15 ...... 101 E4
Lechlade Gdns
  Bournemouth BH7 ...... 206 A4
  Fareham PO15 ...... 130 C2
Leckford Cl
  Portchester PO16 ...... 132 A1
  Southampton SO18 ...... 104 B4
Leckford Rd PO9 ...... 136 A3
Ledbury Rd
  Christchurch BH23 ...... 207 F3
  Cosham PO6 ...... 133 E1
Lederle La PO13 ...... 155 E3
Ledgard Cl BH14 ...... 203 D2
Lee Church La SO51 ...... 76 C4
Lee Ct BH22 ...... 165 E2
Lee Dro SO51 ...... 53 D1
Lee La SO16 ...... 77 D4
Lee Rd PO12 ...... 181 D3
Lee-on-the-Solent Inf Sch
  PO13 ...... 179 F1
Lee-on-the-Solent Jun Sch
  PO13 ...... 179 F1
Leedam Rd BH10 ...... 189 E2
Leelands SO41 ...... 197 E1
Leep La PO12 ...... 181 D1
Lees Cl BH23 ...... 191 E2
Lees La PO12 ...... 181 D3
Lees La N PO12 ...... 181 D3
Leesland CE Inf Sch PO12 ...... 181 D2
Leesland CE Jun Sch PO12 ...... 181 D2
Leesland Rd PO12 ...... 181 D3
Leeson Dr BH22 ...... 165 D4
Leeson Rd BH7 ...... 205 F4
Legg La BH21 ...... 163 E2
Legion Cl BH15 ...... 201 F1
Legion La SO23 ...... 2 B4
Legion Rd Hamworthy BH15 ...... 201 F1
  South Hayling PO11 ...... 185 D2
Leicester Ct PO13 ...... 180 B3
Leicester Rd Poole BH13 ...... 203 F2
  Southampton SO15 ...... 78 B1
Leicester Way SO23 ...... 2 B1
Leigh Comm BH21 ...... 163 F2
Leigh Ct SO50 ...... 55 F2
Leigh Gdns BH21 ...... 163 E2
Leigh House Hospl SO53 ...... 55 E4
Leigh La BH21 ...... 163 F3
Leigh Mansions 10 SO17 ...... 79 D1
Leigh Pk SO41 ...... 197 E2
Leigh Rd
  Chandler's Ford SO53 ...... 55 F2
  Eastleigh SO50, SO53 ...... 55 F2
  Fareham PO16 ...... 131 D1
  Havant PO9 ...... 135 F1
  New Milton BH25 ...... 195 D2
  Southampton SO17 ...... 79 D1
  Wimborne Minster BH21 ...... 163 F2
Leigham Vale Rd BH6 ...... 206 B2
Leighton Ave 7 SO15 ...... 102 A4
Leighton Rd PO13 ...... 103 F2
Leisure The PO13 ...... 155 E2
Leith Ave PO16 ...... 132 B1
Lemon Rd SO15 ...... 102 A4
Lendorber Ave PO6 ...... 158 A4
Lennox Cl
  Chandler's Ford SO53 ...... 55 F4
  Gosport PO12 ...... 181 E1
  Southampton SO16 ...... 77 F3
Lennox Rd N PO5 ...... 182 B1
Lennox Rd S PO5 ...... 182 B1
Lensyd Gdns PO8 ...... 111 F3
Lent Hill Ct 5 SO22 ...... 10 B3
Lentham Cl BH17 ...... 187 E1
Lentune Way SO41 ...... 197 E1
Leofric Ct PO4 ...... 183 E2
Leominster Rd PO6 ...... 133 D1
Leonard Rd PO12 ...... 181 E3
Leonards Ct SO16 ...... 101 E4
Leopold Dr SO32 ...... 83 D4
Leopold St PO4 ...... 182 C1
Lepe Ctry Pk SO45 ...... 178 A1
Lepe Rd SO45 ...... 178 A2
Lerryn Rd PO13 ...... 155 E1
Leslie Loader Ct SO50 ...... 56 A2
Leslie Loader House SO19 ...... 103 F4
Leslie Rd Bournemouth BH9 ...... 204 C4
  Poole BH14 ...... 203 D2
Lester Ave PO9 ...... 135 E1
Lester Rd PO12 ...... 181 E1
Lester Sq BH24 ...... 143 E4
Leven Ave BH4 ...... 204 B3
Leven Cl Bournemouth BH4 ...... 204 B3
  North Baddesley SO53 ...... 55 D4
Leventhorpe Ct PO12 ...... 181 E2
Leveson Cl PO12 ...... 180 C2
Levet's La 5 BH15 ...... 202 A1
Leviathan Cl PO14 ...... 179 E3

Lewens Cl BH21 ...... 163 E2
Lewens La BH21 ...... 163 E2
Lewes Cl SO50 ...... 56 A3
Lewesdon Dr BH18 ...... 186 C2
Lewin Cl SO21 ...... 56 C4
Lewins Wlk SO31 ...... 104 C1
Lewis Cl SO45 ...... 125 E1
Lewis House 17 SO14 ...... 103 D3
Lewis Rd PO10 ...... 137 D2
Lewis Silkin Way SO16 ...... 78 A2
Lewry Cl SO30 ...... 105 E4
Lexby Rd SO40 ...... 101 D3
Lexden Gdns PO11 ...... 184 C2
Leybourne Ave
  Bournemouth BH10 ...... 189 E2
  Southampton SO18 ...... 104 A4
Leybourne Cl BH10 ...... 189 E3
Leydene Ave BH8 ...... 190 C1
Leydene Cl BH8 ...... 190 C1
Leyland Cl PO12 ...... 181 D2
Leyland Rd BH12 ...... 188 C1
Leyside BH23 ...... 207 F3
Lichen Way SO40 ...... 101 F1
Lichfield Ct PO13 ...... 180 B3
Lichfield Rd
  Locks Heath PO14 ...... 129 E2
  Portsmouth PO3 ...... 183 D3
Liddel Way SO53 ...... 55 D3
Liddiards Way PO7 ...... 134 C2
Lidiard Gdns PO4 ...... 183 D1
Lightfoot Lawn PO4 ...... 183 E2
Lilac Cl BH24 ...... 141 D4
Lilac Rd SO16 ...... 79 D2
Lilley Cl SO40 ...... 101 F1
Lilliput CE Fst Sch BH14 ...... 214 B4
Lilliput Ct BH14 ...... 203 D2
Lilliput Rd BH14 ...... 214 B4
Lily Ave PO7 ...... 134 A1
Limberline Rd PO3 ...... 158 A2
Limberline Spur PO3 ...... 158 A3
Lime Ave SO19 ...... 104 A3
Lime Cl Colden Common SO21 ...... 57 D4
  Hythe SO45 ...... 125 F1
  Poole BH15 ...... 202 C3
  Southampton SO19 ...... 104 A3
Lime Gdns SO30 ...... 80 B2
Lime Gr Cosham PO6 ...... 133 D1
  Hordle SO41 ...... 211 E4
  South Hayling PO11 ...... 184 B2
Lime Kiln La SO45 ...... 150 A3
Lime Kiln Lane
  Mobile Home Pk SO45 ...... 150 A3
Lime St SO14 ...... 103 D2
Lime Tree Cl SP6 ...... 92 C3
Lime Tree House SO41 ...... 197 F2
Lime Wlk Botley SO30 ...... 105 F4
  Hythe SO45 ...... 125 F1
Limekiln La
  Bishop's Waltham SO32 ...... 59 F2
  East Meon GU32 ...... 64 B4
Limes Cl GU33 ...... 20 C2
Limes The Gosport PO13 ...... 155 E1
  Havant PO9 ...... 159 F4
  Marchwood SO40 ...... 102 A1
  Waterlooville PO7 ...... 134 B2
Limetree Wlk 8 SO23 ...... 11 E4
Limited Rd BH9 ...... 190 A1
Lin Brook Dr BH24 ...... 117 E1
Linacre Rd SO19 ...... 104 B3
Linbrook Ct BH24 ...... 117 D1
Linbrook View BH24 ...... 117 D1
Lincoln Ave Bournemouth BH1 ...... 205 E3
  Christchurch BH23 ...... 191 F1
Lincoln Cl Locks Heath PO14 ...... 129 E2
  Romsey SO51 ...... 28 A1
Lincoln Ct Gosport PO13 ...... 180 B3
  Southampton SO15 ...... 78 C1
  West End SO30 ...... 80 B1
Lincoln Rd Poole BH12 ...... 203 E4
  Portsmouth PO1 ...... 182 C3
Lincoln Rise PO8 ...... 112 A2
Lincolns Rise SO50 ...... 31 D1
Lind Cl PO7 ...... 134 C2
Lind Rd PO12 ...... 181 E1
Linda Gr PO8 ...... 111 F2
Linda Rd SO45 ...... 151 D2
Lindbergh Cl PO13 ...... 180 B3
Lindbergh Rd BH21 ...... 165 D4
Lindbergh Rise PO15 ...... 129 F3
Linden Cl Ferndown BH22 ...... 165 E1
  Shedfield SO32 ...... 84 A3
Linden Ct Locks Heath SO31 ...... 129 E2
  Ringwood BH24 ...... 140 C4
  12 Romsey SO51 ...... 52 C4
  West End SO30 ...... 80 A2
Linden Dr GU33 ...... 20 C2
Linden Gdns
  Hedge End SO30 ...... 105 E3
  Ringwood BH24 ...... 140 C4
Linden Gr
  Chandler's Ford SO53 ...... 55 E4
  Gosport PO12 ...... 181 D2
  South Hayling PO11 ...... 185 D2
Linden Lea SO16 ...... 132 B1
Linden Rd
  Bournemouth BH9 ...... 190 A2
  Ferndown BH22 ...... 165 E1
  Poole BH12 ...... 203 E3

Linden Rd Continued
  Romsey SO51 ...... 52 C4
  Southampton SO16 ...... 78 A2
Linden Way Havant PO9 ...... 135 F2
  Lymington SO41 ...... 197 E2
  Waterlooville PO8 ...... 112 B3
Linden Wlk SO52 ...... 53 F3
Lindens Cl PO10 ...... 136 C1
Lindens The BH23 ...... 192 B2
Lindisfarne Cl PO6 ...... 158 A4
Lindley Ave PO4 ...... 183 D1
Lindsay House 35 PO5 ...... 182 B1
Lindsay Manor 10 BH12 ...... 204 A2
Lindsay Pk 15 BH12 ...... 204 A2
Lindsay Rd Poole BH13 ...... 204 A2
  Southampton SO19 ...... 104 C3
Lindum Ct 3 BH12 ...... 204 A2
Lindway PO13 ...... 129 D3
Lineside BH23 ...... 207 E4
Linford Cl BH25 ...... 195 D2
Linford Cres SO16 ...... 78 B2
Linford Ct PO9 ...... 135 E4
Linford House BH24 ...... 117 F2
Linford Rd BH24 ...... 117 E1
Ling Dale SO16 ...... 78 C4
Ling Rd BH12 ...... 188 A1
Lingdale Pl 3 SO17 ...... 103 D4
Lingdale Rd BH6 ...... 206 B3
Lingfield Ct PO1 ...... 182 A2
Lingfield Grange BH4 ...... 204 A2
Lingwood Ave BH23 ...... 207 F3
Lingwood Cl SO16 ...... 78 C4
Lingwood Wlk SO16 ...... 78 C4
Linhorns La BH25 ...... 195 D3
Link Rd Ringwood BH24 ...... 141 E4
  Southampton SO16 ...... 77 F2
Link Rise BH21 ...... 186 C3
Link The PO7 ...... 112 A1
Link Way PO14 ...... 179 E3
Linkenholt Way PO9 ...... 135 E2
Linklater Path PO1 ...... 182 B4
Links Cl PO9 ...... 113 D1
Links Dr BH23 ...... 191 E1
Links La
  Rowland's Castle PO9 ...... 113 D1
  South Hayling PO11 ...... 184 B2
  Winchester SO22 ...... 1 B1
Links Rd Poole BH14 ...... 203 E1
Links The PO13 ...... 155 E1
Links View Ave BH23 ...... 203 F1
Links View Way SO16 ...... 78 C3
Linkside Ave BH4 ...... 205 F4
Linmead Dr BH11 ...... 189 D3
Linnet Cl Petersfield GU31 ...... 41 E1
  Ringwood BH24 ...... 141 E4
  Waterlooville PO8 ...... 111 F2
Linnet Ct Gosport PO12 ...... 180 C3
  New Milton BH25 ...... 194 C2
Linnet Rd BH17 ...... 201 F4
Linnet Sq SO50 ...... 55 E1
Linnets The
  Portchester PO16 ...... 155 F4
  Totton SO40 ...... 100 B4
Linnies La SO41 ...... 196 A4
Linthorpe Rd BH15 ...... 202 C2
Linwood Cl SO45 ...... 126 A1
Linwood Rd BH9 ...... 205 D4
Linwood Sch BH9 ...... 205 D4
Lion St PO1 ...... 182 A3
Lion Terr PO1 ...... 182 A3
Lionheart Cl BH11 ...... 188 B3
Lionheart Way SO31 ...... 105 D1
Lions Hall 23 SO22 ...... 10 C4
Lions La BH24 ...... 139 E3
Lions Wood BH24 ...... 139 F2
Liphook House 38 PO9 ...... 136 A3
Lipizzaner Fields SO31 ...... 129 D4
Lippen La SO32 ...... 36 C2
Lisbon Rd SO15 ...... 102 B3
Lisle Cl Lymington SO41 ...... 197 E2
  Winchester SO22 ...... 10 A3
Lisle Court Rd SO41 ...... 198 B2
Lisle Ct SO22 ...... 10 C3
Lisle Way PO10 ...... 136 C2
Liss Rd PO4 ...... 182 C2
Liss Schs GU33 ...... 21 D2
Liss Sta GU33 ...... 20 C2
Litchfield Cres SO18 ...... 79 F1
Litchfield Rd
  Southampton SO18 ...... 79 F1
  Winchester SO22 ...... 1 B2
Litchford Rd BH25 ...... 195 E2
Lith Ave PO8 ...... 112 B4
Little Abshot Rd PO14 ...... 153 D4
Little Anglesey PO12 ...... 181 D1
Little Anglesey Rd PO12 ...... 181 D1
Little Arthur St PO2 ...... 182 C4
Little Ashton La SO32 ...... 59 F2
Little Barn Pl GU33 ...... 21 D2
Little Barrs Dr BH25 ...... 195 D2
Little Bull La SO32 ...... 83 E1
Little Burn SO41 ...... 172 A1
Little Cnr PO7 ...... 111 D2
Little Coburg St 65 PO1 ...... 182 B3
Little Croft Rd BH12 ...... 203 D3
Little Ct Poole BH14 ...... 214 B4
  Poole, Canford Cliffs BH13 ...... 214 C4
Little Dene Copse SO41 ...... 197 D1
Little Dewlands BH31 ...... 114 B3
Little Dro SP6 ...... 70 C4
Little Forest
  Mansions 10 BH1 ...... 205 D2
Little Forest Rd BH4 ...... 204 C3
Little Fosters BH13 ...... 214 C3
Little Gays PO14 ...... 179 D3
Little George St PO1 ...... 182 A4
Little Gr PO12 ...... 181 D1
Little Green Orch PO12 ...... 181 D1
Little La BH23 ...... 167 F1

Little Hambrook St PO5 ...... 182 A2
Little Holbury Park
  Mobile Home Pk SO45 ...... 150 A3
Little Hyden La PO8 ...... 88 A4
Little Kimble Wlk SO30 ...... 105 E3
Little La 181 D1
Little Lance's Hill SO19 ...... 103 F3
Little Lonnen BH21 ...... 163 F4
Little Mead PO7 ...... 111 D2
Little Minster St 28 SO23 ...... 11 D4
Little Oak Rd SO16 ...... 78 C2
Little Park Cl SO30 ...... 105 D3
Little Park Farm Rd PO15 ...... 129 E3
Little Park Mansions PO17 ...... 107 F2
Little Quob La SO30 ...... 80 C1
Little Reynolds SO40 ...... 100 B3
Little Shore La SO32 ...... 83 E4
Little Southsea St PO5 ...... 182 A2
Little Toller SO16 ...... 78 C4
Little Woodfalls Dr SP5 ...... 47 E2
Littlecroft Ave BH9 ...... 190 A2
Littledown Ave BH7 ...... 205 F4
Littledown Dr BH7 ...... 205 F4
Littlegreen Ave PO9 ...... 136 A2
Littlegreen Sch PO18 ...... 90 C2
Littlemead Ct BH17 ...... 202 A4
Littlemeads SO51 ...... 52 B4
Littlemill La SP6 ...... 68 B3
Littlemoor Ave BH11 ...... 188 B2
Littlepark Ave PO9 ...... 135 D2
Littleton Gr PO9 ...... 135 F2
Littleton La SO21 ...... 1 A3
Littleton Rd SO22 ...... 1 A2
Littlewood Gdns
  Locks Heath SO31 ...... 128 C2
  West End SO30 ...... 80 B1
Liverpool Ct PO13 ...... 180 B3
Liverpool Rd Gosport PO14 ...... 154 C3
  Portsmouth PO1 ...... 182 C3
Liverpool St SO14 ...... 103 D4
Livesay Gdns PO1 ...... 182 C3
Livingston Rd BH12 ...... 203 E3
Livingstone Ct PO13 ...... 180 B3
Livingstone Rd
  Bournemouth BH5 ...... 206 A3
  Christchurch BH23 ...... 207 E4
  Portsmouth PO5 ...... 182 B2
  Southampton SO15 ...... 103 D3
  Wimborne Minster BH21 ...... 163 F2
Llewellin Cl BH16 ...... 201 E4
Llewellin Ct BH16 ...... 201 E4
Lloyd Ave SO40 ...... 101 F1
Loane Rd SO19 ...... 103 F2
Lobelia Ct PO7 ...... 135 D3
Lobelia Rd SO16 ...... 79 E3
Locarno Rd PO3 ...... 158 A1
Loch Rd BH14 ...... 203 F3
Lock App PO6 ...... 157 D4
Lock View PO6 ...... 157 D4
Lock's Cotts SO45 ...... 125 E3
Locke Rd SO30 ...... 105 E4
Lockerley Cl SO41 ...... 197 F1
Lockerley Cres SO16 ...... 77 F1
Lockerley Endowed
  CE Prim Sch SO51 ...... 5 D1
Lockerley Rd PO9 ...... 136 A2
Lockhams Rd SO32 ...... 106 C4
Locks Heath Ctr SO31 ...... 129 D2
Locks Heath Jun & Inf Schs
  SO31 ...... 129 D1
Locks Rd SO31 ...... 129 D2
Locksheath Cl PO9 ...... 135 E3
Locksheath Park Rd SO31 ...... 129 D1
Locksley Dr SO50 ...... 165 E2
Locksley Rd SO50 ...... 55 F1
Locksway Rd PO4 ...... 183 E2
Lockswood Rd SO31 ...... 128 C2
Lockyer's Cty Mid Sch BH21 ...... 186 B4
Lockyers Dr BH22 ...... 165 F3
Lode Hill SP5 ...... 47 D4
Loders Cl BH17 ...... 187 E2
Lodge Ave PO6 ...... 158 A4
Lodge Cl BH14 ...... 203 F2
Lodge Ct BH14 ...... 203 F2
Lodge Dr SO45 ...... 126 A1
Lodge Gdns PO12 ...... 181 D2
Lodge Hill PO17 ...... 109 D3
Lodge Rd
  Christchurch BH23 ...... 206 C4
  Havant PO9 ...... 135 D1
  Locks Heath SO31 ...... 129 D2
  Lymington SO41 ...... 197 D2
  Southampton SO14 ...... 103 D4
Lodge The
  Southampton SO15 ...... 102 C4
  Waterlooville PO7 ...... 135 D3
Lodge Vale SO51 ...... 51 D1
Lodgebury Cl PO10 ...... 161 F4
Lodsworth Cl PO8 ...... 88 B2
Loewy Cres BH12 ...... 188 B1
Lofting Cl SO50 ...... 56 C1
Logan Cl SO16 ...... 77 F3
Lomax Cl SO30 ...... 81 E1
Lombard Ave BH6 ...... 206 B3
Lombard Ct PO1 ...... 182 A2
Lombard St PO1 ...... 182 A2
Lombardy Cl Gosport PO13 ...... 155 F1
  Verwood BH31 ...... 115 D1
Lombardy Rise PO7 ...... 134 C3
Lomer La SP6, BH24 ...... 93 E2
Lomond Cl PO2 ...... 182 B4
Lomond Rd 157 E1
London Ave PO2 ...... 182 C4
London Ct Gosport PO13 ...... 180 B3
  Gosport, Alverstoke PO12 ...... 181 D1
London La BH23 ...... 167 F1

London Rd Clanfield PO8 ...... 88 B2
  Cosham PO7 ...... 134 B2
  Hill Brow GU33 ...... 21 D1
  Horndean PO8 ...... 88 B2
  Kings Worthy SO23 ...... 2 A3
  Petersfield GU31 ...... 41 D3
  Portsmouth PO2 ...... 157 F2
  Southampton SO15 ...... 103 D3
  Steep GU31 ...... 41 E3
  Waterlooville PO7, PO6 ...... 134 B2
London Tavern
  Cvn Pk The BH24 ...... 141 E4
Lone Barn La SO32 ...... 60 C4
Lone Pine Cvn Pk BH22 ...... 165 F2
Lone Pine Dr BH22 ...... 165 F2
Lone Pine Way BH22 ...... 165 F1
Lone Valley PO7 ...... 134 B2
Long Acre Ct PO1 ...... 182 C4
Long Beech Dr SO40 ...... 100 B3
Long Cl Downton SP5 ...... 46 C4
  Winchester SO22 ...... 10 C3
Long Copse SO45 ...... 150 C2
Long Copse Ct PO10 ...... 136 C2
Long Copse La PO10 ...... 137 D2
Long Curtain Rd PO5 ...... 182 A1
Long Down GU31 ...... 41 D2
Long Dr Gosport PO13 ...... 155 E1
  West End SO30 ...... 80 C1
Long La Bursledon SO31 ...... 105 D1
  Holbury SO45 ...... 150 B3
  Marchwood SO40 ...... 101 E1
  Ringwood BH24 ...... 141 D2
  Wimborne Minster BH21 ...... 163 F4
Long Lane Cl SO45 ...... 150 B2
Long Priors SO22 ...... 37 D3
Long Rd Bournemouth BH10 ...... 189 E3
  Soberton SO32 ...... 85 E3
Long Water Dr PO12 ...... 181 E1
Long Wlk Itchen Abbas SO21 ...... 2 C2
  Portsmouth PO1 ...... 182 B4
Longacre GU33 ...... 21 D2
Longacre Dr BH22 ...... 165 E2
Longacres PO14 ...... 129 E2
Longbarrow Cl BH8 ...... 191 D1
Longbridge Cl SO40 ...... 76 B1
Longbridge Ct SO40 ...... 76 B1
Longbridge House 51 PO5 ...... 182 B2
Longbridge Pk SO19 ...... 103 E2
Longclose Rd SO30 ...... 105 E4
Longcroft PO9 ...... 135 F1
Longdean Cl 1 PO6 ...... 133 D1
Longdown Dairy Farm SO40 ...... 100 B1
Longespee Rd BH21 ...... 187 F4
Longfield Ave PO14 ...... 154 C4
Longfield Dr
  Bournemouth BH11 ...... 189 D3
  Ferndown BH22 ...... 189 F4
Longfield Rd Emsworth PO10 ...... 136 C2
  Fair Oak SO50 ...... 57 E1
  Hordle SO41 ...... 196 A1
  Winchester SO23 ...... 11 E4
Longfleet CE Comb Sch
  BH15 ...... 202 B2
Longfleet Rd BH15 ...... 202 C2
Longhouse Gn 9 SO23 ...... 11 E4
Longlands Rd PO10 ...... 161 E4
Longleat Gdns
  New Milton BH25 ...... 194 C2
  Southampton SO16 ...... 78 A2
Longmead GU33 ...... 20 C2
Longmead Ave SO50 ...... 56 B2
Longmead Ct PO9 ...... 159 F4
Longmead Gdns PO9 ...... 159 F4
Longmead Rd Burley BH24 ...... 142 C2
  1 Southampton SO18 ...... 80 A1
Longmeadow Gdns SO45 ...... 126 A2
Longmeadow La BH17 ...... 201 F4
Longmore Ave SO19 ...... 103 E1
Longmore Cres SO19 ...... 103 E1
Longmynd Dr PO14 ...... 154 B4
Longridge Rd SO30 ...... 105 E3
Longs La PO14 ...... 154 B2
Longshore Way PO4 ...... 183 E2
Longspee Sch BH17 ...... 202 B4
Longstaff Gdns PO16 ...... 130 C2
Longstock Cl SO19 ...... 127 D4
Longstock Cres SO40 ...... 100 C4
Longstock Rd PO9 ...... 136 A3
Longstone House PO9 ...... 136 A2
Longstone Marina Hts PO4 ...... 183 E2
Longwood Ave PO6 ...... 112 A2
Longwood Dean La
  SO32, SO23 ...... 34 A3
Lonnen Rd BH21 ...... 164 A4
Lonnen Wood Cl BH21 ...... 164 A4
Lonsdale Ave Cosham PO6 ...... 158 A4
  Portchester PO16 ...... 156 B3
Lonsdale Rd BH3 ...... 204 C3
Loose Hanger SP5 ...... 47 F2
Loperwood SO40 ...... 76 A1
Loperwood La
  Netley Marsh SO40 ...... 76 A1
  Ower SO40 ...... 76 A1
  Totton SO40 ...... 76 A1
Loraine Ave BH23 ...... 209 E4
Lord Cl BH17 ...... 202 C4
Lord Montgomery Way PO1 ...... 182 A2
Lord Mountbatten Cl SO18 ...... 79 F2
Lord Wilson Sch SO31 ...... 128 C2
Lord's Hill Ctr E SO16 ...... 77 F2
Lord's Hill Ctr W SO16 ...... 77 F2
Lord's Hill Way SO16 ...... 78 A3
Lordington Cl PO6 ...... 158 A4
Lords Ct 61 PO1 ...... 182 B3
Lords St PO1 ...... 182 B3

Lordswood SO50 .... 56 C4
Lordswood SO16 .... 78 B2
Lordswood Ct SO16 .... 78 B2
Lordswood Gdns SO16 .... 78 B2
Lordswood Rd SO16 .... 78 B2
Loreille Cl SO16 .... 77 F4
Loring House **7** PO2 .... 157 F2
Lorne Park Rd BH1 .... 205 D2
Lorne Pl SO18 .... 104 A4
Lorne Rd PO5 .... 182 C2
Lortemore Pl **7** SO51 .... 52 C4
Loughwood Cl SO50 .... 56 A3
Louis Flagg House **15** PO5 ..... 182 B2
Lovage Gdns SO40 .... 100 B4
Lovage Way PO8 .... 88 B1
Lovatt Gr PO15 .... 130 B2
Love La Milford on Sea SO41 ...... 211 E3
  Petersfield GU31 .... 41 D2
  Romsey SO51 .... 52 C4
  Twyford SO23 .... 32 A3
  Woodgreen SP6 .... 70 C4
Lovedean La Horndean PO8 ...... 111 F3
  Waterlooville PO8 .... 111 F3
Lovedon La SO23 .... 2 B4
Lovett Rd PO3 .... 158 A2
Lovett Wlk SO22 .... 1 B2
Lowcay Rd PO5 .... 182 C1
Lowden Cl SO22 .... 10 B2
Lower Alfred St **8** SO14 .... 103 D3
Lower Ashley Rd BH25 .... 195 E1
Lower Banister St **11** SO15 ... 102 C3
Lower Bartons SP6 .... 69 F1
Lower Baybridge La SO21 .... 33 E1
Lower Bellfield PO14 .... 153 F4
Lower Bere Wood PO7 .... 134 C4
Lower Blandford Rd BH18 .... 187 D2
Lower Brook St **12** SO23 .... 11 D4
Lower Brookfield Rd PO1 .... 182 C3
Lower Brownhill Rd SO16 .... 77 E2
Lower Buckland Rd SO41 .... 197 E3
Lower Canal Wlk SO14 .... 103 D2
Lower Chase Rd Shedfield SO32 83 F2
  Swanmore SO32 .... 83 F2
Lower Church Path PO1 .... 182 B3
Lower Church Rd PO14 .... 129 E2
Lower Common La BH21 .... 139 D4
Lower Common Rd SO51 .... 50 C2
Lower Crabbick La PO7 .... 110 A3
Lower Densome Wood SP6 ...... 70 C4
Lower Derby Rd PO2 .... 157 E1
Lower Drayton La PO6 .... 158 A4
Lower Duncan Rd SO31 .... 129 D3
Lower Farlington Rd PO6 .... 158 C4
Lower Forbury Rd **9** PO5 ...... 182 B2
Lower Golf Links Rd BH18 .... 187 D3
Lower Gr SP6 .... 45 D1
Lower Grove Rd PO9 .... 160 A4
Lower Heyshott GU31 .... 41 D2
Lower La SO32 .... 83 E4
Lower Lamborough La SO24 .... 14 B3
Lower Mead GU31 .... 41 D2
Lower Mead End Rd SO41 .... 171 F1
Lower Moors Rd SO21 .... 31 F1
Lower Mortimer Rd SO19 .... 103 E2
Lower Mullin's La SO45 .... 125 F2
Lower New Rd SO30 .... 80 B1
Lower Northam Rd SO30 .... 105 E4
Lower Pennington La SO41 ...... 212 B4
Lower Quay Rd PO16 .... 155 D4
Lower Quay Cl PO16 .... 155 D4
Lower Quay Rd PO16 .... 155 D4
Lower Rd PO9 .... 135 E1
Lower Sandy Down La SO41 .... 173 E2
Lower Spinney SO31 .... 152 B4
Lower St SO51 .... 28 A4
Lower St Helens Rd SO30 .... 105 E3
Lower Stanmore La SO23 .... 10 C3
Lower Swanwick Rd SO31 .... 128 B4
Lower Vicarage Rd SO19 .... 103 E2
Lower Wardown GU31 .... 41 D2
Lower William St SO14 .... 103 E3
Lower Wingfield St **50** PO1 . 182 B3
Lower Woodside SO41 .... 212 C4
Lower York St SO14 .... 103 E3
Lowesmore Ct BH14 .... 203 E2
Lowestoft Rd PO6 .... 133 E1
Loweswater House **21** PO6 . 133 D1
Lowford Hill SO31 .... 104 C1
Lowland Rd PO7 .... 110 C2
Lowry Gdns SO19 .... 104 B1
Lowther Gdns **3** BH8 .... 205 E3
Lowther Rd BH8 .... 205 D3
Loxwood Rd PO8 .... 111 F3
Luard Ct PO9 .... 136 A1
Lucas Cl SO16 .... 77 F3
Lucas Rd Poole BH15 .... 202 A1
  Poole, Upper Parkstone BH12 .. 203 E3
Luccombe Pl SO15 .... 78 B1
Luccombe Rd SO15 .... 78 B1
Lucerne Ave Bournemouth BH6 206 B3
  Waterlooville PO7 .... 111 E1
Lucerne Gdns SO30 .... 105 D3
Lucerne Rd SO41 .... 211 E2
Luckham Cl BH9 .... 190 A1
Luckham Gdns BH9 .... 190 B1
Luckham Pl BH9 .... 190 A1
Luckham Rd BH9 .... 190 A1
Luckham Rd E BH9 .... 190 A1
Lucknow St PO1 .... 182 C3
Lucky La SO41 .... 174 A1
Ludcombe PO7 .... 110 C3
Ludlow Inf Sch SO19 .... 103 F2
Ludlow Jun Sch SO19 .... 103 F2
Ludlow Rd Cosham PO6 .... 133 E1
  Southampton SO19 .... 103 F2

Ludwell's La SO32 .... 83 F2
Lugano Cl PO7 .... 111 E1
Lukin Dr SO16 .... 77 E3
Lulworth Ave BH15 .... 201 F1
Lulworth Bsns Pk SO40 .... 76 C1
Lulworth Cl
  Chandler's Ford SO53 .... 55 D2
  Hamworthy BH15 .... 201 F1
  South Hayling PO11 .... 185 D3
  Southampton SO16 .... 77 F1
Lulworth Cres BH15 .... 201 F1
Lulworth Gn SO16 .... 77 F1
Lulworth Rd PO13 .... 179 F1
Lumby Dr SO24 .... 14 D4
Lumby Drive Cvn Pk **3** BH24 141 D4
Lumley Gdns PO10 .... 161 D4
Lumley Rd PO10 .... 137 D1
Lumley Terr PO10 .... 137 D1
Lumsden Ave SO15 .... 102 B4
Lumsden Mans **3** SO15 .... 102 B4
Lumsden Rd PO4 .... 183 E2
Lundy Cl SO16 .... 77 F3
Lundy Wlk PO14 .... 154 A2
Lunedale Rd SO45 .... 149 F4
Lupin Rd SO16 .... 79 E3
Luscombe Rd BH14 .... 203 E1
Luther Rd BH9 .... 204 C4
Lutman St PO10 .... 136 C2
Luton Rd SO19 .... 104 A2
Luxton Cl SO30 .... 105 F4
Luzborough La SO51 .... 53 E3
Lyburn Cl SO16 .... 78 B2
Lyburn Ct SO16 .... 78 B2
Lyburn House SP5 .... 73 D4
Lyburn Rd SP5 .... 48 C1
Lych Gate Ct BH24 .... 141 E4
Lychgate Dr PO8 .... 112 A4
Lychgate Gn PO14 .... 154 B3
Lydden Ct PO13 .... 155 E1
Lydford Gdns BH11 .... 189 D1
Lydford Rd BH11 .... 189 D1
Lydgate SO40 .... 100 B4
Lydgate Cl SO19 .... 104 B2
Lydgate Gn SO19 .... 104 B2
Lydgate Rd SO19 .... 104 B2
Lydgate The SO41 .... 211 D3
Lydiard Cl SO50 .... 56 A3
Lydlinch Cl BH22 .... 165 E1
Lydlynch Inf Sch SO40 .... 100 C4
Lydlynch Rd SO40 .... 100 C4
Lydney Cl PO6 .... 157 E4
Lydney Rd SO31 .... 128 C2
Lydwell Cl BH11 .... 188 C3
Lyell Rd PO12 .... 203 E3
Lymbourn Rd PO9 .... 136 A1
Lyme Cl SO50 .... 55 F3
Lyme Cres BH23 .... 208 C4
Lymefields SO41 .... 211 F3
Lymer La SO16 .... 77 E3
Lymer Villas SO16 .... 77 E3
Lymington Cath Sch SO41 ...... 197 F2
Lymington CE Inf Sch SO41 .... 197 E2
Lymington Hospl SO41 .... 197 F2
Lymington Infmy &
  Day Hospl SO41 .... 197 F2
Lymington Jun Sch SO41 .... 197 E2
Lymington Pier Sta SO41 .... 198 A2
Lymington Rd
  Barton on Sea BH25 .... 195 E1
  Brockenhurst SO42 .... 146 A1
  Christchurch BH23 .... 208 C4
  Milford on Sea SO41 .... 211 F3
Lymington Town Sta SO41 ...... 197 F2
Lymore La SO41 .... 211 F3
Lymore Valley SO41 .... 211 F3
Lynch SO22 .... 1 C1
Lynch La GU32 .... 37 E2
Lyndale Cl SO41 .... 211 F3
Lyndale Rd SO31 .... 129 E2
Lynden PO14 .... 154 A4
Lynden Gate SO19 .... 104 A2
Lynden CE Inf Sch SO43 .... 121 F3
Lyndhurst Cl
  South Hayling PO11 .... 185 D2
  Winchester SO22 .... 1 B2
Lyndhurst Hill SO40 .... 98 C4
Lyndhurst House PO9 .... 135 F3
Lyndhurst Jun Sch PO2 .... 157 F1
Lyndhurst Rd Ashurst SO40 .... 100 A1
  Bransgore BH23 .... 193 E3
  Brockenhurst SO42 .... 146 A1
  Burley BH24 .... 143 E3
  Burton BH23 .... 193 E3
  Cadnam SO40 .... 98 C4
  Christchurch BH23 .... 193 E1
  Gosport PO12 .... 181 D2
  Landford SP5 .... 49 E2
  Portsmouth PO2 .... 157 F1
Lyndock Cl SO19 .... 103 F1
Lyndock Pl SO19 .... 103 F1
Lyndon Ct BH23 .... 191 F1
Lyndum Cl GU32 .... 40 C2
Lyne Pl PO8 .... 112 A3
Lyne's La BH24 .... 140 C4
Lynford Ave SO22 .... 1 C1
Lynford Way SO22 .... 1 C1
Lynn Cl SO18 .... 80 A2
Lynn Rd Poole BH17 .... 187 F1
  Portsmouth PO2 .... 182 C4
Lynric Cl BH25 .... 210 A4
Lynton Cres BH23 .... 191 E2
Lynton Ct SO40 .... 100 C3
Lynton Gdns PO16 .... 130 C2
Lynton Gr PO3 .... 183 D4
Lynton Rd Hedge End SO30 .... 105 E4
  Petersfield GU32 .... 40 C2
Lynwood Ave PO8 .... 111 E2
Lynwood Cl BH22 .... 165 E4

Lynwood Ct
  Lymington SO41 .... 197 E2
  Winchester SO22 .... 1 C1
Lynwood Dr BH21 .... 187 F4
Lynx Cl SO50 .... 56 C1
Lyon Ave BH25 .... 195 D2
Lyon Rd BH12 .... 188 C1
Lyon St SO14 .... 103 D3
Lysander Cl BH23 .... 208 B4
Lysander Way PO7 .... 135 D4
Lyse Cl GU33 .... 20 C2
Lysses Ct PO16 .... 131 E1
Lyster Rd SP6 .... 70 A1
Lystra Rd BH9 .... 190 A2
Lytchett Dr BH18 .... 187 D2
Lytchett Way BH16 .... 201 D3
Lyteltane Rd SO41 .... 197 E1
Lytham Rd
  Broadstone BH18 .... 187 D2
  Southampton SO18 .... 80 A1
Lythe La GU32 .... 40 A3
Lytton Rd
  Bournemouth BH1 .... 205 E3
  Hythe SO45 .... 126 A1

Mabey Ave BH10 .... 189 E1
Mabey Cl PO12 .... 181 E1
Mablethorpe Rd PO6 .... 133 F1
Macandrew Rd BH13 .... 214 C4
Macarthur Cres SO18 .... 104 A4
Macaulay Ave PO6 .... 132 C1
Macaulay Rd BH18 .... 187 D2
Macklin House **16** SO22 .... 10 C4
Maclaren Rd SO40 .... 189 F2
Maclean Rd BH11 .... 188 C2
Macnaghten Rd SO18 .... 103 E4
Madden Cl PO12 .... 180 C2
Maddison St **5** SO14 .... 102 C2
Maddoxford La SO32 .... 82 A1
Maddoxford Way SO32 .... 81 F1
Madeira Rd
  Bournemouth BH1 .... 205 D2
  Poole BH14 .... 203 E3
  Portsmouth PO2 .... 157 F2
Madeline Cl PO12 .... 203 D4
Madeline Cres BH12 .... 203 D4
Madeline Rd GU31 .... 40 C2
Madison Ave BH1 .... 205 E3
Madison Cl PO13 .... 180 C4
Madison Ct **10** PO16 .... 131 E1
Madrisa Ct SO41 .... 197 E2
Mafeking Rd PO4 .... 182 C2
Maffey Ct SO30 .... 106 A4
Mag's Barrow BH22 .... 165 F1
Magazine La SO40 .... 102 A2
Magdala Rd Cosham PO6 .... 157 F4
  South Hayling PO11 .... 184 C2
Magdalen Ct **19** PO2 .... 157 F2
Magdalen Hill SO23 .... 11 D4
Magdalen La BH23 .... 207 D3
Magdalen Mews **41** SO23 .... 11 D4
Magdalen Rd PO2 .... 157 F2
Magdalene Way PO14 .... 129 E1
Magennis Cl PO13 .... 180 B4
Magna Cl BH11 .... 188 C3
Magna Gdns BH11 .... 188 C3
Magna Rd
  Bournemouth BH11 .... 188 B4
  Oakley BH11 .... 188 B4
Magnolia Cl
  Bournemouth BH6 .... 207 D3
  Fareham PO14 .... 154 C4
  Hythe SO45 .... 125 E2
  Verwood BH31 .... 115 E2
Magnolia Gr SO50 .... 57 F1
Magnolia House BH10 .... 189 F2
Magnolia Rd SO19 .... 103 F3
Magnolia Terr PO7 .... 134 C3
Magnolia Way PO8 .... 112 B2
Magpie Cl BH8 .... 190 B2
Magpie Dr SO40 .... 100 B4
Magpie Gdns SO19 .... 104 B2
Magpie Gr BH25 .... 194 C1
Magpie La
  Eastleigh SO50 .... 55 F1
  Lee-on-the-Solent PO13 .... 179 F2
Magpie Rd PO8 .... 113 E4
Magpie Wlk PO8 .... 111 E2
Maiden La SO41 .... 197 F1
Maidford Gr PO3 .... 158 B2
Maidment Cl BH11 .... 188 C2
Maidstone Cres PO6 .... 133 F1
Main Rd
  Colden Common SO21 .... 32 A1
  Compton(Hants) SO21 .... 31 D2
  Compton(Hants) SO21 .... 31 E3
  Fawley SO45 .... 150 B3
  Gosport PO13 .... 155 E3
  Hermitage PO10 .... 161 E4
  Hythe SO45 .... 125 E3
  Littleton SO22 .... 1 A3
  Marchwood SO40 .... 101 F1
  Otterbourne SO21 .... 31 D2
  Owslebury SO21 .... 33 D2
  Portsmouth PO1 .... 181 F3
  Portsmouth PO1 .... 182 A2
  Southbourne PO18 .... 161 E4
  Totton SO40 .... 100 C2
Mainstone SO51 .... 52 B3
Mainstream Ct SO50 .... 56 B2
Maisemore Gdns PO10 .... 160 B4
Maitland Cres PO1 .... 182 B4
Maitland St **14** PO1 .... 182 B4
Maitlands The BH2 .... 204 B1
Maizemore Wlk **21** PO13 .... 179 F1
Majestic Rd SO16 .... 77 D2
Majorca Mansions **11** BH2 . 204 C2
Malan Cl BH17 .... 202 C4

Malcolm Cl
  Chandler's Ford SO53 .... 30 C1
  Locks Heath SO31 .... 129 D2
Malcolm Rd SO53 .... 30 C1
Malcomb Cl BH6 .... 207 D2
Malcroft Mews SO40 .... 102 A1
Maldon Cl SO50 .... 56 B2
Maldon Rd **5** Cosham PO6 . 157 E4
  Southampton SO19 .... 103 F2
Malibres Rd SO53 .... 55 F4
Malin Cl Southampton SO16 ..... 77 F2
  Stubbington PO14 .... 154 A2
Malins Rd PO2 .... 182 B4
Mall The Burley BH24 .... 143 D2
  Chandler's Ford SO53 .... 55 F4
  Portsmouth PO2 .... 157 E1
Mallard Bldgs **6** BH25 .... 195 D2
Mallard Cl
  Bishop's Waltham SO32 .... 83 D4
  Bournemouth BH8 .... 190 B1
  Christchurch BH23 .... 208 A3
  Hordle SO41 .... 196 A2
  Romsey SO51 .... 52 C4
Mallard Gdns Gosport PO13 ... 155 D1
  Hedge End SO30 .... 81 E1
Mallard Rd
  Bournemouth BH8 .... 190 B1
  Portsmouth PO4 .... 183 D3
  Rowland's Castle PO9 .... 113 D1
  Wimborne Minster BH21 ...... 164 B3
Mallards Rd SO31 .... 127 F4
Mallards The Fareham PO16 ... 131 D2
  Havant PO9 .... 159 F4
Mallory Cl BH23 .... 207 F4
Mallory Cres PO16 .... 131 D2
Mallow Cl Broadstone BH18 ... 186 C2
  5 Cosham PO6 .... 157 F4
  Waterlooville PO7 .... 134 C3
Mallow Rd SO30 .... 105 D3
Mallows The BH25 .... 195 E2
Malmesbury Cl SO50 .... 57 E1
Malmesbury Gdns SO22 .... 1 B1
Malmesbury Park Pl **7** BH8 . 205 E3
Malmesbury Park Rd BH8 ...... 205 D3
Malmesbury Pk Prim Sch
  BH8 .... 205 D3
Malmesbury Pl SO15 .... 102 B4
Malmesbury Rd Romsey SO51 .. 52 C4
  Southampton SO15 .... 102 B4
  St Leonards BH24 .... 139 F2
Maloney Mews PO11 .... 185 F1
Maloren Way BH22 .... 139 D1
Malory Cl SO19 .... 104 B3
Malt House **22** SO22 .... 10 C4
Malt La SO32 .... 83 E4
Malta Rd PO2 .... 182 C4
Malthouse PO15 .... 202 B1
Malthouse Cl
  Itchen Abbas SO21 .... 2 C2
  Romsey SO51 .... 52 C4
Malthouse Cotts SO16 .... 77 D4
Malthouse Gdns SO40 .... 101 F1
Malthouse La PO16 .... 131 D1
Malthouse Rd PO2 .... 182 B4
Maltings The
  Bournemouth BH11 .... 188 C3
  Fareham PO16 .... 131 E1
  Petersfield GU31 .... 40 C2
  Poole BH15 .... 202 C2
Malus Cl PO14 .... 154 C4
Malvern Bsns Ctr SO16 .... 78 B1
Malvern Cl
  Bishop's Waltham SO32 .... 83 E4
  Bournemouth BH9 .... 190 A2
Malvern Ct Bournemouth BH9 . 190 A1
  2 Christchurch BH23 .... 207 F4
Malvern Dr SO45 .... 125 E2
Malvern Gdns SO30 .... 81 E1
Malvern Mews PO13 .... 136 C1
Malvern Rd Bournemouth BH9 . 190 A1
  Gosport PO12 .... 180 C3
  Hill Brow GU33 .... 21 D1
  Portsmouth PO5 .... 182 B1
  Southampton SO16 .... 78 B1
Malvern Terr SO16 .... 78 B1
Malwood Ave SO16 .... 78 B2
Malwood Cl PO9 .... 136 A3
Malwood Gdns SO40 .... 100 B4
Malwood Rd SO45 .... 126 A2
Malwood Rd W SO45 .... 125 F2
Manaton Way SO30 .... 81 D1
Manchester Ct PO13 .... 180 B3
Manchester Rd
  6 Netley SO31 .... 127 D3
  Portsmouth PO1 .... 182 C3
  Sway SO41 .... 172 A2
Manchester Terr PO10 .... 137 D2
Mancroft Ave PO14 .... 179 E3
Mandale Cl BH11 .... 189 D3
Mandale Rd BH11 .... 188 C2
Mandela Way SO15 .... 102 C3
Manderley SO41 .... 211 F2
Manley Rd SO31 .... 104 C1
Manners La PO4 .... 182 C2
Manners Rd PO4 .... 182 C2
Manning Ave BH23 .... 193 E1
Manning's Heath Rd BH12 ..... 188 A1
Manningford Ct SO23 .... 2 A2
Mannings Heath
  Works BH12 .... 188 A1
Mannington Pl **19** BH2 ...... 204 C2
Mannington Way BH22 .... 138 B1
Manns Cl SO18 .... 80 B1
Mannyngham Way SO51 .... 27 C4
Manor Ave BH12 .... 188 B1

Manor Cl Bursledon SO31 .... 104 C1
  Ferndown BH22 .... 165 F3
  Fordingbridge SP6 .... 69 F1
  9 Havant PO9 .... 135 F1
  Milford on Sea SO41 .... 211 E3
  Totton SO40 .... 100 C3
  Wickham PO17 .... 108 A2
  Winchester SO23 .... 11 D4
Manor Cres Bursledon SO31 ... 104 C1
  Cosham PO6 .... 158 A4
Manor Ct Havant PO9 .... 135 F1
  Locks Heath PO14 .... 129 E2
  Ringwood BH24 .... 140 C4
  Verwood BH31 .... 114 C3
Manor Farm Cl
  4 Bishopstoke SO50 .... 56 C1
  New Milton BH25 .... 194 C1
Manor Farm Ctry Pk SO30 ..... 105 E2
Manor Farm Gr **3** SO50 ...... 56 C1
Manor Farm La SO51 .... 6 C1
Manor Farm Rd
  Bournemouth BH10 .... 189 E4
  Fordingbridge SP6 .... 69 E1
  Southampton SO18 .... 79 E1
Manor Flats SO21 .... 31 F3
Manor Gdns Ringwood BH24 ... 140 C4
  Southbourne PO10 .... 137 E1
  1 Verwood BH31 .... 114 C3
Manor House Ave SO15 .... 101 F3
Manor Inf Sch Holbury SO45 .. 150 A2
  Portsmouth PO3 .... 182 C4
Manor La BH31 .... 114 C3
Manor Lodge Rd PO9 .... 113 D1
Manor Mews PO6 .... 158 B4
Manor Park Ave PO3 .... 183 D4
Manor Park House **14** SO14 103 F4
Manor Pk BH15 .... 202 A3
Manor Rd Bishopstoke SO50 .... 56 C1
  Bournemouth BH1 .... 205 E2
  Chilworth SO16 .... 54 B1
  Christchurch BH23 .... 207 D3
  Durley SO32 .... 82 B4
  East Tytherley SP5 .... 4 C4
  Holbury SO45 .... 150 B2
  Hythe SO45 .... 125 D2
  Milford on Sea SO41 .... 211 E3
  New Milton BH25 .... 195 D2
  North Hayling PO11 .... 184 C3
  Portsmouth PO3 .... 182 C4
  Ringwood BH24 .... 141 D4
  South Hayling PO11 .... 184 C3
  Southbourne PO10 .... 137 E1
  Twyford SO21 .... 31 F3
  Verwood BH31 .... 114 C3
Manor Rd N SO19 .... 103 F2
Manor Rd S SO19 .... 103 F2
Manor Terr Bursledon SO31 .... 104 C1
  Durley SO32 .... 82 C4
Manor Villas PO17 .... 108 A2
Manor Way
  Lee-on-the-Solent PO13 .... 179 F1
  Lee-on-the-Solent PO13 .... 179 F1
  South Hayling PO11 .... 185 D1
  Southbourne PO10 .... 137 E1
  Verwood BH31 .... 114 C4
Manor Wks SO40 .... 101 D4
Mansard Ct BH13 .... 214 A2
Mansbridge Prim Sch SO18 ... 79 F2
Mansbridge Rd
  Eastleigh SO50 .... 56 A1
  Southampton SO18 .... 79 F2
Mansel Cl BH12 .... 204 B4
Mansel Ct SO16 .... 77 E1
Mansel Inf Sch SO16 .... 77 E1
Mansel Jun Sch SO16 .... 77 E1
Mansel Rd E SO16 .... 77 F1
Mansel Rd W SO16 .... 77 E1
Mansell Cl SO45 .... 125 F1
Mansfield Ave BH14 .... 203 E2
Mansfield Cl Ferndown BH22 .. 165 E1
  Poole BH14 .... 203 E2
Mansfield Rd
  Bournemouth BH9 .... 189 F1
  Gosport PO13 .... 180 B4
  Poole BH14 .... 203 E2
  Ringwood BH24 .... 140 C4
Mansion Ct **2** PO4 .... 182 C1
Mansion Rd
  1 Portsmouth PO4 .... 182 C1
  Southampton SO15 .... 102 B3
Manston Ct SO16 .... 77 F2
Mansvid Ave PO6 .... 158 A4
Mantle Cl PO13 .... 180 B4
Mantle Sq PO2 .... 157 D1
Manton Cl BH15 .... 201 F2
Manton Rd BH15 .... 201 F2
Maple Cl Barton on Sea BH25 . 210 A4
  Bursledon SO31 .... 127 F4
  Christchurch BH23 .... 208 C4
  Emsworth PO10 .... 136 C1
  Fareham PO15 .... 130 B1
  Lee-on-the-Solent PO13 .... 179 F1
  Romsey SO51 .... 53 E3
Maple Cres PO8 .... 88 B3
Maple Ct SO19 .... 103 F1
Maple Dr Denmead PO7 .... 111 D2
  Ferndown BH22 .... 165 E4
  Kings Worthy SO23 .... 2 A4
Maple Gdns SO40 .... 100 B3
Maple House SO16 .... 78 C4
Maple Lodge BH16 .... 201 E4
Maple Rd Bournemouth BH9 ... 204 C4
  Hythe SO45 .... 150 A4
  Poole BH15 .... 202 B2
  Portsmouth PO5 .... 182 B1
  Southampton SO18 .... 103 F4
Maple Sq SO50 .... 55 F1
Mapleleaf Gdns **1** SO50 .... 56 A1

Maples The SO53 .... **55** E4
Mapleton Rd SO30 .... **105** E3
Mapletree Ave PO8 .... **112** B2
Maplewood Cl SO40 .... **100** B3
Maplin Rd SO16 .... **77** E1
Mapperton BH17 .... **188** A1
Marabout Cl BH23 .... **207** E4
Maralyn Ave PO7 .... **134** C3
Marathon Pl SO50 .... **57** D1
Marbream Cl SP6 .... **69** E1
Marchesi Ct PO14 .... **154** B2

Marchwood-By-Pass
  Hythe SO40 .... **124** C4
  Marchwood SO40 .... **124** C4
  Totton SO40 .... **101** D2
Marchwood CE Inf Sch SO40 . **124** C4
Marchwood Ct PO12 .... **180** B2
Marchwood Ind Pk SO40 ...... **102** A2
Marchwood Jun Sch SO40 ..... **101** F1

Marchwood Rd
  Bournemouth BH10 .... **189** E2
  Havant PO9 .... **135** F3
  Southampton SO15 .... **102** A3
  Totton SO40 .... **101** E2
Marchwood Terr SO40 .... **101** F1
Marcus Cl SO50 .... **57** D1
Mardale Rd SO16 .... **101** E4
Mardale Wlk SO16 .... **101** E4
Marden Paddock SO42 .... **145** F1
Marden Way GU31 .... **41** D2
Mardon Cl SO18 .... **79** F3
Mare La SO21 .... **32** C3
Margam Ave SO19 .... **103** F3
Margards La BH31 .... **114** C3
Margaret Cl PO7 .... **111** E1
Margarita Rd PO15 .... **130** C1
Margate Rd PO5 .... **182** B2
Margery's Ct *20* PO1 .... **182** A3
Marian Cl BH21 .... **186** B2
Marian Rd BH21 .... **186** B2
Marianne Cl SO15 .... **101** F3

Marianne Rd
  Poole BH12 .... **204** B4
  Wimborne Minster BH21 ... **164** A4
Marie Ave SP5 .... **46** B4
Marie Ct *5* PO7 .... **134** C4
Marie Rd SO19 .... **104** B2
Marigold Cl PO15 .... **130** C1

Marina Bldgs *3* PO12 ... **181** D2
Marina Cl PO10 .... **161** D4

Marina Ct
  21 Bournemouth BH5 ..... **205** E2
  Christchurch BH23 .... **209** D4
Marina Dr BH14 .... **203** D1
Marina Gr Portchester PO16 .. **156** B3
  Portsmouth PO3 .... **183** D4
Marina Keep PO6 .... **157** D3
Marina The BH5 .... **205** F2
Marina Towers *24* BH5 .. **205** F2

Marina View
  6 Christchurch BH23 ...... **207** E3
  Netley SO31 .... **126** C4
Marine Cotts *20* PO12 ..... **181** D3
Marine Ct Barton on Sea BH25 . **209** E4
  Portsmouth PO4 .... **183** D1
Marine Dr BH25 .... **209** F4
Marine Dr E BH25 .... **210** A3
Marine Par SO14 .... **103** D2
Marine Parade E PO13 .... **179** F1
Marine Parade W PO13 .... **179** E1
Marine Rd BH6 .... **206** B2
Marine Wlk PO11 .... **185** E2
Mariner's Cl SO31 .... **128** A2

Mariners Ct
  Christchurch BH23 .... **208** A3
  Lymington SO41 .... **197** F1
Mariners Mews *1* SO45 .... **126** A2
Mariners Way Gosport PO12 . **181** E2
  Locks Heath SO31 .... **128** B1
Mariners Wlk PO4 .... **183** D3
Marion BH23 .... **207** D4
Marion Rd PO4 .... **182** C1
Maritime Ave SO40 .... **102** A2
Maritime Mus SO14 .... **102** C2
Maritime Way SO14 .... **103** D1
Maritime Wlk SO14 .... **103** D1
Marjoram Cres PO8 .... **112** A2
Mark Anthony Ct PO11 .... **184** C2
Mark Cl Portsmouth PO3 ..... **157** F2
  Southampton SO15 .... **102** A4
Mark Ct PO7 .... **134** C4
Mark Way SO51 .... **4** B2
Mark's La BH25 .... **195** D3
Mark's Rd PO14 .... **179** F3
Markall Cl SO24 .... **14** B3
Marken Cl SO31 .... **128** C2
Market Bldgs SO16 .... **79** E2
Market Cl BH15 .... **202** B1
Market La SO23 .... **11** D4
Market Par PO9 .... **135** F1
Market Pl Fordingbridge SP6 ... **69** E1
  Ringwood BH24 .... **140** C4
  Romsey SO51 .... **52** C4
  10 Southampton SO14 ... **103** D2
Market St Eastleigh SO50 ..... **56** A1
  Poole BH15 .... **202** A1
  Winchester SO23 .... **11** D4
Market Way BH21 .... **163** E2
Marketway PO1 .... **182** B3
Markham Ave BH10 .... **189** E4
Markham Cl BH10 .... **189** E3
Markham Rd BH9 .... **205** D4
Marks Rd BH9 .... **189** F2
Marks Terr SO32 .... **83** D4
Marks Tey Rd PO14 .... **154** B3
Markway Cl PO10 .... **136** B1
Marlands Lawn *13* PO9 .. **135** E3
Marlands Sh Ctr SO14 .... **102** C2

Marlands Sq *12* SO15 ... **102** C3
Marlborough Cl PO7 .... **134** B3

Marlborough Ct
  21 Bournemouth BH4 ..... **204** B2
  Chandler's Ford SO53 .... **55** D2
  Hythe SO45 .... **125** F1
  7 Poole BH12 .... **204** A2
  1 Waterlooville PO7 ...... **134** C3
  3 Wimborne Minster BH21 . **163** E3
Marlborough Gdns SO30 .... **81** E2
Marlborough Gr PO16 .... **156** B4
Marlborough Mans *2* BH7 . **206** A3
Marlborough Pk PO9 .... **136** B2

Marlborough Pl
  Lymington SO41 .... **197** E3
  Wimborne Minster BH21 ... **163** E3

Marlborough Rd
  Bournemouth BH4 .... **204** B2
  Chandler's Ford SO53 .... **30** C1
  Gosport PO12 .... **180** C3
  Poole BH14 .... **203** E2
  Southampton SO15 .... **102** A4
Marlborough Row PO1 .... **182** A3
Marldell Cl PO9 .... **136** A3
Marles Cl PO13 .... **180** B4
Marley Ave BH25 .... **194** C2
Marley Cl BH25 .... **194** C2
Marley Mount SO41 .... **171** F1
Marlhill Cl SO18 .... **79** F1
Marlin Cl PO13 .... **180** B3
Marline Rd BH12 .... **203** E3
Marlott Rd BH15 .... **202** B3
Marlow Cl PO15 .... **130** C2
Marlow Dr BH23 .... **191** F2
Marlow Rd SO32 .... **83** D4

Marlowe Ct
  Southampton SO19 .... **103** F1
  Waterlooville PO8 .... **111** E1
Marlpit Dr PO14 .... **194** A1
Marlpit La PO15 .... **195** D4
Marls Rd SO30 .... **105** F3
Marlys Rd SO30 .... **81** E1
Marmion Ave PO5 .... **182** B1
Marmion Gn BH23 .... **207** F4
Marmion Rd PO5 .... **182** B1
Marne House *9* PO14 ..... **154** C4
Marne Rd SO18 .... **104** A4
Marnhull Rd BH15 .... **202** B2
Marpet Cl BH11 .... **188** C3
Marples Way PO9 .... **135** E1
Marquis Way BH11 .... **188** B3
Marram Cl SO41 .... **197** F3
Marryat Ct Christchurch BH23 . **209** D4
  7 New Milton BH25 ...... **194** C2
Marryat Rd BH25 .... **194** C2
Marsden Rd PO6 .... **157** D4
Marsh Cl PO6 .... **158** B3
Marsh Gdns SO30 .... **81** E1
Marsh House *20* SO14 .... **103** D2
Marsh La Breamore SP6 ..... **70** A4
  Christchurch BH23 .... **191** F1
  Fawley SO45 .... **151** D2
  Lymington SO41 .... **197** F3
  Southampton SO14 .... **103** D2
  Upton BH16 .... **201** D4
Marsh Par SO45 .... **126** A2
Marsh The SO45 .... **126** A2
Marshal Rd BH17 .... **187** D1
Marshall Rd PO11 .... **185** E1
Marshfield BH21 .... **163** F4
Marshfield Cl SO40 .... **101** E1
Marshfield House PO6 ..... **158** B4
Marshlands Rd PO6 .... **158** B4

Marshwood Ave
  Broadstone BH17 .... **187** F1
  Waterlooville PO7 .... **135** D4
Marston Cl BH25 .... **195** D3
Marston Gr BH23 .... **193** F1
Marston La PO3 .... **158** A2
Marston Rd New Milton BH25 . **195** D3
  2 Poole BH15 .... **202** A1
  Southampton SO19 .... **104** C3
Martello Cl PO12 .... **180** B2
Martello House *10* BH13 . **214** C4
Martello Pk BH13 .... **214** C4
Martello Rd BH13 .... **203** F1
Martello Rd S BH13 .... **214** C4
Martello Towers BH13 ...... **214** C4
Martells Ct PO1 .... **182** A2
Martells The BH25 .... **210** A4
Martha St PO1 .... **182** B3
Martin Ave Denmead PO7 .. **111** D2
  Stubbington PO14 .... **179** E3
Martin Cl Broadstone BH17 .. **201** F4
  Lee-on-the-Solent PO13 ... **179** F2
  Swanmore SO32 .... **84** A2

Martin Kemp-Welch
  Sch The BH12 .... **203** E4
Martin Rd Havant PO9 .... **136** A2
  Portsmouth PO3 .... **183** D4
  Stubbington PO14 .... **179** E3
Martin St SO32 .... **83** D4
Martin's Rd SO42 .... **146** A1
Martindale Ave BH21 .... **164** A3
Martindale Terr SO16 .... **101** F4
Martingale Cl BH16 .... **201** E4
Martins Cl BH22 .... **165** F4
Martins Dr BH22 .... **165** F4
Martins Fields SO21 .... **10** B1
Martins Hill Cl BH23 .... **192** B1
Martins Hill La BH23 .... **192** B1
Martins The SO50 .... **57** E1
Martins Way BH22 .... **165** F4
Martley Gdns SO30 .... **81** E1
Marvic Ct PO9 .... **135** F3
Marvin Cl SO30 .... **105** F4
Marvin Way Hedge End SO30 . **105** E4
  Southampton SO19 .... **104** B3
Marwell Cl BH7 .... **206** A4

Marwell Zoo SO21 .... **57** F4
Mary La BH22 .... **138** B1
Mary Mitchell Cl BH24 .... **140** C4

Mary Rose PO1 .... **181** F3
Mary Rose Cl PO15 .... **130** C2
Mary Rose St The PO1 .... **182** B3
Marybridge Cl SO40 .... **100** C3
Marycourt Co-ed Sch PO12 . **181** D1
Maryfield SO14 .... **103** D2
Maryland Cl SO18 .... **79** F2
Maryland Ct *3* SO41 .... **211** D2
Maryland Gdns SO41 .... **211** D2
Maryland Rd BH16 .... **201** E2
Masefield Ave PO6 .... **132** C1
Masefield Cl SO50 .... **55** F2
Masefield Cres PO8 .... **111** F2
Masefield Gr SO19 .... **104** B3
Mason Moor Prim Sch SO16 . **101** F4
Masseys La SO42 .... **175** E4
Masten Cres PO13 .... **180** B4
Masters Ct BH4 .... **204** B2
Masterson Ct PO14 .... **207** E4
Matapan Rd PO2 .... **157** F2
Matchams La Hurn BH23 ...... **167** D2
  St Leonards BH24 .... **167** D2
Matheson Rd SO16 .... **78** A3
Matilda Pl *5* SO23 .... **11** D4
Matley Gdns SO40 .... **100** A4
Matlock Rd BH12 .... **205** D4
Matthews Cl PO9 .... **135** E2
Matthews La SO42 .... **175** E3
Maturin Cl SO41 .... **197** E2
Maundeville Cres BH23 .... **206** B4
Maundeville Rd BH23 .... **206** C4
Maunsell Way SO30 .... **81** E1
Maureen Cl BH12 .... **203** D4
Mauretania House *15* SO14 . **103** E3
Mauretania Rd SO16 .... **77** D2
Maurice Rd Bournemouth BH8 . **205** E4
  Portsmouth PO4 .... **183** E2
Maury's La SO51 .... **50** B2
Mavis Cres PO9 .... **135** F1
Mavis Rd BH9 .... **190** A1
Maxstoke Cl *22* PO1 .... **182** B3
Maxwell Rd Bournemouth BH9 . **205** D4
  Broadstone BH18 .... **186** C2
  Poole BH13 .... **214** C4
  Portsmouth PO4 .... **183** D2
  Southampton SO19 .... **104** A2
May Ave SO41 .... **197** E3
May Bush La SO32 .... **85** D1
May Cl SO45 .... **150** B2
May Copse SO45 .... **150** B2
May Cres SO45 .... **150** B2

May Gdns
  Bournemouth BH11 .... **188** C2
  Christchurch BH23 .... **194** A1
May La SO41 .... **174** A1
May Rd SO15 .... **102** B4
May Tree Cl SO22 .... **10** B2
May's La PO14 .... **154** B2
Maybray King Way SO18 ..... **104** A4
Maybush Ct *3* SO16 .... **78** A1
Maybush Rd SO16 .... **77** F1
Maycroft Cl *3* SO15 .... **102** C4
Maydman Sq PO3 .... **183** D3
Mayfair BH4 .... **204** B1
Mayfair Ct SO30 .... **106** A3

Mayfair Gdns
  Bournemouth BH11 .... **189** D2
  Southampton SO15 .... **102** C4
Mayfield PO13 .... **179** F1
Mayfield Ave Poole BH14 ..... **203** F2
  Totton SO40 .... **100** C4

Mayfield Cl
  Ferndown BH22 .... **165** E3
  Stubbington PO14 .... **154** B2
Mayfield Dr PO14 .... **165** E3

Mayfield Rd
  Bournemouth BH9 .... **190** A1
  Fordingbridge SP6 .... **69** D1
  Gosport PO12 .... **181** E2
  Portsmouth PO2 .... **157** F1
  Southampton SO17 .... **79** E2
Mayfield Sch PO2 .... **157** F1
Mayfield Sec Sch PO2 ...... **157** F1
Mayfield Way BH22 .... **165** E3
Mayflower Cl
  Chandler's Ford SO53 .... **55** D3
  Lymington SO41 .... **198** A1
  Stubbington PO14 .... **179** E3
Mayflower Ct *14* SO15 ..... **102** C4
Mayflower Dr PO4 .... **183** E3
Mayflower Rd SO15 .... **102** A4
Mayflowers The SO17 .... **79** D2
Mayfly Cl SP6 .... **69** F1
Mayford Rd BH12 .... **204** A3
Mayhall Rd PO3 .... **158** A1
Mayhill La Droxford SO32 ...... **84** C4
  Swanmore SO32 .... **84** C4
Maylands Ave PO4 .... **183** D3
Maylands Rd PO9 .... **135** D1
Mayles Cl PO17 .... **108** A2
Mayles La PO17 .... **107** F1
Mayles Rd PO4 .... **183** D3
Maylings Farm Rd PO16 ...... **130** C2
Maylyn Rd BH16 .... **186** A1
Maynard Cl SO21 .... **155** E2
Maynard Pl PO8 .... **112** A4
Maynard Rd SO40 .... **100** C4
Mayo Cl PO1 .... **182** B4
Maypole Villas SO50 .... **56** A4
Mayridge PO14 .... **129** E2
Mays Firs SP6 .... **47** F1
Maytree Cl Fair Oak SO50 ...... **57** F4
  Locks Heath SO31 .... **129** D2
Maytree Gdns PO8 .... **111** F2
Maytree Inf Sch SO14 ...... **103** D3

Maytree Rd
  Chandler's Ford SO53 .... **30** B1
  16 Fareham PO16 .... **131** D1
  Southampton PO16 .... **104** A3
  Waterlooville PO8 .... **111** F2
Mayvale Cl SO40 .... **101** F1
Mayville High Sch PO5 ..... **182** B1
Mayville Rd BH23 .... **191** D4
McIntyre Rd PO4 .... **204** B4
McWilliam Cl BH23 .... **204** B4
McWilliam Ct SO41 .... **211** D2
McWilliam Rd BH9 .... **190** A1
Meacher Cl SO40 .... **100** C4
Mead Cl Broadstone BH18 .. **187** D1
  Romsey SO51 .... **53** D4
Mead Cres SO18 .... **79** E2

Mead Ct
  Chandler's Ford SO53 .... **55** E3
  Southampton SO16 .... **78** A2
Mead End Rd Denmead PO7 .. **111** D2
  Sway SO41 .... **171** F1

Mead Rd
  Chandler's Ford SO53 .... **55** E3
  Lymington SO41 .... **197** D1
  Winchester SO23 .... **10** C2
Mead The Gosport PO13 .... **155** D2
  Hythe SO45 .... **125** F2
  Liss GU33 .... **20** C2
  Petersfield GU32 .... **40** B1
Mead Way PO14 .... **131** D2
Meadbrook Gdns SO53 .... **55** E3
Meadcroft Cl SO31 .... **152** B4
Meadend Cl PO9 .... **136** A3

Meadow Ave
  Fordingbridge SP6 .... **69** F1
  Locks Heath SO31 .... **129** D2
Meadow Cl Bransgore BH23 . **193** D4
  Burley BH24 .... **142** C1
  Ferndown BH22 .... **165** E1
  Fordingbridge SP6 .... **69** F1
  North Baddesley SO52 .... **54** A2
  Ringwood BH24 .... **141** D4
  Shedfield SO32 .... **83** F2
  Sopley BH23 .... **192** A4
  Totton SO40 .... **100** C3
  West End SO30 .... **80** C1
Meadow Court Cl BH9 ...... **190** A2
Meadow Croft Cl SO21 ...... **31** E2

Meadow Ct
  Bournemouth BH9 .... **190** A2
  2 Emsworth PO10 .... **160** C4
  Fordingbridge SP6 .... **69** F1
  Whiteparish SP5 .... **24** B2
  12 Wimborne Minster BH21 . **163** E2
Meadow Edge PO7 .... **134** A1
Meadow Farm La BH21 .... **186** B4
Meadow Gdns SO32 .... **83** F2

Meadow Gr
  Chandler's Ford SO53 .... **55** E2
  Verwood BH31 .... **115** D3
Meadow La Burton BH23 .... **192** B1
  Hamble-le-Rice SO31 .... **128** A1
Meadow Rd Lymington SO41 . **197** D1
  New Milton BH25 .... **195** D2
  Ringwood BH24 .... **141** D4

Meadow Rise
  Corfe Mullen BH18 .... **186** C3
  Waterlooville PO8 .... **112** A2
Meadow St PO5 .... **182** A2
Meadow Terr *12* PO16 .... **131** D1
Meadow The Denmead PO7 . **110** C2
  Romsey SO51 .... **28** A1
Meadow View Rd BH11 ..... **188** C2

Meadow Way
  Barton on Sea BH25 .... **210** A4
  Fawley SO45 .... **151** D2
  Ringwood BH24 .... **141** D4
  Verwood BH31 .... **115** D3
  Winchester SO22 .... **10** B2
Meadow Wlk Gosport PO13 . **155** D3
  1 Liss GU33 .... **20** C2
  11 Portsmouth PO1 .... **182** B3
Meadowbank BH16 .... **201** E4
Meadowbank Rd PO15 .... **130** B1
Meadowcrest Wood SO42 .... **145** E1
Meadowhead Rd SO16 .... **78** C2

Meadowland
  Christchurch BH23 .... **207** F3
  Kings Worthy SO23 .... **2** A4
Meadowlands Havant PO9 .. **136** A1
  Lymington SO41 .... **197** E2
  Rowland's Castle PO9 .... **113** E2

Meadowlands Jun &
  Inf Sch PO8 .... **111** F3
Meadowmead Ave SO15 ...... **102** A4
Meadows Cl BH16 .... **201** E4
Meadows Rd BH16 .... **201** E4
Meadows The Fareham PO16 . **131** D2
  Lyndhurst SO43 .... **122** A2
  Waterlooville PO7 .... **134** B4
Meadowside Cl SO18 .... **79** F2
Meadowsweet PO7 .... **112** A1
Meadowsweet Rd BH17 ..... **201** F4

Meadowsweet Way
  Cosham PO6 .... **133** E1
  Fair Oak SO50 .... **81** E3

Meads The
  North Baddesley SO53 .... **55** D3
  Romsey SO51 .... **52** B4
Meadway The BH23 .... **193** E1
Mears Rd SO51 .... **57** E1
Meath Cl PO11 .... **185** E1
Medina Cl SO53 .... **55** F3
Medina Ct PO13 .... **179** E2
Medina House PO14 .... **155** D4
Medina Rd Cosham PO6 .... **157** F4
  Southampton SO15 .... **78** A1
Medina Way BH23 .... **208** B3

Medlar Cl Burton BH23 .... **192** B1
  Hedge End SO30 .... **105** E3
Medley Pl *18* SO15 .... **102** A4
Medlicott Way SO32 .... **84** A2
Medstead Rd PO9 .... **135** F2
Medwall Gr SO19 .... **104** B3
Medway Dr SO53 .... **55** D4
Medway Rd BH22 .... **166** A3
Meerut Rd SO42 .... **145** F1
Meeting House La BH24 ...... **140** C4
Megan Ct *19* PO6 .... **157** F4
Megan Rd SO30 .... **80** B1
Megana Way SO51 .... **28** B3
Meggeson Ave SO18 .... **80** A1
Melbourne Rd BH23 .... **191** F1
Melbourne St SO30 .... **105** E3
Melbourne House *30* PO1 . **182** B3
Melbourne Pl PO5 .... **182** B2

Melbourne Rd
  Bournemouth BH8 .... **205** E3
  Christchurch BH23 .... **191** F1
  Hedge End SO30 .... **105** E3
Melbourne St SO14 .... **103** D2
Melbury Ave BH12 .... **203** F4
Melbury Cl Ferndown BH22 .. **165** E2
  Lymington SO41 .... **197** E2
Melbury Ct *19* SO17 .... **79** D1
Melchet Cl SO51 .... **25** D1

Melchet Ct (St Edward's Sch)
  SO51 .... **25** D1
Melchet Rd SO18 .... **104** B4
Melick Cl SO40 .... **101** F1
Mellor Cl *4* PO6 .... **157** E4
Mellstock Rd BH15 .... **202** B3
Melrose Cl PO4 .... **183** D2
Melrose Ct New Milton SO40 . **195** E2
  Totton SO40 .... **76** B1
Melrose Gdns PO12 .... **180** C4
Melrose Rd SO15 .... **78** B1
Melton Ct *14* BH12 .... **204** A2
Melverley Gdns BH21 .... **163** E3
Melville Cl SO16 .... **78** B3

Melville Rd
  Bournemouth BH9 .... **204** C4
  Gosport PO12 .... **181** D4
  Portsmouth PO4 .... **183** E2
Melvin Jones House PO14 ..... **154** B2
Mendip Cl New Milton BH25 .. **195** E1
  Verwood BH31 .... **114** C3
Mendip Ct *4* BH23 .... **207** F4
Mendip Gdns SO45 .... **125** E1

Mendip Rd
  Southampton SO16 .... **101** F4
  Verwood BH31 .... **114** C3
Mendips Rd PO14 .... **154** C4
Mendips Wlk PO14 .... **154** B4
Mengham Ave PO11 .... **185** D1
Mengham Ct PO11 .... **185** D2
Mengham Inf Sch PO11 ..... **185** D2
Mengham Jun Sch PO11 .... **185** D2
Mengham La PO11 .... **185** D2
Mengham Rd PO11 .... **185** D1
Menin House PO15 .... **130** B1
Menslands La Hambledon PO7 . **86** A1
  Soberton PO7 .... **109** F4
Mentone Rd *2* BH14 .... **203** D2
Menzies Cl SO16 .... **77** F3
Meon Cl Clanfield PO8 .... **88** B2
  Gosport PO13 .... **155** D1
  Petersfield GU32 .... **40** C2
  Romsey SO51 .... **53** E4
Meon Cres SO53 .... **55** E3
Meon Ct SO18 .... **104** B4
Meon Gdns SO32 .... **84** A3
Meon House PO14 .... **155** D4
Meon Jun & Inf Schs PO4 .. **183** D2
Meon Rd Bournemouth BH7 .. **206** A4
  Portsmouth PO4 .... **183** D3
  Romsey SO51 .... **53** E4
Meoncross Sch PO14 .... **154** B2

Meonstoke CE Inf &
  1st Year Jun Sch SO32 .... **61** E2
Meonwara Cres GU32 .... **37** E3
Mercer Way SO51 .... **53** D4
Merchants Pl *9* SO23 .... **11** D4
Merchants Wlk *21* SO14 ... **102** C2
Merchistoun Rd PO7 .... **112** B4
Mercury Cl SO16 .... **77** F2
Mercury Gdns SO31 .... **128** A2
Mercury Pl PO7 .... **134** C1
Merdon Ave SO53 .... **55** E4
Merdon Cl SO53 .... **55** E4
Merdon Jun Sch SO53 .... **55** E4
Mere Croft PO15 .... **129** F2
Meredith Cl BH23 .... **207** E4
Meredith Inf Sch PO2 .... **182** C4
Meredith Gdns SO40 .... **100** B3
Meredith Lodge PO2 .... **135** D4
Meredith Rd PO2 .... **157** F2
Meredith Towers SO19 .... **104** C2
Meredun Cl SO21 .... **30** A4
Merepond La GU34 .... **17** F2
Merganser Cl PO12 .... **181** D4
Meriden Cl BH13 .... **214** C4
Meriden Ct *10* SO23 .... **2** A1
Meriden Rd PO5 .... **182** A2
Meridian Ctr *11* PO9 .... **135** F1
Meridians The BH23 .... **206** C3
Merino Way BH22 .... **138** C3
Merlewood Cl BH2 .... **204** C2
Merlewood Ct *19* BH25 ... **195** D2
Merley Dr BH23 .... **209** D4
Merley Fst Sch BH21 .... **163** F1
Merley Gdns BH21 .... **163** F1

Merley House BH21 .... 163 D1
Merley La BH21 .... 163 F1
Merley Park Rd
  Corfe Mullen BH21 .... 186 C4
  Oakley BH21 .... 163 E1
Merley Ways BH21 .... 163 E1
Merlin Cl
  Bishop's Waltham SO32 ...... 83 C4
  Ringwood BH24 .... 141 E3
Merlin Dr PO3 .... 158 A2
Merlin Gdns Hedge End SO30 .. 105 D4
  Portchester PO16 .... 132 A1
Merlin Lodge SO19 .... 103 E2
Merlin Way BH23 .... 208 A3
Mermaid Ct 22 BH5 .... 205 F2
Mermaid Rd PO14 .... 154 C3
Mermaid Way SO14 .... 103 D1
Merrick Way SO14 .... 55 D4
Merridale Rd SO19 .... 103 F3
Merriefield Ave BH18 .... 187 D3
Merriefield Cl BH18 .... 187 D3
Merriefield Dr BH18 .... 187 D3
Merrieleas Cl SO53 .... 55 E4
Merrieleas Dr SO53 .... 55 E4
Merriemeade Cl SO45 .... 125 F1
Merriemeade Par SO45 .... 125 F1
Merrifield BH21 .... 163 F4
Merritown La BH23 .... 190 B4
Merritt Ct SO53 .... 55 E2
Merrivale Ave BH6 .... 206 C3
Merrivale Cl SO45 .... 125 F2
Merrivale Ct PO10 .... 137 E1
Merrivale Rd PO2 .... 157 F2
Merrow Ave BH12 .... 204 A4
Merrow Chase 1 BH13 ...... 214 C4
Merrow Cl PO16 .... 156 A4
Merry Gdns SO52 .... 54 A3
Merryfield PO14 .... 129 E2
Merryfield Ave PO9 .... 135 E3
Merryfield Cl BH23 .... 193 D4
Merryfield Ct BH10 .... 189 E2
Merryfield La BH10 .... 189 E2
Merryfield Rd GU31 .... 41 D2
Merryoak Gn SO19 .... 103 F3
Merryoak Rd SO19 .... 103 F3
Merrytree Cl SO51 .... 50 C2
Merryweather Est BH24 ...... 141 E4
Mersea Gdns SO19 .... 104 A2
Mersham Gdns SO18 .... 104 A4
Merstone Rd PO13 .... 155 E1
Merthyr Ave PO6 .... 158 A4
Merton Ave PO16 .... 156 B3
Merton Cl SP6 .... 69 F2
Merton Cres PO16 .... 156 B3
Merton Ct
  8 Christchurch BH23 .... 209 D4
  3 Poole BH15 .... 202 C2
Merton Gr BH24 .... 140 C4
Merton Rd Portsmouth PO5 .. 182 B1
  Southampton SO17 .... 79 D2
Meryl Rd PO4 .... 183 E4
Mesh Pond SP5 .... 46 B4
Mesh Rd SO51 .... 6 A1
Meteor Rd PO10 .... 161 D2
Methuen Cl 2 BH8 .... 205 E3
  Broadstone BH17 .... 187 D1
  Portsmouth PO4 .... 183 D2
Methuen Rd Bournemouth BH8 .. 205 D3
Methuen St SO14 .... 103 D4
Metuchen Way SO30 .... 105 E2
Mews Ct SO21 .... 31 D2
Mews La SO22 .... 10 C4
Mews The
  1 Blackfield SO45 .... 177 F4
  1 Bournemouth BH2 .... 204 B2
  Chandler's Ford SO53 .... 55 E2
  Gosport PO12 .... 181 F2
  Havant PO9 .... 135 F2
  Petersfield GU31 .... 41 D2
  Rownhams SO16 .... 77 F3
Mewsey Ct PO9 .... 135 E4
Mey Cl PO7 .... 135 D4
Meynell Cl SO50 .... 55 F2
Meyrick Cl BH23 .... 193 D4
Meyrick House 15 PO2 .... 157 E1
Meyrick Park Cres BH3 .... 204 C3
Meyrick Park Mans 5 BH2 .. 204 C2
Meyrick Rd Bournemouth BH1 .. 205 D2
  Havant PO9 .... 135 E1
  Portsmouth PO2 .... 157 E1
Micawber House 12 PO1 .... 182 B4
Michael Crook Cl PO9 .... 135 E2
Michael's Way SO45 .... 125 F2
Michaels Way SO50 .... 57 E1
Michelgrove Rd BH5 .... 205 F2
Michelmersh Cl SO16 .... 77 F3
Michelmersh Gr BH8 .... 190 B1
Michigan Way SO14 .... 100 A4
Mickleham Cl BH12 .... 204 A4
Midanbury Cres SO18 .... 79 F1
Midanbury Ct 10 SO18 .... 103 F4
Midanbury La SO18 .... 103 F4
Midanbury Wlk 1 SO18 ...... 103 F4
Midas Cl PO7 .... 134 C2
Middle Brook BH11 .... 189 D3
Middle Brook St SO23 .... 11 D4
Middle Common Rd SO41 .. 197 D2
Middle Ct PO1 .... 182 C4
Middle La BH24 .... 141 D4
Middle Mead PO14 .... 154 A4
Middle Meadow GU33 .... 21 D2
Middle Park Way PO9 .... 135 E3
Middle Rd
  Bournemouth BH10 .... 189 E3
  Locks Heath SO31 .... 129 D3

Middle Rd Continued
  Lymington SO41 .... 197 E2
  New Milton BH25 .... 195 F4
  North Baddesley SO52 .... 54 C4
  Poole BH15 .... 202 C3
  Southampton SO19 .... 104 A3
  Sway SO41 .... 172 A1
  Sway SO41 .... 195 F4
  Winchester SO22 .... 10 C4
Middle St Portsmouth PO5 .. 182 B2
  Southampton SO14 .... 103 D4
Middlebere Cres BH16 .... 201 E2
Middlebridge St SO51 .... 52 C3
Middlebrook SO32 .... 83 E4
Middlecroft La PO12 .... 180 C3
Middlehill Dr BH21 .... 164 A3
Middlehill Rd BH21 .... 164 A3
Middlesex Rd PO4 .... 183 D2
Middleton Cl Fareham PO14 .. 154 C4
  Southampton SO18 .... 80 A1
Middleton Rd
  Bournemouth BH9 .... 189 F1
  Ringwood BH24 .... 141 D4
Middleton Rise PO8 .... 88 B2
Middleton Wlk 10 PO14 ...... 154 C4
Midfield Cl PO14 .... 154 C4
Midhurst House 57 PO1 ...... 182 B3
Midland Rd BH9 .... 189 F1
Midlands Est SO30 .... 80 B1
Midlington Hill SO32 .... 85 D4
Midlington House SO32 .... 85 D4
Midlington Rd SO32 .... 85 D4
Midway SO45 .... 125 F2
Midway Path BH13 .... 214 B2
Midway Rd PO2 .... 157 F3
Midways PO14 .... 179 E3
Midwood Ave BH8 .... 190 C1
Milbeck Cl PO8 .... 112 A2
Milborne Cres BH12 .... 203 F4
Milbourne Rd BH22 .... 165 E3
Milburn Cl 12 BH4 .... 204 B2
Milburn Rd BH4 .... 204 A2
Milburns The SO51 .... 27 E4
Milbury Cres SO18 .... 104 A3
Milbury House PO6 .... 133 D1
Mildmay Ct 22 SO23 .... 11 D4
Mildmay St SO20 .... 10 B3
Mile End Rd PO2 .... 182 B4
Miles Ct PO11 .... 185 E1
Miles La SO22 .... 9 F2
Miles La SP5 .... 24 B3
Milestone Rd BH15 .... 202 B3
Milford Cl Havant PO9 .... 135 E2
  West Moors BH22 .... 138 C1
Milford Cres SO41 .... 211 F2
Milford Ct Gosport PO12 .... 180 B2
  Milford on Sea SO41 .... 211 F2
  Portsmouth PO4 .... 183 D2
Milford Dr BH11 .... 188 C3
Milford Gdns SO53 .... 55 F3
Milford House SO41 .... 211 F3
Milford on Sea Prim Sch
  SO41 .... 211 F3
Milford Rd
  Barton on Sea BH25 .... 210 A4
  Lymington SO41 .... 197 D1
  Portsmouth PO1 .... 182 B3
Militair House BH31 .... 114 C4
Military Rd Fareham PO16 .. 131 E1
  Gosport PO12 .... 181 D1
  Gosport, Brockhurst PO13 .. 180 C3
  Gosport, Clayhall PO12 ...... 181 E1
  Portsmouth PO3 .... 157 F3
  Portsmouth PO1 .... 182 A4
Milkwood Ct SO40 .... 100 B4
Mill Cl Denmead PO7 .... 111 D2
  North Hayling PO11 .... 159 F1
  Nursling SO16 .... 77 E3
Mill Ct Fordingbridge SP6 .... 69 F1
  Hermitage PO10 .... 161 D4
  4 Southampton SO17 .... 79 E1
Mill End Damerham SP6 .... 68 B2
Mill Gate House 19 PO1 .... 182 A3
Mill Hill SO30 .... 106 A3
Mill Hill Cl BH14 .... 203 D2
Mill House Bsns Ctr SO19 .. 103 E2
Mill House Ctr SO40 .... 101 D4
Mill House Lodge SO50 .... 56 B2
Mill La Boldre SO41 .... 198 C3
  Brockenhurst SO42 .... 146 A1
  Burley BH24 .... 143 E2
  Christchurch BH23 .... 209 D4
  Crouchston SP5 .... 22 B4
  Droxford SO32 .... 61 D1
  Droxford SO32 .... 61 E1
  Durley SO32 .... 82 B2
  Gosport PO12 .... 181 D3
  Havant PO9 .... 159 F3
  Havant, Bedhampton PO9 .. 135 E1
  Hawkley GU33 .... 19 F4
  Hermitage PO10 .... 137 D1
  Hurn BH23 .... 191 D3
  Kings Worthy SO21 .... 2 B3
  Lymington SO41 .... 197 F2
  Minstead SO43 .... 98 C1
  Nursling SO16 .... 76 C2
  Petersfield GU31, GU32 ...... 41 D3
  Poole BH14 .... 203 D3
  Portsmouth PO1 .... 182 B4
  Romsey SO51 .... 52 B4
  Sherfield English SO51 .... 25 F1
  Southwick PO17 .... 133 F2
  Steep GU32 .... 40 C4
  Steep Marsh GU32 .... 19 F1
  Sway SO41 .... 196 C4
  Titchfield PO15 .... 130 A1
  Westbourne PO10 .... 137 D1
  Wickham PO17 .... 108 A3
  Wimborne Minster BH21 .... 163 F3

Mill Meadow SO41 .... 211 E3
Mill Pond Rd PO12 .... 181 D3
Mill Pond The SO45 .... 150 A3
Mill Quay PO10 .... 161 D4
Mill Race View SP5 .... 46 C4
Mill Rd Christchurch BH23 .. 207 D4
  Denmead PO7 .... 111 D2
  Fareham PO16 .... 155 D4
  Gosport PO12 .... 181 D3
  Liss SO32 .... 21 D3
  Portsmouth PO2 .... 157 E1
  Southampton SO15 .... 102 A4
  Totton SO40 .... 101 D4
  Waterlooville PO7 .... 134 C3
  Westbourne PO10 .... 137 D2
Mill Rd N Bournemouth BH8 .. 190 B2
  Bournemouth BH8 .... 190 C2
Mill Rd S BH8 .... 190 B1
Mill Rise SO51 .... 5 E1
Mill Rythe Inf Sch PO11 .... 185 D3
Mill Rythe Jun Sch PO11 .... 185 D3
Mill Rythe La PO11 .... 185 D4
Mill St Broadstone BH21 .... 162 A1
  Eastleigh SO50 .... 56 A2
  Titchfield PO14 .... 154 A4
Mill Way SO40 .... 100 C3
Millais Rd SO19 .... 103 F2
Milland Rd SO23 .... 11 D3
Millbank House
  14 Southampton SO14 ...... 103 E3
  5 Wimborne Minster BH21 .. 163 E3
Millbank St SO14 .... 103 E3
Millbridge Gdns SO19 .... 104 A2
Millbrook Cl
  Chandler's Ford SO53 .... 55 D3
  Liss SO33 .... 21 D2
Millbrook Com Sch SO16 .... 77 F2
Millbrook Dr PO9 .... 136 A3
Millbrook Flyover SO15 .... 101 F4
Millbrook Point Rd SO15 .... 102 A3
Millbrook Rd E SO15 .... 102 B3
Millbrook Rd W SO15 .... 102 A3
Millbrook Sta SO15 .... 102 A3
Millbrook Trad Est SO15 .... 101 E4
Millcourt 6 SO50 .... 57 E1
Miller Cl BH25 .... 195 E2
Miller Dr PO16 .... 130 C1
Miller Rd BH23 .... 207 E4
Millers La SO22 .... 9 F2
Millers Quay House PO16 .. 155 D4
Millers Way SO45 .... 125 F1
Millfield Broadstone BH17 .. 201 F4
  Broadstone BH17 .... 202 A4
  New Milton BH25 .... 194 C2
Millhams Cl BH10 .... 189 D3
Millhams Dr BH10 .... 189 D3
Millhams Rd BH10 .... 189 D3
Millhams St BH23 .... 207 D3
Millhams St N BH23 .... 207 D3
Milliken Cl SO45 .... 150 C1
Mills The PO17 .... 203 F4
Millstream Cl Broadstone BH17 .. 202 A4
  Wimborne Minster BH21 .... 163 E2
Millstream Rise SO51 .... 52 B4
Millstream Trad Est BH24 .. 141 D3
Millverton Ct SO18 .... 104 A4
Millvina Cl SO40 .... 99 F2
Millward Rd SO32 .... 82 A3
Millyford Cl BH25 .... 209 E4
Milne Cl SO45 .... 125 E1
Milne Rd BH17 .... 187 D1
Milner Ct SO15 .... 102 B4
Milner Pl SO22 .... 10 C3
Milner Rd BH4 .... 204 B1
Milnthorpe La SO22 .... 10 C4
Milton Cl BH14 .... 203 E2
Milton Ct Ferndown BH22 .. 165 E3
  Portsmouth PO3 .... 183 D3
Milton Gr Locks Heath SO31 .. 129 D1
  New Milton BH25 .... 195 D1
Milton Mead BH25 .... 194 C1
Milton Par PO7 .... 111 F1
Milton Park Ave PO4 .... 183 D2
Milton Park Jun & Inf Schs
  PO4 .... 183 D2
Milton Rd
  Bournemouth BH8 .... 205 D3
  Eastleigh SO50 .... 56 A3
  Poole BH14 .... 203 E2
  Portsmouth PO3 .... 183 D3
  Southampton SO15 .... 102 C3
  Waterlooville PO7, PO8 ...... 111 F1
  Wimborne Minster BH21 .... 163 E3
Milton St BH8 .... 205 D3
Milverton Cl
  Christchurch BH23 .... 193 F1
  Totton SO40 .... 101 D3
Milverton House 21 PO5 .... 182 B2
Milverton Rd Totton SO40 .. 101 D3
  Winchester SO22 .... 10 C3
Milvil Ct 5 PO13 .... 179 F1
Milvil Rd PO13 .... 179 F1
Mimosa Ave BH21 .... 187 E4
Mimosa Dr SO50 .... 57 F1
Mincingfield La SO32 .... 82 B3
Mincingfield Terr SO32 .... 82 B3
Minden House Fareham PO14 .. 154 C4
  Romsey SO51 .... 53 D4
Minden Way SO22 .... 10 B3
Minerva Ct PO7 .... 134 C1
Minley Ct PO9 .... 136 A3
Minnitt Rd PO12 .... 181 F2
Minstead Ave SO18 .... 104 B4
Minstead Cl SO22 .... 1 B2
Minstead Ct 4 SO17 .... 103 D4
Minstead Rd
  Bournemouth BH10 .... 189 E2
  Portsmouth PO4 .... 183 D2

Minstead Rural Studies Ctr
  SO43 .... 98 A1
Minster Cl PO15 .... 130 B1
Minster Ct 1 SO15 .... 102 B3
Minster La 27 SO23 .... 11 D4
Minster View BH21 .... 163 E3
Minster Way BH16 .... 201 D4
Mint Rd SO43 .... 21 D3
Mint The GU31,GU32 .... 40 C1
Minter's Lepe PO7 .... 134 C2
Mintern Cl SO50 .... 56 B3
Minterne Grange BH14 ...... 214 B4
Minterne Rd
  Bournemouth BH9 .... 190 A1
  Christchurch BH23 .... 207 F3
  Poole BH14 .... 214 B4
Minton Mews BH2 .... 204 C3
Mintys Hill SP6 .... 68 C4
Mintys Yd 4 BH24 .... 141 D3
Mirror SO31 .... 128 C1
Mislingford Rd SO32 .... 84 B2
Missenden Acres SO30 ...... 105 E4
Mission La SO52 .... 112 A2
Mission Rd BH18 .... 187 D1
Misslebrook La SO52 .... 54 B2
Mistletoe Gdns SO31 .... 128 C3
Mitchell Cl
  Barton on Sea BH25 .... 210 A4
  Locks Heath PO15 .... 129 E3
Mitchell Dr SO50 .... 57 E2
Mitchell Point SO31 .... 127 F1
Mitchell Rd Eastleigh SO50 .. 56 A1
  Ferndown BH21 .... 165 D4
  Havant PO9 .... 135 D2
  Poole BH17 .... 202 C4
Mitchell Way
  Eastleigh SO50 .... 79 F3
  Eastleigh SO50 .... 80 A4
  Portsmouth PO3 .... 158 A2
Mitchells Cl Redlynch SP5 .... 47 E3
  Romsey SO51 .... 52 C4
Mitre Copse SO50 .... 56 C1
Mitre Ct 13 PO14 .... 154 C4
Mizen Way PO13 .... 180 B3
Mizzen Ct SO14 .... 103 D1
Moat Cl SO45 .... 150 A2
Moat Ct
  Bournemouth BH4 .... 204 B3
  Gosport PO12 .... 180 B2
Moat Dr PO12 .... 180 B2
Moat Hill SO18 .... 79 F2
Moat La SO41 .... 209 F4
Moat Wlk PO12 .... 180 B2
Mockbeggar La BH24 .... 117 D4
Moffat Rd BH23 .... 207 E4
Moggs Mead GU31 .... 41 D2
Mole Hill PO7 .... 134 C3
Molefields SO41 .... 211 F3
Molesworth Rd PO12 .... 181 E2
Molyneux Rd BH25 .... 195 E2
Momford Rd SO22 .... 10 A2
Mon Cres SO18 .... 104 B4
Monaco Ct BH9 .... 205 D4
Monarch Cl Locks Heath SO31 .. 129 D1
  Waterlooville PO7 .... 135 D4
Monarch Way SO30 .... 80 C1
Monastery Rd SO18 .... 103 F4
Monckton Rd Gosport PO12 .. 181 E1
  Portsmouth PO3 .... 158 A1
Moneyfield Ave PO3 .... 158 A1
Moneyfield La PO3 .... 183 D4
Moneyfly Rd BH31 .... 115 D3
Monk's Hill PO10 .... 137 D3
Monks Brook Cl SO50 .... 55 F1
Monks Brook Ind Pk SO53 .. 55 D3
Monks Cl BH22 .... 166 A4
Monks Ct 10 SO41 .... 197 F1
Monks Hill PO13 .... 179 E2
Monks Orch GU32 .... 40 C3
Monks Pl SO40 .... 100 B3
Monks Rd Netley SO31 ...... 127 D3
  Winchester SO23 .... 2 A1
Monks Way
  Bournemouth BH11 .... 188 B3
  Eastleigh SO50 .... 55 F1
  Southampton SO18 .... 79 F2
  Stubbington PO14 .... 179 D2
Monks Wlk SO45 .... 149 F4
Monks Wood Cl SO16 .... 40 C3
Monkshood Cl BH23 .... 193 D1
Monkswell Gn BH23 .... 207 E3
Monkton Cl BH22 .... 165 E3
Monkton Cres BH12 .... 203 F4
Monkton House PO12 .... 181 D1
Monkton La BH22 .... 100 B3
Monkwood Cl PO9 .... 135 E3
Monkworthy Dr BH24 .... 139 F3
Monmouth Cl
  North Baddesley SO53 .... 55 D3
  Verwood BH31 .... 115 D2
Monmouth Ct
  Lymington SO41 .... 197 F2
  Ringwood BH24 .... 140 C4
Monmouth Dr BH31 .... 115 D2
Monmouth Gdns SO40 ...... 100 B3
Monmouth Rd PO2 .... 157 E1
Monmouth Sq SO22 .... 10 A3
Monnow Gdns SO18 .... 80 A1
Monroe Cl PO12 .... 180 C2
Monsal Ave BH22 .... 165 E2
Montacute Sch BH17 .... 187 E1
Montacute Way BH21 .... 187 F4
Montagu Pk BH23 .... 209 D4
Montagu Rd BH23 .... 209 D4
Montague Ave SO19 .... 104 A2
Montague Cl SO19 .... 104 B2
Montague Gdns GU31 .... 41 E2

Montague Rd
  Bishopstoke SO50 .... 56 B2
  Bournemouth BH5 .... 206 A2
  Portsmouth PO2 .... 157 F1
Montague Wallis Ct 51 PO1 .. 182 A3
Montana Ct PO7 .... 135 D3
Montefiore House SO18 .... 79 E2
Monterey Dr Havant PO9 .. 136 A2
  Hordle SO41 .... 195 F2
  Locks Heath SO31 .... 129 D1
Montfort Cl SO51 .... 53 E4
Montfort College SO51 .... 53 E4
Montfort Hts SO51 .... 53 E4
Montfort Rd SO51 .... 53 E3
Montgomerie Rd PO5 .... 182 B2
Montgomery Ave
  Bournemouth BH11 .... 189 D2
  Totton SO40 .... 100 B4
Montgomery Rd Gosport PO13 .. 155 E2
  Havant PO9 .... 136 A1
  Southampton SO18 .... 104 A4
Montgomery Way SO53 .... 55 D2
Montgomery Wlk PO7 .... 134 B3
Montpelier Cl SO31 .... 129 E2
Montrose Ave PO16 .... 132 C1
Montrose Cl Hedge End SO30 .. 105 F3
  2 Verwood BH31 .... 114 C3
Montrose Dr BH10 .... 189 D1
Montserrat Rd PO13 .... 179 F1
Monument La Boldre SO41 .. 198 A3
  Southwick PO17 .... 132 B2
  Walderton PO10 .... 137 F4
Monxton Gn 11 PO9 .... 136 A3
Moody Rd PO4 .... 179 E3
Moody's Hill SP5 .... 3 E1
Moonhills La SO42 .... 149 D1
Moonrakers BH13 .... 214 C4
Moonrakers Way BH23 ...... 193 F1
Mooncross Ave SO40 .... 100 C2
Moor La SP5 .... 48 B4
Moor Park PO7 .... 112 A1
Moor Rd BH18 .... 187 D3
Moor View Rd BH15 .... 202 C4
Moorcroft Ave BH23 .... 192 B1
Moordown Cl BH9 .... 190 A2
Moordown St John's
  CE Prim Sch BH9 .... 189 F1
Moore Ave BH11 .... 189 D2
Moore Cl BH25 .... 194 C1
Moore Cres SO31 .... 127 E4
Moore Gdns PO12 .... 180 C2
Moorfield Gr BH9 .... 189 F1
Moorfields Rd BH13 .... 214 C4
Moorgreen Hospl SO30 ...... 80 C1
Moorgreen Rd Havant PO9 .. 136 A3
  West End SO30 .... 80 C1
Moorhaven BH22 .... 165 E3
Moorhead Ct SO14 .... 103 E1
Moorhill Gdns SO18 .... 104 C4
Moorhill Rd Burley BH24 .... 143 D1
  West End SO30 .... 104 B4
Moorhills 13 BH21 .... 163 E2
Moorings The
  7 Christchurch BH23 .... 207 D3
  Fareham PO16 .... 155 D4
Moorings Way PO4 .... 183 E3
Moorings Way Inf Sch PO4 .. 183 E3
Moorland Ave BH25 .... 209 F4
Moorland Cl Hythe SO45 .. 125 D2
  Locks Heath SO31 .... 129 D2
Moorland Cres SO16 .... 201 D4
Moorland Gate BH24 .... 141 D3
Moorland Par BH16 .... 201 D4
Moorland Rd
  Bournemouth BH11 .... 205 D2
  Portsmouth PO1 .... 182 C3
Moorland Way BH16 .... 201 D4
Moorlands Cl SO42 .... 145 E1
Moorlands Coll BH23 ...... 192 A3
Moorlands Cres SO18 .... 104 A4
Moorlands Inf Sch SO18 .... 80 A1
Moorlands Rd
  Swanmore SO32 .... 84 A4
  Verwood BH31 .... 114 C4
  West Moors BH22 .... 138 C2
Moorlands Rise BH22 .... 138 C2
Moorlea 11 BH8 .... 205 D3
Moors Cl
  Colden Common SO21 .... 31 F1
  Hurn BH23 .... 191 D4
Moors Valley Ctry Pk BH24 .. 139 E4
Moorside Cl BH11 .... 189 D2
Moorside Rd
  Bournemouth BH11 .... 189 D2
  Corfe Mullen BH21 .... 186 B3
  West Moors BH22 .... 138 C1
  Winchester SO23 .... 2 B1
Moortown Ave PO6 .... 134 B1
Moortown Dr BH21 .... 188 A4
Moortown House BH24 .... 141 D3
Moortown La BH24 .... 141 E2
Moorvale Rd BH9 .... 190 A1
Moot Cl SP5 .... 47 D4
Moot Gdns SP5 .... 46 C3
Moot La Downton SP5 .... 46 C3
  Redlynch SP5 .... 46 C3
Mopley SO45 .... 177 F4
Mopley Cl SO45 .... 177 F4
Morant Ct 14 BH25 .... 195 D2
Morant Rd BH24 .... 117 D1
Morar Rd PO12 .... 181 E4
Moraunt Cl PO12 .... 156 A3
Moraunt Dr PO16 .... 156 A3
Moray Ct 10 BH23 .... 163 D3
Mordaunt Rd SO14 .... 103 D4
Morden Ave PO12 .... 165 E2
Morden Rd BH9 .... 189 F1
Morecombe Ct 10 PO5 ...... 182 B2
Moreland Rd PO12 .... 181 D3

Morelands Ct PO7 .... 134 C2
Morelands Prim Sch PO7 ...... 134 C1
Morelands Rd PO7 .... 134 C2
Morestead Rd Chilcomb SO21 ... 11 F2
  Winchester SO21 .... 11 D2
  Winchester SO21 .... 11 F2
Moreton Rd BH9 .... 190 A2
Morgan Rd Hedge End SO30 ... 105 E3
  Portsmouth PO4 .... 183 E2
Morgan's La SP5 .... 42 A1
Morgan's Vale & Woodfall's
  Prim Sch SP5 .... 47 E4
Morgans Dr PO14 .... 154 B3
Morgans Rise Rd SP5 .... 47 E4
Morgans Vale Rd SP5 .... 47 E4
Moriconium Quay BH15 .... 201 E1
Morington Ct 8 BH8 .... 205 D3
Morland Rd SO15 .... 78 B1
Morley Cl Bournemouth BH5 .. 206 A3
  Burton BH23 .... 192 B2
  Southampton SO19 .... 103 F3
Morley Cres PO8 .... 112 A4
Morley Dr SO32 .... 83 E4
Morley Rd Bournemouth BH5 .. 206 A3
  Portsmouth PO4 .... 183 D1
Morningside Ave PO16 .... 132 C1
Mornington Dr SO22 .... 1 B1
Mornish Rd BH13 .... 203 F1
Morpeth Ave SO40 .... 100 C4
Morris Cl PO13 .... 155 D3
Morris Rd Poole BH17 .... 202 B4
  Southampton SO15 .... 102 C3
Morrison Ave BH12 .... 203 F3
Morse Cl SO31 .... 127 D3
Morshead Cres PO16 .... 130 C2
Mortimer Cl
  Christchurch BH23 .... 208 A3
  Kings Worthy SO23 .... 2 A3
  10 Netley SO31 .... 127 D3
  Totton SO40 .... 76 B1
Mortimer Lawn PO9 .... 135 E4
Mortimer Rd Botley SO30 ... 106 A3
  Bournemouth BH8 .... 190 A1
  Cosham PO6 .... 133 E1
  Southampton SO19 .... 103 F2
Mortimer Way SO52 .... 53 F2
Mortimer's Ind Units SO40 ... 75 F3
Mortimers Dr 10 SO50 .... 57 E1
Mortimers La SO32 .... 58 A2
Mortimore Rd PO12 .... 180 C3
Mosaic Cl SO19 .... 104 C2
Mosdell Rd PO10 .... 161 F4
Mosedale Wlk SO16 .... 101 F4
Moselle Ct SO15 .... 102 B3
Moss Cl GU33 .... 21 D2
Moss Dr SO40 .... 101 F1
Moss Rd SO23 .... 11 D4
Mossleigh Ave SO16 .... 77 F3
Mossley Ave PO12 .... 189 D1
Motcombe Rd BH13 .... 204 A1
Mottisfont Abbey Gdns SO51 ... 5 F2
Mottisfont Abbey (NT) SO51 ... 5 F1
Mottisfont Cl SO15 .... 102 A3
Mottisfont Rd SO50 .... 56 A2
Moulin Ave PO5 .... 182 C1
Mounbatten Ct 8 BH25 ... 194 C2
Mound Cl PO12 .... 181 D2
Mount Ave PO10 .... 195 D1
Mount Cl New Milton BH25 ... 195 D1
  Winchester SO22 .... 1 C2
Mount Dr Chandler's Ford SO53 .. 55 F2
  Fareham PO15 .... 154 A4
Mount Grace Dr BH14 .... 214 B4
Mount Heatherbank 30 BH1 .. 204 C2
Mount Hospl The SO50 .... 56 B3
Mount House Cl 5 SO45 .... 126 A3
Mount La SO51 .... 25 F4
Mount Pleasant
  Christchurch BH23 .... 208 A3
  Denmead PO7 .... 110 C1
  Kings Worthy SO23 .... 2 B3
  Ringwood BH24 .... 141 D4
  Romsey SO51 .... 52 C3
Mount Pleasant Dr BH8 .... 190 C1
Mount Pleasant Ind Pk SO14 103 D4
Mount Pleasant Jun Sch
  SO14 .... 103 D4
Mount Pleasant La
  Lymington SO41 .... 197 D4
  Sway SO41 .... 197 D4
Mount Pleasant Rd
  Gosport PO12 .... 181 D2
  Southampton SO14 .... 103 D3
Mount Rd
  Bournemouth BH11 .... 189 D4
  Poole BH14 .... 203 D3
Mount Temple SO51 .... 53 D4
Mount The Gosport PO13 .... 155 F1
  Ringwood BH24 .... 141 E4
  Southampton SO16 .... 78 C2
Mount View SO50 .... 56 A2
Mount View Rd SO22 .... 10 A2
Mountain Ash Cl SO18 .... 104 A4
Mountbatten Bsns Ctr SO15 ... 102 B3
Mountbatten Cl
  Christchurch BH23 .... 208 A3
  Gosport PO13 .... 155 E2
  Mountbatten St SO22 .... 1 C2
Mountbatten Dr
  Ferndown BH22 .... 165 E3
  Waterlooville PO7 .... 134 B3
Mountbatten Gdns BH8 .. 190 C1
Mountbatten Pl SO23 .... 2 B4
Mountbatten Rd
  Eastleigh SO50 .... 56 A3
  Poole BH13 .... 204 A1
  Totton SO40 .... 100 B4
Mountbatten Sch The SO51 ... 53 E3

Mountbatten Sports Ctr PO2 . 157 E2
Mountbatten Sq PO4 .... 183 D1
Mountbatten Way
  Romsey SO51 .... 52 C4
  Southampton SO15 .... 102 B3
Mountfield SO45 .... 125 F2
Mountjoy Cl BH21 .... 163 F1
Mountview Ave PO16 .... 132 C1
Mountview Rd PO10 .... 137 E1
Mousehole La Hythe SO45 .... 126 A2
  Southampton SO18 .... 103 F4
Mousehole Rd PO6 .... 132 C1
Mowbray Rd SO19 .... 104 A2
Moxhams SP5 .... 69 F1
Moyles Court Sch BH24 .... 117 E3
Mt Pleasant Dr BH23 .... 169 E1
Mt Pleasant Rd BH23 .... 202 B2
Muccleshell Cl PO9 .... 136 A2
Muddyford Rd SP5 .... 47 E4
Mude Gdns BH23 .... 208 A3
Mudeford BH23 .... 208 A3
Mudeford Cty Inf Sch BH23 .. 207 F3
Mudeford Cty Jun Sch BH23 .. 207 F3
Mudeford Green Cl BH23 .... 207 F3
Mudeford La BH23 .... 207 F3
Muir House SO45 .... 125 F1
Muira Est SO14 .... 103 E3
Mulberry Ave Cosham PO6 .. 158 A4
  Stubbington PO14 .... 179 E3
Mulberry Cl PO12 .... 181 D2
Mulberry Ct 4 BH23 .... 207 D4
Mulberry Gdns SP6 .... 93 F4
Mulberry Gr SO41 .... 211 E4
Mulberry La PO6 .... 158 A4
Mulberry Mews SP6 .... 93 F4
Mulberry Rd SO40 .... 101 F1
Mulberry Wlk SO15 .... 102 B4
Mullen Cl SO19 .... 103 F2
Mullins Cl BH12 .... 204 B4
Mullion Cl PO6 .... 157 D4
Mumby Rd PO12 .... 181 D3
Mundays Row PO8 .... 88 B1
Munro Cres SO15 .... 101 F4
Munster Rd Poole BH14 .... 203 E2
  Portsmouth PO2 .... 157 E1
Murefield Rd PO1 .... 182 B3
Muriel Rd PO7 .... 134 C4
Murley Rd BH9 .... 205 D4
Murray Cl Fareham PO15 .... 130 C1
  Southampton SO19 .... 104 C3
Murray Cotts SO32 .... 107 E4
Murray Rd PO8 .... 112 A3
Murray's La PO1 .... 181 F3
Murrills Est PO16 .... 156 C4
Muscliffe Ct 1 PO9 .... 136 A3
Muscliffe La BH9 .... 190 A2
Muscliffe Rd BH9 .... 189 F1
Museum Rd PO1 .... 182 A2
Mussett Cl SO40 .... 100 C4
Mustang Ave PO15 .... 129 E4
My Lords La PO11 .... 185 D2
Myers Cl SO32 .... 84 A3
Myrtle Ave Portchester PO16 .. 156 B4
  Totton SO40 .... 100 B3
Myrtle Cl Gosport PO13 .... 155 D2
  Hordle SO41 .... 195 F2
Myrtle Gr PO3 .... 183 D4
Myrtle Rd
  Bournemouth BH8 .... 205 E3
  Southampton SO16 .... 78 A2
Myvern Cl SO45 .... 150 B2

Nada Rd BH23 .... 193 E1
Nailsworth Rd PO6 .... 133 D1
Nairn Rd
  Bournemouth BH3 .... 204 C3
  Poole BH13 .... 214 C4
Naish Ct PO9 .... 135 E4
Naish Dr PO12 .... 156 A1
Naish Holiday Village BH25 .. 209 E4
Naish Rd BH25 .... 209 F4
Naked Man SO42 .... 171 D4
Namu Rd BH8 .... 189 F1
Nansen Ave BH15 .... 202 B3
Napier Cl PO13 .... 180 B3
Napier Cres PO15 .... 130 B1
Napier Rd Hamworthy BH15 .. 201 E2
  Horndean PO8 .... 112 B3
  Portsmouth PO5 .... 182 B1
  Southampton SO14 .... 104 C3
Narrow La Ringwood BH24 .. 117 E1
  10 Romsey SO51 .... 52 C4
Narvik Rd PO2 .... 157 E2
Naseby Cl PO6 .... 133 D1
Naseby Rd BH9 .... 190 A1
Nash Cl SO45 .... 125 E1
Nash Rd SO45 .... 125 E1
Nashe Cl PO15 .... 130 B2
Nashe House PO15 .... 130 B2
Nashe Way PO15 .... 130 B2
Nasmith Cl PO12 .... 180 B2
Nat Gonella Sq 21 PO12 .... 181 E2
National Motor Mus The
  SO42 .... 148 C1
Nations Hill SO23 .... 2 B3
Nature Quest SO40 .... 123 F4
Navigator's Way SO30 .... 105 E4
Navy Rd PO1 .... 182 A3
Nea Cl BH23 .... 208 B4
Nea Dr BH24 .... 116 A3
Nea Rd BH23 .... 208 C4
Neacroft Cl BH25 .... 209 E4
Neath Way SO53 .... 55 D4
Needles Cl 11 SO41 .... 211 E2
Needles House PO14 .... 155 D4
Needles Point SO41 .... 211 E2

Neelands Gr PO6 .... 156 C4
Neighbourhood Ctr BH17 .... 187 F1
Neilson Cl SO53 .... 55 E4
Nelson Ave Portchester PO16 .. 156 A4
  Portsmouth PO2 .... 157 E1
Nelson Cl Holbury SO45 .... 150 B2
  New Milton BH25 .... 194 C2
  Romsey SO51 .... 52 C4
Nelson Cres PO8 .... 112 B4
Nelson Ct Fareham PO14 .... 154 C3
  Hythe SO45 .... 126 A1
  11 Poole BH15 .... 202 B1
Nelson Dr BH23 .... 207 F3
Nelson House PO12 .... 181 E2
Nelson Ind Pk SO30 .... 81 D1
Nelson La PO16 .... 132 B1
Nelson Pl SO41 .... 197 F2
Nelson Rd Bishopstoke SO50 ... 56 B2
  Bournemouth BH4 .... 204 A2
  Gosport PO12 .... 181 D2
  Poole BH14 .... 204 A2
  Portsmouth PO5 .... 182 B2
  Portsmouth PO1 .... 182 B4
  Southampton SO15 .... 102 B3
  Winchester SO23 .... 11 E3
Nelson's Gdns SO30 .... 81 E2
Nepean Cl PO12 .... 181 D1
Neptune Cl SO16 .... 77 F2
Neptune House 4 PO6 .... 157 F1
Neptune Rd Fareham PO15 .. 130 B1
  Gosport PO12 .... 154 C3
Neptune Way SO14 .... 103 D1
Nerissa Cl PO7 .... 135 D4
Nerquis Cl SO51 .... 53 D4
Nesbitt Cl PO13 .... 155 D2
Nessus St PO2 .... 182 B4
Netherfield Cl PO7 .... 136 A1
Netherhall Gdns BH4 .... 204 B2
Netherhill La Curdridge SO32 ... 82 A1
  Durley SO32 .... 82 A1
Netherton Rd PO12 .... 180 C4
Netherwood Pl BH21 .... 163 D3
Netley Abbey Inf Sch SO31 .. 127 D4
Netley Abbey Jun Sch SO31 .. 127 D4
Netley Cl
  Chandler's Ford SO53 .... 55 D2
  Poole BH15 .... 203 D4
Netley Cliff SO31 .... 127 D3
Netley Court Sch SO31 .... 127 D3
Netley Firs Cl SO19 .... 104 C2
Netley Firs Rd SO30 .... 105 D3
Netley Hill Est SO19 .... 104 C2
Netley Lodge Cl SO31 .... 127 E3
Netley Marsh CE Inf Sch
  SO40 .... 100 A4
Netley Rd 21 Portsmouth PO5 .. 182 B1
  Titchfield PO14 .... 129 E1
Netley Sta SO31 .... 127 E3
Netley Terr 20 PO5 .... 182 B1
Nettlecombe Ave PO4 .... 182 C1
Nettlestone SO31 .... 127 E4
Nettlestone Rd PO4 .... 183 D1
Nettleton Cl BH17 .... 202 C4
Netton Cl SP5 .... 22 A4
Netton St SP5 .... 22 B4
Neva Rd SO18 .... 103 F4
Nevil Shute Rd PO3 .... 158 A2
Neville Ave PO16 .... 156 B3
Neville Cl PO12 .... 181 D2
Neville Gdns PO10 .... 136 C2
Neville Lovett Com Sch PO14 154 C4
Neville Rd PO3 .... 183 D4
New Borough Rd BH21 .... 163 E2
New Brighton Rd PO10 .... 136 C1
New Cliff House SO19 .... 103 F1
New Cliffe Gdns SO30 .... 105 D4
New Coll (Univ of
  Southampton)SO15 .... 102 C4
New Cotts Ashurst SO40 .... 123 F4
  Boldre SO41 .... 199 D3
  Exbury SO45 .... 177 D3
  Fareham PO16 .... 155 D4
  Ferndown BH21 .... 164 C1
  Nursling SO16 .... 77 E1
New Ct BH24 .... 140 C4
New Cut PO11 .... 159 F2
New Down La Cosham PO6 .. 134 A1
  Southwick PO7 .... 134 A1
New Fields Bsns Pk BH17 .... 202 B4
New Forest Dr SO42 .... 145 E1
New Forest Ent Ctr SO40 .... 100 C3
New Harbour Rd BH15 .... 202 A1
New Harbour Rd S BH15 .... 213 D4
New Harbour Rd W BH15 .. 202 A1
New Inn Cotts SO42 .... 175 E3
New Inn La Cadnam SO40 .... 99 D3
  East Boldre SO42 .... 175 E3
New Inn Rd SO40 .... 99 D4
New La Havant PO9 .... 136 A2
  Milford on Sea SO41 .... 211 F2
  New Milton BH25 .... 194 C3
New Marsh House SO45 .... 126 A2
New Merrifield BH21 .... 163 F4
New Milton Inf Sch BH25 ... 195 D1
New Milton Jun Sch BH25 .. 195 D1
New Milton Sta BH25 .... 195 D2
New Orchard BH15 .... 202 A1
New Par Bournemouth BH10 .. 189 F2
  Portchester PO16 .... 156 B4
New Park Rd BH6 .... 206 B4
New Quay Rd BH15 .... 202 A1
New Rd Ashurst SO40 .... 100 B1
  Bishop's Waltham SO32 .... 59 E1
  Blackfield SO45 .... 150 C1
  Bournemouth BH10 .... 189 F3
  Clanfield PO8 .... 88 B3
  Colden Common SO21 .... 31 F1

New Rd Continued
  Fair Oak SO50 .... 57 D1
  Fareham PO16 .... 131 D1
  Ferndown BH22 .... 165 F2
  Havant PO9 .... 135 F1
  Horndean PO8 .... 111 F3
  Hythe SO45 .... 126 A3
  Ibsley BH24 .... 117 D4
  Landford SP5 .... 49 F1
  Littleton SO22 .... 1 A3
  Locks Heath SO31 .... 152 C1
  Meonstoke SO32 .... 61 E2
  Michelmersh SO51 .... 27 E4
  Milford on Sea SO41 .... 212 A2
  Netley SO31 .... 127 D3
  Poole BH12 .... 203 E3
  Portsmouth PO2 .... 182 C4
  Ringwood BH24 .... 141 D2
  Rockbourne SP6 .... 44 C1
  Romsey SO51 .... 53 D4
  Southampton SO14 .... 103 D3
  Southbourne PO10 .... 161 F4
  Swanmore SO32 .... 84 A3
  Swanwick SO31 .... 128 C4
  Westbourne PO10 .... 137 D2
  Woodlands BH21 .... 114 A3
New St Lymington SO41 .... 197 F2
  9 Poole BH15 .... 202 A1
  Ringwood BH24 .... 141 D2
New Street Mews SO41 .... 197 F2
New Town PO16 .... 156 B4
New Valley Rd SO41 .... 211 E3
Newbarn La PO10, PO18 .... 137 F4
Newbarn Rd PO9 .... 135 E2
Newbolt Cl PO8 .... 111 F2
Newbolt Rd 13 Cosham PO6 .. 133 D1
  Portchester PO6 .... 132 C1
Newbridge SO31 .... 127 E3
Newbridge Jun Sch PO1 .... 182 C4
Newbridge Rd SO40 .... 75 D1
Newbridge Way SO41 .... 197 E1
Newbroke Rd PO13 .... 180 C4
Newburgh St SO23 .... 10 C4
Newbury Cl SO50 .... 57 D1
Newbury Dr BH10 .... 189 E1
Newbury Rd SO15 .... 78 B1
Newcastle Cl PO13 .... 180 B3
Newcombe Rd
  Bournemouth BH6 .... 206 C3
  Southampton SO15 .... 102 C3
  West Moors BH22 .... 138 B1
Newcome Rd PO1 .... 182 C3
Newcomen Ct 8 PO2 .... 157 E1
Newcomen Rd PO2 .... 157 E1
Newcroft Gdns BH23 .... 207 D4
Newenham Rd SO41 .... 197 F1
Newfield Rd GU33 .... 21 D3
Newfoundland Dr PO1 .... 182 B1
Newgate La Fareham PO14 .. 155 D2
  Gosport PO14 .... 155 D2
  Stubbington PO14 .... 155 D2
Newgate Lane Ind Est PO14 .. 155 D3
Newland Ave PO12 .... 181 D2
Newlands PO15 .... 130 B1
Newlands Ave SO15 .... 102 B4
Newlands Cl SO45 .... 150 C1
Newlands Copse SO45 .... 150 C1
Newlands Inf Sch SO16 .... 77 F1
Newlands Jun Sch SO16 .... 77 F1
Newlands La Denmead PO7 .. 134 A3
  Southwick PO7 .... 134 A3
Newlands Manor SO41 .... 211 E4
Newlands Rd
  Bournemouth BH7 .... 206 A3
  Christchurch BH23 .... 207 F4
  Fawley SO45 .... 150 C1
  New Milton BH25 .... 195 D1
  Waterlooville PO7 .... 134 B3
Newlands The 2 SO17 .... 79 E1
Newlands Way BH18 .... 186 B2
Newlease Rd PO7 .... 134 C3
Newlyn Way Poole BH12 .... 203 F4
  Portsmouth PO6 .... 157 D4
Newlyn Wlk SO51 .... 28 A1
Newman St SO16 .... 102 A4
Newman's La BH22 .... 138 B2
Newmans Cl BH22 .... 138 C3
Newmans Hill Shedfield PO17 .. 84 B1
  Swanmore PO17 .... 84 B1
Newmarket Cl SO50 .... 81 E4
Newmer Ct PO9 .... 135 E3
Newmorton Rd BH9 .... 190 A2
Newney Cl PO2 .... 157 F2
Newnham Ct 10 PO9 .... 136 A3
Newport Cl SO53 .... 55 D2
Newport La SO51 .... 28 B3
Newport Rd PO2 .... 180 C3
Newstead Rd BH6 .... 206 B2
Newton Bglws SP5 .... 24 A2
Newton CE Prim Sch PO12 .. 181 E3
Newton Cl Stubbington PO14 .. 154 B2
  Whiteparish SP5 .... 24 A2
Newton La Romsey SO51 .... 52 C3
  Whiteparish SP5 .... 24 A2
Newton Morrell BH14 .... 203 D2
Newton Pl PO13 .... 179 F2
Newton Rd
  Barton on Sea BH25 .... 210 A4
  Poole BH13 .... 214 C4
  Southampton SO18 .... 79 F1
  Twyford SO21 .... 32 A4
Newtown Bsns Ctr BH12 .. 203 D4
Newtown Ct SO31 .... 128 C3
Newtown La
  Corfe Mullen BH21 .... 186 B4
  South Hayling PO11 .... 184 C2
  Verwood BH31 .... 115 D3

Newtown Rd Eastleigh SO50 .. 56 A2
  Locks Heath SO31 .... 152 B4
  Sherfield English SO51 .... 26 A2
  Southampton SO19 .... 104 A1
  Verwood BH31 .... 115 D3
Newtown Soberton Inf Sch
  PO17 .... 109 E3
Nichol Rd SO53 .... 30 B1
Nicholas Cl BH23 .... 194 A1
Nicholas Cres PO15 .... 130 C1
Nicholas Gdns
  10 Lee-on-the-Solent PO13 .. 179 F1
  South Hayling PO11 .... 184 C1
Nicholas Gdns BH10 .... 189 C1
Nicholas Rd SO45 .... 177 F4
Nichole Cl PO12 .... 180 C4
Nicholl Pl PO13 .... 155 E1
Nichols Rd SO14 .... 103 D3
Nicholson Cl BH17 .... 202 C4
Nicholson Gdns 35 PO1 .... 182 B3
Nicholson Way PO9 .... 135 F2
Nicholson Wlk SO16 .... 77 E3
Nickel Cl SO23 .... 11 D4
Nickel St PO5 .... 182 A2
Nickleby Gdns SO40 .... 100 A4
Nickleby House 10 PO1 .... 182 B4
Nickleby Rd PO8 .... 88 A3
Nickson Cl SO53 .... 55 D4
Nightingale Ave SO50 .... 55 E1
Nightingale Cl
  Bursledon SO31 .... 127 F4
  Gosport PO12 .... 180 C3
  Romsey SO51 .... 53 D4
  Rowland's Castle PO9 .... 113 D1
  Verwood BH31 .... 115 D3
  West Wellow SO51 .... 50 B2
  Winchester SO22 .... 10 B3
Nightingale Cres SO32 .... 107 F4
Nightingale Ct SO16 .... 78 A2
Nightingale Dr SO40 .... 100 B4
Nightingale Gr SO15 .... 102 B4
Nightingale House SO51 .... 53 D4
Nightingale La 4 BH15 .... 202 B1
Nightingale Mews
  Locks Heath SO31 .... 129 D2
  Netley SO31 .... 127 D3
Nightingale Pk PO9 .... 136 A1
Nightingale Prim Sch SO50 .. 55 E1
Nightingale Rd
  Petersfield GU32 .... 40 B1
  Portsmouth PO5 .... 182 A1
  Southampton SO15 .... 102 B4
Nightingale Wlk SO31 .... 127 E3
Nightingdale Ct 9 SO15 .... 102 B3
Nightjar Cl Broadstone BH17 .. 201 F4
  Horndean PO8 .... 112 A3
Nile Rd SO17 .... 79 D1
Nile St PO10 .... 160 C4
Nimrod Dr PO13 .... 180 B3
Nine Acres GU32 .... 20 A1
Nine Elms La PO16 .... 131 F2
Ninian Cl SO50 .... 57 E1
Ninian Park Rd PO3 .... 158 A1
Niton Cl PO13 .... 155 E1
Noads Cl SO45 .... 125 F1
Noads Way SO45 .... 125 F1
Noadswood Sec Sch SO45 .. 125 F1
Nobbs La PO1 .... 182 A2
Nobes Ave PO13 .... 155 E2
Nobes Cl PO13 .... 155 E1
Noble Cl BH11 .... 188 C1
Noble Rd SO30 .... 105 E3
Nobs Crook SO21 .... 57 D4
Noel Cl SO42 .... 146 A1
Noel Rd BH10 .... 189 D1
Noel The PO15 .... 195 E2
Nomansland & Hamptworth
  CE Sch SP5 .... 73 E4
Nook The Eastleigh SO50 .... 56 A3
  Gosport PO13 .... 155 F1
Noon Gdns BH31 .... 115 D3
Noon Hill Dr BH31 .... 115 D3
Noon Hill Rd BH31 .... 115 D3
Norbury Cl SO53 .... 55 D4
Norbury Gdns SO31 .... 127 F1
Norcliffe Cl BH11 .... 189 D2
Norcliffe Rd SO17 .... 103 D4
Norcroft Ct SO15 .... 78 B1
Nordik Gdns SO30 .... 105 E3
Nore Cres PO10 .... 136 B1
Nore Farm Ave PO10 .... 136 B1
Noreuil Rd GU32 .... 40 B2
Norfolk Ave BH23 .... 191 F1
Norfolk Cres PO11 .... 184 C1
Norfolk Ct SO53 .... 55 E2
Norfolk House PO9 .... 136 A1
Norfolk Mews PO11 .... 184 C1
Norfolk Rd Gosport PO12 .. 180 C4
  Southampton SO15 .... 102 B4
Norfolk St PO5 .... 182 B2
Norgett Way PO16 .... 156 A4
Norham Ave SO16 .... 78 B1
Norham Cl SO16 .... 78 B1
Norland Rd 5 PO4 .... 182 C2
Norlands Dr SO21 .... 31 E2
Norley Cl PO9 .... 135 F3
Norleywood BH23 .... 208 C4
Norleywood Rd SO41 .... 198 C4
Norman Ave BH12 .... 204 A3
Norman Cl PO16 .... 156 B3
Norman Rd 5 PO4 .... 182 C1
Norman Gdns
  Hedge End SO30 .... 105 D3
  Poole BH12 .... 204 A3
Norman House 16 SO14 .. 103 E3

Norman Rd Blackfield SO45 .... **177** F4
 Gosport PO12 .... **181** D3
 Portsmouth PO4 .... **182** C2
 South Hayling PO11 .... **185** D1
 Southampton SO15 .... **102** B3
 Winchester SO23 .... **10** C3
Norman Way PO9 .... **135** E1
Normandy Cl Rownhams SO16 .. **77** F3
 Sway SO41 .... **172** A1
Normandy Ct
 Locks Heath SO31 .... **128** B1
 Wickham PO17 .... **108** A4
Normandy Dr BH23 .... **207** E4
Normandy Gdns PO12 ...... **180** C2
Normandy House SO51 ...... **53** D4
Normandy La SO41 .... **197** F1
Normandy Rd PO2 .... **157** F2
Normandy Way
 Fordingbridge SP6 .... **69** F1
 Hamworthy BH15 .... **201** E1
 Marchwood SO40 .... **102** A1
Normanhurst Ave BH8 ...... **190** C1
Normans SO22 .... **10** C3
Normanton Cl BH23 .... **191** F1
 St Leonards BH24 .... **139** F2
Norris Gdns Havant PO9 ... **160** A4
 New Milton BH25 .... **195** D1
Norris Hill SO18 .... **79** F1
Norrish Rd BH12 .... **203** E3
Norset Rd PO15 .... **130** B1
North Ave
 Bournemouth BH10 .... **189** E3
 Portsmouth PO2 .... **157** F3
North Baddesley
 Inf Sch SO52 .... **54** A2
North Baddesley
 Jun Sch SO52 .... **54** A2
North Battery Rd PO2 .... **157** D1
North Bay PO10 .... **161** D2
North Block SO15 .... **102** B3
North Cl Gosport PO12 ...... **180** C2
 Havant PO9 .... **160** A4
 Lymington SO41 .... **197** F2
 Romsey SO51 .... **28** B1
North Common La
 Landford SP5 .... **49** D3
 Sway SO41 .... **196** C4
North Cres PO11 .... **185** D2
North Cross St PO12 .... **181** E2
North Ct PO1 .... **182** C4
North Dr Littleton SO22 .... **1** A3
 New Milton BH25 .... **170** C1
North East Cl SO19 .... **104** B3
North East Rd SO19 .... **104** A2
North End Ave PO2 .... **157** E4
North End Cl SO53 .... **55** E2
North End Farm Cotts SO24 .. **14** B4
North End Gr PO2 .... **157** E1
North End La SP6, BH24 ...... **93** E2
North Fields Cotts SO21 ...... **32** A4
North Front SO14 .... **103** D3
North Greenlands SO41 ..... **197** E1
North Head SO41 .... **211** D3
North Hill PO16 .... **131** D2
North Hill Cl SO22 .... **1** C1
North Hill Ct SO22 .... **1** C1
North La Beaulieu SO42 ...... **148** C3
 Buriton GU31 .... **65** F3
 Clanfield PO8 .... **88** B4
 East Meon PO8 .... **64** B1
 Nomansland SP5 .... **73** E4
 West Tytherley SP5 .... **4** A4
North Lodge BH14 .... **203** F2
North Millers Dale SO53 ..... **55** D4
North Path SO18 .... **180** B3
North Poulner Rd BH24 ..... **117** D1
North Rd Bournemouth BH7 .. **205** F3
 Brockenhurst SO42 .... **146** A1
 Horndean PO8 .... **88** B1
 Hythe SO45 .... **125** F1
 Kings Worthy SO23 .... **2** A4
 Petersfield GU32 .... **40** C2
 Poole BH14 .... **203** D2
 Southampton SO17 .... **103** E4
North Rd E PO17 .... **133** D3
North Shore Rd PO11 .... **184** B2
North Solent Nature Reserve
 SO45 .... **178** A4
North St Emsworth PO10 ... **136** C1
 Gosport PO12 .... **181** E2
 Havant PO9 .... **135** F1
 Havant, Bedhampton PO9 .. **135** E1
 Lymington SO41 .... **197** E1
 Poole BH15 .... **202** B1
 Portsmouth PO1 .... **182** A3
 51 Portsmouth PO1 .... **182** B3
 Westbourne PO10 .... **137** D2
North Street Arc 10 PO9 .. **135** F1
North Stroud La GU32 .... **39** F2
North Town SO21 .... **32** A4
North Trestle Rd SO45 ...... **151** E3
North View SO22 .... **10** C4
North Wallington PO16 ..... **131** E1
North Walls SO23 .... **11** D4
North Way Gosport PO13 ... **155** E2
 Havant PO9 .... **135** F1
 Locks Heath PO15 .... **129** F2
North Weirs SO42 .... **145** E1
Northam Bsns Ctr 1 SO14 .. **103** E3
Northam Prim Sch SO14 ... **103** E3
Northam Rd SO14 .... **103** D3
Northam St PO1 .... **182** B3
Northampton La SO45 .... **177** F4
Northarbour Rd PO6 .... **157** E4

Northarbour Spur PO6 ...... **157** E4
Northbourne Ave BH10 ..... **189** E3
Northbourne Cl BH10 .... **126** A1
Northbourne Gdns BH10 ... **189** E3
Northbourne Pl BH10 .... **189** E3
Northbourne Rdbt BH10 ... **189** E3
Northbrook Ave SO23 .... **11** E4
Northbrook Cl PO1 .... **182** B4
Northbrook Ct 11 SO23 ...... **11** E4
Northbrook Ind Est SO16 .... **78** B1
Northbrook Rd
 Broadstone BH18 .... **187** D1
 Southampton SO14 .... **103** D3
Northcote Rd
 Bournemouth BH1 .... **205** D2
 Portsmouth PO4 .... **182** C2
 Southampton SO17 .... **79** E1
Northcott Cl PO12 .... **180** C2
Northcroft Rd PO12 .... **180** C3
Northdene Rd SO53 .... **55** E3
Northend La SO23 .... **61** D1
Northern Access Rd SO45 .. **151** E1
Northern Anchorage SO19 .. **103** E2
Northern Bldgs 13 PO6 .... **157** F4
Northern Inf Sch PO16 ...... **132** B1
Northern Jun Sch PO16 .... **132** B1
Northern Par PO2 .... **157** F2
Northern Parade Inf Sch PO2 **157** F2
Northern Parade Mid
 Sch PO2 .... **157** F2
Northern Rd Cosham PO6 ... **157** F4
 Fawley SO45 .... **151** F1
Northerwood Ave SO43 ..... **121** F3
Northerwood Cl SO52 .... **53** F2
Northerwood House SO43 .. **121** F3
Northey Rd BH6 .... **206** C3
Northfield Ave PO14 .... **154** C4
Northfield Cl
 Bishop's Waltham SO32 ...... **59** D1
 Horndean PO8 .... **88** B1
Northfield Park PO16 .... **132** A1
Northfield Rd
 Milford on Sea SO41 .... **211** F3
 Ringwood BH24 .... **117** D1
 Southampton SO18 .... **79** F1
Northfields Farm La PO17 .. **108** A3
Northgate Ave PO2 .... **182** C4
Northlands Cl SO40 .... **100** B4
Northlands Dr SO23 .... **2** A1
Northlands Gdns SO15 ...... **102** C4
Northlands Rd Eastleigh SO50 .. **56** A2
 Romsey SO51 .... **53** E3
 Southampton SO15, SO40 .. **102** C4
 Totton SO40 .... **100** C4
Northleigh Cnr SO18 .... **79** F3
Northleigh La BH21 .... **163** F3
Northmead Dr BH17 .... **201** F4
Northmere Dr BH12 .... **203** F4
Northmere Rd BH12 .... **203** F4
Northmore Cl SO31 .... **129** D3
Northmore Rd SO31 .... **129** D3
Northney La PO11 .... **160** B2
Northney Rd PO11 .... **160** A2
Northolt Gdns SO16 .... **78** A3
Northover BH3 .... **204** C3
Northover La PO11 .... **195** F4
Northover Rd
 Lymington SO41 .... **197** D2
 Portsmouth PO3 .... **183** D4
Northumberland Ct BH24 .. **140** C4
Northumberland Rd
 Portsmouth PO1 .... **182** C3
 Southampton SO14 .... **103** D3
Northways PO14 .... **179** E3
Northwood Cl SO16 .... **79** D3
Northwood La PO11 .... **160** A1
Northwood Rd PO2 .... **157** F3
Northwood Sq 8 PO16 ...... **131** D1
Nortoft Rd BH8 .... **205** D3
Norton Cl Christchurch BH23 .. **207** E4
 Southampton SO19 .... **103** F2
 Southwick PO17 .... **132** C3
 Waterlooville PO7 .... **134** B4
Norton Dr PO16 .... **131** E1
Norton Rd Bournemouth BH9 .. **204** C4
 Southwick PO17 .... **132** C3
Norton Welch Cl SO52 .... **54** A2
Norway Rd PO3 .... **158** A2
Norwich Ave BH2 .... **204** B2
Norwich Ave W BH2 .... **204** B2
Norwich Cl SO31 .... **128** C2
Norwich Ct 12 BH2 .... **204** C2
Norwich Mansions 4 BH2 .. **204** B2
Norwich Pl PO13 .... **179** F2
Norwich Rd
 Bournemouth BH2 .... **204** C2
 Cosham PO6 .... **133** E1
 Southampton SO18 .... **79** E1
Norwood Cty Prim Sch SO50 .. **56** A2
Norwood Pl BH5 .... **206** A3
Nottingham Pl PO13 .... **179** F2
Nouale La BH24 .... **141** E4
Novello Gdns PO7 .... **134** C3
Noyce Dr SO50 .... **57** E1
Noyce Gdns BH8 .... **191** D1
Nuffield Hospl BH5 .... **205** F2
Nuffield Ind Est BH17 .... **202** B4
Nuffield Rd BH17 .... **202** B4
Nugent Rd BH6 .... **207** D2
Nunns Park SP5 .... **24** A2
Nuns Rd SO23 .... **2** A1
Nurse's Path SO21 .... **32** A3
Nursery Field GU33 .... **20** C2
Nursery Gdns
 Chandler's Ford SO53 .... **55** E2
 Romsey SO51 .... **53** D4

Nursery Gdns Continued
 Southampton SO19 .... **104** A3
 Waterlooville PO8 .... **112** A3
 Winchester SO22 .... **10** B1
Nursery Gr SO30 .... **105** E3
Nursery La PO14 .... **179** E3
Nursery Rd
 Bournemouth BH9 .... **190** A2
 Havant PO9 .... **135** E1
 Ringwood BH24 .... **141** D3
 Southampton SO18 .... **79** E1
Nursling CE Prim Sch SO16 .. **77** E3
Nursling Cres PO9 .... **136** A3
Nursling Gr BH8 .... **190** B1
Nursling Ind Est SO16 .... **77** D2
Nursling St SO16 .... **77** E3
Nutash PO14 .... **129** E2
Nutbeem Rd SO50 .... **56** A1
Nutburne House PO6 .... **158** B4
Nutbourne Rd Cosham PO6 .. **158** B4
 South Hayling PO11 .... **185** F1
Nutburn Rd SO52 .... **54** A3
Nutfield Ct SO16 .... **77** F2
Nutfield Pl PO1 .... **182** B3
Nutfield Rd SO16 .... **77** E3
Nuthatch Cl Broadstone BH17 .. **201** F4
 Ferndown BH22 .... **165** D4
 Rowland's Castle PO9 .... **113** D1
Nutley Cl BH11 .... **188** C2
Nutley Rd PO9 .... **135** E3
Nutley Way BH11 .... **188** C2
Nutsey Ave SO40 .... **76** B1
Nutsey Cl SO40 .... **76** C2
Nutsey La SO40 .... **76** C1
Nutshalling Ave SO16 .... **77** F3
Nutshalling Cl SO40 .... **76** B1
Nutwick Rd PO9 .... **136** A2
Nutwood Way SO40 .... **76** C1
Nyewood Ave PO16 .... **132** B1
Nyria Way PO12 .... **181** E2

O' Jays Ind Pk PO3 .... **158** A1
O'Connell Rd SO50 .... **55** F1
Oak Ave BH23 .... **206** B4
Oak Cl Corfe Mullen BH21 .. **186** B3
 Ferndown BH22 .... **165** F1
 Hythe SO45 .... **125** F1
 Lyndhurst SO43 .... **121** F2
 Southampton SO15 .... **101** E4
 Upham SO32 .... **58** C3
 Waterlooville PO8 .... **111** F1
Oak Coppice Cl SO50 .... **57** D1
Oak Ct Fareham PO15 .... **130** B1
 Lymington SO41 .... **197** E1
Oak Dr SO50 .... **57** E1
Oak Gdns SO41 .... **211** E4
Oak Green Way SO18 .... **104** A4
Oak La BH24 .... **141** D4
Oak Lodge 4 PO2 .... **157** E1
Oak Lodge Specl Sch SO45 .. **125** E2
Oak Mews BH12 .... **203** E3
Oak Park Dr PO9 .... **136** A2
Oak Rd Alderholt SP6 .... **92** C3
 Bishop's Waltham SO32 ...... **83** F4
 Bournemouth BH8 .... **205** E3
 Bursledon SO31 .... **127** F4
 Clanfield PO8 .... **88** B3
 Fareham PO15 .... **130** B1
 Hythe SO45 .... **125** F1
 New Milton BH25 .... **195** E2
 Southampton SO19 .... **103** F1
 Upton BH16 .... **201** E3
Oak St PO12 .... **181** E2
Oak Tree Cl SO21 .... **56** C4
Oak Tree Dr Emsworth PO10 .. **136** C2
 Liss GU33 .... **21** D2
Oak Tree Gdns SO30 .... **105** D3
Oak Tree Rd SO18 .... **79** F1
Oak Tree Way SO50 .... **56** A3
Oak Vale SO30 .... **80** A2
Oak Wlk SO50 .... **57** E1
Oakapple Gdns PO6 .... **158** C4
Oakbank Rd Bishopstoke SO50 .. **56** B2
 Southampton SO19 .... **103** E2
Oakcroft La PO14 .... **154** B3
Oakdale Mid Sch BH15 ...... **202** B3
Oakdale Rd BH15 .... **202** C3
Oakdale South Road
 Mid Sch BH15 .... **202** B3
Oakdene Gosport PO13 ...... **155** E1
 6 Southampton SO17 ...... **79** D1
 Totton SO40 .... **100** B4
Oakdene Cl BH21 .... **163** E3
Oakdene Gdns 3 SO50 ...... **57** E1
Oakdown Rd PO14 .... **154** B2
Oakenbrow Hythe SO45 ..... **125** E1
 Sway SO41 .... **172** A1
Oakes The PO14 .... **154** A2
Oakfield Ct PO9 .... **136** A3
Oakfield Prim Sch SO40 ...... **76** C1
Oakfield Rd Cadnam SO40 ... **99** D4
 Poole BH15 .... **202** B3
 Totton SO40 .... **100** C4
Oakfields SO50 .... **56** A4
Oakford Ct BH8 .... **190** B2
Oakgrove Gdns SO50 .... **56** C1
Oakgrove Rd SO50 .... **56** C1
Oakham Grange BH22 ...... **165** F3
Oakhill SO31 .... **105** D1
Oakhill Cl Bursledon SO31 .. **105** D1
 Chandler's Ford SO53 .... **55** F3
Oakhill Ct SO53 .... **55** F3
Oakhill Terr SO31 .... **105** D1
Oakhurst Cl Netley SO31 ... **127** E3
 West Moors BH22 .... **138** C1

Oakhurst Rd
 Southampton SO17 .... **79** D2
 West Moors BH22 .... **138** C1
Oakhurst Way SO31 .... **127** E3
Oakland Dr SO40 .... **101** F1
Oakland Wlk BH22 .... **165** F1
Oaklands Lymington SO41 .. **197** F1
 Waterlooville PO7 .... **135** D3
Oaklands Ave SO40 .... **100** C4
Oaklands Cl Fordingbridge SP6 .. **69** F1
 Verwood BH31 .... **114** C3
 Winchester SO22, SO23 ...... **10** B3
Oaklands Com Sch SO16 ..... **77** F3
Oaklands Gdns PO14 .... **129** E1
Oaklands Gr PO8 .... **111** F2
Oaklands House 9 PO6 ..... **132** C1
Oaklands RC Sec Sch PO7 .. **134** C3
Oaklands Rd Havant PO9 ... **136** A1
 Petersfield GU32 .... **40** C2
Oaklands The SO53 .... **55** E2
Oaklands Way Hythe SO45 .. **125** E1
 Southampton SO16 .... **78** C2
 Titchfield PO14 .... **129** E1
Oaklea Cl PO7 .... **134** A1
Oakleaf Cl SO40 .... **124** C4
Oakleigh Cres SO40 .... **100** C3
Oakleigh Dr SP5 .... **73** E4
Oakleigh Gdns SO51 .... **53** D4
Oakleigh Way BH23 .... **208** C3
Oakley Cl SO45 .... **150** B2
Oakley Gdns BH16 .... **201** D4
Oakley Hill BH21 .... **163** E1
Oakley House
 11 Southampton,
 Banister's Pk SO15 .... **102** C4
 13 Southampton, Shirley SO16 .. **102** A4
Oakley La BH21 .... **163** F1
Oakley Rd Havant PO9 ...... **135** E3
 Mottisfont SO51 .... **5** F2
 Oakley BH21 .... **163** E1
 Southampton SO16 .... **102** A4
Oakley Straight BH21 .... **163** F1
Oakmead Gdns BH11 .... **188** C2
Oakmead Rd BH17 .... **201** F4
Oakmead Sec Sch BH11 .... **188** C2
Oakmeadow Cl PO10 .... **137** D2
Oakmount Ave
 Chandler's Ford SO53 .... **55** E2
 Southampton SO17 .... **79** D1
 Totton SO40 .... **100** C4
Oakmount Dr PO8 .... **111** F1
Oakmount Mansions SO15 .. **78** C1
Oakmount Rd SO53 .... **55** F3
Oakridge Rd SO15 .... **101** E4
Oaks Coppice PO8 .... **112** A3
Oaks The BH24 .... **139** E2
Oaks The Bursledon SO31 .. **127** F4
 Southampton SO19 .... **103** F3
 Verwood BH31 .... **114** C4
Oakshott Dr PO9 .... **136** A3
Oakthorn Cl PO13 .... **180** B3
Oaktree Ct Milford on Sea SO41 .. **211** E2
 Southampton SO16 .... **78** C2
Oaktree Cvn Pk SO30 .... **80** B2
Oaktree Par BH23 .... **169** D1
Oakum House PO3 .... **183** D3
Oakville Mansions 11 SO15 .. **102** C3
Oakwood BH3 .... **204** C4
Oakwood Ave Havant PO9 .. **135** D2
 New Milton BH25 .... **195** E2
 Otterbourne SO21 .... **31** E2
Oakwood Cl
 Bournemouth BH9 .... **190** A1
 Chandler's Ford SO53 .... **30** B1
 Locks Heath SO31 .... **152** B4
 Otterbourne SO21 .... **31** E2
 Romsey SO51 .... **28** B1
Oakwood Ct
 Chandler's Ford SO53 .... **30** B1
 New Milton BH25 .... **195** D2
Oakwood Ctr The PO9 ...... **136** A2
Oakwood Dr SO16 .... **78** B3
Oakwood House SO21 .... **31** E2
Oakwood Inf Sch SO16 .... **78** A3
Oakwood Jun Sch SO16 ...... **78** A3
Oakwood Lodge SO21 .... **31** E2
Oakwood Rd
 Bournemouth BH9 .... **190** A1
 Chandler's Ford SO53 .... **55** E4
 Christchurch BH23 .... **193** F1
 Portsmouth PO2 .... **157** F2
 South Hayling PO11 .... **184** C2
Oakwood Way SO31 .... **128** A2
Oasis Mews BH16 .... **201** D4
Oasis The 12 BH12 .... **204** A2
Oates Rd BH9 .... **189** F1
Oatfield Gdns SO40 .... **76** B1
Oatlands SO51 .... **52** C4
Oatlands Cl SO32 .... **81** F1
Oatlands Rd SO32 .... **81** F1
Oban Rd BH3 .... **204** C4
Obelisk Cl SO19 .... **103** F1
Obelisk Rd SO19 .... **103** F1
Ober Rd SO42 .... **145** E1
Oberfield Rd SO42 .... **145** E1
Oberland Ct SO41 .... **197** E2
Oberon Cl PO7 .... **135** D4
Occupation La PO14 .... **153** F4
Ocean Cl PO15 .... **130** B1
Ocean Ct PO11 .... **184** C2
Ocean Hights 28 BH5 .... **205** F2
Ocean Pk PO3 .... **158** A1
Ocean Rd Gosport PO14 .... **154** C3
 Southampton SO14 .... **103** D1
Ocean Village SO14 .... **103** D1
Ocean Way SO14 .... **103** D1

Octavia Hill SO22 .... **10** B3
Octavia Rd SO18 .... **79** F2
Octavius Ct PO7 .... **112** A1
Odell Cl PO16 .... **130** C2
Odeon Bldgs 10 PO6 .... **157** F4
Odiham Cl
 Chandler's Ford SO53 .... **55** D2
 Southampton SO16 .... **77** F2
Oelander Cl SO31 .... **129** D3
Oglander Rd SO23 .... **2** A1
Ogle Rd SO14 .... **102** C2
Okeford Rd BH18 .... **187** D1
Okement Cl SO18 .... **80** A1
Old Agwi Rd SO45 .... **151** E3
Old Bakery Ct 8 BH15 ...... **202** B1
Old Barn Cl Christchurch BH23 .. **191** E1
 Ringwood BH24 .... **141** E4
Old Barn Cres PO7 .... **86** B1
Old Barn Farm Rd BH21 .... **139** D3
Old Barn Gdns PO8 .... **111** F3
Old Barn Rd BH23 .... **191** E1
Old Bound Rd BH16 .... **201** E3
Old Brickyard Rd SP6 .... **69** D1
Old Bridge Cl SO31 .... **128** A4
Old Bridge House Rd SO31 .. **128** A4
Old Bridge Rd
 Bournemouth BH6 .... **206** B4
 Portsmouth PO4 .... **182** C1
Old Canal PO4 .... **183** D2
Old Christchurch La 35 BH1 .. **204** C2
Old Christchurch Rd
 Bournemouth BH1, BH2 ..... **204** C2
 Hordle SO41 .... **196** B1
Old Coastguard Rd BH13 ... **214** A2
Old Commercial Rd PO1 .... **182** B4
Old Common SO31 .... **129** D2
Old Common Gdns SO31 ... **129** D2
Old Copse Rd PO9 .... **136** A2
Old Cottage Cl SO51 .... **50** C2
Old Courts The SO31 .... **79** D3
Old Cracknore Cl SO40 ...... **102** A1
Old Down La GU32 .... **18** A1
Old Farm Cl BH24 .... **117** E1
Old Farm Copse SO51 .... **50** C2
Old Farm Dr SO18 .... **79** F2
Old Farm La Stubbington PO14 .. **179** E3
 Westbourne PO10 .... **137** E2
Old Farm Rd BH15 .... **202** C3
Old Farm Way PO6 .... **158** C4
Old Farm Wlk SO41 .... **197** E2
Old Farmhouse Mews SO41 .. **197** F3
Old Forge Cl SP6 .... **92** C3
Old Forge Rd SO41 .... **197** E1
Old Forge Rd BH21 .... **164** C3
Old Forge The SO32 .... **107** E4
Old Garden Cl SO31 .... **129** E1
Old Gdns SO22 .... **1** C1
Old Gosport Rd PO16 .... **155** D4
Old Granary The SP5 .... **46** C4
Old Highway Mews BH21 .. **163** E2
Old Hillside Rd SO22 .... **1** B1
Old Ivy La SO18 .... **80** A1
Old Kennels Cl SO22 .... **10** A2
Old Kennels La SO22 .... **10** A2
Old Kiln Rd Hamworthy BH16 .. **201** E3
 Upton BH16 .... **201** E3
Old Litten La GU32 .... **19** E2
Old London Rd PO2 .... **157** F2
Old Lyndhurst Rd SO40 ...... **98** C4
Old Magazine Cl SO40 ...... **101** F1
Old Maltings The SO41 ..... **197** E2
Old Manor Cl BH21 .... **163** E2
Old Manor Farm PO9 .... **135** D1
Old Manor Way PO6 .... **158** A4
Old Market Rd BH21 .... **186** A4
Old Mill House BH24 .... **140** C3
Old Mill La Hambledon PO8 .. **87** E2
 Petersfield GU31 .... **41** D3
Old Mill Way SO16 .... **78** A1
Old Milton Gn BH25 .... **194** C1
Old Milton Rd BH25 .... **195** D1
Old Orchard BH15 .... **202** B1
Old Orchards SO41 .... **197** F1
Old Parsonage Ct SO21 .... **31** E2
Old Pines Cl BH22 .... **165** F2
Old Priory Cl SO31 .... **128** A1
Old Priory Rd BH6 .... **206** C2
Old Rd Gosport PO12 .... **181** D2
 Romsey SO51 .... **53** D4
 Southampton SO14 .... **103** D1
 Wimborne Minster BH21 .... **163** D3
Old Rectory Cl
 Corfe Mullen BH21 .... **186** B4
 Westbourne PO10 .... **137** D2
Old Rectory Rd SO40 .... **101** D3
Old Rectory Gdns SO21 .... **2** B3
Old Rectory La SO21 .... **32** A3
Old Rectory Rd PO6 .... **158** C4
Old Redbridge Rd SO15 .... **101** E4
Old Reservoir Rd PO6 .... **158** B4
Old River Rd PO7 .... **110** C2
Old Road The PO6 .... **157** F3
Old Romsey Rd SO40 .... **98** C4
Old Rope Wlk The BH15 .... **201** F1
Old Ropewalk BH15 .... **202** A1
Old Salisbury La SO51 .... **27** D1
Old Salisbury Rd SO51 .... **75** F4
Old School Cl Ferndown BH22 .. **165** E3
 Netley SO31 .... **127** E4
 Poole BH14 .... **203** D2
Old School Dr PO11 .... **185** D1
Old School Gdns SO30 .... **80** C1
Old School Rd GU33 .... **20** C2
Old School The SO32 .... **83** D4
Old Shamblehurst La SO30 ... **81** E1
Old Spring La SO32 .... **84** A3
Old St PO14 .... **154** A2
Old St John's Mews BH9 ... **189** F2

Old Stacks Gdns BH24 141 E3
Old Star Pl 3 PO1 182 A3
Old Station App SO23 11 D4
Old Swanwick La SO31 128 B4
Old Timbers PO11 184 C2
Old Town Mews 5 BH15 202 B1
Old Turnpike PO16 131 D2
Old Turnpike Bsns Pk PO16 131 D1
Old Van Diemans Rd PO7 134 B3
Old Vicarage Cl BH10 189 F3
Old Vicarage La SO41 196 B4
Old Vineries The SP6 69 E1
Old Wareham Rd
Poole BH12 203 D4
Upton BH16 186 A1
Old Well Cl The SO19 104 B2
Old Winchester Hill La
Warnford SO32, GU32 37 D1
West Meon GU32 37 E1
Old Wymering La PO6 157 F4
Oldbarn Cl SO40 76 B1
Oldbury Ct SO16 77 E1
Oldbury House 49 PO5 182 B2
Oldbury Way PO14 154 B4
Oldenburg SO31 129 D4
Oldgate Gdns 8 PO2 157 F2
Olinda St PO1 182 C3
Olive Cres PO16 156 B3
Olive Rd SO16 78 A2
Oliver Rd Lymington SO41 197 E2
Portsmouth PO4 183 D2
Southampton SO18 79 E2
Oliver's Battery Cres SO22 10 A2
Oliver's Battery Gdns SO22 10 A2
Oliver's Battery Rd N SO22 10 A3
Oliver's Battery Rd S SO22 10 A2
Olivers Cl SO40 100 A4
Olivers Rd BH21 164 A3
Olivers Way BH21 164 A3
Olivia Cl PO7 112 A1
Olympic Way SO50 57 D1
Omdurman Ct 2 SO17 79 D1
Omdurman Rd SO17 79 D1
Omega House 21 PO1 182 B3
Omega St PO1 182 B3
Onibury Cl SO18 80 A1
Onibury Rd SO18 80 A1
Onslow Gdns BH21 163 E3
Onslow House BH21 163 E3
Onslow Rd Portsmouth PO5 182 B1
Southampton SO14 103 D3
Ophir Gdns 1 BH8 205 E3
Ophir Rd Bournemouth BH8 205 D3
Portsmouth PO2 157 F2
Oracle Dr PO7 134 C2
Orange Gr PO13 155 E1
Orange Row PO10 160 C4
Oratory Gdns BH13 214 C4
Orchard Ave
Bishopstoke SO50 56 C1
Poole BH14 202 C1
Orchard Bglws PO17 109 D1
Orchard Cl Christchurch BH23 207 D3
Colden Common SO21 31 F1
Corfe Mullen BH21 186 B4
Edmondsham BH21 91 D2
Fawley SO45 151 D2
Ferndown BH22 165 F3
Fordingbridge SP6 69 F1
Gosport PO12 156 A1
Horndean PO8 112 B3
North Baddesley SO52 53 F3
Ringwood BH24 141 D4
South Hayling PO11 184 C1
Totton SO40 100 C3
Orchard Ct Cadnam SO40 98 C4
Hedge End SO30 105 F4
10 New Milton BH25 195 D2
Verwood BH31 115 D3
Orchard Cvn Pk The SO40 99 E3
Orchard Gdns SP6 69 F1
Orchard Gr New Milton BH25 195 D1
Portchester PO16 156 A4
Waterlooville PO8 111 F2
Orchard House 13 SO14 103 D2
Orchard Inf Sch SO45 125 F1
Orchard Jun Sch SO45 125 F1
Orchard La Corfe Mullen BH21 186 B4
Hermitage PO10 161 D4
Romsey SO51 52 C4
Southampton SO14 103 D2
Orchard Lea Inf Sch PO15 130 C2
Orchard Lea Jun Sch PO15 130 C2
Orchard Leigh 6 BH25 195 D1
Orchard Mead 5 BH24 141 D4
Orchard Mews 2 BH23 207 D3
Orchard Mount 6 BH24 141 D4
Orchard Pl SO14 103 D2
Orchard Rd Fair Oak SO50 57 E1
Gosport PO12 181 D3
Havant PO9 159 F4
Locks Heath SO31 128 C1
Portsmouth PO4 182 C2
Redlynch SP5 47 E3
South Hayling PO11 185 D1
Orchard St BH2 204 C2
Orchard The
Bournemouth BH11 188 B3
Bransgore BH23 193 E4
Chilworth SO16 54 C1
Cosham PO6 157 F4
Denmead PO7 110 C2
Milford on Sea SO41 211 E2
Southampton SO16 79 D3
Orchard Way SO45 125 F1
Orchard Wlk
22 Bournemouth BH2 204 C2
Winchester SO22 1 B1
Orchardlea SO32 84 B2
Orchards Way
Southampton SO17 79 D1
West End SO30 80 B1
Orcheston Rd BH8 205 E3
Orchid Way BH23 207 E4
Ordnance Ct PO3 158 A3
Ordnance Rd Gosport PO12 181 E2
Southampton SO15 103 D3
Ordnance Row PO1 182 A3
Ordnance Way SO40 102 A2
Oregon Cl SO19 104 A2
Orestes Gate BH23 208 A3
Orford Cl BH23 191 E2
Orford Ct 16 PO6 157 F4
Oriana Way SO16 77 D2
Oriel Dr PO14 129 D1
Oriel Rd PO2 157 E1
Orient Dr SO22 1 B2
Oriental Terr SO14 103 D2
Orion Cl Southampton SO16 77 F2
Stubbington PO14 179 E3
Orion Ind Ctr SO18 79 F3
Orkney Cl SO16 77 F2
Orkney Rd PO6 133 F1
Ormesby Dr SO53 30 A1
Ormond Cl SO50 57 D1
Ormonde Rd BH13 204 A1
Ormsby Rd PO5 182 B2
Orpen Rd SO19 104 B2
Orsmond Cl PO7 134 C3
Orwell Cl SO16 77 F1
Orwell Cres PO14 129 E1
Orwell Rd GU32 40 C1
Osborn Cres PO13 155 D2
Osborn Ct PO3 158 A2
Osborn Mall 6 PO16 131 E1
Osborn Rd PO16 131 D1
Osborn Sq 5 PO16 131 E1
Osborne Cl Netley SO31 127 E3
Waterlooville PO7 135 D4
Osborne Ct
7 Milford on Sea SO41 211 E2
Southampton SO17 79 E1
Osborne Dr SO53 55 F3
Osborne Gdns Fair Oak SO50 57 F1
Southampton SO17 79 E1
Osborne House SO51 50 C2
Osborne Rd
Bournemouth BH9 204 C4
Lee-on-the-Solent PO13 179 F1
Locks Heath SO31 152 B4
New Milton BH25 195 D2
Petersfield GU32 40 C2
Poole BH14 203 D2
Portsmouth PO5 182 B1
Totton SO40 101 D4
Wimborne Minster BH21 163 E2
Osborne Rd N SO17 79 E1
Osborne Rd S Fareham PO16 131 D1
Southampton SO17 103 E4
Osborne View Rd PO14 179 D3
Osbourne House 4 BH25 195 D2
Osbourne Rd PO12 181 E3
Osier Cl PO2 157 E2
Oslands La SO31 128 B4
Oslo Towers 6 SO19 126 C4
Osprey Cl Christchurch BH23 208 A3
Cosham PO6 158 C4
Marchwood SO40 101 F1
Southampton SO16 78 A3
Osprey Ct PO16 155 F4
Osprey Dr PO11 185 D2
Osprey Gdns PO13 179 F1
Osprey Quay PO10 161 D4
Ossemsley Manor House
BH23 194 B3
Ossemsley South Dr BH25 194 C4
Osterley Cl SO30 105 F3
Osterly Rd SO19 103 F3
Oswald Cl BH9 189 F1
Oswald Rd BH9 189 F1
Othello Dr PO7 135 D4
Otter Cl Bishopstoke SO50 57 D1
Gosport PO13 180 B3
Upton BH16 201 D3
Verwood BH31 115 D3
Otter Rd BH15 202 C3
Otterbourne BH2 204 B2
Otterbourne CE Prim Sch
SO21 31 D1
Otterbourne Cres PO9 135 E3
Otterbourne Hill SO21 31 E2
Otterbourne House SO21 31 D1
Otterbourne House Gdns
SO21 31 D1
Otterbourne Rd SO21 31 E3
Otters Wlk BH25 195 E3
Ouse Cl SO53 55 D4
Outer Circ SO16 78 A2
Outlands La SO30 106 B4
Outram Rd PO5 182 B2
Outwick Cross SP6 69 F4
Oval Gdns PO12 180 C2
Oval Rd SO51 5 D1
Oval The GU33 20 C2
Over Links Dr BH14 203 E1
Overbrook SO45 125 F2
Overbrook Way SO52 53 F3
Overbury Rd BH14 203 E2
Overcliff Rise SO16 78 C2
Overcliffe Mansions BH1 205 E2
Overcombe Cl BH17 187 F1
Overdell Ct 25 SO15 102 C4
Overstrand Cres SO41 211 E2
Overton Cres PO9 135 E3
Overton Rd PO10 137 F1
Oviat Cl SO40 100 A4
Ovington Ave BH7 206 B4
Ovington Ct SO18 104 B4
Ovington Gdns BH7 206 B4
Ovington Rd SO50 56 A1
Owen Cl PO13 180 B4
Owen Rd SO50 55 F1
Owen St PO4 183 D1
Owen's Rd SO22 1 C1
Ower La SO45 178 C4
Owls Rd Bournemouth BH5 205 F2
Verwood BH31 115 D3
Owlshotts BH13 214 C4
Owslebury Bottom SO21 33 D3
Owslebury Gr PO9 135 F3
Owslebury Prim Sch SO21 33 D2
Oxburgh Cl SO50 55 F3
Oxenwood Gn 8 PO9 135 E3
Oxey Cl BH25 195 D1
Oxford Ave Bournemouth BH6 206 A3
Southampton SO14 103 D3
Oxford Cl PO16 131 D1
Oxford La Bournemouth BH11 189 D3
Swanmore SO32 84 C4
Oxford Rd Bournemouth BH1 205 D2
Gosport PO12 180 C3
Portsmouth PO5 182 C2
Southampton SO14 103 D4
Oxford St SO14 103 D2
Oxford Terr SO41 172 A1
Oxlease Cl SO51 28 A1
Oxleys Cl PO14 154 A4
Oxted Ct PO4 183 D3
Oyster Est The PO6 158 B3
Oyster Mews
5 Emsworth PO10 160 C4
Portsmouth PO1 182 A2
Oyster Quay PO6 157 D4
Oyster St PO1 182 A2
Ozier Rd SO18 80 A1

P.L.P.H. Rd SO45 151 D3
Packridge La SO51 53 F1
Padbury Cl PO2 157 F2
Paddington Cl BH11 188 B2
Paddington Gr BH11 188 B2
Paddington Rd PO2 157 F1
Paddock Cl Ferndown BH21 165 D3
St Leonards BH24 139 F2
Paddock End PO7 110 C2
Paddock Gdns SO41 197 E3
Paddock Gr BH31 115 D3
Paddock The
Brockenhurst SO42 145 F1
Eastleigh SO50 56 A3
Fordingbridge SP6 94 C3
Gosport PO12 181 D2
Kings Worthy SO23 2 B3
Stubbington PO14 154 B2
Totton SO40 76 B1
Paddock Way GU32 40 B1
Paddock Wlk 1 PO6 157 D4
Paddocks Cl BH12 203 D4
Paddocks The
Bournemouth BH10 189 E2
Fawley SO45 151 D2
Padfield Cl BH6 206 C3
Padget Rd BH24 117 E1
Padnell Ave PO8 112 A1
Padnell Inf Sch PO8 112 A1
Padnell Jun Sch PO8 112 A2
Padnell Pl PO8 112 A1
Padnell Rd PO8 112 A2
Padstow Pl SP6 93 F4
Padwell Rd SO14 103 D4
Padwick Ave PO6 158 A4
Padwick Ct PO11 184 C2
Paffard Cl PO13 180 B4
Pages La SO42 175 E3
Paget Cl BH21 164 A4
Paget Rd Bournemouth BH11 189 D2
Gosport PO12 181 D1
Paget St SO14 103 D2
Pagham Cl PO10 161 D4
Pagham Gdns PO11 185 F1
Paignton Ave PO3 183 D4
Paignton Rd SO16 77 F1
Paimpol Pl SO51 52 C3
Pain's Rd PO5 182 B2
Painswick Cl Cosham PO6 157 E4
Locks Heath SO31 128 C3
Painter Cl PO3 158 A2
Painters Field SO23 10 C2
Paisley Rd BH6 206 B3
Palace House SO42 148 C1
Palace La SO42 148 C1
Palace Mews SO32 83 E4
Palfrey Rd BH10 189 E3
Palk Rd PO9 135 E1
Pallant Gdns PO16 131 E1
Pallant The PO9 135 F1
Pallet Cl SO21 56 C4
Pallot Cl SO31 104 C1
Palm Ct 16 PO5 182 B1
Palm Hall Cl SO23 11 E4
Palm Rd SO16 78 A2
Palma Ct BH23 209 D4
Palmer Pl BH25 195 D2
Palmer Rd BH15 202 B3
Palmer's Rd PO10 136 C1
Palmers Cl SO50 57 E1
Palmerston Ave
Christchurch BH23 207 E3
Fareham PO16 131 D1
Palmerston Bsns Pk PO14 155 D4
Palmerston Cl BH16 201 E4
Palmerston Ct 2 SO22 10 C3
Palmerston Dr PO14 155 D4
Palmerston Mans 28 PO5 182 B1
Palmerston Rd
Bournemouth BH1 205 F3
Poole BH14 203 E2
Portsmouth PO5 182 B1
South Hayling PO11 185 D2
Southampton SO14 103 D2
Upton BH16 201 E4
Palmerston Rd Prec 29 PO5 182 B1
Palmerston St SO51 52 C4
Palmerston Way PO12 180 C1
Palmyra Rd PO12 181 D4
Palomino Dr PO15 129 D4
Pamphill CE Fst Sch BH21 162 C3
Pamplyn Cl SO41 197 E2
Pan St 7 PO1 182 B3
Pangbourne Ave PO6 158 A4
Pangbourne Cl SO19 104 A2
Pannall Rd PO12 181 D4
Panorama Rd BH13 214 A2
Pansy Rd SO16 79 D2
Pantheon Rd SO53 55 F4
Pantiles The SP6 69 E1
Panton Cl PO10 136 C2
Panwell Rd SO18 104 A4
Parade Ct PO2 157 F3
Parade The
Barton on Sea BH25 194 C1
5 Bournemouth BH6 206 C2
Broadstone BH17 187 D1
Cadnam SO40 98 C4
Gosport PO13 155 D2
New Milton BH25 195 E2
Portsmouth PO1 182 A3
Paradise La
Bishop's Waltham SO32 83 F3
Netley Marsh SO40 99 E3
Portchester PO16 131 F1
Westbourne PO10 137 D2
Paradise St 17 Poole BH15 202 A1
Portsmouth PO1 182 B3
Parchment St SO23 11 D4
Parchment The PO9 135 F1
Pardoe Cl SO30 105 E3
Pardys Hill BH21 186 B4
Parham Cl BH25 194 C2
Parham Dr SO50 55 F2
Parham Rd
Bournemouth BH10 189 E1
Gosport PO12 181 E3
Parish Ct SO41 197 F2
Parish Rd BH15 202 C2
Park Ave Bournemouth BH10 189 E3
Lymington SO41 197 E2
Waterlooville PO7 134 B2
Winchester SO23 11 D4
Park Cl Brockenhurst SO42 146 A1
Burton BH23 192 B2
Gosport PO12 180 C3
Hythe SO45 126 A2
Lyndhurst SO43 122 A2
Marchwood SO40 101 E1
Milford on Sea SO41 211 F2
New Milton BH25 195 E3
Winchester SO23 2 A1
Park Com Sch PO9 135 E3
Park Cotts PO17 108 A2
Park Court Flats 3 SO15 102 B3
Park Cres PO10 136 B1
Park Ct 14 Milford on Sea SO41 211 E2
North Baddesley SO51 53 E3
12 Petersfield GU32 40 C2
37 Portsmouth PO5 182 B2
1 Winchester SO23 2 A1
Park Dr BH31 114 C4
Park Farm Ave PO15 130 B2
Park Farm Cl PO15 130 B2
Park Farm Rd PO7 134 B2
Park Gate Bsns Ctr SO31 129 D3
Park Gate Cty Prim Sch SO31 129 D2
Park Gate Mews 14 BH2 204 C2
Park Gdns BH23 207 F4
Park Glen SO31 129 E2
Park Gr PO6 157 F4
Park Hill Cl SO45 150 B2
Park House
22 Portsmouth PO5 182 B1
8 Winchester SO23 11 D4
Park Homer Rd BH21 163 F3
Park House Farm Way PO9 135 E3
Park House Prim Sch PO9 135 E3
Park La Alderholt SP6 92 C3
Beaulieu SO41 200 A4
Bournemouth BH10 189 F2
Cosham PO6 158 A4
Droxford SO32 61 D1
Fareham PO14, PO16 131 D1
Havant PO9 135 E2
Havant PO9 135 E4
Holbury SO45 150 A2
Kings Worthy SO21 2 B3
Marchwood SO40 101 E1
Milford on Sea SO41 211 E2
Otterbourne SO21 31 D1
Rowland's Castle PO10 137 E4
Stubbington PO14 154 B2
Swanmore SO32 60 B1
Twyford SO21 32 A3
Wimborne Minster BH21 163 E2
Park Lane Rd BH15 202 C1
Park Mansions 3 PO6 158 A4
Park Par PO9 135 F2
Park Pl BH14 202 C2
Park Rd Barton on Sea BH25 194 C1
Bishop's Waltham SO32 83 D4
Bournemouth BH8 205 D3
Chandler's Ford SO53 55 E4
Denmead PO7 110 C3
Fordingbridge SP6 69 F1
Park Rd Continued
Gosport PO12 181 D2
Lymington SO41 197 E2
Milford on Sea SO41 211 F2
New Milton BH25 195 E3
Poole BH14 202 C2
Portsmouth PO1 182 A3
South Hayling PO11 184 B2
Southampton SO15 102 B3
Southbourne PO10 137 E1
Waterlooville PO7 134 B2
Winchester SO22, SO23 1 C1
Park Rd N PO9 135 F1
Park Rd S PO9 135 F1
Park Royal 17 PO2 157 F2
Park St Gosport PO12 181 D3
Portsmouth PO5 182 A2
Southampton SO15, SO16 102 A4
Park Terr 10 PO12 181 E2
Park The Barton on Sea BH25 209 E4
Droxford SO32 61 D1
Park View Botley SO30 106 A4
Compton(Hants) SO21 31 F3
Hedge End SO30 105 D4
Lockerley SO21 4 C2
Otterbourne SO50 31 D1
9 Poole BH15 202 C2
Portsmouth PO2 157 E2
Rowland's Castle PO9 136 A4
Park View Mews BH25 195 D1
Park Villas SO32 61 D1
Park Vista GU32 38 B1
Park Way Fair Oak SO50 57 F1
Havant PO9 135 F1
West Moors BH22 138 C1
Park Wlk Fareham PO15 130 B2
Southampton SO14 103 D3
Parker Cl PO12 156 A1
Parker Gdns PO7 134 B1
Parker Rd BH9 204 C4
Parkfield House 11 PO6 132 C1
Parkland Cl BH31 115 E2
Parkland Dr BH25 209 F4
Parkland Pl 13 SO17 103 D4
Parklands Locks Heath SO31 129 D2
6 Southampton SO18 79 F1
Totton SO40 101 D4
Parklands Ave PO8 112 A3
Parklands Bsns Pk PO7 110 C2
Parklands Cl
Chandler's Ford SO53 55 E4
Gosport PO12 181 D3
Parkside Christchurch BH23 193 E1
Havant PO9 135 E1
Ringwood BH24 141 D3
Totton SO40 100 C3
Parkside Ave SO16 101 E4
Parkside Gdns BH10 189 F1
Parkside Rd BH14 203 E2
Parkside The SO15 102 A4
Parkstone Ave Poole BH14 203 E2
Portsmouth PO4 182 C1
Parkstone Gram Sch BH17 187 D1
Parkstone Hts Poole BH14 202 C3
Poole BH14 203 D3
Parkstone Rd BH15 202 C2
Parkstone Sta BH14 203 D2
Parkview BH2 204 C2
Parkville Rd SO16 79 E2
Parkway Swanwick PO15 129 F3
Swanwick PO15 129 F4
Parkway Dr BH8 205 F4
Parkway Gdns SO53 55 E4
Parkway The Gosport PO13 155 D1
Southampton SO16 79 D3
Parkwood Cl SO30 105 E4
Parkwood Ctr PO7 134 C4
Parkwood La 14 BH5 206 A3
Parkwood Rd
Bournemouth BH5 206 A2
Wimborne Minster BH21 163 E2
Parley Cl BH22 165 F1
Parley Cty Fst Sch BH22 165 E2
Parley La BH23 190 B4
Parley Rd BH9 190 A1
Parliament Pl SO22 10 B2
Parmiter Dr BH21 163 F2
Parmiter House 45 SO23 11 D4
Parmiter Rd BH21 163 F2
Parmiter Way BH21 163 F2
Parnell Rd SO50 55 F1
Parnholt Rd SO51 7 F2
Parr House 5 BH14 203 D2
Parr Rd PO6 157 E4
Parr St BH14 203 D2
Parry Cl PO6 156 C4
Parry Rd SO19 104 B2
Parsonage Barn La BH24 141 D4
Parsonage Cl
Fordingbridge SP6 69 F1
Petersfield GU32 41 D3
Parsonage Ct 9 BH8 205 D3
Parsonage La SO32 82 A3
Parsonage Park Dr SP6 69 F1
Parsonage Rd
Bournemouth BH1 205 D2
Southampton SO14 103 E3
Parsons Cl PO3 157 F2
Partridge Cl
Christchurch BH23 208 A3
Portchester PO16 155 F4
Partridge Down SO22 10 A2
Partridge Dr BH14 203 E1
Partridge Gdns PO8 111 E2
Partridge Gr BH25 195 D3

Partridge Rd
Brockenhurst SO42 .... 172 C4
Hythe SO45 .... 125 F1
Partridge Wlk BH14 .... 203 D1
Partry Cl SO53 .... 55 D4
Pascoe Cl BH14 .... 203 D2
Passage La SO31 .... 128 A1
Passfield Ave SO50 .... 55 F1
Passfield Cl SO50 .... 55 F1
Passfield Wlk 53 PO9 .... 136 A3
Passford Hill SO41 .... 197 E4
Passingham Wlk PO8 .... 112 A2
Pastures The Cheriton SO24 ...... 14 B3
Denmead PO7 .... 110 C2
Locks Heath PO14 .... 129 E2
Pat Bear Cl SO15 .... 101 E4
Patchins Rd BH16 .... 201 D2
Patchins The BH14 .... 214 B4
Patchway Dr PO14 .... 154 B4
Paternoster House 31 SO23 ...... 11 D4
Paternoster Row 30 SO23 ...... 11 D4
Patricia Cl SO30 .... 80 B1
Patricia Dr SO30 .... 105 E4
Patrick Howard-Dobson Ct
5 PO8 .... 111 F2
Patrick's Cl GU33 .... 21 D2
Patrick's Copse Rd GU33 ...... 21 D2
Paulet Cl SO18 .... 80 A1
Paulet Pl SO22 .... 10 C3
Pauletts La Ower SO40 .... 76 A2
Totton SO40 .... 76 A2
Pauls La SO41 .... 196 C4
Paulsgrove Cty Prim Sch
PO6 .... 157 E4
Paulsgrove Ent Ctr 6 PO6 ... 157 D4
Paulsgrove Ind Ctr PO6 ...... 157 E4
Paulsgrove Jun Sch PO6 ...... 157 E4
Paulsgrove Rd PO2 .... 182 C4
Paulson Cl SO53 .... 55 E4
Paultons Park SO51 .... 75 E3
Pauncefoot Hill SO51 .... 52 B3
Pauncefote Rd BH5 .... 206 A3
Pauntley Rd BH23 .... 207 F3
Pavan Gdns BH10 .... 189 E1
Pavilion Cl SO50 .... 81 E4
Pavilion Ct 20 SO15 .... 102 C4
Pavilion Rd SO30 .... 105 E4
Paxton Cl SO30 .... 105 E3
Paxton Rd PO14 .... 155 D4
Payne Cl BH22 .... 138 C3
Payne's La SO50 .... 57 E2
Payne's Rd SO15 .... 102 B3
Paynes Hay Rd SO51 .... 28 B4
Peace Cl BH23 .... 193 D4
Peach Rd SO16 .... 78 A2
Peacock Cl PO16 .... 155 F4
Peacock La PO1 .... 182 A2
Peacock Pl 3 SO23 .... 11 E4
Peak Cl SO16 .... 101 F4
Peak Dr PO14 .... 154 B4
Peak La
Bishop's Waltham SO32 .... 59 D2
Fareham PO14 .... 154 B4
Peak The PO9 .... 113 E1
Peak Rd PO8 .... 88 A3
Peake New Rd SO32 .... 61 F4
Peakfield PO7 .... 110 C2
Pealsham Gdns SP6 .... 69 F1
Pear Tree Cl Alderholt SP6 ...... 92 C3
Botley SO32 .... 81 F1
Bransgore BH23 .... 193 D4
Pear Tree Dr SP5 .... 73 E4
Pearce Ave BH14 .... 203 D1
Pearce Ct PO12 .... 181 E3
Pearce Gdns BH14 .... 203 D1
Pearce Rd BH16 .... 201 D3
Pearce-Smith BH25 .... 209 F4
Pearl Gdns BH10 .... 189 E2
Pearl Rd BH10 .... 189 E2
Pearmain Dr 4 SO41 .... 197 F1
Pearman Ct SO41 .... 197 E1
Pearson Ave BH14 .... 203 D3
Pearson Gdns BH10 .... 189 E3
Peartree Ave SO19 .... 103 F3
Peartree Cl
Southampton SO19 .... 103 E2
Stubbington PO14 .... 154 B2
West Wellow SO51 .... 50 B2
Peartree Ct
5 Lymington SO41 .... 197 F1
Southampton SO19 .... 103 F2
Peartree Rd Hythe SO45 ...... 125 F1
Southampton SO19 .... 103 E2
Pebble Cl PO11 .... 185 D1
Pebble Ct SO40 .... 101 F1
Pebmarsh Rd 8 PO6 .... 157 E4
Peckham Ave BH25 .... 195 D1
Pedham Cl PO4 .... 183 D2
Pedlars Wlk BH24 .... 140 C4
Pedula Way SO50 .... 56 C3
Peel Cl Poole BH12 .... 203 E3
Romsey SO51 .... 28 B1
Peel Common Jun &
Inf Schs PO13 .... 155 D1
Peel Rd PO12 .... 181 E2
Peel St SO14 .... 103 E3
Peewit Hill SO31 .... 105 D2
Peewit Hill Cl SO31 .... 105 D2
Pegasus Ave SO41 .... 196 A1
Pegasus Ct Gosport PO13 .... 180 B3
Hamble-le-Rice SO31 .... 127 F1
Southampton SO16 .... 77 F2
Pegasus Ct Bournemouth BH1 .. 205 D3
8 New Milton SO41 .... 195 D2
Peggotty House 17 PO1 ..... 182 B4

Pegham Ind Pk PO15 .... 130 A3
Pelham Cl BH23 .... 207 E3
Pelham Rd Gosport PO12 ..... 181 D3
Portsmouth PO5 .... 182 B2
Pelham Terr 2 PO10 .... 161 D4
Pelican Cl PO15 .... 130 B1
Pelican Cl SO21 .... 30 A4
Pelican Mead BH24 .... 141 E3
Pelican Rd PO14 .... 154 C3
Pembers Cl SO50 .... 57 E1
Pemberton Rd SO43 .... 122 A3
Pembrey Cl SO16 .... 78 A3
Pembridge Rd SP6 .... 70 A1
Pembroke Cl Eastleigh SO50 ... 55 F3
Portsmouth PO1 .... 182 A2
Romsey SO51 .... 52 C4
Totton SO40 .... 101 D4
Pembroke Cres PO14 .... 179 D3
Pembroke Ct
11 Christchurch BH23 ...... 209 D4
Gosport PO13 .... 155 E1
Southampton SO17 .... 79 D1
Pembroke Rd
Bournemouth BH4 .... 204 A1
Poole BH12 .... 203 E4
Portsmouth PO1 .... 182 A2
Southampton SO19 .... 104 A2
Pembury Rd Havant PO9 ...... 160 A4
Stubbington PO14 .... 154 B2
Pemerton Rd SO22 .... 1 B2
Penarth Ave PO6 .... 158 A4
Pencraig BH13 .... 204 A2
Pendennis Rd PO6 .... 132 C1
Pendle Cl SO16 .... 101 F4
Pendle Gn SO51 .... 4 C1
Pendleton Gdns SO45 .... 150 C1
Penelope Ct 18 BH23 .... 209 D4
Penelope Gdns SO31 .... 104 C1
Penfords Paddock SO32 ...... 83 E4
Pengelly Ave BH10 .... 189 F3
Penhale Gdns PO14 .... 129 D1
Penhale Inf Sch PO1 .... 182 C3
Penhale Rd PO1 .... 182 C3
Penhale Way SO40 .... 100 C3
Penhurst Rd PO9 .... 135 D1
Peninsula Rd SO22 .... 10 C4
Peninsula Sq 25 SO22 .... 10 C4
Penistone Cl SO19 .... 104 A1
Penjar Ave PO7 .... 134 B2
Penk Ridge PO9 .... 158 C4
Penn Cl SO53 .... 194 C1
Penn Ct BH21 .... 138 B1
Penn Hill Ave BH14 .... 203 E2
Penn Way PO12 .... 180 C2
Pennant Hills PO9 .... 135 D1
Pennant Park PO16 .... 131 E2
Pennant Way BH23 .... 207 F4
Penner Rd PO9 .... 159 F4
Pennerley Ct PO9 .... 135 E4
Pennine Cl 8 BH23 .... 207 F4
Pennine Gdns SO45 .... 125 E1
Pennine House SO16 .... 101 F4
Pennine Rd SO16 .... 101 F4
Pennine Way
Chandler's Ford SO53 .... 55 E2
Lee-on-the-Solent PO13 ...... 180 A2
Verwood BH31 .... 114 C3
Pennine Wlk PO14 .... 154 C4
Pennington CE Jun Sch
SO41 .... 197 E2
Pennington Cl
Colden Common SO21 .... 56 C4
Lymington SO41 .... 197 E1
West Moors BH22 .... 138 B1
Pennington Cres BH22 .... 138 B1
Pennington Cross SO41 ...... 197 E1
Pennington Inf Sch SO41 .... 197 E2
Pennington Oval SO41 .... 197 D1
Pennington Rd BH22 .... 138 B1
Pennington Way PO15 .... 130 B2
Penns Rd GU32 .... 40 C2
Penny Hedge BH25 .... 210 A4
Penny La
6 Bournemouth BH7 .... 205 F2
Hermitage PO10 .... 161 D4
Penny Pl PO7 .... 134 C2
Penny St PO1 .... 182 A2
Penny's Cl SP6 .... 69 F2
Penny's Cnr SO41 .... 195 F2
Penny's Cres SP6 .... 69 F2
Penny's Ct BH22 .... 165 E3
Penny's La SP6 .... 69 F2
Penny's Wlk BH22 .... 165 E3
Pennycress SO31 .... 128 C1
Pennywell Gdns BH25 .... 195 E2
Penrhyn Ave PO6 .... 158 A4
Penrhyn Cl SO50 .... 55 F3
Penrith Cl BH31 .... 114 C3
Penrith Ct SO16 .... 101 F4
Penrith Rd BH5 .... 206 A2
Penrose Cl 11 PO2 .... 157 E1
Penrose Rd BH22 .... 165 E3
Penshurst Way SO50 .... 56 A3
Pentagon BH15 .... 202 B3
Pentagon The SO45 .... 151 D1
Pentere Rd PO8 .... 112 A3
Pentire Ave SO15 .... 78 B1
Pentire Way SO15 .... 78 B1
Pentland Cl SO45 .... 125 E1
Pentland Rise PO16 .... 132 B1
Penton Cl PO9 .... 158 A4
Penton Pl 8 SO23 .... 11 D3
Penton Rd SO21 .... 32 A4
Pentridge Way SO40 .... 100 C3
Penwood Gn 44 PO9 .... 136 A3
Peper Harow PO8 .... 112 A3

Peppard Cl SO18 .... 104 A4
Peppercorn Way SO30 .... 81 E2
Pepys Ave SO19 .... 104 B3
Pepys Cl Gosport PO12 .... 181 D1
Portsmouth PO4 .... 182 C2
Percival Rd PO2 .... 182 C4
Percy Cl SO45 .... 125 F3
Percy Rd Bournemouth BH5 ... 205 F2
Gosport PO12 .... 181 E2
Portsmouth PO4 .... 182 C2
Southampton SO16 .... 102 A4
Peregrine Cl SO40 .... 100 B3
Peregrine Rd BH23 .... 208 A3
Peregrines The PO16 .... 155 F4
Pergin Cres BH17 .... 202 A4
Pergin Way BH17 .... 202 A4
Pern Dr SO30 .... 106 A4
Peronne Cl PO3 .... 157 F3
Peronne Rd PO3 .... 157 F3
Perran Rd SO16 .... 77 E1
Perry Gdns BH15 .... 202 B1
Perry's Ct SO40 .... 102 A1
Perryfield Gdns BH7 .... 206 A4
Perrywood Cl SO45 .... 150 B2
Perrywood Gdns SO40 .... 100 A4
Perseus Pl PO7 .... 134 C2
Pershore Cl SO31 .... 129 D2
Persian Dr PO15 .... 129 D4
Persley Rd BH10 .... 189 F2
Perth Cl BH23 .... 191 F1
Perth House 31 PO1 .... 182 B3
Perth Rd Gosport PO13 .... 155 E2
Portsmouth PO4 .... 183 D2
Pervin Rd PO6 .... 157 F4
Pesthouse La SO32 .... 85 E2
Peter Ashley Activity Ctr
PO7 .... 134 B1
Peter Ashley Rd PO6 .... 134 B1
Peter Grant Way BH22 .... 165 E3
Peter Symonds' Coll SO22 ..... 1 C1
Peterborough Ct PO13 .... 180 B3
Peterborough Rd Cosham PO6 ... 133 F1
Southampton SO14 .... 103 D4
Peters Cl Locks Heath SO31 ... 128 C2
Upton BH16 .... 201 E3
Peters Rd SO31 .... 128 C2
Peterscroft Ave SO40 .... 100 A1
Petersfield Bsns Pk GU32 ..... 40 B2
Petersfield House 41 PO1 .... 182 B3
Petersfield Hospl GU32 .... 40 C2
Petersfield Inf Sch GU32 ..... 40 C2
Petersfield La PO8 .... 88 B4
Petersfield Pl BH7 .... 206 A4
Petersfield Rd
Bournemouth BH7 .... 206 A4
Buriton GU31 .... 65 E3
Cheriton SO24 .... 14 B2
Havant PO9 .... 136 A3
Winchester SO21, SO23 .... 11 E4
Petersfield Sch The GU32 ..... 40 C1
Petersfield Sta GU32 .... 40 C2
Petersgate Inf Sch PO8 .... 88 B2
Petersham Rd BH17 .... 202 A4
Petit Rd BH9 .... 190 A2
Petrie Rd PO13 .... 179 F1
Petticoat La SP5 .... 47 F4
Pettinger Gdns SO17 .... 103 E4
Petty Cl SO51 .... 53 D3
Pettycot Cres PO13 .... 155 D2
Petworth Gdns
Eastleigh SO50 .... 56 A3
Southampton SO16 .... 78 B3
Petworth Rd PO3 .... 183 D3
Petwyn Cl BH22 .... 166 A3
Pevensey Cl SO16 .... 77 E1
Peverell Rd BH16 .... 201 D2
Peverells Rd SO53 .... 55 F4
Peverells Wood Ave SO53 ..... 55 F4
Peverells Wood Cl SO53 .... 55 F3
Peveril Cl BH24 .... 139 F3
Peveril Rd SO19 .... 103 F2
Pewsey Pl SO15 .... 78 B1
Phelipps Rd BH21 .... 186 C3
Philip Rd PO7 .... 134 C3
Phillimore Rd SO16 .... 79 E2
Phillips Cl SO16 .... 77 F3
Philpott Dr SO40 .... 101 F1
Phoenix Bldgs PO3 .... 158 A1
Phoenix Cl SO31 .... 105 D1
Phoenix Park SO50 .... 56 B1
Phoenix Pru SO45 .... 149 F4
Phoenix Sq PO2 .... 157 F2
Phoenix Way PO13 .... 155 E1
Phyldon Cl BH12 .... 203 D3
Phyldon Rd BH12 .... 203 D3
Pickard Rd BH22 .... 165 F4
Pickering Cl BH18 .... 187 D1
Picket Cl SP6 .... 69 F1
Pickford Rd BH9 .... 189 F1
Pickwick Cl SO40 .... 100 A4
Pickwick House 13 PO1 ..... 182 B4
Picton House 53 PO5 .... 182 B2
Pier Head Rd PO2 .... 157 D1
Pier Rd PO1 .... 182 A2
Pier St PO13 .... 179 F1
Pig Shoot La BH23 .... 190 C3
Pigeon House La PO7 .... 133 E2
Pikes Hill SO43 .... 121 F3
Pikes Hill Ave SO43 .... 121 F3
Pilands Wood Rd SO31 ...... 127 F4
Pilchards Ave SO50 .... 57 D2
Pilford Heath Rd BH21 ...... 164 A4
Pilgrim Park Homes Cvn Pk
BH24 .... 141 E4
Pilgrim Pl SO18 .... 79 F2
Pilgrim's Cl BH25 .... 195 E2
Pilgrims Cl SO53 .... 55 D3

Pilgrims Gate SO22 .... 1 C1
Pilgrims Sch The SO23 .... 11 D4
Pilgrims Way
Broadstone BH17 .... 202 A4
Stubbington PO14 .... 179 D3
Pill Hill SP5 .... 24 A2
Pilley Bailey SO41 .... 174 A1
Pilley Gn SO41 .... 174 A1
Pilley Hill SO41 .... 173 F1
Pilley St SO41 .... 174 A1
Pilning Cl PO14 .... 154 B4
Pilot Hight Rd BH11 .... 189 D2
Pilsdon Dr BH17 .... 187 F2
Pimpern Cl BH17 .... 187 F1
Pimpernel Cl SO31 .... 128 C1
Pine Ave Bournemouth BH6 ... 206 B2
Poole BH13 .... 203 F3
Pine Cl Ashurst SO40 .... 100 B2
Barton on Sea BH25 .... 209 F4
Ferndown BH22 .... 165 E4
Hythe SO45 .... 125 F1
Landford SP5 .... 49 E1
North Baddesley SO52 .... 53 F3
Winchester SO21, SO22 .... 10 A2
Pine Cotts GU33 .... 21 D4
Pine Cres
Chandler's Ford SO53 .... 30 B1
Christchurch BH23 .... 208 C4
Pine Ct PO10 .... 136 C2
Pine Dr Clanfield PO8 .... 88 B3
Poole BH13 .... 203 F2
Southampton SO18 .... 104 B4
St Leonards BH24 .... 139 F2
Pine Dr E SO18 .... 104 C4
Pine Glen Ave BH22 .... 165 E4
Pine Gr PO9 .... 136 A1
Pine Grange 4 BH1 .... 205 D2
Pine House SO16 .... 78 C4
Pine Lodge 16 BH13 .... 214 C4
Pine Manor Rd BH24 .... 139 E3
Pine Mansions 3 BH1 .... 205 E2
Pine Park Mans 18 BH13 ... 204 A2
Pine Rd Alderholt SP6 .... 92 C3
Bishop's Waltham SO32 .... 83 E4
Bournemouth BH9 .... 205 D4
Broadstone BH21 .... 162 C1
Chandler's Ford SO53 .... 55 E4
Romsey SO51 .... 53 E3
Pine Tree Cl BH21 .... 163 E3
Pine Tree Gdns PO8 .... 112 A1
Pine Tree Glen BH4 .... 204 B3
Pine Trees Cl PO14 .... 154 B4
Pine View Cl Redlynch SP5 ..... 47 E2
Upton BH16 .... 201 E3
Pine View Rd BH31 .... 114 B4
Pine Way SO16 .... 78 C4
Pine Wlk Chilworth SO16 ...... 78 C4
Liss GU33 .... 21 D3
Locks Heath SO31 .... 129 D3
Verwood BH31 .... 115 D3
Pinebeach Ct BH13 .... 214 B4
Pinecliff Rd BH13 .... 214 D4
Pinecliffe Ave BH6 .... 206 B2
Pinecliffe Rd BH25 .... 209 E4
Pinefield Rd SO18 .... 79 F1
Pinegrove Rd SO19 .... 103 F2
Pineholt Cl BH24 .... 140 A3
Pinehurst
10 Milford on Sea SO41 .... 211 E2
13 Southampton SO17 .... 79 D1
Pinehurst Ave BH23 .... 207 F3
Pinehurst Cl PO7 .... 112 B1
Pinehurst Rd
Southampton SO16 .... 78 C4
West Moors BH22 .... 138 C1
Pinelands Cl SO16 .... 78 B2
Pinelands Rd SO16 .... 78 C4
Pines The Fordingbridge SP6 ..... 70 B1
Poole BH13 .... 204 A1
Portchester PO16 .... 132 A1
Southampton SO16 .... 78 A2
Pineside BH9 .... 205 D4
Pinesprings Dr BH18 .... 186 C1
Pinetops Cl SO41 .... 197 D2
Pinetree Wlk BH17 .... 201 F4
Pineview Cl SO31 .... 105 D1
Pinewood Gosport PO13 ...... 155 F1
Southampton SO16 .... 78 C3
Pinewood Ave
Bournemouth BH10 .... 189 E3
Havant PO9 .... 135 D2
Pinewood Cl
Bournemouth BH10 .... 189 E3
Christchurch BH23 .... 194 A1
Romsey SO51 .... 28 B1
Stubbington PO14 .... 154 B2
Upton BH16 .... 201 D4
Pinewood Cres SO45 .... 126 A1
Pinewood Dr SO45 .... 126 A1
Pinewood Gdns BH22 .... 165 E4
Pinewood Lodge 6 PO16 .... 131 D1
Pinewood Park SO19 .... 104 C3
Pinewood Rd
Christchurch BH23 .... 193 F1
Ferndown BH22 .... 165 E4
Hordle SO41 .... 195 F2
Poole BH13, BH16 .... 204 A1
St Leonards BH24 .... 139 F2
Upton BH16 .... 201 D4
Pink Rd PO2 .... 182 C4
Pinkney La SO43 .... 121 F2
Pinks Hill PO16 .... 131 E1
Pinsley Dr PO17 .... 133 D3
Pinto Cl PO15 .... 129 E4
Pipers Ash BH24 .... 141 E4
Pipers Cl SO40 .... 100 B3
Pipers Dr BH23 .... 208 A4

Pipers Mead PO8 .... 88 A3
Pipers Wood Ind Est PO7 ... 134 B4
Piping Cl SO21 .... 56 C4
Piping Gr 5 SO21 .... 56 C4
Piping Rd SO21 .... 56 C4
Pipit Cl Gosport PO12 .... 181 D4
Horndean PO8 .... 112 A3
Pippin Cl Christchurch BH23 ... 191 F1
6 Lymington SO41 .... 197 F1
Pirelli St SO15 .... 102 C2
Pirrie Cl SO15 .... 78 B1
Pit Hill La PO7 .... 86 C1
Pitcairn Mews PO4 .... 183 D1
Pitchponds Rd SO31 .... 152 B4
Pitcroft La SO31 .... 65 F3
Pitcroft Rd PO2 .... 157 E1
Pitmore Cl SO50 .... 56 A4
Pitmore La SO41 .... 172 B1
Pitmore Rd SO50 .... 56 A4
Pitmore Spcl Sch SO53 .... 55 F4
Pitreavie Rd PO6 .... 157 F3
Pitt Rd SO15 .... 102 B3
Pitt Rdbt SO22 .... 10 A3
Pitter Cl SO22 .... 1 A3
Pittmore Rd BH23 .... 192 B1
Pitts Deep La SO41 .... 199 E2
Pitts Pl BH25 .... 195 E1
Pitwines Cl BH15 .... 202 B1
Pitymoor La PO17 .... 133 D2
Place Cres PO7 .... 134 C3
Place House Cl PO15 .... 130 B1
Place La SO21 .... 31 F4
Plaitford Gr PO9 .... 135 E3
Plaitford Wlk SO16 .... 77 F1
Plant Park Rd BH24 .... 140 B1
Plantaganet Cres BH11 ...... 188 B3
Plantation Cl
Broadstone BH17 .... 187 E1
Lymington SO41 .... 197 E2
Plantation Ct
Christchurch BH23 .... 194 A1
Marchwood SO40 .... 101 F1
Plantation Dr
Christchurch BH23 .... 194 A1
Marchwood SO40 .... 101 F1
Plantation Rd
Broadstone BH17 .... 187 E1
Hill Brow GU33 .... 21 D1
West Wellow SO51 .... 74 B4
Plantation The SO32 .... 82 C1
Plants Cl SO51 .... 51 D1
Plassey Cres BH10 .... 189 E3
Platform Rd SO14 .... 103 D1
Platoff Rd SO41 .... 212 C4
Player Ct SP6 .... 69 F2
Players Cres SO40 .... 100 C3
Playfair Rd PO5 .... 182 B2
Playfields Dr BH12 .... 203 F3
Plaza Par 14 SO51 .... 52 C4
Pleasance Way BH25 .... 194 C2
Pleasant La PO10 .... 161 E1
Pleasant Rd PO4 .... 183 D2
Plecy Cl PO22 .... 165 E1
Plemont Cl BH12 .... 188 C1
Pless Rd SO41 .... 211 D3
Plough La SO32 .... 85 E1
Plough Way SO22 .... 10 B2
Plover Cl Southampton SO16 ... 78 C4
Stubbington PO14 .... 179 D3
Plover Dr SO41 .... 211 F2
Plover Rd SO40 .... 100 B4
Plover Reach PO4 .... 183 D3
Plovers Down SO22 .... 10 A2
Plovers Rd PO8 .... 112 A4
Plumer Rd BH17 .... 187 D1
Plumley Wlk PO9 .... 135 E4
Plumpton Gdns PO3 .... 158 A2
Plumpton Gr PO7 .... 112 A1
Plymouth Dr PO14 .... 154 A2
Plymouth St PO1 .... 182 B2
Pococks La GU33 .... 19 F4
Poets Way SO22 .... 10 B4
Pointout Cl SO16 .... 78 C2
Pointout Rd SO16 .... 78 C2
Pokesdown Prim Sch BH5 ... 206 A3
Pokesdown Sta BH7 .... 206 A3
Poles La Hursley SO21 .... 30 B3
Lymington SO41 .... 197 F1
Otterbourne SO21 .... 31 D2
Police Station La SO32 .... 61 D1
Police Training Ctr SO31 ..... 127 E2
Pollards Moor Rd SO40 .... 75 D1
Pollesden Cl SO53 .... 55 D4
Polygon Ct SO15 .... 102 C3
Polygon Sch (Annexe) The
SO16 .... 78 A2
Polygon Special Sch The
SO15 .... 102 C3
Polygon The SO15 .... 102 C3
Pomona Cl BH22 .... 165 E3
Pompey's La BH22 .... 165 D1
Pond Cl Marchwood SO40 ..... 101 F1
New Milton BH25 .... 195 D2
Pond Cotts GU32 .... 39 E1
Pond La PO8 .... 88 A3
Pond Piece PO7 .... 110 C2
Pond Rd SO31 .... 128 C3
Pondhead Cl SO45 .... 150 B2
Pondside Flats SO42 .... 148 C1
Pondside La
Bishop's Waltham SO32 .... 59 E1
Bishop's Waltham SO32 .... 83 E1
Ponsonby House 54 PO5 ..... 182 B2
Ponsonby Rd BH14 .... 203 E2
Pony Dr BH16 .... 201 E4
Pook La Fareham PO17 .... 131 E2
Havant PO9 .... 160 A4
Pooksgreen SO40 .... 101 D4
Poole Commerce Ctr BH12 ... 203 F3
Poole Gram Sch BH17 .... 187 E1

Poole High Sch BH15 ..... 202 B2
Poole Hill BH2 ..... 204 C2
Poole Hospl BH15 ..... 202 B2
Poole La BH11 ..... 189 D3
Poole Rd
  Bournemouth BH2, BH4 ..... 204 B2
  Poole BH12 ..... 204 A2
  Southampton SO19 ..... 103 F2
  Upton BH16, BH17 ..... 201 E4
  Wimborne Minster BH21 ..... 163 E2
Poole Sta BH15 ..... 202 B2
Popes La Totton SO40 ..... 100 C4
  Uppham SO32 ..... 58 B2
Popes Rd BH15 ..... 202 B3
Popham Ct PO9 ..... 135 E3
Poplar Cl Bransgore BH23 ..... 193 E4
  Christchurch BH23 ..... 209 D4
  6 Poole BH15 ..... 202 A1
  Wimborne Minster BH21 ..... 163 E3
Poplar Cres BH24 ..... 141 D4
Poplar Dr Fareham PO14 ..... 154 C4
  Marchwood SO40 ..... 101 E1
Poplar Gr PO11 ..... 185 D2
Poplar La BH23 ..... 193 E4
Poplar Rd New Milton BH25 ..... 195 E4
  Southampton SO19 ..... 103 F3
Poplar Way Hedge End SO30 ..... 105 E3
  North Baddesley SO52 ..... 53 F3
  Ringwood BH24 ..... 141 D4
Poplars The SO32 ..... 83 F2
Poppy Cl Christchurch BH23 ..... 208 B4
  Locks Heath SO31 ..... 128 C1
Poppy Rd SO16 ..... 79 E3
Poppyfields SO53 ..... 55 D3
Porchester Ct 12 BH1 ..... 205 D3
Porchester Pl BH8 ..... 205 D3
Porchester Rd
  Bournemouth BH8 ..... 205 D3
  Southampton SO19 ..... 103 F2
Porlock Rd SO16 ..... 77 E1
Port La Hursley SO21 ..... 30 B4
  Winchester SO23 ..... 10 A1
Port Royal St PO1 ..... 182 B3
Port Way PO6 ..... 157 D4
Portal Rd Bishopstoke SO50 ..... 56 B2
  Gosport PO13 ..... 155 E2
  Southampton SO19 ..... 104 A2
  Totton SO40 ..... 100 B4
  Winchester SO23 ..... 11 D3
Portarlington Cl BH2 ..... 204 B1
Portarlington Rd BH4 ..... 204 B1
Portchester Castle PO16 ..... 156 C3
Portchester Com Sch PO16 ..... 156 B4
Portchester La PO17 ..... 132 B2
Portchester Rd
  Portchester PO16 ..... 156 A4
  Portsmouth PO2 ..... 182 A4
Portchester Rise SO50 ..... 56 A4
Portchester Sch BH7 ..... 206 A4
Portchester Sta PO16 ..... 156 B4
Portcreek Cotts PO6 ..... 158 A3
Portelet Cl BH12 ..... 188 B1
Portelet House SO16 ..... 77 E2
Portelet Pl SO30 ..... 105 E3
Porter Rd BH17 ..... 202 A4
Porter's La SO14 ..... 102 C2
Porters La BH21 ..... 164 B3
Portersbridge St SO51 ..... 52 C4
Portesham Gdns BH9 ..... 190 A2
Portesham Way BH17 ..... 187 F2
Porteus Cres SO53 ..... 55 F3
Portfield Cl BH23 ..... 207 D4
Portfield Rd
  Christchurch BH23 ..... 207 D4
  Portsmouth PO3 ..... 158 A2
Portfield Sch
  Christchurch BH23 ..... 207 D3
  Christchurch BH23 ..... 207 D4
Portland Bldgs 5 PO12 ..... 181 E2
Portland Dr PO12 ..... 180 B2
Portland House 24 PO12 ..... 181 E2
Portland Rd
  Bournemouth BH9 ..... 205 D4
  Portsmouth PO5 ..... 182 B1
  Waterlooville PO7 ..... 134 C4
Portland Sq 5 GU33 ..... 20 C2
Portland St Fareham PO16 ..... 131 D1
  Portsmouth PO1 ..... 182 A3
  Southampton SO14 ..... 102 C2
Portland Terr
  27 Portsmouth PO5 ..... 182 B1
  Southampton SO14 ..... 102 C2
Portland's Cl GU31 ..... 41 D3
Portman Cres BH5 ..... 206 A2
Portman Rd BH7 ..... 205 F3
Portman Terr BH5 ..... 206 A2
Portobello Gr PO16 ..... 132 C1
Portsdown Ave BH6 ..... 158 B4
Portsdown Cty Prim Sch PO6 ..... 157 F4
Portsdown Hill Rd
  Cosham PO6 ..... 133 D1
  Havant PO9 ..... 135 D1
  Portchester PO17 ..... 132 B1
Portsdown Prim Sch PO6 ..... 157 F4
Portsdown Rd PO16 ..... 156 C4
Portsmouth Cath (CE) PO1 ..... 182 A3
Portsmouth Cath(RC) PO1 ..... 182 A2
Portsmouth Coll PO3 ..... 183 E4
Portsmouth Gram Sch PO1 ..... 182 A2
Portsmouth Harbour Sta PO1 ..... 181 F3
Portsmouth High Sch for Girls PO5 ..... 182 A1
Portsmouth High Sch for Girls(Juns) PO5 ..... 182 B1
Portsmouth Print Workshop PO1 ..... 182 B4

Portsmouth Rd
  Bursledon SO31 ..... 105 D1
  Colden Common SO50, SO21 ..... 57 E1
  Cosham PO6 ..... 157 F4
  Horndean PO8 ..... 112 A3
  Lee-on-the-Solent PO13 ..... 180 A2
  Southampton SO19, SO31 ..... 104 B1
  Waterlooville PO8 ..... 112 A3
Portsmouth & Southsea Sta PO1 ..... 182 B3
Portsview Ave PO16 ..... 132 C1
Portsview Gdns PO16 ..... 132 B1
Portswood Ave SO17 ..... 103 D4
Portswood Ctr 38 SO17 ..... 79 D1
Portswood Dr BH9 ..... 190 A2
Portswood Pk SO17 ..... 103 D4
Portswood Prim Sch SO17 ..... 79 E1
Portswood Rd Havant PO9 ..... 135 E3
  Portsmouth PO2 ..... 157 F3
  Southampton SO17 ..... 79 E1
Portuguese Fireplace SO43 ..... 120 C2
Portview Rd SO18 ..... 79 F1
Portway Cl SO18 ..... 104 A4
Portway La SO51 ..... 153 F3
Posbrook La PO14 ..... 153 F3
Posbrooke Rd PO4 ..... 183 D2
Post Office Bldgs BH9 ..... 204 C4
Post Office La 6 Poole BH15 ..... 202 B1
  St Leonards BH24 ..... 140 A3
Post Office Rd
  41 Bournemouth BH1 ..... 204 C2
  Waterlooville PO7 ..... 134 B3
Postern Cl PO16 ..... 156 B4
Postern Ct 14 SO14 ..... 102 C2
Potash Terr 6 PO9 ..... 135 F1
Potterdale House 17 PO6 ..... 133 D1
Potteries The PO16 ..... 131 D2
Potterne Way BH21 ..... 115 D2
Potters Ave PO16 ..... 131 D2
Potters Field GU33 ..... 21 D2
Potters Heron Cl SO51 ..... 29 F2
Potters Heron La SO51 ..... 29 F2
Potters Way BH14 ..... 203 E1
Pottery Rd BH14 ..... 203 D1
Poulner Cl SO19 ..... 104 A1
Poulner Ct PO9 ..... 135 E3
Poulner Hill BH24 ..... 141 F4
Poulner Inf & Jun Schs BH24 ..... 117 E1
Poulner Mobile Home Pk BH24 ..... 117 E1
Poulner Pk BH24 ..... 117 E1
Pound Cl Gosport PO13 ..... 180 B4
  Poole BH15 ..... 202 C3
  Ringwood BH24 ..... 141 D4
Pound Cotts SO32 ..... 61 E3
Pound Gate Dr PO14 ..... 153 E2
Pound La Ampfield SO51 ..... 29 D1
  Ashurst SO40 ..... 100 C2
  Bournemouth BH10 ..... 189 E3
  Burley BH24 ..... 142 C1
  Cadnam SO40 ..... 75 E1
  3 Christchurch BH23 ..... 207 D3
  Damerham SP6 ..... 68 A3
  Meonstoke SO32 ..... 61 E3
  North Baddesley SO51 ..... 29 D1
  Plaitford SO51 ..... 50 B3
  Poole BH15 ..... 202 C3
  Sherfield English SO51 ..... 25 F1
Pound Lea PO14 ..... 185 D3
Pound St Bursledon SO31 ..... 104 C1
  Kings Worthy SO23 ..... 2 B4
  Lymington SO41 ..... 197 D1
Pound St SO18 ..... 104 A4
Pound Tree Rd SO14 ..... 103 D2
Pounds Terr PO1 ..... 182 A3
Powell Cres SO40 ..... 100 C3
Powell Rd BH14 ..... 203 D2
Powell Sq 11 PO1 ..... 182 A3
Power Rd PO1 ..... 182 C3
Powerscourt Rd
  Barton on Sea BH25 ..... 209 F4
  Portsmouth PO2 ..... 182 C4
Powis Cl BH25 ..... 195 D2
Powlett Rd SO41 ..... 197 F2
Poyner Cl PO16 ..... 131 D1
Poynings Pl PO1 ..... 182 A2
Precosa Rd SO30 ..... 105 F3
Precinct The 10 PO7 ..... 134 C4
Premier Ctr The SO51 ..... 53 E3
Premier Par SO18 ..... 79 F2
Premier Way SO51 ..... 53 E3
Preshaw Cl SO16 ..... 78 B2
Preshaw Est SO32 ..... 35 D2
Presseys Cnr SP6 ..... 93 D4
Preston Cl BH16 ..... 201 E4
Preston La BH23 ..... 192 B2
Preston Rd Poole BH15 ..... 202 B3
  Portsmouth PO2 ..... 182 C4
Preston Way BH23 ..... 208 B4
Prestwood Cl BH25 ..... 194 C1
Prestwood Rd SO30 ..... 105 E3
Pretoria Rd Hedge End SO30 ..... 105 D3
  Portsmouth PO4 ..... 182 C2
Prettyjohn House PO4 ..... 183 D1
Pricketts Hill PO17 ..... 108 A3
Prideaux-Brune Ave PO13 ..... 155 E2
Priest Croft SO45 ..... 150 C1
Priest Croft Dr SO45 ..... 150 C1
Priest La PO17 ..... 192 A4
Priestlands SO51 ..... 52 C4
Priestlands Cl SO40 ..... 100 A3
Priestlands La SO41 ..... 197 E2
Priestlands Pl SO41 ..... 197 E2
Priestlands Rd SO41 ..... 197 E2
Priestlands Sec Sch SO41 ..... 197 E1
Priestley Cl SO40 ..... 100 B4

Priestley Rd BH10 ..... 189 D1
Priestwood Cl SO18 ..... 104 B4
Primate Rd PO14 ..... 129 E1
Primrose Cl Gosport PO13 ..... 155 E3
  Hedge End SO30 ..... 105 E3
  North Baddesley SO52 ..... 54 C2
Primrose Ct PO7 ..... 135 D3
Primrose Gdns BH17 ..... 186 C1
Primrose La Rake GU33 ..... 21 E2
  Redlynch SP5 ..... 47 E3
Primrose Rd SO16 ..... 79 D2
Primrose Terr SO32 ..... 59 E1
Primrose Way
  Christchurch BH23 ..... 208 B4
  Corfe Mullen BH21 ..... 186 C4
  Locks Heath SO31 ..... 128 C1
  Romsey SO51 ..... 28 B1
Prince Albert Rd PO4 ..... 183 D2
Prince Alfred St PO12 ..... 181 D2
Prince George St PO1 ..... 182 A3
Prince George's St PO9 ..... 135 F1
Prince of Wales Ave SO15 ..... 102 A4
Prince of Wales Cl PO7 ..... 135 D4
Prince of Wales Rd
  Bournemouth BH4 ..... 204 B2
  3 Poole PO12 ..... 181 E2
Prince Rd Gosport PO14 ..... 154 C3
  Rownhams SO16 ..... 77 F3
Prince Regent 45 PO5 ..... 182 B2
Prince William Ct 8 SO50 ..... 56 C1
Prince's Bldgs 10 SO23 ..... 11 D4
Prince's Mead Sch SO22 ..... 10 C3
Prince's Pl New Milton BH25 ..... 195 E2
  Portsmouth PO1 ..... 182 B4
Prince's Rd SO51 ..... 52 C4
Prince's St Portsmouth PO1 ..... 182 B4
  Southampton SO14 ..... 103 E3
Princes Cl
  Bishop's Waltham SO32 ..... 83 D4
  Redlynch SP5 ..... 47 F4
Princes Cotts GU33 ..... 63 E4
Princes Cres SO43 ..... 122 A3
Princes Ct Lyndhurst SO43 ..... 122 A3
  6 Poole BH12 ..... 204 A2
  2 Southampton SO14 ..... 103 E3
Princes Dr PO7 ..... 112 A1
Princes Hill SP5 ..... 47 F4
Princes House 3 SO14 ..... 103 E3
Princes Pl SO23 ..... 10 C3
Princes Rd Ferndown BH22 ..... 165 E3
  Petersfield GU32 ..... 40 B2
  Southampton SO15 ..... 102 B3
Princess Anne Hospl SO16 ..... 78 A2
Princess Ave BH23 ..... 207 D3
Princess Cl SO30 ..... 80 C1
Princess Ct 7 SO23 ..... 11 D4
Princess Gdns PO8 ..... 112 B4
Princess Rd Ashurst SO40 ..... 100 A1
  Bournemouth BH4 ..... 204 A2
  Poole BH12 ..... 204 A2
Pringles Cl BH22 ..... 165 F3
Pringles Dr BH22 ..... 165 F3
Prinstead Cl 7 SO23 ..... 11 D3
Prinstead Cres PO6 ..... 158 B4
Prinsted La SO21 ..... 161 E4
Prinsted Wlk PO14 ..... 154 B4
Priors Barton SO23 ..... 10 C3
Priors Cl Christchurch BH23 ..... 208 B4
  Southbourne PO10 ..... 137 F1
Priors Dean Rd SO22 ..... 1 B2
Priors Hill La SO31 ..... 127 F1
Priors Leaze La PO18 ..... 137 F1
Priors Rd BH17 ..... 202 A4
Priors Way SO22 ..... 10 A2
Priors Wlk 6 BH21 ..... 163 D3
Priorsdean Ave PO3 ..... 183 D3
Priorsdean Cres PO9 ..... 135 E2
Priory Ave SO17 ..... 79 E1
Priory CE Prim Sch The BH23 ..... 207 D3
Priory Cl
  Bishop's Waltham SO32 ..... 83 D4
  Southampton SO17 ..... 79 E1
Priory Cres PO4 ..... 183 D2
Priory Ct
  Bishop's Waltham SO32 ..... 83 D4
  Portchester PO6 ..... 156 C4
  2 Portsmouth PO5 ..... 182 C2
Priory Gdns Portchester PO16 ..... 156 B4
  Waterlooville PO7 ..... 111 F1
  West Moors BH22 ..... 166 A4
Priory House
  Christchurch BH23 ..... 207 E3
  16 Southampton SO14 ..... 103 D3
Priory Ind Pk BH23 ..... 208 A4
Priory Quay BH23 ..... 207 E3
Priory Rd Bournemouth BH2 ..... 204 C1
  Eastleigh SO50 ..... 55 F1
  Fareham PO15, PO17 ..... 130 B1
  Gosport PO12 ..... 181 D4
  Netley SO31 ..... 127 D3
  Portsmouth PO4 ..... 183 D1
  Southampton SO17 ..... 103 E4
  West Moors BH22 ..... 166 A4
Priory Sec Sch PO5 ..... 182 C2
Priory View 5 BH23 ..... 207 D3
Priory View Pl BH9 ..... 190 A2
Priory View Rd
  Bournemouth BH9 ..... 190 A2
  Burton BH23 ..... 192 B1
Private Rd SO41 ..... 197 F3
Privet Rd BH9 ..... 204 C4
Privett House PO1 ..... 182 A3
Privett Pl PO12 ..... 180 C2
Privett Rd Fareham PO15 ..... 130 B1
  Froxfield GU32 ..... 18 C1
  Gosport PO12 ..... 180 C2
  Waterlooville PO7 ..... 134 C2

Prochurch Rd PO8 ..... 112 A2
Proctor Cl SO19 ..... 104 B3
Proctor Dr SO52 ..... 53 F2
Proctor La PO1 ..... 182 C3
Promenade BH2 ..... 208 A3
Promenade Ct 4 PO13 ..... 179 F1
Promenade The
  Emsworth PO10 ..... 160 C4
  Hythe SO45 ..... 126 A3
  19 Portsmouth PO1 ..... 157 E1
Prospect La PO9 ..... 136 A3
Prospect Pl
  Chandler's Ford SO50 ..... 55 F3
  Hythe SO45 ..... 126 A3
Prospect Rd PO1 ..... 182 B4
Prosperous St 15 BH15 ..... 202 B1
Provene Cl SO32 ..... 83 F2
Provene Gdns SO32 ..... 83 F2
Providence Ct 8 PO1 ..... 182 B4
Providence Hill SO31 ..... 105 D3
Provost St SP6 ..... 69 F1
Pruetts La GU33 ..... 20 C1
Prunus Cl Ferndown BH22 ..... 165 D4
  Southampton SO16 ..... 78 B3
Prunus Dr BH22 ..... 165 D4
Pudbrook House SO30 ..... 106 A3
Pudbrooke Gdns SO30 ..... 105 D4
Pudding La SO23 ..... 2 A3
Puddletown Cres BH17 ..... 187 F1
Puffin Cl SO16 ..... 78 A3
Puffin Cres PO14 ..... 154 A2
Puffin Gdns PO13 ..... 155 D2
Puffin Wlk PO8 ..... 111 E2
Pug's Hole SP5 ..... 4 A3
Pulens Cl GU31 ..... 41 E2
Pulens La GU31 ..... 41 D2
Pullman Ct BH22 ..... 138 B1
Pullman Way BH24 ..... 141 D3
Pump La PO13 ..... 155 E1
Pundle Green Est SO40 ..... 99 D3
Punsholt La SO24 ..... 16 C3
Purbeck Ave BH15 ..... 201 F1
Purbeck Cl BH16 ..... 201 E4
Purbeck Ct
  Bournemouth BH5 ..... 206 A2
  3 Christchurch BH23 ..... 207 F4
Purbeck Dr Fareham PO14 ..... 154 B4
  Verwood BH31 ..... 114 C3
Purbeck Hts BH14 ..... 203 D3
Purbeck Rd
  Barton on Sea BH25 ..... 209 E4
  Bournemouth BH2 ..... 204 C1
Purbeck St PO1 ..... 182 A3
Purbeck Wlk PO14 ..... 154 B4
Purbrook Chase Prec PO7 ..... 134 C2
Purbrook Cl SO16 ..... 78 B2
Purbrook Gdns PO7 ..... 134 B3
Purbrook Heath Rd PO7 ..... 134 A3
Purbrook House PO7 ..... 134 B3
Purbrook Inf Sch PO7 ..... 134 B3
Purbrook Jun Sch PO7 ..... 134 B3
Purbrook Park Sec Sch PO7 ..... 134 B2
Purbrook Rd PO1 ..... 182 C3
Purbrook Way PO9 ..... 135 E3
Purcell Cl PO7 ..... 134 C3
Purcell Rd SO19 ..... 104 B2
Purchase Rd BH12 ..... 204 B4
Purewell BH23 ..... 207 E3
Purewell Cl BH23 ..... 207 F3
Purewell Cross BH23 ..... 207 F3
Purewell Cross Rd BH23 ..... 207 E4
Purewell Ct 11 BH23 ..... 207 F4
Purkess Cl SO53 ..... 55 E4
Purkiss Cl SO40 ..... 99 E3
Purley Way SO51 ..... 50 A2
Purrocks The GU32 ..... 40 C3
Purvis Gdns SO19 ..... 104 A1
Pussex La BH23 ..... 191 D4
Putmans La GU31 ..... 66 C4
Pycroft Cl
  North Hayling PO11 ..... 160 B2
  Southampton SO19 ..... 104 A3
Pye Cl BH21 ..... 186 C4
Pye Cnr BH21 ..... 163 D2
Pye La BH21 ..... 91 F3
Pye St PO1 ..... 182 B3
Pylands La SO31 ..... 105 D2
Pyle Cl PO8 ..... 112 A2
Pylewell Rd SO45 ..... 126 A2
Pyramid Ctr PO3 ..... 158 A2
Pyramids L Ctr The PO5 ..... 182 B1
Pyrford Cl Gosport PO12 ..... 180 C2
  Waterlooville PO7 ..... 111 F1
Pyrford Gdns 1 SO41 ..... 197 F1
Pyrford Mews SO41 ..... 197 F1
Pytchley Cl PO14 ..... 179 D3

Quadra Point PO3 ..... 158 A2
Quadrangle The
  Eastleigh SO50 ..... 56 A2
  North Baddesley SO51 ..... 53 E3
Quadrant SP6 ..... 93 F4
Quail Way PO8 ..... 112 A3
Quaker Ct BH24 ..... 140 C2
Quantock Ct 7 BH23 ..... 207 F4
Quantock Rd SO16 ..... 101 F4
Quantocks The SO45 ..... 125 E1
Quarely Rd PO9 ..... 135 D3
Quarr House SO41 ..... 172 A4
Quarry Chase 7 BH4 ..... 204 B2
Quarry Cl PO14 ..... 164 A4
Quarry Dr BH21 ..... 164 A4
Quarry Rd
  Wimborne Minster BH21 ..... 164 A4
  Winchester SO23 ..... 11 E4
Quarterdeck Ave PO2 ..... 157 D1
Quarterjack Mews 2 BH21 ..... 163 E2
Quartremaine Rd PO3 ..... 158 A2

Quavey Rd SP5 ..... 47 F3
Quay Haven SO31 ..... 128 A4
Quay Hill SO41 ..... 197 F2
Quay House SO41 ..... 128 A1
Quay La Gosport PO12 ..... 181 F2
  Gosport, Elson PO12 ..... 156 A1
Quay Point 20 BH15 ..... 202 B1
Quay Rd Christchurch BH23 ..... 207 D3
  Lymington SO41 ..... 197 F2
Quay St Fareham PO16 ..... 131 E1
  Lymington SO41 ..... 197 F2
Quay The Hamble-le-Rice SO31 ..... 128 A1
  Poole BH15 ..... 202 B1
Quayle Dr BH11 ..... 188 C3
Quayside SO18 ..... 103 E4
Quayside Commerce Ctr PO16 ..... 155 D4
Quayside Rd Fawley SO45 ..... 151 F1
  Southampton SO18 ..... 103 E4
Quayside Wlk SO40 ..... 101 F2
Quebec Gdns SO31 ..... 104 C1
Queen Alexandra Hospl PO6 ..... 157 F4
Queen Anne Dr BH21 ..... 187 F4
Queen Anne's Dr PO9 ..... 135 E1
Queen Elizabeth Ave SO41 ..... 197 E2
Queen Elizabeth Ct
  Southampton SO17 ..... 79 E2
  Wimborne Minster BH21 ..... 163 D2
Queen Elizabeth Cty Pk GU31 ..... 65 D2
Queen Elizabeth's Sch BH21 ..... 162 C3
Queen Katherine Rd SO41 ..... 197 F2
Queen Mary Ave BH9 ..... 189 F1
Queen Mary Rd PO16 ..... 156 B4
Queen Rd PO14 ..... 154 C3
Queen St Emsworth PO10 ..... 161 D4
  Lymington SO41 ..... 197 E2
  Portsmouth PO1 ..... 182 A3
  Twyford SO21 ..... 31 F3
  Woodgreen SP6 ..... 47 D1
Queen's Ave BH23 ..... 207 D3
Queen's Cl SO51 ..... 53 D4
Queen's Cres PO5 ..... 182 B2
Queen's Ct SO15 ..... 102 C3
Queen's Gr PO5 ..... 182 B2
Queen's Inclosure Prim Sch PO7 ..... 112 A1
Queen's Par Lyndhurst SO43 ..... 122 A3
  8 Waterlooville PO7 ..... 134 C4
Queen's Park Ave BH8 ..... 205 E4
Queen's Park Gdns BH8 ..... 205 E4
Queen's Park Rd BH8 ..... 205 E4
Queen's Park S Dr BH8 ..... 205 E4
Queen's Park W Dr BH8 ..... 205 E4
Queen's Pl 32 PO5 ..... 182 B2
Queen's Rd
  Bournemouth BH4 ..... 204 B2
  Chandler's Ford SO53 ..... 30 B1
  Christchurch BH23 ..... 207 F3
  Corfe Mullen BH21 ..... 186 B3
  Fareham PO16 ..... 131 D1
  Gosport PO12 ..... 181 E2
  Locks Heath SO31 ..... 152 B4
  Poole BH14 ..... 203 E2
  Portsmouth PO1 ..... 181 F3
  Southampton SO15 ..... 78 B1
  Waterlooville PO7 ..... 111 F1
  Winchester SO23 ..... 10 B1
Queen's Terr SO14 ..... 103 D2
Queen's Way Portsmouth PO5 ..... 182 B2
  Southampton SO14 ..... 103 D2
Queens Cl Hythe SO45 ..... 126 A2
  Lee-on-the-Solent PO13 ..... 179 F1
  West Moors BH22 ..... 138 B1
Queens Cres Horndean PO8 ..... 112 B4
  Stubbington BH24 ..... 154 B2
Queens Ct
  5 Bournemouth BH4 ..... 204 B2
  Bournemouth, Charminster BH9 ..... 205 D4
  New Milton BH25 ..... 195 E2
Queens Gdns
  Bournemouth BH2 ..... 204 B2
  Fordingbridge SP6 ..... 69 F1
Queens Gr New Milton BH25 ..... 195 E2
  Waterlooville PO7 ..... 134 B3
Queens House 15 SO14 ..... 103 D2
Queens Keep 17 PO5 ..... 182 B1
Queens Mead SO22 ..... 10 B3
Queens Par PO12 ..... 180 C2
Queens Rd Ferndown BH22 ..... 165 E4
  Lee-on-the-Solent PO13 ..... 179 F1
  Lyndhurst SO43 ..... 122 A3
  Petersfield GU32 ..... 40 B2
Queens Ride SO52 ..... 53 F2
Queens View SO31 ..... 127 D3
Queens Wa BH24 ..... 141 D4
Queensbury Mansions 7 BH1 ..... 205 D2
Queensland Rd BH5 ..... 206 A3
Queensmead 4 BH21 ..... 163 E3
Queenstown Rd SO15 ..... 102 B3
Queensway
  New Milton BH25 ..... 194 C2
  North Hayling PO11 ..... 160 A2
Queensway The PO16 ..... 156 A4
Queenswood Ave BH8 ..... 190 C1
Queenswood Dr BH22 ..... 165 E4
Querida Cl SO31 ..... 128 B4
Quilter Cl SO19 ..... 104 B2
Quince La BH21 ..... 163 F3
Quinton Cl Christchurch BH23 ..... 208 C4
  Portsmouth PO1 ..... 182 B2
Quintrell Ave PO16 ..... 156 A4

Quob La SO30 .... 80 C2
Quomp The BH24 .... 141 D4

R L Stevenson Ave BH4 ...... 204 A2
Racecourse View SO43 .... 121 F3
Rachel Cl SO50 .... 57 C1
Rachel Madocks Sch PO8 .... 111 E2
Racton Ave PO6 .... 158 A4
Racton Rd PO10 .... 136 C2
Radcliffe Ct 9 SO14 .... 103 E4
Radcliffe Rd SO14 .... 103 D3
Radclyffe Rd PO16 .... 131 E1
Radipole Rd BH17 .... 188 A1
Radley Cl SO30 .... 81 E1
Radnor St PO5 .... 182 B2
Radstock Rd SO19 .... 103 F2
Radway Cres SO15 .... 102 B4
Radway Rd SO15 .... 78 C1
Raeburn Cl SO24 .... 14 B3
Raeburn Dr SO30 .... 105 E4
Raglan Cl SO53 .... 55 D2
Raglan Ct 3 Eastleigh SO50 .... 56 A3
Gosport PO12 .... 181 D2
Locks Heath SO31 .... 129 D3
Raglan Gdns BH11 .... 189 D1
Raglan St PO1 .... 182 B3
Raglan Terr PO10 .... 137 D1
Ragmore La GU32 .... 18 C3
Rails La PO11 .... 185 E1
Railway Cotts
Southampton SO15 .... 101 E4
West Meon GU32 .... 37 E2
West Tisted GU34 .... 17 E3
Railway Flats PO1 .... 182 C3
Railway Terr SO42 .... 172 C4
Railway Triangle Ind Est PO6 .... 158 A3
Railway View PO1 .... 182 B3
Railway View Rd SO17 ...... 103 E4
Rainbow Pl SO15 .... 102 B3
Rake Bsns Pk GU33 .... 21 F2
Rake CE Prim Sch GU33 .... 21 F3
Rake Rd GU33 .... 21 D2
Raleigh Cl Christchurch BH23 .... 207 F3
New Milton BH25 .... 194 C2
Ringwood BH24 .... 141 E4
Raleigh House 25 PO1 ...... 182 A3
Raleigh Rd BH12 .... 188 C1
Raleigh Wlk PO13 .... 180 B3
Raley Rd SO31 .... 129 D1
Ralph La SO51 .... 28 A1
Ralph Rd BH21 .... 186 C4
Ramalley La SO53 .... 55 D4
Rambler Dr PO13 .... 180 B3
Ramblers Way PO7 .... 112 B1
Ramillies House
11 Fareham PO14 .... 154 C4
15 Gosport PO12 .... 181 E2
Ramley Rd SO41 .... 197 D2
Rampart Gdns PO3 .... 157 F3
Rampart Rd SO18 .... 103 E4
Rampart Row PO12 .... 181 F2
Rampart The SO41 .... 197 E3
Rams Wlk GU32 .... 40 C2
Ramsay Pl PO13 .... 155 E1
Ramsay Rd Kings Worthy SO23 .... 2 B4
South Hayling PO11 .... 185 D2
Ramsdale Ave PO9 .... 135 E3
Ramsdean Rd GU32 .... 39 F1
Ramshill GU31 .... 41 D2
Rances Way SO22 .... 10 C3
Randall Cl SO40 .... 76 B1
Randall Rd SO53 .... 30 B1
Randall's La BH24 .... 142 C3
Randalls Hill BH16 .... 186 A1
Randolph Rd
2 Bournemouth BH1 .... 205 F2
Poole BH14 .... 203 E3
Portsmouth PO2 .... 157 F1
Randolph St SO15 .... 102 B4
Ranelagh Ct
Christchurch BH23 .... 208 C4
8 Southampton SO17 ...... 103 C4
Ranelagh Gdns SO15 ...... 102 C4
Ranelagh Rd
Christchurch BH23 .... 208 C4
Havant PO9 .... 135 E1
Portsmouth PO2 .... 157 E1
Range Gdns SO19 .... 104 A2
Range Gn PO2 .... 157 E2
Ranmore Ct SO45 .... 125 E2
Rannoch Cl PO15 .... 130 C2
Ransome Cl PO14 .... 153 F4
Ranvilles Jun & Inf
Schs PO14 .... 154 B4
Ranvilles La PO14 .... 154 A4
Rapson Cl PO6 .... 133 E1
Rareridge La SO32 .... 83 F4
Ratcliffe Rd Hedge End SO30 .... 105 E4
Hythe SO45 .... 125 F1
Rattigan Gdns PO15 .... 129 E4
Ravana Ct 4 BH8 .... 205 D3
Raven Cl PO13 .... 180 B3
Raven Croft 30 PO5 .... 182 B2
Raven Rd SO14 .... 103 D3
Raven Sq SO50 .... 55 E1
Raven Way BH23 .... 208 A3
Ravens Cl PO14 .... 179 C3
Ravens Way SO41 .... 211 E2
Ravenscourt Rd
Bournemouth BH6 .... 206 B3
Lymington SO41 .... 197 E1
Ravenscroft Cl SO41 ...... 104 C1
Ravenscroft Way SO32 .... 81 F1
Ravensdale Cl BH12 .... 203 E3
Ravenshall BH2 .... 204 B1

Ravenswood PO14 .... 129 E2
Ravenswood Gdns 6 PO5 .... 182 B1
Ravine Ct BH13 .... 214 C4
Ravine Gdns 5 BH13 ...... 214 C4
Ravine Rd Bournemouth BH5 .... 206 A2
Poole BH13 .... 214 C4
Raymond Cl Holbury SO45 .... 150 B2
Verwood BH31 .... 115 D3
West End SO30 .... 80 C2
Raymond Rd Portchester PO6 .. 132 C1
Southampton SO15 .... 102 B4
Rayners Gdns SO16 .... 79 E2
Raynes Rd PO13 .... 180 A2
Reading Room La SO32 .... 106 B4
Readon Cl GU31 .... 41 D2
Readon House GU31 .... 41 D2
Rebbeck Rd BH7 .... 206 A3
Recess The SO50 .... 56 A3
Record Rd PO10 .... 136 C1
Recreation Cotts SO51 ...... 50 C2
Recreation Rd BH12 .... 203 F3
Rectory Ave BH21 .... 162 B1
Rectory Cl Gosport PO12 .... 181 D1
Stubbington PO14 .... 154 B2
Rectory Ct SO30 .... 105 F4
Rectory Hill SP5 .... 3 E2
Rectory La Breamore SP6 .... 46 A1
Meonstoke SO32 .... 61 E3
Rectory Rd Havant PO9 .... 159 F4
Poole BH15 .... 202 B3
Red Barn Ave PO17 .... 132 B1
Red Barn Cty Prim Sch PO16 .. 156 B4
Red Barn La PO15, PO16 .... 130 C2
Red Hill Cres SO53 .... 78 C2
Red Hill Way SO16 .... 78 C2
Red Horn Cl BH16 .... 201 E2
Red House Mews SO41 .... 197 F2
Red La
Compton(Hants) SO21 ...... 31 F4
Corfe Mullen BH21 .... 186 A4
Owslebury SO21 .... 58 A3
West Tytherley SP5 .... 4 A4
Red Leaves SO32 .... 83 F1
Red Lodge SO53 .... 55 D2
Red Lodge Sch SO16 .... 78 C2
Red Oaks Cl BH22 .... 165 D4
Red Roofs BH22 .... 165 F2
Redan Cl BH23 .... 208 C4
Redan The PO12 .... 181 E1
Redbreast Rd BH9 .... 190 A2
Redbreast Rd N BH9 ...... 190 A2
Redbridge Com Sch SO16 .... 101 D4
Redbridge Flyover SO15 .... 101 E4
Redbridge Gr PO9 .... 135 E2
Redbridge Hill SO16 .... 77 F1
Redbridge La SO16 .... 77 E2
Redbridge Prim Sch SO16 .... 101 D4
Redbridge Rd SO15 .... 101 E4
Redbridge Sta SO15 ...... 101 E4
Redbridge Towers SO16 .... 101 E4
Redcar Ave PO3 .... 158 A1
Redcar St SO15 .... 102 A4
Redcliffe Cl BH23 .... 192 B2
Redcote Cl SO18 .... 104 A4
Redcotts La BH21 .... 163 D3
Redcotts Rd BH21 .... 163 D3
Redcourt SO16 .... 78 C2
Redcroft La SO31 .... 105 D1
Redfords The SO40 .... 76 C1
Redhill Ave BH9 .... 189 F2
Redhill Cl
Bournemouth BH10 ...... 189 F2
Southampton SO16 .... 78 C2
Redhill Cres BH9 .... 189 F2
Redhill Ct
Bournemouth BH10 ...... 189 F2
Bournemouth BH9 .... 190 A2
Redhill Dr BH10 .... 189 F2
Redhill House 55 PO1 ...... 182 B3
Redhill Rd PO9 .... 113 D1
Redhill Rdbt BH10 .... 189 F2
Redhoave Rd BH17 .... 187 F1
Redhouse Park Gdns PO12 .. 180 C4
Redlands BH12 .... 203 F3
Redlands Dr SO19 .... 103 F3
Redlands Gr PO4 .... 183 E2
Redlands La Emsworth PO10 .. 136 C2
Fareham PO16, PO14 ...... 154 C4
Redlands Prim Sch PO16 .... 155 D4
Redlynch CE Sch SP5 ...... 48 A3
Redmans View BH31 .... 114 C3
Redmoor Cl SO19 .... 103 F3
Rednal House 23 PO1 ...... 182 B3
Redoubt Ct PO14 .... 154 C3
Redrise Cl SO45 .... 150 B2
Redsails BH13 .... 214 A4
Redshank Cl BH17 .... 186 C1
Redshank Rd PO8 .... 112 A4
Redvers Cl SO41 .... 197 E1
Redvers Rd BH23 .... 207 F4
Redward Rd SO16 .... 77 F3
Redwing Ct PO4 .... 183 E3
Redwing Gdns SO40 .... 100 B4
Redwing Rd PO8 .... 88 B2
Redwood Cl Hythe SO45 .... 125 E2
Lymington SO41 .... 197 E3
Ringwood BH24 .... 141 D4
West End SO30 .... 80 B1
Redwood Ct 3 PO7 .... 134 C4
Redwood Dr Ferndown BH22 .. 165 E4
Portchester PO16 .... 156 A4
Redwood Gdns SO40 ...... 100 B4
Redwood Gr PO9 .... 136 A2
Redwood Lodge 4 PO16 .... 131 D1

Redwood Rd BH16 .... 201 D4
Redwood Way SO16 .... 79 D3
Reed Dr SO40 .... 100 C4
Reedmace Cl PO7 .... 135 D3
Reeds La Liss GU33 .... 21 E3
Rake GU33 .... 21 E3
Reeds Meadow GU32 .... 39 E2
Reeds Pl PO12 .... 181 D3
Reeds Rd PO12 .... 181 D4
Reeves Cl SO51 .... 50 C2
Reeves Way SO31 .... 104 C1
Regal Cl PO6 .... 157 F4
Regency Ct PO9 .... 159 F4
Regency Gdns PO7 .... 134 B3
Regency Pl BH24 .... 141 D4
Regent Cl SO21 .... 31 E2
Regent Ct
24 Southampton SO17 ...... 79 C1
17 Winchester SO23 .... 2 A1
Regent Dr BH7 .... 205 F4
Regent House SO30 .... 81 E2
Regent Mews GU32 .... 40 B2
Regent Pl PO5 .... 182 A2
Regent Rd SO53 .... 55 E3
Regent St Portsmouth PO1 .. 182 B3
Southampton SO14 .... 102 C2
Regent Way BH23 .... 207 D3
Regent's Gr 1 SO15 ...... 102 A4
Regent's Park Gdns SO15 .. 102 A4
Regent's Park Rd SO15 .... 102 A4
Regents Ct 6 SO16 .... 102 A4
Regents Gate SO31 .... 128 C3
Regents Park Girls
Sch SO16 .... 102 A4
Reginald Rd PO4 .... 183 D2
Reid St BH23 .... 207 D4
Reigate House 54 PO1 ...... 182 B3
Relay Rd PO7 .... 134 B4
Reldas The PO1 .... 182 A2
Reliant Cl SO53 .... 55 D3
Rempstone Rd BH21 ...... 187 E4
Renault Dr BH18 .... 187 D1
Renda Rd SO45 .... 150 B2
Renny Rd PO1 .... 182 C3
Renouf Cl SO41 .... 197 E2
Renown Cl SO53 .... 55 D3
Renown Gdns PO8 .... 111 F3
Renown House 14 PO12 .... 181 E2
Repton Cl PO12 .... 180 C2
Repton Gdns SO30 .... 81 E1
Reservoir La
Hedge End SO30 .... 105 D3
Petersfield GU32 .... 40 C3
Resolution House 13 PO12 .. 181 E2
Rest-a-Wyle Ave PO11 .... 185 D3
Restharrow BH1, ... 205 D2
Retreat Rd BH21 .... 163 E2
Retreat The Eastleigh SO50 .. 56 A2
Portsmouth PO5 .... 182 B2
Totton SO40 .... 101 D3
Revenge Ct PO4 .... 183 E3
Revenge House 12 PO12 .... 181 E2
Rewlands Dr SO22 .... 1 B2
Rex Est SO53 .... 55 E3
Reynard Ct BH15 .... 202 C2
Reynolds Cl SO53 .... 53 D3
Reynolds Dale SO40 ...... 100 B3
Reynolds Rd Fair Oak SO50 .. 57 E1
Gosport PO12 .... 181 E1
Southampton SO15 .... 102 B4
Rhinefield Cl
Bishopstoke SO50 .... 56 C1
Brockenhurst SO42 ...... 145 F1
Havant PO9 .... 135 E2
Rhinefield Ornamental Dr
SO42 .... 144 C3
Rhinefield Rd
Brockenhurst SO42 ...... 145 E1
New Milton BH25 .... 170 C1
Rhiners Cl SO41 .... 172 A1
Rhyme Hall Mews SO45 .... 151 D2
Rhys Ct PO4 .... 183 D2
Ribble Cl Broadstone BH18 .. 187 D1
Chandler's Ford SO53 ...... 55 E3
Ribble Ct SO16 .... 77 F1
Ricardo Cres BH23 .... 208 A3
Rice Gdns BH16 .... 201 E2
Rice Terr BH16 .... 201 E2
Richard Cl BH16 .... 201 D4
Richard Gr PO12 .... 156 A1
Richard Moss House 6 SO23 .. 11 D4
Richards Cl SO31 .... 129 D2
Richards Ct 13 SO15 .... 78 A1
Richlans Rd SO30 .... 105 E3
Richmond Cl
Chandler's Ford SO53 ...... 30 B1
South Hayling PO11 ...... 184 C2
Totton SO40 .... 76 A1
Richmond Ct
15 Bournemouth BH5 ...... 205 F2
12 Milford on Sea SO41 .... 211 E2
7 New Milton BH25 ...... 195 D2
Richmond Dr PO11 ...... 184 C2
Richmond Gdns
Bournemouth BH1 ...... 204 C2
Southampton SO17 .... 79 D1
Waterlooville PO7 .... 134 B3
Richmond Hall 6 SO17 ...... 79 E1
Richmond Hill BH1, BH2 .... 204 C2
Richmond Hill Dr BH2 .... 204 C2
Richmond House
34 Portsmouth PO1 ...... 182 A3
6 Southampton SO15 .... 102 B3
Richmond La SO51 .... 28 A1
Richmond Park Ave BH8 .... 205 E4
Richmond Park Cl BH8 .... 205 E4
Richmond Park Cres BH8 .. 205 E4
Richmond Park Rd BH8 .... 205 E4

Richmond Pl PO1 .... 182 A3
Richmond Rd Gosport PO12 .. 181 D2
Lee-on-the-Solent PO13 .... 179 F1
Poole BH14 .... 203 E2
Portsmouth PO5 .... 182 B1
Southampton SO15 .... 102 B3
Wimborne Minster BH21 .. 163 E2
Richmond Rise
Bournemouth BH8 ...... 205 E3
Portchester BH8 .... 132 B1
Richmond St SO14 .... 103 D2
Richmond Wood Rd BH8 .. 205 E4
Richville Rd SO16 .... 102 A4
Ridding Cl SO15 .... 78 B1
Riders Inf Sch PO9 .... 135 F3
Riders Jun Sch PO9 .... 135 F3
Riders La PO9 .... 135 F2
Ridge Cl PO8 .... 88 B2
Ridge Common La GU32 .... 40 B3
Ridge La Botley SO30 ...... 106 B2
Romsey SO51 .... 76 B4
Ridge The SP5 .... 47 E3
Ridge Top La GU32 .... 39 F3
Ridgefield Gdns BH23 ...... 208 B4
Ridgemede Cty Jun
Sch SO32 .... 83 E4
Ridgemount Ave SO16 ...... 78 C3
Ridgemount Gdns BH15 .... 201 F2
Ridgemount La SO16 .... 78 C3
Ridgeway Broadstone BH18 .. 187 D2
Corfe Mullen BH21 .... 186 B4
Ferndown BH22 .... 189 F4
Winchester SO22 .... 10 B3
Ridgeway Cl
Chandler's Ford SO53 ...... 55 F3
Cosham PO6 .... 132 C1
Fair Oak SO50 .... 57 E2
Ridgeway House Sch SO19 .. 103 F3
Ridgeway The SO41 .... 197 E1
Ridgeway The PO16 .... 131 F1
Ridgewood Cl SO45 ...... 125 E2
Ridings The Fair Oak SO50 .. 57 D1
Liss GU33 .... 21 D2
Portsmouth PO2 .... 157 F2
Shedfield SO32 .... 83 D2
Ridley Cl SO45 .... 150 B2
Ridley Rd BH9 .... 204 C4
Ridout Cl BH10 .... 189 D1
Rigby Rd SO17 .... 103 D4
Riggs Gdns BH11 .... 188 C1
Rigler Rd BH15 .... 202 A1
Rimbury Way BH23 .... 207 D4
Rimington Gdns 1 SO51 .... 28 A1
Rimington Rd PO8 .... 111 F2
Ring The SO16 .... 78 C4
Ringbury SO41 .... 197 E3
Ringlet Way 6 SO23 .... 11 E4
Ringwood CE Inf Sch
BH24 .... 141 D4
Ringwood Rd SO52 .... 53 F3
Ringwood House PO9 ...... 135 F3
Ringwood Jun Sch BH24 .. 141 D3
Ringwood Rd Alderholt SP6 .. 93 D2
Bournemouth BH11 ...... 188 C2
Bransgore BH23 .... 193 E3
Burley BH24 .... 142 C3
Christchurch BH23 ...... 194 A1
Ferndown BH22 .... 165 E2
Fordingbridge SP6 .... 94 A2
Fordingbridge SP6 .... 94 B2
Netley Marsh SO40 ...... 100 B4
Poole BH12,BH14 .... 203 D4
Portsmouth PO4 .... 183 D2
Sopley BH23 .... 192 A4
St Leonards BH24 .... 139 E1
Three Legged Cross BH22 .. 138 C4
Totton SO40 .... 100 B4
Verwood BH31 .... 115 D3
Ringwood Sch BH24 ...... 141 D4
Ringwood Terr SO42 ...... 146 A1
Ringwood Waldorf Sch BH24 .. 140 B3
Ripley Gr PO3 .... 183 D4
Ripon Rd BH9 .... 190 A1
Ripplewood SO40 .... 102 A1
Ripstone Gdns SO17 ...... 79 D2
Rise The Brockenhurst SO42 .. 145 F1
Waterlooville PO7 .... 134 B3
Ritchie Cl PO11 .... 185 D2
Ritchie Cl SO19 .... 104 A2
Ritchie Pl BH22 .... 138 B2
Ritchie Rd BH11 .... 189 D2
Rival Moor Rd GU31 .... 41 E1
River Cl BH21 .... 163 E3
River Ct SO41 .... 197 F2
River Gdns SO41 .... 211 F2
River Gr SO31 .... 128 A1
River La PO15 .... 130 B3
River Mews SO50 .... 56 B2
River Park L Ctr SO23 .... 2 A1
River Pk BH6 .... 206 C3
River St PO10 .... 137 D2
River View House SO19 .... 103 E2
River View Rd SO18 .... 79 E1
River Way Christchurch BH23 .. 191 E1
Havant PO9 .... 136 A2
River Wlk SO18 .... 79 F2
River's St PO5 .... 182 B2
Riverbourne Ct SO18 ...... 103 E4
Riverdale Ave PO7 .... 135 D4
Riverdale Cl SP6 .... 69 F1
Riverdale Cotts PO16 .... 131 E2
Riverdale La BH23 .... 207 D3
Riverdene Pl SO18 .... 103 E4
Riverhead Cl PO4 .... 183 D3
Riverlea Rd BH23 .... 207 D3
Rivermead Cl SO51 .... 52 B4
Rivermead Ct PO10 ...... 137 D2

Rivermead Gdns BH23 .... 191 F1
Riverpark Ct SO18 .... 79 E1
Rivers Reach SO41 .... 197 F2
Riverside 9 BH21 .... 163 E2
Riverside Cl SO19 .... 126 C4
Riverside Gdns PO9 ...... 135 F1
Riverdale Rd BH6 .... 207 D2
Riverside Bishopstoke SO50 .. 56 B2
Bournemouth BH10 ...... 189 F2
Ringwood BH24 .... 140 C3
Riverside Ave
Bournemouth BH7 ...... 191 E1
Fareham PO16 .... 131 E2
Riverside Bsns Pk SO41 .... 197 F2
Riverside Cl Cadnam SO40 .. 99 E3
Liss GU33 .... 20 C2
Riverside Cotts SO21 ...... 31 F3
Riverside Ct SO18 .... 103 E4
Riverside Gdns SO51 .... 52 C3
Riverside House 44 SO23 .. 11 D4
Riverside La BH6 .... 206 C3
Riverside Mews PO17 ...... 108 A2
Riverside Park BH23 ...... 207 D3
Riverside Pk BH21 .... 163 E2
Riverside Rd
Bournemouth BH6 ...... 206 C3
West Moors BH22 .... 138 B1
Riverside Sch PO7 .... 134 C2
Riverside Terr PO16 .... 131 E1
Riverside Wlk GU31 .... 41 D2
Riverslea Mews BH23 ...... 207 E3
Riverview SO40 .... 100 C3
Riverview Terr SO31 ...... 128 B4
Riviera Ct
3 Bournemouth BH2 ...... 204 B2
3 Poole BH13 .... 214 C4
Rivrea 22 BH1 .... 205 D2
Road View PO2 .... 182 B4
Roads Hill PO8 .... 88 A1
Robere House SO19 ...... 103 E2
Robert Cecil Ave SO18 ...... 79 F2
Robert Mack Ct 32 PO1 .... 182 A3
Robert Whitworth Dr
1 SO51 .... 52 C4
Roberts Cl Hordle SO41 .... 196 C1
Wickham PO17 .... 108 A2
Roberts La BH17 .... 202 A4
Roberts Rd
Bournemouth BH7 ...... 206 A3
Broadstone BH17 .... 187 D1
Gosport PO12 .... 180 C3
Hythe SO45 .... 125 F2
Southampton SO15 .... 102 C3
Totton SO40 .... 100 C3
Robertshaw House SO43 .. 121 F3
Robin Cres BH25 .... 194 B3
Robin Ct SO15 .... 102 C4
Robin Gdns Totton SO40 .. 100 B4
Waterlooville PO8 .... 111 E2
Robin Gr BH25 .... 194 C1
Robin Sq SO50 .... 55 E1
Robina Cl PO7 .... 135 D4
Robinia Gn SO16 .... 78 B3
Robins Cl PO14 .... 154 B2
Robins Ct 8 BH21 .... 163 E2
Robins Meadow PO14 ...... 129 E1
Robins Way BH23 .... 208 A3
Robinson Ct PO16 .... 132 B1
Robinson Rd PO14 .... 179 D3
Robinson Way PO3 .... 158 B2
Robinswood Dr BH22 ...... 165 E4
Robsall Cl PO12 .... 203 F4
Robville St BH6 .... 206 A3
Roche Court (Boundary
Oak Prep Sch) PO17 ...... 131 E3
Rochester Ct PO13 .... 180 B3
Rochester Rd
Bournemouth BH11 ...... 189 D2
Portsmouth PO4 .... 182 C2
Rochester St SO14 .... 103 E3
Rochford Rd PO6 .... 157 E4
Rockall Cl SO16 .... 77 F3
Rockbourne Cl PO9 .... 135 E2
Rockbourne Gdns BH25 .... 209 E4
Rockbourne La
Damerham SP6 .... 68 B4
Rockbourne SP6 .... 68 B4
Rockbourne Rd SO22 .... 1 B2
Rockery Cl SO45 .... 125 E2
Rockford Cl BH6 .... 206 C2
Rockford House SO50 ...... 57 D1
Rockingham Way PO16 .... 156 A4
Rockleigh Dr SO40 .... 100 B3
Rockleigh Rd SO16 .... 78 B2
Rockley Rd BH15 .... 201 F1
Rockpit Cotts GU33 .... 21 D2
Rockram Cl SO40 .... 99 D4
Rockram Gdns SO45 ...... 125 E2
Rockstone La SO14 .... 103 D3
Rockstone Pl SO15 .... 102 C3
Rockville Dr PO7 .... 134 C4
Rodbard House SO31 ...... 104 C1
Rodbourne Cl SO41 .... 211 E4
Rodfield La SO24 .... 13 E3
Rodlease La SO41 .... 173 F1
Rodney Cl Gosport PO13 .. 180 B3
Poole BH12 .... 204 A4
Rodney Ct Christchurch BH23 .. 208 A3
Poole BH15 .... 202 B1
Southampton SO19 .... 104 B2
Rodney Dr BH23 .... 207 F3
Rodney House 27 PO12 .... 181 E2
Rodney Rd PO4 .... 183 D2
Rodney Way PO8 .... 112 A3
Rodway Rd PO1 .... 163 E2
Rodwell Cl BH10 .... 189 E3
Roebuck Cl Cosham PO6 .. 157 F4
New Milton BH25 .... 195 D2

Roeshot Cres BH23 .... 193 F1
Roeshot Hill BH23 .... 193 E1
Roewood Cl SO45 .... 150 B2
Roewood Rd SO45 .... 150 B2
Rogate Gdns PO16 .... 132 B1
Rogate House **48** PO1 .... 182 B3
Roger Penny Way
  Brook SO43, SP6 .... 73 A1
  Fordingbridge, Bramshaw SP6 .... 72 B3
  Fordingbridge, Godshill SP6 ...... 71 D3
Rogers Cl Bishopstoke SO50 ...... 56 C2
  Gosport PO12 .... 181 D3
Rogers House PO13 .... 179 F1
Rogers Mead PO11 .... 159 F2
Rogers Rd SO50 .... 56 C2
Roker Way SO50 .... 57 D1
Roland Cl PO8 .... 112 A3
Rollestone Rd SO45 .... 150 B1
Rolls Dr BH6 .... 207 D2
Roman Cl SO53 .... 55 F4
Roman Ct PO10 .... 137 E1
Roman Dr SO16 .... 78 C4
Roman Gdns SO45 .... 125 E1
Roman Gr PO16 .... 156 B3
Roman House SO18 .... 103 E4
Roman Hts BH12 .... 186 C4
Roman Meadow SP5 .... 46 C4
Roman Quay SP6 .... 69 F1
Roman Rd Chilworth SO16 ...... 78 C4
  Corfe Mullen BH18 .... 186 C3
  Havant PO10 .... 136 B1
  Holbury SO45 .... 150 A3
  Hythe SO45 .... 125 E1
  Twyford SO21 .... 32 A3
Roman Row SO32 .... 83 E4
Roman Way Havant PO9 ...... 135 E1
  Hythe SO45 .... 125 E1
  Pamphill BH21 .... 162 B3
Romans' Rd **1** SO23 .... 11 D3
Romford Rd SO31 .... 152 B4
Romill Cl SO30 .... 80 A2
Romney Cl BH10 .... 189 F2
Romney Rd BH10 .... 189 F2
Romsey Abbey CE Prim Sch
  SO51 .... 52 C4
Romsey Ave Portchester PO16 .. 156 A4
  Portsmouth PO3 .... 183 D3
Romsey Cl SO50 .... 56 A2
Romsey Ct
  9 New Milton BH25 .... 194 C2
  10 Southampton SO15 .... 102 B3
Romsey Hospl SO51 .... 53 D4
Romsey Ind Est SO51 .... 52 C4
Romsey Inf Sch SO51 .... 52 C4
Romsey Jun Sch SO51 .... 53 D4
Romsey Lodge **7** SO15 ...... 78 A1
Romsey Rd Cadnam SO40 ...... 75 F3
  Eastleigh SO50 .... 56 A2
  Horndean PO8 .... 88 B1
  King's Somborne SO51 ...... 6 B4
  Lyndhurst SO43 .... 121 F3
  Ower SO40 .... 75 F2
  Rownhams SO16 .... 77 F2
  Southampton SO16 .... 77 F2
  West Wellow SO51 .... 51 D2
  Whiteparish SP5 .... 24 C2
  Winchester SO22, SO23 ...... 10 B3
Romsey Sch The SO51 .... 52 C4
Romsey Sta SO51 .... 52 C4
Romyns Ct PO10 .... 130 C1
Ronald Bowker Ct **1** SO22 .... 10 C4
Ronald Pugh Ct SO18 .... 79 F2
Rook Hill Rd BH23 .... 208 B3
Rookcliff **13** SO41 .... 211 E2
Rookcliff Way SO41 .... 211 E2
Rookery Ave Swanwick SO31 .. 129 D4
  Swanwick PO15 .... 129 E4
Rookery Cotts SP5 .... 3 E2
Rookery La SP5 .... 45 F1
Rookery The PO10 .... 137 D1
Rookes Cl PO8 .... 112 A3
Rookes La SO41 .... 197 E1
Rookesbury Park Sch PO17 .. 108 B2
Rookley SO31 .... 127 E4
Rooksbridge SO45 .... 125 E2
Rooksbury Croft PO9 .... 136 A3
Rooksway Gr PO16 .... 155 F4
Rookwood **3** SO41 .... 211 E2
Rookwood Cl SO50 .... 56 A3
Rookwood View PO7 .... 110 C3
Roosevelt Cres BH11 .... 189 D3
Rope Hill SO41 .... 173 E1
Rope Wlk SO31 .... 128 A1
Ropers La BH16 .... 201 E4
Ropley Cl SO19 .... 127 E4
Ropley Ct PO11 .... 184 C2
Ropley Rd Bournemouth BH7 .. 206 B4
  47 Havant PO9 .... 136 A3
Rosamund Ave BH21 .... 163 F1
Roscrea Cl BH6 .... 207 D2
Roscrea Dr BH6 .... 207 D2
Rose Cl Hedge End SO30 ...... 105 E4
  Hythe SO45 .... 126 A1
Rose Cott PO8 .... 112 B4
Rose Cres BH15 .... 202 C3
Rose Ct BH15 .... 202 C2
Rose Gdn The BH23 .... 191 E1
Rose Gdns BH9 .... 190 A2
Rose Hill PO8 .... 112 A3
Rose Rd Southampton SO14 .... 103 D4
  Totton SO40 .... 101 D3
Rosebank Cl SO16 .... 77 F3
Rosebank Lodge SO16 ...... 77 F3
Rosebay Cl SO50 .... 81 E3
Rosebay Ct **4** PO7 .... 134 C3
Rosebery Ave Cosham PO6 .. 158 A4
  Hythe SO45 .... 126 A1

Rosebery Cl BH31 .... 115 E3
Rosebery Cres SO50 .... 56 A3
Rosebery Rd BH5 .... 206 A3
Rosebrook Ct **16** SO18 ...... 103 F4
Rosebud Ave BH9 .... 190 A1
Rosedale Ave SO51 .... 53 D4
Rosedale Cl
  3 Christchurch BH23 ...... 207 F3
  Titchfield PO14 .... 153 F4
Rosehill Cl BH23 .... 169 D1
Rosehill Dr BH23 .... 169 D1
Roselands Waterlooville PO8 .. 112 A3
  West End SO30 .... 104 B4
Roselands Cl SO50 .... 57 D2
Roselands Gdns SO17 ...... 79 D1
Roseleigh Dr SO40 .... 100 C3
Rosemary Ct **14** BH23 ...... 209 D4
Rosemary Gdns
  Hedge End SO30 .... 105 E3
  Poole BH12 .... 203 D4
Rosemary La **18** PO1 ...... 182 A3
Rosemary Rd BH12 .... 203 D4
Rosemary Way PO8 .... 112 A3
Rosemary Wlk **17** PO13 .. 179 F1
Rosemoor Gr SO53 .... 30 A1
Rosemount Rd BH4 .... 204 A1
Rosendale Rd SO53 .... 55 E2
Rosery The PO12 .... 181 D1
Rosetta Rd PO4 .... 183 D2
Rosewall Rd SO16 .... 77 F2
Rosewarne Ct **28** SO23 ...... 2 A1
Rosewood PO13 .... 155 F1
Rosewood Gdns
  Clanfield PO8 .... 88 B3
  Marchwood SO40 .... 102 A1
  New Milton BH25 .... 194 C2
Rosina Cl PO7 .... 135 D4
Roslin Gdns BH3 .... 204 B4
Roslin Rd BH3 .... 204 C4
Roslin Rd S BH3 .... 204 C4
Roslyn House **19** PO5 ...... 182 B2
Rosoman Cl SO19 .... 103 F2
Rosoman Rd SO19 .... 103 F2
Ross Gdns
  Bournemouth BH11 .... 188 B3
  Southampton SO16 .... 78 A1
Ross Glades BH3 .... 204 C3
Ross Mews **2** SO31 ...... 127 D3
Ross Rd BH24 .... 117 E1
Ross Way PO13 .... 179 F2
Rossan Ave SO31 .... 152 B4
Rossendale Ave SO18 ...... 103 F4
Rossington Way SO18 ...... 103 F4
Rossiters La SO40 .... 99 F3
Rossley Cl SO52 .... 193 F1
Rossley Cl SO52 .... 54 A2
Rossmore Rd BH12 .... 203 E4
Rossmore Sh Par BH12 ...... 203 D4
Rostrevor La **3** PO4 ...... 182 C1
Rostron Cl SO18 .... 80 A1
Rosyth Rd SO18 .... 103 F4
Rotary Cl BH21 .... 163 F4
Rotary Ct SO31 .... 127 D3
Rotary House SO15 .... 102 B4
Rothbury Cl
  Southampton SO19 .... 104 A2
  Totton SO40 .... 76 B1
Rothbury Park BH25 .... 195 D1
Rother Cl Petersfield GU31 .... 41 E2
  West End SO30 .... 80 A1
Rother Dale SO19 .... 104 C2
Rother House SO31 .... 20 C2
Rotherbank Farm La GU33 .. 21 D3
Rothercombe La GU32 ...... 40 A2
Rotherfield Rd
  Bournemouth BH5 .... 206 A2
  Christchurch BH23 .... 194 A1
Rotherley **1** GU32 .... 40 C2
Rotherwick Cl PO9 .... 136 A3
Rothesay Dr BH23 .... 208 C4
Rothesay Rd
  Bournemouth BH4 .... 204 B3
  Gosport PO12 .... 181 D4
Rothbury Dr SO53 .... 55 D3
Rothschild Cl SO19 .... 103 F1
Rothville Pl SO53 .... 30 A1
Rothwell Cl PO6 .... 133 D1
Rotterdam Dr BH23 .... 207 E4
Rotterdam Towers **8** SO19 .. 126 C4
Roughdown La SO45 .... 150 B1
Roumelia La BH5 .... 205 F2
Round Hill SP6 .... 69 F1
Roundabouts The GU33 ...... 21 D3
Roundcopse SO45 .... 125 D2
Roundhaye Rd BH11 .... 188 C3
Roundhill Ct SO18 .... 80 A1
Roundhouse Ct PO11 .... 185 D1
Roundhouse Dr SO40 .... 100 A3
Roundhouse Meadow PO10 . 161 D4
Roundhuts Rise **4** SO23 .... 11 E4
Roundway PO7 .... 134 C4
Roundways BH11 .... 188 C2
Routs Way SO16 .... 77 F4
Row The SP5 .... 47 E4
Row Wood La PO13 .... 155 D1
Rowallan Ave PO13 .... 180 B4
Rowan Ave PO8 .... 112 A1
Rowan Cl Bursledon SO31 .... 127 F4
  Christchurch BH23 .... 208 B4
  Lee-on-the-Solent PO13 ...... 179 F1
  Romsey SO51 .... 53 E3
  Southampton SO16 .... 78 A2
  St Leonards BH24 .... 139 E2
  Swanmore SO32 .... 84 A2
  Sway SO41 .... 172 A1
  Totton SO40 .... 100 B3
Rowan Ct Portsmouth PO4 .. 182 C2
  Southampton SO19 .... 103 F2

Rowan Dr Broadstone BH17 .. 186 C1
  Christchurch BH23 .... 208 B4
  Verwood BH31 .... 115 D2
Rowan Gdns SO30 .... 105 E3
Rowan Rd PO9 .... 136 A2
Rowan Tree Cl GU33 .... 21 D2
Rowan Way PO14 .... 154 B4
Rowans Pk SO41 .... 197 E2
Rowans The SO40 .... 101 F1
Rowarbow Cl BH17 .... 187 E1
Rowborough Rd SO18 ...... 103 F4
Rowbury Rd PO9 .... 135 E3
Rowden Cl SO51 .... 50 C1
Rowe Asheway SO31 .... 128 C2
Rowena Rd BH6 .... 206 C3
Rowes Alley PO1 .... 181 F2
Rowes La SO41 .... 199 D4
Rowhay La SO32 .... 58 B3
Rowhill Dr SO45 .... 125 E2
Rowin Cl PO11 .... 185 E1
Rowland Ave BH15 .... 202 C3
Rowland Ct PO15 .... 130 C1
Rowland Rd PO6 .... 132 C1
Rowlands Castle Rd PO8 .... 112 C3
Rowlands Castle St John's
  CE Prim Sch PO9 .... 136 A4
Rowlands Castle Sta PO9 .. 113 E1
Rowlands Cl SO53 .... 55 D2
Rowlands Hill BH21 .... 163 E3
Rowlands Wlk **2** SO18 ...... 80 A1
Rowley Cl SO30 .... 105 E4
Rowley Ct SO30 .... 105 E4
Rowley Dr SO30 .... 105 E4
Rowlings Rd SO22 .... 1 B2
Rowner Cl PO13 .... 155 D1
Rowner Jun & Inf Schs PO13 . 155 E1
Rowner La PO13 .... 155 E1
  Gosport, Rowner PO13 ...... 180 B4
Rowner Rd Gosport PO13 .... 155 D1
  Stubbington PO13 .... 155 D1
Rownhams CE Prim Sch SO16 . 77 F3
Rownhams Cl SO16 .... 77 F3
Rownhams La SO16 .... 77 F2
Rownhams La SO52 .... 53 F1
Rownhams Rd
  Bournemouth BH8 .... 190 B2
  Havant PO9 .... 135 E3
  North Baddesley SO52 ...... 54 A2
  Southampton SO16 .... 77 F2
Rownhams Rd N SO16 ...... 77 F3
Rownhams Way SO16 ...... 77 F3
Roxan Ct **9** SO15 .... 102 C4
Roxburgh House SO31 .... 129 D2
Royal Arc **5** BH7 .... 205 F2
Royal Bournemouth
  Gen Hospl The BH23 ...... 191 D1
Royal Crescent Rd SO14 .... 103 D2
Royal Ct Chandler's Ford SO53 . 55 E3
  Southampton SO17 .... 79 E1
Royal Gate PO4 .... 183 D1
Royal Gdns PO9 .... 113 D1
Royal Greenjackets
  Mus The SO23 .... 10 C4
Royal Hampshire Cty Hospl
  SO22 .... 10 B4
Royal Hampshire
  Regiment Mus SO22 ...... 10 C4
Royal London Pk SO30 ...... 105 D4
Royal Marines Mus PO4 .... 183 D1
Royal Naval Cotts PO17 .... 132 C3
Royal Naval Hospl Haslar
  PO12 .... 181 E1
Royal Oak Rd BH10 .... 189 E3
Royal South Hants Hospl
  SO14 .... 103 D3
Royal Sovereign Ave PO14 .... 155 D3
Royal Victoria Ctry Pk SO31 .. 127 E2
Royal Victoria Hospl BH2 .. 204 B2
Royal Way PO7 .... 135 D4
Royden La SO41 .... 173 E2
Roydon Cl SO22 .... 10 C3
Royster Cl BH17 .... 187 E1
Royston Ave SO50 .... 56 A3
Royston Cl SO17 .... 79 D1
Royston Ct SO40 .... 76 C1
Royston Dr BH21 .... 163 E3
Royston Pl BH25 .... 210 B4
Rozel Ct SO16 .... 77 F2
Rozel Manor BH13 .... 204 A1
Rozelle Cl SO22 .... 1 A1
Rozelle Rd BH14 .... 203 E2
Rubens Cl BH25 .... 195 D2
Ruby Rd SO19 .... 104 A3
Rudd Lane SO51 .... 27 F4
Rudgewick Cl PO16 .... 156 A4
Rudmore Rd PO2 .... 182 B4
Rudmore Sq PO2 .... 182 B4
Ruffield Cl SO22 .... 1 B1
Rufford Cl SO50 .... 56 A3
Rufford Gdns BH6 .... 206 C3
Rufus Cl
  Chandler's Ford SO53 ...... 55 F4
  Rownhams SO16 .... 77 E3
Rufus Ct SO43 .... 122 A3
Rufus Gdns SO40 .... 100 B4
Rufus Stone SO43 .... 98 A3
Rugby Rd Broadstone BH17 .. 187 D1
  Portsmouth PO5 .... 182 C2
Rumbridge Gdns SO40 ...... 101 D4
Rumbridge St SO40 .... 101 D3
Runnymede Fareham PO15 .. 130 C2
  West End SO30 .... 80 B1
Runnymede Ave BH11 ...... 188 C3
Runton Rd BH12 .... 203 F3
Runway The BH23 .... 208 A4
Rushall La BH21 .... 186 A3
Rushcombe Cty Fst
  Sch BH21 .... 186 B3

Rushcombe Way BH21 ...... 186 C3
Rushes Farm GU32 .... 40 C2
Rushes Rd GU32 .... 40 C2
Rushes The SO40 .... 101 F1
Rushford Warren BH23 ...... 207 F2
Rushington Ave SO40 ...... 100 C3
Rushington Bsns Pk SO40 .. 100 C3
Rushington La SO40 .... 100 C3
Rushmere Gate PO7 .... 86 B1
Rushmere La PO7 .... 110 C4
Rushmere Rd BH6 .... 206 B4
Rushmere Wlk **3** PO9 ...... 135 E3
Rushpole Ct SO45 .... 125 E2
Rushton Ceres BH3 .... 204 C3
Ruskin Ave BH9 .... 190 A2
Ruskin Rd Eastleigh SO50 .... 56 A3
  Portsmouth PO4 .... 183 D2
Ruskin Way PO8 .... 111 F2
Rusland Cl SO53 .... 55 D4
Russel Rd BH10 .... 189 E3
Russell Bldgs PO16 .... 156 B4
Russell Churcher Ct PO12 .. 180 C4
Russell Ct PO13 .... 179 F1
Russell Cotes Art Gall & Mus
  BH1 .... 205 D1
Russell Cotes Rd BH1 ...... 205 D1
Russell Ct **3** BH25 .... 195 D2
Russell Dr BH23 .... 207 E3
Russell Gdns
  Hamworthy BH15 .... 201 E2
  St Leonards BH24 .... 140 A3
Russell Pl Fareham PO16 .... 131 D1
  Southampton SO17 .... 79 D1
Russell Rd Havant PO9 ...... 135 F2
  Lee-on-the-Solent PO13 ...... 179 F1
  Winchester SO23 .... 2 A1
Russell St Gosport PO12 .... 181 D3
  21 Southampton SO14 .... 103 D2
Russell Way GU31 .... 41 D1
Russet Cl Ferndown BH22 .. 165 E3
  9 Lymington SO41 ...... 197 F1
Russet House SO30 .... 105 D3
Russett Cl SO32 .... 84 A2
Rustan Cl Fair Oak SO50 .... 57 E1
  Hedge End SO30 .... 105 D3
Rutland Ct SO18 .... 104 A4
Rutland Gdns SO31 .... 105 D1
Rutland Manor **9** BH12 .. 204 A2
Rutland Rd
  Bournemouth BH9 .... 205 D4
  Christchurch BH23 .... 191 F1
Rutland Way SO18 .... 80 A1
Ruxley Cl SO45 .... 150 B2
Ryall Rd BH17 .... 187 E1
Ryan Cl BH22 .... 165 E4
Ryan Gdns
  Bournemouth BH11 .... 189 D3
  Ferndown BH22 .... 165 E4
Rydal Cl Christchurch BH23 .. 191 E2
  20 Cosham PO6 .... 133 D1
Rydal House **22** PO6 ...... 133 D1
Rydal Mews BH21 .... 163 E3
Rydal Rd PO12 .... 181 D4
Ryde Pl PO13 .... 180 A2
Ryde Terr SO14 .... 103 D2
Rye Dale SO40 .... 100 B2
Rye Paddock La SO45 ...... 151 D2
Ryecroft Havant PO9 .... 136 A1
  Titchfield PO14 .... 129 E1
Ryecroft Rd BH11 .... 188 C3
Ryedown La SO51 .... 51 F2
Ryefield Cl GU31 .... 41 E2
Ryefield Cotts GU31 .... 41 F1
Rylandes Ct SO16 .... 77 F2

Sabre Rd PO10 .... 161 D2
Sackville St PO5 .... 182 B2
Saddle Cl BH17 .... 164 B3
Saddlers Cl SO50 .... 56 A3
Saddlers La SO45 .... 126 A1
Sadlers Wlk PO10 .... 161 D4
Saffron Cl SO31 .... 128 C1
Saffron Dr BH23 .... 208 A4
Sage Cl PO7 .... 135 D3
Sages La GU34 .... 17 E3
Sailors La SO32 .... 60 B4
Sainsbury Lodge PO1 ...... 182 C3
Saints Cl BH21 .... 138 C4
St Adlem's CE Comb Sch
  BH12 .... 204 A3
St Agatha's Cl SO22 .... 128 A2
St Agathas Way **10** PO1 .. 182 B3
St Alban's Ave BH8 .... 205 E4
St Alban's CE Prim Sch PO9 .. 136 A2
St Alban's Cres BH8 .... 205 D4
St Alban's Rd
  Bournemouth BH8 .... 205 D4
  Havant PO9 .... 136 A2
  Portsmouth PO4 .... 182 C2
  Southampton SO14 .... 103 D3
St Albans Ct PO13 .... 180 B3
St Aldhelm's BH14 .... 203 F2
St Aldhelm's BH13 .... 203 F2
St Aldhelm's Rd BH13 ...... 203 F2
St Andrew Cl PO8 .... 88 B1
St Andrew's Bldgs SO31 .. 128 A1
St Andrew's Rd
  Cosham PO6 .... 158 C4
  Gosport PO12 .... 181 D2
  Portsmouth PO5 .... 182 B2
  South Hayling PO11 ...... 185 D1
St Andrews Rd BH23 .... 207 D3
St Andrews Cl
  Michelmersh SO51 .... 27 E3
  North Baddesley SO52 ...... 53 F3
St Andrews Gn SO32 .... 61 E3
St Andrews House **18** SO17 .. 103 D4
St Andrews Park SO50 ...... 81 E3

St Andrews Rd
  Broadstone BH18 .... 187 D3
  Southampton SO14 .... 103 D3
St Ann's Cres PO12 .... 181 D3
St Ann's Ct **1** BH1, ... 205 F3
St Ann's Hospl BH13 .... 214 C3
St Ann's Rd BH2 .... 112 B4
St Anne's Ave BH6 .... 206 C3
St Anne's Convent RC
  Girls Sch SO15 .... 102 C3
St Anne's Gdns SO19 .... 103 F1
St Anne's Gr PO14 .... 154 C4
St Anne's Rd Portsmouth PO4 .. 182 C2
  Southampton SO19 .... 103 F1
  Upton BH16 .... 201 D4
St Annes Cl SO22 .... 10 B2
St Annes Gdns SO41 .... 197 E2
St Annes House SO51 .... 52 C3
St Annes La SO32 .... 107 F4
St Annes Mews **16** SO14 .... 103 D4
St Anns Ct **7** SO17 .... 79 D1
St Anthony's RC Prim Sch
  PO14 .... 129 E1
St Anthony's Rd BH2 .... 204 C3
St Aubin's Ave SO19 .... 104 A3
St Aubin's Park PO11 ...... 184 B2
St Aubyns Ct **3** BH15 ...... 202 A1
St Aubyns La BH24 .... 117 F1
St Augustin's Rd BH2 ...... 204 C3
St Augustine Gdns SO17 .... 79 E1
St Augustine Rd PO4 ...... 182 C2
St Austell Cl SO50 .... 56 C2
St Barbara Way PO2 .... 157 F2
St Barbe Cl SO51 .... 53 D3
St Bartholomew's Gdns PO5 .. 182 B2
St Bede CE Prim Sch SO23 ...... 2 A1
St Bede's Ct **28** SO23 ...... 2 A1
St Bernard House **24** SO14 .... 103 D2
St Birinus Rd SP5 .... 47 E3
St Blaize Rd SO51 .... 53 E4
St Boniface Ct SO32 .... 54 A2
St Bonnet Dr SO32 .... 83 E4
St Brelade Pl SO16 .... 77 E2
St Brelades BH14 .... 203 E1
St Brelades Ave BH12 ...... 188 B1
St Catherine St PO5 .... 182 B1
St Catherine's Par BH23 .. 191 F1
St Catherine's RC Prim Sch
  BH21 .... 164 A3
St Catherine's Rd
  Bournemouth BH6 .... 206 C2
  South Hayling PO11 ...... 184 B2
  Southampton SO18 .... 79 F1
  Winchester SO23 .... 11 D3
St Catherine's Way BH23 .. 191 E2
St Catherines BH21 .... 163 E2
St Catherines Ct PO11 ...... 184 B2
St Catherines Rd SO50 ...... 56 A3
St Catherines View SO30 .. 105 D3
St Catherines Way
  Portchester PO16 .... 131 F1
  Winchester SO23 .... 11 E3
St Chad's Ave PO2 .... 157 F1
St Christopher Ave PO16 .. 131 E2
St Christopher's Rd PO9 .. 135 E2
St Christophers Cl SO42 .. 54 A2
St Christophers Gdns PO13 .. 155 E1
St Christophers Hospl PO16 .. 131 D2
St Christophers Sch SO18 .. 103 F4
St Clair Rd BH13 .... 214 C4
St Clares Ave PO9 .... 135 E4
St Clement St
  Winchester SO22 .... 10 C4
  23 Winchester SO23 .... 11 D4
St Clement & St John
  CE First Sch BH8 .... 205 E3
St Clement's Gdns BH1 .... 205 E3
St Clement's Rd BH8 .... 205 E3
St Clements Cl SO51 .... 52 C4
St Clements La BH15 .... 202 A1
St Clements Rd BH15 ...... 203 D4
St Colman's Ave PO6 ...... 158 A4
St Cross Ct **4** SO22 .... 10 C3
St Cross Mede SO22 .... 10 C2
St Cross Rd SO22 .... 10 C3
St Cuthberts Cl SO31 .... 129 D2
St Cuthberts La SO31 .... 129 D2
St Cyres Meml Cotts SO41 .. 197 F3
St David's Cl SO40 .... 76 B1
St David's Ct
  3 Bournemouth BH1, .. 205 F3
  Gosport PO13 .... 180 B3
  North Baddesley SO52 ...... 54 A2
St David's Rd Clanfield PO8 .. 88 B3
  Upton BH16 .... 201 D4
St Davids Rd SO31 .... 128 C2
St Denys **28** BH25 .... 195 D1
St Denys Ind Est SO17 ...... 103 E4
St Denys Prim Sch SO17 .... 79 E1
St Denys Rd SO17, SO18 ...... 79 E1
St Denys' Sta SO17 .... 103 E4
St Denys Wlk **6** PO9 ...... 135 E3
St Edmondsbury Ct PO13 .. 180 B3
St Edmund Cl PO14 .... 129 D1
St Edmund's Rd SO16 ...... 102 A4
St Edmunds RC Sch PO1 .. 182 B3
St Edward's RC/CE
  Comp Sch SO23 .... 202 C4
St Edward's Rd
  Gosport PO12 .... 181 D2
  Portsmouth PO5 .... 182 B2
St Edward's Terr **5** PO12 .. 181 D3
St Edwards Rd SO31 .... 127 D4

St Elizabeth's Ave SO18 104 A4
St Evox Cl SO16 77 F3
St Faith's CE Prim Sch SO22 10 C3
St Faith's Cl PO12 181 D3
St Faith's Rd
Portsmouth PO1 182 B3
Winchester SO22 10 C3
St Francis Ave SO18 104 A4
St Francis CE Prim Sch SO53 55 D3
St Francis Cl SO45 177 F4
St Francis Ct 2 PO2 157 F2
St Francis Pl PO9 135 F2
St Francis Rd Blackfield SO45 177 F4
Gosport PO12 181 E1
St Francis Specl Sch PO14 154 B4
St Gabriel's Rd SO18 104 A4
St George Cl SO31 104 C1
St George RC Sch (Boys) SO17 79 E3
St George's Almshouses
11 BH15 202 A1
St George's Ave
Bournemouth BH8 205 E4
Havant PO9 136 A1
Poole BH12 203 D4
St George's Beneficial CE Prim Sch PO1 182 A3
St George's Bsns Ctr 28 PO1 182 A3
St George's Cl
Bournemouth BH8 205 E4
Christchurch BH23 208 B4
St George's Cotts SP6 47 E2
St George's Cres SP6 69 F1
St George's Ct
2 Bournemouth BH1, 205 F3
North Baddesley SO52 54 A2
Portsmouth PO5 182 A2
St George's Dr BH22 165 E2
St George's Rd Cosham PO6 157 F4
Portsmouth PO1 182 A2
Portsmouth, Southsea PO4 183 D1
South Hayling PO11 184 B2
St George's Sq SO32 83 E4
St George's St
Southampton SO14 103 D2
Winchester SO23 11 D4
St George's Way PO1 182 A3
St George's Wlk 11 PO7 134 C4
St Georges Cl BH23 193 D4
St Georges Cotts Martin SP6 43 E2
Woodgreen SP6 70 C4
St Georges Ct PO16 155 D4
St Georges House 20 SO17 103 D4
St Georges Mans 18 BH5 205 F2
St Georges Rd
Fordingbridge SP6 69 F1
Locks Heath SO31 128 C2
St Georges Sq PO1 182 A3
St Giles Cl SO23 11 D4
St Giles Way PO8 88 B1
St Helen's Cl PO4 182 C1
St Helen's Par PO4 182 C1
St Helen's Rd Gosport PO12 180 C2
South Hayling PO11 184 B2
St Helena Gdns SO18 79 F2
St Helena Way PO16 156 B4
St Helens Mews 8 SO50 57 E1
St Helier Pl SO16 77 F2
St Helier Rd BH12 188 B1
St Hellen's Rd PO6 158 B4
St Hermans Mans PO11 185 E1
St Hermans Rd PO11 185 E1
St Hilda Ave PO8 88 B1
St Hubert Rd PO8 88 B1
St Ives Cty Fst Sch BH24 140 A3
St Ives End Rd BH24 140 A2
St Ives Gdns BH2 204 C3
St Ives Park BH24 140 A3
St Ives Wood BH24 140 A3
St James CE Fst Sch SP6 93 D3
St James CE Prim Sch
Bournemouth BH7 206 A3
Emsworth PO10 136 C1
West End SO30 80 C1
St James Cl Clanfield PO8 88 B2
7 Poole BH15 202 A1
St James House 23 SO14 103 D2
St James Hospl PO4 183 E3
St James' La SO22 10 C4
St James Pk (Cvn Pk) SO53 55 D4
St James' Rd PO10 136 C1
St James Rd
Ferndown BH21 165 D3
Sway SO41 172 B1
West End SO30 80 B1
St James' Terr SO22 10 C4
St James' Villas SO22 10 C4
St James Way PO16 156 B4
St James's 20 BH5 205 F2
St James's Cl SO15 78 B1
St James's Park Rd SO16 78 B1
St James's Rd
Portsmouth PO5 182 B2
Southampton SO15 102 B4
St James's Sq BH5 206 A3
St James's St PO1 182 A3
St John the Baptist CE Inf Sch PO14 129 E1
St John The Baptist CE Prim Sch SO32 83 F1
St John's Ave PO7 134 C2
St John's Cl Gosport PO12 181 D3
Wimborne Minster BH21 163 E2
St John's Coll PO5 182 B2
St John's Ctr SO30 105 D3
St John's Ct
4 Bournemouth BH1, 205 F3
North Baddesley SO52 54 A2
16 Portsmouth PO2 157 E1
St John's Gdns BH9 189 F1
St John's Hill BH21 163 E3
St John's Hospl (N)
21 SO23 11 D4
St John's Hospl (S)
32 SO23 11 D4
St John's Rd
Bournemouth BH5 205 F2
Christchurch BH23 207 D3
Cosham PO6 158 A4
Eastleigh SO50 56 A2
Havant PO9 135 E2
Hedge End SO30 105 D3
Locks Heath SO31 129 D1
Poole BH15 202 B2
Southbourne PO10 137 E1
Winchester SO23 11 D4
St John's St Hythe SO45 126 A2
Winchester SO23 11 D4
St Johns CE Fst Sch BH21 163 E2
St Johns CE Prim Sch PO12 181 D4
St Johns Cl
Rownhams SO16 77 F4
South Hayling PO11 184 C1
St Johns Ct SO40 101 F1
St Johns Dr SO40 101 F1
St Johns Gdns SO51 52 C4
St Johns Glebe SO16 77 F3
St Johns Inf Sch SO14 102 C2
St Johns La SO32 107 F4
St Johns Mews SO31 129 E2
St Johns RC Prim Sch PO1 182 B3
St Johns Rd BH25 195 D4
St Johns Sq 19 PO12 181 D3
St Joseph Cl SO31 129 D2
St Joseph's Mews PO5 182 B2
St Joseph's RC Prim Sch BH23 208 A4
St Joseph's RC Sch BH12 203 F4
St Jude's CE Prim Sch PO1 182 A2
St Jude's RC Prim Sch PO14 130 C1
St Julien's Hospl Almshouses SO14 103 D1
St Just Cl BH22 165 E2
St Katharine's CE Prim Sch BH6 207 D2
St Katherine's CE Prim Sch BH6 206 A2
St Kitts House 4 PO6 132 C1
St Lawrence Cl SO30 81 E1
St Lawrence Rd
Eastleigh SO50 56 A2
31 Southampton SO14 103 D2
St Ledger's Pl BH1 205 E3
St Ledger's Rd BH8 205 E3
St Leonard's Ave PO11 185 D2
St Leonard's Rd
Bournemouth BH8 205 D3
Winchester SO23 11 E3
St Leonards Cl PO15 129 F2
St Leonards Hospl BH24 139 E1
St Leonards Way BH24 139 E2
St Lucia House 2 PO6 132 C1
St Luke's CE Prim Sch BH9 204 C4
St Luke's CE Sec Sch PO1 182 B3
St Luke's Rd
Bournemouth BH3 204 C4
Gosport PO12 181 D3
St Lukes Cl SO30 81 E1
St Margaret's Almshouses BH21 163 D3
St Margaret's Ave BH23 207 D3
St Margaret's Cl SO18 104 A4
St Margaret's Cotts SO32 59 E1
St Margaret's Rd
Bishopstoke SO50 56 B2
Bournemouth BH10 189 E1
Poole BH15 202 B2
St Margarets BH2 204 C3
St Margarets Cl BH21 163 D3
St Margarets Hill BH21 163 D3
St Margarets House
6 SO16 102 C4
St Margarets La PO14 129 F1
St Margarets Rd PO11 185 D2
St Mark's CE Jun Sch SO15 102 B4
St Mark's Cl PO12 181 D1
St Mark's Pl PO12 181 D1
St Mark's Prim Sch BH10 189 E1
St Mark's Rd
Bournemouth BH11 189 D2
Gosport PO12 181 D1
Portsmouth PO2 157 E1
St Marks Cl SO53 30 C1
St Marks Ct 11 PO12 181 D3
St Marks Rd SO41 197 D2
St Martin Cl SO23 11 D4
St Martin's Cl
Bishopstoke SO50 56 B2
Southampton SO16 77 F2
St Martin's House 15 PO5 182 B1
St Martins Ind Est SO23 11 D4
St Martins Rd BH16 201 D4
St Mary Gr SO41 196 A1
St Mary Magdalen Almshouses 35 SO23 11 D4
St Mary St SO22 10 B3
St Mary's SO51 52 C3
St Mary's Ave PO12 181 D1
St Mary's Church Cl SO18 79 E2
St Mary's Cl
Droxford SO32 61 D1
Kings Worthy SO21 2 B3
Redlynch SP5 47 F2
St Mary's Coll
Southampton SO18 103 F4
Winchester SO23 11 D3
St Mary's Ct BH6 206 C2
St Mary's House PO1 182 C3
St Mary's Hospl East Wing PO3 183 D3
St Mary's Hospl West Wing PO1 182 C3
St Mary's Maternity Hospl BH15 202 B2
St Mary's Mews BH22 165 E2
St Mary's Pl SO14 103 D2
St Mary's Prim Sch SO14 103 D2
St Mary's RC Prim Sch PO12 181 D3
St Mary's Rd
Bishopstoke SO50 56 B2
Bournemouth BH1 205 E3
Ferndown BH22 165 E3
Liss GU33 20 C2
Netley SO31 127 E3
Poole BH15 202 C2
Portsmouth PO1 182 C3
South Hayling PO11 184 C2
Southampton SO14 103 D3
Stubbington PO14 154 B2
St Mary's St SO14 103 D2
St Mary's Terr SO21 32 A3
St Marys Cl BH23 193 E4
St Matthew's Rd PO6 157 F4
St Matthews Cl 20 SO14 103 D3
St Matthews Ct PO12 181 E3
St Matthews Rd SO22 1 B1
St Merrin's Cl BH10 189 E2
St Michael's 2 BH2 204 B2
St Michael's CE Mid Sch BH21 163 F4
St Michael's CE Prim Sch BH2 204 B2
St Michael's Ct 27 PO6 133 D1
St Michael's Gdns 20 SO22 10 C4
St Michael's Gr PO14 154 C4
St Michael's House 8 PO14 154 C4
St Michael's Mews 16 BH2 204 C2
St Michael's Pass SO23 11 D3
St Michael's Pl 18 BH2 204 C2
St Michael's Rd
Bournemouth BH2 204 C1
Havant PO9 135 E2
Portsmouth PO1 182 A2
Winchester SO22 10 C3
St Michael's Sq 16 SO14 102 C2
St Michael's St 18 SO14 102 C2
St Michaels Cl Blackfield SO45 150 C1
Verwood BH31 114 C3
St Michaels Ct 1 BH6 206 B2
St Michaels Rd
Locks Heath SO31 129 D1
Totton SO40 100 C4
Verwood BH31 114 C2
St Michaels Way PO8 88 B1
St Monica Inf Sch SO19 104 A2
St Monica Jun Sch SO19 104 A2
St Monica Rd SO19 104 A2
St Nicholas Ave PO13 180 B4
St Nicholas Flats 17 PO2 157 E1
St Nicholas' Rd PO9 135 E2
St Nicholas Rise SO23 2 A3
St Nicholas Row PO17 108 A2
St Nicholas St PO1 182 A2
St Osmund's Rd BH14 203 E2
St Patrick's Ct SO52 54 A2
St Patrick's La Liss GU33 21 E3
Rake GU33 21 E3
St Patrick's RC Prim Sch SO19 103 F2
St Paul's Hill SO22 10 C4
St Paul's Hospl SO22 10 C4
St Paul's La BH1 205 D2
St Paul's Pl BH1 205 D2
St Paul's Rd
Bournemouth BH1 205 D2
Locks Heath SO31 128 C3
Portsmouth PO5 182 A2
St Paul's Sq PO5 182 A2
St Pauls Pl 11 SO22 10 C4
St Pauls RC Prim Sch PO6 157 D4
St Peter St SO23 11 D4
St Peter's Ave PO11 160 B1
St Peter's Cres 36 BH1 204 C2
St Peter's Ct
17 Petersfield GU32 40 C2
7 Poole BH14 203 D2
St Peter's Gr PO5 182 B2
St Peter's RC Prim Sch PO7 134 C4
St Peter's RC Sch BH7 206 A4
St Peter's RC Sec Sch BH6 206 C2
St Peter's Rd
Bournemouth BH1 205 D2
Petersfield GU32 40 C2
Poole BH14 203 D2
St Peter's Sq 6 PO10 160 C4
St Peter's St SO32 83 E4
St Peter's Wlk 38 BH1 204 C2
St Peters Cl SO32 106 B4
St Peters Ct
Bournemouth BH1 205 D2
4 Emsworth PO10 161 D4
St Peters Rd PO11 160 B2
St Philip's Way SO18 104 A4
St Piran's Ave PO3 183 D4
St Quentin House 12 PO14 154 C4
St Richards Gdns PO7 134 B3
St Ronan's Ave PO4 182 C1
St Ronan's Rd PO4 182 C1
St Saviors Cl BH7 206 B4
St Sebastian Cres PO16 131 D2
St Simon Cl SO31 129 D2
St Simon's Rd PO5 182 B1
St Stephen's Ct 6 BH2 204 C2
St Stephen's Rd
Bournemouth BH2 204 C2
Portsmouth PO2 182 C4
Winchester SO22 1 B1
St Stephen's Way 27 BH2 204 C2
St Stephens La BH31 115 D4
St Swithun Cl SO32 83 D4
St Swithun St SO23 11 D4
St Swithun Wells (RC) Prim Sc SO53 55 F3
St Swithun's Cl SO51 28 B1
St Swithun's RC Prim Sch PO5 182 B1
St Swithun's Rd
Bournemouth BH1 205 D2
Portsmouth PO2 157 F1
St Swithun's Rd S BH1 205 D2
St Swithun's Sch SO23 11 E4
St Swithuns Ct 5 SO14 103 D3
St Theresas Cl PO9 135 E2
St Thomas Ave PO11 184 B2
St Thomas Cl PO16 131 E2
St Thomas Ct 7 SO50 57 E1
St Thomas Garnet's RC Sch BH5 206 A3
St Thomas More's RC Prim Sch PO9 135 E2
St Thomas' Pas 24 SO22 10 C4
St Thomas Pk SO41 197 E2
St Thomas St
Winchester SO22 10 C4
24 Winchester SO23 11 D4
St Thomas's Cl BH10 189 F1
St Thomas's Ct PO1 182 A2
St Thomas's Rd PO12 181 D4
St Thomas's St
Lymington SO41 197 F2
Portsmouth PO1 182 A2
St Tristan Cl SO31 129 D1
St Ursula Gr PO5 182 B2
St Valerie Rd
Bournemouth BH2 204 C3
Gosport PO12 181 D2
St Vigor Way
Colden Common SO21 31 F1
Colden Common SO21 57 D4
St Vincent Coll PO12 181 D3
St Vincent Cres PO8 112 A3
St Vincent L Ctr PO12 181 E3
St Vincent Rd Gosport PO12 181 D3
Portsmouth PO5 182 B1
St Vincent St PO5 182 A2
St Walburga's RC Prim Sch BH9 190 A1
St Winifred's Rd
Bournemouth BH2 204 C3
Southampton SO16 78 B1
St Winifred's Sch SO17 79 D1
Salcombe Ave PO3 158 A1
Salcombe Cl SO53 55 D2
Salcombe Cres SO40 100 C3
Salcombe Rd
Southampton SO15 102 B4
Totton SO40 100 C3
Salcot Rd SO23 2 A1
Salem St SO15 78 B1
Salerno Dr PO12 180 C2
Salerno House
Fareham PO14 154 C4
Romsey SO51 53 D4
Salerno Pl BH15 201 E1
Salerno Rd Portsmouth PO2 157 E2
Southampton SO16 78 B2
Salet Way PO7 112 A1
Salisbury Cl SO50 56 A2
Salisbury Ct 2 SO50 56 A2
Salisbury Rd Awbridge SO51 52 A3
Bournemouth BH1 205 F2
Breamore SP6 70 A3
Burton BH23 192 A3
Cosham PO6 158 A4
Fordingbridge SP6 70 A1
Fordingbridge SP6 70 A3
Fordingbridge, Ibsley SP6 94 A1
Ibsley BH24 116 C3
Ower SO40 76 B2
Poole BH14 203 E3
Portsmouth PO4 182 C1
Ringwood BH24 116 C3
Sopley, Burton BH23 192 B2
Sopley, Winkton BH23 192 A3
Southampton SO17 79 D2
Totton SO40 76 B2
West Wellow SO51 50 B2
Salisbury Road Arc SO40 100 C4
Salisbury St
Fordingbridge SP6 69 F1
6 Southampton SO15 102 C3
Salisbury Terr PO13 179 F1
Salmon Dr SO50 56 C1
Salt La Upham SO32 & SO24 34 C2
Upham SO32 & SO24 34 C2
Salt Meat La PO12 181 E3
Salter Rd BH13 214 B2
Salterns Ave PO4 183 D3
Salterns Cl PO11 185 E2
Salterns Ct BH14 214 A4
Salterns Est PO16 155 D4
Salterns La Bursledon SO31 128 A4
Fareham PO16 155 D4
South Hayling PO11 185 E2
Salterns Point BH14 214 A4
Salterns Rd Poole BH14 203 D2
Stubbington PO14 179 D2
Salterns Specl Sch SO40 101 D4
Salterns Way BH14 214 A4
Salters Acres SO22 1 B2
Salters La SO22 1 A1
Saltgrass La SO41 212 A2
Saltings Rd BH16 201 D3
Saltings The Cosham PO6 158 C4
Havant PO9 159 F3
Saltmarsh La PO11 184 C3
Saltmarsh Rd SO14 103 D2
Saltmead SO17 79 E1
Salvia Cl PO7 135 D3
Salwey Rd SO30 105 E3
Samber Cl SO41 197 E2
Sampan Cl SO31 128 C1
Samphire Cl SO41 197 F3
Samples Way BH17 202 C4
Sampson Rd Gosport PO14 154 C3
Portsmouth PO1 181 F3
Samson Cl PO13 180 B4
Samson Rd BH15 201 E1
Samuel Rd PO1 182 C3
San Diego Rd PO12 181 D3
San Remo Towers 23 BH5 205 F2
Sancreed Rd BH12 203 F4
Sancroft BH21 164 A1
Sand Cl SO51 50 C2
Sandbanks Bsns Ctr BH13 214 A2
Sandbanks Rd BH14 203 D1
Sandbourne Rd
Bournemouth BH4 204 B1
Poole BH15 202 B2
Sandcroft Cl PO12 180 C2
Sandecotes Rd BH14 203 E2
Sandell Ct SO16 79 D3
Sanderling Rd PO4 183 E3
Sanderlings BH24 141 E3
Sanderlings The PO11 185 D1
Sandford Ave PO12 180 B2
Sandford Cl BH9 190 B2
Sandford Way BH18 186 C1
Sandhill Way PO13 180 A3
Sandhills Cl BH17 187 E1
Sandhurst Dr BH21 139 D4
Sandhurst Rd SO15 102 C3
Sandilands Way SO45 126 A1
Sandisplatt PO14 154 B4
Sandle Copse SP6 69 D1
Sandleford Rd PO9 135 E4
Sandleheath Ind Est SP6 69 D1
Sandleheath Rd SP6 92 C4
Sandlewood Cl Clanfield PO8 88 B3
Totton SO40 100 B4
Sandmartin Cl BH25 209 F4
Sandown Cl PO12 180 B2
Sandown Rd
Christchurch BH23 207 F3
Cosham PO6 157 F4
Southampton SO15 78 A1
Sandpiper Cl
Broadstone BH17 186 C1
Horndean PO8 112 A4
Marchwood SO40 101 F1
Sandpiper Rd SO16 78 A3
Sandpipers PO3 158 C4
Sandpit La Beaulieu SO41 199 E3
Poole BH15 202 B2
Sandport Gr PO16 156 A4
Sandringham Cl
Bournemouth BH9 190 A2
North Baddesley SO52 54 C2
Sandringham Ct
Bournemouth BH8 205 E3
Southampton, Millbrook SO15 102 A3
21 Southampton, Westwood Pk SO17 79 D1
Sandringham Gdns BH9 190 A2
Sandringham House 2 PO7 134 C3
Sandringham La PO1 182 C3
Sandringham Rd
Fareham PO14 154 A4
Petersfield GU32 40 C2
Poole BH14 203 E2
Portsmouth PO1 182 C3
Southampton SO18 79 F1
Sandsbury La GU32 40 B3
Sandy Beach Est PO11 185 F1
Sandy Brow PO7 134 B2
Sandy Cl Petersfield GU31 41 E2
Wimborne Minster BH21 164 A4
Sandy Down SO41 173 E2
Sandy La Abbotswood SO51 28 A2
Bournemouth BH6 206 A3
Christchurch BH23 191 F1
Fair Oak SO50 57 E1
Lyndhurst SO43 121 F2
North Baddesley SO52 54 A3
Pamphill BH21 162 A3
Rake GU33 21 F2
Redlynch SP5 47 F4
Shedfield SO32 83 E1
St Leonards BH24 140 A3
Three Legged Cross BH21 114 C1
Titchfield PO14 153 F4
Upton BH16 201 D3
Verwood BH31 115 D3
Wimborne Minster BH21 164 A4
Sandy Mead Rd BH8 190 C1
Sandy Plot BH23 207 E4
Sandy Point Rd PO11 185 F1
Sandy Way BH10 189 F2
Sandycroft SO31 152 B4
Sandyfield Cres PO8 111 F2
Sandyhurst Cl BH17 187 E1
Sanross Cl PO14 179 D3
Santoy BH13 214 B3
Sapphire Ridge PO7 135 D4
Saracen Cl SO41 197 E1
Saracens Rd SO53 55 F4
Sarah Cl BH7 206 A4

Sarah Robinson House **39** PO1 .... 182 A3
Sarah Sands Cl BH23 .... 207 E4
Sarisbury CE Jun Sch SO31 .... 128 C3
Sarisbury Gate SO31 .... 129 D3
Sarisbury Inf Sch SO31 .... 128 C3
Sark Rd BH12 .... 203 E4
Sarnia Ct SO16 .... 77 F2
Sarum Ave BH22 .... 138 C2
Sarum Cl SO22 .... 10 B4
Sarum Ct BH14 .... 203 E2
Sarum Rd
  Chandler's Ford SO53 .... 55 F3
  Winchester SO22 .... 10 A4
Sarum Road Hospl SO22 .... 10 A4
Sarum St **14** BH15 .... 202 A1
Sarum View SO22 .... 10 A4
Sarum Wlk SO41 .... 197 E3
Satchell La SO31 .... 128 A2
Saturn Cl SO16 .... 77 F2
Saulfland House BH23 .... 208 B4
Saulfland Pl BH23 .... 208 B4
Saulford Dr BH23 .... 208 B4
Saunders House PO16 .... 132 C1
Saunders La SO51 .... 26 C3
Saunders Mews PO4 .... 183 D1
Savernake Cl Gosport PO13 .... 155 E1
  9 Romsey SO51 .... 28 A1
Saville Cl Bishopstoke SO50 .... 56 B3
  Gosport PO12 .... 180 C2
Saville Ct **17** BH21 .... 163 E2
Saville Gdns PO16 .... 131 D2
Savoy Bldgs **20** PO16 .... 131 D1
Sawyer Cl SO22 .... 1 A1
Saxholm Cl SO16 .... 78 C3
Saxholm Dale SO16 .... 78 C3
Saxholm Way SO16 .... 78 C3
Saxley Ct PO9 .... 135 E3
Saxon Cl Horndean PO8 .... 88 B2
  Locks Heath SO31 .... 128 C1
  Portchester PO16 .... 132 A1
Saxon Gdns SO30 .... 105 D3
Saxon House **17** SO14 .... 103 E3
Saxon King Gdns BH6 .... 207 D2
Saxon Meadow SP5 .... 46 C4
Saxon Pl SO41 .... 197 E3
Saxon Rd Blackfield SO45 .... 150 C1
  Southampton SO15 .... 102 B3
  Winchester SO23 .... 2 A1
Saxon Shore Inf Sch PO6 .... 156 C4
Saxon Sq Sh Ctr **4** BH23 .... 207 D3
Saxon Way Alderholt SP6 .... 93 D3
  Romsey SO51 .... 53 D4
Saxon Wlk SO53 .... 55 F3
Saxonbury Rd BH6 .... 206 C3
Saxonford Rd BH23 .... 208 B4
Saxonhurst SP5 .... 47 D4
Saxonhurst Cl BH10 .... 189 F3
Saxonhurst Gdns BH10 .... 189 F2
Saxonhurst Rd BH10 .... 189 F2
Sayers Rd SO30 .... 56 C2
Scafell Ave PO14 .... 154 B4
Scallows La SO51 .... 50 C3
Scantabout Ave SO53 .... 55 F4
Scantabout Prim Sch SO53 .... 55 F4
Scarf Rd BH17 .... 202 C4
Scarff Ct PO11 .... 185 D1
Scholars' Wlk PO6 .... 158 B4
School Cl SO53 .... 55 D3
School Hill SO32 .... 85 E3
School La Boldre SO41 .... 197 F4
  Bournemouth BH11 .... 189 D3
  Bransgore BH23 .... 169 F2
  Chandler's Ford SO53 .... 55 D3
  Compt(Sussex) PO18 .... 90 C1
  Denmead PO7 .... 110 B3
  Emsworth PO10 .... 160 C4
  Hamble-le-Rice SO31 .... 128 A1
  Kings Worthy SO23 .... 2 A3
  3 Liss GU33 .... 20 C2
  Lymington SO41 .... 197 F2
  Michelmersh SO51 .... 6 B1
  Milford on Sea SO41 .... 211 F3
  Petersfield GU32 .... 41 D3
  Poole BH15 .... 202 B3
  Ringwood BH24 .... 141 D4
  Southbourne PO10 .... 161 F4
  St Leonards BH24 .... 140 A2
  Three Legged Cross BH21 .... 138 C4
  Westbourne SO32 .... 137 D3
  Wimborne Minster BH21 .... 163 D3
School Pl SO19 .... 103 F2
School Rd Bransgore BH23 .... 169 F2
  Bursledon SO31 .... 128 A4
  Fawley SO45 .... 151 D2
  Gosport PO12 .... 155 F1
  Havant PO9 .... 135 F1
  Hythe SO45 .... 126 A2
  Nomansland SP5 .... 73 E4
  Redlynch SP5 .... 48 A3
  Romsey SO51 .... 28 B1
  Totton SO40 .... 101 D3
  Twyford SO21 .... 31 F3
  West Wellow SO51 .... 50 C1
  Wickham SO32 .... 108 A2
Schooner Way
  Locks Heath SO31 .... 128 C1
  Portsmouth PO4 .... 183 E3
Scimitars The PO14 .... 154 A2
Scivier's La SO32 .... 58 B1
Scotland Cl SO50 .... 57 F1
Scotney Ct **8** PO9 .... 136 A3
Scott Cl Poole BH12 .... 188 C1
  Stubbington PO14 .... 154 B2
Scott House **2** PO2 .... 157 E1
Scott Rd Eastleigh SO50 .... 55 F1
  Poole BH12 .... 188 C1
  Portsmouth PO1 .... 181 F3

Scott Rd Continued
  Portsmouth PO1 .... 182 A2
  Portsmouth, Hilsea PO3 .... 157 F3
  Southampton SO19 .... 103 F1
Scott's Gn SO21 .... 57 D4
Scott's Gn BH23 .... 207 F4
Scotter Rd Bishopstoke SO50 .... 56 B2
  Bournemouth BH7 .... 206 A3
Scotter Sq SO50 .... 56 B2
Scotts Cl SO21 .... 57 D4
Scotts Hill La BH23 .... 207 E4
Scratchface La Havant PO9 .... 135 D1
  Waterlooville PO7 .... 134 C2
Scullards La **1** SO14 .... 102 C2
Sea Crest Rd PO13 .... 179 F1
Sea Front PO11 .... 184 C2
Sea Front Est PO11 .... 185 D1
Sea Grove Ave PO11 .... 185 D1
Sea Kings PO14 .... 179 D3
Sea La PO13 .... 179 E2
Sea Life Ctr PO5 .... 182 B1
Sea Mill Gdns **24** PO1 .... 182 A3
Sea Pines **9** SO41 .... 211 E2
Sea Point **8** BH13 .... 214 C4
Sea Rd
  Barton on Sea BH25 .... 209 F4
  Bournemouth, Boscombe
    BH5, BH6 .... 205 F2
  Bournemouth, Southbourne BH6 .... 206 C2
  Milford on Sea SO41 .... 211 F2
  Southampton SO19 .... 103 E2
Sea View Cotts PO10 .... 160 C4
Sea View Est SO31 .... 127 D3
Sea View Rd Cosham PO6 .... 134 B1
  Poole BH12 .... 203 D3
  South Hayling PO11 .... 185 E2
  Upton BH16 .... 201 D4
Seabank Cl BH16 .... 201 D4
Seabird Way PO16 .... 155 D4
Seabourne Pl **12** BH5 .... 206 A3
Seabourne Rd BH5 .... 206 A3
Seacombe Gn SO16 .... 77 E1
Seacombe Rd BH13 .... 214 A2
Seacroft Ave BH25 .... 209 F4
Seafarers Wlk PO11 .... 185 F1
Seafield Cl BH25 .... 209 F4
Seafield Dr BH6 .... 206 C3
Seafield Park Rd PO14 .... 179 D3
Seafield Rd
  Barton on Sea BH25 .... 209 F4
  Bournemouth BH6 .... 206 B2
  Christchurch BH23 .... 208 B4
  Portchester PO16 .... 156 A4
  Portsmouth PO3 .... 158 A1
  Southampton SO16 .... 77 F2
Seafield Terr PO12 .... 181 E2
Seafields PO10 .... 160 C4
Seaford Cl SO31 .... 104 C1
Seagarth Cl SO16 .... 78 B2
Seagarth La SO16 .... 78 B2
Seager's Ct PO1 .... 181 F2
Seagrove Rd PO2 .... 157 E1
Seagull Cl PO4 .... 183 E3
Seagull La PO10 .... 136 C1
Seagull Rd BH8 .... 190 B1
Seagulls The PO13 .... 180 A2
Seahorse Wlk PO12 .... 181 E3
Seamans La SO43 .... 98 B2
Seamead PO14 .... 179 E2
Seamoor La BH4 .... 204 A2
Seamoor Rd BH4 .... 204 A2
Searles Hill SO21 .... 32 A3
Seathwaite House **28** PO6 .... 133 D1
Seaton Ave PO3 .... 183 D4
Seaton Cl Christchurch BH23 .... 209 D4
  Lymington SO41 .... 197 F3
  Stubbington PO14 .... 179 E3
  West End SO18 .... 80 B1
Seaton Rd BH23 .... 209 D4
Seatown Cl BH17 .... 188 A1
Seaview Ave PO16 .... 132 C1
Seaview Ct Gosport PO12 .... 180 B2
  14 Lee-on-the-Solent PO13 .... 179 F1
Seaview Rd
  Barton on Sea BH25 .... 209 E4
  Christchurch BH23 .... 194 B1
Seaward Ave BH25 .... 209 F4
Seaward Gdns SO19 .... 103 E2
Seaward Rd Hythe SO45 .... 126 A2
  Southampton SO19 .... 103 F2
Seaward Tower PO12 .... 181 F2
Seaway BH25 .... 210 A4
Seaway Ave BH23 .... 208 B4
Seaway Cres PO4 .... 183 E2
Seaway Gr PO16 .... 156 B4
Seawinds SO41 .... 211 D3
Sebastian Gr PO7 .... 135 D4
Second Ave Cosham PO6 .... 157 F4
  Cosham, Farlington PO6 .... 158 C4
  Emsworth PO9 .... 136 A1
  Southampton SO15 .... 101 E4
  Southbourne PO10 .... 161 E4
Second Marine Ave BH25 .... 210 A3
Second St SO45 .... 150 C4
Sedberg House SO16 .... 77 E1
Sedbergh Rd SO16 .... 77 E1
Seddul-Bahr SO30 .... 80 C3
Sedgefield Cl
  Portchester PO6 .... 156 C4
  Totton SO40 .... 100 B4
Sedgeley Gr PO12 .... 181 D4
Sedgemead SO31 .... 127 D3
Sedgemead Ct SO31 .... 127 D3
Sedgewick Cl PO13 .... 180 B4
Sedgewick Ct SO50 .... 56 B2
Sedgewick Rd
  Bishopstoke SO50 .... 56 B2
  Southampton SO19 .... 104 B3

Sedgley Cl PO5 .... 182 B2
Sedgley Rd BH9 .... 204 C4
Seed Warehouse The
  16 BH15 .... 202 B1
Segars La SO21 .... 31 F3
Segensworth East (Ind Est)
  PO15 .... 129 E3
Segensworth Rd PO15 .... 129 F2
Segensworth West (Ind Est)
  PO15 .... 129 E3
Selangor Ave PO10 .... 136 B1
Selborne Ave Havant PO9 .... 135 E3
  Southampton SO18 .... 104 B4
Selborne Ct **3** SO51 .... 28 A1
Selborne Pl SO22 .... 10 B3
Selborne Rd SO40 .... 100 B4
Selborne Wlk SO18 .... 104 B4
Selbourne Dr SO50 .... 56 A2
Selbourne Gdns PO12 .... 180 C2
Selbourne Rd PO9 .... 135 F1
Selbourne Terr PO1 .... 182 C3
Selby Cl BH18 .... 187 D2
Seldon Cl SO22 .... 10 A2
Seldown BH15 .... 202 B2
Seldown Bridge BH15 .... 202 B1
Seldown La BH15 .... 202 B2
Seldown Rd BH15 .... 202 B2
Self Rd BH15 .... 202 A1
Selfridge Ave BH6 .... 207 D3
Selfridge Cl BH6 .... 207 D3
Selhurst House **32** PO1 .... 182 B3
Selhurst Way SO50 .... 57 E1
Seliot Cl BH15 .... 202 B3
Selkirk Cl BH21 .... 163 F1
Sellwood Rd SO31 .... 127 E3
Sellwood Way BH25 .... 209 E4
Selsdon Ave SO51 .... 53 D4
Selsey Ave Gosport PO12 .... 181 D4
  Portsmouth PO4 .... 183 D1
Selsey Cl South Hayling PO11 .... 185 F1
  Southampton SO16 .... 77 F1
Selsmore Ave PO11 .... 185 E1
Selsmore Rd PO11 .... 185 D2
Selwood Pk BH10 .... 189 E4
Selworth La SO32 .... 85 D2
Selworthy Cl BH14 .... 203 D1
Selwyn Ct **20** BH6 .... 157 F4
Selwyn Gdns SO50 .... 56 A3
Sengana Cl SO30 .... 105 F3
Senlac Rd SO51 .... 53 D4
Sennen Pl PO6 .... 157 D4
Sentinal Ct BH15 .... 202 C2
Sentinel Cl PO7 .... 112 A1
Seps 4 Rd SO45 .... 151 E2
September Cl SO30 .... 80 B1
Serle Cl SO40 .... 100 A4
Serle Gdns SO40 .... 100 B3
Sermon Rd SO22 .... 1 A1
Serpentine Rd
  Fareham PO16 .... 131 D1
  Poole BH15 .... 202 B2
  26 Portsmouth PO5 .... 182 B1
  Waterlooville PO7 .... 134 B2
Service Rd PO13 .... 157 E4
Set Thorns Rd SO41 .... 172 B1
Setley Gdns BH8 .... 190 C2
Setters Cl SO21 .... 56 C4
Settle Cl SO16 .... 102 A4
Settlers Cl **34** PO1 .... 182 B3
Sevenoaks Dr BH7 .... 206 A4
Sevenoaks Rd PO6 .... 157 F4
Severn Cl Cosham PO6 .... 133 D1
  Portchester PO16 .... 156 A4
Severn Rd Ferndown BH22 .... 166 A3
  Southampton SO16 .... 101 F4
Severn Way SO30 .... 80 B1
Seward Ave BH6 .... 206 B2
Seward Rise SO51 .... 53 E4
Seymour Cl
  Chandler's Ford SO53 .... 55 F3
  Portsmouth PO2 .... 182 B4
  Totton SO40 .... 76 B1
Seymour House SO16 .... 78 B2
Seymour La SO52 .... 53 F2
Seymour Rd
  Lee-on-the-Solent PO13 .... 180 A2
  Ringwood BH24 .... 117 D1
  Southampton SO16 .... 78 B2
Shackleton House **2** PO2 .... 157 F1
Shackleton Rd PO13 .... 180 B4
Shackleton Sq BH23 .... 169 D1
Shadwell Ct **9** PO2 .... 157 E1
Shadwell Rd PO2 .... 157 F1
Shaftesbury Ave
  Chandler's Ford SO53 .... 55 E2
  Southampton SO17 .... 79 D1
  Waterlooville PO7 .... 134 C2
Shaftesbury Cl BH22 .... 138 C1
Shaftesbury Rd Gosport PO12 .... 181 E2
  Poole BH15 .... 202 B2
  West Moors BH22 .... 138 C1
Shaftesbury St SP6 .... 69 F1
Shaftsbury Rd
  Bournemouth BH8 .... 205 E3
  Portsmouth PO5 .... 182 B1
Shaggs Meadow SO43 .... 122 A3
Shakespeare Ave SO17 .... 103 D4
Shakespeare Bsns Ctr **1**
  SO50 .... 56 A2
Shakespeare Cty Jun Sch
  SO50 .... 56 A2
Shakespeare Dr SO40 .... 76 B1
Shakespeare Gdns PO8 .... 111 F2
Shakespeare Mews PO14 .... 154 A4
Shakespeare Rd
  Bournemouth BH6 .... 206 B4
  Eastleigh SO50 .... 56 A2

Shakespeare Rd Continued
  Portsmouth PO1 .... 182 C4
  Wimborne Minster BH21 .... 163 E3
Shakespeare Road Cty
  Inf Sc SO50 .... 56 A3
Shalbourne Rd PO12 .... 181 D4
Shalcombe SO31 .... 127 E4
Shalden Cl SO16 .... 78 B3
Shaldon Rd **18** PO9 .... 136 A3
Shales Rd SO18 .... 104 A4
Shallow La SO41 .... 197 F4
Shallows The SP6 .... 70 B4
Shamblehurst La N
  Hedge End SO30 .... 81 E2
  West End SO32 .... 81 E2
Shamblehurst La S SO30 .... 81 E1
Shamblehurst Prim Sch SO30 .... 105 E4
Shamrock Cl PO12 .... 181 E2
Shamrock Ct **3** BH21 .... 163 E2
Shamrock Rd SO19 .... 103 E2
Shamrock Villas **9** SO17 .... 79 E1
Shamrock Way SO45 .... 126 A3
Shanklin Cres SO15 .... 78 B1
Shanklin Rd
  Portsmouth PO4 .... 182 C2
  Southampton SO15 .... 78 B1
Shannon Cl PO15 .... 130 B1
Shannon House **28** SO14 .... 103 E3
Shannon Rd Gosport PO14 .... 155 D3
  Stubbington PO14 .... 154 A2
Shannon Way SO53 .... 55 D3
Shapland Ave BH11 .... 188 C3
Shappen Hill La BH24 .... 142 C1
Shapton Cl SO45 .... 150 A2
Shapwick Rd BH15 .... 202 A1
Shard Cl BH31 .... 115 D3
Sharlands Cl BH18 .... 187 D2
Sharon Ct PO12 .... 181 D3
Sharon Rd SO30 .... 80 B1
Sharp Rd BH12 .... 204 A4
Sharp's Copse Inf Sch PO9 .... 136 A3
Sharp's Copse Jun Sch PO9 .... 136 A3
Sharp's Rd PO9 .... 136 A3
Sharpley Cl SP6 .... 69 F2
Sharpness Cl PO14 .... 154 B4
Sharps Cl PO3 .... 158 A2
Sharvells Rd SO41 .... 211 E3
Shavard La SO32 .... 61 E3
Shaves La SO32 .... 195 D3
Shaw Cl Totton SO40 .... 100 B4
  West End SO18 .... 80 A1
Shaw Rd BH24 .... 117 E1
Shawcross Ind Pk PO3 .... 158 A3
Shawfield Rd PO9 .... 160 A4
Shawford Cl SO16 .... 78 C2
Shawford Gdns BH8 .... 190 B1
Shawford Gr PO9 .... 135 E3
Shawford Rd BH8 .... 190 B2
Shawford Sta SO21 .... 31 F1
Shayer Rd SO15 .... 78 B1
Shear Hill GU31 .... 41 D3
Sheardley La SO32 .... 62 A1
Shearer Rd PO1 .... 182 C4
Shears Brook Cl BH23 .... 169 D1
Shears Rd SO50 .... 56 C2
Shearwater Ave PO16 .... 155 F4
Shearwater Cl PO13 .... 155 D1
Shearwater Ct PO11 .... 185 E1
Shearwater Dr PO6 .... 158 C4
Sheep Pond La SO32 .... 61 D2
Sheep St GU32 .... 40 C2
Sheepwash La PO7 .... 133 F4
Sheet Prim Sch GU32 .... 41 D3
Sheffield Cl SO50 .... 56 B3
Sheffield Ct PO13 .... 180 B3
Sheffield Rd PO1 .... 182 C3
Sheiling Sch The BH24 .... 140 B3
Shelbourne Cl BH8 .... 205 E3
Shelbourne Rd BH8 .... 205 D3
Sheldrake Gdns Hordle SO41 .... 196 A2
  Southampton SO16 .... 78 A3
Sheldrake Rd BH23 .... 208 A3
Shelford Rd PO4 .... 183 D3
Shell Ct SO40 .... 101 F1
Shellcroft SO31 .... 152 B4
Shelley Ave PO6 .... 132 C1
Shelley Cl Bournemouth BH1, ... 205 F3
  Christchurch BH23 .... 208 B4
  St Leonards BH24 .... 139 F3
  Winchester SO21, SO22 .... 10 B4
Shelley Ct Ferndown BH22 .... 165 E3
  Southampton SO15 .... 102 C3
Shelley Gdns
  Bournemouth BH1 .... 205 F3
  Waterlooville PO8 .... 111 F2
Shelley Hamlets BH23 .... 208 B4
Shelley Hill BH23 .... 208 B4
Shelley House **15** BH25 .... 195 D1
Shelley La SO51 .... 75 F4
Shelley Rd
  Bournemouth BH1, BH7 .... 205 F3
  Eastleigh SO50 .... 55 F1
  Poole BH12 .... 203 E3
  Southampton SO19 .... 104 C3
  Totton SO40 .... 76 B1
Shelley Rd E BH7 .... 205 F3
Shelley Way SO41 .... 211 E2
Shelly Park(B'mth & Poole
  Coll of Art & Design) BH5 .... 205 F2
Shelton Rd BH6 .... 206 B3
Shenley Cl PO15 .... 130 B1
Shenstone Ct **18** BH25 .... 195 D1
Shepards Cl PO14 .... 154 B4
Shepheard's Way PO12 .... 181 E1
Shepherd Cl BH23 .... 193 F1
Shepherds Cl Cadnam SO40 .... 99 E3
  Winchester SO22 .... 10 A1
Shepherds Down Sch SO21 .... 31 E3

Shepherds Hey Rd SO40 .... 76 A1
Shepherds Hill BH24 .... 116 B3
Shepherds La
  Compton(Hants) SO21 .... 31 E1
  Ibsley BH24 .... 116 A3
Shepherds Purse Cl SO31 .... 128 C1
Shepherds Rd Cadnam SO40 .... 99 E3
  Winchester SO23 .... 11 E4
Shepherds Way
  Bournemouth BH7 .... 206 A4
  Nursling SO16 .... 77 E3
Sheppard Cl PO8 .... 112 A3
Sheppards Field **4** BH21 .... 163 D3
Sherborn Cres BH17 .... 188 A1
Sherborne Ct SO50 .... 56 A3
Sherborne Dr BH22 .... 165 E2
Sherborne House Sch SO53 .... 55 E4
Sherborne Rd SO17 .... 79 D2
Sherborne Way SO30 .... 105 E3
Sherbrooke Cl SO23 .... 2 B4
Sherecroft Gdns SO30 .... 106 A4
Sherfield Ave PO9 .... 136 A3
Sherfield Cl BH8 .... 190 B3
Sherfield English La SO51 .... 50 B3
Sherfield House **26** SO15 .... 102 C4
Sheridan Cl
  Southampton SO19 .... 104 B3
  Winchester SO22 .... 10 B3
Sheridan Gdns
  Swanwick PO15 .... 129 E4
  Totton SO40 .... 100 B4
Sheringham Rd Cosham PO6 .... 133 E1
  Poole BH12 .... 203 F3
Sherley Gn SO31 .... 105 D1
Sherrin Cl BH15 .... 202 B3
Sherringham Cl SO45 .... 151 D2
Sherwin Wlk PO12 .... 181 D2
Sherwood Ave Ferndown BH22 .... 165 E2
  Hedge End SO30 .... 105 E2
  Poole BH14 .... 203 D2
Sherwood Cl Liss GU33 .... 21 D4
  Southampton SO16 .... 78 C2
Sherwood Dr BH31 .... 115 D3
Sherwood Gdns SO31 .... 128 C2
Sherwood Rd
  Chandler's Ford SO53 .... 30 C1
  Gosport PO12 .... 181 D2
Sherwood Way SO45 .... 177 F4
Shetland Cl Cosham PO6 .... 133 F1
  Totton SO40 .... 100 A4
Shillinglee PO7 .... 134 C2
Shillingstone Dr BH9 .... 190 A2
Shillito Rd BH12 .... 203 F3
Shingle Bank Dr SO41 .... 211 E2
Shinwell Ct **14** SO15 .... 78 A1
Ship Leopard St **12** PO1 .... 182 A3
Shipbuilding Rd PO1 .... 181 F4
Shipcote La SO32 .... 59 E1
Shipley Rd SO21 .... 32 A4
Shipstal Cl BH16 .... 201 E2
Shipton Gn PO9 .... 135 E3
Shire Cl Swanwick PO15 .... 129 D4
  Waterlooville PO7 .... 112 B1
Shires Copse BH6 .... 206 C2
Shires The SO30 .... 105 D3
Shires Wlk SO40 .... 100 A4
Shirley Ave Southampton PO4 .... 183 E2
  Southampton SO15 .... 102 B4
Shirley Cl Bransgore BH23 .... 169 D1
  West Moors BH22 .... 138 C1
Shirley High St SO15, SO16 .... 102 A4
Shirley Holms Boldre SO41 .... 173 D1
  Sway SO41 .... 173 D1
Shirley Inf Sch SO15 .... 78 B1
Shirley Park Rd SO16 .... 102 A4
Shirley Rd
  Bournemouth BH9 .... 190 A1
  Poole BH12 .... 203 D3
  Portsmouth PO5 .... 182 C1
  Southampton SO15 .... 102 B4
  Upton BH16 .... 201 E4
Shirley Towers SO15 .... 102 B4
Shirley Warren Prim
  Sch SO16 .... 78 A1
Shirrel Ct PO12 .... 180 B2
Shoblands Way SO45 .... 126 A1
Shoe La SO32 .... 58 C3
Sholing Ct PO9 .... 135 E3
Sholing Inf Sch SO19 .... 104 A3
Sholing Jun Sch SO19 .... 104 A3
Sholing Rd SO19 .... 103 F2
Sholing Sec Sch (Girls)
  SO19 .... 104 A2
Sholing Sta SO19 .... 103 F1
Shoot Hill Denmead PO17 .... 109 E2
  Southwick PO17 .... 109 E2
Shoot La Gosport PO13 .... 180 A4
  Lee-on-the-Solent PO13 .... 180 A4
Shooters Hill Cl SO19 .... 104 A2
Shop La SO31 .... 104 C1
Shore Ave Portsmouth PO4 .... 183 D3
  Upton BH16 .... 201 E1
Shore Cl Milford on Sea SO41 .... 211 E2
  Upton BH16 .... 201 E1
Shore Cres SO32 .... 83 E4
Shore Gdns BH16 .... 201 D3
Shore La
  Bishop's Waltham SO32 .... 83 E4
  Upton BH16 .... 201 E1
Shore Rd Hythe SO45 .... 126 A2
  Locks Heath SO31 .... 128 B1
  Poole BH13 .... 214 B3
Shoreacres BH13 .... 214 B2
Shorefield Cres SO41 .... 211 E3
Shorefield Cvn Pk SO41 .... 211 D3

Shorefield Rd
Marchwood SO40 .... 101 F1
Milford on Sea SO41 .... 211 D3
Shorefield Way SO41 .... 211 E3
Shorehaven PO6 .... 156 C4
Shorewell SO31 .... 127 E4
Shorewood Cl SO31 .... 128 C1
Short Cl BH12 .... 204 A4
Short Hill Nomansland SP5 ..... 73 D4
Romsey SO51 .... 28 B1
Short Rd PO14 .... 179 D3
Short Row PO1 .... 182 A3
Shorts Cl BH23 .... 192 B1
Shorts Rd SO50 .... 57 E1
Shotterfield Terr GU33 .... 20 C2
Shotters Hill SO30 .... 80 B1
Shotts La SO41 .... 198 C2
Shottsford Rd BH15 .... 202 B3
Shraveshill Cl SO40 .... 76 B1
Shrubb's Ave SO41 .... 197 F2
Shrubbery Cl PO16 .... 156 B4
Shrubbery The PO12 .... 180 C4
Shrubbs Hill Gdns SO43 .... 121 F2
Shrubbs Hill SO43 .... 121 F2
Shrubland Cl SO18 .... 104 A4
Sibland Cl PO14 .... 154 B4
Sicily House PO14 .... 154 C4
Sidings The Downton SP5 .... 47 D4
Netley SO31 .... 127 E3
Sidlesham Cl PO11 .... 185 F1
Sidmouth Ave PO3 .... 183 D4
Sidney Gdns BH9 .... 190 A2
Sidney Smith Ct BH17 .... 187 F1
Silchester Cl BH2 .... 204 C3
Silchester Rd PO3 .... 183 D4
Silhouette Ct PO11 .... 185 E1
Silkin Gdns SO40 .... 100 B3
Silkstead Ave PO9 .... 135 F3
Silkstead La SO21 .... 30 C4
Sillen La SP6 .... 43 D2
Silver Birch Ave PO14 .... 154 C4
Silver Birch Cl Liss GU33 .... 21 D2
Poole BH12 .... 204 A2
Southampton SO19 .... 104 B2
Silver Birches SO31 .... 127 E4
Silver Bsns Pk BH23 .... 207 F4
Silver Hill SO23 .... 11 D4
Silver St Christchurch BH23 ... 207 D3
Hordle SO41 .... 196 B3
Lyndhurst SO43 .... 121 E3
Portsmouth PO5 .... 182 A2
Silver Way BH23 .... 208 C4
Silverdale BH25 .... 210 A4
Silverdale Cl BH18 .... 186 C2
Silverdale Cres SP6 .... 93 D3
Silverdale Ct SO15 .... 102 C4
Silverdale Rd SO15 .... 102 C4
Silverlock Cl PO2 .... 182 B4
Silverlock Pl PO10 .... 137 D3
Silvers End SO45 .... 126 A1
Silvers Wood SO40 .... 76 B1
Silversands Gdns PO11 .... 185 D1
Silverthorne Way PO7 .... 134 B4
Silvertrees PO10 .... 136 C1
Silverwood Cl Oakley BH21 ... 163 E1
Winchester SO22, SO23 .... 10 B3
Silvester Rd PO8 .... 111 F1
Silwood Cl SO22 .... 1 B1
Simmonds Gr PO11 .... 185 E2
Simmonds Rd BH15 .... 202 B3
Simmons Cl SO30 .... 105 E4
Simnel St SO14 .... 102 C2
Simon Cl SO19 .... 104 C4
Simon Way SO19 .... 104 C3
Simonds Cl SO23 .... 2 A1
Simpson Cl PO16 .... 156 B4
Simpson Rd PO2 .... 157 E1
Sinah La PO11 .... 184 B2
Sinclair Ct BH14 .... 203 D2
Sinclair Inf Sch SO16 .... 78 A3
Sinclair Jun Sch SO16 .... 78 A3
Sinclair Rd SO16 .... 78 A3
Singleton Dr BH10 .... 189 E1
Singleton Gdns PO8 .... 88 B2
Sir George's Rd SO15 .... 102 B3
Sir Harold Hillier Gardens
& Arboretum SO51 .... 28 B2
Sirdar House SO17 .... 79 E2
Sirdar Rd SO17 .... 79 E2
Siskin Cl
Bishop's Waltham SO32 .... 83 D4
Ferndown BH22 .... 165 D4
Southampton SO16 .... 78 A3
Siskin Gr PO7 .... 135 D3
Siskin Inf Sch PO13 .... 180 B3
Siskin Jun Sch PO13 .... 180 B3
Sissinghurst Cl SO19 .... 104 A1
Sissinghurst Rd PO16 .... 156 A4
Siverdale Dr PO7 .... 111 E2
Siward House GU32 .... 40 C2
Six Dials SO14 .... 103 D3
Six Oaks Rd SO52 .... 54 A2
Sixpenny Cl
Locks Heath PO14 .... 129 D1
Poole BH12 .... 203 F4
Sixth Ave PO6 .... 157 F4
Sizer Way SO45 .... 125 D2
Skew Rd PO17 .... 132 B1
Skinner St BH15 .... 202 B1
Skintle Gr SO21 .... 56 C4
Skipper Way PO13 .... 180 A3
Skipton Cl BH8 .... 187 D1
Skipton Rd SO53 .... 55 E2
Sky End La SO41 .... 196 A1
Skys Wood Rd SO52 .... 54 C3

Slab La Redlynch SP5 .... 47 E3
West Wellow SO51 .... 50 C2
Slade Cl SO41 .... 196 A2
Slade's La BH10 .... 204 B4
Slades Farm Hostel BH11 ..... 189 E1
Slades Farm Rd BH10 .... 189 E1
Slades Farm Specl Sch
BH10 .... 189 E1
Slades Hill SO45 .... 150 C1
Slater App PO2 .... 157 D1
Sleepbrook Cl BH31 .... 114 C3
Sleeper's Hill SO22 .... 10 B3
Sleeper's Hill Rd SO22 .... 10 B3
Sleepers Delle Gdns SO22 ..... 10 C3
Sleepers Hill Gdns SO22 .... 10 B3
Sleight La BH21 .... 186 A4
Slepe Cres BH12 .... 203 F4
Slindon Cl PO8 .... 88 B3
Slindon Gdns PO9 .... 135 F1
Slindon St PO1 .... 182 B3
Slingsby Cl PO1 .... 182 A2
Slinn Rd BH23 .... 207 F4
Slip Way BH15 .... 202 A1
Slipper Rd PO10 .... 161 D4
Slipway The PO6 .... 157 D4
Sloane Ave SO45 .... 150 B2
Sloane Ct SO45 .... 150 B2
Sloane Park SO32 .... 107 E4
Sloane Stanley Ct SO12 .... 181 D3
Slocum House PO12 .... 181 E2
Sloe Tree Cl PO14 .... 129 E1
Slough La BH16 .... 201 D3
Smallcuts Ave PO10 .... 137 E1
Smeaton St PO2 .... 157 E1
Smeeton Rd PO13 .... 179 F1
Smith Cl SO45 .... 150 C1
Smith Gr SO30 .... 105 E3
Smith La PO10 .... 161 E1
Smith St PO12 .... 181 D3
Smith's Field SO51 .... 28 A1
Smithe Cl SO50 .... 56 A2
Smithfield Pl BH9 .... 189 F1
Smiths La SO32 .... 107 F4
Smithson Cl BH12 .... 204 B4
Smithy La BH25 .... 194 C3
Smithy The PO7 .... 110 C2
Smugglers La BH21 .... 163 F4
Smugglers La N BH23 .... 193 F1
Smugglers La S BH23 .... 208 C4
Smugglers Reach BH23 .... 208 A3
Smugglers Wood Rd BH23 .... 193 E1
Smythe Rd SO19 .... 104 B2
Snailing La GU33 .... 20 B4
Snails La BH24 .... 117 D2
Snakemoor La Durley SO32 ..... 81 F3
Fair Oak SO32 .... 81 F3
Snapdragon Cl SO31 .... 128 C1
Snape Cl PO13 .... 180 B4
Snellgrove Cl SO40 .... 76 B1
Snellgrove Pl SO40 .... 76 B1
Snooks La SO41 .... 198 A3
Snowdon Dr PO14 .... 154 C4
Snowdon Rd BH4 .... 204 B2
Snowdrop Gdns BH23 .... 193 D1
Soake Rd PO7 .... 111 D2
Soalwood La GU32 .... 39 F4
Soberton House SO17 .... 79 D1
Soberton Rd
Bournemouth BH8 .... 205 E3
Havant PO9 .... 135 F2
Soberton Towers SO32 .... 85 E3
Soldridge Cl PO9 .... 136 A3
Solent Ave Lymington SO41 ... 198 A2
Southampton SO19 .... 104 C3
Solent Bsns Pk PO15 .... 129 F4
Solent Cl Chandler's Ford SO53 .. 55 F3
Lymington SO41 .... 197 F2
Solent Ct
Milford on Sea SO41 .... 211 E2
Southampton SO19 .... 103 F1
Solent Ctr PO15 .... 129 F4
Solent Dr Barton on Sea BH25 .. 210 A4
Hythe SO45 .... 125 F2
Locks Heath SO31 .... 152 B3
South Hayling PO11 .... 184 C1
Solent House Fareham PO14 .. 155 D4
Havant PO9 .... 136 A2
Solent Homes SO19 .... 104 C3
Solent Hts
Lee-on-the-Solent PO13 .... 179 F1
Portsmouth PO4 .... 183 E2
Solent Ind Ctr SO15 .... 102 B3
Solent Ind Est SO30 .... 81 D1
Solent Inf Sch PO6 .... 158 B4
Solent Jun Sch PO6 .... 158 B4
Solent Lodge SO19 .... 195 D1
Solent Meadows SO31 .... 128 A1
Solent Pines SO41 .... 211 D2
Solent Rd
Barton on Sea BH25 .... 209 E4
Bournemouth BH6 .... 207 D2
Christchurch BH23 .... 194 A1
Cosham PO6 .... 158 B4
Havant PO9 .... 135 F1
Hythe SO45 .... 149 F4
Southampton SO15 .... 102 C2
Stubbington PO14 .... 179 D3
Solent View Boldre SO41 ...... 198 A2
Bournemouth BH6 .... 207 D2
Fawley SO45 .... 178 C4
Solent View Sch SO41 .... 197 F4
Solent Village PO15 .... 129 F3
Solent Way Gosport PO12 ..... 180 C2
Milford on Sea SO41 .... 211 F2
Solihull House PO5 .... 182 A2
Solly Cl BH12 .... 203 F4
Solomons La SO32 .... 83 F1
Solona Cl SO53 .... 55 F4

Solway House SO14 .... 103 E3
Somborne Ct SO17 .... 79 D1
Somborne Dr PO9 .... 135 F3
Somborne House SO19 .... 103 F1
Somerby Rd BH15 .... 202 B3
Somerford Ave BH23 .... 208 A4
Somerford Bsns Ctr BH23 ..... 208 A4
Somerford Cl SO19 .... 104 A3
Somerford Ct BH23 .... 208 C4
Somerford Cty Inf Sch BH23 . 207 F4
Somerford Cty Jun Sch BH23 . 207 F4
Somerford Rd BH23 .... 207 F4
Somerford Way BH23 .... 207 F3
Somerley Rd BH9 .... 205 D4
Somerley View BH24 .... 141 D4
Somers Cl SO22 .... 10 B3
Somers Park Prim Sch PO1 ... 182 B3
Somers Rd Portsmouth PO1 ... 182 B2
Portsmouth PO1 .... 182 B3
Somers Rd N PO1 .... 182 C3
Somerset Ave SO18 .... 104 B4
Somerset Cres SO53 .... 55 E2
Somerset Ct SO15 .... 102 B3
Somerset Rd
Bournemouth BH7 .... 206 A3
Christchurch BH23 .... 206 C4
Portsmouth PO5 .... 182 B1
Southampton SO17 .... 79 E1
Somerset Terr SO15 .... 102 B3
Somerstown Flats PO9 .... 136 A1
Somerton Ave SO18 .... 104 A4
Somerton Cl BH25 .... 195 E2
Somervell Cl PO12 .... 181 D1
Somervell Dr PO16 .... 131 D2
Somerville Ct BH25 .... 194 C2
Somerville Pl PO2 .... 157 E1
Somerville Rd
Bournemouth BH2 .... 204 B2
Kings Worthy SO23 .... 2 B4
Ringwood BH24 .... 141 E4
Sommers Ct SO19 .... 103 E2
Sonnet Way PO7 .... 135 D4
Sonning Way BH8 .... 190 A1
Soper's La BH23 .... 207 D3
Sopers La BH17 .... 187 D1
Sopley Cl BH25 .... 209 E4
Sopley Ct PO9 .... 136 A3
Sopley Farm Bldgs BH23 ...... 192 A3
Sopley Prim Sch BH23 .... 168 B1
Sopwith Cl BH23 .... 208 A3
Sopwith Cres BH21 .... 163 F1
Sopwith Way SO31 .... 128 C4
Sorrel Cl Romsey SO51 .... 28 B1
Waterlooville PO7 .... 135 D3
Sorrel Dr PO15 .... 129 E4
Sorrel Gdns BH18 .... 186 C1
Sorrell Cl SO31 .... 128 C1
Sorrell Ct BH23 .... 208 A4
Sorrell Way BH23 .... 208 A4
South Ave Fawley SO45 .... 150 C4
New Milton BH25 .... 195 D1
Portsmouth PO2 .... 157 F2
South Baddesley CE Prim
Sch SO41 .... 198 C3
South Baddesley Rd SO41 ..... 198 A2
South Bay Rd SO41 .... 161 D2
South Cl Gosport PO12 .... 180 C1
Havant PO9 .... 160 A4
Romsey SO51 .... 28 B1
South Cliff Rd BH2 .... 204 C1
South Cross St PO12 .... 181 E2
South Ct SO31 .... 127 F1
South Downs Coll PO7 .... 135 D2
South Dr SO22 .... 1 A2
South East Cres SO19 .... 104 A2
South East Rd SO19 .... 104 A2
South End Cl SO21 .... 30 A4
South Front Romsey SO51 .... 52 C4
Southampton SO14 .... 103 D2
South Grove SO41 .... 197 F2
South Hampshire
Ind Pk SO40 .... 76 B1
South Haven Cl BH16 .... 201 D2
South Hill Alderholt SP6 .... 93 D3
Droxford SO32 .... 85 D4
Southampton SO16 .... 79 D2
South Kinson Dr BH11 .... 189 D2
South La Buriton GU31 .... 65 E2
Clanfield PO8 .... 88 A3
Clanfield, Chalton PO8 .... 89 D2
Downton SP5 .... 46 C4
Horndean PO8 .... 89 D2
Nomansland SP5 .... 73 E4
Southbourne PO10 .... 137 F1
Westbourne PO10 .... 137 E2
South Lodge Fareham PO15 ... 130 A1
Poole BH13 .... 214 D4
South Mill Rd SO15 .... 102 A4
South Millers Dale SO53 .... 55 D4
South Normandy PO1 .... 182 A2
South Par Portsmouth PO5 ..... 182 B1
Totton SO40 .... 100 C4
South Park Rd BH12 .... 204 A4
South Pl SO41 .... 180 A2
South Rd Bournemouth BH1 ... 205 F3
Corfe Mullen BH21 .... 186 C3
Cosham PO6 .... 158 B4
Poole BH15 .... 202 B1
Portsmouth PO1 .... 182 C4
South Hayling PO11 .... 184 C2
Southampton SO17 .... 103 E4
South Road Comb Sch
BH15 .... 202 B1
South St Eastleigh SO50 .... 80 A4
Emsworth PO10 .... 160 C4
Gosport PO12 .... 181 D2
Havant PO9 .... 135 F1

South St Continued
Hythe SO45 .... 126 A2
Lymington SO41 .... 197 E1
Portsmouth PO5 .... 182 B2
Titchfield PO14 .... 153 F4
South Stoneham House SO18 .. 79 E2
South Sway La SO41 .... 196 B4
South Terr PO1 .... 182 A3
South Trestle Rd SO45 .... 151 E3
South View
Bournemouth BH2 .... 204 C3
Winchester SO22 .... 10 C4
South View Pl BH2 .... 204 C2
South View Rd
Christchurch BH23 .... 207 D3
Southampton SO15 .... 102 B4
Winchester SO22 .... 10 A2
South Way PO15 .... 129 F2
South Weirs SO42 .... 172 B4
South Western Cres BH14 .... 205 E2
Southampton
Airport (Parkway) Sta SO18 .. 79 F3
Southampton Central Sta
SO15 .... 102 C3
Southampton City Coll SO14 .. 103 D2
Southampton
(Eastleigh) Airport SO50 ...... 80 A4
Southampton Gen Hospl SO16 . 78 A1
Southampton Hill PO14 .... 153 F4
Southampton House PO9 ...... 136 A3
Southampton Inst
(City Campus) SO14 .... 103 D2
Southampton Inst of H Ed
Marine Ops Ctr SO40 .... 102 A1
Southampton Oceanography
Ctr SO14 .... 103 D1
Southampton Rd
Cadnam SO40 .... 98 C4
Cadnam, Bartley SO40 .... 99 D4
Cosham PO6 .... 157 E4
Eastleigh SO50 .... 56 A1
Fareham PO14, PO16 .... 131 D1
Fareham PO14, PO15 .... 154 A4
Fordingbridge SP6 .... 70 A1
Hythe SO45 .... 125 F2
Locks Heath PO14 .... 129 E2
Lymington SO41 .... 197 E2
Lyndhurst SO43 .... 122 A3
North Baddesley SO51 .... 53 D3
Ringwood BH24 .... 140 C4
Romsey SO51 .... 53 D3
Southampton St SO15 .... 102 C3
Southbourne Ave
Cosham PO6 .... 158 A4
Hermitage PO10 .... 161 D4
Holbury SO45 .... 150 B2
Southbourne Coast Rd BH6 ... 206 C2
Southbourne Cross Roads
BH6 .... 206 C2
Southbourne Cty Jun &
Inf Sch PO10 .... 161 F4
Southbourne Gr BH6 .... 206 B2
Southbourne Halt PO10 .... 161 F4
Southbourne Overcliff Dr
BH6 .... 206 B2
Southbourne Rd
Bournemouth BH5, BH6 .... 206 B2
Lymington SO41 .... 197 E2
Southbourne Sands BH6 .... 206 B2
Southbrook Cl Havant PO9 ..... 159 F4
Poole BH17 .... 188 A1
Southbrook Mews SO32 .... 83 E4
Southbrook Rd Havant PO9 ... 159 F4
Southampton SO15 .... 102 C3
Southcliff PO13 .... 179 F2
Southcliff Rd SO14 .... 103 D4
Southcliffe House SO14 .... 103 D3
Southcliffe Rd
Barton on Sea BH25 .... 209 E4
Christchurch BH23 .... 208 B3
Southcote Rd BH1 .... 205 E2
Southcroft Rd PO12 .... 180 C3
Southdale Ct SO53 .... 55 E3
Southdene Rd SO53 .... 55 E3
Southdown Ct BH23 .... 207 F4
Southdown Rd
Compton(Hants) SO21 .... 31 E3
Cosham PO6 .... 158 A4
Horndean PO8 .... 88 B2
Southdown View PO7 .... 111 E1
Southdown Way SO22 .... 138 C1
Southend La SO32 .... 109 E4
Southern Ave BH22 .... 139 D1
Southern Gdns SO40 .... 100 C4
Southern La BH25 .... 209 F4
Southern Oaks BH25 .... 194 C1
Southern Rd
Bournemouth BH6 .... 206 B2
Fawley SO45 .... 151 F1
Lymington SO41 .... 197 E2
Southampton SO15 .... 102 C2
West End SO30 .... 80 C1
Southernhay Rd PO7 .... 110 C2
Southernhay Rd BH31 .... 115 D3
Southey Rd BH23 .... 207 F4
Southfield BH24 .... 141 D3
Southfield La BH24 .... 143 E1
Southfield Mews BH24 .... 141 D3
Southfield Wlk PO9 .... 135 E4
Southfields Cl SO32 .... 83 E4
Southgate St SO23 .... 10 C1
Southgate Villas SO23 .... 10 C4
Southill Ave BH12 .... 203 F4
Southill Gdns BH9 .... 190 A1
Southill Rd Bournemouth BH9 . 190 A1
Poole BH12 .... 203 E4
Southlands Cosham PO6 .... 158 A4
Lymington SO41 .... 197 E1

Southlands Ave
Bournemouth BH6 .... 206 C2
Corfe Mullen BH21 .... 186 C3
Southlands Cl BH21 .... 186 B3
Southlands Ct BH18 .... 187 D2
Southlands Sch SO41 .... 197 F4
Southlawns Wlk BH25 .... 194 C1
Southlea Ave BH6 .... 206 C2
Southleigh Gr PO11 .... 184 C2
Southleigh Rd Emsworth PO9 . 136 B2
Havant PO9 .... 136 B2
Southmead Rd PO15 .... 130 C1
Southmoor La PO9 .... 159 E4
Southsea Castle PO5 .... 182 B1
Southsea Inf Sch PO4 .... 182 C1
Southsea Terr PO5 .... 182 A2
Southview SO32 .... 61 D1
Southville Rd BH5 .... 206 A3
Southwater PO13 .... 179 F1
Southway PO13 .... 155 E2
Southways PO14 .... 179 E3
Southwick Ave PO16 .... 132 C1
Southwick Cl SO22 .... 1 B2
Southwick Ct SO14 .... 155 D3
Southwick Hill Rd PO6 .... 133 F1
Southwick Pl BH6 .... 206 B4
Southwick Rd
Bournemouth BH6 .... 206 B3
Cosham PO7, PO17 .... 133 C1
Denmead PO7 .... 110 C2
Southwick PO17 .... 108 B2
Wickham PO17 .... 108 B2
Southwood Ave
Bournemouth BH6 .... 206 B2
Christchurch BH23 .... 194 A1
Southwood Cl
Christchurch BH23 .... 194 A1
Ferndown BH22 .... 165 E3
Southwood Ct BH23 .... 194 A1
Southwood Gdns SO31 .... 128 C2
Southwood Rd
Portsmouth PO2 .... 157 F2
South Hayling PO11 .... 185 E1
Sovereign Bsns Ctr BH15 ..... 202 A3
Sovereign Cl
Bournemouth BH7 .... 205 F4
Portsmouth PO4 .... 183 E3
Sovereign Cres PO14 .... 129 D1
Sovereign Ct SO17 .... 79 D1
Sovereign Ctr BH1 .... 205 F3
Sovereign Dr
Hedge End SO30 .... 105 E3
Portsmouth PO4 .... 183 E3
Sovereign La PO7 .... 134 C2
Sovereign Sq BH7 .... 205 F2
Sovereign Way SO50 .... 55 F3
Soverign Dr SO30 .... 105 F3
Sowden Cl SO30 .... 105 D4
Sowley La SO41 .... 199 E3
Spa Rd SO14 .... 102 C2
Spain Bldgs GU32 .... 40 C2
Spain The GU32 .... 40 C2
Spalding Rd SO19 .... 104 C3
Spaniard's La SO51 .... 53 D2
Sparkford Cl
Bournemouth BH7 .... 206 A4
Winchester SO22 .... 10 C3
Sparkford Rd SO22 .... 10 C4
Sparrow Cl PO8 .... 111 F2
Sparrow Ct PO13 .... 179 F2
Sparrow Sq SO50 .... 55 E1
Sparrowgrove SO21 .... 31 E2
Sparsholt Ct PO9 .... 135 D2
Sparsholt Rd
Southampton SO19 .... 126 C4
Winchester SO21 .... 9 E2
Spartan Cl Stubbington PO14 . 154 B3
Thorney Island PO10 .... 161 D2
Spartina Dr SO41 .... 197 F3
Spear Rd SO14 .... 103 D4
Specks La PO4 .... 183 D3
Speedwell Cl
Chandler's Ford SO53 .... 55 D3
Locks Heath SO31 .... 128 C1
Speedwell Dr BH23 .... 208 A4
Speggs Wlk SO30 .... 105 E3
Speltham Hill PO7 .... 86 B1
Spencer Cl PO11 .... 185 D2
Spencer Ct
New Milton BH25 .... 195 D1
Stubbington PO14 .... 179 F3
Spencer Dr PO13 .... 179 F1
Spencer Gdns PO8 .... 111 F2
Spencer Rd
Bournemouth BH1 .... 205 E2
Eastleigh SO50 .... 55 F1
Emsworth PO10 .... 136 C2
New Milton BH25 .... 195 D1
Poole BH13 .... 214 C4
Portsmouth PO4 .... 182 C1
Southampton SO19 .... 104 B3
Spenlow Cl PO2 .... 182 B4
Spenser Cl SO31 .... 152 B4
Spetisbury Cl BH9 .... 190 A2
Spice Quay PO1 .... 182 A2
Spicer Cl SO22 .... 10 C4
Spicer La BH1 .... 188 C3
Spicer St PO1 .... 182 B3
Spicer's Hill SO40 .... 100 C3
Spicer's Way SO40 .... 100 C3
Spicewood PO15 .... 130 C1
Spinacre BH25 .... 210 A4
Spindle Cl Broadstone BH18 .. 186 C1
Havant PO9 .... 136 B2
Spindle Warren PO9 .... 136 B2
Spindlewood Cl
Barton on Sea BH25 .... 195 D1
Southampton SO16 .... 79 D3

Spindlewood Way SO40 ..... 124 C4
Spinnaker Cl Gosport PO13 ..... 180 B4
  South Hayling PO11 ..... 184 C2
Spinnaker Grange PO11 ..... 160 B2
Spinnaker View PO9 ..... 135 D1
Spinners Cl BH22 ..... 138 C1
Spinney Cl St Leonards BH24 ..... 139 E2
  Waterlooville PO8 ..... 111 F2
Spinney Dale SO45 ..... 126 A1
Spinney Gdns SO45 ..... 126 A1
Spinney The
  Compton(Hants) SO21 ..... 31 E3
  Denmead PO7 ..... 110 C2
  Fair Oak SO50 ..... 57 D1
  Gosport PO13 ..... 155 E1
  Portchester PO16 ..... 131 F1
  Southampton SO16 ..... 79 D3
  St Leonards BH24 ..... 139 F3
  Totton SO40 ..... 76 B1
  Waterlooville PO8 ..... 112 A3
Spinney Way BH25 ..... 195 D3
Spinney Wlk SO18 ..... 79 F2
Spinneys La BH22 ..... 165 E3
Spinningfield House 4 GU32 .. 40 C2
Spitfire Ct SO19 ..... 103 E2
Spitfire End 7 SO23 ..... 11 E4
Spitfire Link SO23 ..... 11 E4
Spitfire Loop SO50 ..... 80 A4
Spitfire Rdbt SO23 ..... 11 E4
Spitfire Way SO31 ..... 127 F1
Spithead Ave PO12 ..... 181 E1
Spithead House PO14 ..... 155 D4
Spithead Hts PO12 ..... 183 E2
Spittlefields BH24 ..... 141 D4
Spouts La SO51 ..... 50 B3
Spring Cl Fair Oak SO50 ..... 57 E1
  Southampton SO19 ..... 103 F2
Spring Cres SO17 ..... 103 D4
Spring Ct Poole BH12 ..... 203 E3
  17 Southampton SO15 ..... 102 C3
Spring Firs SO19 ..... 103 F2
Spring Garden La PO12 ..... 181 E3
Spring Gdns
  1 Emsworth PO10 ..... 161 D4
  North Baddesley SO52 ..... 54 A2
  Poole BH12 ..... 203 E3
  Portsmouth PO1 ..... 182 A3
Spring Gr SO31 ..... 105 D1
Spring House Cl SO21 ..... 32 A1
Spring La Bishopstoke SO50 ..... 56 B2
  Colden Common SO21 ..... 31 F1
  New Milton BH25 ..... 195 E1
  Swanmore SO32 ..... 84 A3
Spring Pl 5 SO51 ..... 52 C4
Spring Rd
  Bournemouth BH1 ..... 205 E3
  2 Hythe SO45 ..... 126 A2
  Locks Heath SO31 ..... 128 C3
  Lymington SO41 ..... 198 A2
  Southampton SO19 ..... 103 F2
  Waterlooville PO8 ..... 112 A2
Spring St PO1 ..... 182 B3
Spring The PO7 ..... 110 C2
Spring Vale Swanmore SO32 ..... 84 A2
  Waterlooville PO8 ..... 112 A2
Spring Wlk 12 PO1 ..... 182 B3
Springbank Rd BH7 ..... 205 F4
Springbourne Ct BH1 ..... 205 E3
Springbourne Mews BH1 ..... 205 E3
Springcroft PO13 ..... 155 D3
Springdale Ave BH18 ..... 186 C3
Springdale Ct SO40 ..... 100 C4
Springdale Fst Sch BH18 ..... 186 C2
Springdale Gr BH18 ..... 186 C2
Springdale Rd BH18 ..... 186 C2
Springfield 2 GU33 ..... 20 C2
Springfield Ave
  Bournemouth BH6 ..... 207 D2
  Christchurch BH23 ..... 191 E4
  Holbury SO45 ..... 150 B2
Springfield Cl Havant PO9 ..... 135 D1
  Lymington SO41 ..... 198 A2
  Verwood BH31 ..... 114 C3
Springfield Cres
  Poole BH14 ..... 203 D2
  Redlynch SP5 ..... 47 E3
Springfield Ct SO19 ..... 103 F1
Springfield Dr SO40 ..... 100 C3
Springfield Gdns BH25 ..... 195 E1
Springfield Gr SO45 ..... 150 B2
Springfield Rd Poole BH14 ..... 203 D2
  Verwood BH31 ..... 114 C3
Springfield Sch PO6 ..... 158 B4
Springfield Way PO14 ..... 179 E3
Springfields Cl 3 SO21 ..... 31 F1
Springford Cl SO16 ..... 78 A2
Springford Cres SO16 ..... 78 A2
Springford Gdns SO16 ..... 78 A2
Springford Rd SO16 ..... 78 A2
Springhill RC Prim Sch SO15.. 102 C3
Springhill Rd SO53 ..... 55 E3
Springles La PO15 ..... 130 A3
Springvale Ave
  Bournemouth BH7 ..... 206 A4
  Kings Worthy SO23 ..... 2 A3
Springvale Rd SO23 ..... 2 A4
Springwater Cl BH11 ..... 189 D2
Springwater Rd BH11 ..... 189 D2
Springwood Ave PO7 ..... 134 C3
Spruce Ave PO7 ..... 135 D4
Spruce Cl Broadstone BH17 ..... 186 C1
  Locks Heath SO31 ..... 152 B4
Spruce Dr
  Southampton SO19 ..... 104 C3
  Totton SO40 ..... 100 A4
Spruce Wlk 22 PO13 ..... 179 F1
Spur Cl BH21 ..... 164 B3
Spur Hill Ave BH14 ..... 203 E2

Spur Rd Cosham PO6 ..... 157 F4
  Poole BH14 ..... 203 E2
  Waterlooville PO7 ..... 134 C4
Spur The Gosport PO12 ..... 180 C1
  Wickham PO17 ..... 108 A2
Spurgeon Rd BH7 ..... 206 A3
Spurlings Rd PO17 ..... 131 E2
Square The
  Bournemouth BH2 ..... 204 C2
  Compt(Sussex) PO18 ..... 90 C1
  Fawley SO45 ..... 151 D2
  Gosport PO12 ..... 181 E4
  Hamble-le-Rice SO31 ..... 128 A1
  Lymington SO41 ..... 197 E2
  Petersfield GU32 ..... 40 C2
  Sherfield English SO51 ..... 26 A2
  Southbourne PO10 ..... 161 E4
  Titchfield PO14 ..... 153 F4
  Westbourne PO10 ..... 137 D2
  Wickham PO17 ..... 108 A2
  Wimborne Minster BH21 ..... 163 D3
  Winchester SO23 ..... 11 D4
Squarey Cl SP5 ..... 46 C3
Squires Wlk
  Southampton SO19 ..... 103 F1
  3 Southampton SO19 ..... 126 C4
Squirrel Cl 7 SO50 ..... 56 C1
Squirrel Dr SO19 ..... 104 A2
Squirrel Wlk BH31 ..... 114 C3
Squirrel's Cl BH23 ..... 191 E1
Squirrels Wlk SO45 ..... 125 F1
Stable Cl PO14 ..... 129 E1
Stables The SO31 ..... 129 D1
Stacey Cl BH12 ..... 203 E4
Stacey Ct PO9 ..... 135 E4
Stacey Gdns BH8 ..... 190 C1
Staff Rd SO50 ..... 6 A1
Stafford Rd
  Bournemouth BH1 ..... 205 D2
  Petersfield GU32 ..... 40 C3
  Portsmouth PO5 ..... 182 B2
  Southampton SO15 ..... 102 B3
Stag Bsns Pk BH24 ..... 141 D3
Stag Cl Bishopstoke SO50 ..... 56 C1
  New Milton BH25 ..... 194 C2
Stag Gates SO45 ..... 150 C1
Stagbrake Cl SO45 ..... 150 A2
Stags La SO21 ..... 33 D3
Stagshorn Rd PO8 ..... 112 B4
Stainer Cl SO19 ..... 104 B2
Staith Rd SO19 ..... 104 B3
Stake's La SO32 ..... 59 F4
Stakes Hill Inf Sch PO7 ..... 134 C3
Stakes Hill Rd PO7 ..... 134 C3
Stakes La SO32 ..... 58 C2
Stakes Rd PO7 ..... 134 B2
Stalbridge Dr BH22 ..... 165 E2
Stalbridge Rd BH17 ..... 202 A4
Stalham Rd BH12 ..... 203 F3
Stallards La BH24 ..... 140 C4
Stalybridge Cl SO31 ..... 129 D3
Stamford Ave PO11 ..... 184 C2
Stamford Lodge PO11 ..... 184 C2
Stamford Rd BH6 ..... 206 B3
Stamford St PO1 ..... 182 C3
Stamford Way SO50 ..... 57 E1
Stampsey Ct 5 PO2 ..... 157 E1
Stamshaw Cl 14 PO2 ..... 157 E1
Stamshaw Inf Sch PO2 ..... 157 E1
Stamshaw Jun Sch PO2 ..... 157 E1
Stanbridge Earls Sch SO51 ..... 27 D2
Stanbridge La SO51 ..... 27 D2
Stanbridge Rd PO9 ..... 136 A2
Standard Way PO16 ..... 131 F2
Standford St SO14 ..... 103 D2
Standing Hill SP5 ..... 3 F4
Stanfield Cl BH12 ..... 203 E4
Stanfield Rd
  Bournemouth BH9 ..... 204 C4
  Ferndown BH22 ..... 165 E3
  Poole BH12 ..... 203 E4
Stanford Ct PO6 ..... 157 E4
Stanford Ct 51 Havant PO9 ..... 136 A3
  Southampton SO19 ..... 104 B2
Stanford Hill SO41 ..... 197 E2
Stanford Rd SO41 ..... 197 E2
Stanford Rise SO41 ..... 172 A1
Stanhope Rd PO1 ..... 182 B3
Stanier Way SO30 ..... 81 E1
Staniforth Ct BH23 ..... 207 E3
Stanley Ave PO3 ..... 183 D4
Stanley Cl Croucheston SP5 ..... 22 A4
  Fareham PO15 ..... 130 C1
  Gosport PO12 ..... 156 A1
  Verwood BH31 ..... 115 D3
Stanley Ct Bournemouth BH1 .. 205 E3
  Poole BH15 ..... 202 B3
Stanley Green Cres Ind Est
  BH15 ..... 202 B3
Stanley Green Fst Sch BH15 .. 202 B3
Stanley Green Rd BH15 ..... 202 B3
Stanley La PO5 ..... 182 B1
Stanley Pearce House BH17 .. 187 E1
Stanley Rd
  Bournemouth BH1 ..... 205 E3
  Christchurch BH23 ..... 209 D4
  Emsworth PO10 ..... 161 D4
  Holbury SO45 ..... 150 B2
  Lymington SO41 ..... 198 A1
  Poole BH15 ..... 202 B1
  Portsmouth PO2 ..... 157 E1
  Southampton SO17 ..... 79 E1
  Totton SO40 ..... 76 B1
Stanley St PO5 ..... 182 B1
Stanmore La SO22 ..... 10 B3
Stanmore Prim Sch SO22 ..... 10 C3
Stannington Cl BH25 ..... 195 D1

Stannington Cres SO40 ..... 100 C4
Stannington Way SO40 ..... 100 C4
Stanpit BH23 ..... 207 F3
Stanstead Rd SO50 ..... 55 F2
Stansted Cl PO9 ..... 113 E1
Stansted Cres PO9 ..... 136 A3
Stansted Ct PO9 ..... 113 E1
Stansted Rd PO5 ..... 182 C2
Stanswood Rd
  Blackfield SO45 ..... 178 B3
  Fawley SO45 ..... 178 B3
  Havant PO9 ..... 135 E3
Stanton Bldgs 20 SO15 ..... 102 A4
Stanton Lacy 17 BH13 ..... 214 C4
Stanton Rd
  Bournemouth BH10 ..... 189 E1
  Petersfield GU32 ..... 40 C2
  Southampton SO15 ..... 102 A4
Stanton Road Ind
  Est 21 SO15 ..... 102 A4
Stapehill Abbey Gdns BH21 .. 164 C3
Stapehill Cres BH21 ..... 164 B3
Stapehill Rd BH21 ..... 164 C2
Staple Ash La GU32 ..... 39 E4
Staple Cl PO7 ..... 111 E1
Staple Close La BH15 ..... 202 B3
Staple Cross Burton BH23 ..... 207 F4
  Southwick PO17 ..... 132 A4
Staple Gdns SO23 ..... 10 C4
Staplecross La BH23 ..... 207 E4
Stapleford Ave BH22 ..... 165 F3
Stapleford Cl SO51 ..... 28 A1
Stapleford La SO32 ..... 81 F3
Staplehurst Cl SO19 ..... 104 A1
Staplers Reach PO13 ..... 155 D1
Stapleton Rd PO3 ..... 183 D4
Staplewood La Ashurst SO40 .. 124 B4
  Marchwood SO40 ..... 124 B4
Star Cotts PO17 ..... 108 A2
Star La BH24 ..... 140 C4
Stares Cl PO13 ..... 180 B4
Starina Gdns PO7 ..... 135 D4
Starling Sq SO50 ..... 56 C1
Station App Broadstone BH18 .. 187 D2
  1 Portsmouth PO1 ..... 182 A3
Station Cl PO17 ..... 108 A2
Station Cotts SO42 ..... 123 E1
Station Hill Bursledon SO31 .. 128 A4
  Curdridge SO30 ..... 106 B4
  Eastleigh SO50 ..... 56 A2
  Winchester SO21, SO23 ..... 10 C4
Station La SO53 ..... 55 E3
Station Rd Alderholt SP6 ..... 92 C3
  Bishop's Waltham SO32 ..... 83 E4
  Burley SO43 ..... 170 B4
  Bursledon SO31 ..... 128 A4
  Christchurch BH23 ..... 207 D4
  Christchurch, Highcliffe BH23 .. 193 F1
  Cosham PO6 ..... 158 B4
  Fordingbridge SP6 ..... 69 E1
  Gosport PO12 ..... 180 C4
  Hamworthy BH15 ..... 202 A1
  Liss GU33 ..... 20 C2
  Locks Heath SO31 ..... 129 D3
  Netley SO31 ..... 127 E3
  New Milton BH25 ..... 195 D1
  Nursling SO16 ..... 77 D3
  Petersfield GU31, GU32 ..... 40 C2
  Poole BH14 ..... 203 D2
  Portchester PO16 ..... 156 B4
  Portsmouth PO3 ..... 183 D4
  Romsey SO51 ..... 52 C4
  Soberton SO32 ..... 85 E4
  South Hayling PO11 ..... 184 C4
  Southampton, Redbridge SO15 .. 101 E4
  Southampton, Sholing SO19 .. 103 F4
  Sway SO41 ..... 172 A1
  Verwood BH31 ..... 114 C4
  West Meon GU32 ..... 37 E2
  West Moors BH22 ..... 138 B1
  Wickham PO17 ..... 108 A1
  Wimborne Minster BH21 ..... 163 E2
Station Rd N SO40 ..... 101 D4
Station Rd S SO40 ..... 101 D4
Station St Lymington SO41 ..... 197 F2
  Portsmouth PO1 ..... 182 B3
Station Terr BH21 ..... 163 E2
Staunton BH2 ..... 204 C1
Staunton Ave PO11 ..... 184 B2
Staunton Ctry Pk Havant PO9.. 135 F4
  Rowland's Castle PO9 ..... 136 A4
Staunton Park Sec Sch PO9 .. 136 A4
Staunton Rd PO9 ..... 135 F1
Staunton St PO1 ..... 182 B3
Stead Cl PO11 ..... 185 D2
Stedman Rd BH5 ..... 206 A3
Steel St PO5 ..... 182 A2
Steele Cl SO53 ..... 55 E2
Steele Dro SP6 ..... 70 C4
Steels La SP6 ..... 68 B2
Steep CE Prim Sch GU32 ..... 40 C4
Steep Cl Portchester PO16 ..... 132 B1
  Southampton SO18 ..... 104 B4
Steepdene BH14 ..... 203 D2
Steeple Cl BH17 ..... 187 E2
Steeple Way PO14 ..... 129 E2
Steepleton Rd BH18 ..... 187 E2
Steerforth PO2 ..... 182 B4
Stein Rd PO10 ..... 137 E1
Steinbeck Cl PO15 ..... 129 E1
Stella Ct
  19 Christchurch BH23 ..... 209 D4
  Southampton SO16 ..... 78 B2
Stem La BH25 ..... 194 C2
Stenbury Way SO31 ..... 127 E4
Stenhurst Rd BH15 ..... 202 C3
Step Terr SO22 ..... 10 C4
Stephen Cl PO8 ..... 112 A4

Stephen Langton Dr BH11 ..... 188 C2
Stephen Martin Gdns SP6 ..... 69 E1
Stephen Rd PO15 ..... 130 C1
Stephens Ct SO51 ..... 52 C3
Stephens Wlk BH24 ..... 140 C4
Stephenson Cl PO12 ..... 181 D1
Stephenson Rd SO40 ..... 76 B1
Stephenson Way SO30 ..... 81 D2
Steplake La SO51 ..... 25 E1
Steplake Rd SO51 ..... 50 B4
Stepnell Reach BH16 ..... 201 E4
Sterte Ave BH15 ..... 202 A2
Sterte Ave W BH15 ..... 202 A2
Sterte Cl BH15 ..... 202 B2
Sterte Ct BH15 ..... 202 A2
Sterte Espl BH15 ..... 202 B2
Sterte Ind Est BH15 ..... 202 A2
Sterte Rd BH15 ..... 202 B2
Steuart Rd SO18 ..... 103 E4
Stevenson Cres BH14 ..... 203 F2
Stevenson Rd BH6 ..... 207 D2
Stevensons Cl 4 BH21 ..... 163 E2
Steventon Rd SO18 ..... 104 B4
Stewart Cl 5 BH8 ..... 205 E3
Stewart House SO53 ..... 30 B1
Stewart Pl PO1 ..... 182 C4
Stewart Rd BH8 ..... 205 D3
Stewarts Gn PO7 ..... 86 B2
Stewarts Way BH22 ..... 165 F4
Stibbs Way BH23 ..... 169 E1
Stillmore Rd BH11 ..... 188 B2
Stinchar Dr SO53 ..... 55 D3
Stinsford Cl BH9 ..... 190 A2
Stinsford La SO18 ..... 202 B4
Stinsford Rd BH17 ..... 187 E1
Stirling Ave PO7 ..... 134 C4
Stirling Cl New Milton BH25 .. 195 D2
  Totton SO40 ..... 77 D1
Stirling Cres Hedge End SO30 .. 81 E1
  Totton SO40 ..... 101 D4
Stirling Ct
  Bournemouth BH4 ..... 204 B1
  Portsmouth PO15 ..... 130 C2
  21 New Milton BH25 ..... 195 D2
Stirling Rd BH3 ..... 204 C4
Stirling St PO2 ..... 182 B4
Stirling Way BH23 ..... 208 A3
Stirling Wlk SO51 ..... 52 C4
Stirrup Cl Upton BH16 ..... 201 E4
  Wimborne Minster BH21 ..... 164 B3
Stoborough Dr BH18 ..... 187 D1
Stock La SP5 ..... 49 E3
Stock's Cross SO43 ..... 73 F2
Stock's La SO32 ..... 61 F3
Stockbridge Cl Havant PO9 ..... 136 A3
  Poole BH17 ..... 188 A1
Stockbridge Rd SO21, 22, 23 .... 1 B4
Stocker Pl PO13 ..... 155 E1
Stockers Ave SO22 ..... 1 B1
Stockheath La PO9 ..... 135 F2
Stockheath Rd PO9 ..... 135 F2
Stockheath Way PO9 ..... 135 F2
Stockholm Dr SO30 ..... 105 E3
Stockley Cl SO45 ..... 150 B2
Stocks Heath La PO9 ..... 135 F2
Stockton Cl SO30 ..... 105 E4
Stoddart Ave SO19 ..... 103 F3
Stodham La GU33 ..... 20 C1
Stoke Common Rd SO50 ..... 56 C3
Stoke Gdns PO12 ..... 181 D4
Stoke Hts SO50 ..... 57 D2
Stoke Park Dr SO50 ..... 56 B2
Stoke Park Inf Sch SO50 ..... 56 C1
Stoke Park Jun Sch SO50 ..... 56 C1
Stoke Park Rd SO50 ..... 56 B2
Stoke Rd Gosport PO12 ..... 181 D4
  Southampton SO16 ..... 78 A1
  Winchester SO23 ..... 2 A2
Stoke Wood Cl SO50 ..... 57 D1
Stoke Wood Rd BH3 ..... 204 C3
Stokes Ave BH15 ..... 202 B2
Stokes Bay Rd PO12 ..... 180 C1
Stokesay Cl SO45 ..... 150 A4
Stokeway 4 PO12 ..... 181 E2
Stone Gdns BH8 ..... 191 D1
Stone La 5 Gosport PO12 ..... 181 D2
  Wimborne Minster BH21 ..... 163 D3
Stone Sq PO12 ..... 135 F2
Stone St PO5 ..... 182 A2
Stone Terr SO50 ..... 31 D1
Stonechat Cl Ferndown BH22 .. 165 D4
  Petersfield GU31 ..... 41 E1
Stonechat Ct BH23 ..... 207 F4
Stonechat Dr SO40 ..... 100 A4
Stonechat Rd PO8 ..... 112 A4
Stonecrop Cl
  Broadstone BH18 ..... 186 C1
  Locks Heath SO31 ..... 152 B4
Stoneham Cemetery Rd SO18 .. 79 F2
Stoneham Cl Petersfield GU32 .. 40 B2
  Southampton SO16 ..... 79 D3
Stoneham Ct SO16 ..... 79 D3
Stoneham Gdns SO31 ..... 104 C1
Stoneham La Chilworth SO50 .. 79 F4
  Southampton SO16 ..... 79 E3
Stoneham Pk GU32 ..... 40 B2
Stoneham Way SO16, SO18 ..... 79 F3
Stonehills SO45 ..... 151 E2
Stoneleigh 13 BH13 ..... 214 C4
Stoneleigh Ave SO41 ..... 195 F2
Stoneleigh Cl PO16 ..... 156 A4
Stoner Hill Rd GU32 ..... 19 D1
Stoners Cl PO13 ..... 155 D2
Stoney La SO22 ..... 1 B1
Stony La Burton BH23 ..... 192 B3
  Froxfield GU32 ..... 18 C1
  Portsmouth PO1 ..... 182 A3

Stony La S BH23 ..... 207 E3
Stonymoor Cl SO45 ..... 150 B2
Stopples La SO41 ..... 195 F2
Storrington Rd PO8 ..... 88 B3
Story La BH18 ..... 187 D2
Stour Cl Ferndown BH21 ..... 164 B2
  West End SO18 ..... 80 A2
  West Wellow SO51 ..... 50 B2
Stour Rd Bournemouth BH8 ..... 205 E3
  Christchurch BH23 ..... 207 D3
Stour View Gdns BH21 ..... 162 C1
Stour Way BH23 ..... 191 E1
Stour Wlk Bournemouth BH8 .. 190 B2
  18 Wimborne Minster BH21 .. 163 E2
Stourbank Rd BH23 ..... 207 D3
Stourcliffe Ave BH6 ..... 206 B2
Stourcroft Dr BH23 ..... 191 F1
Stourfield Fst & Jun Schs
  BH6 ..... 206 B3
Stourfield Rd BH5 ..... 206 A2
Stourpaine Rd BH17 ..... 187 E1
Stourton Ct 17 BH4 ..... 204 B2
Stourvale Ave BH24 ..... 206 B4
Stourvale Gdns SO53 ..... 55 E3
Stourvale Pl 10 BH5 ..... 206 A3
Stourvale Rd BH5,BH6 ..... 206 B3
Stourwood Ave BH6 ..... 206 B2
Stourwood Mans 4 BH6 ..... 206 B2
Stourwood Rd BH6 ..... 206 B2
Stouts La BH9 ..... 169 D1
Stow Cres PO15 ..... 130 B1
Stowe Rd PO4 ..... 183 D2
Stradbrook BH23 ..... 155 D1
Stragwyne Cl SO52 ..... 53 F3
Straight Mile The
  Ampfield SO51 ..... 28 C1
  North Baddesley SO51 ..... 28 C1
Strand SO14 ..... 103 D2
Strand St BH15 ..... 202 B1
Strand The PO11 ..... 185 E1
Stratfield Dr SO53 ..... 30 A1
Stratfield Gdns PO9 ..... 135 E4
Stratfield Pk PO7 ..... 134 B4
Stratford Cl SO22 ..... 194 C2
Stratford Ct 9 SO23 ..... 2 A1
Stratford House 47 PO5 ..... 182 B2
Stratford Pl Eastleigh SO50 ..... 56 A2
  Lymington SO41 ..... 197 E3
Stratford Rd PO7 ..... 135 D4
Strathmore Dr BH31 ..... 115 D3
Strathmore Rd
  Bournemouth BH9 ..... 190 A2
  Gosport PO12 ..... 181 E2
Stratton Cl PO9 ..... 157 E4
Stratton Rd Bournemouth BH9 .. 190 B2
  Southampton SO15 ..... 78 B1
  Winchester SO23 ..... 11 E4
Strawberry Fields
  East Boldre SO42 ..... 175 E3
  Hedge End SO30 ..... 105 D3
Strawberry Hill SO31 ..... 128 C2
Streamleaze PO14 ..... 129 E1
Street End SO52 ..... 54 A3
Street The SP5 ..... 24 A2
Streets La BH24 ..... 141 E2
Strete Mount 18 BH23 ..... 207 F4
Stretton Ct BH14 ..... 203 D2
Stride Ave PO3 ..... 183 D3
Strides La BH24 ..... 140 C4
Strides Way SO40 ..... 100 A4
Strode Gdns BH24 ..... 140 A3
Strode Rd PO2 ..... 157 E1
Strongs Cl SO51 ..... 53 D4
Stroud Cl BH21 ..... 164 A3
Stroud End GU32 ..... 40 A2
Stroud Gdns BH23 ..... 207 F3
Stroud Green La PO14 ..... 154 B3
Stroud La BH23 ..... 207 F3
Stroud Park Ave BH23 ..... 207 F3
Stroud Sch The SO51 ..... 53 F4
Strouden Ave BH8 ..... 205 E4
Strouden Court Prec PO9 ..... 135 E4
Strouden Ct PO9 ..... 135 E4
Strouden Rd BH9 ..... 190 A1
Stroudley Ave PO6 ..... 158 B3
Stroudley Way SO30 ..... 81 E1
Stroudwood Rd Fair Oak SO32 .. 58 A2
  Havant PO9 ..... 136 A2
Struan Cl BH24 ..... 139 F3
Struan Ct BH24 ..... 140 A3
Struan Dr BH24 ..... 140 A3
Struan Gdns BH24 ..... 139 F3
Stuart Bridgewater House
  SO18 ..... 104 A4
Stuart Cl Stubbington PO14 ..... 179 E3
  Upton BH16 ..... 201 D4
Stuart Cres SO22 ..... 10 C3
Stuart Ct 7 PO6 ..... 157 F4
Stuart Rd BH23 ..... 209 D4
Stubbermere PO10 ..... 136 C4
Stubbington Ave PO2 ..... 157 F1
Stubbington Gn PO14 ..... 154 B2
Stubbington La PO14 ..... 179 E4
Stubbington Study Ctr PO14 .. 179 E2
Stubbington Way SO50 ..... 57 E1
Stubbs Dro SO30 ..... 105 E4
Stubbs Rd SO19 ..... 104 B1
Stuckton Rd SP6 ..... 94 A4
Student Village BH12 ..... 204 B4
Studland Cl SO16 ..... 77 E1
Studland Dr SO41 ..... 211 E4
Studland Rd
  Bournemouth BH4 ..... 204 B1
  Lee-on-the-Solent PO13 ..... 179 F1
  Southampton SO16 ..... 77 E1

Studley Ave SO45 ..... 150 B2
Studley Cl BH23 ..... 209 E4
Studley Ct BH25 ..... 209 E4
Sturminster House ② SO16 ..... 78 A1
Sturminster Rd BH9 ..... 190 A2
Styles The SP5 ..... 22 B4
Submarine Mus PO12 ..... 181 F2
Sudbury Rd PO6 ..... 157 E4
Suetts La SO32 ..... 83 F4
Suffolk Ave Christchurch BH23 .. 191 F1
  Southampton SO15 ..... 102 B4
Suffolk Cl
  Chandler's Ford SO53 ..... 55 E1
  Wimborne Minster BH21 ..... 164 B3
Suffolk Dr
  Chandler's Ford SO53 ..... 55 E1
  Swanwick PO15 ..... 129 D4
Suffolk Gr SO53 ..... 55 E1
Suffolk Rd Bournemouth BH2 .... 204 B2
  Bournemouth BH2 ..... 204 C2
  Portsmouth PO4 ..... 183 D2
Suffolk Rd S BH2 ..... 204 B2
Sullivan Cl PO6 ..... 156 C4
Sullivan Rd SO19 ..... 104 B2
Sullivan Way PO7 ..... 134 C3
Sultan Rd Emsworth PO10 ..... 136 C1
  Portsmouth PO1, PO2 ..... 182 B4
Sumar Cl PO14 ..... 154 B3
Summer Field Cl BH21 ..... 164 A2
Summerbee First Sch BH8 .... 190 B1
Summerbee Jun Sch BH8 ..... 190 B1
Summerbee Sec Sch BH8 ..... 190 B1
Summercroft Way BH22 ..... 138 C2
Summerfield Cl BH23 ..... 192 B1
Summerfield Ct SO53 ..... 158 A2
Summerfield Gdns SO16 ..... 79 E3
Summerfields
  Bournemouth BH7 ..... 205 F4
  Locks Heath SO31 ..... 129 D1
Summerhill Rd PO8 ..... 112 A2
Summerlands BH22 ..... 165 E3
Summerlands Rd SO50 ..... 57 E1
Summerlands Wlk 42 PO9 .... 136 A3
Summers Ave BH11 ..... 189 D3
Summers La BH23 ..... 192 B1
Summers St SO14 ..... 103 E3
Summersfield GU33 ..... 20 C2
Summertrees Ct BH25 ..... 195 E2
Summit Way SO18 ..... 79 F1
Sumner Rd GU31 ..... 65 E3
Sun St PO1 ..... 182 A3
Sunbeam Way PO12 ..... 181 D2
Sunbury Cl
  8 Bournemouth BH2 ..... 204 C2
  Fareham PO15 ..... 130 C2
Suncourt Villas PO12 ..... 180 C4
Sunderland Dr BH23 ..... 208 A4
Sunderton La PO8 ..... 88 B3
Sundew Cl BH25 ..... 195 E2
Sundew Rd BH18 ..... 186 C1
Sundridge Cl PO6 ..... 157 F4
Sunningdale
  Christchurch BH23 ..... 206 C3
  Hythe SO45 ..... 125 F2
  7 Poole BH15 ..... 202 C2
Sunningdale Cl
  8 Bishopstoke SO50 ..... 56 C1
  Gosport PO13 ..... 155 E1
Sunningdale Cres BH10 ..... 189 E2
Sunningdale Gdns
  Broadstone BH18 ..... 187 D3
  Southampton SO18 ..... 104 A4
Sunningdale Rd
  Portchester PO16 ..... 156 B4
  Portsmouth PO3 ..... 183 E4
Sunny Hill Ct BH12 ..... 203 E3
Sunny Hill Rd BH12 ..... 203 E3
Sunny Way SO40 ..... 100 C4
Sunny Wlk PO1 ..... 182 A3
Sunnybank Dr BH21 ..... 164 A3
Sunnybank Rd BH21 ..... 164 A3
Sunnybank Way BH21 ..... 164 A3
Sunnydown Rd SO22 ..... 10 A2
Sunnyfield Rd BH25 ..... 210 A4
Sunnyheath PO9 ..... 135 F2
Sunnyhill Rd BH6 ..... 206 B3
Sunnymead Dr PO7 ..... 111 E1
Sunnymoor Rd BH11 ..... 189 D1
Sunnyside Rd BH12 ..... 203 E3
Sunnyside Wlk PO9 ..... 135 E4
Sunridge Cl BH12 ..... 204 A3
Sunset Ave SO40 ..... 100 C4
Sunset Lodge BH13 ..... 204 A1
Sunset Rd SO40 ..... 100 C4
Sunshine Ave PO11 ..... 185 D1
Suntrap Gdns PO11 ..... 185 D1
Sunvale Cl SO19 ..... 104 A2
Sunwood Rd PO9 ..... 135 E3
Surbiton Rd SO50 ..... 56 A3
Surrey Cl Christchurch BH23 .. 191 F1
  Totton SO40 ..... 100 B3
Surrey Ct SO15 ..... 102 B3
Surrey Gdns BH4 ..... 204 B2
Surrey House SO53 ..... 55 E2
Surrey House Inf Sch SO19 .. 104 B2
Surrey Rd
  Bournemouth BH2, BH4 ..... 204 A4
  Chandler's Ford SO53 ..... 55 E2
  Poole BH12 ..... 204 A4
  Southampton SO19 ..... 103 E1
Surrey Rd S BH4 ..... 204 B2
Surrey St PO1 ..... 182 B3
Sussex Cl BH9 ..... 190 A2

Sussex Gdns GU31 ..... 40 C1
Sussex Pl
  34 Portsmouth PO5 ..... 182 B2
  4 Portsmouth PO1 ..... 182 B3
Sussex Rd
  Chandler's Ford SO53 ..... 55 E2
  Petersfield GU31 ..... 41 D1
  Portsmouth PO5 ..... 182 B2
  Southampton SO14 ..... 103 D2
Sussex St SO23 ..... 10 C4
Sussex Terr 33 PO5 ..... 182 B2
Sutherland Ave BH18 ..... 186 C3
Sutherland Cl 6 SO51 ..... 28 A1
Sutherland Ct SO53 ..... 55 E3
Sutherland Rd
  Portsmouth PO4 ..... 182 C2
  Southampton SO16 ..... 77 F3
Sutherlands Way SO53 ..... 55 D4
Sutton Cl Poole BH17 ..... 188 A1
  Portsmouth PO3 ..... 158 A2
  Waterlooville PO8 ..... 111 E2
Sutton Gdns SO23 ..... 11 D4
Sutton Pl SO42 ..... 146 A1
Sutton Rd Bournemouth BH9 .... 190 A1
  Totton SO40 ..... 76 C1
  Waterlooville PO8 ..... 111 E2
Swale Dr SO53 ..... 55 D4
Swallow Cl Broadstone BH17 .. 201 F4
  Havant PO9 ..... 136 A1
  Totton SO40 ..... 100 A3
Swallow Ct Clanfield PO8 ..... 88 A3
  Lee-on-the-Solent PO13 ..... 179 F2
Swallow Dr SO41 ..... 211 F2
Swallow Sq SO50 ..... 55 E1
Swallow Wood PO16 ..... 131 D2
Swallow Way BH21 ..... 164 A4
Swan Cl Emsworth PO10 ..... 161 D4
  Swanwick SO31 ..... 128 B4
Swan Ct Bursledon SO31 ..... 128 B4
  Gosport PO13 ..... 155 D2
Swan Ctr The SO50 ..... 56 A1
Swan Gn 8 BH23 ..... 207 D3
Swan La SO23 ..... 10 C4
Swan Mead BH24 ..... 141 E3
Swan Quay Portchester PO16 .. 155 E4
  Southampton SO14 ..... 103 E4
Swan St SO32 ..... 40 C2
Swanage Cl SO19 ..... 103 F2
Swanage Rd PO13 ..... 179 F1
Swancote PO16 ..... 155 F4
Swanley Cl SO50 ..... 56 A3
Swanmore Ave SO19 ..... 104 B2
Swanmore Bsns Pk SO32 ..... 83 F3
Swanmore CE Prim Sch SO32 . 84 A3
Swanmore Cl
  Bournemouth BH7 ..... 206 A4
  Winchester SO22 ..... 1 B2
Swanmore Park House SO32 .. 84 B4
Swanmore Rd
  Bournemouth BH7 ..... 206 A4
  Droxford SO32 ..... 84 C4
  Havant PO9 ..... 135 E4
  Swanmore SO32 ..... 84 A3
  Swanmore, Droxford SO32 ..... 84 A4
Swanmore Sec Sch SO32 ..... 84 A2
Swans Wlk PO11 ..... 185 D2
Swansbury Dr BH8 ..... 191 D1
Swanton Gdns SO53 ..... 55 D4
Swanwick Bsns Ctr SO31 ..... 128 B4
Swanwick La SO31 ..... 128 C4
Swanwick Shore Rd SO31 ..... 128 B4
Swanwick Sta SO31 ..... 129 D3
Swarraton Rd PO9 ..... 136 A2
Sway Ct Havant PO9 ..... 136 A3
  Sway SO41 ..... 196 B4
Sway Gdns BH8 ..... 190 B1
Sway Park Ind Est SO41 ..... 172 A1
Sway Rd Brockenhurst SO42 .. 172 C4
  Hordle SO41 ..... 197 D3
  Lymington SO41 ..... 197 D3
  New Milton BH25 ..... 195 E3
Sway St Luke's CE Prim Sch
  SO41 ..... 172 A1
Sway Sta SO41 ..... 172 A1
Swaythling Prim Sch SO17 .... 79 D2
Swaythling Rd Havant PO9 .... 135 E3
  West End SO18,SO30 ..... 80 A1
Swaythling Sta SO18 ..... 79 E2
Swedish Houses SO41 ..... 198 C4
Sweep The BH24 ..... 140 C4
Sweetbriar Gdns PO7 ..... 134 C3
Sweethills Cres PO15 ..... 129 E4
Sweyns Lease SO42 ..... 175 E3
Swift Cl Broadstone BH17 ..... 201 F4
  Eastleigh SO50 ..... 55 E1
  Horndean PO8 ..... 112 A4
  Lee-on-the-Solent PO13 ..... 179 F2
  Winchester SO22 ..... 10 B3
Swift Gdns SO19 ..... 103 E1
Swift Hollow SO19 ..... 103 E1
Swift Rd Southampton SO19 .. 103 E1
  Thorney Island PO10 ..... 161 D2
Swinburn Gdns PO8 ..... 111 F2
Swincombe Rise SO18 ..... 80 A1
Swiss Rd PO7 ..... 134 C4
Switch House Rd SO45 ..... 151 F1
Swivelton La PO17 ..... 132 A2
Sword Cl Clanfield PO8 ..... 88 A3
  Gosport PO12 ..... 180 C1
Sword Sands Rd PO3 ..... 183 E4
Swordfish Dr BH23 ..... 208 A4
Sycamore Ave SO53 ..... 30 B1
Sycamore Cl
  Broadstone BH17 ..... 186 C1
  Bursledon SO31 ..... 127 F4
  Christchurch BH23 ..... 206 B4
  Clanfield PO8 ..... 88 B3
  Gosport PO13 ..... 155 F1

Sycamore Cl Continued
  Milford on Sea SO41 ..... 211 E3
  North Baddesley SO52 ..... 53 F3
  Romsey SO51 ..... 53 E3
  Titchfield PO14 ..... 129 E1
  Waterlooville PO8 ..... 111 F2
Sycamore Ct BH24 ..... 117 E1
Sycamore Dr Holbury SO45 .... 150 A3
  Kings Worthy SO23 ..... 2 A4
  South Hayling PO11 ..... 184 C2
Sycamore Rd
  Bishop's Waltham SO32 ..... 83 F4
  Hordle SO41 ..... 195 F2
  Hythe SO45 ..... 125 F2
  Southampton SO16 ..... 78 A1
Sycamore Wlk SO30 ..... 105 F4
Sycamores The 4 SO45 ..... 126 A2
Sydenham Ct PO1 ..... 182 C3
Sydenham Terr
  Portsmouth PO1 ..... 182 C3
  Westbourne PO10 ..... 137 D3
Sydling Cl BH17 ..... 188 A1
Sydmanton Cl SO51 ..... 53 D3
Sydmonton Ct 2 PO9 ..... 136 A3
Sydney Ave SO31 ..... 127 F2
Sydney House 33 PO1 ..... 182 B3
Sydney Rd Bishopstoke SO50 .. 56 B2
  Broadstone BH18 ..... 187 D2
  Christchurch BH23 ..... 191 F1
  Gosport PO12 ..... 181 D2
  Southampton SO15 ..... 78 A1
Syers Cl GU33 ..... 20 C2
Syers Rd GU33 ..... 20 C2
Sylmor Gdns BH9 ..... 190 A1
Sylvan Ave SO19 ..... 104 B3
Sylvan Cl Hordle SO41 ..... 196 A1
  St Leonards BH24 ..... 139 E2
Sylvan Dr SO52 ..... 53 F2
Sylvan Fst Sch BH12 ..... 203 D3
Sylvan La SO31 ..... 128 A1
Sylvan Rd BH12 ..... 203 D3
Sylvan View PO7 ..... 134 C3
Sylvans The SO45 ..... 125 E2
Sylvia Cres SO40 ..... 76 C1
Symes Rd Hamworthy BH15 ... 201 F2
  Romsey SO51 ..... 53 D4
Symonds Cl SO53 ..... 55 E2
Symonds St SO23 ..... 11 D4
Sywell Cres PO3 ..... 158 B2

Tadburn Cl
  Chandler's Ford SO53 ..... 55 E3
  Romsey SO51 ..... 53 D4
Tadburn Gn SO51 ..... 52 C3
Tadburn Rd SO51 ..... 53 D3
Tadden Cotts BH21 ..... 162 B4
Tadden Wlk BH18 ..... 186 C1
Tadfield Cres SO51 ..... 53 D4
Tadfield Rd SO51 ..... 53 D4
Tadhurst House 24 PO1 ..... 182 B3
Tait Cl BH17 ..... 202 C4
Tait Pl PO13 ..... 155 E1
Talbot Ave BH3 ..... 204 C4
Talbot Cl Havant PO9 ..... 135 E2
  Southampton SO16 ..... 78 C2
Talbot Comb Sch BH12 ..... 204 A4
Talbot Ct Bournemouth BH9 ... 189 F1
  11 Southampton SO14 ..... 103 D2
Talbot Dr Christchurch BH23 .. 193 F1
  Poole BH12 ..... 204 A4
Talbot Heath Sch BH4 ..... 204 B3
Talbot Hill Rd BH9 ..... 204 B4
Talbot House Prep Sch BH4 .. 204 C4
Talbot Meadows SO40 ..... 100 A4
Talbot Mews BH10 ..... 189 D1
Talbot Rd Bournemouth BH9 .. 204 B4
  Havant PO9 ..... 135 E2
  Hythe SO45 ..... 125 F1
  Portsmouth PO4 ..... 182 C2
Talbot Rdbt BH3 ..... 204 B4
Talbot Rise BH10 ..... 189 E1
Talisman Bsns Ctr SO31 ..... 129 D3
Tall Trees BH14 ..... 203 D3
Talland Rd PO14 ..... 129 D1
Tallywater Hill GU32 ..... 18 B2
Tamar Cl Ferndown BH22 ..... 166 A3
  Portchester PO16 ..... 132 A1
Tamar Down PO7 ..... 135 D4
Tamar Gdns SO18 ..... 80 A1
Tamar Gr SO45 ..... 125 F2
Tamarisk Cl Portsmouth PO4 .. 183 E2
  Stubbington PO14 ..... 179 E3
  Waterlooville PO7 ..... 135 D3
Tamarisk Gdns SO18 ..... 103 F4
Tamarisk Rd SO30 ..... 105 D4
Tamella Rd SO30 ..... 105 F3
Tammys Turn PO14 ..... 154 A4
Tamorisk Dr SO40 ..... 100 B3
Tamworth Ct 10 PO12 ..... 181 D2
Tamworth Rd
  Bournemouth BH7 ..... 205 F3
  Portsmouth PO3 ..... 183 D3
Tan Howse Cl BH7 ..... 206 A4
Tanfield La PO17 ..... 108 A3
Tanfield Pk PO17 ..... 108 A2
Tangier La SO32 ..... 83 D4
Tangier Rd PO3 ..... 183 D4
Tanglewood Fareham PO16 ... 131 D2
  Marchwood SO40 ..... 100 A1
Tanglewood Cl PO7 ..... 134 B2
Tanglewood Ct 11 BH25 ..... 195 D2
Tanglewood Lodge BH17 .... 201 F4
Tangley Wlk PO9 ..... 136 A3
Tangmere Cl BH23 ..... 208 A3
Tangmere Dr SO16 ..... 78 A2
Tangmere Pl BH17 ..... 202 C4
Tangyes Cl PO14 ..... 154 B2

Tanhouse Cl SO30 ..... 105 E3
Tanhouse La Botley SO30 ..... 105 E2
  Hedge End SO30 ..... 105 E3
Tankerdale La GU33 ..... 41 E4
Tankerton Cl 2 PO6 ..... 157 F4
Tankerville Rd SO19 ..... 103 E2
Tankerville Sch SO50 ..... 56 A2
Tanner St 20 SO23 ..... 11 D4
Tanner's Brook Way SO15 .... 101 F3
Tanner's La PO7 ..... 111 D3
Tanner's Ridge PO7 ..... 134 C2
Tanneries Ind Est The PO9 .... 135 F1
Tanners Brook Inf Sch SO15 .. 101 F4
Tanners Brook Jun Sch SO15 . 101 F4
Tanners La Boldre SO41 ..... 199 D2
  Gosport PO14 ..... 154 C3
  West Wellow SO51 ..... 51 E4
Tanners Rd SO52 ..... 54 A2
Tanners The PO14 ..... 129 E1
Tansy Cl PO7 ..... 135 D3
Tansy Meadow SO52 ..... 54 C2
Tanyards The SO53 ..... 30 A1
Taplin Dr SO30 ..... 105 E4
Taplings Cl SO22 ..... 1 B2
Taplings Rd SO22 ..... 1 B2
Tapper Ct SO21 ..... 163 F2
Taranto Rd SO16 ..... 78 B2
Tarbery Cres PO8 ..... 112 B4
Tardif House SO16 ..... 78 A1
Target Rd PO2 ..... 157 E1
Tarius Cl PO13 ..... 155 E2
Tarleton Rd PO6 ..... 133 D1
Tarn Dr BH17 ..... 201 F4
Tarn Rise PO8 ..... 88 B1
Tarrant Cl BH17 ..... 187 F1
Tarrant Gdns PO9 ..... 135 E2
Tarrant Rd BH9 ..... 190 A2
Tasman Cl
  Christchurch BH23 ..... 206 C4
  Southampton SO14 ..... 103 D1
Tasman Ct SO14 ..... 103 D1
Taswell Rd PO5 ..... 182 B1
Tatchbury La SO40 ..... 99 F4
Tatchbury Mount Hospl SO40 . 76 A1
Tate Ct SO15 ..... 101 E4
Tate Mews SO15 ..... 101 E4
Tate Rd SO15 ..... 101 E4
Tates Rd Hythe SO45 ..... 126 A1
  Hythe SO45 ..... 126 A2
Tatnam Rd BH15 ..... 202 B2
Tattenham Rd SO42 ..... 172 C4
Tattershall Cres PO16 ..... 156 A4
Tatum Cres BH15 ..... 202 B2
Tatwin Cl SO19 ..... 104 B3
Tatwin Cres SO19 ..... 104 B3
Taunton Coll SO15 ..... 78 C1
Taunton Dr SO18 ..... 104 A4
Taunton Row SO53 ..... 55 E2
Tavell's La SO40 ..... 101 F1
Tavells Cl SO40 ..... 101 F1
Taverner Cl BH15 ..... 202 B1
Taverners Ct SO19 ..... 104 B2
Tavistock Cl 4 SO51 ..... 28 A1
Tavistock Gdns PO9 ..... 136 A1
Tavy Cl SO53 ..... 55 D3
Taw Dr SO53 ..... 55 D3
Tawny Owl Cl PO14 ..... 154 A2
Taylor Cl SO19 ..... 103 E1
Taylor Dr BH8 ..... 190 B2
Taylor Rd PO12 ..... 181 E1
Taylor's Bldgs 22 BH15 ..... 202 B1
Taylors Cnr SO23 ..... 2 A3
Teachers Way SO45 ..... 150 A2
Teak Cl BH13 ..... 214 D4
Teal Cl Portchester PO16 ..... 155 F4
  South Hayling PO11 ..... 185 D2
  Totton SO40 ..... 100 B4
Teal Wlk PO13 ..... 155 D2
Teapot Row PO4 ..... 183 D1
Teasel Way BH22 ..... 138 C1
Teazle Cl GU31 ..... 41 E1
Tebourba Cotts SO41 ..... 172 A1
Tebourba Dr PO12 ..... 181 D2
Tebourba House 6 PO14 ..... 154 C4
Tebourba Way
  Curdridge SO30 ..... 106 B4
  Southampton SO16 ..... 101 F4
  Southampton SO15 ..... 102 A4
Ted Kelly Ct 29 PO1 ..... 182 A3
Tedder Cl BH11 ..... 189 D2
Tedder Gdns BH11 ..... 189 D2
Tedder Rd
  Bournemouth BH11 ..... 189 D2
  Gosport PO13 ..... 155 E2
  Southampton SO18 ..... 104 A4
Tedder Way SO40 ..... 100 B4
Teddington Rd PO4 ..... 183 D2
Tees Cl SO53 ..... 55 D4
Tees Farm Rd SO21 ..... 56 C4
Tees Gr 2 SO21 ..... 56 C4
Teg Down GU31 ..... 41 D2
Teg Down Meads SO22 ..... 1 B1
Teglease Gn PO9 ..... 135 E4
Teignmouth Rd
  Gosport PO12 ..... 180 C4
  Portsmouth PO3 ..... 183 D4
Telegraph Rd SO30 ..... 80 C1
Telephone Rd PO4 ..... 182 C2
Telford Rd Ferndown BH21 .... 165 D4
  Portsmouth PO2 ..... 157 F2
Teme Cres SO16 ..... 101 F4
Teme Rd SO16 ..... 101 F4
Tempest Ave PO7 ..... 135 D4
Templar Ct 27 SO14 ..... 103 D4
Templars Mede SO53 ..... 55 D2
Templars Way SO53 ..... 55 D2
Temple Gdns SO19 ..... 103 F1
Temple La GU32 ..... 63 F4

Temple Rd Liss GU33 ..... 21 D3
  Southampton SO19 ..... 103 F1
Temple St PO1 ..... 182 B3
Templecombe Rd SO50 ..... 56 C1
Templemere PO14 ..... 154 A4
Templer Cl BH11 ..... 188 C1
Templeton Cl PO2 ..... 157 F2
Tenby Cl SO18 ..... 104 A4
Tenby Dr SO53 ..... 55 D2
Tench Way SO51 ..... 52 C4
Tennyson Cl
  Bishop's Waltham SO32 ..... 83 F4
  Holbury SO45 ..... 150 A3
Tennyson Cres PO7 ..... 111 E1
Tennyson Ct
  27 Southampton SO17 ..... 79 D1
  37 Southampton SO17 ..... 79 D1
Tennyson Gdns PO16 ..... 131 D1
Tennyson Rd
  Bournemouth BH9 ..... 189 F1
  Eastleigh SO50 ..... 55 F1
  1 Poole BH14 ..... 203 D2
  Portsmouth PO2 ..... 182 C4
  Southampton SO17 ..... 79 D1
  Totton SO40 ..... 76 B1
  Wimborne Minster BH21 ..... 163 E3
Tensing Cl PO16 ..... 131 D2
Tensing Rd BH23 ..... 207 F4
Tenterton Ave SO19 ..... 104 A1
Terence Ave BH17 ..... 187 E1
Terence Rd BH21 ..... 186 B3
Terminus Terr SO14 ..... 103 D2
Tern Cl SO45 ..... 126 A1
Tern Ct BH6 ..... 206 B3
Tern Wlk PO13 ..... 155 D2
Terrace Rd BH2 ..... 204 C2
Terrace The
  Damerham SP6 ..... 68 B3
  Rockbourne SP6 ..... 68 C4
Terrier Cl SO30 ..... 81 E2
Terrington Ave BH23 ..... 193 F1
Terriote Cl SO53 ..... 55 E4
Test Cl GU32 ..... 40 C1
Test House SO51 ..... 52 B4
Test La Nursling SO16 ..... 77 D1
  Southampton SO16 ..... 77 D1
Test Rd SO14 ..... 126 A4
Test Valley Bsns Ctr SO51 .... 77 E1
Test Valley Bsns Pk SO52 .... 54 A3
Testbourne Ave SO40 ..... 100 B4
Testbourne Cl SO40 ..... 100 B4
Testbourne Rd SO40 ..... 100 B3
Testcombe Rd PO12 ..... 181 D2
Testlands Ave SO16 ..... 77 E3
Testwood Ave SO40 ..... 76 C1
Testwood Cres SO40 ..... 76 B1
Testwood La SO40 ..... 101 D4
Testwood Pl SO40 ..... 101 D4
Testwood Rd Havant PO9 ..... 135 E3
  Southampton SO15 ..... 102 A3
Testwood Sch SO40 ..... 76 C1
Tethering Dro SP6 ..... 47 E2
Tetney Cl SO16 ..... 77 F2
Tetsome Cotts PO17 ..... 130 C4
Teviot House 9 SO14 ..... 103 E3
Teviot Rd BH15 ..... 55 D3
Tewkesbury Ave
  Fareham PO15 ..... 130 B2
  Gosport PO12 ..... 181 D4
Tewkesbury Cl PO6 ..... 157 E4
Texas Dr PO12 ..... 10 A2
Thackeray Mall 24 PO16 ..... 131 D1
Thackeray Rd SO17 ..... 103 D4
Thackeray Sq 4 PO16 ..... 131 E1
Thacking Gr 3 SO21 ..... 56 C4
Thames Alley 13 BH15 ..... 202 A1
Thames Cl
  Ferndown BH22 ..... 166 A3
  West End SO18 ..... 80 A2
Thames Ct 1 PO8 ..... 111 F2
Thames Dr PO15 ..... 130 B2
Thames Mews 12 BH15 ..... 202 A1
Thames St SO14 ..... 202 A1
Thamesmead Cl PO12 ..... 180 C4
Thatchers La Boldre SO41 ..... 198 C4
  Sopley BH23 ..... 168 C2
Theatre Mews 2 PO5 ..... 182 B1
Theobald Rd BH23 ..... 191 D4
Theseus Rd PO13 ..... 179 E2
Thessaly Ct 17 BH5 ..... 205 F2
Thetchers Ct BH25 ..... 195 D3
Thetford Gdns SO53 ..... 55 D4
Thetford Rd Gosport PO12 .... 180 C4
  Poole BH12 ..... 203 F3
Thicket The Gosport PO13 .... 155 F1
  Portchester PO16 ..... 131 F1
  Portsmouth PO5 ..... 182 B2
  Romsey SO51 ..... 53 E3
  Waterlooville PO7 ..... 134 B2
Third Ave Cosham PO6 ..... 157 F4
  Havant PO9 ..... 136 A1
  Southampton SO15 ..... 101 F3
Thirlmere SO50 ..... 55 F1
Thirlmere Cl PO14 ..... 154 B2
Thirlmere House 28 PO6 ..... 133 D1
Thirlmere Rd SO16 ..... 77 F1
Thirlstane Firs SO53 ..... 55 D2
Thistle Rd SO30 ..... 105 D3
Thistlebarrow Rd BH7 ..... 205 F3
Thistledown PO8 ..... 112 A3
Thistledowne Gdns PO10 .... 161 D4
Thomas Cl SO40 ..... 100 B3
Thomas Lewis Way SO17 ..... 79 E1
Thomas Lockyer Cl BH31 .... 115 D3
Thomas St 3 PO1 ..... 182 B3
Thompson's La SO21 ..... 57 E4
Thoresby Ct BH25 ..... 194 C2

Thorn Cl Eastleigh SO50 ...... 56 A3
Petersfield GU31 ...... 41 E1
Thorn Rd PO17 ...... 187 E2
Thornbrake Rd PO12 ...... 181 E2
Thornbury **15** BH4 ...... 204 B2
Thornbury Ave SO15 ...... 102 C4
Thornbury Cl PO14 ...... 154 B4
Thornbury House **10** PO6 ...... 132 C1
Thornbury Hts SO53 ...... 30 C1
Thornbury Rd BH6 ...... 207 D2
Thornbury Wood SO53 ...... 30 C1
Thornby Ct PO3 ...... 158 A2
Thorncliffe Cl PO2 ...... 157 F2
Thorncombe Cl
Bournemouth BH9 ...... 190 A2
Broadstone BH17 ...... 187 F1
Thorncroft Rd PO1 ...... 182 C3
Thornden Sec Sch SO53 ...... 55 F4
Thorndike Cl SO16 ...... 78 A1
Thorndike Rd SO16 ...... 77 F1
Thorne Cl BH31 ...... 114 C3
Thorne Way BH21 ...... 139 D3
Thorner's Homes,
Centre Ct **10** SO15 ...... 102 A4
Thorner's Homes,
North Ct **9** SO15 ...... 102 A4
Thorner's Homes,
South Ct **11** SO15 ...... 102 A4
Thorner's Homes,
West Ct **12** SO15 ...... 102 A4
Thorners Ct **8** SO15 ...... 102 C3
Thorness Cl SO16 ...... 77 E1
Thorney Cl PO14 ...... 154 B4
Thorney Island Cty Prim Sch
PO10 ...... 161 D2
Thorney Old Park PO10 ...... 161 E1
Thorney Rd Hermitage PO10 ...... 161 D3
Thorney Island PO10 ...... 161 D3
Thorney View PO11 ...... 160 B1
Thornfield Cl PO8 ...... 88 B1
Thornfield Dr BH23 ...... 193 F1
Thorngate Ct **7** PO12 ...... 181 D3
Thorngate Way **22** PO12 ...... 181 E2
Thornham La PO10 ...... 161 E3
Thornham Rd BH25 ...... 195 E2
Thornhill Ave SO19 ...... 104 B3
Thornhill Cl SO45 ...... 150 C1
Thornhill Inf Sch SO19 ...... 104 B3
Thornhill Jun Sch SO19 ...... 104 B3
Thornhill Park Rd SO18 ...... 104 C4
Thornhill Rd Blackfield SO45 ...... 150 C1
Southampton SO16 ...... 78 B2
Thorni Ave PO15 ...... 130 B2
Thornleigh Rd SO19 ...... 103 F1
Thornley Rd BH10 ...... 189 E2
Thorns La SO41 ...... 199 F3
Thornton Ave SO31 ...... 128 B1
Thornton Cl Corfe Mullen BH21 ...... 186 B3
Waterlooville PO7 ...... 134 A1
Thornton Rd PO12 ...... 181 D4
Thornycroft Ave SO19 ...... 103 E1
Thorogood Ct **4** BH15 ...... 202 C2
Thorold Ct SO18 ...... 79 F1
Thorold Rd
Chandler's Ford SO53 ...... 30 C1
Southampton SO18 ...... 79 F1
Three Acre Dr BH25 ...... 209 F4
Three Acres PO7 ...... 111 D2
Three Cross Rd BH21, BH22 ...... 138 C3
Three Horse Shoes La GU34 ...... 16 C1
Three Legged Cross
Cty First Sch BH21 ...... 114 C1
Three Oaks SO19 ...... 104 C3
Three Tun **21** PO1 ...... 182 A3
Threefield La SO14 ...... 103 D2
Thresher Cl PO7 ...... 112 B1
Throop Cl BH8 ...... 191 D1
Throop Rd BH8 ...... 190 C2
Throopside Ave BH9 ...... 190 B2
Thrush Rd PO8 ...... 188 B1
Thrush Wlk PO8 ...... 111 F2
Thruxton Ct SO19 ...... 103 F3
Thruxton Rd PO9 ...... 135 E3
Thurbern Rd PO2 ...... 157 F1
Thurmell Cl SO30 ...... 105 E2
Thurmell Wlk SO30 ...... 105 E2
Thurmond Cres SO22 ...... 10 B3
Thurmond Rd SO22 ...... 10 B3
Thursby Rd BH23 ...... 193 F1
Thurston Ct SO53 ...... 55 E4
Thwaite Rd BH12 ...... 204 A3
Tichborne Rd Eastleigh SO50 ...... 80 A4
Southampton SO18 ...... 104 B4
Tichborne Way PO13 ...... 155 E1
Tichbourne House SO30 ...... 105 E4
Tickleford Dr SO19 ...... 104 A1
Tickner St SO30 ...... 105 F3
Tidcombe Gn PO9 ...... 135 E4
Tidemill Cl BH23 ...... 207 D4
Tides Reach SO18 ...... 103 E4
Tideway Gdns PO4 ...... 183 E2
Tidworth Rd PO9 ...... 135 F2
Tiffany Cl SO41 ...... 195 F2
Tiffield Cl PO3 ...... 158 B2
Tilbrook Rd SO15 ...... 102 A4
Tilburg Rd BH23 ...... 207 E4
Tilden Rd SO21 ...... 31 E3
Tilebarn La SO42 ...... 173 D3
Tilford Rd PO8 ...... 111 F3
Tillingbourn PO14 ...... 129 E2
Tillinton Gdns PO8 ...... 88 B2
Tilmore Gdns GU32 ...... 40 C3
Tilmore Rd GU32 ...... 40 C3
Timberlane PO7 ...... 134 B2
Timberley La SP5 ...... 48 A3
Timberly Cl SO45 ...... 150 B2

Timbers The PO15 ...... 130 B1
Timor Cl PO15 ...... 129 E4
Timothy Cl BH10 ...... 189 E3
Timpson Rd PO1 ...... 182 C3
Timsbury Cres PO9 ...... 135 F1
Timsbury Ct SO19 ...... 103 F2
Timsbury Dr SO16 ...... 77 F1
Timson Cl SO40 ...... 100 B3
Tincleton Gdns BH9 ...... 190 A2
Tindale Rd SO16 ...... 77 F1
Tinker Alley SO50 ...... 80 A4
Tinkers Cross SP6 ...... 69 F2
Tinneys St SP5 ...... 47 E2
Tintagel Cl SO16 ...... 78 B3
Tintagel Way PO6 ...... 157 D4
Tintern Cl PO6 ...... 133 D1
Tintern Gr **18** SO15 ...... 102 C3
Tintern Rd PO12 ...... 181 D2
Tipner Gn PO2 ...... 157 E2
Tipner La PO2 ...... 157 E2
Tipner Rd PO2 ...... 157 E1
Tiptoe Gn **9** PO9 ...... 136 A3
Tiptoe Prim Sch SO41 ...... 195 E4
Tiptoe Rd BH25 ...... 171 D1
Tipton House **12** PO5 ...... 182 B2
Tiptree Cl SO50 ...... 56 A3
Tisted Ct **34** PO9 ...... 136 A3
Titchborne Cl PO9 ...... 135 E3
Titchfield Hill PO14 ...... 154 A4
Titchfield House **45** PO1 ...... 182 B3
Titchfield Industries PO14 ...... 154 A4
Titchfield La PO15, PO17 ...... 107 E2
Titchfield Park Rd PO15 ...... 129 E2
Titchfield Prim Sch PO14 ...... 129 F1
Titchfield Rd PO14 ...... 154 A3
Tithe Barn SO41 ...... 197 F3
Tithe The PO7 ...... 110 C2
Tithelands La SO24 ...... 15 F2
Tithewood Cl SO53 ...... 30 A1
Titus Gdns PO7 ...... 135 D4
Tiverton Ct
24 Bournemouth BH4 ...... 204 B2
1 Fareham PO16 ...... 131 E1
Tivoli Cl SO53 ...... 55 F4
Toby St **9** PO1 ...... 182 B3
Todber Cl BH11 ...... 188 C2
Tokar St PO4 ...... 183 D1
Tokio Rd PO3 ...... 158 A1
Tollard Cl BH12 ...... 203 F4
Tollbar Way SO30 ...... 81 D1
Tollerford Rd BH17 ...... 187 E1
Tollgate SO15 ...... 55 E1
Tollgate Rd SO31 ...... 128 B4
Tollgate Ests SO51 ...... 27 D2
Tollgate The **20** SO23 ...... 2 A1
Tolpuddle Gdns BH9 ...... 190 A2
Tolstoi Rd BH11 ...... 203 D3
Toms La BH24 ...... 118 A4
Tonbridge St PO5 ...... 182 B1
Tonge Rd BH11 ...... 189 D3
Tonnant Cl PO14 ...... 179 E3
Toogoods Way SO16 ...... 77 E3
Toomer Cl SO45 ...... 150 C1
Toothill Rd SO51 ...... 53 E1
Top La BH24 ...... 141 D4
Topaz Gr PO7 ...... 135 D4
Topiary Gdns SO31 ...... 129 D2
Tor Cl Portchester PO16 ...... 131 F1
Waterlooville PO7 ...... 134 C2
Tor Way GU31 ...... 41 D2
Torbay Rd BH14 ...... 203 E2
Torberry Dr GU31 ...... 41 D1
Torch Cl SO50 ...... 57 D1
Torcross Cl SO19 ...... 103 F1
Torfrida Ct PO4 ...... 183 E2
Tormead SO45 ...... 125 F2
Tornay Gr SO52 ...... 53 F2
Toronto Pl PO12 ...... 181 D3
Toronto Rd PO2 ...... 182 C4
Torquay Ave Gosport PO12 ...... 181 D4
Southampton SO15 ...... 102 B4
Torque Cl SO19 ...... 104 C2
Torre Cl SO50 ...... 56 A3
Torridge Gdns SO18 ...... 80 A2
Torrington Cl SO19 ...... 104 A2
Torrington Rd PO2 ...... 157 F2
Tortworth Cl PO14 ...... 154 B4
Torwood Gdns SO50 ...... 56 C1
Tosson Cl SO16 ...... 101 F4
Totland Cl SO16 ...... 101 F4
Totland Ct **8** SO41 ...... 211 E2
Totland Rd Cosham PO6 ...... 157 F4
Gosport PO13 ...... 155 C1
Totmel Rd BH17 ...... 188 A1
Totnes Cl SO50 ...... 55 F3
Tottehale Cl SO52 ...... 53 F2
Tottenham Rd PO1 ...... 182 C3
Totton By Pass SO40 ...... 101 D4
Totton Coll SO40 ...... 100 B4
Totton Recn Ctr SO40 ...... 100 B4
Totton Sta SO40 ...... 101 D4
Totton Western By-Pass
SO40 ...... 100 B3
Totton Wlk **5** PO9 ...... 135 E3
Tournerbury La PO11 ...... 185 D2
Tourney Rd BH11 ...... 188 C3
Tovey Pl SO23 ...... 2 B4
Towans The BH13 ...... 214 B2
Tower Cl PO12 ...... 180 B2
Tower Ct Bournemouth BH2 ...... 204 C1
Locks Heath SO31 ...... 128 B1
6 Winchester SO22 ...... 10 C4
Tower Gdns SO19 ...... 103 F1
Tower House SO19 ...... 103 F1
Tower Ind Est The SO50 ...... 56 B1
Tower La Eastleigh SO50 ...... 56 B1
Wimborne Minster BH21 ...... 163 E3
Tower Pl SO30 ...... 80 B1

Tower Rd Bournemouth BH1 ...... 205 F3
Poole BH13 ...... 204 A1
Portsmouth PO5 ...... 182 C2
Winchester SO22 ...... 10 C4
Tower Rd W BH13 ...... 204 A1
Tower St Emsworth PO10 ...... 161 D4
Portsmouth PO1 ...... 181 F2
Winchester SO23 ...... 10 C4
Tower The **16** PO12 ...... 181 D3
Towers Farm BH21 ...... 186 B4
Towers Gdn PO9 ...... 159 F3
Towers Way BH21 ...... 186 B4
Town Hall Rd PO9 ...... 135 F1
Town La GU32 ...... 41 D3
Town Quay Portsmouth PO1 ...... 181 F2
Southampton SO14 ...... 102 C1
Town St PO1 ...... 182 B3
Towngate Bridge BH15 ...... 202 B2
Towngate Sh Ctr **1** BH15 ...... 202 B2
Townhill Inf Sch SO18 ...... 80 A1
Townhill Jun Sch SO18 ...... 80 A1
Townhill Park House (The
Gregg Sch) SO18 ...... 80 A2
Townhill Way
Southampton SO18 ...... 80 A1
West End SO18 ...... 80 A1
Townsend Cl BH11 ...... 189 D3
Townsend Prim Sch BH8 ...... 191 D1
Townsville Rd BH9 ...... 190 A1
Towpath Mead PO4 ...... 183 E2
Toynbee Cl SO50 ...... 56 A2
Toynbee Rd SO50 ...... 56 A2
Toynbee Sec Sch SO53 ...... 55 F3
Tozer Cl BH11 ...... 188 C1
Tracey Ct BH23 ...... 209 D4
Trafalgar Ct SO53 ...... 55 E2
Trafalgar Ct Christchurch BH23 ...... 207 F3
Fareham PO14 ...... 154 C4
33 Portsmouth PO5 ...... 182 B1
Trafalgar Pl Lymington SO41 ...... 197 F2
Portsmouth PO1 ...... 182 C3
Trafalgar Rd Bournemouth BH9 ...... 204 C4
Southampton SO15 ...... 102 B3
Trafalgar Sq PO12 ...... 181 D3
Trafalgar St SO23 ...... 10 C4
Trafalgar Way SO45 ...... 126 A1
Trafford Way SO50 ...... 57 E1
Trampers La PO17 ...... 109 D2
Tranby Rd SO19 ...... 103 F2
Tranmere Cl SO41 ...... 197 F1
Tranmere Rd PO4 ...... 183 E2
Treadwheel Rd PO8 ...... 113 D3
Treagore Rd SO40 ...... 76 B1
Trearnan Cl SO16 ...... 101 F4
Treble Cl SO22 ...... 10 A2
Tredegar Rd PO4 ...... 183 D2
Tree Hamlets BH16 ...... 201 E3
Tree Side Way PO7 ...... 111 F1
Treebys Cl BH23 ...... 192 B1
Treeside BH23 ...... 193 E1
Treeside Ave SO40 ...... 101 D4
Treeside Rd SO15 ...... 102 B4
Treetops **9** BH13 ...... 214 C4
Trefoil Cl PO7 ...... 135 D4
Trefoil Way BH23 ...... 208 B4
Tregaron Ave PO6 ...... 158 A4
Tregonwell Rd BH2 ...... 204 C1
Treloar Rd PO11 ...... 185 F1
Treloen Ct **3** BH8 ...... 205 D3
Treloyhan Cl SO53 ...... 55 E2
Tremona Ct SO16 ...... 78 A1
Tremona Rd SO16 ...... 78 A1
Trenley Cl SO45 ...... 150 B2
Trent Cl SO18 ...... 79 F1
Trent House **25** SO14 ...... 103 E3
Trent Rd SO18 ...... 79 F1
Trent Way Ferndown BH22 ...... 166 A3
Lee-on-the-Solent PO13 ...... 179 F1
West End SO30 ...... 80 B1
Trent Wlk PO6 ...... 156 A4
Trentham Ave BH7 ...... 206 A4
Trentham Cl BH7 ...... 206 A4
Tresillian Cl BH23 ...... 194 A1
Tresillian Gdns SO18 ...... 80 A1
Tresillian Way BH23 ...... 194 A1
Trevis Rd PO4 ...... 183 E2
Trevone **15** BH25 ...... 195 D2
Trevone Cl SO40 ...... 100 C3
Trevor Rd PO4 ...... 182 C2
Trevose Cl
Chandler's Ford SO53 ...... 55 E2
Gosport PO13 ...... 155 E1
Trevose Cres SO53 ...... 55 E3
Trevose Way PO14 ...... 129 D1
Triangle Gdns SO16 ...... 77 E2
Triangle La PO14 ...... 153 F3
Triangle The
Bournemouth BH2 ...... 204 C2
Upton BH16 ...... 201 D4
Whiteparish SP5 ...... 24 A2
Tribe Rd PO12 ...... 181 D3
Tricketts La BH22 ...... 165 F3
Tricorn The PO1 ...... 182 B3
Trigon Rd BH15 ...... 202 B4
Trimaran Rd SO31 ...... 128 C1
Trimm's Dro SP6 ...... 70 C4
Trimmer's Ct PO1 ...... 181 F2
Trinadad House **1** PO6 ...... 132 C1
Trinidad Cres BH12 ...... 203 E4
Trinidad Fst Sch BH12 ...... 203 E4
Trinidad House BH12 ...... 203 E4
Trinity **2** BH1 ...... 205 D2
Trinity Cl PO12 ...... 181 F2
Trinity Ct Chandler's Ford SO53 ...... 55 E3
2 Southampton SO15 ...... 102 B3
Totton SO40 ...... 76 C1
Trinity Gdns PO16 ...... 131 D1
Trinity Gr PO12 ...... 181 F2

Trinity Ind Est SO15 ...... 101 F4
Trinity Rd Bournemouth BH1 ...... 205 D2
Southampton SO14 ...... 103 D3
Trinity St PO16 ...... 131 D1
Tripps End Cvn Site SO30 ...... 105 E4
Tristan Cl SO45 ...... 178 C4
Triton Ctr The SO51 ...... 53 E3
Triumph Cl PO15 ...... 130 B1
Triumph Rd PO14 ...... 154 C3
Troak Cl PO13 ...... 207 F4
Trojan Way PO7 ...... 134 C2
Troon Cres PO6 ...... 134 B1
Troon Rd BH18 ...... 187 D3
Trooper Bottom GU32 ...... 19 D2
Trosnant Inf Sch PO9 ...... 135 F2
Trosnant Jun Sch PO9 ...... 135 F2
Trosnant Rd PO9 ...... 135 F1
Trotters La BH21 ...... 164 A3
Trotts La Marchwood SO40 ...... 101 E1
Totton SO40 ...... 101 E2
Trowbridge Cl SO16 ...... 77 F3
Truman Rd BH11 ...... 189 D3
Truro Ct PO13 ...... 180 B3
Truro Rd PO6 ...... 132 C1
Truro Rise SO50 ...... 56 C2
Truscott Ave BH9 ...... 205 D4
Trussell Cl SO22 ...... 1 B2
Trussell Cres SO22 ...... 1 B2
Trystworthy **10** BH2 ...... 204 C2
Tuckers Cl SO22 ...... 201 F1
Tucks Cl BH23 ...... 193 D4
Tuckton Cl BH6 ...... 206 B2
Tuckton Rd BH6 ...... 206 C2
Tudor Ave PO10 ...... 136 C2
Tudor Cl Alderholt SP6 ...... 93 D3
Gosport PO12 ...... 180 B4
Portchester PO16 ...... 132 A1
South Hayling PO11 ...... 184 C1
Totton SO40 ...... 100 B4
Tudor Cres PO6 ...... 157 F3
Tudor Ct Bournemouth BH1 ...... 205 D3
18 Cosham PO6 ...... 157 F4
18 Fareham PO14 ...... 154 C4
Poole BH15 ...... 202 C3
8 Portsmouth PO5 ...... 182 B1
Tudor Gdns SO30 ...... 105 D3
Tudor House (Mus) SO14 ...... 102 C2
Tudor Rd BH18 ...... 187 D2
Tudor Way SO23 ...... 2 A4
Tudor Wood Cl SO16 ...... 78 C2
Tuffin Cl SO16 ...... 77 E3
Tukes Ave PO13 ...... 155 D2
Tulip Gdns Havant PO9 ...... 135 E1
Locks Heath SO31 ...... 128 C2
Tulip Rd SO16 ...... 79 E2
Tumulus Cl SO19 ...... 104 C2
Tunstall Rd SO19 ...... 104 C2
Tunworth Ct PO9 ...... 136 A3
Tupman House **18** PO1 ...... 182 B4
Tuppenny La PO10 ...... 161 E4
Turbary Ct
Bournemouth BH12 ...... 189 D1
Ferndown BH22 ...... 165 F3
Upton BH16 ...... 201 E4
Turbary Hts BH11 ...... 188 C1
Turbary Park Ave BH11 ...... 189 D1
Turbary Rd BH22 ...... 165 F3
Turbary Ret Pk BH11 ...... 188 C2
Turbury Cl PO14 ...... 203 E4
Turbury Rd BH12 ...... 203 E4
Turf Croft Ct BH23 ...... 194 A1
Turk's La BH14 ...... 203 D1
Turlin Moor Fst Sch BH16 ...... 201 E2
Turlin Moor Mid Sch BH16 ...... 201 E2
Turlin Rd BH16 ...... 201 E2
Turner Ave PO13 ...... 180 C4
Turner Rd PO1 ...... 182 B4
Turners Farm Cres SO41 ...... 196 A1
Turners Oak Ct SO15 ...... 78 B1
Turnpike Way SO30 ...... 105 D4
Turnstone Gdns SO16 ...... 78 A3
Turnworth Ct BH18 ...... 187 E2
Turtle Cl PO14 ...... 154 A2
Turvy King Ct PO7 ...... 110 C2
Tuscan Wlk SO53 ...... 55 F3
Tuscany Way PO7 ...... 135 D4
Tussocks The SO40 ...... 101 F1
Tutland Rd SO52 ...... 53 F2
Tutt's La SO51 ...... 50 C2
Tweed Cl SO53 ...... 55 D4
Tweed La SO41 ...... 197 E4
Tweedale Rd BH9 ...... 190 B2
Twemlow Ave BH14 ...... 202 C2
Twiggs End Cl SO31 ...... 128 C2
Twiggs La SO40 ...... 124 C4
Twiggs Lane End SO40 ...... 124 B3
Twin Oaks SO19 ...... 103 F2
Twin Oaks Cl BH18 ...... 187 D2
Twittens Way **13** PO9 ...... 135 F1
Twyford Ave
Portsmouth PO2 ...... 157 E1
Southampton SO15 ...... 78 B1
Twyford CE Prim Sch SO21 ...... 31 F3
Twyford Cl BH8 ...... 190 B1
Twyford Ct **15** SO23 ...... 2 A1
Twyford Dr PO13 ...... 179 F1
Twyford Rd SO50 ...... 56 A3
Twyford Sch SO21 ...... 32 A3
Twyford Way BH17 ...... 188 A1
Twynham Ave BH23 ...... 207 D4
Twynham Cl SP5 ...... 46 C3
Twynham Comp Sch BH23 ...... 207 D3
Twynham Rd BH6 ...... 206 C2
Twynhams Hill SO32 ...... 108 A4
Tyler Ct PO9 ...... 135 F3
Tylers Cl SO41 ...... 197 E3
Tyleshades The SO51 ...... 53 D3
Tyne Cl SO53 ...... 55 D3

Tynedale Cl Bournemouth BH9 ...... 190 A2
Gosport PO12 ...... 180 C4
Tyneham Ave BH12 ...... 203 E4
Tyneham Cl BH12 ...... 203 E4
Tyrells La BH24 ...... 142 C2
Tyrrel Lawn PO9 ...... 135 E4
Tyrrel Rd SO19 ...... 55 E4
Tyrrell Gdns BH8 ...... 191 D1
Tyrrell Rd PO9 ...... 135 E4
Tyrrells Ct BH23 ...... 169 D1
Tyseley Rd PO1 ...... 182 B2
Tytherley Gn **19** PO9 ...... 136 A3
Tytherley Gr BH8 ...... 190 B1
Tytherley Rd SO18 ...... 104 B4

Uddens Dr BH21 ...... 164 B4
Uddens Trad Est BH21 ...... 164 C3
Ullswater SO50 ...... 56 A1
Ullswater Ave SO18 ...... 80 A1
Ullswater House **15** PO6 ...... 133 D1
Ullswater Rd Oakley BH21 ...... 163 E1
Southampton SO16 ...... 77 F1
Undercliff Dr BH1, BH5 ...... 205 E1
Undercliff Gdns SO16 ...... 78 C2
Underdown Ave PO7 ...... 134 B1
Undershore SO41 ...... 197 F3
Undershore Rd SO41 ...... 198 A2
Underwood Rd
Bishopstoke SO50 ...... 56 C2
Southampton SO16 ...... 78 C2
Unicorn Rd
Lee-on-the-Solent PO13 ...... 179 E2
Portsmouth PO1 ...... 182 A3
Union La SO32 ...... 61 D1
Union Pl PO1 ...... 182 B3
Union Rd Havant PO9 ...... 135 F1
Southampton SO14 ...... 103 E3
Union St
Fareham PO16 ...... 131 E1
8 Portsmouth PO5 ...... 182 A3
Winchester SO23 ...... 11 D4
Univ of Portsmouth PO1 ...... 182 A3
Univ of Portsmouth
(Langstone Campus) PO4 ...... 183 E3
Univ of Portsmouth
(Milton Campus) PO4 ...... 183 D2
University Cres SO17 ...... 79 D2
University Parkway SO16 ...... 54 B1
University Rd SO17 ...... 79 D2
Unwin Cl SO19 ...... 103 E1
Upham CE Prim Sch SO32 ...... 58 C3
Upham St SO32 ...... 58 B3
Uphill Rd SO22 ...... 1 B3
Upland La GU33 ...... 20 A4
Uplands Ave BH25 ...... 210 A4
Uplands Cl PO16 ...... 166 A4
Uplands Cres PO16 ...... 131 D1
Uplands Prim Sch PO16 ...... 131 D2
Uplands Rd
Bournemouth BH8 ...... 190 B1
Cosham PO6 ...... 158 B4
Denmead PO7 ...... 110 B3
Rowland's Castle PO9 ...... 113 E1
West Moors BH22 ...... 139 D1
Winchester SO22 ...... 1 C2
Uplands Sch SH14 ...... 203 E2
Uplands Way SO17 ...... 79 D1
Uplyme Cl BH17 ...... 188 A1
Uppark (NT) GU31 ...... 90 C4
Upper Arundel St PO1 ...... 182 B3
Upper Banister St **1** SO15 ...... 102 C3
Upper Barn Copse SO50 ...... 57 D2
Upper Bere Wood PO7 ...... 134 C4
Upper Brook Dr SO31 ...... 128 C1
Upper Brook St SO23 ...... 11 D4
Upper Brownhill Rd SO16 ...... 77 F2
Upper Bugle St SO14 ...... 102 C2
Upper Church Rd SO32 ...... 107 F4
Upper Common Rd SO41 ...... 196 C2
Upper Crabbick La PO7 ...... 110 B3
Upper Crescent Rd SO52 ...... 53 F3
Upper Deacon Rd SO19 ...... 104 B3
Upper Golf Links Rd BH18 ...... 187 D3
Upper Gordon Rd BH23 ...... 194 A1
Upper Heyshott GU31 ...... 41 D2
Upper High St SO23 ...... 10 C4
Upper Hinton Rd BH1 ...... 204 C2
Upper House Ct PO17 ...... 108 A2
Upper Market St SO50 ...... 56 A2
Upper Mead Ct **9** SO50 ...... 57 E1
Upper Moors Rd SO21 ...... 56 C4
Upper Mount GU33 ...... 20 C2
Upper Mullins La SO45 ...... 125 F2
Upper New Rd SO30 ...... 80 B1
Upper Northam Cl SO30 ...... 105 D3
Upper Northam Rd
Hedge End SO30 ...... 104 C3
Hedge End SO30 ...... 105 D3
Upper Norwich Rd **18** BH2 ...... 204 C2
Upper Old St PO14 ...... 154 A2
Upper Piece PO7 ...... 111 D2
Upper Rd BH12 ...... 203 E3
Upper Shaftesbury Ave SO17 ...... 79 D1
Upper Shirley Ave SO15 ...... 78 B1
Upper Spinney SO31 ...... 152 B4
Upper St Helens Rd SO30 ...... 105 D3
Upper St Michael's Gr PO14 ...... 154 C4
Upper Terrace Rd BH2 ...... 204 C2
Upper Toothill Rd SO16 ...... 77 F4
Upper Wardown GU31 ...... 41 D2
Upper Weston La SO19 ...... 104 A1
Upper Wharf PO16 ...... 155 E4
Uppleby Rd BH12 ...... 203 E3

Upton Cl Havant PO9 ... 135 E4
Upton BH16 ... 201 D4
Upton Cres SO16 ... 77 E3
Upton Cross Mobile
 Home Pk BH16 ... 201 E4
Upton Ct BH16 ... 201 E4
Upton Ctry Pk BH17 ... 201 F3
Upton Cty Inf Sch BH16 ... 201 D4
Upton Cty Jun Sch BH16 ... 201 D4
Upton Grey Cl SO22 ... 1 B2
Upton Heath Est BH16 ... 201 E4
Upton House 1 SO16 ... 78 A1
Upton La SO16 ... 77 E3
Upton Rd Broadstone BH17 ... 202 A4
 Poole BH17 ... 201 F4
Upton Way BH18 ... 186 C2
Upwey Ave BH15 ... 201 F2
Utrecht Ct BH23 ... 207 E4

Vadne Gdns PO12 ... 181 D3
Vaggs La Hordle SO41 ... 195 F3
 New Milton SO41 ... 195 E4
Vale Cl BH14 ... 203 F2
Vale Dr SO18 ... 79 F1
Vale Gr PO12 ... 181 D4
Vale Lodge BH1 ... 205 E3
Vale Mansions 4 BH1 ... 205 E2
Vale Rd Bournemouth BH1 ... 205 E2
 Poole BH14 ... 203 F2
 Redlynch SP5 ... 47 E3
 Winchester SO23 ... 11 E3
Vale The Horndean PO8 ... 88 B1
 Hythe SO45 ... 125 F2
 Locks Heath SO31 ... 129 D1
 Petersfield GU32 ... 41 D3
 Portsmouth PO5 ... 182 B1
Valencia Cl BH23 ... 191 E2
Valentine Ave SO19 ... 104 B2
Valentine Cl PO15 ... 130 B1
Valentine Ct
 Southampton SO19 ... 104 B2
 Waterlooville PO7 ... 135 D4
Valerian Cl SO50 ... 81 E3
Valerian Rd SO30 ... 105 E3
Valetta Park PO10 ... 160 C4
Valetta Rd PO10 ... 161 E1
Valette Rd BH9 ... 190 A2
Valiant Rd PO10 ... 161 E1
Valiant Way BH23 ... 208 A4
Valley Cl Blackfield SO45 ... 150 C1
 Christchurch BH23 ... 191 F2
 Colden Common SO21 ... 56 C4
 Redlynch SP5 ... 47 E3
 Waterlooville PO7 ... 134 B2
Valley Ct The 4 SO22 ... 10 B3
Valley La BH23 ... 169 F2
Valley Park Dr PO8 ... 88 B2
Valley Rd Bournemouth BH8 ... 190 C2
 Chandler's Ford SO53 ... 55 E4
 Littleton SO22 ... 1 A3
 Totton SO40 ... 100 C3
Valley Rise SO31 ... 128 C2
Valley The SO22 ... 10 B3
Valley View Poole BH12 ... 204 A4
 Southampton SO19 ... 104 A2
 Southampton SO19 ... 104 A3
Valleydene SO45 ... 125 F1
Vallis Cl BH15 ... 202 B1
Valsheba Dr PO14 ... 179 D3
Valview Mobile Home Pk
 SO41 ... 195 F4
Vanburgh Way SO53 ... 30 A1
Vanguard Rd
 Bournemouth BH8 ... 190 C1
 Poole BH15 ... 202 B1
 Southampton SO18 ... 104 A4
Vanstone Rd PO13 ... 180 B4
Vardy Cl SO19 ... 104 B2
Varna Rd SO15 ... 102 B3
Varsity Rd PO10 ... 161 E1
Vaudrey Cl SO15 ... 78 B1
Vaughan Cl SO19 ... 104 C3
Vaughan Rd SO45 ... 125 E2
Vauxhall Way GU32 ... 40 C2
Veal's La SO40 ... 125 D4
Vear's La SO21 ... 57 D4
Vecta Cl BH23 ... 208 B3
Vectis Ct SO16 ... 78 C2
Vectis Rd
 Barton on Sea BH25 ... 209 E4
 Gosport PO12 ... 180 C2
Vectis Way PO6 ... 157 F4
Velder Ave PO4 ... 183 D3
Vellan Ct SO16 ... 77 E1
Velmore Rd SO53 ... 55 D2
Velsheda Ct 2 SO45 ... 126 A3
Velvet Lawn Rd BH25 ... 194 C2
Venator Pl BH21 ... 163 E3
Venerable Rd PO14 ... 155 D3
Vengeance Rd PO13 ... 179 F2
Venice Cl PO7 ... 135 D4
Venning Ave BH11 ... 188 C3
Ventnor Ct SO16 ... 79 E3
Ventnor Rd Gosport PO13 ... 155 D2
 Portsmouth PO4 ... 182 C2
Ventnor Way PO16 ... 131 F1
Ventry Cl BH13 ... 203 F2
Ventura Ctr The BH16 ... 201 E3
Ventura Pl BH16 ... 201 E3
Venture Ct PO3 ... 158 A3
Venture Ind Pk PO3 ... 158 A3
Venture Rd SO16 ... 54 B1
Verbena Cres PO8 ... 112 A2
Verbena Way SO30 ... 105 E3
Verdon Ave SO31 ... 127 F2

Verger Cl PO14 ... 129 E2
Verity Cres BH17 ... 188 A1
Vermont Cl SO16 ... 78 C2
Vermont Sch SO16 ... 78 C2
Vernalls Cl BH10 ... 189 E3
Vernalls Gdns BH10 ... 189 E3
Verne Rd BH31 ... 115 D3
Verney Cl BH11 ... 189 D2
Verney Rd BH11 ... 189 D2
Vernham Rd SO22 ... 1 C1
Verno La BH23 ... 193 E3
Vernon Ave PO4 ... 183 D3
Vernon Cl
 Bishop's Waltham SO32 ... 59 E1
 Gosport PO12 ... 181 D3
Vernon Ct 3 PO2 ... 157 F1
Vernon Hill SO32 ... 59 E1
Vernon Mews PO4 ... 183 D3
Vernon Rd Gosport PO12 ... 181 D3
 Portsmouth PO3 ... 158 A1
Vernon Wlk 5 SO15 ... 102 C3
Verona Ave BH6 ... 206 B3
Verona Rd SO53 ... 55 F3
Veronica Cl 31 BH1 ... 204 C2
Verulam Rd Poole BH14 ... 202 C2
 Southampton SO14 ... 103 D4
Verwood Cres BH6 ... 207 D2
Verwood First Sch BH31 ... 114 D3
Verwood Ind Est BH31 ... 115 D3
Verwood Rd Havant PO9 ... 136 A3
 Ibsley BH24 ... 116 A1
 St Leonards BH24 ... 140 B4
 Three Legged Cross BH21 ... 114 C1
 Verwood BH21 ... 114 A4
 Woodlands BH21 ... 114 A4
Veryan PO15 ... 130 C1
Vespasian Ct SO18 ... 103 E4
Vespasian Rd SO18 ... 103 E4
Vespasian Way SO53 ... 55 F4
Vesta Way SO53 ... 55 F4
Vetch Cl BH23 ... 208 B4
Vian Cl PO13 ... 155 E2
Vian Ct 14 BH25 ... 194 C2
Vian Rd PO7 ... 134 C3
Vicarage Cotts BH8 ... 190 C2
Vicarage Dr SO30 ... 105 D3
Vicarage Farm SO50 ... 57 E3
Vicarage Gdns SO41 ... 196 A1
Vicarage La Cadnam SO40 ... 75 D1
 Curdridge SO32 ... 106 B4
 Hambledon PO7 ... 86 B2
 Hordle SO41 ... 196 A1
 Stubbington PO14 ... 154 B2
 Swanmore SO32 ... 84 B3
Vicarage Park SP5 ... 47 E3
Vicarage Rd
 Bournemouth BH9 ... 189 F1
 Marchwood SO40 ... 101 F1
 Poole BH15 ... 202 B3
 Redlynch SP5 ... 48 A3
 Verwood BH31 ... 114 C3
Vicarage Way BH23 ... 192 B1
Vice La SO51 ... 74 A2
Viceroy Rd SO19 ... 104 A2
Vickers Cl BH8 ... 191 D1
Vickery Way BH23 ... 207 E4
Victena Rd SO50 ... 57 E1
Victor Ct SO19 ... 104 B3
Victor Rd Portsmouth PO1 ... 182 C4
 Thorney Island PO10 ... 161 E1
Victor St SO15 ... 78 A1
Victoria Ave
 Bournemouth BH9 ... 189 F1
 South Hayling PO11 ... 184 C2
 Waterlooville PO7 ... 134 A2
Victoria Bldgs SO32 ... 83 D4
Victoria Cl
 Corfe Mullen BH21 ... 186 B3
 Locks Heath PO14 ... 129 D1
Victoria Cottage Hospl PO10 ... 160 C4
Victoria Cres BH12 ... 203 E3
Victoria Ct Durley SO32 ... 82 B4
 South Hayling PO11 ... 184 C2
Victoria Gdns
 Ferndown BH22 ... 165 E3
 Fordingbridge SP6 ... 69 E1
 Ringwood BH24 ... 141 D3
Victoria Glade SO31 ... 127 E3
Victoria Gr PO5 ... 182 B2
Victoria House 11 PO16 ... 131 D1
Victoria Hospl ... 163 D3
Victoria Park Rd BH9 ... 189 F1
Victoria Pl
 Bournemouth BH1 ... 205 E3
 6 Gosport PO12 ... 181 D2
 2 Lymington SO41 ... 197 F1
 Romsey SO51 ... 52 C4
 Wimborne Minster BH21 ... 163 D3
Victoria Rd
 Bishop's Waltham SO32 ... 83 D4
 Bournemouth BH1 ... 205 E3
 Christchurch BH23 ... 207 F3
 Eastleigh SO50 ... 56 A3
 Emsworth PO10 ... 136 C1
 Ferndown BH22 ... 165 E3
 Fordingbridge SP6 ... 69 E1
 Milford on Sea SO41 ... 211 E2
 Netley SO31 ... 127 D3
 North Hayling PO11 ... 159 F1
 Poole BH12 ... 203 E3
 Portsmouth PO1 ... 182 A3
 Southampton SO19 ... 103 E1
 Waterlooville PO7 ... 134 C4
 Wimborne Minster BH21 ... 163 D3
 Winchester SO23 ... 1 C1
Victoria Rd N PO5 ... 182 B2
Victoria Rd S PO5 ... 182 B1

Victoria Sch BH13 ... 203 F2
Victoria Sq PO13 ... 179 F1
Victoria St Gosport PO12 ... 181 E3
 Portsmouth PO1 ... 182 B4
 Southampton SO14 ... 103 E3
Victoria Terr Hermitage PO10 ... 137 D1
 Southbourne PO10 ... 161 E4
 Westbourne PO10 ... 137 D2
Victoria Wlk SO30 ... 80 C1
Victory Cl
 Chandler's Ford SO53 ... 55 D3
 West Moors BH22 ... 139 D3
Victory Cotts SO31 ... 128 B4
Victory Cres SO15 ... 102 A3
Victory Ct Gosport PO13 ... 155 E1
 3 Lee-on-the-Solent PO13 ... 179 F1
Victory Gn PO2 ... 157 E1
Victory Rd
 17 Portsmouth PO1 ... 182 A3
 Southampton SO15 ... 102 A3
 Stubbington PO14 ... 179 E3
Victory Sq SO15 ... 102 A3
Victory Trad Est PO3 ... 158 A1
Victory Way SO16 ... 77 F4
Viewside Cl BH21 ... 186 B3
Viking Cl Blackfield SO45 ... 177 F4
 Bournemouth BH6 ... 207 D2
 Southampton SO16 ... 77 F2
 Stubbington PO14 ... 154 A2
Viking Way
 Bournemouth BH6 ... 207 D2
 Christchurch BH23 ... 208 A3
 Horndean PO8 ... 88 B2
Vikings The SO51 ... 53 D4
Villa Gdns PO7 ... 134 C4
Village Ctr SO40 ... 101 F1
Village Gate PO14 ... 153 F4
Village Rd PO12 ... 180 C1
Village St GU31 ... 41 D3
Ville de Paris Rd PO14 ... 155 D3
Villette Cl BH23 ... 192 A1
Villiers Rd Hythe SO45 ... 149 F4
 Portsmouth PO5 ... 182 B1
 Southampton SO15 ... 102 B4
Vimoutiers Ct SP6 ... 69 F1
Vimy House 3 PO14 ... 154 C4
Vince Cl BH11 ... 189 D3
Vincent Ave SO16 ... 78 B1
Vincent Cl 2 BH25 ... 195 D1
Vincent Gr PO16 ... 156 B4
Vincent Rd 1 BH25 ... 195 D1
Vincent St SO15 ... 102 B4
Vincent's Gr SO15 ... 102 A4
Vincent's Wlk SO14 ... 103 D2
Vine Bank SO18 ... 104 A4
Vine Cl Bournemouth BH7 ... 206 A4
 Locks Heath SO31 ... 128 B2
Vine Coppice PO7 ... 134 C2
Vine Ct 21 PO6 ... 157 F4
Vine Farm Cl BH12 ... 204 B4
Vine Farm Rd BH12 ... 204 A4
Vine Hill BH21 ... 162 C3
Vine House SO31 ... 129 D3
Vine Rd SO16 ... 78 A2
Vinegar Hill SO41 ... 211 E3
Vineries Cl BH21 ... 163 F3
Vineries The BH21 ... 163 F3
Vinery Gdns SO16 ... 78 B1
Vinery Rd SO16 ... 78 B1
Vinery The BH25 ... 195 D1
Vineside PO13 ... 155 F1
Vineyard Cl SO19 ... 103 E2
Vineyards The SO52 ... 54 A2
Vinnells La GU32 ... 37 E3
Vinneys Cl BH23 ... 192 B1
Vinson Rd GU33 ... 21 D2
Violet Ave PO14 ... 179 D3
Violet Cl SO53 ... 55 D3
Violet Farm Cl BH21 ... 186 B4
Violet La BH21 ... 195 D2
Violet Rd SO16 ... 79 D2
Virginia Cl BH12 ... 203 E4
Virginia Park Rd PO12 ... 180 C3
Viscount Ct BH11 ... 188 B3
Viscount Dr BH23 ... 208 A3
Viscount Wlk BH11 ... 188 B3
Vista Marina BH13 ... 214 B3
Vita Rd PO2 ... 157 F2
Vitre Gdns SO41 ... 197 F1
Vivash Rd PO1 ... 182 C3
Vixen Cl PO14 ... 179 D3
Vixen Wlk BH25 ... 195 D3
Vokes Cl SO19 ... 104 A3
Vulcan Cl SO15 ... 101 F3
Vulcan Rd Portsmouth PO1 ... 182 A2
 Southampton SO15 ... 101 F3
 Thorney Island PO10 ... 161 E1
Vulcan Way BH23 ... 208 A4
Vyse La 20 SO14 ... 102 C2

Wade Court Rd PO9 ... 160 A4
Wade La PO9 ... 160 A4
Wadham Rd PO2 ... 157 E1
Wadhurst Gdns SO19 ... 127 D4
Wadhurst Rd SO30 ... 105 E3
Wagtail Dr BH25 ... 194 C1
Wagtail Way PO16 ... 155 F4
Wainscot Rd PO4 ... 183 D1
Wainsford Cl SO41 ... 197 D1
Wainsford Rd Hordle SO41 ... 196 C1
 Lymington SO41 ... 196 C1
Wainwright Cl PO6 ... 158 B3
Wainwright Gdns SO30 ... 81 D2
Wait End Rd PO7 ... 134 C3
Waite End Prim Sch PO7 ... 134 C3
Wake Lawn PO4 ... 183 E2

Wakefield Ave
 Bournemouth BH10 ... 189 F3
 Fareham PO15 ... 130 C2
Wakefield Ct 6 SO18 ... 80 A1
Wakefield Rd SO18 ... 80 A1
Wakeford 18 SO51 ... 52 C4
Wakefords Way PO9 ... 136 A3
Wakely Gdns BH11 ... 189 D3
Wakely Rd BH11 ... 189 D3
Walberant Bldgs 9 PO2 ... 157 F2
Walberton Ave PO6 ... 158 A4
Walberton Ct 1 PO6 ... 158 A4
Walcheren Pl BH15 ... 201 E2
Walcott Ave BH23 ... 191 F1
Waldegrave Cl SO19 ... 103 E1
Walden Gdns PO8 ... 112 A4
Walden Rd PO2 ... 157 E1
Walditch Gdns BH17 ... 187 F1
Waldren Cl BH15 ... 202 C1
Wales St SO23 ... 11 D4
Walford Bldgs PO3 ... 183 D4
Walford Gdns BH21 ... 163 E3
Walford Mill Craft Ctr BH21 ... 163 D3
Walford Rd PO6 ... 133 E1
Walhampton Hill SO41 ... 198 A3
Walhampton Sch SO41 ... 198 A3
Walker Gdns SO30 ... 81 E1
Walker Pl PO13 ... 155 E1
Walker Rd PO2 ... 157 E1
Walker's Lane S SO45 ... 177 F4
Walkers Cl SO50 ... 57 E1
Walkers La N SO45 ... 150 C1
Walkford La BH25 ... 194 B2
Walkford Rd BH23 ... 194 B1
Walkford Way BH23 ... 194 A1
Walkwood Ave BH7 ... 206 A4
Wall Cl SO42 ... 175 E3
Wallace Rd Broadstone BH18 ... 187 D2
 Portsmouth PO2 ... 182 C4
 Southampton SO19 ... 103 F1
Wallington Ct PO14 ... 154 C3
Wallington Dr SO53 ... 55 D4
Wallington Hill 8 PO16 ... 131 E1
Wallington Shore Rd
 Fareham PO16 ... 131 E1
 14 Portchester PO16 ... 131 E1
Wallington Way PO16 ... 131 E1
Wallis Bglws PO12 ... 180 C2
Wallis Gdns PO7 ... 111 F1
Wallis Rd
 Bournemouth BH10 ... 189 D1
 Waterlooville PO7 ... 111 F1
Walliscott Rd BH11 ... 189 D1
Wallisdean Ave PO14 ... 154 C4
Wallisdean Jun & Inf Schs
 PO14 ... 154 C4
Wallisdean Rd PO3 ... 183 D4
Wallisdown Rd BH10, BH11 ... 204 B4
Wallrock Wlk PO10 ... 136 C2
Walmer Cl SO50 ... 56 A4
Walmer Rd PO1 ... 182 C3
Walnut Ave SO18 ... 79 F3
Walnut Cl
 Chandler's Ford SO53 ... 30 B1
 16 New Milton BH25 ... 194 C2
 Southampton SO16 ... 77 F1
Walnut Dr PO14 ... 179 D3
Walnut Gr SO16 ... 77 F1
Walnut Tree Cl PO11 ... 184 C2
Walnut Tree Dr PO10 ... 137 F2
Walpole La SO31 ... 128 C4
Walpole Rd
 Bournemouth BH1 ... 205 F3
 Gosport PO12 ... 181 D2
 Winchester SO22 ... 10 B3
Walpole Terr 9 PO12 ... 181 D2
Walsall Rd PO3 ... 183 D3
Walsford Rd BH4 ... 204 B3
Walsingham Cl PO6 ... 133 E1
Walsingham Dene BH7 ... 205 F4
Walsingham Gdns SO18 ... 79 F2
Waltham Cl Droxford SO32 ... 61 D1
 Portchester PO16 ... 132 B1
Waltham Cres SO16 ... 78 B2
Waltham Rd BH7 ... 206 A3
Waltham St PO5 ... 182 A2
Walton Cl Gosport PO12 ... 181 D2
 Waterlooville PO7 ... 134 C3
Walton Ct Fareham PO15 ... 130 B2
 Portsmouth PO1 ... 182 A2
Walton Pl SO22 ... 10 B3
Walton Rd
 Bournemouth BH10 ... 189 E1
 Cosham PO6 ... 158 B3
 Gosport PO12 ... 181 D2
 Poole BH15 ... 203 D3
 Southampton SO19 ... 104 B2
Waltons Ave SO45 ... 150 B2
Wandesford Pl PO12 ... 156 A1
Wangfield La SO32 ... 82 B1
Wansbeck Cl SO53 ... 55 D3
Wanstead Cl BH24 ... 117 D1
War Meml Hospl ... 181 D2
 Milford on Sea SO41 ... 211 F2
Warbler Cl Hamworthy BH16 ... 201 D4
 Horndean PO8 ... 112 A4
 Southampton SO16 ... 78 A3
Warblington Ave PO9 ... 136 A1
Warblington Cl SO53 ... 55 D2
Warblington Ct PO12 ... 182 A2
Warblington Halt PO9 ... 136 A1
Warblington Rd PO10 ... 160 C4
Warblington Sch PO9 ... 136 A1
Warblington St PO1 ... 182 A2
Warborne La SO41 ... 198 A4

Warbrook Ct 22 PO9 ... 136 A3
Warburton Cl SO19 ... 104 C2
Warburton Rd Poole BH17 ... 202 C4
 Southampton SO19 ... 104 C2
Warburton Way PO8 ... 88 B2
Ward Cres PO10 ... 137 D2
Ward Ct PO11 ... 184 C1
Ward House 38 PO1 ... 182 A3
Ward Rd PO4 ... 183 D1
Warden Cl SO30 ... 80 B1
Wardens Cl PO11 ... 184 C3
Warders Ct 15 PO12 ... 181 D3
Wardle Rd SO50 ... 56 B4
Wardroom Rd PO2 ... 157 D1
Wareham Ct PO1 ... 182 A3
Wareham Rd Broadstone BH21 ... 186 B2
 Upton BH21 ... 186 B2
Warfield Ave PO7 ... 134 C4
Warfield Cres PO7 ... 134 C4
Warland Way BH21 ... 186 C4
Warlock Cl SO19 ... 104 B2
Warmwell Cl
 Bournemouth BH9 ... 190 A2
 Poole BH17 ... 187 F1
Warnborough Ct 6 PO9 ... 136 A3
Warner Ct 11 SO23 ... 2 A1
Warnes La BH24 ... 142 C1
Warnford Cl PO12 ... 180 C2
Warnford Cres PO9 ... 135 E3
Warnford Rd BH6, BH7 ... 206 B4
Warren Ave
 Chandler's Ford SO53 ... 55 F3
 Christchurch BH23 ... 207 F3
 Portsmouth PO4 ... 183 D3
 Southampton SO16 ... 78 A1
Warren Cl Chandler's Ford SO53 . 55 F3
 South Hayling PO11 ... 184 C1
 Southampton SO16 ... 78 A1
 St Leonards BH24 ... 140 B3
Warren Cres SO16 ... 78 A1
Warren Dr BH24 ... 140 B3
Warren Edge Cl BH6 ... 206 C2
Warren Edge Ct BH6 ... 206 C2
Warren Edge Rd BH6 ... 206 C2
Warren Gdns SO51 ... 28 A1
Warren La Beaulieu SO42 ... 200 C4
 Colemore GU32 ... 19 D3
 Froxfield GU32 ... 19 D3
 Owslebury SO21 ... 33 F4
 St Leonards BH24 ... 140 B3
Warren Park Prim Sch PO9 ... 135 E4
Warren Pk SO41 ... 211 D3
Warren Pl SO40 ... 76 B1
Warren Rd
 Bournemouth BH4 ... 204 A1
 Liss GU33 ... 21 D4
 Poole BH14 ... 203 E2
 Winchester SO23 ... 11 E4
Warren The SO45 ... 150 A3
Warren Wlk BH22 ... 165 D4
Warrior Bsns Ctr The PO6 ... 158 C4
Warrior Cl SO53 ... 55 D2
Warrior Pk SO53 ... 55 D2
Warrys Cl SO45 ... 150 A4
Warsash Cl PO9 ... 135 F3
Warsash Ct SO31 ... 128 B1
Warsash Gr PO13 ... 155 D1
Warsash Maritime
 Ctr (Soton Inst) SO31 ... 152 B4
Warsash Rd SO31 ... 129 D1
Warton Cl SO42 ... 175 E3
Warwick Ave BH25 ... 195 D2
Warwick Cl
 Chandler's Ford SO53 ... 55 D2
 Lee-on-the-Solent PO13 ... 180 A2
 13 Winchester SO23 ... 2 A1
Warwick Cres PO5 ... 182 B2
Warwick Ct
 14 Bournemouth BH5 ... 205 F2
 4 Emsworth PO10 ... 160 C4
 14 Winchester SO23 ... 2 A1
Warwick House 21 SO14 ... 103 E3
Warwick Pl
 3 Bournemouth BH7 ... 206 A3
 West Wellow SO51 ... 50 C2
Warwick Rd
 Bournemouth BH7 ... 206 A3
 Poole BH14 ... 203 E2
 Southampton SO15 ... 78 B1
 Totton SO40 ... 100 C4
Warwick Way PO17 ... 108 A2
Wasdale Cl PO8 ... 88 B1
Washbrook Rd PO6 ... 133 E1
Washington Ave BH8 ... 205 E3
Washington Ct PO4 ... 183 D3
Washington Rd
 Emsworth PO10 ... 136 C1
 Portsmouth PO2 ... 182 B4
Wastwater House 25 PO6 ... 133 D1
Watcombe Rd BH6 ... 206 B3
Water Cl SO23 ... 11 D4
Water La
 Bournemouth BH6 ... 206 B4
 Hythe SO45 ... 125 F1
 Totton SO40 ... 100 C4
 Winchester SO23 ... 11 D4
Water Lane Farm BH10 ... 189 F3
Water Tower Rd BH18 ... 187 E2
Water's Edge SO30 ... 105 D3
Waterbeech Dr SO30 ... 105 E4
Waterberry Dr PO7 ... 111 E1
Waterditch Rd
 Bransgore BH23 ... 193 D2
 Burton BH23 ... 193 D2
Waterford Cl Lymington SO41 ... 197 F2
 Poole BH14 ... 203 D1
Waterford Ct SO41 ... 197 E1
Waterford Gdns BH23 ... 209 D4

Waterford La SO41 ...... 197 F1
Waterford Lodge BH23 ...... 208 A3
Waterford Pl BH23 ...... 209 D4
Waterford Rd
  Christchurch BH23 ...... 209 D4
  New Milton BH25 ...... 195 E2
Watergate PO12 ...... 181 F2
Waterhouse La SO15 ...... 102 A4
Waterhouse Way SO15 ...... 102 A4
Waterlock Gdns PO4 ...... 183 E2
Waterloo Cl PO8 ...... 111 E2
Waterloo House BH17 ...... 187 D1
Waterloo Ind Est SO30 ...... 81 D1
Waterloo Rd
  Bournemouth BH9 ...... 204 C4
  Broadstone BH17 ...... 202 B4
  Corfe Mullen BH21 ...... 186 A3
  Gosport PO12 ...... 181 E1
  Havant PO9 ...... 135 F1
  Lymington SO41 ...... 197 F2
  Southampton SO15 ...... 102 B3
Waterloo Spcl Sch PO7 ...... 134 C4
Waterloo St SO15 ...... 182 B2
Waterloo Terr SO15 ...... 102 C3
Waterloo Way BH24 ...... 141 D3
Watermans La SO45 ...... 125 F1
Watermead GU21 ...... 207 D3
Watermead Rd PO6 ...... 158 C4
Watermill Rd BH23 ...... 207 D4
Waters Edge
  Lee-on-the-Solent PO13 ...... 179 F1
  Poole BH13 ...... 214 B3
Waters Edge Gdns PO10 ...... 160 C4
Waters Gn SO42 ...... 146 A1
Waters Green Ct SO42 ...... 146 A1
Waters The PO17 ...... 130 C3
Watersedge Rd [2] PO6 ...... 157 D4
Watershed Cl [2] PO6 ...... 133 D1
Watership Dr BH24 ...... 141 E3
Waterside Christchurch BH23 ...... 207 F2
  [4] Hythe SO45 ...... 126 A3
Waterside Cl BH24 ...... 117 D1
Waterside Gdns PO16 ...... 131 E1
Waterside La PO16 ...... 156 C3
Waterside Rd SO51 ...... 28 A1
Waterside Sch
  Portsmouth, Milton PO4 ...... 183 E2
  Portsmouth, Tipner PO2 ...... 157 D2
Waterside Sq SO45 ...... 125 F3
Watersmeet Fareham PO16 ...... 155 D4
  [36] Winchester SO23 ...... 11 D4
Waterston Cl BH17 ...... 187 E1
Waterworks Rd Cosham PO6 ...... 158 B4
  Otterbourne SO21 ...... 31 E2
  Petersfield GU32 ...... 41 D3
Watery La
  Christchurch BH23 ...... 208 A4
  Upton BH16 ...... 201 D4
Watkin Rd
  [19] Bournemouth BH5 ...... 205 F2
  Hedge End SO30 ...... 81 E1
Watley Cl SO16 ...... 77 E3
Watley La SO21 ...... 32 A3
Watson Wlk SO40 ...... 100 B4
Watton Cl BH8 ...... 191 D1
Watton La SO32 ...... 61 F1
Watton Rd SO45 ...... 150 B2
Watts Cl SO16 ...... 77 F2
Watts Rd Hedge End SO30 ...... 105 E4
  Portsmouth PO1 ...... 182 B4
Wavell Ave BH17 ...... 187 D1
Wavell Rd Bournemouth BH11 ...... 189 D2
  Gosport PO13 ...... 155 E2
  Southampton SO18 ...... 104 A4
Wavell Way SO22 ...... 10 B3
Wavendon Ave BH25 ...... 209 F4
Waveney Cl PO13 ...... 179 F1
Waveney Gn SO16 ...... 77 F1
Waverley Ave SO31 ...... 127 E3
Waverley Cl
  Fordingbridge SP6 ...... 69 F2
  Romsey SO51 ...... 28 A1
Waverley Cres BH15 ...... 202 B3
Waverley Ct SO31 ...... 127 E3
Waverley Gr PO4 ...... 182 C1
Waverley House [12] BH25 ...... 195 D1
Waverley Path PO12 ...... 180 C2
Waverley Rd
  Bournemouth BH1 ...... 205 D2
  Cosham PO6 ...... 158 B4
  Fordingbridge SP6 ...... 69 F2
  New Milton BH25 ...... 195 D1
  Portsmouth PO4 ...... 182 C1
  Southampton SO15 ...... 102 B3
Wayfarer Cl
  Locks Heath SO31 ...... 128 C1
  Portsmouth PO4 ...... 183 E3
Wayfarers PO13 ...... 180 B4
Wayground Rd BH21 ...... 162 C1
Waylands Pl SO30 ...... 105 D2
Wayman Rd BH21 ...... 186 C3
Wayne Rd BH12 ...... 203 D3
Waynflete Cl SO32 ...... 83 E4
Waynflete Pl SO22 ...... 10 B3
Wayside Cl SO41 ...... 211 E3
Wayside Rd
  Bournemouth BH6 ...... 206 C2
  St Leonards BH24 ...... 166 C4
Wayte St PO6 ...... 157 F4
Waytown BH17 ...... 187 E1
Weald Cl SO31 ...... 129 D2
Weardale Rd SO53 ...... 55 E2
Weavers Cl BH22 ...... 138 C1
Weavers Gn PO9 ...... 136 B2
Weavers Pl SO53 ...... 55 D4
Weavills Rd SO50 ...... 57 D1
Webb Cl PO11 ...... 185 D1
Webb La PO11 ...... 185 D1

Webb Rd PO16 ...... 156 B3
Webb's Way BH11 ...... 188 C1
Webbers Way PO12 ...... 181 E1
Webbs Cl BH24 ...... 139 E3
Webbs Way BH24 ...... 139 F3
Webburn Gdns SO18 ...... 80 A2
Webster Rd
  Bournemouth BH9 ...... 190 A2
  Winchester SO22 ...... 1 A1
Wedgewood Cl
  Holbury SO45 ...... 150 B2
  Stubbington BH24 ...... 179 D3
Wedgewood Way PO8 ...... 111 F1
Wedgwood Dr BH14 ...... 203 D1
Wedgwood Gdns BH23 ...... 169 E1
Wedmore Cl SO22 ...... 10 A2
Weeke Manor Cl SO22 ...... 1 B1
Weeke Prim Sch SO22 ...... 1 B1
Weevil La PO12 ...... 181 E3
Weirs The [4] SO23 ...... 11 D3
Welbeck Ave SO17 ...... 79 D1
Welch Ct SO18 ...... 80 A1
Welch Rd Gosport PO12 ...... 181 D4
  Portsmouth PO4 ...... 182 C1
Welch Way SO16 ...... 77 F3
Welchwood Cl PO8 ...... 111 F3
Weldon Ave BH11 ...... 188 C3
Well Cl BH25 ...... 194 C1
Well Copse Cl PO8 ...... 88 B1
Well Hill PO7 ...... 110 B4
Well House Cl SP6 ...... 45 D2
Well House La SO22 ...... 1 C3
Well La Hamble-le-Rice SO31 ...... 128 A1
  Poole BH15 ...... 202 B2
  Swanmore SO32 ...... 84 A4
Well Meadow PO9 ...... 135 F3
Welland Gdns SO18 ...... 80 A1
Welland Gn SO16 ...... 101 F4
Welland Rd BH21 ...... 163 E2
Wellands Rd SO43 ...... 122 A3
Wellbrook Gdns SO53 ...... 55 D4
Weller House [18] PO1 ...... 182 B4
Wellers Cl SO40 ...... 100 A4
Welles Rd SO53 ...... 55 E3
Wellesley Ave BH23 ...... 208 B4
Wellesley Cl PO7 ...... 134 C4
Wellington Ave
  Christchurch BH23 ...... 208 B4
  Southampton SO18 ...... 104 A4
Wellington Cl Horndean PO8 ...... 112 B3
  Hythe SO45 ...... 125 E1
Wellington Ct
  [7] Bournemouth, Deane Pk BH8 ...... 205 D3
  Bournemouth, Westbourne BH2 ...... 204 B2
  [7] Havant PO9 ...... 135 F1
  New Milton BH25 ...... 195 D2
  Southampton SO15 ...... 102 B3
  West End SO30 ...... 80 B1
Wellington Gr PO16 ...... 156 B4
Wellington Pk SO30 ...... 81 D1
Wellington Pl SO40 ...... 98 C4
Wellington Rd
  Bournemouth BH1, BH8 ...... 205 D3
  Poole BH14 ...... 203 E2
  Southampton SO18 ...... 79 F1
Wellington St PO5 ...... 182 B2
Wellington Way [9] PO7 ...... 134 C4
Wellman Ct SO31 ...... 78 C2
Wellow Cl Havant PO9 ...... 135 E2
  Southampton SO18 ...... 104 B4
Wellow Ct [11] SO18 ...... 103 F4
Wellow Cty Prim Sch SO51 ...... 50 C2
Wellow Dro SO51 ...... 50 C4
Wellow Gdns PO14 ...... 129 E1
Wellow Wood Rd SO51 ...... 50 B4
Wellowbrook Cl SO53 ...... 55 D3
Wells Cl PO15 ...... 129 E4
Wells Pl SO16 ...... 56 A1
Wells Rd SO50 ...... 56 A1
Wellsmoor PO14 ...... 129 E1
Wellspring Gdns PO9 ...... 113 E2
Wellsworth La PO9 ...... 113 E2
Wembley Gr PO6 ...... 158 A3
Wembley Way SO50 ...... 57 E1
Wendleholme Nature Reserve SO31 ...... 128 B2
Wendover Cl BH25 ...... 194 C1
Wendover Rd PO9 ...... 135 F1
Wenlock Ct [9] BH23 ...... 207 F4
Wensley Gdns PO10 ...... 136 C2
Wentwood Gdns BH25 ...... 195 E1
Wentworth BH14 ...... 214 B4
Wentworth Ave BH5 ...... 206 A2
Wentworth Ct BH5 ...... 206 A2
Wentworth Coll BH5 ...... 206 A2
Wentworth Dr
  Broadstone BH18 ...... 187 D3
  Christchurch BH23 ...... 206 C3
  Horndean PO8 ...... 112 A4
Wentworth Gdns
  Holbury SO45 ...... 150 B2
  Southampton SO19 ...... 104 A1
Wentworth Gr SO45 ...... 150 B2
Wentworth Grange SO22 ...... 10 C3
Wescott Way BH11 ...... 188 C2
Wesley Cl
  [8] Bournemouth BH8 ...... 205 E3
  Southampton SO19 ...... 104 B2
Wesley Ct PO1 ...... 182 C3
Wesley Gr PO3 ...... 158 A2
Wesley Grange [33] BH4 ...... 204 B2
Wesley Rd
  Kings Worthy SO23 ...... 2 B1
  Poole BH12 ...... 203 E3
  Wimborne Minster BH21 ...... 163 F3
Wessex Ave BH25 ...... 195 D1
Wessex Cl Blackfield SO45 ...... 177 F4
  Christchurch BH23 ...... 208 B4

Wessex Ct
  Southampton, Sholing SO19 ...... 104 A2
  [7] Southampton, Westwood Pk SO17 ...... 103 D4
Wessex Dr SO22 ...... 1 C1
Wessex Est BH24 ...... 141 D4
Wessex Gate Ind Est PO8 ...... 112 B3
Wessex Gdns Portchester PO16 ...... 156 A4
  Romsey SO51 ...... 53 D4
Wessex La SO18 ...... 79 E2
Wessex Nuffield Hospl SO53 ...... 31 D1
Wessex Rd Horndean PO8 ...... 88 B2
  Poole BH14 ...... 203 D2
  Ringwood BH24 ...... 141 D4
Wessex Trad Ctr BH12 ...... 203 D4
Wessex Way
  Bournemouth BH8 ...... 205 E3
  Colden Common SO21 ...... 57 D4
West Ave BH21 ...... 138 C4
West Bargate [2] SO14 ...... 102 C2
West Battery Rd PO2 ...... 157 D1
West Bay Rd SO15 ...... 102 B3
West Block SO15 ...... 102 B3
West Borough BH21 ...... 163 D3
West Butts St [1] BH15 ...... 202 A1
West Cl Lymington SO41 ...... 197 D1
  Verwood BH31 ...... 114 B3
West Cliff Cotts BH2 ...... 204 C1
West Cliff Gdns BH2 ...... 204 C1
West Cliff Mews BH2 ...... 204 C1
West Cliff Rd BH2, BH4 ...... 204 B1
West Close Ct BH6 ...... 207 D2
West Close House BH6 ...... 207 D2
West Common SO45 ...... 177 F3
West Ct Portsmouth PO1 ...... 182 C4
  Portsmouth, Southsea PO4 ...... 183 D2
  Southampton SO19 ...... 103 F1
West Downs Cl PO16 ...... 131 D2
West Dr SO50 ...... 56 B2
West End Cl SO22 ...... 10 C4
West End Cotts [13] PO16 ...... 131 D1
West End Rd Hedge End SO31 ...... 104 A4
  Southampton SO18 ...... 104 A4
West End Terr SO22 ...... 10 C4
West Gr SP6 ...... 69 F1
West Haye Rd PO11 ...... 185 E1
West Hayes Lymington SO41 ...... 197 F2
  Winchester SO22 ...... 10 B4
West Hill Cl SO15 ...... 102 C3
West Hill Dr Hythe SO45 ...... 125 F3
  Winchester SO22 ...... 10 C4
West Hill Pk SO22 ...... 10 B4
West Hill Pl [11] BH2 ...... 204 C2
West Hill Rd BH2 ...... 204 C1
West Hoe La SO32 ...... 83 F4
West Horton Cl SO50 ...... 56 C1
West Horton La SO50 ...... 56 C1
West Howe Cl BH11 ...... 189 D2
West Howe Ind Est BH11 ...... 188 C2
West La Hordle SO41 ...... 196 C1
  North Baddesley SO52 ...... 53 F3
  North Hayling PO11 ...... 184 C3
  South Hayling PO11 ...... 184 C3
West Links SO53 ...... 55 E1
West Lodge PO13 ...... 179 E2
West Mansions [8] BH4 ...... 204 B2
West Marlands Rd SO14 ...... 102 C3
West Meon CE Prim Sch GU32 ...... 37 E3
West Moors Mid Sch BH22 ...... 138 C1
West Moors Oakhurst Fst Sch BH22 ...... 138 C1
West Moors Rd
  Ferndown BH22 ...... 165 E4
  Three Legged Cross BH21 ...... 138 C4
  West Moors BH22 ...... 138 B3
West Moors St Mary's CE Fst Sch BH22 ...... 138 B2
West Overcliff Dr BH4 ...... 204 B1
West Park La SP6 ...... 68 B3
West Park Rd SO15 ...... 102 C3
West Point PO13 ...... 179 F1
West Quay Rd
  Poole BH15 ...... 202 A1
  Southampton SO15 ...... 102 C2
West Rd
  Bournemouth BH5 ...... 206 A2
  Bransgore BH23 ...... 193 D4
  Emsworth PO10 ...... 160 C4
  Fawley SO45 ...... 150 B4
  Hedge End SO30 ...... 104 C3
  Hythe SO45 ...... 125 E1
  Milford on Sea SO41 ...... 211 D3
  Southampton, Old Docks SO14 ...... 103 D1
  Southampton, Woolston SO19 ...... 103 F1
West Row BH21 ...... 163 D2
West Row Mews BH21 ...... 163 D2
West St
  Emsworth PO10 ...... 160 C4
  Fareham PO14, PO16, PO17 ...... 131 D1
  Fordingbridge SP6 ...... 69 F1
  Hambledon PO7 ...... 86 B1
  Havant PO9 ...... 135 F1
  Hythe SO45 ...... 125 F3
  Poole BH15 ...... 202 A1
  Portchester PO16 ...... 156 B4
  Portsmouth PO1 ...... 181 F2
  Ringwood BH24 ...... 140 C4
  Soberton SO32 ...... 85 E3
  Southampton SO14 ...... 102 C2
  Southwick PO17 ...... 132 C3
  Titchfield PO14 ...... 153 F4
  Wimborne Minster BH21 ...... 163 D3
West Station Terr BH24 ...... 204 B2
West Tytherley CE Prim Sch SP5 ...... 4 A4
West View Cotts PO10 ...... 137 F1

West View Rd
  Christchurch BH23 ...... 207 F3
  Poole BH15 ...... 202 B2
West Way Bournemouth BH9 ...... 190 A2
  Broadstone BH18 ...... 187 D2
  Locks Heath PO15 ...... 129 F2
  Lymington SO41 ...... 197 E1
West Way Cl BH9 ...... 190 A1
West Wing SO31 ...... 127 D4
Westbeams Rd SO41 ...... 172 A1
Westborn Rd PO16 ...... 131 D1
Westbourne Ave
  Emsworth PO10 ...... 137 D1
  Holbury SO45 ...... 150 B2
Westbourne Cl
  Bournemouth BH4 ...... 204 B2
  Emsworth PO10 ...... 137 D1
Westbourne Cres SO17 ...... 79 D1
Westbourne Ct [4] PO9 ...... 135 F1
Westbourne Cty Prim Sch PO10 ...... 137 D2
Westbourne Mans [9] SO17 ...... 79 D1
Westbourne Park Rd BH4 ...... 204 A1
Westbourne Rd
  Emsworth PO10 ...... 137 A2
  Portsmouth PO4 ...... 182 C4
  Westbourne PO10 ...... 137 D2
Westbroke Gdns SO51 ...... 27 F1
Westbrook Cl SO31 ...... 129 D3
Westbrook Ctr The PO7 ...... 112 A1
Westbrook Gr PO7 ...... 134 B2
Westbrook Rd PO16 ...... 156 B3
Westbrook Way SO18 ...... 79 E2
Westbrooke Cl PO8 ...... 112 A3
Westbury C [30] PO6 ...... 133 D1
Westbury Cl
  Barton on Sea BH25 ...... 210 A4
  Bransgore BH23 ...... 193 D4
  Christchurch BH23 ...... 193 E1
  Cosham PO6 ...... 133 D1
Westbury Ct Hedge End SO30 ...... 105 E3
  [10] Poole BH14 ...... 203 D2
Westbury Mall [22] PO16 ...... 131 D1
Westbury Rd Fareham PO16 ...... 131 D1
  Ringwood BH24 ...... 141 D4
  Southampton SO15 ...... 101 F4
Westbury Sq [23] PO16 ...... 131 D1
Westby Rd BH5 ...... 205 F2
Westcliff Cl SO13 ...... 179 F2
Westcliff Mews SO19 ...... 103 E2
Westcliff Wlk SO45 ...... 125 F3
Westcot Rd SO45 ...... 150 A2
Westcroft Par [16] BH25 ...... 195 D1
Westcroft Park BH18 ...... 187 E2
Westcroft Rd PO12 ...... 180 C3
Westdown Rd BH11 ...... 189 D3
Westerham Cl PO6 ...... 157 F4
Westerham Rd BH4 ...... 204 A2
Westering SO51 ...... 53 E4
Westerleigh BH4 ...... 204 B1
Westerley Cl SO31 ...... 128 C1
Western Ave
  Barton on Sea BH25 ...... 209 E4
  Bournemouth BH10 ...... 189 D4
  Emsworth PO10 ...... 160 B4
  Poole BH13 ...... 203 F1
  Southampton SO15 ...... 102 A3
Western CE Prim Sch SO22 ...... 10 B4
Western Cl BH10 ...... 189 E3
Western Com Hospl SO16 ...... 77 F1
Western Ct [14] PO16 ...... 131 D1
Western District Cut SO15 ...... 102 B4
Western Downland CE Prim Sch
  Damerham SP6 ...... 68 B2
  Rockbourne SP6 ...... 44 C1
Western Espl SO14 ...... 102 C2
Western Par Emsworth PO10 ...... 160 C4
  Portsmouth PO5 ...... 182 A1
Western Rd
  Chandler's Ford SO53 ...... 30 C1
  Cosham PO6 ...... 157 E4
  Fareham PO16 ...... 131 D1
  Fawley SO45 ...... 151 F1
  Havant PO9 ...... 135 F1
  Liss GU33 ...... 20 C2
  Lymington SO41 ...... 197 E2
  Poole, Branksome Pk BH13 ...... 204 A1
  Poole, Canford Cliffs BH13 ...... 214 C4
  West End SO30 ...... 80 B1
  Winchester SO22 ...... 10 C4
Western Terr PO2 ...... 157 E1
Western Way Fareham PO16 ...... 131 D1
  Gosport PO12 ...... 180 C1
Westerngate BH13 ...... 204 A2
Westfield [11] BH21 ...... 163 D3
Westfield Ave Fareham PO14 ...... 154 C4
  South Hayling SO41 ...... 184 C2
Westfield Cl Fair Oak SO50 ...... 81 E4
  Hamble-le-Rice SO31 ...... 127 F1
  Wimborne Minster BH21 ...... 163 F4
Westfield Cnr SO18 ...... 79 F3
Westfield Comm SO31 ...... 127 F1
Westfield Cres SO53 ...... 55 E2
Westfield Dro SO45 ...... 34 C4
Westfield Gdns BH23 ...... 193 D4
Westfield House SO18 ...... 79 F2
Westfield Ind Est
  Gosport PO12 ...... 181 D2
  Horndean PO8 ...... 112 B4
Westfield Jun Sch PO6 ...... 156 C4
Westfield Oaks PO11 ...... 184 C1
Westfield Rd
  Bournemouth BH6 ...... 206 C2
  Chandler's Ford SO53 ...... 55 E2
  Gosport PO12 ...... 181 D2
  Littleton SO22 ...... 1 A3
  Lymington SO41 ...... 198 A1

Westfield Rd Continued
  Portsmouth PO4 ...... 183 D2
  Southampton SO15 ...... 102 A4
  Totton SO40 ...... 100 C4
Westgate PO14 ...... 179 E3
Westgate Mews SO30 ...... 80 C1
Westgate Park BH4 ...... 204 A2
Westgate Sec Sch SO22 ...... 1 C1
Westgate St [18] SO14 ...... 102 C2
Westgrove PO10 ...... 160 C4
Westham Ct BH17 ...... 187 F2
Westheath Rd BH18 ...... 187 D2
Westland Dr PO7 ...... 134 C2
Westland Gdns PO12 ...... 181 D2
Westlands Ct BH23 ...... 193 D4
Westlands Gr PO16 ...... 156 B4
Westley Cl SO22 ...... 1 B1
Westley Gr PO14 ...... 154 C4
Westmarch Ct [1] SO17 ...... 79 E1
Westmead Cl PO11 ...... 184 C2
Westminster BH25 ...... 209 F4
Westminster Gate SO22 ...... 10 A3
Westminster Gdns PO14 ...... 129 E2
Westminster Pl PO1 ...... 182 B4
Westminster Rd
  Milford on Sea SO41 ...... 211 D2
  Poole BH13 ...... 204 A1
Westminster Rd E BH13 ...... 204 A1
Westmoreland Ct SO41 ...... 195 F2
Westmorland Way SO53 ...... 55 F3
Weston Ave PO4 ...... 183 C4
Weston Cl SO19 ...... 103 F1
Weston Cres SO18 ...... 104 B4
Weston Dr BH1 ...... 205 D2
Weston Grove Rd SO19 ...... 103 E1
Weston Homes [11] SO19 ...... 126 C4
Weston House [12] GU32 ...... 40 C2
Weston La Buriton GU32 ...... 65 E4
  Nursling SO16 ...... 77 D2
  Southampton SO19 ...... 103 F1
Weston Par SO19 ...... 126 C4
Weston Park Inf Sch SO19 ...... 104 A1
Weston Park Jun Sch SO19 ...... 104 A1
Weston Park Sec Sch (Boys) SO19 ...... 104 A1
Weston Rd Eastleigh SO50 ...... 56 A2
  Petersfield GU31 ...... 41 D3
  Wimborne Minster BH21 ...... 163 F4
Weston Shore Inf Sch SO19 ...... 126 C4
Westons La [9] BH15 ...... 202 B1
Westover Prim Sch PO3 ...... 183 D4
Westover Rd
  Bournemouth BH1 ...... 204 C2
  Milford on Sea SO41 ...... 211 C2
  Portsmouth PO3 ...... 183 D4
  Southampton SO16 ...... 101 E4
Westquay House [8] PO16 ...... 131 E1
Westray Hall BH4 ...... 204 B1
Westridge Ct [39] SO17 ...... 79 D1
Westridge Rd SO17 ...... 103 D4
Westrow Gdns SO15 ...... 102 C4
Westrow Rd SO15 ...... 102 C4
Westside View PO7 ...... 111 E1
Westview Rd SO22 ...... 1 A1
Westward Rd SO30 ...... 105 E4
Westways Cosham PO6 ...... 158 C4
  Stubbington PO14 ...... 179 E3
Westways Cl SO16 ...... 77 E3
Westwood Ave BH22 ...... 165 E3
Westwood Cl PO10 ...... 137 D1
Westwood Ct
  [11] Southampton SO17 ...... 103 D4
  Totton SO40 ...... 76 C1
Westwood Gdns SO53 ...... 55 F4
Westwood Mansions [28] SO17 ...... 79 D1
Westwood Rd
  Lyndhurst SO43 ...... 121 F3
  Netley SO31 ...... 127 D4
  Portsmouth PO2 ...... 157 F2
  Southampton SO17 ...... 103 D4
Westwood View SO24 ...... 14 C1
Westwoods & Glendene Pk BH25 ...... 194 B3
Wetherby Cl BH18 ...... 187 D1
Wetherby Ct SO40 ...... 100 A4
Wetherby Gdns SO40 ...... 100 A4
Weyhill Havant PO9 ...... 135 E3
  Portchester PO16 ...... 132 B1
Weyman's Ave BH10 ...... 189 E3
Weymans Dr BH10 ...... 189 E3
Weymouth Ave SO40 ...... 180 C4
Weymouth Rd Poole BH14 ...... 203 E3
  [18] Portsmouth PO2 ...... 157 E1
Whaddon Chase PO14 ...... 179 D3
Whaddon Ct BH25 ...... 135 E3
Whaddon La
  Colden Common SO21 ...... 58 A4
  Owslebury SO21 ...... 33 D2
Whale Island Way PO2 ...... 157 D2
Whalesmead Cl SO50 ...... 56 C1
Whalesmead Rd SO50 ...... 56 C1
Whaley Rd PO2 ...... 157 D1
Wharf Cl BH12 ...... 203 F3
Wharf Hill SO23 ...... 11 D3
Wharf Mill [2] SO23 ...... 11 D3
Wharf Rd Portsmouth PO2 ...... 182 B4
  Southampton SO19 ...... 103 E2
Wharfdale Rd
  Bournemouth BH4 ...... 204 B2
  Poole BH12 ...... 203 F3
Wharncliffe Ct BH23 ...... 208 C4
Wharncliffe Gdns BH23 ...... 209 D4
Wharncliffe House SO19 ...... 103 E2

Wharncliffe Rd
Bournemouth BH5 ... 205 E2
Christchurch BH23 ... 209 D4
Southampton SO19 ... 103 C2
Whartons CI SO40 ... 100 B2
Whartons La SO40 ... 100 B2
Whatleigh CI BH15 ... 202 B1
Wheatcroft Rd PO13 ... 179 F1
Wheatear Dr GU31 ... 41 E1
Wheatears Dr SO51 ... 50 C2
Wheatland CI SO22 ... 10 B3
Wheatlands PO14 ... 129 E2
Wheatlands Ave PO11 ... 185 F1
Wheatlands Cres PO11 ... 185 F1
Wheatley Gn [12] PO9 ... 135 E3
Wheaton Grange BH4 ... 204 B2
Wheaton Rd BH7 ... 206 A3
Wheatsheaf Ct SO30 ... 105 D3
Wheatsheaf Dr PO8 ... 111 E4
Wheatstone Rd PO4 ... 182 C2
Wheeler CI PO12 ... 181 D3
Wheelers La BH11 ... 188 B3
Wheelers Wlk SO45 ... 177 F4
Wheelwright Mews SP5 ... 46 C4
Whernside CI SO16 ... 101 F4
Wherwell Ct [43] PO9 ... 136 A3
Whichers CI PO9 ... 136 A4
Whichers Gate Rd PO9 ... 136 A4
Whiitemoor La SO40 ... 75 F2
Whimbrel CI PO4 ... 183 E3
Whimbrel Ct BH23 ... 208 A3
Whinchat CI Fareham PO15 ... 130 B2
Southampton SO16 ... 78 A3
Whincroft CI PO12 ... 165 F4
Whincroft Dr BH22 ... 165 F3
Whinfield Rd SO45 ... 149 F4
Whinwhistle Rd SO51 ... 51 D1
Whippingham CI PO6 ... 157 E4
Whistler CI SO19 ... 104 B2
Whistler Rd SO19 ... 104 B2
Whitaker Cres SO41 ... 197 E2
Whitby Ave BH18 ... 187 D1
Whitby CI BH23 ... 191 E2
Whitby Cres BH18 ... 187 D1
Whitby CI [4] SO41 ... 211 D2
Whitby Rd SO41 ... 211 D2
Whitchurch Ave BH18 ... 187 E2
Whitchurch Ct SO19 ... 103 F2
Whitcombe CI SO40 ... 100 C4
Whitcombe Gdns PO1 ... 182 C3
White Barn Cres SO41 ... 196 A2
White Beam Rise PO8 ... 88 B3
White CI BH15 ... 203 D4
White Cloud Pk [7] PO4 ... 182 C2
White Cloud PI [8] PO4 ... 182 C2
White Dirt La PO8 ... 88 B2
White Farm CI BH10 ... 204 B4
White Gates SO32 ... 82 A3
White Harmony Acres Ind Est
SO30 ... 80 C3
White Hart La Cadnam SO40 ... 98 C4
Portchester PO16 ... 156 B4
White Hart Rd Fair Oak SO50 ... 57 E1
[4] Gosport PO12 ... 181 D2
Portsmouth PO1 ... 182 A2
White Heather Ct [1] SO45 ... 126 A3
White Horse Crossroads
GU32 ... 18 C3
White Horse Dr BH15 ... 202 B3
White Horse La PO7 ... 111 D3
White Horses BH25 ... 209 F4
White House Gdns
Petersfield GU32 ... 40 C3
Southampton SO15 ... 102 A3
White Knights BH25 ... 209 F4
White La SO21 ... 32 A4
White Ladies CI PO9 ... 136 A1
White Lion Ctyd BH24 ... 140 C4
White Lion Wlk PO12 ... 181 E3
White Lodge BH15 ... 202 C2
White Lodge Gdns PO16 ... 130 C2
White Oak Wlk [36] PO9 ... 136 A3
White Rd SO50 ... 56 B2
White Row SP5 ... 46 B4
White Swan Rd PO1 ... 182 A3
White Way SO32 ... 61 D4
White Wings House PO7 ... 110 C2
White's Rd SO19 ... 104 A3
Whiteacres CI [17] PO12 ... 181 D3
Whitebeam CI
Colden Common SO21 ... 57 D4
[2] Fareham PO14 ... 154 C4
Waterlooville PO8 ... 112 B3
Whitebeam Rd SO30 ... 105 E3
Whitebeam Way
North Baddesley SO52 ... 54 A3
Verwood BH31 ... 115 D3
Whitechimney Row PO10 ... 137 D2
Whitecliff Cres BH14 ... 203 D1
Whitecliff Rd BH14 ... 202 C1
Whitecliffe Ave PO3 ... 183 D4
Whitecliffe Ct PO12 ... 180 B2
Whitecroft SO45 ... 126 A1
Whitecross CI BH17 ... 187 F2
Whitecross Gdns [14] PO2 ... 157 F2
Whitefield Lodge [1] BH25 ... 195 D2
Whitefield Rd Holbury SO45 ... 150 B2
New Milton BH25 ... 195 D1
Poole BH14 ... 203 D1
Whitehall BH23 ... 207 D3
Whitehart Fields BH24 ... 141 E4
Whitehaugh Ct [1] SO50 ... 56 B2
Whitehaven Horndean PO8 ... 112 B3
Portchester PO16 ... 156 A4

Whitehaven Home Pk SO45 ... 177 F4
Whitehayes CI BH23 ... 192 B1
Whitehayes Rd BH23 ... 192 B1
Whitehill CI SO18 ... 104 B4
Whitehorn Dr SP5 ... 73 E4
Whitehouse Rd BH21 ... 163 F1
Whitelands Bransgore BH23 ... 169 E2
Droxford SO32 ... 85 D4
Whitelaw Rd SO15 ... 102 A4
Whiteleaf La PO7 ... 86 B4
Whitelegg Way BH10 ... 189 F3
Whiteley La
Locks Heath PO15 ... 129 F3
Swanwick SO31 ... 106 B1
Whiteley Way PO15 ... 129 E3
Whitemoor Rd SO42 ... 145 E1
Whitenap CI SO51 ... 53 D3
Whitenap La SO51 ... 53 E3
Whiteparish All Saints
CE Prim Sch SP5 ... 24 A2
Whites Ct [18] PO2 ... 157 E1
Whites Hill SO21 ... 33 D2
Whites La SO45 ... 151 D2
Whiteshoot SP5 ... 47 F2
Whiteshoot Hill SP5 ... 47 F2
Whitestone CI SO16 ... 101 F4
Whitethorn Rd PO11 ... 185 D2
Whitewater Rise SO45 ... 125 F1
Whiteways BH23 ... 163 F3
Whitfield Park BH24 ... 140 A3
Whitingham Ct [8] BH5 ... 206 A3
Whitley CI PO10 ... 137 D3
Whitley Way BH25 ... 195 D3
Whitmore La BH21 ... 114 A4
Whitsbury CI BH8 ... 190 B1
Whitsbury Cross SP6 ... 69 E4
Whitsbury Rd
Fordingbridge SP6 ... 69 F2
Havant PO9 ... 136 A3
Whitstable Rd PO6 ... 157 F4
Whittington CI SO45 ... 125 F2
Whittington Ct PO10 ... 160 C4
Whittle Ave PO15 ... 129 E3
Whittle Rd BH21 ... 164 C4
Whittles Way BH15 ... 202 A1
Whitwell SO31 ... 127 E4
Whitwell Rd PO4 ... 182 C1
Whitworth CI PO12 ... 181 D2
Whitworth Cres SO18 ... 103 E4
Whitworth CI SO18 ... 103 E4
Whitworth Rd
Gosport PO12 ... 181 D3
Portsmouth PO2 ... 182 C4
Southampton SO18 ... 103 E4
Whyke Ct [2] PO9 ... 135 F1
Whyte CI SO45 ... 150 A2
Whyteways SO50 ... 56 A2
Wick 1 Ind Est BH25 ... 194 C1
Wick 2 Ind Est BH25 ... 194 C1
Wick CI BH25 ... 194 C1
Wick Dr BH25 ... 194 C1
Wick Farm BH6 ... 207 D3
Wick La
Bournemouth BH6 ... 207 D3
Christchurch BH23 ... 207 D3
Downton SP5 ... 46 A4
Wicket Rd BH10 ... 189 E3
Wicket The SO45 ... 125 F1
Wickfield Ave BH23 ... 207 D3
Wickfield CI BH23 ... 207 D3
Wickford House BH23 ... 207 D3
Wickham CE Prim Sch PO17 ... 108 A2
Wickham Croft PO17 ... 108 A2
Wickham Ct Ferndown BH22 ... 165 F3
Gosport PO12 ... 180 B2
Wickham Dr BH21 ... 186 B2
Wickham House
[17] Southampton SO17 ... 79 D1
[38] Southampton SO17 ... 79 D1
Wickham Rd
Bournemouth BH7 ... 206 A3
Droxford SO32 ... 85 D4
Fareham PO16,PO17 ... 131 D3
Wickham St PO1 ... 182 A3
Wicklea Rd BH6 ... 207 D2
Wicklow Dr SO53 ... 55 D3
Wickmeads Rd BH6 ... 207 D3
Wickor CI PO10 ... 137 D1
Wickor Way PO10 ... 137 D1
Wicor Mill La PO16 ... 156 A4
Wicor Path PO16 ... 156 B3
Wicor Prim Sch PO16 ... 156 A4
Widbury Rd SO41 ... 197 E1
Widden CI SO41 ... 172 A1
Widdicombe Ave BH14 ... 203 F1
Wide La SO18 ... 79 F3
Wide Lane CI SO42 ... 145 F1
Widecombe Dr SO45 ... 125 F2
Widgeon CI Gosport PO12 ... 181 D4
Southampton SO16 ... 78 A3
Widgeon Ct PO16 ... 155 F4
Widget CI BH11 ... 189 D1
Widlers La SO32 ... 58 C3
Widley Court Dr PO6 ... 158 A4
Widley Ct [4] Cosham PO6 ... 158 A4
Fareham PO14 ... 155 D3
Widley Gdns PO7 ... 134 B2
Widley Rd Cosham PO6 ... 158 A4
Portsmouth PO2 ... 157 E1
Widley Wlk PO7 ... 133 F2
Widworthy Dr BH18 ... 186 C3
Wield CI PO12 ... 135 E2
Wigan Cres PO9 ... 135 D1
Wight View PO11 ... 185 E1
Wight Wlk BH22 ... 165 F1
Wightway Mews SO31 ... 128 B1
Wigmore House [84] PO1 ... 182 B3

Wilberforce CI [2] SO22 ... 10 B3
Wilberforce Rd Gosport PO12 ... 181 E1
[36] Portsmouth PO5 ... 182 B2
Wilby La PO3 ... 158 B2
Wild Arum Way SO52 ... 54 C3
Wild Cherry Way SO53 ... 55 D3
Wild Grounds Nature
Reserve PO13 ... 180 B3
Wild Ridings PO14 ... 154 B4
Wild Rose Cres SO31 ... 128 C1
Wildburn CI SO40 ... 76 B1
Wilde CI SO40 ... 100 B4
Wildern CI SO31 ... 128 C2
Wildern La SO30 ... 105 E4
Wildern Sec Sch SO30 ... 105 E4
Wilderness Hts SO18 ... 80 B1
Wilderton Rd BH13 ... 203 F2
Wilderton Rd W BH13 ... 204 A2
Wildfell CI PO4 ... 182 A1
Wildground Inf Sch SO45 ... 125 F1
Wildground Jun Sch SO45 ... 125 F1
Wildmoor Wlk PO9 ... 136 A3
Widown Gdns BH6 ... 207 D2
Widown Rd BH6 ... 207 D2
Wilfred Rd BH5 ... 205 F2
Wilkins CI PO8 ... 88 A3
Wilkins Way SO45 ... 202 A1
Wilkinson Dr BH8 ... 191 D1
Wilkinson House PO4 ... 183 D1
Wilks CI SO16 ... 77 E3
Willersley CI PO6 ... 133 E1
Willett Rd BH21 ... 163 D1
William Booth House [37] PO1 ... 182 A3
William CI
Christchurch BH23 ... 194 A1
Stubbington PO14 ... 179 E3
William Ct [17] BH23 ... 209 D4
William George Ct [9] PO13 ... 179 F1
William Gilpin CE Prim Sch
SO41 ... 173 F1
William Macleod Way SO16 ... 78 A1
William Price Gdns PO16 ... 131 D1
William Rd
Bournemouth BH7 ... 205 F3
Lymington SO41 ... 197 F3
William St SO14 ... 103 D3
William's Ind Pk BH21 ... 194 C1
Williams CI Gosport PO13 ... 180 B4
Holbury SO45 ... 150 B2
Williams Rd PO3 ... 158 A2
Willis Ave SO52 ... 54 A2
Willis Rd Gosport PO12 ... 181 E2
Portsmouth PO1 ... 182 B3
Southampton SO16 ... 79 E3
Willis Way BH15 ... 202 A3
Willis Waye SO23 ... 2 B3
Willow Ave SP6 ... 69 F1
Willow CI
Bournemouth BH4 ... 204 A3
Havant PO9 ... 136 A1
Hedge End SO30 ... 105 E3
St Leonards BH24 ... 139 E2
Upton BH16 ... 201 E3
West End SO30 ... 80 C2
Willow Ct
Bournemouth BH7 ... 206 B3
Fareham PO14 ... 130 B1
Southampton SO15 ... 78 A2
Willow Dr Christchurch BH23 ... 207 D3
Marchwood SO40 ... 124 C4
Ringwood BH24 ... 141 D3
Wimborne Minster BH21 ... 164 B3
Willow Gdns
North Baddesley SO52 ... 53 F3
Westbourne PO10 ... 137 D2
Willow Gn SO21 ... 57 D4
Willow Gr [11] SO50 ... 57 E1
Willow Herb CI SO31 ... 128 C1
Willow La BH23 ... 169 E2
Willow Lodge [1] BH1 ... 205 E2
Willow Mead
Bournemouth BH8 ... 190 B2
Hedge End SO30 ... 105 D4
Willow Pk BH14 ... 203 D2
Willow PI
Christchurch BH23 ... 207 E3
Gosport PO12 ... 181 D3
Willow Rd
Bishop's Waltham SO32 ... 83 F4
Liss GU33 ... 21 D2
Willow Tree Ave PO8 ... 112 A1
Willow Tree Gdns PO14 ... 154 C4
Willow Tree House SO41 ... 197 E1
Willow Tree Rise BH11 ... 189 D2
Willow Tree Wlk SO19 ... 104 A2
Willow Way
Christchurch BH23 ... 207 D3
Ferndown BH22 ... 165 E4
Willow Wood Rd PO11 ... 185 D2
Willowdale CI GU32 ... 40 A2
Willowdene Havant PO9 ... 135 D2
New Milton BH25 ... 195 E2
Willows The
Barton on Sea BH25 ... 210 A4
Chandler's Ford SO53 ... 55 E2
Denmead PO7 ... 110 C2
Wills CI BH21 ... 186 B2
Wills Rd BH12 ... 203 F2
Wills Way SO51 ... 53 D3
Willwood CI BH17 ... 187 F2
Wilmcote Gdns [20] PO1 ... 182 B3
Wilmcote House [19] PO1 ... 182 B3
Wilmer Rd SO50 ... 56 A1
Wilmington CI SO18 ... 79 F2
Wilmott CI PO12 ... 180 C3
Wilmott La PO12 ... 180 C3
Wilmur Cres BH15 ... 202 C3

Wilson Ct Fair Oak SO50 ... 81 E4
Fordingbridge SP6 ... 69 F1
Wilson Gr PO5 ... 182 C2
Wilson Rd Bournemouth BH1 ... 205 F3
Poole BH14 ... 203 E2
Portsmouth PO2 ... 157 E1
Wilson St SO14 ... 103 E3
Wilton Ave SO15 ... 102 C3
Wilton CI
Christchurch BH23 ... 191 E1
Gosport PO12 ... 180 C2
Wilton Cres SO15 ... 78 B1
Wilton Ct SO15 ... 102 B4
Wilton Dr PO8 ... 112 A3
Wilton Gdns
New Milton BH25 ... 194 C2
Southampton SO15 ... 78 B1
Wilton PI PO5 ... 182 B1
Wilton Rd
Bournemouth BH7 ... 205 F3
Southampton SO15 ... 78 B1
Wilton Terr PO5 ... 182 B1
Wiltshire Gdns BH23 ... 192 C4
Wiltshire Rd Bransgore BH23 ... 192 C4
Chandler's Ford SO53 ... 55 E2
Wiltshire St PO5 ... 182 A2
Wilverley Ave
Bournemouth BH8 ... 190 C1
Havant PO9 ... 136 A2
Wilverley CI SO41 ... 197 D1
Wilverley PI SO45 ... 150 C1
Wilverley Rd
Brockenhurst SO42 ... 145 F1
Brockenhurst, Wootton BH25 ... 170 C2
Christchurch BH23 ... 208 A4
Wimbledon Park Rd PO5 ... 182 B1
Wimborne Cty Fst Sch BH21 ... 163 D3
Wimborne House SO16 ... 77 F1
Wimborne Inf & Jun Schs
PO4 ... 183 D2
Wimborne Rd
Bournemouth BH10,11,2,3,9 ... 204 C3
Bournemouth, Kinson
BH10,11,2,3,9 ... 189 E3
Broadstone BH21 ... 162 C1
Poole BH15 ... 202 B3
Portsmouth PO4 ... 183 D2
Wimborne Minster BH21 ... 163 D3
Wimborne Minster BH21 ... 163 F3
Wimborne Rd E BH22 ... 165 E3
Wimborne Rd W
Ferndown BH21 ... 164 B3
Wimborne Minster BH21 ... 164 B3
Wimpole CI [65] PO1 ... 182 B3
Wimpole St PO1 ... 182 B3
Wimpson Gdns SO16 ... 77 F1
Wimpson La SO16 ... 101 F4
Wincanton Way PO7 ... 112 A1
Winchcombe Rd PO6 ... 133 D1
Winchelsea Sch BH12 ... 188 B1
Winchester CI [4] SO31 ... 127 D3
Winchester Coll SO22 ... 10 C3
Winchester Coll (New Hall)
SO23 ... 11 D3
Winchester Ct Gosport PO13 ... 180 B3
[5] Romsey SO51 ... 28 A1
Southampton SO15 ... 78 B1
Winchester Hill SO51 ... 53 D4
Winchester PI [3] BH15 ... 202 B1
Winchester Rd
Bishop's Waltham SO32 ... 83 D4
Botley SO30 ... 81 F2
Chandler's Ford SO53 ... 55 F4
Durley SO32 ... 81 F2
Fair Oak SO32,SO50 ... 81 F2
Langrish GU32 ... 39 F2
New Milton BH25 ... 195 E2
North Baddesley SO51 ... 28 B1
Owslebury SO21,SO32 ... 58 B2
Petersfield GU32 ... 39 F2
Portsmouth PO2 ... 182 C4
Romsey SO51 ... 28 B1
Romsey SO51 ... 52 C4
Shedfield SO32 ... 83 F1
Southampton SO16 ... 78 B1
Upham SO32 ... 58 B2
Winchester Sch of Art SO23 ... 11 D4
Winchester St
Botley SO30 ... 106 A4
[4] Southampton SO15 ... 102 C3
Winchester Sta SO22 ... 10 C4
Winchester Way SO40 ... 100 B4
Winchfield CI SO19 ... 104 A1
Winchfield Cres PO9 ... 135 E2
Winchfield House PO12 ... 181 F2
Wincombe CI BH22 ... 165 E2
Wincombe Dr BH22 ... 165 E2
Windbury Rd SO16 ... 77 F1
Windermere Ave
Southampton SO16 ... 77 F1
Stubbington PO14 ... 154 B2
Windermere Gdns SO40 ... 100 C4
Windermere House [5] PO6 ... 157 D4
Windermere Rd
Bournemouth BH3 ... 205 D2
Portsmouth PO2 ... 157 F2
West End SO30 ... 80 A1
Windfield Dr SO51 ... 53 D4
Windgreen Est BH21 ... 186 C4
Windham Mews BH1 ... 205 E3
Windham Rd BH1 ... 205 E3
Windhill Field PO7 ... 111 D2
Windmill CI Clanfield PO8 ... 88 B3
[5] Milford on Sea SO41 ... 211 E3
St Leonards BH24 ... 140 B2
Windmill Copse SO45 ... 125 F1
Windmill Gr PO16 ... 156 B3

Windmill La
Bursledon SO31 ... 105 D1
St Leonards BH24 ... 140 B2
Windover CI SO19 ... 104 B3
Windrush Gdns PO7 ... 134 B4
Windrush Rd SO16 ... 101 F4
Windrush Way SO45 ... 126 A2
Windsor CI Hordle SO41 ... 195 F2
St Leonards BH24 ... 139 F2
Windsor Ct
[5] Christchurch BH23 ... 209 D4
[9] Cosham PO6 ... 157 F4
Poole BH14 ... 203 D2
[18] Southampton, Bitterne SO18 ... 103 F4
Southampton, Millbrook SO15 ... 102 A3
[5] Southampton, Westwood Pk
SO17 ... 103 D2
Windsor Gate SO50 ... 56 A3
Windsor House
[25] Portsmouth PO1 ... 182 B3
[18] Winchester SO23 ... 11 D4
Windsor La [24] PO5 ... 182 B2
Windsor Rd
Bournemouth BH5 ... 205 F2
Christchurch BH23 ... 206 C4
Cosham PO6 ... 157 F4
Gosport PO12 ... 181 D2
Petersfield GU32 ... 40 C2
Poole BH14 ... 203 D2
Portchester PO16 ... 156 B3
Windsor Way SO45 ... 93 D3
Windward Ct [11] PO12 ... 181 E2
Wine Cross PO17 ... 109 D1
Winecross PO17 ... 109 D1
Winfield Way PO10 ... 136 C2
Winfrid House SO40 ... 100 B4
Winfrith Cres BH12 ... 203 F4
Winfrith Way SO16 ... 77 E3
Wingate Dr SO19 ... 104 A3
Wingate Rd
Gosport PO12 ... 155 F1
Totton SO40 ... 100 B4
Wingfield Ave
Christchurch BH23 ... 193 E1
Poole BH15 ... 202 B3
Wingfield Ct BH1 ... 205 E2
Wingfield St PO1 ... 182 B4
Wingrove Rd SO40 ... 100 B2
Winifred CI SO50 ... 57 E2
Winifred Rd Poole BH15 ... 202 C3
Waterlooville PO7 ... 134 C4
Winkfield Row PO8 ... 112 A3
Winkle St SO14 ... 103 D1
Winkton CI Burton BH23 ... 192 B2
Havant PO9 ... 135 E2
Winkton House BH23 ... 192 B2
Winn Ct SO17 ... 102 C4
Winn Mansions [25] SO17 ... 79 D1
Winn Rd SO17 ... 79 D1
Winnal Ind Est [9] SO23 ... 11 D3
Winnall CI SO23 ... 2 B1
Winnall Manor Rd SO23 ... 11 E4
Winnall Prim Sch SO23 ... 11 E4
Winnall Trad Est SO23 ... 11 E4
Winnall Valley Rd SO23 ... 11 E4
Winnards CI BH22 ... 165 F1
Winnards Pk SO31 ... 128 B2
Winnham Dr PO16 ... 132 A1
Winnington PO15 ... 130 B2
Winnington CI PO15 ... 130 B2
Winscombe Ave PO8 ... 112 A1
Winsford Ave SO50 ... 57 D1
Winsford CI Bishopstoke SO50 ... 57 D1
Christchurch BH23 ... 193 E1
Winsford Gdns SO50 ... 57 D1
Winslade Rd Havant PO9 ... 135 E3
Winchester SO22 ... 1 B2
Winsley Ave BH6 ... 206 B2
Winslow CI PO6 ... 158 B4
Winsor CI PO11 ... 185 E1
Winsor Ct SO50 ... 56 B2
Winsor La SO40 ... 99 F4
Winsor Rd Cadnam SO40 ... 75 E1
Totton SO40 ... 101 D3
Waterlooville PO7 ... 111 E1
Winspit CI BH15 ... 201 F2
Winstanley Rd Nursling SO16 ... 77 F3
Portsmouth PO2 ... 157 F1
Winston Ave BH12 ... 204 A3
Winston Churchill Ave PO5 ... 182 B2
Winston CI
Eastleigh SO50 ... 56 A2
South Hayling PO11 ... 184 C2
Winston Ct
[1] Christchurch BH23 ... 207 D4
[20] New Milton BH25 ... 195 D1
Winston Gdns BH12 ... 204 A3
Winston Par [22] BH25 ... 195 D1
Winston Pk BH12 ... 204 A3
Winston Rd BH9 ... 190 A2
Winston Way PO14 ... 141 D4
Winstone Bldgs SO16 ... 78 C2
Winstone Cres SO52 ... 54 A2
Winter Rd PO4 ... 183 D2
Winterbourne CI BH15 ... 202 B2
Winterbourne Rd
Cosham PO6 ... 132 C1
Poole BH15 ... 202 B3
Romsey SO51 ... 28 A1
Winterhayes CI BH17 ... 187 F2
Winterhill Rd PO6 ... 157 E4
Winters CI SO45 ... 150 B2
Winters Hill
Bishop's Waltham SO32 ... 82 C4
Durley SO32 ... 82 C4
Winters Rd SO32 ... 84 A1
Winterslow Dr PO9 ... 135 F3
Winton CI SO41 ... 197 F2

Winton Ct
  [11] Petersfield GU32 ...... 40 C2
  West End SO30 ...... 80 B1
Winton Prim Sch BH9 ...... 189 F1
Winton Rd Petersfield GU32 ...... 40 C2
  Portsmouth PO2 ...... 157 F1
Winton Sch for Boys (Annex)
  BH9 ...... 189 F1
Winton Sec Sch BH10 ...... 189 E1
Winton St [12] SO14 ...... 103 D3
Winton Way
  Bournemouth BH10 ...... 189 E1
  New Milton BH25 ...... 195 D3
Wisbech Way SO41 ...... 195 F2
Wisborough Rd PO5 ...... 182 C1
Wises Ct PO12 ...... 181 F2
Wish Pl PO5 ...... 182 C2
Wishart Gdns SO41 ...... 190 A3
Wistaria House BH10 ...... 189 F2
Wisteria Dr BH31 ...... 115 E2
Witchampton Cl PO9 ...... 136 A3
Witchampton Rd BH18 ...... 186 C1
Witham Cl SO53 ...... 55 D3
Withedwood Ave SO15 ...... 102 B4
Witherbed La
  Locks Heath PO15 ...... 129 E2
  Locks Heath PO15 ...... 129 F3
Withermoor Rd BH9 ...... 204 C4
Withers La SO42 ...... 175 E4
Withewood Mans [2] SO15 ...... 102 B4
Withies Rd PO13 ...... 180 B4
Withingham Rd BH13 ...... 203 F2
Withington Cl PO6 ...... 133 D1
Withy Cl SO51 ...... 52 C4
Witley BH14 ...... 214 B4
Witley Rd PO8 ...... 111 F3
Witney Rd BH17 ...... 187 C1
Witt Rd SO50 ...... 57 E1
Wittensford La SO43 ...... 98 B4
Wittering Rd
  South Hayling PO11 ...... 185 F1
  Southampton SO16 ...... 78 A2
Witts Hill SO18 ...... 79 F1
Woburn Cl SO50 ...... 56 A3
Woburn Ct PO13 ...... 179 F1
Woburn Rd SO16 ...... 78 B3
Wode Cl PO8 ...... 88 B2
Wodehouse Rd SO19 ...... 103 F2
Woking Rd BH14 ...... 203 F2
Wolfe Cl Christchurch BH23 ...... 207 E4
  Winchester SO22 ...... 10 B3
Wollaston Rd BH6 ...... 206 C2
Wollaton Cres BH22 ...... 165 E2
Wollaton Rd BH22 ...... 165 E2
Wollstonecraft Rd [25] BH5 ...... 205 F2
Wolseley Rd Poole BH12 ...... 203 E3
  Southampton SO15 ...... 102 B4
Wolsey Way SO41 ...... 211 E3
Wolterton Rd BH12 ...... 204 A3
Wolverley Ct
  [16] Bournemouth BH4 ...... 204 B2
  Southampton SO16 ...... 78 B2
Wolverton Rd
  Bournemouth BH7 ...... 205 F3
  Havant PO9 ...... 135 F3
  Southampton SO14 ...... 103 D3
Wolvesey Pl SO53 ...... 55 D2
Wolvesey Terr [3] SO23 ...... 11 D3
Wonderholm Par BH11 ...... 189 D1
Wonston Ct PO9 ...... 136 A3
Wonston Rd SO16 ...... 78 A2
Wood Cl SO19 ...... 104 B2
Wood End Rd BH24 ...... 141 F3
Wood End Way SO53 ...... 55 D3
Wood Glade Cl SO40 ...... 101 F1
Wood House La SO41 ...... 174 A1
Wood La
  Bournemouth BH11 ...... 188 C3
  Bramdean SO24 ...... 15 F3
  Milford on Sea SO41 ...... 211 E2
  Southwick PO17 ...... 133 D3
Wood Lark Gdns GU31 ...... 41 E2
Wood Lawn Cl BH25 ...... 209 F4
Wood Lodge SO40 ...... 76 A1
Wood Rd SO40 ...... 100 A1
Wood View BH21 ...... 164 A4
Wood's Cnr BH24 ...... 143 E3
Woodacre Gdns BH22 ...... 165 F2
Woodberry La PO9 ...... 136 C4
Woodbourne Cl
  Fareham PO15 ...... 130 B1
  Liss GU33 ...... 21 D2
Woodbury BH1 ...... 205 D1
Woodbury Ave
  Bournemouth BH8 ...... 190 C1
  Havant PO9 ...... 159 F4
  Petersfield GU32 ...... 40 C3
Woodbury Cl BH23 ...... 191 F2
Woodcock La SO41 ...... 196 A2
Woodcocks Cres BH7 ...... 206 A4
Woodcot Cres PO9 ...... 136 A3
Woodcot Prim Sch PO13 ...... 155 D2
Woodcote Cotts SO24 ...... 15 E2
Woodcote Dr BH16 ...... 201 D3

Woodcote La PO14 ...... 155 D2
Woodcote Rd SO17 ...... 79 E2
Woodcroft La PO8 ...... 111 F3
Woodend Rd BH9 ...... 204 C4
Wooderson Cl SO50 ...... 57 D2
Woodfern SP6 ...... 70 B1
Woodfield Ave PO6 ...... 134 C1
Woodfield Cotts GU32 ...... 19 D2
Woodfield Dr SO22 ...... 10 A3
Woodfield Gdns BH23 ...... 193 E1
Woodfield Park Rd PO10 ...... 161 D4
Woodfield Rd BH11 ...... 189 D3
Woodford Cl BH24 ...... 141 E4
Woodford House PO15 ...... 130 B1
Woodford Rd BH1 ...... 205 E2
Woodgason La PO11 ...... 160 B1
Woodgreen Ave PO9 ...... 135 E2
Woodgreen Dr BH11 ...... 188 B2
Woodgreen Rd SO22 ...... 1 B2
Woodgreen Wlk SO40 ...... 76 A1
Woodhall Way PO15 ...... 130 C2
Woodhay Wlk [13] PO9 ...... 136 A3
Woodhayes Ave BH23 ...... 193 F1
Woodhill Prep Sch SO30 ...... 105 F4
Woodhill Sch SO53 ...... 55 E4
Woodhouse La
  Hedge End SO30 ...... 105 F4
  Rowland's Castle PO8,PO9 ...... 113 E2
Woodington Cl PO9 ...... 136 A3
Woodington Rd SO51 ...... 51 E3
Woodlake Cl BH17 ...... 187 E1
Woodland Ave BH5 ...... 206 A2
Woodland Cl
  Southampton SO18 ...... 104 B4
  West Wellow SO51 ...... 51 D1
Woodland Ct BH7 ...... 205 F3
Woodland Drove SO21 ...... 32 A2
Woodland Mans BH14 ...... 203 D3
Woodland Mews SO30 ...... 80 B1
Woodland Pl [18] SO15 ...... 102 C4
Woodland St PO1 ...... 182 C3
Woodland Vale SO19 ...... 104 A2
Woodland View
  Bursledon SO31 ...... 127 F4
  Horndean BH26 ...... 111 F3
Woodland Way
  Christchurch BH23 ...... 208 B4
  Milford on Sea SO41 ...... 211 E2
Woodland Wlk
  Bournemouth BH5 ...... 206 A2
  Ferndown BH22 ...... 165 F4
Woodlands PO16 ...... 131 E1
Woodlands Ave
  Emsworth PO10 ...... 136 C2
  Hamworthy BH15 ...... 201 F2
Woodlands Cl
  Bransgore BH23 ...... 193 D4
  Chandler's Ford SO53 ...... 30 B1
  Gosport PO13 ...... 180 B3
  Hythe SO45 ...... 125 F1
  Locks Heath SO31 ...... 128 C3
Woodlands Com Sch SO18 ...... 104 B4
Woodlands Cres BH15 ...... 201 F2
Woodlands Ct Hythe SO45 ...... 125 F1
  [18] Winchester SO23 ...... 2 A1
Woodlands Dr SO31 ...... 127 E3
Woodlands Dro SO40 ...... 99 F2
Woodlands Gdns [8] SO51 ...... 28 A1
Woodlands La Liss GU33 ...... 21 D2
  South Hayling PO11 ...... 184 C3
Woodlands Prim Sch PO8 ...... 111 E2
Woodlands Rd Ashurst SO40 ...... 99 F2
  Barton on Sea BH25 ...... 209 F4
  Brockenhurst SO42 ...... 172 C4
  Netley Marsh SO40 ...... 99 F2
Woodlands The
  Chandler's Ford SO53 ...... 30 A1
  Kings Worthy SO23 ...... 2 B3
Woodlands Way
  Bursledon SO31 ...... 127 F4
  Havant PO9 ...... 135 F2
  New Milton BH25 ...... 195 D3
  North Baddesley SO52 ...... 53 F2
  Southampton SO15 ...... 102 C4
  St Leonards BH24 ...... 139 F2
Woodlane Cl SO24 ...... 15 E3
Woodlea Cl SO22 ...... 1 C1
Woodlea Gdns SO30 ...... 80 C1
Woodlea House SO53 ...... 55 E2
Woodlea Way SO51 ...... 29 F1
Woodleaze Cl BH18 ...... 187 D3
Woodleigh Cl PO9 ...... 136 B2
Woodley Cl SO51 ...... 28 B1
Woodley Close Flats SO51 ...... 28 B1
Woodley Gdns SO41 ...... 197 E3
Woodley La SO51 ...... 28 A1
Woodley Rd Gosport PO12 ...... 181 E2
  Southampton SO19 ...... 103 E2
Woodley Way SO51 ...... 28 B1
Woodling Cres SP6 ...... 70 B1
Woodlinken Cl BH31 ...... 115 D2
Woodlinken Dr BH31 ...... 115 D3
Woodlinken Way BH31 ...... 115 E2

Woodmancote La PO10 ...... 137 F2
Woodmancote Rd PO4 ...... 183 D2
Woodmill La SO18 ...... 79 F1
Woodmoor Cl SO40 ...... 102 A1
Woodpath PO5 ...... 182 B2
Woodpath House [35] PO5 ...... 182 B2
Woodpecker Cl Havant PO9 ...... 136 A1
  Verwood BH31 ...... 114 C3
Woodpecker Copse SO31 ...... 129 D2
Woodpecker Dr
  Broadstone BH17 ...... 201 F4
  Marchwood SO40 ...... 101 F1
  Winchester SO22 ...... 1 B1
Woodpecker Way SO50 ...... 55 E1
Woodrising SO19 ...... 214 A2
Woodrisings The BH2 ...... 204 B2
Woodroffe Wlk PO10 ...... 136 C2
Woodrow PO7 ...... 110 C2
Woodrush Cres SO31 ...... 128 C1
Woods House [5] GU32 ...... 40 C2
Woods View Rd BH9 ...... 204 B4
Woodsedge PO7 ...... 135 D3
Woodside
  Brockenhurst SO42 ...... 173 D4
  Chilworth SO16 ...... 54 C1
  Gosport PO13 ...... 155 D3
Woodside Ave Eastleigh SO50 ...... 56 A3
  Lymington SO41 ...... 197 F1
Woodside Cl Ferndown BH22 ...... 165 F3
  [13] Lymington SO41 ...... 197 F1
  Marchwood SO40 ...... 101 F1
Woodside Cres SO16 ...... 54 C1
Woodside Ct [21] SO17 ...... 103 D4
Woodside Gdns SO40 ...... 100 B2
Woodside La SO41 ...... 197 F1
Woodside Rd
  Bournemouth BH5 ...... 206 A2
  Eastleigh SO50 ...... 55 F2
  Ferndown BH22 ...... 165 F3
  North Baddesley SO52 ...... 53 F2
  Poole BH14 ...... 203 E2
  Southampton SO17 ...... 103 D4
  West Moors BH22 ...... 138 B2
Woodside Way SO30 ...... 105 D3
Woodstock Ave PO8 ...... 112 A3
Woodstock Cl Fareham PO15 ...... 130 C1
  Hedge End SO30 ...... 105 E3
  Poole BH14 ...... 203 D1
Woodstock Dr SO17 ...... 79 D1
Woodstock La BH24 ...... 141 D3
Woodstock Rd
  Burton BH23 ...... 192 B1
  Gosport PO12 ...... 181 E2
  Havant PO9 ...... 135 E1
  Poole BH14 ...... 203 D1
Woodthorpe Gdns SO31 ...... 128 C3
Woodvale PO15 ...... 130 B1
Woodvale Gdns BH25 ...... 195 E2
Woodview Cl SO16 ...... 79 D3
Woodville Dr PO1 ...... 182 A2
Woodville Rd Fawley SO45 ...... 151 D2
  Havant PO9 ...... 135 D1
Woodward Cl PO12 ...... 180 C2
Woofferton Rd PO6 ...... 133 D1
Wool Rd BH12 ...... 203 D4
Woolfield La GU34 ...... 18 A2
Woolford Cl [1] SO22 ...... 10 B3
Woolley House [15] SO14 ...... 103 D3
Woolmer Ct [35] PO9 ...... 136 A3
Woolmer La BH24 ...... 117 D1
Woolmer St PO10 ...... 136 C2
Woolner Ave Cosham PO6 ...... 158 A4
  Petersfield GU32 ...... 40 C2
Woolsbridge Ind Est BH21 ...... 139 D3
Woolsbridge Rd BH24 ...... 139 F3
Woolslope Cl BH22 ...... 138 C1
Woolslope Gdns BH22 ...... 138 C1
Woolslope Rd BH22 ...... 138 C1
Woolston Ct PO12 ...... 180 B2
Woolston Inf Sch SO19 ...... 103 F1
Woolston Rd Havant PO9 ...... 135 E3
  Netley SO31 ...... 127 E4
Woolston Sch (Annexe) SO19 ...... 103 F2
Woolston Sec Sch SO19 ...... 103 F2
Woolston Sta SO19 ...... 103 E2
Woolven Cl BH14 ...... 203 D3
Woolwich Cl SO31 ...... 104 C1
Wootton SO31 ...... 127 E4
Wootton Farm Rd BH25 ...... 170 C1
Wootton Gdns BH1 ...... 205 D2
Wootton Mount BH1 ...... 205 D2
Wootton Rd
  Lee-on-the-Solent PO13 ...... 180 A2
  New Milton BH25 ...... 195 E4
Wootton Rough BH25 ...... 195 D4
Wootton St PO6 ...... 157 F4
Worbarrow Gdns BH12 ...... 203 E4
Worcester Ct PO13 ...... 180 B3
Worcester Pl
  [7] Lymington SO41 ...... 197 F1
  Southampton SO19 ...... 104 A1
Wordsworth Ave
  Bournemouth BH8 ...... 190 C1
  Portchester PO6 ...... 132 C1

Wordsworth Cl
  Bishop's Waltham SO32 ...... 83 F4
  Winchester SO22 ...... 10 B4
Wordsworth Inf Sch SO15 ...... 78 A1
Wordsworth Rd SO15 ...... 78 B1
Worgret Rd BH15 ...... 202 B4
Workhouse La GU32 ...... 38 B1
Worldham Rd PO9 ...... 136 A3
Worrell Dr BH12 ...... 203 E4
Worsley Rd PO5 ...... 182 B2
Worsley St PO4 ...... 183 D1
Worthing Ave PO12 ...... 180 C4
Worthing Rd PO5 ...... 182 B2
Worthington Cres BH14 ...... 203 D2
Worthy Ct [46] PO9 ...... 136 A3
Worthy House SO16 ...... 78 A1
Worthy Rd
  New Milton BH25 ...... 195 D1
  Winchester SO23 ...... 2 A1
Wortley Rd BH23 ...... 209 D4
Wraxall Cl BH17 ...... 187 E1
Wraysbury Park Dr SO16 ...... 136 C2
Wren Cl
  Christchurch BH23 ...... 208 A3
  New Milton BH25 ...... 194 C1
  Ringwood BH24 ...... 141 E3
  Winchester SO22 ...... 10 B3
Wren Cres BH12 ...... 204 A3
Wren Gdns SP6 ...... 93 D3
Wren Rd SO50 ...... 55 F1
Wrenway PO16 ...... 155 F4
Wrexham Gr PO8 ...... 88 A1
Wright Way SO45 ...... 151 F1
Wright's Hill SO19 ...... 104 A1
Wrights Wlk SO31 ...... 104 C1
Wroxham Rd BH12 ...... 203 F3
Wryneck Cl SO16 ...... 78 A3
Wuthering Hghts SO22 ...... 10 C3
Wyatts Cl BH21 ...... 186 B3
Wyatts La BH21 ...... 186 B3
Wyborn Cl PO11 ...... 185 D1
Wych La PO13 ...... 155 D2
Wychwood Cl BH2 ...... 204 C2
Wychwood Dr
  Blackfield SO45 ...... 177 F4
  Bournemouth BH2 ...... 204 C2
Wychwood Gr SO53 ...... 55 F4
Wychwood Grange [1] BH2 ...... 204 C2
Wycliffe Rd
  Bournemouth BH9 ...... 204 C4
  Southampton SO18 ...... 80 A1
Wycote Rd PO13 ...... 155 D2
Wyeford Cl [4] PO9 ...... 136 A3
Wyelands Ave BH21 ...... 164 B3
Wykeham Ave PO2 ...... 157 F1
Wykeham Cl Netley SO31 ...... 127 D3
  Poole BH17 ...... 202 C4
  Southampton SO16 ...... 78 C2
Wykeham Field PO17 ...... 108 A2
Wykeham House Sch PO16 ...... 131 E1
Wykeham Ind Est The SO23 ...... 2 B2
Wykeham Lodge BH13 ...... 214 C3
Wykeham Pl
  Lymington SO41 ...... 197 F2
  Winchester SO22 ...... 10 B3
Wykeham Rd
  [3] Netley SO31 ...... 127 D3
  Portsmouth PO2 ...... 157 F1
Wyld Green La GU33 ...... 21 D3
Wylds La GU34 ...... 65 E4
Wyllie Rd PO2 ...... 157 F2
Wylye Ct SO18 ...... 80 A2
Wymering La PO6 ...... 133 F1
Wymering Manor Cl [9] PO6 ...... 157 E4
Wymering Rd PO2 ...... 182 C4
Wyn Sutcliffe Ct PO4 ...... 183 D2
Wyncombe Rd BH5 ...... 206 A3
Wyndcliffe Rd PO4 ...... 182 C2
Wyndham Cl
  Christchurch BH23 ...... 194 A1
  Waterlooville PO8 ...... 112 A2
Wyndham Ct SO15 ...... 102 C3
Wyndham Mews PO1 ...... 182 A2
Wyndham Pl [14] SO15 ...... 102 C3
Wyndham Rd
  Christchurch BH23 ...... 194 A1
  Poole BH14 ...... 203 D2
Wynford Ind Est
  Abbotswood SO51 ...... 27 F2
  Michelmersh SO51 ...... 27 F2
Wynford Rd
  Bournemouth BH9 ...... 190 A2
  Poole BH14 ...... 203 E2
Wynne Cl BH18 ...... 186 C2
Wynter Cl BH7 ...... 205 F4
Wynter Rd SO18 ...... 104 A4
Wynton Way PO15 ...... 130 B2
Wynyards Gap SO52 ...... 53 F2
Wyre Cl SO53 ...... 55 D3
Wyvern Cl
  Chandler's Ford SO53 ...... 55 E3
  Poole BH12 ...... 203 E4
Wyvern Sch The SO50 ...... 57 E1

Yaldhurst Ct [12] PO9 ...... 136 A3
Yaldhurst La SO41 ...... 197 D2
Yapton St PO1 ...... 182 B3
Yarborough Rd PO5 ...... 182 B2
Yardlea Cl PO9 ...... 113 D1
Yardley Cl PO3 ...... 158 B2
Yardley Rd SO30 ...... 105 E3
Yarmouth Cl BH12 ...... 204 A3
Yarmouth Gdns [11] SO15 ...... 78 A1
Yarmouth Rd BH12 ...... 203 F3
Yarrell Mead SO41 ...... 197 D2
Yarrells Cl BH16 ...... 201 E3
Yarrells Dr BH16 ...... 201 D4
Yarrells La BH16 ...... 201 E3
Yarrells Sch BH16 ...... 201 D4
Yarrow Cl BH23 ...... 208 A4
Yarrow Rd BH12 ...... 203 D4
Yarrow Way SO31 ...... 128 C1
Yateley Cl PO9 ...... 135 E3
Yaverland SO31 ...... 127 E3
Yeatminster Rd BH17 ...... 187 F1
Yeatton House SO41 ...... 196 A1
Yelverton Ave SO45 ...... 150 A4
Yelverton Rd [33] BH1 ...... 204 C2
Yeo Ct PO4 ...... 183 E2
Yeoman Pk SO16 ...... 77 E1
Yeoman Ind Pk BH8 ...... 190 C1
Yeomans Rd BH8 ...... 190 C2
Yeomans Way
  Bournemouth BH8 ...... 190 C1
  Totton SO40 ...... 100 C4
Yeovil Chase SO18 ...... 104 A4
Yeovilton Cl SO41 ...... 196 C1
Yerville Gdns SO41 ...... 195 F2
Yew La BH25 ...... 195 E2
Yew Rd SO18 ...... 104 A4
Yew Tree Ave PO8 ...... 112 A1
Yew Tree Cl Fair Oak SO50 ...... 57 E2
  Hedge End SO30 ...... 105 D3
  Wimborne Minster BH21 ...... 163 E3
Yew Tree Ct
  Fordingbridge SP6 ...... 93 F4
  Locks Heath PO15 ...... 129 E3
  [30] New Milton BH25 ...... 195 D1
Yew Tree Dr PO15 ...... 129 D4
Yew Tree Gdns PO7 ...... 110 C2
Yew Tree Pl GU33 ...... 21 D2
Yew Tree Rd PO11 ...... 185 D4
Yews The PO8 ...... 112 B4
Yewside PO13 ...... 155 F1
Yewtree La SO16 ...... 77 E2
Yoells Cres PO8 ...... 111 F3
Yoells La PO8 ...... 111 F3
Yokesford Hill SO51 ...... 27 F2
Yokesford Hill Est SO51 ...... 27 F3
Yonge Cl SO50 ...... 56 A2
York Ave BH25 ...... 195 D2
York Bldgs SO14 ...... 103 D2
York Cl
  Broadstone BH18 ...... 187 D1
  Christchurch BH23 ...... 206 C4
  Fair Oak SO50 ...... 81 E4
  North Baddesley SO52 ...... 54 C2
  Petersfield GU32 ...... 40 B2
  Southampton SO14 ...... 103 E3
  Totton SO40 ...... 101 D4
York Cres PO13 ...... 180 A2
York Dro
  Nomansland SP5 ...... 73 E4
  Southampton SO18 ...... 104 A4
York Gdns PO16 ...... 156 C3
York House
  [26] Gosport PO12 ...... 181 E2
  [7] Southampton SO14 ...... 103 E3
  [32] Winchester SO23 ...... 2 A1
York Pl
  Bournemouth BH7 ...... 206 A3
  [17] New Milton BH25 ...... 195 D2
  Portsmouth PO1 ...... 182 A3
York Rd
  Bournemouth BH1 ...... 205 D2
  Broadstone BH18 ...... 187 D1
  Eastleigh SO50 ...... 80 A4
  Netley SO31 ...... 127 D3
  Southampton SO15 ...... 102 B4
York Terr PO3 ...... 157 F3
Yorke St PO5 ...... 182 B2
Yorke Way SO31 ...... 127 F2
Yorkwood GU33 ...... 20 C2
Youngbridge Ct PO14 ...... 155 D4
Youngs Rd BH11 ...... 189 D3
Yves Mews PO5 ...... 182 B1

Zamek Cl BH11 ...... 189 D3
Zetland Ct BH4 ...... 204 A1
Zetland Rd
  Cosham PO6 ...... 158 B4
  Gosport PO12 ...... 181 D3
Zeus La PO7 ...... 134 C2
Zinnia Cl BH10 ...... 189 F1

STREET ATLASES
ORDER FORM

STREET ATLAS Bedfordshire
Unique comprehensive coverage

BEST BUY AUTO EXPRESS

Includes Luton and St Neots

PHILIP'S

STREET ATLAS Lanca
COMPLETE COUNTY

STREET ATLAS Northamptonshire
Plus town maps of Banbury, Buckingham, Rugby and Stamford

BEST BUY AUTO EXPRESS

Unique comprehensive coverage

Includes Market Harborough

PHILIP'S

STREET ATLAS Surrey
Dorking, Epsom, Guildford, Kingston, Leatherhead and Woking at extra-large-scale

Unique comprehensive coverage

BEST BUY AUTO EXPRESS

Includes Heathrow and Gatwick Airports

PHILIP'S

The Street Atlases are available from all good bookshops or by mail order direct from the publisher. Orders can be made in the following ways. **By phone** Ring our special Credit Card Hotline on **01933 443863** during office hours (9am to 5pm) or leave a message on the answering machine, quoting your full credit card number plus expiry date and your full name and address. **By post or fax** Fill out the order form below (you may photocopy it) and post it to: **Philip's Direct, 27 Sanders Road, Wellingborough, Northants NN8 4NL** or fax it to: **01933 443849.** Before placing an order by post, by fax or on the answering machine, please telephone to check availability and prices.

COLOUR LOCAL ATLASES	PAPERBACK	Quantity @ £3.50 each	£ Total
CANNOCK, LICHFIELD, RUGELEY		☐ 0 540 07625 2 ➤	
DERBY AND BELPER		☐ 0 540 07608 2 ➤	
NORTHWICH, WINSFORD, MIDDLEWICH		☐ 0 540 07589 2 ➤	
PEAK DISTRICT TOWNS		☐ 0 540 07609 0 ➤	
STAFFORD, STONE, UTTOXETER		☐ 0 540 07626 0 ➤	
WARRINGTON, WIDNES, RUNCORN		☐ 0 540 07588 4 ➤	

COLOUR REGIONAL ATLASES	HARDBACK	SPIRAL	POCKET	
	Quantity @ £10.99 each	Quantity @ £8.99 each	Quantity @ £4.99 each	£ Total
MERSEYSIDE	☐ 0 540 06480 7	☐ 0 540 06481 5	☐ 0 540 06482 3 ➤	
	Quantity @ £12.99 each	Quantity @ £8.99 each	Quantity @ £5.99 each	£ Total
BERKSHIRE	☐ 0 540 06170 0	☐ 0 540 06172 7	☐ 0 540 06173 5 ➤	
	Quantity @ £12.99 each	Quantity @ £9.99 each	Quantity @ £4.99 each	£ Total
DURHAM	☐ 0 540 06365 7	☐ 0 540 06366 5	☐ 0 540 06367 3 ➤	
	Quantity @ £12.99 each	Quantity @ £9.99 each	Quantity @ £5.50 each	£ Total
GREATER MANCHESTER	☐ 0 540 06485 8	☐ 0 540 06486 6	☐ 0 540 06487 4 ➤	
TYNE AND WEAR	☐ 0 540 06370 3	☐ 0 540 06371 1	☐ 0 540 06372 X ➤	
	Quantity @ £12.99 each	Quantity @ £9.99 each	Quantity @ £5.99 each	£ Total
BEDFORDSHIRE	☐ 0 540 07801 8	☐ 0 540 07802 6	☐ 0 540 07803 4 ➤	
BIRMINGHAM & WEST MIDLANDS	☐ 0 540 07603 1	☐ 0 540 07604 X	☐ 0 540 07605 8 ➤	
BUCKINGHAMSHIRE	☐ 0 540 07466 7	☐ 0 540 07467 5	☐ 0 540 07468 3 ➤	
CHESHIRE	☐ 0 540 07507 8	☐ 0 540 07508 6	☐ 0 540 07509 4 ➤	
DERBYSHIRE	☐ 0 540 07531 0	☐ 0 540 07532 9	☐ 0 540 07533 7 ➤	
EDINBURGH & East Central Scotland	☐ 0 540 07653 8	☐ 0 540 07654 6	☐ 0 540 07656 2 ➤	
NORTH ESSEX	☐ 0 540 07289 3	☐ 0 540 07290 7	☐ 0 540 07292 3 ➤	
SOUTH ESSEX	☐ 0 540 07294 X	☐ 0 540 07295 8	☐ 0 540 07297 4 ➤	
GLASGOW & West Central Scotland	☐ 0 540 07648 1	☐ 0 540 07649 X	☐ 0 540 07651 1 ➤	
NORTH HAMPSHIRE	☐ 0 540 07471 3	☐ 0 540 07472 1	☐ 0 540 07473 X ➤	

COLOUR REGIONAL ATLASES

	HARDBACK	SPIRAL	POCKET	£ Total
	Quantity @ £12.99 each	Quantity @ £9.99 each	Quantity @ £5.99 each	
SOUTH HAMPSHIRE	☐ 0 540 07476 4	☐ 0 540 07477 2	☐ 0 540 07478 0	➤ ☐
HERTFORDSHIRE	☐ 0 540 06174 3	☐ 0 540 06175 1	☐ 0 540 06176 X	➤ ☐
EAST KENT	☐ 0 540 07483 7	☐ 0 540 07276 1	☐ 0 540 07287 7	➤ ☐
WEST KENT	☐ 0 540 07366 0	☐ 0 540 07367 9	☐ 0 540 07369 5	➤ ☐
LEICESTERSHIRE	☐ 0 540 07854 9	☐ 0 540 07855 7	☐ 0 540 07856 5	➤ ☐
NORTHAMPTONSHIRE	☐ 0 540 07745 3	☐ 0 540 07746 1	☐ 0 540 07748 8	➤ ☐
OXFORDSHIRE	☐ 0 540 07512 4	☐ 0 540 07513 2	☐ 0 540 07514 0	➤ ☐
SURREY	☐ 0 540 07794 1	☐ 0 540 07795 X	☐ 0 540 07796 8	➤ ☐
EAST SUSSEX	☐ 0 540 07306 7	☐ 0 540 07307 5	☐ 0 540 07312 1	➤ ☐
WEST SUSSEX	☐ 0 540 07319 9	☐ 0 540 07323 7	☐ 0 540 07327 X	➤ ☐
WARWICKSHIRE	☐ 0 540 07560 4	☐ 0 540 07561 2	☐ 0 540 07562 0	➤ ☐
SOUTH YORKSHIRE	☐ 0 540 06330 4	☐ 0 540 07667 8	☐ 0 540 07669 4	➤ ☐
WEST YORKSHIRE	☐ 0 540 07671 6	☐ 0 540 07672 4	☐ 0 540 07674 0	➤ ☐
	Quantity @ £14.99 each	Quantity @ £9.99 each	Quantity @ £5.99 each	£ Total
LANCASHIRE	☐ 0 540 06440 8	☐ 0 540 06441 6	☐ 0 540 06443 2	➤ ☐
NOTTINGHAMSHIRE	☐ 0 540 07541 8	☐ 0 540 07542 6	☐ 0 540 07543 4	➤ ☐
	Quantity @ £14.99 each	Quantity @ £10.99 each	Quantity @ £5.99 each	£ Total
STAFFORDSHIRE	☐ 0 540 07549 3	☐ 0 540 07550 7	☐ 0 540 07551 5	➤ ☐

BLACK AND WHITE REGIONAL ATLASES

	HARDBACK	SOFTBACK	POCKET	£ Total
	Quantity @ £11.99 each	Quantity @ £8.99 each	Quantity @ £3.99 each	
BRISTOL & AVON	☐ 0 540 06140 9	☐ 0 540 06141 7	☐ 0 540 06142 5	➤ ☐
	Quantity @ £12.99 each	Quantity @ £9.99 each	Quantity @ £4.99 each	£ Total
CARDIFF, SWANSEA & GLAMORGAN	☐ 0 540 06186 7	☐ 0 540 06187 5	☐ 0 540 06207 3	➤ ☐

Name...

Address...

....

....

....

.........................Postcode.....................

◆ Add £2 postage and packing per order

◆ All available titles will normally be dispatched within 5 working days of receipt of order but please allow up to 28 days for delivery

☐ Please tick this box if you do not wish your name to be used by other carefully selected organisations that may wish to send you information about other products and services

Registered Office: 2-4 Heron Quays, London E14 4JP
Registered in England number: 3597451

Total price of order £ ☐

(including postage and packing at £2 per order)

I enclose a cheque/postal order, for £ ☐

made payable to *Octopus Publishing Group Ltd,*

or please debit my ☐ Mastercard ☐ American Express

☐ Visa   account by £ ☐

Account no

☐☐☐☐ ☐☐☐☐ ☐☐☐☐ ☐☐☐☐

Expiry date ☐☐ ☐☐

Signature..

Post to: Philip's Direct, 27 Sanders Road, Wellingborough, Northants NN8 4NL

Ordnance Survey

MOTORING ATLAS
Britain

Updated annually

The best-selling *OS Motoring Atlas Britain* uses unrivalled and up-to-date mapping from the Ordnance Survey digital database. The exceptionally clear mapping is at a large scale of 3 miles to 1 inch (Orkney/Shetland Islands at 5 miles to 1 inch).

A special feature of the atlas is its wealth of tourist and leisure information. It contains comprehensive directories, including descriptions and location details, of the properties of the National Trust in England and Wales, the National Trust for Scotland, English Heritage and

Historic Scotland. There is also a useful diary of British Tourist Authority Events listing more than 300 days out around Britain during the year.

Available from all good bookshops or direct from the publisher:
Tel: 01933 443863

The atlas includes:

- ◆ 112 pages of fully updated mapping
- ◆ 45 city and town plans
- ◆ 8 extra-detailed city approach maps
- ◆ route-planning maps
- ◆ restricted motorway junctions
- ◆ local radio information
- ◆ distances chart
- ◆ county boundaries map
- ◆ multi-language legend